TOTAL Braves ®

EDITED BY
JOHN THORN, PETE PALMER,
MICHAEL GERSHMAN, DAVID PIETRUSZA
AND DAN SCHLOSSBERG

PENGUIN BOOKS

PENGUIN BOOKS
Published by the Penguin Group
Penguin Books USA Inc., 375 Hudson Street,
New York, New York 10014, U.S.A.
Penguin Books Ltd, 27 Wrights Lane,
London W8 5TZ, England
Penguin Books Australia Ltd, Ringwood,
Victoria, Australia
Penguin Books Canada Ltd, 10 Alcorn Avenue,
Toronto, Ontario, Canada M4V 3B2
Penguin Books (N.Z.) Ltd, 182–190 Wairau Road,
Auckland 10, New Zealand

Penguin Books Ltd, Registered Offices:
Harmondsworth, Middlesex, England

First published in Penguin Books 1996

10 9 8 7 6 5 4 3 2 1

Official Publication – Major League Baseball

ISBN 0 14 02.5729 2

Printed in the United States of America
Set in Times Roman
Designed by Marc Cheshire with Ray Shaw

Contents

Acknowledgments

The appearance of *Total Braves* marks the first time the editors have created a team-oriented book using concepts originally developed for *Total Baseball*, the official encyclopedia of Major League Baseball. It could not have been published without the assistance of a dedicated group of writers, researchers, and editorial/production staff. The principal contributors are credited on the preceding title page and in the table of contents.

Al Silverman, our editor, made a major contribution in shaping the book and providing wise editorial counsel. His colleagues in Penguin's art, editorial, and production departments — Dolores Reilly, Susan VanOmmeren, and Jessie Reyes — were consistently helpful under exceedingly tight deadlines and helped shepherd this book through the production process in an amazingly short period of time.

The publishing department of Major League Baseball played a key role in bringing this project to fruition, and our thanks go to Michael Bernstein for editorial oversight and to his staff — Dana Williams, Samantha Fahrer, and Rich Pilling — for adding to the book's editorial and visual impact. On the image front, our thanks also go to Bryan Reilly of Photo File and Todd Radom for their All-Star efforts on the cover.

In its fabled history, the Braves franchise has had a long line of distinguished pitchers and players. We were fortunate to have stories about them from Bob Carroll, Eliot Cohen, Henry Hecht, and Havelock Hewes on historic Braves, as well as stories from Bob Klapisch and Matt Silverman on current Braves heroes.

Courier Corporation, which printed Total Baseball, did its usual yeoman job in turning our words into finished form in record time. Our thanks go to Dave Barton for overseeing the project and Bill Topaz, Tom Osenton, and Peter Clifford for their continued support.

We were fortunate to extend our relationship with Starkey & Henricks, which has been the typographer for every edition of *Total Baseball*. To Peter and Doug Bird and their extraordinary, beleaguered staff go our admiration and gratitude.

For research help, particularly into the years before 1920, we extend heartfelt thanks (alphabetically) to SABR colleagues Bill Carle, Bob McConnell, David Neft, Bob Tiemann, and Frank Williams. Bill helped us with biographical data, especially debut dates. Bob McConnell lent his personal expertise and his knowledge of the John Tattersall research collection to clear up a variety of perplexing areas. David supplied us with heretofore unknown RBI data for the National League of 1880-1885 and inspired us by his example, as the man who headed the Information Concepts, Inc., team that produced *The Baseball Encyclopedia* of 1969. Bob Tiemann provided game scores and sites for a host of pre-1900 games that were most helpful in deriving, for the first time, home-road stats for the nineteenth century; he also headed the SABR research project that yielded new National Association data. For *Total Braves* in particular, Bob supplied performance and attendance data for Boston in 1871-1888. And Frank continued his remarkable efforts in correcting pitcher won-lost records before 1920.

CHAPTER 1

The 1995 Championship Season

Dan Schlossberg

No team has ever appeared in postseason play four straight times without winning the World Series. While the Atlanta Braves kept that record intact by beating the Cleveland Indians in the 1995 Fall Classic, it wasn't easy.

Although they had advanced to the World Series in both 1991 and 1992, and the National League Championship Series in 1993, the Braves had always been burdened by an unreliable bullpen. That problem evaporated in 1995 when Mark Wohlers, a young flamethrower previously victimized by erratic control and wavering concentration, suddenly started pitching like the second coming of Goose Gossage. After a rocky start, he saved 21 consecutive games between May 15 and September 3, finally finishing with a 7–3 record, 2.09 ERA, and 90 strikeouts in 64⅔ innings (a nine-inning average of 12.53). In his final 57 appearances, Wohlers' ERA was 1.37.

Maddux and Glavine, and Pray for . . .

Confident the bullpen could hold their leads, Greg Maddux and Tom Glavine continued to establish themselves as baseball's best righty-lefty tandem since Don Drysdale and Sandy Koufax ended their run with the Dodgers 29 years earlier. Maddux, a control artist whose .905 winning percentage (19–2) was a record for anyone with at least 20 decisions, won the NL's Cy Young Award for a record fourth straight season (the last two by unanimous vote). He also became the first pitcher since Walter Johnson (1918–19) to post back-to-back earned run averages below 1.80 and the first National League righthander to win three straight ERA titles since Grover Cleveland Alexander (1915–17). At the same time, the Atlanta Braves star extended his road winning streak to a record 18 games.

Only one other pitcher, Hall of Fame southpaw Steve Carlton, had ever won four Cy Youngs, but none were consecutive. Maddux, on the other hand, may have to create more room on his trophy shelf. The 6-0, 175-pound righthander lost only three times in 1995: once to each of Atlanta's three postseason opponents (though only once in postseason play). In addition to his 1.63 ERA, Maddux led the league in wins and complete games (10), tied for tops in innings (209⅔) and shutouts (3), and placed third in strikeouts (181).

Along the way, Maddux managed to throw his first career one-hitter (Jeff Bagwell homered in the eighth), hold hitters to a .197 batting average, and work 51 straight walkfree innings en route to a nine-inning season's base-on-balls average of 0.99. In his last 20 regular-season starts on the road, the one-time Cub staff leader has an 18–0 record and 0.99 ERA.

When he's on, Maddux not only throws five pitches for strikes but places every pitch exactly where he wants it. "Every hitter has a pitch he can't handle," said Mets manager Dallas Green, who was president of the Cubs when Maddux was a second-round draft choice (behind Drew Hall) in 1984. " 'Maddux' knows exactly where that pitch is and he puts the ball right there."

The Maddux arsenal includes a sinker, slider, cut fastball, curveball, and circle change. He'll throw any pitch on any count, work his way out of jams with double-play balls, and help his own cause with Gold Glove defense. He's won the fielding award six years in a row.

Maddux capped his offseason by becoming the first pitcher to be selected Associated Press Baseball Player of the Year, an award started in 1988. He received 30 votes, six more than runner-up Albert Belle, the Cleveland outfielder.

But awards make little impact on Maddux, a soft-spoken Las Vegas resident who hides his clean-cut visage behind Clark Kent glasses and an average build that shows no hint of his superhuman abilities. "When you win a Cy Young," he explained, "you go home and you're the only one who's happy. In 1995, it was more special because everyone in the clubhouse, the front office, and the city of Atlanta got to share in it."

If there were an award for modesty, Maddux would win that too. Asked if he'd like to become the first pitcher since Bob Gibson of the 1968 Cardinals to win the Most Valuable Player Award, he shook his head.

"I just pitch," he said. "One of the few things you can control is the effort you put into a game. I expect my effort to be as good next year, and as long as I play, as it has been the last six years. If I pitch as well as I can, the numbers will follow."

Maddux not only finished the 1995 regular season with a 17–1 record and 21 consecutive scoreless innings but allowed only one run in the middle innings (fourth, fifth, and sixth) all year. An 8–1 ratio of strikeouts to walks helped him average a meager 12.5 pitches per inning. On the road, his numbers were even more staggering: 13–0 with a 1.12 ERA.

Before Maddux did it last year, only Sandy Koufax had won back-to-back unanimous decisions in Cy Young balloting. He finished third in a close MVP race with Barry Larkin and Dante Bichette but probably would have won if the Atlanta bullpen hadn't blown three of his early-season leads Even MVP voters couldn't have ignored a 22–2 record. But Greg Maddux is used to be being ignored.

The native Texan likes to get lost on the golf course, behind a Nintendo screen, or in the anonymity of the crowds in Las Vegas. His father, a one-time fast-pitch softball star who taught the game to Greg and older brother Mike Maddux, is still a part-time poker dealer.

Maddux, who turns 30 early in the 1996 season, has filled out since his big-league bow in September 1986, but he retains his boyish good looks. "If you see him walk down the street," said former teammate Terry Pendleton, now with the Marlins, "you wouldn't think Cy Young. But give him a baseball, and hitters just want to leave."

They have the same reaction to Glavine, the last NL pitcher to win a Cy Young before Maddux. In 1995, the 29-year-old southpaw joined Lew Burdette (1957) as the only Braves to win World Series MVP awards after he and Wohlers combined on a 1–0 one-hitter in the decisive sixth game. Glavine had also won Game 2, following a two-hitter by Maddux in the opener.

With 91 wins over the last five seasons, Glavine has more wins than any other pitcher (runner-up Maddux has 90). A model of consistency, he has ranked among the league's top five winners in each of those five seasons. He also has more victories than any lefty over the past eight (122). Glavine yields fewer hits than innings, averages less than three walks per game, and keeps the ball in the park. Because he paints the outside corner with his fastball, slider, curve, and circle change, he's especially effective against righthanded hitters.

The book on Glavine says get him early or don't get him at all. His ERA in the first inning last year was 7.76; outside of the first, it was 2.28. Start the game in the second inning and Glavine might be the man with multiple Cy Youngs on his trophy shelf. He's still the only Brave with both a Cy Young and a World Series MVP award. Neither Maddux nor Hall of Fame lefthander Warren Spahn, generally considered the greatest pitchers in franchise history, can make that claim.

But things weren't always was so rosy. When Glavine first reached the majors nine years ago, the Braves were so bad Atlanta fans were hoping for the return of General Sherman. After a 2–4 rookie season, Glavine staggered through a 7–17 campaign in 1988.

"At the time, it wasn't any fun," he said. "But that season taught me a lot about myself and what I needed to do as a pitcher to be successful. It also helped me deal with failure. You're going to fail in this game; you're going to have bad games. That season taught me things won't always go my way. I had two choices: give in or fight my way out of it."

Glavine fought. He's had few rough spots since, despite pitching with a cracked rib in 1992 and battling shoulder problems that lingered nearly three years. By 1995, with his shoulder back to its rookie-year strength, Glavine's velocity showed marked improvement. So did his record.

He finished with a rush, going 11–3 with a 2.80 ERA in 18 starts after June 26 to wind up with a 16–7 record. Only a bad first inning on the last day of the season at New York kept Glavine from an ERA below 3.00 (he finished at 3.08).

His postseason numbers were even better: 0–0 and 2.57 against Colorado in the Division Series and 0–0 and 1.29 against Cincinnati in the NL Championship Series (he pitched seven one-run innings against Pete Schourek in the opener), before finishing with a flourish in the World Series.

The Campaign

Although the 1995 Braves ranked next-to-last in the league with a .250 batting average, their combination of pitching and power helped them win a league-high 90 games. That gave them a club-record 21-game margin over the Philadelphia Phillies and New York Mets, who tied for second in the National League East.

As usual, the Braves started slowly. With spring training cut to three weeks instead of the usual six by the 232-day player strike (a walkout that had wiped out the 1994 postseason), the pitchers were rested but rusty. After not pitching competitively since the previous August, the Atlanta staff allowed 4.8 runs per game in April—easily its worst month of the season.

Before the Braves warmed with the weather, they spent the spring in second place, finishing both May and June four games behind Philadelphia. But a 20–7 July tied the team record for wins in any month, enabling Atlanta to take an eight-game lead into August. Half of those July wins came in the team's last at-bat, a growing Atlanta trademark. The Braves eventually led the league with 25 last-at-bat victories during the regular season.

Newcomer Chipper Jones, a switch-hitting shortstop who had missed all of 1994 after a spring training knee injury, was one of those responsible. Three of his 23 homers won games in the ninth inning. Jones led all major-league rookies with 86 RBI (one short of Earl Williams's 1971 Atlanta rookie record), 87 runs scored, 140 games played, and 524 at-bats—all while batting third and playing third, a new position he assumed after a crash course of 11 exhibition games. He also homered twice, including the game-winner in the ninth, in Game 1 of the Division Series against the Colorado Rockies. But he lost the NL Rookie of the Year voting in a close decision to Dodger pitcher Hideo Nomo.

Sophomores Javy Lopez, the No. 1 catcher, and Ryan Klesko, converted from first base to left field, also helped the Braves hit 168 home runs, second in the National League. Lopez, a fine clutch hitter who averaged .361 after the All-Star break, won Game 2 of the Championship Series against Cincinnati with a three-run, tenth-inning homer, while Klesko homered in each of the three World Series games played in Cleveland.

Leadoff man Marquis Grissom, acquired from Montreal in April for three players plus cash, was also instrumental in Atlanta's 11–3 postseason record. He hit safely in all 14 games, slammed three home runs, stole five bases, and provided his usual strong defense in center field. With three straight Gold Gloves, Grissom and Maddux (six in a row) have monopolized the fielding award.

First baseman Fred McGriff hit 27 regular-season homers, then four more in postseason play, while rightfielder David Justice—bothered by shoulder problems all season—saved the best of his 25 1995 homers for last. It came in the sixth inning of World Series Game 6, giving Glavine the only run he needed.

The Postseason

The 1–0 win was sweet justice for the Braves, who had lost Game 7 and the 1991 World Series when the Minnesota Twins managed to plate the only run of the game in the tenth. Bullpen failures beset the Braves in '92, when they lost the Series to Toronto in six games, and in '93, when the Phillies needed the same number of games to win the NLCS.

The 1995 Braves, however, could not be denied. They came within a whisker of sweeping the entire postseason, blowing a fine ninth-inning scoring chance in the deadlocked Division Series Game 3 (won in 10 innings by the Rockies) and a 6–5, eighth-inning lead in World Series Game 3 (ended by the Indians in the eleventh).

Atlanta even uncovered unexpected postseason heroes. Late-season acquisition Mike Devereaux won MVP honors in the NLCS after hitting a three-run, seventh-inning homer in Game 4 and lefthanded pitcher Steve Avery—who had struggled all year—worked six two-hit innings in the same game and six three-hit innings in Game 4 of the World Series.

The relatively easy victory in the Fall Classic was also unexpected: Cleveland had led the majors with a .291 batting average (baseball's best in 45 years), 840 runs scored, and 207 home runs, 20 more than its previous club record. Against an Atlanta pitching staff that had led the majors with a 3.44 ERA, however, the Indians managed a meager .179 average and 19 runs in six games — an average of 3.2 runs per game by a team used to scoring six per contest. Only Kenny Lofton's ninth-inning single in the opener prevented the Braves from posting bookend one-hitters in the first and last games of the Series.

Cleveland was Atlanta's most formidable opponent. With a 100–44 record, the Indians had flattened all opposition, finishing a record 30 games ahead of the Kansas City Royals in the AL Central Division. Then the Tribe swept three straight from the Boston Red Sox in the Division Series and silenced Seattle's big hitters in a thrilling six-game AL Championship Series.

That set the stage: Cleveland's power against Atlanta's pitching. With the first two and last two games scheduled in Atlanta but the middle three set for Cleveland, the Braves had the home-field advantage. But local fans, disappointed by losses in the previous three postseasons, failed to match the enthusiasm of the audience at Jacobs Field, watching their team compete in the World Series for the first time in 41 years.

That bothered some of the Braves—and Justice summarized their feelings when he complained to a reporter from the *Atlanta Journal-Constitution* before Game 6. After succeeding long-time local hero Dale Murphy and winning NL Rookie of the Year honors in 1990, Justice had become one of the team leaders—and a participant in the recent postseason disappointments.

Game Six

But the fans, still reluctant to forgive the players for the 232-day strike that had wiped out the 1994 World Series, responded to the rightfielder by displaying dozens of homemade signs during the sixth game. Their jeers turned to cheers only when Justice delivered his lone home run of the postseason—a solo shot against southpaw reliever Jim Poole. Advantage Atlanta.

All Tom Glavine had to do was hold off the most formidable offense in the major leagues. "I knew there was a lot riding on that game but I just tried to relax," he said weeks later. "I tried to treat it like any other game. There wasn't that much pressure on me because it wasn't a do-or-die situation. Had we lost, we still would've had another chance in Game 7 the next night.

"I thought about what I did the first time I faced those guys and what adjustments I needed to make. I tried not to think about what winning the game might mean to our organization, the city, and the fans."

After spending the day with his wife and daughter, Glavine went out and pitched the game of his life. The only blemish was a leadoff bloop single by backup catcher Tony Pena in the sixth. Glavine fanned eight and walked three in eight innings but left for a pinch hitter after telling manager Bobby Cox he didn't have enough left for the ninth. But his 2–0 record, 1.29 ERA, four hits allowed, and 11 strikeouts in 14 innings were more than enough to make him World Series MVP.

Though he's started the All-Star Game twice and won 20 games three years in a row, Glavine will always be remembered for Game 6 of the 1995 World Series. He had pitched four two-hitters previously but had only three shutouts (including the first in the history of Denver's Coors Field last year) during the last three regular seasons combined.

"It's hard to explain what it feels like," said Glavine, whose 1987 arrival in Atlanta made him the senior man of the World Champions eight years later. "It's something I dreamed about as a kid. After all our near-misses the last few years and the bitterness of losing two World Series, that dream became more real. It's something I'll never forget and hopefully will experience again."

At the Helm

Unlike the 1991 and 1993 Atlanta teams that needed to win on the final weekend of the season, last year's crew prospered in the postseason after a well-planned program of September rest. With the Braves comfortably ahead of their NL East competition, manager Bobby Cox and pitching coach Leo Mazzone decided a rested staff would have a better chance to win in October. The team's 11–3 postseason record proved them right.

Cox deserves much of the credit for Atlanta's first World Championship. He was Braves' general manager from 1985–90, when many of its current stars were scouted, signed, or acquired in trades. Cox began his second term as Atlanta field pilot on June 22, 1990.

"If you can't play for Bobby, you've got a problem," Glavine said. "He's every bit a players' manager. He's very simple in what he wants: show up on time, be ready to play, and give it 100 per cent. If you do that, he's in your corner. He treats you like a man and expects you to respect what he wants. You just go out there and play hard."

Cox banks heavily on a bench populated by defensive specialists, pinch-hitters, and pinch-runners. One of them, Rafael Belliard, was the only major-leaguer to play in the five postseasons from 1990–95—the first with Pittsburgh, the last four with Atlanta. Known for his sure hands and strong arm at shortstop, Belliard is one of the weakest hitters in baseball. He hasn't even hit a home run since 1987—a record for futility he extends every year. But he's a giant with a glove on his hand. Subbing for the injured Jeff Blauser, Belliard went 0–for–16 during the 1995 World Series. But he made two key plays that might have made a difference.

With Game 1 tied, 1–1, in the seventh, the Braves loaded the bases when the first three hitters walked. Then Luis Polonia, another valuable Atlanta reserve, hit a hard grounder at normally sure-handed shortstop Omar Vizquel. He bobbled the potential double-play ball, getting only a force at second while allowing Fred McGriff to score and leaving runners at the corners.

Cox came out to argue that Vizquel never had possession and the bases should still be loaded. While he was jawing with umpire Bruce Froemming, however, the manager decided to gamble. With Belliard, a better bunter than hitter, due to bat, Cox called for a squeeze. Belliard executed, catching the Cleveland defense by surprise. Justice scored and Polonia moved to second. Then Maddux ended the inning by grounding out.

"You hate to take Raffy out because of the defense he gives you," Cox said. "But we would have had to put a pinch hitter in there if Luis hadn't gotten the first run home." The run scored by Belliard's bunt made the difference in a one-run game—just as his running catch of a foul fly kept the dangerous Lofton off the bases in the ninth inning of the finale.

With Cox at the helm over the last five years, Atlanta has won 454 games—more than any other team in the majors. Level-headed and patient, he's supportive of his players and quick to credit his coaches. And he never presses the panic button.

Although he's considered a conservative in many quarters, Cox is actually one of baseball's more creative managers. He and pitching coach Leo Mazzone, for example, were the first to suggest their starters throw twice between starts. According to Tom Glavine, "The combination of Bobby and Leo is as good as it gets. They're very conscientious about their pitchers and don't run guys out there and get them hurt.

"Some people think throwing twice between starts is too much but I don't believe that. When Bobby and Leo first started the program, it was something new and I wasn't real sure I wanted to do it either. But since I've been on the program, my shoulder has been feeling better and stronger. As a direct result of throwing a little more and exercising, I've had less and less problems. At the same time, I've gotten better as a pitcher because I understand my mechanics better. It's no different than anything else: if you're a golfer, the more you get to the driving range, the better your swing is going to be."

Under Mazzone, a talkative West Virginian who spent his entire nine-year pitching career in the minors, the Braves have led the National League in earned run average three times in the last four years, missing only with a second-place finish in 1994. They led the majors in both 1993 and 1995.

Bobby Cox also gets strong support from former ma-

jor-league managers Pat Corrales, his first-base coach, and Jimy Williams, who coaches third. Clarence Jones, the hitting coach, and Ned Yost, who runs the bullpen, complete the Cox staff. All get along well, though Cox has been trying to think of ways to eliminate smoking during their meetings.

Like Sparky Anderson, Bobby Cox was a big-league regular for one year: as third baseman for the New York Yankees in 1968. Plagued by bad knees, he hit .229 with seven home runs, eventually retiring from the active ranks at age 30 three years later.

Before 1995, he was part of one World Championship team—as first base coach for the 1977 Yankees. He managed the Braves from 1978–81, laying the groundwork for the team's 1982 NL West title, and the Toronto Blue Jays from 1982–85, taking the former expansion team to its first AL East title in his last year.

Chosen AL Manager of the Year by The Associated Press in 1985, he became the first man to win the award in both leagues when he won it again with the 1991 Braves. That was the first full year of his second term, when he guided the Braves on their historic worst-to-first odyssey (the 1990 team had finished last).

By 1991, Cox had given up his dual role as manager and general manager. Hired as GM after the 1985 season, Cox stayed in the front office until June 22, 1990, when team president Stan Kasten asked him to return to the field. Four months later, when Kasten convinced Kansas City general manager John Schuerholz to accept the same job in Atlanta, Cox agreed to remain field manager only.

In the Front Office

Schuerholz quickly showed in Atlanta why he had won a World Series, two pennants, and six divisional crowns with the Royals. An executive with an uncanny sense of timing, he signed seven free agents, plugging holes in the young 1990 team he had inherited. The biggest acquisition was third baseman Terry Pendleton, unwanted anywhere else after hitting .230 for St. Louis. He immediately blossomed into a batting champion, Most Valuable Player, and leader of the 1991 team that went from worst to first.

Two years later, Schuerholz lured Maddux from the Cubs after his first Cy Young season, then watched him win three more in a row. Prior to the 1995 season, he let Pendleton walk when he knew Chipper Jones was ready to jump into his spot.

Schuerholz also showed he knows how to trade. In 1993, when he acquired McGriff from San Diego for the successful stretch drive, he surrendered three minor-leaguers but refused to include Klesko. In '94, he traded Deion Sanders to Cincinnati for Roberto Kelly, a much-needed righthanded hitter. But his *coup de grace* came in April 1995, when Schuerholz persuaded the Montreal Expos, Atlanta's top rivals of the year before, to exchange Gold Glove centerfielder Marquis Grissom for Kelly, Tony Tarasco, minor-leaguer Esteban Yan, and cash.

During the World Championship season, Schuerholz hardly had time to sit on his hands. He rebuilt the bench, adding Devereaux from the White Sox and Polonia from the Yankees, and reacquired 1991 stretch-drive hero Alejandro Pena, a veteran relief pitcher, from the Florida Marlins.

After the 1995 World Series, he outbid several other clubs to sign McGriff for another four years. He also gave Grissom a new, four-year deal, keeping the nucleus of the 1995 club intact. Since the arrival of the former Baltimore schoolteacher, the Braves have posted the best record in baseball: 454–290 and a winning percentage of .610.

It's been more of a roller-coaster ride for Bill Bartholomay, who's been Chairman of the Board since the Braves came to Atlanta in 1966. He's seen the team win five NL West flags, one NL East title, three pennants, and a World Series. But he's seen some tough times too.

Bartholomay, part of the original LaSalle Corporation that purchased the Milwaukee Braves in 1962 and brought it to Atlanta four years later, has been with the team as owner or director for 34 years. He's also been active on the Commissioner's Executive Council, the Ownership and Restructuring committees, and the Commissioner Search committee.

Schuerholz, Bartholomay, and Kasten answer to one man: R.E. (Ted) Turner, founder of Turner Broadcasting. Once an activist owner who was fined and suspended for tampering, Turner has turned over control of his two sports teams—the Braves and the NBA's Atlanta Hawks—to Kasten, who serves as president of both. Turner's time is almost completely devoted to his expanding cable empire, although he's also an active environmentalist and world-class yachtsman.

Turner revolutionized the TV news industry 16 years ago when he started CNN, the first all-news station, and later added CNN Headline News. His stations also include TNT, TBS, and SportSouth, plus a long list of related companies in the film and entertainment world.

Nothing, however, matches the entertainment provided by the 1995 Atlanta Braves.

CHAPTER 2

The Braves History

Dan Schlossberg

When they beat the Cleveland Indians in the 1995 World Series, the Braves became the first team to win a World Championship in three different cities. They had won previously as the Boston Braves in 1914 and the Milwaukee Braves in 1957. That's not many titles for a team that traces its origins to 1871, but the Braves have filled their many lean years with players whose individual accomplishments superseded those of the club.

Hank Aaron, who spent all but his last two years with the team, hit 755 home runs, more than anyone else in baseball history. He and Eddie Mathews, also a Hall of Famer with more than 500 career homers, combined for a record 863 home runs during the time they were teammates, from 1954–66. Mathews was the only man to play for the Braves in all three of their home cities and also the only man to play for, coach , and manage the team.

Pitcher Warren Spahn, who spent only his last year wearing other uniforms, won 363 games, more than any other lefthanded pitcher, and had 13 seasons with 20 or more victories. Had the Braves been a better ballclub during his long tenure, Phil Niekro might have topped Spahn's total. A righthander whose knuckleball tantalized National League hitters, he too won most of his 318 games while working for the Braves.

Like Niekro, Dale Murphy never played in the World Series. But he did win consecutive Most Valuable Player Awards—the only Brave ever to do that. In 1995, his No. 3 jersey was retired, joining previously retired numbers belonging to Aaron (44), Mathews (41), Spahn (21), and Niekro (35) prominently displayed at Atlanta-Fulton County Stadium. When the Braves shift to their new ballpark in 1997, they'll have to leave room for the numbers of current pitching heroes Greg Maddux (31) and Tom Glavine (47).

The original founders of the franchise would have been amazed by the many changes in the game. They never dreamed of night baseball, domed ballparks, artificial turf, or jet travel from coast to coast; their vision was simply to make baseball a paying proposition.

Baseball was a much simpler game in the 1860s, when the New York Game of Base Ball, played according to Knickerbocker Club rules, took hold in New England, banishing the Massachusetts version to oblivion.

Spectator interest boomed so much in the years after the Civil War that Harry Wright, a former Knickerbocker player, gathered top ballplayers from the Northeast to form the Cincinnati Red Stockings, the first openly professional team. Wright was not only the team's creator but its manager and centerfielder.

Though the average Red Stocking of 1869 did not earn more than $1,000 that year, the players were more concerned with pride than price: they went undefeated in 60 games (with one tie) and did not lose until June 14 of the following year. Only once did Cincinnati fail to score 16 or more runs in a game and one of their decisions was a 103–8 triumph over the Buckeyes of Columbus, Ohio. Like the 1995 Atlanta Braves, the team was hosted by the President in a special White House reception.

Professional Baseball Comes to Boston

When Cincinnati decided to disband its team in 1871, however, Wright and three of his players fled to Boston, where they helped form a team in the new National Association of Professional Baseball Players, the first professional league.

Importing their nickname, the new Boston Red Stockings won four pennants in five years. But the league was unable to survive constant player and franchise shifting, the obvious influence of gamblers and other unsavory characters, and the competitive imbalance that was a product of Boston's superiority.

Boston pitcher Albert Goodwill Spalding, who had posted a 55–5 record the year before, then jumped from Boston to Chicago, along with three other Boston stars (Ross Barnes, Cal McVey, and Deacon White). There Spalding collaborated with White Stockings owner William A. Hulbert to form the National League of Professional Baseball Clubs, an eight-team circuit with a 70-game schedule.

Although Boston's "Big Four" propelled Chicago to the NL's first pennant, the Boston Red Stockings became a prominent member of the new league, capturing championships in each of the next two seasons and then again in 1883.

Boston even landed the league's best player when Chicago agreed to sell Mike (King) Kelly for $10,000—a huge sum at that time—on February 14, 1887. A two-time batting king known for his daring baserunning, Kelly was not only a versatile and flamboyant star but an innovator credited with creating the hit-and-run play, hook slide, and finger signs for catchers.

A year after his purchase had stunned the baseball world, Boston owner A.H. Soden sent the White Stockings another $10,000 for star pitcher John Clarkson. In 1889, Clarkson and Kelly helped Boston draw 295,000 fans and make a profit of $100,000—not bad for a team that played only 128 games (for comparison, the Braves drew just 84,938 during the war-shortened season of 1918).

With several stars on its roster, Boston won eight NL pennants in all before the turn of the century. It also changed its nickname to Beaneaters, a title directly related to the team's host city and not easily confused with the Cincinnati Reds of the American Association, a rival major league that competed in 1882–91.

Because schedules, rules, and league formats changed so frequently during the game's early years, records of the time may be difficult to place in a modern context. But several are worth noting.

Pitcher Kid Nichols, a righthanded control artist who worked without a windup, won 27 games as an 1890 rookie, then started a seven-year streak of at least 30 wins per season.

Neither the .440 batting average by Hugh Duffy in 1894 nor the 1,221 runs scored by the team that year have been surpassed during the modern era that began with the advent of the American League in 1901, not even with the expansion of the schedule to 162 games.

The Beaneaters of the 1890s were a great team. But hard times were just around the corner. After leading the National League in 1898 and finishing second a year later, the Boston Nationals began a steady decline—partially because of money woes triggered when local fans showed a preference for their crosstown American League rivals.

The team's 14-year snooze near the bottom of the National League standings included an embarrassing 66½-game deficit in 1906 and a 108-loss season in 1909. They did not even acquire their Braves nickname until 1912, when new owner Jim Gaffney, a contractor with connections to New York's Tammany Hall political machine, showed no reservations about swiping its Indian-head logo. By that time, Boston's AL club had revived the old Red Stockings nickname and shortened it to Red Sox—abandoning previous titles of Pilgrims, Puritans, and Somersets (after owner Charles Somers).

For most of the five-year period prior to Gaffney's purchase, Boston's National League team had been called the Doves—after owners George and John Dovey. Unfortunately, it also played like the peaceful birds, usually surrendering without a fight. The nickname changed again—to Rustlers—after New York attorney William Hepburn Russell bought the club in 1911. Gaffney not only brought the Braves nickname to Beantown but immediately began improving the team and its ballpark.

In 1912 the richer Red Sox opened Fenway Park, a facility far superior to the long-time home of the Braves, South End Grounds. The only Boston ballpark ever to feature a double-decked grandstand, South End Grounds had a seating capacity of only 11,000—hardly enough to accommodate the crowds demanding Braves' tickets during their "miracle" season of 1914. The team began borrowing Fenway Park (capacity 33,871), then returned the favor by letting the Red Sox host World Series games at the larger Braves Field (capacity 43,500) in 1915–16.

The Bosox utilized Braves Field again for the first Sunday game in city history, on April 28, 1929. The Braves had been scheduled to begin Sunday ball there a week earlier but bad weather intervened. The Red Sox chose the location only after they received advance word of a planned protest at Fenway Park. (In 1946, the teams reversed roles. The Braves switched to Fenway for the final time after fans attending the Braves Field opener found that fresh paint recently applied to the seats had not dried properly. The event became known in Boston as "the wearing of the green," even though the town's traditional lusty celebration of St. Patrick's Day had passed a month earlier.)

Boston's tenure at South End Grounds had lasted 44 years—interrupted only on May 15, 1894 after rowdy fans in the cheap right-field seats (25 cents apiece) started a fire in the stands during a game against the arch-rival Baltimore Orioles, led by John McGraw. What began as a small blaze quickly spread, in three hours devouring 170 nearby buildings as well as the wooden ballpark. When the park was reopened two months later, it had only two of its original six flag-topped spires. During reconstruction, the team played most of its games at Congress Street Grounds, previously the home of Boston-based teams in three ill-fated major leagues: the Union Association (1884), the Players League (1890), and the American Association (1891).

Two weeks after the Beaneaters moved into their temporary home, second baseman Bobby Lowe became the first big-leaguer to hit four home runs in a game. After fanning in his first at-bat, Lowe—helped by a left-field fence only 250 feet away—hit four straight homers, two of them in the third inning.

Such an explosion would have been much more difficult at the odd-shaped South End Grounds, with dimensions of 250–440–255, or cavernous Braves Field, where the original measurements were 402–520–402—with the distance to right-center a mind-boggling 550 feet. Winds whipping in off the Charles River made conditions even less conducive to the long ball.

Although there were lots of inside-the-park homers, including two in a 1919 game by Rabbit Maranville (the first time that ever happened), only seven balls cleared the fences before the park was remodeled to accommodate newly acquired slugger Rogers Hornsby in 1928. Hornsby, who spent most of that year—his only one in Boston—as player-manager, won the batting title but hit only 21 homers, not many for him.

The Miracle Braves

In addition to the new nickname and new ballpark, James Gaffney gave his team the gift of a quick pennant. After he made George Stallings manager in 1913, the once moribund ballclub sprang from eighth place to fifth. But it was buried in the standings again by the middle of the following season before the first stirrings of the Miracle Braves.

The 1914 campaign was marked by a slow start and fast finish. Reeling from a 4–18 start, the Braves stood last, 15 games behind, with a 26–40 record on July 3. Then they lost a doubleheader—and even an exhibition game against a soap-manufacturing company. They seemed barely able to blow bubbles.

The Braves didn't actually vacate the basement until July 19. But their 51–16 (.761) second-half featured a 34–10 finish (.773) that gave them a comfortable margin over the second-place Giants. Led by MVP-to-be Johnny Evers, signed to play second base after his release as player-manager of the Cubs, Boston finally caught New

York on August 23, then exchanged leads several times before sprinting to the finish line.

Dick Rudolph and Bill James won 26 games each, while the scrappy keystone combination of Evers and Maranville turned 143 double plays, most in the National League. Maranville, a 5'5" shortstop who would spend 15 of his 23 seasons with the Braves, was one of only four players remaining from the team Stallings had inherited the year before.

Stallings, a highly superstitious sort who went wild whenever he saw paper on the field, was also an innovative pilot who pioneered such devices as platooning and playing the percentages. A master at developing and evaluating players, Stallings had juggled 46 players in his first Boston season while assembling the team that would stage the best worst-to-first turnaround within the same season. It was the only pennant he ever won.

The Philadelphia Athletics were heavily favored to win the 1914 World Series. The players were so sure of themselves that Chief Bender, Philadelphia's top pitcher, had disobeyed manager Connie Mack's directive to scout the Braves, though Boston scouts had secretly observed the Athletics. Stallings, a master psychologist, predicted his upstarts—in their first winning season since 1902—would sweep the defending World Champions, and the Braves had more than enough momentum to neutralize Philadelphia's confidence.

After Boston battered Bender in the opener, the tone was set. A lost fly ball in the ninth gave the Braves their second win, enabling them to return home with a 2–0 cushion. Each team scored twice in the tenth inning of Game 3, which ended two innings later on a double, a walk, a bunt, and an error. Boston's two-run fifth in the finale gave the Braves a 3–1 win and the first sweep in World Series history. Catcher Hank Gowdy was the hitting hero with a .545 average, but the real story was Boston's pitching: Philadelphia got only five earned runs in four games and batted a composite .172.

The upset was prodigious: Mack's men had won the World Series in three of the previous four years and had posted baseball's best record (99–53) in 1914. They had the American League's batting champion and home run king, three starting pitchers destined for Cooperstown, and the famed $100,000 infield of Stuffy McInnis, Eddie Collins, Jack Barry, and Home Run Baker.

After the debacle (or miracle, depending on one's rooting interest), Philadelphia, forced to sell its stars to keep them from jumping to the rival Federal League, did not return to postseason play for 15 years. The Boston Braves, however, were gone more than twice that long. After a third-place finish in 1915, the Braves went into a deep-freeze that lasted well past the Second World War.

They made history, however, when they played a 26-inning, 1–1 tie—still the longest game in big-league annals—against the Brooklyn Dodgers on May 1, 1920. Using only three baseballs between them, pitchers Joe Oeschger of the Braves and Leon Cadore of the Dodgers went the route but were immediately sorry: the former had to brush his teeth lefthanded because he couldn't raise his pitching arm and the latter spent 36 straight hours in bed.

Nine years later, owner Emil Fuchs, an attorney and former New York City magistrate, named himself to suc-

ceed Hornsby as manager. Before the season opener, Fuchs issued a prophetic statement: "I don't think our club can do any worse with me than it has for the last few years."

He was wrong.

The Bad Old Days

Under the German-born Fuchs, whose only baseball experience was a stint as a semipro catcher, the Braves dropped into the NL cellar for the first time since 1924. There was good reason for the players to take their orders from third-base coach Johnny Evers. When Maranville suggested a squeeze play during one contest, Fuchs said, "We'll win honorably or not at all."

Bill McKechnie, who took over in 1930, won NL pennants in three different cities. But Boston wasn't one of them.

The team hit rock bottom in 1935, when it signed a fat, over-the-hill Babe Ruth to a $25,000 contract as a player, assistant manager, and vice president. In reality, he was supposed to be a fan attraction who might help Judge Fuchs overcome pressing financial problems. Though Ruth's double and home run off Carl Hubbell thrilled a record Opening Day crowd of 25,000 at Braves Field, the magic didn't last. Ruth had one more outburst— a three-homer game at Pittsburgh's Forbes Field May 25—before quitting June 2 with a .181 average, 6 home runs, and 12 runs batted in.

Even Wally Berger's league leadership in home runs (34) and RBIs (130) didn't help the Braves avoid a season of disastrous dimensions: it won 38 and lost 115, a twentieth century record for futility unmatched until the expansion New York Mets of 1962 went 40–120 (and the Braves won-lost percentage was *still* lower than that of the Mets). At season's end, Boston stood 61½ games behind. Fuchs, who had lost more than $1 million during his ownership, had to forfeit his majority share of the stock and the league had to seize temporary control of the team.

Bob Quinn, the new team president, knew he had to change the team's image but had little working capital. He came up with a name-the-team contest designed to regenerate fan interest. The team became known as the Bees. And the official title of Braves Field became National League Park, though Quinn convinced fans to call it "the Beehive."

The Bees had no sting, however, and the changes were scrapped after five straight second-division finishes. Even Casey Stengel, later regarded as a managerial genius for winning 10 pennants in 12 years with the New York Yankees, couldn't light the team's fire.

Stengel arrived in 1938, the same year that Cincinnati southpaw Johnny VanderMeer victimized the Braves in the first of his consecutive no-hitters, on June 11. Stengel's six-season tenure had few other highlights. His winning percentage in Boston was .432 (373–491), as opposed to his career managerial mark of .508 (1,905–1,842).

When Warren Spahn arrived under his watch in 1942, Stengel made the worst prediction of his lengthy career: he said the kid lefthander had no future in the majors. More than twenty years later, an aging Spahn pitched for the Stengel-led New York Mets. Ten years after that horrendous season, when both men had Hall of Fame plaques, Spahn said, "I'm probably the only guy who played for Stengel before and after he was a genius."

Stengel would long remember one of two starts Spahn made for him in Boston. On September 26, with the lefty leading the Giants 5–2 in the seventh, youngsters admitted free for 10 pounds of scrap metal (vital to the war effort) stormed the field. Umpire Ziggy Sears forfeited the game to New York, but all player records counted. Spahn got credit for a complete game but no decision and had to wait four more years for his first major-league win.

Things were so bad for Stengel's Braves that the *Boston Record* actually praised the motorist who ran him down—fracturing his leg and idling him for two months—just prior to the 1943 campaign. Stengel was gone after that season, while Spahn was off to war. He later became the only player to receive a battlefield commission during World War II.

Though the 1944 Braves finished 40 games behind, the foundation of a better future was laid when the club was purchased by Lou Perini and two fellow contractors, collectively known as "the Three Little Steam Shovels." Stuck with an assortment of 4-F's, minor-leaguers, and has-beens, they couldn't do much with a team whose ace pitcher was 19-game loser Jim Tobin. But the knuckleballer completed 28 of 36 starts and became the first man to hit a home run and pitch a no-hitter in the same game. He hit five other homers that season, including three in a game—the only time a pitcher has ever done that.

A year later, Boston outfielder Tommy Holmes hit in 37 consecutive games—a modern National League record that stood until 1978, when Pete Rose hit in 44 straight.

New manager Billy Southworth, lured from the Cardinals with a three-year contract, got much-needed pitching help in 1946 when Spahn and Johnny Sain returned from military service. Sain completed a league-high 24 games while placing second with 20 wins and a 2.21 earned run average, while Spahn finally won his first big-league game at age 25.

Spahn and Sain

Two years later, with the Braves bidding for their first pennant since 1914, the pair formed such a potent 1–2 pitching punch that Southworth started them 16 times in 26 games after September 3. Sain finished second to Stan Musial in the voting for Most Valuable Player—an award won the year before by newly acquired Boston third baseman Bob Elliott.

Sain led the league with 24 wins, 28 complete games, and 314⅔ innings pitched, inspiring pundits to say Boston's pitching rotation was "Spahn & Sain & pray for rain." Elliott knocked in 100 runs, shortstop Alvin Dark became the first Brave named NL Rookie of the Year, and the team led the league in both batting and earned run average.

But Boston couldn't duplicate its postseason heroics of 1914. Although Spahn and Sain produced one victory apiece against Bill Veeck's Cleveland Indians, that wasn't enough. With Bob Lemon winning twice, the six-game

World Series went to Cleveland—an outcome that would reverse itself when the teams met again 47 years later.

Even Southworth, the magician who had won three pennants and two World Series with St. Louis, couldn't sustain the winning spirit of 1948. In fact, a series of slumps and crippling injuries—including a sore arm that limited Sain to a 10–17 record—made the manager so uptight that he was sent home for a "rest" on August 16, 1949. When angry players voted him only a half-share of the money they had received for coming in fourth (a first-division finish in the eight-team league), Commissioner Happy Chandler reversed their decision.

Sain's return to health and Spahn's second straight season of 21 wins helped Southworth close the gap to eight games in 1950, but the Braves still finished fourth. The team had to do without Dark and Eddie Stanky, the fine DP tandem who were dealt to the Giants, but compensated with a strong performance from rookie centerfielder Sam Jethroe, who had 18 homers and a league-high 35 stolen bases.

The first black player in Boston's baseball history, Jethroe became the second Brave in three years to win NL Rookie of the Year honors. He had only one other good season, however, and was out of the majors before the Braves bolted Boston for Milwaukee just prior to the 1953 campaign.

The move had been brewing for a long time. While attendance was booming at Fenway Park, home of the high-scoring Red Sox, the Braves had been struggling at the turnstiles as well as in the standings. After drawing 487,475 in 1951, things got off to an ominous start in '52 with a pathetic Opening Day "crowd" of 4,694. When the last home game drew 8,822, it was the second largest attendance of the year.

The Boston Braves lost their last games at home and on the road, with the Brooklyn Dodgers beating Jim Wilson both times. The date of the last home game, September 21, would live in Braves' infamy: exactly 23 years and two moves later, only 6,858 spectators showed up for Fan Appreciation Night in Atlanta.

For the 1952 team, the season's highlight occurred off the field: on June 14, the ballclub paid the Indianapolis Clowns of the Negro American League $10,000 for the contract of a skinny infielder named Henry Louis Aaron. The '52 Braves finished seventh, 32 games behind. Nobody had a good year, though rookies Lew Burdette and Eddie Mathews gave strong hint of better things to come—in greener pastures.

The Milwaukee Braves

Burdette and Mathews made their major impact in Milwaukee, where the Braves relocated in the middle of 1953 spring training. After asking the league for permission to shift on March 13, Perini got it five days later—by unanimous vote. The first franchise shift in major league baseball since the Baltimore Orioles became the New York Highlanders (later Yankees) in 1903 was wildly successful. Welcomed to Wisconsin with open arms, the team had to fight its way through the throng of 12,000 fans who showed up at the Milwaukee railroad station to welcome it home from spring training.

The Cinderella swing from doormats to darlings worked wonders: the Braves shook off their 1952 malaise and began to create a baseball miracle. Under the command of Jolly Cholly Grimm, the team rode the league's best pitching staff to a second-place finish, 13 games behind, and drew 1,826,297 fans, then a National League record. Everyone seemed delighted with Milwaukee County Stadium—a park with far cozier dimensions (320–404–320) than Braves Field. The old home of the Braves was not finished, however: it was purchased by Boston University for $500,000.

Meanwhile, in Milwaukee, Mathews hit a career-high 47 homers, still a franchise record (later tied by Hank Aaron in Atlanta), and knocked in 135 runs, another club record. Mathews led the league in homers, rookie Bill Bruton led in steals (26), and Spahn finished first in victories (23) and ERA (a career-best 2.10). Newcomer Joe Adcock, a big first baseman acquired from Cincinnati, showed he could hit home runs anywhere. On April 29, he became the first player to homer into the distant center-field bleachers of New York's Polo Grounds, more than 483 feet from home plate.

A year later, Adcock produced a one-game power explosion that stands alone in baseball history. On July 31, 1954, the muscular righthanded hitter collected four home runs and a double, good for 18 total bases, in a nine-inning game against the Brooklyn Dodgers at Ebbets Field. Adcock, who had never played baseball before his Louisiana State basketball coach suggested he try the sport, produced his home runs on a Don Newcombe fastball in the second, an Erv Palica slider in the fifth, a Pete Wojey curve in the seventh, and a Johnny Podres fastball in the ninth. Two of the home runs and the double were hit on first pitches, while the other two homers came on second pitches. Two were solo shots, one came with two on, and one with one on, giving the 6'4" slugger seven runs batted in. The Braves won the game, 15–7. Eddie Mathews said afterward that Adcock's hardest hit of the day was his third-inning double off Palica. It missed clearing the left-center field wall by inches.

Adcock credited a coach and a catcher for helping him carve a niche in the record books. Coach Johnny Cooney had told Adcock to "be sure and get under it" when aiming at the Ebbets Field power alley, 350 feet away in left center, while substitute backstop Charlie White had given Adcock a bat after the slugger broke his own the day before.

Adcock, who went on to hit 23 homers in 133 games for the 1954 Braves, did much of his damage against the Dodgers: eight extra-base hits, including five home runs, in the July series alone. Beaned in the head by Clem Labine the next day, Adcock was saved by his batting helmet, which the Braves had made mandatory earlier that season. Examining the seam marks on Adcock's headpiece, Brooklyn team physician Dr. Frank Zorn called the helmet "the greatest invention since the cotton gin."

Neither Mathews nor Aaron, a 1954 rookie, ever duplicated Adcock's feat. In fact, the only Brave to do it in the modern era was Bob Horner, whose 1986 four-homer game in Atlanta was unique because his team managed to lose.

Adcock went on to hit 336 home runs, 239 of them for the Milwaukee Braves, while teaming with Mathews and Aaron in one of the most formidable slugging trios the game has ever seen. Mathews, Aaron, Adcock, and Frank Thomas even become the first teammates to hit four consecutive home runs (a feat duplicated by American League teams in 1963 and 1964). It happened in the seventh inning of a game against the Cincinnati Reds on June 8, 1961.

A is for Aaron

By that time, Aaron was a well-established slugger. But he wasn't expected to become a home run hitter when he first surfaced as a 20-year-old infielder at the Bradenton, Fla. spring training home of the Braves in 1954. In fact, the idea of Aaron hitting more home runs than Babe Ruth seemed as far-fetched as the thought of an actor becoming President of the United States.

Scheduled for another year in the minors to polish his erratic defense at second base, Aaron got his break when Bobby Thomson suffered his. Thomson, a hard-hitting outfielder acquired from the Giants just before spring training, suffered a severe ankle fracture while trying to slide during an exhibition game on March 13. The following day, Grimm gave Aaron his first start—in left field. The rookie responded with three hits, including a home run, and never left the lineup. When Thomson returned, Aaron shifted to right, where he made No. 44 famous.

Once a poor-fielding shortstop who batted cross-handed, Aaron hit a modest .280 with 13 home runs and 69 RBIs in 1954, suffering his only serious injury when he also broke an ankle sliding. But his line-drive stroke was connecting with increasing frequency and he played in his first of 24 All-Star games (a record shared with Willie Mays and Stan Musial) a year later.

By the time he retired after the 1976 campaign, Aaron had more homers, more runs batted in, more extra-base hits, and more total bases than anyone in baseball history. He ranks second in runs scored (tied with Ruth), and third in hits. Willie, Mickey & the Duke don't even fit into the equation.

Durability was Aaron's trademark: for 16 straight seasons from 1955 through 1970, he never played in less than 145 games. He also produced a record 15 seasons in which he hammered at least 30 home runs (Ruth had 13). He and Willie Mays remain the only players with both 3,000 hits and 500 home runs (though Eddie Murray could join them in 1996). Aaron scored at least 100 runs in 15 different seasons and amassed 300 total bases just as often. He even stole 20 or more bases in six different seasons. In addition to all his other feats, it is Aaron—not Mays or the father-and-son Bonds tandem—who remains the only player in National League history to hit 40 homers and steal 30 bases in the same season (1963).

Ten years later, Aaron, Darrell Evans, and Davey Johnson became the only trio of teammates to hit at least 40 home runs apiece in the same season. (Johnson, a first-year Brave acquired from Baltimore for 1971 NL Rookie of the Year Earl Williams, hit 42 as a second baseman to tie the 1922 record of Rogers Hornsby.)

Aaron's 40-homer outburst at age 39 in 1973 set the stage for his final assault on Ruth's record the following year. It also extended another record, the mark for home runs by brothers. The Aarons, not the DiMaggio or Alou threesomes, hit more home runs than any other brother combination (768). Tommie Aaron, unfairly expected to be a carbon copy of his famous older brother and teammate, never got the playing time he might have elsewhere. The outfielder-first baseman, who hit the first Atlanta-Fulton County Stadium homer during a 1965 exhibition game, later left his own legacy as a top minor-league manager, opening a path for future black pilots Frank Robinson, Don Baylor, and Dusty Baker, among others.

Just as Tommie's abilities as a player were never appreciated, Hank's abilities as a five-tools star were overshadowed by his home run heroics. Even sportswriters don't remember him as a base-stealer or a man who won three straight Gold Gloves for his outfield play. That fact became painfully apparent with the announcement of the 1982 voting for enshrinement in the Baseball Hall of Fame: nine nincompoops left Aaron's name off their ballots. No player has even been elected with a unanimous vote, but who could have been more deserving than the career home run king?

Aaron, normally a quiet superstar, was openly unhappy with the vote, but it was hardly the most difficult moment of his career. He had had to endure spring training segregation and, years later, an avalanche of racial hate mail. Even during the '70s, an alarming number of white fans reacted angrily to the idea of a black man breaking the most revered white-held record in sports.

Against such adversity, however, Aaron prevailed. A model of durability, he sustained only one disabling injury (the broken ankle) in a career that lasted 23 seasons. He reached 40 home runs in eight different seasons, topped 100 RBIs in 11, and three times finished a season with double digits in doubles, triples, and home runs.

Aaron's name deserves its first place in baseball's player register. He won two batting crowns, four home run crowns, and four RBI titles, while leading the National League in slugging four times, runs scored three times, and hits twice. A 30/30 performer in 1963, Aaron was even more prolific in 1971, while fighting advancing athletic age and brittle body parts. At 37, Aaron was hobbling around on an injured knee, the result of a 1970 collision with catcher Dick Dietz. But he eliminated the source of his suffering after rival slugger Willie McCovey—bedeviled by similar problems—showed Aaron his knee brace. What worked well for Willie worked wonders for Henry.

In just 139 games, eight of them as a pinch hitter, Aaron hit a career-high 47 homers, knocked in 118 runs, compiled a .327 batting average, and recorded a .669 slugging percentage—at that time the best in the NL since Stan Musial's .702 in 1948.

For Aaron, that season was the turning point in the race for Ruth's record. He "slipped" to 34 homers the next year, then managed a final season of 40 that left him one shy of the mark—and a whole winter to think about it.

Anxious to disperse the hordes of media members who chronicled his every move, Aaron tied Ruth with his first swing of the 1974 campaign, at Cincinnati's Riverfront Stadium. No. 715—the record-breaker—came in the fourth inning of Atlanta's first home game, on April 8, against Los Angeles lefthander Al Downing.

With the strain of The Chase at an end, Aaron simply played out the string. With his skills and motivation fading and the team out of pennant contention, he hit only 18 more homers for the Braves, who obliged his request to let him finish his career where he had started it, in Milwaukee.

In two years as designated hitter of the American League's Milwaukee Brewers, Aaron added 22 more homers, swelling his career count to 755—41 more than Ruth and 95 more than Mays. But he also lost five points off his career batting average, which wound up at .305.

Beyond Aaron, Ruth, and Mays, no one else has reached 600 homers. Even 500 remains an elusive goal: only 14 players, including the three at the top, have reached that plateau. But none hit home runs with the consistency of Hank Aaron. Whenever big home runs were needed, Aaron delivered:

Sixteen home runs with the bases loaded. The eleventh-inning homer that gave Milwaukee its first pennant in 1957. Three homers against the Yankees as the Milwaukee Braves won their only World Championship that fall. Three more as the Atlanta Braves lost three straight playoff games to the 1969 Miracle Mets. Even a rare All-Star homer before the Atlanta home folks in 1972.

Alternately called The Hammer (because of his bat) or Bad Henry (because he was bad news to opposing pitchers), Aaron won only one MVP award, after spearheading the World Championship season of 1957. Even in 1959, the year he said was his best, he was spurned by the voters. Ignoring Aaron's .355 average, 223 hits, and 400 total bases, MVP electors picked Ernie Banks, shortstop of the fifth-place Chicago Cubs, for the second consecutive year. Mathews was runner-up.

Playing in a larger city, or for a better ballclub, would have given Aaron more publicity—and probably more awards. But he preferred to do his job in a quiet, efficient way, cherishing his privacy and keeping to himself as much as possible. Opposing players even said he looked like he was falling asleep at home plate.

That was hardly the case. Aaron was a team man who not only swung a powerful bat but performed anywhere the need arose. He played all three outfield positions, as well as first and second, during his long career. But he made everything look too easy. Aaron always played second fiddle to the flamboyant Mays, epitomized by his basket catches and squeaky, high-pitched voice, or the brittle Mantle, a wounded hero always searching for a triumphant return. Nor did Aaron command the loyalty of the Brooklyn legions who idolized every move made by Duke Snider.

Constant comparisons to the legendary Ruth reduced Aaron's image even further. Except for their uncanny proximity in the zodiac (Aaron's February 5 birthday is one day before Ruth's), the two sluggers had little in common. Ruth supporters consider Aaron as much a record usurper as Roger Maris, whose 61 home runs in 1961 put him one up on Ruth's previous single-season record.

The Maris objections may be valid: he took advantage of expansion-diluted pitching to deliver the only 40-homer season of his career. But Aaron was always Mr. Consistency. While Ruth had four 50-homer seasons, and Mays and Mantle had two apiece, Aaron never exceeded

47. In addition, Ruth never faced the handicaps of night baseball, coast-to-coast travel, constant pitching changes, or media pressure—not to mention the deluge of hate mail that engulfed Henry Aaron. Ruth also had the twin advantages of batting lefthanded (there are more right-handed pitchers) and having Lou Gehrig follow him in the batting order. Considering those differences, Aaron's lone advantage—3,000 more times at-bat—pales in significance.

Three years before the Braves moved to Dixie, Aaron got some unexpected help: new manager Bobby Bragan moved him from fourth to third in the lineup. That helped Aaron average more at-bats per season. He also received solid support from the other Braves' sluggers who surrounded him in the lineup, ranging from Mathews and Adcock early in his career to Joe Torre, Orlando Cepeda, Earl Williams, Dusty Baker, and Darrell Evans later. None was a Lou Gehrig, to be sure, but none was a pushover either.

That Championship Season

Considering that Aaron, Mathews, Spahn, and Burdette were all at their peak in 1957, it's hardly surprising that the Braves won their only Milwaukee World Championship that fall. Aaron, who had won the 1956 batting title, won the other two-thirds of the elusive Triple Crown when he hit 44 homers and knocked in 132 runs for the '57 Braves. His homer won the pennant (and the MVP award) and he had three more against the favored Yankees in the World Series.

Fred Haney, who had succeeded Grimm as manager the previous summer, produced a 95–59 record by relying on two left-right tandems: Mathews & Aaron and Spahn & Burdette. But the midseason additions of second baseman Red Schoendienst, relief pitcher Don McMahon, and outfielders Wes Covington and Bob Hazle also helped.

Hazle, filling in for the injured Billy Bruton, hit so well during his two-month stay that he picked up the nickname Hurricane, after a devastating storm—also named Hazel—hit the U.S. East Coast. Like the real thing, Hazle burned out quickly after his rampage. But he lasted long enough to hit .403 with seven homers, 12 doubles, and 27 RBI in 134 at-bats, spanning 41 games. After 114 listless at-bats the following year, Hurricane Hazle's career was becalmed.

Schoendienst, who had arrived from the Giants on the June 15 trading deadline (for Bobby Thomson, Ray Crone, and Danny O'Connell), led the league in hits, while Covington clouted 21 homers in 96 games. Spahn led the league with 21 wins and 18 complete games, tied for second with a 2.69 ERA, and ranked second with four shutouts and 271 innings pitched. He was rewarded with the only Cy Young Award (then given to only one pitcher per year) of his 21-year career.

In the World Series, however, everyone took a back seat to Burdette, who had become a Brave when the Yankees needed Johnny Sain for a late-season pennant drive in 1951. Duplicating a feat last performed by Cleveland's Stan Coveleski in 1920, Burdette pitched three route-going complete games. Two of them were shutouts, giving the fidgety righthander 24 consecutive scoreless

innings against one of the heaviest-hitting teams of all.

Burdette won the second, fifth, and seventh games—the last one an emergency assignment, on two days' rest, after Spahn was felled by the flu. He yielded seven hits in each of his last two starts, winning 1–0 and 5–0. Spahn was the other Milwaukee winner, going all the way in a 7–5 game that lasted 10 innings and had a most unusual ending.

With the Yankees ahead, 5–4, reserve first baseman Nippy Jones, who had spent most of the previous five years in the minors, led off as a pinch hitter for Spahn. After he backed away from an inside pitch, Jones told home-plate umpire Augie Donatelli that a Tommy Byrne pitch had hit him. Donatelli disagreed, but changed his mind after Jones showed him a smudge of black shoe-polish on the ball.

Schoendienst advanced pinch runner Felix Mantilla with a bunt before Johnny Logan doubled off reliever Bob Grim, tying the game. With first base open but Aaron up next, Casey Stengel elected to pitch to the slumping Mathews, who had gone 1-for-11. On a 2–2 count, the slump ended. The home run tied the Series at two games and gave Milwaukee its first World Series win at home. Burdette, on three days' rest, outdueled Whitey Ford the next day, setting the stage for the teams to split the final two games at Yankee Stadium.

A year later, the Yankees got their revenge, becoming the second team to recover from a 3–1 deficit in the World Series. Milwaukee won the first two games, 4–3 in 10 innings and 13–5, but lost a 4–0 verdict to Don Larsen, author of the 1956 World Series perfect game, in Game 3. After Spahn tosses a two-out, 3–0 shutout in the fourth game, the Braves seemed headed for their second World Championship in a row.

But Bob Turley's 7–0 shutout in Game 5 and six innings of two-hit relief in Game 7 cemented the Yankees' comeback. They won by beating both Spahn and Burdette in Milwaukee, 4–3 in a ten-inning Game 6, and 6–2 in Game 7.

That was a disappointing finish for the 1958 Braves, who had been almost as strong as their '57 counterparts. They led the league with a .266 batting average, 3.21 earned run average, and 72 complete games, but hit 32 fewer homers than they had the year before. With Spahn and Burdette both in the 20-win circle, Milwaukee was able to withstand injuries to fellow starters Gene Conley and Bob Buhl, who went from a combined 27 wins in 1957 to 5 in 1958. The team's first-place margin was still eight games, the same as it had been in 1957.

The Braves actually came close to winning four pennants in a row. After finishing a single game behind the Brooklyn Dodgers in 1956 and winning successive flags in 1957–58, Milwaukee tied for the top with the underdog Dodgers, by then based in Los Angeles, in 1959. That forced a best-of-three playoff under National League rules of the time.

Although surprise starter Carlton Willey pitched a strong game for the Braves in the opener at Milwaukee County Stadium, the Dodgers prevailed, 3–2, on a John Roseboro homer. Their hero was rookie righthander Larry Sherry, who yielded four hits in 7⅔ innings of relief and did not allow a runner past first base.

Burdette, who had beaten the Dodgers twice while

winning 21 games during the regular season, took a 5–2 lead into the second game, at the cavernous Los Angeles Coliseum. Mathews had the big hit: a home run that gave him NL leadership in that department with 46, one more than Ernie Banks. In the ninth, however, consecutive singles by Wally Moon, Duke Snider, and Gil Hodges loaded the bases with none out. Manager Fred Haney hailed a string of relievers—Don McMahon, Joey Jay, and even Spahn—who couldn't stop the uprising.

The game went into extra innings, ending only when backup shortstop Felix Mantilla, subbing for the injured Johnny Logan, made a two-out throwing error that gave the Dodgers the winning run against Bob Rush in the twelfth. It was the only time in five tie-breaking playoffs (including one under the two-division format in 1980) that the Dodgers escaped defeat.

Spahnie, the Kitten, and Knucksie

The Braves, on the other hand, seemed determined to self-destruct whenever they reached the postseason. After blowing a 3–1 lead in the 1958 World Series and failing to win a game in the '59 playoffs, the team suffered consecutive sweeps in the 1969 and 1982 National League Championship Series, best-of-five contests to determine World Series opponents. They also lost the first game of the 1991 NLCS—giving them a 12-game losing streak in postseason play.

Just getting to postseason play proved to be a problem after 1958. Although the '59 team led the National League in homers, complete games, and shutouts, it won only 86 games, a fact not lost on the 20,000 spectators who bought tickets to the playoff opener. An almost identical turnout had come to County Stadium on the foggy night of May 26 for a game against Pittsburgh. Little did they know they would be witnesses to history.

Harvey "the Kitten" Haddix, a veteran lefthander then in his first season with the Pirates, retired the first 36 Braves but had to work into the thirteenth inning of a scoreless duel with Burdette. That's when the magic suddenly ended. Leadoff man Felix Mantilla became the first Braves baserunner when Don Hoak made a bad throw from third base. Mathews bunted him to second and Aaron was purposely passed, setting up a potential double play.

Adcock then hit the ball over the fence in right-center, but Aaron, rounding second as Mantilla scored the winning run, proceeded directly into the dugout. Adcock, in his home run trot, was then ruled out for passing Aaron on the basepaths. His three-run homer became a one-run double and the Braves won, 1–0. Haddix, who would finish the year with a 12–12 record, had yielded only one hit, 11 less than Burdette, but lost the best-pitched game in baseball history.

Milwaukee gave its fans many other memorable moments that season, with Aaron posting a career-high .355 average, Mathews winning the home run crown, and Spahn and Burdette tying for the league lead with 21 victories each. But the poor fan support was a portent of things to come.

As age started to catch up to some of its key performers, the team sunk slowly in the standings, finishing second in 1960, fourth in 1961, fifth in 1962, and sixth in 1963, followed by two more fifth-place seasons. Neither Charlie Dressen, Birdie Tebbetts, nor Bobby Bragan could stem the tide—or induce the fickle fans to support their one-time idols. The only no-hitters of Spahn's career, plus his 23–7 season at age 42, attracted some attention, as did Aaron's Triple Crown bid of 1963, but the natives were getting restless.

Part of the problem was management's decision to dump many of the old heroes, including Adcock, Logan, Bruton, Burdette, and Buhl, as well as some of the best prospects, notably Juan Pizarro and Joey Jay. One of the best trades—Mel Roach for Frank Thomas on May 9, 1961—became one of the worst when Thomas was sent to the New York Mets for Gus Bell and $125,000 on November 28. Milwaukee also did the fledgling Houston Colts a favor by selling them star reliever Don McMahon, another player who was still productive.

Plagued by poor personnel decisions, the '62 Braves posted their worst batting average since the team was based in Boston. Spahn, the primary victim, was helpless to preserve his six-year streak of 20-win seasons despite a league-high 22 complete games and solid 3.04 ERA. The team finished fifth, Tebbetts lost his job, and even the owner had seen enough.

On November 16, the Perini Corporation threw in the towel after 19 seasons, selling the team to a Chicago-based syndicate called the LaSalle Corporation. The price was $5.5 million—just a shade more than Fred McGriff's current salary.

Two years later, with attendance of less than a million for the third straight season, the National League granted the group permission to relocate in Atlanta for 1966.

Spahn would not go with them. After a 6–13 season in 1964, the team sold him to the Mets for $1. Bragan, who had had a falling out with the great lefthander, said that was all Spahn was worth.

Angry fans pinned the blame on the manager, who had allowed Spahn to go all the way in a 16-inning duel with San Francisco ace Juan Marichal at cold, windswept Candlestick Park on July 2, 1963. The 42-year-old Spahn threw 200 pitches before Willie Mays won the game with a home run on pitch 201.

If Spahn strained his arm during the four-hour, ten-minute struggle, it didn't show that season. His record, which had fallen to 11–4 that night, wound up at 23–7, with seven shutouts, a 2.60 earned run average, and a league-high 22 complete games in 33 starts.

But how could a pitcher fall so far so fast? Spahn, traditionally a slow starter, went 5–4 to open the '64 season but was suddenly hit so hard that he was taken out of the rotation after the All-Star break. His pride stung, the pitcher complained bitterly. But he won only one more game in a Milwaukee uniform.

Insisting he could still pitch, Spahn became a player-coach for Casey Stengel's 1965 Mets, who had also reactivated catching great Yogi Berra. "I don't know if we'll be the oldest battery in baseball history but we'll certainly be the ugliest," Spahn said.

His good humor wouldn't last: in 1965, his last major-league season, he went 4–12 in New York and 3–4 with San Francisco. His 4.01 ERA, though nearly a full run higher than Spahn's career mark of 3.05, was far better than the 5.29 mark he had posted the year before.

Still refusing to face Father Time, Spahn pitched three games in the Mexican League in 1966 and three more in the minors a year later, when he used himself as a pitcher while serving as Tulsa manager. All that did was delay his Hall of Fame eligibility, since candidates must be retired five years before they can be considered. Spahn eventually made it on his first try—unlike Mathews, who had to wait five years.

The high-kicking lefthander left behind a rich legacy. Had he not lost more than three seasons to wartime military service, Spahn almost certainly would have joined Cy Young and Walter Johnson as the only 400-game winners in baseball history. His 363 wins, 10 short of the National League record shared by Christy Mathewson and Grover Cleveland Alexander, included 63 shutouts and 5,246 innings pitched. Six of his thirteen 20-win seasons were consecutive, as were all four of his strikeout crowns.

Those crowns came early in his career, when Spahn's best pitch was his fastball. As his velocity faded with age, the crafty lefthander learned to make a smooth transition to the screwball. The makeover worked: Spahn led the National League in wins eight times, complete games nine times, and ERA three times. When he pitched his second no-hitter five days after turning 40 in 1961, he became the second-oldest man (behind Cy Young) to throw one. It followed his first by only seven months, six of which comprised the off-season.

By the time he finally retired, the high-kicking southpaw ranked in the career Top 10 in wins, innings, shutouts, and a dozen other categories. He even matched his career win total with 363 base hits, including 35 home runs, an NL record for a pitcher.

Though filling Spahn's shoes seemed like an insurmountable task for the Braves, the team somehow managed to find another future 300-game winner in Phil Niekro. Ironically, his first year in Milwaukee was Spahn's last.

Used only sparingly his first three seasons, Niekro was actually returned to Richmond briefly because the Braves had nobody who could catch his dancing knuckleball—a dangerous pitch for a reliever who often entered the game with the winning run on second or third.

During the 1967 campaign, however, Niekro got his break when manager Billy Hitchcock needed an emergency starter. The team had traded catchers with the Cardinals—heavy-hitting Gene Oliver for good-field, no-hit Bob Uecker—specifically to help the young righthander.

Niekro made the most of the moment, tossing a two-hit shutout, and went on to lead the National League with a 1.87 ERA, best of his career. He later topped the NL in innings pitched and complete games four times, victories twice, and strikeouts once. Niekro was a 20-game winner three times but a 20-game loser twice—once during one of his 20-win seasons.

Like Spahn, Niekro was a victim of circumstances: he could have crashed the 400-win barrier had the Braves been a better ballclub during his 20-year tenure with the team. Except for divisional titles in 1969 and 1982, however, the ballclub usually behaved like the Bad News Braves while Knucksie wore its uniform.

Though Niekro lasted well past his 40th birthday, the ballclub was anxious to avoid a repeat of Spahn's sudden burnout. After falling from 17–4 in 1982 to 11–10 a year later, Niekro was released. But he was far from through. He won 32 games (including his 300th) for the Yankees over the next two seasons and even made the American League All-Star team. Then he won 18 more for Cleveland before the Braves, realizing their mistake, brought him back for a "farewell game" at age 48 in 1987. Finally retiring after 24 seasons, Niekro had been the oldest man to play regularly in the major leagues. Only three men ever pitched more innings.

One of Niekro's 268 wins for the Braves was the team's first no-hitter since Spahn's 1961 gem against San Francisco. The only other Atlanta Brave to pitch an individual no-hitter would be Kent Mercker, who victimized the Dodgers in his first start of 1994 (Mercker, Mark Wohlers, and Alejandro Pena had pitched a combined no-hit game three years earlier).

By the time they retired, Phil and Joe Niekro had won 539 games, more than the Deans, Perrys, or any other pair of baseball brothers. But they were Atlanta teammates only in 1973–74, when the Braves—in one of their most ill-advised transactions—plucked Joe out of their bullpen and packed him off to Houston. He not only became a solid, front-line starter but the biggest winner in Astros' history. From 1980–87, Joe Niekro won 104 games, four more than his older brother.

Joe also had a 5–4 advantage in games started against Phil. The difference came in 1976, when Joe beat Phil in a one-run game by hitting the only home run of his career.

Phil was a better hitter. In fact, his home run at San Diego on the final Friday of the 1982 season helped the Braves win the NL West. Tasting the title, Niekro went 11–1 down the stretch (losing only to Joe) to finish with a 17–4 record and career-best .810 winning percentage, an Atlanta record before Greg Maddux posted a .905 mark in 1995.

Mathews, Murphy, and Memorable Moments

Niekro's best year was 1969, when he won a career-high 23 games and watched untimely storms wash out two other large leads. Only a 25-win season by Tom Seaver prevented Niekro from winning the Cy Young Award. He would have settled for a World Series ring instead but couldn't get past Seaver and the Mets in the very first NL Championship Series. Niekro had won five of his last six, helping the Braves play .769 ball in September and finish three games ahead of the Giants and four ahead of the Reds.

But 46-year-old reliever Hoyt Wilhelm, the first relief artist to reach the Hall of Fame, wasn't eligible for the playoffs because he'd arrived in Atlanta eight days after the deadline for postseason roster eligibility. Wilhelm's two wins, four saves, and 0.75 ERA down the stretch had been instrumental in Atlanta's ability to win 17 of its last 20, including 10 in a row. The clincher came September 30, in a game Niekro started but Wilhelm finished. But the pairing of the two best knuckleballers in baseball history was short-lived.

The relief Niekro needed in the playoff opener never

came. He yielded five runs in the eighth, turning a 5–4 Atlanta lead into a defeat that set the tone for the series. Though he didn't pitch well either, Seaver got the win.

Pundits who had predicted pitching would dominate the playoffs were proven wrong again the next day. The Mets, who had reached the postseason on the strength of their young arms, pounded Atlanta, 11–6, pinning the loss on 18-game winner Ron Reed. He didn't survive the second frame, but five relievers weren't much better. Pat Jarvis was equally ineffective in Game 3, losing a 7–4 decision to a 22-year-old reliever named Nolan Ryan (seven strikeouts, three hits, and two walks in seven innings). Niekro would have to wait 13 years—a baseball eternity—to reach the playoffs again.

While Niekro was languishing in the bullpen during his early years with the Braves, the team's top starter had been a hard-throwing righthander named Tony Cloninger. With Burdette gone and Spahn going in 1964, Cloninger became the ace of the Milwaukee staff, leading the team with 19 victories. He was even better during the lame-duck year of 1965, when he went 24–11 with a 3.29 ERA for a ballclub that finished fifth with an 86–76 record (making the Milwaukee Braves the only major-league team never to finish a season with a losing record).

Atlanta's first Opening Day pitcher, Cloninger worked all 13 innings of a 3–2 loss to Pittsburgh on a cold April night. The 25-year-old righthander was never the same again. He finished with a 14–11 record—the last time he won more than he lost for the Braves—but managed to become the only player in National League history and the only pitcher in major-league history to hit two grand-slams in one game.

Even Cloninger, who had hit two home runs in a game against the Mets on June 16, couldn't have foreseen his explosion of July 3, 1966. Starting in San Francisco against journeyman Joe Gibbon, Cloninger was staked to an early lead when batterymate Joe Torre delivered a three-run, first-inning homer.

Before he got to pitch, Cloninger got to bat—with the bases loaded. With reliever Bob Priddy on the mound for the Giants, the Atlanta pitcher hit the ball over the fence, swelling the lead to 7–0. He connected again off Ray Sadecki in the fourth, then collected a club-record ninth RBI with a run-scoring single off Sadecki in the eighth. No other pitcher has ever been so prolific at the plate.

He hit five of his 11 career homers in 1966, finishing with 23 RBI in 39 games. Cloninger and Don Newcombe of the Dodgers remain the only pitchers ever to produce a pair of two-homer games in the same season.

Cloninger helped the first edition of the Atlanta Braves hit 207 home runs, a franchise record, but the pitching staff couldn't keep pace. The Braves had imported Aaron, Mathews, Torre, Rico Carty, and Felipe Alou from Milwaukee, but Cloninger and Wade Blasingame were fading and Niekro was still a not-ready-for-prime-time player.

Not long into the season, it was obvious that the biggest falling star belonged to Mathews. Unable to generate his former power with any consistency, he was reduced to a platoon role by Bobby Bragan but didn't hesitate to voice his disagreement.

On August 9, the night Bragan was fired, new manager Billy Hitchcock ended the policy and penciled Mathews into the lineup against future Hall of Famer Sandy Koufax, also a lefthander. An overflow crowd watched Alou and Jim Lefebvre exchange solo homers, sending the game into the bottom of the ninth in a 1–1 tie. With one out and an 0–2 count, Mathews connected off Koufax, triggering a wild celebration that would not be repeated until Aaron hit his 715th home run eight years later.

For Mathews, it was his last hurrah. On New Year's Eve, he was traded to Houston (along with Arnie Umbach and Sandy Alomar, Sr.) in an inexplicable deal for the forgettable Dave Nicholson and Bob Bruce. The handwriting had been on the wall for a month, since the Braves had obtained slick-fielding third baseman Clete Boyer from the Yankees on November 29.

Like Spahn before him and Aaron after him, Mathews left a long trail of accomplishments. The seventh player to reach 500 career homers, he hit more than 30 nine years in a row and topped 40 four times. He not only produced two home run crowns and five 100-RBI seasons but became the most prolific power-hitting third baseman, for both a season and a career, until Mike Schmidt broke both records.

Mathews even managed a grand-slam against Spahn in the veteran southpaw's first appearance against his old team, on May 20, 1965. With Wade Blasingame holding the Mets to one hit, the home run provided more than enough margin for a 7–1 victory.

Mathews also realized an ambition Spahn didn't: to become manager of the Braves. Replacing Luman Harris, who had guided the Braves to their first division crown in 1969, Mathews was at the helm when a controversy erupted over Aaron's race with Ruth.

The Braves had been scheduled to open the 1974 season in Cincinnati but the team wanted Aaron to break Ruth's record at home. Since he needed only one to tie and two to top, management decreed that Aaron would not play in the Cincinnati series.

That didn't sit well with Commissioner Bowie Kuhn, who decided that Aaron's benching would run contrary to "the best interests of baseball." After considerable soul-searching, plus consultations with Aaron and chairman of the board Bill Bartholomay, Mathews agreed to comply—at least for the opener.

Aaron, anxious to end a winter of waiting, responded with a home run against Jack Billingham on his first swing of the season, on a 3–1 count. On April 4, 1974, Hank Aaron had tied Babe Ruth's record of 714 home runs. It was the only time in Aaron's long career that he hit a home run on Opening Day.

Hitting the home run was probably less difficult for Aaron than writing his name on the lineup card had been for Mathews. He desperately wanted his long-time friend to celebrate the record-breaking moment in front of Braves fans but knew his job could be in jeopardy if he defied the Commissioner's Office.

Aaron helped ease the strain by going 0–2 with a walk after his first-inning homer in the opener. With wet weather easing his decision, Mathews held Aaron out of Game 2, scheduled for Saturday afternoon after an off-day Friday. But a telephone call from Kuhn to Mathews ordered Aaron into the Sunday lineup.

Every time he came to bat, Mathews rooted against him—or at least against the possibility that he might hit a home run. On the field, however, neither Mathews nor Aaron ever gave less than 100 per cent effort. On April 7, the baseball gods smiled: Aaron took two called third strikes and hit an infield grounder before leaving the game.

If he could hit a home run during the 11-game homestand that began the next night, Aaron's ordeal would be over. And so would the ordeal of Eddie Mathews, who didn't want another confrontation with the Commissioner when the team hit the road again. Fortunately for both men, Aaron obliged immediately. After taking a five-pitch walk from Al Downing in the second inning, Aaron batted again in the fourth. On a 1–0 count, he saw a fastball he liked, swung, and deposited it into the waiting glove of pitcher Tom House in the Braves bullpen. The time was 9:07 P.M.

For Mathews, it was the highlight of his career as Atlanta manager; he was replaced by the gentlemanly Clyde King, a former Brooklyn relief pitcher, with the team one game over .500 on July 21. King's club played .603 ball the rest of the way to finish a surprising third. Niekro led the league with 20 wins, 18 complete games, and 302⅓ innings pitched; waiver-wire acquisition Buzz Capra posted a league-low 2.28 ERA; and Ralph (the Roadrunner) Garr finished first with a .353 average, 214 hits, and 17 triples.

Aaron put a cap on the season October 2 when he homered in his last at-bat—connecting for his 733rd home run as a Brave (and as a National Leaguer) against Cincinnati's Rawly Eastwick. It was the perfect ending to a bookend season for Aaron, whose Atlanta farewell had featured home runs in his first and last at-bats. Aaron had previously hit the last home run by a Milwaukee Brave, against Philadelphia's Ray Culp on September 20, 1965.

Even though his retirement as an active player would be postponed two more years, Aaron's decision to take off his Braves uniform struck a sentimental chord in Atlanta. Originally reluctant to play in the Deep South because of perceived racial problems, Aaron found Atlanta such a progressive city that he moved his family there. Worshipped by fans and respected by rivals, he discovered Atlanta-Fulton County Stadium was an even friendlier home-run target than Milwaukee's park. Its altitude—at 1,057 feet baseball's highest before Colorado joined the league—and its original dimensions of 325–402–325 were perfect for power-hitting. Years later, Aaron admitted the ballpark was probably the biggest factor in his ability to top Ruth.

Aaron's last season with the Braves coincided with the club's drafting and signing of his eventual successor. Dale Murphy was a high-school catcher in Portland, Ore. when the Braves made him the fifth overall selection in the 1974 amateur draft. Initially regarded as "the next Johnny Bench" because of his great power as both a hitter and a thrower, Murphy was still a catcher when he reached the big leagues. He even caught a one-hitter by Niekro in 1979.

But Murphy developed a catcher's version of Steve Blass disease—a phobia about throwing the ball back to the pitcher. In addition, his bad knees were not suited to the constant squatting and up-and-down movements required by the position. He moved to first base briefly, then blossomed into an All-Star after becoming an outfielder—first in left, then in center, and eventually in right, where the team could take advantage of his powerful throwing arm.

Manager Bobby Cox, the man who moved Murphy to the outfield in 1980, wasn't around to reap the benefits when the slugging tandem of Murphy and third baseman Bob Horner led the Braves to the 1982 NL West title.

At the press conference announcing the ouster of the popular Cox, club owner Ted Turner concocted one of the best quotes of his colorful career. "If Bobby Cox weren't the man being fired," he said, "he'd be the best man for the job."

Cox, whose first term as manager stretched from 1978–81, proved Turner right during his second stint, which started in 1990. In between, he spent four years as manager of the Toronto Blue Jays and five as general manager of the Braves, building the foundation of the ballclub that would blossom into baseball's best team of the '90s.

For manager in 1982, however, the Braves reached into their past to bring back Joe Torre, whom they had traded to the Cardinals for Orlando Cepeda during 1969 spring training after a salary dispute. The former slugger, who caught Warren Spahn's 300th victory in 1961, had spent the previous five years managing the New York Mets.

Torre's main contribution to the Braves was convincing Murphy he could be far more productive by abandoning his pull-hitting style and using all fields. Murphy proved him right by immediately winning consecutive MVP awards under Torre, who had won the award himself while playing for the 1971 Cardinals.

A durable performer who enjoyed his best years in center, Murphy led the National League in home runs, RBI, and slugging twice each. He played all 162 games four years in a row, won five Gold Gloves for defensive excellence, and made the All-Star team seven times. A devout Mormon known for his soft-spoken demeanor, he even won fans in rival dugouts and ballparks.

But he usually let his bat speak for him. In 1982, the year the Braves opened with a 13-game winning streak (a record later tied by the Milwaukee Brewers), Murphy tied for the league lead with 109 RBIs, hit 36 homers to finish one short of league-leader Dave Kingman, won his first Gold Glove, and stole 23 bases.

He became Atlanta's first 30/30 man a year later with 36 homers, 30 steals, a league-best 121 RBIs, a club-record 113 runs scored, and a .302 batting average. With 21 of 24 first-place votes—a better margin than he'd had the year before— Murphy became the fourth NL player to win consecutive MVPs (Ernie Banks, Joe Morgan, and Mike Schmidt had done it previously and Barry Bonds has done it since).

With Horner idled by a broken wrist on August 15, Murphy nearly carried the club by himself. But the Dodgers proved too strong and the Braves finished second, three games behind.

He didn't let down in '84 either, hitting 36 homers for the third straight year, leading the league in total bases and slugging, and finishing third in runs batted in. Had the Cubs not won a surprise divisional title in the NL East, Murphy might have won an unprecedented third straight MVP. Instead, the award went to Chicago's Ryne Sandberg.

Atlanta's chances to reach the playoffs had evaporated on May 29 when Horner, the brawny but brittle slugger who never played in the minors, broke his wrist again. The team also missed Niekro, its long-time pitching ace. With only Rick Mahler and Pascual Perez to lead the staff, Atlanta tied for second, 12 games off the pace. Torre, the fall guy, got the ax and the team's free-fall, which had started as a simple snowball, became an avalanche.

Even Murphy, with 37 homers in '85 and a career-peak 44 two years later, couldn't stop the slide. His power production declined for three straight years before he was finally traded to Philadelphia on August 4, 1990. After spending his entire 15-year career in Atlanta, Murphy missed playing in the World Series by only one year.

The '70s and '80s

The Braves of the late '80s were like the Braves of the late '70s—with one important difference. Though teams of both decades lost embarrassing numbers of games, the Bobby Cox administration was spending its dollars on player development rather than over-the-hill free agents.

From 1976–79, Atlanta finished last four years in a row. Things got so bad that Turner—hoping to stop a 16-game losing streak—made himself manager on May 11, 1977. Incumbent Dave Bristol was sent on an alleged scouting mission, while the outspoken television magnate took a seat in the dugout. Atlanta lost anyway, 2–1, and NL president Chub Feeney ended the episode by finding a rule that prohibited managers from owning stock in their teams.

Bristol returned for the remainder of the season but lost his job in September after the team finished with a 61–101 record, its worst since the Braves created their own depression in 1935.

Atlanta's average annual attendance during the '70s was 851,916, worst in the National League. But those who did show helped Rico Carty become the first write-in candidate to crack the All-Star lineup; saw San Diego's Nate Colbert tie Stan Musial's record with five same-day home runs; and witnessed Aaron's 715th home run.

Although Native Americans might not agree, the most respectable promotion of the period was the performance of Chief Noc-a-Homa, an Indian who did a pregame victory dance on the mound, raced to his teepee in the bleachers, and reappeared for war whoops after every home-team home run.

The teepee had been a fixture in Milwaukee too but never encountered the trouble it had in both of the team's first two title seasons. In 1969, it caught fire when a smoke bomb used to create celebratory smoke signals for a home run ignited the canvas. The Indian occupant tried to douse the flames with beer, Coke, other beverages and even a broom but finally had to use an extinguisher. In 1982, management removed the teepee to create additional seating room during the team's title drive in August. The Braves immediately lost 19 of their next 21 and plunged 10½ games in the standings before superstitious fans demanded and received its restoration.

During the 1970s, however, Noc-a-Homa had little to cheer about. Among those acquired by Atlanta during that dark age were pitchers Denny McLain, Blue Moon Odom, Gary Gentry, Andy Messersmith, and Mike Marshall and sluggers Jim Wynn, Willie Montanez, Gary Matthews, and Jeff Burroughs. Most had seen their best years long before they arrived in Atlanta.

Desperate for pitching help, the Braves even brought *Ball Four* author Jim Bouton back to the big leagues for the first time in eight years. The one-time Yankee star had developed a decent knuckleball but won only one of his five starts for the '78 Braves before his career was back in mothballs for keeps.

In fact, the only good pitchers on the staff that year were Niekro, who had only a 19–18 record despite a 2.88 ERA (the Braves were blanked in his last three starts), and bearded closer Gene Garber. On August 1, rookie lefty Larry McWilliams teamed with Garber to end the 44-game hitting streak of Cincinnati's Pete Rose. Disappointed that he wouldn't be able to continue his pursuit of the record 56-game streak by Joe DiMaggio, Rose blamed McWilliams and Garber for pitching "like it was the seventh game of the World Series."

For them, it was. Except for Horner's home run off Bert Blyleven in his first big-league game on June 16, the team had few other highlights. Horner later became the first man to win College Player of the Year and Rookie of the Year honors in the same season.

The following season, Niekro led the league with 44 starts, 23 complete games, 342 innings pitched, and 21 victories to accompany his 3.39 ERA. But he also led the league with 20 losses, four more than Garber, whose 1979 loss total remains a record for a relief pitcher.

Atlanta's pitching and defense both ranked last in the league but help was on the way. Trade acquisitions Chris Chambliss, a first baseman, and Doyle Alexander, a veteran righthanded pitcher, fueled the team's rise to fourth place, 11 games from the top, in 1980. The Braves also got 22 saves from Rick Camp, who had missed all of the previous year after elbow surgery. With Horner and Murphy combining for 68 homers, the Braves achieved their first plus .500 season since 1974.

Attendance broke the million mark again and things seemed to be on the upswing. But that was before a midyear player strike lasting seven weeks, plus Atlanta's sudden inability to hit, left the '81 team floundering and cost Cox his job. The Braves had added ancient pitcher Gaylord Perry and overrated outfielder Claudell Washington for '81 and, like Al Hrabosky and Andy Messersmith before them, they were overpaid and underproductive.

The 1982 team won, in part, because of solid contributions from rookies Brett Butler, a centerfielder, and Steve Bedrosian, a hard-throwing relief pitcher. Horner, Murphy, and Chambliss had big years, Washington contributed more than expected, and Niekro pitched like Superman down the stretch, notching his only shutouts in his final two starts. The combined 41 saves of Garber and Bedrosian gave the Braves an unbeatable bullpen.

But the Braves' starting pitching couldn't sustain the punishment of postseason play. When Niekro's 1–0 lead in the opener was washed away in the fifth—just three outs from becoming official—Atlanta's fate was sealed.

Pascual Perez lost to Bob Forsch, 7–0, in the "new" Game 1, while the weary Niekro left after six innings of Game 2 with a 3–2 lead. When Garber gave up the tying run in the ninth and winning run in the tenth, Atlanta faced an 0–2 deficit in the best-of-five series. It was settled the next day, when the Cardinals knocked Camp out of the box in the second inning. Atlanta would not return to postseason play until 1991—after years of careful rebuilding by Bobby Cox.

In 1985, the year he returned from exile in Toronto, the Braves finished fifth for rookie manager Eddie Haas. Unpopular for his many rules and regulations, Haas did not complete the season. But he was around for the strangest game in Braves' history.

On July 4, after an 84-minute rain delay at the start, the Mets and Braves played 19 innings in a game that included 45 hits, 23 walks, 22 strikeouts, five errors, 37 men left on base, and **615** pitches. Forty-three players saw action. There were also two more rain delays, adding to the eventual game time of eight hours, fifteen minutes.

The weather made short work of New York starter Dwight Gooden, en route to a 24–4 season that would earn him the NL's Cy Young Award. He left with a lead his bullpen couldn't hold.

In fact, both bullpens had bad nights. The Braves twice matched leads taken by the Mets in extra innings. The second time, in the eighteenth inning, they did it in a most unusual way. Reliever Rick Camp, who had allowed New York's lead run in the top half of the inning, came to bat with two men out, nobody on base, and nobody left on the bench to pinch hit. The game seemed lost, since Camp was one of the worst-hitting pitchers in baseball history (an .060 career average). He picked that moment, however, to hit the only home run of his eight-year career—on an 0–2 pitch to boot!

Running the bases for the first time apparently wore him out; the Mets battered Camp for a five-spot in the top of the nineteenth. The Braves almost pulled it out again, scoring twice and bringing the potential tying run to the plate. But Camp, whose spot in the order had come around again, reverted to form. The Mets won, 16–13.

With little other excitement that summer, Haas was probably glad to get away. The 1988 Braves went 54–106 for a woeful "winning" percentage of .338—only the sixth time in their century-plus of existence they had done that poorly. Most of the players were too old (Ted Simmons, Ken Griffey Sr.), too young (Tom Glavine, John Smoltz), or too brittle (Bruce Sutter), and the able-bodied could hardly field their positions (Ozzie Virgil, Lonnie Smith). The double-play combination of Ron Gant, a rookie slugger playing out of position at second base, and Andres Thomas was an embarrassment. The Braves finished last in on-base percentage, runs scored, stolen bases, and saves but first in errors.

Chuck Tanner, probably the most optimistic manager in baseball history, was fired in midseason for the first time in his 18-year dugout career. A former outfielder who had homered in his first big-league at-bat for the 1955 Milwaukee Braves, Tanner had been wildly successful as a manager with both the White Sox and Pirates. But Atlanta proved to be his Waterloo.

When former catcher Russ Nixon fared no better during two years on the job, Cox came back for his second stint at the request of team president Stan Kasten. With his previously demonstrated integrity and cordial relations with players, fans, and media, Cox now became the beneficiary of his own player development system.

The Glory Years

The 1990 season turned out to be a washout as early as April. First baseman Nick Esasky, an expensive free-agent slugger, failed to knock in a single run during a nine-game Atlanta career ended by a devastating attack of vertigo. He was through at age 30. Projected closer Mike Stanton, a 23-year-old lefty who had blazed his way through the farm system the year before, also spent the year on the sidelines—thanks to a serious shoulder injury that limited him to seven innings of work.

Of those who could play, nobody could catch the ball. As a result, rookie lefty Steve Avery went 3–11 with a 5.64 earned run average and Glavine, the previous year's ace, managed only a 10–12 record and 4.28 ERA in his fourth season. But hope was starting to peek over the horizon.

David Justice, a lefthanded hitter with a sweet swing, took Dale Murphy's right-field job in August and delivered 20 home runs over the final two months, an outburst that earned him Rookie of the Year honors. Gant liked his switch to the outfield so much that he delivered a .300 average and 30/30 season. And Smoltz, a 23-year-old righthander whose slider complemented his blazing fastball, blossomed into a 14-game winner.

Though it finished last for the third straight year and fourth in the last five, the team did improve its winning percentage. And it played better baseball for Cox (.412) than it had for the outspoken Nixon (.385). During his five-year stint as an executive, Cox had planted the seeds for historic seasons to come. He had also realized the chance to nurture them to maturity.

Asked to choose between his two jobs at the end of the 1990 campaign, Cox chose to stay in uniform. With the general manager's chair vacant, the Braves selected John Schuerholz after a lengthy search. The Cox-Schuerholz combine turned out to be a match made in baseball heaven.

"The strength of the club when I got there was clearly pitching," Schuerholz said. "What we tried to do was upgrade the defense. If you have better defense, good pitchers can make good pitches and know guys will catch the ball.

"We especially wanted to improve the infield defense. By signing Terry Pendleton, Rafael Belliard, and Sid Bream, we did that. We also added some speed to the ballclub with Otis Nixon, and he played good defense for us in center field."

Schuerholz signed a total of seven free agents, also adding catcher Mike Heath, outfielder Deion Sanders, and pitcher Juan Berenguer.

"We didn't think we had a choice," admitted Schuerholz, who came to Atlanta after spending nine years in a similar position with the Kansas City Royals. "We knew we had to make dramatic changes in the way the team was structured. We felt like whatever we did—assuming we did our homework right and used good judgment—we would clearly improve the ballclub by one degree or another. We certainly didn't expect that we would be able to create a roster that went from worst to first, but we knew we would be better. We also knew we would improve immediately."

At the All-Star break, the Braves stood third, nine-and-a-half games behind the front-running Los Angeles Dodgers. But it wasn't long before Atlanta bypassed struggling Cincinnati and made the National League West a two-team race.

After eleven ties or lead changes during the closing weeks of the campaign, the Braves finally clinched on the next-to-last day. When they also won a seven-game National League Championship Series against the favored Pittsburgh Pirates, the Braves became the first team in NL history to jump from last place one year to first place the next.

The turnaround took a lot of planning—plus multiple gambles. "It was a challenge getting things together, but it wasn't a challenge in terms of the ability that was here," Schuerholz says. "This organization had been signing and developing players. The pipeline was filled with talented young people, all coming to the major leagues at one time. The nucleus for a championship was already in place. What Bobby and I had to do was find some missing pieces and parts that would fit properly with the guys we already had."

Cox agreed. "We invested big into the farm system, hired more scouts, signed more players, and didn't lose anyone due to lack of money or anything like that," said the manager. "Even in 1990, we knew we had good pitching but didn't have anybody who could catch it behind them. That's when John came in and picked up Bream, Belliard, and Pendleton, and then added Otis Nixon the next spring. The defense made our pitching and we've been strong ever since."

Trading Dale Murphy, the two-time MVP, generated considerable controversy for Cox before the booming bat of David Justice silenced the critics. "It had to be done," Cox said. "Murf had been a fixture in Atlanta for years but it was just time to make a decision. David was a rightfielder and had to play. Fortunately, it worked out well for us."

Force-feeding the young pitchers was also a source of controversy for Cox—especially for fans who had watched Glavine post a 7–17 season and Smoltz struggle through a 2–7 log during the dismal Summer of 1988.

"It wasn't that they pitched that bad," says Cox, who denies the youngsters were rushed. "If our club had been a little better behind them, their stats would have been much better. I thought they pitched well and got their feet wet. I thought it was good for them."

The Free Agents

What was really good for them was the addition of Terry Pendleton, who replaced the good-hit, no-field Jim Presley at third base. Since Pendleton had hit only .230 with six homers for St. Louis the previous year, the market for his services was limited. But the Braves knew he could still supply strong defense.

According to Schuerholz, "Nobody expected him to go from .230 to .330 as a hitter. But we liked his professionalism, his work ethic, his winning spirit, and the way he handled himself professionally all along the way in his career. He was not only a real pro but an excellent defensive third baseman—that was one of the primary things we were looking for. He fit the bill for us."

Pendleton's performance, more than any other factor, put the Braves over the top. He not only played the best third base of his career but led the league with a career-high .319 batting average and 187 hits, 22 of them home runs. He was rewarded with the Most Valuable Player Award.

"Terry certainly did better than what was expected of him," said Cox. "We never thought we were signing the MVP or batting champion. But he won the award in '91 and was runner-up the following year. That was pretty darn good for a guy who was considered to be just about washed up."

Only the Yankees and Braves pursued Pendleton, who preferred to stay in the National League. "We didn't think he was through at all," Cox recalled. "Terry had hit a lot of balls to the track in St. Louis and we kept track of those. There were 22 in one year that would have been home runs in Atlanta if you figure out the dimensions. We obviously thought he had some hitting skills left. Even if he didn't and hit only .260, that would have been fine too because we needed his defense."

Although his Atlanta tenure was relatively short (four years), Pendleton still ranks near the top of the list when experts discuss the best free-agent signings of all time. "He could be No. 1," Cox conceded.

The 1991 signees also helped the team off the field. "All the guys we brought in had played in winning programs," Schuerholz points out. "Terry had played in St. Louis, and Sid and Raffy had played for winning teams in Pittsburgh. Those guys knew how to win. While they were playing well and contributing on the field, it was also important to have them in the clubhouse, leading the way with their mannerisms and professionalism. It was impressive for our young guys to see how they went about their work."

Like Pendleton, Nixon was a defensive standout whose sudden improvement at the plate was an added bonus. "We went after him for his defensive capabilities and speed," says Schuerholz. "Pitching, defense, and speed were our three components. The fact that Otis hit better was a tribute to him and our coaches for working with him. He really got to be a smarter player and learned to utilize the skills he had better through working with our coaching staff."

The changes worked wonders. Pendleton replaced Presley at third, Belliard succeeded Andres Thomas at short, and Bream replaced a 1990 first-base rotation that had included Tommy Gregg, Francisco Cabrera, Mike Bell, Jody Davis, Presley, and even Justice. With Nixon in center, Gant shifted to left, supplanting Lonnie Smith.

Pendleton, Justice, and Gant—enjoying his second straight 30/30 campaign—supplied the bulk of the offense, while Nixon, a .228 lifetime hitter acquired from Montreal during spring training, surprised with a .297 mark and club-record 72 stolen bases.

As predicted, the stronger defense bolstered the pitching. Atlanta's team ERA dropped from 4.58 to 3.49 and the won-lost record jumped from 65–97 in 1990 to 94–68. Glavine won 20 games and the Cy Young Award, while Avery won 18, veteran Charlie Leibrandt posted 15, and Smoltz turned a 2–11 start into a 12–2 finish after consulting a sports psychologist. He pitched the division clincher, the pennant clincher, and what could have been the World Series clincher, absent Jack Morris.

The young starters developed new-found confidence in their veteran bullpen. Once again, Atlanta scouts had seen things others didn't. But Berenguer, 36, and Pena, 32, didn't let age interfere with performance: Berenguer, never a closer before, and late-season trade acquisition Alejandro Pena, previously a middle man, combined for 28 saves.

"Juan came in and did a job," Schuerholz remembered. "He did exactly what he had to do. It seemed like every time we needed a relief pitcher that year, the one we got at the time was the one we needed. When we needed to replace Juan to improve the bullpen, Pena was available. He hadn't pitched much for the Mets, who had relegated him to a deep bullpen role. But our guys liked the way he threw. He came in and did a great job for us— he was a lifesaver. He became a dominant closer for the short time he was with us."

The pitching seemed to improve as the season wore on. There were three 1–0 games in the playoffs, marked by Atlanta's uncanny ability to hold Pittsburgh scoreless over its final 27 innings at Three Rivers Stadium. Avery, at 21 the baby of the staff, won his final five to finish 18–8, then pitched a record 16⅓ scoreless innings against the Pirates to win playoff MVP honors.

In the World Series against the Minnesota Twins—the American League's first worst-to-first team—the Braves endured three extra-inning games, four that went down to the final pitch, and five one-run decisions. Game 7 went ten innings before the Twins pushed across the only run.

An eighth-inning baserunning blunder by Lonnie Smith proved crucial. After stroking a leadoff single against Minnesota ace Jack Morris, Smith could have scored when Pendleton followed with a drive into the left-field corner. But he saw neither the ball nor the frantic arm-waving of Atlanta third-base coach Jimy Williams. Instead, Smith saw a perfectly executed decoy by Minnesota's rookie second baseman Chuck Knoblauch.

Smith's hesitation enabled him only to reach third, while the bewildered Pendleton, running behind him, was forced to stop at second. Both men held while Gant grounded out and Justice was intentionally passed. Sid Bream than banged into an inning-ending double-play. It was the first extra-inning Game 7 since 1924 and the first with a 1–0 score since 1962.

Back to the World Series

Determined to reach the World Series again, the 1992 Braves again relied on a combination of pitching, power, and speed. After overcoming their usual lethargic start (a 20–27 record, seven games off the pace, on May 26), the team caught fire, winning nearly 75 per cent of its games over the next three months. Both the Braves and Glavine had 13-game winning streaks, the former tying the 1982 club record and the latter establishing a new twentieth century team standard.

En route to a 98-win season, a modern club record that would fall the next year, the Braves led the league with 138 home runs and a 3.14 ERA. With Pittsburgh the playoff opponent again, Atlanta took the first two games at home, 5–1 and 13–5. But rookie knuckleballer Tim

Wakefield outpitched Glavine to win Game 3, 3–2. Smoltz beat Pirate ace Doug Drabek for the second time, 6–4 in the fifth game, but the Pirates stunned Avery—the Game 2 winner and 1991 hero—with a first-inning knockout the next night. With journeyman Bob Walk working a three-hitter on the Pittsburgh side, another Glavine-Wakefield match was set for Game 6.

The Atlanta lefthander, who had started his second consecutive All-Star Game three months earlier (the first to do that since Robin Roberts in 1954-55), was not up to the task. Pitching with a slow-healing cracked rib, he had lost five of his last six regular-season starts and had not been especially sharp in Game 3, yielding seven hits, three walks, and a hit batsmen in 6⅓ innings.

He was even worse in Game 6, surrendering six hits and eight runs (seven earned) while hitting a batter without retiring a batter, in a nightmarish second inning. Wakefield, touched only for two home runs by Justice, cruised to a complete-game, 13–4 victory.

When Drabek took a 2–0 shutout into the ninth inning of Game 7, media members covering the game voted Wakefield the NLCS MVP. But they hadn't counted on Atlanta's capacity for coming back.

After Pendleton's leadoff double, Justice grounded to Jose Lind, normally a sure-handed second baseman. But he bobbled the ball, allowing Justice to reach and upsetting Drabek so much that he walked Bream. Pittsburgh manager Jim Leyland decided he's seen enough and summoned closer Stan Belinda.

Gant's long smash to left looked like it might clear the fence for a pennant-winning grand-slam but Barry Bonds hauled it in, converting the shot into a sacrifice fly. Damon Berryhill walked, reloading the bases but creating the strong possibility of a double play that would give Pittsburgh the pennant.

Power-hitting Brian Hunter, a productive pinch hitter against lefthanders, needed only a fly ball to tie the game. Instead, he popped out to second against the righthanded Belinda. With reliever Jeff Reardon due to bat, Bobby Cox turned to the last man on the bench, backup catcher Francisco Cabrera.

A free-swinging righthanded hitter who had spent most of the year at Atlanta's Richmond farm club, Cabrera was also used most often against lefties. But he was a fastball hitter with a demonstrated flair for the dramatic: his two-out, three-run, ninth-inning homer against hard-throwing Cincinnati closer Rob Dibble during the 1991 stretch drive had tied a game the Braves eventually won. He'd also hit two home runs and a single during 10 regular-season at-bats in 1992.

Exercising enormous patience, Cabrera let the count drift to 2 –1. A walk would tie the game but the entire ballpark knew Cabrera was itching to swing at the first decent offering. He did, serving a single to left on a Belinda fastball, scoring Justice and sending Bream—the slowest runner on the team—toward a date with destiny.

The throw from Bonds arrived in time for catcher Mike LaValliere to try a swipe tag, but Bream touched the corner of the plate first. Skip Caray went ballistic behind the radio mike, shouting, "Braves win! Braves win! Braves win!" It was easily the most dramatic moment in the history of the Atlanta Braves.

By contrast, the World Series was almost anticlimactic.

Glavine, recovered from his mauling in NLCS Game 6 four days earlier, beat Toronto with a 3–1 four-hitter in the opener. Then the Jays exploited Atlanta's shaky bullpen, tying Game 2 in the ninth and winning it in the tenth, 5–4, and winning Game 3 by pushing across a run in the bottom of the ninth to win by a score of 3–2. Reardon, far removed from his prime as one of baseball's best late-inning relievers, served up both game-winning hits.

When Jimmy Key outpitched Glavine, 2–1, in Game 4, the Braves were in serious trouble. They staved off the inevitable when the arm of Smoltz and the bat of Lonnie Smith (grand-slam home run) beat Jack Morris, who had joined Toronto as a free agent, in Game 5. But David Cone and six relievers outlasted Avery and four others, 4–3 in eleven innings, enabling the Blue Jays to bring the World Series trophy north of the border for the first time.

For the second year in a row, regular starter Charlie Leibrandt had lost Game 6 of the World Series in an extra-inning relief role. But Bobby Cox had no one else he could trust.

Leibrandt would not pitch for Atlanta again. Minutes after the Braves secured the signature of free agent Greg Maddux on a five-year, $28 million contract in December, they sent Leibrandt to the Texas Rangers for minor-league slugger Jose Oliva. Although Leibrandt had won 15 games for the 1992 Braves, Maddux would win 20 the next year—and the Braves would need every one of them.

Close but No Cigar

When the Braves had last seen Barry Bonds, he was sitting in left field with his head buried in his cupped hands, stunned by Atlanta's ninth-inning uprising in the final game of the 1992 NLCS. He knew he had just played his last game for the Pirates, who could not afford to match the offers the star outfielder would receive as a free agent.

After San Francisco secured his services with a six-year, $42 million deal that including the hiring of his father Bobby as hitting coach, Bonds went west. His third MVP season—and second in succession—was almost enough to put the Giants into the playoffs. Only a sensational second-half rally by the Braves prevented it.

Even with Glavine headed toward his third straight 20-win season and Maddux en route toward his second straight Cy Young Award, the Braves had trouble keeping pace with the Giants. Their usual slow start didn't help.

Sensing he needed a star even to think about catching San Francisco, John Schuerholz sent three prospects to San Diego for slugging first baseman Fred McGriff on July 18. The minute he showed up two days later, both the pressbox and the ballclub caught fire. A McGriff homer in his first game helped turn a 5–0 deficit into an 8–5 victory and the Braves realized, for the first time, that they had a chance. But it was a longshot, at best.

Ten games behind on July 22, they went 51–17 (a .750 percentage) with McGriff to finish with a franchise-record 104 victories, enough for a one-game margin of victory over the Giants. Only a San Francisco loss to Los Angeles on the last day of the season prevented a one-game divisional playoff in Candlestick Park.

After winning five of six from San Francisco in a home-and-away series that started in late August, Atlanta finally caught the Giants on September 10. The streaking Braves took advantage of a San Francisco slump to ease into a four-game lead but had given it all back by September 28.

An Atlanta loss and San Francisco win on that date left the teams tied. The next day, the Braves won and the Giants lost, putting the Braves up by one. On September 30, however, Atlanta lost to Houston again while San Francisco beat Colorado to forge a tie heading into the final weekend.

The Braves beat the Rockies twice while the Giants won two in a row from Los Angeles, keeping the tie intact with one day left. But the Dodgers, remembering how the Giants had whooped it up after their last-day win over L.A. had swung the 1982 title to Atlanta, were determined to wreak revenge on their arch-rivals.

Journeyman pitcher Kevin Gross did the job, as Glavine completed the sweep of the Rockies for his career-best 22nd victory. The Giants had won 14 of their last 18 but it wasn't enough. They went home for the winter with 103 wins but no postseason invitation. This fact helped to instigate reform of the playoff structure, ultimately scheduled to commence in 1994.

Atlanta had led the league with 169 home runs and a 3.14 team ERA while finishing second in defense with a .983 percentage. Maddux and Glavine gave the Braves their first pair of 20-game winners since Spahn and Burdette in 1959, while McGriff, Justice, and Gant topped 100 RBIs each—the first time three Braves had done that in a season since Aaron, Carty, and Cepeda in 1970.

The Braves even had four 15-game winners (Maddux, Glavine, Avery, and Smoltz) for the first time this century and a .300-hitting shortstop (Jeff Blauser) for the first time since Alvin Dark was NL Rookie of the Year for the Boston Braves of 1948.

Turnstiles cranked at a record pace (3,884,720) and the Braves won the more games than any of the 27 other clubs. But the day-to-day pressure of the last "pure" pennant race had taken the wind out of their sails, and it was the Phillies, not the Braves, who advanced to the World Series. For the second straight time, the Braves outscored their postseason opponent but still managed to lose. (In 1992, Atlanta had scored 20 runs, four more than Toronto, but lost the six-game World Series by dropping four one-run games.)

In 1993 the Braves scored more runs than Philadelphia (33–23) and produced far better pitching (3.15 ERA vs. Philly's 4.75). But three one-run losses contributed to another six-game defeat. Again, the culprit was the bullpen.

After losing the ten-inning opener, 4-3, the Braves rebounded for 14-3 and 9-4 victories. A rare error by Mark Lemke handed the Phils two unearned runs—and a 2-1 victory over Smoltz—in Game 4. One night later, relievers Greg McMichael and Mark Wohlers threw gasoline onto the fire by yielding late solo gopherballs, giving Philadelphia another 4-3 win that went ten innings. Atlanta had tied the first and fifth games with ninth-inning rallies, only to watch its bullpen blow both games anyway.

With Maddux on the mound for Game 6 at Veterans Stadium and Glavine slated to work the next night, the Braves knew they still had a good chance. But that began to change after light-hitting Mickey Morandini smashed a line drive off Maddux's leg in the first inning.

Normally a control artist who yields few runs, hits, or walks, Maddux pitched like a Goliath struck by David's slingshot. In just 5⅔ innings, he gave up six runs, two of them on a Dave Hollins homer, six hits, and four walks. Philadelphia, with the third-best record in the National League, subsequently lost a six-game World Series to Toronto while the Braves wondered what went wrong.

Part of their problem was a misguided divisional alignment that paid no attention to geographical realities. Chicago and St. Louis should have been in the NL West from the start, with Cincinnati and Atlanta in the National League East. But the New York Mets had refused to agree to the original proposal for divisional alignment after the 1968 campaign unless the St. Louis Cardinals—then the reigning NL champions—were in their division. Since the Cards and Cubs were traditional rivals, the Braves and Reds agreed to go into the NL West on an "experimental" basis. That experiment, like the American League's 1973 introduction of the designated hitter, lasted more than two dozen years.

When the leagues split into three divisions, however, the NL's early mistake was rectified. Atlanta went into the five-team National League East, Cincinnati was placed in a five-team Central Division, and the four NL West teams breathed a collective sigh of relief that the Braves were gone.

The league's new "balanced" schedule meant the Braves would play virtually an equal number of games against each opponent, a far cry from the two-division format that involved 18 games against intra-divisional rivals but only 12 against opposite-division clubs.

All those years in the same division with the Dodgers, Giants, Astros, and Reds may have deprived the Braves of several divisional crowns. Whenever the West was strong or the East was weak, Braves fans chafed under the NL's operating arrangement.

Pitching Is the Future for Atlanta

The Braves' fortunes changed in the 1990s because management finally realized, early in the Bobby Cox regime as general manager, that pitching is more important than power—even in a ballpark once known as "the Launching Pad."

The organization started stockpiling quality arms, drafting Kent Mercker in 1986 and both Steve Avery and Mark Wohlers in 1988, acquiring little-known Double-A righthander John Smoltz from Detroit in 1987, and adding Pedro Borbon, Jr. (1989) and Greg McMichael (1991) from other organizations. By the mid-'90s, all those moves had paid off. A team that once tried to outslug its opponents suddenly found it more satisfying to outpitch them.

Atlanta's pitching was so powerful in 1994 that fans were convinced the team would finally win its first World Series since 1957. The Braves won 13 of their first 14 games, but then struggled, slipping six games behind the Montreal Expos by the time the player strike froze the schedule on August 12.

Fred McGriff became the ninth man to produce seven straight 30-homer seasons, rookie regulars Javy Lopez and Ryan Klesko brought bright hopes for the future, and Maddux led the league with 202 innings, 10 complete games, and 16 wins (tying Montreal's Ken Hill). He also started the All-Star Game, won by the National League, 8–7 in ten innings, after McGriff hit a titanic two-run, game-tying pinch-homer off Lee Smith with one out in the bottom of the ninth. McGriff became the first Brave ever named All-Star MVP.

But individual heroics weren't enough to keep the Braves in first place. The team's changing of the guard had become painfully obvious: before the season even started, Bream, Berryhill, and Nixon became free agents, Cabrera split for Japan, and Gant was released after suffering a compound fracture of his right leg in a February motorcycle accident.

Still, the Braves were closer to the top when the strike stopped play than they had been on the same date the year before. Had the walkout not wiped out the last seven weeks, as well as the postseason, Atlanta might have made its usual late-summer rush.

Series Rings Before Olympic Rings

That's exactly what happened in 1995 after the players came back, ending the longest work stoppage in the history of professional sports after 232 days. The one thing the Braves hadn't foreseen was angry fan reaction. Glavine, whose vocal defense of the Players Association had made him a frequent uninvited visitor to Atlanta living rooms via TV and radio, was even booed on Opening Day for the first time.

Only a World Championship season could quiet the critics. The 1995 Braves rose to the occasion.

Still, the twice-burned fans were reluctant to throw the team their full support. When Justice knocked them in the newspaper before World Series Game 6, one showed up at the park with a plaque that read, "Justice: Hope Your Bat's as Big as Your Mouth."

It was. The rightfielder smacked the game-winning homer, Glavine pitched a one-hitter for eight innings, and the bullpen didn't blow the lead. Atlanta saluted its first World Champions with a ticker-tape parade that drew 750,000 fans into the streets. Atlanta was in love with its Braves again.

The Braves moved into the second half of the decade as the most powerful team in the major leagues, loaded with pitching, power, and a productive farm system. They planned to move into their new downtown stadium after the 1996 Olympics and make as many memories there as they had in their three previous ballparks.

Designed to resemble the grand old fields of another age, the newest stadium in the majors will house the oldest team. The bronze Hank Aaron statue that stood for years at the entrance to Fulton County Stadium will grace its plaza and there will be ample room inside to display retired uniform numbers.

For a team with such a rich history, that is a top priority.

CHAPTER 3

The Braves in Postseason Play

Frederick Ivor-Campbell

The tradition of major league postseason play traces back to 1871, the first year there was a professional league. National Association teams in the 1870s typically followed the conclusion of their championship (regularly scheduled) season with exhibition games against amateur clubs. In the 1880s nearly every major league club played a couple of weeks of postseason games, generally against major- and minor-league teams they hadn't faced during the regular season. In the twentieth century there had been (until 1994) a World Series every year for ninety years, prefaced since 1969 by League Championship Series to determine the American and National League winners. In 1995 a new round of championship play came into being, the Divisional Playoffs.

The early World Series had their beginnings in 1884. Two years earlier, the champions of the National League and the brand-new American Association played a pair of postseason contests (in which each team recorded a shutout against the other). Some would like to call these games the first World Series, but no one in 1882 saw them as more than exhibition games. In fact, because the NL didn't yet recognize the legitimacy of the AA and forbade its clubs to play those of the new league, the NL champion Chicago White Stockings had to release their players from their season contracts so they could face AA champion Cincinnati as technically independent players.

That winter the two major leagues made their peace, and although a proposed series between the 1883 NL and AA titlists was called off, the 1884 champion Providence Grays (NL) and the Metropolitan Club of New York (AA) played three games "for the championship of the United States." The winning Grays were acclaimed in the press as "champions of the world," and the World Series was born.

The brief 1884 Series set the stage for more elaborate World Series to follow. From 1885 through 1890 the NL and AA pennant-winners met in Series that ranged in length from six games to fifteen.

The demise of the AA after the 1891 season caused a one-year gap in World Series play. When the National League expanded from eight clubs to twelve the next year (by absorbing four teams from the defunct AA), it divided the regular season into two halves, with the first-half winner playing the winner of the second half for the world title. Boston defeated Cleveland in the first official World Series, but the unpopular divided season was not repeated (that is, until the strike year of 1981).

Two years later a new World Series scheme was devised when one William C. Temple offered a prize cup to the winner of a postseason series between the first- and second-place finishers in the NL. For four years these best-of-seven Temple Cup games served as the officially recognized world championship. But by the end of four lopsided Series (only one of which was won by the pennant-winning club), fan interest—never robust—had declined so much that the trophy was returned to its donor and the series abandoned.

The upgrading of the American League from minor- to major-league status in 1901 made a return to interleague World Series play theoretically possible, but it was not until after the NL and AL had made peace in 1903 that the first modern Series was contested. The owners of NL champion Pittsburgh and AL champion Boston arranged a best-of-nine postseason Series in 1903, which proved both popular and financially successful—a firm foundation for future Series.

Key to the Statistics

The statistics in this section of *Total Braves* are standard—there is little point in applying newer analytical measures to performances that run to seven games or fewer. We do offer, however, stats that were not standard at the time, such as earned run averages for years before 1912 and runs batted in before 1920 (which were determined from box scores and play-by-plays) and saves before 1969. We present the cumulative box score for each Braves World Series in accordance with modern practice.

The length of the World Series varied from three games in 1884 all the way up to fifteen in 1887 and ten the following year. The best-of-seven format came in with the Temple Cup Series of 1894 and has been the norm for World Series ever since (excepting 1900, 1903, and 1919–1921). In recent years this format has become the norm for League Championship Series as well. The new Playoffs are best-of-five.

If a player appeared at more than one position during the Series, the number of games he played at each is noted (for example, a man who divided seven games at shortstop and third base would carry the notation *ss-4, 3b-3*). Other abbreviations are as follows:

POS	Position	SB	Stolen Bases
AVG	Batting average	W	Wins
G	Games	L	Losses
AB	At bats	ERA	Earned run average
R	Runs	GS	Games started
H	Hits	CG	Complete games
2B	Doubles	SHO	Shutouts
3B	Triples	SV	Saves
HR	Home runs	IP	Innings pitched
RB	Runs batted in	ER	Earned runs
BB	Bases on Balls	SO	Strikeouts

Interleague squabbling prevented a World Series in 1891, and the AA folded before the next season. Four AA clubs were taken into the NL, expanding the NL to twelve teams. To create a postseason championship series, the regular season was divided in half, with first-half winner Boston meeting second-half victor Cleveland for both the league and world titles.

The first game, in Cleveland, was a pitching and fielding classic. Boston's Jack Stivetts and Cleveland's Cy Young blanked the opposition for eleven innings before darkness halted the game. Young yielded just six hits and Stivetts four—all singles. Just as remarkable in an era when errors were commonplace, Cleveland committed only one and Boston none; several outstanding plays were made in the field.

Boston center fielder Hugh Duffy was the offensive and defensive star of Game Two. He drove in three of the Beaneaters' four runs (with a fly out, a triple, and a double), and scored the fourth himself after tripling a second time. And in the bottom of the ninth he snared a leadoff liner with a great running catch. As it was, Cleveland scored once in the inning to pull within a run of a tie; Duffy's catch prevented a certain tie and a possible Cleveland win. Game Three was just as close. Pitchers Stivetts and Young each gave up two early runs, but then blanked their foes until the seventh inning, when Boston's Tommy McCarthy singled in Stivetts (who had doubled) with what proved the winning run.

The Series moved to Boston for the next three games. In Game Four, Boston ace Kid Nichols shut out the Spiders, scattering seven hits and fanning eight. Cleveland's Nig Cuppy yielded only six hits, but one was a home run ball to Hugh Duffy for two runs in the third inning, and another was a two-run single to Joe Quinn in the sixth. Cleveland pitcher John Clarkson helped his own cause the next day with a three-run homer in the Spider's six-run second inning. But Boston pitcher Jack Stivetts—with the score now 7–5 Cleveland in the sixth—tripled in a run and scored the tying run. In the seventh, Stivetts scored Boston's twelfth (and final) run after singling, while holding Cleveland scoreless through the final four innings.

Two days later the Beaneaters brought the Series to an end with their fifth straight win. The Spiders scored first, with a three-run third, but pitcher Kid Nichols held them

scoreless after that and singled home Boston's tying and go-ahead runs himself as the Beaneaters tagged Cy Young for eight runs over the final six innings.

Boston Beaneaters, 5; Cleveland Spiders, 0; tie, 1

BOS (N)

PLAYER/POS	AVG	G	AB	R	H	2B	3B	HR	RB	BB	SO	SB
Charlie Bennett, c	.286	2	7	2	2	0	0	1	1	0	2	1
Hugh Duffy, of	.462	6	26	3	12	3	2	1	9	1	0	3
Charlie Ganzel, c	.500	2	8	1	4	0	0	0	2	1	0	0
King Kelly, c	.000	2	8	0	0	0	0	0	0	0	2	1
Herman Long, ss	.222	6	27	4	6	0	0	0	1	0	0	2
Bobby Lowe, of	.130	6	23	8	3	0	0	0	0	1	2	1
Tommy McCarthy, of	.381	6	21	2	8	2	0	0	2	6	1	3
Billy Nash, 3b	.167	6	24	3	4	0	0	0	4	2	3	2
Kid Nichols, p	.286	2	7	1	2	0	0	0	2	0	1	1
Joe Quinn, 2b	.286	6	21	2	6	1	1	0	4	1	2	0
Harry Staley, p	.000	1	4	0	0	0	0	0	0	0	3	0
Jack Stivetts, p	.250	3	12	3	3	1	1	0	1	0	2	0
Tommy Tucker, 1b	.261	6	23	2	6	0	0	1	2	0	1	0
TOTAL	.265		211	31	56	7	4	3	28	12	19	14

PITCHER	W	L	ERA	G	GS	CG	SV	SHO	IP	H	ER	BB	SO
Kid Nichols	2	0	1.00	2	2	2	0	1	18.0	17	2	4	13
Harry Staley	1	0	3.00	1	1	1	0	0	9.0	10	3	1	0
Jack Stivetts	2	0	0.93	3	3	3	0	1	29.0	21	3	7	17
TOTAL	5	0	1.29	6	6	6	0	2	56.0	48	8	12	30

CLE (N)

PLAYER/POS	AVG	G	AB	R	H	2B	3B	HR	RB	BB	SO	SB
Jesse Burkett, of	.320	6	25	3	8	1	0	0	1	0	2	4
Cupid Childs, 2b	.409	6	22	3	9	0	2	0	0	5	1	0
John Clarkson, p	.250	2	8	1	2	0	0	1	3	0	1	0
Nig Cuppy, p	.000	1	3	0	0	0	0	0	0	0	2	0
George Davis, 3b-2	.167	3	6	0	1	0	0	0	0	0	1	0
Jimmy McAleer, of	.182	6	22	0	4	0	0	0	1	2	2	1
Ed McKean, ss	.440	6	25	2	11	0	0	0	6	1	3	0
Jack O'Connor, of	.136	6	22	1	3	0	0	0	0	2	3	0
Patsy Tebeau, 3b	.000	5	18	1	0	0	0	0	0	0	2	1
Jake Virtue, 1b	.125	6	24	1	3	0	0	0	0	2	5	1
Cy Young, p	.091	3	11	1	1	0	0	0	0	0	5	0
Chief Zimmer, c	.261	6	23	2	6	1	1	0	2	0	3	0
TOTAL	.230		209	15	48	2	3	1	13	12	30	7

PITCHER	W	L	ERA	G	GS	CG	SV	SHO	IP	H	ER	BB	SO
John Clarkson	0	2	5.29	2	2	2	0	0	17.0	24	10	5	9
Nig Cuppy	0	1	1.13	1	1	1	0	0	8.0	6	1	4	1
Cy Young	0	2	3.00	3	3	3	0	1	27.0	26	9	3	9
TOTAL	0	5	3.46	6	6	6	0	1	52.0	56	20	12	19

GAME 1 AT CLE OCT 17

CLE	000 000 000 00	0	4	1
BOS	000 000 000 00	0	6	0

Pitchers: YOUNG vs STIVETTS
Attendance: 6,000
(Game called at end of eleventh, darkness)

GAME 2 AT CLE OCT 18

BOS	101 010 010	4	10	2
CLE	001 100 001	3	10	2

Pitchers: STALEY vs CLARKSON
Attendance: 6,700

GAME 3 AT CLE OCT 19

CLE	200 000 000	2	8	0
BOS	110 000 10X	3	9	2

Pitchers: YOUNG vs STIVETTS
Attendance: 5,000

GAME 4 AT BOS OCT 21

CLE	000 000 000	0	7	3
BOS	002 002 00X	4	6	0

Pitchers: CUPPY vs NICHOLS
Home Runs: Duffy-BOS
Attendance: 6,547

GAME 5 AT BOS OCT 22

CLE	060 010 000	7	9	4
BOS	000 324 30X	12	14	3

Pitchers: CLARKSON vs STIVETTS
Home Runs: Clarkson-CLE, Tucker-BOS
Attendance: 3,466

GAME 6 AT BOS OCT 24

CLE	003 000 000	3	10	5
BOS	002 211 11X	8	11	5

Pitchers: YOUNG vs NICHOLS
Home Runs: Bennett-BOS
Attendance: 2,300

Boston had edged Baltimore in a close race for the NL pennant, but the Orioles turned the tables on the Beaneaters in Temple Cup play. The Series was a high-scoring affair, the winner of each game averaging eleven runs, the loser eight.

The opener, in Boston, set the tone for the games. Baltimore sent four runners across the plate in the top of the first inning, and Boston followed in its half with three. The Beaneaters recorded only twelve hits in the game to the Orioles' twenty, but they also received seven walks from Baltimore hurler Jerry Nops, and five of those runners scored. The lead switched back and forth in the middle innings, but Boston scored two final runs in the eighth and hung on for a 13–12 win.

Baltimore's Joe Corbett gave up sixteen hits (one a home run) and four walks in Game Two as Boston scored eleven times. But Boston's two pitchers, Fred Klobedanz and Jack Stivetts, were even more generous, handing out seventeen hits (including three homers—one of them to opposing pitcher Corbett, who also hit a double and two singles) and five walks as the Orioles evened the Series with their thirteen-run attack.

Game Three was the Series' lowest in run production, with Baltimore scoring four in the second inning and another four in the third for an 8–3 win. But rain ended the game before Boston could complete its time at bat in the last of the eighth, which erased from the record four more Oriole runs scored earlier in the inning. Rather than waste the two free days before the Series resumed in Baltimore, the two clubs played a pair of exhibition games in Worcester and Springfield, Massachusetts. Baltimore won them both, 11–10 and 8–6.

The Orioles continued their roll in Series Game Four, with another close but high-scoring victory, 12–11. It looked at first like a blowout as Baltimore scored six runs in the first inning and five more in the second. But Ted Lewis relieved Boston starter Jack Stivetts and held Baltimore to just one further run as the Beaneaters fought back to within one run of a tie before faltering in the ninth.

Boston batters hit Oriole Bill Hoffer safely fifteen times in Game Five, but only three Beaneaters scored. Baltimore, with two fewer hits, garnered six more runs than Boston and, with their fourth win, the right to hold the cup for another year. But attendance at the final

game was so small the embarrassed Baltimore management refused to release the figures, and the league gave the cup back to Mr. Temple rather than sponsor another unprofitable Series. There was no postseason championship contest in 1898 or 1899.

Baltimore Orioles, 4; Boston Beaneaters, 1

BAL (N)

PLAYER/POS	AVG	G	AB	R	H	2B	3B	HR	RBI	BB	SO	SB
Frank Bowerman, c-1,1b-1	.500	2	8	2	4	0	1	0	4	0	0	0
Boileryard Clarke, c	.563	4	16	5	9	1	1	1	4	1	0	0
Joe Corbett, p	.667	2	6	2	4	1	0	1	2	0	1	0
Jack Doyle, 1b	.526	5	19	7	10	2	0	0	9	0	1	2
Bill Hoffer, p	.250	2	8	2	2	1	0	0	0	0	0	0
Hughie Jennings, ss	.318	5	22	5	7	2	0	0	3	4	0	0
Willie Keeler, of	.391	5	23	5	9	2	0	0	2	4	0	0
Joe Kelley, of	.313	4	16	7	5	3	0	0	5	5	0	0
John McGraw, 3b	.300	5	20	6	6	1	1	0	6	7	0	0
Jerry Nops, p	.286	2	7	0	2	0	0	0	1	1	5	0
Tom O'Brien, of	.400	1	5	2	2	1	0	0	0	0	0	0
Heinie Reitz, 2b	.250	5	20	4	5	1	0	1	4	2	0	0
Jake Stenzel, of	.381	5	21	7	8	1	1	0	3	2	0	2
TOTAL	.382		191	54	73	16	4	3	43	26	7	4

PITCHER	W	L	ERA	G	GS	CG	SV	SHO	IP	H	ER	BB	SO
Joe Corbett	1	0	9.00	2	1	1	0	0	12.0	21	12	8	5
Bill Hoffer	2	0	3.38	2	2	2	0	0	16.0	25	6	4	2
Jerry Nops	1	1	12.86	2	2	1	0	0	14.0	23	20	9	3
TOTAL	4	1	8.14	6	5	4	0	0	42.0	69	38	21	10

BOS (N)

PLAYER/POS	AVG	G	AB	R	H	2B	3B	HR	RBI	BB	SO	SB
Marty Bergen, c	.500	1	4	0	2	0	0	0	1	0	1	1
Jimmy Collins, 3b	.182	5	22	2	4	0	0	0	4	1	0	0
Hugh Duffy, of	.524	5	21	6	11	2	0	0	7	1	0	0
Billy Hamilton, of	.500	4	16	6	8	1	0	0	2	5	3	2
Charlie Hickman, p-1,of-1	.250	1	4	0	1	1	0	0	1	0	0	0
Fred Klobedanz, p	1.000	2	5	3	5	0	0	0	0	0	0	0
Fred Lake, c	.000	1	3	0	0	0	0	0	0	0	1	0
Ted Lewis, p	.500	3	6	1	3	1	0	0	1	1	0	0
Herman Long, ss	.286	5	21	4	6	1	1	1	5	2	2	1
Bobby Lowe, 2b	.391	5	23	6	9	2	0	0	6	1	0	1
Kid Nichols, p	.000	1	3	0	0	0	0	0	0	1	0	0
Chick Stahl, of	.381	5	21	6	8	1	0	0	6	3	2	2
Jack Stivetts, p-2,of-1	.000	3	7	1	0	0	0	0	0	1	0	1
Jim Sullivan, p	.000	1	1	0	0	0	0	0	0	0	0	0
Fred Tenney, 1b	.286	5	21	4	6	0	0	0	2	4	1	2
George Yeager, c	.500	3	12	2	6	1	1	0	2	2	0	0
TOTAL	.365		189	41	69	10	2	1	38	21	10	10

PITCHER	W	L	ERA	G	GS	CG	SV	SHO	IP	H	ER	BB	SO
Charlie Hickman	0	1	3.60	1	1	0	0	0	5.0	7	2	2	0
Fred Klobedanz	0	1	9.35	2	1	0	0	0	8.2	12	9	8	0
Ted Lewis	1	1	6.00	3	1	0	0	0	12	18	8	9	4
Kid Nichols	0	0	12.00	1	1	0	0	0	6.0	14	8	0	3
Jack Stivetts	0	1	18.47	2	1	0	0	0	6.1	16	13	7	0
Jim Sullivan	0	0	3.00	1	0	0	0	0	3.0	6	1	0	0
TOTAL	1	4	9.00	10	5	0	0	0	41.0	73	41	26	7

GAME 1 AT BOS OCT 4

```
BAL    401  023  200    12 20  4
BOS    300  125  02X    13 12  4
```
Pitchers: NOPS vs Nichols, LEWIS (7)
Attendance: 9,600

GAME 2 AT BOS OCT 5

```
BAL    130  160  110    13 17  2
BOS    002  620  100    11 16  3
```
Pitchers: CORBETT vs KLOBEDANZ, Stivetts (5)
Home Runs: Reitz-BAL, Clarke-BAL, Corbett-BAL, Long-BOS
Attendance: 6,500

GAME 3 AT BOS OCT 6

```
BAL    044  000  0       8  9  2
BOS    003  000  0       3 10  2
```
Pitchers: HOFFER vs LEWIS, Klobedanz
Attendance: 5,000
(Game called in eighth, rain)

GAME 4 AT BAL OCT 9

```
BOS    000  024  320    11 16  3
BAL    650  001  00X    12 14  3
```
Pitchers: STIVETTS, Lewis (3) vs NOPS, Corbett (7)
Attendance: 2,500

GAME 5 AT BAL OCT 11

```
BOS    020  000  001     3 15  3
BAL    023  000  22X     9 13  2
```
Pitchers: HICKMAN, Sullivan (7) vs HOFFER
Attendance: 700

The Athletics, easy winners of their fourth pennant in five years, were clear favorites over Boston. But the "Miracle Braves"—who moved from last place to first between July 18 and August 25 and kept going to take the pennant by 10½ games—had the momentum and swept the Series.

Boston pitcher Dick Rudolph (who won 27 games during the season) limited the A's to five hits and an unearned run, to take the opener behind the Braves' heavy hitting, 7–1. But the rest of the games were not won so easily.

Philadelphia's Eddie Plank held the Braves scoreless through eight innings of Game Two, and gave up only one run in the ninth. But the Braves' Bill James (26–7 during the season) allowed only two hits and no runs at all.

Game Three was a seesaw affair not settled until the twelfth inning. Through ten innings, starters Lefty Tyler of Boston and Joe Bush of the A's traded runs. Philadelphia scored one in the top of the first, but Braves' catcher Hank Gowdy doubled in the tying run in the second. The teams traded runs again in the fourth, but no one else crossed the plate until the tenth, when Frank Baker's bases-loaded single drove in two. For the third time, the Braves came back to tie it up. Gowdy opened the last of the tenth with the Series' only home run, and after a walk and single, a sacrifice fly knotted the score. Bill James came on to pitch no-hit ball through the eleventh and twelfth. Bush remained in for the A's, retiring the side in the eleventh. But an inning later Gowdy opened with his third crucial hit of the game, a double. Les Mann replaced him as runner, and after a walk, bunt, and wild throw to third, Mann scampered home with the winning run.

Two of Connie Mack's most promising young pitchers, Bob Shawkey and Herb Pennock (who would later find stardom as New York Yankees), shared the A's pitching in Game Four, and gave up only six hits between them. But a walk and an error led to a Boston run in the fourth, and although Shawkey himself doubled in the tying run a half inning later, two more Braves scored in the last of the fifth on Johnny Evers's single. Pennock came on to pitch three innings of shutout relief, but Rudolph held the A's hitless over the final four innings to preserve his second win and the Braves' crown.

Boston Braves (NL), 4; Philadelphia Athletics (AL), 0

BOS (N)

PLAYER/POS	AVG	G	AB	R	H	2B	3B	HR	RB	BB	SO	SB
Ted Cather, of	.000	1	5	0	0	0	0	0	0	0	1	0
Joe Connolly, of	.111	3	9	1	1	0	0	0	1	1	1	0
Charlie Deal, 3b	.125	4	16	1	2	2	0	0	0	0	0	2
Josh Devore, ph	.000	1	1	0	0	0	0	0	0	0	1	0
Johnny Evers, 2b	.438	4	16	2	7	0	0	0	2	2	2	1
Larry Gilbert, ph	.000	1	0	0	0	0	0	0	0	1	0	0
Hank Gowdy, c	.545	4	11	3	6	3	1	1	3	5	1	1
Bill James, p	.000	2	4	0	0	0	0	0	0	0	4	0
Les Mann, of-2	.286	3	7	1	2	0	0	0	1	0	1	0
Rabbit Maranville, ss	.308	4	13	1	4	0	0	0	3	1	1	2
Herbie Moran, of	.077	3	13	2	1	1	0	0	0	1	1	1
Dick Rudolph, p	.333	2	6	1	2	0	0	0	0	1	1	0
Butch Schmidt, 1b	.294	4	17	2	5	0	0	0	2	0	2	1
Lefty Tyler, p	.000	1	3	0	0	0	0	0	0	0	1	0
Possum Whitted, of	.214	4	14	2	3	0	1	0	2	3	1	1
TOTAL	.244		135	16	33	6	2	1	14	15	18	9

PITCHER	W	L	ERA	G	GS	CG	SV	SHO	IP	H	ER	BB	SO
Bill James	2	0	0.00	2	1	1	0	1	11.0	2	0	6	9
Dick Rudolph	2	0	0.50	2	2	2	0	0	18.0	12	1	4	15
Lefty Tyler	0	0	3.60	1	1	0	0	0	10.0	8	4	3	4
TOTAL	4	0	1.15	5	4	3	0	1	39.0	22	5	13	28

PHI (A)

PLAYER/POS	AVG	G	AB	R	H	2B	3B	HR	RB	BB	SO	SB
Frank Baker, 3b	.250	4	16	0	4	2	0	0	2	1	3	0
Jack Barry, ss	.071	4	14	1	1	0	0	0	0	1	3	1
Chief Bender, p	.000	1	2	0	0	0	0	0	0	0	0	0
Joe Bush, p	.000	1	5	0	0	0	0	0	0	0	2	0
Eddie Collins, 2b	.214	4	14	0	3	0	0	0	1	2	1	1
Jack Lapp, c	.000	1	1	0	0	0	0	0	0	0	0	0
Stuffy McInnis, 1b	.143	4	14	2	2	1	0	0	0	3	3	0
Eddie Murphy, of	.188	4	16	2	3	2	0	0	0	2	2	0
Rube Oldring, of	.067	4	15	0	1	0	0	0	0	0	5	0
Herb Pennock, p	.000	1	1	0	0	0	0	0	0	0	0	0
Eddie Plank, p	.000	1	2	0	0	0	0	0	0	0	1	0
Wally Schang, c	.167	4	12	1	2	1	0	0	0	1	4	0
Bob Shawkey, p	.500	1	2	0	1	1	0	0	1	0	1	0
Amos Strunk, of	.286	2	7	0	2	0	0	0	0	0	2	0
Jimmy Walsh, of-2	.333	3	6	0	2	1	0	0	1	3	1	0
Weldon Wyckoff, p	1.000	1	1	0	1	1	0	0	0	0	0	0
TOTAL	.172		128	6	22	9	0	0	5	13	28	2

PITCHER	W	L	ERA	G	GS	CG	SV	SHO	IP	H	ER	BB	SO
Chief Bender	0	1	10.13	1	1	0	0	0	5.1	8	6	2	3
Joe Bush	0	1	3.27	1	1	1	0	0	11.0	9	4	4	4
Herb Pennock	0	0	0.00	1	0	0	0	0	3.0	2	0	2	3
Eddie Plank	0	1	1.00	1	1	1	0	0	9.0	7	1	4	6
Bob Shawkey	0	1	3.60	1	1	0	0	0	5.0	4	2	2	0
Weldon Wyckoff	0	0	2.45	1	0	0	0	0	3.2	3	1	1	2
TOTAL	0	4	3.41	6	4	2	0	0	37.0	33	14	15	18

GAME 1 AT PHI OCT 9

BOS	020	013	010	7	11	2
PHI	010	000	000	1	5	0

Pitchers: RUDOLPH vs BENDER, Wyckoff (6)
Attendance: 20,562

GAME 2 AT PHI OCT 10

BOS	000	000	001	1	7	1
PHI	000	000	000	0	2	1

Pitchers: JAMES vs PLANK
Attendance: 20,562

GAME 3 AT BOS OCT 12

PHI	100 100 000	200	4	8	2
BOS	010 100 000	201	5	9	1

Pitchers: BUSH vs Tyler, JAMES (11)
Home Runs: Gowdy-BOS
Attendance: 35,520

GAME 4 AT BOS OCT 13

PHI	000	010	000	1	7	0
BOS	000	120	00X	3	6	0

Pitchers: SHAWKEY, Pennock (6) vs RUDOLPH
Attendance: 34,365

Boston outpitched and outhit Cleveland, and the clubs tied in runs scored. But the Braves scored most of their runs in one game, and the Indians, spreading theirs more evenly, took the Series. Boston ace Johnny Sain dueled Bob Feller in the opener. Feller gave up only two singles, but one of them followed a walk and a sacrifice (and a controversial pickoff play at second, in which the Boston runner was ruled safe although photos later showed him clearly out) and drove in the game's only run. Both teams registered eight hits in Game Two, but Cleveland's led to four runs, while Indian hurler Bob Lemon held Boston to just one—and that was unearned.

Cleveland's rookie sensation Gene Bearden shut out the Braves on five hits in Game Three as the Series moved to Cleveland's huge Municipal Stadium. Bearden himself, after doubling in the third, scored on a Boston error what proved to be the winning run. A record 81,897 fans saw Sain face Steve Gromek in Game Four. Only five Indians hit Sain safely, but a first-inning single and double put Cleveland on the board, and Larry Doby's home run two innings later made the score 2–0. Boston's Marv Rickert homered in the seventh to narrow Cleveland's lead, but that ended the scoring.

Another attendance record was set at Game Five as 86,288 fans gathered to watch Bob Feller sew up the title for Cleveland. They went home disappointed. In a game that featured five of the Series' eight home runs, Boston jumped ahead on Bob Elliott's three-run blast in the first. Dale Mitchell opened Cleveland's half of the inning with a home run, but Elliott neutralized it in the third with his second homer. The Indians drove out Boston starter Nelson Potter with four runs in the fourth inning (three coming on Jim Hegan's homer). But Warren Spahn (who had lost Game Two) hurled one-hit shutout relief over the final five frames as his Braves tied the game on Bill Salkeld's homer in the sixth, and blew out Feller and two relievers with six runs in the seventh. The fourth Indian pitcher, Satchel Paige (in his only World Series appearance), retired two batters to end the inning, but the damage had been done.

A day later though, back in Boston, Cleveland edged the Braves 4–3 for the title. Gene Bearden's relief pitching allowed two inherited baserunners to score in the eighth, but halted Boston's rally one run short of a tie.

Cleveland Indians (AL), 4; Boston Braves (NL), 2

CLE (A)

PLAYER/POS	AVG	G	AB	R	H	2B	3B	HR	RB	BB	SO	SB
Gene Bearden, p	.500	2	4	1	2	1	0	0	0	0	1	0
Ray Boone, ph	.000	1	1	0	0	0	0	0	0	0	1	0
Lou Boudreau, ss	.273	6	22	1	6	4	0	0	3	1	1	0
Russ Christopher, p	.000	1	0	0	0	0	0	0	0	0	0	0
Allie Clark, of	.000	1	3	0	0	0	0	0	0	0	1	0
Larry Doby, of	.318	6	22	1	7	1	0	1	2	2	4	0
Bob Feller, p	.000	2	4	0	0	0	0	0	0	0	2	0
Joe Gordon, 2b	.182	6	22	3	4	0	0	1	2	1	2	1
Steve Gromek, p	.000	1	3	0	0	0	0	0	0	0	1	0
Jim Hegan, c	.211	6	19	2	4	0	0	1	5	1	4	1
Wally Judnich, of	.077	4	13	1	1	0	0	0	1	1	4	0
Ken Keltner, 3b	.095	6	21	3	2	0	0	0	0	2	3	0
Bob Kennedy, of	.500	3	2	0	1	0	0	0	0	1	0	1	0
Ed Klieman, p	.000	1	0	0	0	0	0	0	0	0	0	0
Dale Mitchell, of	.174	6	23	4	4	1	0	1	1	2	0	0
Bob Muncrief, p	.000	1	0	0	0	0	0	0	0	0	0	0
Satchel Paige, p	.000	1	0	0	0	0	0	0	0	0	0	0
Hal Peck, of	.000	1	0	0	0	0	0	0	0	0	0	0
Eddie Robinson, 1b	.300	6	20	0	6	0	0	0	1	1	0	0
Al Rosen, ph	.000	1	1	0	0	0	0	0	0	0	0	0
Joe Tipton, ph	.000	1	1	0	0	0	0	0	0	0	1	0
Thurman Tucker, of	.333	1	3	1	1	0	0	0	0	1	0	0
TOTAL	.199		191	17	38	7	0	4	16	12	26	2

PITCHER	W	L	ERA	G	GS	CG	SV	SHO	IP	H	ER	BB	SO
Gene Bearden	1	0	0.00	2	1	1	1	1	10.2	6	0	1	4
Russ Christopher	0	0	INF	1	0	0	0	0	0.0	2	1	0	0
Bob Feller	0	2	5.02	2	2	1	0	0	14.1	10	8	5	7
Steve Gromek	1	0	1.00	1	1	1	0	0	9.0	7	1	1	2
Ed Klieman	0	0	INF	1	0	0	0	0	0.0	1	3	2	0
Bob Lemon	2	0	1.65	2	2	1	0	0	16.1	16	3	7	6
Bob Muncrief	0	0	0.00	1	0	0	0	0	2.0	1	0	0	0
Satchel Paige	0	0	0.00	1	0	0	0	0	0.2	0	0	0	0
TOTAL	4	2	2.72	11	6	4	1	1	53.0	43	16	16	19

BOS (N)

PLAYER/POS	AVG	G	AB	R	H	2B	3B	HR	RB	BB	SO	SB
Red Barrett, p	.000	2	0	0	0	0	0	0	0	0	0	0
Vern Bickford, p	.000	1	0	0	0	0	0	0	0	0	0	0
Clint Conatser, of	.000	2	4	0	0	0	0	0	1	0	0	0
Alvin Dark, ss	.167	6	24	2	4	1	0	0	0	0	2	0
Bob Elliott, 3b	.333	6	21	4	7	0	0	2	5	2	2	0
Tommy Holmes, of	.192	6	26	3	5	0	0	0	1	0	0	0
Phil Masi, c	.125	5	8	1	1	1	0	0	1	0	0	0
Frank McCormick, 1b-1	.200	3	5	0	1	0	0	0	0	0	2	0
Mike McCormick, of	.261	6	23	1	6	0	0	0	2	0	4	0
Nelson Potter, p	.500	2	2	0	1	0	0	0	0	0	1	0
Marv Rickert, of	.211	5	19	2	4	0	0	1	2	0	4	0
Connie Ryan, ph	.000	2	1	0	0	0	0	0	0	0	1	0
Johnny Sain, p	.200	2	5	0	1	0	0	0	0	0	0	0
Bill Salkeld, c	.222	5	9	2	2	0	0	1	1	5	1	0
Ray Sanders, ph	.000	1	1	0	0	0	0	0	0	0	0	0
Sibby Sisti, 2b	.000	2	1	0	0	0	0	0	0	0	0	0
Warren Spahn, p	.000	3	4	0	0	0	0	0	1	0	0	0
Eddie Stanky, 2b	.286	6	14	0	4	1	0	0	1	7	1	0
Earl Torgeson, 1b	.389	5	18	2	7	3	0	0	1	2	1	1
Bill Voiselle, p	.000	2	2	0	0	0	0	0	0	0	0	0
TOTAL	.230		187	17	43	6	0	4	16	16	19	1

PITCHER	W	L	ERA	G	GS	CG	SV	SHO	IP	H	ER	BB	SO
Red Barrett	0	0	0.00	2	0	0	0	0	3.2	1	0	0	1
Vern Bickford	0	1	2.70	1	1	0	0	0	3.1	4	1	5	1
Nelson Potter	0	0	8.44	2	1	0	0	0	5.1	6	5	2	1
Johnny Sain	1	1	1.06	2	2	2	0	1	17.0	9	2	0	9
Warren Spahn	1	1	3.00	3	1	0	0	0	12.0	10	4	3	12
Bill Voiselle	0	1	2.53	2	1	0	0	0	10.2	8	3	2	2
TOTAL	2	4	2.60	12	6	2	0	1	52.0	38	15	12	26

GAME 1 AT BOS OCT 6

CLE	000	000	000	0	4	0
BOS	000	000	01X	1	2	2

Pitchers: FELLER vs SAIN
Attendance: 40,135

GAME 2 AT BOS OCT 7

CLE	000	210	001	4	8	1
BOS	100	000	000	1	8	3

Pitchers: LEMON vs SPAHN, Barrett (5), Potter (8)
Attendance: 39,633

GAME 3 AT CLE OCT 8

BOS	000	000	000	0	5	1
CLE	001	100	00X	2	5	0

Pitchers: BICKFORD, Voiselle (4), Barrett (8) vs BEARDEN
Attendance: 70,306

GAME 4 AT CLE OCT 9

BOS	000	000	100	1	7	0
CLE	101	000	00X	2	5	0

Pitchers: SAIN vs GROMEK
Home Runs: Doby-CLE, Rickert-BOS
Attendance: 81,897

GAME 5 AT CLE OCT 10

BOS	301	001	600	11	12	0
CLE	100	400	000	5	6	2

Pitchers: Potter, SPAHN (4) vs FELLER, Klieman (7), Christopher (7), Paige (7), Muncrief (8)
Home Runs: Elliott-BOS (2), Mitchell-CLE, Hegan-CLE, Salkeld-BOS
Attendance: 86,288

GAME 6 AT BOS OCT 11

CLE	001	002	010	4	10	0
BOS	000	100	020	3	9	0

Pitchers: LEMON, Bearden (8) vs VOISELLE, Spahn (8)
Home Runs: Gordon-CLE
Attendance: 40,103

Atlanta's Hank Aaron homered in each game and drove in a series-high seven runs. But the "Miracle Mets" as a team outhomered the Braves six to five, outhit them by seventy-two percentage points, and scored nearly twice as many runs.

Twice in the first game the Braves came from behind to lead by a run, but in the top of the eighth, five New York hits and poor Atlanta fielding buried starter Phil Niekro under five runs. In Game Two, home runs by Tommie Agee and Ken Boswell helped New York take an early 8–0 lead that even Aaron's three-run homer in the fifth couldn't damage.

In the third game the lead changed hands three times on home runs. Aaron began the barrage with a two-run shot in the first inning. Agee's homer in the third followed by Boswell's for two runs in the fourth put the Mets ahead—until Orlando Cepeda's two-run homer in the fifth gave Atlanta another lead. But in the bottom of the fifth, Met rookie Wayne Garrett's two-run blast reversed the lead one last time and, after four final shutout innings by twenty-two-year-old reliever Nolan Ryan, the Mets had swept to their first pennant.

New York Mets (East), 3;
Atlanta Braves (West) 0

NY (E)

PLAYER/POS	AVG	G	AB	R	H	2B	3B	HR	RB	BB	SO	SB
Tommie Agee, of	.357	3	14	4	5	1	0	2	4	2	5	2
Ken Boswell, 2b	.333	3	12	4	4	0	0	2	5	1	2	0
Wayne Garrett, 3b	.385	3	13	3	5	2	0	1	3	2	2	1
Rod Gaspar, of	.000	3	0	0	0	0	0	0	0	0	0	0
Gary Gentry, p	.000	1	0	0	0	0	0	0	0	0	0	0
Jerry Grote, c	.167	3	12	3	2	1	0	0	1	1	4	0
Bud Harrelson, ss	.182	3	11	2	2	1	1	0	3	1	2	0
Cleon Jones, of	.429	3	14	4	6	2	0	1	4	1	2	2
Jerry Koosman, p	.000	1	2	1	0	0	0	0	0	1	2	0
Ed Kranepool, 1b	.250	3	12	2	3	1	0	0	1	1	2	0
J. C. Martin, ph	.500	2	2	0	1	0	0	0	2	0	0	0
Tug McGraw, p	.000	1	0	0	0	0	0	0	0	0	0	0
Nolan Ryan, p	.500	1	4	1	2	0	0	0	0	0	1	0
Tom Seaver, p	.000	1	3	0	0	0	0	0	0	0	0	0
Art Shamsky, of	.538	3	13	3	7	0	0	0	1	0	3	0
Ron Taylor, p	.000	2	0	0	0	0	0	0	0	0	0	0
Al Weis, 2b	.000	3	1	0	0	0	0	0	0	0	0	0
TOTAL	.327		113	27	37	8	1	6	24	10	25	5

PITCHER	W	L	ERA	G	GS	CG	SV	SHO	IP	H	ER	BB	SO
Gary Gentry	0	0	9.00	1	1	0	0	0	2.0	5	2	1	1
Jerry Koosman	0	0	11.57	1	1	0	0	0	4.2	7	6	4	5
Tug McGraw	0	0	0.00	1	0	0	1	0	3.0	1	0	1	1
Nolan Ryan	1	0	2.57	1	0	0	0	0	7.0	3	2	2	7
Tom Seaver	1	0	6.43	1	1	0	0	0	7.0	8	5	3	2
Ron Taylor	1	0	0.00	2	0	0	1	0	3.1	3	0	0	4
TOTAL	3	0	5.00	7	3	0	2	0	27.0	27	15	11	20

ATL (W)

PLAYER/POS	AVG	G	AB	R	H	2B	3B	HR	RB	BB	SO	SB
Hank Aaron, of	.357	3	14	3	5	2	0	3	7	0	1	0
Tommie Aaron, ph	.000	1	1	0	0	0	0	0	0	0	0	0
Felipe Alou, ph	.000	1	1	0	0	0	0	0	0	0	0	0
Bob Aspromonte, ph	.000	3	3	0	0	0	0	0	0	0	0	0
Clete Boyer, 3b	.111	3	9	0	1	0	0	0	3	2	3	0
Jim Britton, p	.000	1	0	0	0	0	0	0	0	0	0	0
Rico Carty, of	.300	3	10	4	3	2	0	0	0	3	1	0
Orlando Cepeda, 1b	.455	3	11	2	5	2	0	1	3	1	2	1
Bob Didier, c	.000	3	11	0	0	0	0	0	0	0	2	0
Paul Doyle, p	.000	1	0	0	0	0	0	0	0	0	0	0
Gil Garrido, ss	.200	3	10	0	2	0	0	0	0	1	1	0
Tony Gonzalez, of	.357	3	14	4	5	1	0	1	2	1	4	0
Sonny Jackson, ss	.000	1	0	0	0	0	0	0	0	0	0	0
Pat Jarvis, p	.000	1	2	0	0	0	0	0	0	0	2	0
Mike Lum, of-1	1.000	2	2	0	2	1	0	0	0	0	0	0
Felix Millan, 2b	.333	3	12	2	4	1	0	0	0	3	0	0
Gary Neibauer, p	.000	1	0	0	0	0	0	0	0	0	0	0
Phil Niekro, p	.000	1	3	0	0	0	0	0	0	0	1	0
Milt Pappas, p	.000	1	1	0	0	0	0	0	0	0	1	0
Ron Reed, p	.000	1	0	0	0	0	0	0	0	0	0	0
George Stone, p	.000	1	1	0	0	0	0	0	0	0	1	0
Bob Tillman, c	.000	1	0	0	0	0	0	0	0	0	0	0
Cecil Upshaw, p	.000	3	1	0	0	0	0	0	0	0	1	0
TOTAL	.255		106	15	27	9	0	5	15	11	20	1

PITCHER	W	L	ERA	G	GS	CG	SV	SHO	IP	H	ER	BB	SO
Jim Britton	0	0	0.00	1	0	0	0	0	0.1	0	0	1	0
Paul Doyle	0	0	0.00	1	0	0	0	0	1.0	2	0	1	3
Pat Jarvis	0	1	12.46	1	1	0	0	0	4.1	10	6	0	6
Gary Neibauer	0	0	0.00	1	0	0	0	0	1.0	0	0	0	1
Phil Niekro	0	1	4.50	1	1	0	0	0	8.0	9	4	4	4
Milt Pappas	0	0	11.57	1	0	0	0	0	2.1	4	3	0	4
Ron Reed	0	1	21.60	1	1	0	0	0	1.2	5	4	3	3
George Stone	0	0	9.00	1	0	0	0	0	1.0	2	1	0	0
Cecil Upshaw	0	0	2.84	3	0	0	0	0	6.1	5	2	1	4
TOTAL	0	3	6.92	11	3	0	0	0	26.0	37	20	10	25

GAME 1 AT ATL OCT 4

NY	020 200 050	9	10	1
ATL	012 010 100	5	10	2

Pitchers: SEAVER, Taylor (8) vs NIEKRO, Upshaw (9)
Home Runs: Gonzalez-ATL, H.Aaron-ATL
Attendance: 50,122

GAME 2 AT ATL OCT 5

NY	132 210 200	11	13	1
ATL	000 150 000	6	9	3

Pitchers: Koosman, TAYLOR (5), McGraw (7) vs REED, Doyle (2), Pappas (3), Britton (6), Upshaw (6), Neibauer (9)
Home Runs: Agee-NY, Boswell-NY, H.Aaron-ATL, Jones-NY
Attendance: 50,270

GAME 3 AT NY OCT 6

ATL	200 020 000	4	8	1
NY	001 231 00X	7	14	0

Pitchers: JARVIS, Stone (5), Upshaw (6) vs Gentry, RYAN (3)
Home Runs: H.Aaron-ATL, Agee-NY, Boswell-NY, Cepeda-ATL, Garrett-NY
Attendance: 53,195

The official records show Atlanta ahead and threatening only once in a three-game series swept by the Cardinals. But in the original Game One, Phil Niekro held a slim 1–0 Atlanta lead in the fifth inning when rain wiped out the game just before it could become official.

In the first official game, the Braves scored nothing at all as Bob Forsch held them to three hits. Atlanta's Pascual Perez gave up only one run through the first five innings, but the Cardinals exploded for five runs in the sixth to put the game away. Following another rainout, Niekro tried again in Game Two. He gave up a run in the first, but Atlanta came back with three before he yielded a second run in the sixth. Gene Garber, who relieved Niekro, gave up the tying run in the eighth and lost the game in the bottom of the ninth on Ken Oberkfell's RBI liner over the center fielder's head.

Joaquin Andujar shut out the Braves through six innings of Game Three before giving up two runs in the seventh. But by then St. Louis had scored five times. Bruce Sutter retired the last seven Braves in relief of Andujar, and the Cardinals had their pennant.

St. Louis Cardinals (East), 3; Atlanta Braves (West), 0

STL (E)

PLAYER/POS	AVG	G	AB	R	H	2B	3B	HR	RB	BB	SO	SB
Joaquin Andujar, p	.000	1	1	0	0	0	0	0	0	0	1	0
Doug Bair, p	.000	1	0	0	0	0	0	0	0	0	0	0
Steve Braun, ph	.000	1	1	0	0	0	0	0	0	0	0	0
Bob Forsch, p	.667	1	3	1	2	0	0	0	1	0	0	0
David Green, of	1.000	2	1	1	1	0	0	0	0	0	0	0
George Hendrick, of	.308	3	13	2	4	0	0	0	2	1	2	0
Keith Hernandez, 1b	.333	3	12	3	4	0	0	0	1	2	3	0
Tommy Herr, 2b	.231	3	13	1	3	1	0	0	0	1	2	0
Willie McGee, of	.308	3	13	4	4	0	2	1	5	0	5	0
Ken Oberkfell, 3b	.200	3	15	1	3	0	0	0	2	0	0	0
Darrell Porter, c	.556	3	9	3	5	3	0	0	1	5	2	0
Lonnie Smith, of	.273	3	11	1	3	0	0	0	1	0	1	0
Ozzie Smith, ss	.556	3	9	0	5	0	0	0	3	3	0	1
John Stuper, p	.000	1	1	0	0	0	0	0	0	0	0	0
Bruce Sutter, p	.000	2	1	0	0	0	0	0	0	0	0	0
TOTAL	.330		103	17	34	4	2	1	16	12	16	1

PITCHER	W	L	ERA	G	GS	CG	SV	SHO	IP	H	ER	BB	SO
Joaquin Andujar	1	0	2.70	1	1	0	0	0	6.2	6	2	2	4
Doug Bair	0	0	0.00	1	0	0	0	0	1.0	2	0	3	0
Bob Forsch	1	0	0.00	1	1	1	0	1	9.0	3	0	0	6
John Stuper	0	0	3.00	1	1	0	0	0	6.0	4	2	1	4
Bruce Sutter	1	0	0.00	2	0	0	1	0	4.1	0	0	0	1
TOTAL	3	0	1.33	6	3	1	1	1	27.0	15	4	6	15

ATL (W)

PLAYER/POS	AVG	G	AB	R	H	2B	3B	HR	RB	BB	SO	SB
Steve Bedrosian, p	.000	2	0	0	0	0	0	0	0	0	0	0
Bruce Benedict, c	.250	3	8	1	2	1	0	0	0	2	1	0
Brett Butler, of-1	.000	2	1	0	0	0	0	0	0	0	0	0
Rick Camp, p	.000	1	0	0	0	0	0	0	0	0	0	0
Chris Chambliss, 1b	.000	3	10	0	0	0	0	0	0	1	0	0
Gene Garber, p	.000	2	1	0	0	0	0	0	0	0	0	0
Terry Harper, of	.000	1	1	1	0	0	0	0	0	0	0	0
Bob Horner, 3b	.091	3	11	0	1	0	0	0	0	0	2	0
Glenn Hubbard, 2b	.222	3	9	1	2	0	0	0	1	0	3	0
Rick Mahler, p	.000	1	0	0	0	0	0	0	0	0	0	0
Donnie Moore, p	.000	2	0	0	0	0	0	0	0	0	0	0
Dale Murphy, of	.273	3	11	1	3	0	0	0	0	0	2	1
Phil Niekro, p	.000	1	0	0	0	0	0	0	1	0	0	0
Pascual Perez, p	.000	2	3	0	0	0	0	0	0	0	1	0
Biff Pocoroba, ph	.000	1	1	0	0	0	0	0	0	0	0	0
Rafael Ramirez, ss	.182	3	11	1	2	0	0	0	1	1	1	0
Jerry Royster, of-3,3b-1	.182	3	11	0	2	0	0	0	0	0	2	0
Bob Walk, p	.000	1	0	0	0	0	0	0	0	0	0	0
Claudell Washington, of	.333	3	9	0	3	0	0	0	0	2	2	0
Larry Whisenton, ph	.000	2	2	0	0	0	0	0	0	0	1	0
TOTAL	.169		89	5	15	1	0	0	3	6	15	1

PITCHER	W	L	ERA	G	GS	CG	SV	SHO	IP	H	ER	BB	SO
Steve Bedrosian	0	0	18.00	2	0	0	0	0	1.0	3	2	1	2
Rick Camp	0	1	36.00	1	1	0	0	0	1.0	4	4	1	0
Gene Garber	0	1	8.10	2	0	0	0	0	3.1	4	3	1	3
Rick Mahler	0	0	0.00	1	0	0	0	0	1.2	3	0	2	0
Donnie Moore	0	0	0.00	2	0	0	0	0	2.2	2	0	0	1
Phil Niekro	0	0	3.00	1	1	0	0	0	6.0	6	2	4	5
Pascual Perez	0	1	5.19	2	1	0	0	0	8.2	10	5	2	4
Bob Walk	0	0	9.00	1	0	0	0	0	1.0	2	1	1	1
TOTAL	0	3	6.04	12	3	0	0	0	25.1	34	17	12	16

GAME 1 AT STL OCT 7

ATL	000	000	000	0	3	0
STL	001	005	01X	7	13	1

Pitchers: PEREZ, Bedrosian (6), Moore (6), Walk (8) vs FORSCH
Attendance: 53,008

GAME 2 AT STL OCT 9

ATL	002	010	000	3	6	0
STL	100	001	011	4	9	1

Pitchers: Niekro, GARBER (7) vs Stuper, Bair (7), SUTTER (8)
Attendance: 53,408

GAME 3 AT ATL OCT 10

STL	040	010	001	6	12	0
ATL	000	000	200	2	6	1

Pitchers: ANDUJAR, Sutter (7) vs CAMP, Perez (2), Moore (5), Mahler (7), Bedrosian (8), Garber (9)
Home Runs: McGee-STL
Attendance: 52,173

Pitching dominated this back-and-forth series which featured four shutouts, including three 1–0 games. Three times Atlanta hurlers blanked Pittsburgh on the Pirates' home grounds, including a pair of must-win victories that brought the Braves back from the brink of defeat. Andy Van Slyke opened the series scoring with a first-inning Pirate home run. Pirate starter Doug Drabek held the Braves scoreless through six innings of the opener, before injuring himself on the basepath. By the time David Justice homered in the ninth for Atlanta's only score, the Pirates had the game well in hand.

Atlanta evened the series with its first of three shutouts in Game Two behind the pitching of young Steve Avery and (for the final ⅔ inning) Alejandro Pena, and the bat and glove of Mark Lemke. The Braves' second baseman doubled home that game's only run in the sixth inning and prevented a Pittsburgh run from scoring in the eighth with a diving stop of a grounder up the middle. In Atlanta for Game Three, the Braves took the series lead with a 10–3 route that featured home runs by Ron Gant, Greg Olson, and Sid Bream. (Orlando Merced and Derek Bell homered for Pittsburgh.)

Game Four was much closer; this time three Pirate runs brought them victory. The Braves took a quick lead with two first-inning runs, but Pittsburgh scored once in the second and tied the game in the fifth on a throwing error as Pirate pitching shut down Atlanta's offense. In the top of the tenth, Andy Van Slyke led off with a walk. With two away he stole second, and then scored what proved the winning run on Don Slaught's double. With the series even again, Atlanta lost a run in Game Five when David Justice was ruled out for missing third base as he dashed home from second. An inning later the Pirates parlayed a walk and a pair of singles into the only run they would need to carry the series advantage back to Pittsburgh.

In Game Six, though, the Braves returned the favor, tying the series once more with a gem of their own. Avery and Pena combined for their second 1–0 victory, holding Atlanta to just four singles. Drabek held the Braves scoreless into the ninth, when Olson doubled home the game's only run.

In the finale, Braves starter John Smoltz enjoyed a three-run lead when he took the mound in the bottom of the first inning. Rookie first baseman Brian Hunter (who had homered for two of the first-inning runs) doubled in an additional Atlanta run in the fifth. Meanwhile Smoltz stopped the Pirates on six hits to bring the Braves their first pennant since their move to Atlanta in 1966.

Atlanta Braves (West), 4; Pittsburgh Pirates (East), 3

ATL (W)

PLAYER/POS	AVG	G	AB	R	H	2B	3B	HR	RB	BB	SO	SB
Steve Avery, p	.143	2	7	0	1	0	0	0	0	0	4	0
Rafael Belliard, ss	.211	7	19	0	4	0	0	0	1	3	3	0
Jeff Blauser, ss	.000	2	2	0	0	0	0	0	0	0	0	0
Sid Bream, 1b	.300	4	10	1	3	0	0	1	3	0	1	0
Jim Clancy, p	.000	1	0	0	0	0	0	0	0	0	0	0
Ron Gant, of	.259	7	27	4	7	1	0	1	3	2	4	7
Tom Glavine, p	.250	2	4	0	1	0	0	0	0	0	2	0
Tommy Gregg, ph	.250	4	4	0	1	0	0	0	0	0	2	0
Brian Hunter, 1b	.333	5	18	2	6	2	0	1	4	0	2	0
David Justice, of	.200	7	25	4	5	1	0	1	2	3	7	0
Charlie Leibrandt, p	.000	1	1	0	0	0	0	0	0	0	0	0
Mark Lemke, 2b	.200	7	20	1	4	1	0	0	1	4	0	0
Kent Mercker, p	.000	1	0	0	0	0	0	0	0	0	0	0
Keith Mitchell, of	.000	5	4	0	0	0	0	0	0	0	1	0
Greg Olson, c	.333	7	24	3	8	1	0	1	4	4	3	1
Alejandro Pena, p	.000	4	0	0	0	0	0	0	0	0	0	0
Terry Pendleton, 3b	.167	7	30	1	5	1	1	0	1	1	3	0
Lonnie Smith, of	.250	7	24	3	6	3	0	0	0	4	5	2
John Smoltz, p	.200	2	5	0	1	0	0	0	0	1	4	1
Mike Stanton, p	.000	3	0	0	0	0	0	0	0	0	0	0
Jeff Treadway, 2b	.333	1	3	0	1	0	0	0	0	0	0	0
Jerry Willard, ph	.000	2	2	0	0	0	0	0	0	0	1	0
Mark Wohlers, p	.000	3	0	0	0	0	0	0	0	0	0	0
TOTAL	.231		229	19	53	10	1	5	19	22	42	11

PITCHER	W	L	ERA	G	GS	CG	SV	SHO	IP	H	ER	BB	SO
Steve Avery	2	0	0.00	2	2	0	0	0	16.1	9	0	4	17
Jim Clancy	0	0	0.00	1	0	0	0	0	0.1	0	0	0	0
Tom Glavine	0	2	3.21	2	2	0	0	0	14.0	12	5	6	11
Charlie Leibrandt	0	0	1.35	1	1	0	0	0	6.2	8	1	3	6
Kent Mercker	0	1	13.50	1	0	0	0	0	0.2	1	1	2	0
Alejandro Pena	0	0	0.00	4	0	0	3	0	4.1	1	0	0	4
John Smoltz	2	0	1.76	2	2	1	0	1	15.1	14	3	3	15
Mike Stanton	0	0	2.45	3	0	0	0	0	3.2	4	1	3	3
Mark Wohlers	0	0	0.00	3	0	0	0	0	1.2	3	0	1	1
TOTAL	4	3	1.57	19	7	1	3	1	63.0	51	11	22	57

PIT (E)

PLAYER/POS	AVG	G	AB	R	H	2B	3B	HR	RB	BB	SO	SB
Stan Belinda, p	.000	3	0	0	0	0	0	0	0	0	0	0
Jay Bell, ss	.414	7	29	2	12	2	0	1	1	0	10	0
Barry Bonds, of	.148	7	27	1	4	1	0	0	0	2	4	3
Bobby Bonilla, of	.304	7	23	2	7	2	0	1	6	2	0
Steve Buechele, 3b	.304	7	23	2	7	2	0	0	4	6	0
Doug Drabek, p	.200	2	5	0	1	1	0	0	1	0	2	0
Cecil Espy, ph	.000	2	2	0	0	0	0	0	0	0	2	0
Bob Kipper, p	.000	1	0	0	0	0	0	0	0	0	0	0
Bill Landrum, p	.000	1	0	0	0	0	0	0	0	0	0	0
Mike LaValliere, c	.333	3	6	0	2	0	0	0	1	2	0	0
Jose Lind, 2b	.160	7	25	0	4	0	0	0	3	0	6	0
Roger Mason, p	.000	3	1	0	0	0	0	0	0	0	1	0
Lloyd McClendon, 1b-1	.000	3	2	0	0	0	0	0	0	1	0	0
Orlando Merced, 1b-2	.222	3	9	1	2	0	0	1	1	0	1	0
Bob Patterson, p	.000	1	0	0	0	0	0	0	0	0	0	0
Gary Redus, 1b	.158	5	19	1	3	0	0	0	1	4	2
Rosario Rodriguez, p	.000	1	0	0	0	0	0	0	0	0	0	0
Don Slaught, c	.235	6	17	0	4	0	0	0	1	1	4	0
John Smiley, p	.000	2	0	0	0	0	0	0	0	0	0	0
Zane Smith, p	.000	2	5	0	0	0	0	0	0	0	4	0
Randy Tomlin, p	.000	1	2	0	0	0	0	0	0	0	0	0
Andy Van Slyke, of	.160	7	25	3	4	2	0	1	2	5	5	1
Gary Varsho, ph	.500	2	2	0	1	0	0	0	0	0	1	0
Bob Walk, p	.000	3	2	0	0	0	0	0	0	0	2	0
Curtis Wilkerson, ph	.000	4	4	0	0	0	0	0	0	0	3	0
TOTAL	.224		228	12	51	10	0	3	11	22	57	6

PITCHER	W	L	ERA	G	GS	CG	SV	SHO	IP	H	ER	BB	SO
Stan Belinda	1	0	0.00	3	0	0	0	0	5.0	0	0	3	4
Doug Drabek	1	1	0.60	2	2	1	0	0	15.0	10	1	5	10
Bob Kipper	0	0	4.50	1	0	0	0	0	2.0	2	1	0	1
Bill Landrum	0	0	9.00	1	0	0	0	0	1.0	2	1	2	2
Roger Mason	0	0	0.00	3	0	0	1	0	4.1	3	0	1	2
Bob Patterson	0	0	0.00	1	0	0	0	0	2.0	1	0	0	3
Rosario Rodriguez	0	0	27.00	1	0	0	0	0	1.0	1	3	3	1
John Smiley	0	2	23.63	2	2	0	0	0	2.2	8	7	1	3
Zane Smith	1	1	0.61	2	2	0	0	0	14.2	15	1	3	10
Randy Tomlin	0	0	3.00	1	1	0	0	0	6.0	6	2	2	1
Bob Walk	0	0	1.93	3	0	0	1	0	9.1	5	2	3	5
TOTAL	3	4	2.57	20	7	1	2	0	63.0	53	18	22	42

GAME 1 AT PIT OCT 9

ATL	000	000	001	1	5	1
PIT	102	001	01X	5	8	1

Pitchers: GLAVINE, Wohlers (7), Stanton (8) vs DRABEK, Walk (7)
Home Runs: Van Slyke-PIT, Justice-ATL
Attendance: 57,347

GAME 2 AT PIT OCT 10

ATL	000	001	000	1	8	0
PIT	000	000	000	0	6	0

Pitchers: AVERY, Pena (9) vs SMITH, Mason (8), Belinda (9)
Attendance: 57,533

GAME 3 AT ATL OCT 12

PIT	100	100	100	3	10	2
ATL	411	000	13X	10	11	0

Pitchers: SMILEY, Landrum (3), Patterson (4), Kipper (6), Rodriguez (8), Stanton (7), Wohlers (8), Pena (8)
Home Runs: Merced-PIT, Bell-PIT, Gant-ATL, Olson-ATL, Bream-ATL
Attendance: 50,905

GAME 4 AT ATL OCT 13

PIT	010	010	000	1	3	11	1
ATL	200	000	000	0	2	7	1

Pitchers: Tomlin, Walk (7), BELINDA (9) vs Leibrandt, Clancy (7), Stanton (8), MERCKER (10), Wohlers (10)
Attendance: 51,109

GAME 5 AT ATL OCT 14

PIT	000	010	000	1	6	2
ATL	000	000	000	0	9	1

Pitchers: SMITH, Mason (8) vs GLAVINE, Pena (9)
Attendance: 51,109

GAME 6 AT PIT OCT 16

ATL	000	000	001	1	7	0
PIT	000	000	000	0	4	0

Pitchers: AVERY, Pena (9) vs DRABEK
Attendance: 54,508

GAME 7 AT PIT OCT 17

ATL	300	010	000	4	6	1
PIT	000	000	000	0	6	0

Pitchers: SMOLTZ vs SMILEY, Walk (1), Mason (6), Belinda (8)
Home Runs: Hunter-ATL
Attendance: 46,932

By any measure, this World Series was one of the great ones. Five of the seven games were decided by a single run, three of them—including Games Six and Seven—in extra innings.

The opener in Minnesota gave no indication of the suspense to come, as the Twins opened up a 4–0 lead in the fifth inning en route to a 5–2 win. Game Two proved more difficult. Chili Davis put the Twins in front with a two-run homer in the first inning, but in the fifth Atlanta tied the score. Braves hurler Tom Glavine but lost the game when the Twins' Scott Leius lofted a homer to lead off the eighth.

Minnesota took a quick lead in Game Three, but Atlanta tied the game an inning later, and went ahead on solo homers by David Justice in the fourth inning and Lonnie Smith in the fifth. Home runs by Kirby Puckett and Chili Davis in the fifth and sixth re-tied the score, which remained at 4–4 into the last of the eleventh inning, when Justice scored from second on Mark Lemke's two-out single. Lemke's heroics also made the difference in Game Four. Mike Pagliarulo drove in a pair of runs for Minnesota with a single in the second and a home run in the seventh, but Braves Terry Pendleton and Lonnie Smith neutralized the runs with solo homers in the third and seventh. Lemke came to bat in the bottom of the ninth with one out and the score still 2–2. He tripled, and scored in a tight play to even the Series.

In Game Five the Braves assaulted five Minnesota pitchers for fourteen runs and the Series lead, but when play returned to Minnesota for Game Six the Twins revived with two first-inning runs. In the third inning Puckett prevented two Atlanta runs with a leaping catch above the wall, but in the fifth, Atlanta's Terry Pendleton evened the score with a two-run homer. Later in the inning the Twins regained the lead on Puckett's sacrifice fly. Atlanta knotted the score again in the seventh, at 2–2. In the last of the eleventh, leadoff batter Puckett lined the ball over the wall near where he had earlier made his game-saving catch.

No one scored through 9½ innings of Game Seven as Minnesota's Jack Morris dueled John Smoltz, Mike Stanton, and Alejandro Pena. If the Braves had scored in the eighth as they could have, they would have won the game and the crown. Lonnie Smith singled to lead off the inning and could have come around on Terry Pendleton's double to the wall in left center. But, decoyed by the Twins' middle infielders into thinking there was a play at second, he paused just long enough after passing second to en-

able him to advance only to third. No one was out, but a grounder to first, an intentional walk to load the bases, and a smart 3–2–3 double play ended the Braves' threat.

Thus the game was still scoreless in the last of the tenth when Dan Gladden hustled his way into a broken-bat double and moved to third on Chuck Knoblauch's sacrifice bunt. Then, after the bases were loaded intentionally, pinch hitter Gene Larkin lobbed a hit over the head of the drawn-in left fielder. Gladden came home with the title for Minnesota.

Minnesota Twins (AL), 4; Atlanta Braves (NL), 3

MIN (A)

PLAYER/POS	AVG	G	AB	R	H	2B	3B	HR	RB	BB	SO	SB
Rick Aguilera, p	.000	4	1	0	0	0	0	0	0	0	0	0
Steve Bedrosian, p	.000	3	0	0	0	0	0	0	0	0	0	0
Jarvis Brown, of-2,dh-1	.000	3	2	0	0	0	0	0	0	0	0	0
Randy Bush, of-2	.250	3	4	0	1	0	0	0	0	0	1	0
Chili Davis, dh-4,of-1	.222	6	18	4	4	0	0	2	4	2	3	0
Scott Erickson, p	.000	2	1	0	0	0	0	0	0	0	1	0
Greg Gagne, ss	.167	7	24	1	4	1	0	1	3	0	7	0
Dan Gladden, of	.233	7	30	5	7	2	2	0	0	3	4	2
Mark Guthrie, p	.000	4	0	0	0	0	0	0	0	0	0	0
Brian Harper, c	.381	7	21	2	8	2	0	0	1	2	2	0
Kent Hrbek, 1b	.115	7	26	2	3	1	0	1	2	2	6	0
Chuck Knoblauch, 2b	.308	7	26	3	8	1	0	0	2	4	2	4
Gene Larkin, dh-1	.500	4	4	0	2	0	0	0	1	0	0	0
Terry Leach, p	.000	2	0	0	0	0	0	0	0	0	0	0
Scott Leius, 3b	.357	7	14	2	5	0	0	1	2	1	2	0
Shane Mack, of	.130	6	23	0	3	1	0	0	1	0	7	0
Jack Morris, p	.000	3	2	0	0	0	0	0	0	0	1	0
Al Newman, 3b-2,2b-1,ss-1	.500	4	2	0	1	0	1	0	1	0	0	0
Junior Ortiz, c	.200	3	5	0	1	0	0	0	0	0	1	0
Mike Pagliarulo, 3b	.273	6	11	1	3	0	0	1	2	1	2	0
Kirby Puckett, of	.250	7	24	4	6	0	1	2	4	5	7	1
Paul Sorrento, 1b-1	.000	3	2	0	0	0	0	0	0	1	2	0
Kevin Tapani, p	.000	2	1	0	0	0	0	0	0	0	0	0
David West, p	.000	2	0	0	0	0	0	0	0	0	0	0
Carl Willis, p	.000	4	0	0	0	0	0	0	0	0	0	0
TOTAL	.232		241	24	56	8	4	8	24	21	48	7

PITCHER	W	L	ERA	G	GS	CG	SV	SHO	IP	H	ER	BB	SO
Rick Aguilera	1	1	1.80	4	0	0	2	0	5.0	6	1	1	3
Steve Bedrosian	0	0	5.40	3	0	0	0	0	3.1	3	2	0	2
Scott Erickson	0	0	5.06	2	2	0	0	0	10.2	10	6	4	5
Mark Guthrie	0	1	2.25	4	0	0	0	0	4.0	3	1	4	3
Terry Leach	0	0	3.86	2	0	0	0	0	2.1	2	1	0	2
Jack Morris	2	0	1.17	3	3	1	0	1	23.0	18	3	9	15
Kevin Tapani	1	1	4.50	2	2	0	0	0	12.0	13	6	2	7
David West	0	0	INF	2	0	0	0	0	0.0	2	4	4	0
Carl Willis	0	0	5.14	4	0	0	0	0	7.0	6	4	2	2
TOTAL	4	3	3.74	26	7	1	2	1	67.1	63	28	26	39

ATL (N)

PLAYER/POS	AVG	G	AB	R	H	2B	3B	HR	RB	BB	SO	SB
Steve Avery, p	.000	2	3	0	0	0	0	0	0	0	2	0
Rafael Belliard, ss	.375	7	16	0	6	1	0	0	4	1	2	0
Jeff Blauser, ss	.167	5	6	0	1	0	0	0	0	1	1	0
Sid Bream, 1b	.125	7	24	0	3	2	0	0	3	4	0	0
Francisco Cabrera, c-1	.000	3	1	0	0	0	0	0	0	0	0	0
Jim Clancy, p	.000	3	1	0	0	0	0	0	0	0	1	0
Ron Gant, of	.267	7	30	3	8	0	1	0	4	2	3	1
Tom Glavine, p	.000	2	2	0	0	0	0	0	0	0	0	0
Tommy Gregg, ph	.000	4	3	0	0	0	0	0	0	0	2	0
Brian Hunter, 1b-4,of-4	.190	7	21	2	4	1	0	1	3	0	2	0
David Justice, of	.259	7	27	5	7	0	0	2	6	5	5	2
Charlie Leibrandt, p	.000	2	0	0	0	0	0	0	0	0	0	0
Mark Lemke, 2b	.417	6	24	4	10	1	3	0	4	2	4	0
Kent Mercker, p	.000	2	0	0	0	0	0	0	0	0	0	0
Keith Mitchell, of	.000	3	2	0	0	0	0	0	0	0	1	0
Greg Olson, c	.222	7	27	3	6	2	0	0	1	5	4	1
Alejandro Pena, p	.000	3	0	0	0	0	0	0	0	0	0	0
Terry Pendleton, 3b	.367	7	30	6	11	3	0	2	3	3	1	0
Randy St. Claire, p	.000	1	0	0	0	0	0	0	0	0	0	0
Lonnie Smith, dh-4,of-3	.231	7	26	5	6	0	0	3	3	3	4	1
John Smoltz, p	.000	2	2	0	0	0	0	0	0	0	1	0
Mike Stanton, p	.000	5	0	0	0	0	0	0	0	0	0	0
Jeff Treadway, 2b-1	.250	3	4	1	1	0	0	0	0	1	2	0
Jerry Willard, ph	.000	1	0	0	0	0	0	0	0	1	0	0
Mark Wohlers, p	.000	3	0	0	0	0	0	0	0	0	0	0
TOTAL	.253		249	29	63	10	4	8	29	26	39	5

PITCHER	W	L	ERA	G	GS	CG	SV	SHO	IP	H	ER	BB	SO
Steve Avery	0	0	3.46	2	2	0	0	0	13.0	10	5	1	8
Jim Clancy	1	0	4.15	3	0	0	0	0	4.1	3	2	4	2
Tom Glavine	1	1	2.70	2	2	1	0	0	13.1	8	4	7	8
Charlie Leibrandt	0	2	11.25	2	1	0	0	0	4.0	8	5	1	3
Kent Mercker	0	0	0.00	2	0	0	0	0	1.0	0	0	0	0
Alejandro Pena	0	1	3.38	3	0	0	0	0	5.1	6	2	3	7
Randy St. Claire	0	0	9.00	1	0	0	0	0	1.0	1	1	0	0
John Smoltz	0	0	1.26	2	2	0	0	0	14.1	13	2	1	11
Mike Stanton	1	0	0.00	5	0	0	0	0	7.1	5	0	2	7
Mark Wohlers	0	0	0.00	3	0	0	0	0	1.2	2	0	2	1
TOTAL	3	4	2.89	25	7	1	0	0	65.1	56	21	21	48

GAME 1 AT MIN OCT 19

ATL	000	001	010	2	6 1
MIN	001	031	00X	5	9 1

Pitchers: LEIBRANDT, Clancy (5), Wohlers (7), Stanton (8) vs MORRIS, Guthrie (8), Aguilera (8)
Home Runs: Gagne-MIN, Hrbek-MIN
Attendance: 55,108

GAME 2 AT MIN OCT 20

ATL	010	010	000	2	8 1
MIN	200	000	01X	3	4 1

Pitchers: GLAVINE vs TAPANI, Aguilera (9)
Home Runs: Davis-MIN, Leius-MIN
Attendance: 55,145

GAME 3 AT ATL OCT 22

MIN	100	000	120	000	4	10 1
ATL	010	120	000	001	5	8 2

Pitchers: Erickson, West (5), Leach (5), Bedrosian (6), Willis (8), Guthrie (10), AGUILERA (12) vs Avery, Pena (8), Stanton (10), Wohlers (12), Mercker (12), CLANCY (12)
Home Runs: Justice-ATL, Smith-ATL, Puckett-MIN, Davis-MIN
Attendance: 50,878

GAME 4 AT ATL OCT 23

MIN	010	000	100	2	7 0
ATL	001	000	101	3	8 0

Pitchers: Morris, Willis (7), GUTHRIE (8), Bedrosian (9) vs Smoltz, Wohlers (8), STANTON (8)
Home Runs: Pendleton-ATL, Pagliarulo-ATL, Smith-ATL
Attendance: 50,878

GAME 5 AT ATL OCT 24

MIN	000	003	011	5	7 1
ATL	000	410	63X	14	17 1

Pitchers: TAPANI, Leach (5), West (7), Bedrosian (7), Willis (8) vs GLAVINE, Mercker (6), Clancy (7), St. Claire (9)
Home Runs: Justice-ATL, Smith-ATL, Hunter-ATL
Attendance: 50,878

GAME 6 AT MIN OCT 26

ATL	000	020	100	00	3 9 1
MIN	200	010	000	01	4 9 0

Pitchers: Avery, Stanton (7), Pena (9), LEIBRANDT (11) vs Erickson, Guthrie (7), Willis (7), AGUILERA (10)
Home Runs: Pendleton-ATL, Puckett-MIN
Attendance: 55,155

GAME 7 AT MIN OCT 27

ATL	000	000	000	0	0 7 0
MIN	000	000	001	1	1 10 0

Pitchers: Smoltz, Stanton (8), PENA (9) vs MORRIS
Attendance: 55,118

Atlanta opened the series with a pair of one-sided wins but Pittsburgh pulled out a close victory in Game Three. After a third loss, the Piartes pummelled the Braves for two wins even more lopsided than their losses in the first two games. With the series now even, the stage was set for what turned out to be one of the most dramatic finishes in postseason history.

In Game One Pirate Jose Lind spoiled John Smoltz's shutout with his first home run of the season in the eighth inning. But by then the Braves had scored five times and held victory firmly in hand. Game Two was even easier. By the time the Pirates came up with four runs in the seventh inning (ending Steve Avery's LCS-record streak of scoreless innings at 22⅓), Atlanta had already compiled two four-run innings of their own (one of them on Ron Gant's grand slam). The Braves added five more runs in the last of the seventh to put the game out of reach.

At home for Game Three, the Pirates pulled themselves together behind the five-hit pitching of rookie knuckleballer Tim Wakefield. Sid Bream's solo homer in the fourth inning gave Atlanta a 1–0 lead, but Pirate Don Slaught homered to even the score an inning later and a pair of sixth-inning doubles put the Pirates ahead. Ron Gant's homer for Atlanta in the top of the seventh tied the score again, but a single, double, and sacrifice fly in the bottom of the inning put Pittsburgh on top to stay.

A 6–4 loss in Game Four brought the Pirates to the brink of elimination, but in Game Five they counterattacked, driving out Atlanta starter Steve Avery in the first inning with five hits (four of them doubles) and four runs, on their way to a 7–1 victory. With their feet still at the chasm's edge, the Pirates unloaded on Atlanta's Tom Glavine for eight runs in the second inning of Game Six before the first out was recorded, and pushed the assault to a 13–4 conclusion and a tied series.

While the Pirates scored single runs in the first and sixth innings of the final game, Pirate starter Doug Drabek (who had taken losses in Games One and Four) held Atlanta scoreless through eight innings. Then, in the last of the ninth, leadoff Brave Terry Pendleton doubled. He moved to third as David Justice reached on a grounder bobbled by the usually sure-handed second baseman Jose Lind. A walk to Sid Bream filled the bases. Stan Belinda replaced Drabek on the mound and retired Ron Gant on a fly to left, but Pendleton scored Atlanta's first run after the catch. Damon Berryhill walked to reload the bases, and pinch hitter Brian Hunter popped out. Had there been

no error, the game would have been over, with Pittsburgh waving the pennant. Instead, little-used pinch hitter Francisco Cabrera lined the ball safely to left, scoring Justice with the tying run and Bream with a repeat pennant for Atlanta.

Atlanta Braves (West), 4; Pittsburgh Pirates (East), 3

ATL (W)

PLAYER/POS	AVG	G	AB	R	H	2B	3B	HR	RB	BB	SO	SB
Steve Avery, p	.000	3	2	0	0	0	0	0	0	1	0	1	0
R. Belliard, ss-3,2b-1	.000	4	2	1	0	0	0	0	0	1	0	0
Damon Berryhill, c	.167	7	24	1	4	1	0	0	1	3	2	0
Jeff Blauser, ss	.208	7	24	3	5	0	1	1	4	3	2	0
Sid Bream, 1b	.273	7	22	5	6	3	0	1	2	3	0	0
Francisco Cabrera, ph	.500	2	2	0	1	0	0	0	2	0	0	0
Marvin Freeman, p	.000	3	0	0	0	0	0	0	0	0	0	0
Ron Gant, of	.182	7	22	5	4	0	0	2	6	4	4	1
Tom Glavine, p	.000	2	2	0	0	0	0	0	0	0	0	0
Brian Hunter, 1b-2	.200	3	5	1	1	0	0	0	0	0	1	0
David Justice, of	.280	7	25	5	7	1	0	2	6	6	2	0
Charlie Leibrandt, p	.000	2	1	0	0	0	0	0	0	0	1	0
Mark Lemke, 2b-7,3b-1	.333	7	21	2	7	1	0	0	2	5	3	0
Javier Lopez, c	.000	1	1	0	0	0	0	0	0	0	0	0
Kent Mercker, p	.000	2	0	0	0	0	0	0	0	0	0	0
Otis Nixon, of	.286	7	28	5	8	2	0	0	2	4	4	3
Terry Pendleton, 3b	.233	7	30	2	7	2	0	0	3	0	2	0
Jeff Reardon, p	.000	3	0	0	0	0	0	0	0	0	0	0
Deion Sanders, of-3	.000	4	5	0	0	0	0	0	0	0	3	0
Lonnie Smith, ph	.333	6	6	1	2	0	1	0	1	0	0	0
Pete Smith, p	.000	2	1	0	0	0	0	0	0	0	0	0
John Smoltz, p	.286	3	7	1	2	0	0	0	1	0	2	1
Mike Stanton, p	1.000	5	1	1	1	1	0	0	1	0	0	0
Jeff Treadway, 2b-1	.667	3	3	1	2	0	0	0	0	0	1	0
Mark Wohlers, p	.000	3	0	0	0	0	0	0	0	0	0	0
TOTAL	.244		234	34	57	11	2	6	32	29	28	5

PITCHER	W	L	ERA	G	GS	CG	SV	SHO	IP	H	ER	BB	SO
Steve Avery	1	1	9.00	3	2	0	0	0	8.0	13	8	2	3
Marvin Freeman	0	0	14.73	3	0	0	0	0	3.2	8	6	2	1
Tom Glavine	0	2	12.27	2	2	0	0	0	7.1	13	10	3	2
Charlie Leibrandt	0	0	1.93	2	0	0	0	0	4.2	4	1	3	3
Kent Mercker	0	0	0.00	2	0	0	0	0	3.0	1	0	1	1
Jeff Reardon	1	0	0.00	3	0	0	1	0	3.0	0	0	2	3
Pete Smith	0	0	2.45	2	0	0	0	0	3.2	2	1	3	3
John Smoltz	2	0	2.66	3	3	0	0	0	20.1	14	6	10	19
Mike Stanton	0	0	0.00	5	0	0	0	0	4.1	2	0	2	5
Mark Wohlers	0	0	0.00	3	0	0	0	0	3.0	2	0	1	2
TOTAL	4	3	4.72	28	7	0	1	0	61.0	59	32	29	42

PIT (E)

PLAYER/POS	AVG	G	AB	R	H	2B	3B	HR	RB	BB	SO	SB
Stan Belinda, p	.000	2	0	0	0	0	0	0	0	0	0	0
Jay Bell, ss	.172	7	29	3	5	2	0	1	4	3	4	0
Barry Bonds, of	.261	7	23	5	6	1	0	1	2	6	4	1
Alex Cole, of	.200	4	10	2	2	0	0	0	1	3	2	0
Danny Cox, p	.000	2	0	0	0	0	0	0	0	0	0	0
Doug Drabek, p	.000	3	6	0	0	0	0	0	0	1	4	0
Cecil Espy, of	.667	4	3	0	2	0	0	0	0	0	1	0
Carlos Garcia, 2b	.000	1	1	0	0	0	0	0	0	0	0	0
Danny Jackson, p	.000	1	0	0	0	0	0	0	0	0	0	0
Jeff King, 3b	.241	7	29	4	7	4	0	0	2	0	1	0
Mike LaValliere, c	.200	3	10	1	2	0	0	0	0	0	3	0
Jose Lind, 2b	.222	7	27	5	6	2	1	1	5	1	4	0
Roger Mason, p	.000	2	0	0	0	0	0	0	0	0	0	0
Lloyd McClendon, of	.727	5	11	4	8	2	0	1	4	4	1	0
Orlando Merced, 1b	.100	4	10	0	1	1	0	0	2	2	4	0
Denny Neagle, p	.000	2	0	0	0	0	0	0	0	0	0	0
Bob Patterson, p	.000	2	0	0	0	0	0	0	0	0	0	0
Gary Redus, 1b	.438	5	16	4	7	4	1	0	3	2	3	0
Don Slaught, c	.333	5	12	5	4	1	0	1	5	6	3	0
Randy Tomlin, p	.000	2	0	0	0	0	0	0	0	0	0	0
Andy Van Slyke, of	.276	7	29	1	8	3	1	0	4	1	5	0
Gary Varsho, of-1	.500	2	2	0	1	0	0	0	1	0	0	0
Tim Wakefield, p	.000	2	6	1	0	0	0	0	0	0	0	0
Bob Walk, p	.000	2	5	0	0	0	0	0	0	0	1	0
John Wehner, ph	.000	2	2	0	0	0	0	0	0	0	2	0
TOTAL	.255		231	35	59	20	3	5	32	29	42	1

PITCHER	W	L	ERA	G	GS	CG	SV	SHO	IP	H	ER	BB	SO
Stan Belinda	0	0	0.00	2	0	0	0	0	1.2	2	0	0	2
Danny Cox	0	0	0.00	2	0	0	0	0	1.1	1	0	1	1
Doug Drabek	0	3	3.71	3	3	0	0	0	17.0	18	7	7	10
Danny Jackson	0	1	21.60	1	1	0	0	0	1.2	4	4	2	0
Roger Mason	0	0	0.00	2	0	0	0	0	3.1	0	0	2	1
Denny Neagle	0	0	27.00	2	0	0	0	0	1.2	4	5	3	0
Bob Patterson	0	0	5.40	2	0	0	0	0	1.2	3	1	1	1
Randy Tomlin	0	0	6.75	2	0	0	0	0	2.2	5	2	1	0
Tim Wakefield	2	0	3.00	2	2	2	0	0	18.0	14	6	5	7
Bob Walk	1	0	3.86	2	1	1	0	0	11.2	6	5	7	6
TOTAL	3	4	4.45	20	7	3	0	0	60.2	57	30	29	28

GAME 1 AT ATL OCT 6

PIT	000 000 010	1	5	1
ATL	010 210 10X	5	8	0

Pitchers: DRABEK, Patterson (5), Neagle (7), Cox (8) vs SMOLTZ, Stanton (9)
Home Runs: Lind-PIT, Blauser-ATL
Attendance: 51,971

GAME 2 AT ATL OCT 7

PIT	000 000 410	5	7	0
ATL	040 040 50X	13	14	0

Pitchers: JACKSON, Mason (2), Walk (3), Tomlin (5), Neagle (7), Patterson (7), Belinda (8) vs AVERY, Freeman (7), Stanton (7), Wohlers (8), Reardon (9)
Home Runs: Gant-ATL
Attendance: 51,975

GAME 3 AT PIT OCT 9

ATL	000 100 100	2	5	0
PIT	000 011 10X	3	8	1

Pitchers: GLAVINE, Stanton (7), Wohlers (8) vs WAKEFIELD
Home Runs: Bream-ATL, Gant-ATL, Slaught-PIT
Attendance: 56,610

GAME 4 AT PIT OCT 10

ATL	020 022 000	6	11	1
PIT	021 000 100	4	6	1

Pitchers: SMOLTZ, Stanton (7), Reardon (9) vs DRABEK, Tomlin (5), Cox (6), Mason (7)
Attendance: 57,164

GAME 5 AT PIT OCT 11

ATL	000 000 010	1	3	0
PIT	401 001 10X	7	13	0

Pitchers: AVERY, Smith (1), Leibrandt (5), Freeman (6), Mercker (8) vs WALK
Attendance: 52,929

GAME 6 AT ATL OCT 13

PIT	080 041 000	13	13	1
ATL	000 100 102	4	9	1

Pitchers: WAKEFIELD vs GLAVINE, Leibrandt (2), Freeman (5), Mercker (7), Wohlers (9)
Home Runs: Bell-PIT, Bonds-PIT, McClendon-PIT, Justice-ATL (2)
Attendance: 51,975

GAME 7 AT ATL OCT 14

PIT	100 001 000	2	7	1
ATL	000 000 003	3	7	0

Pitchers: DRABEK, Belinda (9) vs Smoltz, Stanton (7), Smith (7), Avery (7), REARDON (9)
Attendance: 51,975

Atlanta outscored Toronto in the Series 20 runs to 16, but the Blue Jays eked out four one-run victories to bring Canada its first world baseball championship. In the fourth inning of Game One, Atlanta's Tom Glavine gave up a leadoff homer to Joe Carter for the game's first run, but held the Jays to just one single the rest of the way. For five innings, meanwhile, Toronto starter Jack Morris shut out the Braves. But in the top of the sixth he gave up a deciding three-run homer to catcher Damon Berryhill. The next night, though, down 4–5 in the ninth inning, Toronto pinch hitter Derek Bell drew a walk from Braves closer Jeff Reardon, and pinch hitter Ed Sprague lined Reardon's first pitch over the left field wall.

Toronto moved ahead with another close victory in Game Three, the first World Series game ever played outside the United States. Atlanta threatened in the fourth inning when, with two on and none out, David Justice drove the ball to deep center. But in the defensive play of the Series, center fielder Devon White leaped high to snare the ball. Baserunner Terry Pendleton was ruled out for passing Deion Sanders on the basepath, and third baseman Kelly Gruber tagged Sanders, who was diving back into second base, to complete what seemed to be a triple play. The umpire didn't see the tag, however, and called Sanders safe. Still, no Brave scored, and Blue Jay Joe Carter homered for the game's first run in the last of the fourth. Atlanta tied the game in the sixth and took the lead in the top of the eighth. Gruber homered to re-tie it in the bottom of the inning, and after the Jays had filled the bases in the last of the ninth, Candy Maldonado tagged Reardon for a hit over the drawn-in outfield to bring home the winning run.

The Jays pushed their Series advantage to 3–1 in Game Four. Catcher Pat Borders opened the Toronto third with a home run, and Gruber scored from second on Devon White's seventh-inning single to push the Blue Jay lead to 2-0. The Braves got to Toronto starter Jimmy Key for a run in the eighth, but relievers Duane Ward and Tom Henke combined to stop them from scoring again.

In the fifth game the Blue Jays twice came from one run down to even the score. But in the fifth inning, after the Braves had once again built a one-run lead, Lonnie Smith extended it with a grand slam home run that sent the Series back to Atlanta.

Toronto Blue Jays (AL), 4; Atlanta Braves (NL), 2

TOR (A)

PLAYER/POS	AVG	G	AB	R	H	2B	3B	HR	RB	BB	SO	SB
Roberto Alomar, 2b	.208	6	24	3	5	1	0	0	0	3	3	2
Derek Bell, ph	.000	2	1	1	0	0	0	0	0	1	0	0
Pat Borders, c	.450	6	20	2	9	3	0	1	3	2	1	0
Joe Carter, of-4	.273	6	22	2	6	2	0	2	3	3	2	1
David Cone, p	.500	2	4	0	2	0	0	0	1	1	0	0
Mark Eichhorn, p	.000	1	0	0	0	0	0	0	0	0	0	0
Alfredo Griffin, ss	.000	2	0	0	0	0	0	0	0	0	0	0
Kelly Gruber, 3b	.105	6	19	2	2	0	0	1	1	2	5	1
Juan Guzman, p	.000	1	0	0	0	0	0	0	0	0	0	0
Tom Henke, p	.000	3	0	0	0	0	0	0	0	0	0	0
Jimmy Key, p	.000	2	1	0	0	0	0	0	0	0	0	0
Manuel Lee, ss	.105	6	19	1	2	0	0	0	0	1	2	0
Candy Maldonado, of-5	.158	6	19	1	3	0	0	1	2	2	5	0
Jack Morris, p	.000	2	2	0	0	0	0	0	0	0	2	0
John Olerud, 1b	.308	4	13	2	4	0	0	0	0	0	4	0
Ed Sprague, 1b-1	.500	3	2	1	1	0	0	1	2	1	0	0
Todd Stottlemyre, p	.000	4	0	0	0	0	0	0	0	0	0	0
Pat Tabler, ph	.000	2	2	0	0	0	0	0	0	0	0	0
Mike Timlin, p	.000	2	0	0	0	0	0	0	0	0	0	0
Duane Ward, p	.000	4	0	0	0	0	0	0	0	0	0	0
David Wells, p	.000	4	0	0	0	0	0	0	0	0	0	0
Devon White, of	.231	6	26	2	6	1	0	0	2	0	6	1
Dave Winfield, of-3,dh-3	.227	6	22	0	5	1	0	0	3	2	5	0
TOTAL	.230		196	17	45	8	0	6	17	18	33	5

PITCHER	W	L	ERA	G	GS	CG	SV	SHO	IP	H	ER	BB	SO
David Cone	0	0	3.48	2	2	0	0	0	10.1	9	4	8	8
Mark Eichhorn	0	0	0.00	1	0	0	0	0	1.0	0	0	0	0
Juan Guzman	0	0	1.13	1	1	0	0	0	8.0	8	1	1	7
Tom Henke	0	0	2.70	3	0	0	2	0	3.1	2	1	2	1
Jimmy Key	2	0	1.00	2	1	0	0	0	9.0	6	1	0	6
Jack Morris	0	2	8.71	2	2	0	0	0	10.1	13	10	6	12
Todd Stottlemyre	0	0	0.00	4	0	0	0	0	3.2	4	0	0	4
Mike Timlin	0	0	0.00	2	0	0	1	0	1.1	0	0	0	0
Duane Ward	2	0	0.00	4	0	0	0	0	3.1	1	0	1	6
David Wells	0	0	0.00	4	0	0	0	0	4.1	1	0	2	3
TOTAL	4	2	2.80	25	6	0	3	0	54.2	44	17	20	48

ATL (N)

PLAYER/POS	AVG	G	AB	R	H	2B	3B	HR	RB	BB	SO	SB
Steve Avery, p	.000	2	1	0	0	0	0	0	0	0	1	0
Rafael Belliard, ss-3,2b-1	.000	4	0	0	0	0	0	0	0	0	0	0
Damon Berryhill, c	.091	6	22	1	2	0	0	1	3	1	11	0
Jeff Blauser, ss	.250	6	24	2	6	0	0	0	0	1	9	2
Sid Bream, 1b	.200	5	15	1	3	0	0	0	0	4	0	0
Francisco Cabrera, ph	.000	1	1	0	0	0	0	0	0	0	0	0
Ron Gant, of-3	.125	4	8	2	1	1	0	0	0	1	2	2
Tom Glavine, p	.000	2	2	0	0	0	0	0	0	1	0	0
Brian Hunter, 1b-3	.200	4	5	0	1	0	0	0	2	0	1	0
David Justice, of	.158	6	19	4	3	0	0	1	3	6	5	1
Charlie Leibrandt, p	.000	1	0	0	0	0	0	0	0	0	0	0
Mark Lemke, 2b	.211	6	19	0	4	0	0	0	2	1	3	0
Otis Nixon, of	.296	6	27	3	8	1	0	0	1	1	3	5
Terry Pendleton, 3b	.240	6	25	2	6	2	0	0	2	1	5	0
Jeff Reardon, p	.000	2	0	0	0	0	0	0	0	0	0	0
Deion Sanders, of	.533	4	15	4	8	2	0	0	1	2	1	5
Lonnie Smith, dh-3	.167	5	12	1	2	0	0	1	5	1	4	0
Pete Smith, p	.000	1	1	0	0	0	0	0	0	0	1	0
John Smoltz, p-2	.000	3	3	0	0	0	0	0	0	0	2	0
Mike Stanton, p	.000	4	0	0	0	0	0	0	0	0	0	0
Jeff Treadway, ph	.000	1	1	0	0	0	0	0	0	0	0	0
Mark Wohlers, p	.000	2	0	0	0	0	0	0	0	0	0	0
TOTAL	.220		200	20	44	6	0	3	19	20	48	15

PITCHER	W	L	ERA	G	GS	CG	SV	SHO	IP	H	ER	BB	SO
Steve Avery	0	1	3.75	2	2	0	0	0	12.0	11	5	3	11
Tom Glavine	1	1	1.59	2	2	2	0	0	17.0	10	3	4	8
Charlie Leibrandt	0	1	9.00	1	0	0	0	0	2.0	3	2	0	0
Jeff Reardon	0	1	13.50	2	0	0	0	0	1.1	2	2	1	1
Pete Smith	0	0	0.00	1	0	0	0	0	3.0	3	0	0	0
John Smoltz	1	0	2.70	2	2	0	0	0	13.1	13	4	7	12
Mike Stanton	0	0	0.00	4	0	0	1	0	5.0	3	0	2	1
Mark Wohlers	0	0	0.00	2	0	0	0	0	0.2	0	0	1	0
TOTAL	2	4	2.65	16	6	2	1	0	54.1	45	16	18	33

Toronto scored a run in the first inning of Game Six. Atlanta tied the game in the third, but Candy Maldonado's leadoff homer in the fourth restored the advantage to Toronto. In the bottom of the ninth, the Braves scrabbled back to tie it up again. The score remained knotted at 2–2 until the top of the eleventh, when Toronto's Dave Winfield delivered runners from second and first with a two-out double into the left field corner. As it turned out, the Jays needed both runs, for Atlanta scored in the bottom of the eleventh. But with two out and the potential tying run on third, Otis Nixon, attempting a bunt single, just failed to reach safely, and the Series was over.

GAME 1 AT ATL OCT 17

TOR	000	100	000	1	4 0
ATL	000	003	00X	3	4 0

Pitchers: MORRIS, Stottlemyre (7), Wells (8) vs GLAVINE
Home Runs: Carter-TOR, Berryhill-ATL
Attendance: 51,763

GAME 2 AT ATL OCT 18

TOR	000	020	012	5	9 2
ATL	010	120	000	4	5 1

Pitchers: Cone, Wells (5), Stottlemyre (7), WARD (8), Henke (9) vs Smoltz, Stanton (8), REARDON (8)
Home Runs: Sprague-TOR
Attendance: 51,763

GAME 3 AT TOR OCT 20

ATL	000	001	010	2	9 0
TOR	000	100	011	3	6 1

Pitchers: AVERY, Wohlers (9), Stanton (9), Reardon (9) vs Guzman, WARD (9)
Home Runs: Carter-TOR, Gruber-TOR
Attendance: 51,813

GAME 4 AT TOR OCT 21

ATL	000	000	010	1	5 0
TOR	001	000	10X	2	6 0

Pitchers: GLAVINE vs KEY, Ward (8), Henke (9)
Home Runs: Borders-TOR
Attendance: 52,090

GAME 5 AT TOR OCT 22

ATL	100	150	000	7	13 0
TOR	010	100	000	2	6 0

Pitchers: SMOLTZ, Stanton (7) vs MORRIS, Wells (5), Timlin (7), Eichhorn (8), Stottlemyre (9)
Home Runs: Justice-ATL, L.Smith-ATL
Attendance: 52,268

GAME 6 AT ATL OCT 24

TOR	100	100	000 02	4	14 1
ATL	001	000	001 01	3	8 1

Pitchers: Cone, Stottlemyre (7), Wells (7), Ward (8), Henke (9), KEY (10), Timlin (11) vs Avery, P.Smith (5), Stanton (8), Wohlers (9), LEIBRANDT (10)
Home Runs: Maldonado-TOR
Attendance: 51,763

Atlanta outhit the Phillies by 47 percentage points, outscored them by ten runs, and yielded 1.6 fewer earned runs per game. But the Phillies won the pennant. In the opener, Philadelphia starter Curt Schilling fanned ten batters—including the first five he faced—and left the game after eight innings with a 3–2 lead. An errant throw by Phillie third baseman Kim Batiste (who had just entered the game to strengthen the defense) set up an unearned tying run in the ninth inning. But in the last of the tenth, after John Kruk had doubled, Batiste redeemed himself with a game-winning hit down the left field line, and was carried off the field on his teammates' shoulders.

While the Philadelphia offense remained steady over the next two games, the Braves erupted for 28 runs, quadrupling the Phillies' seven. By the time Philadelphia scored its first runs in the fourth inning of Game Two, Atlanta had already sent eight men across the plate. In Game Three the Phillies scored first, and held a 2–0 lead before the Braves destroyed them with five runs in the sixth inning and four more in the seventh.

Game Four featured only four fewer hits than Game Three, but ten fewer runs, as Philadelphia evened the series with its second close win. Phillie starter Danny Jackson yielded nine hits and a pair of walks in 7⅔ innings, but only one second-inning run. In the top of the fourth, Darren Daulton, who had reached on an infield error, took third on Milt Thompson's double and scored on Kevin Stocker's two-out single. Pitcher Jackson then singled home Thompson with what proved the winning run.

In the fifth game, Curt Schilling held Atlanta to four hits through eight innings, and carried a 3–0 lead into the bottom of the ninth. But when a walk and infield error put the first two men on, Mitch Williams relieved Schilling and gave up a trio of singles which tied the game. In the top of the tenth inning, though, Lenny Dykstra's solo homer restored the Phillies' lead, and veteran reliever Larry Andersen blanked the Braves in the bottom of the tenth—striking out the final two batters—to preserve the win.

After their two narrow wins on the road, the Phillies clinched the pennant with relative ease when the series returned to Philadelphia for Game Six. Darren Daulton's two-out double in the third inning put the Phillies up 2–0. Atlanta scored once in the fifth, but Dave Hollins' two-run homer in the last of the fifth increased the Phillies' lead to three runs, and Mickey Morandini's two-out two-run triple

Philadelphia Phillies (East), 4; Atlanta Braves (West), 2

PHI (E)

PLAYER/POS	AVG	G	AB	R	H	2B	3B	HR	RB	BB	SO	SB
Larry Andersen, p	.000	3	0	0	0	0	0	0	0	0	0	0
Kim Batiste, 3b	1.000	4	1	0	1	0	0	0	1	0	0	0
Wes Chamberlain, of-2	.364	4	11	1	4	3	0	0	1	1	3	0
Darren Daulton, c	.263	6	19	2	5	1	0	1	3	6	3	0
Mariano Duncan, 2b	.267	3	15	3	4	0	2	0	0	0	5	0
Lenny Dykstra, of	.280	6	25	5	7	1	0	2	2	5	8	0
Jim Eisenreich, of-5	.133	6	15	0	2	1	0	0	1	0	2	0
Tommy Greene, p	.000	2	0	1	0	0	0	0	0	1	0	0
Dave Hollins, 3b	.200	6	20	2	4	1	0	2	4	5	4	1
Pete Incaviglia, of	.167	3	12	2	2	0	0	1	1	0	3	0
Danny Jackson, p	.250	1	4	0	1	0	0	0	1	0	3	0
Ricky Jordan, ph	.000	2	1	0	0	0	0	0	0	0	1	0
John Kruk, 1b	.250	6	24	4	6	2	1	1	5	4	5	0
Tony Longmire, ph	.000	1	1	0	0	0	0	0	0	0	1	0
Roger Mason, p	.000	2	0	0	0	0	0	0	0	0	0	0
Mickey Morandini, 2b	.250	4	16	1	4	0	1	0	2	0	3	1
Terry Mulholland, p	.000	1	2	0	0	0	0	0	0	0	1	0
Todd Pratt, c	.000	1	1	0	0	0	0	0	0	0	1	0
Ben Rivera, p	.000	1	0	0	0	0	0	0	0	0	0	0
Curt Schilling, p	.000	2	5	0	0	0	0	0	0	0	2	0
Kevin Stocker, ss	.182	6	22	0	4	1	0	0	1	2	5	0
Bobby Thigpen, p	.000	2	0	0	0	0	0	0	0	0	0	0
Milt Thompson, of-5	.231	6	13	2	3	1	0	0	0	1	2	0
David West, p	.000	3	0	0	0	0	0	0	0	0	0	0
Mitch Williams, p	.000	4	0	0	0	0	0	0	0	0	0	0
TOTAL	.227		207	23	47	11	4	7	22	26	51	2

PITCHER	W	L	ERA	G	GS	CG	SV	SHO	IP	H	ER	BB	SO
Larry Andersen	0	0	15.43	3	0	0	1	0	2.1	4	4	1	3
Tommy Greene	1	1	9.64	2	2	0	0	0	9.1	12	10	7	7
Danny Jackson	1	0	1.17	1	1	0	0	0	7.2	9	1	2	6
Roger Mason	0	0	0.00	2	0	0	0	0	3.0	1	0	0	2
Terry Mulholland	0	1	7.20	1	1	0	0	0	5.0	9	4	1	2
Ben Rivera	0	0	4.50	1	0	0	0	0	2.0	1	1	1	2
Curt Schilling	0	0	1.69	2	2	0	0	0	16.0	11	3	5	19
Bobby Thigpen	0	0	5.40	2	0	0	0	0	1.2	1	1	1	3
David West	0	0	13.50	3	0	0	0	0	2.2	5	4	2	5
Mitch Williams	2	0	1.69	4	0	0	2	0	5.1	6	1	2	5
TOTAL	4	2	4.75	21	6	0	3	0	55.0	59	29	22	54

ATL (W)

PLAYER/POS	AVG	G	AB	R	H	2B	3B	HR	RB	BB	SO	SB
Steve Avery, p	.500	2	4	1	2	1	0	0	0	0	1	0
Rafael Belliard, 2b-1,ss-1	.000	2	1	1	0	0	0	0	0	0	1	0
Damon Berryhill, c	.211	6	19	2	4	0	0	1	3	1	5	0
Jeff Blauser, ss	.280	6	25	5	7	1	0	2	4	4	7	0
Sid Bream, 1b	1.000	1	1	1	1	0	0	0	0	0	0	0
Francisco Cabrera, c-1	.667	3	3	0	2	0	0	0	1	0	1	0
Ron Gant, of	.185	6	27	4	5	3	0	0	3	2	9	0
Tom Glavine, p	.000	1	3	0	0	0	0	0	0	0	0	0
David Justice, of	.143	6	21	2	3	1	0	0	4	3	3	0
Mark Lemke, 2b	.208	6	24	2	5	2	0	0	4	1	6	0
Greg Maddux, p	.250	2	4	1	1	0	0	0	0	0	1	0
Fred McGriff, 1b	.435	6	23	6	10	2	0	1	4	4	7	0
Greg McMichael, p	.000	4	0	0	0	0	.	0	0	0	0	0
Kent Mercker, p	.000	5	0	0	0	0	0	0	0	0	0	0
Otis Nixon, of	.348	6	23	3	8	2	0	0	4	5	6	0
Greg Olson, c	.333	2	3	0	1	1	0	0	0	0	1	0
Bill Pecota, ph	.333	4	3	1	1	0	0	0	0	1	1	0
Terry Pendleton, 3b	.346	6	26	4	9	1	0	1	5	0	2	0
Deion Sanders, of-1	.000	5	3	0	0	0	0	0	0	0	1	0
John Smoltz, p	.000	1	1	0	0	0	0	0	0	0	1	0
Mike Stanton, p	.000	1	0	0	0	0	0	0	0	0	0	0
Tony Tarasco, of	.000	2	1	0	0	0	0	0	0	0	1	0
Mark Wohlers, p	.000	4	0	0	0	0	0	0	0	0	0	0
TOTAL	.274		215	33	59	14	0	5	32	22	54	0

PITCHER	W	L	ERA	G	GS	CG	SV	SHO	IP	H	ER	BB	SO
Steve Avery	0	0	2.77	2	2	0	0	0	13.0	9	4	6	10
Tom Glavine	1	0	2.57	1	1	0	0	0	7.0	6	2	0	5
Greg Maddux	1	1	4.97	2	2	0	0	0	12.2	11	7	7	11
Greg McMichael	0	1	6.75	4	0	0	0	0	4.0	7	3	2	1
Kent Mercker	0	0	1.80	5	0	0	0	0	5.0	3	1	2	4
John Smoltz	0	1	0.00	1	1	0	0	0	6.1	8	0	5	10
Mike Stanton	0	0	0.00	1	0	0	0	0	1.0	1	0	1	0
Mark Wohlers	0	1	3.38	4	0	0	0	0	5.1	2	2	3	10
TOTAL	2	4	3.15	20	6	0	0	0	54.1	47	19	26	51

an inning later pushed the score to 6–1, driving out Atlanta starter Greg Maddux. Atlanta's Jeff Blauser brought the score to 6–3 with a home run in the seventh inning, but Phillie relievers David West and Mitch Williams set the Braves down in order in the final two innings.

GAME 1 AT PHI OCT 6

ATL	001 100 001 0	3	9 0
PHI	100 101 000 1	4	9 1

Pitchers: Avery, Mercker (7), McMICHAEL (9) vs Schilling, WILLIAMS (9)
Home Runs: Incaviglia-PHI
Attendance: 62,012

GAME 2 AT PHI OCT 7

ATL	206 010 041	14	16 0
PHI	000 200 001	3	7 2

Pitchers: MADDUX, Stanton (8), Wohlers (9) vs GREENE, Thigpen (3), Rivera (4), Mason (6), West (8), Andersen (9)
Home Runs: Blauser-ATL, McGriff-ATL, Pendleton-ATL, Berryhill-ATL, Dykstra-PHI, Hollins-PHI
Attendance: 62,436

GAME 3 AT ATL OCT 9

PHI	000 101 011	4	10 1
ATL	000 005 40X	9	12 0

Pitchers: MULHOLLAND, Mason (6), Andersen (7), West (7), Thigpen (8) vs GLAVINE, Mercker (8), McMichael (9)
Home Runs: Kruk-PHI
Attendance: 52,032

GAME 4 AT ATL OCT 10

PHI	000 200 000	2	8 1
ATL	010 000 000	1	10 1

Pitchers: JACKSON, Williams (8) vs SMOLTZ, Mercker (7), Wohlers (8)
Attendance: 52,032

GAME 5 AT ATL OCT 11

PHI	100 100 001 1	4	6 1
ATL	000 000 003 0	3	7 1

Pitchers: Schilling, WILLIAMS (9), Andersen (10) vs Avery, Mercker (8), McMichael (9), WOHLERS (10)
Home Runs: Dykstra-PHI, Daulton-PHI
Attendance: 52,032

GAME 6 AT PHI OCT 13

ATL	000 010 200	3	5 3
PHI	002 022 00X	6	7 1

Pitchers: MADDUX, Mercker (6), McMichael (7), Wohlers (7) vs GREENE, West (8), Williams (9)
Home Runs: Blauser-ATL, Hollins-PHI
Attendance: 62,502

Pitching-rich Atlanta's appearance in the division playoffs surprised few, but the hard-hitting expansion Rockies made history by reaching the postseason in just their third year of existence.

Two individuals shared the spotlight in Game One: Braves rookie third baseman Chipper Jones and Rockies manager Don Baylor, but for wildly different reasons. Jones collected two homers and made a spectacular stop to rob Andres Galarraga of a double. Baylor was less fortunate. He ran out of hitters in the bottom of the ninth—having to use pitcher Lance Painter as his last batter—after Jones homered with two outs in the top of the inning. Atlanta won 5–4.

Atlanta trailed 4–3 going into the top of the ninth in Game Two, but came thundering back with four runs as Mike Mordecai pinch homered and Rockies second baseman Eric Young botched a routine ground ball. The Braves triumphed 7–4, taking a 2-0 lead in the series.

In Game Three Atlanta came through in the ninth once more on pinch hitter Luis Polonia's two-strike run-scoring single, and the game went into extra innings. But Colorado bounced back to score twice in the tenth on Dante Bichette's double down the left field line and run-scoring singles by Andres Galarraga and Vinny Castilla (who had homered in the sixth).

Cy Young Award winners battled in Game Four as Greg Maddux and Bret Saberhagen started, but Saberhagen was ineffective and Atlanta eliminated the Rockies with a 10–4 win. Maddux struck out seven and walked none before leaving for a pinch hitter in the seventh inning. Not helping Saberhagen was a controversial "safe" call on a play in which he attempted to cover first. Fred McGriff followed the play with the first of his two homers in the contest.

Atlanta had reached the NLCS for the fourth straight time—a National League record—and would now face Cincinnati in the NLCS.

Atlanta Braves (East), 3; Colorado Rockies (West), 1

ATL (E)

PLAYER/POS	AVG	G	AB	R	H	2B	3B	HR	RB	BB	SO	SB
Steve Avery, p	.000	1	0	0	0	0	0	0	0	0	0	0
Rafael Belliard, ss	.000	4	5	1	0	0	0	0	0	0	1	0
Jeff Blauser, ss	.000	3	6	0	0	0	0	0	0	1	3	0
Pedro Borbon, p	.000	1	0	0	0	0	0	0	0	0	0	0
Brad Clontz, p	.000	1	0	0	0	0	0	0	0	0	0	0
Mike Devereaux, of-3	.200	4	5	1	1	0	0	0	0	0	0	0
Tom Glavine, p	.333	1	3	0	1	0	0	0	0	0	1	0
Marquis Grissom, of	.524	4	21	5	11	2	0	3	4	0	3	2
Chipper Jones, 3b	.389	4	18	4	7	2	0	2	4	2	2	0
David Justice, of	.231	4	13	2	3	0	0	0	0	5	2	0
Ryan Klesko, of	.467	4	15	5	7	1	0	0	1	0	3	0
Mark Lemke, 2b	.211	4	19	3	4	1	0	0	1	1	3	0
Javy Lopez, c	.444	3	9	0	4	0	0	0	3	0	3	0
Greg Maddux, p	.167	2	6	1	1	0	0	0	0	0	1	0
Fred McGriff, 1b	.333	4	18	4	6	0	0	2	6	2	3	0
Greg McMichael, p	.000	3	0	0	0	0	0	0	0	0	0	0
Kent Mercker, p	.000	1	0	0	0	0	0	0	0	0	0	0
Mike Mordecai, ss-1	.667	2	3	1	2	1	0	0	2	0	0	0
Charlie O'Brien, c	.200	2	5	0	1	0	0	0	0	1	1	0
Alejandro Pena, p	.000	3	0	0	0	0	0	0	0	0	0	0
Luis Polonia, ph	.333	3	3	0	1	0	0	0	2	0	1	1
Dwight Smith, ph	.667	4	3	0	2	1	0	0	1	0	0	0
John Smoltz, p	.000	1	2	0	0	0	0	0	0	0	0	0
Mark Wohlers, p	.000	3	0	0	0	0	0	0	0	0	0	0
TOTAL	.331		154	27	51	8	0	7	24	12	27	3

PITCHER	W	L	ERA	G	GS	CG	SV	SHO	IP	H	ER	BB	SO
Steve Avery	0	0	13.50	1	0	0	0	0	0.2	1	1	0	1
Pedro Borbon	0	0	0.00	1	0	0	0	0	1.0	1	0	0	3
Brad Clontz	0	0	0.00	1	0	0	0	0	1.1	1	0	0	3
Tom Glavine	0	0	2.57	1	1	0	0	0	7.0	5	2	1	3
Greg Maddux	1	0	4.50	2	2	0	0	0	14.0	19	7	2	7
Greg McMichael	0	0	6.75	3	0	0	0	0	1.1	1	1	2	1
Kent Mercker	0	0	0.00	1	0	0	0	0	0.1	0	0	0	0
Alejandro Pena	2	0	0.00	3	0	0	0	0	3.0	3	0	1	2
John Smoltz	0	0	7.94	1	1	0	0	0	5.2	5	5	1	6
Mark Wohlers	0	1	6.75	3	0	0	2	0	2.2	6	2	2	4
TOTAL	3	1	4.38	17	4	0	2	0	37.0	41	18	9	29

COL (E)

PLAYER/POS	AVG	G	AB	R	H	2B	3B	HR	RB	BB	SO	SB
Jason Bates, 2b-1,3b-1	.250	4	4	0	1	0	0	0	0	0	0	0
Dante Bichette, of	.588	4	17	6	10	3	0	1	3	1	3	0
Ellis Burks, of	.333	2	6	1	2	1	0	0	2	0	1	0
Vinny Castilla, 3b	.467	4	15	3	7	1	0	3	6	0	1	0
Andres Galarraga, 1b	.278	4	18	1	5	1	0	0	2	0	6	0
Joe Girardi, c	.125	4	16	0	2	0	0	0	0	0	2	0
Darren Holmes, p	.000	3	0	0	0	0	0	0	0	0	0	0
Trenidad Hubbard, ph	.000	3	2	0	0	0	0	0	0	0	0	0
Mike Kingery, of	.200	4	10	1	2	0	0	0	0	0	1	0
Curt Leskanic, p	.000	3	0	0	0	0	0	0	0	0	0	0
Mike Munoz, p	.000	4	0	0	0	0	0	0	0	0	0	0
J Owens, c	.000	1	1	0	0	0	0	0	0	0	1	0
Lance Painter, p-1	.000	2	2	0	0	0	0	0	0	0	1	0
Steve Reed, p	.000	3	0	0	0	0	0	0	0	0	0	0
Armando Reynoso, p	.000	1	0	0	0	0	0	0	0	0	0	0
Kevin Ritz, p	.000	2	2	0	0	0	0	0	0	0	1	0
Bruce Ruffin, p	.000	4	0	0	0	0	0	0	0	0	0	0
Bret Saberhagen, p	.000	1	1	0	0	0	0	0	0	0	1	0
Bill Swift, p	.000	1	3	0	0	0	0	0	0	0	2	0
Mark Thompson, p	.000	1	0	0	0	0	0	0	0	0	0	0
John Vanderwal, ph	.000	4	4	0	0	0	0	0	0	0	2	0
Larry Walker, of	.214	4	14	3	3	0	0	1	3	3	4	1
Walt Weiss, ss	.167	4	12	1	2	0	0	0	0	3	2	1
Eric Young, 2b	.438	4	16	3	7	1	0	1	2	2	2	1
TOTAL	.287		143	19	41	7	0	6	18	9	29	3

PITCHER	W	L	ERA	G	GS	CG	SV	SHO	IP	H	ER	BB	SO
Darren Holmes	1	0	0.00	3	0	0	0	0	1.2	6	0	0	2
Curt Leskanic	0	1	6.00	3	0	0	0	0	3.0	3	2	0	4
Mike Munoz	0	1	13.50	4	0	0	0	0	1.1	4	2	1	1
Lance Painter	0	0	5.40	1	1	0	0	0	5.0	5	3	2	4
Steve Reed	0	0	0.00	3	0	0	0	0	2.2	2	0	1	3
Armando Reynoso	0	0	0.00	1	0	0	0	0	1.0	2	0	0	0
Kevin Ritz	0	0	7.71	2	1	0	0	0	7.0	12	6	3	5
Bruce Ruffin	0	0	2.70	4	0	0	0	0	3.1	3	1	2	2
Bret Saberhagen	0	1	11.25	1	1	0	0	0	4.0	7	5	1	3
Bill Swift	0	0	6.00	1	1	0	0	0	6.0	7	4	2	3
Mark Thompson	0	0	0.00	1	0	0	1	0	1.0	0	0	0	0
TOTAL	1	3	5.75	24	4	0	1	0	36.0	51	23	12	27

GAME 1 AT COL OCT 3

ATL	001	002	011	5	12	1
COL	000	300	010	4	13	4

Pitchers: Maddux, McMichael (8), PENA (8), Wohlers (9) vs Ritz, Reed (6), Ruffin (7), Munoz (8), Holmes (8), LESKANIC (9)
Home Runs: Grissom-ATL, Jones-ATL (2), Castilla-COL
Attendance: 50,040

GAME 2 AT COL OCT 4

ATL	101	100	004	7	13	1
COL	000	003	010	4	8	2

Pitchers: Glavine, Avery (8), PENA (8), Wohlers (9) vs Painter, Reed (6), Ruffin (7), Leskanic (8), MUNOZ (9), Holmes (9)
Home Runs: Grissom-ATL (2), Walker-COL
Attendance: 50,040

GAME 3 AT ATL OCT 6

COL	102	002	000	2	7	9	0
ATL	000	300	101	0	5	11	0

Pitchers: Swift, Reed (7), Munoz (7), Leskanic (7), Ruffin (8), HOLMES (9), Thompson (10) vs Smoltz, Clontz (6), Borbon (8), McMichael (9), WOHLERS (10), Mercker (10)
Home Runs: Young-COL, Castilla-COL
Attendance: 51,300

GAME 4 AT ATL OCT 7

COL	003	001	000	4	11	1
ATL	004	213	00X	10	15	0

Pitchers: SABERHAGEN, Ritz (5), Munoz (6), Reynoso (7), Ruffin (8) vs MADDUX, Pena (8)
Home Runs: Bichette-COL, Castilla-COL, McGriff-ATL (2)
Attendance: 50,027

Both the Braves and the Reds had moved through the National League's first-ever division series with ease, with Atlanta knocking off Colorado 3–1 and Cincinnati sweeping the Dodgers 3–1.

In Game One a scant crowd of only 40,382 Riverfront Stadium patrons saw the Braves edge the Reds 2–1 in extra innings. Atlanta prevailed despite failing to move a runner past second base until the ninth inning, as the Reds' Pete Schourek held the Braves to four singles through eight. Atlanta broke through in the eleventh on Mike Devereaux's pinch-hit single—a feat which helped earn him NLCS MVP honors.

Game Two was another extra inning affair as Atlanta cracked the game open with four in the tenth to triumph 6–2. In that inning the Braves loaded the bases, scoring their first run on Mark Portugal's wild pitch. Javier Lopez followed with a three-run homer off the left-field foul screen.

Game Three remained scoreless until the sixth, when catcher Charlie O'Brien homered to left off David Wells, scoring Fred McGriff and Mike Devereaux. Chipper Jones followed with a two-run homer to complete the Braves' scoring.

Game Four saw a 6–0 Atlanta win, completing the first National League postseason sweep since 1982. Steve Avery allowed just three singles, two of which failed to make it out of the infield. Mike Devereaux delivered the key blow, a three-run homer to left in the seventh.

Atlanta—seeking its first Series win since 1957—would now face Cleveland, making its first Fall Classic appearance since 1954.

Atlanta Braves (East), 4;
Cincinnati Reds (Central), 0

ATL (E)

PLAYER/POS	AVG	G	AB	R	H	2B	3B	HR	RBI	BB	SO	SB
Steve Avery, p	.500	2	2	0	1	0	0	0	0	0	0	0
Rafael Belliard, ss	.273	4	11	1	3	0	0	0	0	0	3	0
Jeff Blauser, ss	.000	1	4	0	0	0	0	0	0	1	2	0
Brad Clontz, p	.000	1	0	0	0	0	0	0	0	0	0	0
Mike Devereaux, of	.308	4	13	2	4	1	0	1	5	1	2	0
Tom Glavine, p	.000	1	1	0	0	0	0	0	0	1	0	0
Marquis Grissom, of	.263	4	19	2	5	0	1	0	0	1	4	0
Chipper Jones, 3b	.438	4	16	3	7	0	0	1	3	3	1	1
David Justice, of	.273	3	11	1	3	0	0	0	1	2	1	0
Ryan Klesko, of-3	.000	4	7	0	0	0	0	0	0	3	4	0
Mark Lemke, 2b	.167	4	18	2	3	0	0	0	1	1	0	0
Javy Lopez, c	.357	3	14	2	5	1	0	1	3	0	1	0
Greg Maddux, p	.000	1	3	0	0	0	0	0	0	0	1	0
Fred McGriff, 1b	.438	4	16	5	7	4	0	0	0	3	0	0
Greg McMichael, p	.000	3	0	0	0	0	0	0	0	0	0	0
Mike Mordecai, ss-1	.000	2	2	0	0	0	0	0	0	0	1	0
Charlie O'Brien, c-1	.400	2	5	1	2	0	0	1	3	0	1	0
Alejandro Pena, p	.000	3	0	0	0	0	0	0	0	0	0	0
Luis Polonia, of-1	.500	3	2	0	1	0	0	0	0	1	0	0
Dwight Smith, ph	.000	2	2	0	0	0	0	0	0	0	0	0
John Smoltz, p	.333	1	3	0	1	0	0	0	0	0	1	1
Mark Wohlers, p	.000	4	0	0	0	0	0	0	0	0	0	0
TOTAL	.282		149	19	42	6	1	4	17	16	22	2

PITCHER	W	L	ERA	G	GS	CG	SV	SHO	IP	H	ER	BB	SO
Steve Avery	1	0	0.00	2	1	0	0	0	6.0	2	0	4	6
Brad Clontz	0	0	0.00	1	0	0	0	0	0.1	1	0	0	0
Tom Glavine	0	0	1.29	1	1	0	0	0	7.0	7	1	2	5
Greg Maddux	1	0	1.13	1	1	0	0	0	8.0	7	1	2	4
Greg McMichael	1	0	0.00	3	0	0	1	0	2.2	0	0	1	2
Alejandro Pena	0	0	0.00	3	0	0	0	0	3.0	2	0	1	4
John Smoltz	0	0	2.57	1	1	0	0	0	7.0	7	2	2	2
Mark Wohlers	1	0	1.80	4	0	0	0	0	5.0	2	1	0	8
TOTAL	4	0	1.15	16	4	0	1	0	39.0	28	5	12	31

CIN (W)

PLAYER/POS	AVG	G	AB	R	H	2B	3B	HR	RBI	BB	SO	SB
Eric Anthony, ph	.000	2	1	0	0	0	0	0	0	1	1	0
Bret Boone, 2b	.214	4	14	1	3	0	0	0	0	1	2	0
Jeff Branson, 3b	.111	4	9	2	1	1	0	0	0	0	2	1
Jeff Brantley, p	.000	2	0	0	0	0	0	0	0	0	0	0
Dave Burba, p	.000	2	0	0	0	0	0	0	0	0	0	0
Hector Carrasco, p	.000	1	0	0	0	0	0	0	0	0	0	0
Mariano Duncan, 1b-1	.000	3	3	0	0	0	0	0	0	1	1	0
Ron Gant, of	.188	4	16	1	3	0	0	0	1	0	3	0
Lenny Harris, ph	1.000	3	2	0	2	0	0	0	1	0	0	1
Xavier Hernandez, p	.000	1	0	0	0	0	0	0	0	0	0	0
Thomas Howard, of-3	.250	4	8	0	2	1	0	0	1	2	0	0
Mike Jackson, p	.000	3	0	0	0	0	0	0	0	0	0	0
Barry Larkin, ss	.389	4	18	1	7	2	1	0	0	1	1	1
Darren Lewis, of	.000	2	1	0	0	0	0	0	0	0	0	0
Mark Lewis, 3b	.250	2	4	0	1	0	0	0	0	1	1	0
Hal Morris, 1b	.167	4	12	0	2	1	0	0	1	1	1	1
Mark Portugal, p	.000	1	0	0	0	0	0	0	0	0	0	0
Reggie Sanders, of	.125	4	16	0	2	0	0	0	0	2	10	0
Benito Santiago, c	.231	4	13	0	3	0	0	0	0	2	3	0
Pete Schourek, p	.000	2	5	0	0	0	0	0	0	0	4	0
John Smiley, p	.000	1	1	0	0	0	0	0	0	0	0	0
Eddie Taubensee, c-1	.500	2	2	0	1	0	0	0	0	0	0	0
Jerome Walton, of	.000	2	7	0	0	0	0	0	0	0	2	0
David Wells, p	.500	1	2	0	1	0	0	0	0	0	0	0
TOTAL	.209		134	5	28	5	1	0	4	12	31	4

PITCHER	W	L	ERA	G	GS	CG	SV	SHO	IP	H	ER	BB	SO
Jeff Brantley	0	0	0.00	2	0	0	0	0	2.2	0	0	2	1
Dave Burba	0	0	0.00	2	0	0	0	0	3.2	3	0	4	0
Hector Carrasco	0	0	0.00	1	0	0	0	0	1.1	1	0	0	3
Xavier Hernandez	0	0	27.00	1	0	0	0	0	0.2	3	2	0	0
Mike Jackson	0	1	23.14	3	0	0	0	0	2.1	5	6	4	1
Mark Portugal	0	1	36.00	1	0	0	0	0	1.0	3	4	1	0
Pete Schourek	0	1	1.26	2	2	0	0	0	14.1	14	2	3	13
John Smiley	0	0	3.60	1	1	0	0	0	5.0	5	2	0	1
David Wells	0	1	4.50	1	1	0	0	0	6.0	8	3	2	3
TOTAL	0	4	4.62	14	4	0	0	0	37.0	42	19	16	22

GAME 1 AT CIN OCT 10

ATL	000 000 001 01	2	7	0
CIN	000 100 000 00	1	8	0

Pitchers: Glavine, Pena (8), WOHLERS (9), Clontz (11), Avery (11), McMichael (11) vs Schourek, Brantley (9), JACKSON (11)
Attendance: 40,382

GAME 2 AT CIN OCT 11

ATL	100 100 000 4	6	11	1
CIN	000 020 000 0	2	9	1

Pitchers: Smoltz, Pena (8), McMICHAEL (9), Wohlers (10) vs Smiley, Burba (6), Jackson (8), Brantley (9), PORTUGAL (10)
Home Runs: Lopez-ATL
Attendance: 44,624

GAME 3 AT ATL OCT 13

CIN	000 000 011	2	8	0
ATL	000 003 20X	5	12	1

Pitchers: WELLS, Hernandez (7), Carrasco (7) vs MADDUX, Wohlers (9)
Home Runs: O'Brien-ATL, Jones-ATL
Attendance: 51,424

GAME 4 AT ATL OCT 14

CIN	000 000 000	0	3	1
ATL	001 000 50X	6	12	1

Pitchers: SCHOUREK, Jackson (7), Burba (7) vs AVERY, McMichael (7), Pena (8), Wohlers (9)
Home Runs: Devereaux-ATL
Attendance: 52,067

The Indians and Braves met for a rematch of their tussle in the 1948 World Series, but this time the transplanted Braves went home with the honors.

Game One quickly established that Atlanta's vaunted pitching staff was no myth. Perennial Cy Young Award winner Greg Maddux used just 95 pitches in shutting down the hard-hitting Indians. Only three runners reached against him, on opposite field singles by Kenny Lofton and Jim Thome, and on an error by Rafael Belliard. Cleveland starter Orel Hershiser tired in the seventh and walked two, leading to the second and third Atlanta runs and his first loss after seven straight postseason victories.

In Game Two Atlanta took a 2–0 series lead as catcher Javier Lopez anticipated a Dennis Martinez fastball on the outside part of the plate. He hammered it to straight-away center field for a two-run homer, shattering a 2–2 tie and providing the Braves with all the margin they would need for a 4–3 win. Earlier Cleveland's 39-year-old Eddie Murray garnered a two-run homer of his own off starter Tom Glavine.

The Indians' bats finally came alive in Game Three's 7–6 win. It looked like the Tribe would be facing a 3–0 deficit, as they trailed 6–5 in the bottom of the eighth. But in that inning Kenny Lofton (who reached base six times in the contest) scored the tying run on Sandy Alomar's first hit of the series. In the eleventh Eddie Murray singled off Alejandro Pena's first pitch to score pinch-runner Alvaro Espinoza with the winning run.

Atlanta's Ryan Klesko and Cleveland's Albert Belle traded solo sixth-inning homers in Game Four to set up a 1–1 tie going into the top of the seventh. Atlanta then scored three runs on Luis Polonia's run-scoring double and David Justice's two-out, two-RBI single to center to break the contest open and ultimately give Atlanta a 5–2 win.

The Tribe stayed alive in Game Five as Jim Thome singled in the go-ahead run in the sixth and provided a crucial insurance run with an eighth inning homer. Ryan Klesko nicked Jose Mesa for a two-run homer in the ninth—the third straight game in which he'd homered—but it wasn't enough.

With a 3–2 lead in the Series and Greg Maddux waiting to pitch Game Seven, the Braves had little to worry about in Game Six. Key to their victory were two players with something to prove: Tom Glavine, who had survived Atlanta's horrible days in the late 1980s, and David Justice, who was taking heat

for comments he had made about Atlanta fans' lack of spirit. Glavine allowed only a sixth inning single to Tony Pena, walked three and struck out eight. Justice brought home the game's only run with a sixth inning homer off reliever Jim Poole.

The Braves now had their first World Championship since 1957 and had become the first franchise to win the crown in three different cities—Boston, Milwaukee, and Atlanta.

Atlanta Braves (NL), 4; Cleveland Indians (AL), 2

ATL (N)

PLAYER/POS	AVG	G	AB	R	H	2B	3B	HR	RB	BB	SO	SB
Steve Avery, p	.000	1	0	0	0	0	0	0	0	0	0	0
Rafael Belliard, ss	.000	6	16	0	0	0	0	0	0	1	4	0
Pedro Borbon, p	.000	1	0	0	0	0	0	0	0	0	0	0
Brad Clontz, p	.000	2	0	0	0	0	0	0	0	0	0	0
Mike Devereaux, of-4,dh-1	.250	5	4	0	1	0	0	0	0	1	2	1	0
Tom Glavine, p	.000	2	4	0	0	0	0	0	0	0	1	2	0
Marquis Grissom, of	.360	6	25	3	9	1	0	0	1	1	3	3
Chipper Jones, 3b	.286	6	21	3	6	3	0	0	1	4	5	0
David Justice, of	.250	6	20	3	5	1	0	1	5	5	5	1	0
Ryan Klesko, of-3,dh-3	.313	6	16	4	5	0	0	3	4	3	4	0
Mark Lemke, 2b	.273	6	22	1	6	0	0	0	0	3	2	0
Javy Lopez, c	.176	6	17	1	3	2	0	1	3	1	1	0
Greg Maddux, p	.000	2	3	0	0	0	0	0	0	0	1	0
Fred McGriff, 1b	.261	6	23	5	6	2	0	2	3	3	5	1
Greg McMichael, p	.000	3	0	0	0	0	0	0	0	0	0	0
Kent Mercker, p	.000	1	0	0	0	0	0	0	0	0	0	0
Mike Mordecai, ss-2,dh-1	.333	3	3	0	1	0	0	0	0	0	1	0
Charlie O'Brien, c	.000	2	3	0	0	0	0	0	0	0	1	0
Alejandro Pena, p	.000	2	0	0	0	0	0	0	0	0	0	0
Luis Polonia, of-4	.286	6	14	3	4	1	0	1	4	1	3	1
Dwight Smith, ph	.500	3	2	0	1	0	0	0	0	1	0	0
John Smoltz, p	.000	1	0	0	0	0	0	0	0	0	0	0
Mark Wohlers, p	.000	4	0	0	0	0	0	0	0	0	0	0
TOTAL	.244		193	23	47	10	0	8	23	25	34	5

PITCHER	W	L	ERA	G	GS	CG	SV	SHO	IP	H	ER	BB	SO
Steve Avery	1	0	1.50	1	1	0	0	0	6.0	3	1	5	3
Pedro Borbon	0	0	0.00	1	0	0	1	0	1.0	0	0	0	2
Brad Clontz	0	0	2.70	2	0	0	0	0	3.1	2	1	0	2
Tom Glavine	2	0	1.29	2	2	0	0	0	14.0	4	2	6	11
Greg Maddux	1	1	2.25	2	2	1	0	0	16.0	9	4	3	8
Greg McMichael	0	0	2.70	3	0	0	0	0	3.1	3	1	2	2
Kent Mercker	0	0	4.50	1	0	0	0	0	2.0	1	1	2	2
Alejandro Pena	0	1	9.00	2	0	0	0	0	1.0	3	1	2	0
John Smoltz	0	0	15.43	1	1	0	0	0	2.1	6	4	2	4
Mark Wohlers	0	0	1.80	4	0	0	2	0	5.0	4	1	3	3
TOTAL	4	2	2.67	19	6	1	3	0	54.0	35	16	25	37

CLE (A)

PLAYER/POS	AVG	G	AB	R	H	2B	3B	HR	RB	BB	SO	SB
Sandy Alomar, c	.200	5	15	0	3	2	0	0	1	0	2	0
Ruben Amaro, of-1	.000	2	2	0	0	0	0	0	0	0	1	0
Paul Assenmacher, p	.000	4	0	0	0	0	0	0	0	0	0	0
Carlos Baerga, 2b	.192	6	26	1	5	2	0	0	4	1	1	0
Albert Belle, of	.235	6	17	4	4	0	0	2	4	7	5	0
Alan Embree, p	.000	4	0	0	0	0	0	0	0	0	0	0
Alvaro Espinoza, 3b-1	.500	2	2	1	1	0	0	0	0	0	0	0
Orel Hershiser, p	.000	2	2	0	0	0	0	0	0	0	1	0
Ken Hill, p	.000	2	0	0	0	0	0	0	0	0	0	0
Wayne Kirby, of-2	.000	3	1	0	0	0	0	0	0	0	1	0
Kenny Lofton, of	.200	6	25	6	5	1	0	0	0	3	1	6
Dennis Martinez, p	.000	2	3	0	0	0	0	0	0	0	1	0
Jose Mesa, p	.000	2	0	0	0	0	0	0	0	0	0	0
Eddie Murray, 1b-3,dh-3	.105	6	19	1	2	0	0	1	3	5	4	0
Charles Nagy, p	.000	1	0	0	0	0	0	0	0	0	0	0
Tony Pena, c	.167	2	6	0	1	0	0	0	0	0	0	0
Herb Perry, 1b	.000	3	5	0	0	0	0	0	0	0	2	0
Jim Poole, p	.000	2	1	0	0	0	0	0	0	0	0	0
Manny Ramirez, of	.222	6	18	2	4	0	0	1	2	4	5	1
Paul Sorrento, 1b-2	.182	5	11	0	2	1	0	0	0	0	4	0
Julian Tavarez, p	.000	5	0	0	0	0	0	0	0	0	0	0
Jim Thome, 3b	.211	6	19	1	4	1	0	1	2	2	5	0
Omar Vizquel, ss	.174	6	23	3	4	0	1	0	1	3	5	1
TOTAL	.179		195	19	35	7	1	5	17	25	37	8

PITCHER	W	L	ERA	G	GS	CG	SV	SHO	IP	H	ER	BB	SO
Paul Assenmacher	0	0	6.75	4	0	0	0	0	1.1	1	1	3	3
Alan Embree	0	0	2.70	4	0	0	0	0	3.1	2	1	2	2
Orel Hershiser	1	1	2.57	2	2	0	0	0	14.0	8	4	4	13
Ken Hill	0	1	4.26	2	1	0	0	0	6.1	7	3	4	1
Dennis Martinez	0	1	3.48	2	2	0	0	0	10.1	12	4	8	5
Jose Mesa	1	0	4.50	2	0	0	1	0	4.0	5	2	1	4
Charles Nagy	0	0	6.43	1	1	0	0	0	7.0	8	5	1	4
Jim Poole	0	1	3.86	2	0	0	0	0	2.1	1	1	0	1
Julian Tavarez	0	0	0.00	5	0	0	0	0	4.1	3	0	2	1
TOTAL	2	4	3.57	24	6	0	1	0	53.0	47	21	25	34

GAME 1 AT ATL OCT 21

CLE	100	000	001	2	2	0
ATL	010	000	20X	3	3	2

Pitchers: HERSHISER, Assenmacher (7), Tavarez (7), Embree (8) vs MADDUX
Home Runs: McGriff-ATL
Attendance: 51,876

GAME 2 AT ATL OCT 22

CLE	020	000	100	3	6	2
ATL	002	002	00X	4	8	2

Pitchers: MARTINEZ, Embree (6), Poole (7), Tavarez (8) vs GLAVINE, McMichael (7), Pena (7), Wohlers (8)
Home Runs: Murray-CLE, Lopez-ATL
Attendance: 51,877

GAME 3 AT CLE OCT 24

ATL	100	001	130	00	6	12	1
CLE	202	000	110	01	7	12	2

Pitchers: Smoltz, Clontz (3), Mercker (5), McMichael (7), Wohlers (8), PENA (11) vs Nagy, Assenmacher (8), Tavarez (8), MESA (9)
Home Runs: McGriff-ATL, Klesko-ATL
Attendance: 43,584

GAME 4 AT CLE OCT 25

ATL	000	001	301	5	11	1
CLE	000	001	001	2	6	0

Pitchers: AVERY, McMichael (7), Wohlers (9), Borbon (9) vs HILL, Assenmacher (7), Tavarez (8), Embree (8)
Home Runs: Belle-CLE, Ramirez-CLE, Klesko-ATL
Attendance: 43,578

GAME 5 AT CLE OCT 26

ATL	000	110	002	4	7	0
CLE	200	002	01X	5	8	1

Pitchers: MADDUX, Clontz (8) vs HERSHISER, Mesa (9)
Home Runs: Belle-CLE, Thome-CLE, Polonia-ATL, Klesko-ATL
Attendance: 43,595

GAME 6 AT ATL OCT 28

CLE	000	000	000	0	1	1
ATL	000	001	00X	1	6	0

Pitchers: Martinez, POOLE (5), Hill (7), Embree (7), Tavarez (8), Assenmacher (8) vs GLAVINE, Wohlers (9)
Home Runs: Justice-ATL
Attendance: 51,875

CHAPTER 4

Baseball in Atlanta

David Pietrusza

Atlanta's baseball history predated the arrival of the big leagues by over three-quarters of a century. The memories are fading now, but in their time the old Atlanta Crackers were as good a minor league team as ever laced up spikes, winning seventeen pennants, a professional baseball record bettered only by the New York Yankees' eighteen championships.

Baseball in Atlanta can be traced to at least 1866, when two teams, the Atlantas and the Gate City Nine, did battle in a monumental four-and-a-half hour contest, with Gate City triumphing 127–29. The discouraged Atlantas did the only honorable thing and disbanded, but the Gate Cities went on tour of the South, posting a 29–1 record, and spreading the gospel of baseball throughout Dixie.

The city's professional diamond history dates back to 1885, when Atlanta was one of the charter members of the original Southern League. *Atlanta Constitution* editor Henry W. Grady, originator of the concept of the "New South," served as league president and trumpeted league news on the paper's front page. Grady had a lot to report: Atlanta (60–31) edged out Peach State rival Augusta (68–36) for the pennant, triumphing by benefit of a higher won-lost percentage even though Augusta had won eight more games during the regular season.

Catcher-manager George McVey's squad should have won the pennant. It was loaded with past and future major leaguers. In 1886 McVey moved on to Nashville, but the team (then simply called the "Atlantas") captured its second pennant. McVey, however, must have suspected something about the state of Atlanta baseball: the city left the Southern League at season's end, not returning until 1889.

The league folded at the end of the 1889 season, but when it returned to action in 1892, Atlanta was again among its franchises. In the 1890s the team suffered from a definite identity crisis. In 1892 it was known as the Firecrackers, in 1893 as the Windjammers, and in 1894 once more as the Atlantas. The club again collapsed after 1894, but returned to the fold in 1896—this time (at last) as the Crackers. The team now had a new ballpark, 1,000–seat Piedmont Park, built at the city's Exposition Grounds and rented by the ballclub for $600 a year. But the Atlanta and Birmingham teams folded in June, and the league itself collapsed at season's end. When the league re-formed in 1898, it was without Atlanta.

In the new century the Southern Association, a much more stable entity, replaced the rickety old Southern League. Atlanta would be one of its flagship franchises, but when the SA began play in 1901, Atlanta was not among its members. In 1902, however, the Selma Christians relocated to Atlanta, and the city began an SA tradition that would last uninterrupted until 1961.

Atlanta's team was then known as the Firemen and sported wild striped stockings, large dark colored collars, and mustachioed manager Ed Pabst, a former major league outfielder. Atlanta's first SA entry finished a mediocre fourth, with a 55–63 record.

In 1903 the club finally became the Crackers for good. In 1904 the team featured future Brooklyn great Nap Rucker and a second baseman from Tennessee who wasn't hitting well, but who kept busy writing articles for the *Atlanta Constitution*.

Recalled Rucker: "One day the manager said to this boy, 'Why don't you quit and be a sports editor? You write better than you play second base.' "

The player—Grantland Rice—took that advice. "And he became a great one, didn't he?" said Rucker.

It was Rice, in fact, who had discovered Rucker and had originally recommended him to Atlanta manager Abner Powell. Rice didn't have to feel too bad about not making the Crackers. Rucker couldn't, either. Control problems plagued him, and Powell sent him down to Augusta—where the southpaw pitched a no-hitter and roomed with Ty Cobb.

In 1904 Piedmont Park's capacity was doubled to 2,000 seats, but it remained too small to accommodate large weekend crowds. Two years later 8,000–seat Ponce de Leon Park was built for $40,000 on Ponce de Leon Boulevard near the Georgia Railway and Electric Company trolley line. (Like all contemporary Southern ballparks, the facility featured separate seating for black patrons.) That same year the Crackers' Frank Smith went 31–10, becoming the first SA pitcher to reach the 30–win mark.

Atlanta won its first SA pennant in 1907, with Cracker outfielder Dode Paskert, a future National Leaguer, pacing the circuit with 6 homers.

Atlanta finished just third in 1910, but made the record books anyway. With the season winding to a close, the Crackers and the Mobile Sea Gulls decided to see just how fast they could play a regulation game. Players ran on and off the field like Olympians; batters swung at whatever they could reach. The result was professional baseball's shortest nine-inning game: all thirty-two minutes of it. By the way, Mobile won 2–1 as it turned a triple play and pushed across the winning run in the top of the ninth.

The year 1919 was an important one for Atlanta baseball. At Chattanooga's Andrews Field on June 23, the Crackers played the longest contest (in terms of innings) in Association history. Atlanta and Chattanooga battled to a 23-inning 2–2 tie. Atlanta third baseman Jimmy Dykes flawlessly handled a record 22 chances—11 assists and 11 putouts. Both Chattanooga's Rube Marshall and Atlanta's Ray Roberts went the distance.

The 1919 Crackers also won a pennant, beating the rival Little Rock Travelers by seven games. The season, however, ended on a distinctly sour note. The Columbia Comers, champions of the Class C South Atlantic League, brashly challenged the Crackers to a postseason series, presumably for the championship of Georgia. The lower-level Comers humiliated the Crackers four games to one.

On September 23, 1923, wooden Ponce de Leon Park burnt down. The team finished its schedule at Georgia Tech's Grant Field and moved into a $250,000 rebuilt concrete-and-steel park the following spring. When it opened, this new facility was known as Spiller Park after the team's owner at the time, Tell J. Spiller. It reverted to its old name only after the 1932 season.

The club had to wait until 1925 for another flag. That season individual Crackers players dominated league batting statistics. Wilbur Good, a diminutive 39-year-old former major league outfielder, led the Southern Association with a .379 average and 236 hits, the latter the all-time league record. Another Atlanta outfielder, Nick "Tomato Face" Cullop, a great minor league slugger, paced the circuit with 30 homers, while Frank Zoeller led with 131 runs. George Pipgras (who started the year with Atlanta but moved over to Nashville in midseason) paced the SA with 141 strikeouts.

The Depression hit Atlanta baseball particularly hard. In 1932 the club finished seventh, 37½ games back, and lost $70,000 in the process. That October 18 the franchise was surrendered to Crackers bondholders.

But Atlanta rebounded quickly. The Crackers' next pennant arrived in 1935 as manager Eddie Moore's team posted a 91–60 mark. Atlanta's Harry Kelly (23–13) led the SA with a 2.50 ERA. By now the minors were employing the Shaughnessy Playoff system, and Atlanta swept Nashville and New Orleans in the postseason. That year, aided by the relatively new phenomenon of night baseball, the Crackers one evening drew an SA record 19,266 fans to Ponce de Leon Park.

Atlanta repeated in 1936 as the team bolted out of the shoot with a 26–4 start, on its way to a 94–59 record, drawing 301,000 fans in the bargain—a total that even outpaced the major league St. Louis Browns (93,267), Boston Braves (232,754), Philadelphia Phillies (249,219), and Philadelphia A's (285,173).

Little Rock won the SA flag in 1937, but Atlanta won again in 1938. The latter year was a banner one for Atlanta baseball as Major Trammell Scott took over as Southern Association president and moved league offices to the Georgia metropolis.

Atlanta's 1938 player-manager was Paul Richards. A catcher, Richards hit .316 as he guided the team to both pennant and playoff wins. Crackers' lefthander Tom Sunkel led the SA with 21 wins, 178 strikeouts, and a 2.33 ERA, while Atlanta third baseman Johnny Hill paced the league with a .338 average and earned a promotion to the Boston Bees in the process.

In 1939 Atlanta (still managed by Richards) fell to fourth, but remarkably finished just two games back in one of the tightest pennant races in association history.

Richards was still at the helm when Atlanta captured the 1941 SA pennant by 15 games as Cracker first baseman Les Burge led the circuit with 38 homers and 146 RBI. But in the postseason finals Larry Gilbert's second-place Nashville Vols upset Atlanta, four games to three.

The Southern Association was one of the few minor leagues to operate during World War II, and that was good news for Atlanta fans as their club captured pennants in both 1944 and 1945. A new manager was at the helm, however, in 1945, Hall of Famer Kiki Cuyler. The 1945 Crackers featured SA batting and RBI champ third baseman Ted Cieslak (.364, 120 RBIs) and victory and ERA leader Lew Carpenter (22 wins, 1.82). Atlanta, however, fell to New Orleans in the first round of the Shaughnessy Playoffs.

The good luck continued after war's end. Atlanta won its third straight pennant in 1946, paced by Association leaders Lloyd Gearhart (with 139 runs), Earl McGowan (22 wins) and William Ayers (1.95 ERA). Ayers (21–10) and Shelby Kinney (20–9) also were 20-game winners, the first time an SA club boasted three 20-game winners since 1906. This time the club took both pennant and playoffs.

Cuyler's club fell to fifth in 1947, but you would never have known it at the gate as a league-leading 404,584 fans poured into Ponce de Leon Park. Cuyler was replaced as manager in 1949 by Cliff Dapper, who gave way the following season to Dixie Walker. Walker rewarded fans with another pennant, and a league-leading 395,696 fans paid their way through the gates.

That year, Crackers owner Earl Mann decided Ponce de Leon Park's dimensions were too generous and decided to cut down left field from 365 feet to 330 feet. In left field, however, was the park's scoreboard. Mann wanted to neither block it nor move it, so he planted a two foot high hedge in left field—and prohibited fielders from jumping over it to make a catch. The experiment was a short-lived one.

That same year saw the first integrated games at Ponce de Leon Park as Jackie Robinson and the Brooklyn Dodgers visited for a three game exhibition series. Nearly fifty thousand fans—more than half of them black—attended, breaking the back of a threatened Ku Klux Klan boycott. In the series' last game 25,000 customers jammed the park, nearly twice capacity. The following spring even saw Mann open up the stadium's bleachers for the first time to black patrons so they could view Robinson and the Dodgers' other black stars.

Atlanta had long featured a rich tradition of black baseball, dating back to the Georgia Champions of 1886. But its most notable representative was the Atlanta Black Crackers, who staged their home games at Brown College. For most of their existence, the Black Crackers either played independent ball or were members of the regional Negro Southern League, but for one season, 1938, the club competed in the Negro American League, against such noted teams as the Kansas City Monarchs.

The Black Crackers featured such players as outfielders Big Jim Williams and Alex Crumbley, shortstop Pee Wee Butts, catchers Bill Thomas and Joe Greene, and pitcher Sam "Lefty" Streeter (who when he was with the Montgomery Grey Sox in 1920 pitched a perfect game against the Black Sox). The greatest player to wear a Crackers uniform was Cuban immortal Cristobel Torrienti, who performed with Atlanta at the tail end of his career. "If I should see Torrienti walking up the other side of the street," Indianapolis ABC's manager C. I. Taylor once remarked, "I would say, 'There walks a ballclub.' "

The 1950s witnessed a parade of notable Cracker managers. Dixie Walker was replaced by Whitlow Wyatt in midseason of 1951 as the team tumbled into the second division, but returned the following year to lead it to a second place finish. The next year Wyatt was succeeded by Gene Mauch, who in turn was replaced in 1954 by a returning Wyatt.

The madness seemed to have its method as Wyatt led the 1954 Crackers to the pennant in a close race over Danny Murtaugh's New Orleans Pelicans. More significant than the pennant, however, was the presence on Atlanta's opening day roster of hard-hitting Nat Peeples.

Peeples was black, and he was not only the Crackers' first black player, he was the first in the entire Southern Association. He hit .467 in spring training, and Wyatt remarked, "I just can't pass over a boy who has the kind of spring Nat has had. Right now he's the best outfielder I've got."

But when the season started, Peeples sat on the bench. After appearing in just two games with four hitless at-bats he was demoted to Jacksonville, where he replaced a young prospect named Hank Aaron.

No other black ever appeared in a Crackers uniform—or with any other Southern Association team in its entire history.

The club tumbled to seventh in 1955 as three other managers fought to end the free-fall. Their third 1955 skipper, Clyde King, returned in 1956, leading the team to another pennant. Buddy Bates replaced King in 1957, but the team kept on winning, edging Memphis by a half-game for the pennant and winning the playoffs over Chattanooga and Nashville.

The team finished in the second division in 1958 and landed in the basement in 1959. But as the Crackers fell, an unlikely scenario was unfolding. Branch Rickey was plotting a third major league, the Continental League, and Atlanta was one of its franchises. On December 8, 1959 an Atlanta group consisting of Joe Fine, Eaton Chalkley, and Hughes Spalding, Jr. was admitted to Continental League membership. At the time Atlanta was still smaller than Kansas City, the smallest city with a big league club.

The Continental League was not to be, although the threat of its existence helped speed American League expansion in 1961 and National League expansion the following year.

Meanwhile, in 1960 another Walker was at the Crackers' helm, future long-time Mets coach Rube Walker, who guided the club to a half-game pennant win over Shreveport. Leading the SA with 19 wins and 251 strike-outs was Atlanta southpaw Pete Richert.

The club fell to fourth under Walker in 1961, and attendance plummeted to just 59,061. By now the Southern Association was dying. It closed its doors at season's end, ending a grand tradition.

Baseball, however, did not leave Atlanta. The Crackers found a home in the International League in 1962 and moved out of Ponce de Leon Park after the 1964 season and into brand-new Atlanta-Fulton County Stadium. The Crackers' IL record was hardly glorious. The club won no pennants, and when it finished dead last as a Twins farm-club in 1964 it drew just 68,537 fans. Yet just two years later, the Braves moved from Milwaukee to Atlanta, bestowing on the city the big league status it had long enjoyed in national terms.

CHAPTER 5

Braves Greats

Michael Gershman

★ Hank Aaron ★

One of the greatest hitters of all time, Henry Aaron combined exceptional natural physical ability and lightning-quick reflexes with a professorial study of opposing pitchers to break Babe Ruth's "unbreakable" record of 714 home runs, surpassing Ruth's record by 41.

Aaron made waves well beyond baseball. That he moved almost overnight from a segregated environment into the white Major League Baseball world had a deep impact on him. And, when he realized he could utilize his talents as a springboard to speak out against and hopefully reduce racial intolerance and inequality, he became more than just a highly skilled athlete; he became a man with a mission.

Never in a rush, always quiet and dignified, Aaron played without the flash of Willie Mays, the fire of Roberto Clemente, or the haughtiness of Frank Robinson. As a result, he failed to receive the recognition due him until his exploits were already of Hall of Fame caliber. And those exploits mounted, cumulatively, year after year after year.

Aaron averaged 33 homers per year, hit more than 20 home runs in 20 consecutive years, and scored more than 100 runs 15 times, including a record 13 consecutive seasons. His consistently excellent performance and his longevity added up to still-standing records of 755 lifetime home runs, 2,297 runs batted in, 1,477 extra-base hits, and 6,856 total bases. Not surprisingly, he was selected as an All-Star 21 times. For his career he batted .305 and slugged .555.

As a hitter, Aaron's style was unique. Counter to conventional baseball wisdom, his incredibly strong wrists made it possible for him to aggressively hit off his *front* foot. He claimed that his hitting style was the result of batting bottle caps with a broom as a youngster. "A bottle cap will swerve at the last instant," he said. "You've got to go out and get it."

His approach to hitting was scientific but not technical. As Aaron described it, "Ted Williams concentrated on the things he had to do himself. I concentrated on the pitcher. I didn't stay up nights worrying about my weight distribution or the location of my hands or the turn of my hips; I stayed up thinking about the pitcher I was going to face the next day." That constant study may explain why he hit 17 home runs, his best against any single pitcher, off Dodger Hall of Famer Don Drysdale.

The success of his relaxed style confounded many observers. Some misjudged him as lazy. An article on Aaron in *Time* magazine was titled "The Talented Shuffler."

According to *Time*, "Thinking, Aaron likes to imply, is dangerous. But by now everyone knows that Aaron is not as dumb as he looks when he shuffles around the field." But as Lonnie Wheeler, Aaron's collaborator on his autobiography, *I Had a Hammer*, reflected, "It was odd that Joe DiMaggio was also quiet and deliberate, and yet in DiMaggio's case these traits were perceived as dignity and grace, which translated into American heroism. In Aaron's case, the same qualities translated into comparative invisibility."

Aaron's rise from Alabama teenager to major league star happened quickly. In 1952, at age 18, he signed with the Negro League Indianapolis Clowns for $200 a month and played shortstop. He batted cross-handed then, but, no one on the Clowns bothered with his style, probably thinking it was part of the show. The truly competitive era of the Negro Leagues had ended with the integration of the majors. The Clowns were barnstormers like their basketball counterparts, the Harlem Globetrotters, and featured players with names such as King Tut and Spec Bebop. Why they were called the Indianapolis Clowns was a mystery to Aaron. "We never made it to Indiana the whole time I was with the team."

He did make it to Wisconsin, however, playing for the Braves's farm team at Eau Claire. After observing Aaron at the plate May 25, 1952, Braves scout Dewey Griggs suggested he uncross his hands to hit and wrote to Braves General Manager John Mullen, "This boy could be the answer." Mullen moved quickly to pay Indianapolis $7,500 for the young infielder.

Aaron played 87 games for Eau Claire in 1952, hitting .336 with nine home runs and 61 RBIs. The following year Aaron, outfielder Horace Garner, and infielder Felix Mantilla were sent to Class A Jacksonville to break the color line in the South Atlantic League, also known as the Sally League, in the Deep South of the early 1950s.

Every day Aaron and his black teammates were subjected to the worst kinds of racial epithets and threats. But it was here that Aaron's baseball skills began to dent those long-standing barriers. Playing second base, Aaron led the league in runs, hits, doubles, RBIs, batting average, putouts, and assists and was chosen Most Valuable Player.

Aaron was expected to play the 1954 season at either Class AAA Toledo or AA Atlanta, but, when his hero, Bobby Thomson, broke a leg in spring training, Aaron replaced him in the lineup. His first game was against the Red Sox in Sarasota, Florida. He came to the plate against pitcher Ike Delock, who had given up a prodigious minor league homer to Aaron the year before. Aaron said, "I cracked one over a row of trailers that bordered that outfield fence — hit it so hard that Ted Williams came

Note: The names of Hall of Fame members are set off by stars (★).

running out from the clubhouse wanting to know who it was that could make a bat sound that way when it hit a baseball."

On their way North to begin the season, the Braves toured with the Dodgers. The black players from both teams stayed at the same "colored" hotels, and Aaron always made a point of hanging around Jackie Robinson's room, where Don Newcombe, Joe Black, Jim Gilliam, and Roy Campanella would gather to play cards and talk. Aaron paid close attention to what they had to say about everything from pitchers to restaurants to how to handle sensitive racial situations. "Those hotel rooms were my college," Aaron said.

"Being around the Dodgers made me realize that I could never be just another major league player," he told Lonnie Wheeler. "I was a black player, and that meant I would be separate most of the time from most of the players on the team. It meant I'd better be good, or I'd be gone . . . And it meant that I had a choice. Either I could forget that I was black and just smile and go along with the program until my time was up, or I could never forget that I was black. After hearing Jackie Robinson and the other Dodgers, there was only one way to make that choice.

"If there's a single reason why the black players of the '50s and '60s were so much better than the white players in the National League, I believe it's because we had to be. And we knew we had to be."

That rookie year, in 122 games, Aaron batted .280 with 13 homers and 69 RBI. But the next year marked a new era for both Aaron and the Braves. It was the first of 20 years in which he would hit 20 or more home runs. It was also the first season he batted .300, a mark that he would achieve 13 more times, and the first of his 11 seasons of 100-plus RBI totals.

In 1955 and 1956 the Braves finished second, and Aaron put up impressive numbers, leading the league in batting average in 1956. But 1957 was the real breakthrough year for Aaron and the Braves. He delivered a league-leading 44 homers and 132 RBI and batted .322, tying for third place in the NL with Frank Robinson.

With St. Louis challenging in a wintry late September, Aaron hit an eleventh-inning homer that clinched the pennant for the Braves. "I galloped around the bases, and when I touched home plate the whole team was there to pick me up and carry me off the field . . . I had always dreamed about a moment like Bobby Thomson had in '51, and this was it." After Aaron's career ended he said this had been his most satisfying. Milwaukee set an NL season attendance record, and Aaron was elected Most Valuable Player.

The Braves were underdogs in the 1957 World Series, and their opponents, the supposedly invincible Yanks, let them know it. Mickey Mantle referred to Milwaukee as "bush league." But the Braves had the last laugh, winning in seven games as Aaron led all hitters in runs, hits, homers, batting average, and RBIs.

In 1958 Aaron batted .326 with 30 homers and 95 RBIs as the Braves easily won the pennant. The Yankees were out for revenge, however, and despite Aaron's .333 World Series batting average, he drove in only two runs. The Yanks prevailed in seven games.

Aaron won his second batting title in 1959, but the

Braves blew their chance to make it three straight World Series appearances when they lost two games of a best-of-three playoff to the Dodgers. Although Aaron maintained his standard of excellence, recording consecutive years of 39, 40, 34, 45, and 44 home runs from 1959 through 1963, Milwaukee's fortunes plummeted. When the team moved to Atlanta in 1966, things changed forever for Aaron.

In his autobiography, *If I Had a Hammer*, Aaron reflected on the move. "Atlanta changed me as a hitter and a person at the same time. The real world made me angrier and hungrier than I had been as a young Milwaukee Brave . . . I was tired of being invisible. I was the equal of any ballplayer in the world, dammit, and if nobody was going to give me my due, it was time to grab for it."

He hit 44 and 39 homers in his first two years there. By then, he was 34 years old and had 481 lifetime home runs, seemingly a universe away from Babe Ruth's mark.

The 1967 season was an unhappy one. The Braves had traded away his good friend Eddie Mathews, with whom he set numerous two-teammate home run records. The pitching-dominated 1968 season didn't make him feel any better. Batting statistics plummeted throughout baseball, and Aaron's 86 RBIs were the fewest since his rookie season.

In spring training the following year the Braves invited Satchel Paige along as a good will gesture so that he could earn his major league pension. Aaron looked around at all the youngsters and felt "as old as Satchel." He began to think of retirement.

Then legendary baseball historian Lee Allen pulled him aside. Allen explained the place Aaron was about to create for himself in baseball history. With his second home run that season, he would pass Mel Ott. He had a good chance to get more at bats than anyone else in history, and, with 2,792 lifetime hits, he had an excellent chance to reach the 3,000 level attained by only eight players. Aaron listened and realized he could not only set records but also make himself heard.

His first objective was to reach 3,000 hits. When Aaron smacked No. 3,000 in 1970 he joined Ty Cobb, Stan Musial, Eddie Collins, Tris Speaker, Honus Wagner, Nap Lajoie, Cap Anson, and Paul Waner. Despite this achievement, lack of recognition still plagued him. When he sent the 3,000-hit ball to the Hall of Fame, they put it away in a back room.

The quest to match Ruth subsequently became an obsession. The Babe's career home run record still seemed unreachable, and Willie Mays was nearly 100 homers ahead of Aaron. But, in 1971, at the age of 37, Aaron hit a career-best 47 home runs. At the same time he hit .327 and drove in 118 runs. He signed a two-year contract that made him the first player to earn $200,000 a year. He surpassed Musial for lifetime leadership in total bases in September 1972 and finished the season 41 home runs behind Ruth's magical 714.

Even 22 years later, it is hard to comprehend the enmity that Hank Aaron inspired as he closed in on Ruth's sanctified record. Atlanta police had to assign a bodyguard to him, and Aaron told sportswriters about the hate mail he'd received. It became big news, and before long Aaron was receiving more supportive letters than threatening ones. At the end of the year he received a plaque from the

U.S. Post Office for having received the most mail of any nonpolitician during the year — 930,000 letters.

Aaron had finished 1973 with 40 homers, leaving him at 713, one behind Ruth, and the next year began with a minor brouhaha. The Braves wanted to hold Aaron out of the lineup for their first three road games so he could tie and break Ruth's record in Atlanta. But the commissioner's office and many sportswriters felt that such maneuvering was a travesty. Ordered to play at least two of the games, Aaron hit homer No. 714 off Jack Billingham in his first at bat of the season. He sat out the second game, and in the third he struck out twice and grounded out once against Clay Kirby.

Aaron's tie-breaking home run was registered at home against Al Downing of the Dodgers. In Aaron's first at bat, Downing had walked him. When Aaron finally came around to score, he broke Mays's NL record for runs. But no one noticed. The Dodgers were ahead, 3-1, in the fourth and Aaron was again at bat. With a man on first, Downing didn't want to walk him again. Aaron deposited a low slider into the Braves' bullpen in left field for home run number 715. Teammates, fans, and Aaron's mother met him at the plate. The game was halted for a brief ceremony, and the next time Aaron batted the stands had nearly emptied.

Aaron ended the season with 733 homers. In 1975 he was traded to the AL Milwaukee Brewers, where he added 22 more for a career total of 755 home runs. Aaron once said, "I believed, and I still do, that there was a reason why I was chosen to break the record. It's my task to carry on where Jackie Robinson left off."

Aaron became a vice president of the Braves and a leading spokesman for better opportunities for Blacks in baseball. He sponsors the Hank Aaron Scholarship Program, and serves on the boards of foundations involved with cystic fibrosis, cancer, leukemia, sickle-cell anemia, the Salvation Army, the Boy Scouts, and Big Brothers/Big Sisters. The last player from the Negro Leagues to play in the white majors, he left a legacy much greater than his remarkable statistics on the field.

Joe Adcock

In the Golden Era of the 1950s, the National League featured a trio of hard-hitting first basemen — Gil Hodges, Ted Kluszewski, and a soft-spoken Louisiana slugger named Joe Adcock.

Signed by the Cincinnati Reds following an impressive stint at Louisiana State University, Adcock, who stood 6′4″ and weighed 220, advanced rapidly through the Reds' system, but ultimately his progress was blocked by the presence of Ted Kluszewski, who had more power and hit for a higher average. In 1951 and 1952 Adcock played in Cincinnati but had to be shifted to the outfield. He demanded a trade, and the Reds were happy to oblige him, sending him to the Boston Braves in early 1953.

Soon enough, the Braves packed Adcock up along with the rest of their luggage and set up shop in Milwaukee. His first season with the Braves was impressive, capped by his massive home run into the Polo Grounds' center field bleachers on April 29. Only Henry Aaron and Lou Brock would ever duplicate his feat.

Adcock's biggest day in baseball came at cozy Ebbets Field on July 31, 1954. In the second inning he homered off Brooklyn's Don Newcombe. The next inning he faced Erv Palica and doubled off the left-center fence. In the fifth he faced Palica again and homered into the upper deck. In the seventh he clipped Pete Wojey for yet another four-bagger.

In the ninth, Adcock came to the plate again. Southpaw Johnny Podres went 2-0 on Adcock, who was determined to swing at anything near the plate. On a pitch that was over his head, Adcock clubbed the ball into the center field bleachers and put himself into the record books — not only for four homers in a single game but also for most total bases in one game, 18.

"On my first three home runs," said Adcock, "I was swinging away in a carefree fashion. But on the last one I went to the plate tensed, aiming to poke one. Perhaps the strangest part of the day was I hit four home runs and only swung the bat five times." The next day he doubled in his first at bat.

Adcock played on the great Braves teams of the 1950s — clubs that boasted Hank Aaron, Eddie Mathews, Warren Spahn, Lew Burdette, and Del Crandall. Adcock could hold his own with any of them. During the eight years he and Hammerin' Hank were teammates, Adcock actually averaged more home runs per at bat than Aaron.

Nonetheless, Adcock paid proper homage to the future home run king. "Trying to sneak a pitch past Hank Aaron," Joe one said, "is like trying to sneak the sunrise past a rooster." On June 8, 1961, Mathews, Aaron, Adcock, and Frank Thomas homered in succession.

An Adcock "home run" took center stage again in May 1959. Burdette and the Pirates' Harvey Haddix locked horns in a 12-inning duel of shutout baseball with Haddix working on a perfect game. In the bottom of the thirteenth, Felix Mantilla reached on an error, and Henry Aaron walked. Adcock then dispatched a ball through the evening fog and over the fence.

In a bizarre twist, however, he would not be officially credited with a home run. Aaron had gotten as far as second. Thinking the ball had gone for a double and the winning run had scored, Aaron trotted, head down, off the field. Adcock — also oblivious to events — continued circling the bases and was called out for passing Aaron. He only got credit for a double.

During the course of his career Adcock hit 10 grand slams, had 28 multiple-homer games, and was the first player to homer over the grandstand roof at Ebbets Field. "I was a guess hitter," he once modestly explained, "and anybody who says he isn't just won't admit the truth. It's always better to be lucky than good."

In 1967 club owner Gabe Paul hired Adcock to manage the Cleveland Indians. The Tribe finished eighth, and Adcock was not rehired. He managed two more years in the minors before leaving the game. Adcock then settled down on a 288-acre farm in his hometown of Coushatta, Louisiana, to devote his time to horse breeding.

Wally Berger

Until Eddie Mathews and Hank Aaron arrived in the 1950s, Wally Berger was the greatest slugger ever to wear a Braves uniform and hit more than twice as many homers at Braves Field than any other Boston Brave.

If that criterion is limited to members of the Boston Braves, Berger still comes out on top. From 1930 through 1936 the righthander was practically the only home run threat the Braves could muster. In 1935, for example, he hammered 34 homers to lead the National League. Significantly, the second-most prolific home run hitter on the club was Babe Ruth, who hit six before he retired in May.

Berger was born in Chicago but grew up in San Francisco playing sandlot baseball. In high school he played third base on a team that featured future Hall of Famer Joe Cronin at second. In 1927 Berger signed his first professional contract with Pocatello of the Utah-Idaho League and became an outfielder. When he hit .385 with 24 home runs in 92 games, he was brought back home to play for San Francisco's Pacific Coast League team.

Although Berger tore up Coast League pitching for the next two seasons, he was not brought up to the majors for even the traditional "cup of coffee." His rights were owned by the Chicago Cubs, whose 1930 team boasted an outfield of Riggs Stephenson, Hack Wilson, and Kiki Cuyler, each of whom would hit .300 with more than 100 RBIs that year.

Before the 1930 season opened, Berger was traded to Boston. He rewarded his new employers with one of the best rookie seasons on record, hitting .310 with 38 home runs and 119 RBIs. His home run total as a rookie, though tied by Frank Robinson in 1956, stood as the major league record until Mark McGwire bested it in 1987. (It remains the National League record for a freshman.)

Although he never surpassed his rookie home run total in any other year, Berger hit between 17 and 34 home runs for each of the next six seasons. He also batted over .300 four times with the Braves, with a career-high .323 in 1931. He batted in more than 100 runs four times, with a league-leading 130 in 1935. A reliable center fielder, he led the league's outfielders in fielding average in 1932, started in center for the National League in the first three All-Star Games (1933-35), and was also named to the squad in 1936.

In 1933 Berger missed almost three weeks of the season due to illness but almost single-handedly pulled the Braves into the first division for the first time in a dozen years. He hit .313 with 106 RBIs, and his 27 homers were exactly half his team's total for the season. He finished third in the voting for the NL's Most Valuable Player.

Two factors make Berger's record all the more impressive. First, during his entire time with Boston, he had virtually no "protection." Pitchers could always pitch around him because there was never a long-ball threat coming up behind him. The second-highest homer total for a Brave during those seven years was only 13, hit by Gene Moore in 1936, and only two other batters had seasons with double figures in home runs.

Another factor working against Berger was the Braves' ballpark. Braves Field had the most distant fences in the National League. A right-handed pull hitter, Berger was challenged by a distance of 350 feet down the left field line. Although he hit 105 homers at Braves Field, more than any other player in history, one can only wonder how many he might have hit in more friendly confines, such as Wrigley Field.

A shoulder injury in 1936 reduced Berger's hitting ability, and in 1937 he was traded to the New York Giants. Playing only part time, he helped them win the 1937 NL pennant with a dozen homers. In 1938 he was sent on to Cincinnati, where he helped the Reds win a pennant in 1939. Released after two games in 1940, he signed with the Phillies but didn't finish the season. After hitting only .241 for Los Angeles of the Pacific Coast League, he retired in 1941.

Tommy Bond

Just think what a 40-game winner would be worth today and imagine the value of someone who pulled off that feat three years in a row. Tommy Bond did it for the Red Stockings (Braves) in 1877, 1878, and 1879.

Not only was Bond the last pitcher to win 40 or more games three consecutive years, but he was also the first to capture pitching's "Triple Crown," leading the National League in victories (40), strikeouts (170), and ERA (2.11) in 1877 for the Red Stockings.

Bond had been a decent pitcher in the NL's predecessor, the National Association. With the Brooklyn Atlantics and the Hartford Dark Blues, Bond was particularly impressive against the Red Stockings, the league's best club. He holds the distinction of being the last pitcher to defeat Boston at home. This may not seem like much of an honor, but, after Bond bested them on September 30, 1874, Boston won its last 39 home games before the National Association expired, at the end of the 1875 season.

Bond had learned the curveball from the pitch's reputed inventor, Arthur "Candy" Cummings, and put it to good use when he joined the Red Stockings in 1877, where he was the NL's ERA leader in 1879 with a 1.96 mark. His overall major league record was 193 victories, 115 losses, and a 2.25 ERA.

After retiring from the mound in 1882, Bond briefly managed Worcester and then umpired in the New England League. He went on to coach at Harvard, where his charges included Hall of Famers John Clarkson and Tim Keefe. He attempted a comeback with the ill-fated Union Association and pitched briefly in the minors for Indianapolis, Memphis, and Brockton. At the time of his death in 1941 Bond was the last surviving player from 1876, the National League's first season.

Lew Burdette

Lew Burdette is the only Braves pitcher to win three games in a single World Series, and, it was against the team that had originally signed him — the New York Yankees. Each game was a seven-hitter, two were shutouts, and Burdette's World Series ERA was a minuscule 0.67.

Burdette had been signed by the Yankees in 1950 and had worked his way up the chain in such places as Norfolk, Amsterdam, Quincy, and Kansas City. On August 30, 1951, New York traded him to the Boston Braves for veteran hurler Johnny Sain and threw in $50,000 to sweeten the deal.

Burdette was an extraordinarily consistent pitcher with the 1950s Braves. With the exception of the 1955 season (he was 13-8), from 1953 to 1961 he never won fewer than 15 games nor more than 21. In 1956 he was tops in the National League with an ERA of 2.70. In 1959 he tied for the league lead with 21 victories.

His biggest moment, without a doubt, was that historic 1957 World Series. In Game 1 Warren Spahn took a loss, but in Game 2 Burdette shut down Casey Stengel's Yankee squad, 4-2. In Game 5 Burdette came back with a 1-0 whitewash and was on the mound again with just two days' rest for the deciding Game 7.

"I'll be all right. In 1953 I once relieved in 16 games out of 22. I'm bigger, stronger, and dumber now," Burdette calmly reassured worried Milwaukee fans. Burdette was right on the money. He again shut out the Yankees on just seven hits, becoming the first pitcher to toss two World Series shutouts since Christy Mathewson accomplished it in 1905.

How did "Squirrel" (short for "Squirrel Jaw") Burdette enjoy such mastery? "I exploit the greed of all hitters," was his explanation. More cynical observers had another theory: the spitter. Although Burdette earnestly denied all charges, columnist Jim Murray once quipped that if Burdette ever received a Cy Young Award, the trophy should take the form of a spittoon. Burdette retorted, "Let them think I throw it. That gives me an edge because it's another pitch they have to worry about.

"They talk as if all you had to do to throw a spitter was to crank up and throw one," Burdette explained in 1957. "Don't they know it's the hardest pitch to control? It takes a lot of practice and you just don't throw one when you figure it might get the hitter out. I'd love to use it, if I knew how." he said without a grin. "Burleigh Grimes told me five years ago not to monkey around with it, but to let them think I threw it. That's what I've done."

The Yankees got their revenge in the 1958 Fall Classic when they beat Burdette in two out of three decisions. The following year Burdette won 21. His most famous victory that year was his 1-0, 13-inning win over Pittsburgh's Harvey Haddix after Haddix had hurled 12 perfect innings. On August 18, 1960, Burdette himself approached perfection as he pitched a no-hitter versus the Phillies. He faced only 27 batters; after walking Tony Gonzalez in the fifth, he induced the next batter to hit into a double play.

He was traded to the Cardinals in 1963, and was then sold to the Phillies in 1965 before finishing his career with California. Upon leaving the game in 1967, Burdette worked as a public relations specialist for an Athens, Georgia, cable television company before retiring to Florida.

Rico Carty

Rico Carty once "homered" twice in the same at bat, with Toronto of the International League in 1963. The first four-bagger was disallowed because time had been called. Carty returned to the batter's box and promptly hit another ball into the seats.

That incident prefigured the rest of Rico Carty's career. If something bad could happen to him, it would — but, after it did, Carty, a lifetime .299 hitter, would usually go right on hitting as if nothing had ever happened.

Carty was born in San Pedro de Macoris in the Dominican Republic, a region famous for producing exceptional ballplayers. Originally a boxer, he switched to baseball, became a catcher, and was so impressive that he was signed by 10 different clubs. Not scouted but *signed*. Because Carty hadn't actually accepted money from any of the 10 teams, National Association President George Trautman ruled that Carty could sign with whomever he wanted. He chose the Braves, hung up his catcher's gear, and became an outfielder.

After two at bats with the Braves at the end of the 1963 season, Carty went to spring training with the big club in 1964. He struggled initially, but on the advice of hitting coach Dixie Walker began waiting on pitches "until the last second." As a result Carty enjoyed a freshman year that he felt should have earned him Rookie of the Year honors over Dick Allen. Their numbers are worth examining.

Carty hit .330 with 28 doubles, four triples, 22 homers, and 88 RBIs in 455 at bats for the highest-scoring team in the league. Allen, meanwhile, hit .318 with 38 doubles, a league-leading 13 triples, 29 homers, and 91 RBIs in 632 at bats, but also committed an embarrassing 41 errors at third base.

In 1965 Carty suffered chronic back problems and missed half the season. A specially designed shoe helped to correct the situation, and he hit .326 the following year as a regular player. In 1967, however, Carty missed 18 games with an injured shoulder after a baseline collision with Ron Hunt and hit only .255.

Once, during spring training in 1968, Carty jokingly pretended that he didn't feel well. The team physician, taking Carty seriously, found that the ballplayer had a slight fever and that his appetite was abnormal. As it turned out, Carty was in the early stages of tuberculosis and missed the entire season. He came back as strong as ever in 1969 — except for his shoulder, which he dislocated seven times. Atlanta won the NL West in the first year of division play and Carty hit .342 in 104 games, driving in 58 runs in only 304 at bats.

Carty avoided mishap in 1970 and won the NL batting crown with a whopping .366 average, 25 homers, and 101 RBIs in only 478 at bats. Since then, only Tony Gwynn's .370 in 1987 and Andres Galarraga's .370 in 1993 have been better in the NL.

In 1971 in a now-familiar scenario, Carty collided with Matty Alou and fractured his kneecap while playing in the Dominican Winter League. He missed the whole season. To compound matters, his newly opened Atlanta restaurant, the "Rico Carty Open Pit Barbecue," burned down, and the better part of Carty's losses were not covered by fire insurance.

As if Carty hadn't endured enough misfortune, he was stopped and attacked by Atlanta police officers in August 1971 while driving his Dominican brother-in-law home. The officers kept beating and kicking him in what appeared to be a racially motivated assault until they realized who he was. Fortunately, fears that Carty's vision might be damaged were unfounded.

True to form, he came back in 1972, although not as strong as before, hitting .277 in 86 games. More importantly, he failed to get along with Manager Eddie Mathews, so he was traded to Texas right after the season.

In Texas he was injured again, and again he didn't get along with his manager (Whitey Herzog). He was sold to the Cubs in August, and a month later was shipped off to Oakland.

Oakland released him in December, and Carty played with Cordoba of the Mexican League in 1974, batting .354. On August 17, 1974, he made it back to the majors with Cleveland and revived his career. As the Tribe's designated hitter he batted .363 in 33 games that season and then .308 and .310 in the next two seasons. In March 1978 he was traded to Toronto, who dealt him back to Oakland in August. He returned to the Blue Jays that October on waivers, and his last year was 1979, when he hit .256 as a 40-year-old.

"I never gave up when things were bad," Carty said. "Not one moment. I think that's what helped me. My positive thinking."

Since leaving the major leagues Carty has been associated with the Dominican League and holds the honorary rank of general in the Dominican Army.

★ John Clarkson ★

John Clarkson once won 49 games in a season for the Braves, pitching 620 innings.

"John Clarkson never had a superior as a pitcher and never will," said infielder Fred Pfeffer of his former teammate. "He was a master of control. I believe he could put a ball where he wanted it nine times out of ten. He had everything any pitcher ever had as well. His speed was something terrific, and he could throw any curve. However, his favorite pitch was a drop, something like the spitball of today, although he delivered it without the ointment necessary nowadays." In 12 major league seasons, Clarkson won 328 games (an average of 27 wins a season) including a 53-win season in 1885, the second highest season win total in major league history after Providence hurler Charles "Old Hoss" Radbourn's 59 in 1884.

Clarkson, the son of a jeweler, was born on July 1, 1861, in Cambridge, Massachusetts. His two pitching brothers, Arthur "Dad" Clarkson and Walter Clarkson, also distinguished themselves on major league diamonds.

John started the 1884 season playing for the Saginaw, Michigan, team, where White Sox player-manager Adrian "Cap" Anson discovered him. Anson once said of Clarkson, "Scold him, find fault with him and he could not pitch at all. Praise him, and he was unbeatable. In knowing exactly what kind of ball a batter could not hit and in his ability to serve up just that kind of ball, I don't think I have ever seen the equal of Clarkson." The right-hander, who had already recorded 10 shutouts in 40 starts for Saginaw, won 10 games in Chicago and struck out 517 that year.

Although he had several excellent seasons, Clarkson's 1885 numbers are almost superhuman. In addition to his 53-16 record and 1.85 ERA, he completed 68 games, pitched 623 innings, struck out 308, and tossed 10 shutouts and one no-hitter. In a battle of future Hall of Famers, Clarkson no-hit Providence and Charley Radbourn, 4-0, on July 27. He gave up no walks and was denied a perfect game only because five batters reached base on five errors.

The White Sox moundsman also had a sense of humor. One afternoon, as the skies darkened and the umpire refused to stop the game on account of darkness, Clarkson wound up and threw a lemon to the plate. When his catcher showed the umpire that the batters were no longer facing a ball, the umpire relented and declared the game a draw.

After the 1887 season Clarkson demanded to be sold to Boston in order to be closer to home. The Boston Red Stockings, as the Braves were then known, bought Clarkson that winter from Chicago for $10,000. After winning 33 games in 1888, Clarkson was dazzling in 1889, winning pitching's Triple Crown by leading the league with 49 wins, 284 strikeouts, a 2.73 ERA, 620 innings pitched, eight shutouts, and 68 complete games. Clarkson died of pneumonia in 1909 and was inducted into the Hall of Fame in 1963.

★ Jimmy Collins ★

Jimmy Collins spent six seasons with the Boston Beaneaters (Braves) as the league's leading third baseman although he started out as an outfielder.

During an 1895 matchup between the Baltimore Orioles and the Colonels in Louisville, seven consecutive Orioles bunted the ball toward third baseman Walter Preston, and, seven times, Preston clumsily played the ball into a base hit. After the seventh bunt, Louisville Manager John J. McCloskey called Fred Clarke in from left field and offered him $50 more a month to play third base. Clarke balked. He had played shortstop early in his career and knew he belonged in the outfield. "Why don't you move that fellow Collins from center field?" he asked. "I understand he played third base at Buffalo."

Jimmy Collins, on loan from Boston, was hastily summoned to the infield. As he later recalled, "McGraw bunted and I came in as fast as I dared, picked up the ball, and threw it underhanded to first base. He was out. Keeler tried it and I nailed him by a step. I had to throw out four bunters in a row before the Orioles quit bunting." The barehanded pickup and underhand throw are standard today; a third baseman who cannot make the play will not keep his position for long. Yet, in 1895, it was revolutionary.

Collins completely recast the position of third base with that play and with other innovations. Before he came along, third basemen stood close to the base; some even kept one foot on the bag. Collins noticed that most balls were hit to the third baseman's left, so he moved away from the foul line to lessen the gap between himself and the shortstop, realizing that he was quick enough to grab balls hit down the third base line. He also played in close on bunting situations, trusting that his reflexes were fast enough to stop the ball should the batter suddenly swing out.

Collins had begun his career with Buffalo of the Eastern League in 1893. A solid 5 feet 9 inches tall and 178 pounds, he threw and batted righthanded. At Buffalo he played a little third base but was mainly an outfielder. He hit .353 for the Buffs in 1894, and in 1895 Boston purchased his contract and brought him to the National League.

The veteran club had no place for him to play, however, and after appearing in 11 games and batting only .211 he was sold to Louisville for $1,500. There Collins hit a respectable .273, but his third base play was the talk of the league. When he rapped out four hits and handled 16 fielding chances faultlessly in a game against his old team, the Boston fans howled about the one that got away.

Collins didn't get away for long, however. The deal that sent him to Louisville included a provision that gave Boston the right to buy back his contract at the end of the season for the same price. Boston exercised its option and demonstrated its faith in Collins by dealing Billy Nash, the third baseman for 10 seasons, to Philadelphia.

Along with Collins, the Beaneaters featured three other future Hall of Famers — pitcher Kid Nichols and outfielders Hugh Duffy and Billy Hamilton. The club's infield was perhaps the best ever up to that time. Collins played third, acrobatic Herman Long played shortstop, reliable Bobby Lowe covered second, and slick-fielding Fred Tenney played first. Collins hit a career-high .346 in his first season back in Boston and finished second in the league in RBIs with 132, but an ankle injury limited him to just 84 games.

In the close 1897 pennant race the Beaneaters wrested the NL championship from the Orioles by two games, and they repeated as pennant winners in 1898, widening their margin over Baltimore to six games. Collins was again outstanding, batting .328, leading the league with 15 home runs, and finishing second in RBIs with 111.

Boston might have won a third consecutive pennant in 1899 except for a maneuver that is now illegal: the Orioles' owner purchased the Brooklyn club and combined the two squads in Baltimore to produce a powerhouse. Boston finished second.

Despite Boston's success on the field and at the gate, the team's owners were notoriously cheap. Their ballpark was falling apart, and their players were underpaid. In 1901 the American League declared itself a major league and began waving money at the NL players. Many Boston players leapt at the chance, including Collins. His brilliant third base play was not lost to the fans, though; he signed with the city's AL team as player-manager for $5,500 a year. Within a few seasons he earned $10,000 a year plus 10 percent of the gate, nearly $18,000 one year.

It was a fabulous salary for the time, and Collins earned it. In his first two AL seasons he hit .332 and .322, and Boston finished second and third. This early success, combined with the NL Beaneaters' fall to the second division, made the AL club Boston's more popular team. In 1903 Collins's men won the American League pennant.

After two years of bitter acrimony, the National and American Leagues agreed to live in peace. Barney Dreyfuss, owner of the NL champion Pittsburgh Pirates, and Boston owner Henry Killea agreed to a postseason "world's series" to settle the championship of baseball. Pittsburgh had won three straight pennants and was a slight favorite, but by the time the Series was played, illness and injuries had left the Pirates with only one reliable pitcher, righthander Deacon Phillippe.

In the best-of-nine affair Phillippe won three of the first four games before he tired. Boston pitchers Cy Young and Bill Dinneen took over, and Boston won in eight games to become the first true world champions.

In 1904 Boston successfully defended its AL title in a close race with the New York Highlanders. However, New York Giants owner John T. Brush and Manager John McGraw refused to play their NL champion in a second World Series.

The Boston club aged rapidly after 1904, and Collins wasn't immune to the rigors of time. After the team tumbled in the standings for two straight seasons, he was replaced as manager, although he began the 1907 season as the regular third baseman. In July he was traded to Connie Mack's Philadelphia Athletics. Collins finished the year, then slumped to .217 before retiring from the major leagues after the 1908 season. During 14 seasons he had cracked out exactly 2,000 hits for a batting average of .294.

Collins continued to play and manage in the minors through 1911. When he retired, he lived comfortably for 20 years because of his real estate investments in the Buffalo area. The Great Depression all but wiped him out, however, and he went to work for the city as a park inspector. He died in Buffalo in 1943, and two years later the Old Timer's Committee named him to the Hall of Fame, the first third baseman to be inducted.

Del Crandall

No team pursued Brooklyn with the ferocity that the Braves did in the 1950s, and Del Crandall was one of their most ferocious players.

On a club that featured Hall of Famers Hank Aaron, Eddie Mathews, and Warren Spahn, Crandall helped turn the Braves into a National League power with his hitting and catching skills, and he became one of the league's top catchers of his era.

From 1953 through 1960, the team's first eight seasons in Milwaukee, the Braves went to the World Series twice, took second place five times, and finished third once. That was when Crandall was in his prime. He went to the All-Star Game seven times, missing only in 1957. He was named to the *Sporting News* Major League All-Star Team in 1958 and 1960. He captured Gold Gloves for defensive excellence in 1958, 1959, and 1960 while averaging 70 RBIs and more than 19 home runs per season.

Crandall's career spanned 16 years, five clubs, and two homes for the Braves franchise. He compiled a lifetime batting average of .254 and hit 179 home runs, often batting second in the order. After catching more than 100 games for eight straight seasons he lost playing time because of a sore arm and the emergence of a young catcher named Joe Torre.

The 6-foot-1 Crandall was born in Ontario, California, and was signed for a small bonus out of Fullerton (California) High School. He played in the Western Association, the American Association, and the III League during his brief minor league career. In 1949 Crandall reached the majors with the Braves, who were still in Boston. He saw action as a backup in 1950, and after a two-year hitch was given a regular job when the franchise relocated to Milwaukee.

In 1953 Crandall hit .272 with 15 homers and 51 RBIs as the Braves won 92 games, their most since the "miracle" season of 1914, but they still finished 13 games behind pennant-winning Brooklyn. Although he never topped .242 during the next three years, Crandall belted 63 homers during that span. In 1955 he hit a career-high 26 round-trippers, including three grand slams.

In 1957 Milwaukee finally captured a pennant, winning 95 games and finishing eight games ahead of St. Louis. Crandall hit only 15 homers with 46 RBIs during the season, but Aaron and Mathews combined for 76 home runs and Spahn won 21 games. Crandall played in six of the seven World Series games that year, going 4-for-19 with a home run as the Braves beat the Yankees on the strength of three complete-game victories by Lew Burdette.

In 1958 Crandall and the Braves were back in the World Series, once again facing the Yankees. Crandall had six hits in 25 at bats for a .240 average, and Milwaukee won three of the first four games. But New York stormed back, and after Crandall's home run in the sixth inning of the final game tied the score, 2-2, the Yankees scored four runs in the eighth to wrap up the Series.

In 1959 Crandall enjoyed another productive season, belting 21 homers and driving in 77 runs. The Braves finished in a regular-season tie with the Dodgers, then lost the best-of-three playoff. Manager Fred Haney called Crandall the most valuable man on the team.

In 1960, at age 30, Crandall batted .294 with a career-high 77 RBIs. He also caught the second and third no-hitters of his career. On August 18 Crandall was behind the plate when Burdette no-hit Philadelphia. Less than a month later Spahn pitched the first of his two career no-no's, shutting down the Phillies, 4-0. After an arm injury limited him to only 15 games in 1961, Crandall delivered one more standout season in 1962. He won his eighth and final All-Star berth, captured his fourth Gold Glove, and was named to the *Sporting News* NL All-Star team.

But by then his skills were beginning to decline. In December 1963 he was traded to the Giants in a seven-player deal that sent Felipe Alou to Milwaukee. He spent 1965 with Pittsburgh, and finished his career in the American League with Cleveland.

After his playing days were over Crandall tried his hand at managing, without much success. Crandall replaced Dave Bristol as the Milwaukee Brewers' manager in 1972 and held the job through 1975. In 1983 at age 53 he took over for Rene Lachemann in Seattle and was replaced by Chuck Cottier the following season.

Alvin Dark

A shortstop with the Boston Braves in 1948, Dark was a vital cog on three pennant-winning teams.

Nicknamed "Blackie" because of his jet-black hair, Dark had starred in football at Louisiana State University and was drafted by the Philadelphia Eagles. Instead he took a $50,000 bonus from Boston, became Rookie of the Year for the pennant-winning Braves in 1948, and finished third in MVP balloting.

In December 1949, Dark and his keystone teammate, Eddie "the Brat" Stanky, were traded to the Giants, and

Dark was promptly named team captain by Manager Leo Durocher. With Dark at shortstop the Giants won pennants in 1951 and 1954. In the 1951 World Series against the Yankees Dark hit .417; against Cleveland in post-season play in 1954 the steady Dark hit .412.

Dark was traded to the Cardinals, Cubs, Phillies, and the now-Milwaukee Braves. Meanwhile, the Giants had moved to San Francisco and were looking for a new manager. In October 1960 they sent infielder Andre Rodgers to the Braves to acquire Dark — not to play, but to manage.

In 1962, his second year as a manager, he steered the Giants to a pennant, but Dark was frustrated by the second-guessing that came with the job. "There are surprisingly few real students of the game of baseball, partly because everybody, my 83-year-old mother included, thinks they learned all there was to know about it at puberty. Baseball is very beguiling that way."

He was fired after the 1964 season and became the A's manager at the start of the 1966 season, tangled with owner Charlie Finley, and didn't finish the season. After he spent four unsuccessful years managing in Cleveland, Finley gave him a second chance in 1974. Dark won another world championship that year and then was fired despite another first-place finish in 1975. Signed to manage the Padres in 1977, he lasted one season and hasn't returned to the majors since.

★ Hugh Duffy ★

Diminutive Boston outfielder Hugh Duffy holds the all-time record for the best single-season batting average — a .440 mark set in 1894.

It was a year for exceptional averages: the Phillies had a .400-hitting outfield, and the National League maintained a batting mark of .309, also the highest ever. Yet, for his efforts Duffy received only a raise of $12.50 per month to $2,700 annually. "No one thought much of averages in those days. I didn't realize I had hit that much until the official averages were published months later," he recalled a half century later.

Duffy was originally a mill worker who supplemented his income by playing ball on Saturdays and Sundays. He entered Organized Baseball with Hartford of the Eastern (International) League in 1886 and then split the 1887 season between Springfield of the Eastern League and Salem-Lowell of the New England League.

By 1888 he was with Cap Anson's Chicago White Stockings, although Anson was not impressed with Duffy's 5-foot-7-inch frame. "Where's the rest of you?" sneered Anson. "This is all there is," Duffy coolly replied. Anson kept him but wouldn't speak to him for the next two months.

In 1890 Duffy jumped to the Players League, along with many other National League stars. When it disbanded he signed with Boston's American Association franchise. After the 1891 season the AA also folded, and Duffy joined Boston's NL club, where he had his career year in 1894. Not only did he hit .440, but he also went hitless in only 17 games that season, had 12 four-hit games, and got five hits in a game twice, a feat he accomplished five other times in his career. Getting off to a slow start — he was hitting just .260 in early May — Duffy got hot and stayed that way for the remainder of the season. He led the National League in home runs (18) and did so again in 1897 (11).

Duffy played for Milwaukee in 1901, its first year as an American League franchise. The following year the club moved to St. Louis and became the Browns, but Duffy remained behind and served as player-manager for Milwaukee's entry in a new Western League. He returned to the National League in 1904 as the Phillies' player-manager, a position he held through 1906.

In 1910 and 1911 he managed the White Sox; he then went back to manage Milwaukee (now in the American Association) before returning to the NL as a scout for the Braves in 1917. In 1920 he managed Toronto of the International League, and in 1921 and 1922 he managed in the majors again when he took charge of the Red Sox.

He was inducted into the Hall of Fame in 1945 and stayed with Boston as a scout and coach until his death in 1954.

Bob Elliott

Bob Elliott, a Braves MVP in the '40s, came up to the majors with the Pittsburgh Pirates in 1939, hit .289 lifetime, and was named to the 1941 National League All-Star team, but he was something less than a gazelle in the outfield.

In 1942 Manager Frankie Frisch moved the awkward-fielding Elliott to third base and told him, "It's an easy position to play, Bob. I even played it myself. All you need is a strong arm and a strong chest. Whatever I couldn't stop with my glove I stopped with my chest. Playing the outfield wears out your legs. You can play third base on a dime, no running or nothing. It will add five years to your playing career."

Frisch tirelessly hit grounders to Elliott during practice. One day a ball hit Elliott squarely between the eyes and knocked him out. As he regained consciousness, Elliott muttered, "Hey, Frank, remember what you told me about third base adding five years to my career? Well, I think I lost three of those five extra years already."

Elliott survived and went on to have a long and fruitful career in the majors, mostly with the Braves. Along the way he spoiled three no-hitters, mastered third base well enough to lead the league in fielding one year, and was named to seven All-Star teams.

The Pirates traded Elliott to the Boston Braves after the 1946 season for Billy Herman, who became their manager. The swap became known as one of the worst in Buc history in 1947 when Elliott hit 22 home runs, had 113 RBIs, batted .317 with a .517 slugging percentage, won the Most Valuable Player Award, and the next year led the Braves to a pennant. Elliott was so valuable to his mates that they nicknamed him "Mr. Team."

He was traded to the New York Giants for the 1952 season and split 1953, his last season as a player, between the St. Louis Browns and the Chicago White Sox. Elliott later managed in the minor leagues, and in 1960 he took the reins of the awful Kansas City Athletics. He later worked for a beer distributor. He died of a ruptured vein in his windpipe in 1966.

Darrell Evans

Like fine wine, third baseman Darrell Evans seemed to get better with age. He became, at 38, the oldest player to win a home run title and the second-oldest to hit 40 homers in a season as he put a cap on a fine career that saw him collect 414 homers. When he retired, only three players — Mike Schmidt, Dave Kingman, and Reggie Jackson — had exceeded his homer total and not yet been inducted into the Hall of Fame.

Oddly enough, as a youth Evans was not a home run hitter. His father stressed the idea of simply making contact, and not until he was a sophomore in high school did the younger Evans hit a homer. "I lined one over the right fielder's head and made it around the bases before he could catch up," Evans admitted. "I don't know if it would have gone over any fences, so I don't know if you can call it a 'real' home run. But it still felt good." A source of inspiration for Evans was Ted Williams's *The Science of Hitting*, which father and son Evans would review nightly. "I take that book out to this day — still look at it every winter," Evans said in 1985. "That man knows what hitting is all about."

Evans signed with the Kansas City A's in the secondary phase of the June 1967 free-agent draft. He had previously been selected by the Cubs, Yankees, Tigers, and Phillies but had opted to remain enrolled at Pasadena City College.

He divided his first professional season between Peninsula of the Carolina League, the Bradenton A's of the Gulf Coast Rookie League, and Leesburg of the Florida State League. Although he played only 14 games with Bradenton, he was selected as the Gulf Coast League's 1967 Player of the Year based on his prodigious .489 batting average.

Evans spent that winter with the Marines. "I signed up in the reserves and spent six months at a marine camp in San Diego," Evans recalled. "I went in as a 178-pound weakling and came out over 200 pounds. It was the best thing that ever happened to me. They built me into a man."

After spending 1968 with Birmingham in the Southern League, Evans was drafted by the Atlanta Braves, who seasoned him at Shreveport and Richmond. The Braves concentrated on changing Evans's batting style. "I was strong enough but I didn't know how to pull the ball," he said. "(Eddie) Mathews taught me how to do it. He was a hitting instructor in the Braves' system and he showed me how to turn my body, how to shift my weight, how to lay back on the ball, how to be patient — and how to pull it. He did more for me than anyone else in my career."

Evans's path to Fulton County Stadium, however, seemed to be blocked by the presence of Clete Boyer at third. "Then, Boyer and (General Manager Paul) Richards had their big feud, and they got rid of Clete. The third base job was mine . . . all I had to do was keep it," Evans recalled.

Keep it he did. With Atlanta in 1973, Evans hit 41 home runs, Hank Aaron slugged 40, and Davey Johnson had 43, the first and only time in major league history that three teammates have hit 40 or more.

Evans hit for power but not for average and was a

career .248 hitter, so he could easily be stereotyped as a free-swinging slugger. Actually, he was quite selective at the plate, and during the course of his career walked more times than he struck out, 1,605 versus 1,410 and he led the National League twice in bases on balls.

Evans contended, "Drawing walks has always been one of my weapons. They've helped me as a hitter. I played on teams with Aaron and Willie McCovey and they taught me that, to hit home runs, you had to be selective. You have to prove to the pitcher that he has to throw you strikes."

Atlanta traded Evans to San Francisco in June 1976 for first baseman-outfielder Willie Montanez and three other players. In eight and a half years in San Francisco, Evans hit more than 20 homers in a season only once; that was in 1983, his final year with the Giants.

He signed with the Tigers that December, shifted between first base and designated hitter, and, eventually, regained his Atlanta-style power. In 1984 he finally saw postseason play, hitting .300 in the American League Championship Series, and, in 1985 he hit a league-leading 40 homers.

At age 40 in 1987 he hit 34 homers, topping Hank Sauer's previous record of 26 at that age. He hit 22 homers in 1988 but found no major league club willing to sign him for the following season.

He signed a minor league contract with Richmond, the Atlanta Braves' International League farm team, and made the big club that spring, but only in a pinch-hitting, spare-part capacity. "I don't know if you really accept it,"Evans said of part-time duty. "You deal with it. It's tough to back off and say you've got to be satisfied with what's going on."

That was his last season. He served as the Tigers minor league batting coach and Yankees batting coach before retiring from baseball.

★ Johnny Evers ★

Best known as part of the Cubs's Tinker-to-Evers-to-Chance double play combination, Johnny Evers had an MVP season with the Braves in 1914.

That was the year Evers and his mates went from last place in August to win the National League pennant going away. In Game 4 of the 1914 World Series Evers scored the Braves's first run and knocked in the other two, as Boston swept Connie Mack's heavily favored Athletics. Evers, known more for his glove and his brains than his bat, hit a lusty .438 in the Series.

He was smart enough to use the rule book to wrest the 1908 National League pennant from the Giants. But, for those who saw him play, "the Crab" was a baseball maniac who had no truck for other players, umpires, reporters, or fans. Tinker and Evers had a fight early in their careers and played side by side for many years without speaking to each other.

Tinker may have considered himself lucky because, when Evers did speak, he rarely had anything nice to say. Of sportswriters Evers commented, "A ballplayer has two reputations, one with the players and one with the fans. The first is based on ability. The second the newspapers give him." Of fans Evers said, "The spectators take for

granted really wonderful catches and unless the outfielder is compelled to climb a tree, turn a double somersault, leap over a 10-foot bleacher fence, or do something equally sensational, he scarcely attracts attention."

But Evers saved his worst vitriol for umpires and suffered numerous suspensions. Cubs owner Charles Murphy offered Evers a new suit if he would go two weeks without being ejected from a game. Evers won the suit but was expelled the day after collecting his prize.

Evers's worst arguments were with umpire Bill Klem. In late 1909 he got into a real doozy with Klem. Evers said he would leave the settlement of the issue to the league office. "That suits me," Klem replied.

"I'll bet you five bucks you don't show up," challenged Evers. "You're on," Klem replied. Evers showed up but Klem did not. After that, whenever Klem umpired a Cubs game, Evers would scream about the five dollars Klem owed him and draw the figure 5 in the dirt with his bat at home plate. Finally, the two met on a car of a train between Chicago and Pittsburgh and Klem paid off. He made Evers write out a receipt, which he then proceeded to tear into pieces.

Evers's nightly habit was to curl up in bed with the baseball rule book, the *Sporting News*, and two candy bars. In 1908 his research paid off when he played a key role in "the Merkle Boner."

On September 4, 1908, Evers complained to umpire Hank O'Day after Warren Gill of the Pirates ran off the field without touching second base in a force situation when the winning run had scored — common practice of the time. O'Day said that if the play happened again he would call it. On September 23 the Giants Fred Merkle failed to touch second base, Evers secured a ball, and made the force out. Merkle was called out, and the game was ruled a tie, necessitating the first one-game playoff to decide a pennant; the Cubs won, meaning that Evers's "heads-up" play cost the Giants the pennant.

Evers was born in Troy, New York, in 1881, and played minor league ball in Troy before coming to the Cubs in 1902. The left-handed hitter is generously listed at 5-foot-9 and 125 pounds; when he reported to the Cubs the team did not have a small enough uniform for him.

A career .270 hitter, Evers was known more for his glove than his bat. Yet he did have his moments at the plate. He hit .350 in the 1907 World Series and became a better hitter in 1908 when he began to use his size to draw walks and better pitches. His .300 average in 1908 was a career high at that point, and he again hit .350 in the 1908 World Series with five runs scored.

Evers was a thief on the bases early in his career. In 1906 he and Frank Chance combined for 106 stolen bases, and they still rank among the best NL stolen base duos in a season. On June 16, 1907, Evers stole four bases in one game. He swiped 36 bases in 1908, 28 in 1909, and 28 in 1910.

But a series of personal tragedies enveloped Evers in 1910. Late in the season he was the driver in an accident that killed his best friend. A few weeks later Evers lost his life savings when his business partner invested in two shoe stores that went belly-up. During the off-season Evers had a nervous breakdown and soon after he caught pneumonia. Then his daughter died.

Evers played sparingly in 1911 and hit only .226. He

came back in 1912 to have his best offensive season of his career, batting .341 with a league-leading .431 on-base percentage. He was appointed player-manager of the Cubs in 1913, batted .284, and led the team to a third-place finish, but he was traded to the Braves in February 1914 for second baseman Bill Sweeney and cash.

But Evers, who had averaged more than 30 steals a season in his early years, was slowing down and hit only .216 with five steals in 1916. Early in the 1917 season, his last full one in the majors, Evers was waived to the Phillies.

In 1921 he returned to manage the Cubs, but he was replaced in midseason after a 41-55 start. The cross-town White Stockings hired him to manage their club in 1924. The team finished in the cellar, and Eddie Collins replaced him the following season.

After retiring from Major League Baseball, Evers operated a sporting goods store in Albany, New York, and he was hired as superintendent of the city's Bleeker Stadium. In 1938 he was to appear on a radio program and did not know that Tinker was also scheduled to be there. When the two former combatants met, they fell into each other's arms. "Both of us could hardly keep from crying," Evers remembered.

In 1942 Evers suffered a stroke and was no longer able to walk. He was inducted into the Hall of Fame with Joe Tinker and Frank Chance in 1946. Evers died in 1947, at age 65.

Ralph Garr

Ralph "the Roadrunner" Garr, who won the National League batting title in 1974 with a .353 average and used his speed to compile a lifetime .306 average, traced his natural hitting talents to his genes — his mother's.

"She played softball when she was growing up, and, man, could she hit!" Garr said. "She never did any running or anything. All she did was hit the long ball. I just know I inherited my ability to hit from her."

Garr starred at football at Grambling State University, where he received a degree in physical education. He also hit .582, the highest average at that point in the history of the National Intercollegiate Athletic Association.

The Braves selected him in the third round of the June 1967 draft, and his stops on the way to the majors included Austin, Shreveport, and Richmond. At Austin in 1967, he paced the Texas League in stolen bases with 32. With Richmond, he led the International League with a .329 average and 63 stolen bases in 1969, and a .386 mark with 39 steals in 1970.

At Austin the Braves converted Garr from a second baseman to an outfielder, partly to take advantage of his speed and partly for other reasons. "When they moved me from second base to the outfield," Garr admitted, "I think they were trying to keep me from getting hurt."

Garr was no bargain in left field either, and with Hank Aaron, Felipe Alou, and Tony Gonzalez in the Atlanta outfield, he spent most of 1970 back in Richmond. Adding to his problems was a contract disagreement with Atlanta General Manager Paul Richards. But when Garr got his chance in 1971, he was an immediate hit. He batted .343 with 219 hits, one of three 200-hit seasons.

When he led the NL in batting in 1974 with .353, he was also the league leader in hits at 214 and triples at 17.

In 1975 he again led the league in triples, with 11. Reds scout Ray Shore said in 1971, "Garr is the fastest player in the game between home and first. I don't care who you name. Garr is a step faster."

Hank Aaron agreed, "They claim Mantle was fast, but Ralph gets down to first faster than anybody I ever saw." The Braves thought so much of his nickname, they paid Warner Brothers for permission to call Garr "Roadrunner II," one of the few times in baseball history that a nickname has actually been copyrighted.

One thing Garr never did much of was walk. He finished with only 246 bases on balls in 1,317 games. "People think I swing wild and crazy," he once said. "I do. But I look for certain pitches in certain spots and try to hit that way. I'm a guess hitter. I try to think some up there, but I don't think it's good to think too much."

He was traded to the White Sox after the 1975 season and finished his career with the Angels, retiring after the 1980 reason with a .306 lifetime average. Following his playing days, Garr became a minor league baserunning and batting instructor, as well as a scout for the Braves.

Tom Glavine

If anyone deserved to be the winning pitcher in the deciding game of the 1995 World Series for the Atlanta Braves, it was Tom Glavine, the human link between the dismal teams of the late 1980s and the ballclub that made the playoffs for four straight seasons.

When the young left-hander arrived in Atlanta the city's feeling for the team could be summed up by a crude banner: "Go Braves — and take the Falcons with you." Now the Braves are world champs, winning in their third try.

Growing up in Concord, Massachusetts, Glavine's favorite sport was hockey, and his major league career began like a slam into the boards. He had a .292 winning percentage (7-17), his first full season in the big leagues for 54-106 Atlanta in 1988. It was a very different story seven years later. Still six months shy of his thirtieth birthday, Glavine was nothing short of brilliant in the sixth game of the 1995 World Series; he pitched a 1-0 one-hitter against Cleveland to clinch the first title in Atlanta history and won the Most Valuable Player award to boot.

"I've seen Tommy throw a lot of great games, but given the circumstances and the pressure on us all, he was about as good as I've ever seen him," Atlanta pitching coach Leo Mazzone said of Glavine's Game 6 performance. "What he did was put the stamp on five great years of pitching."

Glavine's great seasons, not coincidentally, began about the same time the Braves became contenders in 1991. After back-to-back 65-97 seasons, Atlanta turned the tables on the National League West and dropped its three-year hold on the cellar like a bad habit. The Braves weren't satisfied just being contenders. They pursued, caught, then overtook the Los Angeles Dodgers the final week of the season to win the division by one game.

A lot of that credit goes to Terry Pendleton, who came

over from St. Louis and earned NL MVP honors, but it was Glavine who provided the guiding light for a very young and very talented pitching staff. He was among the league leaders in almost every category, tying for the league lead in wins (20) and complete games (nine), while posting a 2.52 earned run average, 192 strikeouts, and a .645 winning percentage. Perhaps his most impressive feat was beating out Greg Maddux, then of the Chicago Cubs, for the Cy Young Award. No one else has had a chance since.

Glavine started the 1992 season with a two-hitter. His buddy and number two man in the rotation John Smoltz came back with a retort that not only summed up the Braves' pitching situation, but also the expectations people were beginning to have for them. "Thanks for leaving me an out," Smoltz told Glavine. "Now I just have to throw a one-hitter, not a no-hitter."

Glavine actually had a better year in 1992, again winning 20 games, but increasing his winning percentage to .714, allowing only six home runs and tying for the league lead with five shutouts. Of course, Maddux was also having quite a year in Chicago, and he won the Cy Young.

Glavine again went to the World Series, again pitched well, but the Braves again lost the close ones. (All eight of Atlanta's World Series losses to both Minnesota and Toronto in 1991-92 were by one run.) So the Braves made the best pitching staff in baseball better. Maddux was signed as a free agent, and Glavine (22-6, .786 winning percentage, 239 innings) nearly beat him out for the Cy Young. Atlanta, however, could not get by Philadelphia in the playoffs.

The following season, Glavine's record slipped to 13-9, his ERA ballooned to 3.97, and Montreal ran away with the newly configured National League East. Then the baseball strike hit. Glavine's face was often on television as he worked with the Players Union — some people came to resent that, but they could not resent what Glavine did on the baseball field once the game returned.

Despite the shortened 1995 season, Glavine put together a 16-7 record (.695 winning percentage) and returned his name to its rightful spot among the league leaders in ERA (3.08) and innings pitched (198). The Braves also returned to their rightful spot in first place, winning the NL East by 21 games, and beating both Colorado and Cincinnati in four games to get back to the World Series.

Maddux started the Series with a two-hitter, and Glavine allowed three hits in six innings in Game 2 as the Braves beat the Indians for the second straight night by one run. When Maddux lost Game 5 to send the series back to Atlanta, the ball was in Glavine's hand.

What about the Atlanta fans, who were all but demanding a championship? What of the public disillusioned by the strike? What about owner Ted Turner and Jane Fonda sitting right next to the dugout? "Just thinking about such things," says Glavine, "is enough to drive you crazy."

All Glavine did was drive Cleveland crazy, carrying a no-hitter into the sixth inning before allowing a bloop single. And with the Braves clinging to a 1-0 lead just three outs away from the ever elusive title, Tom Glavine, the team's first star, did what he felt was best for Atlanta.

"I wanted to win this game as badly as any in my life, but I felt I had to fight my emotions and keep my ego in check," Glavine says. "I had trouble getting loose [in the eighth] and I didn't make that many good pitches."

Mark Wohlers, who was in high school when Glavine made his debut in Atlanta, got the last three outs and was the man everyone mobbed when it was all over. Glavine was the MVP, though, and he finally got the World Series ring that had been well deserved but so long in coming.

Hank Gowdy

Hank Gowdy was one of the better catchers of the first half of the twentieth century, and he finished tenth in Hall of Fame balloting for 1955 and 1956. Every player who finished above him in those years has since been enshrined.

He came to the majors in 1910 with the New York Giants but was traded to the Boston Doves (Braves) in the same year. He didn't become a regular until 1914, when he appeared in 128 games for the "Miracle Braves" while batting .243.

The Braves's manager that year, George Stallings, had a favorite word for his players — "Bonehead!" When one of them made an inexcusable error, a not infrequent occurrence, Stallings would bellow: "Bonehead!"

One day, in a late inning of a close game, Stallings called on Gowdy to pinch hit, but he didn't do it directly. Instead, he pointed to the Boston bench, in Gowdy's general direction, and said, "Now, you bonehead, get up there with a bat and see if you can hit the ball." Seven Braves, Gowdy included, made for the bat rack.

Although he was always a better defensive backstop than a batter, Gowdy was the unexpected hitting star in Boston's 1914 World Series sweep of the Philadelphia Athletics, when he batted .545 with one home run and three RBI.

The first major leaguer to enlist during World War I, he missed the 1918 season while fighting in France. He was traded back to the Giants during the 1923 season and helped New York win pennants in that year and the next. He was the goat in the 1924 World Series against Washington. In the twelfth inning of Game 7, he stepped on his mask while pursuing a foul popup hit by Senator catcher Muddy Ruel. The ball dropped safely. Given a second chance, Ruel doubled and eventually came around to score the winning run.

After that Gowdy was strictly a backup catcher. He was traded back to the Braves in 1929 and retired after the 1930 season.

In his later years he would never forget the memories of 1914 and that magical World Series. After the Braves had won the Series, a grateful Braves fan wrote Gowdy:

> When you're down on your luck and feeling fit
> For the hospital or the grave.
> Just think of a chap who wouldn't quit,
> Hank Gowdy, the Boston Brave.

★ Billy Hamilton ★

Using the rare combination of the ability to get on base and the ability to steal one, Billy Hamilton scored 152 runs in a season twice for the Braves and set a major league record of 192 runs for the Phillies in 1894, one of four seasons in which he led the league in runs scored.

During his 14-year career Hamilton led the NL five times in bases on balls, five times in on-base percentage, and twice in batting average. With a record augmented by 912 career stolen bases, including five basestealing titles and three consecutive 100-plus steal seasons, he compiled the highest ratio of runs scored to games played (1.06) in major league history.

Nicknamed "Sliding Billy," the slight, 5-foot-6-inch outfielder was fearless on the basepaths, often colliding with larger men. Playing for the Philadelphia Phillies against the Baltimore Orioles in September 1894, he had a particularly hard collision with the opposing catcher, 250-pound Wilbert Robinson. An account of the incident stated that "after being trampled upon and severely stunned by Hughie Jennings at second base, Hamilton made a grand run for home on Bobby Lowe's single, collided with Baltimore's fleshy backstop, and falling heavily, pluckily crawled toward the base, almost fainting as he touched it."

After hitting in 46 consecutive games, the Worcester, Massachusetts, native finished the 1894 season with a .404 batting average, and his league-leading .523 on-base percentage is the sixth-best single-season percentage on record. Traded to the Boston Beaneaters (Braves) after the 1895 season for Billy Nash, Hamilton rejected a large contract offer to skip to the American League Boston team and remained with the Beaneaters through 1901.

After he retired from the majors Hamilton played in both the New England and the Tri-State Leagues through 1910. In 1909, at age 45, he led the New England League in batting with a .332 average. He went on to manage in Fall River, Springfield, and Worcester (where he owned a piece of the team) and also scouted for the Red Sox.

In 1937 Hamilton contacted the *Sporting News* after he had been mentioned in an article. "I'll have you know sir," he wrote, "that I was and will be the greatest stealer of all times. I stole over 100 bases many years, and, if they ever re-count the record, I would get my just reward."

He got his just reward posthumously. Sliding Billy died in 1940 at age 74 and was inducted into the Hall of Fame in 1961.

Tommy Holmes

When Pete Rose broke Tommy Holmes's modern National League hitting streak in 1978, an appreciative and tearful Holmes came onto the field and thanked him for "making people remember me." But how could they have forgotten him?

During the 1945 season, when Holmes hit safely in 37 consecutive games, his performance was truly remarkable. The Braves outfielder hit .352 with 117 RBIs, 125 runs scored, and 15 stolen bases. He led the league with 47 doubles, 224 hits, a .577 slugging average, and 28 home runs. In 636 at bats, he struck out only nine times. In 11 seasons, Holmes hit .302 and struck out only 122 times in 4,992 at bats, the fourth-best ratio of all time.

Holmes was born and reared in Brooklyn, New York. His father, once a boxer, envisioned Tommy as a future boxing champion. While still in elementary school, the

youngster gave boxing exhibitions at neighborhood schools and clubs. When he turned to baseball, he credited his batting success to his boxing training. "It helped develop my arms and wrists, which figure in batting," Holmes later claimed. "Punching the bag also develops coordination, another factor in hitting."

A left-handed hitter, Holmes played first base at Brooklyn Technical High School. The Dodgers ignored him, and after graduation he played for the semipro Brooklyn Bay Parkways. Finally, Yankee scout Paul Krichell spotted him, and Holmes signed with New York in 1937.

In the outfield, Holmes made the jump to professional baseball look easy. He hit .320 with 25 home runs and 111 RBIs during his rookie season with Norfolk of the Piedmont League. In 1938 with Binghamton, he led the Eastern League with a .368 batting average before moving up to Newark in the International League (IL) in 1939.

In Newark Holmes's career stalled. Although he hit better than .300 in three seasons with the Bears, twice leading the IL in hits, he was a victim of the numbers game. The Yankees' outfielders included Joe DiMaggio, Tommy Henrich, Charley Keller, and George Selkirk. There simply wasn't any room on the talent-rich Yankees.

In the winter of 1941 he was traded to the Boston Braves for infielder Buddy Hassett and cash. Holmes quickly became a fixture in the outfield and a particular favorite of the fans in the right center field "Jury Box" at Braves Field.

After three seasons of hitting .278, .270, and .309, Holmes broke out in 1945. Between June 6 and July 8 he hit safely in 37 consecutive games, then the third-longest streak in NL history, behind Wee Willie Keeler's 44 and Bill Dahlen's 42. Despite accumulating the best offensive statistics in the league, and the best of his career, Holmes was beaten out for the MVP Award by the Cubs' Phil Cavarretta, although the *Sporting News* did select Holmes as its NL MVP.

Although he followed with three consecutive seasons hitting above .300, Holmes never again approached the heights of 1945. After banging out 28 home runs in 1945, he never hit more than 9 in any other season, and he never came close to 100 RBIs. However, he did have a 20-game hitting streak in 1946 and another 20-gamer in 1949.

Holmes hit .325 when the Braves won the NL pennant in 1948 and was part of an all-.300-hitting outfield (Jeff Heath hit .319 and Mike McCormick batted .303). But Holmes slumped in the World Series against Cleveland, managing only five hits in 26 at bats. As the Braves declined in the next few seasons, so did Holmes's average. He never hit better than .300 again in his career.

In 1951 the Braves offered him a job as manager of Hartford in the Eastern League. For the first two months of the season, the 34-year-old Holmes led Hartford into the first division and hit .319 as a part-time outfielder. Then the Braves fired Manager Billy Southworth and convinced Holmes to take over. He directed the Braves to a surprising fourth-place finish, and he appeared in 27 games, mostly in a pinch-hitter's role. But when the club dropped to seventh place the next year, he was replaced in midseason by Charley Grimm.

Holmes signed with Brooklyn as a pinch hitter and played on a second championship team when the Dodgers captured the pennant in 1952. Retiring as a player, he took a series of minor league managerial jobs and appeared in 24 games for Elmira in 1954. He became a Dodger scout in 1958, then took over as director of the Greater New York Sandlot Baseball Foundation and became a salesman for various metal products. In 1973 the Mets hired Holmes as the community relations director for their own youth baseball program, which sent an astounding 65 players to the major leagues. He also worked as an executive in a sporting goods company before retiring.

Bob Horner

Power-hitting Bob Horner appeared to be on the verge of greatness when he hit 23 homers for the Braves and won the 1978 National League Rookie of the Year Award.

Although he never quite lived up to his spectacular entrance into the major leagues, Horner did hit 218 homers in just ten seasons, including four in a single game on July 6, 1986. He retired in 1988 with a better home run ratio than Hall of Famers Reggie Jackson, Ernie Banks, and Mel Ott.

Horner, who set state home run records at Apollo High School in Glendale, Arizona, was drafted by the Oakland Athletics in the fifteenth round of the June 1975 draft, but he elected to attend Arizona State. As a sophomore in 1977, he led the Sun Devils to the College World Series, where he was named Most Valuable Player. He was also honored as an All-American second baseman. The following season he collected an NCAA-record 25 homers and was named the *Sporting News* College Player of the Year.

Atlanta rewarded that performance by making Horner the first choice in the June 1978 free-agent draft. The Braves originally planned on sending the slugging infielder to Savannah of the Southern League, but once Horner visited Fulton County Stadium, he thought he could start swinging in the majors. "When you see guys like Johnny Bench or George Foster on *Monday Night Baseball*, they look like supermen," said Horner. "Down there I saw for myself how they look and what they do. They looked just like me."

Horner and his agent, Bucky Hoy, persuaded Atlanta to start him with the big club — and to give him a signing bonus of $175,000. Horner started out by homering off Bert Blyleven in his first major league contest. He played 89 games at third base and ended the season with one homer for every 14.04 at bats, the best ever by a Rookie of the Year. "Another Harmon Killebrew," said Montreal Manager Dick Williams — and he was not alone in his opinion.

In 1979 Horner tangled with Braves owner Ted Turner over his salary. When Horner and agent Hoy pointed out that Horner's huge signing bonus should be counted as part of his 1978 base salary — and that Turner could not cut that salary by more than 20 percent — they won a huge financial victory, but, in the process, they alienated Turner. Horner followed up the fracas on Opening Day by breaking an ankle. Nonetheless, he responded with a solid year — 33 homers, 98 RBI — and signed a new three-year, $1-million contract.

Horner started off the first 10 days of the 1980 season with an .059 start, and Turner tried to demote the third

baseman to Richmond. Horner refused to go and was suspended, knocking three weeks out of his season. Nonetheless, Horner finished the year with a .268 batting average and a career-high 35 homers.

In 1982 Horner and Dale Murphy combined for 68 homers and 206 RBIs. The Braves won the NL West on the final day of the season, propelling them into the National League Championship Series against the St. Louis Cardinals. Atlanta was swept in the three-game Series, and Horner hit only .091.

Horner was known to some teammates as "Piggy," and he battled weight problems throughout his career. In January 1983, when he signed a four-year, $6-million Braves contract, it contained $400,000 in weight clauses. He was also susceptible to injury. In August 1983 he broke a bone in his right wrist. He missed most of the 1984 season when he broke the navicular bone in that same wrist.

In 1985 Horner played 40 games at first base. The following season he made a permanent move across the diamond and led NL first basemen in putouts, double plays, and total chances. At the plate he hit 27 homers and drove in a team-leading 87 runs.

Following the 1986 campaign, Horner was offered a two-year, $3-million contract from Atlanta — which represented a $300,000 cut in salary. When no other club bettered the Braves' offer, the 30-year-old Horner signed a one-year, $2.4-million pact with the Yakult Swallows of the Japan Central League. Swallows ownership prophesied that Horner would deliver 50 homers, and when six of his first seven hits were homers (including three in one game), the prediction seemed justified. He ended up hitting 31 homers, not 50, and batted .327 in 99 games.

He also ended up unhappy in Japan. "I don't have any funny anecdotes," he said. "Life last year was not amusing." Despite a three-year, $10-million offer to stay in Japan, he decided to return to the United States.

When first baseman Jack Clark left St. Louis for the Yankees prior to the 1988 season, Horner saw his chance and made overtures to Cardinals management. Manager Whitey Herzog's initial response was, "I don't want Horner." But the Cards tendered him a contract calling for a $950,000 base salary with a $500,000 bonus if he played in at least 135 games.

Hampered in part by the spacious dimensions of Busch Stadium, Horner never got untracked and retired after appearing in only 60 games. He was only 31 years old.

Joey Jay

One of the early bonus babies, Joey Jay pitched for 13 years in the big leagues, seven of them with the Braves. He won 21 games in both 1961 and 1962, was once named to the National League All-Star team, and beat the New York Yankees in a World Series game. But, in the end, he is remembered principally for his accomplishments as a youngster and for the way baseball took advantage of his youth.

In 1947 at age 12, Jay, very tall for his age, enrolled in the newly established Little League program in Middletown, Connecticut. The parents of other children petitioned to bar him from competition because of his size, but they failed. Ironically, Jay's talent at that age did not equal his stature; it was not until he reached high school that everyone knew he was destined for the majors. In fact, Jay became the first Little League graduate to make it in the big time.

Although he always vowed that his own experience with organized baseball for kids was a positive one, Jay was appalled at the abuses he saw in Little League programs everywhere. Years later he wrote a magazine article, "Don't Trap Your Son in Little League Madness." Although it was published some 30 years ago, its message hits home today. "I didn't want my son trapped in this Little League madness," Jay wrote. "I discouraged him from joining this year. Instead, he'll be riding his bike, going on camping trips, and occasionally playing pickup ball like anyone his age."

At age 17, Jay himself signed a $40,000 contract with the Milwaukee Braves and thus became a "bonus baby" and had to spend two years on a major league roster under the rules at the time. The ill-conceived rule was designed to stop wealthy clubs from signing up all the good young talent, but it penalized the players in terms of experience. Jay said, "That was a terrible rule. I got none of the experience I needed, and I took up a spot on the roster someone more deserving should have had. And what a drag I was on the ballclub."

In Jay's case, the bonus signing resulted in seven years in a Braves' uniform with only two wins in the first four years and 22 thereafter. Actually, he was beginning to deliver on his promise in 1958, when he was a veteran but still only 22 years old. Until he broke a finger on his pitching hand in midseason, Jay was 7-5 and had a sparkling 2.14 ERA.

When he seemed to be treading water the next two seasons, the Braves traded him to Cincinnati along with another highly touted pitching prospect, Juan Pizzaro, in exchange for shortstop Roy McMillan. The Reds then sent Pizzaro and pitcher Cal McLish to the White Sox for third baseman Gene Freese in the trade that transformed the sixth-place Reds of 1960 into champs in 1961.

Overnight Jay became a new pitcher. Given a regular spot in the rotation, he led the NL in wins, with 21, and in shutouts, with four. He became the ace of a surprising Reds staff that also boasted significant contributions from Bob Purkey and Jim O'Toole. Cincinnati won the pennant handily only to fall to the Yankees in the World Series in five games, even with Mickey Mantle sidelined with a leg injury. Jay was the only Reds pitcher to win a game, four-hitting the Bronx Bombers, 6-2, in Game 2.

The Reds made a run for a second pennant in 1962. On August 25, Cincinnati won for the eighteenth time in 21 tries, and Jay won his twentieth to put his club within three games of first place. The Reds eventually faded, and the Dodgers and Giants, tied at season's end, played a three-game playoff that San Francisco won.

Jay ended the season with a 21-14 record, and his success was due partially to varying his windup in an attempt to foil the basestealing abilities of Dodgers shortstop Maury Wills and outfielder Willie Davis.. Sometimes he would come to a full stop at his waist; sometimes he would hurry his windup; other times, particularly with speedy runners aboard, he would use no windup at all.

His approach foiled the Dodgers on occasion, but NL

managers complained. The following year the rules committee mandated a complete stop at the belt — a stipulation that in later years Luis Tiant and others would find ways of circumventing. The resourceful Jay suffered one of the worst turnarounds in big league pitching history, tumbling from 21-14 to 7-18 for the 1963 season.

Jay was barely a .500 pitcher for the balance of his stay with Cincinnati. After three more years with the Reds, Jay returned to the Braves in 1966, their first season in Atlanta. He posted an 0-4 record and then retired after the season.

Sam Jethroe

Sam Jethroe is one of baseball's little-known desegregation pioneers, often overlooked amid the contributions of both Jackie Robinson, the first African-American to take the field in the National League, and Larry Doby, the first in the American League. But Jethroe definitely deserves credit as a trailblazer in his own right, having been the first black man to play for the Boston Braves.

Like many black stars in those early days of integrating the majors, Jethroe arrived after he was well into his prime, but he still showed enough ability to win the NL Rookie of the Year Award in 1950. In three big league seasons and a fourth in which he played only two games, Jethroe hit .261, with 49 homers and 181 RBIs. He averaged 27 doubles and eight triples per full season in the majors.

Jethroe was born on January 20, 1922, in East St. Louis, Illinois. Twenty years later, he was playing for the Cleveland Buckeyes, a Negro League team with which he would spend seven seasons. A switch-hitting outfielder who threw righthanded, Jethroe was nicknamed "Jet" for running at speeds so overwhelming that opponents worked on special strategies to contain him. He was also a fine hitter and led the Negro Leagues in hitting in 1942, 1944, and 1945.

Meanwhile, social forces were building for blacks to play in the majors, although most cities lacked the will or courage to make the move. But, in 1945, a Boston councilman put pressure on the Red Sox to grant Black players a tryout. It took place on April 16, with Red Sox coaches Hugh Duffy and Larry Woodall taking a look at Jethroe, Jackie Robinson, and Philadelphia Stars second baseman Marvin Williams. The tryout was a charade, though, as general manager Eddie Collins did not even attend.

In 1945, Brooklyn Dodger executive Branch Rickey made the move, signing Robinson to break the color line. With the initial step having been taken, blacks slowly began to appear in the minor leagues with more frequency. In 1949 the Dodgers added Jethroe to the roster of their Montreal club in the International League.

There, Jethroe displayed the talent of a pioneer. As the leadoff man for the Royals, he created such havoc that opposing Manager Paul Richards sometimes intentionally walked the pitcher in front of him just to prevent Jethroe from tearing around the bases.

Jethroe's statistics compared favorably to those posted by Robinson in Montreal in 1946. He finished the 1949 season with 207 hits, including 19 triples, and scored 154 runs. These numbers and Boston's narrow losses in the

1948 and 1949 pennant races suggest that history might have been different had the Red Sox signed Jethroe in 1945.

Following the 1949 season, the Braves acquired Jethroe from the Dodgers for $100,000. In 1950 the 28-year-old Jethroe finally got his chance to play in the major leagues and was one of the big stories in the Braves' camp. Despite his speed and ability to hit, his throwing was not up to par for a center fielder, and his defensive instincts left something to be desired; he played too deep, preferring, as many ballplayers do, to come in on a ball rather than go back.

Despite these flaws, and the fact that the social climate was not always comfortable for black athletes, Jethroe became one of the better players in the National League. He won the basestealing crown, with 35, scored 100 runs, and batted .273, with 18 homers and 58 RBIs. In those early days of the Rookie of the Year Award, he was the third black to capture the honor in four years.

Jethroe was even better in 1951, repeating his stolen base title win and batting .280, with 101 runs scored, 29 doubles, 10 triples, 18 homers, and 65 RBIs. In 1952 his performance fell off, as he hit only .232 and struck out 112 times.

After spending 1953 in the minors, Jethroe went to Pittsburgh during the off-season as part of a blockbuster deal in which the Braves sent six players, plus money, to the Pirates for infielder Danny O'Connell. Jethroe played only two games for Pittsburgh, and his career was over.

David Justice

With the home crowd booing him, with the words he had used to criticize Atlanta Braves fans a day earlier burning in his ears, and with a world championship hanging in the balance, David Justice put his money where his mouth is.

"If we don't win, they'll probably burn our houses down," Justice said of Braves fans before Game 6 of the 1995 World Series. "If we get down 1-0 tonight, they'll probably boo us out of the stadium."

Actually the game was scoreless in the bottom of the sixth when Justice stepped up to the plate — and he heard plenty of boos. The 29-year-old right fielder crushed a fastball high and deep into the Atlanta night off Cleveland southpaw Jim Poole. It proved to be the only run in a 1-0 one-hit masterpiece by Braves pitchers Tom Glavine and Mark Wohlers. With one swing, Justice, who led all hitters with 5 RBI for the Series, had won back the fans and helped bring the Braves their first championship since 1957 — when the team was in Milwaukee.

When Justice arrived in Atlanta as the everyday right fielder in 1990, the Braves were the worst team in the National League and would finish last in their division that season for the third consecutive year. Justice's Rookie of the Year performance — .282 average, 28 home runs, 78 RBI, and a .535 slugging percentage — was a sign that the team's future was brighter than its past.

Overlooked in that litany of freshman stats was the fact that Justice hit .351 and 11 home runs with runners on base. That ability to hit in the clutch — and hit with power in the clutch — was one of the factors that enabled the

Braves to top their division four of the next five seasons.

In 1991, his second full season with the Braves, a lineup that had once featured only Justice, Ron Gant and Jeff Blauser, now included Terry Pendleton, Sid Bream and Otis Nixon. At the same time, the promising pitching staff came to maturity and the Braves rocketed through the standings. In a dogfight with the Los Angeles Dodgers, the Braves — a team that had lost 97 games the previous year — passed L.A. the final week of the season and claimed the NL West by one game.

Seemingly overmatched by the Pirates in the Championship Series, the Braves rallied from a three games to two deficit — in Pittsburgh, no less — to shut out the Bucs in the final two games and earn a trip to the World Series.

Against the Minnesota Twins, Justice led everyone with six RBI and had two of his team's five stolen bases in the 1991 Series, but the Twins won the final two games in extra innings at the Metrodome. Justice's average slipped to .256 in 1992, but the Braves were just as tough. Atlanta clinched the NL West by eight games, and beat the Pirates for the pennant in Game 7 as Justice scored the tying run in the bottom of the ninth moments before Bream slid home with the winner.

The World Series again found the Braves matched up in a dogfight, this time against the Toronto Blue Jays. The Braves were struggling, and Justice hit just .167 through the first four games of the Series when he announced on his morning radio show that his team's performance in a 2-1 loss was reminiscent of a "spring training game." Manager Bobby Cox described Justice's statement as "a crock." When he stepped up to the plate with a tie score in the fourth inning of Game 5, Justice showed this was no "B squad game" by cracking a fastball off the bunting in the second deck of the SkyDome against eventual Series MVP Jack Morris.

The Braves won that game and brought the World Series back to Atlanta, only to see it end again in extra innings. Dave Winfield, whose double drove in two runs in the top of the 11th in Game 6, said it best: "The Atlanta Braves, they're like . . . like trying to hold water back with your hands. It just keeps coming through."

Justice came through like never before in 1993. He crushed a career-high 40 home runs, 120 RBI, played in his first All-Star Game, and was a newly-married man. He married vivacious movie actress Halle Berry, who, like Justice, had grown up in a single-parent household. His mother, Nettie, showered him with so much love and attention in their Cincinnati home that he had her name tattooed on his arm. Berry, a big fan of Justice's, has his name tattooed on her derriere.

After the Braves overtook the San Francisco Giants for the NL West title the last week of the 1993 season, Justice was tattooed by the Philadelphia Phillies pitching staff. He batted a meek .143 as the Phils snatched the pennant in six games.

Following a disappointing 1994 season cut short by the strike, Atlanta dominated the newly-configured NL East in 1995 after the Phillies faded in the summer heat. Injuries kept Justice fading in and out of the lineup, but he still managed 24 home runs and 78 RBI in only 411 at bats. In the most important at bat of his career, he ended a long siege of frustration for Atlanta, for the Braves, for himself and made everyone forget his comments and remember only his heroic actions.

★ King Kelly ★

Michael Joseph "King" Kelly was king of the one-liners. During one game in the late nineteenth century while managing Boston, Kelly saw an opposing batter lift a foul ball toward his bench and realized that it would fall in front of his fielders. Thinking quickly, he leapt off the bench, yelled, "Kelly now catching for Boston," and caught the ball for out number three.

Kelly often outwitted the opposition, usually by twisting the rules in some clever way. In another instance, the score was tied in extra innings as darkness fell on a National League field. With two outs in the bottom of the twelfth the batter scorched a drive to right field. Kelly, the right fielder, took off like a shot, raced over, jumped, and clasped both hands together, apparently making a remarkable catch. As Kelly ran off the field the umpire called the game because of darkness. Later, a teammate asked Kelly how far the ball was hit. "How the hell would I know?" he said. "It was a mile over my head."

Kelly was born in Troy, New York, on New Year's Eve, 1857. He went on to spend most of his life celebrating the New Year. When asked once if he drank on the field, he answered that it depended on the length of the game.

At age 15 he began playing baseball professionally for the independent Troy Haymakers. A versatile athlete, Kelly could play any position. In 1876 he joined the Paterson, New Jersey, Olympics. The next year he moved to Ohio and played for the Columbus Buckeyes. The Cincinnati Red Stockings of the NL signed him in 1878. Playing primarily in the outfield, he hit .283. The following season he batted .348 and scored 78 runs in 77 games.

In 1880 Chicago Manager Cap Anson induced Kelly to join the White Stockings, who brought a pennant to the Windy City. Kelly's arrival and the team's sudden success were no coincidence. In the seven seasons Kelly played for the White Stockings they won five pennants. Anson assembled some excellent players during this time, men such as George Gore, Tom Burns, Ned Williamson, Abner Dalrymple, Silver Flint, John Clarkson, Larry Corcoran, and Fred Goldsmith. Anson himself was the best player on the team, but Kelly ran a close second.

At 5-foot-10 and 170 pounds, Kelly was strikingly handsome, the stereotypical "man about town." He wore the latest fashions, carried a cane, twiddled his mustache at the Chicago ladies, and captivated all with his Irish wit and his willingness to buy a round for the house. He played baseball by day, partied by night, and seldom slept in his own bed. The only thing he consumed faster and in greater quantity than alcohol was Cap Anson's patience. The manager was not complimenting Kelly when he said, "There's not a man alive who can drink Mike Kelly under the table."

Yet Anson knew that Kelly would always show up to play. He led the NL in doubles in 1881 and 1882, in runs scored from 1884 through 1886, and in batting average in 1884 and 1886. But it was his knack for winning games with intelligent and sometimes outrageous play that was his claim to fame.

Although Kelly usually played in the outfield, Anson often put him behind the plate in important games so he could be closer to the action. On one occasion Kelly was behind the plate with two outs and a runner on third base. The batter grounded to the shortstop, who threw to first for a bang-bang play. Coming in from third, the runner saw Kelly drop his mitt, apparently indicating the end of the inning, and he slowed down. But the batter at first was in fact safe. The infielder whipped the ball to Kelly, who caught it barehanded and tagged the runner for the third out.

Because of his reputation for cleverness Kelly was later credited with originating signs between the catcher and pitcher and with inventing the hit-and-run play. Both ideas were probably developed by other players, but Kelly was certainly one of the first to use them.

Kelly's baserunning alone was worth the price of admission. He knew just when to run, and he perfected a hook slide that often allowed him to elude tags. He also wouldn't hesitate to kick the ball out of an infielder's glove. During one game umpire "Honest John" Kelly called the King out on a close play. Kelly plucked the loose baseball from beneath his body, looked up, and said, "If I'm out, John, what's this?"

The fans yelled, "Slide, Kelly, slide!" as soon as he reached base. An enterprising songwriter eventually turned the cheer into a song that enjoyed great popularity, particularly in Chicago.

During Kelly's 16 years in the majors he played 758 games in the outfield, 583 as catcher, 96 at third base, 90 at shortstop, 53 at second base, and 25 at first base. He even made 12 pitching appearances, compiling a record of 2-2. Fans not only didn't know where to find Kelly on the diamond, but also they often didn't know what to expect from him at the plate.

He hit only .255 in 1883, but in 1884 his average jumped 99 points and he led the league. In 1885 it dropped to .288, but the following season he raised it by 100 points and again led the league.

After hitting .388 in 1886 and leading the White Sox to another pennant, Kelly was sold to Boston. The city of Chicago was stunned. Anson was certainly fed up with Kelly's drinking, but it was Boston who had instigated the deal. Player contracts had often been peddled before, but no player of Kelly's stature had ever been sold.

Before the deal was made White Stockings President A. G. Spalding asked Kelly if he would consent to the sale. "Horses are sold," said Kelly, "not ballplayers." His contract with Chicago was for $3,000 a year, minus numerous fines levied by Anson. Spalding told him he'd make more money with Boston. Responded Kelly, "If you can get me $5,000, I don't care a damn if you sell me for a hundred thousand."

The deal was made, but when Kelly met with the Boston owners he was offered only $2,000, the limit imposed by the club. After a number of negotiations Kelly finally signed for $2,000 in salary and a $3,000 fee that allowed Boston to use his photograph. The $10,000 sale price was unprecedented for a single player, but the Chicago fans couldn't cheer for greenbacks. In 1887 they virtually boycotted the White Stocking games, turning out in full force only when Boston was in town.

In 1887 Kelly played well, batting .322 and scoring 120

runs. But his presence brought dissension to the Boston team. "Honest John" Morrill had been a member of the club since 1876 and its manager and captain since 1882. He was retained as manager, but Kelly was named the field captain, a more prestigious position at the time. This division of authority led to rancor, and Morrill no more approved of Kelly's lifestyle than had Anson. The team finished a disappointing fifth.

In 1888 Morrill was named captain and the Boston owners sent another $10,000 to Chicago for pitcher John Clarkson. The $20,000 battery of Clarkson and Kelly moved Boston to only fourth place, although Clarkson won 33 games and Kelly hit .318 to lead the club.

Before the 1889 season Boston played an exhibition game with local semipro stars. Kelly led the Boston pros, while poor Morrill was designated captain of the semipros. Morrill was outraged, made a fuss about it, and was sold to Washington. James A. Hart was named manager and Kelly was reinstated as captain. Many Boston rooters blamed Kelly for driving away the popular Morrill, but he won back some support by leading the league in doubles and batting .294. Clarkson won 49 games and the team jumped to second place.

After years of unresolved grievances, in 1890 the NL players revolted and formed their own league. Kelly, one of the league's most famous players, was offered a small fortune to remain in the NL, but he remained loyal to the players. He managed Boston's Players League team to a pennant and hit .326. It was the only Players League pennant ever awarded, for the league collapsed after a single season.

At the same time, Kelly's indulgent lifestyle was beginning to catch up with him. Although he played in the majors for three more seasons and appeared intermittently on two more Boston pennant winners, Kelly was only a bloated shadow of his former self.

He played briefly in the minor leagues and later opened a saloon in New York, but it didn't prosper. He also appeared on the stage, reciting Ernest L. Thayer's *Casey at the Bat.* He was on his way to Boston to appear at the Palace Theater in November 1894 when he was stricken with pneumonia. As they carried his stretcher into the hospital, the attendants tripped and dumped Kelly on the floor. "That's my last slide," he said. A few days later he died.

As a representative of baseball's misty past, Kelly is often regarded as a lovable scamp. Nonetheless, there remains his .308 career batting average, 1,357 runs scored, 1,813 hits in 1,455 games, five pennants with the White Stockings and another in the Players League, and the recognition of his contemporaries that he was one of the greatest players of his age. In 1945 Kelly was inducted into the Hall of Fame.

Johnny Logan

Johnny Logan was the shortstop for the Milwaukee Braves during their back-to-back pennant winning years from 1957 to 1958. He had a gift for baseball and a talent for malapropisms. Asked to name the greatest player of all time, Logan responded, "I'd have to go with the immoral Babe Ruth."

Logan was a four-time All-Star and a scrapper at shortstop, carrying on in the tradition of tough-guy middle infielders such as Leo Durocher, Dick Bartell, and Eddie Stanky. Angered once over a pitch he considered a beanball, the 5-foot-11, 175-pound Logan took on Don Drysdale, giving away 7 inches and 40 pounds. (Fortunately for Logan, other players separated them.)

Logan starred with the Milwaukee Brewers of the American Association and gained the nickname "Yatcha" (Ukrainian for John) from the local ethnic populace. Promoted to the Boston Braves in 1951, Logan played behind Buddy Kerr for a season and then took over at short in 1952, leading National League shortstops in fielding.

His fielding prowess began with quick, sure hands and decent range, which made up for an average arm. He led NL shortstops in fielding through 1954, topped the league in assists four times, total chances per game three times, putouts once, and errors twice.

Logan kept making the plays when he changed infields after the Braves moved to Milwaukee in 1953. He was picked for his first All-Star team in 1955 at County Stadium, and, in front of the hometown fans, singled in his first All-Star at bat, driving in the first run of the NL's comeback from a 5-0 deficit to a 12-inning, 6-5 win.

That season he set career highs with 83 RBIs, an NL-leading 37 doubles, 58 walks, and a .297 batting average. He also set season highs in slugging and on-base percentage, and, on August 30, he hit one of the Braves' NL-record-setting eight home runs against the Pittsburgh Pirates.

In the 1957 World Series against the New York Yankees, Logan handled 38 chances flawlessly and delivered a solo home run in the third inning of Game 2, that gave Milwaukee a 2-1 lead in what was ultimately Lew Burdette's 4-2 win. Batting second in the lineup between double play partner Red Schoendienst and Eddie Mathews, Logan had two hits in Game 3 and scored on Hank Aaron's two-run homer in the Braves' 12-3 loss.

In Game 4 Logan walked leading off the fourth and scored on Aaron's three-run shot, part of a four-run inning that gave Milwaukee a 4-1 lead. But the Yankees rallied in the ninth to tie the score and force extra innings. Jerry Coleman grounded out to short leading off the tenth, allowing Logan to set a new World Series shortstop assist record. But the Yankees scored once that inning to go on top, 5-4.

In the bottom of the tenth, Yankee pitcher Tommy Byrne hit pinch hitter Vernal "Nippy" Jones on the foot — at least, a shoe polish stain on the ball convinced home plate umpire Augie Donatelli that it did — putting the tying run on first. After Schoendienst sacrificed pinch runner Felix Mantilla to second, Logan doubled into the left field corner off reliever Bob Grim, driving home the tying run. Mathews then homered to right for a 7-5 Milwaukee win. In Game 7 Logan reached base three times, on two Yankee errors and an infield hit, and scored once in Burdette's third win of the Series.

In the 1958 repeat World Series, Logan doubled in his first at bat. Dropped to eighth in the order in Game 2, Logan singled in a run and scored on Burdette's homer in Milwaukee's seven-run first, as the Braves took a 2-0 lead over the Yankees. In Game 4 Logan, batting second again, got Schoendienst home from third when shortstop Tony

Kubek booted his grounder, and Logan doubled and scored in the eighth, backing Warren Spahn's two-hit, 3-0 win.

Logan went hitless in Games 5 and 6. He committed a pair of harmless errors in Game 6, and he walked and scored in the bottom of the tenth as a Braves' rally fell a run short in a 4-3 loss. In Game 7 he went hitless as the Yankees avenged their 1957 Series loss.

In 1959 the Braves nearly made it three pennants in a row, finishing in a tie with the Los Angeles Dodgers. Logan's walk in the second inning of the playoff opener sparked a two-run rally, but the Dodgers came back to win, 3-2. In Game 2 Logan had two hits and scored once as the Braves built a 4-2 lead, but he left the game after getting flattened by L.A.'s Norm Larker while completing a 3-6-3 double play. The Dodgers rallied from a 5-2 ninth-inning deficit to tie the score. In the bottom of the twelfth, Logan's replacement at short, Felix Mantilla, threw late and wild to first, allowing the winning run to score.

Logan remained the Braves' regular at short through the 1960 season. Then, on June 15, 1961, the Braves replaced him with Roy McMillan and traded Logan to Pittsburgh for outfielder Gino Cimoli. He remained a backup there for three seasons.

Logan currently works as a Brewers scout, where he maintains his gift for saying the right thing in the wrong way. Logan once said of an acquaintance, "I know the name but I can't replace the face." Informed that a box score depriving him of a hit was a typographical error, Logan said, "The hell it was. That was a clean base hit."

Herman Long

In 1889 Beaneaters (Braves) shortstop Herman Long made 117 errors. Today he would never have the chance to make so many without being booted back to the minors — or worse.

But the game was different in 1889, when Long's numerous miscues didn't even lead the league. In more than 16 major league seasons he accumulated an astonishing 1,070 errors at shortstop alone, plus another 6 when he filled in at other positions. Add his minor league bobbles, and he probably made more errors than any other man in baseball history.

Yet the "Earl of Errors" was regarded as one of the best shortstops of his day, and many authorities place him at the top of the list. Long may have botched a lot of balls, but he also covered more ground than any of his counterparts. Many of his misses came on balls that other shortstops could only salute from afar. Long was spectacularly acrobatic as he pursued batted balls, cutting off some hits with moves more likely to be seen at the circus. He ranks second all-time in total chances per game. The outstanding plays that occasionally resulted from his attempts made the extra errors worthwhile.

Fielders of the 1890s labored under atrocious conditions. Gloves were rudimentary pieces of leather that offered minimal hand protection. The often lopsided baseballs bounced in unpredictable ways. Most diamonds were not much more than converted rock quarries. The field in Boston, where Long played half his games, was particularly hazardous. And hard-hearted scorekeepers of the day ruled any touch of the ball that did not produce an out an error.

Long was born in Chicago in 1866 to German immigrants. He became a professional ballplayer with Arkansas City of the Kansas State League in 1887. Two years later he played shortstop and hit .275 with Kansas City of the American Association.

When the Boston Beaneaters of the National League hired Frank Selee in 1890 as manager, he paid Kansas City $6,200 for Long's contract. A tremendous judge of baseball talent, Selee also acquired outfielder-second baseman Bobby Lowe, first baseman and leadoff hitter Tommy Tucker, and pitcher Kid Nichols. With Hugh Duffy and Tommy McCarthy and a few veterans, Selee's Beaneaters won three consecutive pennants starting in 1891.

Long, a compact 5-foot-8 and 160 pounds, collected errors but also made great plays. One day he couldn't quite reach a ball with his glove, so he stuck out his foot, deflected the ball into the air with his toe, caught it, and threw the runner out. And unlike most shortstops even in the 1890s, he hit with power. A left-handed batter, he socked 10 homers in 139 games in 1891, fourth highest in the league. His 129 runs scored placed second in the NL. In 1892 he was second in the league with 33 doubles. And in 1893 he led the NL with 149 runs scored.

One of those runs may have won the pennant for Boston. Pittsburgh was making a determined run for the flag, but, in a collision at home plate, Long ran into catcher Connie Mack and broke his leg. The Pittsburgh fans insisted there was no play at the plate. Long argued that Mack had illegally blocked his way, and that the backstop bore the broken leg to prove it.

Selee's Beaneaters played rugged but smart baseball. They pioneered the hit-and-run play, stole signs, and are credited with other innovations. Right fielder Tommy McCarthy regularly let flyballs drop and then turned double plays. But by 1894 the Baltimore Orioles were playing equally smart baseball and outdoing Boston in dirty tricks.

It helped that Boston was growing old and that the Orioles were the best-hitting team in the league. Boston fell in the standings as the Orioles swept to pennants from 1894 through 1896. But Long had three of his best seasons during those years, hitting over .300 each season. In 1896 he had his best season at bat, hitting .343 with 100 RBIs and 105 runs scored.

The Beaneaters were back in top form by 1897. Their infield combination of newcomer Fred Tenney at first, Bobby Lowe at second, future Hall of Famer Jimmy Collins at third, and Long at short is often cited as the Nineteenth Century's best. Long hit .322 in 1897, and the Beaneaters copped another pennant. The following year, as Boston won its fifth flag of the decade, Long's batting average fell to .265, but he batted in 99 runs and scored an equal number.

He posted his second 100-RBI season in 1899. But Brooklyn had put together a super team, adding most of the old Oriole stars to their own, and Boston was simply outmanned. Although Long led the NL with 12 home runs, he was starting to slip. Ironically, as his range decreased at shortstop he became more sure-handed. In 1901 and 1902 he led all NL shortstops in fielding.

Like so many other stars, Long jumped to the new American League in 1903. But he could no longer hit. After playing a single game with Mack's Philadelphia Athletics in 1904, he was released.

In 16 seasons he averaged .277 and collected 2,127 hits, 1,455 runs scored, 1,055 RBIs, and a respectable 92 home runs. Long managed in the minors through 1905, but he contracted tuberculosis, moved to Colorado for his health, and died there in 1909.

Greg Maddux

It's hard to imagine that Atlanta's Greg Maddux ever had a problem with major league hitters.

Yet the four-time Cy Young Award winner, who will not turn 30 until the first month of the 1996 season, was hit hard his first two seasons. He went a combined 8-18 with the Chicago Cubs in the 1986-87 seasons and his earned run average was over 5.00. Then again, Sandy Koufax went seven years before he won more than 11 games or struck out more than 200 batters.

Koufax and Maddux proceeded to become the only two pitchers to have four straight years with ERAs of under 2.40. Koufax, who went on to the Hall of Fame, won the Cy Young Award three times with the Los Angeles Dodgers. In 1995 Maddux became the only pitcher to win four consecutive Cy Young Awards, one in 1992 with Chicago, the last three with the Braves, and will surely follow Koufax to the Hall of Fame in Cooperstown.

"I think he's got a gift," says Brave teammate Tom Glavine, the last man to win the Cy Young before it became Maddux's personal statue. "He's able to notice things in the course of a game that no one else can."

Even though Maddux's fastball only moves 85-87 miles per hour (about 10 mph less than Gibson, Seaver, Feller or Koufax), he mixes his "heater" with four other pitches to lead the league in strikeouts for four straight years. "I don't think I understand hitting any better than I did four years ago," he says. "I'm just making better pitches at certain times."

He gambles on the mound, but he hedges his bets and usually comes out on top. In pitching, he's "the house" and hitters are just throwing their money away. On the mound, he is as cool as a blackjack dealer. In fact, he's the son of a second-career blackjack dealer. Maddux came to Las Vegas to stay as a 10-year-old in 1976 after having lived in Texas, Indiana, North Dakota, California and Spain as an Air Force brat.

When he was 15, Maddux learned to throw more from the side than over the top and to switch from a four-seam fastball to a two-seamer. The ball began to dance like Fred Astaire, and Maddux took it from there. Both Greg and brother Mike Maddux made their major league debuts in 1986.

Few could have predicted Greg Maddux's domination after a 2-4 start and a 6-14 sophomore year. In 1988, however, Maddux arrived; his ERA dropped nearly 2.5 runs per game, he gave up fewer gopher balls, and his strikeouts increased substantially. He also began a streak in which he would average 250 innings except for the strike-shortened 1994 season.

His breakthrough year was 1992, when he pitched in

the All-Star Game, lead the league in wins with 20, and reduced his home runs allowed from 18 to 7. When it was time to pick a new team as a free agent in 1993, Maddux spurned the New York Yankees and their extra $6 million to come to Atlanta and get a chance to pitch in the World Series.

When Atlanta lost to Philadelphia in the playoffs that year, that chance went out the window — although he won his second straight Cy Young Award with a 20-10 record, 267 strikeouts and 2.36 ERA (nearly identical numbers to his previous season in Chicago). He was on pace to better those numbers and get another shot at the World Series in 1994, but the baseball strike ended his season, as well as everyone else's. The powers that be gave out awards, despite the incomplete season, and his 16-6 record, 202 strikeouts and minuscule 1.56 ERA were more than enough to claim the Cy Young.

Maddux's year was 1995. He put together a 19-2 season, 1.63 ERA, and 10 complete games to lead the league in each category. The carry-over of the strike resulted in trimming 18 games from the schedule to deny him not only of 20 wins, but 200 strikeouts for the eighth straight year (he was third in the league with 181). Most important, though, he not only reached the World Series, but won it as the Braves defeated the Indians, four games to two.

Although Maddux lost his second start of the Series, he started things off with a two-hitter in the only complete game of the Fall Classic. "He doesn't seem dominating," says Cleveland third baseman Jim Thome, "then you look up on the scoreboard and you've got one hit and it's the eighth inning."

★ Rabbit Maranville ★

When the "Miracle Braves" of 1914 rose from last place to win the pennant, much of the credit went to Walter James Vincent "Rabbit" Maranville.

Maranville was considered a defensive genius in his time as Bill James concluded in his *Historical Baseball Abstract*: "After hitting .266 in 1920 with one home run, Maranville was traded for three players and $15,000, and the fans were outraged. The perception that he was an extraordinarily valuable defensive player, whether accurate or not, was the perception of his own time, not something that was created after the fact."

He was also a perennial league leader in jokes and pranks, a natural clown who had more fun, on and off the field, than anybody who ever played the game. Always a fan favorite, the shortstop had sure hands that snatched up balls. He was the kind of guy you wanted to have on your ballclub — until you tired of his waggish behavior. That's why he played for five different National League teams during his 23-year career.

For several years after his election to the Hall of Fame in 1954 it was common for baseball fans who had never seen him play to laugh at the choice. After all, Maranville was a lifetime .258 hitter who hit a grand total of 28 home runs during his career. Nevertheless, he belongs in the Hall. Maranville set major league career records at shortstop in several categories including most chances, most putouts, most assists, and most years leading the league in putouts. Among NL shortstops, he holds the record for most years with 500 or more assists and most years leading the league in assists. For the record, he led the NL in fielding four times, putouts six times, assists four times, and chances per game three times.

In 1914, only his second full season in the majors, Maranville was an important addition to baseball history. His new double-play partner at second base was the "Crab," the legendary Johnny Evers, who had been released by the Cubs after the 1913 season.

With the 33-year-old Evers and the 23-year-old Maranville anchoring the defense, the Boston Braves did something remarkable: 11½ games out and in last place on July 16, they won the pennant by 10½ games and swept Connie Mack's powerful A's in the World Series. Maranville hit only .246 during the season, but he batted .308 with three RBI during the Series.

The Rabbit kept things lively with the Pirates, Cubs, Dodgers, and Cards before he rejoined the Braves for the last six years of his career. One time, during a beanball brawl with the Cubs, the diminutive Maranville tried several times to get into the action but kept getting pushed away. Frustrated, he went to the first base coach's box and began to shadowbox. As he described it, "I got so excited that I gave myself an uppercut and knocked myself out." Turning their attention to Maranville's antics, the fans ignored the fight on the field. The next morning Commissioner Kenesaw Mountain Landis called Maranville to his office to compliment him for preventing a riot.

While Maranville played for the Pirates he sang tenor in a barbershop quartet with Charlie Grimm, George "Possum" Whitted, and James "Cotton" Tierney. The quartet would sing at the mention of beer. Imitating the flappers of the day, the four liked to take batting practice with their socks rolled down.

A late-season collapse had cost the Pirates the 1921 pennant, and, when Bucs manager Bill "Deacon" McKechnie took over in the middle of the 1922 season, he decided to share a room with Maranville and his original roommate, Moses "Chief" Yellowhorse, in hopes of keeping the pair under control.

During the first night of the experiment McKechnie went out for a movie, came home about 10 p.m., and heard both men snoring away. He might have thought his babysitting job was going to be easy. What happened, of course, was that the two wild men had gone out early and had drunk their fill. McKechnie began to undress and opened a closet door, whereupon a flock of pigeons flew out in his face. Emitting a startled roar, he awakened Maranville, who commented, "Hey, Bill, don't open that other closet. You just let out the Chief's pigeons. Mine are over there."

Other tales about Maranville abound. A thirsty Jim Thorpe once hung the shortstop out of a hotel window by his ankles while demanding a drink. On another occasion, Maranville stole second by diving between the legs of startled umpire Hank O'Day. And once, while demonstrating a hook slide in a vaudeville act, his vigorous effort took him all the way across the stage into the orchestra pit, over the shoulder of the first violinist, and into a large bass drum.

Despite his antics, Maranville knew his baseball. When Leo Durocher's family moved to Springfield, Massachusetts, Leo's father bragged so much about his son to Maranville that the shortstop just had to meet Leo, then a teenager. Maranville gave the diminutive Durocher lessons on how a small player had to behave. He also gave Durocher his first baseball glove and even cut out the leather in the pocket for him.

Great one-on-one, Maranville tried his hand at managing the Cubs in 1925, but he was no disciplinarian and lasted only 53 games. After the Dodgers released him in 1926 the Cards picked him up and sent him to the minors. The next year he spoke these immortal words: "The national consumption of alcoholic beverages took a sharp downturn after May 24, 1927. That's the day I quit drinking."

After he was brought back to the majors in 1928 he filled a big hole for the Cards at shortstop, played 112 games, and formed a sensational double play combination with Frankie Frisch. Some (including Maranville himself) say that he was the main reason the Cards won the pennant that year.

Maranville was back with the Braves in 1929 and ended his career with them. Late in the 1933 season the 42-year-old was trying to swipe home as part of a double steal when he shattered two bones in his left leg. The injury kept him out of baseball for the entire 1934 season, and he played in only 23 games the next year, his last in the big leagues.

As a 44-year-old player-manager for minor league Elmira in 1936, he hit .323. He also managed in Montreal, Albany, and Springfield, and retired from the game in 1941. He later ran baseball clinics for the Hearst newspapers. He died in 1954.

★ Eddie Mathews ★

Eddie Mathews was once the greatest power-hitting third baseman in baseball history. And, even after Philadelphia's Mike Schmidt came along, Mathews's 512 homers and 1,453 RBIs secured a place for him in baseball's pantheon.

When Mathews was coming up with the Braves in 1952, Paul Waner said it best: "There's nothing I can teach that boy about swinging a bat. He's perfect." Ty Cobb agreed. "I've only known three or four perfect swings in my time. This lad has one of them."

The Texas-born Mathews grew up in Santa Barbara, California, and was a good enough football player to be offered scholarships to USC, UCLA, and several other schools. Mathews rejected them all for two reasons: one, he hated studying, and two, he was determined to play baseball.

All but two of the major league clubs were scouting him, and he had numerous offers. The largest offer came from the Dodgers — a $10,000 bonus and another $20,000 for his family. But there was a catch. The bonus baby rules then in force mandated that any free agent signed for $6,000 or more would have to spend two years in the majors right off the bat — with no guarantee of starting even in the minors.

Neither Mathews nor his father saw any point in that. They scanned the list of proposals and saw that the club with the oldest third baseman was the Braves. Bob Elliott, the 1947 MVP, was 32. Mathews was not eligible to sign with any team until the day after his high school class graduated. So at 12:01 a.m. on June 19, 1949, he signed with Braves scout Johnny Moore for $5,999.

Mathews joined the Braves in Chicago and found out that he had made the right choice in deciding to go to the minors. "I couldn't touch the ball, not even in batting practice," he recalled. The Braves assigned him to High Point-Thomasville in the Class D Carolina State League where he hit .363 with 17 homers in just 43 games.

His fielding was atrocious, but the Braves promoted Mathews to Atlanta of the Southern Association in 1950. Mathews started slowly but finished with 32 homers and 106 RBIs. At season's end he was promoted to Milwaukee in the American Association, and, in his first at bat there, the 19-year-old hit a grand slam.

Mathews faced the military draft, however, so he enrolled in the Navy after the season. But only a few weeks after Mathews enlisted, his father was diagnosed with tuberculosis, and Mathews received a dependency discharge.

He got his chance after one more year in the minors. Elliott had staged a holdout in 1952 and was traded to the Giants on April 8. Again Mathews started slowly at bat and his fielding was still deficient. To make matters worse he failed to get along with Boston's combative sportswriting community. The personable Elliott had been one of their favorites, but they were lucky to get a grunt out of Mathews in response to a question. Said one writer: "The Braves traded away Bob Elliott, who averaged nearly 100 RBIs a season for five years, to make room for a mere babe who belongs back in the baseball nursery."

Mathews turned it around that season, even though he led the National League in strikeouts with 115. His first homer came off lefty Ken Heintzelman at Philadelphia's Shibe Park, and, by the end of the season, he'd hit 25. The last three came at Ebbets Field on the next-to-last day of the season, which made him the first rookie to hit three homers in a single game.

That was the Braves' last season in Boston and Mathews did not have fond memories of his one year there. "About the only people who seemed to be interested in the Braves," he said, "were the 50 or so gamblers who always congregated in the first-base section of the stands."

In Milwaukee the introverted and often sullen Mathews found an entirely different atmosphere. Baseball was the biggest thing to hit Wisconsin since bratwurst, and, while the players were showered with adulation, Mathews didn't consider this an ideal situation. Despite personal problems with all the media attention, he led the National League with a career-high 47 homers and drove in a career-high 135 runs, the first of three straight 40-homer, 100-RBI seasons.

From 1952 through 1959 Mathews led all major leaguers with 299 home runs. In 1957 the Milwaukee Braves won their only World Series, beating the Yankees in seven games. Mathews pulled out Game 4 with a tenth-inning homer off Bob Grim, and his infield single drove in the only run in Game 5.

But what mattered most to him was his backhand stab of Bill Skowron's bases-loaded one-hopper for the last out of Game 7. "That play ranked right up there with breaking the 500 home run barrier," Mathews said. "I'd

made better plays, but that big one in the spotlight stamped me the way I wanted to be remembered."

In 1962 Mathews tore ligaments and tendons in his shoulder while swinging against the Houston Colt 45s' Turk Farrell. "The injury was slow to heal,"Mathews said, "and even after it did, I became a defensive hitter and developed some bad batting habits."

He was only 31 when he hurt his shoulder; however, after that injury, he hit only 23 homers in both 1963 and 1964. He had one more high-quality season in 1965. He hit 32 homers with 95 RBIs in the Braves' last year in Milwaukee. Mathews moved with the Braves to Atlanta and hit only 16 homers with 53 RBIs in 1966. He was traded to Houston after the season, and the Astros traded him to Detroit in August 1967. He retired after only 52 at bats with the Tigers in 1968.

A coach for the Braves in 1971 and 1972, he replaced Luman Harris as the Atlanta manager in August 1972 but was fired after 99 games in 1974. In 1978 Mathews was elected to the Hall of Fame. "The Hall of Fame is something I never thought about when I was playing," Mathews said. "But this is it for me. I don't know what else there is to do after being elected."

★ Tommy McCarthy ★

Tommy McCarthy's election to the Baseball Hall of Fame by the Veterans Committee of 1946 is one of the shrine's mysteries.

Certainly he was not chosen on the basis of his career statistics, and a suggestion that his plaque was placed among the immortals because the committee thought it was voting for another player altogether is no doubt apocryphal.

To give McCarthy his due, he was a regular on two pennant winners: St. Louis in 1888 and the Boston Beaneaters (Braves) in 1892. A swift baserunner, he led the American Association with 83 steals in 1890 and was considered an ace outfielder during his time, although that can't be proven by his .897 career fielding average. Still, when he and Hugh Duffy played in the same Boston outfield from 1892 though 1895, they were called "the Heavenly Twins" for their artistry in corralling flyballs.

McCarthy was particularly known for trapping short flies in right field and turning them into double plays. He did hit over .340 three times and drove in 126 runs for Boston in 1894. He concluded his above-average but unspectacular career with Brooklyn in 1896.

Fred McGriff

He was swimming merrily along in free agency waters this winter, floating by this team, then that team, everyone lusting for baseball's most dangerous home run hitter. It wasn't a question of how much cash Fred McGriff could collect in the 1995 off-season, but, whose uniform did he feel like wearing in 1996? Talk about a man who could pick his next employer.

After all, McGriff is one of only nine players to hit 30 home runs in seven straight seasons — and the other eight are already Hall of Famers. If the Braves ever have their own Hall of Fame, McGriff is a shoo-in for election. Since Atlanta acquired McGriff from the Padres in mid-summer 1993, they're 92 games over .500 (209-117), and finally won their first World Series since 1957.

No wonder McGriff returned to the Braves for four more years — through the year 1999. The team's attachment to him — both professionally and emotionally — was too strong, even with the capable Ryan Klesko seemingly ready to inherit first base any day now. That means there'll be four more years of watching McGriff's long, gorgeous swing at Atlanta-Fulton County Stadium, which of course also means trouble for National League pitchers.

McGriff showed signs of greatness as far back as 1987, when was just a rookie with the Blue Jays. McGriff hit 20 home runs in the span of 107 games, including a monstrous homer off Rick Rhoden into the 13th row of the upper deck at Yankee Stadium. It was estimated to have traveled 480 feet, which, at the time, was the longest HR at the Stadium since it had been refurbished in 1976. That blast had real significance for McGriff, since it came against George Steinbrenner's team, and it was Steinbrenner whom McGriff had always considered a neighbor growing up in Tampa.

Actually, McGriff was once a Steinbrenner employee, having been selected by the Yankees in the 23rd round of the 1981 draft. McGriff had set numerous records at Jefferson High School in Tampa — marks which would eventually be broken by Mariner-turned Yankee Tino Martinez. But despite McGriff obvious skill, there was no room for him in Steinbrenner's fiefdom. That's because they already had a hot shot, left-handed-hitting first baseman named Don Mattingly.

So the Yankees swallowed hard and traded McGriff and Dale Murray to the Blue Jays in 1982, in exchange for Dave Collins and Mike Morgan. McGriff spent the next four years struggling through Toronto's farm system. In 1988, he finally made the Yankees look bad, becoming the Jays' regular first baseman and embarking on an incredible home run streak which has earned him not only respect from his peers, but at times, even awe.

"Fred's swing is a beautiful thing to watch," says teammate David Justice. "Maybe the media and the fans don't give him enough credit, but the players do. You talk to people in baseball, believe me, they'll tell you Freddie is one of the best." McGriff's manager Bobby Cox adds, simply, "Fred is a great, great player."

His reign of terror began in earnest in 1988, when McGriff smoked 34 home runs for the Jays and also led American League first basemen with a .997 fielding percentage. Even though he's maintained high fielding percentages ever since, most of the talk revolves around his swing. McGriff releases his top hand, just as White Sox hitting coach Walt Hrniak teaches his students, but, upon contact, McGriff waves his bat, twirling it through the air in a manner that is impossible to duplicate and even harder for him to explain.

"I really don't try to swing that way; it just happens," McGriff says. "Basically, when I'm at the plate, I try to keep my head down and get extension through the strike zone. The rest happens on its own. I can't believe that some young hitters are actually trying to copy me now."

Why not? All McGriff did in 1989 was lead the American League in homers in 1989 with 36, then move on to win an HR crown in the National League, too. On December 5, 1990, Joe McIlvaine, the newly-named general manager of the Padres completed the most historic deal of the decade, sending Joe Carter and Robbie Alomar to the Blue Jays in exchange for McGriff and Tony Fernandez.

Of course, nothing changed for McGriff: he kept hitting home runs at a furious pace, crushing 31 for the Padres in 91 and then leading the NL with 35 in 1992. But a funny thing happened to McGriff on the way to greatness: no one was noticing. The problem was going from one developing team to another, but either one was ready to blossom. The Blue Jays clubs of the 80s were still a few years shy of the early 90s dominance, and when McGriff landed in San Diego, he was the centerpiece of another franchise running in place.

As frustrated as McGriff might've been, he never showed it. The baseball community is in agreement on this one: McGriff is the kindest superstar man in the game, a man so humble that Bobby Cox says, "he's someone who's actually embarrassed by his talent."

Finally, though, the world is getting a long look at this home run factory. Who could forget the historic debut with the Braves on July 18, 1993? The Padres were looking to lighten their payroll, and McGriff was more than happy to leave. So there he was, standing in his new home, Fulton County Stadium . . . which had caught on fire that same day. The club-level tier was burning, a metaphor almost too perfect to be coincidental.

McGriff hit a home run in his third at-bat with the Braves, and they've been in the postseason every season since. Tom Glavine says, "it's almost mind-boggling the kind of difference Fred has made since he got here."

It's been nine years since McGriff started going crazy at the plate. Nine years of that graceful swing. Nine years, 289 home runs. No one in baseball has more homers since 1987 than Fred McGriff. Every pitcher knows the book on him: quiet man, loud bat.

★ Bill McKechnie ★

Hall of Fame manager Bill McKechnie skippered four National League teams for long stretches and won pennants for the Pirates, Cardinals, and Reds but came up empty in an eight-year stretch as head man of the Braves.

William Boyd McKechnie was born into a devout Methodist-Episcopal family near Pittsburgh in 1886. His upbringing, his conservative lifestyle, and the fact that he sang for 25 years in a Methodist choir earned him the nickname "Deacon." He began playing baseball professionally in 1906 in Washington, Pennsylvania. During the next four years he played the infield for teams in Wheeling, West Virginia, and Canton, Ohio.

The Pittsburgh Pirates gave him a three-game trial in 1907, and from 1910 through 1912 he was their utility man. The 5-foot-10, 160-pound switch hitter never hit better than .247 for the Pirates, but he was a good fielder and was considered an intelligent player.

Late in the 1912 season he was sent down to St. Paul of the American Association. He spent 1913 with St. Paul, the Boston Braves, and the New York Highlanders (later Yankees). When Highlander Manager Frank Chance was asked why he spent so much time off the field with McKechnie, he answered, "Because he knows more baseball than all the rest of my team put together."

McKechnie jumped to Indianapolis of the upstart Federal League in 1914, where he played third base and hit an uncharacteristic .304. The franchise moved to Newark in 1915, and McKechnie was named manager early in the season. He compiled a 54-45 record and moved the team up in the standings, but the league disbanded at the end of the season.

In 1916 McKechnie signed with the Giants, where he tied the major league record for most times caught stealing in a game with three failed attempts. He was soon traded to Cincinnati in a deal that sent Christy Mathewson to the Reds as manager. After two rather undistinguished years as a utility infielder, McKechnie was sold to Pittsburgh.

In 1918, a year in which many baseball stars were either in the service or engaged in defense industries, McKechnie was the Pirates' regular third baseman. He retired in 1919 but came back as a reserve in 1920 before finishing his playing career with Minneapolis of the American Association in 1921. In 11 major league seasons McKechnie played in 845 games and batted .251.

When he took over as manager of the Pirates in 1922, they were in fifth place and going nowhere. Despite becoming ensnared in the machinations of colorful players like Rabbit Maranville (see Maranville's profile for the pigeon anecdote), McKechnie's mixture of patient understanding, firm but fair discipline, and solid baseball strategy helped lift the team to a tie for third by the end of the season. Two more third-place finishes followed in 1923 and 1924, and, in 1925 they won the National League pennant.

That team included three Hall of Famers — third baseman Pie Traynor and outfielders Max Carey and Kiki Cuyler. Pittsburgh faced defending world champion Washington in the World Series. With a pitching staff that included Walter Johnson and Stan Coveleski, the Senators were slight favorites to win. They started strong, taking a 3-1 Series lead, but Pittsburgh came back to win the last three games and claim their first title since 1909.

Although the Pirates added Paul Waner, another great hitter, to their lineup in 1926, they fell back to third place. Many of Pittsburgh's problems stemmed from the hiring of blunt-spoken Fred Clarke as McKechnie's adviser. His caustic comments provoked a small revolt among the players, and McKechnie was fired after the season.

McKechnie joined the St. Louis coaching staff in 1927. The Cards had won the 1926 pennant under Rogers Hornsby, who had then been traded to the New York Giants for Frankie Frisch. When new Manager Bob O'Farrell failed to bring the Cardinals another pennant he was fired, and McKechnie was installed as manager for 1928.

The Cardinal roster included such hitters as Frisch, Chick Hafey, and Jim Bottomley, but they didn't gel until McKechnie plugged a hole at shortstop with his old nemesis Maranville. The Giants and Cubs finished strong, but the Cardinals won the 1928 race to give McKechnie his second pennant in four years. In the World Series the Redbirds squared off against a New York Yankees team that boasted Babe Ruth, Lou Gehrig, Tony Lazzeri, and other fearsome sluggers. It was no contest; New York won in a four-game sweep.

Cardinal ownership overreacted and demoted McKechnie to manager of their Rochester farm club. Crushed, he ran for the office of tax collector in Wilkinsburg, Pennsylvania, vowing to give up baseball if he won. He lost. Midway through the 1929 season Cardinals owner Sam Breadon realized his mistake and brought McKechnie back. Although the Cardinals posted a winning record, they still finished fourth.

McKechnie accepted a position as the Boston Braves' manager in 1930 and remained there through 1937. He took the perennially last-place Braves and, with very little talent on hand, turned them into a respectable ballclub.

In 1933 and 1934 the team actually posted a winning record and finished fourth, the franchise's only first-division finishes between 1921 and 1946. McKechnie was particularly adept at handling pitchers. In 1937 he turned aging minor league hurlers Lou Fette and Jim Turner into "rookie" 20-game winners to spur the Braves to a fifth-place finish and earn himself Manager of the Year honors.

In 1938 he took over as manager of the Cincinnati Reds, who had finished last in 1937. Two years later they won the pennant. McKechnie's Reds featured solid defense and the pitching of Bucky Walters, a converted infielder, and Paul Derringer, a righthander who'd had a losing record before McKechnie took over. The two men became stars under him. The 1939 team lost to the Yankees in the World Series but in 1940 defeated favored Detroit in seven games.

McKechnie's strengths as a manager were summed up by Johnny Vander Meer, the Reds pitcher who threw two consecutive no-hitters under McKechnie: "I can sincerely say that I was proud to play for him. He was one of the greatest individuals I have ever met in my life, either on the field or off. Ballplayers never feared McKechnie; they respected him.

"He had a remarkable ability for evoking respect; a great handler of men. He was the most outstanding defensive manager I ever saw. We were not noted as a heavy-hitting team, so all his skills and insights were directed toward defense, from handling his pitchers to positioning his men in the field. He was so skillful at doing these things that we never had to score too many runs to win. McKechnie knew how to hold on to a one or two-run lead better than any other manager."

The Reds stayed in contention for several more seasons, but by 1945 most of their better players were gone. When the club finished sixth in 1946, McKechnie was let go. In 25 years as a manager, he produced two world champions, four pennants, and a 1,899-1,724 record.

McKechnie turned down several managerial offers to sign as a coach with the Cleveland Indians from 1946 through 1949. As Lou Boudreau's right-hand man, he was given much of the credit for developing Bob Lemon into a winning pitcher and Larry Doby into an outstanding center fielder. His sage advice and steady personality were of great help to Boudreau in 1948 when Cleveland won the pennant and World Series.

After coaching for Boudreau at Boston in 1952 and 1953, McKechnie retired to Florida. In 1962, three years before his death, he was elected to the Hall of Fame.

Dale Murphy

A complete player during his prime, Dale Murphy ranked among the premier sluggers of the 1980s and was the winner of back-to-back National League Most Valuable Player Awards in 1982 and 1983. He won five Gold Glove awards, belted at least 20 home runs for eight consecutive seasons, and, unfortunately like many of the game's great sluggers, was also one of the top strikeout victims of all time.

Murphy, a devout Mormon, was an All-City and All-State catcher at Woodrow Wilson High School in Portland, Oregon. The Braves designated him with the fifth pick in the first round of the June 1974 draft. Murphy batted .254 with five home runs and 31 RBIs in the Appalachian League that summer. In 1975 he hit .228 with five homers, 20 doubles, and 48 RBIs in the Class A West Carolinas League, playing first base in addition to catcher. His play won him a spot on the league's All-Star team.

Murphy moved up to Class AA Savannah in 1976, hitting 12 home runs, knocking in 55 runs, and batting .267 in 104 games. Late in the season he was promoted to Class AAA Richmond, where he hit four homers in 50 at bats while catching and playing the outfield. That earned him a call-up by the Braves, and he went two-for-four with two RBIs in his big league debut, September 13, 1976, at Dodger Stadium.

Murphy spent a full season at Richmond in 1977, putting together the kind of year the Braves had hoped for, with 22 homers, a league-leading 90 RBIs, 249 total bases, 33 doubles, and a .305 batting average. Exciting behind the plate, too, the lean 6-foot-4 Murphy led the circuit in putouts, double plays, and passed balls. He earned his second September promotion to Atlanta, batting .316 in 18 games, and the Braves figured they had the next Johnny Bench.

But he caught just 21 games in 1978, becoming instead the Braves starting first baseman; he caught just 21 games that season. He batted only .226 and led the NL in strikeouts as well as in errors at first, but he hit 23 homers and drove in 79 runs. In 1979 Murphy opened the season at catcher, but again logged most of his playing time at first base. Although he played 47 fewer games than he did in 1978, he still hit 21 home runs — including a 3-homer game May 18 — with 57 RBI.

That season convinced Braves Manager Bobby Cox that Murphy had a future in the major leagues, but, not as a catcher. "He was so big, and he had such a powerful throwing arm, it was hard to get it organized to make a good throw," Cox recalled. "That's the only reason he was converted. And he became a great outfielder, not a good one."

Opening 1980 in his third position in three years, Murphy played left field and made the All-Star team. He led the NL in strikeouts again, but his long swing also produced 33 homers, third in the league, mostly to the opposite field. Murphy and Bob Horner became a devastating one-two punch in the Braves lineup, combining for 479 homers during their nine seasons together.

The 1981 Opening Day lineup had Murphy in center field, where he showed good speed, fine instincts, and a strong arm. He won five straight Gold Gloves starting in 1982 while shifting between left and center. After slumping in the strike-shortened 1981 campaign, Murphy became a star in 1982. He played in every game, as he would for four straight seasons, a streak that ran to 740 games, the twelfth longest on record.

In 1982 Murphy tied for the NL lead with 109 RBI, was the league runner-up with 36 homers and 113 runs, ranked third with 303 total bases, fourth with 93 walks, batted .281, and stole 23 bases in 34 tries. He was elected to start the All-Star Game by the fans for the first of five straight seasons.

The Braves, under .500 during each half of the 1981 campaign, won 13 straight games to start 1982 and held on to take the NL West flag. But Murphy had just three singles in the playoffs against the St. Louis Cardinals. The Braves scratched out only five runs and were swept in three games. In the NL MVP vote, Murphy won comfortably over Cardinals outfielder Lonnie Smith.

In 1983 Murphy became the fourth back-to-back NL MVP winner, and at 27, the youngest player to win the award in consecutive seasons. His record: a career-high .302, a career-high 121 RBI (best in the NL), and a .540 slugging percentage. He finished second with 131 runs scored, had 318 total bases, and hit 36 homers. Murphy also stole 30 bases in 34 tries, becoming the sixth player in major league history, and the first NL player since Bobby Bonds 10 years earlier, with 30 homers and 30 steals in the same season. The Braves finished second in the division, their best showing during the rest of Murphy's tenure.

As the Braves fell in the standings, Murphy kept hitting. He became Atlanta's lone bright light in the basement. He was involved with numerous charities and, in the midst of baseball's scandals and greed, maintained his All-America hero image. In 1984 Murphy led the NL with a .547 slugging percentage and 303 total bases, and tied Mike Schmidt for the home run lead with 36. He finished ninth in the MVP voting.

Murphy won the home run title outright in 1985 with 37 and knocked in 111 runs, his fourth straight season with at least 36 homers and 100 RBI. He also led the circuit with 118 runs and 90 walks, reached double figures in stolen bases for the fifth consecutive season, and batted .300 for the second and final time, despite tying for the NL lead with 141 strikeouts.

In 1986 Murphy dramatically extended his consecutive-game streak. On April 29 he cut his hand bracing himself against the fence after making a catch. The cut required nine stitches, and it was expected to keep him out of action for at least a week. But the next night, he came off the bench to homer. He extended the streak two more months before taking a day off July 9 and ending a run that had begun September 27, 1981. Murphy's run of 30-homer, 100-RBI seasons also came to an end in 1986. He had 29 homers, 83 RBI, and batted .265 — his lowest mark since 1981.

Murphy switched to right field in 1987 and his offense rebounded with career highs of 44 homers and 115 walks, as he batted .295. But in 1988 Murphy's output fell again. Although he showed up on the leader board in power categories, he batted only .226 and was no longer a dominant offensive player.

He had arthroscopic surgery on his right knee after the season and returned to center field, but his numbers fell further in 1989. One of the season's few highlights came during a July 27 win over the San Francisco Giants. Murphy hit two home runs in the sixth inning, and his six RBIs in the inning tied an NL record.

Despite the poor finish, Murphy was the second leading home run hitter of the 1980s with 308 to Mike Schmidt's 313, was second in RBIs with 929, and ranked fifth with 1,553 hits. He played in 1,537 of his teams' 1,557 games. At 98.7 percent, his attendance rate was the ninth best for any 10-year period.

At 34 years old, Murphy was still one of the most popular players in the game, and his fans and colleagues hoped he would return to his previous heights. The Braves cashed in his remaining trade value on August 3, 1990, sending him to the Philadelphia Phillies, with pitcher Tommy Greene for pitcher Jeff Parrett and others. Ironically, the Braves won their first of three straight NL West titles the season following the trade of their signature player.

Murphy played regularly for the Phillies in 1991. Though he didn't advertise his Mormon faith and rarely took offense to vile locker-room banter, his presence did lead some of his earthier teammates to watch their language in the clubhouse. He had knee surgery again in 1992 and played just 18 games, leaving him two home runs short of the 400-mark.

The Phillies re-signed him for 1993, but had no room on their roster and traded him to the expansion Colorado Rockies. There he played just 26 games before retiring in late May after batting .143 with no homers, leaving his career total at 398.

Murphy finished with 31 career multihomer games, and he becomes eligible for the Hall of Fame in 1998. Does anyone think he won't make it?

★ Kid Nichols ★

Amos Rusie, Cy Young, and Charles "Kid" Nichols were the three greatest pitchers of the nineteenth century.

Rusie was the premier strikeout artist of the time. Young continued to pitch for another decade and retired with untouchable career totals. But, in the 1890s, Nichols was the winningest pitcher in the game, collecting 30 more victories than Young and 64 more than Rusie. Moreover, he was the only one of the three to pitch his team to a pennant during that decade, and he did it five times.

The slender righthander delivered a basic overhand fastball from a windup so simple it was almost nonexistent. "Many a pitcher uses an elaborate windup,"he said in 1901, "and I have been repeatedly asked to adopt one. I have persistently refused. I don't approve of it because it interferes with the control of the ball. It's a useless exertion on the arm; and as far as confusing the batter is concerned, it doesn't always work."

Charles Augustus Nichols was born in Madison, Wisconsin, in 1869. He first gained attention as a pitcher in 1886 while hurling for the Blue Avenue Club, an amateur team in Kansas City. In 1887 he turned professional with Kansas City of the Western League and won 21 games. He split the next season between Kansas City and Memphis, then pitched spectacularly in 1889 for Omaha of the Western Association, going 36-12. Frank Selee, his manager at Omaha, was hired to manage Boston's National League team in 1890, and he brought Nichols with him.

Selee faced a difficult task in Boston. Although the club had finished second in the NL in 1889, most of its best players had jumped to the rebel Players League in 1890. But Selee, an astute judge of talent, purchased first baseman Tommy Tucker from Baltimore, versatile Bobby Lowe from Milwaukee, and shortstop Herman Long from Kansas City. Then he installed Nichols as the ace of the pitching staff.

Nichols, nicknamed "Kid" because of his youth and his slender build, went 27-19 with a 2.23 earned run average. He completed all 47 of his starts and led the league with seven shutouts.

The Boston entry won the Players League pennant in 1890, but the league collapsed after one season. The American Association then put a team in Boston for 1891. It, too, won the pennant then folded at the end of the season. In the meantime Selee's Beaneaters (Braves) took the National League pennant, winning 23 of 30 September games to clinch the flag despite not having a .300 hitter. Nichols went 30-17, while veteran John Clarkson, in his last great year, was 33-19. Because of interleague squabbles, no World Series was held between the NL and AA winners, preventing what would have been an all-Boston affair.

The Beaneaters were even better in 1892. Outfielder Hugh Duffy added some heavy hitting, and Nichols improved his record to 35-16. That year the NL divided the season into two halves, declaring that the winners of each half would meet at the end of the season in a "World Series." Boston won the first half by a big margin and finished the year with the best overall record, but Cleveland collected the second-half crown. In the postseason series, Boston knocked off Cleveland without a loss. Nichols pitched the final game, defeating Cy Young.

In 1893 the pitching distance was increased from 50 feet to 60 feet 6 inches, adversely affecting many pitchers. Nichols's strikeout total was cut in half, from 187 to 94, and his ERA went up by more than half a run. Yet the Kid remained one of the league's most effective hurlers, going 34-14. Boston coasted to its third straight pennant.

Under Frank Selee the Beaneaters were the smartest team in baseball, pioneering such plays as the hit-and-run and cleverly skirting or ignoring the rules whenever possible. But from 1894 through 1896, as injuries and age caught up with the Beans, they were exceeded in trickery by the Baltimore Orioles. Boston finished well behind the champion Orioles, but Nichols remained superb. He won 32 games in 1894, 26 in 1895, and a league-high 30 in 1896.

Selee rebuilt the club in 1897, and the pennant race that season was a battle between the Beaneaters and the Orioles. Boston took the pennant by two games, paced by Nichols's 31-11 record. The pitcher also led the league in innings pitched, with 368, and in victories. The National League, still seeking some sort of postseason event, had instituted the Temple Cup Series in 1894, in which the second-place team played the pennant winner. The Series was anticlimactic, however, and the pennant winner seldom took it seriously. When Baltimore defeated Boston

— the third time in four years that the second-place club had won — the Series was discontinued.

Selee's Beaneaters won the pennant again in 1898. Nichols led the league in wins for the third straight year with a 31-12 record, the seventh time he'd registered at least 30 victories. In 1899 the Beaneaters finished second to Brooklyn, a team made up of many former Orioles. Nichols slumped to 21-19. His slide continued in 1900, when he had his first losing season, going 13-16.

Boston's owners were notoriously cheap. When the American League declared itself a major league in 1901, many of the Beaneaters jumped to the new circuit for better wages. Nichols stuck it out and pitched well, earning 19 wins, but was released at the end of the season in a cost-cutting move. He became pitcher-manager of Kansas City of the Western League and won 48 games in two seasons.

In 1904 he returned to the NL and won 21 games as the St. Louis pitcher-manager. The Cardinals were owned by a pair of brothers, Frank and Stanley Robison. Frank had hired Nichols, but the pitcher didn't get along with Stanley, who fired him as manager early in 1905. The team kept Nichols as a pitcher, but when Stanley tried to humiliate him by ordering him to serve as gate attendant before a game, Nichols balked and was released. He won a few more games for the Phillies then retired.

In his career he won 361 games, sixth all-time, with 531 complete games in 561 starts. After retiring, Nichols and Cubs shortstop Joe Tinker opened a string of bowling alleys in Kansas City. Nichols became one of the finest bowlers in the area, winning a championship trophy at age 64. He also dabbled in real estate and the motion picture business. In 1949, four years before his death at age 83, he was enshrined in the Hall of Fame.

Phil Niekro

Phil Niekro and his knuckleball kept going, and going, and going. Niekro pitched with the Braves for two decades in Milwaukee and Atlanta. He won more than 300 games and lost more games than any other National League pitcher in the modern era.

Phil and his brother, Joe, hold the record for most wins by a brother combination in major league history. They had a total of 539 major league victories, better than the Deans and the Perrys. Joe, despite collecting 221 of those wins, was never accorded the acclaim of his brother, but Phil did teach his younger brother the knuckleball, substantially extending his career.

Niekro was born on April 1, 1939, in Blaine, Ohio. Joe was born five and a half years later. The Niekros grew up in coal country, in the Appalachian foothills of eastern Ohio, down the road from pro basketball Hall of Famer John Havlicek.

Niekro's father was a fastball pitcher in the industrial leagues. While playing catch when Phil was 10 or 11 years old, his father threw him a knuckleball as a joke. The knuckler eluded young Niekro, but it fascinated him and he wanted to learn how to throw it. By the time he reached high school, Niekro had become so proficient with the pitch that his father could no longer catch it.

The Milwaukee Braves were sufficiently interested in Niekro and his knuckleball to sign him for a $500 bonus. Niekro put in his time in the minors and saw the country. He played at Wellsville in the New York-Penn League, McCook in the Nebraska State League, Jacksonville in the South Atlantic League, Louisville in the American Association, Austin in the Texas League, and Denver in the Pacific Coast League.

Niekro, recalled writer Pat Jordan, who pitched with Niekro in 1959, was "the tenth pitcher on the staff. At first he appeared only in the last innings of hopelessly lost games. He was inefficient because he could not throw his knuckleball over the plate, and preferred instead, to deal up one of his other pitches, all of which were deficient."

Mastery of the knuckleball came slowly but surely. When Niekro reached the Braves to stay in 1965, their last year in Milwaukee before moving to Atlanta, he was a relief pitcher. He made 41 appearances, only one start, and saved six games. By 1967, 20 of Niekro's appearances were as a starting pitcher. He won 11 games that season, while losing 9, and led the NL in ERA with a 1.87 mark. Although he would make an occasional relief appearance throughout his career, after 1967 he was used primarily as a starter.

"When I first came up," Niekro said years later, "I felt like a kid. I looked at guys like (teammates) Warren Spahn, Eddie Mathews, Hank Aaron as men. I felt I had to throw only strikes. If I dropped the ball covering first base, I thought I'd be cut from the team."

Soon Niekro was the ace of the Braves staff. In 1969 he won 23 games as the Braves captured the first NL West title. He struck out 193 batters versus only 57 walks. Niekro started but lost Game 1 of the first National League Championship Series to Tom Seaver, as the Mets swept the Braves in three games.

Niekro struggled in 1970, losing 18 games and seeing his ERA soar to 4.27. He developed a sore arm after two more mediocre seasons, and Atlanta Manager Eddie Mathews moved him to the bullpen to start 1973.

Niekro eventually returned to the rotation, and on August 5, 1973, he pitched a no-hitter against the San Diego Padres, the first no-hitter by a Braves pitcher since Warren Spahn recorded one in 1961. "Knucksie" finished the season with a 13-10 record, a 3.31 ERA, and four saves.

In 1974 Niekro won 20 games again for the Braves, tying for the league lead in victories. He also led the league in complete games, with 18, and innings pitched, with 302. Brother Joe was a relief pitcher on that Braves squad, going 3-2 with a 3.56 ERA. However, at season's end, he was sold to Houston for $35,000.

Brother Phil won 15 games in 1975 and 17 in 1976, but the Braves finished with more than 90 losses in each season. In 1977 Atlanta lost 101 games and finished in the NL West basement. Niekro lost a league-leading 20 of those games, yet he led the league again in strikeouts, complete games, and innings. He led the NL in complete games and innings for the next two years as well, pitching more than 300 innings both times.

In 1978 Niekro was 19-18; he was now 40 years old and his days as a 20-win pitcher appeared to be over. The Braves stayed at the bottom in 1979, losing 94 games and finishing 24 games behind first-place Cincinnati. But Niekro somehow managed to win 21 games, and he is the last player in the major leagues to win 20 games for a last-place team. Niekro also lost 20 games to become the first pitcher since 1906 to win and lose at least 20 games in the same season. He pitched a whopping 342 innings that season, including a career-high 23 complete games.

Always a strong fielder, Niekro won NL Gold Glove awards in 1978, 1979, and 1980, and added two more in 1982 and 1983. The ups and downs on the mound continued for Niekro during the next few seasons, however. He was 15-18 in 1980, then led the NL in winning percentage with .810, when he went 17-4 in 1982. The Braves won the NL West that season, and Niekro started Game 2 of the NLCS against St. Louis. He had a no-decision, however, and the Cardinals swept the Braves.

Following the 1983 season, Niekro, now age 44, was released by the Braves. He signed with the New York Yankees and won 16 games in each of two seasons in the Bronx. He won his 300th game in a Yankee uniform in 1985, forgoing the knuckleball until the last two pitches of the game. Niekro left the Yankees following that season and signed with the Cleveland Indians at the start of the 1986 campaign.

The Indians traded him to Toronto on August 9, 1987, and they released him on August 31. Niekro recalled that it wasn't easy for Toronto Manager Jimy Williams to let him go: "Jimy looked me in the eye and said, 'Releasing a Hall of Famer like you is the hardest thing I ever had to do.' From the look on his face, I believed him."

Niekro was re-signed by Atlanta on September 23, 1987, for one last appearance in a Braves uniform. He started a game and lasted until he loaded the bases in the fourth inning. The show was over but he still wasn't ready to leave. "They released me because of my age not my talent," he said.

Niekro won 121 games after age 40, the most wins by anyone over that age in baseball history. He left the game with 318 wins and 274 losses, a modern NL record. Thanks to the knuckleball, he also set an NL career record for wild pitches, with 200.

Phil Niekro might have won many more games had he pitched for a contending organization. The Braves were perennial also-rans throughout the 1970s, and often afforded Niekro little or no run support. Niekro's 49 shutout losses are the third most in major league history; he trails only Nolan Ryan and Walter Johnson. Niekro also holds the record for most seasons, with 24, played without appearing in a World Series.

"I've taken my shots of cortisone in the arm, and Lord knows, I've had my share of aches and pains," he once said. "I feel it's remarkable to have played so long and only been on the disabled list once." The Braves honored Niekro by retiring his uniform No. 35.

★ Jim O'Rourke ★

"Orator Jim" O'Rourke helped inspire the reserve clause and was one of the leading home run hitters of his day. He led the National Association, a forerunner of the National League, in home runs in 1874 (5) and 1875 (6).

Such low numbers amaze modern fans; but the ball was far less lively then than it is today, and teams played only half the number of games. O'Rourke's six homers in 1875 represented 14.2 percent of the 42 hit by the entire league, which compares favorably with 1920 when Babe Ruth's 54 homers represented 14.6 percent of the 369 hit in the American League.

A versatile, verbose, and very good nineteenth-century ballplayer, he played in more than 100 major league games at each of six different positions — left field, center, right, third base, first base, and catcher. His tendency to make long-winded pronouncements earned him the nickname "Orator, but he could also hit, averaging .310 in 19 major league seasons and playing a lead role on eight different championship teams.

O'Rourke was born in 1850 in Bridgeport, Connecticut, the son of an Irish farmer. When his father died, young Jim became the family breadwinner and played ball only after completing his daily chores. When he was offered a professional contract, his mother would not allow him to sign until the team agreed to provide the family with a farm laborer to take over his duties.

O'Rourke's professional career began in 1872 when he played shortstop with the Middletown Mansfields of the National Association, hitting .330 in 23 games. In 1873 O'Rourke joined the Boston Red Stockings, the NA pennant winners the year before.

The Irish were not regarded highly in Boston at the time, so Manager Harry Wright suggested that O'Rourke change his name. The player replied proudly, "Mr. Wright, I would rather die than give up my father's name. A million dollars would not tempt me." His fine play soon won over the Boston fans.

Solidly built at 5-foot-8 and 185 pounds, O'Rourke batted and threw righthanded. In his first season with the Red Stockings (forerunners of the Braves). He hit .350, but his batting average dropped to .316 in 1874 and .291 in 1875, although he led the NA in home runs.

The National League was formed in 1876, and the Red Stockings team was a charter member. But four Boston stars jumped to the Chicago White Stockings and led them to the pennant. O'Rourke, however, remained loyal to Boston and Wright.

The first National League game was played on April 22, 1876, when Philadelphia played host to Boston. Philadelphia pitcher Lon Knight retired the first two men he faced before O'Rourke cracked a single to left, the first hit in National League history. He went on to hit .327 in the league's inaugural season.

By 1877 Wright's team was back on top. O'Rourke, a team leader both on and off the field, hit .362, the fourth best in the league, and led the circuit in runs scored and on-base percentage. Although he slumped to .278 in 1878, he still led the Red Stockings in hitting. Despite weak offense Boston won its second consecutive pennant on the strength of its pitching and defense.

In 1879 George Wright, the Boston shortstop and younger brother of Harry, jumped to Providence to become the Grays' player-manager. O'Rourke was also unhappy in Boston because his employers taxed the players $20 per season for uniforms and 50 cents a day for travel maintenance. Although sympathetic fans chipped in to pay the fees, a disgruntled O'Rourke followed the younger Wright to Providence. (The defections of George Wright and O'Rourke led Boston owner Arthur H. Soden to propose the inclusion of a reserve clause in player contracts.)

O'Rourke followed the move with one of his best seasons, hitting .348 and again leading the league in on-base percentage. With the pennant at stake, Providence beat Boston in four of the last six games to capture the flag and, remarkably, O'Rourke's sixth championship in seven seasons.

O'Rourke returned to Boston in 1880 and led the NL again with six home runs. He became manager of the Buffalo Bisons in 1881, and in 1884 led the NL with 162 hits and batted .347. Dealt to the New York Giants in 1885, O'Rourke led the NL with 16 triples.

In 1888 and 1889 he once again found himself on a pennant-winning team. The Giants included six future Hall of Famers: pitchers Tim Keefe and Mickey Welch, catcher Buck Ewing, first baseman Roger Connor, shortstop John Montgomery Ward, and O'Rourke. After each pennant win the Giants went on to defeat the American Association champions in the World Series.

In 1890 O'Rourke and many other baseball stars jumped to the Players League, a circuit created and run by the players in response to their grievances with the NL and AA owners. In August of that year O'Rourke, at age 38, had one of his best seasons for New York's PL team, batting .360 with 115 RBIs. When the league collapsed after only one season, he returned to the Giants for two more seasons and retired as player-manager with Washington in 1893.

Eleven years later at age 52, O'Rourke visited the Polo Grounds. Giants Manager John McGraw let him catch New York's pennant-clinching win. O'Rourke singled once in four trips to the plate.

In his four NA seasons O'Rourke averaged .318. Including his 1904 appearance he played for another 18 seasons in the NL and 1 in the PL, averaging .310 and collecting 2,304 hits, 1,446 runs, and 1,010 RBIs.

After retiring as a player in 1893, he worked as an umpire in the NL for one season and managed the Bridgeport entry in the Connecticut League from 1897 through 1908, taking over as league president from 1907 to 1913. One day Manager O'Rourke got into an argument with an umpire. His orator's skill deserted him, and he let fly with some four-letter words. Suddenly realizing what he had done, he turned to the crowd and gravely announced that President O'Rourke was fining Manager O'Rourke for using profanity.

One of Bridgeport's leading citizens, O'Rourke also earned a law degree from Yale. On a frigid New Year's Day in 1919 he insisted on walking into Bridgeport, contracted pneumonia, and died. In 1945 he was named to the Hall of Fame.

★ Charley Radbourn ★

Charley "Old Hoss" Radbourn won 20 or more games for the Braves four times, but that was nothing compared with what he did one season for the Providence Grays.

During the 1884 season, Radbourn won 59 games, six more wins than any other pitcher has collected in a season. Although he pitched well in several other seasons, once winning 48, he might have been forgotten were it not for that one unbelievable year that was probably responsible for his 1939 induction into the Baseball Hall of Fame.

Radbourn was a great pitcher who was apparently difficult to like. The *Providence Journal-Bulletin* dubbed the hard-drinking player "Lord Radbourn" and called him "erratic, capricious, and ill-tempered."

In 1880, his first season in the major leagues, an injured arm limited him to part-time infielding for Buffalo. His arm recovered in 1881, and he won 25 games with the Providence Grays, sharing mound duty with John Montgomery Ward.

In 1882 he finished 33-20, leading the league in shutouts and strikeouts. He was outstanding again in 1883; he led in appearances and in victories, with 48, and ranked second in complete games, innings pitched, strikeouts, and earned run average.

Radbourn was notably suspicious, even paranoid, and it was his suspicious personality that brought about his great 1884 season. Early in the season he shared Providence pitching duties with 21-year-old Bill Sweeney, another righthander who was considered something of a phenomenon. Radbourn was apparently jealous of the youngster and disliked Sweeney.

At midseason, Old Hoss was suspended by his team. One account claims the suspension resulted from "improper conduct," and another claims he was suspended for cursing his catcher and firing a baseball at him so hard that it knocked him flat. (Radbourn thought the catcher, who'd just dropped a third strike, deserved it.)

Just after Radbourn's suspension, Sweeney jumped the Providence team and joined St. Louis of the outlaw Union Association. The Grays were left with only one pitcher — the suspended Radbourn. Thinking quickly, Radbourn offered to pitch the rest of the season for a small bonus and the right to become a free agent after the season ended. Providence management had no recourse but to agree, and the suspension was dropped.

Old Hoss didn't actually pitch every remaining game (several position players filled in), but he did pitch most of the Grays' games, including a stretch from August 21 to September 15 that encompassed most of a 20-game Providence winning streak that won the team the pennant. His 678⅔ innings pitched for the season are only an inning and a third short of the record set by Cincinnati's Will White in 1879.

A three-game playoff series for the baseball world championship (which some consider the first World Series) was arranged that same year with the American Association champions, the New York Mets. Radbourn's mastery continued: he pitched and won all three games and allowed only three hits. For all his efforts, including the postseason, he won 62 games and was paid $3,000.

He also managed to lead the National League in ERA that year. Of course, the rules of the day mandated that pitchers throw underhanded, a style Radbourn continued to use after overhand tosses were made legal because the underhanded pitches put less strain on his arm.

Even so, his big year took a toll on his arm. Some days, Old Hoss came to the park unable even to comb his hair with his right hand. He would apply hot towels to the arm for a couple of hours and then toss around an iron ball. Then he'd switch to a baseball and would throw it at ever-increasing distances until he could get it to the plate. He would pitch nine innings — usually more effectively than did his opponent.

Although he won more than 20 games in each of his next three seasons, pitching for Providence and then Boston, he lost almost as often as he won. His strikeout totals decreased sharply. By 1888 his arm seemed gone, but he came back to post a 20-11 mark in 1889 and go 27-12 with Boston's Players League team in 1890.

Retiring after the 1891 season, Radbourn operated a combination pool hall and saloon in Bloomington, Indiana. He lost an eye in a hunting accident in 1894 and spent the last years of his life as a recluse in a back room of his saloon. He died in 1897.

Johnny Sain

Spahn and Sain
And two days of rain

When the Braves won a pennant in 1948 Johnny Sain won 24 to lead the league, and Warren Spahn pitched in with 15 wins, hence this refrain that Boston fans sang and Braves fans today still recognize.

Sain, who some years later would later rejoin Atlanta as a pitching coach, won 20 games four times. His father taught him how to throw a curveball when he was a boy. He used the curve and slider to get to the majors in 1942, and in his first game he retired all nine men he faced. "I noticed they started taking me seriously," he said. But after 40 appearances he was drafted into the armed services and joined the Navy.

Returning to the big leagues as a 28-year-old, Sain was eager to learn. He credited Casey Stengel and Billy Southworth, his first two managers in Boston, as major influences. An intelligent player, Sain knew how to help himself with the bat, both as a hitter and as a bunter. In his 11 years, he struck out only 20 times. In 1946 he barely missed a no-hitter against the Reds when a ninth-inning pop fly fell among a crowd of Braves. He finished that season 20-14, and his 24 complete games were the most by any NL pitcher.

The following year he repeated his 20-win feat, winning 21 and losing 12. He and Warren Spahn became the workhorses of the Boston staff: each won 21 games, no other pitcher won a dozen. Sain also demonstrated his hitting skills. Along with his 20 wins, he batted .347, and is one of only 29 pitchers to pull off this unusual defense-offense "double."

In 1948 Spahn and Sain joined forces to pitch the Braves to the World Series. Sain won 24 and also led the NL with 28 complete games, and 314.2 innings pitched. (Spahn was third). Sain also led the NL in sacrifice hits, the first pitcher ever to do so.

Sain was at the plate for one of the most debated calls in World Series history in Game 1 of the 1948 Classic against Cleveland. He and Bob Feller had both been nearly unhittable into the eighth inning, allowing a total of four hits between them. With pinch-runner Phil Masi on second in the last of the eighth, Feller spun and fired to Lou Boudreau, apparently picking Masi off, but the runner was called safe. The next batter, Tommy Holmes, singled in Masi with the game's only run. Cleveland came back to win the Series in six games.

In 1949 the veteran Braves collapsed under the weight of their age (only two of the 1948 regulars were under 31),

and Sain won only 10 games while losing 17. Sain won 20 again in 1950, but a shoulder injury hampered his effectiveness in 1951, and on August 30, 1951, with a 5-13 record, he was sent to the Yankees for $50,000. New York also threw in the erratic young arm of Lew Burdette.

Sain appeared in only seven games for the Yanks at the tail end of the season, but his 2-1 record was deemed important enough by his teammates to earn him a full World Series share. Sain became a vital cog for Casey Stengel's creatively managed team. He won 11 games in 1952 and 14 in 1953 as a swingman. Stengel even used him as a pinch hitter. Once Sain batted for Joe Collins, who already had two hits in the game, and drove a liner over Minnie Minoso's head in left field to drive in the winning run.

Between the 1951 and 1952 seasons Sain's shoulder problem persisted, so he tried a then-new X-ray therapy,. The experimental treatment worked so well for Sain that he became an advocate for it. At Sain's urging, Eddie Lopat tried it, too. Later, Whitey Ford subjected himself to the treatment — five times. Mel Stottlemyre had it done six times.

Sain made a career-high 45 appearances in 1954, all in relief, and he led the league with 22 saves. He and Enos Slaughter were traded to Kansas City in May of 1955, and Sain finished his playing career that year.

In 1959 he joined the Athletics as their pitching coach, and he stayed in the game for another three decades as a pitching coach. He schooled a number of hurlers who had never won 20 games in a season until he joined their team. And they would never win 20 again after he left.

The pitchers included Whitey Ford, Ralph Terry, and Jim Bouton of the Yankees; Mudcat Grant and Jim Kaat of the Twins; Earl Wilson and Denny McLain of the Tigers; and Wilbur Wood and Stan Bahnsen of the White Sox. Dave Boswell and Jim Perry of Minnesota applied Sain's teachings and won 20 soon after he was gone, and Detroit's Mickey Lolich won 20 shortly after Sain left and gave the coach credit.

Although teaching the slider was one of Sain's specialties (learning the pitch rejuvenated Whitey Ford's career and helped McLain and Kaat), he taught much more. For one thing, he didn't believe that running was the key to good pitching, which endeared him to most hurlers immediately. He was also one of the first to have the next day's pitcher chart the hitters. He rarely visited the mound to talk to a pitcher and seldom spoke to one during the game, unless the pitcher asked a question. Sain believed in preparation and focus, so he spent his time getting pitchers ready and did not disturb them with suggestions once they were on the mound.

"Pitching coaches don't change pitchers," Sain said. "We just stimulate their thinking." He stressed rehearsal and practice to make the correct moves automatic — part of the subconscious mind, as he described it. When he first met a pitcher, he would hit fungoes and watch how the pitcher threw the ball back to him. "That will generally be his natural way of throwing and the way he should pitch," Sain said.

Jim Bouton called him "the greatest pitching coach who ever lived." In fact, one time when the Yankees wouldn't give Sain a $2,500 raise, causing him to quit, Bouton called and said he would have paid the $2,500 to keep Sain on the team. Mickey Lolich put it this way: "Johnny Sain loves pitchers. Maybe he doesn't love baseball so much, but he loves pitchers. Only he understands them."

Sain's coaching resume reads like this: 1959, Kansas City Athletics; 1961-63, New York Yankees; 1965-66, Minnesota Twins; 1967-69, Detroit Tigers; 1970, California Angels; 1971-75, Chicago White Sox; 1977 and *1985-86, Atlanta.* Five of the teams he coached won pennants, although he frequently clashed with managers.

Like all experts, Sain believed completely in his way of doing things. Yankee Manager Ralph Houk feared that Sain was after his job. And old-school Detroit Manager Mayo Smith couldn't figure out Sain's way of thinking. One day Sain had other business to attend to, and Smith made the pitchers run. When Sain returned, he asked Smith, "Are we going to go with what made this staff lead the league in complete games last year, or with what hasn't worked here in 25 years?" When Smith traded Dick Radatz, Sain's pet pupil, to Montreal, Sain quit.

John Smoltz

The Tigers traded Detroit native John Smoltz to Atlanta and went to the playoffs once. The Atlanta Braves, who got Smoltz for Doyle Alexander, have now been there four times.

The Tigers swapped the promising Smoltz in the heat of the 1987 stretch run. Alexander went 9-0 after the trade as Detroit overtook the Blue Jays to win the American League East, but he was hit hard in the playoffs. Alexander lost twice in the championship series and was knocked out in the second inning of the deciding game as the favored Tigers lost to the Twins in five games.

Smoltz never beat the Twins, either, but he allowed only two runs in 14 innings in the 1991 World Series against them. He even matched Jack Morris zero for zero for eight innings in the seventh game of the World Series, before the Twins prevailed in 10 innings, 1-0.

Alexander's career was over by 1989, the same year Smoltz's was just beginning. In his first full year in the majors, he went 12-11 with a 2.94 ERA for an Atlanta team that lost 97 games. He proved he had the right stuff by going 14-11 the following year for a team that lost 97 times again. Dodgers Hall of Fame pitcher Don Drysdale said of him, "If Smoltz has his stuff and he's throwing the way he can throw, he's as tough as anybody in baseball."

In 1991, Smoltz and Atlanta's entire pitching staff became as tough as anybody in baseball. Tom Atlanta's starting four — Glavine, Steve Avery, Charlie Leibrandt and Smoltz — won 67 games, two more wins than the entire *team* had in 1989 or 1990. The Braves rallied the final week of the season to beat the Dodgers for the National League West title.

Smoltz won twice in the NLCS against the Pittsburgh Pirates; he pitched a complete game six-hitter in the deciding seventh game at Three Rivers Stadium to give the Braves their first pennant since the team moved to Atlanta in 1966. He pitched equally well in the World Series, but ran into another hot pitcher, Jack Morris, who was a single run better in the deciding game.

The next season was a similar story. Smoltz pitched well, going 15-12, leading the league in strikeouts (215), and recording a career-best 2.85 ERA in 246 innings. The Braves also did well, winning the division by eight games to set up another NLCS with Pittsburgh.

This time Smoltz pitched three times in the playoffs, beating the Pirates and Doug Drabek in Games 1 and 4 and again getting the nod in the deciding seventh game. He allowed only two runs, but Drabek kept the Braves scoreless until a ninth-inning error gave Atlanta a chance. Then Francisco Cabrera's two-out, two-run single sent the Braves to the World Series for the second straight year.

Smoltz won once against Toronto in the World Series, but was denied a second victory in Game 2 when reliever Jeff Reardon surrendered a two-run home run to Ed Sprague in the ninth. The Braves would lose the Series four days later. "There's no worse way to lose," Smoltz said afterwards. "To get beat four games to two, when we know it could have just as easily been the other way around."

It would take Smoltz and the Braves two more years to get another chance at the World Series. In between, there were two frustrating seasons.

Smoltz went 15-11 in 1993, but he surrendered 23 home runs and 100 walks to go with a 3.62 ERA. The Braves rallied late in the season to overtake the San Francisco Giants and clinched the division on the final day of the season to go to the playoffs for the third year in a row. Smoltz got one start against the Philadelphia Phillies and surrendered only two unearned runs but suffered his first postseason loss as the Braves fell in six games.

The Braves languished six games behind the Montreal Expos and Smoltz was 6-10 with a 4.14 ERA when the 1994 season was called to a halt by the strike. The players came back in 1995 and so did Smoltz. His return to form saw his ERA plummet (3.18), his strikeouts soar (193), and his team make it to the World Series for the first time since 1992.

Smoltz pitched once in the Series against Cleveland and was knocked out in the third inning. "I honestly didn't think I made that many bad pitches," he said of his outing. "They just hit them where our fielders weren't."

He didn't get his first World Series loss because the Braves rallied to tie it, even though Atlanta eventually lost in extra innings. Smoltz was set to pitch in Game 7, but Tom Glavine's 1-0 one-hitter in Game 6 ended the Series.

In the 27-year-old Smoltz's seven-plus years in Atlanta, his team has gone from the worst team in baseball to world champions. The way people perceive Atlanta has changed along with it. "I am in no way comparing our team to Notre Dame," he says. "But, when everybody plays Notre Dame, they're not just playing a college football team, you know?"

★ Warren Spahn ★

The winningest lefthander in Major League Baseball history, Warren Spahn won 20 games 13 different times, a mark equaled only by Christy Mathewson. He recorded 63 shutouts, the National League record for a lefthander, and produced a lifetime ERA of 3.09.

A consummate competitor, Spahn once observed,

"When I'm pitching I feel I'm down to the essentials. Two men, with one challenge between them, and what better challenge than between pitcher and hitter."

Born and raised in Buffalo, New York, Spahn started his baseball career playing first base for the junior squad of Buffalo's Lake City Athletic Club while his father held down third base for the senior team. Later, both father and son performed in the same infield. Spahn wanted to play first base for his South Park High School team, but since the incumbent was already All-City, Spahn thought it best to switch to the mound.

In 1940 he signed with the Boston Braves and was assigned to Bradford of the Class D PONY League. No bonus was involved. If there had been a bonus, the Braves might have thought they had wasted their money. That first year Spahn injured his arm twice, and he worked only 66 innings. But the next year Spahn graduated to Evansville of the 3-I League, where he led the league with 19 wins, a .760 won-lost percentage, and a 1.83 ERA.

Spahn started the 1942 season with the big league club, and saw Braves pitcher Jim Tobin hit two home runs on Opening Day. Spahn concluded that he wanted to be that type of pitcher. Boston Manager Casey Stengel had other ideas for Spahn, however. When the rookie refused to throw a brushback pitch at Brooklyn shortstop Pee Wee Reese, Stengel demoted him to Hartford of the Eastern League. There Spahn went 17-12 with a 1.96 ERA. "It was the worst mistake I ever made," Stengel later admitted.

Spahn didn't return to Boston in 1943. He was drafted into the Army and assigned to the 176th Combat Engineers Battalion. Spahn fought in the Battle of the Bulge and participated in the taking of the key Rhine crossing bridge at Remagen, Germany. Several of his company were lost when the bridge finally collapsed. He received a Bronze Star, as well as a Purple Heart for being hit with shrapnel.

Spahn's bravery won him a battlefield commission, but the honor also cost him six more months in the Army and an additional three months out of his baseball career. He spent the extended time in Germany with the Army of Occupation, replacing a fellow officer who had been killed.

Many have speculated about how many more games Spahn might have won in the majors had he not spent 3½ seasons in the Army, but Spahn approached the topic philosophically. "People say that my absence from the big leagues may have cost me a chance to win 400 games," he reflected. "But I don't know about that. I matured a lot in three years, and I think I was better equipped to handle major league hitters at 25 than I was at 22. Also, I pitched until I was 44. Maybe I wouldn't have been able to do that otherwise."

Spahn returned to Boston in July 1946 and quickly emerged as one of the top pitchers in the league. In 1947 he won 21 games and led the NL in ERA. In 1948 he was a key member of the Braves' "Spahn and Sain and Two Days of Rain" pitching staff.

On Labor Day Spahn and Sain opposed the Dodgers in a twin bill. Spahn, who had gotten off to a very slow start that year, pitched 14 innings and won the first game on a 2-1 five-hitter. In the second game Sain shut out Brooklyn, 4-0. No games were scheduled for the following two days, and then it did indeed rain. Spahn and Sain won the next two games, followed by a day off, and Boston's two other starters split a doubleheader. Sain and Spahn then defeated Chicago on September 14 and 15. The team had another day off. Then the two staff aces took the mound again and won a pair of games against Pittsburgh.

Exhausted from this stretch drive, Spahn started and lost Game 2 of the World Series. He won Game 5 in relief, but surrendered a run in two innings of relief as Cleveland won Game 6 and the Series.

Although he wasn't known as a strikeout artist, Spahn led the NL in that category from 1949 through 1952. On June 14, 1952, he struck out 18 batters in a 15-inning contest against Chicago. After the Braves moved to Milwaukee in 1953 he helped the club win two more pennants and a world championship. He won the Cy Young Award in 1957 and beat the Yankees twice in the 1958 World Series.

Spahn was a true craftsman on the mound, much more a pitcher than a thrower. "A pitcher needs two pitches — one they're looking for and one to cross 'em up," he once observed. Batters could take a "comfortable oh-for-four" against Spahn. Hitters would get around enough to hit the ball, but not well enough to do any real damage. They would be only slightly off. "Hitting is timing. Pitching is upsetting timing," Spahn theorized.

Spahn did not record any no-hitters until late in his career, when he cemented his reputation as an ageless wonder by pitching two of them. At age 39, at Milwaukee's County Stadium, he no-hit the Phillies for his twentieth win of the 1960 season, the eleventh time he had reached that number. He struck out 15 batters, his career high for nine innings.

The following year Spahn did it again. Five days after his fortieth birthday he no-hit San Francisco, defeating them, 1-0. "It was so easy, it was pathetic,"commented Spahn. "Everything went my way and they kept guessing wrong. But let's face it, I was just plain lucky. I walked a man twice to start an inning — a cardinal sin with a one-run lead — not once, but twice, and got away with it." Of course, what Spahn didn't mention is that after both walks he took care of the baserunners personally by starting double plays. Later that season Spahn notched his 300th career victory, defeating the Cubs, 2-1, on a six-hitter.

Spahn was one of baseball's better hitting pitchers, with 35 lifetime home runs, the NL record for a hurler and fourth-best on the all-time list. In 1958 he became one of the few pitchers to bat .300 and record 20 wins in the same season.

Toward the end of his career Spahn was sent to the last-place Mets, where he briefly served as a pitcher-coach under Casey Stengel. Spahn and fellow Mets player-coach Yogi Berra teamed up for a historic battery. "I don't think we're the oldest battery, but we're certainly the ugliest," remarked Berra. At about that time Stan Musial said, "I don't think Spahn will ever get into the Hall of Fame. He'll never stop pitching." But he did retire from playing, in 1965, after going 3-4 for the San Francisco Giants.

After leaving the majors Spahn coached for the Mexico City Tigers and also pitched a few games in Mexico. Some criticized Spahn for continuing to pitch at his age. "I don't care what the public thinks," said Spahn. "I'm pitching because I enjoy pitching."

Spahn served as a pitching coach first for the Cleveland Indians and later in Japan with the Hiroshima Carp from 1973 to 1978, before retiring to his ranch in Hartshorne, Oklahoma. Following the death of his first wife he returned to the game for two seasons as a minor league pitching instructor in the Angel organization.

He was elected to the Hall of Fame in 1973, his first year of eligibility.

Eddie Stanky

Branch Rickey once said that Eddie Stanky "can't hit, he can't run, he can't field, he can't throw. He can't do a goddamn thing — but beat you."

The fiery little infielder with a knack for drawing walks was nicknamed "the Brat." He went to the World Series with three different teams and, according to many accounts, made life miserable for opponents and teammates alike.

He broke into the majors with the Cubs in 1943 and was traded to the Dodgers in June 1944. In three full seasons in Brooklyn Stanky led the league in walks twice, in on-base percentage once, and in runs scored once. In both 1945 and 1946 he had more walks than hits. He repeated the feat in 1951, and is the only player in major league history to record more hits than walks in three separate seasons.

The Dodgers traded Stanky to the Braves before the 1948 season, and, although he spent two months on the disabled list with a broken ankle, Stanky helped the Braves win a pennant in 1948. He hit a career-high .320 during the season, then walked seven times in the World Series and recorded a .524 on-base percentage, but Cleveland beat Boston in six games.

There was dissension in the Braves clubhouse in 1949, and some felt that Stanky's outspoken manner had contributed to Manager Billy Southworth's breakdown. Despite hitting .285 that year, Stanky was traded to the Giants after the season, where he was reunited with Manager Leo Durocher, his former skipper in Brooklyn.

Stanky and Durocher had seemed to inspire each other in Brooklyn, and it happened again in New York. In 1951 Stanky slammed a career-high 14 homers and was part of "The Miracle of Coogan's Bluff." After Bobby Thomson hit his dramatic three-run homer to win the NL pennant, Stanky celebrated by hopping on Durocher's back in the third base coaching box. But Stanky was disappointed in his third World Series in as many tries, as the Giants were beaten by the Yankees in six games.

He was traded to the Cardinals in December 1951 and became their playing manager. The team finished third in 1952, and Stanky was named the *Sporting News* Manager of the Year. He retired as a player after the 1953 season with a career .268 batting average.

He managed in the minor leagues in 1956 and coached for Cleveland in 1957 and 1958. Stanky was assistant to the general manager in St. Louis from 1959 through 1964 and served as the Mets' farm director in 1965. He was named manager of the White Sox in 1966 and finished fourth that season.

Chicago won 89 games in 1967, but Stanky was fired in

1968. He coached at the University of South Alabama until June 1977, when he replaced Frank Lucchesi as the Rangers' manager. In one of the briefest managerial tenures of all time, the usually tenacious Stanky won his first game in Texas and abruptly quit.

★ Casey Stengel ★

Warren Spahn pitched for Casey Stengel with the Braves in 1942 and with the Mets in 1965. Spahn's comment on the experience was, "I'm the only man who played for Casey Stengel before and after he was a genius."

Stengel was a genius when he won seven World Series with the Yankees. Before and after, he was the game's most colorful character, a man who would start stories like this: "Now take Ty Cobb, who is dead at the present time."

Stengel left behind too many stories, too many laughs, too many outrageous stunts, and too many run-on sentences that started at Point A and meandered through the rest of the alphabet. His version of the English language even developed a name — Stengelese. Asked why he never visited Montreal, Stengel answered, "Because then there'd be two languages I couldn't speak—French and English."

From 1910, when he signed his first pro contract, until 1965, when a broken hip forced him to retire as the Mets' manager, Charles Dillon Stengel, "the Ol' Perfessor," was consumed by baseball. Stengel was born in 1890 in Kansas City, and his nickname Casey was derived from K.C.

He began playing semipro ball when he was still in high school. In 1910 he was shipped to Kankakee, a Class C team, for his first pro season. Less than three years later, he was playing for the Brooklyn Dodgers. Besides his gift of gab, he was a good left-handed hitter with decent power and above-average speed.

He spent the winter after his first two years in the minors studying dentistry at Western Dental College in Kansas City and undoubtedly would have become a dentist if he had washed out of baseball. Stengel was known as the kind of student who stuck a cigar in the corner of a corpse's mouth in anatomy class. He also established his reputation as a clown par excellence in the minors. At Montgomery, his last stop before the majors, he noticed a manhole in right field, and while everyone's attention was elsewhere one day, he pried off the cover and hid under it. When a batter hit a flyball to right, he popped out and nonchalantly caught the ball.

Arriving in Brooklyn, Stengel came up with a novel solution to some hazing. Tradition prevented rookies from getting batting practice swings, so he handed out business cards as an introduction and requested that he be allowed to take his turn. On July 17, 1912, Stengel made his major league debut and singled four times. He stayed with Brooklyn through 1917, hitting .316 in 1914 and driving in a career-high 73 runs in 1917.

In January 1918 he was traded to the Pirates. In his first game back at Ebbets Field, he was booed unmercifully by the home fans. Undaunted, he found a sparrow, tucked it under his cap just before his next at bat, and when the crowd let loose with another round of boos, he doffed his cap, and the boos turned to waves of laughter.

After two years in Pittsburgh and a year and a half in Philadelphia, Stengel landed in New York with the Giants, where he met John McGraw, who was to become his greatest influence. McGraw already had the status of a legend, and from him Stengel learned about the virtues of platooning. Stengel also learned from McGraw how to motivate players and how important it was to be flexible, in game strategy or in planning the club roster during the off-season.

Stengel, whose playing career was winding down in the mid-1920s, had his greatest moments on the field in the 1923 World Series against the Yankees, as the Giants lost their bid to become the first team to win three straight Series. He won Game 1 with an inside-the-park home run with two outs in the ninth — the first Series homer hit in the new Yankee Stadium. Then he won Game 3 with a seventh-inning homer off "Sad Sam" Jones that broke a scoreless tie.

Following the Series, New York traded Stengel to the Boston Braves. He hit .280 in 1924 but played only 12 games in 1925. He left the majors then to become a player-manager and club president for Worcester of the Eastern League. He managed in the minors until 1934, when he was named manager of the Brooklyn Dodgers. The best of his three years there was his first, when the Dodgers won 71 games. When he was fired, or as Stengel might have phrased it, "discharged," he hooked up with the Boston Braves, who became the Bees for four years and then reverted to Braves, for six years through 1943.

The Braves were another poor team, finishing in seventh place four times and recording a winning record only once. Stengel missed the first 47 games of the 1943 season in Boston, having suffered a broken leg when a taxicab hit him. A local columnist indicated the level of esteem he had for the manager when he wrote, "The man who did the most for baseball in Boston was the motorist who ran down Stengel and kept him away from the Braves for two months." Stengel was discharged at the end of the season.

Stengel was now age 53 and without a job for the first time in 33 years. Early the following season, the Cubs hired Charlie Grimm as their manager. Grimm, who owned a piece of the club, promptly hired Stengel to replace himself as manager of the Class AAA Milwaukee Brewers. Bill Veeck, the Brewers' principal owner, was somewhere in the South Pacific fighting a war, and the move was made without his knowledge. When Veeck found out, he was livid; he considered Stengel a talentless clown.

For once, Veeck was wrong. Stengel led the Brewers to a pennant, and for good measure, the team set an attendance record. After being named Minor League Manager of the Year with the Oakland Oaks in 1948, Stengel got his big break. Yankee General Manager George Weiss had first met Stengel in 1916, and they had become friends while they both worked in the Eastern League. Weiss always thought Stengel was a first-rate manager and had tried to convince Lee MacPhail to hire Stengel as New York's manager in 1947. When MacPhail sold his interest in the Yankees, Weiss took over the front office and one year later he hired Stengel to manage the team.

New York fans were shocked to hear that the Yankees had hired Stengel because the club was the most pompous and staid operation in baseball. Stengel told some reporters after he was hired, "I didn't get the job through friendship. The Yankees represent an investment of millions of dollars. They don't hand out jobs like this just because they like your company. I know I can make people laugh and some of you think I'm a damn fool, (but) I got the job because the people here think I can produce for them." He did indeed. His teams won 10 pennants and seven World Series in 12 years, including an unprecedented five straight World Series in Stengel's first five seasons on the job. It was the greatest run by any manager in the game's history.

His best year was probably that first one. The 1949 Yankees were devastated by an incredible run of injuries. Joe DiMaggio, who had a bum heel, didn't play his first game until June 28. Stengel juggled his lineup and somehow got the Yanks home by one game after they beat the Red Sox in the last two games of the season at Yankee Stadium. A humble Stengel said, "I couldn't have done it without my players."

Stengel's eye for talent was exceptional. He insisted that Yogi Berra be force-fed into the lineup as the everyday catcher, and let him learn the subtleties of the position on the job. Stengel's pre-spring training Instructional School for Yankee minor leaguers was the genesis of the Instructional League. His ability to platoon the right players at the right time was uncanny. He would make moves that baffled people, going against the percentage time and time again, yet he was almost always right. The lessons he learned from McGraw were finally paying off.

In *Stengel: His Life and Times*, the definitive biography, Robert Creamer writes that Stengel "had the kind of understanding of a situation that is often described as intuitive —immediate comprehension of a problem and its solution without recourse to orderly, reasoned analysis — but that is probably just rapid-fire, computer-speed deduction derived from long experience. The best chess players occasionally play this way, making moves they can't immediately explain or justify; Stengel did the same in baseball."

He also kept having a good time. After Bill Veeck installed the first exploding scoreboard in Comiskey Park, Stengel smuggled in firecrackers for the Yankees' next visit to Chicago. When Yankee Clete Boyer hit the team's first homer that day, Stengel and his players set the fireworks off on the dugout steps, and he danced a jig.

After the Yankees lost the 1960 World Series to the Pirates in seven games, Yankee owners Del Webb and Dan Topping discharged Stengel and Weiss. Stengel was 70 years old, and the Yankees had Ralph Houk ready to step in. Houk was a favorite of the players and Stengel was certainly not. He had a cruel streak that surfaced at times, and his sarcastic comments had devastated many a player.

The Yankees held a press conference to announce that Stengel was leaving the team, claiming he was retiring. He put everyone straight: "They paid me off in full and told me my services are not desired any longer by this club." Later that day Stengel said, "I'll never make the mistake of being 70 again."

After sitting out the 1961 season, he was back in 1962 with the expansion Mets, hired by his old buddy, George

Weiss. The 1962 Mets were the worst team in baseball history. They went 40-120 and played some of the most bizarre baseball ever witnessed. They won only 51 and 53 games the next two seasons, but despite their failures on the field, they were a phenomenal success off the field.

Everywhere he went, Stengel sold the "Amazing Mets" and the game of baseball. He talked about "the Youth of America," who would one day turn the Mets into champions. He talked about "the New Breed" of Mets fans who flocked to the Polo Grounds and then to Shea Stadium. He talked before the games, he talked after the games, he talked in bars, he talked in airports, he talked in hotels, he talked anywhere he could find a person willing to listen. If he fell asleep on the bench every so often, what did it matter? He was in his mid-70s and his most important work was being done off the field.

Stengel managed his last game on July 24, 1965, though he didn't bow out quietly. That night at Toots Shor's restaurant he attended a party to honor the invitees for the next day's Old Timer's Game. He fell, breaking his left hip. A few weeks later, Stengel retired officially after 3,766 games, 1,905 wins, and 1,842 losses as a manager. He won 10 pennants, which tied him with his mentor, John McGraw, for the most in major league history.

The next year Stengel was elected to the Hall of Fame, and both the Mets and Yankees retired his uniform No. 37. Stengel died at his Glendale, California, home on September 29, 1975.

Joe Torre

Joe Torre was a Brave for the first eight years of his major league career. After conquering a weight problem, he won the National League Most Valuable Player award as a Cardinal, and added the word "svelte" to hundreds of sportswriters' vocabularies.

Torre began his career at St. Francis Prep in Brooklyn, New York, where he played third base. His father scouted for the Milwaukee Braves and later for the Baltimore Orioles, and his older brother, Frank, played first base for the Braves. So it was no surprise that Joe signed with Milwaukee in 1959.

With Eddie Mathews occupying third, the Braves converted Torre into a catcher. His bat, however, was his ticket to the majors. In 1960, his first season of pro ball, Torre won the Class A Northern League batting title, hitting .344. Late that season he was promoted to Milwaukee and singled off Harvey Haddix in his first major league at bat.

Torre spent barely a month of 1961 at Milwaukee's Class AAA club, batting .342 to earn a permanent promotion to the Braves. He played 113 games in 1961, filling in when regular catcher Del Crandall was injured. In 1962 he and Crandall shared catching duties, and the next year Torre began playing first base when he wasn't behind the plate in order to get his bat in the lineup. That season he even made two outfield appearances. Torre was selected to the NL All-Star team for five straight seasons, starting in 1963, and he had four more consecutive selections, starting in 1970.

When Crandall was traded to San Francisco in an eight-player deal that brought Felipe Alou to Milwaukee for the 1964 season, Torre became the Braves' regular catcher. He led NL receivers with a .995 fielding average and flowered as a power hitter, with 36 doubles, 20 homers, 109 RBIs, and a .321 batting average. He also led the league in grounding into double plays, a dubious distinction he'd achieve again in 1965, 1967, and 1968. He finished fifth in the 1964 NL MVP voting and received a smattering of votes the next two years.

In 1965 Torre slammed 27 homers. He was one of an NL-record six 20-home run hitters on the Braves, an arsenal matched only by the 1961 Yankees, 1964 Twins, and 1986 Tigers. He also won his only Gold Glove and hit a two-run homer in the first inning of the All-Star Game.

The Braves moved to Atlanta in 1966 and led the NL in home runs for the second straight season. Torre batted .315 and was one of the team's three 30-home run hitters, socking a career-high 36. He suffered a broken cheekbone in April 1968, missing three weeks, which caused a drop in his power numbers. But he led NL catchers in fielding percentage for the second time.

On St. Patrick's Day 1969, the Braves traded Torre to St. Louis for first baseman Orlando Cepeda, the 1967 NL MVP and a team leader for the back-to-back NL champion Cardinals. Torre replaced Cepeda at first base, fielded better, outhit him by 32 points, and knocked in 13 more runs. But the Braves scrambled from behind to win the inaugural NL West flag while the favored Cardinals were never in the NL East race.

Torre began the 1970 season behind the plate and made the All-Star team as a catcher. But when Shannon left the lineup, Torre shifted to third base, a position he hadn't played since high school. He finished with yet another banner year at the plate, setting career highs with a .325 average, second-best in the NL, and 203 hits, including 57 for extra bases. He also knocked in 100 runs, his best power output in four years. The Cardinals decided that Torre would be their regular third baseman.

To prepare for the new assignment, Torre put himself on the popular Stillman water diet: lots of protein, no carbohydrates, and eight glasses of water a day. He dropped more than 20 pounds before spring training and had his best season in the majors. He led both leagues with 230 hits, 137 RBIs, 352 total bases, and a .363 average, winning the National League MVP over Willie Stargell. Torre clouted 24 homers that season but never again hit more than 13 or knocked in more than 81 runs in any of his six remaining major league seasons.

After playing mainly at third base in 1972, he shifted across the diamond to first base for the next two years. During the 1974 World Series the New York Mets continued their habit of collecting longtime players for their troublesome third base position. They acquired Torre for veteran pitcher Ray Sadecki and youngster Tommy Moore.

The Mets soon learned that Torre had slowed down. In his first year in New York, Torre grounded into an NL-record four double plays in a nine-inning game, tying the major league mark first set 30 years earlier by Leon "Goose" Goslin. During his career, Torre hit into 284 double plays, ninth on the all-time list.

After a dreadful 1975 Torre batted .306 as a semiregular in 1976, playing first more often than third. But he was no longer a power threat. On May 31, 1977, the Mets fired

Manager Joe Frazier and appointed Torre, who remained on the roster as a player until June 18.

Skipper Torre allegedly approved of the unpopular deal sending Tom Seaver to Cincinnati. The Mets played slightly better under Torre but finished last, as they would the next two seasons. They jumped to fifth in 1980 but still lost 95 games. New York came within four games of .500 in the second half of 1981, yet Torre was fired by Mets General Manager Frank Cashen after the season.

In 1982 Torre replaced Bobby Cox in Atlanta, and with the blossoming of Dale Murphy and a healthy Bob Horner, the Braves started the season 13-0 and won the NL West division. It was Torre's only career title. In the playoffs against the St. Louis Cardinals, rain erased Phil Niekro's 1-0 lead in the opener. The Braves lost the replay and the next two. They were NL West runners-up the next two seasons, and Torre was fired.

Torre then became a broadcaster for the California Angels but, on August 1, 1990, he took over the last-place St. Louis team. He led the Cards to a surprising second-place finish in 1991, and the 1992 team held first place briefly in May before falling to second.

In 1993 the Cards appeared poised to challenge the Phillies for the NL East flag. They began a late July series in Philadelphia four games behind but dropped three straight and faded to third. Their 87-75 finish left Torre 94 games under .500 in a dozen years as a manager. He also managed the Cardinals in 1994 and took over as manager of the New York Yankees after the 1995 season.

Torre has logged 31 years in the majors as a player and manager without reaching the World Series, a drought surpassed only by Gene Mauch.

★ Vic Willis ★

Vic Willis was a 20-game winner four times for the Beaneaters (Braves) and, in 1902, also established a modern record by pitching 45 complete games. The durable righthander pitched 300 or more innings in each of eight seasons and averaged 7.8 innings per game in 513 games, 471 of them starts.

Possessed of an excellent curveball, which he used to maximum advantage, Willis began his baseball career in 1895 with Harrisburg of the Pennsylvania State League. In 1896 and 1897 he pitched for Syracuse of the Eastern (now International) League, going 10-6 and 21-16. In 1898 he came up to the big leagues with the Beaneaters. and helped pitch them to a pennant with a 24-13 record as a rookie.

Willis managed to beat the sophomore jinx, and 1899 was his best year. He was 27-8, and, on August 7, he no-hit Washington, defeating Bill Dinneen, 7-1. After an off-year (9-16), he came back strong to go 20-17 for a fifth-place team, and the next year he was 27-19, led the league in innings pitched and strikeouts and set the complete game record.

By then, the Beaneaters were on the way down as a franchise, and the 1903-1905 teams were mired in sixth and seventh place. Willis contributed to that slide, and his 29 losses in 1905 remain the modern record for a season. Of course, he was not alone. That year's Boston staff featured three other 20-game losers.

That might have been the end of it for Willis except that he was traded to Pittsburgh after the 1905 season; the Pirates saw him as the potential key to wresting the NL pennant away from John McGraw's Giants, with whom Pittsburgh were engaged in a particularly bitter and personal feud. That strategy finally paid off with a World Championship in 1909, when Willis went 22-11 for the Bucs.

Willis won 20 games for the Pirates four straight years and had his last hurrah in 1910, going 9-12 for the St. Louis Cardinals. He chalked up to a 249-205 lifetime record with a 2.63 ERA and recorded 50 career shutouts. He died in Elkton, Maryland, in 1947 and was elected to the Hall of Fame in 1995.

★ George Wright ★

During the late 1860s and early 1870s George Wright was undoubtedly the best baseball player in the country.

He played on numerous championship teams, managed one himself, and was responsible for several innovations that changed the way the game was played. He also founded a nationally known sporting goods company and was important in advancing several other sports in America.

George Wright was born in New York in 1847 and was taught cricket by his father. The game was played regularly at Elysian Fields in Hoboken, New Jersey, where baseball was played as well, so Wright grew up playing both sports. By age 15 he was an assistant pro with the St. George Cricket Club. He then moved to Philadelphia and in 1865 was both a pro for the Philadelphia Cricket Club and shortstop for the Philadelphia Olympians.

At the time, baseball was supposed to be an amateur sport, although many players were paid under the table. Wright's amateur status was not affected by his job with the cricket club because it was considered a teaching position. In 1867, Wright was the captain of the Washington, D.C., Nationals. He was listed on the roster as a government clerk, but the address of his office was a public park!

By this time Wright was regarded as one of the best players in the country. He had remarkably soft hands and perfected a style of catching the ball with his elbows bent to cushion the shock. He supposedly pulled off the first hidden ball trick and often trapped short fly balls to create double plays. In 1911, when Honus Wagner was at the height of his career, the *New York Journal*'s Sam Crane called Wright "the best shortstop ever."

In 1869 Harry Wright, who had moved to Cincinnati, was given the task of putting together the first openly professional team. His first call was for his younger brother. George Wright was paid $1,400 for the season, $200 more than Harry paid himself for managing and playing center field.

The Cincinnati Red Stockings toured from coast to coast, defeating all comers. Precisely how many games they played is in dispute because some games against lesser town teams were apparently not counted in the official record. One source credits Wright with a .629 batting average with 49 home runs in 57 games, while another claims he hit .518 with 59 homers in 52 games.

To be fair, much of the opposition was second rate. The Red Stockings often won by such scores as 53–9 and 48–12, and many games were played on fields with no outfield fences. Whenever he hit the ball over an outfielder or between fielders, the speedy Wright could circle the bases.

The Red Stockings were not the first completely professional team, of course; they were merely the first to admit it. Their undefeated record, though, helped make professionalism respectable. When they lost a couple of games on their 1870 tour, interest in the team waned, but many cities responded with the desire to field their own professional teams.

In 1871 the National Association, the first professional league, was formed. Harry Wright moved to Boston and organized a new Red Stockings team which was the forerunners of the Braves, and George tagged along as star shortstop. Although Boston narrowly missed winning the first NA pennant, the club followed with four straight flags, winning each one more easily than the last.

Boston's continued success destroyed interest in the NA's pennant races, and the league faced a number of other problems. In 1876, the National League was formed. Harry Wright's Red Stockings were charter members, but they lost the initial pennant to the Chicago White Stockings, a team that had signed four of Boston's stars.

Again the competition was improved, and George Wright's days as a great slugger were over. In seven NL seasons, he batted only .256. He remained a superior fielder, however, and helped Boston win pennants in 1877 and 1878. In 1879, after a dispute with the Boston owners, he jumped to the Providence Grays as player-manager. In his only year as manager, Wright's Grays finished five games ahead of Harry Wright's Red Stockings and won the NL pennant, George Wright's seventh in eight years.

In 1871 Wright opened a sporting goods business in Boston and in 1879 took Henry A. Ditson as a partner. Although Wright returned to the Red Stockings in 1880 and was active through 1882, he played very little, as Wright & Ditson was becoming a major sporting goods concern. Through his business, Wright played a large part in making tennis popular in the United States and in introducing Canadian ice hockey here. He also introduced golf to Boston and laid out the city's first course.

His interest in baseball remained strong, and he served on the commission that wrongly identified Abner Doubleday as the inventor of baseball. Eventually the National League issued him pass No. 1, and he was a frequent guest at major league games. He was elected to the Hall of Fame in 1937, the year he died at age 90.

★ Harry Wright ★

William Henry "Harry" Wright was saluted on his death in 1895 by legendary baseball writer and promoter Henry Chadwick, who proclaimed, "There is no doubt that Harry Wright was the father of professional base ball playing."

A pioneer who was instrumental in evolving the game from genteel sporting club to professionalism, Wright helped keep the game clean and then became a legendary manager. His brother, George, was the superior ballplayer, but Harry was the brains of the duo.

Wright instituted dozens of innovations, including the backup system, whereby fielders back up each other and pitchers back up bases; pregame batting practice; and, fungoing flyballs to outfielders before a game. He invented hand signals and was the first to reposition his defensive players to suit the style of the batsman. He introduced the double steal, and, in 1870, his catcher became the first player to wear a glove; five years later he helped originate the face mask for catchers.

Wright even influenced how the players looked. He abandoned the old practice of tying the pants at the cuffs so they wouldn't interfere with running. Instead, he put his men in flannel knickers, and the brightly colored socks his Cincinnati team wore led to the nickname of Red Stockings. Not all his innovations took hold. For example, he frequently had his team take the field by marching nine abreast to first before running, with each peeling out of formation, to take their positions.

Not surprisingly, Wright was an early student of statistics. He devised his own detailed box scores and pored over them in search of ways to improve his team's chances. In fact, so much time spent studying the notes may have caused him to temporarily lose his sight for a year in 1890.

But perhaps Wright's most significant contribution to the early game was his total dedication to fairness and good sportsmanship. According to historian David Voigt, Wright "believed the British standards of sportsmanship should dominate organized baseball." One of Wright's teams went down to defeat in one of the game's most dramatic losses because of his belief in absolute fairness.

In 1870, after Cincinnati had won about 60 consecutive games, the ballclub faced the Brooklyn Excelsiors, the most powerful team in the East. After nine innings the score was tied, 7-7, and both clubs were ready to call it a day, in the custom of the time. But Wright insisted the game be played to a finish. His team lost in the eleventh inning, ending the most storied winning streak in baseball history and establishing the East Coast teams as forces to be reckoned with.

Wright understood the business side of the game, too. In the earliest days of the game the captain did what the field manager does today. The manager acted as general manager, accountant, and traveling secretary. Devising a schedule was a demanding task at that time, because formal leagues did not exist. As early as 1869 Wright wrote to a friend about his scheduling frustrations, "Base ball is business now, Nick, and I am trying to arrange our games to make them successful and make them pay, irrespective of my feelings, and to the best of my ability."

The story of baseball's Wright brothers begins in England. Harry and George were just youngsters when their father, a star cricket player, was hired by the St. George Cricket Club in New York City in the early 1850s. In America, both boys took after their father, becoming quality cricketers. By age 19 Harry was a professional bowler, the cricket equivalent of the pitcher, for St. George's famous Dragonslayers.

Harry learned the jeweler's trade, but, before long, he and George were collecting salaries playing for Alexander Cartwright's Knickerbockers. Harry accepted an offer to be a player and instructor for the Cincinnati Cricket Club in 1865 while his brother stayed in New York.

In 1869 the town fathers of Cincinnati decided that having a baseball team would be good for their growing city. So they hired Harry Wright as manager and told him to acquire quality players. Although the 1869 Red Stockings may not have been the first team to field paid players, the ballplayers were the first "to make no bones about their professionalism," historian Mark Alvarez said.

Harry signed his brother George and several other excellent players. The team playing for Cincinnati in 1869 had only one player from the city on the roster. In 1870 the Red Stockings began a triumphant national tour during which they won every one of their 60 games.

By the time the National Association was formed in 1871, Wright had become an important figure. He took most of the Red Stocking talent with him to Boston, and although his team finished third in the NA's first year, they won the pennant the next four seasons.

But the Association was a rough-and-tumble organization, loose in structure and lacking central power. The threat of gamblers hung over everything they did. The league's first champions, the Philadelphia Athletics, hung their championship pennant in their favorite saloon. That kind of behavior didn't sit well with Wright.

When businessman William Hulbert decided a new league was necessary, he consulted Wright on structure, rules, and franchise locations. Wright was the secretary at the first meeting of the National League when it was organized in late 1875.

Hulbert signed "the Big Four" of Wright's team —

pitcher Ross Barnes and utility men Al Spalding, Cal McVey, and Deacon White — to his Chicago ballclub. The White Stockings went on to win the first NL crown. Wright's Boston Red Stockings finished fourth, and the manager even made a token field appearance. Wright was oh-for-three in 1876, and finished his major league career oh-for-seven with two strikeouts.

Wright bounced back in 1877 and 1878, taking the league flag both times behind stars Jim O'Rourke, George Wright, and ace hurler Tommy Bond, who won 40 games to lead the league both years. George moved to Providence for the 1879 season and his team took the crown while Harry's dropped to second.

Wright was fired by notorious Boston owner Arthur Soden after a sixth-place finish and some player grumbling in 1880. He moved to Providence as manager for two years, then finished his managerial career in 1893 after 10 years as head man for Philadelphia. Wright was appointed director of league umpires after he left managing, but the post was largely honorary.

Wright's all-time record as a manager was 1,000 wins, 825 losses. But numbers don't do the man justice. With his immaculate chin whiskers and ever-professional demeanor, Wright was a unique figure in the game of that era. Baseball at the time was still a rough game; umpires often took their lives into their hands when they made calls that were unpalatable to the home crowd. But according to historian Harold Seymour, "about the only manager who didn't go after umpires was old Harry Wright."

In 1953 Wright was elected into the Hall of Fame.

CHAPTER 6

The Braves Index

Aaron, Hank (O) Mil-N 54-65, Atl-N 66-74, Mil-A 75-76

Aaron, Tommie (1) Mil-N 62-63, 65, Atl-N 68-71

Abbaticchio, Ed (S) Phi-N 1897-98, Bos-N 03-05, 10, Pit-N 07-10

Abernathy, Ted (P) Was-A 55-57, 60, Cle-A 63-64, Chi-N 65-66, 69-70, Atl-N 66, Cin-N 67-68, StL-N 70, KC-A 70-72

Acker, Jim (P) Tor-A 83-86, 89-91, Atl-N 86-89, Sea-A 92

Adcock, Joe (1) Cin-N 50-52, Mil-N 53-62, Cle-A 63, LA-A 64, Cal-A 65-66

Addis, Bob (O) Bos-N 50-51, Chi-N 52-53, Pit-N 53

Addy, Bob (O) Rok-n 1871, Phi-n 1873, 1875, Bos-n 1873, Har-n 1874, Chi-N 1876, Cin-N 1877

Aderholt, Morrie (O) Was-A 39-41, Bro-N 44-45, Bos-N 45

Aker, Jack (P) KC-A 64-67, Oak-A 68, Sea-A 69, NY-A 69-72, Chi-N 72-73, Atl-N 74, NY-N 74

Akers, Bill (3) Det-A 29-31, Bos-N 32

Aldrich, Jay (P) Mil-A 87, 89, Atl-N 89, Bal-A 90

Alexander, Doyle (P) LA-N 71, Bal-A 72-76, NY-A 76, 82-83, Tex-A 77-79, Atl-N 80, 86-87, SF-N 81, Tor-A 83-86, Det-A 87-89

Allen, Frank (P) Bro-N 12-14, Pit-F 14-15, Bos-N 16-17

Allen, Myron (2) NY-N 1883, Bos-N 1886, Cle-a 1887, KC-a 1888

Allen, Bob (S) Phi-N 1890-94, Bos-N 1897, Cin-N 00

Alomar, Sandy (S) Mil-N 64-65, Atl-N 66, NY-N 67, Chi-A 67-69, Cal-A 69-74, NY-A 74-76, Tex-A 77-78

Alou, Felipe (O) SF-N 58-63, Mil-N 64-65, Atl-N 66-69, Oak-A 70-71, NY-A 71-73, Mon-N 73, Mil-A 74

Alvarez, Jose (P) Atl-N 81-82, 88-89

Anderson, Bill (P) Bos-N 25

Andrews, Nate (P) StL-N 37, 39, Cle-A 40-41, Bos-N 43-45, Cin-N 46, NY-N 46

Andrews, Stan (C) Bos-N 39-40, Bro-N 44-45, Phi-N 45

Annis, Bill (O) Bos-N 1884

Antonelli, Johnny (P) Bos-N 48-50, Mil-N 53, 61, NY-N 54-57, SF-N 58-60, Cle-A 61

Asmussen, Tom (C) Bos-N 07

Aspromonte, Ken (2) Bos-A 57-58, Was-A 58-60, Cle-A 60-62, LA-A 61, Mil-N 62, Chi-N 63

Aspromonte, Bob (3) Bro-N 56, LA-N 60-61, Hou-N 62-68, Atl-N 69-70, NY-N 71

Asselstine, Brian (O) Atl-N 76-81

Assenmacher, Paul (P) Atl-N 86-89, Chi-N 89-93, NY-N 93, Chi-A 94, Cle-A 95

Atwell, Toby (C) Chi-N 52-53, Pit-N 53-56, Mil-N 56

Aubrey, Harry (S) Bos-N 03

Autry, Al (P) Atl-N 76

Autry, Chick (1) Cin-N 07, 09, Bos-N 09

Averill, Earl (O) Cle-A 29-39, Det-A 39-40, Bos-N 41

Avery, Steve (P) Atl-N 90-95

Avila, Bobby (2) Cle-A 49-58, Bal-A 59, Bos-A 59, Mil-N 59

Babich, Johnny (P) Bro-N 34-35, Bos-N 36, Phi-A 40-41

Bagwell, Bill (O) Bos-N 23, Phi-A 25

Bailey, Gene (O) Phi-A 17, Bos-N 19-20, Bos-A 20, Bro-N 23-24

Bailey, Fred (O) Bos-N 16-18

Bailey, Harvey (P) Bos-N 1899-1900

Bailey, Ed (C) Cin-N 53-61, SF-N 61-63, 65, Mil-N 64, Chi-N 65, Cal-A 66

Baker, Dusty (O) Atl-N 68-75, LA-N 76-83, SF-N 84, Oak-A 85-86

Balas, Mike (P) Bos-N 38

Bales, Lee (2) Atl-N 66, Hou-N 67

Ball, Jim (C) Bos-N 07-08

Bancroft, Dave (S) Phi-N 15-20, NY-N 20-23, 30, Bos-N 24-27, Bro-N 28-29

Banks, Bill (P) Bos-N 1895-96

Bannon, Jimmy (O) StL-N 1893, Bos-N 1894-96

Barbare, Walter (S) Cle-A 14-16, Bos-A 18, Pit-N 19-20, Bos-N 21-22

Barber, Steve (P) Bal-A 60-67, NY-A 67-68, Sea-A 69, Chi-N 70, Atl-N 70-72, Cal-A 72-73, SF-N 74

Barberich, Frank (P) Bos-N 07, Bos-A 10

Barclay, George (O) StL-N 02-04, Bos-N 04-05

Barker, Len (P) Tex-A 76-78, Cle-A 79-83, Atl-N 83-85, Mil-A 87

Barkley, Red (S) StL-N 37, Bos-N 39, Bro-N 43

Barnes, Jesse (P) Bos-N 15-17, 23-25, NY-N 18-23, Bro-N 26-27

Barnes, Ross (2) Bos-n 1871-75, Chi-N 1876-77, Cin-N 1879, Bos-N 1881

Barnes, Virgil (P) NY-N 19-20, 22-28, Bos-N 28

Barnicle, George (P) Bos-N 39-41

Barrett, Red (P) Cin-N 37-40, Bos-N 43-45, 47-49, StL-N 45-46

Barrett, Frank (P) StL-N 39, Bos-A 44-45, Bos-N 46, Pit-N 50

Barrett, Johnny (O) Pit-N 42-46, Bos-N 46

Barrett, Marty (C) Bos-N 1884, Ind-n 1884

Barrett, Dick (P) Phi-A 33, Bos-N 34, Chi-N 43, Phi-N 43-45

Barron, Red (O) Bos-N 29

Barrows, Frank (O) Bos-n 1871

Barry, Shad (O) Was-N 1899, Bos-N 00-01, Phi-N 01-04, Chi-N 04-05, Cin-N 05-06, StL-N 06-08, NY-N 08

Bass, Doc (H) Bos-N 18

Batchelder, Joe (P) Bos-N 23-25

Bates, Johnny (O) Bos-N 06-09, Phi-N 09-10, Cin-N 11-14, Chi-N 14, Bal-F 14

Beall, Bob (1) Atl-N 75, 78-79, Pit-N 80

Beals, Tommy (2) Oly-n 1871-72, Was-n 1873, Bos-n 1874-75, Chi-N 1880

Beard, Mike (P) Atl-N 74-77

Beauchamp, Jim (1) StL-N 63, 70-71, Hou-N 64-65, 70, Mil-N 65, Atl-N 67, Cin-N 68-69, NY-N 72-73

Beaumont, Ginger (O) Pit-N 1899-1906, Bos-N 07-09, Chi-N 10

Beazley, Johnny (P) StL-N 41-42, 46, Bos-N 47-49

Beck, Fred (O) Bos-N 09-10, Cin-N 11, Phi-N 11, Chi-F 14-15

Becker, Beals (O) Pit-N 08, Bos-N 08-09, NY-N 10-12, Cin-N 13, Phi-N 13-15

Bedell, Howie (O) Mil-N 62, Phi-N 68

Bedrosian, Steve (P) Atl-N 81-85, 93-95, Phi-N 86-89, SF-N 89-90, Min-A 91

Behenna, Rick (P) Atl-N 83, Cle-A 83-85

Bell, Gus (O) Pit-N 50-52, Cin-N 53-61, NY-N 62, Mil-N 62-64

Bell, Les (3) StL-N 23-27, Bos-N 28-29, Chi-N 30-31

Bell, Mike (1) Atl-N 90-91

Bell, Terry (H) KC-A 86, Atl-N 87

Belliard, Rafael (S) Pit-N 82-90, Atl-N 91-95

Belloir, Rob (S) Atl-N 75-78

Benedict, Bruce (C) Atl-N 78-89

Benge, Ray (P) Cle-A 25-26, Phi-N 28-32, 36, Bro-N 33-35, Bos-N 36, Cin-N 38

Bennett, Charlie (C) Mil-N 1878, Wor-N 1880, Det-N 1881-88, Bos-N 1889-93

Benton, Larry (P) Bos-N 23-27, 35, NY-N 27-30, Cin-N 30-34

Berenguer, Juan (P) NY-N 78-80, KC-A 81, 92, Tor-A 81, Det-A 82-85, SF-N 86, Min-A 87-90, Atl-N 91-92

Bergen, Marty (C) Bos-N 1896-99

Berger, Wally (O) Bos-N 30-37, NY-N 37-38, Cin-N 38-40, Phi-N 40

Bergh, John (C) Phi-N 1876, Bos-N 1880

Berres, Ray (C) Bro-N 34, 36, Pit-N 37-40, Bos-N 40-41, NY-N 42-45

Berroa, Geronimo (O) Atl-N 89-90, Cin-N 92, Fla-N 93, Oak-A 94-95

Berryhill, Damon (C) Chi-N 87-91, Atl-N 91-93, Bos-N 94, Cin-N 95

Betts, Huck (P) Phi-N 20-25, Bos-N 32-35

Bickford, Vern (P) Bos-N 48-52, Mil-N 53, Bal-A 54

Bielecki, Mike (P) Pit-N 84-87, Chi-N 88-91, Atl-N 91-92, 94, Cle-A 93, Cal-A 95

Birdsall, Dave (O) Bos-n 1871-73

Blackaby, Ethan (O) Mil-N 62, 64

Blackburn, Earl (C) Pit-N 12, Cin-N 12-13, Bos-N 15-16, Chi-N 17

Blackburne, Lena (3) Chi-A 10, 12, 14-15, 27, 29, Cin-N 18, Bos-N 19, Phi-N 19

Blanchard, Johnny (O) NY-A 55, 59-65, KC-A 65, Mil-N 65

Blanche, Al (P) Bos-N 35-36

Blankenship, Kevin (P) Atl-N 88, Chi-N 88-90

Blanks, Larvell (S) Atl-N 72-75, 80, Cle-A 76-78, Tex-A 79

Blasingame, Wade (P) Mil-N 63-65, Atl-N 66-67, Hou-N 67-72, NY-A 72

Blauser, Jeff (S) Atl-N 87-95

Blocker, Terry (O) NY-N 85, Atl-N 88-89

Boeckel, Tony (3) Pit-N 17, 19, Bos-N 19-23

Boever, Joe (P) StL-N 85-86, Atl-N 87-90, Phi-N 90-91, Hou-N 92, Oak-A 93, Det-A 93-95

Boggs, Ray (P) Bos-N 28

Boggs, Tommy (P) Tex-A 76-77, 85, Atl-N 78-83

Bolling, Frank (2) Det-A 54, 56-60, Mil-N 61-65, Atl-N 66

Bond, Tommy (P) Atl-n 1874, Har-n 1875-76, Bos-N 1877-81, Wor-N 1882, Bos-U 1884, Ind-a 1884

Bonnell, Barry (O) Atl-N 77-79, Tor-A 80-83, Sea-A 84-86

Bonner, Frank (2) Bal-N 1894-95, StL-N 1895, Bro-N 1896, Was-N 1899, Cle-A 02, Phi-A 02, Bos-N 03

Bool, Al (C) Was-A 28, Pit-N 30, Bos-N 31

Boone, Ray (1) Cle-A 48-53, Det-A 53-58, Chi-A 58-59, KC-A 59, Mil-N 59-60, Bos-A 60

Borbon, Pedro (P) Atl-N 92-93, 95

Borden, Joe (P) Phi-n 1875, Bos-N 1876

Boultes, Jake (P) Bos-N 07-09

Bouton, Jim (P) NY-A 62-68, Sea-A 69, Hou-N 69-70, Atl-N 78

Bowerman, Frank (C) Bal-N 1895-98, Pit-N 1898-99, NY-N 00-07, Bos-N 08-09

Boyd, Bob (1) Chi-A 51, 53-54, Bal-A 56-60, KC-A 61, Mil-N 61

Boyer, Clete (3) KC-A 55-57, NY-A 59-66, Atl-N 67-71

Boyle, Buzz (O) Bos-N 29-30, Bro-N 33-35

Bradford, Larry (P) Atl-N 77, 79-81

Bradley, Foghorn (P) Bos-N 1876

Brady, King (P) Phi-N 05, Pit-N 06-07, Bos-A 08, Bos-N 12

Brady, Bob (C) Bos-N 46-47

Brady, Bill (P) Bos-N 12

Brain, Dave (3) Chi-A 01, StL-N 03-05, Pit-N 05, Bos-N 06-07, Cin-N 08, NY-N 08

Brandt, Ed (P) Bos-N 28-35, Bro-N 36, Pit-N 37-38

Bransfield, Kitty (C) Bos-N 1898, Pit-N 01-04, Phi-N 05-11, Chi-N 11

Braun, John (P) Mil-N 64

Braxton, Garland (P) Bos-N 21-22, NY-A 25-26, Was-A 27-30, Chi-A 30-31, StL-A 31, 33

Bray, Buster (O) Bos-N 41

Bream, Sid (1) LA-N 83-85, Pit-N 85-90, Atl-N 91-93, Hou-N 94

Breazeale, Jim (1) Atl-N 69, 71-72, Chi-A 78

Bridwell, Al (S) Cin-N 05, Bos-N 06-07, 11-12, NY-N 08-11, Chi-N 13, StL-F 14-15

Britton, Jim (P) Atl-N 67-69, Mon-N 71

Brizzolara, Tony (P) Atl-N 79, 83-84

Daley, Bill (P) Bos-N 1889, Bos-P 1890, Bos-a 1891
Daly, Joe (C) Phi-a 1890, Cle-N 1891, Bos-N 1892
Dam, Bill (O) Bos-N 09
Daniels, Jack (O) Bos-N 52
Dark, Alvin (S) Bos-N 46, 48-49, NY-N 50-56, StL-N 56-58, Chi-N 58-59, Phi-N 60, Mil-N 60
Davey, Mike (P) Atl-N 77-78
Davidson, Ted (P) Cin-N 65-68, Atl-N 68
Davis, George (P) NY-A 12, Bos-N 13-15
Davis, Jody (C) Chi-N 81-88, Atl-N 88-90
Davis, Daisy (P) StL-a 1884, Bos-N 1884-85
Davis, Mark (P) Phi-N 80-81, 93, SF-N 83-87, SD-N 87-89, 93-94, KC-A 90-92, Atl-N 92
Davis, Trench (H) Pit-N 85-86, Atl-N 87
Dayley, Ken (P) Atl-N 82-84, StL-N 84-90, Tor-A 91, 93
Deal, Charlie (3) Det-A 12-13, Bos-N 13-14, StL-F 15, StL-A 16, Chi-N 16-21
Dealy, Pat (C) Stp-U 1884, Bos-N 1885-86, Was-N 1887, Syr-a 1890
Deasley, Pat (C) Bos-N 1881-82, StL-a 1883-84, NY-N 1885-87, Was-N 1888
Dedmon, Jeff (P) Atl-N 83-87, Cle-A 88
Delahanty, Jim (O) Chi-N 01, NY-N 02, Bos-N 04-05, Cin-N 06, StL-N 07, Was-A 07-09, Det-A 09-12, Bro-F 14-15
DeLa Hoz, Mike (3) Cle-A 60-63, Mil-N 64-65, Atl-N 66-67, Cin-N 69
Delaney, Art (P) StL-N 24, Bos-N 28-29
Demaree, Al (P) NY-N 12-14, 17-18, Phi-N 15-16, Chi-N 17, Bos-N 19
Demaree, Frank (O) Chi-N 32-33, 35-38, NY-N 39-41, Bos-N 41-42, StL-N 43, StL-A 44
DeMerit, John (O) Mil-N 57-59, 61, NY-N 62
DeMontreville, Gene (2) Pit-N 1894, Was-N 1895-97, Bal-N 1898-99, Chi-N 1899, Bro-N 00, Bos-N 01-02, Was-A 03, StL-A 04
Denson, Drew (1) Atl-N 89, Chi-A 93
Dessau, Rube (P) Bos-N 07, Bro-N 10
Detweiler, Ducky (3) Bos-N 42, 46
Devereaux, Mike (O) LA-N 87-88, Bal-A 89-94, Chi-A 95, Atl-N 95
Devine, Adrian (P) Atl-N 73, 75-76, 78-79, Tex-A 77, 80
Devlin, Art (3) NY-N 04-11, Bos-N 12-13
DeVogt, Rex (C) Bos-N 13
Devore, Josh (O) NY-N 08-13, Cin-N 13, Phi-N 13-14, Bos-N 14
Dexter, Charlie (O) Lou-N 1896-99, Chi-N 00-02, Bos-N 02-03
Diaz, Carlos (P) Atl-N 82, NY-N 82-83, LA-N 84-86
Dickson, Walt (P) NY-N 10, Bos-N 12-13, Pit-F 14-15
Didier, Bob (C) Atl-N 69-72, Det-A 73, Bos-A 74
Diehl, Ernie (O) Pit-N 03-04, Bos-N 06, 09
Diehl, George (P) Bos-N 42-43
Dietz, Dick (1) SF-N 66-71, LA-N 72, Atl-N 73
Dignan, Steve (O) Bos-N 1880, Wor-N 1880
Dillard, Don (O) Cle-N 59-62, Mil-N 63, 65
DiMaggio, Vince (O) Bos-N 37-38, Cin-N 39-40, Pit-N 40-44, Phi-N 45-46, NY-N 46
Dinneen, Bill (P) Was-N 1898-99, Bos-N 00-01, Bos-A 02-07, StL-A 07-09
Dittmer, Jack (2) Bos-N 52, Mil-N 53-56, Det-A 57
Dobson, Pat (P) Det-A 67-69, SD-N 70, Bal-A 71-72, Atl-N 73, NY-A 73-75, Cle-A 76-77
Dolan, Cozy (O) Bos-N 1895-96, 05-06, Chi-N 00-01, Bro-N 01-02, Chi-A 03, Cin-N 03-05
Doll, Art (P) Bos-N 35-36, 38
Donlin, Mike (O) StL-N 1899-1900, Bal-A 01, Cin-N 02-04, NY-N 04-06, 08, 11, 14, Bos-N 11, Pit-N 12
Donnelly, Ed (P) Bos-N 11-12
Donnelly, Blix (P) StL-N 44-46, Phi-N 46-50, Bos-N 51
Donovan, Patsy (O) Bos-N 1890, Bro-N 1890, 06-07, Lou-N 1891, Was-a 1891, 04, Was-N 1892, Pit-N 1892-99, StL-N 00-03
Donovan, Dick (P) Bos-N 50-52, Det-A 54, Chi-A 55-60, Was-A 61, Cle-A 62-65
Donovan, Bill (P) Bos-N 42-43
Dorner, Gus (P) Cle-A 02-03, Cin-N 06, Bos-N 06-09
Doyle, Paul (P) Atl-N 69, Cal-N 70, 72, SD-N 70
Drabowsky, Moe (P) Chi-N 56-60, Mil-N 61, Cin-N 62, KC-A 62-65, 69-70, Bal-A 66-68, 70, StL-N 71-72, Chi-A 72
Dreesen, Bill (3) Bos-N 31
Dresser, Bob (P) Bos-N 02
Drews, Frank (2) Bos-N 44-45

Dudra, John (2) Bos-N 41
Duffy, Hugh (O) Chi-N 1888-89, Chi-P 1890, Bos-a 1891, Bos-N 1892-1900, Mil-A 01, Phi-N 04-06
Dugan, Joe (3) Phi-A 17-21, Bos-A 22, NY-A 22-28, Bos-N 29, Det-A 31
Dugey, Oscar (2) Bos-N 13-14, 20, Phi-N 15-17
Dunlap, Bill (O) Bos-N 29-30
Earley, Tom (P) Bos-N 38-42, 45
Eason, Mal (P) Chi-N 00-02, Bos-N 02, Det-A 03, Bro-N 05-06
Easterly, Jamie (P) Atl-N 74-79, Mil-A 81-83, Cle-A 83-87
Eave, Gary (P) Atl-N 88-89, Sea-A 90
Eayrs, Eddie (O) Pit-N 13, Bos-N 20-21, Bro-N 21
Eckhardt, Ox (H) Bos-N 32, Bro-N 36
Edelman, John (P) Mil-N 55
Eden, Mike (2) Atl-N 76, Chi-A 78
Edwards, Foster (P) Bos-N 25-28, NY-A 30
Egan, Dick (2) Cin-N 08-13, Bro-N 14-15, Bos-N 15-16
Eichelberger, Juan (P) SD-N 78-82, Cle-A 83, Atl-N 88
Eichhorn, Mark (P) Tor-A 82, 86-88, 92-93, Atl-N 89, Cal-N 90-92, Bal-A 94
Eilers, Dave (P) Mil-N 64-65, NY-N 65-66, Hou-N 67
Elliott, Rowdy (C) Bos-N 10, Chi-N 16-18, Bro-N 20
Elliott, Glenn (P) Bos-N 47-49
Elliott, Jumbo (P) StL-A 23, Bro-N 25, 27-30, Phi-N 31-34, Bos-N 34
Elliott, Bob (3) Pit-N 39-46, Bos-N 47-51, NY-N 52, StL-A 53, Chi-A 53
Emmerich, Bob (O) Bos-N 23
English, Gil (3) NY-N 31-32, Det-A 36-37, Bos-N 37-38, Bro-N 44
Errickson, Dick (P) Bos-N 38-42, Chi-N 42
Esasky, Nick (1) Cin-N 83-88, Bos-A 89, Atl-N 90
Estock, George (P) Bos-N 51
Etchison, Buck (1) Bos-N 43-44
Evans, Chick (P) Bos-N 09-10
Evans, Darrell (3) Atl-N 69-76, 89, SF-N 76-83, Det-A 84-88
Evers, Johnny (2) Chi-N 02-13, Bos-N 14-17, 29, Phi-N 17, Chi-A 22
Falcone, Pete (P) SF-N 75, StL-N 76-78, NY-N 79-82, Atl-N 83-84
Fallenstein, Ed (P) Phi-N 31, Bos-N 33
Farrell, Doc (S) NY-N 25-27, 29, Bos-N 27-29, StL-N 30, Chi-N 30, NY-A 32-33, Bos-A 35
Farrell, Kerby (1) Bos-N 43, Chi-A 45
Felix, Gus (O) Bos-N 23-25, Bro-N 26-27
Ferguson, George (P) NY-N 06-07, Bos-N 08-11
Fernandez, Nanny (3) Bos-N 42, 46-47, Pit-N 50
Ferrell, Wes (P) Cle-A 27-33, Bos-A 34-37, Was-A 37-38, NY-A 38-39, Bro-N 40, Bos-N 41
Fette, Lou (P) Bos-N 37-40, 45, Bro-N 40
Fillingim, Dana (P) Phi-A 15, Bos-N 18-23, Phi-N 25
Fischer, Hank (P) Mil-N 62-65, Atl-N 66, Cin-N 66, Bos-A 66-67
Fischlin, Mike (R) Hou-N 77-78, 80, Cle-A 81-85, NY-A 86, Atl-N 87
Fisher, Tom (P) Bos-N 04
Fitzberger, Charlie (H) Bos-N 28
Fitzpatrick, Ed (2) Bos-N 15-17
Flaherty, Patsy (P) Lou-N 1899, Pit-N 00, 04-05, Chi-A 03-04, Bos-N 07-08, 11, Phi-N 10
Fletcher, Elbie (1) Bos-N 34-35, 37-39, 49, Pit-N 39-43, 46-47
Foley, Curry (O) Bos-N 1879-80, Buf-N 1881-83
Ford, Gene (P) Bos-N 36, Chi-A 38
Ford, Hod (2) Bos-N 19-23, 32-33, Phi-N 24, Bro-N 25, Cin-N 26-31, StL-N 32
Ford, Wenty (P) Atl-N 73
Forster, Terry (P) Chi-A 71-76, Pit-N 77, LA-N 78-82, Atl-N 83-85, Cal-A 86
Foster, Leo (S) Atl-N 71, 73-74, NY-N 76-77
Fournier, Jack (1) Chi-A 12-17, NY-A 18, StL-N 20-22, Bro-N 23-26, Bos-N 27
Fox, John (P) Bos-N 1881, Bal-a 1883, Pit-a 1884, Was-N 1886
Fox, Terry (P) Mil-N 60, Det-A 61-66, Phi-N 66
Francona, Tito (1) Bal-A 56-57, Chi-A 58, Det-A 58, Cle-A 59-64, StL-N 65-66, Phi-N 67, Atl-N 67-69, Oak-A 69-70, Mil-A 70
Frankhouse, Fred (P) StL-N 27-30, Bos-N 30-35, 39, Bro-N 36-38
Fraser, Chick (P) Lou-N 1896-98, Cle-N 1898, Phi-N 1899-1900, 02-04, Phi-A 01, Bos-N 05, Cin-N 06, Chi-N 07-09

Frasier, Vic (P) Chi-A 31-33, 39, Det-A 33-34, Bos-N 37
Freeman, Jimmy (P) Atl-N 72-73
Freeman, Buck (O) Was-a 1891, Was-N 1898-99, Bos-N 00, Bos-A 01-07
Freeman, Marvin (P) Phi-N 86, 88-90, Atl-N 90-93, Col-N 94-95
Freigau, Howard (S) StL-N 22-25, Chi-N 25-27, Bro-N 28, Bos-N 28
Frias, Pepe (S) Mon-N 73-78, Atl-N 79, Tex-A 80, LA-N 80-81
Frisbee, Charlie (O) Bos-N 1899, NY-N 00
Frisella, Danny (P) NY-N 67-72, Atl-N 73-74, SD-N 75, StL-N 76, Mil-A 76
Frock, Sam (P) Bos-N 07, 10-11, Pit-N 09-10
Fuller, John (O) Atl-N 74
Funk, Frank (P) Cle-A 60-62, Mil-N 63
Gabler, Frank (P) NY-N 35-37, Bos-N 37-38, Chi-A 38
Gabrielson, Len (1) Mil-N 60, 63-64, Chi-N 64-65, SF-N 65-66, Cal-A 67, LA-N 67-70
Gallagher, Dave (O) Cle-A 87, Chi-A 88-90, Bal-A 90, Cal-A 91, 95, NY-N 92-93, Atl-N 94, Phi-N 95
Gallagher, Gil (S) Bos-N 22
Gammons, Daff (O) Bos-N 01
Gant, Ron (O) Atl-N 87-93, Cin-N 95
Ganzel, Charlie (C) Stp-U 1884, Phi-N 1885-86, Det-N 1886-88, Bos-N 1889-97
Garber, Gene (P) Pit-N 69-70, 72, KC-A 73-74, 87-88, Phi-N 74-78, Atl-N 78-87
Garcia, Damaso (2) NY-A 78-79, Tor-A 80-86, Atl-N 88, Mon-N 89
Garms, Debs (O) StL-A 32-35, Bos-N 37-39, Pit-N 40-41, StL-N 43-45
Garr, Ralph (O) Atl-N 68-75, Chi-A 76-79, Cal-A 79-80
Garrett, Adrian (O) Atl-N 66, Chi-N 70, 73-75, Oak-A 71-72, Cal-A 75-76
Garrido, Gil (S) SF-N 64, Atl-N 68-72
Garry, Jim (P) Bos-N 1893
Gaston, Cito (O) Atl-N 67, 75-78, SD-N 69-74, Pit-N 78
Gastright, Hank (P) Col-a 1889-91, Was-N 1892, Pit-N 1893, Bos-N 1893, Bro-N 1894, Cin-N 1896
Gatewood, Aubrey (P) LA-N 63-64, Cal-A 65, Atl-N 70
Gautreau, Doc (2) Phi-A 25, Bos-N 25-28
Gearin, Dinty (P) NY-N 23-24, Bos-N 24
Geier, Phil (O) Phi-N 1896-97, Cin-N 00, Phi-A 01, Mil-A 01, Bos-N 04
Geiger, Gary (O) Cle-A 58, Bos-A 59-65, Atl-N 66-67, Hou-N 69-70
Genewich, Joe (P) Bos-N 22-28, NY-N 28-30
Gentile, Sam (H) Bos-N 43
Gentry, Gary (P) NY-N 69-72, Atl-N 73-75
George, Lefty (P) StL-A 11, Cle-A 12, Cin-N 15, Bos-N 18
Geraghty, Ben (2) Bro-N 36, Bos-N 43-44
Gervais, Lefty (P) Bos-N 13
Getz, Gus (3) Bos-N 09-10, Bro-N 14-16, Cin-N 17, Cle-A 18, Pit-N 18
Getzien, Charlie (P) Det-N 1884-88, Ind-N 1889, Bos-N 1890-91, Cle-N 1891, StL-N 1892
Gibson, Frank (C) Det-A 13, Bos-N 21-27
Giggie, Bob (P) Mil-N 59-60, KC-A 60, 62
Gilbert, Larry (O) Bos-N 14-15
Gilbreath, Rod (2) Atl-N 72-78
Gillenwater, Carden (O) StL-N 40, Bro-N 43, Bos-N 45-46, Was-A 48
Ging, Billy (P) Bos-N 1899
Giovanola, Ed (2) Atl-N 95
Gladu, Roland (3) Bos-N 44
Glavine, Tom (P) Atl-N 87-95
Glenn, Ed (O) Ric-a 1884, Pit-a 1886, KC-a 1888, Bos-N 1888
Glossop, Al (2) NY-N 39-40, Bos-N 40, Phi-N 42, Bro-N 43, Chi-N 46
Goggin, Chuck (2) Pit-N 72-73, Atl-N 73, Bos-A 74
Goldsmith, Hal (P) Bos-N 26-28, StL-N 29
Gomez, Luis (S) Min-A 74-77, Tor-A 78-79, Atl-N 80-81
Gonder, Jesse (C) NY-A 60-61, Cin-N 62-63, NY-N 63-65, Mil-N 65, Pit-N 66-67
Gonzalez, Tony (O) Cin-N 60, Phi-N 60-68, SD-N 69, Atl-N 69-70, Cal-A 70-71
Gonzalez, Mike (C) Bos-N 12, Cin-N 14, StL-N 15-18, 24-25, 31-32, NY-N 19-21, Chi-N 25-29
Good, Gene (O) Bos-N 06
Good, Ralph (P) Bos-N 10

Joost, Eddie (3) Cin-N 36-37, 39-42, Bos-N 43, 45, Phi-A 47-54, Bos-A 55
Jordan, Buck (1) NY-N 27, 29, Was-A 31, Bos-N 32-37, Cin-N 37-38, Phi-N 38
Jorgensen, Mike (1) NY-N 68, 70-71, 80-83, Mon-N 72-77, Oak-A 77, Tex-A 78-79, Atl-N 83-84, StL-N 84-85
Justice, David (O) Atl-N 89-95
Kahle, Bob (H) Bos-N 38
Kahn, Owen (R) Bos-N 30
Kaiser, Al (O) Chi-N 11, Bos-N 11-12, Ind-F 14
Kamp, Ike (P) Bos-N 24-25
Kane, Tom (2) Bos-N 38
Karl, Andy (P) Bos-A 43, Phi-N 43-46, Bos-N 47
Keating, Ray (P) NY-A 12-16, 18, Bos-N 19
Keister, Bill (2) Bal-N 1896, 1899, Bos-N 1898, StL-N 00, Bal-A 01, Was-A 02, Phi-N 03
Kelleher, John (H) StL-N 12, Bro-N 16, Chi-N 21-23, Bos-N 24
Kelley, Joe (O) Bos-N 1891, 08, Pit-N 1892, Bal-N 1892-98, Bro-N 1899-1901, Bal-A 02, Cin-N 02-06
Kelley, Dick (P) Mil-N 64-65, Atl-N 66-68, SD-N 69, 71
Kelley, Tom (P) Cle-A 64-67, Atl-N 71-73
Kelly, Jim (O) Pit-N 14, Pit-F 15, Bos-N 18
Kelly, Joe (O) Pit-N 14, Chi-N 16, Bos-N 17-19
Kelly, King (C) Cin-N 1878-79, Chi-N 1880-86, Bos-N 1887-89, 1891-92, Bos-P 1890, 1891, Bos-a 1891, NY-N 1893
Kelly, Mike (O) Atl-N 94-95
Kelly, Roberto (O) NY-A 87-92, Cin-N 93-94, Atl-N 94, Mon-N 95, LA-N 95
Kenney, Art (P) Bos-N 38
Keough, Marty (1) Bos-A 56-60, Cle-A 60, Was-A 61, Cin-N 62-65, Atl-N 66, Chi-N 66
Kerfeld, Charlie (P) Hou-N 85-87, 90, Atl-N 90
Kerr, Buddy (S) NY-N 43-49, Bos-N 50-51
Kester, Rick (P) Atl-N 68-70
Kibbie, Hod (2) Bos-N 25
Kiley, John (P) Was-a 1884, Bos-N 1891
Killen, Frank (P) Mil-a 1891, Was-N 1892, 1898-99, Pit-N 1893-98, Bos-N 1899, Chi-N 00
King, Lee (H) Phi-A 16, Bos-N 19
King, Hal (C) Hou-N 67-68, Atl-N 70-71, Tex-A 72, Cin-N 73-74
Kirke, Jay (O) Det-A 10, Bos-N 11-13, Cle-A 14-15, NY-N 18
Kittridge, Malachi (C) Chi-N 1890-97, Lou-N 1898-99, Was-N 1899, Bos-N 01-03, Was-A 03-06, Cle-A 06
Klaus, Billy (S) Bos-N 52, Mil-N 53, Bos-A 55-58, Bal-A 59-60, Was-A 61, Phi-N 62-63
Klesko, Ryan (O) Atl-N 92-95
Klimchock, Lou (1) KC-A 58-61, Mil-N 62-65, Was-A 63, NY-N 66, Cle-A 68-70
Kline, Ron (P) Pit-N 52, 55-59, 68-69, StL-N 60, LA-N 61, Det-A 61-62, Was-A 63-66, Min-A 67, SF-N 69, Bos-A 69, Atl-N 70
Kline, Steve (P) NY-A 70-74, Cle-A 74, Atl-N 77
Kling, Johnny (C) Chi-N 00-08, 10-11, Bos-N 11-12, Cin-N 13
Klobedanz, Fred (P) Bos-N 1896-99, 02
Klopp, Stan (P) Bos-N 44
Klusman, Billy (2) Bos-N 1888, StL-a 1890
Kluttz, Clyde (C) Bos-N 42-45, NY-N 45-46, StL-N 46, Pit-N 47-48, StL-A 51, Was-A 51-52
Knetzer, Elmer (P) Bro-N 09-12, Pit-F 14-15, Bos-N 16, Cin-N 16-17
Knight, Jack (P) StL-N 22, Phi-N 25-26, Bos-N 27
Knothe, Fritz (3) Bos-N 32-33, Phi-N 33
Knotts, Joe (C) Bos-N 07
Kolb, Gary (O) StL-N 60, 62-63, Mil-N 64-65, NY-N 65, Pit-N 68-69
Komminsk, Brad (O) Atl-N 83-86, Mil-A 87, Cle-A 89, SF-N 90, Bal-A 90, Oak-A 91
Konetchy, Ed (1) StL-N 07-13, Pit-N 14, Pit-F 15, Bos-N 16-18, Bro-N 19-21, Phi-N 21
Konstanty, Jim (P) Cin-N 44, Bos-N 46, Phi-N 48-54, NY-A 54-56, StL-N 56
Kopacz, George (1) Atl-N 66, Pit-N 70
Kopf, Larry (2) Cle-A 13, Phi-A 14-15, Cin-N 16-17, 19-21, Bos-N 22-23
Koppe, Joe (S) Mil-N 58, Phi-N 59-61, LA-A 61-64, Cal-A 65
Koslo, Dave (P) NY-N 41-42, 46-53, Bal-A 54, Mil-N 54-55
Kowalik, Fabian (P) Chi-A 32, Chi-N 35-36, Phi-N 36, Bos-N 36
Kowitz, Brian (O) Atl-N 95
Kraft, Clarence (1) Bos-N 14
Krausse, Lew (P) KC-A 61, 64-67, Oak-A 68-69, Mil-N 70-71, Bos-A 72, StL-N 73, Atl-N 74

Kremers, Jimmy (C) Atl-N 90
Kroh, Rube (P) Bos-A 06-07, Chi-N 08-10, Bos-N 12
Krsnich, Mike (O) Mil-N 60, 62
Kruger, Art (H) Cin-N 07, Cle-A 10, 10, Bos-N 10, KC-F 14-15
Kuczek, Steve (H) Bos-N 49
Kuhns, Charlie (3) Pit-N 1897, Bos-N 1899
LaCorte, Frank (P) Atl-N 75-79, Hou-N 79-83, Cal-A 84
Lacy, Lee (2) LA-N 72-78, Atl-N 76, Pit-N 79-84, Bal-A 85-87
Ladd, Hi (O) Pit-N 1898, Bos-N 1898
Lake, Fred (C) Bos-N 1891, 1897, 10, Lou-N 1894, Pit-N 1898
Lakeman, Al (1) Cin-N 42-47, Phi-N 47-48, Bos-N 49, Det-A 54
LaManna, Frank (P) Bos-N 40-42
Lampe, Henry (P) Bos-N 1894, Phi-N 1895
Lane, Hunter (3) Bos-N 24
Lanfranconi, Walt (P) Chi-N 41, Bos-N 47
Lanning, Johnny (P) Bos-N 36-39, 47, Pit-N 40-43, 45-46
Lansing, Gene (P) Bos-N 22
Larker, Norm (1) LA-N 58-61, Hou-N 62, Mil-N 63, SF-N 63
Larsen, Swede (2) Bos-N 36
LaRussa, Tony (2) KC-A 63, Oak-A 68-71, Atl-N 71, Chi-N 73
Lary, Frank (P) Det-A 54-64, NY-N 64-65, Mil-N 64, Chi-A 65
Latham, Juice (1) Bos-n 1875, NH-n 1875, Lou-N 1877, Phi-a 1882, Lou-a 1883-84
Lau, Charlie (C) Det-A 56, 58-59, Mil-N 60-61, Bal-A 61-67, KC-A 63-64, Atl-N 67
Lauterborn, Bill (2) Bos-N 04-05
Lawson, Al (P) Bos-N 1890, Pit-N 1890
Lawson, Bob (P) Bos-N 1901, Bal-A 02
Leach, Freddy (O) Phi-N 23-28, NY-N 29-31, Bos-N 32
Leary, Jack (P) Bos-N 1880, Det-N 1881, Pit-a 1882, Bal-a 1882-83, Lou-a 1883, Alt-U 1884, CP-U 1884
Lee, Hal (O) Bro-N 30, Phi-N 31-33, Bos-N 33-36
Lee, Bill (P) Chi-N 34-43, 47, Phi-N 43-45, Bos-N 45-46
Lefler, Wade (H) Bos-N 24, Was-N 24
Legett, Lou (C) Bos-N 29, Bos-A 33-35
Leibrandt, Charlie (P) Cin-N 79-82, KC-A 84-89, Atl-N 90-92, Tex-A 93
Lemaster, Denny (P) Mil-N 62-65, Atl-N 66-67, Hou-N 68-71, Mon-N 72
Lemke, Mark (2) Atl-N 88-95
Leon, Max (P) Atl-N 73-78
Leonard, Andy (O) Oly-n 1871, Bos-n 1872-75, Bos-N 1876-78, Cin-N 1880
Leverett, Dixie (P) Chi-A 22-24, 26, Bos-N 29
Lewis, Ted (P) Bos-N 1896-1900, Bos-A 01
Lewis, Fred (O) Bos-N 1881, Phi-N 1883, StL-a 1883-84, StL-U 1884, StL-N 1885, Cin-a 1886
Lewis, Bill (C) StL-N 33, Bos-N 35-36
Liddle, Don (P) Mil-N 53, NY-N 54-56, StL-N 56
Liese, Fred (H) Bos-N 10
Lilliquist, Derek (P) Atl-N 89-90, SD-N 90-91, Cle-A 92-94, Bos-A 95
Linares, Rufino (O) Atl-N 81-82, 84, Cal-A 85
Lindaman, Vive (P) Bos-N 06-09
Lindemann, Ernie (P) Bos-N 07
Linden, Walt (C) Bos-N 50
Lindquist, Carl (P) Bos-N 43-44
Littlefield, Dick (P) Bos-A 50, Chi-A 51, Det-A 52, StL-A 52-53, Bal-A 54, Pit-N 54-56, StL-N 56, NY-N 56, Chi-N 57, Mil-N 58
Litwhiler, Danny (O) Phi-N 40-43, StL-N 43-44, 46, Bos-N 46-48, Cin-N 48-51
Livingston, Mickey (C) Was-A 38, Phi-N 41-43, Chi-N 43, 45-47, NY-N 47-49, Bos-N 49, Bro-N 51
Loane, Bob (O) Was-A 39, Bos-N 40
Logan, Johnny (S) Bos-N 51-52, Mil-N 53-61, Pit-N 61-63
Logan, Bob (P) Bro-N 35, Det-A 37, Chi-N 37-38, Cin-N 41, Bos-N 45
Lombardi, Ernie (C) Bro-N 31, Cin-N 32-41, Bos-N 42, NY-N 43-47
Long, Herman (S) KC-a 1889, Bos-N 1890-1902, NY-A 03, Det-A 03, Phi-N 04
Long, Red (P) Bos-N 02
Lopata, Stan (C) Phi-N 48-58, Mil-N 59-60
Lopez, Al (C) Bro-N 28, 30-35, Bos-N 36-40, Pit-N 40-46, Cle-A 47
Lopez, Javy (C) Atl-N 92-95

Lord, Bris (O) Phi-A 05-07, 10-12, Cle-A 09-10, Bos-N 13
Lovett, Tom (P) Phi-a 1885, Bro-a 1889, Bro-N 1890-91, 1893, Bos-N 1894
Low, Fletcher (3) Bos-N 15
Lowe, Bobby (2) Bos-N 1890-1901, Chi-N 02-03, Pit-N 04, Det-A 04-07
Lucas, Red (P) NY-A 23, Bos-N 24-25, Cin-N 26-33, Pit-N 34-38
Luecken, Rick (P) KC-A 89, Atl-N 90, Tor-A 90
Lum, Mike (O) Atl-N 67-75, 79-81, Cin-N 76-78, Chi-N 81
Luque, Dolf (P) Bos-N 14-15, Cin-N 18-29, Bro-N 30-31, NY-N 32-35
Lush, Billy (O) Was-N 1895-97, Bos-N 01-02, Det-A 03, Cle-A 04
Lyons, Al (P) NY-A 44, 46-47, Pit-N 47, Bos-N 48
Lyons, Steve (O) Bos-A 85-86, 91-93, Chi-A 86-90, Atl-N 92, Mon-N 92
MacFayden, Danny (P) Bos-A 26-32, NY-A 32-34, Cin-N 35, Bos-N 35-39, 43, Pit-N 40, Was-A 41
Macha, Mike (3) Atl-N 79, Tor-A 80
Mack, Joe (1) Bos-N 45
MacKenzie, Ken (P) Mil-N 60-61, NY-N 62-63, StL-N 63, SF-N 64, Hou-N 65
Macon, Max (1) StL-N 38, Bro-N 40, 42-43, Bos-N 44, 47
MacPherson, Harry (P) Bos-N 44
Madden, Kid (P) Bos-N 1887-89, Bos-P 1890, Bos-a 1891, Bal-a 1891
Madden, Tommy (O) Bos-N 06, NY-A 10
Maddox, Jerry (3) Atl-N 78
Maddux, Greg (P) Chi-N 86-92, Atl-N 93-95
Magee, Sherry (O) Phi-N 04-14, Bos-N 15-17, Cin-N 17-19
Maggert, Harl (O) Bos-N 38
Maguire, Freddie (2) NY-N 22-23, Chi-N 28, Bos-N 29-31
Mahler, Mickey (P) Atl-N 77-79, Pit-N 80, Cal-A 81-82, Mon-N 85, Det-A 85, Tex-A 86, Tor-A 86
Mahler, Rick (P) Atl-N 79-88, 91, Cin-N 89-90, Mon-N 91
Mahoney, Mike (P) Bos-N 1897, StL-N 1898
Mains, Willard (P) Chi-N 1888, Cin-a 1891, Mil-a 1891, Bos-N 1896
Majeski, Hank (3) Bos-N 39-41, NY-A 46, Phi-A 46-49, 51-52, Chi-A 50-51, Cle-A 52-55, Bal-A 55
Malarkey, John (P) Was-N 1894-96, Chi-N 1899, Bos-N 02-03
Malkmus, Bobby (2) Mil-N 57, Was-A 58-59, Phi-N 60-62
Mallon, Les (2) Phi-N 31-32, Bos-N 34-35
Maloney, Charlie (P) Bos-N 08
Mangum, Leo (P) Chi-A 24-25, NY-N 28, Bos-N 32-35
Mann, Kelly (C) Atl-N 89-90
Mann, Les (O) Bos-N 13-14, 19-20, 24-27, Chi-F 15, Chi-N 16-19, StL-N 21-23, Cin-N 23, NY-N 27-28
Manning, Jim (O) Bos-N 1884-85, Det-N 1885-87, KC-a 1889
Manning, Jack (O) Bos-n 1873, 1875, Bal-n 1874, Har-n 1874, Bos-N 1876, 1878, Cin-N 1877, 1880, Buf-N 1881, Phi-N 1883-85, Bal-a 1886
Manno, Don (O) Bos-N 40-41
Mantilla, Felix (2) Mil-N 56-61, NY-N 62, Bos-A 63-65, Hou-N 66
Manville, Dick (P) Bos-N 50, Chi-N 52
Marak, Paul (P) Atl-N 90
Maranville, Rabbit (S) Bos-N 12-20, 29-33, 35, Pit-N 21-24, Chi-N 25, Bro-N 26, StL-N 27-28
Marquard, Rube (P) NY-N 08-15, Bro-N 15-20, Cin-N 21, Bos-N 22-25
Marquez, Luis (O) Bos-N 51, Chi-N 54, Pit-N 54
Marriott, William (3) Chi-N 17, 20-21, Bos-N 25, Bro-N 26-27
Marshall, Mike (P) Det-A 67, Sea-A 69, Hou-N 70, Mon-N 70-73, LA-N 74-76, Atl-N 76-77, Tex-A 77, Min-A 78-80, NY-N 81
Marshall, Willard (O) NY-N 42, 46-49, Bos-N 50-52, Cin-N 52-53, Chi-A 54-55
Marshall, Doc (C) Phi-N 04, NY-N 04, 04, 06, Bos-N 04, StL-N 06-08, Chi-N 08, Bro-N 09
Martel, Doc (1) Phi-N 09, Bos-N 10
Martin, Billy (H) NY-A 50-53, 55-57, KC-A 57, Det-A 58, Cle-A 59, Cin-N 60, Mil-N 61, Min-A 61
Martin, Jack (3) NY-A 12, Bos-N 14, Phi-N 14
Martin, Ray (P) Bos-N 43, 47-48
Martin, Billy (S) Bos-N 14

Ruthven, Dick (P) Phi-N 73-75, 78-83, Atl-N 76-78, Chi-N 83-86
Ryan, Connie (2) NY-N 42, Bos-N 43-44, 46-50, Cin-N 50-51, 54, Phi-N 52-53, Chi-A 53
Ryan, Cyclone (P) NY-a 1887, Bos-N 1891
Ryan, Jack (C) Lou-a 1889-91, Bos-N 1894-96, Bro-N 1898, Bal-N 1899, StL-N 01-03, Was-A 12-13
Ryan, Rosy (P) NY-N 19-24, Bos-N 25-26, NY-A 28, Bro-N 33
Sadecki, Ray (P) StL-N 60-66, 75, SF-N 66-69, NY-N 70-74, 77, Atl-N 75, KC-A 75-76, Mil-A 76
Sadowski, Ed (C) Bos-A 60, LA-A 61-63, Atl-N 66
Sadowski, Bob (P) Mil-N 63-65, Bos-A 66
Sain, Johnny (P) Bos-N 42, 46-51, NY-A 51-55, KC-A 55
St.Claire, Ebba (C) Bos-N 51-52, Mil-N 53, NY-N 54
St.Claire, Randy (P) Mon-N 84-88, Cin-N 88, Min-A 89, Atl-N 91-92, Tor-A 94
Salkeld, Bill (C) Pit-N 45-47, Bos-N 48-49, Chi-A 50
Salvo, Manny (P) NY-N 39, Bos-N 40-43, 43, Phi-N 43
Sample, Bill (O) Tex-A 78-84, NY-A 85, Atl-N 86
Samuel, Amado (S) Mil-N 62-63, NY-N 64
Sanders, Deion (O) NY-A 89-90, Atl-N 91-94, Cin-N 94-95, SF-N 95
Sanders, Ray (1) StL-N 42-45, Bos-N 46, 48-49
Sandlock, Mike (3) Bos-N 42, 44, Bro-N 45-46, Pit-N 53
Santorini, Al (P) Atl-N 68, SD-N 69-71, StL-N 71-73
Sauer, Ed (O) Chi-N 43-45, StL-N 49, Bos-N 49
Sawatski, Carl (C) Chi-N 48, 50, 53, Chi-A 54, Mil-N 57-58, Phi-N 58-59, StL-N 60-63
Scalzi, Johnny (H) Bos-N 31
Scarsella, Les (1) Cin-N 35-37, 39, Bos-N 40
Schacht, Sid (P) StL-A 50-51, Bos-N 51
Schacker, Hal (P) Bos-N 45
Schafer, Harry (3) Bos-n 1871-75, Bos-N 1876-78
Schellhase, Al (C) Bos-N 1890, Lou-a 1891
Schmidt, Butch (1) NY-A 09, Bos-N 13-15
Schmidt, Jason (P) Atl-N 95
Schneider, Dan (P) Mil-N 63-64, Atl-N 66, Hou-N 67, 69
Schoendienst, Red (2) StL-N 45-56, 61-63, NY-N 56-57, Mil-N 57-60
Schreiber, Hank (3) Chi-A 14, Bos-N 17, Cin-N 19, NY-N 21, Chi-N 26
Schueler, Ron (P) Atl-N 72-73, Phi-N 74-76, Min-A 77, Chi-A 78-79
Schuler, Dave (P) Cal-A 79-80, Atl-N 85
Schulmerich, Wes (O) Bos-N 31-33, Phi-N 33-34, Cin-N 34
Schulte, Johnny (C) StL-A 23, 32, StL-N 27, Phi-N 28, Chi-N 29, Bos-N 32
Schulte, Jack (S) Bos-N 06
Schultz, Joe (2) Bos-N 12-13, Bro-N 15, Chi-N 15, Pit-N 16, StL-N 19-24, Phi-N 24-25, Cin-N 25
Schuster, Bill (3) Pit-N 37, Bos-N 39, Chi-N 43-45
Schwall, Don (P) Bos-A 61-62, Pit-N 63-66, Atl-N 66-67
Schwind, Art (3) Bos-N 12
Scott, Jack (P) Pit-N 16, Bos-N 17, 19-21, Cin-N 22, NY-N 22-23, 25-26, 28-29, Phi-N 27
Seibold, Socks (P) Phi-A 15-17, 19, Bos-N 29-33
Sellers, Rube (O) Bos-N 10
Sexton, Frank (P) Bos-N 1895
Seymour, Cy (O) NY-N 1896-1900, 06-10, Bal-A 01-02, Cin-N 02-06, Bos-N 13
Shannon, Joe (O) Bos-N 15
Shannon, Red (2) Bos-N 15, Phi-A 17-21, Bos-A 19, Was-A 20, Chi-N 26
Sharpe, Bud (1) Bos-N 05, 10, Pit-N 10
Sharperson, Mike (3) Tor-A 87, LA-N 87-93, Atl-N 95
Shaw, Al (C) Det-A 01, Bos-A 07, Chi-A 08, Bos-N 09
Shaw, Bob (P) Det-A 57-58, Chi-A 58-61, KC-A 61, Mil-N 62-63, SF-N 64-66, NY-N 66-67, Chi-N 67
Shay, Marty (2) Chi-N 16, Bos-N 24
Shean, Dave (2) Phi-A 06, Phi-N 08-09, Bos-N 09-10, 12, Chi-N 11, Cin-N 17, Bos-A 18-19
Shearer, Ray (O) Mil-N 57
Sheely, Earl (1) Chi-A 21-27, Pit-N 29, Bos-N 31
Shemo, Steve (2) Bos-N 44-45
Sherdel, Bill (P) StL-N 18-30, 32, Bos-N 30-32
Shields, Steve (P) Atl-N 85-86, KC-A 86, Sea-A 87, NY-A 88, Min-A 89
Shires, Art (1) Chi-A 28-30, Was-A 30, Bos-N 32

Shoffner, Milt (P) Cle-A 29-31, Bos-N 37-39, Cin-N 39-40
Shoun, Clyde (P) Chi-N 35-37, StL-N 38-42, Cin-N 42-44, 46-47, Bos-N 47-49, Chi-A 49
Shupe, Vince (1) Bos-N 45
Siemer, Oscar (C) Bos-N 25-26
Simmons, Al (O) Phi-A 24-32, 40-41, 44, Chi-A 33-35, Det-A 36, Was-A 37-38, Bos-N 39, Cin-N 39, Bos-A 43
Simmons, Ted (1) StL-N 68-80, Mil-N 81-85, Atl-N 86-88
Sinatro, Matt (C) Atl-N 81-84, Oak-A 87-88, Det-A 89, Sea-A 90-92
Siner, Hosea (3) Bos-N 09
Singleton, Elmer (P) Bos-N 45-46, Pit-N 47-48, Was-A 50, Chi-N 57-59
Sisk, Doug (P) NY-N 82-87, Bal-A 88, Atl-N 90-91
Sisler, George (1) StL-A 15-22, 24-27, Was-A 28, Bos-N 28-30
Sisti, Sibby (2) Bos-N 39-42, 46-52, Mil-N 53-54
Skok, Craig (P) Bos-A 73, Tex-A 76, Atl-N 78-79
Slagle, Jimmy (O) Was-N 1899, Phi-N 00-01, Bos-N 01, Chi-N 02-08
Slaughter, Enos (O) StL-N 38-42, 46-53, NY-A 54-59, KC-A 55-56, Mil-N 59
Sleater, Lou (P) StL-A 50-52, Was-A 52, KC-A 55, Mil-N 56, Det-A 57-58, Bal-A 58
Small, Hank (1) Atl-N 78
Smalley, Roy (S) Chi-N 48-53, Mil-N 54, Phi-N 55-58
Smith, Edgar (O) Bos-N 1883
Smith, Pop (2) Cin-N 1880, Cle-N 1881, Buf-N 1881, Wor-N 1881, Phi-a 1882, Lou-a 1882, Col-a 1883-84, Pit-a 1885-86, Pit-N 1887-89, Bos-N 1889-90, Was-a 1891
Smith, Earl (C) NY-N 19-23, Bos-N 23-24, Pit-N 24-28, StL-N 28-30
Smith, Elmer (O) Cin-a 1886-89, Pit-N 1892-97, 01, Cin-N 1898-1900, NY-N 00, Bos-N 01
Smith, Fred (3) Bos-N 13, Buf-F 14-15, Bro-F 15, StL-N 17
Smith, Harry (C) Phi-A 01, Pit-N 02-07, Bos-N 08-10
Smith, Jack (O) StL-N 15-26, Bos-N 26-29
Smith, Jack (P) LA-N 62-63, Mil-N 64
Smith, Stub (S) Bos-N 1898
Smith, Red (3) Bro-N 11-14, Bos-N 14-19
Smith, Jimmy (2) Chi-F 14-15, Bal-F 15, Pit-N 16, NY-N 17, Bos-N 18, Cin-N 19, Phi-N 21-22
Smith, Dwight (O) Chi-N 89-93, Cal-A 94, Bal-A 94, Atl-N 95
Smith, Ken (1) Atl-N 81-83
Smith, Lonnie (O) Phi-N 78-81, StL-N 82-85, KC-A 85-87, Atl-N 88-92, Pit-N 93, Bal-A 93-94
Smith, Pete (P) Atl-N 87-93, NY-N 94, Cin-N 95
Smith, Bob (P) Bos-N 23-30, 33-37, Cin-N 31-32, Cin-N 33
Smith, Tom (P) Bos-N 1894, Phi-N 1895, Lou-N 1896, StL-N 1898
Smith, Zane (P) Atl-N 84-89, Mon-N 89-90, Pit-N 90-94, Bos-A 95
Smoltz, John (P) Atl-N 88-95
Snodgrass, Fred (O) NY-N 08-15, Bos-N 15-16
Snyder, Pop (C) Was-n 1873, Bal-n 1874, Phi-n 1875, Lou-N 1876-77, Bos-N 1878-79, 1881, Cin-a 1882-86, Cle-a 1887-88, Cle-N 1889, Cle-P 1890, Was-a 1891
Solomon, Eddie (P) LA-N 73-74, Chi-N 75, StL-N 76, Atl-N 77-79, Pit-N 80-82, Chi-A 82
Sommers, Pete (C) NY-a 1887, Bos-N 1888, Chi-N 1889, Ind-N 1889, NY-N 1890, Cle-N 1890
Sosa, Elias (P) SF-N 72-74, StL-N 75, Atl-N 75-76, LA-N 76-77, Oak-A 78, Mon-N 79-81, Det-A 82, SD-N 83
Southworth, Bill (3) Mil-N 64
Southworth, Billy (O) Cle-A 13, 15, Pit-N 18-20, Bos-N 21-23, NY-N 24-26, StL-N 26-27, 29
Sowders, Bill (P) Bos-N 1888-89, Pit-N 1889-90
Spahn, Warren (P) Bos-N 42, 46-52, Mil-N 53-64, NY-N 65, SF-N 65
Spalding, Al (P) Bos-n 1871-75, Chi-N 1876-78
Spangler, Al (O) Mil-N 59-61, Hou-N 62-65, Cal-A 65-66, Chi-N 67-71
Speck, Cliff (P) Atl-N 86
Spencer, Chet (O) Bos-N 06
Sperber, Ed (O) Bos-N 24-25
Spikes, Charlie (O) NY-A 72, Cle-A 73-77, Det-A 78, Atl-N 79-80
Spohrer, Al (C) NY-N 28, Bos-N 28-35
Spratt, Harry (S) Bos-N 11-12
Staehle, Marv (2) Chi-A 64-67, Mon-N 69-70, Atl-N 71

Stafford, General (O) Buf-P 1890, NY-N 1893-97, Lou-N 1897-98, Bos-N 1898-99, Was-N 1899
Stahl, Chick (O) Bos-N 1897-1900, Bos-A 01-06
Staley, Harry (P) Pit-N 1888-89, 1891, Pit-P 1890, Bos-N 1891-94, StL-N 1895
Stanky, Eddie (2) Chi-N 43-44, Bro-N 44-47, Bos-N 48-49, NY-N 50-51, StL-N 52-53
Stanley, Joe (O) Was-N 1897, Was-A 02, 05-06, Bos-N 03-04, Chi-N 09
Stanton, Mike (P) Atl-N 89-95, Bos-A 95
Starr, Charlie (2) StL-A 05, Pit-N 08, Bos-N 09, Phi-N 09
Starr, Ray (P) StL-N 32, NY-N 33, Bos-N 33, Cin-N 41-43, Pit-N 44-45, Chi-N 45
Steinfeldt, Harry (3) Cin-N 1898-1905, Chi-N 06-10, Bos-N 11
Stem, Fred (1) Bos-N 08-09
Stemmeyer, Bill (P) Bos-N 1885-87, Cle-a 1888
Stengel, Casey (O) Bro-N 12-17, Pit-N 18-19, Phi-N 20-21, NY-N 21-23, Bos-N 24-25
Stewart, Joe (P) Bos-N 04
Stivetts, Jack (P) StL-a 1889-91, Bos-N 1892-98, Cle-N 1899
Stocksdale, Otis (P) Was-N 1893-95, Bos-N 1895, Bal-N 1896
Stone, George (P) Atl-N 67-72, NY-N 73-75
Stout, Allyn (P) StL-N 31-33, Cin-N 33-34, NY-N 35, Bos-N 43
Stovey, Harry (O) Wor-N 1880-82, Phi-a 1883-89, Bos-P 1890, Bos-N 1891-92, Bal-N 1892-93, Bro-N 1893
Strand, Paul (P) Bos-N 13-15, Phi-A 24
Street, Gabby (C) Cin-N 04-05, 05, Bos-N 05, Was-A 08-11, NY-A 12, StL-N 31
Streit, Oscar (P) Bos-N 1899, Cle-A 02
Strincevich, Nick (P) Bos-N 40-41, Pit-N 41-42, 44-48, Phi-N 48
Stripp, Joe (3) Cin-N 28-31, Bro-N 32-37, StL-N 38, Bos-N 38
Strobel, Allie (2) Bos-N 05-06
Stryker, Dutch (P) Bos-N 24, Bro-N 26
Stultz, George (P) Bos-N 1894
Sturgeon, Bobby (2) Chi-N 40-42, 46-47, Bos-N 48
Sullivan, Andy (S) Bos-N 04
Sullivan, Denny (C) Pro-N 1879, Bos-N 1880
Sullivan, Jim (P) Bos-N 1891, 1895-97, Col-a 1891
Sullivan, John (O) Bos-N 20-21, Chi-N 21
Sullivan, Joe (P) Det-A 35-36, Bos-N 39-41, Pit-N 41
Sullivan, Marty (O) Chi-N 1887-88, Ind-N 1889, Bos-N 1890-91, Cle-N 1891
Sullivan, Mike (P) Was-N 1889, 1894, Chi-N 1890, Phi-a 1891, NY-N 1891, 1896-97, Cin-N 1892-93, Cle-N 1894-95, Bos-N 1898-99
Sullivan, Billy (C) Bos-N 1899-1900, Chi-A 01-12, 14, Det-A 16
Surkont, Max (P) Chi-A 49, Bos-N 50-52, Mil-N 53, Pit-N 54-56, StL-N 56, NY-N 56-57
Sutcliffe, Butch (C) Bos-N 38
Sutter, Bruce (P) Chi-N 76-80, StL-N 81-84, Atl-N 85-86, 88
Sutton, Ezra (3) Cle-n 1871-72, Ath-n 1873-75, Phi-N 1876, Bos-N 1877-88
Sweasy, Charlie (2) Oly-n 1871, Cle-n 1872, Bos-n 1873, Bal-n 1874, Atl-n 1874, RS-n 1875, Cin-N 1876, Pro-N 1878
Sweeney, Bill (2) Chi-N 07, 14, Bos-N 07-13
Swift, Bill (P) Pit-N 32-39, Bos-N 40, Bro-N 41, Chi-A 43
Taber, John (P) Bos-N 1890
Talcott, Roy (P) Bos-N 43
Tanner, Chuck (O) Mil-N 55-57, Chi-N 57-58, Cle-A 59-60, LA-A 61-62
Tarasco, Tony (O) Atl-N 93-94, Mon-N 95
Tate, Pop (C) Bos-N 1885-88, Bal-a 1889-90
Taylor, Ben (1) StL-A 51, Det-A 52, Mil-N 55
Taylor, Ed (3) Bos-N 26
Taylor, Zack (C) Bro-N 20-25, 35, Bos-N 26-29, NY-N 27, Chi-N 29-33, NY-A 34
Taylor, Hawk (O) Mil-N 57-58, 61-63, NY-N 64-67, Cal-A 67, KC-A 69-70
Tenney, Fred (1) Bos-N 1894-1907, 11, NY-N 08-09
Tepedino, Frank (1) NY-A 67, 69-72, Mil-A 71, Atl-N 73-75
Terry, Zeb (S) Chi-A 16-17, Bos-N 18, Pit-N 19, Chi-N 20-22
Theiss, Duane (P) Atl-N 77-78
Thevenow, Tommy (S) StL-N 24-28, Phi-N 29-30, Pit-N 31-35, 38, Cin-N 36, Bos-N 37
Thiel, Bert (P) Bos-N 52

CHAPTER 7

The Player Register

The Braves Player Register consists of the central batting, baserunning, and fielding statistics of every man who has batted for the team since 1871, excepting those men who were primarily pitchers. A pitcher's complete batting record, however, is included for those pitchers who also, over the course of their careers, played in 100 or more games at another position—including pinch hitter—or played in more than half of their total major league games at a position other than pitcher, or played more games at a position other than pitcher in at least one year. (Pitcher batting is also expressed in Batting Wins in the Pitcher Batting column of the Braves Pitcher Register.)

The players are listed alphabetically by surname and, when more than one player bears the name, alphabetically by *given* name—not by "use name," by which we mean the name that may have been applied to him during his playing career. This is the standard method of alphabetizing used in other biographical reference works, and in the case of baseball it makes it easier to find a lesser-known player with a common surname like Smith or Johnson. On the whole, we have been conservative in ascribing nicknames, doing so only when the player was in fact known by that name during his playing days.

Each page of the Player Register is topped at the corner by a finding aid: in capital letters, the surname of, first, the player whose entry heads up the page and, second, the player whose entry concludes it. Another finding aid is the use of boldface numerals to indicate a league-leading total in those categories in which a player is truly attempting to excel (no boldface is given to the "leaders" in batter strikeouts, times caught stealing, at bats, or games played). An additional finding aid is an asterisk alongside the team for which a player appeared in postseason competition, thus making for easy cross-reference to the earlier section on postseason play. Additional symbols denote All Star Game selection and/or play; these appear to the right of the team/league column. Condensed type appears occasionally throughout this section; it has no special significance but is designed simply to accommodate unusually wide figures, such as the 4.000 slugging average of a man who, in his only at bat of the year, hit a home run.

The record for each man who played in more than one season as a Brave is given in a line for each season, plus a career total line and a Braves total line. Refer to the preceding Player Index, and ultimately to *Total Baseball*, for complete seasonal data for Braves when they wore the uniforms of other clubs. If a man played for another team in addition to the Braves, only his total for the Braves is shown in a given year. And a man who played in only one year will have no additional career total line, since it would be identical to his seasonal listing.

Batting records for the National Association are included in The Player Register because the editors, like most baseball historians, regard it as a major league, inasmuch as it was the only professional league of its day and supplied the National League of 1876 with most of its players. In *Total Braves*, we benefit from the SABR research project which to date has produced extra-base hits, corrected averages, walks, and some stolen bases, strikeouts, and other data heretofore unavailable; fielding data for the NA is as yet not available. Unless Major League Baseball reverses the position it adopted in 1969 and restores the NA to official major-league status, we will continue the practice of carrying separate totals lines for the National Association years rather than integrating them into the career marks of those players whose major league tenures began before 1876 and concluded in that year or later.

Gaps remain elsewhere in the official record of baseball and in the ongoing process of sabermetric reconstruction. The reader will note occasional blank elements in biographical lines, or in single-season columns; these are not typographical lapses but signs that the information does not exist or has not yet been found. In the totals lines of many players, an underlined figure indicates that the total reflects partial data, such as caught stealing for a man whose career covers the National League of 1918–1930 (during which this data was available only for 1920–1925), or batter strikeouts for a man whose career spanned both sides of the year 1909.

For a discussion of which data is missing for particular years, see "The History of Major League Baseball Statistics" in *Total Baseball*. Here is a quick summation of the missing data:

Hit batters, 1897–1908 NL/AL, 5 percent missing;

Caught stealing, 1886–1914, 1916 for players with fewer than 20 stolen bases, 1917–1919, 1926–1950 NL; 1886–1891 AA; 1890 PL; 1901–1913, 1916 for players with fewer than 20 stolen bases, 1917–1919 AL (1927 data, missing from the first edition, is now 90 percent complete); 1914–15 FL;

Sacrifice hit, 1908–1930, 1939 (in these years fly balls scoring runners counted as sacrifice hits, and in 1927–1930 fly balls advancing runners to any base counted as sacrifices);

Sacrifice fly, 1908–1930, 1939 (counted but inseparable from sacrifice hits), 1940–1953 (not counted);

Runs batted in, 1882–1887, 1890 AA; 1884 UA;

Strikeouts for batters, 1882–1888, 1890 AA; 1884 UA; 1897–1909 NL; 1901-1912 AL.

For a key to the team and league abbreviations used in the Player Register, flip to the last page of this volume. For a guide to the other procedures and abbreviations employed in the Player Register, review the comments on the prodigiously extended playing record below.

Looking at the biographical line for any player, we see first his use name in full capitals, then his given name and nickname (and any other name he may have used or been born with, such as the matronymic of a Latin American player). His date and place of birth follow "b" and his date

YEAR	TM/L	G	AB	R	H	2B	3B	HR	RBI	BB	SO	AVG	OBP	SLG	PRO+	BR/A	SB	CS	SBR	FA	FR	G/POS	TPR
■ KID DE LEON	Ponce de Leon, Juan "Castilian Kid" (also played in 1874 as Kid Madrid) b: 3/13/1460, Madrid, Spain d: 2/25/1968, St. Augustine, Fl. BR/TR, 5'11", 173 lbs. Deb: 5/21/1874 FMUCH																						
1874	Bos-n	52	277	73	94	7	4	1	14	2		.339	.342	.400	111	4						*2-52	0.2
1875	Bos-n	2	3	1	1	0	0	0		0		.333	.333	.333	95	0						/S-2	0.0
1883	Bos-N	28	121	12	33	2	1	1		8		.273	.318	.331	101	2				.901	0	C-16,O-10/S	0.0
1884	Bos-N	87	375	76	108	12	5	2		11		.288	.309	.358	128	-0	0			.914	0	1-63,O-15/C	0.9
1890	Bos-N	1	1	1	0	0	0	0	0	0		—	—	—	—	0	0			.000	0	/2-1	0.0
1908	Bos-N	9	31	5	9	3	0	0	2	0		.290	.290	.387	113	0	0			.899	-1	/3-8	0.0
1909	Bos-N	148	541	73	165	27	19	4	85	26		.305	.343	.447	146	26	20			.920	-5	*3-141	3.0
1910	Bos-N	146	561	83	159	25	15	2	75	34		.283	.329	.392	123	13	21			.934	3	*3-144	2.4
1911	Bos-N	148	592	96	198	40	4	11	115	50		.334	.379	.505	157	38	38			.912	-8	*3-147	3.3
1912	Bos-N	149	577	116	200	40	21	10	130	50		.347	.404	.541	171	50	40			.930	9	*3-149	5.4
1913	Bos-N	149	564	116	190	34	9	12	117	63	31	.337	.413	.493	171	48	34			.927	7	*3-148	6.1
1916	Bos-N	100	360	46	97	23	2	10	52	36	30	.269	.344	.428	130	12	15			.931	3	3-98	2.1
1917	Bos-N	146	553	57	156	24	2	6	71	48	27	.282	.345	.365	109	6	18			.940	11	*3-145	2.7
1918	Bos-N	126	504	65	154	24	5	6	62	38	13	.306	.357	.409	138	20	8			.943	11	*3-122	3.4
1956	*Mil-N☆	141	567	70	166	22	1	10	83	44	18	.293	.346	.388	100	-0	13	6	0	.944	-2	3-140	0.9
1957	*Mil-N★	94	330	46	97	16	2	9	71	26	12	.294	.353	.436	98	-2	8	5	-1	.955	13	3-92	1.6
1966	*Atl-N†	69	234	30	65	12	3	7	36	15	14	.278	.327	.444	98	-2	1	3	-2	.940	-8	3-67	-0.4
Total	2 n	54	280	74	95	7	4	1	14	2		.339	.348	.404	110	4						*2-52/S-2	0.2
Total	21	1694	6489	981	1983	329	100	100	992	502	184	.306	.354	.446	130	246	235	34		.938	41	*3-1409,1-126/CSO2R	35.6
Team	15	1541	5911	892	1797	304	89	90	899	449	145	.304	.353	.448	132	210	216	14		.937	32	*3-1257,1-126/CSO2R	31.4

and place of death follow "d." Years through 1900 are expressed fully, in four digits, and years after 1900 are expressed in their last two digits.

Then comes the player's manner of batting and throwing, abbreviated for a lefthanded batter who throws right as BL/TR (a switch-hitter would be shown as BB for "bats both" and a switch thrower as TB for "throws both").

Next, and for most players last, is the player's debut date in the major leagues.

Some players continue in major league baseball after their playing days are through, as managers, coaches, or even umpires. A player whose biographical line concludes with an M served as a major league manager, not necessarily with the Braves; one whose line bears a C served as a major league coach; and one with a U served as a umpire. (In the last case we have placed a U on the biographical line only for those players who umpired in at least six games in a year, for in the nineteenth century—and especially in the years of the National Association—literally hundreds of players were pressed into service as umpires for a game or two. It would be misleading to accord such players the same code we give to Bob Emslie or Babe Pinelli.) The select few who have been enshrined in the Baseball Hall of Fame at Cooperstown, NY, are noted with an H. Also on this line is an F to denote family connection—father-son-grandson or brother.

The explanations for the statistical column heads follow; for more technical information about formulas and calculations, see the next-to-last page. The vertical rules in the column-header line separate the stats into seven logical groupings: year, team, league; fundamental counting stats for batters; hits and plate appearances broken out into their component counting stats; basic calculated averages; sabermetric figures of more complex calculation; baserunning stats; fielding stats and Total Player Rating.

Newly found hit-by-pitch data for batters in the 1897-1908 period is reflected in their on base percentages. We have also made an upward adjustment to overall league performance in the Federal League of 1914-15 and the Union Association of 1884 (thus lowering individual ratings), because while both leagues are regarded as major leagues, there can be no doubt that their caliber of play was not equivalent to that in the rival leagues of those years. Suffice it to say here that league at bats were reduced to 80 percent for the UA and 90 percent for the FL. Few Braves extended their careers into the UA or FL.

YEAR   Year of play

*   Denotes postseason play, World Series or League Championship Series

TM/L   Team and League

★   Named to All Star Game, played

☆   Named to All Star Game, did not play

†   Named to All Star Game, replaced because of injury

G   Games

AB   At-bats

R   Runs

H   Hits (Bases on balls were counted as hits by scorers in 1887, but in *Total Braves* they are not figured as times at bat, nor as hits.)

2B   Doubles

3B   Triples

HR   Home Runs

RBI   Runs Batted In

BB   Bases on Balls (Bases on balls were counted as outs by scorers in 1876, but in *Total Braves* they are not figured as times at bat nor as outs.)

SO   Strikeouts

AVG   Batting Average (Figured as hits over at-bats; mathematically meaningless averages created through a division by zero are rendered as dashes; see Kid De Leon's entry for 1908. League leaders in this category, as in others in the Player Register, are noted by bold type. However, some bold-face leaders in batting average will have lower marks than other batters who are not credited with having won a championship; for a full explanation of the reasoning for this anomaly, see "The History of Major League Baseball Statistics" in *Total Baseball*.

OBP   On Base Percentage (See comments for AVG)

SLG   Slugging Average

PRO⁺ Production Plus, or Adjusted Production (On Base Percentage plus Slugging Average, normalized to league average and adjusted for home-park factor.) See comments for /A.

BR/A Batting Runs (Linear Weights measure of runs contributed beyond what a league-average batter or team might have contributed, defined as zero. Occasionally the curious figure of -0 will appear in this column, or in the columns of other Linear Weights measures of batting, baserunning, fielding, and the TPR. This "negative zero" figure signifies a run contribution that falls below the league average, but to so small a degree that it cannot be said to have cost the team a run. The "/A" signifies that the measure has been adjusted for home-park factor and normalized to league average. A mark of 100 is a league-average performance. Pitcher batting is removed from all league batting statistics before normalization, for a variety of reasons. Three-year averages are employed for batting park factors. If a team moved or the park changed dramatically, then two-year averages are employed; if the park was used for only one year, then of course only that run-scoring data is used.)

SB   Stolen Bases (for 1886 to the present, plus partial data for the NA years, 1871-75.)

CS   Caught Stealing (Available 1915, 1916 for players with 20 or more stolen bases, 1920–1925, 1951–date NL; 1914–1915, 1916 for players with 20 or more stolen bases, 1920 to date AL with scattered data still missing from 1927.)

SBA   Stolen Base Average (Stolen bases divided by attempts; availability dependent upon CS as shown above.)

SBR   Stolen Base Runs (This is a Linear Weights measure of runs contributed *beyond* what a league-average base stealer might have gained, defined as zero and calculated on the basis of a 66.7 percent success rate, which computer simulations have shown to be the break-even point beyond which stolen bases have positive run value to the team. The presence of a figure in the SBR column in the Player Register is dependent upon the availability of CS as shown above. Lifetime Stolen Base Runs are not totaled where data is incomplete, but seasonal SBRs are reflected in the seasonal Total Player Ratings, which in turn are added to form the lifetime Total Player Rating.)

FA   Fielding Average, often called Fielding Percentage as well (putouts plus assists divided by putouts plus assists plus errors, here calculated only for the position at which a man played the most games in a season or career.)

FR   Fielding Runs (The Linear Weights measure of runs saved *beyond* what a league-average player at that position might have saved, defined as zero; this stat is calculated to take account of the particular demands of the different positions; see next-to-last page for formulas.)

G/POS Positions played (This is a ranking from left to right by frequency of the positions played in the field or at designated hitter. An asterisk to the left of the position indicates, generally, that in a given year the man played about two-thirds of his team's scheduled games at that position; more precisely, it is figured at 20 games in 1871, 30 in 1872, 35 in 1873, 40 in 1874, and 50 in 1875; two-thirds of the scheduled games in 1876-1900, and 100 or more games since. When a slash separates positions, the man played those positions listed to the left of the slash in 10 or more games and the positions to the right of the slash in fewer than 10 games. If there is no slash, he played all positions listed in 10 or more games. For the lifetime line, the asterisk signifies 1,000 games and the slash marks a dividing point of 100 games. A player's POS column will list him as a pinch runner or pinch hitter in only those years in which he appeared at no other position. New to this edition are listings of the number of games played at the individual's two most common positions. The positions and their abbreviations are)

1:	First base	P:	Pitcher
2:	Second base	D:	Designated hitter
S:	Shortstop	R:	Runner (pinch)
3:	Third base	H:	Hitter (pinch)
O:	Outfield	M:	Manager (playing)
C:	Catcher		

TPR   Total Player Rating (This is the sum of a player's Adjusted Batting Runs, Fielding Runs, and Base Stealing Runs, minus his positional adjustment, all divided by the Runs Per Win factor for that year—generally around 10, historically in the 9–11 range. In the lifetime line, the TPR is the sum of the seasonal TPRs. For men who were primarily pitchers but whose extent of play at other positions warrants a listing in the Player Register as well as the Pitcher Register, the TPR may be listed as 0.0; this signifies that their batting records are summed up in the Total Pitcher Index [TPI] column of the Pitcher Register.) A broader and more sophisticated computation of the positional adjustment to Batting Runs has improved the accuracy and reasonableness of the method, by which the TPR of those who play skill positions like shortstop and second base tend to be boosted and the TPR of the sluggers who customarily play first base and left field are generally diminished. Because games in left, center, and right fields are now available for all outfielders, center fielders no longer need be compared to an average of the regular center fielders and now may be set against all the men who played center, thus tending to elevate their Fielding Runs. Because Hit Batsmen data is now available for the 1903–1908 period, plus considerable data for the years 1897–1902, men like Frank Chance, who was hit over 100 times in his career, increase their Batter Ratings perceptibly. And for players who were both batters and pitchers, the method of allocating Wins between TPR and TPI (Total Pitcher Index) was improved. Previously, if a pitcher pitched in over half his games, all his batting was included with his pitcher rating (TPI); if he pitched in less than half his games, his Batting Wins were thrown over to his batter rating (TPR), with his TPI including only his Pitching Wins and Pitcher Defense. The new method prorates batting proportionally with the number of games pitched. In addition, fielding ratings at nonpitching positions for players who pitched in over half their games, previously omitted, are now part of the Total Baseball Ranking.

Total   For players whose careers include play in the National Association as well as other major leagues, two totals are given, as described above and as illustrated in Kid De Leon's record, where the record of his years in the National Association is shown alongside the notation "Total 2 n," where *2* stands for the number of years totaled and *n* stands for National Association. For players whose careers began in 1876 or later, the lifetime record is shown alongside the notation "Total x," where *x* stands for the number of post-1875 years totaled. Note the underlined entries in the record for Kid De Leon, reflecting the partial data for RBI, batter strikeouts, stolen bases, and times caught stealing.

Team   The totals for a player while he was a Brave, from the Boston Red Stockings of 1876 onward. In cases where a player served two or more teams in the NA, he will receive an additional Team line, such as "Team 2n."

■ **HANK AARON** Aaron, Henry Louis "Hammerin' Hank" b: 2/5/34, Mobile, Ala. BR/TR, 6', 180 lbs. Deb: 4/13/54 FH

YEAR	TM/L	G	AB	R	H	2B	3B	HR	RBI	BB	SO	AVG	OBP	SLG	PRO+	BR/A	SB	CS	SBR	FA	FR	G/POS	TPR
1954	Mil-N	122	468	58	131	27	6	13	69	28	39	.280	.325	.447	105	1	2	2	-1	.970	-2	*O-116	-0.6
1955	Mil-N★	153	602	105	189	**37**	9	27	106	49	61	.314	.369	.540	144	36	3	1	0	.967	6	*O-126,2-27	3.8
1956	Mil-N★	153	609	106	**200**	**34**	14	26	92	37	54	**.328**	.369	.558	154	**43**	2	4	-2	.962	10	*O-152	4.4
1957	*Mil-N★	151	615	**118**	198	27	6	**44**	**132**	57	58	.322	.379	.600	170	58	1	1	-0	.983	2	*O-150	5.0
1958	*Mil-N★	153	601	109	196	34	4	30	95	59	49	.326	.387	.546	157	47	4	1	1	.984	2	*O-153	4.1
1959	Mil-N★	154	629	116	**223**	46	7	39	123	51	54	**.355**	.406	**.636**	**188**	**75**	8	0	2	.982	-2	*O-152/3-5	**6.6**
1960	Mil-N★	153	590	102	172	20	11	40	**126**	60	63	.292	.359	.566	160	46	16	7	1	.982	9	*O-153/2-2	4.8
1961	Mil-N★	155	603	115	197	**39**	10	34	120	56	64	.327	.386	.594	**165**	**54**	21	9	1	.982	12	*O-154/3-2	**5.6**
1962	Mil-N★	156	592	127	191	28	6	45	128	66	73	.323	.393	.618	171	58	15	7	0	.980	8	*O-153/1-1	5.5
1963	Mil-N★	161	631	**121**	201	29	4	**44**	**130**	78	94	.319	.394	**.586**	**180**	**64**	31	5	**6**	.979	-1	*O-161	6.5
1964	Mil-N★	145	570	103	187	30	2	24	95	62	46	.328	.394	.514	152	40	22	4	4	.983	11	*O-139,2-11	5.1
1965	Mil-N★	150	570	109	181	**40**	1	32	89	60	81	.318	.384	.560	161	45	24	4	5	.987	10	*O-148	5.5
1966	Atl-N★	158	603	117	168	23	1	**44**	**127**	76	96	.279	.360	.539	144	35	21	3	5	.988	9	*O-158/2-2	4.3
1967	Atl-N★	155	600	**113**	184	37	3	**39**	109	63	97	.307	.373	**.573**	169	**52**	17	6	2	.979	12	*O-152/2-1	6.1
1968	Atl-N★	160	606	84	174	33	4	29	86	64	62	.287	.356	.498	154	39	28	5	5	.991	14	*O-151,1-14	**5.5**
1969	*Atl-N★	147	547	100	164	30	3	44	97	87	47	.300	.398	.607	177	56	9	10	-3	.982	6	*O-144/1-4	5.2
1970	Atl-N★	150	516	103	154	26	1	38	118	74	63	.298	.389	.574	146	33	9	0	3	.977	5	*O-125,1-11	3.2
1971	Atl-N★	139	495	95	162	22	3	47	118	71	58	.327	.414	**.669**	**190**	58	1	1	-0	.996	-8	1-71,O-60	4.2
1972	Atl-N★	129	449	75	119	10	0	34	77	92	55	.265	.391	.514	142	27	4	0	1	.987	1	*1-109,O-15	1.9
1973	Atl-N★	120	392	84	118	12	1	40	96	68	51	.301	.406	.643	173	39	1	1	-0	.977	2	*O-105	3.7
1974	Atl-N★	112	340	47	91	16	0	20	69	39	29	.268	.343	.491	126	11	1	0	0	.986	-4	O-89	0.3
Total	23	3298	12364	2174	3771	624	98	755	2297	1402	1383	.305	.377	.555	156	914	240	73	28	.980	101	*O-2760,1-210,D/23	89.8
Team	21	3076	11628	2107	3600	600	96	733	2202	1297	1294	.310	.380	.567	159	915	240	71	29	.980	102	*O-2756,1-210/23	90.7

■ **TOMMIE AARON** Aaron, Tommie Lee b: 8/5/39, Mobile, Ala. d: 8/16/84, Atlanta, Ga. BR/TR, 6'1", 200 lbs. Deb: 4/10/62 FC

YEAR	TM/L	G	AB	R	H	2B	3B	HR	RBI	BB	SO	AVG	OBP	SLG	PRO+	BR/A	SB	CS	SBR	FA	FR	G/POS	TPR
1962	Mil-N	141	334	54	77	20	2	8	38	41	58	.231	.315	.374	86	-7	6	0	2	.989	2	*1-110,O-42/23	-0.8
1963	Mil-N	72	135	6	27	6	1	1	15	11	27	.200	.260	.281	57	-8	0	3	-2	1.000	-6	1-45,O-14/23	-1.8
1965	Mil-N	8	16	1	3	0	0	0	1	1	2	.188	.235	.188	21	-2	0	0	0	.961	0	/1-6	-0.2
1968	Atl-N	98	283	21	69	10	3	1	25	21	37	.244	.296	.311	82	-6	3	4	-2	.942	-4	O-62,1-28/3	-1.9
1969	*Atl-N	49	60	13	15	2	0	1	5	6	6	.250	.318	.333	82	-1	0	1	-1	1.000	1	1-16/O-8	-0.2
1970	Atl-N	44	63	3	13	2	0	2	7	3	10	.206	.242	.333	50	-5	0	0	0	.955	-2	1-16,O-12	-0.8
1971	Atl-N	25	53	4	12	2	0	0	3	3	5	.226	.268	.264	48	-4	0	0	0	.974	2	1-11/3-7	-0.2
Total	7	437	944	102	216	42	6	13	94	86	145	.229	.293	.327	75	-31	9	8	-2	.990	-7	1-232,O-138/32	-5.9

■ **ED ABBATICCHIO** Abbaticchio, Edward James "Batty" b: 4/15/1877, Latrobe, Pa. d: 1/6/57, Ft.Lauderdale, Fla. BR/TR, 5'11", 170 lbs. Deb: 9/4/1897

YEAR	TM/L	G	AB	R	H	2B	3B	HR	RBI	BB	SO	AVG	OBP	SLG	PRO+	BR/A	SB	CS	SBR	FA	FR	G/POS	TPR
1903	Bos-N	136	489	61	111	18	5	1	46	52		.227	.306	.290	73	-16	23			.934	3	*2-116,S-17	-0.7
1904	Bos-N	154	579	76	148	18	10	3	54	40		.256	.309	.337	103	2	24			.915	2	*S-154	0.9
1905	Bos-N	153	610	70	170	25	12	3	41	35		.279	.326	.374	111	7	30			.919	-12	*S-152/O-1	-0.2
1910	Bos-N	52	178	20	44	4	2	0	10	12	16	.247	.295	.292	68	-7	2			.910	-3	S-46/2-1	-0.9
Total	9	855	3044	355	772	99	43	11	324	289	16	.254	.325	.325	98	-4	142			.949	-59	2-419,S-388/3O	-5.0
Team	4	495	1856	227	473	65	29	7	151	139	16	.255	.313	.332	94	-15	79			.914	-10	S-369,2-117/O	-0.9

■ **JOE ADCOCK** Adcock, Joseph Wilbur b: 10/30/27, Coushatta, La. BR/TR, 6'4", 220 lbs. Deb: 4/23/50 M

YEAR	TM/L	G	AB	R	H	2B	3B	HR	RBI	BB	SO	AVG	OBP	SLG	PRO+	BR/A	SB	CS	SBR	FA	FR	G/POS	TPR
1953	Mil-N	157	590	71	168	33	6	18	80	42	82	.285	.334	.453	110	6	3	2	-0	.991	-4	*1-157	-0.5
1954	Mil-N	133	500	73	154	27	5	23	87	44	58	.308	.367	.520	137	25	1	4	-2	.995	-11	*1-133	0.5
1955	Mil-N	84	288	40	76	14	0	15	45	31	44	.264	.340	.469	118	7	0	2	-1	.990	-5	1-78	-0.4
1956	Mil-N	137	454	76	132	23	1	38	103	32	86	.291	.339	.597	**154**	31	1	0	0	**.995**	-6	*1-129	1.8
1957	*Mil-N	65	209	31	60	13	2	12	38	20	51	.287	.352	.541	146	13	0	0	0	.996	-3	1-56	0.6
1958	*Mil-N	105	320	40	88	15	1	19	54	21	63	.275	.322	.506	125	9	0	0	0	.989	-1	1-71,O-22	0.3
1959	Mil-N	115	404	53	118	19	2	25	76	32	77	.292	.344	.535	141	21	0	0	0	.998	10	1-89,O-21	2.5
1960	Mil-N★	138	514	55	153	21	4	25	91	46	86	.298	.357	.500	142	28	2	2	-1	**.993**	3	*1-136	1.9
1961	Mil-N	152	562	77	160	20	0	35	108	59	94	.285	.355	.507	133	25	2	1	0	**.993**	-5	*1-148	0.8
1962	Mil-N	121	391	48	97	12	1	29	78	50	91	.248	.335	.506	126	13	2	0	1	**.997**	-4	*1-112	0.3
Total	17	1959	6606	823	1832	295	35	336	1122	594	1059	.277	.339	.485	125	210	20	25		.994	-28	*1-1501,O-310	7.3
Team	10	1207	4232	564	1206	197	22	239	760	377	732	.285	.345	.511	133	178	11	11		.994	-25	*1-1109/O-43	7.8

■ **BOB ADDIS** Addis, Robert Gordon b: 11/6/25, Mineral, Ohio BL/TR, 6', 175 lbs. Deb: 9/1/50

YEAR	TM/L	G	AB	R	H	2B	3B	HR	RBI	BB	SO	AVG	OBP	SLG	PRO+	BR/A	SB	CS	SBR	FA	FR	G/POS	TPR
1950	Bos-N	16	28	7	7	1	0	0	2	3	5	.250	.323	.286	66	-1	1			1.000	-2	/O-7	-0.3
1951	Bos-N	85	199	23	55	7	0	1	24	9	10	.276	.308	.327	76	-7	3	2	-0	.982	-0	O-46	-0.9
Total	4	208	534	70	150	22	2	2	47	37	47	.281	.327	.341	84	-12	8	6		.986	-3	O-135	-2.1
Team	2	101	227	30	62	8	0	1	26	12	15	.273	.310	.322	75	-8	4	2		.983	-2	/O-53	-1.2

■ **BOB ADDY** Addy, Robert Edward "Magnet" b: 2/1845, Rochester, N.Y. d: 4/9/10, Pocatello, Idaho BL/TL, 5'8", 160 lbs. Deb: 5/6/1871 M

YEAR	TM/L	G	AB	R	H	2B	3B	HR	RBI	BB	SO	AVG	OBP	SLG	PRO+	BR/A	SB	CS	SBR	FA	FR	G/POS	TPR
1873	Bos-n	31	152	37	54	6	2	1	36	1	0	.355	.359	.441	124	3						*O-31	0.2
Total	4 n	185	843	164	231	33	8	1	58	9	0	.274	.282	.336	91	-11						/O-97,2-80,3S	-1.2
Total	2	89	387	63	108	6	4	0	47	11	5	.279	.299	.315	100	0				.803	5	/O-89	0.2

■ **MORRIE ADERHOLT** Aderholt, Morris Woodrow b: 9/13/15, Mt.Olive, N.C. d: 3/18/55, Sarasota, Fla. BL/TR, 6'1", 188 lbs. Deb: 9/13/39

YEAR	TM/L	G	AB	R	H	2B	3B	HR	RBI	BB	SO	AVG	OBP	SLG	PRO+	BR/A	SB	CS	SBR	FA	FR	G/POS	TPR
1945	Bos-N	31	102	15	34	4	0	2	11	9	6	.333	.387	.431	127	4	3			.984	0	O-24/2-1	0.3
Total	5	106	262	36	70	7	3	3	32	19	29	.267	.317	.351	85	-6	3			.949	-2	/O-45,2-11,3	-1.0

■ **BILL AKERS** Akers, William G. "Bump" b: 12/25/04, Chattanooga, Tenn. d: 4/13/62, Chattanooga, Tenn. BR/TR, 5'11", 178 lbs. Deb: 9/8/29

YEAR	TM/L	G	AB	R	H	2B	3B	HR	RBI	BB	SO	AVG	OBP	SLG	PRO+	BR/A	SB	CS	SBR	FA	FR	G/POS	TPR
1932	Bos-N	36	93	8	24	3	1	1	17	10	15	.258	.330	.344	85	-2	0			.927	-5	3-20/2-5,S	-0.5
Total	4	174	475	64	124	17	9	11	69	63	64	.261	.349	.404	93	-4	7			.936	-6	/S-99,3-46,2	-0.1

■ **MYRON ALLEN** Allen, Myron Smith "Zeke" b: 3/22/1854, Kingston, N.Y. d: 3/8/24, Kingston, N.Y. BR/TR, 5'8", 150 lbs. Deb: 7/19/1883

YEAR	TM/L	G	AB	R	H	2B	3B	HR	RBI	BB	SO	AVG	OBP	SLG	PRO+	BR/A	SB	CS	SBR	FA	FR	G/POS	TPR
1886	Bos-N	1	3	0	0	0	0	0	0	0	1	.000	.000	.000	-99	-1	0			1.000	-0	/2-1	-0.1
Total	4	156	606	89	157	28	14	4	11	45	3	.259	.317	.371	98	-2	30			.903	15	O-150/P-5,3S2	0.9

■ **BOB ALLEN** Allen, Robert Gilman b: 7/10/1867, Marion, Ohio d: 5/14/43, Little Rock, Ark. BR/TR, 5'11", 175 lbs. Deb: 4/19/1890 M

YEAR	TM/L	G	AB	R	H	2B	3B	HR	RBI	BB	SO	AVG	OBP	SLG	PRO+	BR/A	SB	CS	SBR	FA	FR	G/POS	TPR
1897	Bos-N	34	119	33	38	5	0	1	24	18		.319	.409	.387	104	1	1			.924	8	S-32/O-1,2	0.8
Total	7	606	2211	337	532	77	44	14	306	297		.241	.334	.334	88	-32	53			.915	93	S-604/2-1,O	7.8

■ **SANDY ALOMAR** Alomar, Santos Sr. (Conde) b: 10/19/43, Salinas, P.R. BB/TR, 5'9", 155 lbs. Deb: 9/15/64 FC

YEAR	TM/L	G	AB	R	H	2B	3B	HR	RBI	BB	SO	AVG	OBP	SLG	PRO+	BR/A	SB	CS	SBR	FA	FR	G/POS	TPR
1964	Mil-N	19	53	3	13	1	0	0	6	0	11	.245	.245	.264	43	-4	1	0	0	.967	8	S-19	0.6
1965	Mil-N	67	108	16	26	1	1	0	8	4	12	.241	.268	.269	51	-7	12	5	1	.964	14	S-39,2-19	1.0
1966	Atl-N	31	44	4	4	1	0	0	2	1	10	.091	.111	.114	-37	-8	0	0	0	.981	3	2-21/S-5	-0.4
Total	15	1481	4760	558	1168	126	19	13	282	302	482	.245	.291	.288	68	-201	227	80	20	.977	31	*2-1156,S-197/3D1O	-6.9
Team	3	117	205	23	43	3	1	0	16	5	33	.210	.229	.234	30	-19	13	5	1	.967	25	/S-63,2-40	1.2

■ **FELIPE ALOU** Alou, Felipe Rojas (b: Felipe Rojas (Alou)) b: 5/12/35, Haina, D.R. BR/TR, 6', 195 lbs. Deb: 6/8/58 FMC

YEAR	TM/L	G	AB	R	H	2B	3B	HR	RBI	BB	SO	AVG	OBP	SLG	PRO+	BR/A	SB	CS	SBR	FA	FR	G/POS	TPR
1964	Mil-N	121	415	60	105	26	3	9	51	30	41	.253	.310	.395	96	-2	5	2	0	.975	-1	O-92,1-18	-0.9
1965	Mil-N	143	555	80	165	29	2	23	78	31	63	.297	.340	.481	128	19	8	4	0	.980	-4	O-91,1-69/3S	0.8
1966	Atl-N☆	154	666	**122**	**218**	32	6	31	74	24	51	.327	.362	.533	143	36	5	7	-3	.988	1	1-90,O-79/3S	2.7

YEAR	TM/L	G	AB	R	H	2B	3B	HR	RBI	BB	SO	AVG	OBP	SLG	PRO+	BR/A	SB	CS	SBR	FA	FR	G/POS	TPR
1967	Atl-N	140	574	76	157	26	3	15	43	32	50	.274	.320	.408	108	5	6	5	-1	.993	-11	1-85,O-56	-1.7
1968	Atl-N★	160	662	72	**210**	37	5	11	57	48	56	.317	.367	.438	140	32	12	11	-3	.980	8	*O-158	3.2
1969	*Atl-N	123	476	54	134	13	1	5	32	23	23	.282	.320	.345	86	-9	4	6	-2	.989	3	*O-116	-1.6
Total	17	2082	7339	985	2101	359	49	206	852	423	706	.286	.330	.433	114	114	107	67	-8	.979	-37	*O-1531,1-468/3S	-3.4
Team	6	841	3348	464	989	163	20	94	335	188	284	.295	.340	.440	120	81	40	35	-9	.981	-5	O-592,1-262/3S	2.5

■ STAN ANDREWS
Andrews, Stanley Joseph "Polo" (b: Stanley Joseph Andruskewicz) b: 4/17/17, Lynn, Mass. d: 6/10/95, Bradenton, Fla. BR/TR, 5'11", 178 lbs. Deb: 6/11/39

YEAR	TM/L	G	AB	R	H	2B	3B	HR	RBI	BB	SO	AVG	OBP	SLG	PRO+	BR/A	SB	CS	SBR	FA	FR	G/POS	TPR
1939	Bos-N	13	26	1	6	0	0	0	1	1	2	.231	.259	.231	35	-2	0			.857	-2	C-10	-0.4
1940	Bos-N	19	33	1	6	0	0	0	2	0	3	.182	.182	.182	1	-4	1			.944	-1	C-14	-0.5
Total	4	70	149	11	32	2	1	1	12	8	16	.215	.259	.262	46	-11	2			.938	-1	/C-61	-1.1
Team	2	32	59	2	12	0	0	0	3	1	5	.203	.217	.203	16	-7	1			.906	-2	/C-24	-0.9

■ BILL ANNIS
Annis, William Perley b: 3/8/1857, Stoneham, Mass. d: 6/10/23, Kennebunkport, Me BR , 5'7", 150 lbs. Deb: 5/1/1884

YEAR	TM/L	G	AB	R	H	2B	3B	HR	RBI	BB	SO	AVG	OBP	SLG	PRO+	BR/A	SB	CS	SBR	FA	FR	G/POS	TPR
1884	Bos-N	27	96	17	17	2	0	0	3	0	8	.177	.177	.198	18	-9				.897	-3	O-27	-1.2

■ TOM ASMUSSEN
Asmussen, Thomas William b: 9/26/1876, Chicago, Ill. d: 8/21/63, Arlington Heights, Ill. TR , Deb: 8/10/07

YEAR	TM/L	G	AB	R	H	2B	3B	HR	RBI	BB	SO	AVG	OBP	SLG	PRO+	BR/A	SB	CS	SBR	FA	FR	G/POS	TPR
1907	Bos-N	2	5	0	0	0	0	0	0	0		.000	.000	.000	-99	-1	0			1.000	-1	/C-2	-0.3

■ KEN ASPROMONTE
Aspromonte, Kenneth Joseph b: 9/22/31, Brooklyn, N.Y. BR/TR, 6', 180 lbs. Deb: 9/2/57 FM

YEAR	TM/L	G	AB	R	H	2B	3B	HR	RBI	BB	SO	AVG	OBP	SLG	PRO+	BR/A	SB	CS	SBR	FA	FR	G/POS	TPR
1962	Mil-N	34	79	11	23	2	0	0	7	6	5	.291	.349	.316	82	-2	0	1	-1	1.000	-0	2-12/3-6	-0.1
Total	7	475	1483	171	369	69	3	19	124	179	149	.249	.332	.338	82	-33	7	5		.969	-7	2-342/3-56,S10	-1.1

■ BOB ASPROMONTE
Aspromonte, Robert Thomas b: 6/19/38, Brooklyn, N.Y. BR/TR, 6'2", 185 lbs. Deb: 9/19/56 F

YEAR	TM/L	G	AB	R	H	2B	3B	HR	RBI	BB	SO	AVG	OBP	SLG	PRO+	BR/A	SB	CS	SBR	FA	FR	G/POS	TPR
1969	*Atl-N	82	198	16	50	8	1	3	24	13	19	.253	.305	.348	82	-5	0	1	-1	.975	-6	O-24,3-23,S/2	-1.3
1970	Atl-N	62	127	5	27	3	0	0	7	13	13	.213	.286	.236	39	-11	0	0	0	.938	-1	3-30/S-4,1O	-1.1
Total	13	1324	4369	386	1103	135	26	60	457	333	459	.252	.310	.336	86	-84	19	24	-9	.960	-57	*3-1094/O-61,S12	-16.9
Team	2	144	325	21	77	11	1	3	31	26	32	.237	.297	.305	64	-15	0	1	-1	.927	-7	/3-53,O-25,S21	-2.4

■ BRIAN ASSELSTINE
Asselstine, Brian Hanly b: 9/23/53, Santa Barbara, Cal BL/TR, 6'1", 175 lbs. Deb: 9/14/76

YEAR	TM/L	G	AB	R	H	2B	3B	HR	RBI	BB	SO	AVG	OBP	SLG	PRO+	BR/A	SB	CS	SBR	FA	FR	G/POS	TPR
1976	Atl-N	11	33	2	7	0	0	1	3	1	2	.212	.235	.303	49	-2	0	0	0	1.000	-1	/O-9	-0.3
1977	Atl-N	83	124	12	26	6	0	4	17	9	10	.210	.263	.355	57	-8	1	0	0	.983	-2	O-35	-1.1
1978	Atl-N	39	103	11	28	3	3	2	13	11	16	.272	.353	.417	103	0	2	1	0	.968	-5	O-35	-0.7
1979	Atl-N	8	10	1	1	0	0	0	0	1	2	.100	.182	.100	-20	-2	0	0	0	1.000	-0	/O-1	-0.2
1980	Atl-N	87	218	18	62	13	1	3	25	11	37	.284	.322	.394	96	-2	1	3	-2	.962	-9	O-61	-1.5
1981	Atl-N	56	86	8	22	5	0	2	10	5	7	.256	.297	.384	90	-1	1	0	0	.958	-1	O-16	-0.3
Total	6	284	574	52	146	27	4	12	68	38	74	.254	.304	.378	83	-14	5	4	-1	.971	-19	O-157	-4.1

■ TOBY ATWELL
Atwell, Maurice Dailey b: 3/8/24, Leesburg, Va. BL/TR, 5'9.5", 185 lbs. Deb: 4/15/52

YEAR	TM/L	G	AB	R	H	2B	3B	HR	RBI	BB	SO	AVG	OBP	SLG	PRO+	BR/A	SB	CS	SBR	FA	FR	G/POS	TPR
1956	Mil-N	15	30	2	5	1	0	2	7	4	1	.167	.265	.400	80	-1	0	0	0	1.000	-1	C-10	-0.1
Total	5	378	1117	116	290	41	7	9	110	161	84	.260	.357	.333	86	-17	4	5	-2	.980	-5	C-344	-0.9

■ HARRY AUBREY
Aubrey, Harry Herbert "Chub" b: 7/5/1880, St.Joseph, Mo. d: 9/18/53, Baltimore, Md. TR , Deb: 4/22/03

YEAR	TM/L	G	AB	R	H	2B	3B	HR	RBI	BB	SO	AVG	OBP	SLG	PRO+	BR/A	SB	CS	SBR	FA	FR	G/POS	TPR
1903	Bos-N	96	325	26	69	8	2	0	27	18		.212	.264	.249	49	-22	7			.868	-10	S-94/2-1,O	-2.7

■ CHICK AUTRY
Autry, William Askew b: 1/2/1885, Humboldt, Tenn. d: 1/16/76, Santa Rosa, Cal. BL/TL, 5'11", 168 lbs. Deb: 9/18/07

YEAR	TM/L	G	AB	R	H	2B	3B	HR	RBI	BB	SO	AVG	OBP	SLG	PRO+	BR/A	SB	CS	SBR	FA	FR	G/POS	TPR
1909	Bos-N	65	199	16	39	4	0	0	13	21		.196	.279	.216	51	-11	5			.994	5	1-61/O-4	-0.8
Total	2	81	257	22	50	6	0	0	17	24		.195	.269	.218	49	-15	6			.968	4	/1-70,O-11	-1.4

■ EARL AVERILL
Averill, Howard Earl "Rock" b: 5/21/02, Snohomish, Wash. d: 8/16/83, Everett, Wash. BL/TR, 5'9.5", 172 lbs. Deb: 4/16/29 FH

YEAR	TM/L	G	AB	R	H	2B	3B	HR	RBI	BB	SO	AVG	OBP	SLG	PRO+	BR/A	SB	CS	SBR	FA	FR	G/POS	TPR
1941	Bos-N	8	17	2	2	0	0	0	2	1	4	.118	.211	.118	-6	-2	0			1.000	1	/O-4	-0.2
Total	13	1668	6353	1224	2019	401	128	238	1164	774	518	.318	.395	.534	132	296	70			.970	-8	*O-1589	17.6

■ BOBBY AVILA
Avila, Roberto Francisco (Gonzales) b: 4/2/24, Veracruz, Mexico BR/TR, 5'10", 175 lbs. Deb: 4/30/49

YEAR	TM/L	G	AB	R	H	2B	3B	HR	RBI	BB	SO	AVG	OBP	SLG	PRO+	BR/A	SB	CS	SBR	FA	FR	G/POS	TPR
1959	Mil-N	51	172	29	41	3	2	3	19	24	31	.238	.332	.331	84	-4	3	0	1	.967	-12	2-51	-1.1
Total	11	1300	4620	725	1296	185	35	80	467	561	399	.281	.360	.388	104	34	78	52		.979	-64	*2-1168/3-50,OS	3.6

■ BILL BAGWELL
Bagwell, William Mallory "Big Bill" b: 2/24/1896, Choudrant, La. d: 10/5/76, Choudrant, La. BL/TL, 6'1", 175 lbs. Deb: 4/17/23

YEAR	TM/L	G	AB	R	H	2B	3B	HR	RBI	BB	SO	AVG	OBP	SLG	PRO+	BR/A	SB	CS	SBR	FA	FR	G/POS	TPR
1923	Bos-N	56	93	8	27	4	2	2	10	6	12	.290	.333	.441	107	1	0	0	0	1.000	-3	O-22	-0.3
Total	2	92	143	12	42	6	3	2	20	8	14	.294	.331	.420	95	-2	0	0	0	.973	-5	/O-26	-0.7

■ GENE BAILEY
Bailey, Arthur Eugene b: 11/25/1893, Pearsall, Tex. d: 11/14/73, Houston, Tex. BR/TR, 5'8", 160 lbs. Deb: 9/10/17

YEAR	TM/L	G	AB	R	H	2B	3B	HR	RBI	BB	SO	AVG	OBP	SLG	PRO+	BR/A	SB	CS	SBR	FA	FR	G/POS	TPR
1919	Bos-N	4	6	0	2	0	0	0	1	0	2	.333	.333	.333	105	0	1			1.000	0	/O-3	0.0
1920	Bos-N	13	24	2	2	0	0	0	0	3	3	.083	.185	.083	-22	-4	0	1	-1	.929	-2	/O-8	-0.8
Total	5	213	634	95	156	16	7	2	52	63	61	.246	.321	.303	69	-27	13	15		.965	-5	O-172/1-5	-4.8
Team	2	17	30	2	4	0	0	0	1	3	5	.133	.212	.133	1	-4	1	1		.947	-2	/O-11	-0.8

■ FRED BAILEY
Bailey, Frederick Middleton "Penny" b: 8/16/1895, Mt.Hope, W.Va. d: 8/16/72, Huntington, W.Va. BL/TL, 5'11", 150 lbs. Deb: 8/19/16

YEAR	TM/L	G	AB	R	H	2B	3B	HR	RBI	BB	SO	AVG	OBP	SLG	PRO+	BR/A	SB	CS	SBR	FA	FR	G/POS	TPR
1916	Bos-N	6	10	0	1	0	0	0	1	0	3	.100	.100	.100	-40	-2	0			1.000	-0	/O-2	-0.2
1917	Bos-N	50	110	9	21	2	1	1	5	9	25	.191	.270	.255	65	-4	3			.962	-1	O-27	-0.8
1918	Bos-N	4	4	1	1	0	0	0	0	0	1	.250	.250	.250	55	-0	0			.000	0	H	0.0
Total	3	60	124	10	23	2	1	1	6	9	29	.185	.257	.242	57	-6	3			.963	-2	/O-29	-1.0

■ ED BAILEY
Bailey, Lonas Edgar b: 4/15/31, Strawberry Plains, Tenn. BL/TR, 6'2", 205 lbs. Deb: 9/26/53 F

YEAR	TM/L	G	AB	R	H	2B	3B	HR	RBI	BB	SO	AVG	OBP	SLG	PRO+	BR/A	SB	CS	SBR	FA	FR	G/POS	TPR
1964	Mil-N	95	271	30	71	10	1	5	34	34	39	.262	.346	.362	99	1	2	0	1	.982	-10	C-80	-0.5
Total	14	1212	3581	432	915	128	15	155	540	545	577	.256	.358	.429	110	56	17	18		.986	-54	*C-1064/1-5,O	4.6

■ DUSTY BAKER
Baker, Johnnie B b: 6/15/49, Riverside, Cal. BR/TR, 6'2", 187 lbs. Deb: 9/7/68 MC

YEAR	TM/L	G	AB	R	H	2B	3B	HR	RBI	BB	SO	AVG	OBP	SLG	PRO+	BR/A	SB	CS	SBR	FA	FR	G/POS	TPR
1968	Atl-N	6	5	0	2	0	0	0	0	0	1	.400	.400	.400	140	0	0	0	0	.000	-1	/O-3	-0.1
1969	Atl-N	3	7	0	0	0	0	0	0	0	3	.000	.000	.000	-99	-2	0	0	0	1.000	-1	/O-3	-0.3
1970	Atl-N	13	24	3	7	0	0	0	4	2	4	.292	.346	.292	69	-1	0	0	0	.800	-2	O-11	-0.3
1971	Atl-N	29	62	2	14	2	0	0	4	1	14	.226	.238	.258	38	-5	0	1	-1	1.000	-2	O-18	-0.9
1972	Atl-N	127	446	62	143	27	2	17	76	45	68	.321	.388	.504	139	23	4	7	-3	.989	2	*O-123	1.7
1973	Atl-N	159	604	101	174	29	4	21	99	67	72	.288	.364	.454	116	14	24	3	5	.983	10	*O-156	2.3
1974	Atl-N	149	574	80	147	35	0	20	69	71	87	.256	.339	.422	107	5	18	7	1	.981	-18	*O-148	-1.9
1975	Atl-N	142	494	63	129	18	2	19	72	67	57	.261	.349	.421	109	6	12	7	-1	.990	7	*O-136	0.7
Total	19	2039	7117	964	1981	320	23	242	1013	762	926	.278	.351	.432	116	149	137	73	-3	.985	-2	*O-1842/1-61,D	7.5
Team	8	628	2216	311	616	111	8	77	324	253	306	.278	.355	.440	114	40	58	25	2	.984	-6	O-598	1.2

■ LEE BALES
Bales, Wesley Owen b: 12/4/44, Los Angeles, Cal. BB/TR, 5'10.5", 165 lbs. Deb: 8/7/66

YEAR	TM/L	G	AB	R	H	2B	3B	HR	RBI	BB	SO	AVG	OBP	SLG	PRO+	BR/A	SB	CS	SBR	FA	FR	G/POS	TPR
1966	Atl-N	12	16	4	1	0	0	0	0	0	5	.063	.063	.063	-64	-3	0	0	0	1.000	3	/2-7,3-3	0.0
Total	2	31	43	8	4	0	0	0	2	8	12	.093	.235	.093	-3	-6	1	1	-0	.978	1	/2-13,3-3,S	-0.4

■ JIM BALL
Ball, James Chandler b: 2/22/1884, Harford Co., Md. d: 4/7/63, Glendale, Cal. BR/TR, 5'11", 175 lbs. Deb: 9/21/07

YEAR	TM/L	G	AB	R	H	2B	3B	HR	RBI	BB	SO	AVG	OBP	SLG	PRO+	BR/A	SB	CS	SBR	FA	FR	G/POS	TPR
1907	Bos-N	10	36	3	6	2	0	0	3	2		.167	.211	.222	36	-3	0			.963	-2	C-10	-0.4
1908	Bos-N	6	15	1	1	0	0	0	0	1		.067	.125	.067	-39	-2	0			.917	-1	/C-6	-0.3
Total	2	16	51	4	7	2	0	0	3	3		.137	.185	.176	14	-5	0			.949	-2	/C-16	-0.7

YEAR	TM/L	G	AB	R	H	2B	3B	HR	RBI	BB	SO	AVG	OBP	SLG	PRO+	BR/A	SB	CS	SBR	FA	FR	G/POS	TPR

■ **DAVE BANCROFT**   Bancroft, David James "Beauty"   b: 4/20/1891, Sioux City, Iowa   d: 10/9/72, Superior, Wis.   BB/TR, 5'9.5", 160 lbs.   Deb: 4/14/15 MCH

1924	Bos-N	79	319	49	89	11	1	2	21	37	24	.279	.356	.339	91	-3	4	4	-1	.961	-5	S-79,M	-0.1
1925	Bos-N	128	479	75	153	29	8	2	49	64	22	.319	.400	.426	122	18	7	4	-0	.945	10	*S-125,M	3.8
1926	Bos-N	127	453	70	141	18	6	1	44	64	29	.311	.399	.384	122	17	3			.956	-3	*S-123/3-2M	2.7
1927	Bos-N	111	375	44	91	13	4	1	31	43	36	.243	.322	.307	75	-13	5			.939	6	*S-104/3-1M	0.4
Total	16	1913	7182	1048	2004	320	77	32	591	827	487	.279	.355	.358	98	8	145	75		.944	198	*S-1873/2-14,3O	35.2
Team	4	445	1626	238	474	71	19	6	145	208	111	.292	.373	.370	105	19	19	8		.950	8	S-431/3-3	6.8

■ **JIMMY BANNON**   Bannon, James Henry "Foxy Grandpa"   b: 5/5/1871, Amesbury, Mass.   d: 3/24/48, Glen Rock, N.J.   BR/TR, 5'5", 160 lbs.   Deb: 6/15/1893 F

1894	Bos-N	128	494	130	166	29	10	13	114	62	42	.336	.414	.514	114	9	47			.873	18	*O-128/P-1	1.4
1895	Bos-N	123	489	101	171	35	5	6	74	54	31	.350	.420	.479	122	15	28			.879	10	*O-122/P-1	1.3
1896	Bos-N	89	343	52	86	9	5	0	50	32	23	.251	.316	.306	61	-20	16			.901	-1	O-76/2-3,S	-2.2
Total	4	366	1433	292	459	76	24	19	253	152	101	.320	.390	.447	105	5	99			.877	22	O-350/S-7,23P	0.1
Team	3	340	1326	283	423	73	20	19	238	148	96	.319	.392	.447	104	4	91			.881	28	O-326/2-6,S3P	0.5

■ **WALTER BARBARE**   Barbare, Walter Lawrence "Dinty"   b: 8/11/1891, Greenville, S.C.   d: 10/28/65, Greenville, S.C.   BR/TR, 6', 162 lbs.   Deb: 9/17/14

1921	Bos-N	134	550	66	166	22	7	0	49	24	28	.302	.331	.367	89	-9	11	4	1	.957	-17	*S-121/2-8,3	-1.3
1922	Bos-N	106	373	38	86	5	4	0	40	21	22	.231	.272	.265	41	-33	2	0	1	.966	2	2-45,3-38,1	-2.5
Total	8	500	1777	173	462	52	21	1	156	88	121	.260	.297	.315	71	-72	37	16		.959	-21	3-230,S-157/21	-7.2
Team	2	240	923	104	252	27	11	0	89	45	50	.273	.307	.326	69	-42	13	4		.957	-14	S-121/2-53,31	-3.8

■ **GEORGE BARCLAY**   Barclay, George Oliver "Deerfoot"   b: 5/16/1876, Millville, Pa.   d: 4/3/09, Philadelphia, Pa.   TR, 5'10", 162 lbs.   Deb: 4/17/02

1904	Bos-N	24	93	5	21	3	1	0	10	2		.226	.258	.280	68	-4	3			.935	-3	O-24	-0.9
1905	Bos-N	29	108	5	19	1	0	0	7	2		.176	.205	.185	17	-11	2			.854	-5	O-28	-1.8
Total	4	401	1538	167	382	35	15	4	140	62		.248	.286	.298	79	-42	61			.911	-29	O-399	-9.9
Team	2	53	201	10	40	4	1	0	17	4		.199	.230	.229	40	-15	5			.886	-8	/O-52	-2.7

■ **RED BARKLEY**   Barkley, John Duncan   b: 9/19/13, Childress, Tex.   BR/TR, 5'11", 160 lbs.   Deb: 9/2/37

| 1939 | Bos-N | 12 | 11 | 1 | 0 | 0 | 0 | 0 | 1 | 2 | | .000 | .083 | .000 | -82 | -3 | 0 | | | .842 | 4 | /S-7,3-4 | 0.1 |
| Total | 3 | 63 | 163 | 16 | 43 | 9 | 0 | 0 | 21 | 19 | 26 | .264 | .341 | .319 | 75 | -6 | 2 | | | .882 | -3 | /2-31,S-25,3 | -0.5 |

■ **ROSS BARNES**   Barnes, Roscoe Charles   b: 5/8/1850, Mount Morris, Ill.   d: 2/5/15, Chicago, Ill.   BR/TR, 5'8.5", 145 lbs.   Deb: 5/5/1871 U

1871	Bos-n	31	157	66	63	10	9	0	34	13	1	.401	.447	.580	186	17	11					2-16,S-15/3	1.0
1872	Bos-n	45	230	81	97	28	2	1	44	9	4	.422	.444	.574	200	25						*2-45	1.6
1873	Bos-n	60	322	125	137	28	10	3	61	18	2	.425	.456	.602	193	34						*2-47,3-13	2.2
1874	Bos-n	51	259	72	89	12	4	0		8		.344	.363	.421	141	11						*2-52	0.6
1875	Bos-n	78	393	114	142	22	6	1		7		.361	.373	.455	178	29						*2-78	2.3
1881	Bos-n	69	294	42	80	14	1	0	17	16	16	.271	.309	.325	104	2				.854	-0	*S-63/2-7	0.6
Total	5 n	265	1361	458	528	100	31	5	139	55	7	.388	.412	.518	180	116						2-238/S-15,3	7.7
Total	4	234	1032	239	329	45	17	2	111	59	53	.319	.356	.401	143	43				.859	-5	S-124,2-111/P	4.1

■ **JOHNNY BARRETT**   Barrett, John Joseph "Jack"   b: 12/18/15, Lowell, Mass.   d: 8/17/74, Seabrook Beach, N.H.   BL/TL, 5'10.5", 170 lbs.   Deb: 4/14/42

| 1946 | Bos-N | 24 | 43 | 3 | 10 | 3 | 0 | 0 | 6 | 12 | 1 | .233 | .400 | .302 | 100 | 1 | 0 | | | .962 | -3 | O-17 | -0.3 |
| Total | 5 | 588 | 1811 | 303 | 454 | 82 | 32 | 23 | 220 | 265 | 201 | .251 | .349 | .369 | 100 | 5 | 69 | | | .974 | -15 | O-510 | -3.6 |

■ **MARTY BARRETT**   Barrett, Martin F.   b: 11/1860, Port Henry, N.Y.   d: 1/29/10, Holyoke, Mass.   BR/TR, 5'9", 170 lbs.   Deb: 6/24/1884

| 1884 | Bos-N | 3 | 6 | 0 | 0 | 0 | 0 | 0 | 0 | 4 | .000 | .000 | .000 | -99 | -1 | | | | .900 | -1 | /C-3 | -0.2 |
| Total | 1 | 8 | 19 | 1 | 1 | 1 | 0 | 0 | 0 | 1 | 4 | .053 | .100 | .105 | -34 | -3 | | | | .833 | -4 | /C-7,O-1 | -0.6 |

■ **RED BARRON**   Barron, David Irenus   b: 6/21/1900, Clarksville, Ga.   d: 10/4/82, Atlanta, Ga.   BR/TR, 5'11.5", 185 lbs.   Deb: 6/10/29

| 1929 | Bos-N | 10 | 21 | 3 | 4 | 1 | 0 | 0 | 1 | 1 | 4 | .190 | .227 | .238 | 16 | -3 | 2 | | | .929 | 1 | /O-6 | -0.2 |

■ **FRANK BARROWS**   Barrows, Franklin L.   b: 10/22/1846, Hudson, Ohio   d: 2/6/22, Fitchburg, Mass.   Deb: 5/20/1871

| 1871 | Bos-n | 18 | 86 | 13 | 13 | 2 | 1 | 0 | 11 | 0 | 0 | .151 | .151 | .198 | -1 | -11 | 1 | | | | | O-17/2-1 | -0.7 |

■ **SHAD BARRY**   Barry, John C.   b: 10/27/1878, Newburgh, N.Y.   d: 11/27/36, Los Angeles, Cal.   BR/TR,   Deb: 5/30/1899

1900	Bos-N	81	254	40	66	10	7	1	37	13		.260	.301	.366	74	-10	9			.956	-16	O-24,S-18,21/3	-2.4
1901	Bos-N	11	40	3	7	2	0	0	6	2		.175	.233	.225	30	-4	1			.926	-0	O-11	-0.5
Total	10	1100	4014	516	1073	128	47	10	391	279		.267	.321	.330	94	-37	140			.955	-65	O-625,1-295/23S	-14.0
Team	2	92	294	43	73	12	7	1	43	15		.248	.292	.347	69	-14	10			.944	-16	/O-35,S-18,213	-2.9

■ **DOC BASS**   Bass, Williams Capers (also played one game in 1918 under name of Johnson)
b: 12/4/1899, Macon, Ga.   d: 1/12/70, Macon, Ga.   BL/TL, 5'10", 165 lbs.   Deb: 7/29/18

| 1918 | Bos-N | 2 | 1 | 1 | 1 | 0 | 0 | 0 | 0 | 0 | 0 | 1.000 | 1.000 | 1.000 | 533 | 0 | 1 | | | .000 | 0 | /H | 0.1 |

■ **JOHNNY BATES**   Bates, John William   b: 8/21/1882, Steubenville, Ohio   d: 2/10/49, Steubenville, Ohio   BL/TL, 5'7", 168 lbs.   Deb: 4/12/06

1906	Bos-N	140	504	52	127	21	5	6	54	36		.252	.315	.349	110	5	9			.958	-10	*O-140	-1.3
1907	Bos-N	126	447	52	116	18	12	2	49	39		.260	.329	.367	118	9	11			.979	-2	*O-120	0.2
1908	Bos-N	127	445	48	115	14	6	1	29	35		.258	.315	.324	106	3	25			.948	-4	*O-117	-0.6
1909	Bos-N	63	236	27	68	15	3	1	23	20		.288	.354	.390	125	7	15			.945	5	O-60	1.0
Total	9	1154	3913	565	1087	167	73	25	417	503		.278	.367	.377	121	114	187			.955	9	*O-1080	7.3
Team	4	456	1632	179	426	68	26	10	155	130		.261	.324	.353	113	23	60			.958	-11	O-437	-0.7

■ **BOB BEALL**   Beall, Robert Brooks   b: 4/24/48, Portland, Ore.   BB/TL, 5'11", 180 lbs.   Deb: 5/12/75

1975	Atl-N	20	31	2	7	0	0	0	1	6	9	.226	.351	.290	77	-1	0	0	0	.984	-0	/1-8	-0.1
1978	Atl-N	108	185	29	45	8	0	1	16	36	27	.243	.369	.303	81	-3	4	5	-2	.987	-1	1-40/O-8	-0.9
1979	Atl-N	17	15	1	2	2	0	0	1	3	4	.133	.278	.267	46	-1	0	0	0	1.000	0	/1-3	-0.1
Total	4	148	234	32	54	12	0	1	18	45	41	.231	.357	.295	76	-6	4	5	-2	.987	-1	/1-51,O-8	-1.2
Team	3	145	231	32	54	12	0	1	18	45	40	.234	.361	.299	78	-5	4	5	-2	.987	-1	/1-51,O-8	-1.1

■ **TOMMY BEALS**   Beals, Thomas L. (a.k.a. W.Thomas In 1871-1873)   b: 8/1850, New York   d: 10/2/15, San Francisco, Cal.   BR, 5'5", 144 lbs.   Deb: 7/27/1871

1874	Bos-n	19	97	20	19	0	0	0		0		.196	.196	.309	55	-5						2-10/O-8	-0.4
1875	Bos-n	36	164	41	42	1	5	0		2		.256	.265	.323	99	-1						2-31,O-6	-0.1
Total	5 n	111	502	109	126	12	7	0	26	6	2	.251	.260	.343	87	-7						/2-74,O-25,CS	-0.8
Team	2 n	55	261	61	61	4	9	0	0	2	0	.234	.240	.318	82	0				.987	0	/2-41,O-14	-0.5

■ **JIM BEAUCHAMP**   Beauchamp, James Edward   b: 8/21/39, Vinita, Okla.   BR/TR, 6'2", 205 lbs.   Deb: 9/22/63 C

1965	Mil-N	4	3	0	0	0	0	0	0	1	1	.000	.250	.000	-23	-0	0	1	-1	1.000	-0	/1-2	-0.1
1967	Atl-N	4	3	0	0	0	0	0	1	0	0	.000	.000	.000	-99	-1	0	0	0	.000	0	H	-0.1
Total	10	393	661	79	153	18	4	14	90	54	150	.231	.292	.334	76	-22	6	5	-1	.980	-11	1-106/O-78	-4.7
Team	2	8	6	0	0	0	0	0	1	1	1	.000	.143	.000	-56	-1	0	1	-1	1.000	-0	/1-2	-0.2

■ **GINGER BEAUMONT**   Beaumont, Clarence Howeth   b: 7/23/1876, Rochester, Wis.   d: 4/10/56, Burlington, Wis.   BL/TR, 5'8", 190 lbs.   Deb: 4/21/1899

| 1907 | Bos-N | 150 | 580 | 67 | 187 | 19 | 14 | 4 | 62 | 37 | | .322 | .366 | .424 | 148 | 30 | 25 | | | .962 | 5 | *O-149 | 3.2 |
| 1908 | Bos-N | 125 | 476 | 66 | 127 | 20 | 6 | 2 | 52 | 42 | | .267 | .328 | .347 | 117 | 9 | 1 | | | .965 | -1 | *O-121 | 0.4 |

YEAR TM/L		G	AB	R	H	2B	3B	HR	RBI	BB	SO	AVG	OBP	SLG	PRO+	BR/A	SB	CS	SBR	FA	FR	G/POS	TPR
1909	Bos-N	123	407	35	107	11	4	0	60	35		.263	.321	.310	92	-4	12			.969	1	*O-111	-0.8
Total	12	1463	5660	955	1759	182	82	39	617	425		.311	.362	.393	122	151	254			.956	-26	*O-1407/1-2	4.7
Team	3	398	1463	168	421	50	24	6	174	114		.288	.341	.367	122	35	50			.965	5	O-381	2.8

■ **FRED BECK** Beck, Frederick Thomas b: 11/17/1886, Havana, Ill. d: 3/12/62, Havana, Ill. BL/TL, 6'1", 180 lbs. Deb: 4/14/09

YEAR TM/L		G	AB	R	H	2B	3B	HR	RBI	BB	SO	AVG	OBP	SLG	PRO+	BR/A	SB	CS	SBR	FA	FR	G/POS	TPR
1909	Bos-N	96	334	20	66	5	6	2	27	17		.198	.245	.266	56	-18	5			.966	4	O-57,1-33	-1.8
1910	Bos-N	154	571	52	157	32	9	**10**	64	19	55	.275	.307	.415	105	-0	8			.963	2	*O-134,1-19	-0.5
Total	5	635	2130	191	536	78	27	33	251	122	193	.252	.301	.360	85	-54	31			.984	-20	1-332,O-268	-10.0
Team	2	250	905	72	223	37	15	12	91	36	55	.246	.284	.360	88	-18	13			.964	6	O-191/1-52	-2.3

■ **BEALS BECKER** Becker, David Beals b: 7/5/1886, ElDorado, Kan. d: 8/16/43, Huntington Park, Cal. BL/TL, 5'9", 170 lbs. Deb: 4/19/08

YEAR TM/L		G	AB	R	H	2B	3B	HR	RBI	BB	SO	AVG	OBP	SLG	PRO+	BR/A	SB	CS	SBR	FA	FR	G/POS	TPR
1908	Bos-N	43	171	13	47	3	1	0	7	7		.275	.303	.304	96	-1	7			.941	-4	O-43	-0.8
1909	Bos-N	152	562	60	138	15	6	6	24	47		.246	.305	.326	91	-7	21			.932	-2	*O-152	-1.6
Total	8	876	2764	367	763	114	43	45	292	241		.276	.335	.397	112	35	129			.955	-13	O-758/1-2	-1.8
Team	2	195	733	73	185	18	7	6	31	54		.252	.305	.321	92	-8	28			.934	-6	O-195	-2.4

■ **HOWIE BEDELL** Bedell, Howard William b: 9/29/35, Clearfield, Pa. BL/TR, 6'1", 185 lbs. Deb: 4/10/62 C

YEAR TM/L		G	AB	R	H	2B	3B	HR	RBI	BB	SO	AVG	OBP	SLG	PRO+	BR/A	SB	CS	SBR	FA	FR	G/POS	TPR
1962	Mil-N	58	138	15	27	1	2	0	2	11	22	.196	.255	.232	33	-13	1	0	0	.955	-3	O-45	-1.8
Total	2	67	145	15	28	1	2	0	3	12	22	.193	.255	.228	32	-14	1	0	0	.993	-3	/O-45	-1.9

■ **GUS BELL** Bell, David Russell b: 11/15/28, Louisville, Ky. d: 5/7/95, Montogomery, Ohio BL/TR, 6'2", 196 lbs. Deb: 5/30/50 F

YEAR TM/L		G	AB	R	H	2B	3B	HR	RBI	BB	SO	AVG	OBP	SLG	PRO+	BR/A	SB	CS	SBR	FA	FR	G/POS	TPR
1962	Mil-N	79	214	28	61	11	3	5	24	12	17	.285	.323	.435	104	1	0	0	0	.987	-3	O-58	-0.6
1963	Mil-N	3	3	0	1	0	0	0	0	0	0	.333	.333	.333	94	-0	0	0	0	.000	0	H	0.0
1964	Mil-N	3	3	0	0	0	0	0	0	0	1	.000	.000	.000	-99	-1	0	0	0	.000	0	H	-0.1
Total	15	1741	6478	865	1823	311	66	206	942	470	636	.281	.333	.445	102	7	30	31	-10	.985	2	*O-1642	-8.3
Team	3	85	220	28	62	11	3	5	24	12	18	.282	.319	.427	101	-0	0	0	0	.987	-3	/O-58	-0.7

■ **LES BELL** Bell, Lester Rowland b: 12/14/01, Harrisburg, Pa. d: 12/26/85, Hershey, Pa. BR/TR, 5'11", 165 lbs. Deb: 9/18/23

YEAR TM/L		G	AB	R	H	2B	3B	HR	RBI	BB	SO	AVG	OBP	SLG	PRO+	BR/A	SB	CS	SBR	FA	FR	G/POS	TPR
1928	Bos-N	153	591	58	164	36	7	10	91	40	45	.277	.323	.413	96	-6	1			.948	5	*3-153	0.8
1929	Bos-N	139	483	58	144	23	5	9	72	50	42	.298	.364	.422	98	-1	4			.953	-20	*3-127/2-1,S	-1.5
Total	9	896	3239	404	938	184	49	66	509	276	322	.290	.346	.438	102	1	25			.939	-53	3-828/S-44,12	-0.3
Team	2	292	1074	116	308	59	12	19	163	90	87	.287	.342	.417	97	-7	5			.950	-15	3-280/2-1,S	-0.7

■ **MIKE BELL** Bell, Michael Allen b: 4/22/68, Lewiston, N.J. BL/TL, 6'1", 175 lbs. Deb: 5/2/90

YEAR TM/L		G	AB	R	H	2B	3B	HR	RBI	BB	SO	AVG	OBP	SLG	PRO+	BR/A	SB	CS	SBR	FA	FR	G/POS	TPR
1990	Atl-N	36	45	8	11	5	1	1	5	2	9	.244	.292	.467	99	-0	0	1	-1	.981	1	1-24	-0.1
1991	Atl-N	17	30	4	4	0	0	1	1	2	7	.133	.188	.233	17	-3	1	0	0	.975	-0	1-14	-0.4
Total	2	53	75	12	15	5	1	2	6	4	16	.200	.250	.373	67	-4	1	1	-0	.979	1	/1-38	-0.5

■ **TERRY BELL** Bell, Terence William b: 10/27/62, Dayton, Ohio BR/TR, 6', 195 lbs. Deb: 9/3/86

YEAR TM/L		G	AB	R	H	2B	3B	HR	RBI	BB	SO	AVG	OBP	SLG	PRO+	BR/A	SB	CS	SBR	FA	FR	G/POS	TPR
1987	Atl-N	1	1	0	0	0	0	0	0	0	1	.000	.000	.000	-95	-0	0	0	0	.000	0	/H	0.0
Total	2	9	4	0	0	0	0	0	0	2	2	.000	.333	.000	-0	-0	0	0	0	.976	-0	/C-8	0.0

■ **RAFAEL BELLIARD** Belliard, Rafael Leonidas (Matias) b: 10/24/61, Pueblo Nuevo, D.R. BR/TR, 5'6", 160 lbs. Deb: 9/6/82

YEAR TM/L		G	AB	R	H	2B	3B	HR	RBI	BB	SO	AVG	OBP	SLG	PRO+	BR/A	SB	CS	SBR	FA	FR	G/POS	TPR
1991	*Atl-N	149	353	36	88	9	2	0	27	22	63	.249	.297	.286	61	-18	3	1	0	.967	26	*S-145	1.7
1992	*Atl-N	144	285	20	60	6	1	0	14	14	43	.211	.255	.239	38	-23	0	1	-1	.969	**27**	*S-139/2-1	1.0
1993	*Atl-N	91	79	6	18	5	0	0	6	4	13	.228	.291	.291	56	-5	0	0	0	1.000	20	S-58,2-24	1.6
1994	Atl-N	46	120	9	29	7	1	0	9	2	29	.242	.266	.317	50	-9	0	2	-1	.984	-5	S-26,2-18	-1.2
1995	*Atl-N	75	180	12	40	2	1	0	7	6	28	.222	.255	.244	32	-17	2	2	-1	.992	13	S-40,2-32	-0.2
Total	14	989	2068	198	464	45	14	1	135	133	344	.224	.279	.261	49	-140	40	15	3	.973	109	S-773,2-150/3	1.7
Team	5	505	1017	83	235	29	5	0	63	48	176	.231	.274	.269	48	-72	5	6	-2	.973	81	S-408/2-75	2.9

■ **ROB BELLOIR** Belloir, Robert Edward b: 7/13/48, Heidelberg, Ger. BR/TR, 5'10", 155 lbs. Deb: 8/2/75

YEAR TM/L		G	AB	R	H	2B	3B	HR	RBI	BB	SO	AVG	OBP	SLG	PRO+	BR/A	SB	CS	SBR	FA	FR	G/POS	TPR
1975	Atl-N	43	105	11	23	2	1	0	9	7	8	.219	.268	.257	45	-8	0	0	0	.922	-2	S-38/2-1	-0.7
1976	Atl-N	30	60	5	12	2	0	0	4	5	7	.200	.262	.233	39	-5	0	0	0	.929	-1	S-12,3-10/2	-0.5
1977	Atl-N	6	1	2	0	0	0	0	0	0	0	.000	.000	.000	-89	-0	0	0	0	1.000	1	/S-3	0.1
1978	Atl-N	2	1	0	1	1	0	0	0	0	0	1.000	1.000	2.000	647	1	0	0	0	1.000	-0	/S-1,3-1	0.1
Total	4	81	167	18	36	5	1	0	13	12	15	.216	.268	.257	45	-12	0	0	0	.924	-3	/S-54,3-11,2	-1.0

■ **BRUCE BENEDICT** Benedict, Bruce Edwin b: 8/18/55, Birmingham, Ala. BR/TR, 6'1", 190 lbs. Deb: 8/18/78

YEAR TM/L		G	AB	R	H	2B	3B	HR	RBI	BB	SO	AVG	OBP	SLG	PRO+	BR/A	SB	CS	SBR	FA	FR	G/POS	TPR
1978	Atl-N	22	52	3	13	2	0	0	1	6	6	.250	.328	.288	66	-2	0	0	0	.990	2	C-22	0.0
1979	Atl-N	76	204	14	46	11	0	0	15	33	18	.225	.333	.279	64	-9	1	3	-2	.984	1	C-76	-0.8
1980	Atl-N	120	359	18	91	14	1	2	34	28	36	.253	.309	.315	72	-13	3	3	-1	.988	3	*C-120	-0.7
1981	Atl-N★	90	295	26	78	12	1	5	35	33	21	.264	.344	.363	98	-0	1	1	-0	.986	6	C-90	1.0
1982	*Atl-N	118	386	34	95	11	1	3	44	37	40	.246	.317	.303	71	-14	4	4	-1	**.993**	2	*C-118	-0.9
1983	Atl-N★	134	423	43	126	13	1	2	43	61	24	.298	.388	.348	98	2	1	3	-2	.992	9	*C-134	1.5
1984	Atl-N	95	300	26	67	8	1	4	25	34	25	.223	.304	.297	65	-13	1	2	-1	.991	1	C-95	-1.0
1985	Atl-N	70	208	12	42	6	0	0	20	22	12	.202	.281	.231	42	-16	0	1	-1	.989	-2	C-70	-1.6
1986	Atl-N	64	160	11	36	10	1	0	13	15	10	.225	.299	.300	62	-8	1	0	0	.993	-3	C-57	-0.8
1987	Atl-N	37	95	4	14	1	0	1	5	17	15	.147	.277	.189	25	-10	0	1	-1	.989	4	C-35	-0.5
1988	Atl-N	90	236	11	57	7	0	0	19	19	26	.242	.298	.271	61	-11	0	2	-1	.989	8	C-89	0.0
1989	Atl-N	66	160	12	31	3	0	1	6	23	18	.194	.299	.231	52	-9	0	0	0	.995	16	C-65	1.0
Total	12	982	2878	214	696	98	6	18	260	328	251	.242	.322	.299	71	-104	12	20	-8	.990	47	C-971	-2.8

■ **CHARLIE BENNETT** Bennett, Charles Wesley b: 11/21/1854, New Castle, Pa. d: 2/24/27, Detroit, Mich. BR/TR, 5'11", 180 lbs. Deb: 5/1/1878

YEAR TM/L		G	AB	R	H	2B	3B	HR	RBI	BB	SO	AVG	OBP	SLG	PRO+	BR/A	SB	CS	SBR	FA	FR	G/POS	TPR
1889	Bos-N	82	247	42	57	8	2	4	28	21	43	.231	.296	.328	70	-11	7			**.955**	12	C-82	0.6
1890	Bos-N	85	281	59	60	17	2	3	40	72	56	.214	.377	.320	96	1	6			**.959**	10	C-85	1.6
1891	Bos-N	75	256	35	55	9	3	5	39	42	61	.215	.332	.332	84	-6	3			**.960**	14	C-75	1.3
1892	*Bos-N	35	114	19	23	4	0	1	16	27	23	.202	.355	.263	80	-2	6			.948	1	C-35	0.2
1893	Bos-N	60	191	34	40	6	0	4	27	40	36	.209	.352	.304	69	-8	5			.953	-3	C-60	-0.6
Total	15	1062	3821	549	978	203	67	55	533	478	572	.256	.340	.387	118	90	42			.942	57	C-954/O-70,32S1	19.2
Team	5	337	1089	189	235	44	7	17	150	202	219	.216	.343	.316	81	-27	27			.943	33	C-337	3.1

■ **MARTY BERGEN** Bergen, Martin b: 10/25/1871, N.Brookfield, Mass d: 1/19/1900, N.Brookfield, Mass TR, 5'10", 170 lbs. Deb: 4/17/1896 F

YEAR TM/L		G	AB	R	H	2B	3B	HR	RBI	BB	SO	AVG	OBP	SLG	PRO+	BR/A	SB	CS	SBR	FA	FR	G/POS	TPR
1896	Bos-N	65	245	39	66	6	4	4	37	11	22	.269	.309	.376	75	-10	6			.920	6	C-63/1-1	0.2
1897	*Bos-N	87	327	47	81	11	3	2	45	18		.248	.295	.318	58	-21	5			.963	4	C-85/O-1	-0.6
1898	Bos-N	120	446	62	125	16	5	3	60	13		.280	.302	.359	85	-11	9			.962	2	*C-117/1-2	0.2
1899	Bos-N	72	260	32	67	11	3	1	34	10		.258	.290	.335	65	-14	4			.955	3	C-72	-0.5
Total	4	344	1278	180	339	44	15	10	176	52	22	.265	.299	.347	72	-56	24			.954	15	C-337/1-3,O	-0.7

■ **WALLY BERGER** Berger, Walter Antone b: 10/10/05, Chicago, Ill. d: 11/30/88, Redondo Beach, Cal BR/TR, 6'2", 198 lbs. Deb: 4/15/30

YEAR TM/L		G	AB	R	H	2B	3B	HR	RBI	BB	SO	AVG	OBP	SLG	PRO+	BR/A	SB	CS	SBR	FA	FR	G/POS	TPR
1930	Bos-N	151	555	98	172	27	14	38	119	54	69	.310	.375	.614	139	31	3			.966	4	*O-145	2.2
1931	Bos-N	156	617	94	199	44	8	19	84	55	70	.323	.380	.512	143	36	13			.977	11	*O-156/1-1	3.5
1932	Bos-N	145	602	90	185	34	6	17	73	33	66	.307	.346	.468	121	16	5			**.993**	5	*O-134,1-11	1.2
1933	Bos-N★	137	528	84	165	37	8	27	106	41	77	.313	.365	.566	**177**	49	2			.977	4	*O-136	4.7
1934	Bos-N★	150	615	92	183	35	8	34	121	49	65	.298	.352	.546	148	38	2			.978	1	*O-150	3.1
1935	Bos-N★	150	589	91	174	39	4	**34**	**130**	50	80	.295	.355	.548	151	39	3			.965	9	*O-149	4.0

YEAR	TM/L	G	AB	R	H	2B	3B	HR	RBI	BB	SO	AVG	OBP	SLG	PRO+	BR/A	SB	CS	SBR	FA	FR	G/POS	TPR
1936	Bos-N☆	138	534	88	154	23	3	25	91	53	84	.288	.361	.483	134	24	1			.966	7	*O-133	2.5
1937	Bos-N	30	113	14	31	9	1	5	22	11	33	.274	.344	.504	140	6	0			1.000	-2	O-28	0.3
Total	11	1350	5163	809	1550	299	59	242	898	435	694	.300	.359	.522	140	269	36			.974	26	*O-1296/1-13	22.2
Team	8	1057	4153	651	1263	248	52	199	746	346	544	.304	.362	.533	144	239	29			.975	39	*O-1031/1-12	21.5

■ JOHN BERGH
Bergh, John Baptist b: 10/8/1857, Boston, Mass. d: 4/16/1883, Boston, Mass. Deb: 8/5/1876

YEAR	TM/L	G	AB	R	H	2B	3B	HR	RBI	BB	SO	AVG	OBP	SLG	PRO+	BR/A	SB	CS	SBR	FA	FR	G/POS	TPR
1880	Bos-N	11	40	2	8	3	0	0	0	2	5	.200	.238	.275	76	-1				.844	-3	C-11	-0.4
Total	2	12	44	2	8	3	0	0	0	2	7	.182	.217	.250	59	-2				.841	-4	/C-12,O-1	-0.5

■ RAY BERRES
Berres, Raymond Frederick b: 8/31/07, Kenosha, Wis. BR/TR, 5'9", 170 lbs. Deb: 4/24/34 C

YEAR	TM/L	G	AB	R	H	2B	3B	HR	RBI	BB	SO	AVG	OBP	SLG	PRO+	BR/A	SB	CS	SBR	FA	FR	G/POS	TPR
1940	Bos-N	85	229	12	44	4	1	0	14	18	19	.192	.251	.218	32	-21	0			.981	1	C-85	-1.5
1941	Bos-N	120	279	21	56	10	0	1	19	17	20	.201	.247	.247	41	-22	2			**.995**	9	*C-120	-0.6
Total	11	561	1330	96	287	37	3	3	78	76	134	.216	.260	.255	43	-105	4			.989	40	C-551	-4.0
Team	2	205	508	33	100	14	1	1	33	35	39	.197	.249	.234	37	-43	2			.989	10	C-205	-2.1

■ GERONIMO BERROA
Berroa, Geronimo Emiliano Letta (b: Geronimo Emiliano Letta (Berroa)) b: 3/18/65, Santo Domingo, D.R. BR/TR, 6', 165 lbs. Deb: 4/5/89

YEAR	TM/L	G	AB	R	H	2B	3B	HR	RBI	BB	SO	AVG	OBP	SLG	PRO+	BR/A	SB	CS	SBR	FA	FR	G/POS	TPR
1989	Atl-N	81	136	7	36	4	0	2	9	7	32	.265	.301	.338	80	-4	0	1	-1	.971	1	O-34	-0.4
1990	Atl-N	7	4	0	0	0	0	0	0	1	1	.000	.200	.000	-38	-1	0	0	0	1.000	-1	/O-3	-0.2
Total	6	352	1075	154	300	46	5	37	162	116	201	.279	.352	.434	113	21	14	8	-1	.974	2	O-162,D-116/1	1.0
Team	2	88	140	7	36	4	0	2	9	8	33	.257	.297	.329	76	-4	0	1	-1	.972	0	/O-37	-0.6

■ DAMON BERRYHILL
Berryhill, Damon Scott b: 12/3/63, South Laguna, Cal. BB/TR, 6' ", 210 lbs. Deb: 9/5/87

YEAR	TM/L	G	AB	R	H	2B	3B	HR	RBI	BB	SO	AVG	OBP	SLG	PRO+	BR/A	SB	CS	SBR	FA	FR	G/POS	TPR
1991	Atl-N	1	1	0	0	0	0	0	0	0	1	.000	.000	.000	-94	-0	0	0	0	1.000	0	/C-1	0.0
1992	*Atl-N	101	307	21	70	16	1	10	43	17	67	.228	.271	.384	79	-9	0	2	-1	.998	-8	C-84	-1.5
1993	*Atl-N	115	335	24	82	18	2	8	43	21	64	.245	.293	.382	78	-11	0	0	0	.990	9	*C-105	0.3
Total	9	610	1863	158	445	98	6	44	234	119	380	.239	.287	.369	76	-64	3	6	-3	.988	-25	C-539/D-6,1	-6.4
Team	3	217	643	45	152	34	3	18	86	38	132	.236	.282	.383	78	-20	0	2	-1	.994	1	C-190	-1.2

■ DAVE BIRDSALL
Birdsall, David Solomon b: 7/16/1838, New York, N.Y. d: 12/30/1896, Boston, Mass. BR/TR, 5'9", 126 lbs. Deb: 5/5/1871

YEAR	TM/L	G	AB	R	H	2B	3B	HR	RBI	BB	SO	AVG	OBP	SLG	PRO+	BR/A	SB	CS	SBR	FA	FR	G/POS	TPR
1871	Bos-n	29	152	51	46	3	3	0	24	4	4	.303	.321	.362	93	-2	6					*O-26/C-3	-0.1
1872	Bos-n	16	76	11	14	3	0	0	14	1	0	.184	.195	.224	27	-7						C-11/O-5	-0.6
1873	Bos-n	3	12	4	1	0	0	0	1	0	0	.083	.083	.083	-47	-2						/O-3	-0.2
Total	3 n	48	240	66	61	6	3	0	39	5	4	.254	.269	.304	65	-11						/O-34,C-14	-0.9

■ ETHAN BLACKABY
Blackaby, Ethan Allen b: 7/24/40, Cincinnati, O. BL/TL, 5'11", 190 lbs. Deb: 9/6/62

YEAR	TM/L	G	AB	R	H	2B	3B	HR	RBI	BB	SO	AVG	OBP	SLG	PRO+	BR/A	SB	CS	SBR	FA	FR	G/POS	TPR
1962	Mil-N	6	13	0	2	1	0	0	0	1	8	.154	.214	.231	20	-1	0	0	0	1.000	-1	/O-3	-0.2
1964	Mil-N	9	12	0	1	0	0	0	1	1	2	.083	.154	.083	-31	-2	0	0	0	.500	-2	/O-5	-0.4
Total	2	15	25	0	3	1	0	0	1	2	10	.120	.185	.160	-4	-4	0	0	0	.800	-2	/O-8	-0.6

■ EARL BLACKBURN
Blackburn, Earl Stuart b: 11/1/1892, Leesville, Ohio d: 8/3/66, Mansfield, Ohio BR/TR, 5'11", 180 lbs. Deb: 9/17/12

YEAR	TM/L	G	AB	R	H	2B	3B	HR	RBI	BB	SO	AVG	OBP	SLG	PRO+	BR/A	SB	CS	SBR	FA	FR	G/POS	TPR
1915	Bos-N	3	6	0	1	0	0	0	0	2	1	.167	.375	.167	70	-0	0			1.000	-0	/C-3	0.0
1916	Bos-N	47	110	12	30	4	4	0	7	9	21	.273	.328	.382	123	3	2			.972	-1	C-44	0.5
Total	5	71	145	13	38	4	4	0	10	14	27	.262	.327	.345	107	1	4			.954	-2	/C-61	0.3
Team	2	50	116	12	31	4	4	0	7	11	22	.267	.331	.371	120	3	2			.974	-2	/C-47	0.5

■ LENA BLACKBURNE
Blackburne, Russell Aubrey "Slats"
b: 10/23/1886, Clifton Heights, Pa. d: 2/29/68, Riverside, N.J. BR/TR, 5'11", 160 lbs. Deb: 4/14/10 MC

YEAR	TM/L	G	AB	R	H	2B	3B	HR	RBI	BB	SO	AVG	OBP	SLG	PRO+	BR/A	SB	CS	SBR	FA	FR	G/POS	TPR
1919	Bos-N	31	80	5	21	3	1	0	4	6	7	.262	.322	.325	99	-0	3			.948	3	3-24/1-1,2S	0.5
Total	8	550	1807	173	387	39	23	4	139	162	151	.214	.284	.268	67	-69	54			.927	30	S-213,3-180,2/1P	-3.2

■ JOHNNY BLANCHARD
Blanchard, John Edwin b: 2/26/33, Minneapolis, Minn. BL/TR, 6'1", 198 lbs. Deb: 9/25/55

YEAR	TM/L	G	AB	R	H	2B	3B	HR	RBI	BB	SO	AVG	OBP	SLG	PRO+	BR/A	SB	CS	SBR	FA	FR	G/POS	TPR
1965	Mil-N	10	10	1	1	0	0	1	2	2	1	.100	.250	.400	79	-0	0	0	0	.000	-0	/O-1	-0.1
Total	8	516	1193	137	285	36	2	67	200	136	163	.239	.320	.441	109	13	2	0		.987	-25	O-169,C-155/1	-1.6

■ LARVELL BLANKS
Blanks, Larvell b: 1/28/50, Del Rio, Tex. BR/TR, 5'8", 167 lbs. Deb: 7/19/72

YEAR	TM/L	G	AB	R	H	2B	3B	HR	RBI	BB	SO	AVG	OBP	SLG	PRO+	BR/A	SB	CS	SBR	FA	FR	G/POS	TPR
1972	Atl-N	33	85	10	28	5	0	1	7	7	12	.329	.380	.424	117	2	0	0	0	1.000	6	2-18/S-4,3	1.0
1973	Atl-N	17	18	1	4	0	0	0	0	1	3	.222	.263	.222	33	-2	0	0	0	.000	-3	/3-3,2-2,S	-0.4
1974	Atl-N	3	8	0	2	0	0	0	1	0	0	.250	.250	.250	38	-1	0	0	0	.889	-0	/S-2	-0.1
1975	Atl-N	141	471	49	110	13	3	3	38	38	43	.234	.294	.293	61	-25	4	3	-1	.960	-12	*S-129,2-12	-2.5
1980	Atl-N	88	221	23	45	6	0	2	12	16	27	.204	.257	.258	43	-17	1	2	-1	.947	7	S-56,3-43/2	-0.8
Total	9	629	1766	203	446	57	14	20	172	132	178	.253	.306	.335	78	-51	9	7	-2	.957	-66	S-407,2-124/3D	-7.6
Team	5	282	803	83	189	24	3	6	58	62	85	.235	.292	.295	61	-42	5	5	-2	.958	-2	S-193/3-48,2	-2.8

■ JEFF BLAUSER
Blauser, Jeffrey Michael b: 11/8/65, Los Gatos, Cal. BR/TR, 6'1", 180 lbs. Deb: 7/5/87

YEAR	TM/L	G	AB	R	H	2B	3B	HR	RBI	BB	SO	AVG	OBP	SLG	PRO+	BR/A	SB	CS	SBR	FA	FR	G/POS	TPR
1987	Atl-N	51	165	11	40	6	3	2	15	18	34	.242	.328	.352	76	-5	7	3	0	.962	10	S-50	0.9
1988	Atl-N	18	67	7	16	3	1	2	7	2	11	.239	.271	.403	87	-1	0	1	-1	.967	3	/2-9,S-8	0.2
1989	Atl-N	142	456	63	123	24	2	12	46	38	101	.270	.327	.410	107	3	5	2	0	.929	-17	3-78,2-39,S/O	-1.0
1990	Atl-N	115	386	46	104	24	3	8	39	35	70	.269	.338	.409	99	-1	3	5	-2	.961	-3	S-93,2-14/3O	0.2
1991	*Atl-N	129	352	49	91	14	3	11	54	54	59	.259	.360	.409	109	5	5	6	-2	.948	-36	S-85,2-32,3	-2.9
1992	*Atl-N	123	343	61	90	19	3	14	46	46	82	.262	.356	.458	122	10	5	5	-2	.968	-47	*S-106,2-21/3	-3.5
1993	*Atl-N★	161	597	110	182	29	2	15	73	85	109	.305	.405	.436	124	24	16	6	1	.970	-23	*S-161	1.5
1994	Atl-N	96	380	56	98	21	4	6	45	38	64	.258	.333	.382	84	-9	1	3	-2	.970	3	S-96	0.1
1995	*Atl-N	115	431	60	91	16	2	12	31	57	107	.211	.320	.341	73	-16	8	5	-1	.970	-1	*S-115	-0.7
Total	9	950	3177	463	835	156	23	82	356	373	637	.263	.349	.404	101	11	50	36	-7	.966	-110	S-744,2-115,3/O	-5.2

■ TERRY BLOCKER
Blocker, Terry Fennell b: 8/18/59, Columbia, S.C. BL/TL, 6'2", 195 lbs. Deb: 4/11/85

YEAR	TM/L	G	AB	R	H	2B	3B	HR	RBI	BB	SO	AVG	OBP	SLG	PRO+	BR/A	SB	CS	SBR	FA	FR	G/POS	TPR
1988	Atl-N	66	198	13	42	4	2	2	10	10	20	.212	.250	.283	50	-13	1	1	-0	.994	4	O-61	-1.2
1989	Atl-N	26	31	1	7	1	0	0	1	1	5	.226	.250	.258	44	-2	1	0	0	1.000	-2	/O-8,P-1	-0.4
Total	3	110	244	15	50	5	2	2	11	12	27	.205	.242	.266	44	-18	2	1	0	.994	1	/O-74,P-1	-2.0
Team	2	92	229	14	49	5	2	2	11	11	25	.214	.250	.279	49	-15	2	1	0	.994	2	/O-69,P-1	-1.6

■ TONY BOECKEL
Boeckel, Norman Doxie b: 8/25/1892, Los Angeles, Cal. d: 2/16/24, Torrey Pines, Cal. BR/TR, 5'10.5", 175 lbs. Deb: 7/23/17

YEAR	TM/L	G	AB	R	H	2B	3B	HR	RBI	BB	SO	AVG	OBP	SLG	PRO+	BR/A	SB	CS	SBR	FA	FR	G/POS	TPR
1919	Bos-N	95	365	42	91	11	5	1	26	35	13	.249	.317	.315	94	-2	10			.960	-4	3-93	-0.2
1920	Bos-N	153	582	70	156	28	5	3	62	38	50	.268	.314	.349	94	-5	18	15	-4	.936	-7	*3-149/S-3,2	-0.8
1921	Bos-N	153	592	93	185	20	13	10	84	52	41	.313	.370	.441	120	17	20	15	-3	.933	-12	*3-153	1.2
1922	Bos-N	119	402	61	116	19	6	6	47	35	32	.289	.349	.410	99	-1	14	8	-1	.952	-11	*3-106	-0.4
1923	Bos-N	148	568	72	169	32	4	7	79	51	31	.298	.357	.405	105	4	11	8	-2	.939	-10	*3-147/S-1	0.6
Total	6	777	2880	372	813	130	36	27	337	237	218	.282	.339	.381	102	10	90	46		.941	-55	3-755/S-4,2	-1.0
Team	5	668	2509	338	717	110	33	27	298	211	167	.286	.343	.388	104	13	73	46		.942	-43	3-648/S-4,2	0.4

■ FRANK BOLLING
Bolling, Frank Elmore b: 11/16/31, Mobile, Ala. BR/TR, 6'1", 175 lbs. Deb: 4/13/54 F

YEAR	TM/L	G	AB	R	H	2B	3B	HR	RBI	BB	SO	AVG	OBP	SLG	PRO+	BR/A	SB	CS	SBR	FA	FR	G/POS	TPR
1961	Mil-N★	148	585	86	153	16	4	15	56	57	62	.262	.330	.379	93	-6	7	3	0	**.988**	1	*2-148	1.1
1962	Mil-N★	122	406	45	110	17	4	9	43	35	45	.271	.335	.399	99	-1	2	2	-1	**.989**	-9	*2-119	0.1
1963	Mil-N	142	542	73	132	18	2	5	43	41	47	.244	.300	.312	77	-15	2	1	0	.981	-5	*2-141	-0.8
1964	Mil-N	120	352	35	70	11	1	5	34	21	44	.199	.248	.278	48	-24	0	1	-1	**.985**	-9	*2-117	-2.7
1965	Mil-N	148	535	55	141	26	3	7	50	24	41	.264	.295	.363	84	-12	0	4	-2	.976	-16	*2-147	-1.9

YEAR	TM/L	G	AB	R	H	2B	3B	HR	RBI	BB	SO	AVG	OBP	SLG	PRO+	BR/A	SB	CS	SBR	FA	FR	G/POS	TPR
1966	Atl-N	75	227	16	48	7	0	1	18	10	14	.211	.248	.256	40	-18	1	1	-0	.983	-15	2-67	-3.2
Total	12	1540	5562	692	1415	221	40	106	556	462	558	.254	.315	.366	85	-114	40	38	-11	.982	-98	*2-1518	-10.2
Team	6	755	2647	310	654	95	14	42	244	188	253	.247	.300	.341	78	-77	12	12	-4	.984	-54	2-739	-7.4

■ TOMMY BOND Bond, Thomas Henry b: 4/2/1856, Granard, Ireland d: 1/24/41, Boston, Mass. BR/TR, 5'7.5", 160 lbs. Deb: 5/5/1874 MU

YEAR	TM/L	G	AB	R	H	2B	3B	HR	RBI	BB	SO	AVG	OBP	SLG	PRO+	BR/A	SB	CS	SBR	FA	FR	G/POS	TPR
1877	Bos-N	61	259	32	59	4	3	0	30	1	15	.228	.231	.266	54	-14				.937	3	*P-58/O-3	-0.1
1878	Bos-N	59	236	22	50	4	1	0	23	0	9	.212	.212	.237	44	-15				.941	1	*P-59/O-2	-0.1
1879	Bos-N	65	257	35	62	3	1	0	21	6	8	.241	.259	.261	70	-8				**.957**	5	*P-64/O-5,1	-0.2
1880	Bos-N	76	282	27	62	4	1	0	24	8	14	.220	.241	.241	66	-9				.940	13	*P-63,O-26/31	0.0
1881	Bos-N	3	10	0	2	0	0	0	0	0	0	.200	.200	.200	27	-1				1.000	1	/P-3	0.0
Total	2 n	126	536	57	132	23	3	0		1		.246	.248	.300	84	-9						/P-95,O-29,21	0.3
Total	8	361	1441	156	340	32	7	0	121	21	53	.236	.247	.268	64	-59				.927	24	P-322/O-63,31	-1.4
Team	5	264	1044	116	235	15	6	0	98	15	46	.225	.236	.251	58	-46				.945	23	P-247/O-36,13	-0.4

■ BARRY BONNELL Bonnell, Robert Barry b: 10/27/53, Clermont County, O. BR/TR, 6'3", 200 lbs. Deb: 5/4/77

YEAR	TM/L	G	AB	R	H	2B	3B	HR	RBI	BB	SO	AVG	OBP	SLG	PRO+	BR/A	SB	CS	SBR	FA	FR	G/POS	TPR
1977	Atl-N	100	360	41	108	11	0	1	45	37	32	.300	.368	.339	81	-8	7	5	-1	.989	8	O-75,3-32	-0.4
1978	Atl-N	117	304	36	73	11	3	1	16	20	30	.240	.287	.306	59	-17	12	6	0	.984	-9	*O-105,3-15	-3.1
1979	Atl-N	127	375	47	97	20	3	12	45	26	55	.259	.312	.424	92	-5	8	7	-2	.983	-15	*O-124/3-1	-2.7
Total	10	976	3068	363	833	143	24	56	355	229	387	.272	.325	.389	89	-45	64	39	-4	.982	-51	O-859/3-71,D1	-13.0
Team	3	344	1039	124	278	42	6	14	106	83	117	.268	.325	.360	79	-29	27	18	-3	.985	-17	O-304/3-48	-6.2

■ FRANK BONNER Bonner, Frank J b: 8/20/1869, Lowell, Mass. d: 12/31/05, Kansas City, Mo. BR/TR, 5'7.5", 169 lbs. Deb: 4/26/1894

YEAR	TM/L	G	AB	R	H	2B	3B	HR	RBI	BB	SO	AVG	OBP	SLG	PRO+	BR/A	SB	CS	SBR	FA	FR	G/POS	TPR
1903	Bos-N	48	173	11	38	5	0	1	10	7		.220	.262	.266	53	-11	2			.957	-4	2-24,S-22	-1.2
Total	6	246	949	115	244	44	8	4	115	55		.257	.305	.333	73	-38	28			.931	-36	2-190/S-23,3OC	-5.6

■ AL BOOL Bool, Albert J. b: 8/24/1897, Lincoln, Neb. d: 9/27/81, Lincoln, Neb. BR/TR, 5'11", 180 lbs. Deb: 9/29/28

YEAR	TM/L	G	AB	R	H	2B	3B	HR	RBI	BB	SO	AVG	OBP	SLG	PRO+	BR/A	SB	CS	SBR	FA	FR	G/POS	TPR
1931	Bos-N	49	85	5	16	1	0	0	6	9	13	.188	.266	.200	28	-8	0			.989	-2	C-37	-0.9
Total	3	129	308	35	73	13	4	7	53	34	42	.237	.313	.373	71	-15	0			.973	-2	C-104	-1.0

■ RAY BOONE Boone, Raymond Otis "Ike" b: 7/27/23, San Diego, Cal. BR/TR, 6'1", 188 lbs. Deb: 9/3/48 F

YEAR	TM/L	G	AB	R	H	2B	3B	HR	RBI	BB	SO	AVG	OBP	SLG	PRO+	BR/A	SB	CS	SBR	FA	FR	G/POS	TPR
1959	Mil-N	13	15	3	3	0	0	1	2	4	2	.200	.368	.400	114	0	0	0	0	1.000	-0	/1-3	0.0
1960	Mil-N	7	12	3	3	1	0	0	4	5	1	.250	.471	.333	135	1	0	0	0	1.000	0	/1-4	0.1
Total	13	1373	4589	645	1260	162	46	151	737	608	463	.275	.363	.429	115	95	21	19		.958	-46	3-510,S-464,1/2	5.3
Team	2	20	27	6	6	1	0	1	6	9	3	.222	.417	.370	124	1	0	0		1.000	0	/1-7	0.1

■ FRANK BOWERMAN Bowerman, Frank Eugene "Mike" b: 12/5/1868, Romeo, Mich. d: 11/30/48, Romeo, Mich. BR/TR, 6'2", 190 lbs. Deb: 8/24/1895 M

YEAR	TM/L	G	AB	R	H	2B	3B	HR	RBI	BB	SO	AVG	OBP	SLG	PRO+	BR/A	SB	CS	SBR	FA	FR	G/POS	TPR
1908	Bos-N	86	254	16	58	8	1	1	25	13		.228	.274	.280	78	-7	4			.971	-3	C-63,1-11	-0.5
1909	Bos-N	33	99	6	21	2	0	0	4	2		.212	.228	.232	41	-7	0			.928	1	C-27,M	-0.4
Total	15	1045	3401	343	852	102	38	13	392	129		.251	.287	.314	77	-105	81			.963	40	C-826,1-132/2S3PO	0.6
Team	2	119	353	22	79	10	1	1	29	15		.224	.261	.266	67	-14	4			.956	-2	/C-90,1-11	-0.9

■ BOB BOYD Boyd, Robert Richard "The Rope" b: 10/1/25, Potts Camp, Miss. BL/TL, 5'10", 170 lbs. Deb: 9/8/51

YEAR	TM/L	G	AB	R	H	2B	3B	HR	RBI	BB	SO	AVG	OBP	SLG	PRO+	BR/A	SB	CS	SBR	FA	FR	G/POS	TPR
1961	Mil-N	36	41	3	10	0	0	0	3	1	7	.244	.262	.244	38	-4	0	0	0	1.000	1	/1-3	-0.3
Total	9	693	1936	253	567	81	23	19	175	167	114	.293	.351	.388	105	14	9	17		.991	-24	1-475/O-38	-4.6

■ CLETE BOYER Boyer, Cletis Leroy b: 2/9/37, Cassville, Mo. BR/TR, 6', 182 lbs. Deb: 6/5/55 FC

YEAR	TM/L	G	AB	R	H	2B	3B	HR	RBI	BB	SO	AVG	OBP	SLG	PRO+	BR/A	SB	CS	SBR	FA	FR	G/POS	TPR
1967	Atl-N	154	572	63	140	18	3	26	96	39	81	.245	.295	.423	105	1	6	3	0	**.970**	5	*3-150/S-6	0.6
1968	Atl-N	71	273	19	62	7	2	4	17	16	32	.227	.275	.311	75	-8	2	0	1	.981	-0	3-69	-0.9
1969	*Atl-N	144	496	57	124	16	1	14	57	55	87	.250	.330	.371	96	-3	3	7	-3	**.965**	3	*3-141	-0.3
1970	Atl-N	134	475	44	117	14	1	16	62	41	71	.246	.308	.381	79	-15	2	5	-2	.954	12	*3-126/S-5	-0.6
1971	Atl-N	30	98	10	24	1	0	6	19	8	11	.245	.302	.439	101	-0	0	0	0	.961	3	3-25/S-1	0.2
Total	16	1725	5780	645	1396	200	33	162	654	470	931	.242	.301	.372	87	-112	41	28	-5	.965	233	*3-1439,S-186/2O	12.6
Team	5	533	1914	193	467	56	7	66	251	159	282	.244	.305	.384	91	-25	13	15	-5	.966	23	3-511/S-12	-1.0

■ BUZZ BOYLE Boyle, Ralph Francis b: 2/9/08, Cincinnati, Ohio d: 11/12/78, Cincinnati, Ohio BL/TL, 5'11.5", 170 lbs. Deb: 9/11/29 F

YEAR	TM/L	G	AB	R	H	2B	3B	HR	RBI	BB	SO	AVG	OBP	SLG	PRO+	BR/A	SB	CS	SBR	FA	FR	G/POS	TPR
1929	Bos-N	17	57	8	15	2	1	1	2	6	11	.263	.333	.386	81	-2	2			1.000	-0	O-17	-0.3
1930	Bos-N	1	1	0	0	0	0	0	0	0	1	.000	.000	.000	-99	-0	0			.000	-1	/O-1	-0.1
Total	5	366	1343	185	389	58	24	12	125	116	125	.290	.347	.395	105	10	24			.970	6	O-353	-0.0
Team	2	18	58	8	15	2	1	1	2	6	12	.259	.328	.379	78	-2	2			1.000	-1	/O-18	-0.4

■ BOB BRADY Brady, Robert Jay b: 11/8/22, Lewistown, Pa. BL/TR, 6'1", 175 lbs. Deb: 8/24/46

YEAR	TM/L	G	AB	R	H	2B	3B	HR	RBI	BB	SO	AVG	OBP	SLG	PRO+	BR/A	SB	CS	SBR	FA	FR	G/POS	TPR
1946	Bos-N	3	5	0	1	0	0	0	0	1	1	.200	.333	.200	52	-0	0			.857	0	/C-1	0.0
1947	Bos-N	1	1	0	0	0	0	0	0	0	0	.000	.000	.000	-99	-0	0			.000	0	H	0.0
Total	2	4	6	0	1	0	0	0	0	1	1	.167	.286	.167	29	-1	0			.833	0	/C-1	0.0

■ DAVE BRAIN Brain, David Leonard b: 1/24/1879, Hereford, England d: 5/25/59, Los Angeles, Cal. BR/TR, 5'10", 170 lbs. Deb: 4/24/01

YEAR	TM/L	G	AB	R	H	2B	3B	HR	RBI	BB	SO	AVG	OBP	SLG	PRO+	BR/A	SB	CS	SBR	FA	FR	G/POS	TPR
1906	Bos-N	139	525	43	131	19	5	5	45	29		.250	.293	.333	98	-3	11			.917	26	*3-139	2.9
1907	Bos-N	133	509	60	142	24	9	**10**	56	29		.279	.324	.420	134	17	10			.916	25	*3-130/O-3	5.0
Total	7	679	2543	254	641	97	52	27	303	134		.252	.292	.363	101	-10	73			.913	58	3-431,S-165/O21	7.0
Team	2	272	1034	103	273	43	14	15	101	58		.264	.308	.376	116	13	21			.917	50	3-269/O-3	7.9

■ KITTY BRANSFIELD Bransfield, William Edward b: 1/7/1875, Worcester, Mass. d: 5/1/47, Worcester, Mass. BR/TR, 5'11", 207 lbs. Deb: 8/22/1898 U

YEAR	TM/L	G	AB	R	H	2B	3B	HR	RBI	BB	SO	AVG	OBP	SLG	PRO+	BR/A	SB	CS	SBR	FA	FR	G/POS	TPR
1898	Bos-N	5	9	2	2	0	1	0	1	0		.222	.222	.444	85	-0	0			.889	-1	/C-4,1-1	-0.1
Total	12	1330	4999	529	1351	225	75	13	637	221		.270	.304	.353	97	-35	175			.983	-18	*1-1291/C-4	-8.1

■ BUSTER BRAY Bray, Clarence Wilbur b: 4/1/13, Birmingham, Ala. d: 9/4/82, Evansville, Ind. BL/TL, 6', 170 lbs. Deb: 4/18/41

YEAR	TM/L	G	AB	R	H	2B	3B	HR	RBI	BB	SO	AVG	OBP	SLG	PRO+	BR/A	SB	CS	SBR	FA	FR	G/POS	TPR
1941	Bos-N	4	11	2	1	1	0	0	1	1	2	.091	.167	.182	-2	-2	0			1.000	-0	/O-3	-0.2

■ SID BREAM Bream, Sidney Eugene b: 8/3/60, Carlisle, Pa. BL/TL, 6'4", 220 lbs. Deb: 9/1/83

YEAR	TM/L	G	AB	R	H	2B	3B	HR	RBI	BB	SO	AVG	OBP	SLG	PRO+	BR/A	SB	CS	SBR	FA	FR	G/POS	TPR
1991	*Atl-N	91	265	32	67	12	0	11	45	25	31	.253	.317	.423	100	-0	0	3	-2	.996	-0	1-85	-0.7
1992	*Atl-N	125	372	30	97	25	1	10	61	46	51	.261	.344	.414	107	4	6	0	2	.989	-3	*1-120	-0.5
1993	*Atl-N	117	277	33	72	14	1	9	35	31	43	.260	.334	.415	98	-1	4	2	0	.996	5	1-90	-0.1
Total	12	1088	3108	351	819	191	12	90	455	353	450	.264	.340	.420	107	32	50	40		.992	74	1-954/O-2	3.6
Team	3	333	914	95	236	51	2	30	141	102	125	.258	.333	.417	102	3	10	5		.993	2	1-295	-1.3

■ JIM BREAZEALE Breazeale, James Leo b: 10/3/49, Houston, Tex. BL/TR, 6'2", 210 lbs. Deb: 9/13/69

YEAR	TM/L	G	AB	R	H	2B	3B	HR	RBI	BB	SO	AVG	OBP	SLG	PRO+	BR/A	SB	CS	SBR	FA	FR	G/POS	TPR
1969	Atl-N	2	1	1	0	0	0	0	0	2	0	.000	.667	.000	101	0	0	0	0	.833	-0	/1-1	0.0
1971	Atl-N	10	21	1	4	0	0	1	3	0	3	.190	.190	.333	43	-2	0	0	0	1.000	-0	/1-4	-0.2
1972	Atl-N	52	85	10	21	2	0	5	17	6	12	.247	.297	.447	100	-0	0	1	-1	1.000	-2	1-16/3-1	-0.4
Total	4	89	179	20	40	5	0	9	33	16	25	.223	.287	.402	88	-3	0	1	-1	.993	-5	/1-40,D-4,3	-1.1
Team	3	64	107	12	25	2	0	6	20	8	15	.234	.287	.421	91	-2	0	1	-1	.994	-2	/1-21,3-1	-0.6

■ AL BRIDWELL Bridwell, Albert Henry b: 1/4/1884, Friendship, Ohio d: 1/23/69, Portsmouth, Ohio BL/TR, 5'9", 170 lbs. Deb: 4/16/05

YEAR	TM/L	G	AB	R	H	2B	3B	HR	RBI	BB	SO	AVG	OBP	SLG	PRO+	BR/A	SB	CS	SBR	FA	FR	G/POS	TPR
1906	Bos-N	120	459	41	104	9	1	0	22	44		.227	.297	.251	73	-14	6			.930	17	*S-119/O-1	0.8
1907	Bos-N	140	509	49	111	8	2	0	26	61		.218	.309	.242	73	-13	17			**.942**	7	*S-140	-0.4
1911	Bos-N	51	182	29	53	5	0	0	10	33	8	.291	.403	.319	95	0	2			.950	-11	S-51	-0.7

YEAR	TM/L	G	AB	R	H	2B	3B	HR	RBI	BB	SO	AVG	OBP	SLG	PRO+	BR/A	SB	CS	SBR	FA	FR	G/POS	TPR
1912	Bos-N	31	106	6	25	5	1	0	14	5	5	.236	.270	.302	55	-7	2			.936	-6	S-31	-1.0
Total	11	1252	4169	457	1064	95	32	2	348	557	98	.255	.347	.295	87	-45	136			.939	23	*S-1094/2-60,3O1	3.4
Team	4	342	1256	125	293	27	4	0	72	143	13	.233	.316	.261	75	-33	27			.938	7	S-341/O-1	-1.3

■ **STEVE BRODIE** Brodie, Walter Scott b: 9/11/1868, Warrenton, Va. d: 10/30/35, Baltimore, Md. BL/TR, 5'11", 180 lbs. Deb: 4/21/1890

YEAR	TM/L	G	AB	R	H	2B	3B	HR	RBI	BB	SO	AVG	OBP	SLG	PRO+	BR/A	SB	CS	SBR	FA	FR	G/POS	TPR
1890	Bos-N	132	514	77	152	19	9	0	67	66	20	.296	.387	.368	111	8	29			**.953**	3	*O-132	0.6
1891	Bos-N	133	523	84	136	13	6	2	78	63	39	.260	.351	.319	85	-11	25			.951	10	*O-133	-0.4
Total	12	1437	5699	886	1726	191	89	25	900	420	148	.303	.364	.381	102	15	289			.959	48	*O-1420/2-16,3	-2.0
Team	2	265	1037	161	288	32	15	2	145	129	59	.278	.369	.343	98	-3	54			.952	14	O-265	0.2

■ **SIG BROSKIE** Broskie, Sigmund Theodore "Chops" b: 3/23/11, Iselin, Pa. d: 5/17/75, Canton, Ohio BR/TR, 5'11.5", 200 lbs. Deb: 9/11/40

YEAR	TM/L	G	AB	R	H	2B	3B	HR	RBI	BB	SO	AVG	OBP	SLG	PRO+	BR/A	SB	CS	SBR	FA	FR	G/POS	TPR
1940	Bos-N	11	22	1	6	1	0	0	4	1	2	.273	.304	.318	76	-1	0			.935	0	C-11	0.0

■ **DAN BROUTHERS** Brouthers, Dennis Joseph "Big Dan" b: 5/8/1858, Sylvan Lake, N.Y. d: 8/2/32, E.Orange, N.J. BL/TL, 6'2", 207 lbs. Deb: 6/23/1879 H

YEAR	TM/L	G	AB	R	H	2B	3B	HR	RBI	BB	SO	AVG	OBP	SLG	PRO+	BR/A	SB	CS	SBR	FA	FR	G/POS	TPR
1889	Bos-N	126	485	105	181	26	9	7	118	66	6	**.373**	.462	.507	161	42	22			.974	1	*1-126	2.9
Total	19	1673	6711	1523	2296	460	205	106	1296	840	238	.342	.423	.519	170	609	256			.971	-18	*1-1633/O-35,P3	41.1

■ **DRUMMOND BROWN** Brown, Drummond Nicol b: 1/31/1885, Los Angeles, Cal. d: 1/27/27, Parkville, Mo. BR/TR, 6', 180 lbs. Deb: 4/25/13

YEAR	TM/L	G	AB	R	H	2B	3B	HR	RBI	BB	SO	AVG	OBP	SLG	PRO+	BR/A	SB	CS	SBR	FA	FR	G/POS	TPR
1913	Bos-N	15	34	3	11	1	0	1	2	2	9	.324	.361	.441	126	1	0			.960	-4	C-12	-0.2
Total	3	123	319	20	77	14	1	2	33	21	38	.241	.294	.310	64	-17	4			.960	-2	C-100/1-3	-1.2

■ **EDDIE BROWN** Brown, Edward William "Glass Arm Eddie" b: 7/17/1891, Milligan, Neb. d: 9/10/56, Vallejo, Cal. BR/TR, 6'3", 190 lbs. Deb: 9/26/20

YEAR	TM/L	G	AB	R	H	2B	3B	HR	RBI	BB	SO	AVG	OBP	SLG	PRO+	BR/A	SB	CS	SBR	FA	FR	G/POS	TPR
1926	Bos-N	153	612	71	**201**	31	8	2	84	23	20	.328	.355	.415	117	12	5			.965	8	*O-153	1.0
1927	Bos-N	155	558	64	171	35	6	2	75	28	20	.306	.340	.401	106	3	11			.980	3	*O-150/1-1	-0.4
1928	Bos-N	142	523	45	140	28	2	2	59	24	22	.268	.305	.340	72	-22	6			.960	-4	*O-129/1-1	-3.5
Total	7	790	2902	341	878	170	33	16	407	127	109	.303	.334	.400	99	-14	29			.970	13	O-731/1-2	-5.1
Team	3	450	1693	180	512	94	16	6	218	75	62	.302	.334	.387	99	-8	22			.968	6	O-432/1-2	-2.9

■ **FRED BROWN** Brown, Fred Herbert b: 4/12/1879, Ossipee, N.H. d: 2/3/55, Somersworth, N.H. BR/TR, 5'10.5", 190 lbs. Deb: 5/4/01

YEAR	TM/L	G	AB	R	H	2B	3B	HR	RBI	BB	SO	AVG	OBP	SLG	PRO+	BR/A	SB	CS	SBR	FA	FR	G/POS	TPR
1901	Bos-N	7	14	1	2	0	0	0	2	0		.143	.143	.143	-16	-2	0			1.000	0	/O-5	-0.2
1902	Bos-N	2	6	1	2	1	0	0	0	0		.333	.333	.500	155	0	0			1.000	0	/O-2	0.0
Total	2	9	20	2	4	1	0	0	2	0		.200	.200	.250	30	-2	0			1.000	0	/O-7	-0.2

■ **JARVIS BROWN** Brown, Jarvis Ardel b: 3/26/67, Waukegan, Ill. BR/TR, 5'7", 165 lbs. Deb: 7/2/91

YEAR	TM/L	G	AB	R	H	2B	3B	HR	RBI	BB	SO	AVG	OBP	SLG	PRO+	BR/A	SB	CS	SBR	FA	FR	G/POS	TPR
1994	Atl-N	17	15	3	2	1	0	1	1	0	2	.133	.133	.400	31	-2	0	0	0	1.000	-2	/O-9	-0.3
Total	5	155	227	44	46	11	2	1	10	26	49	.203	.304	.282	57	-13	13	7		.978	-26	O-132/D-6	-4.1

■ **LEW BROWN** Brown, Lewis J. "Blower" b: 2/1/1858, Leominster, Mass. d: 1/16/1889, Boston, Mass. BR/TR, 5'10.5", 185 lbs. Deb: 6/17/1876

YEAR	TM/L	G	AB	R	H	2B	3B	HR	RBI	BB	SO	AVG	OBP	SLG	PRO+	BR/A	SB	CS	SBR	FA	FR	G/POS	TPR
1876	Bos-N	45	195	23	41	6	6	2	21	3	22	.210	.222	.333	82	-4				.856	-2	C-45/O-1	-0.4
1877	Bos-N	58	221	27	56	12	8	1	31	6	33	.253	.273	.394	104	0				.897	15	*C-55/1-4	1.6
1883	Bos-N	14	54	5	13	4	1	0	9	3	6	.241	.281	.352	89	-1				.943	-2	1-14	-0.3
Total	7	378	1531	205	379	83	31	10	169	45	155	.248	.269	.362	94	-13				.884	17	C-248,1-118/OP	0.4
Team	3	117	470	55	110	22	15	3	61	12	61	.234	.253	.364	93	-4				.882	12	C-100/1-18,O	0.9

■ **OSCAR BROWN** Brown, Oscar Lee b: 2/8/46, Long Beach, Cal. BR/TR, 6', 175 lbs. Deb: 9/3/69 F

YEAR	TM/L	G	AB	R	H	2B	3B	HR	RBI	BB	SO	AVG	OBP	SLG	PRO+	BR/A	SB	CS	SBR	FA	FR	G/POS	TPR
1969	Atl-N	7	4	2	1	0	0	0	0	0	1	.250	.250	.250	40	-0	0	0	0	1.000	-1	/O-3	-0.1
1970	Atl-N	28	47	6	18	2	1	1	7	7	7	.383	.473	.532	159	4	0	2	-1	.960	-5	O-25	-0.2
1971	Atl-N	27	43	4	9	4	0	0	5	3	8	.209	.261	.302	56	-3	0	0	0	1.000	-2	O-15	-0.5
1972	Atl-N	76	164	19	37	5	1	3	16	4	29	.226	.244	.323	55	-10	0	2	-1	.899	-4	O-59	-1.8
1973	Atl-N	22	58	3	12	3	0	0	0	3	10	.207	.246	.259	37	-5	0	0	0	1.000	2	O-13	-0.4
Total	5	160	316	34	77	14	2	4	28	17	55	.244	.284	.339	68	-13	0	4	-2	.939	-10	O-115	-3.0

■ **SAM BROWN** Brown, Samuel Wakefield b: 5/21/1878, Webster, Pa. d: 11/8/31, Mount Pleasant, Pa. BR/TR, Deb: 4/21/06

YEAR	TM/L	G	AB	R	H	2B	3B	HR	RBI	BB	SO	AVG	OBP	SLG	PRO+	BR/A	SB	CS	SBR	FA	FR	G/POS	TPR
1906	Bos-N	71	231	12	48	6	1	0	20	13		.208	.262	.242	59	-11	4			.970	-1	C-35,O-13,3/12	-1.0
1907	Bos-N	70	208	17	40	6	0	0	14	12		.192	.250	.221	48	-12	0			.970	7	C-63/1-2	0.0
Total	2	141	439	29	88	12	1	0	34	25		.200	.256	.232	54	-24	4			.970	6	/C-98,O-13,312	-1.0

■ **TOM BROWN** Brown, Thomas Tarlton b: 9/21/1860, Liverpool, England d: 10/25/27, Washington, D.C. BL/TR, 5'10", 168 lbs. Deb: 7/6/1882 MU

YEAR	TM/L	G	AB	R	H	2B	3B	HR	RBI	BB	SO	AVG	OBP	SLG	PRO+	BR/A	SB	CS	SBR	FA	FR	G/POS	TPR
1888	Bos-N	107	420	62	104	10	7	9	49	30	68	.248	.299	.369	110	4	46			.896	-3	*O-107	-0.1
1889	Bos-N	90	362	93	84	10	5	2	24	59	56	.232	.341	.304	76	-11	63			.901	3	O-90	-0.9
Total	17	1786	7363	1521	1952	239	138	64	530	748	708	.265	.337	.361	101	9	657			.890	38	*O-1783/P-12	-1.4
Team	2	197	782	155	188	20	12	11	73	89	124	.240	.320	.339	93	-6	109			.899	-1	O-197	-1.0

■ **GEORGE BROWNE** Browne, George Edward b: 1/12/1876, Richmond, Va. d: 12/9/20, Hyde Park, N.Y. BL/TR, 5'10.5", 160 lbs. Deb: 9/27/01

YEAR	TM/L	G	AB	R	H	2B	3B	HR	RBI	BB	SO	AVG	OBP	SLG	PRO+	BR/A	SB	CS	SBR	FA	FR	G/POS	TPR
1908	Bos-N	138	536	61	122	10	6	1	34	36		.228	.276	.274	77	-14	17			.950	4	*O-138	-1.9
Total	12	1102	4300	614	1176	119	55	18	303	259		.273	.318	.339	100	-8	190			.927	-32	*O-1077	-10.4

■ **BILL BRUBAKER** Brubaker, Wilbur Lee b: 11/7/10, Cleveland, Ohio d: 4/2/78, Laguna Hills, Cal. BR/TR, 6'2", 185 lbs. Deb: 9/8/32 F

YEAR	TM/L	G	AB	R	H	2B	3B	HR	RBI	BB	SO	AVG	OBP	SLG	PRO+	BR/A	SB	CS	SBR	FA	FR	G/POS	TPR
1943	Bos-N	13	19	3	8	3	0	0	1	2	2	.421	.476	.579	207	3	0			.778	-1	/3-5,1-3	0.2
Total	10	479	1564	208	413	85	10	22	225	151	239	.264	.333	.373	90	-20	13			.938	2	3-350/2-65,1SO	-0.7

■ **BOB BRUSH** Brush, Robert b: 3/8/1875, Osage, Iowa d: 4/2/44, San Bernardino, Cal. Deb: 4/20/07

YEAR	TM/L	G	AB	R	H	2B	3B	HR	RBI	BB	SO	AVG	OBP	SLG	PRO+	BR/A	SB	CS	SBR	FA	FR	G/POS	TPR
1907	Bos-N	2	2	0	0	0	0	0	0	0		.000	.000	.000	-99	-0	0			1.000	-0	/1-1	-0.1

■ **BILL BRUTON** Bruton, William Haron b: 12/22/25, Panola, Ala. BL/TR, 6'0.5", 169 lbs. Deb: 4/13/53

YEAR	TM/L	G	AB	R	H	2B	3B	HR	RBI	BB	SO	AVG	OBP	SLG	PRO+	BR/A	SB	CS	SBR	FA	FR	G/POS	TPR
1953	Mil-N	151	613	82	153	18	14	1	41	44	100	.250	.306	.330	70	-27	**26**	11	1	.979	8	*O-150	-2.3
1954	Mil-N	142	567	89	161	20	7	4	30	40	78	.284	.336	.365	88	-11	**34**	13	2	.981	1	*O-141	-1.3
1955	Mil-N	149	636	106	175	30	12	9	47	43	72	.275	.325	.403	97	-4	**25**	11	1	.968	15	*O-149	0.4
1956	Mil-N	147	525	73	143	23	**15**	8	56	26	63	.272	.308	.419	99	-3	8	6	-1	.969	3	*O-145	-0.9
1957	Mil-N	79	306	41	85	16	9	5	30	19	35	.278	.322	.438	110	3	11	4	1	.981	1	O-79	0.0
1958	*Mil-N	100	325	47	91	11	3	3	28	27	37	.280	.339	.360	93	-4	4	1	1	.977	-7	O-96	-1.4
1959	Mil-N	133	478	72	138	22	6	6	41	35	54	.289	.339	.397	104	1	13	5	1	.991	4	*O-133	0.0
1960	Mil-N	151	629	**112**	180	27	**13**	12	54	41	97	.286	.332	.428	115	10	22	13	-1	.986	4	*O-149	0.5
Total	12	1610	6056	937	1651	241	102	94	545	482	793	.273	.329	.393	96	-43	207	89	9	.981	68	*O-1561	-4.2
Team	8	1052	4079	622	1126	167	79	48	327	275	536	.276	.325	.391	96	-34	143	64	5	.978	28	*O-1042	-5.0

■ **ART BUES** Bues, Arthur Frederick b: 3/3/1888, Milwaukee, Wis. d: 11/7/54, Whitefish Bay, Wis. BR/TR, 5'11", 184 lbs. Deb: 4/17/13

YEAR	TM/L	G	AB	R	H	2B	3B	HR	RBI	BB	SO	AVG	OBP	SLG	PRO+	BR/A	SB	CS	SBR	FA	FR	G/POS	TPR
1913	Bos-N	2	1	0	0	0	0	0	0	0	1	.000	.000	.000	-98	-0	0			.000	0	/2-1,3-1	0.0
Total	2	16	46	3	10	1	1	0	4	5	7	.217	.294	.283	72	-2	1			.968	-2	/3-13,2-1	-0.4

■ **CHARLIE BUFFINTON** Buffinton, Charles G. b: 6/14/1861, Fall River, Mass. d: 9/23/07, Fall River, Mass. BR/TR, 6'1", 180 lbs. Deb: 5/17/1882 M

YEAR	TM/L	G	AB	R	H	2B	3B	HR	RBI	BB	SO	AVG	OBP	SLG	PRO+	BR/A	SB	CS	SBR	FA	FR	G/POS	TPR
1882	Bos-N	15	50	5	13	1	0	0	4	2	3	.260	.288	.280	83	-1				.615	-1	/O-7,P-5,1	-0.2
1883	Bos-N	86	341	28	81	8	3	1	26	6	24	.238	.251	.287	62	-16				.756	-7	O-51,P-43/1	-1.4
1884	Bos-N	87	352	48	94	18	3	1	39	16	12	.267	.299	.344	102	1				.946	-1	P-67,O-13,1	-0.5
1885	Bos-N	82	338	26	81	12	3	1	33	3	26	.240	.246	.302	79	-8				.912	-0	P-51,O-18,1	-1.1

YEAR	TM/L	G	AB	R	H	2B	3B	HR	RBI	BB	SO	AVG	OBP	SLG	PRO+	BR/A	SB	CS	SBR	FA	FR	G/POS	TPR
1886	Bos-N	44	176	27	51	4	1	1	30	6	12	.290	.313	.341	103	1	3			.968	-6	1-19,P-18/O	-0.7
Total	11	586	2214	245	543	67	16	7	255	91	114	.245	.276	.299	72	-78	14			.916	2	P-414,O-137/1	-5.4
Team	5	314	1257	134	320	43	10	4	132	33	77	.255	.274	.314	84	-23	3			.912	-15	P-184/O-98,1	-3.9

■ JACK BURDOCK

Burdock, John Joseph "Black Jack" b: 4/1852, Brooklyn, N.Y. d: 11/27/31, Brooklyn, N.Y. BR/TR, 5'9.5", 158 lbs. Deb: 5/2/1872 MU

YEAR	TM/L	G	AB	R	H	2B	3B	HR	RBI	BB	SO	AVG	OBP	SLG	PRO+	BR/A	SB	CS	SBR	FA	FR	G/POS	TPR
1878	Bos-N	60	246	37	64	12	6	0	25	3	17	.260	.269	.358	97	-2				**.918**	**21**	*2-60	2.2
1879	Bos-N	84	359	64	86	10	3	0	36	9	28	.240	.258	.284	77	-9				.911	10	*2-84	0.6
1880	Bos-N	86	356	58	90	17	4	2	35	8	26	.253	.269	.340	108	3				**.923**	12	*2-86	1.9
1881	Bos-N	73	282	36	67	12	4	1	24	7	18	.238	.256	.319	84	-5				.911	-11	*2-72/S-1	-1.2
1882	Bos-N	83	319	36	76	6	7	0	27	9	24	.238	.259	.301	79	-7				**.932**	3	*2-83	-0.2
1883	Bos-N	96	400	80	132	27	8	5	88	14	35	.330	.353	.475	145	20				.921	-1	*2-96/M	1.8
1884	Bos-N	87	361	65	97	14	4	6	49	15	52	.269	.298	.380	112	5				**.922**	1	*2-87/3-1	0.7
1885	Bos-N	45	169	18	24	5	0	0	7	8	18	.142	.181	.172	15	-15				.917	-4	2-45	-1.7
1886	Bos-N	59	221	26	48	6	1	0	25	11	27	.217	.254	.253	57	-11	3			.904	-8	2-59	-1.5
1887	Bos-N	65	237	36	61	6	0	0	29	18	22	.257	.320	.283	69	-9	19			.882	-19	2-65	-2.3
1888	Bos-N	22	79	5	16	0	0	0	4	2	5	.203	.232	.203	39	-5	1			.903	0	2-22	-0.4
Total	4 n	227	1038	199	285	41	11	4	48	14	5	.275	.284	.347	97	-6	3					2-128/3-62,SC	-0.7
Total	14	960	3873	578	944	131	40	15	390	128	305	.244	.270	.310	83	-74	32			.912	13	2-956/3-5,S	-2.5
Team	11	760	3029	461	761	115	37	14	349	104	272	.251	.277	.328	90	-36	23			.915	5	2-759/S-1,3	-0.1

■ JOE BURG

Burg, Joseph Peter b: 6/4/1882, Chicago, Ill. d: 4/28/69, Joliet, Ill. BR/TR, 5'10", 150 lbs. Deb: 9/26/10

YEAR	TM/L	G	AB	R	H	2B	3B	HR	RBI	BB	SO	AVG	OBP	SLG	PRO+	BR/A	SB	CS	SBR	FA	FR	G/POS	TPR
1910	Bos-N	13	46	7	15	0	1	0	10	7	12	.326	.415	.370	124	2	5			.867	3	3-12/S-1	0.5

■ DAN BURKE

Burke, Daniel L. b: 10/25/1868, Abington, Mass. d: 3/20/33, Taunton, Mass. BR/TR, 5'10", 190 lbs. Deb: 4/18/1890

YEAR	TM/L	G	AB	R	H	2B	3B	HR	RBI	BB	SO	AVG	OBP	SLG	PRO+	BR/A	SB	CS	SBR	FA	FR	G/POS	TPR
1892	Bos-N	1	4	0	0	0	0	0	0	0	2	.000	.000	.000	-92	-1	0			.900	1	/C-1	0.0
Total	2	42	126	15	22	1	0	0	0	22	2	.175	.307	.183	48	-7	2			.892	-2	/O-29,C-14,1	-0.7

■ FRANK BURKE

Burke, Frank Aloysius b: 2/16/1880, Carbon Co., Pa. d: 9/17/46, Los Angeles, Cal. TR , Deb: 9/14/06

YEAR	TM/L	G	AB	R	H	2B	3B	HR	RBI	BB	SO	AVG	OBP	SLG	PRO+	BR/A	SB	CS	SBR	FA	FR	G/POS	TPR
1907	Bos-N	43	129	6	23	0	1	0	8	11		.178	.243	.194	37	-9	3			.955	-4	O-36	-1.6
Total	2	51	138	8	26	1	2	0	9	12		.188	.253	.225	50	-8	4			.942	-5	/O-40	-1.6

■ JOE BURNS

Burns, Joseph James b: 6/17/16, Bryn Mawr, Pa. d: 6/24/74, Bryn Mawr, Pa. BR/TR, 5'10.5", 175 lbs. Deb: 4/24/43

YEAR	TM/L	G	AB	R	H	2B	3B	HR	RBI	BB	SO	AVG	OBP	SLG	PRO+	BR/A	SB	CS	SBR	FA	FR	G/POS	TPR
1943	Bos-N	52	135	12	28	3	0	1	5	8	25	.207	.262	.252	49	-9	2			.933	-1	3-34/O-4	-1.0
Total	3	111	300	24	69	6	1	2	16	16	50	.230	.274	.277	60	-16	2			.920	-12	/3-56,O-23,21	-3.2

■ PAUL BURRIS

Burris, Paul Robert b: 7/21/23, Hickory, N.C. BR/TR, 6', 190 lbs. Deb: 10/2/48

YEAR	TM/L	G	AB	R	H	2B	3B	HR	RBI	BB	SO	AVG	OBP	SLG	PRO+	BR/A	SB	CS	SBR	FA	FR	G/POS	TPR
1948	Bos-N	2	4	0	2	0	0	0	0	0	0	.500	.500	.500	174	0	0			1.000	1	/C-2	0.1
1950	Bos-N	10	23	1	4	1	0	0	3	1	2	.174	.208	.217	13	-3	0			1.000	1	/C-8	-0.1
1952	Bos-N	55	168	14	37	4	0	2	21	7	19	.220	.256	.280	50	-12	0	0	0	1.000	-4	C-50	-1.4
1953	Mil-N	2	1	0	0	0	0	0	0	0	0	.000	.000	.000	-99	-0	0	0	0	1.000	-0	/C-2	0.0
Total	4	69	196	15	43	5	0	2	24	8	21	.219	.254	.276	47	-14	0	0		1.000	-2	/C-62	-1.4

■ JEFF BURROUGHS

Burroughs, Jeffrey Alan b: 3/7/51, Long Beach, Cal. BR/TR, 6'1", 200 lbs. Deb: 7/20/70

YEAR	TM/L	G	AB	R	H	2B	3B	HR	RBI	BB	SO	AVG	OBP	SLG	PRO+	BR/A	SB	CS	SBR	FA	FR	G/POS	TPR
1977	Atl-N	154	579	91	157	19	1	41	114	86	126	.271	.365	.520	120	16	4	1	1	.974	-4	*O-154	0.6
1978	Atl-N☆	153	488	72	147	30	6	23	77	**117**	92	.301	**.436**	.529	151	38	1	2	-1	.975	-0	*O-146	3.2
1979	Atl-N	116	397	49	89	14	1	11	47	73	75	.224	.349	.348	84	-7	2	2	-1	.963	-1	*O-110	-1.3
1980	Atl-N	99	278	35	73	14	0	13	51	35	57	.263	.349	.453	118	7	1	1	-0	.977	-4	O-73	0.0
Total	16	1689	5536	720	1443	230	20	240	882	831	1135	.261	.359	.439	120	159	16	22	-8	.974	-36	*O-1281,D-269/1	5.2
Team	4	522	1742	247	466	77	8	88	289	311	350	.268	.380	.472	121	54	8	6	-1	.972	-9	O-483	2.5

■ DICK BURRUS

Burrus, Maurice Lennon b: 1/29/1898, Hatteras, N.C. d: 2/2/72, Elizabeth City, N.C BL/TL, 5'11", 175 lbs. Deb: 6/23/19

YEAR	TM/L	G	AB	R	H	2B	3B	HR	RBI	BB	SO	AVG	OBP	SLG	PRO+	BR/A	SB	CS	SBR	FA	FR	G/POS	TPR
1925	Bos-N	152	588	82	200	41	4	5	87	51	29	.340	.396	.449	126	24	8	9	-3	**.990**	1	*1-151	1.2
1926	Bos-N	131	486	59	131	21	1	3	61	37	16	.270	.324	.335	85	-11	4			.991	12	*1-128	-0.6
1927	Bos-N	72	220	22	70	8	3	0	32	17	10	.318	.370	.382	110	3	3			.972	1	1-61	0.1
1928	Bos-N	64	137	15	37	6	0	3	13	19	8	.270	.367	.380	101	1	1			.977	-2	1-32	-0.4
Total	6	560	1760	206	513	87	12	11	211	138	95	.291	.347	.373	97	-6	18	12		.986	7	1-441/O-12	-3.1
Team	4	419	1431	178	438	76	8	11	193	124	63	.306	.365	.393	108	17	16	9		.986	12	1-372	0.3

■ ART BUTLER

Butler, Arthur Edward (b: Arthur Edward Bouthillier)
b: 12/19/1887, Fall River, Mass. d: 10/7/84, Fall River, Mass. BR/TR, 5'9", 160 lbs. Deb: 4/14/11

YEAR	TM/L	G	AB	R	H	2B	3B	HR	RBI	BB	SO	AVG	OBP	SLG	PRO+	BR/A	SB	CS	SBR	FA	FR	G/POS	TPR
1911	Bos-N	27	68	11	12	2	0	0	2	6	6	.176	.263	.206	30	-6	0			.930	-3	3-14/2-4,S	-1.0
Total	6	454	1289	181	311	44	13	3	101	146	102	.241	.323	.303	85	-20	54			.919	-96	S-236/2-85,O3	-10.8

■ BRETT BUTLER

Butler, Brett Morgan b: 6/15/57, Los Angeles, Cal. BL/TL, 5'10", 160 lbs. Deb: 8/20/81

YEAR	TM/L	G	AB	R	H	2B	3B	HR	RBI	BB	SO	AVG	OBP	SLG	PRO+	BR/A	SB	CS	SBR	FA	FR	G/POS	TPR
1981	Atl-N	40	126	17	32	2	3	0	4	19	17	.254	.352	.317	89	-1	9	1	2	.987	-2	O-37	-0.2
1982	*Atl-N	89	240	35	52	2	0	0	7	25	35	.217	.291	.225	44	-17	21	8	2	1.000	-10	O-77	-2.9
1983	Atl-N	151	549	84	154	21	**13**	5	37	54	56	.281	.347	.393	98	-1	39	23	-2	.987	6	*O-143	-0.2
Total	15	2074	7706	1285	2243	268	127	54	552	1078	845	.291	.381	.380	112	166	535	244	14	.992	109	*O-2034/D-1	23.2
Team	3	280	915	136	238	25	16	5	48	98	108	.260	.333	.339	83	-20	69	32	2	.990	-5	O-257	-3.3

■ FRANCISCO CABRERA

Cabrera, Francisco (Paulino) b: 10/10/66, Santo Domingo, D.R. BR/TR, 6'4", 195 lbs. Deb: 7/24/89

YEAR	TM/L	G	AB	R	H	2B	3B	HR	RBI	BB	SO	AVG	OBP	SLG	PRO+	BR/A	SB	CS	SBR	FA	FR	G/POS	TPR
1989	Atl-N	4	14	0	3	2	0	0	0	0	3	.214	.214	.357	59	-1	0	0	0	1.000	-1	/1-2,C-1	-0.2
1990	Atl-N	63	137	14	38	5	1	7	25	5	21	.277	.303	.482	106	1	1	0	0	.990	-2	1-48/C-3	-0.3
1991	*Atl-N	44	95	7	23	6	0	4	23	6	20	.242	.287	.432	94	-1	1	1	-0	.987	-3	C-17,1-14	-0.4
1992	*Atl-N	12	10	2	3	0	0	2	3	1	1	.300	.364	.900	233	2	0	0	0	.000	0	/C-1	0.2
1993	*Atl-N	70	83	8	20	3	0	4	11	8	21	.241	.308	.422	92	-1	0	0	0	1.000	2	1-12/C-2	0.0
Total	5	196	351	32	89	17	1	17	62	21	69	.254	.296	.453	99	-2	2	1	0	.989	-3	/1-76,C-24,D	-0.8
Team	5	193	339	31	87	16	1	17	62	20	66	.257	.298	.460	101	-1	2	1	0	.989	-3	/1-76,C-24	-0.7

■ SAM CALDERONE

Calderone, Samuel Francis b: 2/6/26, Beverly, N.J. BR/TR, 5'10.5", 185 lbs. Deb: 4/19/50

YEAR	TM/L	G	AB	R	H	2B	3B	HR	RBI	BB	SO	AVG	OBP	SLG	PRO+	BR/A	SB	CS	SBR	FA	FR	G/POS	TPR
1954	Mil-N	22	29	3	11	2	0	0	5	4	4	.379	.455	.448	146	2	0	0	0	1.000	3	C-16	0.5
Total	3	91	141	16	41	5	0	1	25	7	13	.291	.324	.348	76	-5	0	0	0	.978	-2	/C-80	-0.4

■ BILL CALHOUN

Calhoun, William Davitte "Mary" b: 6/23/1890, Rockmart, Ga. d: 1/28/55, Sandersville, Ga. BL/TL, 6', 180 lbs. Deb: 4/24/13

YEAR	TM/L	G	AB	R	H	2B	3B	HR	RBI	BB	SO	AVG	OBP	SLG	PRO+	BR/A	SB	CS	SBR	FA	FR	G/POS	TPR
1913	Bos-N	6	13	0	1	0	0	0	0	0	3	.077	.077	.077	-55	-3	0			.970	-0	/1-3	-0.3

■ HANK CAMELLI

Camelli, Henry Richard b: 12/12/14, Gloucester, Mass. BR/TR, 5'11", 190 lbs. Deb: 10/3/43

YEAR	TM/L	G	AB	R	H	2B	3B	HR	RBI	BB	SO	AVG	OBP	SLG	PRO+	BR/A	SB	CS	SBR	FA	FR	G/POS	TPR
1947	Bos-N	52	150	10	29	8	1	1	11	18	18	.193	.280	.280	50	-11	0			.977	6	C-51	-0.2
Total	5	159	376	33	86	15	4	2	26	46	39	.229	.313	.306	70	-15	0			.970	14	C-153	0.5

■ JACK CAMERON

Cameron, John William "Happy Jack" b: 9/1884, Nova Scotia, Can. d: 8/17/51, Boston, Mass. Deb: 9/13/06

YEAR	TM/L	G	AB	R	H	2B	3B	HR	RBI	BB	SO	AVG	OBP	SLG	PRO+	BR/A	SB	CS	SBR	FA	FR	G/POS	TPR
1906	Bos-N	18	61	3	11	0	0	0	4	2		.180	.206	.180	21	-6	0			.852	-1	O-16/P-2	-0.8

■ VIN CAMPBELL

Campbell, Arthur Vincent b: 1/30/1888, St.Louis, Mo. d: 11/16/69, Towson, Md. BL/TR, 6', 185 lbs. Deb: 6/6/08

YEAR	TM/L	G	AB	R	H	2B	3B	HR	RBI	BB	SO	AVG	OBP	SLG	PRO+	BR/A	SB	CS	SBR	FA	FR	G/POS	TPR
1912	Bos-N	145	624	102	185	32	9	3	48	32	44	.296	.334	.391	96	-5	19			.938	0	*O-144	-1.2
Total	6	546	2069	326	642	85	36	15	167	132	156	.310	.357	.408	104	6	92			.929	-17	O-497	-3.6

YEAR	TM/L	G	AB	R	H	2B	3B	HR	RBI	BB	SO	AVG	OBP	SLG	PRO+	BR/A	SB	CS	SBR	FA	FR	G/POS	TPR
■ **RIP CANNELL**	Cannell, Virgin Wirt b: 1/23/1880, S.Bridgton, Maine d: 8/26/48, Bridgton, Maine BL/TR, 5'10.5", 180 lbs. Deb: 4/14/04																						
1904	Bos-N	100	346	32	81	5	1	0	18	23		.234	.286	.254	70	-12	10			.897	-11	O-93	-3.0
1905	Bos-N	154	567	52	140	14	4	0	36	51		.247	.311	.286	80	-13	17			.935	-8	*O-154	-3.0
Total	2	254	913	84	221	19	5	0	54	74		.242	.302	.274	76	-25	27			.923	-19	O-247	-6.0
■ **PAT CAPRI**	Capri, Patrick Nicholas b: 11/27/18, New York, N.Y. d: 6/14/89, New York, N.Y. BR/TR, 6'0.5", 170 lbs. Deb: 7/16/44																						
1944	Bos-N	7	1	1	0	0	0	0	0	0	1	.000	.000	.000	-96	-0	0			1.000	1	/2-1	0.1
■ **RAMON CARABALLO**	Caraballo, Ramon (Sanchez) b: 5/23/69, Rio San Juan, D.R. BB/TR, 5'7", 150 lbs. Deb: 9/9/93																						
1993	Atl-N	6	0	0	0	0	0	0	0	0	0	—	—	—	—	0	0	0	0	1.000	2	/2-5	0.2
Total	2	40	99	10	20	4	1	2	3	6	33	.202	.269	.323	55	-7	3	2	-0	.958	1	/2-29	-0.5
■ **EDDIE CARNETT**	Carnett, Edwin Elliott "Lefty" b: 10/21/16, Springfield, Mo. BL/TL, 6', 185 lbs. Deb: 4/19/41																						
1941	Bos-N	2	0	0	0	0	0	0	0	0	0	—	—	—	—	0	0			.000	0	/P-2	0.0
Total	3	158	530	56	142	25	8	1	67	28	44	.268	.312	.351	91	-7	5			.952	-8	O-104/1-25,P	-2.4
■ **PAT CARNEY**	Carney, Patrick Joseph "Doc" b: 8/7/1876, Holyoke, Mass. d: 1/9/53, Worcester, Mass. BL/TL, 6', 200 lbs. Deb: 9/20/01																						
1901	Bos-N	13	55	6	16	2	1	0	6	3		.291	.339	.364	95	-0	0			.933	-3	O-13	-0.4
1902	Bos-N	137	522	75	141	17	4	2	65	42		.270	.339	.330	105	4	27			.930	-9	*O-137/P-2	-1.4
1903	Bos-N	110	392	37	94	12	4	1	49	28		.240	.297	.298	73	-14	10			.953	-6	O-92,P-10/1	-2.3
1904	Bos-N	78	279	24	57	5	2	0	11	12		.204	.240	.237	49	-17	6			.953	-2	O-71/P-4,1	-2.4
Total	4	338	1248	142	308	36	11	3	131	85		.247	.304	.300	82	-27	43			.942	-20	O-313/P-16,1	-6.5
■ **DIXIE CARROLL**	Carroll, Dorsey Lee b: 5/9/1891, Paducah, Ky. d: 10/13/84, Jacksonville, Fla BL/TR, 5'11", 165 lbs. Deb: 9/12/19																						
1919	Bos-N	15	49	10	13	3	1	0	7	7	1	.265	.379	.367	130	2	5			.921	2	O-13	0.3
■ **CLIFF CARROLL**	Carroll, Samuel Clifford b: 10/18/1859, Clay Grove, Iowa d: 6/12/23, Portland, Ore. BB/TR, 5'8", 163 lbs. Deb: 8/3/1882																						
1893	Bos-N	120	438	80	98	7	5	2	54	88	28	.224	.360	.276	65	-21	29			.917	2	*O-120	-2.1
Total	11	991	3972	729	995	125	47	31	423	361	290	.251	.320	.329	93	-31	197			.905	25	O-991	-3.1
■ **RICO CARTY**	Carty, Ricardo Adolfo Jacobo (b: Ricardo Adolfo Jacobo (Carty)) b: 9/1/39, San Pedro De Macoris, D.R. BR/TR, 6'3", 200 lbs. Deb: 9/15/63																						
1963	Mil-N	2	2	0	0	0	0	0	0	0	2	.000	.000	.000	-99	-1	0	0	0	.000	0	H	-0.1
1964	Mil-N	133	455	72	150	28	4	22	88	43	78	.330	.391	.554	162	37	1	2	-1	.978	1	*O-121	3.3
1965	Mil-N	83	271	37	84	18	1	10	35	17	44	.310	.357	.494	136	12	1	4	-2	.958	1	O-73	0.8
1966	Atl-N	151	521	73	170	25	2	15	76	60	74	.326	.396	.468	137	28	4	6	-2	.971	5	*O-126,C-17/13	2.7
1967	Atl-N	134	444	41	113	16	2	15	64	49	70	.255	.330	.401	110	6	4	3	-1	.959	4	*O-112/1-9	0.3
1969	*Atl-N	104	304	47	104	15	0	16	58	32	28	.342	.405	.549	164	26	0	2	-1	.952	-3	O-79	1.8
1970	Atl-N★	136	478	84	175	23	3	25	101	77	46	**.366**	**.456**	.584	167	48	1	2	-1	.974	3	*O-133	4.2
1972	Atl-N	86	271	31	75	12	2	6	29	44	33	.277	.378	.402	111	5	0	0	0	.979	-1	O-78	0.1
Total	15	1651	5606	712	1677	278	17	204	890	642	663	.299	.372	.464	132	240	21	26	-9	.970	3	O-807,D-650/1C3	17.9
Team	8	829	2746	385	871	137	14	109	451	322	375	.317	.391	.496	143	161	11	19	-8	.968	9	O-722/C-17,13	13.1
■ **PAUL CASANOVA**	Casanova, Paulino (Ortiz) b: 12/21/41, Colon, Matanzas, Cuba BR/TR, 6'4", 200 lbs. Deb: 9/18/65																						
1972	Atl-N	49	136	8	28	3	0	2	10	4	28	.206	.229	.272	38	-11	0	1	-1	.975	-6	C-43	-1.8
1973	Atl-N	82	236	18	51	7	0	7	18	11	36	.216	.254	.335	58	-14	0	2	-1	.977	6	C-78	-0.7
1974	Atl-N	42	104	5	21	0	0	0	8	5	17	.202	.239	.202	23	-11	0	0	0	.986	-1	C-33	-1.1
Total	10	859	2786	214	627	87	12	50	252	101	430	.225	.254	.319	64	-137	2	10	-5	.985	-38	C-811	-15.4
Team	3	173	476	31	100	10	0	9	36	20	81	.210	.243	.288	45	-36	0	3	-2	.978	-1	C-154	-3.6
■ **VINNY CASTILLA**	Castilla, Vinicio (Soria) b: 7/4/67, Oaxaca, Mexico BR/TR, 6'1", 175 lbs. Deb: 9/1/91																						
1991	Atl-N	12	5	1	1	0	0	0	0	0	2	.200	.200	.200	12	-1	0	0	0	1.000	1	S-12	0.1
1992	Atl-N	9	16	1	4	1	0	0	1	1	4	.250	.333	.313	79	-0	0	0	0	.875	0	/3-4,S-4	0.0
Total	5	317	1015	136	297	55	10	44	139	51	161	.293	.331	.497	95	-15	6	14	-7	.958	3	3-150,S-143/21	-0.9
Team	2	21	21	2	5	1	0	0	1	1	6	.238	.304	.286	64	-1	0	0	0	1.000	2	/S-16,3-4	0.1
■ **TED CATHER**	Cather, Theodore Physick b: 5/20/1889, Chester, Pa. d: 4/9/45, Elkton, Md. BR/TR, 5'10.5", 178 lbs. Deb: 9/23/12																						
1914	*Bos-N	50	145	19	43	11	2	0	27	7	28	.297	.338	.400	120	3	7			.953	-9	O-48	-0.8
1915	Bos-N	40	102	10	21	3	1	2	18	15	19	.206	.319	.314	96	-0	2	4	-2	.902	-7	O-32	-1.2
Total	4	201	548	60	138	30	8	2	72	34	90	.252	.300	.347	91	-7	21	4		.938	-21	O-170/1-1,P	-4.1
Team	2	90	247	29	64	14	3	2	45	22	47	.259	.330	.364	110	3	9	4		.933	-16	/O-80	-2.0
■ **WAYNE CAUSEY**	Causey, James Wayne b: 12/26/36, Ruston, La. BL/TR, 5'10.5", 175 lbs. Deb: 6/5/55																						
1968	Atl-N	16	37	2	4	0	1	1	4	0	4	.108	.108	.243	3	-4	0	0	0	1.000	-4	/2-6,S-2,3	-1.0
Total	11	1105	3244	357	819	130	26	35	285	390	341	.252	.335	.341	89	-42	12	12	-4	.969	-42	S-406,2-307,3	-4.9
■ **ORLANDO CEPEDA**	Cepeda, Orlando Manuel (Penne) "Baby Bull" or "Cha Cha" b: 9/17/37, Ponce, P.R. BR/TR, 6'2", 210 lbs. Deb: 4/15/58 C																						
1969	*Atl-N	154	573	74	147	28	2	22	88	55	76	.257	.327	.428	109	6	12	5	1	.994	3	*1-153	-0.3
1970	Atl-N	148	567	87	173	33	0	34	111	47	75	.305	.368	.543	133	25	6	5	-1	.992	3	*1-148	1.3
1971	Atl-N	71	250	31	69	10	1	14	44	22	29	.276	.335	.492	124	7	3	6	-3	.992	2	1-63	0.1
1972	Atl-N	28	84	6	25	3	0	4	9	7	17	.298	.352	.476	122	2	0	0	0	1.000	1	1-22	0.1
Total	17	2124	7927	1131	2351	417	27	379	1365	588	1169	.297	.353	.499	133	338	142	80	-5	.990	-39	*1-1683,O-231,D/3	16.7
Team	4	401	1474	198	414	74	3	74	252	131	197	.281	.345	.486	122	40	21	16	-3	.993	9	1-386	1.2
■ **RICK CERONE**	Cerone, Richard Aldo b: 5/19/54, Newark, N.J. BR/TR, 5'11", 192 lbs. Deb: 8/17/75																						
1985	Atl-N	96	282	15	61	9	0	3	25	29	25	.216	.292	.280	57	-16	0	3	-2	.986	-8	C-91	-2.2
Total	18	1329	4069	393	998	190	15	59	436	320	450	.245	.304	.343	78	-123	6	22	-11	.990	-19	*C-1279/D-11,1P2O3	-10.0
■ **CHET CHADBOURNE**	Chadbourne, Chester James "Pop" b: 10/28/1884, Parkman, Me. d: 6/21/43, Los Angeles, Cal. BL/TR, 5'9", 170 lbs. Deb: 9/17/06																						
1918	Bos-N	27	104	9	27	2	1	0	6	5	5	.260	.300	.298	86	-2	5			.925	-3	O-27	-0.7
Total	5	347	1353	183	345	41	18	2	82	146	83	.255	.333	.316	78	-41	78			.969	10	O-335/2-11,S	-5.1
■ **CHRIS CHAMBLISS**	Chambliss, Carroll Christopher b: 12/26/48, Dayton, O. BL/TR, 6'1", 215 lbs. Deb: 5/28/71 C																						
1980	Atl-N	158	602	83	170	37	2	18	72	49	73	.282	.340	.440	113	9	7	3	0	.993	-2	*1-158	-0.2
1981	Atl-N	107	404	44	110	25	2	8	51	44	41	.272	.345	.403	109	5	4	1	1	.997	7	*1-107	0.7
1982	*Atl-N	157	534	57	144	25	2	20	86	57	57	.270	.340	.436	111	8	7	3	0	.993	14	*1-151	1.5
1983	Atl-N	131	447	59	125	24	3	20	78	63	68	.280	.369	.481	124	15	2	7	-4	.996	0	*1-126	0.5
1984	Atl-N	135	389	47	100	14	0	9	44	58	54	.257	.355	.362	95	-1	1	2	-1	.993	2	*1-109	-0.7
1985	Atl-N	101	170	16	40	7	0	3	21	18	22	.235	.309	.329	74	-6	0	0	0	.997	2	1-39	-0.6
1986	Atl-N	97	122	13	38	8	0	2	14	15	24	.311	.387	.426	117	3	0	2	-1	.993	-2	1-20	-0.1
Total	17	2175	7571	912	2109	392	42	185	972	632	926	.279	.336	.415	108	75	40	35		.993	25	*1-1962/D-24	-4.0
Team	7	886	2668	319	727	140	9	80	366	304	339	.272	.348	.422	109	33	21	18		.994	22	1-710	1.1
■ **DARREL CHANEY**	Chaney, Darrel Lee b: 3/9/48, Hammond, Ind. BB/TR, 6'1", 190 lbs. Deb: 4/11/69																						
1976	Atl-N	153	496	42	125	20	8	1	50	54	92	.252	.327	.331	82	-11	5	7	-3	.950	-0	*S-151/2-1,3	0.4
1977	Atl-N	74	209	22	42	7	2	3	15	17	44	.201	.261	.297	44	-17	0	0	0	.979	4	S-41,2-24	-0.7
1978	Atl-N	89	245	27	55	9	1	3	20	25	48	.224	.296	.306	62	-12	1	0	0	.976	-6	S-77/3-8,2	-1.0

YEAR TM/L	G	AB	R	H	2B	3B	HR	RBI	BB	SO	AVG	OBP	SLG	PRO+	BR/A	SB	CS	SBR	FA	FR	G/POS	TPR
1979 Atl-N	63	117	15	19	5	0	0	10	19	34	.162	.279	.205	32	-11	2	1	0	.945	-3	S-39/2-5,3C	-1.1
Total 11	915	2113	237	458	75	17	14	190	238	471	.217	.297	.288	61	-107	19	18	-5	.959	26	S-621,2-137,3/C	-2.3
Team 4	379	1067	106	241	41	11	7	95	115	218	.226	.302	.305	64	-51	8	8	-2	.960	-5	S-308/2-31,3C	-2.4

■ LARRY CHAPPELL

Chappell, La Verne Ashford b: 2/19/1890, McClusky, Ill. d: 11/8/18, San Francisco, Cal. BL/TR, 6', 186 lbs. Deb: 7/18/13

YEAR TM/L	G	AB	R	H	2B	3B	HR	RBI	BB	SO	AVG	OBP	SLG	PRO+	BR/A	SB	CS	SBR	FA	FR	G/POS	TPR
1916 Bos-N	20	53	4	12	1	1	0	9	2	8	.226	.268	.283	72	-2	1			.957	-2	O-14	-0.5
1917 Bos-N	4	2	0	0	0	0	0	1	0	1	.000	.000	.000	-99	-0	0			.000	-1	/O-1	-0.1
Total 5	109	305	27	69	9	2	0	26	25	42	.226	.289	.269	66	-13	9			.951	-5	/O-83	-2.3
Team 2	24	55	4	12	1	1	0	10	2	9	.218	.259	.273	66	-2	1			.957	-3	/O-15	-0.6

■ BUSTER CHATHAM

Chatham, Charles L b: 12/25/01, West, Tex. d: 12/15/75, Waco, Tex. BR/TR, 5'5", 150 lbs. Deb: 6/1/30

YEAR TM/L	G	AB	R	H	2B	3B	HR	RBI	BB	SO	AVG	OBP	SLG	PRO+	BR/A	SB	CS	SBR	FA	FR	G/POS	TPR
1930 Bos-N	112	404	48	108	20	11	5	56	37	41	.267	.332	.408	80	-13	8			.920	-14	3-92,S-17	-1.8
1931 Bos-N	17	44	4	10	1	0	1	3	6	6	.227	.320	.318	75	-1	0			.762	-6	/S-6,3-6	-0.6
Total 2	129	448	52	118	21	11	6	59	43	47	.263	.331	.400	80	-15	8			.924	-20	/3-98,S-23	-2.4

■ NEIL CHRISLEY

Chrisley, Barbra O'Neil b: 12/16/31, Calhoun Falls, S.C BL/TR, 6'3", 187 lbs. Deb: 4/15/57

YEAR TM/L	G	AB	R	H	2B	3B	HR	RBI	BB	SO	AVG	OBP	SLG	PRO+	BR/A	SB	CS	SBR	FA	FR	G/POS	TPR
1961 Mil-N	10	9	1	2	0	0	0	0	1	1	.222	.300	.222	44	-1	0	0	0	.000	0	H	-0.1
Total 5	302	619	60	130	22	8	16	64	55	62	.210	.277	.349	69	-28	3	3		.975	-0	O-148/1-2,3	-3.7

■ LLOYD CHRISTENBURY

Christenbury, Lloyd Reid "Low"
b: 10/19/1893, Mecklenburg Co., N.C. d: 12/13/44, Birmingham, Ala. BL/TR, 5'7", 165 lbs. Deb: 9/20/19

YEAR TM/L	G	AB	R	H	2B	3B	HR	RBI	BB	SO	AVG	OBP	SLG	PRO+	BR/A	SB	CS	SBR	FA	FR	G/POS	TPR
1919 Bos-N	7	31	5	9	1	0	0	4	2	2	.290	.333	.323	102	0	0			.941	1	/O-7	0.1
1920 Bos-N	65	106	17	22	2	2	0	14	13	12	.208	.300	.264	66	-4	0	1	-1	.895	-7	O-14/S-7,23	-1.2
1921 Bos-N	62	125	34	44	6	2	3	16	21	7	.352	.449	.504	161	12	3	4	-2	.914	-13	2-32/S-2,3	-0.1
1922 Bos-N	71	152	22	38	5	2	1	13	18	11	.250	.337	.329	76	-5	2	4	-2	.946	0	O-32/2-5,3	-0.8
Total 4	205	414	78	113	14	6	4	47	54	32	.273	.362	.365	101	3	5	9		.936	-18	/O-53,2-43,S3	-2.0

■ GINO CIMOLI

Cimoli, Gino Nicholas b: 12/18/29, San Francisco, Cal. BR/TR, 6'2", 200 lbs. Deb: 4/19/56

YEAR TM/L	G	AB	R	H	2B	3B	HR	RBI	BB	SO	AVG	OBP	SLG	PRO+	BR/A	SB	CS	SBR	FA	FR	G/POS	TPR
1961 Mil-N	37	117	12	23	5	0	3	4	11	15	.197	.266	.316	57	-8	1	0	0	.985	-3	O-31	-1.2
Total 10	969	3054	370	808	133	48	44	321	221	474	.265	.317	.383	84	-70	21	6	3	.974	-50	O-909	-16.5

■ EARL CLARK

Clark, Bailey Earl b: 11/6/07, Washington, D.C. d: 1/16/38, Washington, D.C. BR/TR, 5'10", 160 lbs. Deb: 8/17/27

YEAR TM/L	G	AB	R	H	2B	3B	HR	RBI	BB	SO	AVG	OBP	SLG	PRO+	BR/A	SB	CS	SBR	FA	FR	G/POS	TPR
1927 Bos-N	13	44	6	12	1	0	0	3	2	4	.273	.304	.295	66	-2	0			1.000	-1	O-13	-0.3
1928 Bos-N	28	112	18	34	9	1	0	10	4	8	.304	.339	.402	98	-1	0			.987	-1	O-27	-0.3
1929 Bos-N	84	279	43	88	13	3	1	30	12	30	.315	.346	.394	86	-6	6			.978	4	O-74	-0.6
1930 Bos-N	82	233	29	69	11	3	3	28	7	22	.296	.320	.408	77	-9	3			.977	1	O-63	-1.1
1931 Bos-N	16	50	8	11	2	0	0	4	7	4	.220	.316	.260	58	-3	1			.970	1	O-14	-0.3
1932 Bos-N	50	44	11	11	2	0	0	4	2	7	.250	.283	.295	58	-3	1			1.000	-2	O-16	-0.5
1933 Bos-N	7	23	3	8	1	0	0	1	2	1	.348	.400	.391	138	1	0			1.000	-1	/O-6	0.0
Total 8	293	826	122	240	41	7	4	81	37	79	.291	.324	.372	78	-28	11			.981	2	O-222	-3.6
Team 7	280	785	118	233	39	7	4	80	36	76	.297	.331	.380	82	-22	11			.981	1	O-213	-3.1

■ GLEN CLARK

Clark, Glen Ester b: 3/7/41, Austin, Tex. BB/TR, 6'1", 190 lbs. Deb: 6/3/67

YEAR TM/L	G	AB	R	H	2B	3B	HR	RBI	BB	SO	AVG	OBP	SLG	PRO+	BR/A	SB	CS	SBR	FA	FR	G/POS	TPR
1967 Atl-N	4	4	0	0	0	0	0	0	0	1	.000	.000	.000	-99	-1	0	0	0	.000	0	H	-0.1

■ JOSH CLARKE

Clarke, Joshua Baldwin "Pepper" b: 3/8/1879, Winfield, Kan. d: 7/2/62, Ventura, Cal. BL/TR, 5'10", 180 lbs. Deb: 6/15/1898 F

YEAR TM/L	G	AB	R	H	2B	3B	HR	RBI	BB	SO	AVG	OBP	SLG	PRO+	BR/A	SB	CS	SBR	FA	FR	G/POS	TPR
1911 Bos-N	32	120	16	28	7	3	1	4	29	22	.233	.387	.367	103	1	6			.938	4	O-30	0.3
Total 5	223	809	118	193	18	9	5	43	135	22	.239	.351	.302	102	8	51			.949	-9	O-196/2-16,S	-1.1

■ BOILERYARD CLARKE

Clarke, William Jones b: 10/18/1868, New York, N.Y. d: 7/29/59, Princeton, N.J. BR/TR, 5'11.5", 170 lbs. Deb: 5/1/1893

YEAR TM/L	G	AB	R	H	2B	3B	HR	RBI	BB	SO	AVG	OBP	SLG	PRO+	BR/A	SB	CS	SBR	FA	FR	G/POS	TPR
1899 Bos-N	60	223	25	50	3	2	2	32	10		.224	.270	.283	47	-17	2			.940	-1	C-60	-1.2
1900 Bos-N	81	270	35	85	5	2	1	30	9		.315	.344	.359	84	-7	0			.928	7	C-67/1-8	0.6
Total 13	950	3346	394	858	110	32	20	429	176		.256	.310	.326	75	-115	54			.947	-39	C-739,1-193	-7.6
Team 2	141	493	60	135	8	4	3	62	19		.274	.310	.325	67	-24	2			.934	6	C-127/1-8	-0.6

■ BUZZ CLARKSON

Clarkson, James Buster b: 3/13/15, Hopkins, S.C. d: 1/18/89, Jeannette, Pa. BR/TR, 5'11", 210 lbs. Deb: 4/30/52

YEAR TM/L	G	AB	R	H	2B	3B	HR	RBI	BB	SO	AVG	OBP	SLG	PRO+	BR/A	SB	CS	SBR	FA	FR	G/POS	TPR
1952 Bos-N	14	25	3	5	0	0	0	1	3	3	.200	.286	.200	38	-2	0	0	0	.938	-2	/S-6,3-2	-0.4

■ CHET CLEMENS

Clemens, Chester Spurgeon b: 5/10/17, San Fernando, Cal. BR/TR, 6', 175 lbs. Deb: 9/13/39

YEAR TM/L	G	AB	R	H	2B	3B	HR	RBI	BB	SO	AVG	OBP	SLG	PRO+	BR/A	SB	CS	SBR	FA	FR	G/POS	TPR
1939 Bos-N	9	23	2	5	0	0	0	1	1	3	.217	.250	.217	29	-2	1			.867	-1	/O-7	-0.4
1944 Bos-N	19	17	7	3	1	1	0	2	2	2	.176	.263	.353	69	-1	0			1.000	-2	/O-7	-0.3
Total 2	28	40	9	8	1	1	0	3	3	5	.200	.256	.275	46	-3	1			.905	-3	/O-14	-0.7

■ JACK CLEMENTS

Clements, John J. b: 7/24/1864, Philadelphia, Pa. d: 5/23/41, Norristown, Pa. BL/TL, 5'8.5", 204 lbs. Deb: 4/22/1884 M

YEAR TM/L	G	AB	R	H	2B	3B	HR	RBI	BB	SO	AVG	OBP	SLG	PRO+	BR/A	SB	CS	SBR	FA	FR	G/POS	TPR
1900 Bos-N	16	42	6	13	1	0	1	10	3		.310	.370	.405	101	-0	0			.948	1	C-10	0.2
Total 17	1157	4283	619	1226	226	60	77	687	339		.286	.347	.421	115	78	55			.937	-26	*C-1073/O-41,13S	12.7

■ TY CLINE

Cline, Tyrone Alexander b: 6/15/39, Hampton, S.C. BL/TL, 6'0.5", 170 lbs. Deb: 9/14/60

YEAR TM/L	G	AB	R	H	2B	3B	HR	RBI	BB	SO	AVG	OBP	SLG	PRO+	BR/A	SB	CS	SBR	FA	FR	G/POS	TPR
1963 Mil-N	72	174	17	41	2	1	0	10	10	31	.236	.285	.259	58	-9	2	1	0	.992	-0	O-62	-1.3
1964 Mil-N	101	116	22	35	4	2	1	13	8	22	.302	.362	.397	113	2	0	1	-1	.982	-10	O-54/1-6	-1.0
1965 Mil-N	123	220	27	42	5	3	0	10	16	50	.191	.246	.241	37	-18	2	2	-1	.969	-6	O-86/1-5	-2.9
1966 Atl-N	42	71	12	18	0	0	0	6	3	11	.254	.303	.254	56	-4	2	1	0	1.000	-5	O-19/1-6	-1.0
1967 Atl-N	10	8	0	0	0	0	0	0	0	3	.000	.111	.000	-66	-2	0	0	0	1.000	-0	/O-1	-0.2
Total 12	892	1834	251	437	53	25	6	125	153	262	.238	.304	.304	72	-65	22	19		.986	-38	O-548/1-62	-14.2
Team 5	348	589	78	136	11	6	1	39	37	117	.231	.285	.275	59	-31	6	5		.982	-22	O-222/1-17	-6.4

■ OTIS CLYMER

Clymer, Otis Edgar b: 1/27/1876, Pine Grove, Pa. d: 2/27/26, St.Paul, Minn. BB/TR, 5'11", 180 lbs. Deb: 4/14/05

YEAR TM/L	G	AB	R	H	2B	3B	HR	RBI	BB	SO	AVG	OBP	SLG	PRO+	BR/A	SB	CS	SBR	FA	FR	G/POS	TPR
1913 Bos-N	14	37	4	12	3	1	0	6	3	3	.324	.375	.459	135	2	2			.880	-2	O-11	-0.1
Total 6	385	1330	182	355	42	19	2	98	99	21	.267	.322	.332	106	8	83			.939	-24	O-326/2-13,13	-3.3

■ JACK COFFEY

Coffey, John Francis b: 1/28/1887, New York, N.Y. d: 2/14/66, Bronx, N.Y. BR/TR, 5'11", 178 lbs. Deb: 6/23/09

YEAR TM/L	G	AB	R	H	2B	3B	HR	RBI	BB	SO	AVG	OBP	SLG	PRO+	BR/A	SB	CS	SBR	FA	FR	G/POS	TPR
1909 Bos-N	73	257	21	48	4	4	0	20	11		.187	.229	.233	41	-18	2			.896	-12	S-73	-3.2
Total 2	110	368	33	69	5	6	1	26	22		.188	.241	.242	47	-23	6			.908	-9	/S-73,2-23,3	-3.4

■ ED COGSWELL

Cogswell, Edward b: 2/25/1854, England d: 7/27/1888, Fitchburg, Mass. BR/TR, 5'8", 150 lbs. Deb: 7/11/1879

YEAR TM/L	G	AB	R	H	2B	3B	HR	RBI	BB	SO	AVG	OBP	SLG	PRO+	BR/A	SB	CS	SBR	FA	FR	G/POS	TPR
1879 Bos-N	49	236	51	76	8	1	1	18	8	5	.322	.344	.377	135	8				.967	1	1-49	0.7
Total 3	109	496	102	146	16	4	1	32	25	21	.294	.328	.349	121	11				.960	1	1-109	0.4

■ DICK COLE

Cole, Richard Roy b: 5/6/26, Long Beach, Cal. BR/TR, 6'2", 175 lbs. Deb: 4/27/51 C

YEAR TM/L	G	AB	R	H	2B	3B	HR	RBI	BB	SO	AVG	OBP	SLG	PRO+	BR/A	SB	CS	SBR	FA	FR	G/POS	TPR
1957 Mil-N	15	14	1	1	0	0	0	0	3	5	.071	.235	.071	-13	-2	0	0	0	.952	0	2-10/1-1,3	-0.2
Total 6	456	1215	106	303	50	10	2	107	132	124	.249	.324	.312	69	-52	2	3		.961	-19	S-169,2-118,3/1	-5.7

■ WILSON COLLINS

Collins, Cyril Wilson b: 5/7/1889, Pulaski, Tenn. d: 2/28/41, Knoxville, Tenn. BR/TR, 5'9.5", 165 lbs. Deb: 5/12/13

YEAR TM/L	G	AB	R	H	2B	3B	HR	RBI	BB	SO	AVG	OBP	SLG	PRO+	BR/A	SB	CS	SBR	FA	FR	G/POS	TPR
1913 Bos-N	16	3	3	1	0	0	0	0	0	1	.333	.333	.333	89	-0	0			1.000	-4	/O-9	-0.4
1914 Bos-N	27	35	5	9	0	0	0	1	2	8	.257	.297	.257	66	-1	0			.917	-4	O-19	-0.7
Total 2	43	38	8	10	0	0	0	1	2	9	.263	.300	.263	68	-1	0			.926	-8	/O-28	-1.1

YEAR	TM/L	G	AB	R	H	2B	3B	HR	RBI	BB	SO	AVG	OBP	SLG	PRO+	BR/A	SB	CS	SBR	FA	FR	G/POS	TPR
■ JIMMY COLLINS Collins, James Joseph b: 1/16/1870, Buffalo, N.Y. d: 3/6/43, Buffalo, N.Y. BR/TR, 5'9", 178 lbs. Deb: 4/19/1895 MH																							
1895	Bos-N	11	38	10	8	3	0	1	8	4	4	.211	.302	.368	67	-2	0			.714	-2	O-10	-0.4
1896	Bos-N	84	304	48	90	10	9	1	46	30	12	.296	.374	.398	98	-1	10			.909	20	3-80/S-4	1.7
1897	*Bos-N	134	529	103	183	28	13	6	132	41		.346	.400	.482	125	17	14			.917	21	*3-134	3.5
1898	Bos-N	152	597	107	196	35	5	**15**	111	40		.328	.377	.479	138	26	12			.932	15	*3-152	3.8
1899	Bos-N	151	599	98	166	28	11	5	92	40		.277	.335	.386	89	-12	12			.943	21	*3-151	0.9
1900	Bos-N	142	586	104	178	25	5	6	95	34		.304	.352	.394	94	-7	23			.935	10	*3-141/S-1	0.4
Total	14	1726	6796	1055	2000	353	116	65	983	426	32	.294	.344	.409	112	86	194			.929	139	*3-1683/O-28,S2	23.5
Team	6	674	2653	470	821	129	43	34	484	189	16	.309	.365	.429	108	20	71			.929	85	3-658/O-10,S	9.9
■ ZIP COLLINS Collins, John Edgar b: 5/2/1892, Brooklyn, N.Y. d: 12/19/83, Manassas, Va. BL/TL, 5'11", 152 lbs. Deb: 7/31/14																							
1915	Bos-N	5	14	3	4	1	1	0	0	2	1	.286	.375	.500	171	1	1			1.000	0	/O-4	0.2
1916	Bos-N	93	268	39	56	1	6	1	18	18	42	.209	.261	.269	66	-11	4			.947	-6	O-78	-2.4
1917	Bos-N	9	27	3	4	0	1	0	2	0	4	.148	.148	.222	14	-3	0			1.000	1	/O-5	-0.3
Total	5	281	916	124	232	17	14	2	63	58	100	.253	.301	.309	85	-18	15			.946	1	O-245	-3.7
Team	3	107	309	45	64	2	8	1	20	20	47	.207	.258	.275	66	-13	5			.954	-5	/O-87	-2.5
■ PAT COLLINS Collins, Tharon Leslie b: 9/13/1896, Sweet Sprgs., Mo. d: 5/20/60, Kansas City, Kan. BR/TR, 5'9", 178 lbs. Deb: 9/5/19																							
1929	Bos-N	7	5	1	0	0	0	0	2	3	1	.000	.375	.000	2	-1	0			1.000	1	/C-6	0.1
Total	10	543	1204	146	306	46	6	33	168	235	202	.254	.378	.385	98	5	4			.974	-7	C-403/1-5	1.9
■ BILL COLLINS Collins, William Shirley b: 3/27/1882, Chesterton, Ind. d: 6/26/61, San Bernardino, Cal. BB/TR, 6', 170 lbs. Deb: 4/14/10																							
1910	Bos-N	151	584	67	141	6	7	3	40	43	48	.241	.308	.291	72	-21	36			**.977**	13	*O-151	-1.7
1911	Bos-N	17	44	8	6	1	1	0	8	1	8	.136	.156	.205	0	-6	4			1.000	0	O-13/3-1	-0.6
Total	4	228	773	91	173	11	10	3	54	54	75	.224	.287	.276	60	-41	42			.966	7	O-210/3-1	-4.5
Team	2	168	628	75	147	7	8	3	48	44	56	.234	.298	.285	66	-27	40			.979	13	O-164/3-1	-2.3
■ BILL COLLVER Collver, William J. b: 3/21/1867, Clyde, Ohio d: 3/24/1888, Detroit, Mich. Deb: 7/4/1885																							
1885	Bos-N	1	4	0	0	0	0	0	0	0	1	.000	.000	.000	-99	-1				.000	-0	/O-1	-0.1
■ PETE COMPTON Compton, Anna Sebastian "Bash" b: 9/28/1889, San Marcos, Tex. d: 2/3/78, Kansas City, Mo. BL/TL, 5'11", 170 lbs. Deb: 9/6/11																							
1915	Bos-N	35	116	10	28	7	1	1	12	8	11	.241	.290	.345	96	-1	4	1	1	.971	0	O-31	-0.2
1916	Bos-N	34	98	13	20	2	0	0	8	7	7	.204	.264	.224	53	-5	5			.939	-2	O-30	-1.0
Total	6	291	773	78	186	24	8	5	80	65	40	.241	.303	.312	83	-17	26	1		.933	-6	O-208	-3.6
Team	2	69	214	23	48	9	1	1	20	15	18	.224	.278	.290	76	-6	9	1		.956	-2	/O-61	-1.2
■ CLINT CONATSER Conatser, Clinton Astor "Connie" b: 7/24/21, Los Angeles, Cal. BR/TR, 5'11", 182 lbs. Deb: 4/21/48																							
1948	*Bos-N	90	224	30	62	9	3	3	23	32	27	.277	.370	.384	106	3	0			.974	-9	O-76	-0.9
1949	Bos-N	53	152	10	40	6	0	3	16	14	19	.263	.325	.362	89	-3	0			.951	0	O-44	-0.4
Total	2	143	376	40	102	15	3	6	39	46	46	.271	.352	.375	99	0	0			.965	-8	O-120	-1.3
■ FRED CONE Cone, Joseph Frederick b: 5/1848, Rockford, Ill. d: 4/13/09, Chicago, Ill. 5'9.5", 171 lbs. Deb: 5/5/1871																							
1871	Bos-n	19	77	17	20	3	1	0	16	8	2	.260	.329	.325	86	-1	12					O-18	0.0
■ JOCKO CONLON Conlon, Arthur Joseph b: 12/10/1897, Woburn, Mass. d: 8/5/87, Falmouth, Mass. BR/TR, 5'7", 145 lbs. Deb: 4/17/23																							
1923	Bos-N	59	147	23	32	3	0	0	17	11	11	.218	.299	.238	45	-11	0	3	-2	.955	1	2-36/S-6,3	-1.0
■ FRANK CONNAUGHTON Connaughton, Frank Henry b: 1/1/1869, Clinton, Mass. d: 12/1/42, Boston, Mass. BR/TR, 5'9", 165 lbs. Deb: 5/28/1894																							
1894	Bos-N	46	171	42	59	9	2	2	33	16	8	.345	.407	.456	100	-0	3			.892	-3	S-33/C-7,O	-0.1
1906	Bos-N	12	44	3	9	0	0	0	1	3		.205	.271	.205	50	-2	1			.918	-3	S-11/2-1	-0.5
Total	3	146	530	98	150	12	4	4	77	44	15	.283	.344	.343	78	-18	26			.894	-3	/S-98,O-34,C2	-1.7
Team	2	58	215	45	68	9	2	2	34	19	8	.316	.380	.405	93	-3	4			.898	-5	/S-44,C-7,O2	-0.6
■ JOE CONNOLLY Connolly, Joseph Aloysius b: 2/12/1888, N.Smithfield, R.I. d: 9/1/43, Springfield, R.I. BL/TR, 5'7.5", 165 lbs. Deb: 4/10/13																							
1913	Bos-N	126	427	79	120	18	11	5	57	66	47	.281	.379	.410	123	14	18			.954	-8	*O-124	0.1
1914	*Bos-N	120	399	64	122	28	10	9	65	49	36	.306	.393	.494	164	32	12			.974	-5	*O-118	2.2
1915	Bos-N	104	305	48	91	14	8	0	23	39	35	.298	.387	.397	144	18	13	12	-3	.971	-4	O-93	0.7
1916	Bos-N	62	110	11	25	5	2	0	12	14	13	.227	.320	.309	98	0	5			.980	-1	O-31	-0.2
Total	4	412	1241	202	358	65	31	14	157	168	131	.288	.380	.425	139	63	48	12		.967	-17	O-366	2.8
■ JOE CONNOR Connor, Joseph Francis b: 12/8/1874, Waterbury, Conn. d: 11/8/57, Waterbury, Conn. BR/TR, 6'2", 185 lbs. Deb: 9/9/1895 F																							
1900	Bos-N	7	19	2	4	0	0	0	4	2		.211	.286	.211	34	-2	1			.971	2	/C-7	0.1
Total	4	92	271	29	54	7	2	1	22	18		.199	.257	.251	43	-21	8			.952	5	/C-75,O-5,31S2	-0.9
■ RIP CONWAY Conway, Richard Daniel b: 4/18/1896, White Bear Lake, Minn. d: 12/3/71, St.Paul, Minn. BL/TR, 5'6", 160 lbs. Deb: 4/16/18																							
1918	Bos-N	14	24	4	4	0	0	0	2	2	4	.167	.231	.167	23	-2	1			.810	-4	/2-5,3-1	-0.7
■ DUFF COOLEY Cooley, Duff Gordan "Dick" b: 3/14/1873, Dallas, Tex. d: 8/9/37, Dallas, Tex. BL/TR, 5'11", 158 lbs. Deb: 7/27/1893																							
1901	Bos-N	63	240	27	62	13	3	0	27	14		.258	.302	.338	78	-7	5			.943	2	O-53,1-10	-0.9
1902	Bos-N	135	548	73	162	26	8	0	58	34		.296	.339	.372	118	11	27			.952	-6	*O-127/1-7	-0.4
1903	Bos-N	138	553	76	160	26	10	1	70	44		.289	.342	.378	109	6	27			.952	-5	*O-126,1-13	-0.7
1904	Bos-N	122	467	41	127	18	7	5	70	24		.272	.312	.373	115	7	14			.976	-7	*O-116/1-6	-0.8
Total	13	1316	5364	847	1576	180	102	26	557	365		.294	.341	.380	104	20	224			.945	-22	*O-1094,1-184/3CS2	-7.0
Team	4	458	1808	217	511	83	28	6	225	116		.283	.328	.369	109	16	73			.956	-16	O-422/1-36	-2.8
■ JIMMY COONEY Cooney, James Edward "Scoops" b: 8/24/1894, Cranston, R.I. d: 8/7/91, Warwick, R.I. BR/TR, 5'11", 160 lbs. Deb: 9/22/17 F																							
1928	Bos-N	18	51	2	7	0	0	0	3	2	5	.137	.170	.137	-20	-9	1			.982	2	S-11/2-4	-0.6
Total	7	448	1575	181	413	64	16	2	150	76	58	.262	.298	.327	67	-75	30			.974	30	S-400/2-31,3O	-0.6
■ JOHNNY COONEY Cooney, John Walter b: 3/18/01, Cranston, R.I. d: 7/8/86, Sarasota, Fla. BR/TL, 5'10", 165 lbs. Deb: 4/19/21 FMC																							
1921	Bos-N	8	5	0	1	0	0	0	0	0	1	.200	.200	.200	7	-1	0	0	0	1.000	0	/P-8	0.0
1922	Bos-N	4	8	0	0	0	0	0	0	0	1	.000	.000	.000	-99	-2	0	0	0	1.000	0	/P-4	0.0
1923	Bos-N	42	66	7	25	1	0	0	3	4	2	.379	.414	.394	119	2	0	1	-1	1.000	0	P-23,O-11/1	0.2
1924	Bos-N	55	130	10	33	2	1	0	4	9	5	.254	.302	.285	61	-7	0	4	-2	.962	0	P-34,O-16/1	-0.4
1925	Bos-N	54	103	17	33	7	0	0	13	3	6	.320	.346	.388	96	-1	1	0	0	.949	0	P-31/1-3,O	-0.1
1926	Bos-N	64	126	17	38	3	2	0	18	13	7	.302	.367	.357	105	1	6			.996	5	1-31,P-19/O	0.3
1927	Bos-N	10	1	3	0	0	0	0	0	0	0	.000	.000	.000	-99	-0	0			.000	0	H	0.0
1928	Bos-N	33	41	2	7	0	0	0	2	4	3	.171	.244	.171	11	-5	0			1.000	2	P-24/1-3,O	-0.2
1929	Bos-N	41	72	10	23	4	1	0	6	3	3	.319	.355	.403	91	-1	1			1.000	2	O-16,P-14	-0.1
1930	Bos-N	4	3	0	0	0	0	0	0	0	0	.000	.000	.000	-99	-1	0			1.000	1	/P-2	0.0
1938	Bos-N	120	432	45	117	25	5	0	17	22	12	.271	.308	.352	90	-8	2			.982	-10	*O-110,1-13	-2.2
1939	Bos-N	118	368	39	101	8	1	2	27	21	8	.274	.317	.318	77	-12	2			.992	-6	*O-116/1-2	-2.2
1940	Bos-N	108	365	40	116	14	3	0	21	25	9	.318	.363	.373	109	5	4			.992	-1	O-99/1-7	-0.1
1941	Bos-N	123	442	52	141	25	2	0	29	27	15	.319	.358	.385	114	8	3			**.996**	4	*O-111/1-4	0.5

YEAR	TM/L	G	AB	R	H	2B	3B	HR	RBI	BB	SO	AVG	OBP	SLG	PRO+	BR/A	SB	CS	SBR	FA	FR	G/POS	TPR
1942	Bos-N	74	198	23	41	6	0	0	7	23	5	.207	.290	.237	56	-10	2			.984	-14	O-54,1-23	-3.1
Total	20	1172	3372	408	965	130	26	2	219	208	107	.286	.329	.342	87	-63	30	5		.988	-6	O-794,P-159/1	-10.1
Team	15	858	2360	265	676	95	15	2	147	154	77	.286	.332	.342	90	-34	21	5		.989	-18	O-537,P-159/1	-7.4

■ **BILL COONEY** Cooney, William A. "Cush" b: 4/7/1883, Boston, Mass. d: 11/6/28, Roxbury, Mass. TR, Deb: 9/22/09

YEAR	TM/L	G	AB	R	H	2B	3B	HR	RBI	BB	SO	AVG	OBP	SLG	PRO+	BR/A	SB	CS	SBR	FA	FR	G/POS	TPR
1909	Bos-N	5	10	0	3	0	0	0	0	0		.300	.300	.300	82	-0	0			.500	-0	/P-3,2-1,S	0.0
1910	Bos-N	8	12	2	3	0	0	0	1	2	0	.250	.357	.250	74	-0	0			.000	-1	/O-2	-0.1
Total	2	13	22	2	6	0	0	0	1	2	0	.273	.333	.273	78	-1	0			.500	-1	/P-3,O-2,S2	-0.1

■ **GARY COOPER** Cooper, Gary Nathaniel b: 12/22/56, Savannah, Ga. BB/TR, 6'3", 175 lbs. Deb: 8/25/80

YEAR	TM/L	G	AB	R	H	2B	3B	HR	RBI	BB	SO	AVG	OBP	SLG	PRO+	BR/A	SB	CS	SBR	FA	FR	G/POS	TPR
1980	Atl-N	21	2	3	0	0	0	0	0	0	1	.000	.000	.000	-97	-1	2	1	0	1.000	-4	O-13	-0.4

■ **WALKER COOPER** Cooper, William Walker "Walk" b: 1/8/15, Atherton, Mo. d: 4/11/91, Scottsdale, Ariz. BR/TR, 6'3", 210 lbs. Deb: 9/25/40 FC

YEAR	TM/L	G	AB	R	H	2B	3B	HR	RBI	BB	SO	AVG	OBP	SLG	PRO+	BR/A	SB	CS	SBR	FA	FR	G/POS	TPR
1950	Bos-N☆	102	337	52	111	19	3	14	60	30	26	.329	.389	.528	148	23	1			.973	-5	C-88	2.1
1951	Bos-N	109	342	42	107	14	1	18	59	28	18	.313	.367	.518	145	20	1	1	-0	.981	-2	C-90	2.2
1952	Bos-N	102	349	33	82	12	1	10	55	22	32	.235	.282	.361	80	-11	1	0	0	.983	-4	C-89	-1.0
1953	Mil-N	53	137	12	30	6	0	3	16	12	15	.219	.287	.328	64	-8	1	0	0	.983	-5	C-35	-1.0
Total	18	1473	4702	573	1341	240	40	173	812	309	357	.285	.332	.464	116	82	18	1		.977	-63	*C-1223	9.3
Team	4	366	1165	139	330	51	5	45	190	92	91	.283	.339	.452	117	24	4	1		.980	-16	C-302	2.3

■ **VIC CORRELL** Correll, Victor Crosby b: 2/5/46, Washington, D.C. BR/TR, 5'10", 185 lbs. Deb: 10/4/72

YEAR	TM/L	G	AB	R	H	2B	3B	HR	RBI	BB	SO	AVG	OBP	SLG	PRO+	BR/A	SB	CS	SBR	FA	FR	G/POS	TPR
1974	Atl-N	73	202	20	48	15	1	4	29	21	38	.238	.322	.381	92	-2	0	0	0	.988	6	C-59	0.6
1975	Atl-N	103	325	37	70	12	1	11	39	42	66	.215	.307	.360	82	-8	0	2	-1	.973	-2	C-97	-0.8
1976	Atl-N	69	200	26	45	6	2	5	16	21	37	.225	.302	.350	80	-5	0	1	-1	.981	3	C-65	-0.1
1977	Atl-N	54	144	16	30	7	0	7	16	22	33	.208	.317	.403	82	-4	2	3	-1	.973	2	C-49	-0.2
Total	8	410	1132	124	259	60	4	29	125	128	220	.229	.312	.366	83	-26	2	8	-4	.979	18	C-380	-0.2
Team	4	299	871	99	193	40	4	27	100	106	174	.222	.311	.370	84	-20	2	6	-3	.978	9	C-270	-0.5

■ **JOE COSCARART** Coscarart, Joseph Marvin b: 11/18/09, Escondido, Cal. d: 4/5/93, Sequim, Wash. BR/TR, 6', 185 lbs. Deb: 4/26/35 F

YEAR	TM/L	G	AB	R	H	2B	3B	HR	RBI	BB	SO	AVG	OBP	SLG	PRO+	BR/A	SB	CS	SBR	FA	FR	G/POS	TPR
1935	Bos-N	86	284	30	67	11	2	1	29	16	28	.236	.277	.299	59	-17	2			.962	-4	3-41,S-27,2	-1.7
1936	Bos-N	104	367	28	90	11	2	2	44	19	37	.245	.292	.302	64	-19	0			.935	2	3-97/S-6,2	-1.3
Total	2	190	651	58	157	22	4	3	73	35	65	.241	.285	.301	62	-35	2			.943	-3	3-138/S-33,2	-3.0

■ **CHUCK COTTIER** Cottier, Charles Keith b: 1/8/36, Delta, Colo. BR/TR, 5'10.5", 175 lbs. Deb: 4/17/59 MC

YEAR	TM/L	G	AB	R	H	2B	3B	HR	RBI	BB	SO	AVG	OBP	SLG	PRO+	BR/A	SB	CS	SBR	FA	FR	G/POS	TPR
1959	Mil-N	10	24	1	3	1	0	0	1	3	7	.125	.222	.167	6	-3	0	0	0	.976	1	2-10	-0.2
1960	Mil-N	95	229	29	52	8	0	3	19	14	21	.227	.278	.301	63	-12	1	0	0	.968	17	2-92	1.2
Total	9	580	1584	168	348	63	17	19	127	137	248	.220	.284	.317	65	-77	28	10	2	.976	81	2-482/S-34,3	4.8
Team	2	105	253	30	55	9	0	3	20	17	28	.217	.272	.289	57	-15	1	0	0	.969	17	2-102	1.0

■ **ERNIE COURTNEY** Courtney, Edward Ernest b: 1/20/1875, Des Moines, Iowa d: 2/29/20, Buffalo, N.Y. BL/TR, 5'10", Deb: 4/17/02

YEAR	TM/L	G	AB	R	H	2B	3B	HR	RBI	BB	SO	AVG	OBP	SLG	PRO+	BR/A	SB	CS	SBR	FA	FR	G/POS	TPR
1902	Bos-N	48	165	23	36	3	0	0	17	13		.218	.291	.236	62	-7	3			.974	-1	O-39/S-3	-1.1
Total	6	558	1921	226	471	52	17	5	200	188		.245	.321	.298	91	-15	35			.920	-49	3-362/1-75,OS2	-6.2

■ **DEE COUSINEAU** Cousineau, Edward Thomas b: 12/16/1898, Watertown, Mass. d: 7/14/51, Watertown, Mass. BR/TR, 6', 170 lbs. Deb: 10/6/23

YEAR	TM/L	G	AB	R	H	2B	3B	HR	RBI	BB	SO	AVG	OBP	SLG	PRO+	BR/A	SB	CS	SBR	FA	FR	G/POS	TPR
1923	Bos-N	1	2	1	2	0	0	0	2	0	0	1.000	1.000	1.000	447	1	0	0	0	.000	0	/C-1	0.1
1924	Bos-N	3	2	0	0	0	0	0	0	0	0	.000	.000	.000	-99	-1	0	0	0	.500	-1	/C-3	-0.1
1925	Bos-N	1	0	0	0	0	0	0	0	0	0	—	—	—	—	0	0	0	0	.000	0	/C-1	0.0
Total	3	5	4	1	2	0	0	0	2	0	0	.500	.500	.500	174	0	0	0	0	.500	-1	/C-5	0.0

■ **SAM COVINGTON** Covington, Clarence Otto b: 12/17/1892, Henryville, Tenn. d: 1/4/63, Denison, Tex. BL/TR, 6'1", 190 lbs. Deb: 8/25/13 F

YEAR	TM/L	G	AB	R	H	2B	3B	HR	RBI	BB	SO	AVG	OBP	SLG	PRO+	BR/A	SB	CS	SBR	FA	FR	G/POS	TPR
1917	Bos-N	17	66	8	13	2	0	1	10	5	5	.197	.264	.273	69	-2	1			.994	0	1-17	-0.3
1918	Bos-N	3	3	0	1	0	0	0	0	0	0	.333	.333	.333	108	0	0			.000	0	H	0.0
Total	3	40	129	11	23	2	1	1	14	9	11	.178	.237	.233	43	-9	4			.994	3	/1-33	-0.7
Team	2	20	69	8	14	2	0	1	10	5	5	.203	.267	.275	70	-2	1			.994	0	/1-17	-0.3

■ **WES COVINGTON** Covington, John Wesley b: 3/27/32, Laurinburg, N.C. BL/TR, 6'1", 205 lbs. Deb: 4/19/56

YEAR	TM/L	G	AB	R	H	2B	3B	HR	RBI	BB	SO	AVG	OBP	SLG	PRO+	BR/A	SB	CS	SBR	FA	FR	G/POS	TPR
1956	Mil-N	75	138	17	39	4	0	2	16	16	20	.283	.361	.355	100	0	1	0	0	.979	-3	O-35	-0.4
1957	*Mil-N	96	328	51	93	4	8	21	65	29	44	.284	.345	.537	143	18	4	1	1	.981	0	O-89	1.4
1958	*Mil-N	90	294	43	97	12	1	24	74	20	35	.330	.382	.622	175	30	0	0	0	.953	-4	O-82	2.1
1959	Mil-N	103	373	38	104	17	3	7	45	26	41	.279	.331	.397	101	-0	0	1	-1	.962	-3	O-94	-0.8
1960	Mil-N	95	281	25	70	16	1	10	35	15	37	.249	.290	.420	99	-2	1	2	-1	.964	-5	O-72	-1.1
1961	Mil-N	9	21	3	4	1	0	0	0	2	4	.190	.261	.238	36	-2	0	0	0	1.000	-1	/O-5	-0.4
Total	11	1075	2978	355	832	128	17	131	499	247	414	.279	.339	.466	123	86	7	4	-0	.961	-49	O-803	-0.1
Team	6	468	1435	177	407	54	13	64	235	108	181	.284	.339	.473	124	44	6	4	-1	.967	-16	O-377	0.8

■ **BILLY COWAN** Cowan, Billy Rolland b: 8/28/38, Calhoun City, Miss. BR/TR, 6', 170 lbs. Deb: 9/9/63

YEAR	TM/L	G	AB	R	H	2B	3B	HR	RBI	BB	SO	AVG	OBP	SLG	PRO+	BR/A	SB	CS	SBR	FA	FR	G/POS	TPR
1965	Mil-N	19	27	4	5	1	0	0	0	0	9	.185	.185	.222	14	-3	0	0	0	1.000	-2	O-10	-0.5
Total	8	493	1190	131	281	44	8	40	125	50	297	.236	.269	.387	83	-31	17	8	0	.977	-28	O-329/1-25,32S	-7.7

■ **DEL CRANDALL** Crandall, Delmar Wesley b: 3/5/30, Ontario, Cal. BR/TR, 6'1", 195 lbs. Deb: 6/17/49 MC

YEAR	TM/L	G	AB	R	H	2B	3B	HR	RBI	BB	SO	AVG	OBP	SLG	PRO+	BR/A	SB	CS	SBR	FA	FR	G/POS	TPR
1949	Bos-N	67	228	21	60	10	1	4	34	9	18	.263	.291	.368	80	-7	2			.982	7	C-63	0.3
1950	Bos-N	79	255	21	56	11	0	4	37	13	24	.220	.257	.310	52	-19	0			.967	3	C-75/1-1	-1.3
1953	Mil-N†	116	382	55	104	13	1	15	51	33	47	.272	.330	.429	102	0	2	1	0	.986	15	*C-108	1.9
1954	Mil-N☆	138	463	60	112	18	2	21	64	40	56	.242	.306	.425	94	-6	0	3	-2	.989	14	*C-136	1.2
1955	Mil-N★	133	440	61	104	15	2	26	62	40	56	.236	.303	.457	103	-0	2	1	0	.985	-2	*C-131	0.3
1956	Mil-N†	112	311	37	74	14	2	16	48	35	30	.238	.317	.450	110	3	1	2	-1	**.996**	3	*C-109	1.0
1957	*Mil-N	118	383	45	97	11	2	15	46	30	38	.253	.309	.410	98	-2	1	2	-1	.987	-8	*C-102/O-9,1	-0.8
1958	*Mil-N★	131	427	50	116	23	1	18	63	48	38	.272	.351	.457	122	12	4	1	1	**.990**	6	*C-124	2.6
1959	Mil-N★	150	518	65	133	19	2	21	72	46	48	.257	.321	.423	105	2	5	1	1	**.994**	6	*C-146	1.7
1960	Mil-N★	142	537	81	158	14	1	19	77	34	36	.294	.341	.430	118	12	4	6	-2	.988	-15	*C-141	0.3
1961	Mil-N	15	30	3	6	3	0	0	1	1	0	.200	.226	.300	40	-3	0	0	0	1.000	-2	/C-5	-0.4
1962	Mil-N★	107	350	35	104	12	3	8	45	27	24	.297	.351	.417	108	4	3	4	-2	**.994**	-4	C-90/1-5	0.2
1963	Mil-N	86	259	18	52	4	0	3	28	18	22	.201	.253	.251	46	-18	1	4	-2	.991	5	C-75/1-7	-1.4
Total	16	1573	5026	585	1276	179	18	179	657	424	477	.254	.315	.404	97	-35	26	28		.989	61	*C-1479/1-14,O	8.2
Team	13	1394	4583	552	1176	167	17	170	628	374	437	.257	.315	.412	99	-22	25	25		.989	28	*C-1305/1-14,O	5.6

■ **DOC CRANDALL** Crandall, James Otis b: 10/8/1887, Wadena, Ind. d: 8/17/51, Bell, Cal. BR/TR, 5'10.5", 180 lbs. Deb: 4/24/08

YEAR	TM/L	G	AB	R	H	2B	3B	HR	RBI	BB	SO	AVG	OBP	SLG	PRO+	BR/A	SB	CS	SBR	FA	FR	G/POS	TPR
1918	Bos-N	14	28	1	8	0	0	0	2	4	3	.286	.375	.286	107	0	0			1.000	0	/P-5,O-3	0.0
Total	10	500	887	109	253	35	19	9	126	118	94	.285	.372	.398	109	13	9			.962	-18	P-302/2-71,SO1	-1.4

■ **CONNIE CREEDEN** Creeden, Cornelius Stephen b: 7/21/15, Danvers, Mass. d: 11/30/69, Santa Ana, Cal. BL/TL, 6'1", 200 lbs. Deb: 4/28/43

YEAR	TM/L	G	AB	R	H	2B	3B	HR	RBI	BB	SO	AVG	OBP	SLG	PRO+	BR/A	SB	CS	SBR	FA	FR	G/POS	TPR
1943	Bos-N	5	4	0	1	0	0	0	1	1	0	.250	.400	.250	91	0	0			.000	0	H	0.0

■ **FRED CROLIUS** Crolius, Fred Joseph b: 12/16/1876, Jersey City, N.J. d: 8/25/60, Ormond Beach, Fla. Deb: 4/19/01

YEAR	TM/L	G	AB	R	H	2B	3B	HR	RBI	BB	SO	AVG	OBP	SLG	PRO+	BR/A	SB	CS	SBR	FA	FR	G/POS	TPR
1901	Bos-N	49	200	22	48	4	1	1	13	9		.240	.306	.285	66	-9	6			.850	-8	O-49	-2.0
Total	2	58	238	26	58	6	2	1	20	9		.244	.300	.298	69	-9	6			.868	-8	/O-58	-2.2

■ BILL CRONIN
Cronin, William Patrick "Crungy" b: 12/26/02, W.Newton, Mass. d: 10/26/66, Newton, Mass. BR/TR, 5'9", 167 lbs. Deb: 7/4/28

YEAR	TM/L	G	AB	R	H	2B	3B	HR	RBI	BB	SO	AVG	OBP	SLG	PRO+	BR/A	SB	CS	SBR	FA	FR	G/POS	TPR
1928	Bos-N	3	2	1	0	0	0	0	0	1	0	.000	.333	.000	-6	-0	0			1.000	-0	/C-3	0.0
1929	Bos-N	6	9	0	1	0	0	0	0	0	0	.111	.111	.111	-47	-2	0			1.000	1	/C-6	-0.1
1930	Bos-N	66	178	19	45	9	1	0	17	4	8	.253	.277	.315	44	-16	0			.983	7	C-64	-0.4
1931	Bos-N	51	107	8	22	6	1	0	10	7	5	.206	.267	.280	49	-8	0			.941	1	C-50	-0.5
Total	4	126	296	28	68	15	2	0	27	12	13	.230	.269	.294	43	-26	0			.968	9	C-123	-1.0

■ GEORGE CROWE
Crowe, George Daniel "Big George" b: 3/22/21, Whiteland, Ind. BL/TL, 6'2", 212 lbs. Deb: 4/16/52

YEAR	TM/L	G	AB	R	H	2B	3B	HR	RBI	BB	SO	AVG	OBP	SLG	PRO+	BR/A	SB	CS	SBR	FA	FR	G/POS	TPR
1952	Bos-N	73	217	25	56	13	1	4	20	18	25	.258	.329	.382	100	-0	0	1	-1	.985	2	1-55	-0.1
1953	Mil-N	47	42	6	12	2	0	2	6	2	7	.286	.333	.476	115	1	0	0	0	1.000	0	/1-9	0.1
1955	Mil-N	104	303	41	85	12	4	15	55	45	44	.281	.375	.495	135	16	1	0	0	.989	2	1-79	1.3
Total	9	702	1727	215	467	70	12	81	299	159	246	.270	.335	.466	109	20	3	2	-0	.990	4	1-407/2-1	0.3
Team	3	224	562	72	153	27	5	21	81	65	76	.272	.355	.450	121	16	1	1	-0	.988	4	1-143	1.3

■ TERRY CROWLEY
Crowley, Terrence Michael b: 2/16/47, Staten Island, N.Y. BL/TL, 6', 180 lbs. Deb: 9/4/69 C

YEAR	TM/L	G	AB	R	H	2B	3B	HR	RBI	BB	SO	AVG	OBP	SLG	PRO+	BR/A	SB	CS	SBR	FA	FR	G/POS	TPR
1976	Atl-N	7	6	0	0	0	0	0	1	0	0	.000	.000	.000	-94	-2	0	0	0	.000	0	H	-0.2
Total	15	865	1518	174	379	62	1	42	229	222	181	.250	.348	.375	104	13	3	0	1	.980	-13	D-195,O-141/1	-1.7

■ BILL CROWLEY
Crowley, William Michael b: 4/8/1857, Philadelphia, Pa. d: 7/14/1891, Gloucester, N.J. BR/TR, 5'7.5", 159 lbs. Deb: 4/26/1875

YEAR	TM/L	G	AB	R	H	2B	3B	HR	RBI	BB	SO	AVG	OBP	SLG	PRO+	BR/A	SB	CS	SBR	FA	FR	G/POS	TPR
1881	Bos-N	72	279	33	71	12	0	0	31	14	15	.254	.290	.297	89	-3				.880	-1	*O-72	-0.5
1884	Bos-N	108	407	50	110	14	6	6	61	33	74	.270	.325	.378	121	10				.870	-5	*O-108	0.3
Total	7	512	2020	259	537	83	22	8	206	101	178	.266	.301	.341	103	5				.853	-6	O-480/C-34,12S3	-1.2
Team	2	180	686	83	181	26	6	6	92	47	89	.264	.311	.345	109	8				.875	-6	O-180	-0.2

■ WALTON CRUISE
Cruise, Walton Edwin b: 5/6/1890, Childersburg, Ala. d: 1/9/75, Sylacauga, Ala. BL/TR, 6', 175 lbs. Deb: 4/14/14

YEAR	TM/L	G	AB	R	H	2B	3B	HR	RBI	BB	SO	AVG	OBP	SLG	PRO+	BR/A	SB	CS	SBR	FA	FR	G/POS	TPR
1919	Bos-N	73	241	23	52	7	0	1	21	17	29	.216	.267	.257	61	-11	8			.978	-5	O-66	-2.4
1920	Bos-N	91	288	40	80	7	5	1	21	31	26	.278	.352	.347	106	3	5	3	-0	.950	-7	O-82	-1.1
1921	Bos-N	108	344	47	119	16	7	8	55	48	24	.346	.429	.503	154	29	10	8	-2	.963	-6	*O-102/1-2	1.4
1922	Bos-N	104	352	51	98	15	10	4	46	44	20	.278	.360	.412	103	2	4	4	-1	.948	-0	*O-100/1-2	-0.6
1923	Bos-N	21	38	4	8	2	0	0	0	3	2	.211	.268	.263	42	-3	1	0	0	.952	-0	/O-9	-0.4
1924	Bos-N	9	9	4	4	1	0	1	3	0	2	.444	.444	.889	260	2	0	0	0	.000	0	H	0.2
Total	10	736	2321	293	644	83	39	30	272	238	250	.277	.348	.386	114	44	49	15		.962	-45	O-664/1-6	-4.9
Team	6	406	1272	169	361	48	22	15	146	143	103	.284	.358	.392	110	21	28	15		.958	-19	O-359/1-4	-2.9

■ TONY CUCCINELLO
Cuccinello, Anthony Francis "Cooch" or "Chick"
b: 11/8/07, Long Island City, N.Y. d: 9/21/95, Tampa, Fla. BR/TR, 5'7", 160 lbs. Deb: 4/15/30 FC

YEAR	TM/L	G	AB	R	H	2B	3B	HR	RBI	BB	SO	AVG	OBP	SLG	PRO+	BR/A	SB	CS	SBR	FA	FR	G/POS	TPR
1936	Bos-N	150	565	68	174	26	3	7	86	58	49	.308	.374	.402	116	14	1			.971	22	*2-150	4.5
1937	Bos-N	152	575	77	156	36	4	11	80	61	40	.271	.341	.405	112	9	2			.967	-10	*2-151	1.0
1938	Bos-N☆	147	555	62	147	25	2	9	76	52	32	.265	.331	.366	102	0	4			.974	-26	*2-147	-1.7
1939	Bos-N	81	310	42	95	17	1	2	40	26	26	.306	.360	.387	109	4	5			.970	-4	2-80	0.5
1940	Bos-N	34	126	14	34	9	0	0	19	8	9	.270	.319	.341	87	-2	1			.978	1	3-33	0.0
1942	Bos-N	40	104	8	21	3	0	1	8	9	11	.202	.265	.260	55	-6	1			.907	-4	3-20,2-14	-1.0
1943	Bos-N	13	19	0	0	0	0	0	2	3	1	.000	.136	.000	-60	-4	0			.929	0	/3-4,2-2,S	-0.4
Total	15	1704	6184	730	1729	334	46	94	884	579	497	.280	.343	.394	105	41	42			.973	-18	*2-1205,3-468/S	10.8
Team	7	617	2254	271	627	116	10	30	311	217	168	.278	.343	.378	105	14	14			.971	-19	2-544/3-57,S	2.9

■ DICK CULLER
Culler, Richard Broadus b: 1/15/15, High Point, N.C. d: 6/16/64, Chapel Hill, N.C. BR/TR, 5'9.5", 155 lbs. Deb: 9/19/36

YEAR	TM/L	G	AB	R	H	2B	3B	HR	RBI	BB	SO	AVG	OBP	SLG	PRO+	BR/A	SB	CS	SBR	FA	FR	G/POS	TPR
1944	Bos-N	8	28	2	2	0	0	0	0	4	2	.071	.188	.071	-24	-5	0			.904	2	/S-8	-0.2
1945	Bos-N	136	527	87	138	12	1	2	30	50	35	.262	.328	.300	75	-17	7			.954	-8	*S-126/3-6	-1.5
1946	Bos-N	134	482	70	123	15	3	0	33	62	18	.255	.342	.299	82	-9	7			.948	-8	*S-132	-1.1
1947	Bos-N	77	214	20	53	5	1	0	19	19	15	.248	.309	.280	59	-12	1			.967	3	S-77	-0.6
Total	8	472	1527	195	372	39	6	2	99	166	87	.244	.320	.281	68	-62	19			.954	14	S-398/3-32,2	-2.6
Team	4	355	1251	179	316	32	5	2	82	135	70	.253	.327	.291	72	-43	15			.952	-11	S-343/3-6	-3.4

■ JACK CUMMINGS
Cummings, John William b: 4/1/04, Pittsburgh, Pa. d: 10/5/62, W.Mifflin, Pa. BR/TR, 6', 195 lbs. Deb: 9/11/26

YEAR	TM/L	G	AB	R	H	2B	3B	HR	RBI	BB	SO	AVG	OBP	SLG	PRO+	BR/A	SB	CS	SBR	FA	FR	G/POS	TPR
1929	Bos-N	3	6	0	1	0	0	0	1	0	2	.167	.167	.167	-18	-1	0			.667	-1	/C-3	-0.2
Total	4	89	132	15	45	11	1	4	28	12	18	.341	.400	.530	145	8	0			.947	-6	/C-48	0.4

■ BILL CUNNINGHAM
Cunningham, William Aloysius b: 7/30/1895, San Francisco, Cal. d: 9/26/53, Colusa, Cal. BR/TR, 5'8", 155 lbs. Deb: 7/14/21 C

YEAR	TM/L	G	AB	R	H	2B	3B	HR	RBI	BB	SO	AVG	OBP	SLG	PRO+	BR/A	SB	CS	SBR	FA	FR	G/POS	TPR
1924	Bos-N	114	437	44	119	15	8	1	40	32	27	.272	.326	.350	85	-9	8	5	-1	.970	6	*O-109	-1.1
Total	4	318	945	113	270	39	12	9	112	52	48	.286	.326	.381	88	-17	17	13		.982	-8	O-268/2-4,3	-4.3

■ JACK CUSICK
Cusick, John Peter b: 6/12/28, Weehawken, N.J. d: 11/17/89, Edgewood, N.J. BR/TR, 6', 170 lbs. Deb: 4/24/51

YEAR	TM/L	G	AB	R	H	2B	3B	HR	RBI	BB	SO	AVG	OBP	SLG	PRO+	BR/A	SB	CS	SBR	FA	FR	G/POS	TPR
1952	Bos-N	49	78	5	13	1	0	0	6	6	9	.167	.226	.179	14	-9	0	1	-1	.969	-2	S-28/3-3	-1.1
Total	2	114	242	21	42	4	2	2	22	23	38	.174	.245	.231	30	-24	2	2	-1	.958	-4	/S-84,3-3	-2.4

■ BILL DAHLEN
Dahlen, William Frederick "Bad Bill" b: 1/5/1870, Nelliston, N.Y. d: 12/5/50, Brooklyn, N.Y. BR/TR, 5'9", 180 lbs. Deb: 4/22/1891 M

YEAR	TM/L	G	AB	R	H	2B	3B	HR	RBI	BB	SO	AVG	OBP	SLG	PRO+	BR/A	SB	CS	SBR	FA	FR	G/POS	TPR
1908	Bos-N	144	524	50	125	23	2	3	48	35		.239	.296	.307	94	-4	10			.952	**38**	*S-144	4.2
1909	Bos-N	69	197	22	46	6	1	2	16	29		.234	.332	.305	93	-1	4			.908	9	S-49/2-6,3	1.0
Total	21	2443	9031	1589	2457	413	163	84	1233	1064		.272	.358	.382	109	121	547			.927	348	*S-2132,3-223/O2	51.4
Team	2	213	721	72	171	29	3	5	64	64		.237	.306	.307	94	-5	14			.940	47	S-193/2-6,3	5.2

■ BABE DAHLGREN
Dahlgren, Ellsworth Tenney b: 6/15/12, San Francisco, Cal. BR/TR, 6', 190 lbs. Deb: 4/16/35 C

YEAR	TM/L	G	AB	R	H	2B	3B	HR	RBI	BB	SO	AVG	OBP	SLG	PRO+	BR/A	SB	CS	SBR	FA	FR	G/POS	TPR
1941	Bos-N	44	166	20	39	8	1	7	30	16	13	.235	.306	.422	108	1	0			.993	2	1-39/3-5	0.1
Total	12	1137	4045	470	1056	174	37	82	569	390	401	.261	.329	.383	92	-49	18			.990	-44	*1-1030/3-48,SC	-16.9

■ CON DAILY
Daily, Cornelius F. b: 9/11/1864, Blackstone, Mass. d: 6/14/28, Brooklyn, N.Y. BL, 6', 192 lbs. Deb: 6/9/1884 F

YEAR	TM/L	G	AB	R	H	2B	3B	HR	RBI	BB	SO	AVG	OBP	SLG	PRO+	BR/A	SB	CS	SBR	FA	FR	G/POS	TPR
1886	Bos-N	50	180	25	43	4	2	0	21	19	29	.239	.312	.283	85	-2	2			.911	-11	C-49/O-1	-0.7
1887	Bos-N	36	120	12	19	5	0	0	13	9	8	.158	.229	.200	20	-13	7			.889	-2	C-36	-1.0
Total	13	630	2222	280	541	74	22	2	262	208	208	.243	.314	.299	76	-68	94			.912	-43	C-550/O-45,13S2	-5.6
Team	2	86	300	37	62	9	2	0	34	28	37	.207	.279	.250	57	-15	9			.904	-13	/C-85,O-1	-1.7

■ JOE DALY
Daly, Joseph John b: 9/21/1868, Conshohocken, Pa. d: 3/21/43, Philadelphia, Pa. TR, 5'8", 157 lbs. Deb: 9/19/1890 F

YEAR	TM/L	G	AB	R	H	2B	3B	HR	RBI	BB	SO	AVG	OBP	SLG	PRO+	BR/A	SB	CS	SBR	FA	FR	G/POS	TPR
1892	Bos-N	1	0	0	0	0	0	0	0	0	0	—	—	—	—	0	0			1.000	0	/C-1	0.0
Total	3	23	78	8	21	4	1	0	0	3	2	.269	.296	.346	91	-1	1			.909	-6	/O-15,C-10	-0.6

■ BILL DAM
Dam, Elbridge Rust b: 4/4/1885, Cambridge, Mass. d: 6/22/30, Quincy, Mass. Deb: 8/23/09

YEAR	TM/L	G	AB	R	H	2B	3B	HR	RBI	BB	SO	AVG	OBP	SLG	PRO+	BR/A	SB	CS	SBR	FA	FR	G/POS	TPR
1909	Bos-N	1	2	1	1	1	0	0	0	1		.500	.667	1.000	398	1	0			1.000	-0	/O-1	0.1

■ JACK DANIELS
Daniels, Harold Jack "Sour Mash Jack" b: 12/21/27, Chester, Pa. BL/TL, 5'10", 165 lbs. Deb: 4/18/52

YEAR	TM/L	G	AB	R	H	2B	3B	HR	RBI	BB	SO	AVG	OBP	SLG	PRO+	BR/A	SB	CS	SBR	FA	FR	G/POS	TPR
1952	Bos-N	106	219	31	41	5	1	2	14	28	30	.187	.288	.247	51	-14	3	3	-1	.977	-9	O-87	-2.8

■ ALVIN DARK
Dark, Alvin Ralph "Blackie" b: 1/7/22, Comanche, Okla. BR/TR, 5'11", 185 lbs. Deb: 7/14/46 MC

YEAR	TM/L	G	AB	R	H	2B	3B	HR	RBI	BB	SO	AVG	OBP	SLG	PRO+	BR/A	SB	CS	SBR	FA	FR	G/POS	TPR
1946	Bos-N	15	13	0	3	3	0	0	1	0	3	.231	.231	.462	93	-0	0			.905	2	S-12/O-1	0.2
1948	*Bos-N	137	543	85	175	39	6	3	48	24	36	.322	.353	.433	114	9	4			.963	-12	*S-133	0.4
1949	Bos-N	130	529	74	146	23	5	3	53	31	43	.276	.317	.355	85	-13	5			.961	-4	*S-125/3-4	-0.7

YEAR	TM/L	G	AB	R	H	2B	3B	HR	RBI	BB	SO	AVG	OBP	SLG	PRO+	BR/A	SB	CS	SBR	FA	FR	G/POS	TPR
1960	Mil-N	50	141	16	42	6	2	1	18	7	13	.298	.336	.390	106	1	0	0	0	.960	-1	O-25,1-10/32	-0.2
Total	14	1828	7219	1064	2089	358	72	126	757	430	534	.289	.334	.411	98	-30	59	27		.960	-43	*S-1404,3-320/O21P	3.0
Team	4	332	1226	175	366	71	13	7	120	62	95	.299	.334	.395	100	-3	9	0		.961	-14	S-270/O-26,132	-0.3

■ JODY DAVIS

Davis, Jody Richard b: 11/12/56, Gainesville, Ga. BR/TR, 6'3", 210 lbs. Deb: 4/21/81

YEAR	TM/L	G	AB	R	H	2B	3B	HR	RBI	BB	SO	AVG	OBP	SLG	PRO+	BR/A	SB	CS	SBR	FA	FR	G/POS	TPR
1988	Atl-N	2	8	2	2	0	0	1	3	0	1	.250	.250	.625	137	0	0	0	0	1.000	1	/C-2	0.1
1989	Atl-N	78	231	12	39	5	0	4	19	23	61	.169	.247	.242	39	-18	0	0	0	.985	-9	C-72/1-2	-2.6
1990	Atl-N	12	28	0	2	0	0	0	1	3	3	.071	.161	.071	-32	-5	0	0	0	1.000	1	/1-6,C-4	-0.4
Total	10	1082	3585	364	877	164	11	127	490	333	712	.245	.310	.403	91	-48	7	16	-8	.987	-15	*C-1039/1-9	-1.8
Team	3	92	267	14	43	5	0	5	23	26	65	.161	.238	.236	34	-23	0	0	0	.987	-8	/C-78,1-8	-2.9

■ TRENCH DAVIS

Davis, Trench Neal b: 9/12/60, Baltimore, Md. BL/TL, 6'3", 171 lbs. Deb: 6/4/85

YEAR	TM/L	G	AB	R	H	2B	3B	HR	RBI	BB	SO	AVG	OBP	SLG	PRO+	BR/A	SB	CS	SBR	FA	FR	G/POS	TPR
1987	Atl-N	6	3	0	0	0	0	0	0	0	1	.000	.000	.000	-95	-1	0	0	0	.000	0	/H	-0.1
Total	3	23	33	3	4	0	0	0	1	0	5	.121	.121	.121	-32	-6	1	0	0	.867	-1	/O-9	-0.8

■ CHARLIE DEAL

Deal, Charles Albert b: 10/30/1891, Wilkinsburg, Pa. d: 9/16/79, Covina, Cal. BR/TR, 6', 160 lbs. Deb: 7/19/12

YEAR	TM/L	G	AB	R	H	2B	3B	HR	RBI	BB	SO	AVG	OBP	SLG	PRO+	BR/A	SB	CS	SBR	FA	FR	G/POS	TPR
1913	Bos-N	10	36	6	11	1	0	0	3	2	1	.306	.359	.333	96	-0	1			.935	-6	2-10	-0.7
1914	*Bos-N	79	257	17	54	13	2	0	23	20	23	.210	.270	.276	63	-12	4			.948	-5	3-74/S-1	-1.6
Total	10	851	2930	295	752	104	34	11	318	135	121	.257	.293	.327	78	-86	65			.958	41	3-823/2-11,S	-2.6
Team	2	89	293	23	65	14	2	0	26	22	24	.222	.281	.283	67	-12	5			.948	-11	/3-74,2-10,S	-2.3

■ PAT DEALY

Dealy, Patrick E. b: Burlington, Vt. d: 12/16/24, Buffalo, N.Y. BR/TR, 5'8", 145 lbs. Deb: 9/30/1884

YEAR	TM/L	G	AB	R	H	2B	3B	HR	RBI	BB	SO	AVG	OBP	SLG	PRO+	BR/A	SB	CS	SBR	FA	FR	G/POS	TPR
1885	Bos-N	35	130	18	29	4	1	1	9	2	14	.223	.235	.292	72	-4				.903	0	C-29/3-3,OS1	-0.1
1886	Bos-N	15	46	9	15	1	1	0	3	4	4	.326	.380	.391	140	2	5			.929	-2	C-14/O-1	0.2
Total	5	131	469	71	113	14	4	2	30	19	26	.241	.275	.301	74	-17	45			.914	-12	/C-85,S-25,3O1	-1.8
Team	2	50	176	27	44	5	2	1	12	6	18	.250	.275	.318	91	-2	5			.910	-1	/C-43,3-3,OS1	0.1

■ PAT DEASLEY

Deasley, Thomas H. b: 11/17/1857, Ireland d: 4/1/43, Philadelphia, Pa. BR/TR, 5'8.5", 154 lbs. Deb: 5/18/1881 F

YEAR	TM/L	G	AB	R	H	2B	3B	HR	RBI	BB	SO	AVG	OBP	SLG	PRO+	BR/A	SB	CS	SBR	FA	FR	G/POS	TPR
1881	Bos-N	43	147	13	35	5	2	0	8	5	10	.238	.263	.299	80	-3				.914	-4	C-28/O-7,S1	-0.6
1882	Bos-N	67	264	36	70	8	0	0	29	7	22	.265	.284	.295	86	-4				**.958**	2	*C-56,O-14/S	-0.1
Total	8	402	1466	161	358	37	9	0	105	49	89	.244	.271	.282	75	-42	7			.927	28	C-354/O-43,S312	0.8
Team	2	110	411	49	105	13	2	0	37	12	32	.255	.277	.297	84	-7	0			.945	-2	/C-84,O-21,S1	-0.7

■ JIM DELAHANTY

Delahanty, James Christopher b: 6/20/1879, Cleveland, Ohio d: 10/17/53, Cleveland, Ohio BR/TR, 5'10.5", 170 lbs. Deb: 4/19/01 F

YEAR	TM/L	G	AB	R	H	2B	3B	HR	RBI	BB	SO	AVG	OBP	SLG	PRO+	BR/A	SB	CS	SBR	FA	FR	G/POS	TPR
1904	Bos-N	142	499	56	142	27	8	3	60	27		.285	.333	.389	127	15	16			.888	1	*3-113,2-18/OP	1.9
1905	Bos-N	125	461	50	119	11	8	5	55	28		.258	.315	.349	100	-1	12			.962	-7	*O-124/P-1	-1.5
Total	13	1186	4091	520	1159	191	59	19	489	378		.283	.357	.373	121	110	151			.946	-97	2-568,3-296,O/1SP	0.3
Team	2	267	960	106	261	38	16	8	115	55		.272	.324	.370	114	14	28			.957	-7	O-133,3-113/2P	0.4

■ MIKE de la HOZ

de la Hoz, Miguel Angel (Piloto) b: 10/2/38, Havana, Cuba BR/TR, 5'11", 175 lbs. Deb: 7/22/60

YEAR	TM/L	G	AB	R	H	2B	3B	HR	RBI	BB	SO	AVG	OBP	SLG	PRO+	BR/A	SB	CS	SBR	FA	FR	G/POS	TPR
1964	Mil-N	78	189	25	55	7	1	4	12	14	22	.291	.346	.402	109	2	1	1	-0	.968	-4	2-25,3-25/S	0.0
1965	Mil-N	81	176	15	45	3	2	2	11	8	21	.256	.296	.330	75	-6	0	1	-1	.963	-10	S-41,3-22,2/1	-1.6
1966	Atl-N	71	110	11	24	3	0	2	7	5	18	.218	.252	.300	52	-7	0	1	-1	.950	-2	3-30/2-8,S	-1.1
1967	Atl-N	74	143	10	29	3	0	3	14	4	14	.203	.224	.287	46	-10	1	0	0	1.000	-4	2-23,3-22/S	-1.5
Total	9	494	1114	116	280	42	5	25	115	56	130	.251	.292	.365	82	-29	2	3		.936	-28	3-129,2-119,S/O1	-4.9
Team	4	304	618	61	153	16	3	11	44	31	75	.248	.288	.337	75	-21	2	3		.935	-21	/3-99,2-66,S1	-4.2

■ FRANK DEMAREE

Demaree, Joseph Franklin (b: Joseph Franklin Dimaria)
b: 6/10/10, Winters, Cal. d: 8/30/58, Los Angeles, Cal. BR/TR, 5'11.5", 185 lbs. Deb: 7/22/32

YEAR	TM/L	G	AB	R	H	2B	3B	HR	RBI	BB	SO	AVG	OBP	SLG	PRO+	BR/A	SB	CS	SBR	FA	FR	G/POS	TPR
1941	Bos-N	48	113	20	26	5	2	2	15	12	5	.230	.304	.363	91	-2	2			1.000	-4	O-28	-0.7
1942	Bos-N	64	187	18	42	5	0	3	24	17	10	.225	.289	.299	74	-6	2			1.000	4	O-49	-0.6
Total	12	1155	4144	578	1241	190	36	72	591	359	269	.299	.357	.415	110	57	33			.978	-22	*O-1076	-1.3
Team	2	112	300	38	68	10	2	5	39	29	15	.227	.295	.323	80	-8	4			1.000	-1	/O-77	-1.3

■ JOHN DeMERIT

DeMerit, John Stephen "Thumper" b: 1/8/36, West Bend, Wis. BR/TR, 6'1.5", 195 lbs. Deb: 6/18/57

YEAR	TM/L	G	AB	R	H	2B	3B	HR	RBI	BB	SO	AVG	OBP	SLG	PRO+	BR/A	SB	CS	SBR	FA	FR	G/POS	TPR
1957	*Mil-N	33	34	8	5	0	0	0	1	0	8	.147	.147	.147	-22	-6	1	0	0	1.000	-3	O-13	-0.9
1958	Mil-N	3	3	1	2	0	0	0	0	0	0	.667	.667	.667	278	1	0	0	0	1.000	-1	/O-2	0.0
1959	Mil-N	11	5	4	1	0	0	0	0	1	2	.200	.333	.200	51	-0	0	0	0	1.000	-0	/O-4	-0.1
1961	Mil-N	32	74	5	12	3	0	2	5	5	19	.162	.225	.284	36	-7	0	0	0	1.000	0	O-21	-0.8
Total	5	93	132	21	23	3	0	3	7	8	33	.174	.227	.265	32	-13	1	0	0	1.000	-6	/O-49	-2.2
Team	4	79	116	18	20	3	0	2	6	6	29	.172	.220	.250	26	-12	1	0	0	1.000	-4	/O-40	-1.8

■ GENE DeMONTREVILLE

DeMontreville, Eugene Napoleon b: 3/26/1874, St.Paul, Minn. d: 2/18/35, Memphis, Tenn. BR/TR, 5'8", 165 lbs. Deb: 8/20/1894 F

YEAR	TM/L	G	AB	R	H	2B	3B	HR	RBI	BB	SO	AVG	OBP	SLG	PRO+	BR/A	SB	CS	SBR	FA	FR	G/POS	TPR
1901	Bos-N	140	577	83	173	14	4	5	72	17		.300	.321	.364	90	-9	25			**.954**	5	*2-120,3-20	0.1
1902	Bos-N	124	481	51	125	16	5	0	53	12		.260	.278	.314	82	-12	23			.940	-17	*2-112,S-10	-2.5
Total	11	922	3615	537	1096	130	35	17	497	174		.303	.340	.373	97	-21	228			.948	31	2-510,S-379/31O	3.8
Team	2	264	1058	134	298	30	9	5	125	29		.282	.301	.341	87	-21	48			.947	-11	2-232/3-20,S	-2.4

■ DREW DENSON

Denson, Andrew b: 11/16/65, Cincinnati, Ohio BB/TR, 6'5", 210 lbs. Deb: 9/13/89

YEAR	TM/L	G	AB	R	H	2B	3B	HR	RBI	BB	SO	AVG	OBP	SLG	PRO+	BR/A	SB	CS	SBR	FA	FR	G/POS	TPR
1989	Atl-N	12	36	1	9	1	0	0	5	3	9	.250	.308	.278	67	-1	1	0	0	.988	2	1-12	0.0
Total	2	16	41	1	10	1	0	0	5	3	11	.244	.295	.268	60	-2	1	0	0	.977	2	/1-15	-0.1

■ DUCKY DETWEILER

Detweiler, Robert Sterling b: 2/15/19, Trumbauersville, Pa. BR/TR, 5'11", 178 lbs. Deb: 9/12/42

YEAR	TM/L	G	AB	R	H	2B	3B	HR	RBI	BB	SO	AVG	OBP	SLG	PRO+	BR/A	SB	CS	SBR	FA	FR	G/POS	TPR
1942	Bos-N	12	44	3	14	2	1	0	5	2	7	.318	.348	.409	123	1	0			.929	-4	3-12	-0.3
1946	Bos-N	1	1	0	0	0	0	0	0	0	0	.000	.000	.000	-99	-0	0			.000	0	H	0.0
Total	2	13	45	3	14	2	1	0	5	2	7	.311	.340	.400	118	1	0			.956	-4	/3-12	-0.3

■ MIKE DEVEREAUX

Devereaux, Michael b: 4/10/63, Casper, Wyo. BR/TR, 6' ", 195 lbs. Deb: 9/2/87

YEAR	TM/L	G	AB	R	H	2B	3B	HR	RBI	BB	SO	AVG	OBP	SLG	PRO+	BR/A	SB	CS	SBR	FA	FR	G/POS	TPR
1995	*Atl-N	29	55	7	14	3	0	1	8	2	11	.255	.281	.364	67	-3	2	0	1	1.000	-2	O-27	-0.4
Total	9	921	3332	434	856	155	31	97	438	252	570	.257	.311	.409	95	-29	76	53		.988	16	O-895/D-9	-4.2

■ ART DEVLIN

Devlin, Arthur McArthur b: 10/16/1879, Washington, D.C. d: 9/18/48, Jersey City, N.J. BR/TR, 6', 175 lbs. Deb: 4/14/04 C

YEAR	TM/L	G	AB	R	H	2B	3B	HR	RBI	BB	SO	AVG	OBP	SLG	PRO+	BR/A	SB	CS	SBR	FA	FR	G/POS	TPR
1912	Bos-N	124	436	59	126	18	8	0	54	51	37	.289	.367	.367	99	1	11			.992	-1	1-69,S-26,3/O	0.1
1913	Bos-N	73	210	19	48	7	5	0	12	29	17	.229	.328	.310	81	-4	8			.973	9	3-69	0.5
Total	10	1313	4412	603	1185	164	57	10	505	576	105	.269	.364	.338	109	68	285			.938	86	*3-1192/1-75,S2O	20.6
Team	2	197	646	78	174	25	13	0	66	80	54	.269	.354	.348	94	-4	19			.969	8	/3-95,1-69,SO	0.6

■ REX DeVOGT

DeVogt, Rex Eugene b: 1/4/1888, Clare, Mich. d: 11/9/35, Alma, Mich. BR/TR, 5'9", 170 lbs. Deb: 4/17/13

YEAR	TM/L	G	AB	R	H	2B	3B	HR	RBI	BB	SO	AVG	OBP	SLG	PRO+	BR/A	SB	CS	SBR	FA	FR	G/POS	TPR
1913	Bos-N	3	6	0	0	0	0	0	0	0	3	.000	.000	.000	-98	-2	0			.941	1	/C-3	0.0

■ JOSH DEVORE

Devore, Joshua D. b: 11/13/1887, Murray City, Ohio d: 10/6/54, Chillicothe, Ohio BL/TL, 5'6", 160 lbs. Deb: 9/25/08

YEAR	TM/L	G	AB	R	H	2B	3B	HR	RBI	BB	SO	AVG	OBP	SLG	PRO+	BR/A	SB	CS	SBR	FA	FR	G/POS	TPR
1914	*Bos-N	51	128	22	29	4	0	1	5	18	14	.227	.327	.281	82	-2	2			.915	-8	O-42	-1.3
Total	7	601	1874	331	520	58	31	11	149	222	230	.277	.361	.359	103	13	160			.925	-38	O-519	-5.0

■ CHARLIE DEXTER

Dexter, Charles Dana b: 6/15/1876, Evansville, Ind. d: 6/9/34, Cedar Rapids, Iowa BR/TR, 5'7", 155 lbs. Deb: 4/17/1896

YEAR	TM/L	G	AB	R	H	2B	3B	HR	RBI	BB	SO	AVG	OBP	SLG	PRO+	BR/A	SB	CS	SBR	FA	FR	G/POS	TPR
1902	Bos-N	48	183	33	47	3	0	1	18	16		.257	.323	.290	88	-2	16			.901	-4	S-22,2-19/O3	-0.4

YEAR TM/L	G	AB	R	H	2B	3B	HR	RBI	BB	SO	AVG	OBP	SLG	PRO+	BR/A	SB	CS	SBR	FA	FR	G/POS	TPR
1903 Bos-N	123	457	82	102	15	1	3	34	61		.223	.323	.280	75	-12	32			.941	-10	*O-106/S-9,C	-2.7
Total 8	771	2866	429	749	94	24	16	346	198		.261	.318	.328	85	-57	183			.942	-22	O-402,C-116/312S	-8.7
Team 2	171	640	115	149	18	1	4	52	77		.233	.323	.283	79	-14	48			.944	-13	O-113/S-31,2C3	-3.1

■ **BOB DIDIER** Didier, Robert Daniel b: 2/16/49, Hattiesburg, Miss. BB/TR, 6', 190 lbs. Deb: 4/7/69 C

YEAR TM/L	G	AB	R	H	2B	3B	HR	RBI	BB	SO	AVG	OBP	SLG	PRO+	BR/A	SB	CS	SBR	FA	FR	G/POS	TPR
1969 *Atl-N	114	352	30	90	16	1	0	32	34	39	.256	.321	.307	76	-10	1	3	-2	.994	-2	*C-114	-0.9
1970 Atl-N	57	168	9	25	2	1	0	7	12	11	.149	.210	.173	3	-23	1	0	0	.988	1	C-57	-1.9
1971 Atl-N	51	155	9	34	4	1	0	5	6	17	.219	.248	.258	41	-12	0	0	0	1.000	3	C-50	-0.8
1972 Atl-N	13	40	5	12	2	1	0	5	2	4	.300	.349	.400	103	0	0	0	0	1.000	2	C-11	0.2
Total 6	247	751	56	172	25	4	0	51	59	72	.229	.287	.273	55	-45	2	3	-1	.994	6	C-244	-3.0
Team 4	235	715	53	161	24	4	0	49	54	71	.225	.281	.270	52	-45	2	3	-1	.994	3	C-232	-3.4

■ **ERNIE DIEHL** Diehl, Ernest Guy b: 10/2/1877, Cincinnati, Ohio d: 11/6/58, Miami, Fla. BR/TR, 6'1", 190 lbs. Deb: 5/31/03

YEAR TM/L	G	AB	R	H	2B	3B	HR	RBI	BB	SO	AVG	OBP	SLG	PRO+	BR/A	SB	CS	SBR	FA	FR	G/POS	TPR
1906 Bos-N	3	11	1	5	0	1	0	0	0		.455	.455	.636	247	2	0			1.000	0	/O-2,S-1	0.2
1909 Bos-N	1	4	1	2	1	0	0	0	0		.500	.500	.750	274	1	0			.800	1	/O-1	0.1
Total 4	17	55	8	14	1	1	0	4	6		.255	.349	.309	101	0	3			.944	2	/O-11,S-5	0.1
Team 2	4	15	2	7	1	1	0	0	0		.467	.467	.667	255	2	0			.889	1	/O-3,S-1	0.3

■ **DICK DIETZ** Dietz, Richard Allen b: 9/18/41, Crawfordsville, Ind. BR/TR, 6'1", 195 lbs. Deb: 6/18/66

YEAR TM/L	G	AB	R	H	2B	3B	HR	RBI	BB	SO	AVG	OBP	SLG	PRO+	BR/A	SB	CS	SBR	FA	FR	G/POS	TPR
1973 Atl-N	83	139	22	41	8	1	3	24	49	25	.295	.479	.432	143	12	0	0	0	.989	1	1-36,C-20	1.1
Total 8	646	1829	226	478	89	6	66	301	381	402	.261	.392	.425	130	88	4	6		.980	-39	C-528/1-36	7.1

■ **STEVE DIGNAN** Dignan, Stephen E. b: 5/16/1859, Boston, Mass. d: 7/11/1881, Boston, Mass. Deb: 6/1/1880

YEAR TM/L	G	AB	R	H	2B	3B	HR	RBI	BB	SO	AVG	OBP	SLG	PRO+	BR/A	SB	CS	SBR	FA	FR	G/POS	TPR
1880 Bos-N	8	34	4	11	1	0	0	4	0	3	.324	.324	.353	133	1				.684	0	/O-8	0.1

■ **DON DILLARD** Dillard, David Donald b: 1/8/37, Greenville, S.C. BL/TR, 6'1", 200 lbs. Deb: 4/24/59

YEAR TM/L	G	AB	R	H	2B	3B	HR	RBI	BB	SO	AVG	OBP	SLG	PRO+	BR/A	SB	CS	SBR	FA	FR	G/POS	TPR
1963 Mil-N	67	119	9	28	6	4	1	12	5	21	.235	.272	.378	86	-2	0	2	-1	.951	-0	O-30	-0.5
1965 Mil-N	20	19	1	3	0	0	1	3	0	6	.158	.158	.316	30	-2	0	0	0	.000	-0	/O-1	-0.2
Total 6	272	476	59	116	16	5	14	47	32	85	.244	.293	.387	86	-10	0	3	-2	.976	-15	O-121	-3.2
Team 2	87	138	10	31	6	4	2	15	5	27	.225	.257	.370	78	-4	0	2	-1	.951	-1	/O-31	-0.7

■ **VINCE DiMAGGIO** DiMaggio, Vincent Paul b: 9/6/12, Martinez, Cal. d: 10/3/86, N.Hollywood, Cal. BR/TR, 5'11", 183 lbs. Deb: 4/19/37 F

YEAR TM/L	G	AB	R	H	2B	3B	HR	RBI	BB	SO	AVG	OBP	SLG	PRO+	BR/A	SB	CS	SBR	FA	FR	G/POS	TPR
1937 Bos-N	132	493	56	126	18	4	13	69	39	111	.256	.311	.387	98	-4	8			.982	16	*O-130	0.7
1938 Bos-N	150	540	71	123	28	3	14	61	65	134	.228	.313	.369	96	-4	11			.973	13	*O-149/2-1	0.5
Total 10	1110	3849	491	959	209	24	125	584	412	837	.249	.324	.413	108	29	79			.981	71	*O-1081/3-1,S2	5.0
Team 2	282	1033	127	249	46	7	27	130	104	245	.241	.312	.378	97	-8	19			.977	29	O-279/2-1	1.2

■ **JACK DITTMER** Dittmer, John Douglas b: 1/10/28, Elkader, Iowa BL/TR, 6'1", 175 lbs. Deb: 6/17/52

YEAR TM/L	G	AB	R	H	2B	3B	HR	RBI	BB	SO	AVG	OBP	SLG	PRO+	BR/A	SB	CS	SBR	FA	FR	G/POS	TPR
1952 Bos-N	93	326	26	63	7	2	7	41	26	26	.193	.255	.291	53	-21	1	0	0	.982	6	2-90	-1.1
1953 Mil-N	138	504	54	134	22	1	9	63	18	35	.266	.293	.367	75	-20	1	0	0	.965	-29	*2-138	-4.0
1954 Mil-N	66	192	22	47	8	0	6	20	19	17	.245	.322	.380	88	-4	0	1	-1	.977	-3	2-55	-0.4
1955 Mil-N	38	72	4	9	1	1	1	4	4	15	.125	.171	.208	0	-11	0	0	0	.977	-2	2-28	-1.1
1956 Mil-N	44	102	8	25	4	0	1	6	8	8	.245	.300	.314	69	-4	0	0	0	.979	3	2-42	0.0
Total 6	395	1218	117	283	43	4	24	136	77	102	.232	.281	.333	66	-61	2	1	0	.974	-26	2-354/3-3	-6.8
Team 5	379	1196	114	278	42	4	24	134	75	101	.232	.281	.334	66	-60	2	1	0	.974	-25	2-353	-6.6

■ **COZY DOLAN** Dolan, Patrick Henry b: 12/3/1872, Cambridge, Mass. d: 3/29/07, Louisville, Ky. BL/TL, 5'10", 160 lbs. Deb: 4/26/1895

YEAR TM/L	G	AB	R	H	2B	3B	HR	RBI	BB	SO	AVG	OBP	SLG	PRO+	BR/A	SB	CS	SBR	FA	FR	G/POS	TPR
1895 Bos-N	26	83	12	20	4	1	0	7	6	7	.241	.300	.313	54	-6	3			.949	3	P-25/O-1	-0.1
1896 Bos-N	6	14	4	2	0	0	0	0	0	1	.143	.143	.143	-23	-3	0			.765	-0	/P-6	0.0
1905 Bos-N	112	433	44	119	11	7	3	48	27		.275	.322	.353	103	1	21			.946	4	*O-111/P-2,1	0.0
1906 Bos-N	152	549	54	136	20	4	0	39	55		.248	.318	.299	95	-2	17			.928	-2	*O-144/2-7,P1	-1.2
Total 9	830	3174	428	855	99	37	10	315	227	8	.269	.322	.333	94	-27	114			.931	-18	O-723/1-59,P2	-8.5
Team 4	296	1079	114	277	35	12	3	94	88	8	.257	.316	.320	93	-10	41			.916	5	O-256/P-35,21	-1.3

■ **ART DOLL** Doll, Arthur James "Moose" b: 5/7/13, Chicago, Ill. d: 4/28/78, Calumet City, Ill. BR/TR, 6'1", 190 lbs. Deb: 9/21/35

YEAR TM/L	G	AB	R	H	2B	3B	HR	RBI	BB	SO	AVG	OBP	SLG	PRO+	BR/A	SB	CS	SBR	FA	FR	G/POS	TPR
1935 Bos-N	3	10	0	1	0	0	0	0	0	1	.100	.100	.100	-50	-2	0			.867	0	/C-3	-0.2
1936 Bos-N	1	2	0	0	0	0	0	0	0	2	.000	.000	.000	-99	-1	0			1.000	-0	/P-1	0.0
1938 Bos-N	3	1	0	1	0	0	0	0	0	0	1.000	1.000	1.000	501	1	0			1.000	0	/P-3	0.0
Total 3	7	13	0	2	0	0	0	0	0	3	.154	.154	.154	-18	-2	0			1.000	0	/P-4,C-3	-0.2

■ **MIKE DONLIN** Donlin, Michael Joseph "Turkey Mike" b: 5/30/1878, Peoria, Ill. d: 9/24/33, Hollywood, Cal. BL/TL, 5'9", 170 lbs. Deb: 7/19/1899

YEAR TM/L	G	AB	R	H	2B	3B	HR	RBI	BB	SO	AVG	OBP	SLG	PRO+	BR/A	SB	CS	SBR	FA	FR	G/POS	TPR
1911 Bos-N	56	222	33	70	16	1	2	34	22	17	.315	.377	.423	115	4	7			.912	-3	O-56	-0.2
Total 12	1049	3854	669	1282	176	97	51	543	312	39	.333	.386	.468	142	193	213			.924	-37	O-867/1-95,PS	10.6

■ **PATSY DONOVAN** Donovan, Patrick Joseph b: 3/16/1865, County Cork, Ireland d: 12/25/53, Lawrence, Mass. BL/TL, 5'11.5", 175 lbs. Deb: 4/19/1890 M

YEAR TM/L	G	AB	R	H	2B	3B	HR	RBI	BB	SO	AVG	OBP	SLG	PRO+	BR/A	SB	CS	SBR	FA	FR	G/POS	TPR
1890 Bos-N	32	140	17	36	0	0	0	9	8	17	.257	.307	.257	60	-7	10			.891	-5	O-32	-1.2
Total 17	1821	7496	1318	2253	207	75	16	736	453	131	.301	.347	.355	98	-22	518			.941	13	*O-1813	-11.0

■ **BILL DREESEN** Dreesen, William Richard b: 7/26/04, New York, N.Y. d: 11/9/71, Mt.Vernon, N.Y. BL/TR, 5'7.5", 160 lbs. Deb: 5/1/31

YEAR TM/L	G	AB	R	H	2B	3B	HR	RBI	BB	SO	AVG	OBP	SLG	PRO+	BR/A	SB	CS	SBR	FA	FR	G/POS	TPR
1931 Bos-N	48	180	38	40	10	4	1	10	23	23	.222	.310	.339	77	-6	1			.910	-8	3-47	-1.1

■ **FRANK DREWS** Drews, Frank John b: 5/25/16, Buffalo, N.Y. d: 4/22/72, Buffalo, N.Y. BR/TR, 5'10", 175 lbs. Deb: 8/13/44

YEAR TM/L	G	AB	R	H	2B	3B	HR	RBI	BB	SO	AVG	OBP	SLG	PRO+	BR/A	SB	CS	SBR	FA	FR	G/POS	TPR
1944 Bos-N	46	141	14	29	9	1	0	10	25	14	.206	.329	.284	71	-5	0			.959	1	2-46	-0.2
1945 Bos-N	49	147	13	30	4	1	0	19	16	18	.204	.282	.245	47	-10	0			.976	5	2-48	-0.3
Total 2	95	288	27	59	13	2	0	29	41	32	.205	.306	.264	59	-15	0			.967	5	/2-94	-0.5

■ **JOHN DUDRA** Dudra, John Joseph b: 5/27/16, Assumption, Ill. d: 10/24/65, Pana, Ill. BR/TR, 5'11.5", 175 lbs. Deb: 9/7/41

YEAR TM/L	G	AB	R	H	2B	3B	HR	RBI	BB	SO	AVG	OBP	SLG	PRO+	BR/A	SB	CS	SBR	FA	FR	G/POS	TPR
1941 Bos-N	14	25	3	9	3	1	0	3	3	4	.360	.429	.560	185	3	0			.933	0	/2-5,3-5,1S	0.3

■ **HUGH DUFFY** Duffy, Hugh b: 11/26/1866, Cranston, R.I. d: 10/19/54, Boston, Mass. BR/TR, 5'7", 168 lbs. Deb: 6/23/1888 MCH

YEAR TM/L	G	AB	R	H	2B	3B	HR	RBI	BB	SO	AVG	OBP	SLG	PRO+	BR/A	SB	CS	SBR	FA	FR	G/POS	TPR
1892 *Bos-N	147	612	125	184	28	12	5	81	60	37	.301	.364	.410	123	14	51			.942	-9	*O-146/3-2	-0.1
1893 Bos-N	131	560	147	203	23	7	6	118	50	13	.363	.416	.461	123	16	44			.953	-2	*O-131	0.6
1894 Bos-N	125	539	160	**237**	**51**	16	**18**	**145**	66	15	**.440**	.502	**.694**	172	61	48			.927	4	*O-124/S-2	4.3
1895 Bos-N	130	531	110	187	30	6	9	100	63	16	.352	.425	.482	124	18	42			.945	6	*O-130	1.1
1896 Bos-N	131	527	97	158	16	8	5	113	52	19	.300	.365	.389	93	-6	39			.957	0	*O-120/2-9,S	-1.3
1897 *Bos-N	134	550	130	187	25	10	**11**	129	52		.340	.403	.482	125	18	41			.975	-1	*O-129/2-6,S	0.7
1898 Bos-N	152	568	97	169	13	3	8	108	59		.298	.365	.373	106	4	29			.956	2	*O-152/3-1,1C	-0.4
1899 Bos-N	147	588	103	164	29	7	5	102	39		.279	.327	.378	85	-15	26			.970	-4	*O-147	-2.7
1900 Bos-N	55	181	27	55	5	4	2	31	16		.304	.360	.409	100	-1	11			.957	-1	O-49/2-1	-0.5
Total 17	1737	7042	1552	2282	325	119	106	1302	662	211	.324	.384	.449	121	181	574			.943	-10	*O-1681/S-20,23C1	5.5
Team 9	1152	4656	996	1544	220	73	69	927	457	100	.332	.394	.455	119	111	331			.953	-4	*O-1128/2-16,S3C1	1.7

■ **JOE DUGAN** Dugan, Joseph Anthony "Jumping Joe" b: 5/12/1897, Mahanoy City, Pa. d: 7/7/82, Norwood, Mass. BR/TR, 5'11", 160 lbs. Deb: 7/5/17

YEAR TM/L	G	AB	R	H	2B	3B	HR	RBI	BB	SO	AVG	OBP	SLG	PRO+	BR/A	SB	CS	SBR	FA	FR	G/POS	TPR
1929 Bos-N	60	125	14	38	10	0	0	15	8	8	.304	.346	.384	84	-3	0			.918	-9	3-24/S-5,2O	-1.0
Total 14	1447	5410	665	1516	277	46	42	571	250	419	.280	.317	.372	82	-152	37			.957	-107	*3-1048,S-281/2O	-17.5

YEAR	TM/L	G	AB	R	H	2B	3B	HR	RBI	BB	SO	AVG	OBP	SLG	PRO+	BR/A	SB	CS	SBR	FA	FR	G/POS	TPR

■ OSCAR DUGEY   Dugey, Oscar Joseph "Jake"   b: 10/25/1887, Palestine, Tex.   d: 1/1/66, Dallas, Tex.   BR/TR, 5'8", 160 lbs.   Deb: 9/13/13   C

1913	Bos-N	5	8	1	2	0	0	0	1	1	1	.250	.333	.250	67	-0	0			.500	-1	/3-2,2-1,S	-0.1
1914	Bos-N	58	109	17	21	2	0	1	10	10	15	.193	.267	.239	51	-6	10			.933	-2	O-16,2-16/3	-1.0
1920	Bos-N	5	0	2	0	0	0	0	0	0	0	—	—	—	—	—	0	0	0	.000	0	R	0.0
Total	6	195	278	45	54	10	1	1	20	31	38	.194	.277	.248	58	-14	17	1		.915	3	/2-58,O-20,3S	-1.2
Team	3	68	117	20	23	2	0	1	10	11	16	.197	.271	.239	52	-7	10	0		.891	-3	/2-17,O-16,3S	-1.1

■ BILL DUNLAP   Dunlap, William James   b: 5/1/09, Palmer, Mass.   d: 11/29/80, Reading, Pa.   BR/TR, 5'11", 170 lbs.   Deb: 9/2/29

1929	Bos-N	10	29	6	12	0	1	1	4	4	4	.414	.485	.586	171	3	0			.889	-1	/O-9	0.1
1930	Bos-N	16	29	3	2	1	0	0	0	0	6	.069	.069	.103	-61	-8	0			1.000	-1	/O-7	-0.8
Total	2	26	58	9	14	1	1	1	4	4	10	.241	.290	.345	57	-4	0			.939	-2	/O-16	-0.7

■ EDDIE EAYRS   Eayrs, Edwin   b: 11/10/1890, Blackstone, Mass.   d: 11/30/69, Warwick, R.I.   BL/TL, 5'7", 160 lbs.   Deb: 6/30/13

1920	Bos-N	87	244	31	80	5	2	1	24	30	18	.328	.410	.377	133	12	4	3	-1	.950	-4	O-63/P-7	0.1
1921	Bos-N	15	15	0	1	0	0	0	1	0	4	.067	.067	.067	-68	-4	0	0	0	.000	-0	/P-2	0.0
Total	3	114	271	32	83	5	2	1	26	32	23	.306	.388	.351	116	7	4	3		.950	-5	/O-64,P-11	0.0
Team	2	102	259	31	81	5	2	1	25	30	22	.313	.392	.359	121	9	4	3		.950	-5	/O-63,P-9	0.1

■ OX ECKHARDT   Eckhardt, Oscar George   b: 12/23/01, Yorktown, Tex.   d: 4/22/51, Yorktown, Tex.   BL/TR, 6'1", 185 lbs.   Deb: 4/16/32

| 1932 | Bos-N | 8 | 8 | 1 | 2 | 0 | 0 | 0 | 1 | 0 | 1 | .250 | .250 | .250 | 36 | -1 | 0 | | | .000 | 0 | H | -0.1 |
| Total | 2 | 24 | 52 | 6 | 10 | 1 | 0 | 1 | 7 | 5 | 3 | .192 | .263 | .269 | 43 | -4 | 0 | | | .964 | 1 | /O-10 | -0.4 |

■ MIKE EDEN   Eden, Edward Michael   b: 5/22/49, Fort Clayton, Canal Zone   BB/TR, 5'10", 170 lbs.   Deb: 8/2/76

| 1976 | Atl-N | 5 | 8 | 0 | 0 | 0 | 0 | 0 | 1 | 0 | 0 | .000 | .000 | .000 | -94 | -2 | 0 | 0 | 0 | 1.000 | 1 | /2-2 | -0.1 |
| Total | 2 | 15 | 25 | 1 | 2 | 0 | 0 | 0 | 1 | 4 | 0 | .080 | .207 | .080 | -16 | -4 | 0 | 0 | 0 | 1.000 | 0 | /2-6,S-5 | -0.2 |

■ DICK EGAN   Egan, Richard Joseph   b: 6/23/1884, Portland, Ore.   d: 7/7/47, Oakland, Cal.   BR/TR, 5'11", 162 lbs.   Deb: 9/15/08

1915	Bos-N	83	220	20	57	9	1	0	21	28	18	.259	.343	.309	102	2	3	4	-2	.974	-2	O-24,2-22/S13	-0.2
1916	Bos-N	83	238	23	53	8	3	0	16	19	21	.223	.280	.282	76	-7	2			.949	-21	2-59,S-12/3	-3.0
Total	9	917	3080	374	767	87	29	4	292	291	191	.249	.315	.300	82	-69	167	4		.956	-14	2-686,S-135/O31	-9.2
Team	2	166	458	43	110	17	4	0	37	47	39	.240	.311	.295	89	-5	5	4		.947	-23	/2-81,O-24,S31	-3.2

■ ROWDY ELLIOTT   Elliott, Harold B.   b: 7/8/1890, Kokomo, Ind.   d: 2/12/34, San Francisco, Cal.   BR/TR, 5'9", 160 lbs.   Deb: 9/24/10

| 1910 | Bos-N | 3 | 2 | 0 | 0 | 0 | 0 | 0 | 0 | 0 | 0 | .000 | .000 | .000 | -96 | -0 | 0 | | | 1.000 | -0 | /C-1 | -0.1 |
| Total | 5 | 157 | 402 | 36 | 97 | 15 | 5 | 1 | 44 | 19 | 23 | .241 | .281 | .311 | 73 | -14 | 5 | | | .967 | 7 | C-136 | 0.3 |

■ BOB ELLIOTT   Elliott, Robert Irving "Mr. Team"   b: 11/26/16, San Francisco, Cal.   d: 5/4/66, San Diego, Cal.   BR/TR, 6', 185 lbs.   Deb: 9/2/39   MC

1947	Bos-N†	150	555	93	176	35	5	22	113	87	60	.317	.410	.517	148	40	3			**.956**	-2	*3-148	3.7
1948	*Bos-N★	151	540	99	153	24	5	23	100	**131**	57	.283	.423	.474	145	40	6			.945	-10	*3-150	2.8
1949	Bos-N	139	482	77	135	29	5	17	76	90	38	.280	.395	.467	138	28	0			.963	11	*3-130	3.5
1950	Bos-N	142	531	94	162	28	5	24	107	68	67	.305	.386	.512	143	33	2			.952	-17	*3-137	1.3
1951	Bos-N★	136	480	73	137	29	2	15	70	65	56	.285	.371	.448	128	19	2	0	1	.941	-8	*3-127	1.1
Total	15	1978	7141	1064	2061	382	94	170	1195	967	604	.289	.375	.440	124	252	60	2		.947	-37	*3-1365,O-537/S2	18.9
Team	5	718	2588	436	763	145	22	101	466	441	278	.295	.398	.485	141	159	13	0		.951	-26	3-692	12.4

■ BOB EMMERICH   Emmerich, Robert George   b: 8/1/1897, New York, N.Y.   d: 11/22/48, Bridgeport, Conn.   BR/TR, 5'3", 155 lbs.   Deb: 9/22/23

| 1923 | Bos-N | 13 | 24 | 3 | 2 | 0 | 0 | 0 | 2 | 2 | 3 | .083 | .154 | .083 | -37 | -5 | 1 | 1 | -0 | 1.000 | -1 | /O-8 | -0.6 |

■ GIL ENGLISH   English, Gilbert Raymond   b: 7/2/09, Glenola, N.C.   BR/TR, 5'11", 180 lbs.   Deb: 9/20/31

1937	Bos-N	79	269	25	78	5	2	2	37	23	27	.290	.348	.346	98	-1	3			.958	-7	3-71	-0.6
1938	Bos-N	53	165	17	41	6	0	2	21	15	16	.248	.315	.321	84	-4	1			.956	-4	3-43/O-3,2S	-0.7
Total	6	240	791	74	194	22	7	8	90	56	78	.245	.298	.321	72	-31	5			.950	-18	3-174/S-38,2O	-4.2
Team	2	132	434	42	119	11	2	4	58	38	43	.274	.335	.336	92	-5	4			.957	-11	3-114/O-3,2S	-1.3

■ NICK ESASKY   Esasky, Nicholas Andrew   b: 2/24/60, Hialeah, Fla.   BR/TR, 6'3", 205 lbs.   Deb: 6/19/83

| 1990 | Atl-N | 9 | 35 | 2 | 6 | 0 | 0 | 0 | 4 | 4 | 14 | .171 | .256 | .171 | 19 | -4 | 0 | 0 | 0 | .944 | -2 | /1-9 | -0.6 |
| Total | 8 | 810 | 2703 | 336 | 677 | 120 | 21 | 122 | 427 | 314 | 712 | .250 | .332 | .446 | 109 | 31 | 18 | 14 | | .993 | -45 | 1-478,3-230/O | -6.0 |

■ BUCK ETCHISON   Etchison, Clarence Hampton   b: 1/27/15, Baltimore, Md.   d: 1/24/80, E.New Market, Md.   BL/TL, 6'1", 190 lbs.   Deb: 9/22/43

1943	Bos-N	10	19	2	6	3	0	2	2	2	2	.316	.381	.474	148	1	0			.956	-1	/1-6	0.0
1944	Bos-N	109	308	30	66	16	0	8	33	33	50	.214	.292	.344	76	-10	1			.993	-1	1-85	-1.6
Total	2	119	327	32	72	19	0	8	35	35	52	.220	.298	.352	79	-9	1			.991	-2	/1-91	-1.6

■ DARRELL EVANS   Evans, Darrell Wayne   b: 5/26/47, Pasadena, Cal.   BL/TR, 6'2", 205 lbs.   Deb: 4/20/69   C

1969	Atl-N	12	26	3	6	0	0	0	1	1	8	.231	.259	.231	38	-2	0	0	0	.917	-2	/3-6	-0.4
1970	Atl-N	12	44	4	14	1	1	0	9	7	5	.318	.423	.386	112	1	0	0	0	.941	-1	3-12	0.0
1971	Atl-N	89	260	42	63	11	1	12	38	39	54	.242	.343	.431	111	4	2	3	-1	.937	4	3-72/O-3	0.6
1972	Atl-N	125	418	67	106	12	0	19	71	90	58	.254	.391	.419	119	14	4	2	0	.941	9	*3-123	2.3
1973	Atl-N★	161	595	114	167	25	8	41	104	**124**	104	.281	.407	.556	153	45	6	3	0	.953	8	*3-146,1-20	5.2
1974	Atl-N	160	571	99	137	21	3	25	79	**126**	88	.240	.383	.419	119	18	4	2	0	.955	16	*3-160	3.4
1975	Atl-N	156	567	82	138	22	2	22	73	105	106	.243	.364	.406	109	9	12	3	2	.938	23	*3-156/1-3	3.5
1976	Atl-N	44	139	11	24	0	0	1	10	30	33	.173	.309	.194	45	-4	3	0	1	.994	0	1-36/3-7	-1.1
1989	Atl-N	107	276	31	57	6	1	11	39	41	46	.207	.309	.355	87	-4	0	1	-1	.985	6	1-50,3-28	-0.3
Total	21	2687	8973	1344	2223	329	36	414	1354	1605	1410	.248	.364	.431	119	263	98	68	-11	.946	165	*3-1442,1-856,D/OS	34.6
Team	9	866	2896	453	712	98	16	131	424	563	502	.246	.372	.426	116	76	31	14	1	.945	63	3-710,1-109/O	13.2

■ JOHNNY EVERS   Evers, John Joseph "Crab" or "Trojan"   b: 7/21/1881, Troy, N.Y.   d: 3/28/47, Albany, N.Y.   BL/TR, 5'9", 125 lbs.   Deb: 9/1/02   FMCH

1914	*Bos-N	139	491	81	137	20	3	1	40	87	26	.279	.390	.338	118	16	12			**.976**	5	*2-139	2.0
1915	Bos-N	83	241	38	73	4	1	1	22	50	16	.263	.395	.295	109	6	7	8	-3	.959	-1	2-82	0.3
1916	Bos-N	71	241	33	52	4	1	0	15	40	19	.216	.330	.241	80	-4	5			.951	-18	2-71	-2.2
1917	Bos-N	24	83	5	16	0	0	0	13	8	8	.193	.302	.193	56	-4	1			.950	-7	2-24	-1.1
1929	Bos-N	1	0	0	0	0	0	0	0	0	0	—	—	—	—	—	0	0	0	.000	-1	/2-1	0.0
Total	18	1784	6137	919	1659	216	70	12	538	778	142	.270	.356	.334	106	71	324	8		.955	54	*2-1735/3-21,SO	12.9
Team	5	318	1093	157	278	28	5	2	77	190	69	.254	.366	.295	103	14	25	8		.965	-22	2-317	-1.1

■ DOC FARRELL   Farrell, Edward Stephen   b: 12/26/01, Johnson City, N.Y.   d: 12/20/66, Livingston, N.J.   BR/TR, 5'10", 160 lbs.   Deb: 6/15/25

1927	Bos-N	110	424	44	124	13	2	1	58	14	21	.292	.315	.340	82	-12	4			.931	-4	S-57,2-40,3	-0.8
1928	Bos-N	134	483	36	104	14	2	3	43	26	26	.215	.263	.271	42	-42	3			.933	-17	*S-132/2-1	-4.3
1929	Bos-N	5	8	0	1	0	0	0	2	0	1	.125	.125	.125	-39	-2	0			.000	-1	/2-1,S-1	-0.2
Total	9	591	1799	181	467	63	8	10	213	109	120	.260	.306	.320	66	-93	14			.934	-24	S-376,2-118/31	-7.3
Team	3	249	915	80	229	27	4	4	103	40	48	.250	.285	.302	59	-56	7			.932	-21	S-190/2-42,3	-5.3

■ KERBY FARRELL   Farrell, Major Kerby   b: 9/3/13, Leapwood, Tenn.   d: 12/17/75, Nashville, Tenn.   BL/TL, 5'11", 172 lbs.   Deb: 4/24/43   MC

| 1943 | Bos-N | 85 | 280 | 11 | 75 | 14 | 1 | 0 | 21 | 16 | 15 | .268 | .307 | .325 | 84 | -6 | 1 | | | .996 | 2 | 1-69/P-5 | -0.9 |
| Total | 2 | 188 | 676 | 55 | 177 | 25 | 4 | 0 | 55 | 40 | 33 | .262 | .303 | .311 | 80 | -19 | 5 | | | .992 | 1 | 1-166/P-5 | -3.4 |

■ GUS FELIX Felix, August Guenther b: 5/24/1895, Cincinnati, Ohio d: 5/12/60, Montgomery, Ala. BR/TR, 6', 180 lbs. Deb: 4/19/23

YEAR	TM/L	G	AB	R	H	2B	3B	HR	RBI	BB	SO	AVG	OBP	SLG	PRO+	BR/A	SB	CS	SBR	FA	FR	G/POS	TPR
1923	Bos-N	139	506	64	138	17	2	6	44	51	65	.273	.348	.350	88	-8	8	13	-5	.950	0	*O-123/2-5,3	-2.0
1924	Bos-N	59	204	25	43	7	1	1	10	18	16	.211	.275	.270	48	-15	0	3	-2	.950	5	O-51	-1.5
1925	Bos-N	121	459	60	141	25	7	2	66	30	34	.307	.356	.405	103	2	5	5	-2	.972	10	*O-114	0.3
Total	5	583	2046	256	561	91	25	12	230	189	194	.274	.341	.361	89	-31	28	21	-4	.957	11	O-532/2-5,3	-6.2
Team	3	319	1169	149	322	49	10	9	120	99	115	.275	.338	.358	87	-21	13	21	-9	.960	15	O-288/2-5,3	-3.2

■ NANNY FERNANDEZ Fernandez, Froilan b: 10/25/18, Wilmington, Cal. BR/TR, 5'9", 170 lbs. Deb: 4/14/42

YEAR	TM/L	G	AB	R	H	2B	3B	HR	RBI	BB	SO	AVG	OBP	SLG	PRO+	BR/A	SB	CS	SBR	FA	FR	G/POS	TPR
1942	Bos-N	145	577	63	147	29	3	6	55	38	61	.255	.303	.347	92	-8	15			.914	6	3-98,O-44	-0.3
1946	Bos-N	115	372	37	95	15	2	2	42	30	44	.255	.313	.323	79	-10	1			.940	-2	3-81,S-18,O	-1.2
1947	Bos-N	83	209	16	43	4	0	2	21	22	20	.206	.281	.254	44	-17	2			.933	-13	S-62/O-8,3	-2.7
Total	4	408	1356	139	336	59	5	16	145	109	142	.248	.306	.334	80	-38	20			.925	-13	3-237/S-80,O	-4.9
Team	3	343	1158	116	285	48	5	10	118	90	125	.246	.302	.322	78	-34	18			.924	-10	3-185/S-80,O	-4.2

■ WES FERRELL Ferrell, Wesley Cheek b: 2/2/08, Greensboro, N.C. d: 12/9/76, Sarasota, Fla. BR/TR, 6'2", 195 lbs. Deb: 9/9/27 F

YEAR	TM/L	G	AB	R	H	2B	3B	HR	RBI	BB	SO	AVG	OBP	SLG	PRO+	BR/A	SB	CS	SBR	FA	FR	G/POS	TPR
1941	Bos-N	4	4	2	2	0	0	1	2	1	1	.500	.600	1.250	430	2	0			1.000	-0	/P-4	0.0
Total	15	548	1176	175	329	57	12	38	208	129	185	.280	.351	.446	99	-5	2			.975	7	P-374/O-13	0.1

■ MIKE FISCHLIN Fischlin, Michael Thomas b: 9/13/55, Sacramento, Cal. BR/TR, 6'1", 165 lbs. Deb: 9/3/77

YEAR	TM/L	G	AB	R	H	2B	3B	HR	RBI	BB	SO	AVG	OBP	SLG	PRO+	BR/A	SB	CS	SBR	FA	FR	G/POS	TPR
1987	Atl-N	1	0	0	0	0	0	0	0	0	0	—	—	—	—	0	0	0	0	.000	0	/R	0.0
Total	10	517	941	109	207	29	6	3	68	92	142	.220	.293	.273	57	-54	24	13		.959	63	S-268,2-191/31DC	2.7

■ CHARLIE FITZBERGER Fitzberger, Charles Casper b: 2/13/04, Baltimore, Md. d: 1/25/65, Baltimore, Md. BL/TL, 6'1.5", 170 lbs. Deb: 9/11/28

YEAR	TM/L	G	AB	R	H	2B	3B	HR	RBI	BB	SO	AVG	OBP	SLG	PRO+	BR/A	SB	CS	SBR	FA	FR	G/POS	TPR
1928	Bos-N	7	7	0	2	0	0	0	0	0	3	.286	.286	.286	52	-0	0			.000	0	H	0.0

■ ED FITZPATRICK Fitzpatrick, Edward Henry b: 12/9/1889, Lewistown, Pa. d: 10/23/65, Bethlehem, Pa. BR/TR, 5'8", 165 lbs. Deb: 4/17/15

YEAR	TM/L	G	AB	R	H	2B	3B	HR	RBI	BB	SO	AVG	OBP	SLG	PRO+	BR/A	SB	CS	SBR	FA	FR	G/POS	TPR
1915	Bos-N	105	303	54	67	19	3	0	24	43	36	.221	.344	.304	101	3	13	8	-1	.967	-5	2-71,O-29	-0.4
1916	Bos-N	83	216	17	46	8	0	1	18	15	26	.213	.280	.264	70	-7	5			.950	-12	2-46,O-28	-2.2
1917	Bos-N	63	178	20	45	8	4	0	17	12	22	.253	.318	.343	109	2	4			.929	-13	2-22,O-19,3	-1.2
Total	3	251	697	91	158	35	7	1	59	70	84	.227	.319	.301	94	-3	22	8		.956	-30	2-139/O-76,3	-3.8

■ PATSY FLAHERTY Flaherty, Patrick Joseph b: 6/29/1876, Mansfield, Pa. d: 1/23/68, Alexandria, La. BL/TL, 5'8", 165 lbs. Deb: 9/8/1899

YEAR	TM/L	G	AB	R	H	2B	3B	HR	RBI	BB	SO	AVG	OBP	SLG	PRO+	BR/A	SB	CS	SBR	FA	FR	G/POS	TPR
1907	Bos-N	41	115	9	22	3	2	2	11	2		.191	.212	.304	62	-6	1			.907	3	P-27/O-8	-0.1
1908	Bos-N	32	86	8	12	0	2	0	5	6		.140	.196	.186	22	-8	2			.961	2	P-31	0.0
1911	Bos-N	38	94	9	27	3	2	2	20	8	11	.287	.343	.426	106	0	2			.933	-4	O-19/P-4	-0.4
Total	9	235	624	53	123	19	13	6	70	40	11	.197	.247	.298	63	-30	9			.921	11	P-173/O-34	-0.6
Team	3	111	295	26	61	6	6	4	36	16	11	.207	.250	.308	68	-13	5			.927	2	/P-62,O-27	-0.5

■ ELBIE FLETCHER Fletcher, Elburt Preston b: 3/18/16, Milton, Mass. d: 3/9/94, Milton, Mass. BL/TL, 6', 180 lbs. Deb: 9/16/34

YEAR	TM/L	G	AB	R	H	2B	3B	HR	RBI	BB	SO	AVG	OBP	SLG	PRO+	BR/A	SB	CS	SBR	FA	FR	G/POS	TPR
1934	Bos-N	8	4	4	2	0	0	0	0	0	2	.500	.500	.500	182	0	1			.875	-0	/1-1	0.0
1935	Bos-N	39	148	12	35	7	1	1	9	7	13	.236	.271	.318	63	-8	1			.997	2	1-39	-1.0
1937	Bos-N	148	539	56	133	22	4	1	38	56	64	.247	.321	.308	79	-16	3			.993	1	*1-148	-3.2
1938	Bos-N	147	529	71	144	24	7	6	48	60	40	.272	.351	.378	112	8	5			.990	10	*1-146	0.3
1939	Bos-N	35	106	14	26	2	0	0	6	19	5	.245	.365	.264	77	-2	1			.986	-5	1-31	-1.1
1949	Bos-N	122	413	57	108	19	3	11	51	84	65	.262	.396	.402	121	16	1			.991	0	*1-121	1.5
Total	12	1415	4879	723	1323	228	58	79	616	851	495	.271	.384	.390	118	145	32			.993	33	*1-1380	7.7
Team	6	499	1739	214	448	74	15	19	152	226	189	.258	.348	.350	98	-1	12			.991	8	1-486	-3.5

■ CURRY FOLEY Foley, Charles Joseph b: 1/14/1856, Milltown, Ireland d: 10/20/1898, Boston, Mass. TL, 5'10", 160 lbs. Deb: 5/13/1879

YEAR	TM/L	G	AB	R	H	2B	3B	HR	RBI	BB	SO	AVG	OBP	SLG	PRO+	BR/A	SB	CS	SBR	FA	FR	G/POS	TPR
1879	Bos-N	35	146	16	46	3	1	0	17	3	4	.315	.329	.349	121	3				.857	-7	P-21,O-17/1	-0.4
1880	Bos-N	80	332	44	97	13	2	2	31	8	14	.292	.309	.361	130	10				.953	-3	P-36,O-35,1	0.0
Total	5	305	1305	192	373	57	12	6	128	34	83	.286	.304	.362	114	19				.819	-16	O-214/P-69,1	-0.8
Team	2	115	478	60	143	16	3	2	48	11	18	.299	.315	.358	127	13				.919	-11	/P-57,O-52,1	-0.4

■ HOD FORD Ford, Horace Hills b: 7/23/1897, New Haven, Conn. d: 1/29/77, Winchester, Mass. BR/TR, 5'10", 165 lbs. Deb: 9/8/19

YEAR	TM/L	G	AB	R	H	2B	3B	HR	RBI	BB	SO	AVG	OBP	SLG	PRO+	BR/A	SB	CS	SBR	FA	FR	G/POS	TPR
1919	Bos-N	10	28	4	6	0	1	0	3	2	6	.214	.290	.286	77	-1	0			.946	3	/S-8,3-2	0.3
1920	Bos-N	88	257	16	62	12	5	1	30	18	25	.241	.296	.339	86	-5	3	3	-1	.972	15	2-59,S-18/1	1.3
1921	Bos-N	152	555	50	155	29	5	2	61	36	49	.279	.328	.360	87	-11	2	11	-6	**.973**	16	*2-119,S-33	0.5
1922	Bos-N	143	515	58	140	23	9	2	60	30	36	.272	.317	.363	78	-17	2	1	0	.953	-4	*S-115,2-28	-0.8
1923	Bos-N	111	380	27	103	16	7	2	50	31	30	.271	.326	.366	86	-8	1	1	-0	.970	-9	2-95,S-19	-1.4
1932	Bos-N	40	95	9	26	5	2	0	6	6	9	.274	.324	.368	89	-1	0			.984	-3	2-20,S-16/3	-0.2
1933	Bos-N	5	15	0	1	0	0	0	1	3	1	.067	.222	.067	-16	-2	0			1.000	5	/S-5	0.3
Total	15	1446	4833	484	1269	200	55	16	494	351	354	.263	.316	.337	72	-198	21	28		.960	54	S-846,2-589/31	-5.2
Team	7	549	1845	164	493	85	29	7	211	126	156	.267	.318	.356	83	-46	8	16		.973	23	2-321,S-214/13	0.0

■ LEO FOSTER Foster, Leonard Norris b: 2/2/51, Covington, Ky. BR/TR, 5'11", 165 lbs. Deb: 7/9/71

YEAR	TM/L	G	AB	R	H	2B	3B	HR	RBI	BB	SO	AVG	OBP	SLG	PRO+	BR/A	SB	CS	SBR	FA	FR	G/POS	TPR
1971	Atl-N	9	10	1	0	0	0	0	0	0	1	.000	.000	.000	-94	-2	0	0	0	.900	2	/S-3	-0.1
1973	Atl-N	3	6	1	1	1	0	0	0	0	2	.167	.167	.333	33	-1	0	0	0	1.000	-0	/S-1	-0.1
1974	Atl-N	72	112	16	22	2	0	1	5	9	22	.196	.256	.241	38	-9	1	2	-1	.977	-1	S-43,2-10/3O	-0.8
Total	5	144	262	35	52	8	0	2	26	22	44	.198	.263	.252	44	-20	7	3	0	.964	-3	/S-62,2-33,3O	-1.8
Team	3	84	128	18	23	3	0	1	5	9	25	.180	.234	.227	28	-12	1	2	-1	.972	1	/S-47,2-10,3O	-1.0

■ JACK FOURNIER Fournier, John Frank b: 9/28/1889, AuSable, Mich. d: 9/5/73, Tacoma, Wash. BL/TR, 6', 195 lbs. Deb: 4/13/12

YEAR	TM/L	G	AB	R	H	2B	3B	HR	RBI	BB	SO	AVG	OBP	SLG	PRO+	BR/A	SB	CS	SBR	FA	FR	G/POS	TPR
1927	Bos-N	122	374	55	106	18	2	10	53	44	16	.283	.368	.422	121	11	4			.989	0	*1-102	0.4
Total	15	1530	5208	822	1631	252	113	136	859	587	408	.313	.392	.483	143	308	145			.984	20	*1-1313/O-87,P	23.9

■ TITO FRANCONA Francona, John Patsy b: 11/4/33, Aliquippa, Pa. BL/TL, 5'11", 190 lbs. Deb: 4/17/56 F

YEAR	TM/L	G	AB	R	H	2B	3B	HR	RBI	BB	SO	AVG	OBP	SLG	PRO+	BR/A	SB	CS	SBR	FA	FR	G/POS	TPR
1967	Atl-N	82	254	28	63	5	1	6	25	20	34	.248	.305	.346	87	-4	1	0	0	.991	-1	1-56/O-6	-0.9
1968	Atl-N	122	346	32	99	13	1	2	47	51	45	.286	.378	.347	118	10	3	0	1	.978	-8	O-65,1-33	-0.3
1969	Atl-N	51	88	5	26	1	0	2	22	13	10	.295	.386	.375	114	2	0	1	-1	.957	-0	O-15/1-7	0.0
Total	15	1719	5121	650	1395	224	34	125	656	544	694	.272	.346	.403	108	56	46	21		.984	-49	O-911,1-475	-7.0
Team	3	255	688	65	188	19	2	10	94	84	89	.273	.353	.350	107	8	4	1		.991	-9	/1-96,O-86	-1.2

■ BUCK FREEMAN Freeman, John Frank b: 10/30/1871, Catasauqua, Pa. d: 6/25/49, Wilkes-Barre, Pa. BL/TL, 5'9", 169 lbs. Deb: 6/27/1891

YEAR	TM/L	G	AB	R	H	2B	3B	HR	RBI	BB	SO	AVG	OBP	SLG	PRO+	BR/A	SB	CS	SBR	FA	FR	G/POS	TPR
1900	Bos-N	117	418	58	126	19	13	6	65	25		.301	.355	.452	109	2	10			.950	-11	O-91,1-19	-1.4
Total	11	1126	4208	588	1235	199	131	82	713	272		.293	.346	.462	131	152	92			.950	-53	O-837,1-256/P32	3.8

■ HOWARD FREIGAU Freigau, Howard Earl "Ty" b: 8/1/02, Dayton, Ohio d: 7/18/32, Chattanooga, Tenn BR/TR, 5'10.5", 160 lbs. Deb: 9/13/22

YEAR	TM/L	G	AB	R	H	2B	3B	HR	RBI	BB	SO	AVG	OBP	SLG	PRO+	BR/A	SB	CS	SBR	FA	FR	G/POS	TPR
1928	Bos-N	52	109	11	28	8	1	1	17	9	14	.257	.319	.376	86	-3	1			.938	-10	S-14,2-11	-1.0
Total	7	579	1974	224	537	99	25	15	226	138	161	.272	.322	.370	82	-52	32			.940	-11	3-371,S-132/210	-2.7

■ PEPE FRIAS Frias, Jesus Maria (Andujar) b: 7/14/48, San Pedro De Macoris, D.R. BR/TR, 5'10", 159 lbs. Deb: 4/6/73

YEAR	TM/L	G	AB	R	H	2B	3B	HR	RBI	BB	SO	AVG	OBP	SLG	PRO+	BR/A	SB	CS	SBR	FA	FR	G/POS	TPR
1979	Atl-N	140	475	41	123	18	4	1	44	20	36	.259	.292	.320	62	-25	3	2	-0	.954	0	*S-137	-1.0
Total	9	723	1346	132	323	49	8	1	108	49	136	.240	.269	.290	52	-88	12	8		.951	63	S-426,2-186/3O	1.2

YEAR	TM/L	G	AB	R	H	2B	3B	HR	RBI	BB	SO	AVG	OBP	SLG	PRO+	BR/A	SB	CS	SBR	FA	FR	G/POS	TPR
■ CHARLIE FRISBEE	Frisbee, Charles Augustus "Bunt" b: 2/2/1874, Dows, Iowa d: 11/7/54, Alden, Iowa BB/TR, 5'9", 175 lbs. Deb: 6/22/1899																						
1899	Bos-N	42	152	22	50	4	2	0	20	9		.329	.374	.382	98	-1	10			.875	-2	O-40	-0.5
Total	2	46	165	24	52	5	2	0	23	11		.315	.365	.370	94	-2	10			.849	-4	/O-44	-0.8
■ JOHN FULLER	Fuller, John Edward b: 1/29/50, Lynwood, Cal. BL/TL, 6'2", 180 lbs. Deb: 5/9/74																						
1974	Atl-N	3	3	1	1	0	0	0	0	0	0	.333	.333	.333	83	-0	0	0	0	1.000	-0	/O-1	0.0
■ LEN GABRIELSON	Gabrielson, Leonard Gary b: 2/14/40, Oakland, Cal. BL/TR, 6'4", 210 lbs. Deb: 9/9/60 F																						
1960	Mil-N	4	3	1	0	0	0	0	0	1	0	.000	.250	.000	-27	-1	0	0	0	.000	-0	/O-1	-0.1
1963	Mil-N	46	120	14	26	5	0	3	15	8	23	.217	.266	.333	72	-4	1	1	-0	1.000	-3	O-22,1-16/3	-1.0
1964	Mil-N	24	38	0	7	2	0	0	1	1	8	.184	.205	.237	24	-4	1	0	0	1.000	-1	1-12/O-2	-0.5
Total	9	708	1764	178	446	64	12	37	176	145	315	.253	.311	.366	94	-15	20	12	-1	.977	-31	O-455/1-51,3	-7.3
Team	3	74	161	15	33	7	0	3	16	10	31	.205	.251	.304	59	-9	2	1	0	.978	-5	/1-28,O-25,3	-1.6
■ DAVE GALLAGHER	Gallagher, David Thomas b: 9/20/60, Trenton, N.J. BR/TR, 6' ", 180 lbs. Deb: 4/12/87																						
1994	Atl-N	89	152	27	34	5	0	2	14	22	17	.224	.326	.296	62	-8	0	2	-1	.989	-9	O-77/1-1	-1.9
Total	9	794	2081	273	564	100	10	17	190	187	251	.271	.333	.353	90	-26	20	24	-8	.993	-30	O-699/D-12,1	-8.0
■ GIL GALLAGHER	Gallagher, Lawrence Kirby b: 9/5/1896, Washington, D.C. d: 1/6/57, Washington, D.C. BB/TR, 5'8", 155 lbs. Deb: 9/13/22																						
1922	Bos-N	7	22	1	1	1	0	0	2	1	7	.045	.087	.091	-57	-5	0	0	0	.893	-2	/S-6	-0.6
■ DAFF GAMMONS	Gammons, John Ashley b: 3/17/1876, New Bedford, Mass. d: 9/24/63, E.Greenwich, R.I. BR/TR, 5'11", 170 lbs. Deb: 4/23/01																						
1901	Bos-N	28	93	10	18	0	1	0	10	3		.194	.242	.215	30	-8	5			.880	-3	O-23/2-2,3	-1.2
■ RON GANT	Gant, Ronald Edwin b: 3/2/65, Victoria, Tex. BR/TR, 6' ", 192 lbs. Deb: 9/6/87																						
1987	Atl-N	21	83	9	22	4	0	2	9	1	11	.265	.274	.386	69	-4	4	2	0	.972	-0	2-20	-0.3
1988	Atl-N	146	563	85	146	28	8	19	60	46	118	.259	.319	.439	110	6	19	10	-0	.963	-1	*2-122,3-22	1.0
1989	Atl-N	75	260	26	46	8	3	9	25	20	63	.177	.238	.335	61	-14	9	6	-1	.887	3	3-53,O-14	-1.3
1990	Atl-N	152	575	107	174	34	3	32	84	50	86	.303	.359	.539	136	26	33	16	0	.978	7	*O-146	3.0
1991	*Atl-N	154	561	101	141	35	3	32	105	71	104	.251	.341	.496	125	18	34	15	1	.983	8	*O-148	2.4
1992	*Atl-N★	153	544	74	141	22	6	17	80	45	101	.259	.324	.415	102	1	32	10	4	.986	-4	*O-147	-0.2
1993	*Atl-N	157	606	113	166	27	4	36	117	67	117	.274	.348	.510	125	20	26	9	2	.962	-3	*O-155	1.6
Total	8	977	3602	594	949	177	31	176	568	374	708	.263	.336	.476	118	81	180	76	8	.979	12	O-727,2-142/3	9.3
Team	7	858	3192	515	836	158	27	147	480	300	600	.262	.329	.466	114	53	157	68	6	.978	8	O-610,2-142/3	6.2
■ CHARLIE GANZEL	Ganzel, Charles William b: 6/18/1862, Waterford, Wis. d: 4/7/14, Quincy, Mass. BR/TR, 6', 161 lbs. Deb: 9/27/1884 F																						
1889	Bos-N	73	275	30	73	3	5	1	43	15	11	.265	.308	.324	72	-11	13			.927	5	C-39,O-26/1S3	-0.3
1890	Bos-N	38	163	21	44	7	3	0	24	5	6	.270	.300	.350	83	-5	1			.958	3	C-22,O-15/S2	0.1
1891	Bos-N	70	263	33	68	18	5	1	29	12	13	.259	.304	.376	87	-6	7			.956	4	C-59,O-13	0.2
1892	*Bos-N	54	198	25	53	9	3	0	25	18	12	.268	.332	.343	96	-2	7			.933	-6	C-51/O-2,1	-0.4
1893	Bos-N	73	281	50	75	10	2	1	48	22	9	.267	.325	.327	68	-14	6			.952	-2	C-40,O-23,1	-1.1
1894	Bos-N	70	266	51	74	7	6	3	56	19	6	.278	.326	.383	65	-17	1			.897	-5	C-59/1-7,OS2	-1.3
1895	Bos-N	80	277	38	73	2	5	1	52	24	6	.264	.325	.318	61	-17	1			.962	19	C-76/S-2,1	0.7
1896	Bos-N	47	179	28	47	2	0	1	18	9	5	.263	.305	.291	54	-12	2			.989	6	C-41/1-3,S	-0.1
1897	Bos-N	30	105	15	28	4	3	0	14	4		.267	.300	.362	70	-5	2			.942	2	C-27/1-2	0.0
Total	14	786	2984	421	774	91	45	10	412	161	121	.259	.301	.330	73	-120	60			.934	35	C-578,O-100/21S3	-2.7
Team	9	535	2007	291	535	62	32	8	309	128	68	.267	.316	.341	72	-89	40			.946	26	C-414/O-82,1S23	-2.2
■ DAMASO GARCIA	Garcia, Damaso Domingo (Sanchez) b: 2/7/55, Moca, D.R. BR/TR, 6', 170 lbs. Deb: 6/24/78																						
1988	Atl-N	21	60	3	7	1	0	1	4	3	10	.117	.159	.183	-2	-8	1	0	0	.984	-4	2-13	-1.2
Total	11	1032	3914	490	1108	183	27	36	323	130	322	.283	.311	.371	84	-91	203	90		.980	-62	2-960/D-18,S31	-10.4
■ DEBS GARMS	Garms, Debs C. "Tex" b: 6/26/08, Bangs, Tex. d: 12/16/84, Glen Rose, Tex. BL/TR, 5'8.5", 165 lbs. Deb: 8/10/32																						
1937	Bos-N	125	478	60	124	15	8	2	37	37	33	.259	.317	.337	85	-11	2			.977	-8	O-81,3-36	-2.0
1938	Bos-N	117	428	62	135	19	1	0	47	34	22	.315	.371	.364	114	9	4			.985	-7	O-63,3-54/2	0.1
1939	Bos-N	132	513	68	153	24	9	2	37	39	20	.298	.350	.392	107	4	2			.964	-4	O-96,3-37	-0.3
Total	12	1010	3111	438	910	141	39	17	328	288	161	.293	.355	.379	103	13	18			.966	-58	O-501,3-296/S2	-6.5
Team	3	374	1419	190	412	58	18	4	121	110	75	.290	.345	.365	102	2	8			.974	-18	O-240,3-127/2	-2.2
■ RALPH GARR	Garr, Ralph Allen "Road Runner" b: 12/12/45, Monroe, La. BL/TR, 5'11", 197 lbs. Deb: 9/3/68																						
1968	Atl-N	11	7	3	2	0	0	0	0	1	0	.286	.375	.286	100	0	1	0	0	.000	0	H	0.0
1969	Atl-N	22	27	6	6	1	0	0	2	2	4	.222	.276	.259	50	-2	1	1	-0	.857	-1	/O-7	-0.4
1970	Atl-N	37	96	18	27	3	0	0	8	5	12	.281	.317	.313	65	-5	5	2	0	1.000	0	O-21	-0.5
1971	Atl-N	154	639	101	219	24	6	9	44	30	68	.343	.374	.441	122	18	30	14	1	.968	16	*O-153	2.9
1972	Atl-N	134	554	87	180	22	0	12	53	25	41	.325	.361	.430	113	9	25	9	2	.962	-4	*O-131	0.1
1973	Atl-N	148	668	94	200	32	6	11	55	22	64	.299	.324	.415	96	-5	35	11	4	.968	1	*O-148	-0.7
1974	Atl-N★	143	606	87	**214**	24	**17**	11	54	28	52	**.353**	.384	.503	141	30	26	16	-2	.967	-19	*O-139	0.4
1975	Atl-N	151	625	74	174	26	**11**	6	31	44	50	.278	.329	.384	94	-6	14	9	-1	.966	6	*O-148	-0.7
Total	13	1317	5108	717	1562	212	64	75	408	246	445	.306	.340	.416	106	33	172	83	2	.968	-11	*O-1176/D-48	-2.9
Team	8	800	3222	470	1022	132	40	49	247	157	291	.317	.352	.429	111	41	137	62	4	.967	0	O-747	1.1
■ ADRIAN GARRETT	Garrett, Henry Adrian "Pat" b: 1/3/43, Brooksville, Fla. BL/TR, 6'3", 185 lbs. Deb: 4/13/66 FC																						
1966	Atl-N	4	3	0	0	0	0	0	0	0	2	.000	.000	.000	-99	-1	0	0	0	.000	-0	/O-1	-0.1
Total	8	163	276	30	51	8	0	11	37	31	87	.185	.267	.333	71	-11	4	0	1	.959	-5	/D-27,C-25,O1	-1.6
■ GIL GARRIDO	Garrido, Gil Gonzalo b: 6/26/41, Panama City, Pan. BR/TR, 5'8", 160 lbs. Deb: 4/24/64																						
1968	Atl-N	18	53	5	11	0	0	0	2	2	2	.208	.236	.208	34	-4	0	0	0	.987	3	S-17	0.1
1969	*Atl-N	82	227	18	50	5	1	0	10	16	11	.220	.272	.251	47	-16	0	0	0	.973	-11	S-81	-2.1
1970	Atl-N	101	367	38	97	5	4	1	19	15	16	.264	.293	.308	58	-22	0	2	-1	.975	-1	S-80,2-26	-1.3
1971	Atl-N	79	125	8	27	3	0	0	12	15	12	.216	.300	.240	51	-8	0	1	-1	.961	4	S-32,3-28,2	0.0
1972	Atl-N	40	75	11	20	1	0	0	7	11	6	.267	.368	.280	79	-1	1	1	-0	.989	1	2-21,S-10/3	0.0
Total	6	334	872	81	207	14	5	1	51	61	54	.237	.288	.268	53	-55	2	4	-2	.974	-4	S-234/2-65,3	-3.8
Team	5	320	847	80	205	14	5	1	50	59	47	.242	.292	.274	55	-51	1	4	-2	.974	-3	S-220/2-65,3	-3.3
■ CITO GASTON	Gaston, Clarence Edwin b: 3/17/44, San Antonio, Tex. BR/TR, 6'4", 210 lbs. Deb: 9/14/67 MC																						
1967	Atl-N	9	25	1	3	0	1	0	1	0	5	.120	.120	.200	-10	-4	1	0	0	.800	-1	/O-7	-0.5
1975	Atl-N	64	141	17	34	4	0	6	15	17	33	.241	.323	.397	95	-1	1	0	0	.974	-1	O-35/1-1	-0.3
1976	Atl-N	69	134	15	39	4	0	4	25	13	21	.291	.354	.410	109	2	1	0	0	.977	-2	O-28/1-2	-0.1
1977	Atl-N	56	85	6	23	4	0	3	21	5	19	.271	.311	.424	85	-2	1	0	0	1.000	-0	/O-9,1-5	-0.2
1978	Atl-N	60	118	5	27	1	0	1	9	3	20	.229	.248	.263	38	-10	0	0	0	.957	-4	O-29/1-4	-1.5
Total	11	1026	3120	314	799	106	30	91	387	185	693	.256	.300	.397	95	-32	13	7	-0	.970	6	O-773/1-12	-6.7
Team	5	258	503	44	126	13	1	14	71	38	98	.250	.303	.364	79	-15	4	0	1	.963	-8	O-108/1-12	-2.6
■ DOC GAUTREAU	Gautreau, Walter Paul "Punk" b: 7/26/01, Cambridge, Mass. d: 8/23/70, Salt Lake City, Ut BR/TR, 5'4", 129 lbs. Deb: 6/22/25																						
1925	Bos-N	68	279	45	73	13	3	0	23	35	13	.262	.346	.330	81	-7	11	7	-1	.976	-4	2-68	-1.0
1926	Bos-N	79	266	36	71	9	4	0	8	35	24	.267	.356	.331	94	-1	17			.942	-20	2-74	-1.9

YEAR TM/L	G	AB	R	H	2B	3B	HR	RBI	BB	SO	AVG	OBP	SLG	PRO+	BR/A	SB	CS	SBR	FA	FR	G/POS	TPR
1927 Bos-N	87	236	38	58	12	2	0	20	25	20	.246	.321	.314	76	-8	11			.965	-2	2-57	-0.8
1928 Bos-N	23	18	3	5	0	1	0	1	4	3	.278	.409	.389	116	1	1			.750	-1	/2-4,S-1	0.0
Total 4	261	806	122	207	34	10	0	52	99	63	.257	.341	.324	83	-18	40	7		.960	-25	2-207/S-1	-3.8
Team 4	257	799	122	207	34	10	0	52	99	60	.259	.344	.327	85	-16	40	7		.960	-26	2-203/S-1	-3.7

■ PHIL GEIER Geier, Philip Louis "Little Phil" b: 11/3/1875, Washington, D.C. d: 9/25/67, Spokane, Wash. BL/TR, 5'7", 145 lbs. Deb: 8/17/1896

YEAR TM/L	G	AB	R	H	2B	3B	HR	RBI	BB	SO	AVG	OBP	SLG	PRO+	BR/A	SB	CS	SBR	FA	FR	G/POS	TPR
1904 Bos-N	149	580	70	141	17	2	1	27	56		.243	.314	.284	88	-6	18			.933	-3	*O-137/3-7,2S	-1.8
Total 5	349	1315	197	327	30	12	2	102	154		.249	.332	.294	81	-27	54			.932	-16	O-279/2-45,3SC	-5.5

■ GARY GEIGER Geiger, Gary Merle b: 4/4/37, Sand Ridge, Ill. BL/TR, 6', 168 lbs. Deb: 4/15/58

YEAR TM/L	G	AB	R	H	2B	3B	HR	RBI	BB	SO	AVG	OBP	SLG	PRO+	BR/A	SB	CS	SBR	FA	FR	G/POS	TPR
1966 Atl-N	78	126	23	33	5	3	4	10	21	29	.262	.372	.444	124	5	0	1	-1	.982	-9	O-49	-0.6
1967 Atl-N	69	117	17	19	1	1	1	5	20	35	.162	.285	.214	45	-8	1	1	-0	.980	-6	O-38	-1.6
Total 12	954	2569	388	633	91	29	77	283	341	466	.246	.339	.394	98	-6	62	29		.986	8	O-749/1-6,3P	-3.5
Team 2	147	243	40	52	6	4	5	15	41	64	.214	.330	.333	87	-3	1	2		.981	-14	/O-87	-2.2

■ SAM GENTILE Gentile, Samuel Christopher b: 10/12/16, Charlestown, Mass. BL/TR, 5'11", 180 lbs. Deb: 4/24/43

YEAR TM/L	G	AB	R	H	2B	3B	HR	RBI	BB	SO	AVG	OBP	SLG	PRO+	BR/A	SB	CS	SBR	FA	FR	G/POS	TPR
1943 Bos-N	8	4	1	1	1	0	0	0	1	0	.250	.400	.500	162	0	0			.000	0	H	0.0

■ BEN GERAGHTY Geraghty, Benjamin Raymond b: 7/19/12, Jersey City, N.J. d: 6/18/63, Jacksonville, Fla BR/TR, 5'11", 175 lbs. Deb: 4/17/36

YEAR TM/L	G	AB	R	H	2B	3B	HR	RBI	BB	SO	AVG	OBP	SLG	PRO+	BR/A	SB	CS	SBR	FA	FR	G/POS	TPR
1943 Bos-N	8	1	2	0	0	0	0	0	0	0	.000	.000	.000	-99	-0	0			1.000	1	/2-1,S-1,3	0.1
1944 Bos-N	11	16	3	4	0	0	0	0	1	2	.250	.294	.250	52	-1	0			1.000	0	/2-4,3-3	-0.1
Total 3	70	146	16	29	4	0	0	9	9	18	.199	.245	.226	28	-15	4			.922	-6	/S-32,2-14,3	-1.8
Team 2	19	17	5	4	0	0	0	0	1	2	.235	.278	.235	44	-1	0			1.000	1	/2-5,3-4,S	0.0

■ GUS GETZ Getz, Gustave "Gee-Gee" b: 8/3/1889, Pittsburgh, Pa. d: 5/28/69, Keansburg, N.J. BR/TR, 5'11", 165 lbs. Deb: 8/15/09

YEAR TM/L	G	AB	R	H	2B	3B	HR	RBI	BB	SO	AVG	OBP	SLG	PRO+	BR/A	SB	CS	SBR	FA	FR	G/POS	TPR
1909 Bos-N	40	148	6	33	2	0	0	9	1		.223	.228	.236	42	-10	2			.934	0	3-36/2-2,S	-1.0
1910 Bos-N	54	144	14	28	0	1	0	7	6	10	.194	.232	.208	27	-13	2			.915	3	3-22,2-13/OS	-1.1
Total 7	339	1114	85	265	22	9	2	93	24	46	.238	.257	.279	60	-56	41			.942	18	3-271/2-19,SO1	-3.5
Team 2	94	292	20	61	2	1	0	16	7	10	.209	.230	.223	35	-24	4			.927	3	/3-58,2-15,OS	-2.1

■ FRANK GIBSON Gibson, Frank Gilbert b: 9/27/1890, Omaha, Neb. d: 4/27/61, Austin, Tex. BB/TR, 6'0.5", 172 lbs. Deb: 4/22/13

YEAR TM/L	G	AB	R	H	2B	3B	HR	RBI	BB	SO	AVG	OBP	SLG	PRO+	BR/A	SB	CS	SBR	FA	FR	G/POS	TPR
1921 Bos-N	63	125	14	33	5	4	2	13	3	17	.264	.292	.416	90	-2	0	0	0	.979	1	C-41	0.0
1922 Bos-N	66	164	15	49	7	2	3	20	10	27	.299	.339	.421	99	-1	4	1	1	.981	-1	C-29,1-20	-0.1
1923 Bos-N	41	50	13	15	1	0	0	5	7	7	.300	.386	.320	92	-0	0	2	-1	.923	-2	C-20	-0.2
1924 Bos-N	90	229	25	71	15	6	1	30	10	23	.310	.342	.441	113	3	1	1	-0	.972	2	C-46,1-10/3	0.7
1925 Bos-N	104	316	36	88	23	5	2	50	15	28	.278	.313	.402	89	-7	3	3	-1	.968	-2	C-86/1-2	-0.5
1926 Bos-N	24	47	3	16	4	0	0	7	4	6	.340	.392	.426	132	2	0			1.000	2	C-13	0.4
1927 Bos-N	60	167	7	37	1	2	0	19	3	10	.222	.235	.251	33	-16	2			.965	-3	C-47	-1.7
Total 8	471	1155	121	317	57	19	8	146	55	127	.274	.310	.377	86	-28	12	7		.967	-10	C-301/1-32,3O	-2.7
Team 7	448	1098	113	309	56	19	8	144	52	118	.281	.316	.389	90	-21	10	7		.971	-4	C-282/1-32,3	-1.4

■ LARRY GILBERT Gilbert, Lawrence William b: 12/3/1891, New Orleans, La. d: 2/17/65, New Orleans, La. BL/TL, 5'9", 158 lbs. Deb: 4/14/14 F

YEAR TM/L	G	AB	R	H	2B	3B	HR	RBI	BB	SO	AVG	OBP	SLG	PRO+	BR/A	SB	CS	SBR	FA	FR	G/POS	TPR
1914 *Bos-N	72	224	32	60	6	1	5	25	26	34	.268	.347	.371	114	4	3			.979	-0	O-60	0.1
1915 Bos-N	45	106	11	16	4	0	0	4	11	13	.151	.231	.189	29	-9	4	1	1	.941	-2	O-27	-1.3
Total 2	117	330	43	76	10	1	5	29	37	47	.230	.310	.312	88	-5	7	1		.969	-3	/O-87	-1.2

■ ROD GILBREATH Gilbreath, Rodney Joe b: 9/24/52, Laurel, Miss. BR/TR, 6'2", 185 lbs. Deb: 6/17/72

YEAR TM/L	G	AB	R	H	2B	3B	HR	RBI	BB	SO	AVG	OBP	SLG	PRO+	BR/A	SB	CS	SBR	FA	FR	G/POS	TPR
1972 Atl-N	18	38	2	9	1	0	0	1	2	10	.237	.293	.263	54	-2	1	1	-0	1.000	3	/2-7,3-4	0.0
1973 Atl-N	29	74	10	21	2	1	0	2	6	10	.284	.346	.338	84	-1	2	1	0	.960	-0	3-22	-0.2
1974 Atl-N	3	6	2	2	0	0	0	0	2	0	.333	.500	.333	131	0	0	0	0	1.000	0	/2-2	0.1
1975 Atl-N	90	202	24	49	3	1	2	16	24	26	.243	.326	.297	71	-7	5	5	-2	.980	2	2-52,3-10/S	-0.4
1976 Atl-N	116	383	57	96	11	8	1	32	42	36	.251	.331	.329	83	-8	7	7	-2	.975	7	*2-104/3-7,S	0.4
1977 Atl-N	128	407	47	99	15	2	8	43	45	79	.243	.322	.349	71	-16	3	9	-5	.978	3	*2-122/3-1	-1.0
1978 Atl-N	116	326	22	80	13	3	3	31	26	51	.245	.301	.331	69	-14	7	6	-2	.968	-3	3-62,2-39	-1.8
Total 7	500	1436	164	356	45	15	14	125	147	212	.248	.322	.329	74	-48	25	29	-10	.978	11	2-326,3-106/S	-2.9

■ CARDEN GILLENWATER Gillenwater, Carden Edison b: 5/13/18, Riceville, Tenn. BR/TR, 6'1", 178 lbs. Deb: 9/22/40

YEAR TM/L	G	AB	R	H	2B	3B	HR	RBI	BB	SO	AVG	OBP	SLG	PRO+	BR/A	SB	CS	SBR	FA	FR	G/POS	TPR
1945 Bos-N	144	517	74	149	20	2	7	72	73	70	.288	.379	.375	110	9	13			.979	24	*O-140	2.5
1946 Bos-N	99	224	30	51	10	1	1	14	39	27	.228	.342	.295	81	-4	3			.979	1	O-78	-0.6
Total 5	335	1004	129	261	41	7	11	114	153	138	.260	.359	.348	96	-1	20			.979	23	O-296	0.7
Team 2	243	741	104	200	30	3	8	86	112	97	.270	.368	.351	101	5	16			.979	25	O-218	1.9

■ ED GIOVANOLA Giovanola, Edward Thomas b: 3/4/69, Los Gatos, Cal. BL/TR, 5'10", 170 lbs. Deb: 9/10/95

YEAR TM/L	G	AB	R	H	2B	3B	HR	RBI	BB	SO	AVG	OBP	SLG	PRO+	BR/A	SB	CS	SBR	FA	FR	G/POS	TPR
1995 Atl-N	13	14	2	1	0	0	0	0	3	5	.071	.235	.071	-14	-2	0	0	0	1.000	-2	/2-7,3-3,S	-0.4

■ ROLAND GLADU Gladu, Roland Edouard b: 5/10/11, Montreal, Que., Can d: 7/26/94, Montreal, Que., Can. BL/TR, 5'8.5", 185 lbs. Deb: 4/18/44

YEAR TM/L	G	AB	R	H	2B	3B	HR	RBI	BB	SO	AVG	OBP	SLG	PRO+	BR/A	SB	CS	SBR	FA	FR	G/POS	TPR
1944 Bos-N	21	66	5	16	2	1	1	7	3	8	.242	.275	.348	72	-3	0			.891	-5	3-15/O-3	-0.8

■ ED GLENN Glenn, Edward C. "Mouse" b: 9/19/1860, Richmond, Va. d: 2/10/1892, Richmond, Va. BR/TR, 5'10", 160 lbs. Deb: 8/5/1884

YEAR TM/L	G	AB	R	H	2B	3B	HR	RBI	BB	SO	AVG	OBP	SLG	PRO+	BR/A	SB	CS	SBR	FA	FR	G/POS	TPR
1888 Bos-N	20	65	8	10	0	2	0	3	2	8	.154	.203	.215	33	-5	0			.957	2	O-19/3-1	-0.3
Total 3	137	525	66	106	8	11	1	3	24	8	.202	.245	.265	62	-22	20			.867	7	O-136/3-1	-1.6

■ AL GLOSSOP Glossop, Alban b: 7/23/15, Christopher, Ill. d: 7/2/91, Walnut Creek, Cal. BB/TR, 6', 170 lbs. Deb: 9/23/39

YEAR TM/L	G	AB	R	H	2B	3B	HR	RBI	BB	SO	AVG	OBP	SLG	PRO+	BR/A	SB	CS	SBR	FA	FR	G/POS	TPR
1940 Bos-N	60	148	17	35	2	1	3	14	17	22	.236	.315	.324	81	-4	1			.938	6	2-18,3-18/S	0.4
Total 5	309	952	99	199	29	2	15	86	89	105	.209	.280	.291	66	-43	5			.954	6	2-196/S-36,3O	-2.5

■ CHUCK GOGGIN Goggin, Charles Francis b: 7/7/45, Pompano Beach, Fla. BB/TR, 5'11", 175 lbs. Deb: 9/8/72

YEAR TM/L	G	AB	R	H	2B	3B	HR	RBI	BB	SO	AVG	OBP	SLG	PRO+	BR/A	SB	CS	SBR	FA	FR	G/POS	TPR
1973 Atl-N	64	90	18	26	5	0	0	7	9	19	.289	.354	.344	88	-1	0	1	-1	.938	-10	2-19/O-6,SC	-1.1
Total 3	72	99	19	29	5	0	0	7	10	21	.293	.358	.343	90	-1	0	1		.927	-9	/2-22,O-6,SC	-1.1

■ LUIS GOMEZ Gomez, Luis (Sanchez) b: 8/19/51, Guadalajara, Mex. BR/TR, 5'9", 150 lbs. Deb: 4/28/74

YEAR TM/L	G	AB	R	H	2B	3B	HR	RBI	BB	SO	AVG	OBP	SLG	PRO+	BR/A	SB	CS	SBR	FA	FR	G/POS	TPR
1980 Atl-N	121	278	18	53	6	0	0	24	17	27	.191	.240	.212	26	-27	0	4	-2	.968	12	*S-119	-0.8
1981 Atl-N	35	35	4	7	0	0	0	1	6	4	.200	.317	.200	48	-2	0	1	-1	.895	-3	S-21/3-9,2P	-0.5
Total 8	609	1251	108	263	26	5	0	90	86	129	.210	.262	.239	40	-98	6	22	-11	.970	53	S-483/2-58,3DOP	-1.6
Team 2	156	313	22	60	6	0	0	25	23	31	.192	.249	.211	29	-29	0	5	-3	.963	10	S-140/3-9,2P	-1.3

■ JESSE GONDER Gonder, Jesse Lemar b: 1/20/36, Monticello, Ark. BL/TR, 5'10", 190 lbs. Deb: 9/23/60

YEAR TM/L	G	AB	R	H	2B	3B	HR	RBI	BB	SO	AVG	OBP	SLG	PRO+	BR/A	SB	CS	SBR	FA	FR	G/POS	TPR
1965 Mil-N	31	53	2	8	2	0	1	5	4	9	.151	.211	.245	28	-5	0	0	0	.989	5	C-13	0.0
Total 8	395	876	73	220	28	2	26	94	72	184	.251	.312	.377	94	-7	1	2	-1	.981	-15	C-250	-1.4

■ TONY GONZALEZ Gonzalez, Andres Antonio (Gonzalez) b: 8/28/36, Central Cunagua, Cuba BL/TR, 5'9", 170 lbs. Deb: 4/12/60

YEAR TM/L	G	AB	R	H	2B	3B	HR	RBI	BB	SO	AVG	OBP	SLG	PRO+	BR/A	SB	CS	SBR	FA	FR	G/POS	TPR
1969 *Atl-N	89	320	51	94	15	2	10	50	27	22	.294	.358	.447	124	10	3	1	0	.989	2	O-82	0.8
1970 Atl-N	123	430	57	114	18	2	7	55	46	45	.265	.347	.365	86	-8	3	5	-2	.987	-3	*O-119	-1.8
Total 12	1559	5195	690	1485	238	57	103	615	467	706	.286	.353	.413	114	100	79	61	-13	.987	-12	*O-1447	0.4
Team 2	212	750	108	208	33	4	17	105	73	67	.277	.352	.400	101	2	6	6	-2	.988	-1	O-201	-1.0

YEAR	TM/L	G	AB	R	H	2B	3B	HR	RBI	BB	SO	AVG	OBP	SLG	PRO+	BR/A	SB	CS	SBR	FA	FR	G/POS	TPR
■ **MIKE GONZALEZ**	Gonzalez, Miguel Angel (Cordero) b: 9/24/1890, Havana, Cuba d: 2/19/77, Havana, Cuba BR/TR, 6'1", 200 lbs. Deb: 9/28/12 MC																						
1912	Bos-N	1	2	0	0	0	0	0	0	1	1	.000	.333	.000	-5	-0	0			.875	1	/C-1	0.1
Total	17	1042	2829	283	717	123	19	13	263	231	198	.253	.314	.324	81	-71	52			.980	45	C-868/1-60,O	2.9
■ **GENE GOOD**	Good, Eugene J. b: 12/13/1882, Roxbury, Mass. d: 8/6/47, Boston, Mass. BL/TL, 5'6", 130 lbs. Deb: 4/12/06																						
1906	Bos-N	34	119	4	18	0	0	0	0	13		.151	.246	.151	25	-10	2			.873	-2	O-34	-1.6
■ **WILBUR GOOD**	Good, Wilbur David "Lefty" b: 9/28/1885, Punxsutawney, Pa. d: 12/30/63, Brooksville, Fla. BL/TL, 5'6", 165 lbs. Deb: 8/18/05																						
1910	Bos-N	23	86	15	29	5	4	0	11	6	13	.337	.394	.488	150	5	5			.969	5	O-23	0.9
1911	Bos-N	43	165	21	44	9	3	0	15	12	22	.267	.316	.358	82	-5	3			.945	8	O-43	0.1
Total	11	749	2364	324	609	84	44	9	187	190	243	.258	.322	.342	98	-7	104			.942	-8	O-624/P-5	-5.3
Team	2	66	251	36	73	14	7	0	26	18	35	.291	.343	.402	104	1	8			.953	12	/O-66	1.0
■ **ED GOODSON**	Goodson, James Edward b: 1/25/48, Pulaski, Va. BL/TR, 6'3", 185 lbs. Deb: 9/5/70																						
1975	Atl-N	47	76	5	16	2	0	1	8	2	8	.211	.231	.276	39	-6	0	0	0	.990	0	1-13/3-1	-0.7
Total	8	515	1266	108	329	51	2	30	170	63	135	.260	.298	.374	84	-31	1	3		.994	-16	1-176,3-135/O2	-6.2
■ **SID GORDON**	Gordon, Sidney b: 8/13/17, Brooklyn, N.Y. d: 6/17/75, New York, N.Y. BR/TR, 5'10", 185 lbs. Deb: 9/11/41																						
1950	Bos-N	134	481	78	146	33	4	27	103	78	31	.304	.403	.557	160	42	2			.990	6	*O-123,3-10	4.1
1951	Bos-N	150	550	96	158	28	1	29	109	80	32	.287	.383	.500	146	35	2	0	1	.984	-4	*O-122,3-34	2.7
1952	Bos-N	144	522	69	151	22	2	25	75	77	49	.289	.384	.483	144	32	0	4	-2	**.996**	2	*O-142/3-2	2.6
1953	Mil-N	140	464	67	127	22	4	19	75	71	40	.274	.372	.461	123	17	1	1	-0	.977	-1	*O-137	1.0
Total	13	1475	4992	735	1415	220	43	202	805	731	356	.283	.377	.466	130	218	19	5		.985	-19	O-918,3-454/12	15.1
Team	4	568	2017	310	582	105	11	100	362	306	152	.289	.385	.500	143	126	5	5		.987	2	O-524/3-46	10.4
■ **CHARLIE GOULD**	Gould, Charles Harvey b: 8/21/1847, Cincinnati, Ohio d: 4/10/17, Flushing, N.Y. BR/TR, 6', 172 lbs. Deb: 5/5/1871 M																						
1871	Bos-n	31	151	38	43	9	2	2	32	3	1	.285	.299	.411	98	-1	6					*1-30/O-1	0.0
1872	Bos-n	45	214	39	57	7	**8**	0	33	2	3	.266	.273	.374	92	-3						*1-44/O-2	-0.1
Total	4 n	136	616	106	160	24	11	2	65	9	4	.260	.270	.344	89	-9						1-132/O-4,C	-0.4
Total	2	85	349	32	90	9	1	0	24	11	16	.258	.281	.289	101	2				.934	0	/1-85,P-2,O	0.1
Team	2 n	76	365	77	100	16	10	2	65	5	4	.274	.284	.389	95	0				.000	0	/1-74,O-3	-0.1
■ **HANK GOWDY**	Gowdy, Henry Morgan b: 8/24/1889, Columbus, Ohio d: 8/1/66, Columbus, Ohio BR/TR, 6'2", 182 lbs. Deb: 9/13/10 MC																						
1911	Bos-N	29	97	9	28	4	2	0	16	4	19	.289	.324	.371	87	-2	2			.966	-1	1-26/C-1	-0.3
1912	Bos-N	44	96	16	26	6	1	3	10	16	13	.271	.386	.448	126	4	3			.926	-2	C-22/1-7	0.3
1913	Bos-N	3	5	0	3	1	0	0	2	3	2	.600	.750	.800	336	2	0			1.000	-1	/C-2	0.1
1914	*Bos-N	128	366	42	89	17	6	3	46	48	40	.243	.337	.347	104	3	14			.968	-5	*C-115/1-9	0.7
1915	Bos-N	118	316	27	78	15	3	2	30	41	34	.247	.339	.332	108	4	10	4	1	.974	0	*C-114	1.5
1916	Bos-N	118	349	32	88	14	1	1	34	24	33	.252	.311	.307	94	-2	8			.980	3	*C-116	1.0
1917	Bos-N	49	154	12	33	7	0	0	14	15	13	.214	.288	.260	73	-5	2			.969	-1	C-49	-0.2
1919	Bos-N	78	219	18	61	8	1	1	22	19	16	.279	.339	.338	108	2	5			.977	5	C-74/1-1	1.4
1920	Bos-N	80	214	14	52	11	2	0	18	20	15	.243	.314	.313	84	-4	6	1	1	.980	11	C-74	1.3
1921	Bos-N	64	164	17	49	7	2	2	17	16	11	.299	.368	.402	110	3	2	0	1	.981	-1	C-53	0.4
1922	Bos-N	92	221	23	70	11	1	1	27	24	13	.317	.391	.389	107	3	2	1	0	.971	1	C-72/1-1	0.7
1923	Bos-N	23	48	5	6	1	1	0	5	15	5	.125	.354	.188	48	-3	1	1	-0	.982	-2	C-15	-0.4
1929	Bos-N	10	16	1	7	0	0	0	3	0	2	.438	.438	.438	122	1	0			1.000	-0	/C-9	0.0
1930	Bos-N	16	25	0	5	1	0	0	2	3	1	.200	.310	.240	37	-3	0			.972	1	C-15	-0.1
Total	17	1050	2735	270	738	124	27	21	322	311	247	.270	.351	.358	105	25	59	7		.975	5	C-893/1-51	9.3
Team	14	852	2290	216	595	103	20	13	246	248	217	.260	.339	.339	99	3	55	7		.973	6	C-731/1-44	6.4
■ **PEACHES GRAHAM**	Graham, George Frederick b: 3/23/1877, Aledo, Ill. d: 7/25/39, Long Beach, Cal. BR/TR, 5'9", 180 lbs. Deb: 9/14/02 F																						
1908	Bos-N	75	215	22	59	5	0	0	22	23		.274	.361	.298	112	4	4			.955	-3	C-62/2-5	0.8
1909	Bos-N	92	267	27	64	6	3	0	17	24		.240	.302	.285	79	-7	7			.948	-4	C-76/O-6,S3	-0.4
1910	Bos-N	110	291	31	82	13	2	0	21	33	15	.282	.359	.340	100	0	5			.966	-8	C-87/3-2,1O	0.1
1911	Bos-N	33	88	7	24	6	1	0	12	14	5	.273	.373	.364	98	0	2			.912	-5	C-26	-0.3
Total	7	373	999	99	265	34	6	1	85	114	33	.265	.347	.314	95	-3	21			.953	-25	C-298/O-7,231SP	-0.2
Team	4	310	861	87	229	30	6	0	72	94	20	.266	.344	.315	96	-2	18			.952	-19	C-251/O-7,231S	0.2
■ **SID GRAVES**	Graves, Samuel Sidney "Whitey" b: 11/30/01, Marblehead, Mass. d: 12/26/83, Biddeford, Maine BR/TR, 6', 170 lbs. Deb: 7/23/27 F																						
1927	Bos-N	7	20	5	5	1	1	0	2	0	1	.250	.250	.400	78	-1	1			.857	0	/O-5	-0.1
■ **TOMMY GREGG**	Gregg, William Thomas b: 7/29/63, Boone, N.C. BL/TL, 6'1", 190 lbs. Deb: 9/14/87																						
1988	Atl-N	11	29	1	10	3	0	0	4	2	2	.345	.387	.448	132	1	0	0	0	1.000	2	/O-7	0.3
1989	Atl-N	102	276	24	67	8	0	6	23	18	45	.243	.289	.337	76	-9	3	4	-2	.967	-10	O-48,1-37	-2.5
1990	Atl-N	124	239	18	63	13	1	5	32	20	39	.264	.323	.389	90	-3	4	3	-1	.987	-2	1-50,O-20	-0.9
1991	*Atl-N	72	107	13	20	8	1	1	4	12	24	.187	.275	.308	60	-6	2	2	-1	1.000	-2	O-14,1-13	-0.9
1992	Atl-N	18	19	1	5	0	0	1	1	1	7	.263	.300	.421	96	-0	1	0	0	1.000	-1	/O-9	-0.1
Total	8	433	861	85	209	39	2	20	88	70	156	.243	.303	.362	80	-23	13	11		.981	-20	O-150,1-102	-5.7
Team	5	327	670	57	165	32	2	13	64	53	117	.246	.303	.358	82	-17	10	9		.993	-12	1-100/O-98	-4.1
■ **ED GREMMINGER**	Gremminger, Lorenzo Edward "Battleship" b: 3/30/1874, Canton, Ohio d: 5/26/42, Canton, Ohio BR/TR, 6'1", 200 lbs. Deb: 4/21/1895																						
1902	Bos-N	140	522	55	134	20	12	1	65	39		.257	.314	.347	103	1	7			**.951**	3	*3-140	0.6
1903	Bos-N	140	511	57	135	24	9	5	56	31		.264	.313	.376	100	-2	12			.935	16	*3-140	1.5
Total	4	383	1420	140	356	58	24	7	164	89		.251	.301	.340	92	-16	22			.940	2	3-383	-1.0
Team	2	280	1033	112	269	44	21	6	121	70		.260	.314	.361	101	-1	19			.943	19	3-280	2.1
■ **BUDDY GREMP**	Gremp, Lewis Edward b: 8/5/19, Denver, Col. BR/TR, 6'1", 175 lbs. Deb: 9/13/40																						
1940	Bos-N	4	9	0	2	0	0	0	2	0	0	.222	.222	.222	24	-1	0			1.000	-0	/1-3	-0.1
1941	Bos-N	37	75	7	18	3	0	0	10	5	3	.240	.287	.280	63	-4	0			.977	-3	1-21/2-6,C	-0.8
1942	Bos-N	72	207	12	45	11	0	3	19	13	21	.217	.267	.314	71	-8	1			.991	1	1-62/3-1	-1.1
Total	3	113	291	19	65	14	0	3	31	18	24	.223	.271	.302	67	-13	1			.988	-3	/1-86,2-6,C3	-2.0
■ **KEN GRIFFEY**	Griffey, George Kenneth Sr. b: 4/10/50, Donora, Pa. BL/TL, 6', 200 lbs. Deb: 8/25/73 FC																						
1986	Atl-N	80	292	36	90	15	3	12	32	20	43	.308	.353	.503	126	10	12	7	-1	.986	1	O-77/1-1	0.8
1987	Atl-N	122	399	65	114	24	1	14	64	46	54	.286	.361	.456	109	6	4	7	-3	.995	1	*O-107/1-3	0.0
1988	Atl-N	69	193	21	48	5	0	2	19	17	26	.249	.310	.306	74	-6	1	3	-2	.969	-4	O-42,1-11	-1.5
Total	19	2097	7229	1129	2143	364	77	152	859	719	898	.296	.361	.431	118	175	200	83		.981	4	*O-1703,1-172/D	12.4
Team	3	271	884	122	252	44	4	28	115	83	123	.285	.347	.439	107	9	17	17		.987	-3	O-226/1-15	-0.7
■ **TOMMY GRIFFITH**	Griffith, Thomas Herman b: 10/26/1889, Prospect, Ohio d: 4/13/67, Cincinnati, Ohio BL/TR, 5'10", 175 lbs. Deb: 8/28/13																						
1913	Bos-N	37	127	16	32	4	1	1	12	9	8	.252	.301	.323	77	-4	1			.886	1	O-35	-0.4
1914	Bos-N	16	48	3	5	0	0	0	1	2	6	.104	.140	.104	-27	-7	0			.931	3	O-14	-0.6
Total	13	1401	4947	589	1383	208	72	52	619	351	262	.280	.328	.382	102	6	70			.956	-19	*O-1333	-11.3
Team	2	53	175	19	37	4	1	1	13	11	14	.211	.258	.263	50	-11	1			.899	4	/O-49	-1.0

YEAR	TM/L	G	AB	R	H	2B	3B	HR	RBI	BB	SO	AVG	OBP	SLG	PRO+	BR/A	SB	CS	SBR	FA	FR	G/POS	TPR
■ MARQUIS GRISSOM Grissom, Marquis Deon b: 4/17/67, Atlanta, Ga. BR/TR, 5'11", 190 lbs. Deb: 8/22/89																							
1995	*Atl-N	139	551	80	142	23	3	12	42	47	61	.258	.319	.376	81	-16	29	9	3	.994	11	*O-136	-0.4
Total	7	837	3229	510	889	153	26	66	318	255	434	.275	.331	.400	97	-15	295	57		.985	58	O-807	8.1
■ GEORGE GROSSART Grossart, George Albert b: 4/11/1880, Meadville, Pa. d: 4/18/02, Pittsburgh, Pa. Deb: 6/7/01																							
1901	Bos-N	7	26	4	3	0	0	0	1	0		.115	.115	.115	-30	-4	0			1.000	0	/O-7	-0.5
■ TOM GUNNING Gunning, Thomas Francis b: 3/4/1862, Newmarket, N.H. d: 3/17/31, Fall River, Mass. BR/TR, 5'10", 160 lbs. Deb: 7/26/1884 U																							
1884	Bos-N	12	45	4	5	1	1	0	2	1	12	.111	.130	.178	-4	-5				.914	-5	C-12	-0.9
1885	Bos-N	48	174	17	32	3	0	0	15	5	29	.184	.207	.201	34	-12				.877	-7	C-48	-1.5
1886	Bos-N	27	98	15	22	2	1	0	7	3	19	.224	.248	.265	58	-5	3			.892	-5	C-27	-0.6
Total	6	146	537	79	110	12	4	2	46	16	70	.205	.235	.253	50	-32	38			.887	-15	C-146	-3.1
Team	3	87	317	36	59	6	2	0	24	9	60	.186	.209	.218	36	-22	3			.886	-18	/C-87	-3.0
■ DICK GYSELMAN Gyselman, Richard Renald b: 4/6/08, San Francisco, Cal. d: 9/20/90, Seattle, Wash. BR/TR, 6'2", 170 lbs. Deb: 4/20/33																							
1933	Bos-N	58	155	10	37	6	2	0	12	7	21	.239	.272	.303	70	-7	0			.926	6	3-42/2-5,S	0.2
1934	Bos-N	24	36	7	6	1	1	0	4	2	11	.167	.211	.250	25	-4	0			.739	-2	3-15/2-2	-0.5
Total	2	82	191	17	43	7	3	0	16	9	32	.225	.260	.293	61	-11	0			.901	4	/3-57,2-7,S	-0.3
■ EDDIE HAAS Haas, George Edwin b: 5/26/35, Paducah, Ky. BL/TR, 5'11", 178 lbs. Deb: 9/8/57 MC																							
1958	Mil-N	9	14	2	5	0	0	0	1	2	1	.357	.438	.357	124	1	0	0	0	1.000	-0	/O-3	0.0
1960	Mil-N	32	32	4	7	2	0	1	5	5	14	.219	.324	.375	98	-0	0	0	0	1.000	-0	/O-2	-0.1
Total	3	55	70	7	17	3	0	1	10	8	20	.243	.321	.329	80	-2	0	0		1.000	-2	/O-9	-0.4
Team	2	41	46	6	12	2	0	1	6	7	15	.261	.358	.370	106	1	0	0		1.000	-1	/O-5	-0.1
■ MERT HACKETT Hackett, Mortimer Martin b: 11/11/1859, Cambridge, Mass. d: 2/22/38, Cambridge, Mass. BR/TR, 5'10.5", 175 lbs. Deb: 5/2/1883 F																							
1883	Bos-N	46	179	20	42	8	6	2	24	1	48	.235	.239	.380	82	-4				.909	-6	C-44/O-4	-0.7
1884	Bos-N	72	268	28	55	13	2	1	20	2	66	.205	.211	.280	53	-14				.928	12	C-71/3-1	0.3
1885	Bos-N	34	115	9	21	7	1	0	4	2	28	.183	.197	.261	49	-6				.901	5	C-34	0.2
Total	5	256	939	87	203	42	15	8	83	16	225	.216	.231	.318	65	-40	5	0	2	.921	-15	C-242/O-19,13	-3.1
Team	3	152	562	57	118	28	9	3	48	5	142	.210	.217	.308	62	-25	0	0	0	.917	11	C-149/O-4,3	-0.2
■ WALTER HACKETT Hackett, Walter Henry b: 8/15/1857, Cambridge, Mass. d: 10/2/20, Cambridge, Mass. Deb: 4/17/1884 F																							
1885	Bos-N	35	125	8	23	3	0	0	9	3	22	.184	.203	.208	34	-9				.893	-12	2-20,S-15	-1.9
Total	2	138	540	79	124	22	0	1	9	10	22	.230	.244	.276	47	-37				.852	1	S-118/2-20	-3.2
■ ALBERT HALL Hall, Albert b: 3/7/58, Birmingham, Ala. BB/TR, 5'11", 155 lbs. Deb: 9/12/81																							
1981	Atl-N	6	2	1	0	0	0	0	0	1	1	.000	.333	.000	1	-0	0	0	0	.000	-1	/O-2	-0.1
1982	Atl-N	5	0	1	0	0	0	0	0	0	0	—	—	—	—	0	0	0	0	.000	0	/R	0.0
1983	Atl-N	10	8	2	0	0	0	0	0	2	2	.000	.200	.000	-37	-1	1	1	-0	.750	-2	/O-4	-0.4
1984	Atl-N	87	142	25	37	6	1	1	9	10	18	.261	.309	.338	76	-4	6	4	-1	.932	-10	O-66	-1.7
1985	Atl-N	54	47	5	7	0	1	0	3	9	12	.149	.286	.191	34	-4	1	1	-0	.900	-4	O-13	-0.8
1986	Atl-N	16	50	6	12	2	0	0	1	5	6	.240	.309	.280	60	-3	8	3	1	.900	0	O-14	-0.3
1987	Atl-N	92	292	54	83	20	4	3	24	38	36	.284	.370	.411	102	2	33	10	4	.981	3	O-69	0.6
1988	Atl-N	85	231	27	57	7	1	1	15	21	35	.247	.315	.299	73	-7	15	10	-2	.973	2	O-63	-1.0
Total	9	375	805	125	202	37	8	5	53	89	115	.251	.329	.335	80	-20	67	29	3	.958	-15	O-243	-4.2
Team	8	355	772	121	196	35	7	5	52	86	110	.254	.332	.337	80	-18	64	29	2	.960	-12	O-231	-3.7
■ GEORGE HALL Hall, George William b: 3/29/1849, Stepney, England d: 6/11/23, Ridgewood, N.J. BL, 5'7", 142 lbs. Deb: 5/5/1871																							
1874	Bos-n	47	222	58	64	11	7	1		2		.288	.295	.414	117	3						*O-47	0.3
Total	5 n	244	1138	273	351	48	35	10	87	16	1	.308	.318	.438	130	33						O-244/1-1	2.9
Total	2	121	537	104	185	22	21	5	71	20	23	.345	.368	.492	162	35				.837	-7	O-121	2.1
■ JIMMIE HALL Hall, Jimmie Randolph b: 3/17/38, Mt.Holly, N.C. BL/TR, 6', 175 lbs. Deb: 4/9/63																							
1970	Atl-N	39	47	7	10	2	0	2	4	2	14	.213	.245	.383	62	-3	0	0	0	1.000	-6	O-28	-0.9
Total	8	963	2848	387	724	100	24	121	391	287	529	.254	.323	.434	112	40	38	18	1	.982	-17	O-806/1-7	-1.5
■ BILLY HAMILTON Hamilton, William Robert "Sliding Billy" b: 2/16/1866, Newark, N.J. d: 12/16/40, Worcester, Mass. BL/TR, 5'6", 165 lbs. Deb: 7/31/1888 H																							
1896	Bos-N	131	523	152	191	24	9	3	52	**110**	29	.365	**.477**	.463	140	36	83			.934	-11	*O-131	1.2
1897	*Bos-N	127	507	**152**	174	17	5	3	61	**105**		.343	.461	.414	124	24	66			.962	-3	*O-126	1.0
1898	Bos-N	110	417	110	154	16	5	3	50	87		.369	**.480**	.453	**159**	38	54			.904	-15	*O-110	1.4
1899	Bos-N	84	297	63	92	7	1	1	33	72		.310	.446	.350	109	8	19			.952	-2	O-81	-0.1
1900	Bos-N	136	520	103	173	20	5	1	47	107		.333	.449	.396	119	18	32			.947	2	*O-136	0.9
1901	Bos-N	102	348	71	100	11	2	3	38	64		.287	.404	.356	111	8	20			.945	1	O-99	0.1
Total	14	1591	6268	1690	2158	242	94	40	736	1187	218	.344	.455	.432	139	414	912			.926	-5	*O-1584	26.4
Team	6	690	2612	651	884	95	27	14	281	545	29	.338	.456	.412	128	132	274			.942	-29	O-683	4.5
■ HARRY HANEBRINK Hanebrink, Harry Aloysius b: 11/12/27, St.Louis, Mo. BL/TR, 6', 165 lbs. Deb: 5/3/53																							
1953	Mil-N	51	80	8	19	1	1	1	8	6	8	.237	.291	.313	61	-5	1	0	0	.979	4	2-21/3-1	0.0
1957	Mil-N	6	7	0	2	0	0	0	0	1	2	.286	.375	.286	87	-0	0	0	0	1.000	1	/3-2	0.1
1958	*Mil-N	63	133	14	25	3	0	4	10	13	9	.188	.270	.301	56	-9	0	1	-1	.982	-0	O-33/3-7	-1.1
Total	4	177	317	32	71	7	2	6	25	22	31	.224	.279	.315	60	-19	1	1	-0	.959	-2	/2-36,O-34,3	-2.1
Team	3	120	220	22	46	4	1	5	18	20	19	.209	.281	.305	59	-14	1	1	-0	.982	4	/O-33,2-21,3	-1.0
■ JACK HANNIFIN Hannifin, John Joseph b: 2/25/1883, Holyoke, Mass. d: 10/27/45, Northampton, Mass. BR/TR, 5'11", 167 lbs. Deb: 4/19/06																							
1908	Bos-N	90	257	30	53	6	2	2	22	28		.206	.284	.268	78	-6	7			.930	5	3-35,2-22,S/O	0.0
Total	3	158	439	50	94	13	6	3	40	45		.214	.289	.292	84	-8	14			.937	0	/3-48,S-30,12O	-0.8
■ LOU HARDIE Hardie, Louis W. b: 8/24/1864, New York, N.Y. d: 3/5/29, Oakland, Cal. 5'11", 180 lbs. Deb: 5/22/1884																							
1890	Bos-N	47	185	17	42	8	0	3	17	18	36	.227	.296	.319	73	-7	4			.886	-0	C-25,O-15/3S1	-0.5
Total	4	81	300	28	67	10	3	3	21	30	56	.223	.294	.307	71	-12	8			.910	-2	/C-41,O-32,31S	-1.0
■ PINKY HARGRAVE Hargrave, William McKinley b: 1/31/1896, New Haven, Ind. d: 10/3/42, Ft.Wayne, Ind. BB/TR, 5'8.5", 180 lbs. Deb: 5/18/23 F																							
1932	Bos-N	82	217	20	57	14	3	4	33	24	18	.263	.336	.410	103	1	1			.968	-4	C-73	0.1
1933	Bos-N	45	73	5	13	0	0	0	6	5	7	.178	.241	.178	23	-7	1			.957	1	C-25	-0.6
Total	10	650	1601	177	445	91	16	39	265	140	165	.278	.339	.428	98	-8	17			.976	-35	C-442/3-8,O	-1.2
Team	2	127	290	25	70	14	3	4	39	29	25	.241	.313	.352	85	-6	2			.966	-3	/C-98	-0.5
■ GEORGE HARPER Harper, George Washington b: 6/24/1892, Arlington, Ky. d: 8/18/78, Magnolia, Ark. BL/TR, 5'8", 167 lbs. Deb: 4/15/16																							
1929	Bos-N	136	457	65	133	25	5	10	68	69	27	.291	.389	.433	108	7	5			.972	-1	*O-130	-0.3
Total	11	1073	3398	505	1030	158	43	91	528	389	208	.303	.380	.455	118	90	58			.970	-5	O-933	1.1
■ TERRY HARPER Harper, Terry Joe b: 8/19/55, Douglasville, Ga. BR/TR, 6'4", 195 lbs. Deb: 9/12/80																							
1980	Atl-N	21	54	3	10	2	1	0	3	6	5	.185	.279	.259	49	-4	2	1	0	.968	-2	O-18	-0.6
1981	Atl-N	40	73	9	19	1	0	2	8	11	17	.260	.357	.356	100	0	5	1	1	.976	-2	O-27	-0.1
1982	*Atl-N	48	150	16	43	3	0	2	16	14	28	.287	.352	.347	92	-1	7	4	-0	.987	-0	O-41	-0.3

YEAR	TM/L	G	AB	R	H	2B	3B	HR	RBI	BB	SO	AVG	OBP	SLG	PRO+	BR/A	SB	CS	SBR	FA	FR	G/POS	TPR
1983	Atl-N	80	201	19	53	13	1	3	26	20	43	.264	.333	.383	91	-2	6	5	-1	.952	-1	O-60	-0.7
1984	Atl-N	40	102	4	16	3	1	0	8	4	21	.157	.196	.206	12	-12	4	1	1	1.000	4	O-29	-0.9
1985	Atl-N	138	492	58	130	15	2	17	72	44	76	.264	.328	.407	98	-1	9	9	-3	.978	1	*O-131	-0.7
1986	Atl-N	106	265	26	68	12	0	8	30	29	39	.257	.332	.392	94	-2	3	6	-3	.970	-11	O-83	-1.9
Total	8	540	1467	147	371	55	5	36	180	144	248	.253	.323	.371	88	-24	37	28	-6	.976	-16	O-423/D-15	-5.9
Team	7	473	1337	135	339	49	5	32	163	128	229	.254	.322	.369	87	-22	36	27	-5	.975	-12	O-389	-5.2

■ **JOE HARRINGTON** Harrington, Joseph C. b: 12/21/1869, Fall River, Mass. d: 9/13/33, Fall River, Mass. BR/TR, 5'8.5", 162 lbs. Deb: 9/10/1895

YEAR	TM/L	G	AB	R	H	2B	3B	HR	RBI	BB	SO	AVG	OBP	SLG	PRO+	BR/A	SB	CS	SBR	FA	FR	G/POS	TPR
1895	Bos-N	18	65	21	18	0	2	2	13	7	5	.277	.356	.431	95	-1	3			.912	0	2-18	0.0
1896	Bos-N	54	198	25	39	5	3	1	25	19	17	.197	.271	.268	40	-18	2			.816	-10	3-49/S-4,2	-2.3
Total	2	72	263	46	57	5	5	3	38	26	22	.217	.292	.308	54	-19	5			.901	-10	/3-49,2-19,S	-2.3

■ **DAVE HARRIS** Harris, David Stanley "Sheriff" b: 7/14/1900, Summerfield, N.C. d: 9/18/73, Atlanta, Ga. BR/TR, 5'11", 170 lbs. Deb: 4/14/25

YEAR	TM/L	G	AB	R	H	2B	3B	HR	RBI	BB	SO	AVG	OBP	SLG	PRO+	BR/A	SB	CS	SBR	FA	FR	G/POS	TPR
1925	Bos-N	92	340	49	90	8	7	5	36	27	44	.265	.321	.374	84	-9	6	4	-1	.962	8	O-90	-0.7
1928	Bos-N	7	17	2	2	1	0	0	0	2	6	.118	.211	.176	2	-2	0			.833	-1	/O-6	-0.4
Total	7	542	1447	243	406	74	33	32	247	196	245	.281	.368	.444	112	25	28	21		.963	-8	O-381/3-7,12	-0.9
Team	2	99	357	51	92	9	7	5	36	29	50	.258	.315	.364	80	-11	6	4		.956	6	/O-96	-1.1

■ **ROY HARTSFIELD** Hartsfield, Roy Thomas "Spec" b: 10/25/25, Chattahoochee, Ga. BR/TR, 5'9", 165 lbs. Deb: 4/28/50 MC

YEAR	TM/L	G	AB	R	H	2B	3B	HR	RBI	BB	SO	AVG	OBP	SLG	PRO+	BR/A	SB	CS	SBR	FA	FR	G/POS	TPR
1950	Bos-N	107	419	62	116	15	2	7	24	27	61	.277	.322	.372	88	-8	7			.949	-24	2-96	-2.8
1951	Bos-N	120	450	63	122	11	2	6	31	41	73	.271	.333	.344	89	-7	7	2	1	.969	-5	*2-114	-0.5
1952	Bos-N	38	107	13	28	4	3	0	4	5	12	.262	.295	.355	82	-3	0	0	0	.950	-6	2-29	-0.7
Total	3	265	976	138	266	30	7	13	59	73	146	.273	.324	.358	88	-18	14	2		.959	-34	2-239	-4.0

■ **MICKEY HASLIN** Haslin, Michael Joseph b: 10/31/10, Wilkes-Barre, Pa. BR/TR, 5'8", 165 lbs. Deb: 9/7/33

YEAR	TM/L	G	AB	R	H	2B	3B	HR	RBI	BB	SO	AVG	OBP	SLG	PRO+	BR/A	SB	CS	SBR	FA	FR	G/POS	TPR
1936	Bos-N	36	104	14	29	1	2	2	11	5	9	.279	.312	.385	93	-1	0			.892	-5	3-17/2-7	-0.5
Total	6	318	974	125	265	33	8	9	109	59	64	.272	.316	.350	74	-34	8			.927	-15	S-100/2-92,3	-3.8

■ **BUDDY HASSETT** Hassett, John Aloysius b: 9/5/11, New York, N.Y. BL/TL, 5'11", 180 lbs. Deb: 4/14/36

YEAR	TM/L	G	AB	R	H	2B	3B	HR	RBI	BB	SO	AVG	OBP	SLG	PRO+	BR/A	SB	CS	SBR	FA	FR	G/POS	TPR
1939	Bos-N	147	590	72	182	15	3	2	60	29	14	.308	.342	.354	94	-6	13			.985	9	*1-123,O-23	-1.1
1940	Bos-N	124	458	59	107	19	4	0	27	25	16	.234	.273	.293	59	-26	4			.979	7	1-98,O-13	-2.9
1941	Bos-N	118	405	59	120	9	4	1	33	36	15	.296	.354	.346	102	1	10			.991	7	1-99	0.1
Total	7	929	3517	469	1026	130	40	12	343	209	116	.292	.333	.362	92	-40	53			.985	45	1-747,O-114	-7.0
Team	3	389	1453	190	409	43	11	3	120	90	45	.281	.324	.332	85	-30	27			.985	23	1-320/O-36	-3.9

■ **BILL HAWES** Hawes, William Hildreth b: 11/17/1853, Nashua, N.H. d: 6/16/40, Lowell, Mass. BR/TR, 5'10", 155 lbs. Deb: 5/1/1879

YEAR	TM/L	G	AB	R	H	2B	3B	HR	RBI	BB	SO	AVG	OBP	SLG	PRO+	BR/A	SB	CS	SBR	FA	FR	G/POS	TPR
1879	Bos-N	38	155	19	31	3	3	0	9	2	13	.200	.210	.258	52	-8				.828	-3	O-34/C-5	-1.2
Total	2	117	504	99	128	10	7	4	9	7	13	.254	.264	.325	64	-24				.827	-10	/O-92,1-21,C	-3.6

■ **BOB HAZLE** Hazle, Robert Sidney "Hurricane" b: 12/9/30, Laurens, S.C. d: 4/25/92, Columbia, S.C. BL/TR, 6', 190 lbs. Deb: 9/8/55

YEAR	TM/L	G	AB	R	H	2B	3B	HR	RBI	BB	SO	AVG	OBP	SLG	PRO+	BR/A	SB	CS	SBR	FA	FR	G/POS	TPR
1957	*Mil-N	41	134	26	54	12	0	7	27	18	15	.403	.477	.649	214	22	1	3	-2	.906	-5	O-40	1.3
1958	Mil-N	20	56	6	10	0	0	0	5	9	4	.179	.303	.179	34	-5	0	0	0	1.000	-1	O-20	-0.7
Total	3	110	261	37	81	14	0	9	37	32	35	.310	.390	.467	135	14	1	3		.951	-7	/O-75	0.2
Team	2	61	190	32	64	12	0	7	32	27	19	.337	.425	.511	161	17	1	3		.938	-7	/O-60	0.6

■ **JEFF HEATH** Heath, John Geoffrey b: 4/1/15, Ft.William, Ont., Canada d: 12/9/75, Seattle, Wash. BL/TR, 5'11.5", 200 lbs. Deb: 9/13/36

YEAR	TM/L	G	AB	R	H	2B	3B	HR	RBI	BB	SO	AVG	OBP	SLG	PRO+	BR/A	SB	CS	SBR	FA	FR	G/POS	TPR
1948	Bos-N	115	364	64	116	26	5	20	76	51	46	.319	.404	.582	167	33	2			**.991**	-2	*O-106	2.6
1949	Bos-N	36	111	17	34	7	0	9	23	15	26	.306	.389	.613	174	11	0			.983	-2	O-31	0.8
Total	14	1383	4937	777	1447	279	102	194	887	593	670	.293	.370	.509	140	262	56			.972	-20	*O-1299	16.4
Team	2	151	475	81	150	33	5	29	99	66	72	.316	.400	.589	168	44	2			.990	-4	O-137	3.4

■ **MIKE HEATH** Heath, Michael Thomas b: 2/5/55, Tampa, Fla. BR/TR, 5'11", 190 lbs. Deb: 6/3/78

YEAR	TM/L	G	AB	R	H	2B	3B	HR	RBI	BB	SO	AVG	OBP	SLG	PRO+	BR/A	SB	CS	SBR	FA	FR	G/POS	TPR
1991	Atl-N	49	139	4	29	3	1	1	12	7	26	.209	.252	.266	43	-10	0	0	0	.991	-0	C-45	-0.9
Total	14	1325	4212	462	1061	173	27	86	469	278	616	.252	.302	.367	87	-79	54	40		.981	-46	*C-1083,O-215/D31S2	-8.7

■ **DANNY HEEP** Heep, Daniel William b: 7/3/57, San Antonio, Tex. BL/TL, 5'11", 185 lbs. Deb: 8/31/79

YEAR	TM/L	G	AB	R	H	2B	3B	HR	RBI	BB	SO	AVG	OBP	SLG	PRO+	BR/A	SB	CS	SBR	FA	FR	G/POS	TPR
1991	Atl-N	14	12	4	5	1	0	0	3	1	4	.417	.462	.500	161	1	0	1	-1	1.000	-0	/1-1,O-1	0.0
Total	13	883	1961	208	503	96	6	30	229	220	242	.257	.334	.357	95	-12	12	14	-5	.986	-34	O-429,1-131/DP	-7.1

■ **FRANK HEIFER** Heifer, Franklin "Heck" b: 1/18/1854, Reading, Pa. d: 8/29/1893, Reading, Pa. 5'10.5", 175 lbs. Deb: 6/4/1875

YEAR	TM/L	G	AB	R	H	2B	3B	HR	RBI	BB	SO	AVG	OBP	SLG	PRO+	BR/A	SB	CS	SBR	FA	FR	G/POS	TPR
1875	Bos-n	11	51	11	14	0	3	0		0		.275	.275	.392	123	1						/1-7,O-6,P	0.1

■ **HEINIE HELTZEL** Heltzel, William Wade b: 12/21/13, York, Pa. BR/TR, 5'10", 150 lbs. Deb: 7/27/43

YEAR	TM/L	G	AB	R	H	2B	3B	HR	RBI	BB	SO	AVG	OBP	SLG	PRO+	BR/A	SB	CS	SBR	FA	FR	G/POS	TPR
1943	Bos-N	29	86	6	13	3	0	0	5	7	13	.151	.215	.186	17	-9	0			.880	-3	3-29	-1.3
Total	2	40	108	7	17	4	0	0	5	9	16	.157	.229	.194	23	-11	0			.983	-5	/3-29,S-10	-1.6

■ **KEN HENDERSON** Henderson, Kenneth Joseph b: 6/15/46, Carroll, Iowa BB/TR, 6'2", 180 lbs. Deb: 4/23/65

YEAR	TM/L	G	AB	R	H	2B	3B	HR	RBI	BB	SO	AVG	OBP	SLG	PRO+	BR/A	SB	CS	SBR	FA	FR	G/POS	TPR
1976	Atl-N	133	435	52	114	19	0	13	61	62	68	.262	.355	.395	106	5	5	7	-3	.987	-12	*O-122	-1.6
Total	16	1444	4553	595	1168	216	26	122	576	589	763	.257	.346	.396	106	45	86	42		.977	-19	*O-1252/D-30,31	-3.3

■ **SNAKE HENRY** Henry, Frederick Marshall b: 7/19/1895, Waynesville, N.C. d: 10/12/87, Wendell, N.C. BL/TL, 6', 170 lbs. Deb: 9/15/22

YEAR	TM/L	G	AB	R	H	2B	3B	HR	RBI	BB	SO	AVG	OBP	SLG	PRO+	BR/A	SB	CS	SBR	FA	FR	G/POS	TPR
1922	Bos-N	18	66	5	13	4	1	0	5	2	8	.197	.221	.288	32	-7	2	2	-1	.995	1	1-18	-0.7
1923	Bos-N	11	9	1	1	0	0	0	2	1	1	.111	.200	.111	-17	-2	0	0	0	.000	0	H	-0.1
Total	2	29	75	6	14	4	1	0	7	3	9	.187	.218	.267	26	-8	2	2	-1	.978	1	/1-18	-0.8

■ **JOHN HENRY** Henry, John Park "Bull" b: 12/26/1889, Amherst, Mass. d: 11/24/41, Fort Huachuca, Ariz. BR/TR, 6', 180 lbs. Deb: 7/8/10

YEAR	TM/L	G	AB	R	H	2B	3B	HR	RBI	BB	SO	AVG	OBP	SLG	PRO+	BR/A	SB	CS	SBR	FA	FR	G/POS	TPR
1918	Bos-N	43	102	6	21	2	0	0	4	10	15	.206	.283	.225	58	-5	0			.964	1	C-38	-0.1
Total	9	688	1920	161	397	54	15	2	171	244	189	.207	.303	.254	65	-79	55			.978	31	C-629/1-40	0.4

■ **BILLY HERMAN** Herman, William Jennings Bryan b: 7/7/09, New Albany, Ind. d: 9/5/92, W.Palm Beach, Fla. BR/TR, 5'11", 180 lbs. Deb: 8/29/31 MCH

YEAR	TM/L	G	AB	R	H	2B	3B	HR	RBI	BB	SO	AVG	OBP	SLG	PRO+	BR/A	SB	CS	SBR	FA	FR	G/POS	TPR
1946	Bos-N	75	252	32	77	23	1	3	22	43	13	.306	.409	.440	139	14	1			.956	-16	2-44,1-22/3	0.0
Total	15	1922	7707	1163	2345	486	82	47	839	737	428	.304	.367	.407	112	138	67			.967	71	*2-1813/3-71,1	31.7

■ **AL HERMANN** Hermann, Albert Bartel b: 3/28/1899, Milltown, N.J. d: 8/20/80, Lewes, Del. BR/TR, 6', 180 lbs. Deb: 7/17/23

YEAR	TM/L	G	AB	R	H	2B	3B	HR	RBI	BB	SO	AVG	OBP	SLG	PRO+	BR/A	SB	CS	SBR	FA	FR	G/POS	TPR
1923	Bos-N	31	93	2	22	4	0	0	11	0	7	.237	.237	.280	37	-9	3	2	-0	.957	-6	2-15/3-5,1	-1.4
1924	Bos-N	1	1	0	0	0	0	0	0	0	1	.000	.000	.000	-99	-0	0	0	0	.000	0	H	0.0
Total	2	32	94	2	22	4	0	0	11	0	8	.234	.234	.277	36	-9	3	2	-0	.967	-6	/2-15,3-5,1	-1.4

■ **REMY HERMOSO** Hermoso, Angel Remigio b: 10/1/46, Carabobo, Venezuela BR/TR, 5'8", 155 lbs. Deb: 9/14/67

YEAR	TM/L	G	AB	R	H	2B	3B	HR	RBI	BB	SO	AVG	OBP	SLG	PRO+	BR/A	SB	CS	SBR	FA	FR	G/POS	TPR
1967	Atl-N	11	26	3	8	0	0	0	0	2	4	.308	.357	.308	93	-0	1	0	0	.952	1	/S-9,2-2	0.2
Total	4	91	223	25	47	3	1	0	8	14	21	.211	.261	.233	42	-17	6	3	0	.968	12	/2-66,S-15,3	-0.0

■ **JOHN HERRNSTEIN** Herrnstein, John Ellett b: 3/31/38, Hampton, Va. BL/TL, 6'3", 215 lbs. Deb: 9/15/62

YEAR	TM/L	G	AB	R	H	2B	3B	HR	RBI	BB	SO	AVG	OBP	SLG	PRO+	BR/A	SB	CS	SBR	FA	FR	G/POS	TPR
1966	Atl-N	17	18	2	4	0	0	0	1	0	7	.222	.222	.222	24	-2	0	0	0	1.000	-1	/O-5	-0.3
Total	5	239	450	52	99	14	4	8	34	29	115	.220	.272	.322	67	-20	1	2	-1	.983	-26	/O-94,1-91	-5.5

YEAR	TM/L	G	AB	R	H	2B	3B	HR	RBI	BB	SO	AVG	OBP	SLG	PRO+	BR/A	SB	CS	SBR	FA	FR	G/POS	TPR

■ **EARL HERSH**   Hersh, Earl Walter b: 5/21/32, Ebbvale, Md. BL/TL, 6', 205 lbs. Deb: 9/4/56

| 1956 | Mil-N | 7 | 13 | 0 | 3 | 3 | 0 | 0 | 0 | 0 | 5 | .231 | .231 | .462 | 85 | -0 | 0 | 0 | 0 | .000 | -1 | /O-2 | -0.2 |

■ **BUCK HERZOG**   Herzog, Charles Lincoln b: 7/9/1885, Baltimore, Md. d: 9/4/53, Baltimore, Md. BR/TR, 5'11", 160 lbs. Deb: 4/17/08 M

1910	Bos-N	106	380	51	95	20	3	3	32	30	34	.250	.329	.342	92	-4	13			.915	4	*3-105	0.3
1911	Bos-N	79	294	53	91	19	5	5	41	33	21	.310	.398	.459	129	11	26			.934	8	S-74/3-4	2.4
1918	Bos-N	118	473	57	108	12	6	0	26	29	28	.228	.280	.279	74	-15	10			.961	4	2-99,1-12/S	-0.6
1919	Bos-N	73	275	27	77	8	5	1	25	13	11	.280	.327	.356	110	3	16			.953	-14	2-70/1-1	-0.9
Total	13	1493	5284	705	1370	191	75	20	445	427	307	.259	.329	.335	96	-27	312			.954	77	2-490,3-473,S/O1	11.3
Team	4	376	1422	188	371	59	19	9	124	105	94	.261	.328	.348	98	-5	65			.958	2	2-169,3-109/S1	1.2

■ **OTTO HESS**   Hess, Otto C. b: 10/10/1878, Bern, Switzerland d: 2/25/26, Tucson, Ariz. BL/TL, 6'1", 170 lbs. Deb: 8/3/02

1912	Bos-N	33	94	10	23	4	4	0	10	0	26	.245	.245	.372	66	-5	0			.951	-4	P-33	0.0
1913	Bos-N	35	83	9	26	0	1	2	11	7	15	.313	.367	.410	119	2	0			.945	1	P-29	0.0
1914	Bos-N	31	47	5	11	1	0	1	6	1	11	.234	.250	.319	69	-2	0			.947	1	P-14/1-5	-0.1
1915	Bos-N	5	5	1	2	1	0	0	1	0	2	.400	.400	.600	210	1	0			.800	-0	/P-4,1-1	0.0
Total	10	280	714	63	154	21	9	5	58	27	54	.216	.248	.291	64	-33	4			.941	-3	P-198/O-51,1	-1.2
Team	4	104	229	25	62	6	5	3	28	8	54	.271	.295	.380	89	-4	0			.944	-2	/P-80,1-6	-0.1

■ **MIKE HICKEY**   Hickey, Michael Francis b: 12/25/1871, Chicopee, Mass. d: 6/11/18, Springfield, Mass BR/TR, 5'10.5", 150 lbs. Deb: 9/14/1899

| 1899 | Bos-N | 1 | 3 | 0 | 1 | 0 | 0 | 0 | 0 | 0 | | .333 | .333 | .333 | 76 | -0 | 0 | | | .889 | 1 | /2-1 | 0.1 |

■ **CHARLIE HICKMAN**   Hickman, Charles Taylor "Cheerful Charlie" or "Piano Legs"
b: 3/4/1876, Taylortown, Dunkard Township, Pa. d: 4/19/34, Morgantown, W.Va. BR/TR, 5'11.5", 215 lbs. Deb: 9/8/1897

1897	*Bos-N	2	3	1	2	0	0	1	2	0		.667	.667	1.667	475	1	0			1.000	0	/P-2	0.0
1898	Bos-N	19	58	4	15	2	0	0	7	1		.259	.283	.293	62	-3	0			1.000	-1	/O-7,1-6,P	-0.3
1899	Bos-N	19	63	15	25	2	7	0	15	2		.397	.433	.651	178	6	1			.941	-2	P-11/O-7,1	0.1
Total	12	1081	3982	478	1176	217	91	59	614	153		.295	.331	.440	133	145	72			.968	-26	1-394,O-290,23/PS	9.8
Team	3	40	124	20	42	4	7	1	24	3		.339	.369	.508	134	5	1			.958	-3	/P-19,O-14,1	-0.2

■ **BILL HIGGINS**   Higgins, William Edward b: 9/8/1861, Wilmington, Del. d: 4/25/19, Wilmington, Del. TR , 5'9", 155 lbs. Deb: 8/9/1888

| 1888 | Bos-N | 14 | 54 | 5 | 10 | 1 | 0 | 0 | 4 | 1 | 3 | .185 | .200 | .204 | 28 | -4 | 1 | | | .906 | 5 | 2-14 | 0.2 |
| Total | 2 | 82 | 316 | 45 | 76 | 8 | 2 | 0 | 4 | 25 | 3 | .241 | .296 | .278 | 64 | -16 | 8 | | | .943 | 20 | /2-82 | 0.8 |

■ **ANDY HIGH**   High, Andrew Aird "Handy Andy" b: 11/21/1897, Ava, Ill. d: 2/22/81, Toledo, Ohio BL/TR, 5'6", 155 lbs. Deb: 4/12/22 FC

1925	Bos-N	60	219	31	63	11	4	0	28	24	2	.288	.361	.402	104	1	3	5	-2	.979	-9	3-60/2-1	-0.6
1926	Bos-N	130	476	55	141	17	10	2	66	39	9	.296	.351	.387	108	5	4			.962	-6	3-81,2-49	0.5
1927	Bos-N	113	384	59	116	15	9	4	46	26	11	.302	.350	.419	114	6	4			.915	-20	3-89/2-8,S	-0.9
Total	13	1314	4400	618	1250	195	65	44	482	425	130	.284	.350	.388	94	-33	33	25		.956	-125	3-790,2-287/S	-10.2
Team	3	303	1079	145	320	43	20	10	140	89	22	.297	.352	.401	109	12	11	5		.949	-36	3-230/2-58,S	-1.0

■ **OLIVER HILL**   Hill, Oliver Clinton b: 10/16/12, Powder Springs, Ga d: 9/20/70, Decatur, Ga. BL/TR, 5'11", 178 lbs. Deb: 4/19/39

| 1939 | Bos-N | 2 | 2 | 1 | 1 | 1 | 0 | 0 | 0 | 0 | 0 | .500 | .500 | 1.000 | 317 | 1 | 0 | | | .000 | 0 | H | 0.1 |

■ **MIKE HINES**   Hines, Michael P. b: 9/1862, Ireland d: 3/14/10, New Bedford, Mass. BR/TL, 5'10", 176 lbs. Deb: 5/1/1883

1883	Bos-N	63	231	38	52	13	1	0	16	7	36	.225	.248	.290	61	-11				.887	8	C-59/O-7	0.1
1884	Bos-N	35	132	16	23	3	0	0	3	3	24	.174	.193	.197	23	-11				.919	6	C-35	-0.2
1885	Bos-N	14	56	11	13	4	0	0	4	4	5	.232	.283	.304	93	-0				.857	-3	O-14	-0.4
1888	Bos-N	4	16	3	2	0	1	0	2	2	0	.125	.222	.250	49	-1	0			1.000	-0	/O-3,C-1	-0.1
Total	4	120	451	69	91	20	3	0	25	16	67	.202	.229	.259	51	-25	0			.896	9	/C-99,O-24	-0.9
Team	4	116	435	68	90	20	2	0	25	16	65	.207	.235	.262	54	-23	0			.897	11	/C-95,O-24	-0.6

■ **PAUL HINES**   Hines, Paul A. b: 3/1/1852, Washington, D.C. d: 7/10/35, Hyattsville, Md. BR/TR, 5'9.5", 173 lbs. Deb: 4/20/1872

1890	Bos-N	69	273	41	72	12	3	2	48	32	20	.264	.350	.352	97	-2	9			.881	-12	O-69/1-1	-1.4
Total	4 n	178	809	135	250	37	8	2	30	6	1	.309	.314	.382	121	18	0					O-123/2-42,1SC3	1.5
Total	16	1481	6253	1083	1881	368	84	56	751	366	304	.301	.343	.413	133	236	153			.887	-3	*O-1251,1-185/23SP	17.2

■ **JOHN HINTON**   Hinton, John Robert "Red" b: 6/20/1876, Pittsburgh, Pa. d: 7/19/20, Braddock, Pa. BR/TR, 6', 200 lbs. Deb: 6/3/01

| 1901 | Bos-N | 4 | 13 | 0 | 1 | 0 | 0 | 0 | 0 | 0 | 2 | .077 | .200 | .077 | -17 | -2 | 0 | | | .750 | -2 | /3-4 | -0.4 |

■ **JIM HITCHCOCK**   Hitchcock, James Franklin b: 6/28/11, Inverness, Ala. d: 6/23/59, Montgomery, Ala. BR/TR, 5'11", 175 lbs. Deb: 8/24/38 F

| 1938 | Bos-N | 28 | 76 | 2 | 13 | 0 | 0 | 0 | 7 | 2 | 11 | .171 | .192 | .171 | 1 | -10 | 1 | | | .881 | -2 | S-24/3-2 | -1.1 |

■ **RALPH HODGIN**   Hodgin, Elmer Ralph b: 2/10/16, Greensboro, N.C. BL/TR, 5'10", 170 lbs. Deb: 4/19/39

| 1939 | Bos-N | 32 | 48 | 4 | 10 | 1 | 0 | 0 | 4 | 3 | 4 | .208 | .255 | .229 | 33 | -5 | 0 | | | 1.000 | -1 | /O-9 | -0.6 |
| Total | 6 | 530 | 1689 | 198 | 481 | 79 | 24 | 4 | 188 | 97 | 63 | .285 | .330 | .367 | 98 | -10 | 7 | | | .985 | 7 | O-261,3-138 | -1.7 |

■ **STEW HOFFERTH**   Hofferth, Stewart Edward b: 1/27/13, Logansport, Ind. d: 3/7/94, Kouts, Ind. BR/TR, 6'2", 195 lbs. Deb: 4/19/44

1944	Bos-N	66	180	14	36	8	1	0	26	11	5	.200	.246	.261	41	-14	0			.984	0	C-47	-1.2
1945	Bos-N	50	170	13	40	2	0	3	15	14	11	.235	.297	.300	66	-8	1			.980	6	C-45	0.1
1946	Bos-N	20	58	3	12	1	1	0	10	3	6	.207	.246	.259	43	-4	0			1.000	-1	C-15	-0.5
Total	3	136	408	30	88	11	1	4	51	28	22	.216	.268	.277	52	-26	1			.985	6	C-107	-1.6

■ **IZZY HOFFMAN**   Hoffman, Harry C. b: 1/5/1875, Bridgeport, N.J. d: 11/13/42, Philadelphia, Pa. BL/TL, 5'9", 160 lbs. Deb: 4/14/04

| 1907 | Bos-N | 19 | 86 | 17 | 24 | 3 | 1 | 0 | 3 | 6 | | .279 | .326 | .337 | 108 | 1 | 2 | | | .897 | -2 | O-19 | -0.2 |
| Total | 2 | 29 | 116 | 18 | 27 | 4 | 1 | 0 | 4 | 8 | | .233 | .282 | .284 | 79 | -3 | 2 | | | .939 | -1 | /O-28 | -0.6 |

■ **SHANTY HOGAN**   Hogan, James Francis b: 3/21/06, Somerville, Mass. d: 4/7/67, Boston, Mass. BR/TR, 6'1", 240 lbs. Deb: 6/23/25

1925	Bos-N	9	21	2	6	1	1	0	3	1	3	.286	.318	.429	97	-0	0	0	0	1.000	-1	/O-5	-0.1
1926	Bos-N	4	14	1	4	1	1	0	5	0	0	.286	.286	.500	119	0	0			.852	1	/C-4	0.1
1927	Bos-N	71	229	24	66	17	1	3	32	9	23	.288	.324	.410	104	-0	2			.985	2	C-61	0.6
1933	Bos-N	96	328	15	83	7	0	3	30	13	9	.253	.288	.302	75	-12	0			.997	-1	C-95	-0.7
1934	Bos-N	92	279	20	73	5	2	4	34	16	13	.262	.316	.337	81	-8	0			.986	-2	C-90	-0.6
1935	Bos-N	59	163	9	49	8	0	2	25	21	8	.301	.394	.387	120	6	0			.990	-4	C-56	0.4
Total	13	989	3180	288	939	146	12	61	474	220	188	.295	.348	.406	101	1	6	2		.985	-26	C-908/O-5	3.2
Team	6	331	1034	71	281	39	5	12	129	60	56	.272	.322	.354	91	-14	2	0		.987	-6	C-306/O-5	-0.3

■ **WALTER HOLKE**   Holke, Walter Henry "Union Man" b: 12/25/1892, St.Louis, Mo. d: 10/12/54, St.Louis, Mo. BB/TL, 6'1.5", 185 lbs. Deb: 10/6/14 C

1919	Bos-N	137	518	48	151	14	6	0	48	21	25	.292	.325	.342	105	2	19			.993	6	*1-136	0.4
1920	Bos-N	144	551	53	162	15	11	3	64	28	31	.294	.329	.377	107	4	4	11	-5	.991	-3	*1-143	-0.8
1921	Bos-N	150	579	60	151	13	6	3	63	17	41	.261	.284	.337	67	-28	8	11	-4	.997	-1	*1-150	-3.4
1922	Bos-N	105	395	35	115	9	4	0	46	14	23	.291	.317	.334	71	-17	6	8	-3	.993	-4	*1-105	-2.7
Total	11	1212	4456	464	1278	153	58	24	487	191	304	.287	.318	.363	89	-74	81	50		.993	7	*1-1193/P-1	-13.5
Team	4	536	2043	196	579	53	31	6	221	80	120	.283	.313	.349	87	-39	37	30		.994	2	1-534	-6.5

■ **DUTCH HOLLAND**   Holland, Robert Clyde b: 10/12/03, Middlesex, N.C. d: 6/16/67, Lumberton, N.C. BR/TR, 6'1", 190 lbs. Deb: 8/16/32

| 1932 | Bos-N | 39 | 156 | 15 | 46 | 11 | 1 | 1 | 18 | 12 | 20 | .295 | .345 | .397 | 103 | 1 | 0 | | | .990 | 2 | O-39 | 0.0 |

YEAR	TM/L	G	AB	R	H	2B	3B	HR	RBI	BB	SO	AVG	OBP	SLG	PRO+	BR/A	SB	CS	SBR	FA	FR	G/POS	TPR
1933	Bos-N	13	31	3	8	3	0	0	3	3	8	.258	.324	.355	102	0	1			.867	-1	/O-7	-0.2
Total	3	102	315	37	86	26	2	3	34	28	39	.273	.332	.397	95	-3	1			.969	-3	/O-77	-1.0
Team	2	52	187	18	54	14	1	1	21	15	28	.289	.342	.390	103	1	1			.973	1	/O-46	-0.2
■ TOMMY HOLMES	Holmes, Thomas Francis "Kelly" b: 3/29/17, Brooklyn, N.Y. BL/TL, 5'10", 180 lbs. Deb: 4/14/42 M																						
1942	Bos-N	141	558	56	155	24	4	4	41	64	10	.278	.353	.357	110	8	2			.990	15	*O-140	1.7
1943	Bos-N	152	629	75	170	33	10	5	41	58	20	.270	.334	.378	107	5	7			.993	8	*O-152	0.5
1944	Bos-N	155	631	93	195	42	6	13	73	61	11	.309	.372	.456	127	22	4			.991	6	*O-155	2.0
1945	Bos-N†	154	636	125	**224**	**47**	6	**28**	117	70	9	.352	.420	**.577**	**175**	**62**	15			.983	1	*O-154	**5.4**
1946	Bos-N	149	568	80	176	35	6	6	79	58	14	.310	.377	.424	126	19	7			.987	8	*O-146	2.1
1947	Bos-N	150	618	90	**191**	33	3	9	53	44	16	.309	.360	.416	108	7	3			.989	10	*O-147	0.8
1948	*Bos-N★	139	585	85	190	35	7	6	61	46	20	.325	.375	.439	122	17	1			.983	3	*O-137	1.3
1949	Bos-N	117	380	47	101	20	4	8	59	39	6	.266	.337	.403	103	1	1			.987	5	*O-103	0.1
1950	Bos-N	105	322	44	96	20	1	9	51	33	8	.298	.370	.450	122	10	0			1.000	-0	O-88	0.6
1951	Bos-N	27	29	1	5	2	0	0	5	3	4	.172	.250	.241	35	-3	0	0	0	1.000	-1	/O-3,M	-0.4
Total	11	1320	4992	698	1507	292	47	88	581	480	122	.302	.366	.432	122	144	40	0		.989	53	*O-1231	13.5
Team	10	1289	4956	696	1503	291	47	88	580	476	118	.303	.367	.434	123	149	40	0		.989	54	*O-1225	14.1
■ ABIE HOOD	Hood, Albie Larrison b: 1/31/03, Sanford, N.C. d: 10/14/88, Chesapeake, Va. BL/TR, 5'7", 152 lbs. Deb: 7/15/25																						
1925	Bos-N	5	21	2	6	2	0	1	2	1	0	.286	.318	.524	122	0	0	0	0	.920	-4	/2-5	-0.3
■ JOHNNY HOPP	Hopp, John Leonard "Hippity" b: 7/18/16, Hastings, Neb. BL/TL, 5'10", 175 lbs. Deb: 9/18/39 C																						
1946	Bos-N★	129	445	71	148	23	8	3	48	34	34	.333	.386	.440	133	19	21			.981	-1	1-68,O-58	1.2
1947	Bos-N	134	430	74	124	20	2	2	32	58	30	.288	.376	.358	98	1	13			.980	-6	*O-125	-1.1
Total	14	1393	4260	698	1262	216	74	46	458	464	378	.296	.368	.414	113	79	128			.985	-36	O-717,1-479	-1.1
Team	2	263	875	145	272	43	10	5	80	92	64	.311	.381	.400	115	20	34			.986	-7	O-183/1-68	0.1
■ BOB HORNER	Horner, James Robert b: 8/6/57, Junction City, Kan. BR/TR, 6'1", 210 lbs. Deb: 6/16/78																						
1978	Atl-N	89	323	50	86	17	1	23	63	24	42	.266	.321	.539	123	8	0	0	0	.956	6	3-89	1.3
1979	Atl-N	121	487	66	153	15	1	33	98	22	74	.314	.348	.552	132	19	0	2	-1	.930	-7	3-82,1-45	0.8
1980	Atl-N	124	463	81	124	14	1	35	89	27	50	.268	.310	.529	126	13	3	1	0	.935	5	*3-121/1-1	1.7
1981	Atl-N	79	300	42	83	10	0	15	42	32	39	.277	.348	.460	125	9	2	3	-1	.938	-15	3-79	-0.9
1982	*Atl-N★	140	499	85	130	24	0	32	97	66	75	.261	.351	.501	131	20	3	5	-2	.970	-17	*3-137	-0.3
1983	Atl-N	104	386	75	117	25	1	20	68	50	63	.303	.384	.528	140	21	4	2	0	.958	-13	*3-104/1-1	0.7
1984	Atl-N	32	113	15	31	8	0	3	19	14	17	.274	.354	.425	110	2	0	0	0	.965	-1	3-32	0.1
1985	Atl-N	130	483	61	129	25	3	27	89	50	57	.267	.337	.499	123	14	1	1	-0	1.000	-10	1-87,3-40	-0.3
1986	Atl-N	141	517	70	141	22	0	27	87	52	72	.273	.342	.472	116	10	1	4	-2	.995	2	*1-139	0.0
Total	10	1020	3777	560	1047	169	8	218	685	369	512	.277	.344	.499	125	117	14	18	-7	.946	-50	3-684,1-330	2.8
Team	9	960	3571	545	994	160	7	215	652	337	489	.278	.343	.508	126	115	14	18	-7	.946	-50	3-684,1-273	3.1
■ ROGERS HORNSBY	Hornsby, Rogers "Rajah" b: 4/27/1896, Winters, Tex. d: 1/5/63, Chicago, Ill. BR/TR, 5'11", 175 lbs. Deb: 9/10/15 MCH																						
1928	Bos-N	140	486	99	188	42	7	21	94	**107**	41	**.387**	**.498**	**.632**	**204**	**80**	5			.973	-24	*2-140,M	**5.8**
Total	23	2259	8173	1579	2930	541	169	301	1584	1038	679	.358	.434	.577	176	874	135			.965	-91	*2-1561,S-356,3/10	81.1
■ JOE HORNUNG	Hornung, Michael Joseph "Ubbo Ubbo" b: 6/12/1857, Carthage, N.Y. d: 10/30/31, Howard Beach, N.Y. BR/TR, 5'8.5", 164 lbs. Deb: 5/1/1879 U																						
1881	Bos-N	83	324	40	78	12	8	2	25	5	25	.241	.252	.346	90	-4				**.948**	12	*O-83	0.6
1882	Bos-N	85	388	67	117	14	11	1	50	2	25	.302	.305	.402	124	10				**.932**	11	*O-84/1-1	1.8
1883	Bos-N	98	446	**107**	124	25	13	8	66	8	54	.278	.291	.446	117	8				**.936**	7	*O-98/3-1	1.2
1884	Bos-N	115	518	119	139	27	10	7	51	17	80	.268	.292	.400	116	8				.916	3	*O-110/1-6	0.8
1885	Bos-N	25	109	14	22	4	1	1	7	1	20	.202	.209	.284	61	-5				.919	-3	O-25	-0.8
1886	Bos-N	94	424	67	109	12	2	2	40	10	62	.257	.274	.309	80	-10	16			**.948**	7	*O-94	-0.5
1887	Bos-N	98	437	85	118	10	6	5	49	17	28	.270	.302	.355	82	-11	41			**.935**	13	*O-98	0.0
1888	Bos-N	107	431	61	103	11	7	3	53	16	39	.239	.269	.318	85	-8	29			.947	-8	*O-107	-1.9
Total	12	1123	4784	788	1230	172	90	31	564	120	498	.257	.277	.350	91	-64	159			.922	49	*O-1054/1-62,32SP	-4.1
Team	8	705	3077	560	810	115	58	29	341	76	333	.263	.282	.367	98	-12	86			.937	43	O-699/1-7,3	1.2
■ PETE HOTALING	Hotaling, Peter James "Monkey" b: 12/16/1856, Mohawk, N.Y. d: 7/3/28, Cleveland, Ohio BL/TR, 5'8", 166 lbs. Deb: 5/1/1879																						
1882	Bos-N	84	378	64	98	16	5	0	28	16	21	.259	.289	.328	97	-1				.865	2	*O-84	0.1
Total	9	840	3492	590	931	148	63	9	243	224	161	.267	.314	.353	108	38	78			.869	-11	O-825/C-13,23	0.7
■ SADIE HOUCK	Houck, Sargent Perry b: 3/1856, Washington, D.C. d: 5/26/19, Washington, D.C. BR/TR, 5'7", 151 lbs. Deb: 5/1/1879																						
1879	Bos-N	80	356	69	95	24	9	2	49	4	11	.267	.275	.402	117	6				.814	-8	O-47,S-33	-0.2
1880	Bos-N	12	47	2	7	0	0	0	2	0	6	.149	.149	.149	1	-5				.786	-1	O-12	-0.6
Total	8	641	2659	406	666	106	58	4	163	48	75	.250	.269	.338	91	-35	31			.863	39	S-526,O-109/2	1.1
Team	2	92	403	71	102	24	9	2	51	4	17	.253	.260	.372	105	1	0			.808	-9	/O-59,S-33	-0.8
■ BEN HOUSER	Houser, Benjamin Franklin b: 11/30/1883, Shenandoah, Pa. d: 1/15/52, Augusta, Maine BL/TL, 6'1", 185 lbs. Deb: 5/2/10																						
1911	Bos-N	20	71	11	18	1	0	1	9	8	6	.254	.329	.310	73	-2	2			.988	0	1-20	-0.2
1912	Bos-N	108	332	38	95	17	3	8	52	22	29	.286	.332	.428	105	1	1			.986	-3	1-83	-0.3
Total	3	162	472	58	126	21	5	9	68	37	35	.267	.322	.390	96	-4	3			.989	-3	1-129	-0.8
Team	2	128	403	49	113	18	3	9	61	30	35	.280	.332	.407	99	-2	3			.987	-3	1-103	-0.5
■ DEL HOWARD	Howard, George Elmer b: 12/24/1877, Kenney, Ill. d: 12/24/56, Seattle, Wash. BL/TR, 6', 180 lbs. Deb: 4/15/05 F																						
1906	Bos-N	147	545	46	142	19	8	1	54	26		.261	.306	.330	101	-1	17			.911	-12	O-87,2-45,S/1	-1.8
1907	Bos-N	50	187	20	51	4	2	1	13	11		.273	.330	.332	108	2	11			.969	-3	O-45/2-3	-0.3
Total	5	536	1833	199	482	54	22	6	193	111		.263	.318	.326	98	-5	67			.946	-30	O-249,1-187/2SP	-5.5
Team	2	197	732	66	193	23	10	2	67	37		.264	.313	.331	103	1	28			.929	-14	O-132/2-48,S1	-2.1
■ LARRY HOWARD	Howard, Lawrence Rayford b: 6/6/45, Columbus, Ohio BR/TR, 6'3", 200 lbs. Deb: 8/9/70																						
1973	Atl-N	4	8	0	1	0	0	0	0	2	3	.125	.300	.125	20	-1	0	0	0	1.000	-0	/C-2	-0.1
Total	4	133	365	36	86	19	0	6	47	37	85	.236	.306	.337	81	-9	0	1		.986	-4	C-123/O-2,1	-1.0
■ WALT HRINIAK	Hriniak, Walter John b: 5/22/43, Natick, Mass. BL/TR, 5'11", 180 lbs. Deb: 9/10/68 C																						
1968	Atl-N	9	26	0	9	0	0	0	3	0	3	.346	.346	.346	108	0	0	0	0	.967	3	/C-9	0.4
1969	Atl-N	7	7	0	1	0	0	0	0	2	1	.143	.333	.143	38	-0	0	0	0	1.000	-1	/C-6	-0.1
Total	2	47	99	4	25	0	0	0	4	10	15	.253	.333	.253	71	-3	0	0	0	.977	-0	/C-34	-0.1
Team	2	16	33	0	10	0	0	0	3	2	4	.303	.343	.303	92	-0	0	0	0	.971	2	/C-15	0.3
■ GLENN HUBBARD	Hubbard, Glenn Dee b: 9/25/57, Hahn Air Force Base, Germany BR/TR, 5'7", 180 lbs. Deb: 7/14/78																						
1978	Atl-N	44	163	15	42	4	0	2	13	10	20	.258	.309	.319	68	-7	2	1	0	.979	3	2-44	0.0
1979	Atl-N	97	325	34	75	12	0	3	29	27	43	.231	.292	.295	56	-19	0	6	-4	.968	5	2-91	-1.3
1980	Atl-N	117	431	55	107	21	3	9	43	49	69	.248	.325	.374	91	-5	7	5	-1	.978	19	*2-117	2.2
1981	Atl-N	99	361	39	85	13	5	6	33	33	59	.235	.303	.349	82	-8	4	2	0	.991	-4	2-98	-0.7
1982	*Atl-N	145	532	75	132	25	1	9	59	59	62	.248	.327	.350	86	-9	4	3	-1	.983	20	*2-144	1.8
1983	Atl-N★	148	517	65	136	24	6	12	70	55	71	.263	.339	.402	97	-2	3	8	-4	.985	22	*2-148	2.4
1984	Atl-N	120	397	53	93	27	2	9	43	55	61	.234	.333	.380	93	-3	4	1	1	.988	20	*2-117	2.2

YEAR	TM/L	G	AB	R	H	2B	3B	HR	RBI	BB	SO	AVG	OBP	SLG	PRO+	BR/A	SB	CS	SBR	FA	FR	G/POS	TPR
1985	Atl-N	142	439	51	102	21	0	5	39	56	54	.232	.325	.314	75	-13	4	3	-1	.989	**62**	*2-140	5.4
1986	Atl-N	143	408	42	94	16	1	4	36	66	74	.230	.343	.304	76	-11	3	2	-0	.976	**41**	*2-142	3.5
1987	Atl-N	141	443	69	117	33	2	5	38	77	57	.264	.380	.381	98	1	1	1	-0	.986	**28**	*2-139	3.5
Total	12	1354	4441	545	1084	214	22	70	448	539	640	.244	.330	.349	85	-83	35	35	-11	.983	229	*2-1332/D-4	20.2
Team	10	1196	4016	498	983	196	20	64	403	487	570	.245	.331	.351	84	-77	32	32	-10	.983	215	*2-1180	19.0
■ OTTO HUBER Huber, Otto b: 3/12/14, Garfield, N.J. d: 4/9/89, Passaic, N.J. BR/TR, 5'10", 165 lbs. Deb: 6/10/39																							
1939	Bos-N	11	22	2	6	1	0	0	3	0	1	.273	.273	.318	63	-1	0			1.000	-0	/2-4,3-4	-0.1
■ BILL HUNNEFIELD Hunnefield, William Fenton "Wild Bill" b: 1/5/1899, Dedham, Mass. d: 8/28/76, Nantucket, Mass. BB/TR, 5'10", 165 lbs. Deb: 4/17/26																							
1931	Bos-N	11	21	2	6	0	0	0	1	0	2	.286	.286	.286	56	-1	0			.864	2	/3-5,2-4	0.1
Total	6	511	1664	230	452	75	9	9	144	117	111	.272	.322	.344	76	-60	67			.925	-67	S-230,2-204/31	-9.4
■ BRIAN HUNTER Hunter, Brian Ronald b: 3/4/68, Torrance, Cal. BR/TL, 6', 195 lbs. Deb: 5/31/91																							
1991	*Atl-N	97	271	32	68	16	1	12	50	17	48	.251	.298	.450	101	-1	0	2	-1	.988	-4	1-85/O-6	-1.1
1992	*Atl-N	102	238	34	57	13	2	14	41	21	50	.239	.301	.487	113	3	1	2	-1	.997	3	1-92/O-6	0.1
1993	Atl-N	37	80	4	11	3	1	0	8	2	15	.138	.159	.200	-5	-12	0	0	0	.994	0	1-29/O-2	-1.3
Total	5	361	924	113	213	54	5	42	165	68	190	.231	.285	.436	90	-16	3	5	-2	.991	-1	1-289/O-28	-3.7
Team	3	236	589	70	136	32	4	26	99	40	113	.231	.281	.431	92	-9	1	4	-2	.992	-0	1-206/O-14	-2.3
■ JERRY HURLEY Hurley, Jeremiah Joseph b: 6/15/1863, Boston, Mass. d: 9/17/50, Boston, Mass. BR/TR, 6', 190 lbs. Deb: 5/1/1889																							
1889	Bos-N	1	4	0	0	0	0	0	0	0	0	.000	.000	.000	-94	-1	0			.000	-1	/O-1,C-1	-0.2
Total	3	33	92	15	20	4	2	0	8	14	18	.217	.321	.304	72	-3	2			.943	-5	/C-32,O-3,1	-0.5
■ WARREN HUSTON Huston, Warren Llewellyn b: 10/31/13, Newtonville, Mass. BR/TR, 6', 170 lbs. Deb: 6/24/37																							
1944	Bos-N	33	55	7	11	1	0	0	1	8	5	.200	.313	.218	49	-3	0			.979	3	3-20/2-5,S	0.0
Total	2	71	109	12	18	4	0	0	4	10	14	.165	.242	.202	19	-13	0			.964	11	/3-22,2-21,S	-0.1
■ ALEXIS INFANTE Infante, Fermin Alexis (Carpio) b: 12/4/61, Barquisimeto, Venez. BR/TR, 5'10", 175 lbs. Deb: 9/27/87																							
1990	Atl-N	20	28	3	1	1	0	0	0	0	7	.036	.069	.071	-58	-6	0	0	0	.964	4	2-10/3-4,S	-0.2
Total	4	60	55	11	6	1	0	0	0	2	12	.109	.155	.127	-20	-9	1	0		.933	9	/3-17,S-14,2D	0.1
■ SCOTTY INGERTON Ingerton, William John b: 4/19/1886, Peninsula, Ohio d: 6/15/56, Cleveland, Ohio BR/TR, 6'1", 172 lbs. Deb: 4/12/11																							
1911	Bos-N	136	521	63	130	24	4	5	61	39	68	.250	.304	.340	74	-20	6			.942	18	3-58,O-43,12/S	-0.3
■ FRED JACKLITSCH Jacklitsch, Frederick Lawrence b: 5/24/1876, Brooklyn, N.Y. d: 7/18/37, Brooklyn, N.Y. BR/TR, 5'9", 180 lbs. Deb: 6/6/00																							
1917	Bos-N	1	0	0	0	0	0	0	0	0	0	—	—	—	—	0	0			1.000	-0	/C-1	0.0
Total	13	490	1344	160	327	64	12	5	153	201	100	.243	.349	.320	91	-8	35			.978	-14	C-397/1-19,2O3S	1.5
■ GEORGE JACKSON Jackson, George Christopher "Hickory" b: 10/14/1882, Springfield, Mo. d: 11/25/72, Cleburne, Tex. BR/TR, 6'0.5", 180 lbs. Deb: 8/2/11																							
1911	Bos-N	39	147	28	51	11	2	0	25	12	21	.347	.404	.449	128	5	12			.929	-2	O-39	0.1
1912	Bos-N	110	397	55	104	13	5	4	48	38	72	.262	.342	.350	88	-6	22			.943	2	*O-107	-1.0
1913	Bos-N	3	10	2	3	0	0	0	0	0	2	.300	.300	.300	70	-0	0			.875	0	/O-3	0.0
Total	3	152	554	85	158	24	7	4	73	50	95	.285	.357	.375	98	-1	34			.938	-0	O-149	-0.9
■ SONNY JACKSON Jackson, Roland Thomas b: 7/9/44, Washington, D.C. BL/TR, 5'9", 155 lbs. Deb: 9/27/63 C																							
1968	Atl-N	105	358	37	81	8	2	1	19	25	35	.226	.282	.268	66	-14	16	6	1	.952	-17	S-99	-2.4
1969	*Atl-N	98	318	41	76	3	5	1	27	35	33	.239	.318	.289	71	-11	12	7	-1	.961	-23	S-97	-2.6
1970	Atl-N	103	328	60	85	14	3	0	20	45	27	.259	.350	.320	76	-10	11	4	1	.933	-23	S-87	-2.1
1971	Atl-N	149	547	58	141	20	5	2	25	35	45	.258	.304	.324	73	-19	7	6	-2	.980	3	*O-145	-2.7
1972	Atl-N	60	126	20	30	6	3	0	8	7	9	.238	.278	.333	67	-6	1	0	0	.976	-6	S-17,O-10/3	-1.0
1973	Atl-N	117	206	29	43	5	2	0	12	22	13	.209	.288	.252	47	-14	6	3	0	.981	-14	O-56,S-36	-2.7
1974	Atl-N	5	7	0	3	0	0	0	0	0	0	.429	.429	.429	134	0	0	1	-1	1.000	0	/O-1	0.0
Total	12	936	3055	396	767	81	28	7	162	250	265	.251	.310	.303	73	-104	126	51		.949	-104	S-630,O-212/3	-15.6
Team	7	637	1890	245	459	56	20	4	111	169	162	.243	.308	.300	69	-74	53	27		.952	-80	S-336,O-212/3	-13.5
■ SAM JACKSON Jackson, Samuel b: 3/24/1849, Ripon, England d: 8/4/1893, Clifton Springs, N.Y. BR/TR, 5'5.5", 160 lbs. Deb: 5/16/1871																							
1871	Bos-n	16	76	17	17	5	3	0	11	1	4	.224	.234	.368	67	-4	0					2-14/O-1	-0.3
Total	2 n	19	88	17	19	6	3	0	11	1	4	.216	.225	.352	61	-5						/2-14,O-4	-0.4
■ BROOK JACOBY Jacoby, Brook Wallace b: 11/23/59, Philadelphia, Pa. BR/TR, 5'11", 195 lbs. Deb: 9/13/81																							
1981	Atl-N	11	10	0	2	0	0	0	1	0	3	.200	.200	.200	13	-1	0	0	0	1.000	2	/3-3	0.1
1983	Atl-N	4	8	0	0	0	0	0	0	0	1	.000	.000	.000	-93	-2	0	0	0	1.000	-1	/3-2	-0.3
Total	11	1311	4520	535	1220	204	24	120	545	439	764	.270	.337	.405	104	22	16	25	-10	.958	-71	*3-1166,1-153/D2S	-8.1
Team	2	15	18	0	2	0	0	0	1	0	4	.111	.111	.111	-36	-3	0	0	0	1.000	1	/3-5	-0.2
■ DION JAMES James, Dion b: 11/9/62, Philadelphia, Pa. BL/TL, 6'1", 170 lbs. Deb: 9/16/83																							
1987	Atl-N	134	494	80	154	37	6	10	61	70	63	.312	.399	.472	124	19	10	8	-2	**.996**	1	*O-126	1.3
1988	Atl-N	132	386	46	99	17	5	3	30	58	59	.256	.355	.350	98	1	9	9	-3	.987	-12	*O-120	-1.9
1989	Atl-N	63	170	15	44	7	0	1	11	25	23	.259	.357	.318	92	-1	1	3	-2	1.000	-0	O-46/1-8	-0.4
Total	10	911	2696	361	779	142	21	32	266	317	305	.289	.366	.393	108	37	42	38	-10	.986	-50	O-678/D-75,1	-4.8
Team	3	329	1050	141	297	61	11	14	102	153	145	.283	.376	.402	110	19	20	20	-6	.993	-12	O-292/1-8	-1.0
■ BERNIE JAMES James, Robert Byrne b: 9/2/05, Angleton, Tex. d: 8/1/94, San Antonio, Tex. BB/TR, 5'9.5", 150 lbs. Deb: 5/6/29																							
1929	Bos-N	46	101	12	31	3	2	0	9	9	13	.307	.369	.376	89	-2	3			.940	-9	2-32/O-1	-0.9
1930	Bos-N	8	11	1	2	1	0	0	1	0	1	.182	.182	.273	8	-2	0			.941	0	/2-7	-0.1
Total	3	114	237	35	61	6	3	1	20	17	26	.257	.310	.321	70	-10	8			.944	-7	/2-65,S-6,3O	-1.3
Team	2	54	112	13	33	4	2	0	10	9	14	.295	.352	.366	81	-3	3			.940	-9	/2-39,O-1	-1.0
■ SAM JETHROE Jethroe, Samuel "Jet" b: 1/20/18, E.St.Louis, Ill. BB/TR, 6'1", 178 lbs. Deb: 4/18/50																							
1950	Bos-N	141	582	100	159	28	8	18	58	52	93	.273	.338	.442	110	7	**35**			.969	8	*O-141	0.9
1951	Bos-N	148	572	101	160	29	10	18	65	57	88	.280	.356	.460	127	20	**35**	5	**8**	.974	7	*O-140	2.9
1952	Bos-N	151	608	79	141	23	7	13	58	68	112	.232	.318	.357	90	-8	28	9	3	.970	4	*O-151	-0.8
Total	4	442	1763	280	460	80	25	49	181	177	293	.261	.337	.418	108	18	98	14		.971	19	O-433	2.9
Team	3	440	1762	280	460	80	25	49	181	177	293	.261	.337	.418	109	19	98	14		.971	19	O-432	3.0
■ DAVEY JOHNSON Johnson, David Allen b: 1/30/43, Orlando, Fla. BR/TR, 6'1", 180 lbs. Deb: 4/13/65 M																							
1973	Atl-N★	157	559	84	151	25	0	43	99	81	93	.270	.371	.546	140	30	5	3	-0	.966	-3	*2-156	3.7
1974	Atl-N	136	454	56	114	18	0	15	62	75	59	.251	.361	.390	105	5	1	2	-1	.993	7	1-73,2-71	1.0
1975	Atl-N	1	1	0	1	1	0	0	1	0	0	1.000	1.000	2.000	691	1	0	0	0	.000	0	H	0.1
Total	13	1435	4797	564	1252	242	18	136	609	559	675	.261	.343	.404	110	66	33	25	-5	.980	10	*2-1198,1-123/S3	15.6
Team	3	294	1014	140	266	44	0	58	162	156	152	.262	.367	.477	126	36	6	5	-1	.970	4	2-227/1-73	4.8
■ DERON JOHNSON Johnson, Deron Roger b: 7/17/38, San Diego, Cal. d: 4/23/92, Poway, Cal. BR/TR, 6'2", 209 lbs. Deb: 9/20/60 C																							
1968	Atl-N	127	342	29	71	11	1	8	33	35	79	.208	.287	.316	81	-8	0	1	-1	.996	-1	1-97,3-21	-1.8
Total	16	1765	5941	706	1447	247	33	245	923	585	1318	.244	.313	.420	102	9	11	18	-8	.993	-63	1-880,3-332,DO	-14.9

YEAR	TM/L	G	AB	R	H	2B	3B	HR	RBI	BB	SO	AVG	OBP	SLG	PRO+	BR/A	SB	CS	SBR	FA	FR	G/POS	TPR

■ LOU JOHNSON Johnson, Louis Brown "Slick" b: 9/22/34, Lexington, Ky. BR/TR, 5'11", 175 lbs. Deb: 4/17/60

| 1962 | Mil-N | 61 | 117 | 22 | 33 | 4 | 5 | 2 | 13 | 11 | 27 | .282 | .349 | .453 | 116 | 3 | 6 | 1 | 1 | 1.000 | -9 | O-55 | -0.7 |
| Total | 8 | 677 | 2049 | 244 | 529 | 97 | 14 | 48 | 232 | 110 | 320 | .258 | .313 | .389 | 103 | 5 | 50 | 24 | 1 | .981 | -19 | O-606 | -4.2 |

■ RANDY JOHNSON Johnson, Randall Glenn b: 6/10/56, Escondido, Cal. BR/TR, 6'1", 190 lbs. Deb: 4/27/82

1982	Atl-N	27	46	5	11	5	0	0	6	6	4	.239	.352	.348	93	-0	0	1	-1	.955	5	2-13/3-4	0.5
1983	Atl-N	86	144	22	36	3	0	1	17	20	27	.250	.345	.292	73	-5	1	3	-2	.991	10	3-53/2-4	0.4
1984	Atl-N	91	294	28	82	13	0	5	30	21	21	.279	.329	.374	91	-4	4	7	-3	.939	5	3-81	-0.3
Total	3	204	484	55	129	21	0	6	53	47	52	.267	.336	.347	85	-8	5	11	-5	.956	20	3-138/2-17	0.6

■ BOB JOHNSON Johnson, Robert Wallace b: 3/4/36, Omaha, Neb. BR/TR, 5'10", 175 lbs. Deb: 4/19/60

| 1968 | Atl-N | 59 | 187 | 15 | 49 | 5 | 1 | 0 | 11 | 10 | 20 | .262 | .299 | .299 | 80 | -5 | 0 | 0 | 0 | .948 | 1 | 3-48/2-4 | -0.3 |
| Total | 11 | 874 | 2307 | 254 | 628 | 88 | 11 | 44 | 230 | 156 | 291 | .272 | .321 | .377 | 95 | -18 | 24 | 12 | 0 | .956 | -26 | S-201,2-167,31/O | -2.4 |

■ ROY JOHNSON Johnson, Roy Cleveland b: 2/23/03, Pryor, Okla. d: 9/10/73, Tacoma, Wash. BL/TR, 5'9", 175 lbs. Deb: 4/18/29 F

1937	Bos-N	85	260	24	72	8	3	3	22	38	29	.277	.369	.365	110	5	5			.965	-1	O-63/3-1	0.2
1938	Bos-N	7	29	2	5	0	0	0	1	1	5	.172	.200	.172	4	-4	1			.769	-2	/O-7	-0.6
Total	10	1155	4359	717	1292	275	83	58	556	489	380	.296	.369	.437	107	43	135			.938	22	*O-1066/3-1	-0.1
Team	2	92	289	26	77	8	3	3	23	39	34	.266	.354	.346	100	1	6			.948	-3	/O-70,3-1	-0.4

■ JIMMY JOHNSTON Johnston, James Harle b: 12/10/1889, Cleveland, Tenn. d: 2/14/67, Chattanooga, Tenn. BR/TR, 5'10", 160 lbs. Deb: 5/3/11 FC

| 1926 | Bos-N | 23 | 57 | 7 | 14 | 1 | 0 | 1 | 5 | 10 | 3 | .246 | .348 | .316 | 91 | -0 | 2 | | | .865 | -4 | 3-14/2-2,O | -0.3 |
| Total | 13 | 1377 | 5070 | 754 | 1493 | 185 | 75 | 22 | 410 | 391 | 246 | .294 | .347 | .374 | 100 | 7 | 169 | | | .926 | 10 | 3-448,O-354,2S/1 | 3.1 |

■ DICK JOHNSTON Johnston, Richard Frederick b: 4/6/1863, Kingston, N.Y. d: 4/4/34, Detroit, Mich. BR/TR, 5'8", 155 lbs. Deb: 8/12/1884

1885	Bos-N	26	111	17	26	6	3	1	23	0	15	.234	.234	.369	96	-1				.842	1	O-26	0.0
1886	Bos-N	109	413	48	99	18	9	1	57	3	70	.240	.245	.334	78	-12	11			.892	17	*O-109	0.2
1887	Bos-N	127	507	87	131	13	20	5	77	16	35	.258	.281	.393	85	-12	52			.933	25	*O-127	0.9
1888	Bos-N	135	585	102	173	31	18	12	68	15	33	.296	.314	.472	145	27	35			.898	7	*O-135	2.9
1889	Bos-N	132	539	80	123	16	4	5	67	41	60	.228	.285	.301	60	-31	34			.917	-7	*O-132	-3.6
Total	8	746	2992	453	751	109	68	33	386	133	283	.251	.285	.366	87	-63	151			.903	54	O-743/S-4	-2.0
Team	5	529	2155	334	552	84	54	24	292	75	213	.256	.282	.379	93	-28	132			.908	43	O-529	0.4

■ CHARLEY JONES Jones, Charles Wesley "Baby" (b: Benjamin Wesley Rippay) b: 4/30/1850, Alamance Co., N.C. BR/TR, 5'11.5", 202 lbs. Deb: 5/4/1875 U

1879	Bos-N	83	355	85	112	22	10	9	62	29	38	.315	.367	.510	182	31				.933	12	*O-83	3.5
1880	Bos-N	66	280	44	84	15	3	5	37	11	27	.300	.326	.429	159	17				.826	-4	*O-66	1.0
Total	11	881	3687	728	1101	170	98	56	219	237	124	.299	.347	.443	150	206	19			.882	51	O-872/1-11,P	20.7
Team	2	149	635	129	196	37	13	14	99	40	65	.309	.350	.474	172	48	0			.888	8	O-149	4.5

■ CHIPPER JONES Jones, Larry Wayne b: 4/24/72, DeLand, Fla. BB/TR, 6'3", 185 lbs. Deb: 9/11/93

1993	Atl-N	8	3	2	2	1	0	0	0	1	1	.667	.750	1.000	360	1	0	0	0	1.000	1	/S-3	0.2
1995	*Atl-N	140	524	87	139	22	3	23	86	73	99	.265	.355	.450	108	6	8	4	0	.931	3	*3-123,O-20	0.9
Total	2	148	527	89	141	23	3	23	86	74	100	.268	.358	.454	110	8	8	4	0	.750	3	3-123/O-20,S	1.1

■ MACK JONES Jones, Mack "Mack The Knife" b: 11/6/38, Atlanta, Ga. BL/TR, 6'1", 180 lbs. Deb: 7/13/61

1961	Mil-N	28	104	13	24	3	2	0	12	12	28	.231	.322	.298	70	-4	4	4	-1	1.000	-2	O-26	-0.9
1962	Mil-N	91	333	51	85	17	4	10	36	44	100	.255	.354	.420	110	5	5	1	1	.973	-8	O-91	-0.7
1963	Mil-N	93	228	36	50	11	4	3	22	26	59	.219	.318	.342	91	-2	8	4	0	.978	-8	O-80	-1.4
1965	Mil-N	143	504	78	132	18	7	31	75	29	122	.262	.314	.510	127	16	8	2	1	.980	-10	*O-133	0.1
1966	Atl-N	118	417	60	110	14	1	23	66	39	85	.264	.338	.468	120	11	16	10	-1	.981	-3	*O-112/1-1	0.2
1967	Atl-N	140	454	72	115	23	4	17	50	64	108	.253	.357	.434	127	17	10	6	-1	.985	2	*O-126	1.3
Total	10	1002	3091	485	778	132	31	133	415	383	756	.252	.349	.444	120	86	65	40	-5	.976	-35	O-871/1-1	0.4
Team	6	613	2040	310	516	86	22	84	261	214	502	.253	.336	.440	116	43	51	27	-1	.981	-28	O-568/1-1	-1.4

■ NIPPY JONES Jones, Vernal Leroy b: 6/29/25, Los Angeles, Cal. d: 10/3/95, Sacramento, Cal. BR/TR, 6'1", 185 lbs. Deb: 6/8/46

| 1957 | *Mil-N | 30 | 79 | 5 | 21 | 2 | 1 | 2 | 8 | 3 | 7 | .266 | .293 | .392 | 88 | -2 | 0 | 0 | 0 | .994 | -0 | 1-20/O-1 | -0.3 |
| Total | 8 | 412 | 1381 | 146 | 369 | 60 | 12 | 25 | 209 | 71 | 102 | .267 | .304 | .382 | 81 | -40 | 4 | 2 | 0 | .987 | -19 | 1-333/2-16,O | -6.5 |

■ BILL JONES Jones, William Dennis "Midget" b: 4/8/1887, Hartland, N.B., Can. d: 10/10/46, Boston, Mass. BL/TR, 5'6.5", 157 lbs. Deb: 6/20/11

1911	Bos-N	24	51	6	11	2	1	0	3	15	7	.216	.394	.294	89	-0	1			.867	-1	O-18	0.0
1912	Bos-N	3	2	0	1	0	0	0	2	0	1	.500	.500	.500	171	0	0			.000	0	H	0.0
Total	2	27	53	6	12	2	1	0	5	15	8	.226	.397	.302	89	-0	1			.857	-1	/O-18	-0.2

■ EDDIE JOOST Joost, Edwin David b: 6/5/16, San Francisco, Cal BR/TR, 6', 175 lbs. Deb: 9/11/36 M

1943	Bos-N	124	421	34	78	16	3	2	20	68	80	.185	.299	.252	61	-20	5			.945	13	3-67,2-60/S	-0.3
1945	Bos-N	35	141	16	35	7	1	0	9	13	7	.248	.312	.312	73	-5	0			.945	-7	2-19,3-16	-1.1
Total	17	1574	5606	874	1339	238	35	134	601	1043	827	.239	.361	.366	99	18	61			.958	-20	*S-1296,2-166/31	8.4
Team	2	159	562	50	113	23	4	2	29	81	87	.201	.302	.267	64	-25	5			.935	6	/3-83,2-79,S	-1.4

■ BUCK JORDAN Jordan, Baxter Byerly b: 1/16/07, Cooleemee, N.C. d: 3/18/93, Salisbury, N.C. BL/TR, 6', 170 lbs. Deb: 9/15/27

1932	Bos-N	49	212	27	68	12	3	2	29	4	5	.321	.333	.434	109	2	1			.991	-1	1-49	-0.3
1933	Bos-N	152	588	77	168	29	9	4	46	34	22	.286	.327	.386	112	7	4			.991	-3	*1-150	-1.1
1934	Bos-N	124	489	68	152	26	9	2	58	35	19	.311	.358	.413	114	9	3			.989	-1	*1-117	-0.4
1935	Bos-N	130	470	62	131	24	5	5	35	19	17	.279	.307	.383	91	-7	3			.983	1	1-95/3-8,O	-1.6
1936	Bos-N	138	555	81	179	27	5	3	66	45	22	.323	.375	.405	118	14	2			.993	1	*1-136	0.2
1937	Bos-N	8	8	1	2	0	0	0	0	0	0	.250	.250	.250	40	-1	0			.000	0	H	-0.1
Total	10	811	2980	396	890	153	35	17	281	182	109	.299	.340	.391	106	18	20			.990	-12	1-648/3-66,O	-5.7
Team	6	601	2322	316	700	118	31	16	234	137	85	.301	.342	.400	109	25	13			.990	-5	1-547/3-8,O	-3.3

■ MIKE JORGENSEN Jorgensen, Michael b: 8/16/48, Passaic, N.J. BL/TL, 6', 195 lbs. Deb: 9/10/68 M

1983	Atl-N	57	48	5	12	1	0	1	8	8	8	.250	.357	.333	86	-1	0	0	0	1.000	-0	1-19/O-6	-0.1
1984	Atl-N	31	26	4	7	1	0	0	5	3	6	.269	.345	.308	79	-1	0	0	-1	1.000	-0	/1-8,O-4	-0.0
Total	17	1633	3421	429	833	132	13	95	426	532	589	.243	.349	.373	100	10	58	44		.994	21	*1-1052,O-283/D	-3.6
Team	2	88	74	9	19	2	0	1	13	11	14	.257	.353	.324	84	-1	0	1		1.000	-1	/1-27,O-10	-0.4

■ DAVID JUSTICE Justice, David Christopher b: 4/14/66, Cincinnati, Ohio BL/TL, 6'3", 195 lbs. Deb: 5/24/89

1989	Atl-N	16	51	7	12	3	0	1	3	3	9	.235	.291	.353	81	-1	2	1	0	1.000	-1	O-16	-0.3
1990	Atl-N	127	439	76	124	23	2	28	78	64	92	.282	.374	.535	139	23	11	6	-0	.981	-2	1-69,O-61	1.5
1991	*Atl-N	109	396	67	109	25	1	21	87	65	81	.275	.381	.503	138	21	8	8	-2	.968	5	*O-106	2.2
1992	*Atl-N	144	484	78	124	19	5	21	72	79	85	.256	.363	.446	121	14	2	4	-2	.976	14	*O-140	2.5
1993	*Atl-N★	157	585	90	158	15	4	40	120	78	90	.270	.359	.515	129	24	3	5	-2	.985	9	*O-157	2.7
1994	*Atl-N★	104	352	61	110	16	2	19	59	69	45	.313	.428	.531	144	26	2	4	-2	.947	2	*O-102	2.3
1995	*Atl-N	120	411	73	104	17	2	24	78	73	68	.253	.368	.479	118	12	4	2	0	.984	7	*O-120	1.5
Total	7	777	2718	452	741	118	16	154	497	431	470	.273	.375	.498	130	119	32	30	-8	.974	33	O-702/1-69	12.4

YEAR	TM/L	G	AB	R	H	2B	3B	HR	RBI	BB	SO	AVG	OBP	SLG	PRO+	BR/A	SB	CS	SBR	FA	FR	G/POS	TPR

■ BOB KAHLE Kahle, Robert Wayne b: 11/23/15, Newcastle, Ind. d: 12/16/88, Inglewood, Cal. BR/TR, 6', 170 lbs. Deb: 4/21/38

| 1938 | Bos-N | 8 | 3 | 2 | 1 | 0 | 0 | 0 | 0 | 0 | 0 | .333 | .333 | .333 | 93 | -0 | 0 | | | .000 | 0 | H | 0.0 |

■ OWEN KAHN Kahn, Owen Earle "Jack" b: 6/5/05, Richmond, Va. d: 1/17/81, Richmond, Va. BR/TR, 5'11", 160 lbs. Deb: 5/24/30

| 1930 | Bos-N | 1 | 0 | 1 | 0 | 0 | 0 | 0 | 0 | 0 | 0 | — | — | — | — | 0 | 0 | | | .000 | 0 | R | 0.0 |

■ AL KAISER Kaiser, Alfred Edward "Deerfoot" b: 8/3/1886, Cincinnati, Ohio d: 4/11/69, Cincinnati, Ohio BR/TR, 5'9", 165 lbs. Deb: 4/18/11

1911	Bos-N	66	197	20	40	5	2	2	15	10	26	.203	.249	.279	44	-15	4			.922	-6	O-58	-2.4
1912	Bos-N	4	13	0	0	0	0	0	0	0	3	.000	.000	.000	-98	-4	0			.900	0	/O-4	-0.4
Total	3	155	481	58	104	15	7	3	38	34	82	.216	.274	.295	50	-34	16			.917	-12	O-134/1-1	-5.4
Team	2	70	210	20	40	5	2	2	15	10	29	.190	.234	.262	36	-19	4			.921	-6	/O-62	-2.8

■ TOM KANE Kane, Thomas Joseph "Sugar" b: 12/15/06, Chicago, Ill. d: 11/26/73, Chicago, Ill. BR/TR, 5'10.5", 160 lbs. Deb: 8/3/38

| 1938 | Bos-N | 2 | 2 | 0 | 0 | 0 | 0 | 0 | 0 | 2 | 0 | .000 | .500 | .000 | 53 | -1 | 0 | | | 1.000 | -1 | /2-2 | -0.1 |

■ BILL KEISTER Keister, William Hoffman "Wagon Tongue" b: 8/17/1874, Baltimore, Md. d: 8/19/24, Baltimore, Md. BL/TR, 5'5.5", 168 lbs. Deb: 5/20/1896

| 1898 | Bos-N | 10 | 30 | 5 | 5 | 2 | 0 | 0 | 4 | 0 | | .167 | .167 | .233 | 14 | -3 | 0 | | | 1.000 | 1 | /S-4,2-4,O | -0.2 |
| Total | 7 | 621 | 2433 | 400 | 758 | 133 | 63 | 18 | 400 | 90 | | .312 | .349 | .440 | 116 | 43 | 131 | | | .870 | -80 | S-215,2-214,O/3 | -1.8 |

■ JOHN KELLEHER Kelleher, John Patrick b: 9/13/1893, Brookline, Mass. d: 8/21/60, Brighton, Mass. BR/TR, 5'11", 150 lbs. Deb: 7/31/12

| 1924 | Bos-N | 1 | 1 | 0 | 0 | 0 | 0 | 0 | 0 | 0 | 0 | .000 | .000 | .000 | -99 | -0 | 0 | 0 | 0 | .000 | 0 | H | 0.0 |
| Total | 6 | 235 | 703 | 81 | 206 | 29 | 8 | 10 | 89 | 45 | 42 | .293 | .337 | .400 | 92 | -8 | 9 | 16 | | .924 | -0 | /3-98,1-37,2SO | -0.6 |

■ JOE KELLEY Kelley, Joseph James b: 12/9/1871, Cambridge, Mass. d: 8/14/43, Baltimore, Md. BR/TR, 5'11", 190 lbs. Deb: 7/27/1891 MCH

1891	Bos-N	12	45	7	11	1	1	0	3	2	7	.244	.277	.311	63	-2	0			.852	-1	O-12	-0.3
1908	Bos-N	73	228	25	59	8	2	2	17	27		.259	.342	.338	119	6	5			.938	-4	O-51,1-11M	-0.1
Total	17	1853	7006	1421	2220	358	194	65	1194	911	163	.317	.402	.451	132	321	443			.955	20	*O-1465,1-291/32S	20.2
Team	2	85	273	32	70	9	3	2	20	29	7	.256	.332	.333	109	3	5			.917	-5	/O-63,1-11	-0.4

■ JIM KELLY Kelly, James Robert (Also Played Under Real Name Of Robert John Taggert In 1918) b: 2/1/1884, Bloomfield, N.J. d: 4/10/61, Kingsport, Tenn. BL/TR, 5'10.5", 180 lbs. Deb: 4/26/14

| 1918 | Bos-N | 35 | 146 | 19 | 48 | 1 | 4 | 0 | 9 | 9 | 9 | .329 | .376 | .390 | 140 | 7 | 4 | | | .955 | 1 | O-35 | 0.6 |
| Total | 3 | 215 | 714 | 91 | 212 | 15 | 22 | 4 | 57 | 46 | 58 | .297 | .343 | .396 | 106 | 3 | 42 | | | .954 | 15 | O-190 | 0.9 |

■ JOE KELLY Kelly, Joseph Henry b: 9/23/1886, Weir City, Kan. d: 8/16/77, St.Joseph, Mo. BR/TR, 5'10", 175 lbs. Deb: 4/14/14

1917	Bos-N	116	445	41	99	9	8	3	36	26	45	.222	.268	.299	78	-12	21			.946	14	*O-116	-0.6
1918	Bos-N	47	155	20	36	2	4	0	15	6	12	.232	.265	.297	74	-5	12			.933	-0	O-45	-0.8
1919	Bos-N	18	64	3	9	1	0	0	3	6	11	.141	.154	.156	-7	-8	2			.943	0	O-16	-1.1
Total	5	376	1341	129	300	38	22	6	117	80	143	.224	.272	.298	75	-44	66			.945	16	O-362	-5.2
Team	3	181	664	64	144	12	13	3	54	32	68	.217	.257	.285	69	-26	35			.943	13	O-177	-2.5

■ KING KELLY Kelly, Michael Joseph b: 12/31/1857, Troy, N.Y. d: 11/8/1894, Boston, Mass. BR/TR, 5'10", 170 lbs. Deb: 5/1/1878 MH

1887	Bos-N	116	484	120	156	34	11	8	63	55	84	.322	.393	.488	143	29	84			.856	-11	O-61,2-30,C/PS3M	1.7
1888	Bos-N	107	440	85	140	22	11	9	71	31	39	.318	.368	.480	166	32	56			.905	-3	C-76,O-34	3.4
1889	Bos-N	125	507	120	149	41	5	9	78	65	40	.294	.376	.448	122	14	68			.848	-9	*O-113,C-23	0.3
1891	Bos-N	16	52	7	12	1	0	0	5	6	10	.231	.322	.250	60	-3	6			.844	-5	C-11/O-6	-0.6
1892	*Bos-N	78	281	40	53	7	0	2	41	39	31	.189	.287	.235	54	-16	24			.912	-0	C-72/O-2,31P	-0.9
Total	16	1455	5894	1357	1813	359	102	69	950	549	417	.308	.368	.438	136	241	368			.820	1	O-750,C-583/3S21P	24.7
Team	5	442	1764	372	510	105	27	28	258	196	160	.289	.363	.427	125	56	238			.827	-28	O-216,C-206/2P31S	3.9

■ MIKE KELLY Kelly, Michael Raymond b: 6/2/70, Los Angeles, Cal. BR/TR, 6'4", 195 lbs. Deb: 4/5/94

1994	Atl-N	30	77	14	21	10	1	2	9	2	17	.273	.300	.506	103	-0	0	1	-1	.962	-5	O-25	-0.6
1995	Atl-N	97	137	26	26	6	1	3	17	11	49	.190	.260	.314	49	-10	7	3	0	.940	-16	O-83	-2.7
Total	2	127	214	40	47	16	2	5	26	13	66	.220	.274	.383	69	-10	7	4	-0	.946	-21	O-108	-3.3

■ ROBERTO KELLY Kelly, Roberto Conrado (Gray) "Bobby" b: 10/1/64, Panama City, Pan. BR/TR, 6'4", 185 lbs. Deb: 7/29/87

| 1994 | Atl-N | 63 | 255 | 44 | 73 | 15 | 3 | 6 | 24 | 24 | 36 | .286 | .348 | .439 | 101 | 0 | 10 | 3 | 1 | .985 | -2 | O-63 | -0.1 |
| Total | 9 | 962 | 3535 | 495 | 1006 | 173 | 20 | 81 | 395 | 242 | 633 | .285 | .336 | .414 | 105 | 18 | 210 | 74 | 19 | .985 | 28 | O-936/D-6 | 4.4 |

■ MARTY KEOUGH Keough, Richard Martin b: 4/14/35, Oakland, Cal. BL/TL, 6', 180 lbs. Deb: 4/21/56 F

| 1966 | Atl-N | 17 | 17 | 1 | 1 | 0 | 0 | 0 | 1 | 1 | 6 | .059 | .111 | .059 | -50 | -3 | 0 | 0 | 0 | 1.000 | -2 | /1-4,O-3 | -0.6 |
| Total | 11 | 841 | 1796 | 256 | 434 | 71 | 23 | 43 | 176 | 164 | 318 | .242 | .311 | .379 | 86 | -35 | 26 | 19 | -4 | .984 | -25 | O-464,1-130 | -9.0 |

■ BUDDY KERR Kerr, John Joseph b: 11/6/22, Astoria, N.Y. BR/TR, 6'2", 180 lbs. Deb: 9/8/43

1950	Bos-N	155	507	45	115	24	6	2	46	50	50	.227	.296	.310	64	-27	0			.965	2	*S-155	-1.3
1951	Bos-N	69	172	18	32	6	1	0	18	22	20	.186	.282	.227	41	-14	0	0	0	.969	13	S-63/2-5	0.3
Total	9	1067	3631	378	903	145	25	31	333	324	280	.249	.312	.328	76	-123	38	0		.967	92	*S-1038/3-18,2	3.9
Team	2	224	679	63	147	28	6	3	64	72	70	.216	.293	.289	58	-41	0	0		.966	16	S-218/2-5	-1.0

■ HOD KIBBIE Kibbie, Horace Kent b: 7/18/03, Ft.Worth, Tex. d: 10/19/75, Ft.Worth, Tex. BR/TR, 5'10", 150 lbs. Deb: 6/13/25

| 1925 | Bos-N | 11 | 41 | 5 | 11 | 2 | 0 | 0 | 6 | 3 | 6 | .268 | .348 | .317 | 78 | -0 | 0 | 0 | 0 | .904 | -0 | /2-8,S-3 | -0.1 |

■ JOHN KILEY Kiley, John Frederick b: 7/1/1859, Dedham, Mass. d: 12/18/40, Norwood, Mass. BL/TL, 5'7", 147 lbs. Deb: 5/1/1884

| 1891 | Bos-N | 1 | 2 | 0 | 0 | 0 | 0 | 0 | 0 | 1 | 1 | .000 | .500 | .000 | 45 | 0 | 0 | | | 1.000 | 0 | /P-1 | 0.0 |
| Total | 2 | 15 | 58 | 9 | 12 | 2 | 2 | 0 | 4 | 1 | | .207 | .281 | .310 | 102 | 0 | 0 | | | .893 | -4 | /O-14,P-1 | -0.3 |

■ LEE KING King, Edward Lee b: 3/28/1894, Waltham, Mass. d: 9/7/38, Newton Center, Mass. BR/TR, 5'10", 160 lbs. Deb: 6/24/16

| 1919 | Bos-N | 2 | 1 | 0 | 0 | 0 | 0 | 0 | 0 | 0 | 0 | .000 | .000 | .000 | -99 | -0 | 0 | | | .000 | 0 | H | 0.0 |
| Total | 2 | 44 | 145 | 13 | 27 | 1 | 2 | 0 | 8 | 7 | 15 | .186 | .229 | .221 | 37 | -12 | 4 | | | .968 | -10 | /O-22,S-11,32 | -2.5 |

■ HAL KING King, Harold b: 2/1/44, Oviedo, Fla. BL/TR, 6'1", 200 lbs. Deb: 9/6/67

1970	Atl-N	89	204	29	53	8	0	11	30	32	41	.260	.366	.461	113	4	1	0	0	.985	-11	C-62	-0.4
1971	Atl-N	86	198	14	41	9	0	5	19	29	43	.207	.320	.328	79	-5	0	0	0	.983	-2	C-60	-0.5
Total	7	322	683	67	146	26	3	24	82	104	158	.214	.325	.366	93	-6	1	0		.982	-26	C-204	-2.7
Team	2	175	402	43	94	17	0	16	49	61	84	.234	.343	.396	97	-1	1	0		.984	-13	C-122	-0.9

■ JAY KIRKE Kirke, Judson Fabian b: 6/16/1888, Fleischmanns, N.Y d: 8/31/68, New Orleans, La. BL/TR, 6', 195 lbs. Deb: 9/28/10

1911	Bos-N	20	89	9	32	5	5	0	12	2	6	.360	.380	.528	142	4	3			.929	-1	O-14/1-3,2S3	0.3
1912	Bos-N	103	359	53	115	11	4	4	62	9	46	.320	.339	.407	102	-1	7			.903	-2	O-72,3-14/S1	-0.5
1913	Bos-N	18	38	3	9	2	0	0	3	1	6	.237	.293	.289	65	-2	0			.923	2	O-13	0.0
Total	7	320	1148	122	346	49	13	7	148	35	112	.301	.328	.385	103	-0	21			.927	-4	O-142,1-125/32S	-2.1
Team	3	141	486	65	156	18	9	4	77	12	58	.321	.343	.420	106	2	10			.909	-1	/O-99,3-15,1S2	-0.2

■ MALACHI KITTRIDGE Kittridge, Malachi Jeddidah "Jeddidah" b: 10/12/1869, Clinton, Mass. d: 6/23/28, Gary, Ind. BR/TR, 5'7", 170 lbs. Deb: 4/19/1890 M

| 1901 | Bos-N | 114 | 381 | 24 | 96 | 14 | 0 | 2 | 40 | 32 | | .252 | .312 | .304 | 72 | -14 | 2 | | | .984 | 12 | *C-113 | 1.0 |
| 1902 | Bos-N | 80 | 255 | 18 | 60 | 7 | 0 | 2 | 30 | 24 | | .235 | .304 | .286 | 81 | -5 | 4 | | | .981 | 6 | C-72 | 0.9 |

YEAR	TM/L	G	AB	R	H	2B	3B	HR	RBI	BB	SO	AVG	OBP	SLG	PRO+	BR/A	SB	CS	SBR	FA	FR	G/POS	TPR
1903	Bos-N	32	99	10	21	2	0	0	6	11		.212	.291	.232	52	-6	1			.981	5	C-30	0.2
Total	16	1215	4027	375	882	108	31	17	390	314		.219	.277	.274	56	-236	64			.961	47	*C-1196/P-1	-6.7
Team	3	226	735	52	177	23	0	4	76	67		.241	.306	.288	73	-25	7			.982	22	C-215	2.1

■ **BILLY KLAUS** Klaus, William Joseph b: 12/9/28, Fox Lake, Ill. BL/TR, 5'10", 165 lbs. Deb: 4/16/52 F

YEAR	TM/L	G	AB	R	H	2B	3B	HR	RBI	BB	SO	AVG	OBP	SLG	PRO+	BR/A	SB	CS	SBR	FA	FR	G/POS	TPR
1952	Bos-N	7	4	3	0	0	0	0	0	1	1	.000	.200	.000	-42	-1	0	0	0	.500	-1	/S-4	-0.2
1953	Mil-N	2	2	1	0	0	0	0	1	0	0	.000	.000	.000	-99	-1	0	0	0	.000	0	H	-0.1
Total	11	821	2513	357	626	106	15	40	250	331	285	.249	.337	.351	82	-62	14	7	0	.955	-24	S-425,3-272/2O	-5.1
Team	2	9	6	4	0	0	0	0	1	1	1	.000	.143	.000	-60	-1	0	0	0	.500	-1	/S-4	-0.3

■ **RYAN KLESKO** Klesko, Ryan Anthony b: 6/12/71, Westminster, Cal. BL/TL, 6'3", 220 lbs. Deb: 9/12/92

YEAR	TM/L	G	AB	R	H	2B	3B	HR	RBI	BB	SO	AVG	OBP	SLG	PRO+	BR/A	SB	CS	SBR	FA	FR	G/POS	TPR
1992	Atl-N	13	14	0	0	0	0	0	1	0	5	.000	.067	.000	-75	-3	0	0	0	1.000	-1	/1-5	-0.4
1993	Atl-N	22	17	3	6	1	0	2	5	3	4	.353	.450	.765	216	3	0	0	0	1.000	-1	/1-3,O-2	0.2
1994	Atl-N	92	245	42	68	13	3	17	47	26	48	.278	.349	.563	130	10	1	0	0	.921	-11	O-74/1-6	-0.2
1995	*Atl-N	107	329	48	102	25	2	23	70	47	72	.310	.399	.608	157	27	5	4	-1	.942	-10	*O-102/1-4	1.4
Total	4	234	605	93	176	39	5	42	123	76	129	.291	.374	.580	143	37	6	4	-1	.934	-22	O-178/1-18	1.0

■ **LOU KLIMCHOCK** Klimchock, Louis Stephen b: 10/15/39, Hostetter, Pa. BL/TR, 5'11", 180 lbs. Deb: 9/27/58

YEAR	TM/L	G	AB	R	H	2B	3B	HR	RBI	BB	SO	AVG	OBP	SLG	PRO+	BR/A	SB	CS	SBR	FA	FR	G/POS	TPR
1962	Mil-N	8	8	0	0	0	0	0	0	0	2	.000	.000	.000	-99	-2	0	0	0	.000	0	H	-0.2
1963	Mil-N	24	46	6	9	1	0	0	1	0	12	.196	.196	.217	19	-5	0	1	-1	.988	0	1-12	-0.6
1964	Mil-N	10	21	3	7	2	0	0	2	1	2	.333	.364	.429	121	1	0	0	0	1.000	-3	/3-4,2-2	-0.2
1965	Mil-N	34	39	3	3	0	0	0	3	2	8	.077	.122	.077	-42	-7	0	0	0	.923	1	/1-4	-0.7
Total	12	318	669	64	155	21	3	13	69	31	71	.232	.267	.330	63	-35	0	1	-1	.906	-30	/3-70,2-52,1OC	-6.6
Team	4	76	114	12	19	3	0	0	6	3	24	.167	.188	.193	8	-14	0	1	-1	.972	-2	/1-16,3-4,2	-1.7

■ **JOHNNY KLING** Kling, John "Noisy" b: 2/25/1875, Kansas City, Mo. d: 1/31/47, Kansas City, Mo. BR/TR, 5'9.5", 160 lbs. Deb: 9/11/00 FM

YEAR	TM/L	G	AB	R	H	2B	3B	HR	RBI	BB	SO	AVG	OBP	SLG	PRO+	BR/A	SB	CS	SBR	FA	FR	G/POS	TPR
1911	Bos-N	75	241	32	54	8	1	2	24	30	29	.224	.310	.290	63	-12	0			.951	-5	C-71/3-1	-1.0
1912	Bos-N	81	252	26	80	10	3	2	30	15	30	.317	.356	.405	106	2	3			.958	5	C-74,M	1.3
Total	13	1260	4241	474	1151	181	61	20	513	281	114	.271	.318	.357	100	-11	123			.971	3	*C-1168/O-24,13S	11.5
Team	2	156	493	58	134	18	4	4	54	45	59	.272	.333	.349	84	-10	3			.954	-0	C-145/3-1	0.3

■ **BILLY KLUSMAN** Klusman, William F. b: 3/24/1865, Cincinnati, Ohio d: 6/24/07, Cincinnati, Ohio BR/TR, 5'10.5", 185 lbs. Deb: 6/21/1888

YEAR	TM/L	G	AB	R	H	2B	3B	HR	RBI	BB	SO	AVG	OBP	SLG	PRO+	BR/A	SB	CS	SBR	FA	FR	G/POS	TPR
1888	Bos-N	28	107	9	18	4	0	2	11	5	13	.168	.205	.262	47	-6	3			.914	-9	2-28	-1.4
Total	2	43	172	18	36	8	1	3	11	6	13	.209	.236	.320	67	-8	4			.908	-12	/2-43	-1.7

■ **CLYDE KLUTTZ** Kluttz, Clyde Franklin b: 12/12/17, Rockwell, N.C. d: 5/12/79, Salisbury, N.C. BR/TR, 6', 198 lbs. Deb: 4/20/42

YEAR	TM/L	G	AB	R	H	2B	3B	HR	RBI	BB	SO	AVG	OBP	SLG	PRO+	BR/A	SB	CS	SBR	FA	FR	G/POS	TPR
1942	Bos-N	72	210	21	56	10	1	1	31	7	13	.267	.294	.338	86	-4	0			.979	0	C-57	0.0
1943	Bos-N	66	207	13	51	7	0	0	20	15	9	.246	.297	.280	68	-8	0			.973	2	C-55	-0.2
1944	Bos-N	81	229	20	64	12	2	2	19	13	14	.279	.318	.376	91	-3	0			.980	4	C-58	0.4
1945	Bos-N	25	81	9	24	4	1	0	10	2	6	.296	.313	.370	89	-1	0			.987	-0	C-19	-0.1
Total	9	656	1903	172	510	90	8	19	212	132	119	.268	.318	.354	86	-39	5			.978	-3	C-556	-0.9
Team	4	244	727	63	195	33	4	3	80	37	42	.268	.305	.337	83	-17	0			.978	6	C-189	0.1

■ **FRITZ KNOTHE** Knothe, Wilfred Edgar b: 5/1/03, Passaic, N.J. d: 3/27/63, Passaic, N.J. BR/TR, 5'10.5", 180 lbs. Deb: 4/12/32 F

YEAR	TM/L	G	AB	R	H	2B	3B	HR	RBI	BB	SO	AVG	OBP	SLG	PRO+	BR/A	SB	CS	SBR	FA	FR	G/POS	TPR
1932	Bos-N	89	344	45	82	19	1	1	36	39	37	.238	.318	.308	72	-13	5			.947	-3	3-87	-1.0
1933	Bos-N	44	158	15	36	5	2	1	6	13	25	.228	.291	.304	76	-5	1			.978	-7	3-33/S-9	-1.0
Total	2	174	615	70	135	26	3	2	53	58	81	.220	.289	.281	59	-32	8			.953	5	3-152/S-9,2	-1.7
Team	2	133	502	60	118	24	3	2	42	52	62	.235	.309	.307	73	-18	6			.955	-10	3-120/S-9	-2.0

■ **JOE KNOTTS** Knotts, Joseph Steven b: 3/3/1884, Greensboro, Pa. d: 9/15/50, Philadelphia, Pa. BR/TR, Deb: 9/18/07

YEAR	TM/L	G	AB	R	H	2B	3B	HR	RBI	BB	SO	AVG	OBP	SLG	PRO+	BR/A	SB	CS	SBR	FA	FR	G/POS	TPR
1907	Bos-N	3	8	0	0	0	0	0	0	1		.000	.111	.000	-65	-2	0			1.000	-0	/C-3	-0.2

■ **GARY KOLB** Kolb, Gary Alan b: 3/13/40, Rock Falls, Ill. BL/TR, 6', 195 lbs. Deb: 9/7/60

YEAR	TM/L	G	AB	R	H	2B	3B	HR	RBI	BB	SO	AVG	OBP	SLG	PRO+	BR/A	SB	CS	SBR	FA	FR	G/POS	TPR
1964	Mil-N	36	64	7	12	1	0	0	2	6	10	.188	.257	.203	31	-6	3	2	-0	1.000	-6	O-14/3-7,2C	-1.3
1965	Mil-N	24	27	3	7	0	0	0	1	1	6	.259	.286	.259	54	-2	0	0	0	1.000	-3	O-13	-0.5
Total	7	293	450	63	94	9	6	6	29	46	104	.209	.282	.296	65	-21	10	4		.965	-23	O-147/C-20,321	-5.2
Team	2	60	91	10	19	1	0	0	3	7	16	.209	.265	.220	38	-7	3	2		1.000	-8	/O-27,3-7,2C	-1.8

■ **BRAD KOMMINSK** Komminsk, Brad Lynn b: 4/4/61, Lima, Ohio BR/TR, 6'2", 205 lbs. Deb: 8/14/83

YEAR	TM/L	G	AB	R	H	2B	3B	HR	RBI	BB	SO	AVG	OBP	SLG	PRO+	BR/A	SB	CS	SBR	FA	FR	G/POS	TPR
1983	Atl-N	19	36	2	8	2	0	0	4	5	7	.222	.317	.278	62	-2	0	0	0	.944	-1	O-13	-0.3
1984	Atl-N	90	301	37	61	10	0	8	36	29	77	.203	.277	.316	62	-15	18	8	1	.993	-2	O-80	-2.1
1985	Atl-N	106	300	52	68	12	3	4	21	38	71	.227	.316	.327	75	-9	10	8	-2	.959	-4	O-92	-1.9
1986	Atl-N	5	5	1	2	0	0	0	1	0	1	.400	.400	.400	115	0	0	1	-1	1.000	-0	/3-2,O-2	-0.1
Total	8	376	986	140	215	37	5	23	105	114	258	.218	.303	.336	75	-31	39	20	-0	.984	-17	O-329/D-3,3	-6.0
Team	4	220	642	92	139	24	3	12	62	72	156	.217	.298	.319	68	-26	28	17	-2	.972	-7	O-187/3-2	-4.4

■ **ED KONETCHY** Konetchy, Edward Joseph "Big Ed" b: 9/3/1885, LaCrosse, Wis. d: 5/27/47, Ft.Worth, Tex. BR/TR, 6'2.5", 195 lbs. Deb: 6/29/07

YEAR	TM/L	G	AB	R	H	2B	3B	HR	RBI	BB	SO	AVG	OBP	SLG	PRO+	BR/A	SB	CS	SBR	FA	FR	G/POS	TPR
1916	Bos-N	158	566	76	147	29	13	3	70	43	46	.260	.320	.373	117	11	13			.990	9	*1-158	1.5
1917	Bos-N	130	474	56	129	19	13	2	54	36	40	.272	.330	.380	125	13	16			**.994**	2	*1-129	1.1
1918	Bos-N	119	437	33	103	15	5	2	56	32	35	.236	.291	.307	86	-8	5			**.992**	-2	*1-112/O-6,P	-1.6
Total	15	2085	7649	972	2150	344	181	75	992	689	545	.281	.346	.403	121	196	255			.990	59	*1-2073/O-7,P	22.3
Team	3	407	1477	165	379	63	31	7	180	111	121	.257	.315	.355	110	16	34			.992	9	1-399/O-6,P	1.0

■ **GEORGE KOPACZ** Kopacz, George Felix "Sonny" b: 2/26/41, Chicago, Ill. BL/TL, 6'1", 195 lbs. Deb: 9/18/66

YEAR	TM/L	G	AB	R	H	2B	3B	HR	RBI	BB	SO	AVG	OBP	SLG	PRO+	BR/A	SB	CS	SBR	FA	FR	G/POS	TPR
1966	Atl-N	6	9	1	0	0	0	0	0	1	5	.000	.100	.000	-68	-2	0	0	0	.909	-1	/1-2	-0.3
Total	2	16	25	2	3	0	0	0	0	1	10	.120	.154	.120	-25	-4	0	0	0	.964	-1	/1-5	-0.6

■ **LARRY KOPF** Kopf, William Lorenz (a.k.a. Fred Brady In 1913) b: 11/3/1890, Bristol, Conn. d: 10/15/86, Anderson Twp., O. BB/TR, 5'9", 160 lbs. Deb: 9/2/13 F

YEAR	TM/L	G	AB	R	H	2B	3B	HR	RBI	BB	SO	AVG	OBP	SLG	PRO+	BR/A	SB	CS	SBR	FA	FR	G/POS	TPR
1922	Bos-N	126	466	59	124	6	3	1	37	45	22	.266	.332	.298	67	-22	8	9	-3	.944	-14	2-78,S-33,3	-3.1
1923	Bos-N	39	138	15	38	3	1	0	10	13	6	.275	.338	.312	75	-5	0	3	-2	.905	-8	S-37/2-4	-1.0
Total	10	853	3010	349	750	84	30	5	266	242	214	.249	.312	.302	78	-82	72	48	-7	.928	-122	S-664/2-99,3O	-17.8
Team	2	165	604	74	162	9	4	1	47	58	28	.268	.333	.301	69	-26	8	12	-5	.942	-22	/2-82,S-70,3	-4.1

■ **JOE KOPPE** Koppe, Joseph (b: Joseph Kopchia) b: 10/19/30, Detroit, Mich. BR/TR, 5'10", 165 lbs. Deb: 8/9/58

YEAR	TM/L	G	AB	R	H	2B	3B	HR	RBI	BB	SO	AVG	OBP	SLG	PRO+	BR/A	SB	CS	SBR	FA	FR	G/POS	TPR
1958	Mil-N	16	9	3	4	0	0	0	0	1	1	.444	.500	.444	167	1	0	0	0	.833	5	/S-3	0.6
Total	8	578	1606	202	379	61	12	19	141	209	345	.236	.327	.324	76	-50	16	13	-3	.952	29	S-436/2-56,3O	1.1

■ **BRIAN KOWITZ** Kowitz, Brian Mark b: 8/7/69, Baltimore, Md. BL/TL, 5'10", 180 lbs. Deb: 6/4/95

YEAR	TM/L	G	AB	R	H	2B	3B	HR	RBI	BB	SO	AVG	OBP	SLG	PRO+	BR/A	SB	CS	SBR	FA	FR	G/POS	TPR
1995	Atl-N	10	24	3	4	1	0	0	3	2	5	.167	.259	.208	25	-3	0	1	-1	1.000	-2	/O-8	-0.5

■ **CLARENCE KRAFT** Kraft, Clarence Otto "Big Boy" b: 6/9/1887, Evansville, Ind. d: 3/26/58, Fort Worth, Tex. BR/TR, 6', 190 lbs. Deb: 5/1/14

YEAR	TM/L	G	AB	R	H	2B	3B	HR	RBI	BB	SO	AVG	OBP	SLG	PRO+	BR/A	SB	CS	SBR	FA	FR	G/POS	TPR
1914	Bos-N	3	3	0	1	0	0	0	0	0	1	.333	.333	.333	99	-0	0			1.000	0	/1-1	0.0

■ **JIMMY KREMERS** Kremers, James Edward b: 10/8/65, Little Rock, Ark. BL/TR, 6'3", 205 lbs. Deb: 6/5/90

YEAR	TM/L	G	AB	R	H	2B	3B	HR	RBI	BB	SO	AVG	OBP	SLG	PRO+	BR/A	SB	CS	SBR	FA	FR	G/POS	TPR
1990	Atl-N	29	73	7	8	1	1	1	2	6	27	.110	.177	.192	1	-10	0	0	0	.992	-3	C-27	-1.3

YEAR	TM/L	G	AB	R	H	2B	3B	HR	RBI	BB	SO	AVG	OBP	SLG	PRO+	BR/A	SB	CS	SBR	FA	FR	G/POS	TPR

■ MIKE KRSNICH   Krsnich, Michael b: 9/24/31, W.Allis, Wis.   BR/TR, 6'1", 190 lbs.   Deb: 4/23/60 F

1960	Mil-N	4	9	0	3	1	0	0	2	0	0	.333	.333	.444	120	0	0	0	0	1.000	-0	/O-3	0.0
1962	Mil-N	11	12	0	1	1	0	0	2	0	4	.083	.083	.167	-36	-2	0	0	0	1.000	-0	/O-3,1-1,3	-0.3
Total	2	15	21	0	4	2	0	0	4	0	4	.190	.190	.286	28	-2	0	0	0	1.000	-0	/O-6,3-1,1	-0.3

■ ART KRUGER   Kruger, Arthur T. b: 3/16/1881, San Antonio, Tex. d: 11/28/49, Honda, Cal. BR/TR, 6', 185 lbs.   Deb: 4/11/07

| 1910 | Bos-N | 1 | 1 | 0 | 0 | 0 | 0 | 0 | 0 | 0 | 0 | .000 | .000 | .000 | -96 | -0 | 0 | | | .000 | -0 | H | 0.0 |
| Total | 4 | 365 | 1222 | 113 | 283 | 49 | 21 | 6 | 115 | 73 | 88 | .232 | .281 | .321 | 70 | -52 | 38 | | | .968 | -2 | O-344 | -7.5 |

■ STEVE KUCZEK   Kuczek, Stanislaw Leo b: 12/28/24, Amsterdam, N.Y. BR/TR, 6', 160 lbs.   Deb: 9/29/49

| 1949 | Bos-N | 1 | 1 | 0 | 1 | 1 | 0 | 0 | 0 | 0 | 0 | 1.000 | 1.000 | 2.000 | 723 | 1 | 0 | | | .000 | 0 | H | 0.1 |

■ CHARLIE KUHNS   Kuhns, Charles B. b: 10/27/1877, Freeport, Pa. d: 7/15/22, Pittsburgh, Pa. 5'9", 160 lbs.   Deb: 6/4/1897

| 1899 | Bos-N | 7 | 18 | 2 | 5 | 0 | 0 | 0 | 3 | 2 | | .278 | .350 | .278 | 67 | -1 | 0 | | | .813 | -1 | /S-3,3-3 | -0.1 |
| Total | 2 | 8 | 21 | 2 | 5 | 0 | 0 | 0 | 3 | 3 | | .238 | .333 | .238 | 53 | -1 | 0 | | | .733 | -1 | /3-4,S-3 | -0.1 |

■ LEE LACY   Lacy, Leondaus b: 4/10/48, Longview, Tex. BR/TR, 6'1", 175 lbs.   Deb: 6/30/72

| 1976 | Atl-N | 50 | 180 | 25 | 49 | 4 | 2 | 3 | 20 | 6 | 12 | .272 | .299 | .367 | 83 | -4 | 2 | 2 | -1 | .969 | -10 | 2-44/O-5,3 | -1.4 |
| Total | 16 | 1523 | 4549 | 650 | 1303 | 207 | 42 | 91 | 458 | 372 | 657 | .286 | .342 | .410 | 108 | 43 | 185 | 86 | | .983 | -31 | *O-1006,2-275/3DS | -0.3 |

■ HI LADD   Ladd, Arthur Clifford b: 2/9/1870, Willimantic, Conn. d: 5/7/48, Cranston, R.I. BL/TR, 6'4", 180 lbs.   Deb: 7/12/1898

| 1898 | Bos-N | 1 | 4 | 1 | 1 | 0 | 0 | 0 | 0 | 0 | | .250 | .250 | .250 | 41 | -0 | 0 | | | 1.000 | -0 | /O-1 | 0.0 |

■ FRED LAKE   Lake, Frederick Lovett b: 10/16/1866, Nova Scotia, Can. d: 11/24/31, Boston, Mass. BR/TR, 5'10", 170 lbs.   Deb: 5/7/1891 M

1891	Bos-N	5	7	1	1	0	0	0	0	2	4	.143	.333	.143	36	-1	0			1.000	-0	/C-4,O-1	-0.1
1897	*Bos-N	19	62	2	15	4	0	0	5	1		.242	.254	.306	45	-5	2			.970	-1	C-18	-0.4
1910	Bos-N	3	1	0	0	0	0	0	0	1	0	.000	.500	.000	46	0				.000	0	HM	0.0
Total	5	48	125	12	29	6	0	1	16	17	10	.232	.342	.304	68	-5	4			.930	-5	/C-27,2-6,S10	-0.7
Team	3	27	70	3	16	4	0	0	5	4	4	.229	.270	.286	45	-6	2			.971	-2	/C-22,O-1	-0.5

■ AL LAKEMAN   Lakeman, Albert Wesley "Moose" b: 12/31/18, Cincinnati, Ohio d: 5/25/76, Spartanburg, S.C. BR/TR, 6'2", 195 lbs.   Deb: 4/19/42 C

| 1949 | Bos-N | 3 | 6 | 0 | 1 | 0 | 0 | 0 | 0 | 1 | 0 | .167 | .286 | .167 | 26 | -1 | 0 | | | 1.000 | 1 | /1-2 | 0.0 |
| Total | 9 | 239 | 646 | 40 | 131 | 17 | 5 | 15 | 66 | 36 | 137 | .203 | .248 | .314 | 55 | -42 | 0 | | | .974 | -16 | C-167/1-31,P | -5.0 |

■ HUNTER LANE   Lane, James Hunter "Dodo" b: 7/20/1900, Pulaski, Tenn. d: 9/12/94, Memphis, Tenn. BR/TR, 5'11", 165 lbs.   Deb: 5/13/24

| 1924 | Bos-N | 7 | 15 | 0 | 1 | 0 | 0 | 0 | 0 | 1 | 1 | .067 | .125 | .067 | -49 | -3 | 0 | 0 | 0 | .909 | -1 | /3-4,2-1 | -0.4 |

■ NORM LARKER   Larker, Norman Howard John b: 12/27/30, Beaver Meadows, Pa. BL/TL, 6', 200 lbs.   Deb: 4/15/58

| 1963 | Mil-N | 64 | 147 | 15 | 26 | 6 | 0 | 1 | 14 | 24 | 24 | .177 | .301 | .238 | 58 | -7 | 0 | 2 | -1 | .992 | 4 | 1-42 | -0.6 |
| Total | 6 | 667 | 1953 | 227 | 538 | 97 | 15 | 32 | 271 | 211 | 165 | .275 | .351 | .390 | 97 | -3 | 3 | 5 | -2 | .991 | 17 | 1-483/O-82 | -2.3 |

■ SWEDE LARSEN   Larsen, Erling Adeli b: 11/15/13, Jersey City, N.J. BR/TR, 5'11", 170 lbs.   Deb: 6/17/36

| 1936 | Bos-N | 3 | 1 | 0 | 0 | 0 | 0 | 0 | 0 | 0 | 0 | .000 | .000 | .000 | -99 | -0 | 0 | | | 1.000 | -0 | /2-2 | -0.1 |

■ TONY LaRUSSA   LaRussa, Anthony b: 10/4/44, Tampa, Fla. BR/TR, 6'1", 190 lbs.   Deb: 5/10/63 MC

| 1971 | Atl-N | 9 | 7 | 1 | 2 | 0 | 0 | 0 | 0 | 1 | 1 | .286 | .375 | .286 | 84 | -0 | 0 | 0 | 0 | .933 | 0 | /2-9 | 0.1 |
| Total | 6 | 132 | 176 | 15 | 35 | 5 | 2 | 0 | 7 | 23 | 37 | .199 | .295 | .250 | 54 | -11 | 0 | 0 | | .963 | 6 | /2-63,S-18,3 | -0.1 |

■ JUICE LATHAM   Latham, George Warren "Jumbo" b: 9/6/1852, Utica, N.Y. d: 5/26/14, Utica, N.Y. BR/TR, 5'8", 164 lbs.   Deb: 4/19/1875 M

| 1875 | Bos-n | 16 | 77 | 23 | 21 | 4 | 1 | 0 | | | | .273 | .273 | .351 | 110 | 1 | | | | | | 1-16 | 0.0 |
| Total | 4 | 298 | 1277 | 180 | 317 | 30 | 17 | 0 | 22 | 35 | | .248 | .270 | .298 | 82 | -30 | | | | .960 | 1 | 1-276/2-14,S3 | -4.9 |

■ CHARLIE LAU   Lau, Charles Richard b: 4/12/33, Romulus, Mich. d: 3/18/84, Key Colony Beach, Fla. BL/TR, 6', 190 lbs.   Deb: 9/12/56 C

1960	Mil-N	21	53	4	10	2	0	0	2	6	10	.189	.271	.226	41	-4	0	0	0	1.000	5	C-16	0.1
1961	Mil-N	28	82	3	17	5	0	0	5	14	11	.207	.330	.268	65	-4	1	1	-0	.968	-3	C-25	-0.6
1967	Atl-N	52	45	3	9	1	0	1	5	4	9	.200	.265	.289	59	-2	0	0	0	.000	0	H	-0.3
Total	11	527	1170	105	298	63	9	16	140	109	150	.255	.321	.365	89	-17	3	1	0	.988	-21	C-321	-2.7
Team	3	101	180	10	36	8	0	1	12	24	30	.200	.298	.261	57	-10	1	1	-0	.983	2	/C-41	-0.8

■ BILL LAUTERBORN   Lauterborn, William Bernard b: 6/9/1879, Hornell, N.Y. d: 4/19/65, Andover, N.Y. BR/TR, 5'6", 140 lbs.   Deb: 9/20/04

1904	Bos-N	20	69	7	19	2	0	0	2	1		.275	.286	.304	85	-1	1			.943	-3	2-20	-0.4
1905	Bos-N	67	200	11	37	1	1	0	9	12		.185	.238	.200	32	-17	1			.843	-7	3-29,2-23/SO	-2.4
Total	2	87	269	18	56	3	1	0	11	13		.208	.250	.227	45	-18	2			.929	-10	/2-43,3-29,SO	-2.8

■ FREDDY LEACH   Leach, Frederick b: 11/23/1897, Springfield, Mo. d: 12/10/81, Hagerman, Idaho BL/TR, 5'11", 183 lbs.   Deb: 5/24/23

| 1932 | Bos-N | 84 | 223 | 21 | 55 | 9 | 2 | 4 | 29 | 18 | 10 | .247 | .306 | .318 | 71 | -9 | 1 | | | .977 | -2 | O-50 | -1.4 |
| Total | 10 | 991 | 3733 | 543 | 1147 | 196 | 53 | 72 | 509 | 163 | 189 | .307 | .341 | .446 | 101 | -4 | 32 | | | .975 | -5 | O-875/1-25 | -6.7 |

■ JACK LEARY   Leary, John J. b: 1858, New Haven, Conn. TL, 5'11", 186 lbs.   Deb: 8/21/1880

| 1880 | Bos-N | 1 | 3 | 0 | 0 | 0 | 0 | 0 | 0 | 1 | 0 | .000 | .250 | .000 | -7 | -0 | | | | 1.000 | 1 | /O-1,P-1 | 0.0 |
| Total | 5 | 129 | 538 | 56 | 125 | 11 | 9 | 4 | 4 | 10 | 1 | .232 | .246 | .309 | 81 | -11 | | | | .725 | -17 | /S-40,O-40,3P21 | -2.2 |

■ HAL LEE   Lee, Harold Burnham "Sheriff" b: 2/15/05, Ludlow, Miss. d: 9/4/89, Pascagoula, Miss. BR/TR, 5'11", 180 lbs.   Deb: 4/19/30

1933	Bos-N	88	312	32	69	15	9	8	28	18	26	.221	.266	.337	77	-10	1			.977	2	O-87	-1.4
1934	Bos-N	139	521	70	152	23	6	8	79	47	43	.292	.353	.405	111	8	3			.985	5	*O-128/2-4	0.7
1935	Bos-N	112	422	49	128	18	6	0	39	18	25	.303	.333	.374	98	-2	0			.962	6	*O-110	-0.1
1936	Bos-N	152	565	46	143	24	7	3	64	52	50	.253	.318	.336	82	-15	4			.973	-6	*O-150	-2.6
Total	7	752	2750	316	755	144	40	33	323	203	225	.275	.326	.392	95	-25	15			.973	16	O-718/2-4	-4.4
Team	4	491	1820	197	492	80	28	12	210	135	144	.270	.323	.365	93	-20	8			.974	7	*O-475/2-4	-3.4

■ WADE LEFLER   Lefler, Wade Hampton b: 6/5/1896, Cooleemee, N.C. d: 3/6/81, Hickory, N.C. BL/TR, 5'11", 162 lbs.   Deb: 4/16/24

| 1924 | Bos-N | 1 | 1 | 0 | 0 | 0 | 0 | 0 | 0 | 0 | 0 | .000 | .000 | .000 | -99 | -0 | 0 | 0 | 0 | .000 | 0 | H | 0.0 |
| Total | 1 | 6 | 9 | 0 | 5 | 3 | 0 | 0 | 4 | 0 | 1 | .556 | .556 | .889 | 279 | 2 | 0 | 0 | 0 | .963 | -0 | /O-1 | 0.2 |

■ LOU LEGETT   Legett, Louis Alfred "Doc" b: 6/1/01, New Orleans, La. d: 3/6/88, New Orleans, La. BR/TR, 5'10", 166 lbs.   Deb: 5/8/29

| 1929 | Bos-N | 39 | 81 | 7 | 13 | 2 | 0 | 0 | 6 | 3 | 18 | .160 | .190 | .185 | -7 | -14 | 2 | | | .914 | -1 | C-28 | -1.2 |
| Total | 4 | 68 | 124 | 13 | 25 | 3 | 0 | 0 | 8 | 5 | 22 | .202 | .233 | .226 | 16 | -16 | 2 | | | .938 | -1 | /C-47 | -1.4 |

■ MARK LEMKE   Lemke, Mark Alan b: 8/13/65, Utica, N.Y. BB/TR, 5'10", 167 lbs.   Deb: 9/17/88

1988	Atl-N	16	58	8	13	4	0	0	2	4	5	.224	.274	.293	60	-3	0	2	-1	.970	4	2-16	0.1
1989	Atl-N	14	55	4	10	2	1	2	10	5	7	.182	.250	.364	72	-2	0	1	-1	1.000	-2	2-14	-0.4
1990	Atl-N	102	239	22	54	13	0	0	21	21	22	.226	.288	.280	54	-15	0	1	-1	.989	23	3-45,2-44/S	0.9
1991	*Atl-N	136	269	36	63	11	2	2	23	29	27	.234	.305	.312	71	-10	1	2	-1	.978	13	*2-110,3-15	0.4
1992	*Atl-N	155	427	38	97	7	4	6	26	50	39	.227	.308	.304	70	-16	0	3	-2	.984	-10	*2-145,3-13	-2.7
1993	*Atl-N	151	493	52	124	19	2	7	49	65	50	.252	.339	.341	82	-11	1	2	-1	.982	6	*2-150	-0.2
1994	Atl-N	104	350	40	103	15	0	3	31	38	37	.294	.363	.363	88	-5	0	3	-2	.994	7	*2-103	0.5

YEAR TM/L	G	AB	R	H	2B	3B	HR	RBI	BB	SO	AVG	OBP	SLG	PRO+	BR/A	SB	CS	SBR	FA	FR	G/POS	TPR
1995 *Atl-N	116	399	42	101	16	5	5	38	44	40	.253	.327	.356	78	-12	2	2	-1	.990	-11	*2-115	-1.8
Total 8	794	2290	242	565	87	14	25	200	256	227	.247	.322	.330	75	-74	4	16	-8	.986	31	2-697/3-73,S	-3.2
■ ANDY LEONARD Leonard, Andrew Jackson b: 6/1/1846, County Cavan, Ireland d: 8/21/03, Boston, Mass. BR/TR, 5'7", 168 lbs. Deb: 5/5/1871																						
1872 Bos-n	46	243	59	84	8	2	2	44	0	2	.346	.346	.420	128	6						*O-37/3-6,2	0.4
1873 Bos-n	58	302	81	95	12	6	0	58	4	0	.315	.324	.394	102	-2						*O-45,2-12/13	-0.2
1874 Bos-n	71	340	68	109	18	4	0		2		.321	.325	.397	122	6						*O-51,S-11/2	0.5
1875 Bos-n	80	394	87	127	14	6	1		1		.322	.324	.396	143	15						*O-73/S-3,32	1.3
1876 Bos-N	64	303	53	85	10	2	0	27	4	6	.281	.290	.327	103	1				.925	-1	O-35,2-30	0.0
1877 Bos-N	58	272	46	78	5	0	0	27	5	5	.287	.300	.305	88	-4				.875	-4	O-37,S-21	-0.8
1878 Bos-N	60	262	41	68	8	5	0	16	3	19	.260	.268	.328	88	-4				.777	-7	*O-60	-1.3
Total 5 n	286	1427	328	458	60	21	3	132	10	3	.321	.326	.399	121	26						O-216/2-45,S31	2.0
Total 4	215	970	155	259	26	7	1	87	20	41	.267	.282	.311	91	-11				.856	-23	O-132/S-44,23	-3.4
Team 4 n	255	1279	295	415	52	18	3	102	7	2	.324	.328	.400	123	0				.856	0	O-206/2-25,S31	2.0
Team 3	182	837	140	231	23	7	0	70	12	30	.276	.286	.320	93	-8				.856	-11	O-132/2-30,S	-2.1
■ FRED LEWIS Lewis, Frederick Miller b: 10/13/1858, Buffalo, N.Y. d: 6/5/45, Utica, N.Y. BB/TR, 5'10.5", 194 lbs. Deb: 7/2/1881																						
1881 Bos-N	27	114	17	25	6	0	0	9	7	5	.219	.264	.272	72	-3				.837	-2	O-27	-0.6
Total 5	317	1318	224	390	70	13	4	54	60	28	.296	.330	.378	123	32	8	0	2	.866	4	O-316/3-1	2.7
■ BILL LEWIS Lewis, William Henry "Buddy" b: 10/15/04, Ripley, Tenn. d: 10/24/77, Memphis, Tenn. BR/TR, 5'9", 165 lbs. Deb: 6/3/33																						
1935 Bos-N	6	4	1	0	0	0	0	0	1	1	.000	.200	.000	-45	-1	0			.000	0	/C-1	-0.1
1936 Bos-N	29	62	11	19	2	0	0	3	12	7	.306	.419	.339	113	2	0			.967	-4	C-21	-0.1
Total 3	50	101	20	33	3	0	1	11	15	11	.327	.414	.386	124	4	0			.981	-3	/C-30	0.2
Team 2	35	66	12	19	2	0	0	3	13	8	.288	.405	.318	104	1	0			.967	-4	/C-22	-0.2
■ FRED LIESE Liese, Frederick Richard b: 10/7/1885, Wisconsin d: 6/30/67, Los Angeles, Cal. BL/TL, 5'8", 150 lbs. Deb: 4/14/10																						
1910 Bos-N	5	4	0	0	0	0	0	0	1	2	.000	.200	.000	-39	-1	0			.000	0	H	-0.1
■ RUFINO LINARES Linares, Rufino (b: Rufino De La Cruz (Linares)) b: 2/28/51, San Pedro De Macoris, D.R. BR/TR, 6', 170 lbs. Deb: 4/10/81																						
1981 Atl-N	78	253	27	67	9	2	5	25	9	28	.265	.290	.375	85	-6	8	4	0	.963	3	O-60	-0.5
1982 Atl-N	77	191	28	57	7	1	2	17	7	29	.298	.327	.377	92	-2	5	2	0	1.000	0	O-53	-0.3
1984 Atl-N	34	58	4	12	3	0	1	10	6	12	.207	.281	.310	62	-3	0	0	0	.958	1	O-13	-0.3
Total 4	207	545	66	147	21	3	11	63	24	74	.270	.302	.380	88	-10	15	6	1	.977	4	O-128/D-14	-1.1
Team 3	189	502	59	136	19	3	8	52	22	69	.271	.303	.369	85	-11	13	6	0	.976	4	O-126	-1.1
■ WALT LINDEN Linden, Walter Charles b: 3/27/24, Chicago, Ill. BR/TR, 6'1", 190 lbs. Deb: 4/30/50																						
1950 Bos-N	3	5	0	2	1	0	0	0	1	0	.400	.500	.600	201	1	0			1.000	-1	/C-3	0.0
■ DANNY LITWHILER Litwhiler, Daniel Webster b: 8/31/16, Ringtown, Pa. BR/TR, 5'10.5", 198 lbs. Deb: 4/25/40 C																						
1946 Bos-N	79	247	29	72	12	2	8	38	19	23	.291	.347	.453	125	7	1			.985	-3	O-65/3-2	0.1
1947 Bos-N	91	226	38	59	5	2	7	31	25	43	.261	.337	.394	96	-2	1			.976	-6	O-66	-1.0
1948 Bos-N	13	33	0	9	2	0	0	6	4	2	.273	.385	.333	97	0	0			1.000	2	/O-8	0.1
Total 11	1057	3494	428	982	162	32	107	451	299	377	.281	.342	.438	119	78	11			.982	9	O-915/3-20	4.2
Team 3	183	506	67	140	19	4	15	75	48	68	.277	.345	.419	110	6	2			.982	-7	O-139/3-2	-0.8
■ MICKEY LIVINGSTON Livingston, Thompson Orville b: 11/15/14, Newberry, S.C. d: 4/3/83, Newberry, S.C. BR/TR, 6'1.5", 185 lbs. Deb: 9/17/38																						
1949 Bos-N	28	64	6	15	2	1	0	6	3	5	.234	.290	.297	61	-4	0			.977	1	C-22	-0.2
Total 10	561	1490	128	354	56	9	19	153	144	141	.238	.310	.326	82	-37	7			.984	-11	C-483/1-14	-1.8
■ BOB LOANE Loane, Robert Kenneth b: 8/6/14, Berkeley, Cal. BR/TR, 6', 190 lbs. Deb: 7/29/39																						
1940 Bos-N	13	22	4	5	3	0	0	1	2	5	.227	.292	.364	84	-1	2			1.000	0	O-10	0.0
Total 2	16	31	6	5	3	0	0	2	6	9	.161	.297	.258	54	-2	2			.969	2	/O-13	0.0
■ JOHNNY LOGAN Logan, John "Yatcha" b: 3/23/27, Endicott, N.Y. BR/TR, 5'11", 175 lbs. Deb: 4/17/51																						
1951 Bos-N	62	169	14	37	7	1	0	16	18	13	.219	.298	.272	59	-10	0	0	0	.958	4	S-58	-0.2
1952 Bos-N	117	456	56	129	21	3	4	42	31	33	.283	.334	.368	98	-2	1	2	-1	**.972**	18	*S-117	2.4
1953 Mil-N	150	611	100	167	27	8	11	73	41	33	.273	.326	.398	93	-7	2	2	-1	**.975**	21	*S-150	2.3
1954 Mil-N	154	560	66	154	17	7	8	66	51	51	.275	.342	.373	92	-7	2	0	1	**.969**	14	*S-154	2.1
1955 Mil-N★	154	595	95	177	**37**	5	13	83	58	58	.297	.364	.442	118	16	3	3	-1	.963	8	*S-154	3.5
1956 Mil-N	148	545	69	153	27	5	15	46	46	49	.281	.342	.431	113	9	3	0	1	.968	3	*S-148	2.6
1957 *Mil-N☆	129	494	59	135	19	7	10	49	31	49	.273	.321	.401	100	-2	5	0	2	.960	24	*S-129	3.6
1958 *Mil-N★	145	530	54	120	20	0	11	53	40	57	.226	.287	.326	68	-26	1	2	-1	.959	10	*S-144	-0.4
1959 Mil-N☆	138	470	59	137	17	0	13	50	57	45	.291	.372	.411	118	13	1	3	-2	.975	-3	*S-138	2.0
1960 Mil-N	136	482	52	118	14	4	7	42	43	40	.245	.309	.334	82	-12	1	1	-0	.956	2	*S-136	0.0
1961 Mil-N	18	19	0	2	1	0	0	1	1	3	.105	.150	.158	-19	-3	0	0	0	1.000	-0	/S-2	-0.4
Total 13	1503	5244	651	1407	216	41	93	547	451	472	.268	.331	.378	95	-41	19	13	-2	.965	105	*S-1380/3-30	17.3
Team 11	1351	4931	624	1329	207	40	92	521	417	431	.270	.332	.384	97	-31	19	13	-2	.966	100	*S-1330	17.5
■ ERNIE LOMBARDI Lombardi, Ernesto Natali "Schnozz" or "Bocci" b: 4/6/08, Oakland, Cal. d: 9/26/77, Santa Cruz, Cal. BR/TR, 6'3", 230 lbs. Deb: 4/15/31 H																						
1942 Bos-N★	105	309	32	102	14	0	11	46	37	12	**.330**	.403	.482	162	24	1			.980	-16	C-85	1.5
Total 17	1853	5855	601	1792	277	27	190	990	430	262	.306	.358	.460	126	195	8			.979	-113	*C-1544	17.3
■ HERMAN LONG Long, Herman C. "Germany" or "Flying Dutchman" b: 4/13/1866, Chicago, Ill. d: 9/17/09, Denver, Colo. BL/TR, 5'8.5", 160 lbs. Deb: 4/17/1889																						
1890 Bos-N	101	431	95	108	15	3	8	52	40	34	.251	.320	.355	90	-8	49			.898	11	*S-101	0.8
1891 Bos-N	139	577	129	163	21	12	9	76	80	51	.282	.377	.407	115	9	60			.902	15	*S-139	2.8
1892 *Bos-N	151	646	115	181	33	6	6	78	44	36	.280	.334	.378	105	1	57			.889	14	*S-141,O-12/3	1.9
1893 Bos-N	128	552	**149**	159	22	6	6	58	73	32	.288	.376	.382	94	-6	38			.883	16	*S-123/2-5	1.3
1894 Bos-N	104	475	136	154	28	11	12	79	35	17	.324	.375	.505	103	-2	24			.885	3	*S-98/O-5,2	0.5
1895 Bos-N	124	535	109	169	23	10	9	75	31	12	.316	.357	.447	99	-5	35			.891	-7	*S-122/2-2	-0.5
1896 Bos-N	120	501	105	172	26	8	6	100	26	16	.343	.382	.463	115	9	36			.897	10	*S-120	1.9
1897 *Bos-N	107	450	89	145	32	7	3	69	23		.322	.358	.444	105	0	22			.905	-3	*S-107/O-1	0.0
1898 Bos-N	144	589	99	156	21	10	6	99	39		.265	.311	.365	89	-11	20			.923	1	*S-142/2-2	-0.3
1899 Bos-N	145	578	91	153	30	8	6	100	45		.265	.321	.375	83	-17	20			.929	-10	*S-143/1-2	-1.4
1900 Bos-N	125	486	80	127	19	4	**12**	66	44		.261	.325	.391	86	-12	26			.937	-6	*S-125	-0.8
1901 Bos-N	138	518	54	112	14	6	3	68	25		.216	.254	.284	51	-34	20			**.946**	-3	*S-138	-2.5
1902 Bos-N	120	439	40	101	11	0	2	44	31		.230	.282	.269	69	-16	24			**.946**	23	*S-107,2-13	1.5
Total 16	1874	7674	1455	2127	342	97	91	1055	612	261	.277	.335	.383	93	-109	534			.906	94	*S-1794/2-65,O13	6.6
Team 13	1646	6777	1291	1900	295	91	88	964	536	198	.280	.337	.390	94	-91	431			.910	65	*S-1606/2-25,O13	5.2
■ STAN LOPATA Lopata, Stanley Edward "Stash" b: 9/12/25, Delray, Mich. BR/TR, 6'2", 210 lbs. Deb: 9/19/48																						
1959 Mil-N	25	48	0	5	0	0	0	4	3	13	.104	.157	.104	-31	-9	0	0	0	1.000	-3	C-11/1-2	-1.2
1960 Mil-N	7	8	0	1	0	0	0	0	1	3	.125	.222	.125	-2	-1	0	0	0	.944	1	/C-4	0.0
Total 13	853	2601	375	661	116	25	116	397	393	497	.254	.354	.452	115	56	18	11		.986	-15	C-695/1-66	6.5
Team 2	32	56	0	6	0	0	0	4	4	16	.107	.167	.107	-27	-10	0	0		.984	-2	/C-15,1-2	-1.2

■ AL LOPEZ Lopez, Alfonso Ramon b: 8/20/08, Tampa, Fla. BR/TR, 5'11", 165 lbs. Deb: 9/27/28 MH

YEAR	TM/L	G	AB	R	H	2B	3B	HR	RBI	BB	SO	AVG	OBP	SLG	PRO+	BR/A	SB	CS	SBR	FA	FR	G/POS	TPR
1936	Bos-N	128	426	46	103	12	5	7	50	41	41	.242	.311	.343	81	-12	1			.975	10	*C-127/1-1	0.4
1937	Bos-N	105	334	31	68	11	1	3	38	35	57	.204	.281	.269	55	-21	3			.984	8	*C-102	-0.7
1938	Bos-N	71	236	19	63	6	1	1	14	11	24	.267	.305	.314	78	-8	5			.989	3	C-71	-0.1
1939	Bos-N	131	412	32	104	22	1	8	49	40	45	.252	.319	.369	91	-6	1			.986	3	*C-129	0.3
1940	Bos-N	36	119	20	35	3	1	2	17	6	8	.294	.328	.387	102	-0	1			.987	2	C-36	0.4
Total	19	1950	5916	613	1547	206	43	51	652	556	538	.261	.326	.337	83	-133	46			.985	67	*C-1918/3-3,21	4.6
Team	5	471	1527	148	373	54	9	21	168	133	175	.244	.307	.333	79	-47	11			.983	26	C-465/1-1	0.3

■ JAVY LOPEZ Lopez, Javier Torres b: 11/5/70, Ponce, P.R. BR/TR, 6'3", 185 lbs. Deb: 9/18/92

YEAR	TM/L	G	AB	R	H	2B	3B	HR	RBI	BB	SO	AVG	OBP	SLG	PRO+	BR/A	SB	CS	SBR	FA	FR	G/POS	TPR
1992	*Atl-N	9	16	3	6	2	0	0	2	0	1	.375	.375	.500	137	1	0	0	0	1.000	1	/C-9	0.2
1993	Atl-N	8	16	1	6	1	1	1	2	0	2	.375	.412	.750	201	2	0	0	0	.975	2	/C-7	0.4
1994	Atl-N	80	277	27	68	9	0	13	35	17	61	.245	.301	.419	83	-7	0	2	-1	.995	2	C-75	-0.1
1995	*Atl-N	100	333	37	105	11	4	14	51	14	57	.315	.347	.498	117	7	0	1	-1	.988	2	C-93	1.3
Total	4	197	642	68	185	23	5	28	90	31	121	.288	.329	.470	105	3	0	3	-2	.991	7	C-184	1.8

■ BRIS LORD Lord, Bristol Robotham "The Human Eyeball" b: 9/21/1883, Upland, Pa. d: 11/13/64, Annapolis, Md. BR/TR, 5'9", 185 lbs. Deb: 4/21/05

YEAR	TM/L	G	AB	R	H	2B	3B	HR	RBI	BB	SO	AVG	OBP	SLG	PRO+	BR/A	SB	CS	SBR	FA	FR	G/POS	TPR
1913	Bos-N	73	235	22	59	12	1	6	26	8	22	.251	.276	.387	86	-5	7			.914	-10	O-62	-1.9
Total	8	742	2767	379	707	119	49	13	236	175	22	.256	.304	.348	95	-22	74			.957	8	O-713/P-1	-5.3

■ FLETCHER LOW Low, Fletcher b: 4/7/1893, Essex, Mass. d: 6/6/73, Hanover, N.H. BR/TR, 5'10.5", 175 lbs. Deb: 10/7/15

YEAR	TM/L	G	AB	R	H	2B	3B	HR	RBI	BB	SO	AVG	OBP	SLG	PRO+	BR/A	SB	CS	SBR	FA	FR	G/POS	TPR
1915	Bos-N	1	4	1	1	0	1	0	1	0	0	.250	.250	.750	207	0	0			1.000	-0	/3-1	0.0

■ BOBBY LOWE Lowe, Robert Lincoln "Link" b: 7/10/1868, Pittsburgh, Pa. d: 12/8/51, Detroit, Mich. BR/TR, 5'10", 150 lbs. Deb: 4/19/1890 M

YEAR	TM/L	G	AB	R	H	2B	3B	HR	RBI	BB	SO	AVG	OBP	SLG	PRO+	BR/A	SB	CS	SBR	FA	FR	G/POS	TPR
1890	Bos-N	52	207	35	58	13	2	2	21	26	32	.280	.366	.391	112	3	15			.951	-9	S-24,O-15,3	-0.4
1891	Bos-N	125	497	92	129	19	5	6	74	53	54	.260	.342	.354	92	-7	43			.927	-6	*O-107,2-17/S3P	-1.5
1892	*Bos-N	124	475	79	115	16	7	3	57	37	46	.242	.308	.324	84	-11	36			.928	13	O-90,3-14,S2	0.0
1893	Bos-N	126	526	130	157	19	5	14	89	55	29	.298	.369	.433	105	0	22			.936	1	*2-121/S-5	0.4
1894	Bos-N	133	613	158	212	34	11	17	115	50	25	.346	.401	.520	112	8	23			.927	-6	*2-130/S-2,3	0.6
1895	Bos-N	99	412	101	122	12	7	7	62	40	16	.296	.370	.410	94	-5	24			.954	15	*2-99	1.2
1896	Bos-N	73	305	59	98	11	4	2	48	20	11	.321	.371	.403	98	-1	15			.965	25	2-73	2.3
1897	*Bos-N	123	499	87	154	24	8	5	106	32		.309	.355	.419	98	-4	16			.952	-4	*2-123	-0.1
1898	Bos-N	147	559	65	152	11	7	4	94	29		.272	.311	.338	82	-15	12			.958	16	*2-145/S-2	1.0
1899	Bos-N	152	559	81	152	5	9	4	88	35		.272	.316	.335	72	-24	17			.954	3	*2-148/S-4	-1.1
1900	Bos-N	127	474	65	132	11	5	3	71	26		.278	.323	.342	74	-18	15			.951	-7	*2-127	-1.8
1901	Bos-N	129	491	47	125	11	1	3	47	17		.255	.284	.299	63	-24	22			.912	-5	*3-111,2-18	-2.7
Total	18	1818	7064	1131	1929	230	85	71	984	473	213	.273	.325	.360	86	-157	302			.950	70	*2-1313,O-240,3/S1P	-4.1
Team	12	1410	5617	999	1606	186	71	70	872	420	213	.286	.342	.382	90	-100	260			.948	37	*2-1011,O-212,3/SP	-2.1

■ RED LUCAS Lucas, Charles Frederick "The Nashville Narcissus" b: 4/28/02, Columbia, Tenn. d: 7/9/86, Nashville, Tenn. BL/TR, 5'9.5", 170 lbs. Deb: 4/19/23

YEAR	TM/L	G	AB	R	H	2B	3B	HR	RBI	BB	SO	AVG	OBP	SLG	PRO+	BR/A	SB	CS	SBR	FA	FR	G/POS	TPR
1924	Bos-N	33	33	5	11	1	0	0	5	1	4	.333	.353	.364	96	-0	0	0	0	1.000	1	P-27/3-2	0.0
1925	Bos-N	6	20	1	3	0	0	0	2	2	4	.150	.227	.150	-2	-3	0	0	0	.968	0	/2-6	-0.3
Total	16	907	1439	155	404	61	13	3	190	124	133	.281	.340	.347	84	-29	2	0		.981	-14	P-396/2-12,S3O	-0.7
Team	2	39	53	6	14	1	0	0	7	3	8	.264	.304	.283	59	-3	0	0		1.000	1	/P-27,2-6,3	-0.3

■ MIKE LUM Lum, Michael Ken-Wai b: 10/27/45, Honolulu, Hawaii BL/TL, 6', 180 lbs. Deb: 9/12/67 C

YEAR	TM/L	G	AB	R	H	2B	3B	HR	RBI	BB	SO	AVG	OBP	SLG	PRO+	BR/A	SB	CS	SBR	FA	FR	G/POS	TPR
1967	Atl-N	9	26	1	6	0	0	0	1	1	4	.231	.259	.231	42	-2	0	1	-1	.944	1	/O-6	-0.2
1968	Atl-N	122	232	22	52	7	3	3	21	14	35	.224	.280	.319	79	-6	3	5	-2	.976	-9	O-95	-2.4
1969	*Atl-N	121	168	20	45	8	0	1	22	16	18	.268	.332	.333	86	-3	0	0	0	.992	-8	O-89	-1.3
1970	Atl-N	123	291	25	74	17	2	7	28	17	43	.254	.307	.399	83	-8	3	2	-0	.988	-3	O-98	-1.5
1971	Atl-N	145	454	56	122	14	1	13	55	47	43	.269	.344	.390	101	1	0	3	-2	.990	9	*O-125/1-1	0.3
1972	Atl-N	123	369	40	84	14	2	9	38	50	52	.228	.325	.350	84	-7	1	4	-2	.976	4	*O-109/1-2	-1.0
1973	Atl-N	138	513	74	151	26	6	16	82	41	89	.294	.354	.462	116	10	2	5	-2	.991	-3	1-84,O-64	-0.4
1974	Atl-N	106	361	50	84	11	2	11	50	45	49	.233	.321	.366	88	-6	0	2	-1	.994	-5	1-60,O-50	-1.9
1975	Atl-N	124	364	32	83	8	2	8	36	39	38	.228	.303	.327	72	-14	2	4	-2	.992	-1	1-60,O-38	-2.3
1979	Atl-N	111	217	27	54	6	0	6	27	18	34	.249	.306	.359	75	-7	0	2	-1	.998	2	1-51/O-3	-0.9
1980	Atl-N	93	83	7	17	3	0	0	5	18	19	.205	.347	.241	65	-3	0	0	0	1.000	-3	O-19,1-10	-0.7
1981	Atl-N	10	11	1	1	0	0	0	0	2	2	.091	.231	.091	-6	-1	0	0	0	1.000	0	/O-1	-0.1
Total	15	1517	3554	404	877	128	20	90	431	366	506	.247	.322	.370	89	-54	13	29	-14	.986	-29	O-816,1-284	-15.2
Team	12	1225	3089	355	773	114	18	74	365	308	426	.250	.323	.371	89	-46	11	28	-14	.986	-15	O-697,1-268	-12.4

■ BILLY LUSH Lush, William Lucas b: 11/10/1873, Bridgeport, Conn. d: 8/28/51, Hawthorne, N.Y. BB/TR, 5'8", 165 lbs. Deb: 9/3/1895 F

YEAR	TM/L	G	AB	R	H	2B	3B	HR	RBI	BB	SO	AVG	OBP	SLG	PRO+	BR/A	SB	CS	SBR	FA	FR	G/POS	TPR
1901	Bos-N	7	27	2	5	1	1	0	3	3		.185	.267	.296	58	-2	0			.960	3	/O-7	0.0
1902	Bos-N	120	413	68	92	8	1	2	19	76		.223	.346	.262	87	-2	30			.952	11	*O-116/3-1	0.1
Total	7	489	1722	294	429	49	35	8	152	291		.249	.360	.332	107	27	84			.943	24	O-461/3-13,2S	2.6
Team	2	127	440	70	97	9	2	2	22	79		.220	.342	.264	85	-4	30			.952	13	O-123/3-1	0.1

■ STEVE LYONS Lyons, Stephen John b: 6/3/60, Tacoma, Wash. BL/TR, 6'3", 192 lbs. Deb: 4/15/85

YEAR	TM/L	G	AB	R	H	2B	3B	HR	RBI	BB	SO	AVG	OBP	SLG	PRO+	BR/A	SB	CS	SBR	FA	FR	G/POS	TPR
1992	Atl-N	11	14	0	1	0	1	0	1	0	4	.071	.071	.214	-21	-2	0	0	0	1.000	-2	/O-6,2-2	-0.4
Total	9	853	2162	264	545	100	17	19	196	156	364	.252	.304	.340	77	-67	42	32		.979	-4	O-334,3-229,21/DSCP	-9.0

■ MIKE MACHA Macha, Michael William b: 2/17/54, Victoria, Tex. BR/TR, 5'11", 180 lbs. Deb: 4/20/79 F

YEAR	TM/L	G	AB	R	H	2B	3B	HR	RBI	BB	SO	AVG	OBP	SLG	PRO+	BR/A	SB	CS	SBR	FA	FR	G/POS	TPR
1979	Atl-N	6	13	2	2	0	0	0	1	1	5	.154	.214	.154	2	-2	0	0	0	.769	0	/3-3	-0.1
Total	2	11	21	2	2	0	0	0	1	1	6	.095	.136	.095	-33	-4	0	0	0	.773	1	/3-5,C-1	-0.3

■ JOE MACK Mack, Joe John (b: Joseph John Maciarz) b: 1/4/12, Chicago, Ill. BB/TL, 5'11.5", 185 lbs. Deb: 4/17/45

YEAR	TM/L	G	AB	R	H	2B	3B	HR	RBI	BB	SO	AVG	OBP	SLG	PRO+	BR/A	SB	CS	SBR	FA	FR	G/POS	TPR
1945	Bos-N	66	260	30	60	13	1	3	44	34	39	.231	.320	.323	79	-7	1			.991	0	1-65	-1.1

■ MAX MACON Macon, Max Cullen b: 10/14/15, Pensacola, Fla. d: 8/5/89, Jupiter, Fla. BL/TL, 6'3", 175 lbs. Deb: 4/21/38

YEAR	TM/L	G	AB	R	H	2B	3B	HR	RBI	BB	SO	AVG	OBP	SLG	PRO+	BR/A	SB	CS	SBR	FA	FR	G/POS	TPR
1944	Bos-N	106	366	38	100	15	3	3	36	12	23	.273	.296	.355	79	-11	7			.977	-2	1-72,O-22/P	-1.8
1947	Bos-N	1	1	0	0	0	0	0	0	0	0	.000	.000	.000	-99	-0	0			1.000	0	/P-1	0.0
Total	6	226	502	54	133	17	4	3	46	16	32	.265	.288	.333	72	-19	9			.965	-2	/P-81,1-75,O	-2.0
Team	2	107	367	38	100	15	3	3	36	12	23	.272	.296	.354	79	-11	7			.977	-2	/1-72,O-22,P	-1.8

■ TOMMY MADDEN Madden, Thomas Joseph b: 7/31/1883, Philadelphia, Pa. d: 7/26/30, Philadelphia, Pa. BL/TL, 5'11", 160 lbs. Deb: 9/10/06

YEAR	TM/L	G	AB	R	H	2B	3B	HR	RBI	BB	SO	AVG	OBP	SLG	PRO+	BR/A	SB	CS	SBR	FA	FR	G/POS	TPR
1906	Bos-N	4	15	1	4	0	0	0	0	1		.267	.313	.267	83	-0	0			1.000	-0	/O-4	-0.1
Total	2	5	16	1	4	0	0	0	0	1		.250	.294	.250	71	-1	0			.935	-1	/O-4	-0.2

■ JERRY MADDOX Maddox, Jerry Glenn b: 7/28/53, Whittier, Cal. BR/TR, 6'2", 200 lbs. Deb: 6/3/78

YEAR	TM/L	G	AB	R	H	2B	3B	HR	RBI	BB	SO	AVG	OBP	SLG	PRO+	BR/A	SB	CS	SBR	FA	FR	G/POS	TPR
1978	Atl-N	7	14	1	3	0	0	0	1	1	2	.214	.267	.214	32	-1	0	0	0	.909	-0	/3-5	-0.2

■ SHERRY MAGEE Magee, Sherwood Robert b: 8/6/1884, Clarendon, Pa. d: 3/13/29, Philadelphia, Pa. BR/TR, 5'11", 179 lbs. Deb: 6/29/04 U

YEAR	TM/L	G	AB	R	H	2B	3B	HR	RBI	BB	SO	AVG	OBP	SLG	PRO+	BR/A	SB	CS	SBR	FA	FR	G/POS	TPR
1915	Bos-N	156	571	72	160	34	12	2	87	54	39	.280	.350	.392	130	21	15	12	-3	.981	15	*O-135,1-21	2.9
1916	Bos-N	122	419	44	101	17	5	3	54	44	52	.241	.322	.327	104	3	10			.978	-5	*O-120/1-2,S	-1.0

YEAR	TM/L	G	AB	R	H	2B	3B	HR	RBI	BB	SO	AVG	OBP	SLG	PRO+	BR/A	SB	CS	SBR	FA	FR	G/POS	TPR
1917	Bos-N	72	246	24	63	8	4	1	29	13	23	.256	.302	.333	100	-0	7			.954	2	O-65/1-2	-0.3
Total	16	2087	7441	1112	2169	425	166	83	1176	736	359	.291	.364	.427	137	324	441	12		.970	16	*O-1861,1-136/S23	26.5
Team	3	350	1236	140	324	59	21	6	170	111	114	.262	.331	.358	116	23	32	12		.975	12	O-320/1-25,S	1.6

■ HARL MAGGERT

Maggert, Harl Warren b: 5/4/14, Los Angeles, Cal. d: 7/10/86, Citrus Heights, Cal. BR/TR, 6', 190 lbs. Deb: 4/19/38 F

YEAR	TM/L	G	AB	R	H	2B	3B	HR	RBI	BB	SO	AVG	OBP	SLG	PRO+	BR/A	SB	CS	SBR	FA	FR	G/POS	TPR
1938	Bos-N	66	89	12	25	3	0	3	19	10	20	.281	.354	.416	123	3	0			.944	-0	O-10/3-8	0.2

■ FREDDIE MAGUIRE

Maguire, Frederick Edward b: 5/10/1899, Roxbury, Mass. d: 11/3/61, Boston, Mass. BR/TR, 5'11", 155 lbs. Deb: 9/22/22

YEAR	TM/L	G	AB	R	H	2B	3B	HR	RBI	BB	SO	AVG	OBP	SLG	PRO+	BR/A	SB	CS	SBR	FA	FR	G/POS	TPR
1929	Bos-N	138	496	54	125	26	8	0	41	19	40	.252	.284	.337	55	-36	8			.971	8	*2-138/S-1	-2.0
1930	Bos-N	146	516	54	138	21	5	0	52	20	22	.267	.297	.328	53	-40	4			.969	-4	*2-146	-3.2
1931	Bos-N	148	492	36	112	18	2	0	26	16	26	.228	.259	.272	45	-39	3			**.976**	9	*2-148	-2.1
Total	6	618	2120	226	545	90	22	1	163	82	131	.257	.289	.322	57	-140	23			.971	77	2-589/S-1,3	-3.2
Team	3	432	1504	144	375	65	15	0	119	55	88	.249	.280	.313	51	-114	15			.972	13	2-432/S-1	-7.3

■ MIKE MAHONEY

Mahoney, George W. "Big Mike" b: 12/5/1873, Boston, Mass. d: 1/3/40, Boston, Mass. BR , 6'4", 220 lbs. Deb: 5/18/1897

YEAR	TM/L	G	AB	R	H	2B	3B	HR	RBI	BB	SO	AVG	OBP	SLG	PRO+	BR/A	SB	CS	SBR	FA	FR	G/POS	TPR
1897	Bos-N	2	2	1	1	0	0	0	1	0		.500	.500	.500	155	0	0			1.000	0	/C-1,P-1	0.0
Total	2	4	9	1	1	0	0	0	1	0		.111	.111	.111	-36	-2	0			.949	-0	/1-2,P-1,C	-0.2

■ HANK MAJESKI

Majeski, Henry "Heeney" b: 12/13/16, Staten Island, N.Y d: 8/9/91, Staten Island, N.Y. BR/TR, 5'9", 180 lbs. Deb: 5/17/39

YEAR	TM/L	G	AB	R	H	2B	3B	HR	RBI	BB	SO	AVG	OBP	SLG	PRO+	BR/A	SB	CS	SBR	FA	FR	G/POS	TPR
1939	Bos-N	106	367	35	100	16	1	7	54	18	30	.272	.310	.379	91	-6	2			.945	12	3-99	0.7
1940	Bos-N	3	3	0	0	0	0	0	0	0	0	.000	.000	.000	-99	-1	0			.000	0	H	-0.1
1941	Bos-N	19	55	5	8	5	0	0	3	1	13	.145	.161	.236	11	-7	0			.911	1	3-11	-0.6
Total	13	1069	3421	404	956	181	27	57	501	299	260	.279	.342	.398	100	-9	10			.968	49	3-861/2-48,SO	3.2
Team	3	128	425	40	108	21	1	7	57	19	43	.254	.289	.358	79	-14	2			.941	13	3-110	-0.0

■ BOBBY MALKMUS

Malkmus, Robert Edward b: 7/4/31, Newark, N.J. BR/TR, 5'9", 180 lbs. Deb: 6/1/57

YEAR	TM/L	G	AB	R	H	2B	3B	HR	RBI	BB	SO	AVG	OBP	SLG	PRO+	BR/A	SB	CS	SBR	FA	FR	G/POS	TPR
1957	Mil-N	13	22	6	2	0	1	0	0	3	3	.091	.200	.182	4	-3	0	0	0	.972	4	/2-7	0.1
Total	6	268	572	69	123	15	5	8	46	38	90	.215	.266	.301	53	-39	3	5	-2	.982	36	2-114/S-65,3	0.7

■ LES MALLON

Mallon, Leslie Clyde b: 11/21/05, Sweetwater, Tex. d: 4/17/91, Granbury, Tex. BR/TR, 5'8", 160 lbs. Deb: 4/14/31

YEAR	TM/L	G	AB	R	H	2B	3B	HR	RBI	BB	SO	AVG	OBP	SLG	PRO+	BR/A	SB	CS	SBR	FA	FR	G/POS	TPR
1934	Bos-N	42	166	23	49	6	1	0	18	15	12	.295	.354	.343	95	-1	0			.967	-4	2-42	-0.3
1935	Bos-N	116	412	48	113	24	2	2	25	28	37	.274	.322	.357	89	-7	3			.975	-14	2-73,3-36/O	-1.3
Total	4	383	1300	156	368	65	5	8	119	100	117	.283	.336	.359	85	-26	4			.962	-43	2-300/3-44,1SO	-4.9
Team	2	158	578	71	162	30	3	2	43	43	49	.280	.331	.353	91	-8	3			.972	-18	2-115/3-36,O	-1.6

■ KELLY MANN

Mann, Kelly John b: 8/17/67, Santa Monica, Cal. BR/TR, 6'3", 215 lbs. Deb: 9/4/89

YEAR	TM/L	G	AB	R	H	2B	3B	HR	RBI	BB	SO	AVG	OBP	SLG	PRO+	BR/A	SB	CS	SBR	FA	FR	G/POS	TPR
1989	Atl-N	7	24	1	5	2	0	0	1	0	6	.208	.240	.292	50	-2	0	0	0	1.000	2	/C-7	0.1
1990	Atl-N	11	28	2	4	1	0	1	2	0	6	.143	.143	.286	14	-3	0	0	0	1.000	-1	C-10	-0.4
Total	2	18	52	3	9	3	0	1	3	0	12	.173	.189	.288	30	-5	0	0	0	1.000	1	/C-17	-0.3

■ LES MANN

Mann, Leslie "Major" b: 11/18/1893, Lincoln, Neb. d: 1/14/62, Pasadena, Cal. BR/TR, 5'9", 172 lbs. Deb: 4/30/13

YEAR	TM/L	G	AB	R	H	2B	3B	HR	RBI	BB	SO	AVG	OBP	SLG	PRO+	BR/A	SB	CS	SBR	FA	FR	G/POS	TPR
1913	Bos-N	120	407	54	103	24	7	3	51	18	73	.253	.291	.369	86	-9	7			.960	-2	*O-120	-1.7
1914	*Bos-N	126	389	44	96	16	11	4	40	24	50	.247	.292	.375	99	-2	9			.952	13	*O-123	0.6
1919	Bos-N	40	145	15	41	6	4	3	20	9	14	.283	.329	.441	136	6	7			.929	3	O-40	0.6
1920	Bos-N	115	424	48	117	7	8	3	32	38	42	.276	.341	.351	104	3	7	7	-2	.980	3	*O-110	-0.5
1924	Bos-N	32	102	13	28	7	4	0	10	8	10	.275	.333	.422	105	1	1	0	0	1.000	2	O-28	0.1
1925	Bos-N	60	184	27	63	11	4	2	20	5	11	.342	.373	.478	127	7	6	1	1	.992	-2	O-57	0.3
1926	Bos-N	50	129	23	39	8	2	1	20	9	9	.302	.348	.419	116	2	5			.966	-6	O-46	-0.6
1927	Bos-N	29	66	8	17	3	1	0	6	8	3	.258	.338	.333	87	-1	2			.955	-2	O-24	-0.4
Total	16	1498	4716	677	1332	203	106	44	503	324	464	.282	.332	.398	108	43	129	21		.966	-32	*O-1368/S-1	-6.9
Team	8	572	1846	232	504	82	41	16	199	119	212	.273	.322	.388	104	5	44	8		.965	8	O-548	-1.6

■ JIM MANNING

Manning, James H. b: 1/31/1862, Fall River, Mass. d: 10/22/29, Edinburg, Tex. BB/TR, 5'7", 157 lbs. Deb: 5/16/1884 M

YEAR	TM/L	G	AB	R	H	2B	3B	HR	RBI	BB	SO	AVG	OBP	SLG	PRO+	BR/A	SB	CS	SBR	FA	FR	G/POS	TPR
1884	Bos-N	89	345	52	83	8	6	2	35	19	47	.241	.280	.316	88	-5				.878	1	O-73/S-9,23	-0.4
1885	Bos-N	84	306	34	63	8	9	2	27	19	36	.206	.252	.310	84	-5				.898	9	*O-83/S-1	0.2
Total	5	364	1384	188	298	39	25	8	149	107	168	.215	.278	.297	73	-46	68	0	20	.903	-11	O-261/2-72,S3	-5.2
Team	2	173	651	86	146	16	15	4	62	38	83	.224	.267	.313	86	-10	0	0	0	.890	10	O-156/S-10,23	-0.2

■ JACK MANNING

Manning, John E. b: 12/20/1853, Braintree, Mass. d: 8/15/29, Boston, Mass. BR/TR, 5'8.5", 158 lbs. Deb: 4/23/1873 M

YEAR	TM/L	G	AB	R	H	2B	3B	HR	RBI	BB	SO	AVG	OBP	SLG	PRO+	BR/A	SB	CS	SBR	FA	FR	G/POS	TPR
1873	Bos-n	32	159	29	43	5	2	0	22	1	11	.270	.275	.327	71	-7						1-29/O-5	-0.4
1875	Bos-n	77	343	71	94	8	2	1		2		.274	.278	.318	102	-0						*O-58,P-27,13	0.3
1876	Bos-N	70	288	52	76	13	0	2	25	7	5	.264	.281	.330	101	0				.777	-5	*O-56,P-34/S2	-0.5
1878	Bos-N	60	248	41	63	10	1	0	23	10	16	.254	.283	.302	86	-4				.753	-13	*O-59/P-3	-1.9
Total	3 n	152	675	134	197	23	5	1	22	6	11	.292	.298	.345	105	2	1	0	0			/O-63,P-49,12S3	0.5
Total	9	682	2824	430	725	147	31	13	230	176	173	.257	.301	.345	108	33	24	0	7	.844	-40	O-621/P-47,S12	-2.2
Team	2 n	109	502	100	137	13	4	1	22	3	11	.273	.277	.321	91	0	1	0	0	.765	0	/O-63,1-31,P3	-0.1
Team	2	130	536	93	139	23	1	2	48	17	21	.259	.282	.317	94	-4	0	0	0	.765	-18	O-115/P-37,2S	-2.4

■ DON MANNO

Manno, Donald D. b: 5/15/15, Williamsport, Pa. BR/TR, 6'1", 190 lbs. Deb: 9/22/40

YEAR	TM/L	G	AB	R	H	2B	3B	HR	RBI	BB	SO	AVG	OBP	SLG	PRO+	BR/A	SB	CS	SBR	FA	FR	G/POS	TPR
1940	Bos-N	3	7	1	2	0	0	1	4	0	2	.286	.286	.714	177	1	0			1.000	0	/O-2	0.1
1941	Bos-N	22	30	2	5	1	0	0	4	3	7	.167	.242	.200	27	-3	0			1.000	-1	/O-5,3-3,1	-0.5
Total	2	25	37	3	7	1	0	1	8	3	9	.189	.250	.297	56	-2	0			1.000	-1	/O-7,3-3,1	-0.4

■ FELIX MANTILLA

Mantilla, Felix (Lamela) b: 7/29/34, Isabela, P.R. BR/TR, 6', 160 lbs. Deb: 6/21/56

YEAR	TM/L	G	AB	R	H	2B	3B	HR	RBI	BB	SO	AVG	OBP	SLG	PRO+	BR/A	SB	CS	SBR	FA	FR	G/POS	TPR
1956	Mil-N	35	53	9	15	1	1	0	3	1	8	.283	.309	.340	79	-2	0	1	-1	1.000	9	S-15/3-3	0.8
1957	*Mil-N	71	182	28	43	9	1	4	21	14	34	.236	.298	.363	82	-5	2	0	1	.931	6	S-35,2-13/3O	0.5
1958	*Mil-N	85	226	37	50	5	1	7	19	20	20	.221	.285	.345	72	-10	2	0	1	.987	-6	O-43,2-21/S3	-1.6
1959	Mil-N	103	251	26	54	5	0	3	19	16	31	.215	.268	.271	48	-19	6	1	1	.970	4	2-60,S-23/3O	-0.9
1960	Mil-N	63	148	21	38	7	0	3	11	7	16	.257	.295	.365	86	-3	3	1	0	.956	-12	2-26,S-25/O	-1.3
1961	Mil-N	45	93	13	20	3	0	1	5	10	16	.215	.298	.280	58	-6	1	1	-0	.933	-4	S-19,2-10,O/3	-0.9
Total	11	969	2707	360	707	97	10	89	330	256	352	.261	.331	.403	100	-6	27	10	2	.977	-44	2-326,S-180,O3/1	-1.9
Team	6	402	953	134	220	30	3	18	78	68	125	.231	.287	.325	69	-45	14	4	2	.970	-2	2-130,S-122/O3	-3.4

■ RABBIT MARANVILLE

Maranville, Walter James Vincent b: 11/11/1891, Springfield, Mass. d: 1/5/54, New York, N.Y. BR/TR, 5'5", 155 lbs. Deb: 9/10/12 MH

YEAR	TM/L	G	AB	R	H	2B	3B	HR	RBI	BB	SO	AVG	OBP	SLG	PRO+	BR/A	SB	CS	SBR	FA	FR	G/POS	TPR
1912	Bos-N	26	86	8	18	2	0	0	8	9	14	.209	.292	.233	44	-6	1			.929	5	S-26	0.1
1913	Bos-N	143	571	68	141	13	8	2	48	68	62	.247	.330	.308	81	-12	25			.949	15	*S-143	1.7
1914	*Bos-N	156	586	74	144	23	6	4	78	45	56	.246	.306	.326	88	-9	28			.938	**52**	*S-156	**5.9**
1915	Bos-N	149	509	51	124	23	6	2	43	45	65	.244	.308	.324	96	-3	18	12	-2	.941	21	*S-149	3.0
1916	Bos-N	155	604	79	142	16	13	4	38	50	69	.235	.296	.325	94	-5	32	15	1	**.947**	22	*S-155	2.9
1917	Bos-N	142	561	69	146	19	13	3	43	40	47	.260	.312	.357	111	6	27			.947	14	*S-142	3.0
1918	Bos-N	11	38	3	12	0	1	0	3	4	0	.316	.381	.368	134	2	0			.932	2	S-11	0.4
1919	Bos-N	131	480	44	128	18	10	5	43	36	23	.267	.319	.377	113	7	12			.941	**29**	*S-131	**4.7**
1920	Bos-N	134	493	48	131	19	15	1	43	28	24	.266	.305	.371	98	-3	14	11	-2	.948	14	*S-133	2.1
1929	Bos-N	146	560	87	159	26	10	0	55	47	33	.284	.344	.366	79	-18	13			.961	20	*S-145/2-1	1.8
1930	Bos-N	142	558	85	157	26	8	2	43	48	23	.281	.344	.367	75	-22	9			**.965**	-13	*S-138/3-4	-1.7
1931	Bos-N	145	562	69	146	22	5	0	33	56	34	.260	.329	.317	77	-17	9			.949	-24	*S-137,2-11	-2.7

YEAR	TM/L	G	AB	R	H	2B	3B	HR	RBI	BB	SO	AVG	OBP	SLG	PRO+	BR/A	SB	CS	SBR	FA	FR	G/POS	TPR
1932	Bos-N	149	571	67	134	20	4	0	37	46	28	.235	.295	.284	59	-32	4			**.975**	6	*2-149	-1.9
1933	Bos-N	143	478	46	104	15	4	0	38	36	34	.218	.274	.266	59	-25	2			.971	-27	*2-142	-4.7
1935	Bos-N	23	67	3	10	2	0	0	5	3	3	.149	.186	.179	-2	-10	0			.963	-5	2-20	-1.3
Total	23	2670	10078	1255	2605	380	177	28	884	839	756	.258	.318	.340	82	-246	291	93		.952	158	*S-2153,2-513/3	12.9
Team	15	1795	6724	801	1696	244	103	23	558	561	515	.252	.313	.329	84	-148	194	38		.948	130	*S-1466,2-323/3	13.3

■ **LUIS MARQUEZ** Marquez, Luis Angel (Sanchez) "Canena" b: 10/28/25, Aguadilla, P.R. d: 3/1/88, Aguadilla, P.R. BR/TR, 5'10.5", 174 lbs. Deb: 4/18/51

1951	Bos-N	68	122	19	24	5	1	0	11	10	20	.197	.274	.254	46	-9	4	4	-1	1.000	-2	O-43	-1.4
Total	2	99	143	24	26	5	1	0	11	16	24	.182	.278	.231	40	-12	7	4	-0	1.000	-7	/O-61	-2.2

■ **WILLIAM MARRIOTT** Marriott, William Earl b: 4/18/1893, Pratt, Kan. d: 8/11/69, Berkeley, Cal. BL/TR, 6', 170 lbs. Deb: 9/6/17

1925	Bos-N	103	370	37	99	9	1	1	40	28	26	.268	.322	.305	67	-18	3	8	-4	.928	3	3-89/O-1	-1.2
Total	6	265	826	86	220	27	14	4	95	57	55	.266	.317	.347	78	-27	16	10	-1	.925	-9	3-196/2-20,OS	-2.8

■ **WILLARD MARSHALL** Marshall, Willard Warren b: 2/8/21, Richmond, Va. BL/TR, 6'1", 205 lbs. Deb: 4/14/42

1950	Bos-N	105	298	38	70	10	2	5	40	36	5	.235	.319	.332	77	-10	1			.958	1	O-85	-1.2
1951	Bos-N	136	469	65	132	24	7	11	62	48	18	.281	.351	.433	118	11	0	3	-2	**1.000**	-8	*O-136	-0.3
1952	Bos-N	21	66	5	15	4	1	2	11	4	4	.227	.271	.409	89	-1	0	0	0	.938	1	O-16	-0.1
Total	11	1246	4233	583	1160	163	39	130	604	458	219	.274	.347	.423	109	51	14	4		.979	20	*O-1145	1.3
Team	3	262	833	108	217	38	10	18	113	88	27	.261	.333	.395	101	-1	1	3		.979	-6	O-237	-1.6

■ **DOC MARSHALL** Marshall, William Riddle b: 9/22/1875, Butler, Pa. d: 12/11/59, Clinton, Ill. BR/TR, 6', 185 lbs. Deb: 4/15/04

1904	Bos-N	13	43	3	9	0	1	0	2	2		.209	.244	.256	56	-2	2			.955	1	C-10/O-1	0.0
Total	5	261	756	51	159	23	8	2	54	34		.210	.251	.270	64	-34	15			.960	19	C-213/O-23,12	0.3

■ **DOC MARTEL** Martel, Leon Alphonse "Marty" b: 1/29/1883, Weymouth, Mass. d: 10/11/47, Washington, D.C. BR/TR, 6', 185 lbs. Deb: 7/6/09

1910	Bos-N	10	31	0	4	0	0	0	1	2	3	.129	.182	.129	-9	-4	0			.980	-0	1-10	-0.5
Total	2	34	72	1	15	3	1	0	8	6	3	.208	.269	.278	64	-3	0			.960	4	/C-12,1-10	0.2

■ **BILLY MARTIN** Martin, Alfred Manuel b: 5/16/28, Berkeley, Cal. d: 12/25/89, Johnson City, N.Y. BR/TR, 5'11.5", 165 lbs. Deb: 4/18/50 MC

1961	Mil-N	6	6	1	0	0	0	0	0	0	1	.000	.000	.000	-99	-2	0	0	0	.000	0	H	-0.2
Total	11	1021	3419	425	877	137	28	64	333	188	355	.257	.301	.369	81	-96	34	29		.980	-61	2-767,S-118/3O	-10.5

■ **JACK MARTIN** Martin, John Christopher b: 4/19/1887, Plainfield, N.J. d: 7/4/80, Plainfield, N.J. BR/TR, 5'9", 159 lbs. Deb: 4/25/12

1914	Bos-N	33	85	10	18	2	0	0	5	6	7	.212	.264	.235	49	-5	0			.949	0	3-26/1-1,2	-0.5
Total	2	187	608	66	144	13	4	0	43	70	36	.237	.323	.271	71	-21	20			.915	-0	S-148/3-30,21	-0.8

■ **BILLY MARTIN** Martin, William Lloyd b: 2/13/1894, Washington, D.C. d: 9/14/49, Arlington, Va. BR/TR, 5'8.5", 170 lbs. Deb: 10/6/14

1914	Bos-N	1	3	0	0	0	0	0	0	0	0	.000	.000	.000	-99	-1	0			.500	-1	/S-1	-0.2

■ **MARTY MARTINEZ** Martinez, Orlando (Oliva) b: 8/23/41, Havana, Cuba BB/TR, 6'1", 175 lbs. Deb: 5/2/62 MC

1967	Atl-N	44	73	14	21	2	1	0	5	11	11	.288	.388	.342	112	2	0	1	-1	.920	4	S-25/2-9,C31	0.8
1968	Atl-N	113	356	34	82	5	3	0	12	29	28	.230	.292	.261	67	-14	6	6	-2	.955	-5	S-54,3-37,2C	-1.6
Total	7	436	945	97	230	19	11	0	57	70	107	.243	.298	.287	70	-37	7	8		.950	-5	S-157/3-74,2CO1P	-3.2
Team	2	157	429	48	103	7	4	0	17	40	39	.240	.309	.275	75	-12	6	7		.944	-1	/S-79,3-39,2C1	-0.8

■ **PHIL MASI** Masi, Philip Samuel b: 1/6/16, Chicago, Ill. d: 3/29/90, Mt.Prospect, Ill. BR/TR, 5'10", 180 lbs. Deb: 4/23/39

1939	Bos-N	46	114	14	29	7	2	1	14	9	15	.254	.315	.377	92	-2	0			.960	-3	C-42	-0.3
1940	Bos-N	63	138	11	27	4	1	1	14	14	14	.196	.270	.261	50	-10	0			.966	-1	C-52	-0.7
1941	Bos-N	87	180	17	40	8	2	3	18	16	13	.222	.286	.339	79	-6	4			.978	-7	C-83	-0.8
1942	Bos-N	57	87	14	19	3	1	0	9	12	4	.218	.313	.276	74	-3	2			.961	2	C-39/O-4	0.1
1943	Bos-N	80	238	27	65	9	1	2	28	27	20	.273	.347	.345	102	1	7			.991	-6	C-73	0.0
1944	Bos-N	89	251	33	69	13	5	3	23	31	20	.275	.355	.402	108	3	4			.977	-0	C-63,1-12/3	0.6
1945	Bos-N†	114	371	55	101	25	4	7	46	42	32	.272	.348	.418	112	5	9			.980	1	C-95/1-7	1.1
1946	Bos-N★	133	397	52	106	17	5	3	62	55	41	.267	.358	.358	102	2	5			.981	-5	*C-124	0.4
1947	Bos-N★	126	411	54	125	22	4	9	50	47	27	.304	.377	.443	120	12	7			**.989**	-6	*C-123	1.4
1948	*Bos-N★	113	376	43	95	19	0	5	44	35	26	.253	.318	.343	80	-10	2			.988	1	*C-109	-0.2
1949	Bos-N	37	105	13	22	2	0	0	6	14	10	.210	.303	.229	47	-8	1			.993	-2	C-37	-0.7
Total	14	1229	3468	420	917	164	31	47	417	410	311	.264	.344	.370	97	-14	45			.983	-27	*C-1101/1-21,O3	1.7
Team	11	945	2668	333	698	129	25	34	314	302	222	.262	.338	.367	96	-14	41			.982	-24	C-840/1-19,O3	0.9

■ **ROY MASSEY** Massey, Roy Hardee "Red" b: 10/9/1890, Sevierville, Tenn. d: 6/23/54, Atlanta, Ga. BL/TR, 5'11", 170 lbs. Deb: 4/16/18

1918	Bos-N	66	203	20	59	6	2	0	18	23	20	.291	.363	.340	120	5	1			.954	-3	O-45/3-2,1S	0.0

■ **MIKE MASSEY** Massey, William Herbert b: 9/28/1893, Galveston, Tex. d: 10/17/71, Shreveport, La. BB/TR, 6', 195 lbs. Deb: 4/12/17

1917	Bos-N	31	91	12	18	0	0	0	2	15	15	.198	.318	.198	63	-3	2			.900	-8	2-25	-1.1

■ **JOE MATHES** Mathes, Joseph John b: 7/28/1891, Milwaukee, Wis. d: 12/21/78, St.Louis, Mo. BB/TR, 6'0.5", 180 lbs. Deb: 9/19/12

1916	Bos-N	2	0	0	0	0	0	0	0	0	0	—	—	—	—	0	0			.000	-1	/2-2	-0.1
Total	3	32	99	10	27	3	0	0	6	9	11	.273	.339	.303	67	-4	1			.921	-6	/2-25,3-4	-1.1

■ **EDDIE MATHEWS** Mathews, Edwin Lee b: 10/13/31, Texarkana, Tex. BL/TR, 6'1", 200 lbs. Deb: 4/15/52 MCH

1952	Bos-N	145	528	80	128	23	5	25	58	59	115	.242	.320	.447	114	8	6	4	-1	.957	-10	*3-142	-0.5
1953	Mil-N★	157	579	110	175	31	8	**47**	135	99	83	.302	.406	.627	**175**	**64**	1	3	-2	.939	3	*3-157	5.8
1954	Mil-N	138	476	96	138	21	4	40	103	113	61	.290	.428	.603	**177**	57	10	3	1	.966	-2	*3-127,O-10	5.2
1955	Mil-N★	141	499	108	144	23	5	41	101	**109**	98	.289	.417	.601	175	56	3	4	-2	.952	-4	*3-137	4.9
1956	Mil-N☆	151	552	103	150	21	2	37	95	91	86	.272	.376	.518	146	36	6	0	2	.944	-12	*3-150	2.8
1957	*Mil-N★	148	572	109	167	28	9	32	94	90	79	.292	.388	.540	157	47	3	1	0	.964	-2	*3-147	4.8
1958	*Mil-N☆	149	546	97	137	18	1	31	77	85	85	.251	.354	.458	123	18	5	0	2	.955	5	*3-149	2.6
1959	Mil-N★	148	594	118	182	16	8	**46**	114	80	71	.306	.391	.593	172	59	2	1	0	.961	3	*3-148	6.2
1960	Mil-N★	153	548	108	152	19	7	39	124	111	113	.277	.401	.551	**170**	**55**	7	3	0	.950	-13	*3-153	4.2
1961	Mil-N★	152	572	103	175	23	6	32	91	**93**	95	.306	.405	.535	156	48	12	7	-1	.961	-6	*3-151	4.2
1962	Mil-N★	152	536	106	142	25	6	29	90	**101**	90	.265	.383	.496	138	30	4	2	0	.964	2	*3-140/1-7	3.3
1963	Mil-N	158	547	82	144	27	4	23	84	**124**	119	.263	**.400**	.453	147	39	3	4	-2	**.968**	15	*3-121,O-42	5.3
1964	Mil-N	141	502	83	117	19	1	23	74	85	100	.233	.345	.412	112	9	2	2	-1	.962	2	*3-128/1-7	0.9
1965	Mil-N	156	546	77	137	23	0	32	95	73	110	.251	.342	.469	125	18	1	0	0	.956	9	*3-153	2.6
1966	Atl-N	134	452	72	113	21	4	16	53	63	82	.250	.342	.420	109	6	1	1	-0	.946	-2	*3-127	0.1
Total	17	2391	8537	1509	2315	354	72	512	1453	1444	1487	.271	.378	.509	145	559	68	39	-3	.956	-20	*3-2181,1-112/O	51.6
Team	15	2223	8049	1452	2201	338	70	493	1388	1376	1387	.273	.381	.517	147	552	66	35	-1	.956	-13	*3-2130/O-52,1	52.4

■ **BOBBY MATHEWS** Mathews, Robert T. b: 11/21/1851, Baltimore, Md. d: 4/17/1898, Baltimore, Md. BR/TR, 5'5.5", 140 lbs. Deb: 5/4/1871 U

1881	Bos-N	19	71	2	12	2	0	0	4	0	5	.169	.169	.197	15	-7				.818	-4	O-18/P-5	-0.9
1882	Bos-N	45	169	17	38	6	0	0	13	8	18	.225	.260	.260	67	-6				.867	-10	P-34,O-13/S	-0.6
Total	5 n	256	1098	160	234	22	8	0	44	19	5	.213	.226	.248	47	-66	4	0	1			P-255/O-8,3	1.0
Total	10	367	1390	158	267	28	2	1	40	53	45	.192	.222	.217	42	-87	1	0	0	.845	-30	P-323/O-65,3S	-2.9
Team	2	64	240	19	50	8	0	0	17	8	23	.208	.234	.242	53	-13	0	0	0	.878	-14	/P-39,O-31,S	-1.5

YEAR	TM/L	G	AB	R	H	2B	3B	HR	RBI	BB	SO	AVG	OBP	SLG	PRO+	BR/A	SB	CS	SBR	FA	FR	G/POS	TPR

■ GARY MATTHEWS   Matthews, Gary Nathaniel   b: 7/5/50, San Fernando, Cal.   BR/TR, 6'3", 190 lbs.   Deb: 9/6/72

1977	Atl-N	148	555	89	157	25	5	17	64	67	90	.283	.362	.438	101	1	22	8	2	.965	8	*O-145	0.6
1978	Atl-N	129	474	75	135	20	5	18	62	61	92	.285	.369	.462	118	11	8	7	-2	.969	2	*O-127	0.6
1979	Atl-N★	156	631	97	192	34	5	27	90	60	75	.304	.365	.502	125	21	18	6	2	.974	1	*O-156	1.7
1980	Atl-N	155	571	79	159	17	3	19	75	42	93	.278	.328	.419	104	2	11	3	2	.960	-3	*O-143	-0.6
Total	16	2033	7147	1083	2011	319	51	234	978	940	1125	.281	.367	.439	116	164	183	74	11	.968	12	*O-1876/D-39	12.0
Team	4	588	2231	340	643	96	18	81	291	230	350	.288	.356	.456	112	35	59	24	3	.967	8	O-571	2.3

■ GENE MAUCH   Mauch, Gene William "Skip"   b: 11/18/25, Salina, Kan.   BR/TR, 5'10", 165 lbs.   Deb: 4/18/44   M

1950	Bos-N	48	121	17	28	5	0	1	15	14	9	.231	.316	.298	67	-6	1			.968	-1	2-28/3-7,S	-0.5
1951	Bos-N	19	20	5	2	0	0	0	1	7	4	.100	.333	.100	24	-2	0	0	0	1.000	-0	S-10/3-3,2	-0.2
Total	9	304	737	93	176	25	7	5	62	104	82	.239	.335	.312	75	-23	6	0		.958	-10	2-158/S-65,3	-2.1
Team	2	67	141	22	30	5	0	1	16	21	13	.213	.319	.270	61	-8	1	0		.968	-1	/2-30,S-15,3	-0.7

■ DAVE MAY   May, David La France   b: 12/23/43, New Castle, Del.   BL/TR, 5'10.5", 186 lbs.   Deb: 7/28/67   F

1975	Atl-N	82	203	28	56	8	0	12	40	25	27	.276	.361	.493	130	8	1	1	-0	.964	-1	O-53	0.5
1976	Atl-N	105	214	27	46	5	3	3	23	26	31	.215	.303	.308	69	-8	5	1	1	.972	-0	O-60	-1.0
Total	12	1252	3670	462	920	130	20	96	422	344	501	.251	.320	.375	97	-16	60	47	-10	.978	10	*O-1021/D-23	-6.3
Team	2	187	417	55	102	13	3	15	63	51	58	.245	.331	.398	99	-0	6	2	1	.968	-2	O-113	-0.5

■ LEE MAYE   Maye, Arthur Lee   b: 12/11/34, Tuscaloosa, Ala.   BL/TR, 6'2", 190 lbs.   Deb: 7/17/59

1959	Mil-N	51	140	17	42	5	1	4	16	7	26	.300	.338	.436	114	2	2	2	-1	.976	1	O-44	0.0
1960	Mil-N	41	83	14	25	6	0	0	2	7	21	.301	.363	.373	110	1	5	0	2	.968	-1	O-19	0.1
1961	Mil-N	110	373	68	101	11	5	14	41	36	50	.271	.340	.440	112	6	10	1	2	.972	-2	O-96	0.0
1962	Mil-N	99	349	40	85	10	0	10	41	25	58	.244	.296	.358	77	-12	9	3	1	.977	1	O-94	-1.6
1963	Mil-N	124	442	67	120	22	7	11	34	36	52	.271	.331	.428	118	10	14	2	3	.983	-8	*O-111	-0.2
1964	Mil-N	153	588	96	179	**44**	5	10	74	34	54	.304	.347	.447	121	16	5	10	-5	.961	-1	*O-135/3-5	0.3
1965	Mil-N	15	53	8	16	2	0	2	7	2	6	.302	.339	.453	120	1	0	0		.962	1	O-13	0.2
Total	13	1288	4048	533	1109	190	39	94	419	282	481	.274	.324	.410	108	32	59	34	-3	.970	-31	*O-1040/3-6,12	-5.7
Team	7	593	2028	310	568	100	18	51	215	147	267	.280	.333	.423	110	23	45	18	3	.973	-11	O-512/3-5	-1.2

■ EDDIE MAYO   Mayo, Edward Joseph "Hotshot" (b: Edward Joseph Mayoski)   b: 4/15/10, Holyoke, Mass.   BL/TR, 5'11", 178 lbs.   Deb: 5/22/36   C

1937	Bos-N	65	172	19	39	6	1	1	18	15	20	.227	.293	.291	65	-9	1			.956	-4	3-50	-1.1
1938	Bos-N	8	14	2	3	0	0	1	4	1	0	.214	.267	.429	98	-0				.923	2	/3-6,S-2	0.1
Total	9	834	3013	350	759	119	16	26	287	257	175	.252	.323	.328	78	-89	29			.978	3	2-544,3-229/S	-6.3
Team	2	73	186	21	42	6	1	2	22	16	20	.226	.291	.301	67	-9	1			.953	-2	/3-56,S-2	-1.0

■ GENE McAULIFFE   McAuliffe, Eugene Leo   b: 2/28/1872, Randolph, Mass.   d: 4/29/53, Randolph, Mass.   BR/TR, 6'1", 180 lbs.   Deb: 8/17/04

| 1904 | Bos-N | 1 | 2 | 0 | 1 | 0 | 0 | 0 | 0 | 0 | 0 | .500 | .500 | .500 | 217 | 0 | 0 | | | .667 | -0 | /C-1 | 0.0 |

■ JOHNNY McCARTHY   McCarthy, John Joseph   b: 1/7/10, Chicago, Ill.   d: 9/13/73, Mundelein, Ill.   BL/TL, 6'1.5", 185 lbs.   Deb: 9/2/34

1943	Bos-N	78	313	32	95	24	6	2	33	10	19	.304	.327	.438	122	7	1			.996	1	1-78	0.3
1946	Bos-N	2	7	0	1	0	0	0	1	2	0	.143	.333	.143	37	-0	0			1.000	-1	/1-2	-0.1
Total	11	542	1557	182	432	72	16	25	209	96	114	.277	.319	.392	95	-14	8			.990	-5	1-383/O-5,P	-5.4
Team	2	80	320	32	96	24	6	2	34	12	19	.300	.327	.431	120	6	1			.996	0	/1-80	0.2

■ TOMMY McCARTHY   McCarthy, Thomas Francis Michael   b: 7/24/1863, Boston, Mass.   d: 8/5/22, Boston, Mass.   BR/TR, 5'7", 170 lbs.   Deb: 7/10/1884   MH

1885	Bos-N	40	148	16	27	2	0		11	5	25	.182	.209	.196	33	-11				.865	3	O-40	-0.8
1892	*Bos-N	152	603	119	146	19	5	4	63	93	29	.242	.347	.310	91	-6	53			.883	2	*O-152	-1.0
1893	Bos-N	116	462	107	160	28	6	5	111	64	10	.346	.429	.465	128	18	46			.902	3	*O-108/2-7,S	1.3
1894	Bos-N	127	539	118	188	21	8	13	126	59	17	.349	.419	.490	110	7	43			.904	11	*O-127/S-2,2P	0.7
1895	Bos-N	117	452	90	131	13	2	2	73	72	12	.290	.391	.341	83	-10	18			.885	-10	*O-109/2-9	-2.3
Total	13	1275	5128	1069	1496	192	53	44	666	537	163	.292	.364	.376	99	-31	468			.897	45	*O-1189/2-39,3SP	-3.1
Team	5	552	2204	450	652	83	21	24	384	293	93	.296	.382	.385	100	-2	160			.892	9	O-536/2-17,SP	-2.1

■ BILL McCARTHY   McCarthy, William John   b: 2/14/1886, Boston, Mass.   d: 2/4/28, Washington, D.C.   TR ,   Deb: 6/5/05

| 1905 | Bos-N | 1 | 3 | 0 | 0 | 0 | 0 | 0 | 0 | 0 | 0 | .000 | .000 | .000 | -99 | -1 | 0 | | | .667 | -0 | /C-1 | -0.1 |
| Total | 2 | 4 | 11 | 1 | 1 | 0 | 0 | 0 | 0 | 0 | 0 | .091 | .091 | .091 | -43 | -2 | 0 | | | .842 | -1 | /C-4 | -0.3 |

■ JEFF McCLESKEY   McCleskey, Jefferson Lamar   b: 11/6/1891, Americus, Ga.   d: 5/11/71, Americus, Ga.   BL/TR, 5'11", 160 lbs.   Deb: 9/8/13

| 1913 | Bos-N | 2 | 3 | 0 | 0 | 0 | 0 | 0 | 1 | 0 | 1 | .000 | .250 | .000 | -25 | -0 | 0 | | | .750 | -0 | /3-2 | -0.1 |

■ HAL McCLURE   McClure, Harold Murray "Mac"   b: 8/8/1859, Lewisburg, Pa.   d: 3/1/19, Lewisburg, Pa.   BR/TR, 6', 165 lbs.   Deb: 5/10/1882

| 1882 | Bos-N | 2 | 6 | 1 | 2 | 0 | 0 | 0 | | 0 | 1 | .333 | .333 | .333 | 115 | 0 | | | | .750 | -0 | /O-2 | 0.0 |

■ FRANK McCORMICK   McCormick, Frank Andrew "Buck"   b: 6/9/11, New York, N.Y.   d: 11/21/82, Manhassett, N.Y.   BR/TR, 6'4", 205 lbs.   Deb: 9/11/34   C

1947	Bos-N	81	212	24	75	18	2	4	43	11	8	.354	.386	.486	133	9	2			.996	-1	1-46	0.7
1948	*Bos-N	75	180	14	45	9	2	4	34	10	9	.250	.289	.389	84	-5	0			.987	3	1-50	-0.3
Total	13	1534	5723	722	1711	334	26	128	951	399	189	.299	.348	.434	118	125	27			.995	31	*1-1448/2-4,O	5.0
Team	2	156	392	38	120	27	4	6	77	21	17	.306	.341	.441	111	4	2			.992	2	/1-96	0.4

■ MIKE McCORMICK   McCormick, Myron Winthrop   b: 5/6/17, Angels Camp, Cal.   d: 4/14/76, Ventura, Cal.   BR/TR, 6', 200 lbs.   Deb: 4/16/40

1946	Bos-N	59	164	23	43	6	2	1	16	11	7	.262	.309	.341	83	-4	0			.973	-2	O-48	-0.8
1947	Bos-N	92	284	42	81	13	7	3	36	20	21	.285	.332	.412	99	-1	1			.981	-12	O-79	-1.6
1948	*Bos-N	115	343	45	104	22	7	1	39	32	34	.303	.364	.417	112	6	1			.975	-11	*O-100	-1.0
Total	10	748	2325	302	640	100	29	14	215	188	173	.275	.330	.361	90	-33	16			.980	-14	O-653	-8.0
Team	3	266	791	110	228	41	16	5	91	63	62	.288	.341	.399	102	1	2			.977	-25	O-227	-3.4

■ TOM McCREERY   McCreery, Thomas Livingston   b: 10/19/1874, Beaver, Pa.   d: 7/3/41, Beaver, Pa.   BB/TR, 5'11", 180 lbs.   Deb: 6/8/1895

| 1903 | Bos-N | 23 | 83 | 15 | 18 | 2 | 1 | 1 | 10 | 9 | | .217 | .293 | .301 | 72 | -3 | 6 | | | .900 | 0 | O-23 | -0.4 |
| Total | 9 | 799 | 2951 | 464 | 855 | 99 | 76 | 26 | 386 | 308 | | .290 | .359 | .401 | 113 | 54 | 116 | | | .905 | -22 | O-628,1-113/S2P3 | -1.7 |

■ TEX McDONALD   McDonald, Charles E. (b: Charles C. Crabtree)   b: 1/31/1891, Farmersville, Tex.   d: 3/31/43, Houston, Tex.   BL/TR, 5'10", 160 lbs.   Deb: 4/11/12

| 1913 | Bos-N | 62 | 145 | 24 | 52 | 4 | 4 | 0 | 18 | 15 | 17 | .359 | .422 | .441 | 144 | 7 | 4 | | | .869 | -1 | 3-31/2-6,O | 0.8 |
| Total | 4 | 357 | 1019 | 131 | 304 | 45 | 27 | 13 | 135 | 88 | 125 | .298 | .359 | .434 | 110 | 12 | 34 | | | .936 | -22 | O-156/S-48,23 | -1.3 |

■ ED McDONALD   McDonald, Edward C.   b: 10/28/1886, Albany, N.Y.   d: 3/11/46, Albany, N.Y.   BR/TR, 6', 180 lbs.   Deb: 8/5/11

1911	Bos-N	54	175	28	36	7	3	1	21	40	39	.206	.359	.297	78	-4	11			.955	-6	3-53/S-1	-0.9
1912	Bos-N	121	459	70	119	23	6	2	34	70	91	.259	.363	.349	94	-2	22			.940	-2	*3-118	-0.3
Total	3	176	634	98	155	30	9	3	55	110	130	.244	.362	.334	89	-6	33			.945	-7	3-171/S-1	-1.2
Team	2	175	634	98	155	30	9	3	55	110	130	.244	.362	.334	89	-6	33			.945	-7	3-171/S-1	-1.2

■ ODDIBE McDOWELL   McDowell, Oddibe   b: 8/25/62, Hollywood, Fla.   BL/TL, 5'9", 165 lbs.   Deb: 5/19/85

| 1989 | Atl-N | 76 | 280 | 56 | 85 | 18 | 4 | 7 | 24 | 27 | 37 | .304 | .365 | .471 | 134 | 12 | 15 | 10 | -2 | .978 | 5 | O-68 | 1.4 |

YEAR	TM/L	G	AB	R	H	2B	3B	HR	RBI	BB	SO	AVG	OBP	SLG	PRO+	BR/A	SB	CS	SBR	FA	FR	G/POS	TPR
1990	Atl-N	113	305	47	74	14	0	7	25	21	53	.243	.296	.357	74	-11	13	2	3	.971	-6	O-72	-1.6
Total	7	830	2829	458	715	125	28	74	266	294	550	.253	.325	.395	94	-23	169	53		.987	5	O-746/D-12	-2.1
Team	2	189	585	103	159	32	4	14	49	48	90	.272	.329	.412	102	1	28	12		.975	-1	O-140	-0.2

■ FRANK McELYEA McElyea, Frank b: 8/4/18, Hawthorne Twsp., Ill. d: 4/19/87, Evansville, Ill. BR/TR, 6'6", 221 lbs. Deb: 9/10/42

YEAR	TM/L	G	AB	R	H	2B	3B	HR	RBI	BB	SO	AVG	OBP	SLG	PRO+	BR/A	SB	CS	SBR	FA	FR	G/POS	TPR
1942	Bos-N	7	4	2	0	0	0	0	0	0	0	.000	.000	.000	-99	-1	0			1.000	-0	/O-1	-0.1

■ DAN McGANN McGann, Dennis Lawrence "Cap" b: 7/15/1871, Shelbyville, Ky. d: 12/13/10, Louisville, Ky. BB/TR, 6', 190 lbs. Deb: 8/8/1896

YEAR	TM/L	G	AB	R	H	2B	3B	HR	RBI	BB	SO	AVG	OBP	SLG	PRO+	BR/A	SB	CS	SBR	FA	FR	G/POS	TPR
1896	Bos-N	43	171	25	55	6	7	2	30	12	10	.322	.383	.474	118	4	2			.905	-17	2-43	-0.9
1908	Bos-N	135	475	52	114	8	5	2	55	38		.240	.321	.291	97	0	9			.988	5	*1-121/2-9	0.3
Total	12	1436	5222	842	1482	181	100	42	727	429	10	.284	.364	.381	117	122	282			.989	10	*1-1376/2-53	11.4
Team	2	178	646	77	169	14	12	4	85	50	10	.262	.338	.339	104	4	11			.988	-12	1-121/2-52	-0.6

■ CHIPPY McGARR McGarr, James B. b: 5/10/1863, Worcester, Mass. d: 6/6/04, Worcester, Mass. BR/TR, 5'7", 168 lbs. Deb: 7/11/1884 U

YEAR	TM/L	G	AB	R	H	2B	3B	HR	RBI	BB	SO	AVG	OBP	SLG	PRO+	BR/A	SB	CS	SBR	FA	FR	G/POS	TPR
1890	Bos-N	121	487	68	115	12	7	1	51	34	38	.236	.291	.296	66	-23	39			**.933**	-2	*3-115/S-5,O	-1.8
Total	10	826	3253	537	872	116	28	9	294	183	157	.268	.310	.329	70	-144	267			.903	-33	3-538,S-220/2OC	-13.6

■ DAN McGEE McGee, Daniel Aloysius b: 9/29/11, New York, N.Y. d: 12/4/91, Lakehurst, N.J. BR/TR, 5'8.5", 152 lbs. Deb: 7/14/34

YEAR	TM/L	G	AB	R	H	2B	3B	HR	RBI	BB	SO	AVG	OBP	SLG	PRO+	BR/A	SB	CS	SBR	FA	FR	G/POS	TPR
1934	Bos-N	7	22	2	3	0	0	0	1	3	6	.136	.240	.136	4	-3	0			.951	3	/S-7	0.0

■ TIM McGINLEY McGinley, Timothy S. b: Philadelphia, Pa. d: 11/2/1899, Oakland, Cal. 5'9.5", 155 lbs. Deb: 4/30/1875

YEAR	TM/L	G	AB	R	H	2B	3B	HR	RBI	BB	SO	AVG	OBP	SLG	PRO+	BR/A	SB	CS	SBR	FA	FR	G/POS	TPR
1876	Bos-N	9	40	5	6	0	0	0	2	0	1	.150	.150	.150	0	-4				.600	-3	/O-6,C-3	-0.7

■ BEAUTY McGOWAN McGowan, Frank Bernard b: 11/8/01, Branford, Conn. d: 5/6/82, Hamden, Conn. BL/TR, 5'11", 190 lbs. Deb: 4/12/22

YEAR	TM/L	G	AB	R	H	2B	3B	HR	RBI	BB	SO	AVG	OBP	SLG	PRO+	BR/A	SB	CS	SBR	FA	FR	G/POS	TPR
1937	Bos-N	9	12	0	1	0	0	0	0	1	2	.083	.154	.083	-37	-2	0			1.000	-1	/O-2	-0.3
Total	5	375	1208	174	316	58	16	6	108	154	122	.262	.347	.351	80	-33	17			.970	13	O-327	-4.2

■ FRED McGRIFF McGriff, Frederick Stanley b: 10/31/63, Tampa, Fla. BL/TL, 6'3", 215 lbs. Deb: 5/17/86

YEAR	TM/L	G	AB	R	H	2B	3B	HR	RBI	BB	SO	AVG	OBP	SLG	PRO+	BR/A	SB	CS	SBR	FA	FR	G/POS	TPR
1993	*Atl-N	68	255	59	79	18	1	19	55	34	51	.310	.393	.612	163	22	1	0	0	.992	-1	1-66	1.6
1994	Atl-N★	113	424	81	135	25	1	34	94	50	76	.318	.392	.623	156	34	7	3	0	.994	-5	*1-112	1.8
1995	*Atl-N★	144	528	85	148	27	1	27	93	65	99	.280	.365	.489	120	15	3	6	-3	.996	0	*1-144	-0.1
Total	10	1291	4512	788	1284	229	17	289	803	744	1019	.285	.388	.535	148	309	48	29		.992	-22	*1-1183,D-100	18.6
Team	3	325	1207	225	362	70	3	80	242	149	226	.300	.380	.562	141	71	11	9		.994	-6	1-322	3.3

■ STUFFY McINNIS McInnis, John Phalen "Jack" b: 9/19/1890, Gloucester, Mass. d: 2/16/60, Ipswich, Mass. BR/TR, 5'9.5", 162 lbs. Deb: 4/12/09 M

YEAR	TM/L	G	AB	R	H	2B	3B	HR	RBI	BB	SO	AVG	OBP	SLG	PRO+	BR/A	SB	CS	SBR	FA	FR	G/POS	TPR
1923	Bos-N	154	607	70	191	23	9	2	95	26	12	.315	.343	.392	97	-3	7	8	-3	.991	4	*1-154	-1.0
1924	Bos-N	146	581	57	169	23	7	1	59	15	6	.291	.311	.360	83	-15	9	3	1	.994	7	*1-146	-1.7
Total	19	2128	7822	872	2405	312	101	20	1062	380	189	.307	.343	.381	106	35	172	59	16	.993	17	*1-1995/S-55,320	-2.5
Team	2	300	1188	127	360	46	16	3	154	41	18	.303	.327	.376	90	-18	16	11	-2	.992	10	1-300	-2.7

■ BILL McKECHNIE McKechnie, William Boyd "Deacon" b: 8/7/1886, Wilkinsburg, Pa. d: 10/29/65, Bradenton, Fla. BB/TR, 5'10", 160 lbs. Deb: 9/8/07 MCH

YEAR	TM/L	G	AB	R	H	2B	3B	HR	RBI	BB	SO	AVG	OBP	SLG	PRO+	BR/A	SB	CS	SBR	FA	FR	G/POS	TPR
1913	Bos-N	1	4	1	0	0	0	0	0	0	1	.000	.200	.000	-39	-1	0			1.000	0	/O-1	-0.1
Total	11	846	2843	319	713	86	33	8	240	190	199	.251	.301	.313	72	-108	127			.952	22	3-553,2-117/1SO	-7.4

■ RALPH McLEOD McLeod, Ralph Alton b: 10/19/16, N.Quincy, Mass. BL/TL, 6', 170 lbs. Deb: 9/14/38

YEAR	TM/L	G	AB	R	H	2B	3B	HR	RBI	BB	SO	AVG	OBP	SLG	PRO+	BR/A	SB	CS	SBR	FA	FR	G/POS	TPR
1938	Bos-N	6	7	1	2	1	0	0	0	0	2	.286	.286	.429	105	-0	0			1.000	-0	/O-1	0.0

■ MARTY McMANUS McManus, Martin Joseph b: 3/14/1900, Chicago, Ill. d: 2/18/66, St.Louis, Mo. BR/TR, 5'10.5", 160 lbs. Deb: 9/26/20 M

YEAR	TM/L	G	AB	R	H	2B	3B	HR	RBI	BB	SO	AVG	OBP	SLG	PRO+	BR/A	SB	CS	SBR	FA	FR	G/POS	TPR
1934	Bos-N	119	435	56	120	18	0	8	47	32	42	.276	.330	.372	95	-4	5			.964	-5	2-73,3-37	-0.3
Total	15	1831	6660	1008	1926	401	88	120	996	675	558	.289	.357	.430	101	5	126			.965	44	2-927,3-725/1SO	8.8

■ ROY McMILLAN McMillan, Roy David b: 7/17/30, Bonham, Tex. BR/TR, 5'11", 170 lbs. Deb: 4/17/51 MC

YEAR	TM/L	G	AB	R	H	2B	3B	HR	RBI	BB	SO	AVG	OBP	SLG	PRO+	BR/A	SB	CS	SBR	FA	FR	G/POS	TPR
1961	Mil-N	154	505	42	111	16	0	7	48	61	86	.220	.309	.293	65	-25	2	4	-2	**.975**	-0	*S-154	-1.4
1962	Mil-N	137	468	66	115	13	0	12	41	60	53	.246	.338	.350	87	-7	2	2	-1	.972	1	*S-135	0.5
1963	Mil-N	100	320	35	80	10	1	4	29	17	25	.250	.292	.325	78	-9	1	5	-3	.979	7	S-94	0.2
1964	Mil-N	8	13	1	4	0	0	0	2	0	2	.308	.308	.308	73	-0	1	0	0	.933	-1	/S-8	-0.1
Total	16	2093	6752	739	1639	253	35	68	594	665	711	.243	.316	.321	72	-259	41	36		.972	66	*S-2028/3-12,2	-4.6
Team	4	399	1306	144	310	39	1	23	120	138	166	.237	.315	.322	76	-42	6	11		.975	7	S-391	-0.8

■ DINNY McNAMARA McNamara, John Raymond b: 9/16/05, Lexington, Mass. d: 12/20/63, Arlington, Mass. BL/TR, 5'9", 165 lbs. Deb: 7/2/27

YEAR	TM/L	G	AB	R	H	2B	3B	HR	RBI	BB	SO	AVG	OBP	SLG	PRO+	BR/A	SB	CS	SBR	FA	FR	G/POS	TPR
1927	Bos-N	11	9	3	0	0	0	0	0	0	3	.000	.000	.000	-99	-3	0			1.000	0	/O-3	-0.2
1928	Bos-N	9	4	2	1	0	0	0	0	0	1	.250	.250	.250	33	-0	0			1.000	-0	/O-3	-0.1
Total	2	20	13	5	1	0	0	0	0	0	4	.077	.077	.077	-63	-3	0			1.000	0	/O-6	-0.3

■ BILL McTIGUE McTigue, William Patrick "Rebel" b: 1/3/1891, Nashville, Tenn. d: 5/8/20, Nashville, Tenn. BL/TL, 6'1.5", 175 lbs. Deb: 5/2/11

YEAR	TM/L	G	AB	R	H	2B	3B	HR	RBI	BB	SO	AVG	OBP	SLG	PRO+	BR/A	SB	CS	SBR	FA	FR	G/POS	TPR
1911	Bos-N	14	12	1	1	1	0	0	0	0	5	.083	.083	.167	-28	-2	0			.875	-1	P-14	0.0
1912	Bos-N	10	13	2	1	0	0	0	1	1	5	.077	.143	.077	-38	-2	0			1.000	1	P-10	0.0
1913	Bos-N	1	0	0	0	0	0	0	0	0	0	—	—	—	—	0	0			.000	0	R	0.0
Total	4	28	26	3	2	1	0	0	1	1	10	.077	.111	.115	-36	-5	0			.957	0	/P-27	0.0
Team	3	25	25	3	2	1	0	0	1	1	10	.080	.115	.120	-33	-5	0			.947	-0	/P-24	0.0

■ CAL McVEY McVey, Calvin Alexander b: 8/30/1850, Montrose, Iowa d: 8/20/26, San Francisco, Cal BR/TR, 5'9", 170 lbs. Deb: 5/5/1871 M

YEAR	TM/L	G	AB	R	H	2B	3B	HR	RBI	BB	SO	AVG	OBP	SLG	PRO+	BR/A	SB	CS	SBR	FA	FR	G/POS	TPR
1871	Bos-n	29	153	43	**66**	9	5	0	43	1	2	.431	.435	.556	177	14	6					*C-28/O-1	0.9
1872	Bos-n	46	237	56	73	11	3	0	41	0	1	.308	.308	.380	105	-0						*C-40/O-9	0.0
1874	Bos-n	70	341	**91**	**124**	22	4	4		0		.364	.364	.487	159	20						*O-55,C-15	1.6
1875	Bos-n	82	389	88	137	**33**	9	3		1		.352	.354	**.506**	187	32						*1-54,O-17,C/P	2.7
Total	5 n	265	1312	327	473	83	26	10	117	5	5	.361	.363	.486	160	80						C-119/O-88,1S2P3D	6.3
Total	4	265	1199	227	393	52	17	3	172	23	38	.328	.340	.407	140	48				.951	-26	1-128/3-80,CPO2	1.8
Team	4 n	227	1120	278	400	75	21	7	84	2	3	.357	.358	.480	159	0				.000	0	/C-94,O-82,1P	5.2

■ JOE MEDWICK Medwick, Joseph Michael "Ducky" or "Muscles" b: 11/24/11, Carteret, N.J. d: 3/21/75, St.Petersburg, Fla BR/TR, 5'10", 187 lbs. Deb: 9/2/32 H

YEAR	TM/L	G	AB	R	H	2B	3B	HR	RBI	BB	SO	AVG	OBP	SLG	PRO+	BR/A	SB	CS	SBR	FA	FR	G/POS	TPR
1945	Bos-N	66	218	17	62	13	0	0	26	12	12	.284	.325	.344	85	-4	3			1.000	1	O-38,1-15	-0.7
Total	17	1984	7635	1198	2471	540	113	205	1383	437	551	.324	.362	.505	133	310	42			.980	49	*O-1852/1-19	27.1

■ DENIS MENKE Menke, Denis John b: 7/21/40, Algona, Iowa BR/TR, 6', 190 lbs. Deb: 4/14/62 C

YEAR	TM/L	G	AB	R	H	2B	3B	HR	RBI	BB	SO	AVG	OBP	SLG	PRO+	BR/A	SB	CS	SBR	FA	FR	G/POS	TPR
1962	Mil-N	50	146	12	28	3	1	2	16	16	38	.192	.280	.267	49	-10	0	1	-1	.980	5	2-20,3-15/S1O	-0.4
1963	Mil-N	146	518	58	121	16	4	11	50	37	106	.234	.292	.344	83	-11	6	7	-2	.976	12	S-82,3-51,2/1O	0.6
1964	Mil-N	151	505	79	143	29	5	20	65	68	77	.283	.373	.479	137	26	4	2	0	.964	2	*S-141,2-15/3	4.0
1965	Mil-N	71	181	16	44	13	1	4	18	18	28	.243	.315	.392	97	-1	1	3	-2	.967	-7	S-54/1-8,3	-0.7
1966	Atl-N	138	454	55	114	20	4	15	60	71	87	.251	.360	.412	112	9	0	7	-4	.955	-22	*S-106,3-39/1	-0.9
1967	Atl-N	129	418	37	95	14	3	7	39	65	62	.227	.335	.325	91	-3	5	7	-3	.965	-23	*S-124/3-3	-1.8
Total	13	1598	5071	605	1270	225	40	101	606	698	853	.250	.346	.370	104	44	34	54	-22	.961	-58	S-841,3-420,21/O	3.9
Team	6	685	2222	257	545	95	18	59	248	275	398	.245	.334	.384	102	10	16	27	-11	.964	-33	S-516,3-118/21O	0.8

■ BILL MERRITT Merritt, William Henry b: 7/30/1870, Lowell, Mass. d: 11/17/37, Lowell, Mass. BR/TR, 5'7", 160 lbs. Deb: 8/8/1891

YEAR	TM/L	G	AB	R	H	2B	3B	HR	RBI	BB	SO	AVG	OBP	SLG	PRO+	BR/A	SB	CS	SBR	FA	FR	G/POS	TPR
1893	Bos-N	39	141	30	49	6	3	3	26	13	13	.348	.403	.496	128	5	3			.945	-4	C-37/O-2	0.3
1894	Bos-N	10	26	3	6	1	0	0	6	8	0	.231	.412	.269	62	-1	0			.881	1	/C-8,O-1	0.0

YEAR	TM/L	G	AB	R	H	2B	3B	HR	RBI	BB	SO	AVG	OBP	SLG	PRO+	BR/A	SB	CS	SBR	FA	FR	G/POS	TPR
1899	Bos-N	1	2	0	0	0	0	0	0	0		.000	.333	.000	-5	-0	0			1.000	0	/C-1	0.0
Total	8	400	1410	182	383	40	12	8	195	109	71	.272	.327	.334	75	-52	21			.942	-19	C-353/1-18,3O2S	-3.2
Team	3	50	169	33	55	7	3	3	32	21	13	.325	.403	.456	115	3	3			.933	-3	/C-46,O-3	0.3

■ CATFISH METKOVICH
Metkovich, George Michael b: 10/8/20, Angels Camp, Cal. d: 5/17/95, Costa Mesa, Cal. BL/TL, 6'1", 185 lbs. Deb: 7/16/43

YEAR	TM/L	G	AB	R	H	2B	3B	HR	RBI	BB	SO	AVG	OBP	SLG	PRO+	BR/A	SB	CS	SBR	FA	FR	G/POS	TPR
1954	Mil-N	68	123	7	34	5	1	1	15	15	15	.276	.360	.358	94	-1	0	0	0	1.000	1	1-18,O-13	-0.1
Total	10	1055	3585	476	934	167	36	47	373	307	359	.261	.323	.367	91	-49	61	28		.976	-28	O-644,1-289	-12.5

■ CHIEF MEYERS
Meyers, John Tortes b: 7/29/1880, Riverside, Cal. d: 7/25/71, San Bernardino, Cal. BR/TR, 5'11", 194 lbs. Deb: 4/16/09

YEAR	TM/L	G	AB	R	H	2B	3B	HR	RBI	BB	SO	AVG	OBP	SLG	PRO+	BR/A	SB	CS	SBR	FA	FR	G/POS	TPR
1917	Bos-N	25	68	5	17	4	4	0	4	4	4	.250	.311	.426	133	2	0			1.000	7	C-24	1.2
Total	9	992	2834	276	826	120	41	14	363	274	162	.291	.367	.378	117	67	44			.974	-14	C-911	13.4

■ FELIX MILLAN
Millan, Felix Bernardo (Martinez) b: 8/21/43, Yabucoa, P.R. BR/TR, 5'11", 172 lbs. Deb: 6/2/66

YEAR	TM/L	G	AB	R	H	2B	3B	HR	RBI	BB	SO	AVG	OBP	SLG	PRO+	BR/A	SB	CS	SBR	FA	FR	G/POS	TPR
1966	Atl-N	37	91	20	25	6	0	0	5	2	6	.275	.290	.341	74	-3	3	1	0	.973	-2	2-25/S-1,3	-0.4
1967	Atl-N	41	136	13	32	3	3	2	6	4	10	.235	.268	.346	75	-5	0	3	-2	.972	3	2-41	-0.1
1968	Atl-N	149	570	49	165	22	2	1	33	22	26	.289	.323	.340	99	-1	6	6	-2	.980	3	*2-145	1.0
1969	*Atl-N★	162	652	98	174	23	5	6	57	34	35	.267	.311	.345	83	-15	14	3	2	**.980**	-16	*2-162	-1.6
1970	Atl-N†	142	590	100	183	25	5	2	37	35	23	.310	.354	.380	91	-7	16	5	2	.979	-19	*2-142	-1.2
1971	Atl-N★	143	577	65	167	20	8	2	45	37	22	.289	.335	.362	92	-6	11	7	-1	.982	6	*2-141	1.2
1972	Atl-N	125	498	46	128	19	3	1	38	23	28	.257	.294	.313	66	-22	6	4	-1	.987	-16	*2-120	-3.5
Total	12	1480	5791	699	1617	229	38	22	403	318	242	.279	.324	.343	87	-103	67	43	-6	.980	-129	*2-1450/3-1,S	-15.0
Team	7	799	3114	391	874	118	26	14	221	157	150	.281	.321	.349	86	-58	56	29	-1	.980	-41	2-776/3-1,S	-4.6

■ EDDIE MILLER
Miller, Edward Lee b: 6/29/57, San Pablo, Cal. BB/TR, 5'9", 175 lbs. Deb: 9/5/77

YEAR	TM/L	G	AB	R	H	2B	3B	HR	RBI	BB	SO	AVG	OBP	SLG	PRO+	BR/A	SB	CS	SBR	FA	FR	G/POS	TPR
1978	Atl-N	6	21	5	3	1	0	0	2	2	4	.143	.250	.190	22	-2	3	0	1	1.000	-1	/O-5	-0.2
1979	Atl-N	27	113	12	35	1	0	0	5	5	24	.310	.350	.319	78	-3	15	2	3	.988	3	O-27	0.2
1980	Atl-N	11	19	3	3	0	0	0	0	0	5	.158	.158	.158	-11	-3	1	2	-1	1.000	-3	/O-9	-0.8
1981	Atl-N	50	134	29	31	3	1	0	7	7	29	.231	.285	.269	56	-8	23	5	4	.985	-1	O-36	-0.7
Total	7	138	332	63	79	5	2	1	17	19	71	.238	.297	.274	57	-18	49	13	7	.989	-4	/O-95,D-4	-2.0
Team	4	94	287	49	72	5	1	0	14	14	62	.251	.300	.275	58	-16	42	9	7	.988	-3	/O-77	-1.5

■ EDDIE MILLER
Miller, Edward Robert "Eppie" b: 11/26/16, Pittsburgh, Pa. BR/TR, 5'9", 180 lbs. Deb: 9/9/36

YEAR	TM/L	G	AB	R	H	2B	3B	HR	RBI	BB	SO	AVG	OBP	SLG	PRO+	BR/A	SB	CS	SBR	FA	FR	G/POS	TPR
1939	Bos-N	77	296	32	79	12	2	4	31	16	21	.267	.315	.361	88	-6	4			.970	12	S-77	1.3
1940	Bos-N★	151	569	78	157	33	3	14	79	41	43	.276	.330	.418	111	7	8			**.970**	15	*S-151	3.5
1941	Bos-N★	154	585	54	140	27	3	6	68	35	72	.239	.288	.326	76	-20	8			**.966**	12	*S-154	0.4
1942	Bos-N★	142	534	47	130	28	2	6	47	22	42	.243	.279	.337	81	-15	11			**.983**	4	*S-142	-0.2
Total	14	1510	5337	539	1270	263	28	97	640	351	465	.238	.290	.352	80	-160	64			.972	102	*S-1395/2-84,3	4.4
Team	4	524	1984	211	506	100	10	30	225	114	178	.255	.302	.361	89	-34	31			.972	43	S-524	5.0

■ NORM MILLER
Miller, Norman Calvin b: 2/5/46, Los Angeles, Cal. BL/TR, 5'11", 195 lbs. Deb: 9/11/65

YEAR	TM/L	G	AB	R	H	2B	3B	HR	RBI	BB	SO	AVG	OBP	SLG	PRO+	BR/A	SB	CS	SBR	FA	FR	G/POS	TPR
1973	Atl-N	9	8	2	3	1	0	1	6	3	3	.375	.545	.875	267	2	0	0	0	.667	-0	/O-1	0.2
1974	Atl-N	42	41	1	7	1	0	1	5	7	9	.171	.292	.268	55	-2	0	0	0	1.000	-1	/O-4	-0.3
Total	10	540	1364	166	325	68	10	24	159	160	265	.238	.325	.356	95	-9	16	10		.972	-18	O-378/C-2,3	-4.7
Team	2	51	49	3	10	2	0	2	11	10	12	.204	.339	.367	93	-0	0	0		.857	-1	/O-5	-0.1

■ DOC MILLER
Miller, Roy Oscar b: 2/4/1883, Chatham, Ontario, Canada d: 7/31/38, Jersey City, N.J. BL/TL, 5'10.5", 170 lbs. Deb: 5/4/10

YEAR	TM/L	G	AB	R	H	2B	3B	HR	RBI	BB	SO	AVG	OBP	SLG	PRO+	BR/A	SB	CS	SBR	FA	FR	G/POS	TPR
1910	Bos-N	130	482	48	138	27	4	3	55	33	52	.286	.333	.378	103	0	17			.951	-12	*O-130	-1.9
1911	Bos-N	146	577	69	**192**	36	3	7	91	43	43	.333	.379	.442	120	13	32			.961	2	*O-146	0.8
1912	Bos-N	51	201	26	47	8	1	2	24	14	17	.234	.287	.313	63	-11	6			.948	3	O-50	-1.1
Total	5	557	1717	184	507	96	15	12	235	121	149	.295	.343	.390	102	-0	64			.958	-13	O-425	-3.6
Team	3	327	1260	143	377	71	8	12	170	90	112	.299	.347	.397	104	3	55			.955	-7	O-326	-2.2

■ TOM MILLER
Miller, Thomas Royall b: 7/5/1897, Powhatan Court House, Va. d: 8/13/80, Richmond, Va. BL/TR, 5'11", 180 lbs. Deb: 7/29/18

YEAR	TM/L	G	AB	R	H	2B	3B	HR	RBI	BB	SO	AVG	OBP	SLG	PRO+	BR/A	SB	CS	SBR	FA	FR	G/POS	TPR
1918	Bos-N	2	2	0	0	0	0	0	0	0	0	.000	.000	.000	-99	-0	1			.000	0	H	-0.1
1919	Bos-N	7	6	2	2	0	0	0	0	0	1	.333	.333	.333	105	0	0			.000	0	H	0.0
Total	2	9	8	2	2	0	0	0	0	0	1	.250	.250	.250	53	-0	1			.000	0	H	-0.1

■ FRED MITCHELL
Mitchell, Frederick Francis (b: Frederick Francis Yapp)
b: 6/5/1878, Cambridge, Mass. d: 10/13/70, Newton, Mass. BR/TR, 5'9.5", 185 lbs. Deb: 4/27/01 MC

YEAR	TM/L	G	AB	R	H	2B	3B	HR	RBI	BB	SO	AVG	OBP	SLG	PRO+	BR/A	SB	CS	SBR	FA	FR	G/POS	TPR
1913	Bos-N	4	3	0	1	0	0	0	0	0	2	.333	.333	.333	89	-0	0			.000	0	H	0.0
Total	7	201	572	55	120	16	7	0	52	22	2	.210	.245	.262	52	-35	8			.904	-14	/P-97,C-62,13OS2	-2.9

■ KEITH MITCHELL
Mitchell, Keith Alexander b: 8/6/69, San Diego, Cal. BR/TR, 5'10", 180 lbs. Deb: 7/23/91

YEAR	TM/L	G	AB	R	H	2B	3B	HR	RBI	BB	SO	AVG	OBP	SLG	PRO+	BR/A	SB	CS	SBR	FA	FR	G/POS	TPR
1991	*Atl-N	48	66	11	21	0	0	2	5	8	12	.318	.392	.409	118	2	3	1	0	.970	-7	O-34	-0.5
Total	2	94	194	32	50	2	0	7	20	26	34	.258	.348	.376	89	-3	3	1	0	.976	-13	/O-72,D-6	-1.6

■ JOHN MIZEROCK
Mizerock, John Joseph b: 12/8/60, Punxsutawney, Pa. BL/TR, 5'11", 190 lbs. Deb: 4/12/83

YEAR	TM/L	G	AB	R	H	2B	3B	HR	RBI	BB	SO	AVG	OBP	SLG	PRO+	BR/A	SB	CS	SBR	FA	FR	G/POS	TPR
1989	Atl-N	11	27	1	6	0	0	0	2	0	3	.222	.222	.222	27	-3	0	0	0	1.000	1	C-11	-0.2
Total	4	103	231	24	43	9	2	2	24	38	42	.186	.309	.268	64	-10	0	0	0	.979	8	C-101	0.2

■ WILLIE MONTANEZ
Montanez, Guillermo (Naranjo) b: 4/1/48, Catano, P.R. BL/TL, 6'1", 193 lbs. Deb: 4/12/66

YEAR	TM/L	G	AB	R	H	2B	3B	HR	RBI	BB	SO	AVG	OBP	SLG	PRO+	BR/A	SB	CS	SBR	FA	FR	G/POS	TPR
1976	Atl-N	103	420	52	135	14	0	9	64	21	32	.321	.354	.419	112	6	0	4	-2	.986	-6	*1-103	-1.0
1977	Atl-N★	136	544	70	156	31	1	20	68	35	60	.287	.330	.458	97	-3	1	1	-0	.992	-4	*1-134	-1.6
Total	14	1632	5843	645	1604	279	25	139	802	465	751	.275	.331	.402	101	1	32	42	-16	.992	15	*1-1164,O-352/D	-9.5
Team	2	239	964	122	291	45	1	29	132	56	92	.302	.340	.441	103	2	1	5	-3	.989	-10	1-237	-2.6

■ AL MONTGOMERY
Montgomery, Alvin Atlas b: 7/3/20, Loving, N.Mex. d: 4/26/42, Waverly, Va. BR/TR, 5'10.5", 185 lbs. Deb: 6/20/41

YEAR	TM/L	G	AB	R	H	2B	3B	HR	RBI	BB	SO	AVG	OBP	SLG	PRO+	BR/A	SB	CS	SBR	FA	FR	G/POS	TPR
1941	Bos-N	42	52	4	10	1	0	0	4	9	8	.192	.323	.212	55	-3	0			.976	-6	C-30	-0.8

■ JUNIOR MOORE
Moore, Alvin Earl b: 1/25/53, Waskom, Tex. BR/TR, 5'11", 185 lbs. Deb: 8/2/76

YEAR	TM/L	G	AB	R	H	2B	3B	HR	RBI	BB	SO	AVG	OBP	SLG	PRO+	BR/A	SB	CS	SBR	FA	FR	G/POS	TPR
1976	Atl-N	20	26	1	7	1	0	0	2	4	4	.269	.387	.308	93	0	0	0	0	.929	1	/3-6,2-1,O	0.1
1977	Atl-N	112	361	41	94	9	3	5	34	33	29	.260	.324	.343	71	-15	4	5	-2	.942	-4	*3-104/2-1	-2.2
Total	5	289	774	83	204	20	7	7	73	62	71	.264	.320	.335	73	-28	5	10	-5	.936	-14	3-150/O-70,D21	-5.2
Team	2	132	387	42	101	10	3	5	36	37	33	.261	.329	.341	72	-15	4	5	-2	.941	-3	3-110/2-2,O	-2.1

■ GENE MOORE
Moore, Eugene Jr. "Rowdy" b: 8/26/09, Lancaster, Tex. d: 3/12/78, Jackson, Miss. BL/TL, 5'11", 175 lbs. Deb: 9/19/31 F

YEAR	TM/L	G	AB	R	H	2B	3B	HR	RBI	BB	SO	AVG	OBP	SLG	PRO+	BR/A	SB	CS	SBR	FA	FR	G/POS	TPR
1936	Bos-N	151	637	91	185	38	12	13	67	40	80	.290	.335	.449	117	12	6			.977	15	*O-151	2.0
1937	Bos-N☆	148	561	88	159	29	10	16	70	61	73	.283	.358	.456	132	23	11			.978	14	*O-148	3.1
1938	Bos-N	54	180	27	49	8	3	3	19	16	20	.272	.338	.400	114	3	1			.981	1	O-47	0.2
1940	Bos-N	103	363	46	106	24	1	5	39	25	32	.292	.338	.405	110	4	2			.986	6	O-94	0.6
1941	Bos-N	129	397	42	108	17	8	5	43	45	37	.272	.349	.393	114	7	5			.968	4	*O-110	0.5
Total	14	1042	3543	497	958	179	53	58	436	317	401	.270	.333	.400	105	24	31			.975	32	O-914/1-3	0.5
Team	5	585	2138	294	607	116	34	42	238	187	242	.284	.345	.429	119	49	25			.977	40	O-550	6.4

■ EDDIE MOORE
Moore, Graham Edward b: 1/18/1899, Barlow, Ky. d: 2/10/76, Ft.Myers, Fla. BR/TR, 5'7", 165 lbs. Deb: 9/25/23

YEAR	TM/L	G	AB	R	H	2B	3B	HR	RBI	BB	SO	AVG	OBP	SLG	PRO+	BR/A	SB	CS	SBR	FA	FR	G/POS	TPR
1926	Bos-N	54	184	17	49	3	2	0	15	16	12	.266	.325	.304	77	-6	6			.973	-3	2-39,S-14/3	-0.7
1927	Bos-N	112	411	53	124	14	4	1	32	39	17	.302	.364	.363	103	2	5			.947	-2	3-52,2-39,O/S	0.3

YEAR TM/L	G	AB	R	H	2B	3B	HR	RBI	BB	SO	AVG	OBP	SLG	PRO+	BR/A	SB	CS	SBR	FA	FR	G/POS	TPR
1928 Bos-N	68	215	27	51	9	0	2	18	19	12	.237	.299	.307	62	-12	7			.958	6	O-54/2-1	-1.0
Total 10	748	2474	360	706	108	26	13	257	272	121	.285	.359	.366	89	-37	52			.956	-29	2-349,O-145/S3	-4.9
Team 3	234	810	97	224	26	6	3	65	74	41	.277	.338	.335	86	-15	18			.969	1	/2-79,O-70,3S	-1.4
■ **RANDY MOORE**	Moore, Randolph Edward b: 6/21/06, Naples, Tex. d: 6/12/92, Mt.Pleasant, Tex. BL/TR, 6', 185 lbs. Deb: 4/12/27																					
1930 Bos-N	83	191	24	55	9	0	2	34	10	13	.288	.323	.366	69	-10	3			.986	-2	O-34,3-13	-1.2
1931 Bos-N	83	192	19	50	8	1	3	34	13	3	.260	.311	.359	83	-5	1			.952	0	O-29,3-22/2	-0.5
1932 Bos-N	107	351	41	103	21	2	3	43	15	11	.293	.322	.390	94	-3	1			.987	-7	O-41,3-31,1/C	-1.3
1933 Bos-N	135	497	64	150	23	7	8	70	40	16	.302	.356	.425	133	20	3			.979	-0	*O-122,1-10	1.3
1934 Bos-N	123	422	55	120	21	2	7	64	40	16	.284	.346	.393	105	3	2			.965	-2	O-72,1-37	-0.4
1935 Bos-N	125	407	42	112	20	4	4	42	26	16	.275	.319	.373	93	-5	1			.950	0	O-78,1-21	-1.0
Total 10	749	2253	258	627	110	17	27	308	158	85	.278	.326	.378	95	-19	11			.969	-15	O-418/1-90,3C2	-5.5
Team 6	656	2060	245	590	102	16	27	287	144	75	.286	.334	.391	101	0	11			.970	-11	O-376/1-90,3C2	-3.1
■ **HERBIE MORAN**	Moran, John Herbert b: 2/16/1884, Costello, Pa. d: 9/21/54, Clarkson, N.Y. BL/TR, 5'5", 150 lbs. Deb: 4/16/08																					
1908 Bos-N	8	29	3	8	0	0	0	2	2		.276	.364	.276	106	0	1			1.000	2	/O-8	0.3
1909 Bos-N	8	31	8	7	1	0	0	0	5		.226	.333	.258	80	-1	0			1.000	-1	/O-8	-0.1
1910 Bos-N	20	67	11	8	0	0	0	3	13	14	.119	.280	.119	17	-7	6			.958	4	O-20	-0.4
1914 *Bos-N	41	154	24	41	3	1	0	4	17	11	.266	.347	.299	93	-1	4			.940	-8	O-41	-1.1
1915 Bos-N	130	419	59	84	13	5	0	21	66	41	.200	.320	.255	79	-8	16	10	-1	.964	-6	*O-123	-2.3
Total 7	595	2177	300	527	60	26	2	135	264	162	.242	.332	.296	83	-35	103	10		.957	-2	O-584	-7.2
Team 5	207	700	105	148	17	6	0	30	103	66	.211	.324	.253	76	-15	27	10		.962	-7	O-200	-3.6
■ **PAT MORAN**	Moran, Patrick Joseph b: 2/7/1876, Fitchburg, Mass. d: 3/7/24, Orlando, Fla. BR/TR, 5'10", 180 lbs. Deb: 5/15/01 M																					
1901 Bos-N	52	180	12	38	5	1	2	18	3		.211	.228	.283	44	-13	3			.973	-5	C-28,1-13/3SO2	-1.6
1902 Bos-N	80	251	22	60	5	5	1	24	17		.239	.303	.311	88	-3	6			**.982**	1	C-71/1-3,O	0.5
1903 Bos-N	109	389	40	102	25	5	7	54	29		.262	.331	.406	114	6	8			.967	19	*C-107/1-1	3.5
1904 Bos-N	113	398	26	90	11	3	4	34	18		.226	.267	.299	77	-11	10			.957	4	C-72,3-39/1	0.2
1905 Bos-N	85	267	22	64	11	5	2	22	8		.240	.270	.341	83	-7	3			**.986**	13	C-78	1.4
Total 14	818	2634	198	618	102	24	18	262	142		.235	.283	.312	78	-74	55			.976	34	C-697/3-43,1OS2	3.0
Team 5	439	1485	122	354	57	19	16	152	75		.238	.286	.335	86	-29	30			.972	32	C-356/3-43,1OS2	4.0
■ **MIKE MORDECAI**	Mordecai, Michael Howard b: 12/13/67, Birmingham, Ala. BB/TR, 5'11", 175 lbs. Deb: 5/8/94																					
1994 Atl-N	4	4	1	1	0	0	1	3	1	0	.250	.400	1.000	244	1	0	0	0	1.000	-0	/S-4	0.1
1995 *Atl-N	69	75	10	21	6	0	3	11	9	16	.280	.357	.480	115	2	0	0	0	1.000	-2	2-21/1-9,3SO	0.0
Total 2	73	79	11	22	6	0	4	14	10	16	.278	.360	.506	122	2	0	0	0	1.000	-2	/2-21,S-10,13O	0.1
■ **OMAR MORENO**	Moreno, Omar Renan (Quintero) b: 10/24/52, Puerto Armuelles, Panama BL/TL, 6'2", 180 lbs. Deb: 9/6/75																					
1986 Atl-N	118	359	46	84	18	6	4	27	21	77	.234	.276	.351	68	-16	17	16	-5	.970	-3	O-97	-2.7
Total 12	1382	4992	699	1257	171	87	37	386	387	885	.252	.308	.343	79	-146	487	182	37	.982	103	*O-1323/D-2	-5.3
■ **JOE MORGAN**	Morgan, Joseph Michael b: 11/19/30, Walpole, Mass. BL/TR, 5'10", 170 lbs. Deb: 4/14/59 MC																					
1959 Mil-N	13	23	2	5	1	0	0	1	2	4	.217	.280	.261	49	-2	0	0	0	.913	-2	/2-7	-0.4
Total 4	88	187	15	36	5	3	2	10	18	31	.193	.263	.283	49	-13	0	0	0	.944	-3	/3-38,2-7,O	-1.8
■ **ED MORIARTY**	Moriarty, Edward Jerome b: 10/12/12, Holyoke, Mass. d: 9/29/91, Holyoke, Mass. BR/TR, 5'10.5", 180 lbs. Deb: 6/21/35																					
1935 Bos-N	8	34	4	11	2	1	1	1	0	6	.324	.324	.529	136	1	0			.923	-4	/2-8	-0.2
1936 Bos-N	6	6	1	1	0	0	0	0	0	1	.167	.167	.167	-11	-1	0			.000	0	H	-0.1
Total 2	14	40	5	12	2	1	1	1	0	7	.300	.300	.475	114	0	0			.771	-4	/2-8	-0.3
■ **GENE MORIARITY**	Moriarity, Eugene John b: 1/5/1865, Holyoke, Mass. BL/TL, 5'8", 130 lbs. Deb: 6/18/1884																					
1884 Bos-N	4	16	1	1	0	0	0	0	0	8	.063	.063	.063	-61	-3				.714	-1	/O-4	-0.3
Total 3	72	269	26	41	5	3	3	19	4	55	.152	.174	.227	24	-24	7			.822	2	/O-64,3-5,PS	-2.2
■ **JOHN MORRILL**	Morrill, John Francis "Honest John" b: 2/19/1855, Boston, Mass. d: 4/2/32, Boston, Mass. BR/TR, 5'10.5", 155 lbs. Deb: 4/24/1876 M																					
1876 Bos-N	66	278	38	73	5	2	0	26	3	5	.263	.270	.295	87	-4				.857	7	2-37,C-23/O1	0.3
1877 Bos-N	61	242	47	73	5	1	0	28	6	15	.302	.319	.331	101	0				.864	-9	3-30,1-18,O/2	-0.8
1878 Bos-N	60	233	26	56	5	1	0	23	5	16	.240	.256	.270	68	-9				.957	2	*1-59/O-1,3	-0.8
1879 Bos-N	84	348	56	98	18	5	0	49	14	32	.282	.309	.362	118	6				.878	3	3-51,1-33	0.8
1880 Bos-N	86	342	51	81	16	8	2	44	11	37	.237	.261	.348	108	3				.966	0	1-46,3-40/P	0.0
1881 Bos-N	81	311	47	90	19	3	1	39	12	30	.289	.316	.379	123	8				.969	9	*1-74/2-4,P3	1.0
1882 Bos-N	83	349	73	101	19	11	2	54	18	29	.289	.324	.424	137	14				.964	-3	*1-76/S-3,2O3PM	0.3
1883 Bos-N	97	404	83	129	33	16	6	68	15	68	.319	.344	.525	155	25				**.974**	-1	*1-81/O-7,3S2PM	1.4
1884 Bos-N	111	438	80	114	19	7	3	61	30	87	.260	.308	.356	109	5				.971	3	*1-91,2-17/P3OM	-0.2
1885 Bos-N	111	394	74	89	20	7	4	44	64	78	.226	.334	.343	124	14				.969	2	*1-92,2-17/3M	0.5
1886 Bos-N	117	430	86	106	25	6	7	69	56	81	.247	.333	.381	121	13	9			.895	-3	S-55,1-42,2/PM	0.6
1887 Bos-N	127	504	79	141	32	6	12	81	37	86	.280	.330	.438	112	7	19			.984	4	*1-127,M	-0.2
1888 Bos-N	135	486	60	96	18	7	4	39	55	68	.198	.282	.288	81	-9	21			.979	9	*1-133/2-2M	-1.3
Total 15	1265	4912	821	1275	239	80	43	643	358	656	.260	.310	.367	111	68	61			.971	22	1-916,3-138,2/SOCP	0.8
Team 13	1219	4759	800	1247	234	80	41	625	326	632	.262	.310	.371	113	73	49			.971	23	1-875,3-135,2/SOCP	1.6
■ **JIM MORRISON**	Morrison, James Forrest b: 9/23/52, Pensacola, Fla. BR/TR, 5'11", 182 lbs. Deb: 9/18/77																					
1988 Atl-N	51	92	6	14	2	0	2	13	10	13	.152	.235	.239	35	-8	0	1	-1	.933	0	3-20/O-4,P	-0.9
Total 12	1089	3375	371	876	170	16	112	435	213	521	.260	.308	.419	98	-18	50	37		.949	1	3-619,2-324/SDO1P	-1.6
■ **BUBBA MORTON**	Morton, Wycliffe Nathaniel b: 12/13/31, Washington, D.C. BR/TR, 5'10.5", 180 lbs. Deb: 4/19/61																					
1963 Mil-N	15	28	1	5	0	0	0	4	2	3	.179	.258	.179	28	-2	0	0	0	1.000	-1	/O-9	-0.4
Total 7	451	928	117	248	37	8	14	128	111	143	.267	.352	.370	106	10	7	7	-2	.988	-17	O-278/1-4,3	-2.1
■ **DARRYL MOTLEY**	Motley, Darryl De Wayne b: 1/21/60, Muskogee, Okla. BR/TR, 5'9", 196 lbs. Deb: 8/10/81																					
1986 Atl-N	5	10	1	2	1	0	0	0	1	1	.200	.273	.300	55	-1	0	0	0	1.000	-0	/O-3	-0.1
1987 Atl-N	6	8	0	0	0	0	0	1	0	1	.000	.000	.000	-95	-2	0	0	0	1.000	-0	/O-2	-0.3
Total 6	413	1333	156	324	60	10	44	159	67	186	.243	.282	.402	86	-30	19	22	-8	.976	-15	O-380/D-10	-6.4
Team 2	11	18	1	2	1	0	0	1	1	2	.111	.158	.167	-11	-3	0	0	0	1.000	-1	/O-5	-0.4
■ **JOE MOWRY**	Mowry, Joseph Aloysius b: 4/6/08, St.Louis, Mo. d: 2/9/94, St.Louis, Mo. BB/TR, 6', 198 lbs. Deb: 5/13/33																					
1933 Bos-N	86	249	25	55	8	5	0	20	15	22	.221	.273	.293	67	-11	1			.994	1	O-64	-1.5
1934 Bos-N	25	79	9	17	3	0	1	4	3	13	.215	.244	.291	46	-6	0			.976	0	O-20/2-1	-0.7
1935 Bos-N	81	136	17	36	8	1	1	13	11	13	.265	.324	.360	91	-2	0			.970	-7	O-45	-1.0
Total 3	192	464	51	108	19	6	2	37	29	48	.233	.284	.313	71	-19	1			.985	-7	O-129/2-1	-3.2
■ **HEINIE MUELLER**	Mueller, Clarence Francis b: 9/16/1899, Creve Coeur, Mo. d: 1/23/75, DeSoto, Mo. BL/TL, 5'8", 158 lbs. Deb: 9/25/20																					
1928 Bos-N	42	151	25	34	3	1	0	19	17	9	.225	.316	.258	54	-10	1			.985	6	O-41	-0.6
1929 Bos-N	46	93	10	19	2	1	0	11	12	12	.204	.302	.247	39	-9	2			1.000	-4	O-24	-1.3
Total 11	693	2118	296	597	87	37	22	272	168	147	.282	.342	.389	94	-20	37			.960	-11	O-557/1-31	-7.1
Team 2	88	244	35	53	5	2	0	30	29	21	.217	.310	.254	48	-18	3			.989	3	/O-65	-1.9

YEAR	TM/L	G	AB	R	H	2B	3B	HR	RBI	BB	SO	AVG	OBP	SLG	PRO+	BR/A	SB	CS	SBR	FA	FR	G/POS	TPR
■ RAY MUELLER Mueller, Ray Coleman "Iron Man" b: 3/8/12, Pittsburg, Kan. d: 6/29/94, Lower Paxton Township, Pa. BR/TR, 5'9", 175 lbs. Deb: 5/11/35 C																							
1935	Bos-N	42	97	10	22	5	0	3	11	3	11	.227	.250	.371	70	-5	0			.978	-2	C-40	-0.5
1936	Bos-N	24	71	5	14	4	0	0	5	5	17	.197	.250	.254	38	-6	0			.986	-4	C-23	-0.9
1937	Bos-N	64	187	21	47	9	2	2	26	18	36	.251	.317	.353	90	-3	1			.995	2	C-57	0.2
1938	Bos-N	83	274	23	65	8	6	4	35	16	28	.237	.282	.354	82	-8	3			.993	-2	C-75	-0.7
1951	Bos-N	28	70	8	11	2	0	1	9	7	11	.157	.234	.229	27	-7	0	0	0	1.000	3	C-23	-0.4
Total	14	985	2911	281	733	123	23	56	373	250	322	.252	.314	.368	91	-44	14	0		.988	21	C-917	2.7
Team	5	241	699	67	159	28	8	10	86	49	103	.227	.279	.333	72	-29	4	0		.992	-3	C-218	-2.3
■ TIM MURNANE Murnane, Timothy Hayes b: 6/4/1852, Naugatuck, Conn. d: 2/7/17, Boston, Mass. BL/TR, 5'9.5", 172 lbs. Deb: 4/26/1872 M																							
1876	Bos-N	69	308	60	87	4	3	2	34	8	12	.282	.301	.334	109	3				.927	-4	*1-65/O-3,2	-0.2
1877	Bos-N	35	140	23	39	7	1	1	15	6	7	.279	.308	.364	107	1				.815	-1	O-30/1-5	-0.1
Total	4 n	155	683	163	181	12	1	2	23	18	14	.265	.284	.294	83	-14						/O-69,1-65,2	-0.8
Total	4	229	947	173	244	22	7	3	63	44	31	.258	.291	.305	82	-20				.938	-8	1-181/O-50,2	-3.6
Team	2	104	448	83	126	11	4	3	49	14	19	.281	.303	.344	109	4				.927	-4	/1-70,O-33,2	-0.3
■ DALE MURPHY Murphy, Dale Bryan b: 3/12/56, Portland, Ore. BR/TR, 6'5", 215 lbs. Deb: 9/13/76																							
1976	Atl-N	19	65	3	17	6	0	0	9	7	9	.262	.333	.354	89	-1	0	0	0	.974	-0	C-19	0.0
1977	Atl-N	18	76	5	24	8	1	2	14	0	8	.316	.316	.526	108	1	0	1	-1	.954	-2	C-18	-0.1
1978	Atl-N	151	530	66	120	14	3	23	79	42	145	.226	.287	.394	80	-16	11	7	-1	.984	4	*1-129,C-21	-2.1
1979	Atl-N	104	384	53	106	7	2	21	57	38	67	.276	.344	.469	111	5	6	1	1	.980	-9	1-76,C-27	-0.6
1980	Atl-N★	156	569	98	160	27	2	33	89	59	133	.281	.350	.510	133	23	9	6	-1	.985	11	*O-154/1-1	2.8
1981	Atl-N	104	369	43	91	12	1	13	50	44	72	.247	.327	.390	100	0	14	5	1	.981	4	*O-103/1-3	0.2
1982	*Atl-N★	162	598	113	168	23	2	36	**109**	93	134	.281	.380	.507	140	33	23	11	0	.979	-1	*O-162	2.9
1983	Atl-N★	162	589	131	178	24	4	36	**121**	90	110	.302	.396	**.540**	146	38	30	4	7	.985	5	*O-160	4.6
1984	Atl-N★	162	607	94	176	32	8	**36**	100	79	134	.290	.374	**.547**	145	36	19	7	2	.987	1	*O-160	3.4
1985	Atl-N★	162	616	**118**	185	32	2	**37**	111	**90**	141	.300	.390	.539	148	40	10	3	1	.980	-5	*O-161	3.3
1986	Atl-N★	160	614	89	163	29	7	29	83	75	141	.265	.347	.477	118	15	7	7	-2	.981	-4	*O-159	0.4
1987	Atl-N★	159	566	115	167	27	1	44	105	115	136	.295	.420	.580	154	47	16	6	1	.977	12	*O-159	5.4
1988	Atl-N	156	592	77	134	35	4	24	77	74	125	.226	.314	.421	104	3	3	5	-2	.992	18	*O-156	1.4
1989	Atl-N	154	574	60	131	16	0	20	84	65	142	.228	.309	.361	88	-8	3	2	-0	.985	4	*O-151	-0.9
1990	Atl-N	97	349	38	81	14	0	17	55	41	84	.232	.315	.418	94	-3	9	2	2	.981	4	O-97	0.0
Total	18	2180	7960	1197	2111	350	39	398	1266	986	1748	.265	.348	.469	119	203	161	68	8	.983	45	*O-1853,1-209/C	19.3
Team	15	1926	7098	1103	1901	306	37	371	1143	912	1581	.268	.353	.478	123	212	160	67	8	.983	43	*O-1622,1-209/C	20.7
■ DAVE MURPHY Murphy, David Francis "Dirty Dave" b: 5/4/1876, Adams, Mass. d: 4/8/40, Adams, Mass. TR , Deb: 8/28/05																							
1905	Bos-N	3	11	0	2	0	0	0	1	0		.182	.182	.182	9	-1	0			1.000	-2	/S-2,3-1	-0.4
■ FRANK MURPHY Murphy, Francis Patrick b: 4/16/1875, N.Tarrytown, N.Y. d: 11/4/12, Central Islip, N.Y. Deb: 7/2/01																							
1901	Bos-N	45	176	13	46	5	3	1	18	4		.261	.282	.341	73	-7	6			.939	4	O-45	-0.6
■ BUZZ MURPHY Murphy, Robert R. b: 4/26/1895, Denver, Colo. d: 5/11/38, Denver, Colo. BL/TL, 5'8.5", 155 lbs. Deb: 7/14/18																							
1918	Bos-N	9	32	6	12	2	3	1	9	3	5	.375	.429	.719	259	6	0			1.000	-2	/O-9	0.4
Total	2	88	284	25	78	9	7	1	37	22	37	.275	.338	.366	101	0	5			.961	0	/O-82	-0.5
■ JIM MURRAY Murray, James Oscar b: 1/16/1878, Galveston, Tex. d: 4/25/45, Galveston, Tex. BR/TL, 5'10", 180 lbs. Deb: 9/2/02																							
1914	Bos-N	39	112	10	26	4	2	0	12	6	24	.232	.277	.304	73	-4	2			.941	-8	O-32	-1.4
Total	3	82	261	21	53	9	2	3	24	13	24	.203	.244	.287	56	-16	2			.949	-9	/O-69	-2.8
■ IVAN MURRELL Murrell, Ivan Augustus (Peters) b: 4/24/45, Almirante, Panama BR/TR, 6'2", 196 lbs. Deb: 9/28/63																							
1974	Atl-N	73	133	11	33	1	1	2	12	5	35	.248	.275	.316	62	-7	0	0	0	.983	-1	O-32,1-13	-1.0
Total	10	564	1306	126	308	41	15	33	123	44	342	.236	.266	.366	77	-46	20	13		.965	-2	O-343/1-40	-6.9
■ DANNY MURTAUGH Murtaugh, Daniel Edward b: 10/8/17, Chester, Pa. d: 12/2/76, Chester, Pa. BR/TR, 5'9", 165 lbs. Deb: 7/6/41 MC																							
1947	Bos-N	3	8	0	1	0	0	0	0	1	2	.125	.222	.125	-6	-1	0			1.000	-0	/2-2,3-2	-0.1
Total	9	767	2599	263	661	97	21	8	219	287	215	.254	.331	.317	81	-61	49			.975	10	2-631/S-61,3	-1.5
■ HAP MYERS Myers, Ralph Edward b: 4/8/1888, San Francisco, Cal. d: 6/30/67, San Francisco, Cal. BR/TR, 6'3", 175 lbs. Deb: 4/16/10																							
1913	Bos-N	140	524	74	143	20	1	2	50	38	48	.273	.333	.326	87	-8	57			.987	5	*1-135	-0.5
Total	5	377	1251	203	335	42	7	4	116	119	130	.268	.338	.322	81	-31	132			.987	4	1-353/O-2	-3.5
■ BILL NAHORODNY Nahorodny, William Gerard b: 8/31/53, Hamtramck, Mich. BR/TR, 6'2", 200 lbs. Deb: 9/27/76																							
1980	Atl-N	59	157	14	38	12	0	5	18	8	21	.242	.287	.414	91	-2	0	2	-1	.990	-7	C-54/1-1	-1.0
1981	Atl-N	14	13	0	3	1	0	0	2	1	3	.231	.286	.308	67	-1	0	0	0	1.000	0	/C-3,1-1	-0.1
Total	9	308	844	74	203	41	3	25	109	56	118	.241	.292	.385	85	-18	1	4		.983	-17	C-275/1-7,D	-3.3
Team	2	73	170	14	41	13	0	5	20	9	24	.241	.287	.406	89	-3	0	2		.990	-7	/C-57,1-2	-1.1
■ BILLY NASH Nash, William Mitchell b: 6/24/1865, Richmond, Va. d: 11/15/29, E.Orange, N.J. BR/TR, 5'8.5", 167 lbs. Deb: 8/5/1884 MU																							
1885	Bos-N	26	94	9	24	4	0	0	11	2	9	.255	.271	.298	87	-1				.864	-4	3-19/2-8	-0.4
1886	Bos-N	109	417	61	117	11	8	1	45	24	28	.281	.320	.353	108	4	16			.863	-5	*3-90,S-17/O	0.2
1887	Bos-N	121	475	100	140	24	12	6	94	60	30	.295	.376	.434	124	17	43			.884	9	*3-117/O-5	2.3
1888	Bos-N	135	526	71	149	18	15	4	75	50	46	.283	.350	.397	136	22	20			**.913**	26	*3-105,2-31	**4.9**
1889	Bos-N	128	481	84	132	20	2	3	76	79	44	.274	.379	.343	97	-0	26			.905	12	*3-128/P-1	1.4
1891	Bos-N	140	537	92	148	24	9	5	95	74	50	.276	.369	.382	106	2	28			.900	-12	*3-140	-0.3
1892	*Bos-N	135	526	94	137	25	5	4	95	59	41	.260	.338	.350	99	-2	31			**.898**	24	*3-135/O-1	2.5
1893	Bos-N	128	485	115	141	27	6	10	123	85	29	.291	.399	.433	112	8	30			**.923**	3	*3-128	1.0
1894	Bos-N	132	512	132	148	23	6	8	87	91	23	.289	.399	.404	87	-11	20			**.933**	6	*3-132	-0.4
1895	Bos-N	132	508	97	147	23	6	10	108	74	19	.289	.383	.417	99	-2	18			.882	-8	*3-132	-0.7
Total	15	1549	5849	1072	1606	266	87	60	977	803	383	.275	.366	.381	103	29	265			.897	76	*3-1464/2-43,SOP	12.7
Team	10	1186	4561	855	1283	199	69	51	809	598	319	.281	.368	.389	106	37	232			.901	51	*3-1126/2-39,SOP	10.5
■ TOM NEEDHAM Needham, Thomas J. "Deerfoot" b: 4/7/1879, Ireland d: 12/13/26, Steubenville, Ohio BR/TR, 5'10", 180 lbs. Deb: 5/12/04																							
1904	Bos-N	84	269	18	70	12	3	4	19	11		.260	.292	.372	108	1	3			.945	4	C-77/O-1	1.4
1905	Bos-N	83	271	21	59	6	1	2	17	24		.218	.293	.269	70	-10	3			.949	-8	C-77/O-3,1	-1.1
1906	Bos-N	83	285	11	54	8	2	1	12	13		.189	.230	.242	49	-18	3			.959	-2	C-76/2-5,130	-1.3
1907	Bos-N	86	260	19	51	6	2	1	19	18		.196	.264	.246	60	-12	4			.967	-11	C-78/1-1	-1.8
Total	11	523	1491	113	311	50	10	8	117	109		.209	.274	.272	66	-60	20			.962	5	C-465/1-7,203	-1.5
Team	4	336	1085	69	234	32	8	8	67	66		.216	.270	.282	71	-38	13			.955	-17	C-308/2-5,103	-2.8
■ TOMMY NEILL Neill, Thomas White b: 11/7/19, Hartselle, Ala. d: 9/22/80, Houston, Tex. BL/TR, 6'2", 200 lbs. Deb: 9/10/46																							
1946	Bos-N	13	45	8	12	2	0	0	7	2	1	.267	.298	.311	72	-2	0			1.000	-1	O-13	-0.4
1947	Bos-N	7	10	1	2	0	1	0	0	1	2	.200	.333	.400	96	-0	0			1.000	-1	/O-2	-0.1
Total	2	20	55	9	14	2	1	0	7	3	3	.255	.305	.327	77	-2	0			1.000	-2	/O-15	-0.5
■ BERNIE NEIS Neis, Bernard Edmund b: 9/26/1895, Bloomington, Ill. d: 11/29/72, Inverness, Fla. BB/TR, 5'7", 160 lbs. Deb: 4/14/20																							
1925	Bos-N	106	355	47	101	20	2	5	45	38	19	.285	.354	.394	100	-0	8	10	-4	.970	11	O-87	0.1

YEAR	TM/L	G	AB	R	H	2B	3B	HR	RBI	BB	SO	AVG	OBP	SLG	PRO+	BR/A	SB	CS	SBR	FA	FR	G/POS	TPR
1926	Bos-N	30	93	16	20	5	2	0	8	8	10	.215	.277	.312	64	-5	4			.925	2	O-23	-0.5
Total	8	677	1825	297	496	84	18	25	210	201	186	.272	.346	.379	94	-13	46	39		.950	3	O-520/2-1	-5.0
Team	2	136	448	63	121	25	4	5	53	46	29	.270	.338	.377	93	-5	12	10		.962	12	O-110	-0.4

■ **TOMMY NELSON** Nelson, Tom Cousineau b: 5/1/17, Chicago, Ill. d: 9/24/73, San Diego, Cal. BR/TR, 5'11.5", 180 lbs. Deb: 4/17/45

YEAR	TM/L	G	AB	R	H	2B	3B	HR	RBI	BB	SO	AVG	OBP	SLG	PRO+	BR/A	SB	CS	SBR	FA	FR	G/POS	TPR
1945	Bos-N	40	121	6	20	2	0	0	6	4	13	.165	.192	.182	4	-16	1			.910	-3	3-20,2-12	-1.8

■ **GRAIG NETTLES** Nettles, Graig b: 8/20/44, San Diego, Cal. BL/TR, 6', 186 lbs. Deb: 9/6/67 FC

YEAR	TM/L	G	AB	R	H	2B	3B	HR	RBI	BB	SO	AVG	OBP	SLG	PRO+	BR/A	SB	CS	SBR	FA	FR	G/POS	TPR
1987	Atl-N	112	177	16	37	8	1	5	33	22	25	.209	.296	.350	67	-8	1	0	0	.951	-0	3-40/1-6	-0.9
Total	22	2700	8986	1193	2225	328	28	390	1314	1088	1209	.248	.332	.421	110	117	32	36		.961	132	*3-2412/O-73,1DS	21.3

■ **JOHNNY NEUN** Neun, John Henry b: 10/28/1900, Baltimore, Md. d: 3/28/90, Baltimore, Md. BB/TL, 5'10.5", 175 lbs. Deb: 4/14/25 MC

YEAR	TM/L	G	AB	R	H	2B	3B	HR	RBI	BB	SO	AVG	OBP	SLG	PRO+	BR/A	SB	CS	SBR	FA	FR	G/POS	TPR
1930	Bos-N	81	212	39	69	12	2	2	23	21	18	.325	.389	.429	101	1	9			.991	0	1-55	-0.4
1931	Bos-N	79	104	17	23	1	3	0	11	11	14	.221	.302	.288	62	-5	2			.994	-0	1-36	-0.7
Total	6	432	945	171	273	42	17	2	85	110	93	.289	.366	.376	91	-10	41			.987	-7	1-231	-3.3
Team	2	160	316	56	92	13	5	2	34	32	32	.291	.360	.383	89	-4	11			.992	-0	/1-91	-1.1

■ **DAVE NICHOLSON** Nicholson, David Lawrence b: 8/29/39, St.Louis, Mo. BR/TR, 6'2", 215 lbs. Deb: 5/24/60

YEAR	TM/L	G	AB	R	H	2B	3B	HR	RBI	BB	SO	AVG	OBP	SLG	PRO+	BR/A	SB	CS	SBR	FA	FR	G/POS	TPR
1967	Atl-N	10	25	2	5	0	0	0	1	2	9	.200	.259	.200	34	-2	0	0	0	1.000	-0	/O-7	-0.3
Total	7	538	1419	184	301	32	12	61	179	219	573	.212	.320	.381	97	-4	6	10		.974	-19	O-472	-4.9

■ **FRED NICHOLSON** Nicholson, Fred "Shoemaker" b: 9/1/1894, Honey Grove, Tex. d: 1/23/72, Kilgore, Tex. BR/TR, 5'10.5", 173 lbs. Deb: 4/11/17

YEAR	TM/L	G	AB	R	H	2B	3B	HR	RBI	BB	SO	AVG	OBP	SLG	PRO+	BR/A	SB	CS	SBR	FA	FR	G/POS	TPR
1921	Bos-N	83	245	36	80	11	7	5	41	17	29	.327	.370	.490	133	11	5	4	-1	.983	-7	O-59/1-4,2	0.0
1922	Bos-N	78	222	31	56	4	5	2	29	23	24	.252	.336	.342	79	-7	5	7	-3	.915	-4	O-63	-1.7
Total	5	303	794	112	247	34	21	12	107	65	97	.311	.367	.452	124	25	21	17	-4	.950	-11	O-200/1-5,2	-0.2
Team	2	161	467	67	136	15	12	7	70	40	53	.291	.354	.420	107	4	10	11	-4	.946	-11	O-122/1-4,2	-1.7

■ **BUTCH NIEMAN** Nieman, Elmer Le Roy b: 2/8/18, Herkimer, Kan. d: 11/2/93, Topeka, Kan. BL/TL, 6'2", 195 lbs. Deb: 5/2/43

YEAR	TM/L	G	AB	R	H	2B	3B	HR	RBI	BB	SO	AVG	OBP	SLG	PRO+	BR/A	SB	CS	SBR	FA	FR	G/POS	TPR
1943	Bos-N	101	335	39	84	15	8	7	46	39	39	.251	.331	.406	114	5	4			.963	1	O-93	0.2
1944	Bos-N	134	468	65	124	16	6	16	65	47	47	.265	.332	.427	108	4	5			.975	-2	*O-126	-0.4
1945	Bos-N	97	247	43	61	15	0	14	56	43	33	.247	.361	.478	131	10	11			.932	0	O-57	0.7
Total	3	332	1050	147	269	46	14	37	167	129	119	.256	.339	.432	116	20	20			.961	-0	O-276	0.5

■ **MELVIN NIEVES** Nieves, Melvin Ramos b: 12/28/71, San Juan, P.R. BB/TR, 6'2", 186 lbs. Deb: 9/1/92

YEAR	TM/L	G	AB	R	H	2B	3B	HR	RBI	BB	SO	AVG	OBP	SLG	PRO+	BR/A	SB	CS	SBR	FA	FR	G/POS	TPR
1992	Atl-N	12	19	0	4	1	0	0	1	2	7	.211	.286	.263	53	-1	0	0	0	.727	-1	/O-6	-0.3
Total	4	139	319	38	66	8	1	17	46	27	126	.207	.281	.398	79	-10	2	3	-1	.961	-7	O-106/1-2	-2.2

■ **AL NIXON** Nixon, Albert Richard "Humpty Dumpty" b: 4/11/1886, Atlantic City, N.J d: 11/9/60, Opelousas, La. BR/TL, 5'7.5", 164 lbs. Deb: 9/4/15

YEAR	TM/L	G	AB	R	H	2B	3B	HR	RBI	BB	SO	AVG	OBP	SLG	PRO+	BR/A	SB	CS	SBR	FA	FR	G/POS	TPR
1921	Bos-N	55	138	25	33	6	3	1	9	7	11	.239	.281	.348	69	-7	3	2	-0	.980	-2	O-43	-1.1
1922	Bos-N	86	318	35	84	14	4	2	22	9	19	.264	.284	.352	66	-17	6	6	-2	.975	1	O-79	-2.2
1923	Bos-N	88	321	53	88	12	4	0	19	24	14	.274	.334	.336	81	-9	2	3	-1	.987	9	O-80	-0.6
Total	9	422	1345	180	372	60	13	7	118	66	77	.277	.314	.356	78	-45	19	12	-2	.980	2	O-373	-6.6
Team	3	229	777	113	205	32	11	3	50	40	44	.264	.305	.345	73	-32	11	11	-3	.981	8	O-202	-3.9

■ **OTIS NIXON** Nixon, Otis Junior b: 1/9/59, Columbus Co., N.C. BB/TR, 6'2", 180 lbs. Deb: 9/9/83 F

YEAR	TM/L	G	AB	R	H	2B	3B	HR	RBI	BB	SO	AVG	OBP	SLG	PRO+	BR/A	SB	CS	SBR	FA	FR	G/POS	TPR
1991	Atl-N	124	401	81	119	10	1	0	26	47	40	.297	.373	.327	93	-2	72	21	9	.987	1	*O-115	0.6
1992	*Atl-N	120	456	79	134	14	2	2	22	39	54	.294	.349	.346	92	-4	41	18	2	.991	13	*O-111	0.9
1993	*Atl-N	134	461	77	124	12	3	1	24	61	63	.269	.354	.315	80	-11	47	13	6	.990	8	*O-116	0.1
Total	13	1245	3444	605	920	101	16	7	217	382	477	.267	.341	.312	77	-96	444	147	45	.988	-33	*O-1098/D-18,S	-10.7
Team	3	378	1318	237	377	36	6	3	72	147	157	.286	.359	.329	88	-16	160	52	17	.990	22	O-342	1.6

■ **JOE NOLAN** Nolan, Joseph William b: 5/12/51, St.Louis, Mo. BL/TR, 6', 190 lbs. Deb: 9/21/72

YEAR	TM/L	G	AB	R	H	2B	3B	HR	RBI	BB	SO	AVG	OBP	SLG	PRO+	BR/A	SB	CS	SBR	FA	FR	G/POS	TPR
1975	Atl-N	4	4	0	1	0	0	0	0	1	0	.250	.400	.250	80	-0	0	0	0	1.000	-0	/C-1	0.0
1977	Atl-N	62	82	13	23	3	0	3	9	13	12	.280	.379	.427	103	1	1	0	0	1.000	-1	C-19	0.1
1978	Atl-N	95	213	22	49	7	3	4	22	34	28	.230	.339	.347	83	-4	3	2	-0	.979	-6	C-61	-1.0
1979	Atl-N	89	230	28	57	9	3	4	21	27	28	.248	.335	.365	85	-4	1	3	-2	.983	-7	C-74	-1.1
1980	Atl-N	17	22	2	6	1	0	0	2	2	4	.273	.333	.318	80	-1	0	0	0	1.000	1	/C-6	0.1
Total	11	621	1454	156	382	66	10	27	178	164	183	.263	.340	.378	95	-7	7	8	-3	.984	-37	C-444/D-15	-3.4
Team	5	267	551	65	136	20	6	11	54	77	72	.247	.343	.365	87	-9	5	5	-2	.984	-13	C-161	-1.9

■ **DIZZY NUTTER** Nutter, Everett Clarence b: 8/27/1893, Roseville, Ohio d: 7/25/58, Battle Creek, Mich. BL/TR, 5'9", 160 lbs. Deb: 9/7/19

YEAR	TM/L	G	AB	R	H	2B	3B	HR	RBI	BB	SO	AVG	OBP	SLG	PRO+	BR/A	SB	CS	SBR	FA	FR	G/POS	TPR
1919	Bos-N	18	52	4	11	0	0	0	3	4	5	.212	.268	.212	47	-3	1			1.000	2	O-12	-0.3

■ **CHARLIE NYCE** Nyce, Charles Reiff (b: Charles Reiff Nice) b: 7/1/1870, Philadelphia, Pa. d: 5/9/08, Philadelphia, Pa. 5'8", 160 lbs. Deb: 5/28/1895

YEAR	TM/L	G	AB	R	H	2B	3B	HR	RBI	BB	SO	AVG	OBP	SLG	PRO+	BR/A	SB	CS	SBR	FA	FR	G/POS	TPR
1895	Bos-N	9	35	7	8	5	0	2	9	4	2	.229	.325	.543	113	0	0			.889	-1	/S-9	0.0

■ **JOHNNY OATES** Oates, Johnny Lane b: 1/21/46, Sylva, N.C. BL/TR, 5'11", 188 lbs. Deb: 9/17/70 MC

YEAR	TM/L	G	AB	R	H	2B	3B	HR	RBI	BB	SO	AVG	OBP	SLG	PRO+	BR/A	SB	CS	SBR	FA	FR	G/POS	TPR
1973	Atl-N	93	322	27	80	6	0	4	27	22	31	.248	.299	.304	63	-16	1	4	-2	.981	-6	C-86	-2.1
1974	Atl-N	100	291	22	65	10	0	1	21	23	24	.223	.280	.268	52	-19	2	3	-1	.992	12	C-91	-0.5
1975	Atl-N	8	18	0	4	1	0	0	0	1	4	.222	.263	.278	48	-1	0	0	0	1.000	-0	/C-6	-0.2
Total	11	593	1637	146	410	56	2	14	126	141	149	.250	.311	.313	73	-58	11	19		.987	16	C-533	-3.5
Team	3	201	631	49	149	17	0	5	48	46	59	.236	.289	.287	57	-36	3	7		.987	6	C-183	-2.8

■ **KEN OBERKFELL** Oberkfell, Kenneth Ray b: 5/4/56, Highland, Ill. BL/TR, 6', 210 lbs. Deb: 8/22/77

YEAR	TM/L	G	AB	R	H	2B	3B	HR	RBI	BB	SO	AVG	OBP	SLG	PRO+	BR/A	SB	CS	SBR	FA	FR	G/POS	TPR
1984	Atl-N	50	172	21	40	8	1	1	10	15	17	.233	.294	.308	65	-8	1	3	-2	.964	-5	3-45/2-4	-1.6
1985	Atl-N	134	412	30	112	19	4	3	35	51	38	.272	.360	.359	96	-0	1	2	-1	.963	-1	*3-117,2-16	-0.4
1986	Atl-N	151	503	62	136	24	3	5	48	83	40	.270	.376	.360	98	2	7	4	-0	.976	9	*3-130,2-41	1.0
1987	Atl-N	135	508	59	142	29	2	3	48	48	29	.280	.344	.362	83	-11	3	3	-1	.979	-4	*3-126,2-11	-1.8
1988	Atl-N	120	422	42	117	20	4	3	40	32	28	.277	.331	.365	95	-3	4	5	-2	.951	-7	*3-113/2-1	-1.3
Total	16	1602	4874	558	1354	237	44	29	446	546	356	.278	.353	.362	97	-7	62	47	-10	.965	-5	*3-1046,2-402/1SD	-2.2
Team	5	590	2017	214	547	100	14	15	181	229	152	.271	.349	.357	91	-20	16	17	-5	.967	-8	3-531/2-73	-4.1

■ **CHARLIE O'BRIEN** O'Brien, Charles Hugh b: 5/1/60, Tulsa, Okla. BR/TR, 6'2", 195 lbs. Deb: 6/2/85

YEAR	TM/L	G	AB	R	H	2B	3B	HR	RBI	BB	SO	AVG	OBP	SLG	PRO+	BR/A	SB	CS	SBR	FA	FR	G/POS	TPR
1994	Atl-N	51	152	24	37	11	0	8	28	15	24	.243	.324	.474	102	0	0	0	0	.991	3	C-48	0.5
1995	*Atl-N	67	198	18	45	7	0	9	23	29	40	.227	.343	.399	93	-2	0	1	-1	.992	4	C-64	0.5
Total	10	524	1427	144	312	77	3	33	166	145	189	.219	.303	.346	77	-45	1	7	-4	.988	79	C-510	5.7
Team	2	118	350	42	82	18	0	17	51	44	64	.234	.335	.431	97	-2	0	1	-1	.991	6	C-112	1.0

■ **JOHNNY O'BRIEN** O'Brien, John Thomas b: 12/11/30, S.Amboy, N.J. BR/TR, 5'9", 170 lbs. Deb: 4/19/53 F

YEAR	TM/L	G	AB	R	H	2B	3B	HR	RBI	BB	SO	AVG	OBP	SLG	PRO+	BR/A	SB	CS	SBR	FA	FR	G/POS	TPR
1959	Mil-N	44	116	16	23	4	0	1	8	11	15	.198	.273	.259	47	-9	0	0	0	.987	-3	2-37	-0.9
Total	6	339	815	90	204	35	5	4	59	59	82	.250	.307	.320	68	-38	2	2	-1	.974	0	2-248/P-25,S	-2.1

■ **DANNY O'CONNELL** O'Connell, Daniel Francis b: 1/21/27, Paterson, N.J. d: 10/2/69, Clifton, N.J. BR/TR, 6', 180 lbs. Deb: 7/14/50 C

YEAR	TM/L	G	AB	R	H	2B	3B	HR	RBI	BB	SO	AVG	OBP	SLG	PRO+	BR/A	SB	CS	SBR	FA	FR	G/POS	TPR
1954	Mil-N	146	541	61	151	28	4	2	37	38	46	.279	.329	.357	84	-13	2	2	-1	.979	9	*2-103,3-35/1S	0.1
1955	Mil-N	124	453	47	102	15	4	6	40	28	43	.225	.278	.316	60	-27	2	2	-1	.981	16	*2-114/3-7,S	-0.3
1956	Mil-N	139	498	71	119	17	9	2	42	76	42	.239	.344	.321	86	-8	3	3	-1	.985	-6	*2-138/3-4,S	-0.4

YEAR	TM/L	G	AB	R	H	2B	3B	HR	RBI	BB	SO	AVG	OBP	SLG	PRO+	BR/A	SB	CS	SBR	FA	FR	G/POS	TPR
1957	Mil-N	48	183	29	43	9	1	1	8	19	20	.235	.314	.311	74	-7	1	0	0	.982	7	2-48	0.4
Total	10	1143	4035	527	1049	181	35	39	320	431	396	.260	.335	.351	84	-86	48	22	1	.980	67	2-713,3-335/S1	3.5
Team	4	457	1675	208	415	69	18	11	127	161	151	.248	.319	.330	77	-55	8	7	-2	.982	26	2-403/3-46,1S	-0.2

■ **KEN O'DEA** O'Dea, James Kenneth b: 3/16/13, Lima, N.Y. d: 12/17/85, Lima, N.Y. BL/TR, 6', 180 lbs. Deb: 4/21/35

YEAR	TM/L	G	AB	R	H	2B	3B	HR	RBI	BB	SO	AVG	OBP	SLG	PRO+	BR/A	SB	CS	SBR	FA	FR	G/POS	TPR
1946	Bos-N	12	32	4	7	0	0	0	2	8	4	.219	.375	.219	70	-1	0			1.000	-1	C-12	-0.1
Total	12	832	2195	262	560	101	20	40	323	273	251	.255	.338	.374	95	-12	3			.983	26	C-627	4.7

■ **BLUE MOON ODOM** Odom, Johnny Lee b: 5/29/45, Macon, Ga. BR/TR, 6', 185 lbs. Deb: 9/5/64

YEAR	TM/L	G	AB	R	H	2B	3B	HR	RBI	BB	SO	AVG	OBP	SLG	PRO+	BR/A	SB	CS	SBR	FA	FR	G/POS	TPR
1975	Atl-N	15	13	0	1	1	0	0	1	0	5	.077	.077	.154	-36	-2	0	0	0	.944	0	P-15	0.0
Total	13	402	405	76	79	9	2	12	31	19	163	.195	.235	.316	60	-22	6	5		.904	5	P-295	0.0

■ **ROWLAND OFFICE** Office, Rowland Johnie b: 10/25/52, Sacramento, Cal. BL/TL, 6', 170 lbs. Deb: 8/5/72

YEAR	TM/L	G	AB	R	H	2B	3B	HR	RBI	BB	SO	AVG	OBP	SLG	PRO+	BR/A	SB	CS	SBR	FA	FR	G/POS	TPR
1972	Atl-N	2	5	1	2	0	0	0	0	1	2	.400	.500	.400	145	0	0	0	0	1.000	0	/O-1	0.0
1974	Atl-N	131	248	20	61	16	1	3	31	16	30	.246	.292	.355	77	-8	5	3	-0	.994	-25	*O-119	-3.8
1975	Atl-N	126	355	30	103	14	1	3	30	23	41	.290	.339	.361	91	-4	2	2	-1	.967	-6	*O-107	-1.6
1976	Atl-N	99	359	51	101	17	1	4	34	37	49	.281	.352	.368	98	-0	2	8	-4	.986	-3	O-92	-1.2
1977	Atl-N	124	428	42	103	13	1	5	39	23	58	.241	.284	.311	53	-28	2	4	-2	.988	7	*O-104/1-1	-2.7
1978	Atl-N	146	404	40	101	13	1	9	40	22	52	.250	.299	.354	73	-15	8	6	-1	.990	-3	*O-136	-2.5
1979	Atl-N	124	277	35	69	14	2	2	37	27	33	.249	.320	.336	74	-10	5	4	-1	.988	-13	O-97	-2.7
Total	11	899	2413	259	626	101	11	32	242	189	311	.259	.317	.350	79	-66	27	30	-10	.985	-57	O-771/1-1	-16.6
Team	7	752	2076	219	540	87	7	26	211	149	265	.260	.315	.346	77	-65	24	27	-9	.985	-42	O-656/1-1	-14.5

■ **KID O'HARA** O'Hara, James Francis b: 12/19/1875, Wilkes-Barre, Pa. d: 12/1/54, Canton, Ohio BB/TR, 5'7.5", 152 lbs. Deb: 9/15/04

YEAR	TM/L	G	AB	R	H	2B	3B	HR	RBI	BB	SO	AVG	OBP	SLG	PRO+	BR/A	SB	CS	SBR	FA	FR	G/POS	TPR
1904	Bos-N	8	29	3	6	0	0	0	0	4		.207	.303	.207	60	-1	1			.923	0	/O-8	-0.2

■ **DAN O'LEARY** O'Leary, Daniel "Hustling Dan" b: 10/22/1856, Detroit, Mich. d: 6/24/22, Chicago, Ill. BL, 5'10", 165 lbs. Deb: 9/3/1879 M

YEAR	TM/L	G	AB	R	H	2B	3B	HR	RBI	BB	SO	AVG	OBP	SLG	PRO+	BR/A	SB	CS	SBR	FA	FR	G/POS	TPR
1880	Bos-N	3	12	1	3	2	0	0	1	0	3	.250	.250	.417	126	0				1.000	-1	/O-3	-0.1
Total	5	45	181	18	44	3	2	1	5	10	10	.243	.283	.298	62	-9				.843	-2	/O-45	-1.1

■ **JOSE OLIVA** Oliva, Jose (Galvez) b: 3/3/71, San Pedro De Macoris, D.R. BR/TR, 6'1", 150 lbs. Deb: 7/1/94

YEAR	TM/L	G	AB	R	H	2B	3B	HR	RBI	BB	SO	AVG	OBP	SLG	PRO+	BR/A	SB	CS	SBR	FA	FR	G/POS	TPR
1994	Atl-N	19	59	9	17	5	0	6	11	7	10	.288	.364	.678	160	5	0	1	-1	.932	2	3-16	0.6
1995	Atl-N	48	109	7	17	4	0	5	12	7	22	.156	.207	.330	38	-10	0	0	0	.902	-1	3-25/1-1	-1.1
Total	2	89	242	24	43	10	0	13	31	19	56	.178	.243	.380	60	-15	0	1	-1	.932	-2	/3-59,1-3	-1.8
Team	2	67	168	16	34	9	0	11	23	14	32	.202	.264	.452	82	-5	0	1	-1	.914	1	/3-41,1-1	-0.5

■ **GENE OLIVER** Oliver, Eugene George b: 3/22/35, Moline, Ill. BR/TR, 6'2", 225 lbs. Deb: 6/6/59

YEAR	TM/L	G	AB	R	H	2B	3B	HR	RBI	BB	SO	AVG	OBP	SLG	PRO+	BR/A	SB	CS	SBR	FA	FR	G/POS	TPR
1963	Mil-N	95	296	34	74	12	2	11	47	27	59	.250	.323	.416	112	5	4	4	-1	.985	-14	1-55,O-35/C	-1.5
1964	Mil-N	93	279	45	77	15	1	13	49	17	41	.276	.320	.477	120	7	3	7	-3	.982	-6	1-76/C-1	-0.6
1965	Mil-N	122	392	56	106	20	0	21	58	36	61	.270	.336	.482	127	13	5	4	-1	.976	1	C-64,1-52/O	1.5
1966	Atl-N	76	191	19	37	9	1	8	24	16	43	.194	.256	.377	72	-8	2	0	1	.990	11	C-48/1-5,O	0.7
1967	Atl-N	17	51	8	10	2	0	3	6	6	8	.196	.281	.412	97	-0	0	0	0	.968	2	C-14	0.3
Total	10	786	2216	268	546	111	5	93	320	215	420	.246	.317	.427	103	5	24	21	-5	.985	-24	C-382,1-200/O	-2.0
Team	5	403	1209	162	304	58	4	56	184	102	212	.251	.314	.445	112	16	14	15	-5	.983	-5	1-188,C-129/O	0.4

■ **LUIS OLMO** Olmo, Luis Francisco (Rodriguez) (b: Luis Francisco Rodriquez (Olmo)) b: 8/11/19, Arecibo, P.R. BR/TR, 5'11.5", 190 lbs. Deb: 7/23/43

YEAR	TM/L	G	AB	R	H	2B	3B	HR	RBI	BB	SO	AVG	OBP	SLG	PRO+	BR/A	SB	CS	SBR	FA	FR	G/POS	TPR
1950	Bos-N	69	154	23	35	7	1	5	22	18	23	.227	.308	.383	86	-4	3			.974	-9	O-55/3-1	-1.4
1951	Bos-N	21	56	4	11	1	1	0	4	4	4	.196	.250	.250	38	-5	0	1	-1	1.000	-3	O-16	-0.9
Total	6	462	1629	208	458	65	25	29	272	88	128	.281	.319	.405	102	-3	33	1		.968	-34	O-332/3-63,2	-5.1
Team	2	90	210	27	46	8	2	5	26	22	27	.219	.293	.348	74	-9	3	1		.980	-11	/O-71,3-1	-2.3

■ **GREG OLSON** Olson, Gregory William b: 9/6/60, Marshall, Minn. BR/TR, 6', 200 lbs. Deb: 6/27/89

YEAR	TM/L	G	AB	R	H	2B	3B	HR	RBI	BB	SO	AVG	OBP	SLG	PRO+	BR/A	SB	CS	SBR	FA	FR	G/POS	TPR
1990	Atl-N★	100	298	36	78	12	1	7	36	30	51	.262	.333	.379	90	-4	1	1	-0	.987	-7	C-97/3-1	-0.5
1991	•Atl-N	133	411	46	99	25	0	6	44	44	48	.241	.319	.345	82	-9	1	1	-0	.995	3	*C-127	0.0
1992	Atl-N	95	302	27	72	14	2	3	27	34	31	.238	.318	.328	78	-8	2	1	0	.998	7	C-94	0.5
1993	•Atl-N	83	262	23	59	10	0	4	24	29	27	.225	.305	.309	64	-13	1	0	0	.988	-1	C-81	-1.0
Total	5	414	1275	132	309	61	3	20	131	137	157	.242	.319	.342	79	-34	5	3	-0	.992	3	C-402/3-1	-1.0
Team	4	411	1273	132	308	61	3	20	131	137	157	.242	.319	.342	79	-34	5	3	-0	.992	3	C-399/3-1	-1.0

■ **MICKEY O'NEIL** O'Neil, George Michael b: 4/12/1900, St.Louis, Mo. d: 4/8/64, St.Louis, Mo. BR/TR, 5'10", 185 lbs. Deb: 9/12/19 C

YEAR	TM/L	G	AB	R	H	2B	3B	HR	RBI	BB	SO	AVG	OBP	SLG	PRO+	BR/A	SB	CS	SBR	FA	FR	G/POS	TPR
1919	Bos-N	11	28	3	6	0	0	0	1	1	7	.214	.241	.214	39	-2	0			.981	3	C-11	0.2
1920	Bos-N	112	304	19	86	5	4	0	28	21	20	.283	.339	.326	96	-1	4	4	-1	.962	8	*C-105/2-1	1.3
1921	Bos-N	98	277	26	69	9	4	2	29	23	21	.249	.307	.332	73	-11	2	2	-1	.968	8	C-95	0.1
1922	Bos-N	83	251	18	56	5	2	0	26	14	11	.223	.267	.259	38	-23	1	0	0	.978	0	C-79	-1.8
1923	Bos-N	96	306	29	65	7	4	0	20	17	14	.212	.258	.261	39	-27	3	2	-0	.973	14	C-95	-0.9
1924	Bos-N	106	362	32	89	4	1	0	22	14	27	.246	.276	.262	47	-27	4	3	-1	.985	1	*C-106	-2.0
1925	Bos-N	70	222	29	57	6	5	2	30	21	16	.257	.327	.356	81	-6	1	2	-1	.972	-8	C-69	-1.1
Total	9	672	1995	177	475	41	23	4	179	139	127	.238	.292	.288	58	-118	18	13		.972	26	C-654/2-1	-5.7
Team	7	576	1750	156	428	36	20	4	156	111	116	.245	.294	.295	61	-98	15	13		.973	26	C-560/2-1	-4.2

■ **JACK O'NEILL** O'Neill, John Joseph b: 1/10/1873, Galway, Ireland d: 6/29/35, Scranton, Pa. BR/TR, 5'10", 165 lbs. Deb: 4/21/02 F

YEAR	TM/L	G	AB	R	H	2B	3B	HR	RBI	BB	SO	AVG	OBP	SLG	PRO+	BR/A	SB	CS	SBR	FA	FR	G/POS	TPR
1906	Bos-N	61	167	14	30	5	1	0	4	12		.180	.243	.222	46	-10	0			.971	12	C-48/1-2,O	0.6
Total	5	303	945	74	185	24	5	1	74	52		.196	.258	.235	49	-58	20			.974	40	C-280/1-2,O	0.9

■ **JESS ORNDORFF** Orndorff, Jesse Walworth Thayer b: 1/15/1881, Chicago, Ill. d: 9/28/60, Cardiff-By-The- Sea, Cal. BB/TR, 6', 168 lbs. Deb: 4/18/07

YEAR	TM/L	G	AB	R	H	2B	3B	HR	RBI	BB	SO	AVG	OBP	SLG	PRO+	BR/A	SB	CS	SBR	FA	FR	G/POS	TPR
1907	Bos-N	5	17	0	2	0	0	0	0	0		.118	.118	.118	-26	-2	0			.900	-2	/C-5	-0.5

■ **FRANK O'ROURKE** O'Rourke, James Francis "Blackie" b: 11/28/1894, Hamilton, Ont., Can d: 5/14/86, Chatham, N.J. BR/TR, 5'10.5", 165 lbs. Deb: 6/12/12

YEAR	TM/L	G	AB	R	H	2B	3B	HR	RBI	BB	SO	AVG	OBP	SLG	PRO+	BR/A	SB	CS	SBR	FA	FR	G/POS	TPR
1912	Bos-N	61	196	11	24	3	1	0	16	11	50	.122	.177	.148	-10	-30	1			.915	-7	S-59/3-1	-3.3
Total	14	1131	4069	547	1032	196	42	15	430	314	377	.254	.315	.333	68	-189	100			.949	16	3-598,S-289,2/10	-12.0

■ **JIM O'ROURKE** O'Rourke, James Henry "Orator Jim" b: 9/1/1850, Bridgeport, Conn. d: 1/8/19, Bridgeport, Conn. BR/TR, 5'8", 185 lbs. Deb: 4/26/1872 FMUH

YEAR	TM/L	G	AB	R	H	2B	3B	HR	RBI	BB	SO	AVG	OBP	SLG	PRO+	BR/A	SB	CS	SBR	FA	FR	G/POS	TPR
1873	Bos-n	57	280	79	98	22	3	1	46	14	1	.350	.381	.461	135	10						1-32,O-22/C	0.9
1874	Bos-n	70	332	82	105	12	6	**5**		2		.316	.320	.434	130	9						*1-70	0.7
1875	Bos-n	75	364	98	106	16	8	**6**		10		.291	.310	.429	147	16						O-45,3-27/1	1.4
1876	Bos-N	70	312	61	102	17	3	2	43	15	17	.327	.358	.420	156	18				.856	-3	*O-68/1-2,C	1.3
1877	Bos-N	61	265	**68**	96	14	4	0	23	**20**	9	.362	**.407**	.445	162	19				.846	-0	*O-60/1-1	1.4
1878	Bos-N	60	255	44	71	17	7	1	29	5	21	.278	.292	.412	120	4				.860	4	*O-57/1-2,C	0.4
1880	Bos-N	86	363	71	100	20	11	**6**	45	21	8	.275	.315	.441	158	22				.907	-3	O-37,1-19,S3/C	1.8
Total	4 n	225	1076	286	342	53	17	12	61	28	1	.318	.335	.432	137	39	5					1-105/O-67,3SC	3.2
Total	19	1774	7435	1446	2304	414	132	50	1010	481	348	.310	.355	.421	133	286	191			.898	-80	*O-1377,C-209,31/SP2	16.1
Team	3 n	202	976	259	309	50	17	12	46	26	1	.317	.334	.440	138	0	4			.862	0	1-105/O-67,3C	3.0
Team	4	277	1195	244	369	68	25	9	140	61	55	.309	.342	.430	150	63	0			.862	-2	O-222/1-24,SC3	4.9

■ **JOHN O'ROURKE** O'Rourke, John b: 8/23/1849, Bridgeport, Conn. d: 6/23/11, Boston, Mass. BL/TL, 6', 190 lbs. Deb: 5/1/1879 F

YEAR	TM/L	G	AB	R	H	2B	3B	HR	RBI	BB	SO	AVG	OBP	SLG	PRO+	BR/A	SB	CS	SBR	FA	FR	G/POS	TPR
1879	Bos-N	72	317	69	108	17	11	6	**62**	8	32	.341	.357	**.521**	181	26				.882	2	*O-71	2.3

YEAR	TM/L	G	AB	R	H	2B	3B	HR	RBI	BB	SO	AVG	OBP	SLG	PRO+	BR/A	SB	CS	SBR	FA	FR	G/POS	TPR
1880	Bos-N	81	313	30	86	22	8	3	36	18	32	.275	.314	.425	153	17				.871	5	*O-81	1.9
Total	3	230	945	148	279	58	24	11	98	47	64	.295	.329	.442	150	49				.871	4	O-228/1-1	4.3
Team	2	153	630	99	194	39	19	9	98	26	64	.308	.335	.473	168	44				.876	7	O-152	4.2

■ TOM O'ROURKE O'Rourke, Thomas Joseph b: 10/1865, New York, N.Y. d: 7/19/29, New York, N.Y. TR , 5'9", 158 lbs. Deb: 5/11/1887

YEAR	TM/L	G	AB	R	H	2B	3B	HR	RBI	BB	SO	AVG	OBP	SLG	PRO+	BR/A	SB	CS	SBR	FA	FR	G/POS	TPR
1887	Bos-N	22	78	12	12	3	0	0	10	7	6	.154	.233	.192	19	-8	4			.777	-5	C-21/O-1,3	-1.0
1888	Bos-N	20	74	3	13	0	0	0	4	1	9	.176	.187	.176	16	-7	2			.881	1	C-20/O-1	-0.4
Total	3	85	312	32	58	11	0	0	14	21	15	.186	.242	.221	39	-23	8			.867	-15	/C-83,O-2,13	-2.7
Team	2	42	152	15	25	3	0	0	14	8	15	.164	.211	.184	18	-15	6			.830	-4	/C-41,O-2,3	-1.4

■ JIMMY OUTLAW Outlaw, James Paulus b: 1/20/13, Orme, Tenn. BR/TR, 5'8", 168 lbs. Deb: 4/20/37

YEAR	TM/L	G	AB	R	H	2B	3B	HR	RBI	BB	SO	AVG	OBP	SLG	PRO+	BR/A	SB	CS	SBR	FA	FR	G/POS	TPR
1939	Bos-N	65	133	15	35	2	0	0	5	10	14	.263	.315	.278	65	-6	1			.964	-3	O-39/3-2	-1.1
Total	10	650	1974	257	529	79	17	6	184	188	176	.268	.333	.334	85	-39	24			.972	-19	O-390,3-158	-8.5

■ LARRY OWEN Owen, Lawrence Thomas b: 5/31/55, Cleveland, Ohio BR/TR, 5'11", 185 lbs. Deb: 8/14/81

YEAR	TM/L	G	AB	R	H	2B	3B	HR	RBI	BB	SO	AVG	OBP	SLG	PRO+	BR/A	SB	CS	SBR	FA	FR	G/POS	TPR
1981	Atl-N	13	16	0	0	0	0	0	0	1	4	.000	.059	.000	-80	-4	0	0	0	.964	2	C-10	-0.2
1982	Atl-N	2	3	1	1	1	0	0	0	0	1	.333	.333	.667	167	0	0	0	0	1.000	-0	/C-2	0.0
1983	Atl-N	17	17	0	2	0	0	0	1	0	2	.118	.118	.118	-32	-3	0	1	-1	.970	1	C-16	-0.3
1985	Atl-N	26	71	7	17	3	0	2	12	8	17	.239	.316	.366	85	-1	0	0	0	.966	3	C-25	0.2
Total	6	171	352	30	68	11	0	8	30	34	98	.193	.268	.293	51	-24	0	1	-1	.980	29	C-165	1.0
Team	4	58	107	8	20	4	0	2	13	9	24	.187	.250	.280	46	-8	0	1	-1	.967	5	/C-53	-0.3

■ TOM PACIOREK Paciorek, Thomas Marian b: 11/2/46, Detroit, Mich. BR/TR, 6'4", 215 lbs. Deb: 9/12/70 F

YEAR	TM/L	G	AB	R	H	2B	3B	HR	RBI	BB	SO	AVG	OBP	SLG	PRO+	BR/A	SB	CS	SBR	FA	FR	G/POS	TPR
1976	Atl-N	111	324	39	94	10	4	4	36	19	57	.290	.335	.383	97	-1	2	3	-1	.983	-12	O-84,1-12/3	-2.0
1977	Atl-N	72	155	20	37	8	0	3	15	6	46	.239	.267	.348	57	-10	1	0	0	.984	-2	1-32/O-9,3	-1.3
1978	Atl-N	5	9	2	3	0	0	0	0	0	1	.333	.333	.333	78	-0	0	0	0	1.000	-0	/1-2	-0.1
Total	18	1392	4121	494	1162	232	30	86	503	245	704	.282	.328	.415	102	6	55	38	-6	.979	-89	O-794,1-396/D3S	-13.9
Team	3	188	488	61	134	18	4	7	51	25	104	.275	.314	.371	83	-11	3	3	-1	.977	-14	/O-93,1-46,3	-3.4

■ DON PADGETT Padgett, Don Wilson b: 12/5/11, Caroleen, N.C. d: 12/9/80, High Point, N.C. BL/TR, 6', 190 lbs. Deb: 4/23/37

YEAR	TM/L	G	AB	R	H	2B	3B	HR	RBI	BB	SO	AVG	OBP	SLG	PRO+	BR/A	SB	CS	SBR	FA	FR	G/POS	TPR
1946	Bos-N	44	98	6	25	3	0	2	21	5	7	.255	.291	.347	80	-3	0			.939	-6	C-26	-0.8
Total	8	699	1991	247	573	111	16	37	338	141	130	.288	.336	.415	101	1	6			.962	-32	C-251,O-242/1	-3.2

■ ERNIE PADGETT Padgett, Ernest Kitchen "Red" b: 3/1/1899, Philadelphia, Pa. d: 4/15/57, E.Orange, N.J. BR/TR, 5'8", 155 lbs. Deb: 10/3/23

YEAR	TM/L	G	AB	R	H	2B	3B	HR	RBI	BB	SO	AVG	OBP	SLG	PRO+	BR/A	SB	CS	SBR	FA	FR	G/POS	TPR
1923	Bos-N	4	11	3	2	0	0	0	0	2	0	.182	.308	.182	33	-1	0	0	0	.947	2	/S-2,2-1	0.1
1924	Bos-N	138	502	42	128	25	9	1	46	37	56	.255	.310	.347	79	-15	4	9	-4	.967	-10	*3-113,2-29	-2.1
1925	Bos-N	86	256	31	78	9	7	0	29	14	14	.305	.341	.395	96	-2	3	5	-2	.964	-20	2-47,S-18/3	-2.1
Total	5	271	838	84	223	34	17	1	81	61	75	.266	.318	.351	80	-24	8	14	-6	.957	-26	3-149/2-81,S	-4.4
Team	3	228	769	76	208	34	16	1	75	53	70	.270	.320	.360	84	-19	7	14	-6	.962	-28	3-120/2-77,S	-4.1

■ ANDY PAFKO Pafko, Andrew "Handy Andy" or "Pruschka" b: 2/25/21, Boyceville, Wis. BR/TR, 6', 190 lbs. Deb: 9/24/43 C

YEAR	TM/L	G	AB	R	H	2B	3B	HR	RBI	BB	SO	AVG	OBP	SLG	PRO+	BR/A	SB	CS	SBR	FA	FR	G/POS	TPR
1953	Mil-N	140	516	70	153	23	4	17	72	37	33	.297	.347	.455	114	9	2	1	0	.976	-4	*O-139	0.1
1954	Mil-N	138	510	61	146	22	4	14	69	37	36	.286	.339	.427	105	2	1	2	-1	.969	-4	*O-138	-0.8
1955	Mil-N	86	252	29	67	3	5	5	34	7	23	.266	.297	.377	81	-7	1	2	-1	.980	-8	O-58,3-12	-1.9
1956	Mil-N	45	93	15	24	5	0	2	9	10	13	.258	.330	.376	95	-1	0	0	0	.978	-5	O-37	-0.7
1957	*Mil-N	83	220	31	61	6	1	8	27	10	22	.277	.312	.423	102	-0	1	0	0	.982	-6	O-69	-0.9
1958	*Mil-N	95	164	17	39	7	1	3	23	15	17	.238	.309	.348	80	-5	0	0	0	1.000	-14	O-93	-2.2
1959	Mil-N	71	142	17	31	8	2	1	15	14	15	.218	.293	.324	70	-6	0	0	0	.978	-12	O-64	-2.0
Total	17	1852	6292	844	1796	264	62	213	976	561	477	.285	.351	.449	118	141	38	13	4	.984	-21	*O-1570,3-213	4.5
Team	7	658	1897	240	521	74	17	50	249	130	159	.275	.326	.411	99	-8	5	5	-2	.978	-53	O-598/3-12	-8.4

■ MIKE PAGE Page, Michael Randy b: 7/12/40, Woodruff, S.C. BL/TR, 6'2.5", 210 lbs. Deb: 6/30/68

YEAR	TM/L	G	AB	R	H	2B	3B	HR	RBI	BB	SO	AVG	OBP	SLG	PRO+	BR/A	SB	CS	SBR	FA	FR	G/POS	TPR
1968	Atl-N	20	28	1	5	0	0	0	1	1	9	.179	.207	.179	16	-3	0	0	0	1.000	-1	/O-6	-0.5

■ BILL PARKS Parks, William Robert b: 6/4/1849, Easton, Pa. d: 10/10/11, Easton, Pa. BR/TR, 5'8", 150 lbs. Deb: 4/26/1875 M

YEAR	TM/L	G	AB	R	H	2B	3B	HR	RBI	BB	SO	AVG	OBP	SLG	PRO+	BR/A	SB	CS	SBR	FA	FR	G/POS	TPR
1876	Bos-N	1	4	0	0	0	0	0	0	0	0	.000	.000	.000	-98	-1				.750	-0	/O-1	-0.1

■ GENE PATTON Patton, Gene Tunney b: 7/8/26, Coatesville, Pa. BL/TR, 5'10", 165 lbs. Deb: 6/17/44

YEAR	TM/L	G	AB	R	H	2B	3B	HR	RBI	BB	SO	AVG	OBP	SLG	PRO+	BR/A	SB	CS	SBR	FA	FR	G/POS	TPR
1944	Bos-N	1	0	0	0	0	0	0	0	0	0	—	—	—	—	0	0			.000	0	R	0.0

■ BILL PECOTA Pecota, William Joseph b: 2/16/60, Redwood City, Cal. BR/TR, 6'2", 195 lbs. Deb: 9/19/86

YEAR	TM/L	G	AB	R	H	2B	3B	HR	RBI	BB	SO	AVG	OBP	SLG	PRO+	BR/A	SB	CS	SBR	FA	FR	G/POS	TPR
1993	*Atl-N	72	62	17	20	2	1	0	5	2	5	.323	.344	.387	94	-1	1	1	-0	1.000	1	3-23/2-4,O	0.1
1994	Atl-N	64	112	11	24	5	0	2	16	16	16	.214	.313	.313	62	-6	1	0	0	.974	7	3-31/2-1,O	0.2
Total	9	698	1527	223	380	72	11	22	148	160	216	.249	.324	.354	87	-26	52	20		.968	39	3-272,S-177,2/O1DPC	2.9
Team	2	136	174	28	44	7	1	2	21	18	21	.253	.323	.339	73	-7	2	1		.978	9	/3-54,2-5,O	0.3

■ JIM PENDLETON Pendleton, James Edward b: 1/7/24, St.Charles, Mo. BR/TR, 6', 185 lbs. Deb: 4/17/53

YEAR	TM/L	G	AB	R	H	2B	3B	HR	RBI	BB	SO	AVG	OBP	SLG	PRO+	BR/A	SB	CS	SBR	FA	FR	G/POS	TPR
1953	Mil-N	120	251	48	75	12	4	7	27	7	36	.299	.323	.462	108	2	6	5	-1	.961	-13	*O-105/S-7	-1.4
1954	Mil-N	71	173	20	38	3	1	1	16	4	21	.220	.237	.266	33	-17	2	1	0	.950	-4	O-50	-2.3
1955	Mil-N	8	10	0	0	0	0	0	0	0	2	.000	.000	.000	-99	-3	0	0	0	1.000	-0	/S-1,3-1,O	-0.3
1956	Mil-N	14	11	0	0	0	0	0	0	1	3	.000	.083	.000	-80	-3	0	0	0	1.000	-0	/S-3,3-2,12	-0.3
Total	8	444	941	120	240	30	8	19	97	43	151	.255	.292	.365	76	-35	11	6	-0	.959	-26	O-279/3-24,S12	-7.0
Team	4	213	445	68	113	15	5	8	43	12	62	.254	.277	.364	70	-21	8	6	-1	.957	-18	O-156/S-11,321	-4.3

■ TERRY PENDLETON Pendleton, Terry Lee b: 7/16/60, Los Angeles, Cal. BB/TR, 5'9", 180 lbs. Deb: 7/18/84

YEAR	TM/L	G	AB	R	H	2B	3B	HR	RBI	BB	SO	AVG	OBP	SLG	PRO+	BR/A	SB	CS	SBR	FA	FR	G/POS	TPR
1991	*Atl-N	153	586	94	**187**	34	8	22	86	43	70	**.319**	.367	.517	138	28	10	2	2	.950	**28**	*3-148	5.9
1992	*Atl-N★	160	640	98	**199**	39	1	21	105	37	67	.311	.349	.473	123	18	5	2	0	.960	13	*3-158	3.3
1993	*Atl-N	161	633	81	172	33	1	17	84	36	97	.272	.314	.408	91	-10	5	1	1	.959	12	*3-161	0.4
1994	Atl-N	77	309	25	78	18	3	7	30	12	57	.252	.280	.398	73	-13	2	0	1	.950	6	3-77	-0.6
Total	12	1611	6114	772	1673	311	38	125	825	418	805	.274	.321	.398	95	-53	122	55	4	.957	179	*3-1581/O-1	12.9
Team	4	551	2168	298	636	124	13	67	305	128	291	.293	.334	.455	110	23	22	5	4	.956	59	3-544	9.0

■ JOE PEPITONE Pepitone, Joseph Anthony "Pepi" b: 10/9/40, Brooklyn, N.Y. BL/TL, 6'2", 200 lbs. Deb: 4/10/62 C

YEAR	TM/L	G	AB	R	H	2B	3B	HR	RBI	BB	SO	AVG	OBP	SLG	PRO+	BR/A	SB	CS	SBR	FA	FR	G/POS	TPR
1973	Atl-N	3	11	0	4	0	0	0	1	1	1	.364	.417	.364	110	0	0	0	0	.963	-1	/1-3	-0.1
Total	12	1397	5097	606	1315	158	35	219	721	302	526	.258	.303	.432	105	12	41	32	-7	.993	-21	1-953,O-496	-10.4

■ HENRY PEPLOSKI Peploski, Henry Stephen "Pep" b: 9/15/05, Garlin, Poland d: 1/28/82, Dover, N.J. BL/TR, 5'9", 155 lbs. Deb: 9/19/29 F

YEAR	TM/L	G	AB	R	H	2B	3B	HR	RBI	BB	SO	AVG	OBP	SLG	PRO+	BR/A	SB	CS	SBR	FA	FR	G/POS	TPR
1929	Bos-N	6	10	1	2	0	0	0	1	1	3	.200	.273	.200	20	-1	0			1.000	-0	/3-2	-0.1

■ EDDIE PEREZ Perez, Eduardo b: 5/4/68, Ciudad Ojeda, Venez. BR/TR, 6'1", 175 lbs. Deb: 9/10/95

YEAR	TM/L	G	AB	R	H	2B	3B	HR	RBI	BB	SO	AVG	OBP	SLG	PRO+	BR/A	SB	CS	SBR	FA	FR	G/POS	TPR
1995	Atl-N	7	13	1	4	1	0	1	4	0	2	.308	.308	.615	133	1	0	0	0	1.000	3	/C-5,1-1	0.3

■ MARTY PEREZ Perez, Martin Roman b: 2/28/47, Visalia, Cal. BR/TR, 5'11", 160 lbs. Deb: 9/9/69

YEAR	TM/L	G	AB	R	H	2B	3B	HR	RBI	BB	SO	AVG	OBP	SLG	PRO+	BR/A	SB	CS	SBR	FA	FR	G/POS	TPR
1971	Atl-N	130	410	28	93	15	3	4	32	25	44	.227	.273	.307	60	-22	1	2	-1	.955	-14	*S-126/2-1	-2.3
1972	Atl-N	141	479	33	109	13	1	1	28	30	55	.228	.277	.265	50	-31	0	3	-2	.957	-34	*S-141	-5.2
1973	Atl-N	141	501	66	125	15	5	8	57	49	66	.250	.319	.347	79	-14	2	3	-1	.962	-9	*S-139	-0.8
1974	Atl-N	127	447	51	116	20	5	2	34	35	51	.260	.315	.340	80	-12	2	0	1	.985	-9	*2-102,S-14/3	-1.5

YEAR	TM/L	G	AB	R	H	2B	3B	HR	RBI	BB	SO	AVG	OBP	SLG	PRO+	BR/A	SB	CS	SBR	FA	FR	G/POS	TPR
1975	Atl-N	120	461	50	127	14	2	2	34	37	44	.275	.329	.328	80	-12	2	2	-1	.985	-8	*2-116/S-7	-1.5
1976	Atl-N	31	96	12	24	4	0	1	6	8	9	.250	.308	.323	74	-3	0	0	0	.976	-2	2-18,S-17/3	-0.3
Total	10	931	3131	313	771	108	22	22	241	245	369	.246	.303	.316	70	-124	11	17	-7	.958	-59	S-465,2-434/3	-12.0
Team	6	690	2394	240	594	81	16	18	191	184	269	.248	.304	.318	70	-94	7	10	-4	.957	-76	S-444,2-237/3	-11.6

■ GERALD PERRY Perry, Gerald June b: 10/30/60, Savannah, Ga. BL/TR, 6', 190 lbs. Deb: 8/11/83

YEAR	TM/L	G	AB	R	H	2B	3B	HR	RBI	BB	SO	AVG	OBP	SLG	PRO+	BR/A	SB	CS	SBR	FA	FR	G/POS	TPR
1983	Atl-N	27	39	5	14	2	0	1	6	5	4	.359	.432	.487	144	2	0	1	-1	.982	-2	/1-7,O-1	-0.1
1984	Atl-N	122	347	52	92	12	2	7	47	61	38	.265	.378	.372	104	4	15	12	-3	.988	-8	1-64,O-53	-1.2
1985	Atl-N	110	238	22	51	5	0	3	13	23	28	.214	.284	.273	53	-15	9	5	-0	.985	-0	1-55/O-1	-1.9
1986	Atl-N	29	70	6	19	2	0	2	11	8	4	.271	.346	.386	96	-0	0	1	-1	.889	-5	O-21/1-1	-0.7
1987	Atl-N	142	533	77	144	35	2	12	74	48	63	.270	.332	.411	91	-7	42	16	3	.990	-10	*1-136/O-7	-2.4
1988	Atl-N★	141	547	61	164	29	1	8	74	36	49	.300	.344	.400	108	5	29	14	0	.988	1	*1-141	-0.6
1989	Atl-N	72	266	24	67	11	0	4	21	32	28	.252	.339	.338	92	-2	10	6	-1	.987	1	1-72	-0.7
Total	13	1193	3144	383	832	150	11	59	396	328	374	.265	.336	.376	95	-20	142	75	-2	.988	-32	1-656/O-89,D	-10.7
Team	7	643	2040	247	551	96	5	37	246	213	214	.270	.341	.376	95	-12	105	55	-1	.988	-24	1-476/O-83	-7.6

■ DAMON PHILLIPS Phillips, Damon Roswell "Dee" b: 6/8/19, Corsicana, Tex. BR/TR, 6', 176 lbs. Deb: 7/19/42

YEAR	TM/L	G	AB	R	H	2B	3B	HR	RBI	BB	SO	AVG	OBP	SLG	PRO+	BR/A	SB	CS	SBR	FA	FR	G/POS	TPR
1944	Bos-N	140	489	35	126	30	1	1	53	28	34	.258	.301	.329	74	-17	1			.932	-4	3-90,S-60	-1.6
1946	Bos-N	2	2	0	1	0	0	0	0	0	0	.500	.500	.500	182	0	0			.000	0	H	0.0
Total	3	170	575	39	144	32	1	1	59	35	39	.250	.296	.315	70	-23	1			.956	3	/3-90,S-87	-1.3
Team	2	142	491	35	127	30	1	1	53	28	34	.259	.301	.330	74	-17	1			.953	-4	/3-90,S-60	-1.6

■ EDDIE PHILLIPS Phillips, Edward David b: 2/17/01, Worcester, Mass. d: 1/26/68, Buffalo, N.Y. BR/TR, 6', 178 lbs. Deb: 5/4/24

YEAR	TM/L	G	AB	R	H	2B	3B	HR	RBI	BB	SO	AVG	OBP	SLG	PRO+	BR/A	SB	CS	SBR	FA	FR	G/POS	TPR
1924	Bos-N	3	3	0	0	0	0	0	0	0	2	.000	.000	.000	-99	-1	0	0	0	1.000	0	/C-1	-0.1
Total	6	312	997	82	236	54	6	14	126	104	115	.237	.312	.345	72	-41	3	1	0	.980	-27	C-298	-4.7

■ CHARLIE PICK Pick, Charles Thomas b: 4/10/1888, Brookneal, Va. d: 6/26/54, Lynchburg, Va. BL/TR, 5'10", 160 lbs. Deb: 9/20/14

YEAR	TM/L	G	AB	R	H	2B	3B	HR	RBI	BB	SO	AVG	OBP	SLG	PRO+	BR/A	SB	CS	SBR	FA	FR	G/POS	TPR
1919	Bos-N	34	114	12	29	1	1	1	7	7	5	.254	.325	.307	94	-0	4			.924	-2	2-21/3-5,O1	-0.2
1920	Bos-N	95	383	34	105	16	6	2	28	23	11	.274	.320	.363	100	-0	10	16	-7	.952	0	2-94	-0.4
Total	6	367	1278	115	333	39	17	3	86	102	60	.261	.323	.325	95	-8	64	34		.949	14	2-206,3-124/O1	0.7
Team	2	129	497	46	134	17	7	3	35	30	16	.270	.321	.350	99	-1	14	16		.947	-2	2-115/3-5,O1	-0.6

■ DAVE PICKETT Pickett, David T. b: 5/26/1874, Brookline, Mass. d: 4/22/50, Easton, Mass. 5'7.5", 170 lbs. Deb: 7/21/1898

YEAR	TM/L	G	AB	R	H	2B	3B	HR	RBI	BB	SO	AVG	OBP	SLG	PRO+	BR/A	SB	CS	SBR	FA	FR	G/POS	TPR
1898	Bos-N	14	43	3	12	1	0	0	3	6		.279	.380	.302	91	-0	2			.955	-2	O-14	-0.3

■ JACK PIERCE Pierce, Lavern Jack b: 6/2/48, Laurel, Miss. BL/TR, 6', 210 lbs. Deb: 4/27/73

YEAR	TM/L	G	AB	R	H	2B	3B	HR	RBI	BB	SO	AVG	OBP	SLG	PRO+	BR/A	SB	CS	SBR	FA	FR	G/POS	TPR
1973	Atl-N	11	20	0	1	0	0	0	0	1	8	.050	.095	.050	-55	-4	0	0	0	1.000	1	/1-6	-0.4
1974	Atl-N	6	9	1	1	0	0	0	0	1	0	.111	.200	.111	-11	-1	0	0	0	.958	0	/1-2	-0.1
Total	3	70	199	20	42	6	1	8	22	22	48	.211	.296	.372	83	-5	0	0	0	.973	-3	/1-57	-1.2
Team	2	17	29	1	2	0	0	0	0	2	8	.069	.129	.069	-41	-5	0	0	0	.986	1	/1-8	-0.5

■ ANDY PILNEY Pilney, Antone James b: 1/19/13, Frontenac, Kan. BR/TR, 5'11", 174 lbs. Deb: 6/12/36

YEAR	TM/L	G	AB	R	H	2B	3B	HR	RBI	BB	SO	AVG	OBP	SLG	PRO+	BR/A	SB	CS	SBR	FA	FR	G/POS	TPR
1936	Bos-N	3	2	0	0	0	0	0	0	0	1	.000	.000	.000	-99	-1	0			.000	0	H	-0.1

■ JIM PISONI Pisoni, James Pete b: 8/14/29, St.Louis, Mo. BR/TR, 5'10", 169 lbs. Deb: 9/25/53

YEAR	TM/L	G	AB	R	H	2B	3B	HR	RBI	BB	SO	AVG	OBP	SLG	PRO+	BR/A	SB	CS	SBR	FA	FR	G/POS	TPR
1959	Mil-N	9	24	4	4	1	0	0	0	2	6	.167	.231	.208	20	-3	0	0	0	.941	-1	/O-9	-0.4
Total	5	103	189	26	40	3	3	6	20	16	47	.212	.280	.354	71	-8	0	0		.978	-7	/O-98	-1.9

■ BIFF POCOROBA Pocoroba, Biff b: 7/25/53, Burbank, Cal. BB/TR, 5'10", 180 lbs. Deb: 4/25/75

YEAR	TM/L	G	AB	R	H	2B	3B	HR	RBI	BB	SO	AVG	OBP	SLG	PRO+	BR/A	SB	CS	SBR	FA	FR	G/POS	TPR
1975	Atl-N	67	188	15	48	7	1	1	22	20	11	.255	.327	.319	77	-5	0	0	0	.970	-4	C-62	-0.8
1976	Atl-N	54	174	16	42	7	0	0	14	19	12	.241	.316	.282	66	-7	1	0	0	.978	4	C-54	-0.1
1977	Atl-N	113	321	46	93	24	1	8	44	57	27	.290	.398	.445	113	7	3	4	-2	.989	2	*C-100	1.1
1978	Atl-N★	92	289	21	70	8	0	6	34	29	14	.242	.316	.332	73	-10	0	3	-2	.990	1	C-79	-1.0
1979	Atl-N	28	38	6	12	4	0	0	4	7	0	.316	.422	.421	122	1	1	1	-0	.933	0	/C-7	0.2
1980	Atl-N	70	83	7	22	4	0	2	8	11	11	.265	.351	.386	102	0	1	0	0	.934	-1	C-10	0.1
1981	Atl-N	57	122	4	22	4	0	0	8	12	15	.180	.265	.213	36	-10	0	0	0	.938	-5	3-21/C-9	-1.6
1982	*Atl-N	56	120	5	33	7	0	2	22	13	12	.275	.351	.383	101	0	0	0	0	.988	-4	C-36/3-2	-0.3
1983	Atl-N	55	120	11	32	6	0	2	16	12	7	.267	.333	.367	87	-2	0	0	0	.983	-3	C-34	-0.3
1984	Atl-N	4	2	1	0	0	0	0	0	2	0	.000	.500	.000	48	0	0	0	0	.000	0	/H	0.0
Total	10	596	1457	132	374	71	2	21	172	182	109	.257	.342	.351	86	-25	6	8	-3	.982	-9	C-391/3-23	-2.7

■ HUGH POLAND Poland, Hugh Reid b: 1/19/13, Tompkinsville, Ky. d: 3/30/84, Guthrie, Ky. BL/TR, 5'11.5", 185 lbs. Deb: 4/22/43

YEAR	TM/L	G	AB	R	H	2B	3B	HR	RBI	BB	SO	AVG	OBP	SLG	PRO+	BR/A	SB	CS	SBR	FA	FR	G/POS	TPR
1943	Bos-N	44	141	5	27	7	0	0	13	4	11	.191	.214	.241	32	-13	0			.973	-2	C-38	-1.3
1944	Bos-N	8	23	1	3	1	0	0	2	0	1	.130	.130	.174	-14	-3	0			.939	1	/C-6	-0.2
1946	Bos-N	4	6	0	1	1	0	0	0	0	0	.167	.167	.333	40	-1	0			1.000	0	/C-2	0.0
Total	5	83	211	8	39	10	1	0	19	6	16	.185	.207	.242	28	-20	0			.958	-4	/C-55	-2.1
Team	3	56	170	6	31	9	0	0	15	4	12	.182	.201	.235	25	-17	0			.968	-1	/C-46	-1.5

■ LUIS POLONIA Polonia, Luis Andrew (Almonte) b: 10/12/64, Santiago, D.R. BL/TL, 5'8", 155 lbs. Deb: 4/24/87

YEAR	TM/L	G	AB	R	H	2B	3B	HR	RBI	BB	SO	AVG	OBP	SLG	PRO+	BR/A	SB	CS	SBR	FA	FR	G/POS	TPR
1995	*Atl-N	28	53	6	14	7	0	0	2	3	9	.264	.304	.396	81	-2	3	0	1	1.000	-4	O-15	-0.5
Total	9	1095	3957	606	1159	150	56	17	327	313	456	.293	.346	.372	97	-11	283	122		.983	18	O-919,D-101	-0.7

■ TOM POORMAN Poorman, Thomas Iverson b: 10/14/1857, Lock Haven, Pa. d: 2/18/05, Lock Haven, Pa. BL/TR, 5'7", 135 lbs. Deb: 5/5/1880

YEAR	TM/L	G	AB	R	H	2B	3B	HR	RBI	BB	SO	AVG	OBP	SLG	PRO+	BR/A	SB	CS	SBR	FA	FR	G/POS	TPR
1885	Bos-N	56	227	44	54	5	3	3	25	7	32	.238	.261	.326	92	-2				.867	-2	O-56	-0.6
1886	Bos-N	88	371	72	97	16	6	3	41	19	52	.261	.297	.361	103	1	31			.902	6	*O-88	0.4
Total	6	496	2043	396	498	65	43	12	111	102	99	.244	.285	.335	90	-26	165			.885	-4	O-486/P-15,2	-3.5
Team	2	144	598	116	151	21	9	6	66	26	84	.253	.284	.348	99	-1	31			.889	4	O-144	-0.2

■ BOB PORTER Porter, Robert Lee b: 7/22/59, Yuma, Ariz. BL/TL, 5'10", 180 lbs. Deb: 5/13/81

YEAR	TM/L	G	AB	R	H	2B	3B	HR	RBI	BB	SO	AVG	OBP	SLG	PRO+	BR/A	SB	CS	SBR	FA	FR	G/POS	TPR
1981	Atl-N	17	14	2	4	1	0	0	4	2	1	.286	.375	.357	106	0	0	0	0	.000	0	/H	0.0
1982	Atl-N	24	27	1	3	0	0	0	0	1	9	.111	.143	.111	-27	-5	0	0	0	1.000	-1	/O-4,1-1	-0.6
Total	2	41	41	3	7	1	0	0	4	3	10	.171	.227	.195	19	-4	0	0	0	.973	-1	/O-4,1-1	-0.6

■ RAY POWELL Powell, Raymond Reath "Rabbit" b: 11/20/1888, Siloam Springs, Ark. d: 10/16/62, Chillicothe, Mo. BL/TR, 5'9", 160 lbs. Deb: 4/16/13

YEAR	TM/L	G	AB	R	H	2B	3B	HR	RBI	BB	SO	AVG	OBP	SLG	PRO+	BR/A	SB	CS	SBR	FA	FR	G/POS	TPR
1917	Bos-N	88	357	42	97	10	4	4	30	24	54	.272	.318	.356	113	5	12			.976	9	O-88	0.9
1918	Bos-N	53	188	31	40	7	5	0	20	29	30	.213	.321	.303	95	-0	2			.949	-0	O-53	-0.4
1919	Bos-N	123	470	51	111	12	12	2	33	41	79	.236	.303	.326	93	-4	16			.951	1	*O-122	-1.3
1920	Bos-N	147	609	69	137	12	12	6	29	44	83	.225	.282	.314	74	-21	10	18	-8	.956	5	*O-147	-3.8
1921	Bos-N	149	624	114	191	25	**18**	12	74	58	85	.306	.369	.462	125	22	6	17	-8	.954	3	*O-149	0.5
1922	Bos-N	142	550	82	163	22	11	6	37	59	66	.296	.369	.409	105	5	3	12	-6	.980	12	*O-136	0.0
1923	Bos-N	97	338	57	102	20	4	4	38	45	36	.302	.385	.420	117	10	1	6	-3	.941	-4	O-84	-0.3
1924	Bos-N	74	188	21	49	9	1	1	15	21	28	.261	.338	.335	85	-4	1	3	-2	.947	4	O-46	-0.4
Total	9	875	3324	467	890	117	67	35	276	321	461	.268	.336	.375	102	11	51	56		.959	29	O-826	-4.8
Team	8	873	3324	467	890	117	67	35	276	321	461	.268	.336	.375	102	11	51	56		.959	29	O-825	-4.8

YEAR TM/L	G	AB	R	H	2B	3B	HR	RBI	BB	SO	AVG	OBP	SLG	PRO+	BR/A	SB	CS	SBR	FA	FR	G/POS	TPR
■ PHIL POWERS Powers, Phillip B. "Grandmother" b: 7/26/1854, New York, N.Y. d: 12/22/14, New York, N.Y. BR/TR, 5'7", 166 lbs. Deb: 8/31/1878 U																						
1880 Bos-N	37	126	11	18	5	0	0	10	5	15	.143	.176	.183	22	-10				.851	-5	C-37/O-2	-1.4
Total 7	154	570	56	103	12	6	0	12	19	22	.181	.207	.223	40	-37				.877	-2	C-130/O-19,13	-3.2
■ MEL PREIBISCH Preibisch, Melvin Adolphus "Primo" b: 11/23/14, Sealy, Tex. d: 4/12/80, Sealy, Tex. BR/TR, 5'11", 185 lbs. Deb: 9/17/40																						
1940 Bos-N	11	40	3	9	2	0	0	5	2	4	.225	.262	.275	51	-3	0			1.000	1	O-11	-0.3
1941 Bos-N	5	4	0	0	0	0	0	0	1	2	.000	.200	.000	-42	-1	0			1.000	-1	/O-2	-0.2
Total 2	16	44	3	9	2	0	0	5	3	6	.205	.255	.250	42	-3	0			1.000	-0	/O-13	-0.5
■ JIM PRESLEY Presley, James Arthur b: 10/23/61, Pensacola, Fla. BR/TR, 6'1", 200 lbs. Deb: 6/24/84																						
1990 Atl-N	140	541	59	131	34	1	19	72	29	130	.242	.284	.414	85	-13	1	1	-0	.930	-3	*3-133,1-17	-1.7
Total 8	959	3546	413	875	181	14	135	495	210	859	.247	.292	.420	90	-57	9	14		.949	-2	3-911/1-47,DS	-7.8
■ BLONDIE PURCELL Purcell, William Aloysius b: Paterson, N.J. BR/TR, 5'9.5", 159 lbs. Deb: 5/1/1879 M																						
1885 Bos-N	21	87	9	19	1	1	0	3	3	15	.218	.244	.253	63	-3				.840	-3	O-21	-0.7
Total 12	1097	4563	767	1217	177	60	13	310	284	170	.267	.314	.340	103	22	197	0	59	.869	-49	O-995/P-79,3S1C	-4.6
■ BILLY QUEEN Queen, William Eddleman "Doc" b: 11/28/28, Gastonia, N.C. BR/TR, 6'1", 185 lbs. Deb: 4/13/54																						
1954 Mil-N	3	2	0	0	0	0	0	0	0	2	.000	.000	.000	-99	-1	0	0	0	1.000	-0	/O-1	-0.1
■ QUINN Quinn Deb: 9/7/1881																						
1881 Bos-N	1	4	0	0	0	0	0	0	0	0	.000	.000	.000	-99	-1				1.000	-0	/1-1	-0.1
■ JOE QUINN Quinn, Joseph J. b: 12/25/1864, Sydney, Australia d: 11/12/40, St.Louis, Mo. BR/TR, 5'7", 158 lbs. Deb: 4/26/1884 M																						
1888 Bos-N	38	156	19	47	8	3	4	29	2	5	.301	.310	.468	143	7	12			.914	-7	2-38	0.1
1889 Bos-N	112	444	57	116	13	5	2	69	25	21	.261	.308	.327	73	-17	24			.860	-29	S-63,2-47/3	-3.5
1891 Bos-N	124	508	70	122	8	10	3	63	28	28	.240	.288	.313	67	-25	24			.938	-23	*2-124	-3.8
1892 *Bos-N	143	532	63	116	14	1	1	59	35	40	.218	.275	.254	55	-30	17			.951	2	*2-143	-2.4
Total 17	1768	6879	891	1797	228	70	29	794	364	214	.261	.302	.327	73	-265	268			.946	-91	*2-1303,S-135,O1/3	-27.4
Team 4	417	1640	209	401	43	19	10	220	90	94	.245	.291	.312	71	-66	77			.939	-58	2-352/S-63,3	-9.6
■ JOHN RABB Rabb, John Andrew b: 6/23/60, Los Angeles, Cal. BR/TR, 6'1", 180 lbs. Deb: 9/4/82																						
1985 Atl-N	3	2	0	0	0	0	0	0	0	1	.000	.000	.000	-94	-1	0	0	0	.000	-0	/O-1	-0.1
Total 5	108	204	22	46	12	1	4	27	19	53	.225	.291	.353	81	-6	2	1		.966	2	/C-37,1-14,OD	-0.2
■ CHARLEY RADBOURN Radbourn, Charles Gardner "Old Hoss" b: 12/11/1854, Rochester, N.Y. d: 2/5/1897, Bloomington, Ill. BR/TR, 5'9", 168 lbs. Deb: 5/5/1880 H																						
1886 Bos-N	66	253	30	60	5	1	2	22	17	36	.237	.285	.289	78	-6	5			.924	1	P-58/O-6	-0.2
1887 Bos-N	51	175	25	40	2	2	1	24	18	21	.229	.308	.280	64	-8	6			.848	-4	P-50/O-2	-0.1
1888 Bos-N	24	79	6	17	1	0	0	6	3	14	.215	.262	.228	56	-4	4			.895	-1	P-24	0.0
1889 Bos-N	35	122	17	23	1	0	1	13	9	19	.189	.256	.221	32	-11	3			.975	1	P-33/O-2,3	-0.1
Total 12	653	2487	308	585	64	11	9	259	158	244	.235	.283	.281	72	-78	26			.913	-6	P-528,O-118/S123	-2.5
Team 4	176	629	78	140	9	3	4	65	47	90	.223	.283	.266	61	-29	18			.911	-3	P-165/O-10,3	-0.4
■ PAUL RADFORD Radford, Paul Revere "Shorty" b: 10/14/1861, Roxbury, Mass. d: 2/21/45, Boston, Mass. BR/TR, 5'6", 148 lbs. Deb: 5/1/1883																						
1883 Bos-N	72	258	46	53	6	3	0	14	9	26	.205	.232	.252	46	-16				.836	-5	*O-72	-1.9
Total 12	1361	4979	945	1206	176	57	13	417	791	373	.242	.351	.308	92	-8	346			.901	46	O-902,S-356/32P	2.3
■ RAFAEL RAMIREZ Ramirez, Rafael Emilio (Peguero) b: 2/18/58, San Pedro De Macoris, D.R. BR/TR, 6', 185 lbs. Deb: 8/4/80																						
1980 Atl-N	50	165	17	44	6	1	2	11	2	33	.267	.292	.352	76	-5	2	1	0	.949	-10	S-46	-1.1
1981 Atl-N	95	307	30	67	16	2	2	20	24	47	.218	.277	.303	63	-15	7	3	0	.942	-2	S-95	-0.8
1982 *Atl-N	157	609	74	169	24	4	10	52	36	49	.278	.321	.379	91	-7	27	14	-0	.956	17	*S-157	2.4
1983 Atl-N	152	622	82	185	13	5	7	58	36	48	.297	.338	.358	89	-9	16	12	-2	.949	8	*S-152	1.2
1984 Atl-N☆	145	591	51	157	22	4	2	48	26	70	.266	.298	.327	70	-23	14	17	-6	.959	-3	*S-145	-2.0
1985 Atl-N	138	568	54	141	25	4	5	58	20	63	.248	.274	.333	65	-27	2	6	-3	.954	9	*S-133	-0.9
1986 Atl-N	134	496	57	119	21	1	8	33	21	60	.240	.275	.335	64	-25	19	8	1	.952	13	S-86,3-57/O	-0.4
1987 Atl-N	56	179	22	47	12	0	1	21	8	16	.263	.302	.346	68	-8	6	3		.946	-6	S-38,3-12	-1.1
Total 13	1539	5494	562	1432	224	31	53	484	264	621	.261	.297	.342	77	-177	112	75	-11	.953	-64	*S-1386/3-72,2O	-14.1
Team 8	927	3537	387	929	139	21	37	301	173	386	.263	.300	.345	75	-121	93	64	-11	.952	25	S-852/3-69,O	-2.7
■ BILL RAMSEY Ramsey, William Thrace "Square Jaw" b: 10/20/20, Osceola, Ark. BR/TR, 6', 175 lbs. Deb: 4/19/45																						
1945 Bos-N	78	137	16	40	8	0	1	12	4	22	.292	.326	.372	93	-2	1			.963	-7	O-43	-1.0
■ NEWT RANDALL Randall, Newton J. b: 2/3/1880, New Lowell, Ont., Canada d: 5/3/55, Duluth, Minn. BR/TR, 5'10", Deb: 4/18/07																						
1907 Bos-N	75	258	16	55	6	3	0	15	19		.213	.285	.260	71	-8	4			.920	-8	O-73	-2.1
■ MERRITT RANEW Ranew, Merritt Thomas b: 5/10/38, Albany, Ga. BL/TR, 5'10", 180 lbs. Deb: 4/13/62																						
1964 Mil-N	9	17	1	2	0	0	0	0	0	3	.118	.118	.118	-33	-3	0	1	-1	1.000	-1	/C-3	-0.5
Total 5	269	594	68	147	20	9	8	54	42	120	.247	.304	.352	83	-14	3	3		.982	-25	C-144/1-9,O3	-3.8
■ BILL RARIDEN Rariden, William Angel "Bedford Bill" b: 2/4/1888, Bedford, Ind. d: 8/28/42, Bedford, Ind. BR/TR, 5'10", 168 lbs. Deb: 8/12/09																						
1909 Bos-N	13	42	1	6	1	0	0	1	4		.143	.217	.167	18	-4	1			.912	-3	C-13	-0.7
1910 Bos-N	49	137	15	31	5	1	0	14	12	22	.226	.293	.299	70	-5	1			.962	3	C-49	0.2
1911 Bos-N	70	246	22	56	9	0	0	21	21	18	.228	.288	.264	51	-16	3			.952	1	C-65/3-3,2	-0.8
1912 Bos-N	79	247	27	55	3	1	1	14	18	35	.223	.281	.255	46	-18	3			.964	-5	C-73	-1.6
1913 Bos-N	95	246	31	58	9	2	3	30	30	21	.236	.324	.325	84	-5	5			.976	-0	C-87	0.2
Total 12	982	2877	272	682	105	24	7	272	340	251	.237	.320	.298	76	-83	47			.973	8	C-948/3-3,2	0.1
Team 5	306	918	96	206	27	4	5	80	85	96	.224	.294	.279	60	-48	13			.962	-4	C-287/3-3,2	-2.7
■ JOHNNY RAWLINGS Rawlings, John William "Red" b: 8/17/1892, Bloomfield, Iowa d: 10/16/72, Inglewood, Cal. BR/TR, 5'8", 158 lbs. Deb: 4/14/14																						
1917 Bos-N	122	371	39	95	9	4	2	31	38	32	.256	.337	.318	107	4	12			.977	11	2-96,S-17/3O	2.3
1918 Bos-N	111	410	32	85	7	3	0	21	30	31	.207	.265	.239	56	-21	10			.956	2	S-71,2-20,O	-1.8
1919 Bos-N	77	275	30	70	8	2	1	16	16	20	.255	.298	.309	86	-5	10			.961	-12	2-58,O-10/S	-1.7
1920 Bos-N	5	3	0	0	0	0	0	2	0	1	.000	.000	.000	-99	-1	0	0	0	1.000	-1	/2-1	-0.1
Total 12	1080	3719	409	928	122	28	14	303	257	275	.250	.309	.309	70	-153	92	22		.968	3	2-709,S-280/O3	-12.1
Team 4	315	1059	99	250	24	9	3	70	84	84	.236	.298	.284	82	-22	32	0		.973	1	2-175/S-93,O3	-1.3
■ IRV RAY Ray, Irving Burton "Stubby" b: 1/22/1864, Harrington, Me. d: 2/21/48, Harrington, Me. BL/TR, 5'6", 165 lbs. Deb: 7/7/1888																						
1888 Bos-N	50	206	26	51	2	3	2	26	6	11	.248	.272	.316	85	-4	7			.879	-11	S-48/2-3	-1.4
1889 Bos-N	9	33	8	10	1	0	0	2	4	0	.303	.378	.333	94	-0	1			.875	-4	/S-5,3-4	-0.4
Total 4	226	902	154	263	30	13	4	103	86	35	.292	.360	.359	109	11	59			.863	-46	S-151/O-70,32	-2.9
Team 2	59	239	34	61	3	3	2	28	10	11	.255	.288	.322	87	-4	8			.878	-15	/S-53,3-4,2	-1.8
■ FRED RAYMER Raymer, Frederick Charles b: 11/12/1875, Leavenworth, Kan. d: 6/11/57, Los Angeles, Cal. BR/TR, 5'11", 185 lbs. Deb: 4/24/01																						
1904 Bos-N	114	419	28	88	12	3	1	27	13		.210	.236	.260	55	-23	17			.958	7	*2-114	-1.4

YEAR	TM/L	G	AB	R	H	2B	3B	HR	RBI	BB	SO	AVG	OBP	SLG	PRO+	BR/A	SB	CS	SBR	FA	FR	G/POS	TPR
1905	Bos-N	137	498	26	105	14	2	0	31	8		.211	.232	.247	44	-35	15			.949	-18	*2-134/1-1,O	-5.5
Total	3	371	1380	95	301	40	7	1	101	32		.218	.242	.259	51	-85	50			.954	-28	2-251/3-82,S10	-11.0
Team	2	251	917	54	193	26	5	1	58	21		.210	.234	.253	49	-58	32			.954	-11	2-248/O-1,1	-6.9
■ BILLY REED Reed, William Joseph b: 11/12/22, Shawano, Wis. BL/TR, 5'10.5", 175 lbs. Deb: 4/15/52																							
1952	Bos-N	15	52	4	13	0	0	0	0	0	5	.250	.264	.250	45	-4	0	0	0	.931	-7	2-14	-1.0
■ WALLY REHG Rehg, Walter Phillip b: 8/31/1888, Summerfield, Ill. d: 4/5/46, Burbank, Cal. BR/TR, 5'8", 160 lbs. Deb: 4/14/12																							
1917	Bos-N	87	341	48	92	12	6	1	31	24	32	.270	.320	.349	111	4	13			.956	-5	O-86	-0.6
1918	Bos-N	40	133	6	32	5	1	1	12	5	14	.241	.268	.316	81	-3	3			.988	2	O-38	-0.4
Total	7	263	752	85	188	24	11	2	66	50	66	.250	.299	.319	90	-11	26			.965	-12	O-201	-3.7
Team	2	127	474	54	124	17	7	2	43	29	46	.262	.306	.340	103	1	16			.968	-3	O-124	-1.0
■ BOBBY REIS Reis, Robert Joseph Thomas b: 1/2/09, Woodside, N.Y. d: 5/1/73, St.Paul, Minn. BR/TR, 6'1", 175 lbs. Deb: 9/19/31																							
1936	Bos-N	37	60	3	13	2	0	0	5	3	6	.217	.254	.250	39	-5	0			1.000	3	P-35/O-2	-0.1
1937	Bos-N	45	86	10	21	5	0	0	6	13	12	.244	.343	.302	84	-2	2			1.000	-4	O-18/P-4,1	-0.6
1938	Bos-N	34	49	6	9	0	0	0	4	1	3	.184	.200	.184	7	-6	1			1.000	-3	P-16,O-10/SC2	-0.7
Total	6	175	301	32	70	10	2	0	21	25	35	.233	.291	.279	59	-17	5			1.000	-2	/P-69,O-51,312SC	-1.8
Team	3	116	195	19	43	7	0	0	15	17	21	.221	.283	.256	52	-13	3			1.000	-3	/P-55,O-30,1SC2	-1.4
■ PETE REISER Reiser, Harold Patrick b: 3/17/19, St.Louis, Mo. d: 10/25/81, Palm Springs, Cal. BL/TR, 5'11", 185 lbs. Deb: 7/23/40 C																							
1949	Bos-N	84	221	32	60	8	3	8	40	33	42	.271	.369	.443	123	8	3			.980	-1	O-63/3-4	0.4
1950	Bos-N	53	78	12	16	2	0	1	10	18	22	.205	.367	.269	75	-2	1			.979	-2	O-24/3-1	-0.4
Total	10	861	2662	473	786	155	41	58	368	343	369	.295	.380	.450	127	100	87			.979	-1	O-634/3-59,S	7.0
Team	2	137	299	44	76	10	3	9	50	51	64	.254	.368	.398	111	6	4			.979	-2	/O-87,3-5	0.0
■ BILLY RHIEL Rhiel, William Joseph b: 8/16/1900, Youngstown, Ohio d: 8/16/46, Youngstown, Ohio BR/TR, 5'11", 175 lbs. Deb: 4/20/29																							
1930	Bos-N	20	47	3	8	4	0	0	4	2	5	.170	.204	.255	11	-7	0			.947	-4	3-13/2-2	-0.9
Total	4	200	519	61	138	26	8	7	68	43	57	.266	.323	.387	78	-18	2			.949	-8	/3-57,2-50,1OS	-2.0
■ DEL RICE Rice, Delbert b: 10/27/22, Portsmouth, Ohio d: 1/26/83, Buena Park, Cal. BR/TR, 6'2", 190 lbs. Deb: 5/2/45 MC																							
1955	Mil-N	27	71	5	14	0	1	2	7	6	12	.197	.260	.310	53	-5	0	0	0	.981	1	C-22	-0.4
1956	Mil-N	71	188	15	40	9	1	3	17	18	34	.213	.282	.319	65	-10	0	0	0	.983	2	C-65	-0.5
1957	*Mil-N	54	144	15	33	1	1	9	20	17	37	.229	.311	.438	106	1	0	0	0	.992	6	C-48	0.9
1958	Mil-N	43	121	10	27	7	0	1	8	8	30	.223	.271	.306	57	-8	0	0	0	.995	-0	C-38	-0.6
1959	Mil-N	13	29	3	6	0	0	0	1	2	3	.207	.258	.207	28	-3	0	0	0	.956	-0	/C-9	-0.3
Total	17	1309	3826	342	908	177	20	79	441	382	522	.237	.312	.356	78	-122	2	3		.987	25	*C-1249	-4.1
Team	5	208	553	48	120	17	3	15	53	51	116	.217	.283	.340	70	-25	0	0		.986	8	C-182	-0.9
■ HARDY RICHARDSON Richardson, Abram Harding "Old True Blue" b: 4/21/1855, Clarksboro, N.J. d: 1/14/31, Utica, N.Y. BR/TR, 5'9.5", 170 lbs. Deb: 5/1/1879																							
1889	Bos-N	132	536	122	163	33	10	6	79	48	44	.304	.367	.437	117	10	47			.924	13	2-86,O-46	2.3
Total	14	1331	5642	1120	1688	303	126	70	822	377	445	.299	.344	.435	130	186	205			.915	113	2-585,O-544,3/S1CP	27.3
■ LANCE RICHBOURG Richbourg, Lance Clayton b: 12/18/1897, DeFuniak Springs, Fla. d: 9/10/75, Crestview, Fla. BL/TR, 5'10.5", 160 lbs. Deb: 7/4/21																							
1927	Bos-N	115	450	57	139	12	9	2	34	22	30	.309	.342	.389	104	1	24			.953	-4	*O-110	-1.0
1928	Bos-N	148	612	105	206	26	12	2	52	62	39	.337	.399	.428	123	22	11			.972	7	*O-148	1.8
1929	Bos-N	139	557	76	170	24	13	3	56	42	26	.305	.355	.411	93	-6	7			.971	5	*O-134	-1.0
1930	Bos-N	130	529	81	161	23	8	3	54	19	31	.304	.331	.395	77	-20	13			.971	-3	*O-128	-2.8
1931	Bos-N	97	286	32	82	11	6	2	29	19	14	.287	.331	.388	96	-2	9			.981	-3	O-71	-1.0
Total	8	698	2619	378	806	101	51	13	247	174	147	.308	.352	.400	97	-14	65			.970	4	O-631/2-4	-4.9
Team	5	629	2434	351	758	96	48	12	225	164	140	.311	.356	.405	99	-6	64			.969	2	O-591	-4.0
■ LEE RICHMOND Richmond, J Lee b: 5/5/1857, Sheffield, Ohio d: 10/1/29, Toledo, Ohio TL, 5'10", 155 lbs. Deb: 9/27/1879																							
1879	Bos-N	1	6	0	2	0	0	0	1	0	1	.333	.333	.333	118	0				1.000	0	/P-1	0.0
Total	6	251	1018	169	262	29	20	3	110	46	73	.257	.289	.334	94	-7	0			.886	-26	P-191/O-90	-2.0
■ JOHN RICHMOND Richmond, John H. b: 1854, Pennsylvania TR, 5'9", 170 lbs. Deb: 4/22/1875																							
1880	Bos-N	32	129	12	32	3	1	0	9	2	18	.248	.260	.287	88	-2				.844	-12	S-31/O-1	-1.1
1881	Bos-N	27	98	13	27	2	2	1	12	6	7	.276	.317	.367	120	2				.969	-0	O-25/S-2	0.2
Total	7	411	1600	210	385	43	28	5	55	102	76	.241	.288	.312	101	8				.866	-10	S-280,O-133/C	-0.0
Team	2	59	227	25	59	5	3	1	21	8	25	.260	.285	.322	102	1				.836	-12	/S-33,O-26	-0.9
■ JOE RICKERT Rickert, Joseph Francis "Diamond Joe" b: 12/12/1876, London, Ohio d: 10/15/43, Springfield, Ohio BR/TR, 5'10.5", 165 lbs. Deb: 10/12/1898																							
1901	Bos-N	13	60	6	10	1	2	0	1	3		.167	.206	.250	29	-6	1			.974	2	O-13	-0.4
Total	2	15	66	6	11	1	2	0	1	3		.167	.203	.242	27	-6	1			.979	3	/O-15	-0.4
■ MARV RICKERT Rickert, Marvin August "Twitch" b: 1/8/21, Longbranch, Wash. d: 6/3/78, Oakville, Wash. BL/TR, 6'2", 195 lbs. Deb: 9/10/42																							
1948	*Bos-N	3	13	1	3	0	1	0	2	0	1	.231	.286	.385	81	-0	0			1.000	1	/O-3	0.1
1949	Bos-N	100	277	44	81	18	3	6	49	23	38	.292	.347	.444	117	6	1			.981	-0	O-75,1-12	0.2
Total	6	402	1149	139	284	45	9	19	145	88	161	.247	.302	.352	79	-38	4			.976	-12	O-299/1-20	-6.3
Team	2	103	290	45	84	18	4	6	51	23	39	.290	.344	.441	115	5	1			.982	1	/O-78,1-12	0.3
■ ART RICO Rico, Arthur Raymond b: 7/23/1896, Roxbury, Mass. d: 1/3/19, Boston, Mass. BR/TR, 5'9.5", 185 lbs. Deb: 7/31/16																							
1916	Bos-N	4	4	0	0	0	0	0	0	0	0	.000	.000	.000	-99	-1	0			1.000	-0	/C-4	-0.1
1917	Bos-N	13	14	1	4	1	0	0	2	0	2	.286	.286	.357	102	-0	0			.950	-2	C-11/O-2	-0.1
Total	2	17	18	1	4	1	0	0	2	0	2	.222	.222	.278	56	-1	0			.962	-2	/C-15,O-2	-0.2
■ HARRY RICONDA Riconda, Henry Paul b: 3/17/1897, New York, N.Y. d: 11/15/58, Mahopac, N.Y. BR/TR, 5'10", 175 lbs. Deb: 4/19/23																							
1926	Bos-N	4	12	1	2	0	0	0	0	2	2	.167	.286	.167	27	-1	0			.818	-1	/3-4	-0.2
Total	6	243	765	83	189	44	11	4	70	61	91	.247	.309	.349	71	-34	13			.922	7	3-145/2-53,S	-1.5
■ JOHNNY RIDDLE Riddle, John Ludy "Mutt" b: 10/3/05, Clinton, S.C. BR/TR, 5'11", 190 lbs. Deb: 4/17/30 FC																							
1937	Bos-N	2	3	0	0	0	0	0	0	1	0	.000	.250	.000	-29	-1	0			1.000	1	/C-2	0.0
1938	Bos-N	19	57	6	16	1	0	0	2	4	2	.281	.328	.298	81	-1	0			.951	4	C-19	0.3
Total	7	98	214	18	51	4	1	0	11	13	19	.238	.288	.266	51	-15	0			.983	7	/C-98	-0.3
Team	2	21	60	6	16	1	0	0	2	5	2	.267	.323	.283	75	-2	0			.955	5	/C-21	0.3
■ JOE RIGGERT Riggert, Joseph Aloysius b: 12/11/1886, Janesville, Wis. d: 12/10/73, Kansas City, Mo. BR/TR, 5'9.5", 170 lbs. Deb: 5/12/11																							
1919	Bos-N	63	240	34	68	8	5	4	17	25	30	.283	.356	.408	135	10	9			.950	2	O-61	0.9
Total	3	174	558	68	134	18	14	8	44	46	64	.240	.305	.366	98	-2	20			.950	-6	O-150	-1.6
■ JIM RILEY Riley, James Joseph b: 11/10/1886, Buffalo, N.Y. d: 3/25/49, Buffalo, N.Y. BR/TR, 6', 165 lbs. Deb: 8/2/10																							
1910	Bos-N	1	1	0	0	0	0	0	0	1	1	.000	.500	.000	46	0	0			.600	-0	/O-1	0.0
■ CLAUDE RITCHEY Ritchey, Claude Cassius "Little All Right" b: 10/5/1873, Emlenton, Pa. d: 11/8/51, Emlenton, Pa. BB/TR, 5'6.5", 167 lbs. Deb: 4/22/1897																							
1907	Bos-N	144	499	45	127	17	4	2	51	50		.255	.329	.317	103	2	8			**.971**	14	*2-144	1.7

YEAR	TM/L	G	AB	R	H	2B	3B	HR	RBI	BB	SO	AVG	OBP	SLG	PRO+	BR/A	SB	CS	SBR	FA	FR	G/POS	TPR
1908	Bos-N	121	421	44	115	10	3	2	36	50		.273	.361	.325	121	12	7			.967	16	*2-120	3.1
1909	Bos-N	30	87	4	15	1	0	0	3	8		.172	.242	.184	31	-7	1			.959	0	2-25	-0.8
Total	13	1671	5919	708	1618	215	68	18	673	607		.273	.348	.342	101	21	155			.957	19	*2-1478,S-166/O	9.0
Team	3	295	1007	93	257	28	7	4	90	108		.255	.335	.309	104	8	16			.968	30	2-289	4.0

■ MEL ROACH Roach, Melvin Earl b: 1/25/33, Richmond, Va. BR/TR, 6'1", 190 lbs. Deb: 7/31/53

YEAR	TM/L	G	AB	R	H	2B	3B	HR	RBI	BB	SO	AVG	OBP	SLG	PRO+	BR/A	SB	CS	SBR	FA	FR	G/POS	TPR
1953	Mil-N	5	2	1	0	0	0	0	0	0	1	.000	.000	.000	-99	-1	0	0	0	.000	0	/2-1	-0.1
1954	Mil-N	3	4	0	0	0	0	0	0	0	1	.000	.000	.000	-99	-1	0	0	0	1.000	-0	/1-1	-0.1
1957	Mil-N	7	6	1	1	0	0	0	0	0	3	.167	.167	.167	-11	-1	0	0	0	1.000	0	/2-5	-0.1
1958	Mil-N	44	136	14	42	7	0	3	10	6	15	.309	.338	.426	110	1	0	0	0	.993	-2	2-27/O-7,1	0.2
1959	Mil-N	19	31	1	3	0	0	0	0	2	4	.097	.152	.097	-35	-6	0	0	0	.880	1	/2-8,O-4,3	-0.5
1960	Mil-N	48	140	12	42	12	0	3	18	6	19	.300	.333	.450	121	3	0	0	0	.975	-8	O-21,2-20/13	-0.4
1961	Mil-N	13	36	3	6	0	0	1	6	2	4	.167	.250	.250	35	-3	0	0	0	1.000	-2	/O-9,1-2	-0.6
Total	8	227	499	42	119	25	0	7	43	24	75	.238	.278	.331	66	-24	1	0	0	.969	-12	/2-77,O-44,31	-3.5
Team	7	139	355	32	94	19	0	7	34	16	47	.265	.302	.377	88	-7	0	0	0	.969	-10	/2-61,O-41,13	-1.6

■ SKIPPY ROBERGE Roberge, Joseph Albert Armand b: 5/19/17, Lowell, Mass. d: 6/7/93, Lowell, Mass. BR/TR, 5'11", 185 lbs. Deb: 7/18/41

YEAR	TM/L	G	AB	R	H	2B	3B	HR	RBI	BB	SO	AVG	OBP	SLG	PRO+	BR/A	SB	CS	SBR	FA	FR	G/POS	TPR
1941	Bos-N	55	167	12	36	6	0	0	15	9	18	.216	.256	.251	45	-12	0			.978	5	2-46/3-5,S	-0.5
1942	Bos-N	74	172	10	37	7	0	1	12	9	19	.215	.258	.273	57	-10	1			.977	8	2-29,3-27/S	0.0
1946	Bos-N	48	169	13	39	6	2	2	20	7	12	.231	.270	.325	68	-8	1			.973	2	3-48	-0.5
Total	3	177	508	35	112	19	2	3	47	25	49	.220	.261	.283	57	-30	2			.967	15	/3-80,2-75,S	-1.0

■ GENE ROBERTSON Robertson, Eugene Edward b: 12/25/1898, St.Louis, Mo. d: 10/21/81, Fallon, Nev. BL/TR, 5'7", 152 lbs. Deb: 7/4/19

YEAR	TM/L	G	AB	R	H	2B	3B	HR	RBI	BB	SO	AVG	OBP	SLG	PRO+	BR/A	SB	CS	SBR	FA	FR	G/POS	TPR
1929	Bos-N	8	28	1	8	0	0	0	6	1	0	.286	.310	.286	51	-2	1			.875	-2	/3-6,S-1	-0.3
1930	Bos-N	21	59	7	11	1	0	0	7	5	3	.186	.250	.203	12	-8	0			.949	-2	3-17	-0.9
Total	9	656	2200	311	615	100	23	20	249	205	79	.280	.344	.373	83	-58	29			.941	-56	3-571/S-20,2	-7.8
Team	2	29	87	8	19	1	0	0	13	6	3	.218	.269	.230	24	-11	1			.927	-4	/3-23,S-1	-1.2

■ CRAIG ROBINSON Robinson, Craig George b: 8/21/48, Abington, Pa. BR/TR, 5'10", 165 lbs. Deb: 9/9/72

YEAR	TM/L	G	AB	R	H	2B	3B	HR	RBI	BB	SO	AVG	OBP	SLG	PRO+	BR/A	SB	CS	SBR	FA	FR	G/POS	TPR
1974	Atl-N	145	452	52	104	4	6	0	29	30	57	.230	.282	.265	52	-29	11	2	2	.956	-17	*S-142	-2.8
1975	Atl-N	10	17	1	1	0	0	0	0	0	5	.059	.059	.059	-65	-4	0	0	0	1.000	1	/S-7	-0.2
1976	Atl-N	15	17	4	4	0	0	0	3	5	2	.235	.409	.235	81	-0	0	0	0	.952	2	/2-5,S-2,3	0.2
1977	Atl-N	27	29	4	6	1	0	0	1	1	6	.207	.233	.241	25	-3	0	0	0	1.000	6	S-23	0.3
Total	6	292	718	80	157	15	6	0	42	42	107	.219	.265	.256	44	-54	12	4		.956	3	S-233/2-25,3	-2.7
Team	4	197	515	61	115	5	6	0	33	36	70	.223	.278	.256	48	-36	11	2		.959	-8	S-174/2-5,3	-2.5

■ BILL ROBINSON Robinson, William Henry b: 6/26/43, McKeesport, Pa. BR/TR, 6'3", 205 lbs. Deb: 9/20/66 C

YEAR	TM/L	G	AB	R	H	2B	3B	HR	RBI	BB	SO	AVG	OBP	SLG	PRO+	BR/A	SB	CS	SBR	FA	FR	G/POS	TPR
1966	Atl-N	6	11	1	3	0	1	0	3	0	1	.273	.273	.455	96	-0	0	0	0	.800	-1	/O-5	-0.2
Total	16	1472	4364	536	1127	229	29	166	641	263	820	.258	.303	.438	104	4	71	49	-8	.979	-84	*O-1059,1-201,3	-14.8

■ PAT ROCKETT Rockett, Patrick Edward b: 1/9/55, San Antonio, Tex. BR/TR, 5'11", 170 lbs. Deb: 9/17/76

YEAR	TM/L	G	AB	R	H	2B	3B	HR	RBI	BB	SO	AVG	OBP	SLG	PRO+	BR/A	SB	CS	SBR	FA	FR	G/POS	TPR
1976	Atl-N	4	5	0	1	0	0	0	0	0	1	.200	.200	.200	13	-1	0	0	0	1.000	-1	/S-2	-0.2
1977	Atl-N	93	264	27	67	10	0	1	24	27	32	.254	.330	.303	64	-13	1	2	-1	.940	-11	S-84	-1.6
1978	Atl-N	55	142	6	20	2	0	0	4	13	12	.141	.213	.155	4	-18	1	2	-1	.970	-10	S-51	-2.6
Total	3	152	411	33	88	12	0	1	28	40	45	.214	.289	.251	43	-32	2	4	-2	.949	-21	S-137	-4.4

■ GARY ROENICKE Roenicke, Gary Steven b: 12/5/54, Covina, Cal. BR/TR, 6'3", 205 lbs. Deb: 6/8/76 F

YEAR	TM/L	G	AB	R	H	2B	3B	HR	RBI	BB	SO	AVG	OBP	SLG	PRO+	BR/A	SB	CS	SBR	FA	FR	G/POS	TPR
1987	Atl-N	67	151	25	33	8	0	9	28	32	23	.219	.359	.450	107	2	0	0	0	.968	-4	O-44/1-9	-0.3
1988	Atl-N	49	114	11	26	5	0	1	7	8	15	.228	.279	.298	63	-5	0	0	0	1.000	-4	O-35/1-1	-1.1
Total	12	1064	2708	367	670	135	4	121	410	406	428	.247	.354	.434	117	70	16	20	-7	.988	-92	O-918/D-36,13	-5.7
Team	2	116	265	36	59	13	0	10	35	40	38	.223	.327	.385	90	-3	0	0	0	.982	-8	/O-79,1-10	-1.4

■ FRALEY ROGERS Rogers, Fraley W. b: 1850, Brooklyn, N.Y. d: 5/10/1881, New York, N.Y. 5'8", 184 lbs. Deb: 4/30/1872

YEAR	TM/L	G	AB	R	H	2B	3B	HR	RBI	BB	SO	AVG	OBP	SLG	PRO+	BR/A	SB	CS	SBR	FA	FR	G/POS	TPR
1872	Bos-n	45	204	39	58	10	1	1	28	1	4	.284	.288	.358	93	-3						O-42/1-6	0.0
1873	Bos-n	1	6	1	2	2	0	0	2	0	1	.333	.333	.667	172	0						/1-1	0.0
Total	2 n	46	210	40	60	12	1	1	30	1	5	.286	.289	.367	95	-3						/O-42,1-7	0.0

■ RED ROLLINGS Rollings, William Russell b: 3/21/04, Mobile, Ala. d: 12/31/64, Mobile, Ala. BL/TR, 5'11", 167 lbs. Deb: 4/17/27

YEAR	TM/L	G	AB	R	H	2B	3B	HR	RBI	BB	SO	AVG	OBP	SLG	PRO+	BR/A	SB	CS	SBR	FA	FR	G/POS	TPR
1930	Bos-N	52	123	10	29	6	0	0	10	9	5	.236	.288	.285	40	-12	2			.973	3	3-28,2-10	-0.7
Total	3	184	355	36	89	13	2	0	28	27	23	.251	.311	.299	57	-23	5			.947	-5	/3-73,2-16,1O	-2.3

■ ED ROMERO Romero, Edgardo Ralph (Rivera) b: 12/9/57, Santurce, P.R. BR/TR, 5'11", 175 lbs. Deb: 7/16/77

YEAR	TM/L	G	AB	R	H	2B	3B	HR	RBI	BB	SO	AVG	OBP	SLG	PRO+	BR/A	SB	CS	SBR	FA	FR	G/POS	TPR
1989	Atl-N	7	19	1	5	1	0	1	1	0	0	.263	.263	.474	104	-0	0	0	0	.947	5	/2-4,S-2,3	0.5
Total	12	730	1912	218	473	79	1	8	155	140	159	.247	.300	.302	67	-83	9	10		.958	30	S-288,2-192,3/O1D	-2.7

■ PHIL ROOF Roof, Phillip Anthony b: 3/5/41, Paducah, Ky. BR/TR, 6'3", 210 lbs. Deb: 4/29/61 FC

YEAR	TM/L	G	AB	R	H	2B	3B	HR	RBI	BB	SO	AVG	OBP	SLG	PRO+	BR/A	SB	CS	SBR	FA	FR	G/POS	TPR
1961	Mil-N	1	0	0	0	0	0	0	0	0	0	—	—	—	—	0	0	0	0	1.000	0	/C-1	0.0
1964	Mil-N	1	2	0	0	0	0	0	0	0	1	.000	.000	.000	-99	-1	0	0	0	1.000	1	/C-1	0.1
Total	15	857	2151	190	463	69	13	43	210	184	504	.215	.284	.319	73	-77	11	10	-3	.986	58	C-835/1-3,D	1.1
Team	2	2	2	0	0	0	0	0	0	0	1	.000	.000	.000	-99	-1	0	0	0	1.000	1	/C-2	0.1

■ GEORGE ROOKS Rooks, George Brinton McClellan (b: George Brinton Mc Clellan Ruckser)
b: 10/21/1863, Chicago, Ill. d: 3/11/35, Chicago, Ill. BR/TR, 5'11", 170 lbs. Deb: 5/12/1891 F

YEAR	TM/L	G	AB	R	H	2B	3B	HR	RBI	BB	SO	AVG	OBP	SLG	PRO+	BR/A	SB	CS	SBR	FA	FR	G/POS	TPR
1891	Bos-N	5	16	1	2	0	0	0	0	4	1	.125	.300	.125	23	-2	0			1.000	1	/O-5	-0.1

■ VICTOR ROSARIO Rosario, Victor Manuel (Rivera) b: 8/26/66, Hato Mayor Del Rey, D.R. BR/TR, 5'11", 155 lbs. Deb: 9/6/90

YEAR	TM/L	G	AB	R	H	2B	3B	HR	RBI	BB	SO	AVG	OBP	SLG	PRO+	BR/A	SB	CS	SBR	FA	FR	G/POS	TPR
1990	Atl-N	9	7	3	1	0	0	0	0	1	1	.143	.250	.143	10	-1	0	0	0	1.000	1	/S-3,2-1	0.0

■ BOB ROSELLI Roselli, Robert Edward b: 12/10/31, San Francisco, Cal. BR/TR, 5'11", 185 lbs. Deb: 8/16/55

YEAR	TM/L	G	AB	R	H	2B	3B	HR	RBI	BB	SO	AVG	OBP	SLG	PRO+	BR/A	SB	CS	SBR	FA	FR	G/POS	TPR
1955	Mil-N	6	9	1	2	1	0	0	0	1	4	.222	.364	.333	91	-0	0	0	0	.917	0	/C-2	0.0
1956	Mil-N	4	2	1	1	0	0	1	1	0	1	.500	.500	2.000	564	1	0	0	0	1.000	2	/C-3	0.3
1958	Mil-N	1	1	0	0	0	0	0	0	0	0	.000	.000	.000	-99	-0	0	0	0	.000	0	H	0.0
Total	5	68	114	8	25	7	1	2	10	12	31	.219	.305	.351	76	-4	1	0	0	.986	-1	/C-35	-0.3
Team	3	11	12	2	3	1	0	1	1	1	5	.250	.357	.583	153	1	0	0	0	.952	2	/C-5	0.3

■ BUNNY ROSER Roser, John William Joseph "Jack" b: 11/15/01, St.Louis, Mo. d: 5/6/79, Rocky Hill, Conn. BL/TL, 5'11", 175 lbs. Deb: 8/24/22

YEAR	TM/L	G	AB	R	H	2B	3B	HR	RBI	BB	SO	AVG	OBP	SLG	PRO+	BR/A	SB	CS	SBR	FA	FR	G/POS	TPR
1922	Bos-N	32	113	13	27	3	4	0	16	10	19	.239	.306	.336	69	-5	2	1	0	.915	-2	O-32	-1.0

■ CHET ROSS Ross, Chester James b: 4/1/17, Buffalo, N.Y. d: 2/21/89, Buffalo, N.Y. BR/TR, 6'1", 195 lbs. Deb: 9/15/39

YEAR	TM/L	G	AB	R	H	2B	3B	HR	RBI	BB	SO	AVG	OBP	SLG	PRO+	BR/A	SB	CS	SBR	FA	FR	G/POS	TPR
1939	Bos-N	11	31	4	10	1	1	0	0	2	10	.323	.364	.419	118	1	0			1.000	1	/O-8	0.1
1940	Bos-N	149	569	84	160	23	14	17	89	59	127	.281	.352	.460	130	22	4			.962	7	*O-149	2.1
1941	Bos-N	29	50	1	6	1	0	0	4	9	17	.120	.254	.140	14	-6	0			1.000	-1	O-12	-0.7
1942	Bos-N	76	220	20	43	7	2	5	19	16	37	.195	.250	.314	66	-10	0			.992	-1	O-57	-1.5
1943	Bos-N	94	285	27	62	12	2	7	32	26	67	.218	.285	.347	84	-7	1			.977	3	O-73	-0.8
1944	Bos-N	54	154	20	35	9	2	5	26	12	23	.227	.287	.409	91	-3	1			1.000	3	O-38	-0.2
Total	6	413	1309	156	316	53	21	34	170	124	281	.241	.309	.392	100	-3	6			.976	11	O-337	-1.0

YEAR	TM/L	G	AB	R	H	2B	3B	HR	RBI	BB	SO	AVG	OBP	SLG	PRO+	BR/A	SB	CS	SBR	FA	FR	G/POS	TPR
■ RICO ROSSY			Rossy, Elam Jose (Ramos)			b: 2/16/64, San Juan, P.R.			BR/TR, 5'10", 175 lbs.			Deb: 9/11/91										
1991	Atl-N	5	1	0	0	0	0	0	0	0	1	.000	.000	.000	-94	-0	0	0	0	.000	0	/S-1	0.0
Total	3	110	236	31	51	12	1	3	24	29	32	.216	.307	.314	69	-10	0	3	-2	.966	6	/S-63,2-27,3	-0.1
■ BAMA ROWELL			Rowell, Carvel William			b: 1/13/16, Citronelle, Ala.			d: 8/16/93, Citronelle, Ala.			BL/TR, 5'11", 185 lbs.			Deb: 9/4/39							
1939	Bos-N	21	59	5	11	2	2	0	6	1	4	.186	.200	.288	32	-6	0			.853	-2	O-16	-0.9
1940	Bos-N	130	486	46	148	19	8	3	58	18	22	.305	.331	.395	105	2	12			.953	-3	*2-115/O-7	0.6
1941	Bos-N	138	483	49	129	23	6	7	60	39	36	.267	.322	.383	102	0	11			.935	-10	*2-112,O-14/3	-0.3
1946	Bos-N	95	293	37	82	12	6	3	31	29	15	.280	.345	.392	108	3	5			.978	-0	O-85	-0.1
1947	Bos-N	113	384	48	106	23	2	5	40	18	14	.276	.310	.385	86	-9	7			.945	-8	*O-100/2-7,3	-2.1
Total	6	574	1901	200	523	95	26	19	217	113	105	.275	.316	.382	95	-20	37			.945	-35	2-246,O-239/3	-4.9
Team	5	497	1705	185	476	79	24	18	195	105	91	.279	.322	.385	98	-11	35			.944	-23	2-234,O-222/3	-2.8
■ ED ROWEN			Rowen, W. Edward			b: 10/22/1857, Bridgeport, Conn.			d: 2/22/1892, Bridgeport, Conn.			5'6", 155 lbs.			Deb: 5/1/1882							
1882	Bos-N	83	327	36	81	7	4	1	43	19	18	.248	.289	.303	90	-3				.885	-12	O-48,C-34/S3	-1.3
Total	3	136	538	68	130	18	5	1	43	31	18	.242	.284	.299	85	-9				.866	-17	/C-82,O-56,S32	-2.0
■ JERRY ROYSTER			Royster, Jeron Kennis			b: 10/18/52, Sacramento, Cal.			BR/TR, 6', 165 lbs.			Deb: 8/14/73 C								
1976	Atl-N	149	533	65	132	13	1	5	45	52	53	.248	.316	.304	72	-19	24	13	-1	.962	17	*3-148/S-2	-0.4
1977	Atl-N	140	445	64	96	10	2	6	28	38	67	.216	.279	.288	47	-33	28	10	2	.953	-29	3-56,S-51,2/O	-5.5
1978	Atl-N	140	529	67	137	17	8	2	35	56	49	.259	.333	.333	78	-15	27	17	-2	.974	-13	2-75,S-60/3	-1.7
1979	Atl-N	154	601	103	164	25	6	3	51	62	59	.273	.341	.349	83	-13	35	8	6	.948	13	3-80,2-77	1.0
1980	Atl-N	123	392	42	95	17	5	1	20	37	48	.242	.309	.319	73	-14	22	13	-1	.948	-11	2-49,3-48,O	-2.6
1981	Atl-N	64	93	13	19	4	1	0	9	7	14	.204	.260	.269	49	-6	7	5	-1	.950	3	3-24,2-13	-0.4
1982	*Atl-N	108	261	43	77	13	2	2	25	22	36	.295	.354	.383	102	1	14	6	1	.943	-2	3-62,O-25,2S	-0.1
1983	Atl-N	91	268	32	63	10	3	3	30	28	35	.235	.307	.328	71	-10	11	7	-1	.940	7	3-47,2-26,OS	-0.4
1984	Atl-N	81	227	22	47	13	2	1	21	15	41	.207	.259	.295	52	-15	6	4	-1	.973	5	2-29,3-17,SO	-0.9
1988	Atl-N	68	102	8	18	3	0	0	1	6	16	.176	.222	.206	22	-10	0	0	0	1.000	-2	O-26,3-10/2S	-1.3
Total	16	1428	4208	552	1049	165	33	40	352	411	534	.249	.318	.333	76	-130	189	95		.951	-19	3-634,2-416,SO/D	-12.7
Team	10	1118	3451	459	848	125	30	23	265	323	418	.246	.312	.319	70	-133	174	83		.955	-11	3-493,2-325,SO	-12.3
■ CHICO RUIZ			Ruiz, Manuel (Cruz)			b: 11/1/51, Santurce, P.R.			BR/TR, 5'11.5", 170 lbs.			Deb: 7/29/78								
1978	Atl-N	18	46	3	13	3	0	0	2	2	4	.283	.313	.348	76	-1	0	0	0	.984	1	2-14/3-1	0.1
1980	Atl-N	25	26	3	8	2	1	0	2	3	7	.308	.379	.462	129	1	0	1	-1	.875	2	3-16/S-4,2	0.2
Total	2	43	72	6	21	5	1	0	4	5	11	.292	.338	.389	95	-0	0	1	-1	.880	3	/3-17,2-16,S	0.3
■ PAUL RUNGE			Runge, Paul William			b: 5/21/58, Kingston, N.Y.			BR/TR, 6', 175 lbs.			Deb: 9/25/81								
1981	Atl-N	10	27	2	7	1	0	0	2	4	4	.259	.355	.296	84	-0	0	0	0	.911	-1	S-10	-0.1
1982	Atl-N	4	2	0	0	0	0	0	0	0	0	.000	.000	.000	-96	-1	0	0	0	.000	0	/H	-0.1
1983	Atl-N	5	8	0	2	0	0	0	1	1	4	.250	.333	.250	59	-0	0	0	0	1.000	-1	/2-2	-0.1
1984	Atl-N	28	90	5	24	3	1	0	3	10	14	.267	.340	.322	81	-2	5	3	-0	.970	10	2-22/S-7,3	0.9
1985	Atl-N	50	87	15	19	3	0	1	5	18	18	.218	.352	.287	76	-0	0	1	-1	.929	1	3-28/S-5,2	0.1
1986	Atl-N	7	8	1	2	0	0	0	0	2	5	.250	.400	.250	79	-0	0	0	0	1.000	2	/2-5	0.2
1987	Atl-N	27	47	9	10	1	0	3	8	5	10	.213	.288	.426	82	-1	0	1	-1	.923	1	3-10/S-9,2	-0.1
1988	Atl-N	52	76	11	16	5	0	0	7	14	21	.211	.333	.276	73	-2	0	0	0	1.000	-1	3-19/2-7,S	-0.4
Total	8	183	345	43	80	13	1	4	26	54	75	.232	.336	.310	77	-9	5	5	-2	.941	13	/3-60,2-40,S	0.4
■ JIM RUSSELL			Russell, James William			b: 10/1/18, Fayette City, Pa.			d: 11/24/87, Pittsburgh, Pa.			BB/TR, 6'1", 181 lbs.			Deb: 9/12/42						
1948	Bos-N	89	322	44	85	18	1	9	54	46	31	.264	.361	.410	110	5	4			.992	6	O-84	0.6
1949	Bos-N	130	415	57	96	22	1	8	54	64	68	.231	.337	.347	88	-6	3			.975	-9	*O-120	-2.1
Total	10	1035	3595	554	959	175	51	67	428	503	427	.267	.360	.400	108	44	59			.981	27	O-942/1-11	2.3
Team	2	219	737	101	181	40	2	17	108	110	99	.246	.347	.374	98	-1	7			.983	-4	O-204	-1.5
■ JOHN RUSSELL			Russell, John William			b: 1/5/61, Oklahoma City, Okla.			BR/TR, 6', 200 lbs.			Deb: 6/22/84								
1989	Atl-N	74	159	14	29	2	0	2	9	8	53	.182	.226	.233	31	-14	0	0	0	.990	-7	C-45,O-14/13P	-2.1
Total	10	448	1087	113	245	50	3	34	129	84	355	.225	.285	.371	79	-32	3	3		.979	-16	C-209,O-119/D13P	-4.5
■ BABE RUTH			Ruth, George Herman "The Bambino" or "The Sultan Of Swat"						b: 2/6/1895, Baltimore, Md.			d: 8/16/48, New York, N.Y.			BL/TL, 6'2", 215 lbs.			Deb: 7/11/14 CH		
1935	Bos-N	28	72	13	13	0	0	6	12	20	24	.181	.359	.431	121	3	0			.952	-4	O-26	-0.2
Total	22	2503	8399	2174	2873	506	136	714	2213	2056	1330	.342	.474	.690	209	1382	123			.968	5	*O-2241,P-163/1	107.6
■ CONNIE RYAN			Ryan, Cornelius Joseph			b: 2/27/20, New Orleans, La.			BR/TR, 5'11", 175 lbs.			Deb: 4/14/42 MC							
1943	Bos-N	132	457	52	97	10	2	1	24	58	56	.212	.301	.249	61	-22	7			.962	-20	*2-100,3-30	-3.8
1944	Bos-N★	88	332	56	98	18	5	4	25	36	40	.295	.364	.416	114	7	13			.974	13	2-80,3-14	2.4
1946	Bos-N	143	502	55	121	28	8	1	48	55	63	.241	.317	.335	84	-11	7			.968	-2	*2-120,3-24	-0.5
1947	Bos-N	150	544	60	144	33	5	5	69	71	60	.265	.351	.371	94	-4	5			.973	-4	*2-150/S-1	0.0
1948	*Bos-N	51	122	14	26	3	0	0	10	21	16	.213	.333	.238	58	-6	0			.966	4	2-40/3-4	0.0
1949	Bos-N	85	208	28	52	13	1	6	20	21	30	.250	.319	.409	99	-1	1			.973	6	3-25,S-18,2/1	0.6
1950	Bos-N	20	72	12	14	2	0	1	6	2	9	.194	.220	.347	82	-2	0			1.000	1	2-20	0.0
Total	12	1184	3982	535	988	181	42	56	381	518	514	.248	.337	.357	90	-48	69			.970	-1	2-980,3-116/S10	0.3
Team	7	669	2237	277	552	107	21	20	202	274	274	.247	.330	.340	86	-38	33			.970	-4	2-526/3-97,S1	-1.3
■ CYCLONE RYAN			Ryan, Daniel R.			b: 1866, Cappagh White, Ireland			d: 1/30/17, Medfield, Mass.			TR, 6', 200 lbs.			Deb: 8/8/1887					
1891	Bos-N	1	1	0	0	0	0	0	0	0	0	.000	.000	.000	-89	-0	0			1.000	0	/P-1	0.0
Total	2	9	33	4	7	1	0	0	0	3	0	.212	.278	.242	48	-2	1			1.000	0	/1-8,P-3	-0.2
■ JACK RYAN			Ryan, John Bernard			b: 11/12/1868, Haverhill, Mass.			d: 8/21/52, Boston, Mass.			BR/TR, 5'10.5", 165 lbs.			Deb: 9/2/1889 C			
1894	Bos-N	53	201	39	54	12	7	1	29	13	16	.269	.313	.413	69	-12	3			.911	0	C-51/1-2	-0.5
1895	Bos-N	49	189	22	55	7	0	0	18	6	6	.291	.313	.328	61	-12	3			.951	1	C-43/2-5,O	-0.5
1896	Bos-N	8	32	2	3	1	0	0	0	0	1	.094	.094	.125	-40	-7	0			.911	2	/C-8	-0.3
Total	13	616	2192	245	476	69	29	4	154	85	80	.217	.249	.281	50	-154	32			.947	-6	C-527/1-42,230S	-10.3
Team	3	110	422	63	112	20	7	1	47	23	23	.265	.299	.353	58	-30	6			.929	4	C-102/2-5,1O	-1.3
■ ED SADOWSKI			Sadowski, Edward Roman			b: 1/19/31, Pittsburgh, Pa.			d: 11/6/93, Garden Grove, Cal.			BR/TR, 5'11", 175 lbs.			Deb: 4/20/60 F			
1966	Atl-N	3	9	1	1	0	0	0	1	1	1	.111	.200	.111	-10	-1	0	0	0	1.000	1	/C-3	-0.1
Total	217	495	55	100	20	1	12	39	39	94		.202	.262	.319	56	-31	5	4		.991	37	C-181	1.0
■ EBBA ST.CLAIRE			St.Claire, Edward Joseph			b: 8/5/21, Whitehall, N.Y.			d: 8/22/82, Whitehall, N.Y.			BB/TR, 6'1", 219 lbs.			Deb: 4/17/51 F			
1951	Bos-N	72	220	22	62	17	2	1	25	12	24	.282	.322	.391	98	-2	2	0	1	.977	3	C-62	0.4
1952	Bos-N	39	108	5	23	2	0	2	4	8	12	.213	.267	.287	56	-7	0	1	-1	.972	4	C-34	-0.2
1953	Mil-N	33	80	7	16	3	0	2	5	9	8	.200	.229	.313	42	-7	0	0	0	.992	3	C-27	-0.3
Total	4	164	450	39	112	23	2	5	40	35	52	.249	.306	.356	81	-13	2	1	0	.978	12	C-139	0.4
Team	3	144	408	34	101	22	2	5	34	23	45	.248	.289	.348	75	-15	2	1	0	.978	10	C-123	-0.1

YEAR	TM/L	G	AB	R	H	2B	3B	HR	RBI	BB	SO	AVG	OBP	SLG	PRO+	BR/A	SB	CS	SBR	FA	FR	G/POS	TPR

■ BILL SALKELD
Salkeld, William Franklin b: 3/8/17, Pocatello, Idaho d: 4/22/67, Los Angeles, Cal. BL/TR, 5'10", 190 lbs. Deb: 4/18/45 F

1948	*Bos-N	78	198	26	48	8	1	8	28	42	37	.242	.378	.414	116	6	1			.990	5	C-59	1.5
1949	Bos-N	66	161	17	41	5	0	5	25	44	24	.255	.417	.379	121	8	1			.980	-4	C-63	0.7
Total	6	356	850	111	232	39	2	31	132	182	101	.273	.402	.433	129	40	6			.979	-11	C-275	4.5
Team	2	144	359	43	89	13	1	13	53	86	61	.248	.396	.398	119	13	2			.985	1	C-122	2.2

■ BILL SAMPLE
Sample, William Amos b: 4/2/55, Roanoke, Va. BR/TR, 5'9", 175 lbs. Deb: 9/2/78

| 1986 | Atl-N | 92 | 200 | 23 | 57 | 11 | 0 | 6 | 14 | 14 | 26 | .285 | .341 | .430 | 105 | 1 | 4 | 2 | 0 | .986 | -8 | O-56/2-1 | -0.8 |
| Total | 9 | 826 | 2516 | 371 | 684 | 127 | 9 | 46 | 230 | 195 | 230 | .272 | .331 | .384 | 98 | -7 | 98 | 31 | | .987 | -19 | O-711/D-19,2 | -3.6 |

■ AMADO SAMUEL
Samuel, Amado Ruperto b: 12/6/38, San Pedro De Macoris, D.R. BR/TR, 6'1", 170 lbs. Deb: 4/10/62

1962	Mil-N	76	209	16	43	10	0	3	20	12	54	.206	.249	.297	47	-16	0	2	-1	.958	-4	S-36,2-28/3	-1.7
1963	Mil-N	15	17	0	3	1	0	0	0	0	4	.176	.176	.235	18	-2	0	1	-1	.786	2	/S-7,2-4	0.0
Total	3	144	368	23	79	18	0	3	25	16	82	.215	.251	.288	49	-26	0	4	-2	.942	-4	/S-77,2-35,3	-1.9
Team	2	91	226	16	46	11	0	3	20	12	58	.204	.244	.292	45	-18	0	3	-2	.939	-2	/S-43,2-32,3	-1.7

■ DEION SANDERS
Sanders, Deion Luwynn b: 8/9/67, Ft.Myers, Fla. BL/TL, 6'1", 195 lbs. Deb: 5/31/89

1991	Atl-N	54	110	16	21	1	2	4	13	12	23	.191	.270	.345	68	-5	11	3	2	.952	-5	O-44	-0.9
1992	*Atl-N	97	303	54	92	6	**14**	8	28	18	52	.304	.347	.495	128	10	26	9	2	.983	-1	O-75	1.1
1993	*Atl-N	95	272	42	75	18	6	6	28	16	42	.276	.323	.452	104	1	19	7	2	.986	0	O-60	0.1
1994	Atl-N	46	191	32	55	10	4	0	21	16	28	.288	.346	.403	93	-2	19	7	2	.980	-2	O-46	-0.3
Total	7	494	1583	249	418	57	36	33	141	121	275	.264	.321	.408	94	-15	127	46	11	.981	-6	O-411/D-4	-1.8
Team	4	292	876	144	243	35	22	22	90	62	145	.277	.329	.443	105	4	75	26	7	.979	-8	O-225	0.0

■ RAY SANDERS
Sanders, Raymond Floyd b: 12/4/16, Bonne Terre, Mo. d: 10/28/83, Washington, Mo. BL/TR, 6'2", 185 lbs. Deb: 4/14/42

1946	Bos-N	80	259	43	63	12	0	6	35	50	38	.243	.368	.359	105	3	0			.988	4	1-77	0.3
1948	*Bos-N	5	4	0	1	0	0	0	2	1	0	.250	.400	.250	81	-0	0			.000	0	H	0.0
1949	Bos-N	9	21	0	3	1	0	0	4	5	3	.143	.280	.190	30	-2	0			.984	2	/1-7	0.0
Total	7	630	2182	321	597	114	19	42	329	328	216	.274	.370	.401	115	50	8			.991	-22	1-596	-0.6
Team	3	94	284	43	67	13	0	6	37	55	47	.236	.362	.345	99	1	0			.987	6	/1-84	0.3

■ MIKE SANDLOCK
Sandlock, Michael Joseph b: 10/17/15, Old Greenwich, Conn. BB/TR, 6'1", 185 lbs. Deb: 9/19/42

1942	Bos-N	2	1	0	1	0	0	0	0	0	0	1.000	1.000	1.000	496	0	0			.000	0	/S-2	0.1
1944	Bos-N	30	30	1	3	0	0	0	2	5	3	.100	.250	.100	1	-4	0			.956	7	3-22/S-7	0.3
Total	5	195	446	34	107	19	2	2	31	38	45	.240	.304	.305	66	-21	2			.989	30	C-128/S-31,32	1.6
Team	2	32	31	2	4	0	0	0	2	5	3	.129	.270	.129	14	-3	0			.956	7	/3-22,S-9	0.4

■ ED SAUER
Sauer, Edward "Horn" b: 1/3/19, Pittsburgh, Pa. d: 7/1/88, Thousand Oaks, Cal BR/TR, 6'1", 188 lbs. Deb: 9/17/43 F

| 1949 | Bos-N | 79 | 214 | 26 | 57 | 12 | 0 | 3 | 31 | 17 | 34 | .266 | .323 | .364 | 89 | -4 | 0 | | | .972 | -7 | O-71 | -1.4 |
| Total | 4 | 189 | 457 | 45 | 117 | 25 | 2 | 5 | 57 | 33 | 77 | .256 | .309 | .352 | 83 | -11 | 3 | | | .981 | -10 | O-132 | -2.6 |

■ CARL SAWATSKI
Sawatski, Carl Ernest "Swats" b: 11/4/27, Shickshinny, Pa. d: 11/24/91, Little Rock, Ark. BL/TR, 5'10", 210 lbs. Deb: 9/29/48

1957	*Mil-N	58	105	13	25	4	0	6	17	10	15	.238	.316	.448	110	1	0	0	0	.986	6	C-28	0.8
1958	Mil-N	10	10	1	1	0	0	0	1	2	5	.100	.250	.100	-3	-1	0	0	0	1.000	1	/C-3	-0.1
Total	11	633	1449	133	351	46	5	58	213	191	251	.242	.333	.401	92	-16	2	0		.988	-32	C-457/O-1	-2.8
Team	2	68	115	14	26	4	0	6	18	12	20	.226	.310	.417	100	-0	0	0	0	.987	7	/C-31	0.7

■ JOHNNY SCALZI
Scalzi, John Anthony b: 3/22/07, Stamford, Conn. d: 9/27/62, Port Chester, N.Y BR/TR, 5'7", 170 lbs. Deb: 6/19/31

| 1931 | Bos-N | 2 | 1 | 0 | 0 | 0 | 0 | 0 | 0 | 0 | 1 | .000 | .000 | .000 | -99 | -0 | 0 | | | .000 | 0 | H | 0.0 |

■ LES SCARSELLA
Scarsella, Leslie George b: 11/23/13, Santa Cruz, Cal. d: 12/17/58, San Francisco, Cal BL/TL, 5'11", 185 lbs. Deb: 9/15/35

| 1940 | Bos-N | 18 | 60 | 7 | 18 | 1 | 3 | 0 | 8 | 3 | 5 | .300 | .344 | .417 | 115 | 1 | 2 | | | .986 | -1 | 1-15 | -0.1 |
| Total | 5 | 265 | 898 | 109 | 255 | 34 | 16 | 6 | 109 | 37 | 70 | .284 | .315 | .378 | 92 | -13 | 13 | | | .988 | -4 | 1-197/O-14 | -3.7 |

■ HARRY SCHAFER
Schafer, Harry C. "Silk Stocking" b: 8/14/1846, Philadelphia, Pa. d: 2/28/35, Philadelphia, Pa. BR/TR, 5'9.5", 143 lbs. Deb: 5/5/1871

1871	Bos-n	31	149	38	42	7	5	0	28	3	1	.282	.296	.396	94	-2	13					*3-31/2-1	-0.3
1872	Bos-n	48	226	50	66	12	5	1	37	0	8	.292	.292	.403	106	0						*3-43/O-5	-0.2
1873	Bos-n	60	295	65	79	8	3	2	43	3	1	.268	.275	.336	73	-12						*3-47,O-13	-1.1
1874	Bos-n	71	325	69	84	13	3	1		0		.258	.258	.326	80	-8						*3-71	-0.7
1875	Bos-n	51	216	47	62	9	0	0		0		.287	.287	.329	108	1						*3-50/O-1	0.1
1876	Bos-N	70	286	47	72	11	0	0	35	4	11	.252	.262	.290	82	-5				.810	3	*3-70	0.0
1877	Bos-N	33	141	20	39	5	2	0	13	0	7	.277	.277	.340	90	-2				.621	-12	O-23/3-9,S	-1.3
1878	Bos-N	2	8	0	1	0	0	0	0	0	1	.125	.125	.125	-16	-1				1.000	-1	/O-2	-0.2
Total	5 n	261	1211	269	333	49	16	4	108	6	10	.275	.279	.352	89	-21						3-242/O-19,2	-2.2
Total	3	105	435	67	112	16	2	0	48	4	19	.257	.264	.303	83	-8				.810	-9	/3-79,O-25,S	-1.5

■ AL SCHELLHASE
Schellhase, Albert Herman "Schelley" b: 9/13/1864, Evansville, Ind. d: 1/3/19, Evansville, Ind. BR/TR, 5'8", 148 lbs. Deb: 5/7/1890

| 1890 | Bos-N | 9 | 29 | 1 | 4 | 0 | 0 | 0 | 1 | 1 | 10 | .138 | .167 | .138 | -10 | -4 | 0 | | | .778 | -1 | /O-5,C-2,S3 | -0.4 |
| Total | 2 | 16 | 49 | 5 | 7 | 0 | 0 | 0 | 2 | 2 | 12 | .143 | .176 | .143 | -7 | -7 | 3 | | | .922 | -1 | /C-9,O-5,3S | -0.6 |

■ BUTCH SCHMIDT
Schmidt, Charles John "Butcher Boy" b: 7/19/1886, Baltimore, Md. d: 9/4/52, Baltimore, Md. BL/TL, 6'1.5", 200 lbs. Deb: 5/11/09

1913	Bos-N	22	78	6	24	2	1	14	2	5		.308	.333	.423	113	1	1			.983	1	1-22	0.1
1914	*Bos-N	147	537	67	153	17	9	1	71	43	55	.285	.350	.356	111	8	14			.990	3	*1-147	0.7
1915	Bos-N	127	458	46	115	26	7	2	60	36	59	.251	.318	.352	107	4	3	10	-5	.987	-4	*1-127	-1.0
Total	4	297	1075	119	292	45	18	4	145	81	119	.272	.335	.358	109	12	18	10		.988	-1	1-296/P-1	-0.2
Team	3	296	1073	119	292	45	18	4	145	81	119	.272	.335	.359	110	12	18	10		.988	-1	1-296	-0.2

■ RED SCHOENDIENST
Schoendienst, Albert Fred b: 2/2/23, Germantown, Ill. BB/TR, 6', 170 lbs. Deb: 4/17/45 MCH

1957	*Mil-N★	93	394	56	122	23	4	6	32	23	7	.310	.349	.434	117	8	3	3	-1	.987	4	2-92/O-2	1.9
1958	*Mil-N	106	427	47	112	23	1	1	24	31	21	.262	.314	.328	77	-15	3	1	0	**.987**	1	*2-105	-0.7
1959	Mil-N	5	3	0	0	0	0	0	0	0	0	.000	.000	.000	-99	-1	0	0	0	.667	-0	/2-4	-0.1
1960	Mil-N	68	226	21	58	9	1	1	19	17	13	.257	.311	.319	79	-7	1	0	0	.964	-17	2-62	-1.9
Total	19	2216	8479	1223	2449	427	78	84	773	606	346	.289	.338	.387	93	-82	89	27	11	.983	88	2-1834,0-123/S3	10.6
Team	4	272	1050	124	292	55	6	8	75	71	41	.278	.326	.365	92	-14	6	4	-1	.981	-13	2-263/O-2	-0.8

■ HANK SCHREIBER
Schreiber, Henry Walter b: 7/12/1891, Cleveland, Ohio d:2/23/68, Indianapolis, Ind. BR/TR, 5'11", 165 lbs. Deb: 4/14/14

| 1917 | Bos-N | 2 | 7 | 1 | 2 | 0 | 0 | 0 | 0 | 0 | 1 | .286 | .286 | .286 | 80 | -0 | 0 | | | 1.000 | -1 | /S-1,3-1 | -0.1 |
| Total | 5 | 36 | 91 | 10 | 18 | 5 | 0 | 0 | 6 | 1 | 16 | .198 | .207 | .253 | 34 | -8 | 0 | | | .986 | 6 | /3-22,S-8,2O | -0.1 |

■ WES SCHULMERICH
Schulmerich, Edward Wesley b: 8/21/01, Hillsboro, Ore. d: 6/26/85, Corvallis, Ore. BR/TR, 5'11", 210 lbs. Deb: 5/1/31

1931	Bos-N	95	327	36	101	17	7	2	43	28	30	.309	.363	.422	115	7	0			.966	-4	O-87	-0.3
1932	Bos-N	119	404	47	105	22	5	11	57	27	61	.260	.314	.421	99	-1	5			.968	3	*O-101	-0.5
1933	Bos-N	29	85	10	21	6	1	1	13	5	10	.247	.289	.376	97	-1	0			.980	1	O-21	-0.1
Total	4	429	1442	169	417	73	20	27	192	118	197	.289	.347	.424	109	15	7			.971	-6	O-375	-1.0
Team	3	243	816	93	227	45	13	14	113	60	101	.278	.331	.417	105	5	5			.968	-1	O-209	-0.9

YEAR	TM/L	G	AB	R	H	2B	3B	HR	RBI	BB	SO	AVG	OBP	SLG	PRO+	BR/A	SB	CS	SBR	FA	FR	G/POS	TPR

■ JOHNNY SCHULTE   Schulte, John Clement b: 9/8/1896, Fredericktown, Mo. d: 6/28/78, St.Louis, Mo. BL/TR, 5'11", 190 lbs. Deb: 4/18/23 C

| 1932 | Bos-N | 10 | 9 | 1 | 2 | 0 | 0 | 1 | 2 | 2 | 1 | .222 | .364 | .556 | 149 | 1 | | | 0 | 1.000 | 1 | C-10 | 0.2 |
| Total | 5 | 192 | 374 | 59 | 98 | 15 | 4 | 14 | 64 | 76 | 49 | .262 | .388 | .436 | 112 | 8 | | | 1 | .957 | -2 | C-140/1-1 | 1.5 |

■ JACK SCHULTE   Schulte, John Herman Frank b: 11/15/1881, Cincinnati, Ohio d: 8/17/75, Roseville, Mich. BR/TR, 5'9", 180 lbs. Deb: 8/19/06

| 1906 | Bos-N | 2 | 7 | 0 | 0 | 0 | 0 | 0 | 0 | 0 | 0 | .000 | .000 | .000 | -99 | -2 | | | 0 | 1.000 | -1 | /S-2 | -0.3 |

■ JOE SCHULTZ   Schultz, Joseph Charles Sr. "Germany" b: 7/24/1893, Pittsburgh, Pa. d: 4/13/41, Columbia, S.C. BR/TR, 5'11.5", 172 lbs. Deb: 9/28/12 F

1912	Bos-N	4	12	1	3	1	0	0	4	0	2	.250	.250	.333	58	-1			0	.824	-0	/2-4	-0.1
1913	Bos-N	9	18	2	4	0	0	0	1	2	7	.222	.333	.222	59	-1			0	1.000	-1	/O-5,2-1	-0.1
Total	11	703	1959	235	558	83	19	15	249	116	102	.285	.327	.370	93	-21			35	.966	-43	O-411/3-55,21S	-9.3
Team	2	13	30	3	7	1	0	0	5	2	9	.233	.303	.267	60	-2			0	.842	-0	/O-5,2-5	-0.2

■ BILL SCHUSTER   Schuster, William Charles "Broadway Bill" b: 8/4/12, Buffalo, N.Y. d: 6/28/87, ElMonte, Cal. BR/TR, 5'9", 164 lbs. Deb: 9/29/37

| 1939 | Bos-N | 2 | 3 | 0 | 0 | 0 | 0 | 0 | 0 | 0 | 1 | .000 | .000 | .000 | -99 | -1 | | | 0 | .833 | -0 | /S-1,3-1 | -0.1 |
| Total | 5 | 123 | 261 | 27 | 61 | 11 | 3 | 1 | 17 | 23 | 23 | .234 | .296 | .310 | 72 | -10 | | | 6 | .954 | 11 | /S-76,2-9,3 | 0.6 |

■ ART SCHWIND   Schwind, Arthur Edwin b: 11/4/1889, Ft.Wayne, Ind. d: 1/13/68, Sullivan, Ill. BB/TR, 5'8", 150 lbs. Deb: 10/3/12

| 1912 | Bos-N | 1 | 2 | 0 | 1 | 0 | 0 | 0 | 0 | 0 | 0 | .500 | .500 | .500 | 171 | 0 | | | 0 | .000 | 0 | /3-1 | 0.0 |

■ SOCKS SEIBOLD   Seibold, Harry b: 4/3/1896, Philadelphia, Pa. d: 9/21/65, Philadelphia, Pa. BR/TR, 5'8.5", 162 lbs. Deb: 9/18/15

1929	Bos-N	33	70	6	20	2	0	0	9	6	6	.286	.342	.314	67	-3			0	**1.000**	-1	P-33	0.0
1930	Bos-N	36	90	6	19	2	0	1	5	6	6	.211	.260	.267	29	-11			0	.941	-3	P-36	0.0
1931	Bos-N	33	70	3	9	0	0	0	2	1	9	.129	.141	.129	-28	-13			0	**1.000**	0	P-33	0.0
1932	Bos-N	28	46	2	7	0	0	0	0	2	0	.152	.188	.152	-8	-7			0	1.000	2	P-28	0.0
1933	Bos-N	11	9	0	1	0	0	0	0	2	2	.111	.273	.111	14	-1			0	1.000	0	P-11	0.0
Total	9	207	395	27	76	7	1	1	27	25	43	.192	.242	.223	25	-42			1	.982	-5	P-191/S-7,O	-0.8
Team	5	141	285	17	56	4	0	1	18	17	23	.196	.242	.221	20	-34			0	.986	-1	P-141	0.0

■ RUBE SELLERS   Sellers, Oliver b: 3/7/1881, Duquesne, Pa. d: 1/14/52, Pittsburgh, Pa. BR/TR, 5'10", 180 lbs. Deb: 8/12/10

| 1910 | Bos-N | 12 | 32 | 3 | 5 | 0 | 0 | 0 | 2 | 6 | 5 | .156 | .289 | .156 | 29 | -3 | | | 1 | 1.000 | -2 | /O-9 | -0.6 |

■ CY SEYMOUR   Seymour, James Bentley b: 12/9/1872, Albany, N.Y. d: 9/20/19, New York, N.Y. BL/TL, 6', 200 lbs. Deb: 4/22/1896

| 1913 | Bos-N | 39 | 73 | 2 | 13 | 2 | 0 | 0 | 10 | 7 | 7 | .178 | .250 | .205 | 33 | -6 | | | 2 | .950 | 0 | O-18 | -0.7 |
| Total | 16 | 1528 | 5682 | 737 | 1723 | 229 | 96 | 52 | 799 | 354 | 32 | .303 | .347 | .405 | 117 | 95 | | | 222 | .945 | 81 | *O-1333,P-140/132 | 10.4 |

■ JOE SHANNON   Shannon, Joseph Aloysius b: 2/11/1897, Jersey City, N.J. d: 7/28/55, Jersey City, N.J. BR/TR, 5'11", 170 lbs. Deb: 7/7/15 F

| 1915 | Bos-N | 5 | 10 | 3 | 2 | 0 | 0 | 0 | 1 | 0 | 3 | .200 | .200 | .200 | 22 | -1 | | | 0 | .750 | -0 | /O-4,2-1 | -0.1 |

■ RED SHANNON   Shannon, Maurice Joseph b: 2/11/1897, Jersey City, N.J. d: 4/12/70, Jersey City, N.J. BB/TR, 5'11", 170 lbs. Deb: 10/7/15 F

| 1915 | Bos-N | 1 | 3 | 0 | 0 | 0 | 0 | 0 | 0 | 0 | 0 | .000 | .000 | .000 | -99 | -1 | | | 0 | .857 | 1 | /2-1 | 0.0 |
| Total | 7 | 310 | 1070 | 124 | 277 | 38 | 22 | 0 | 91 | 109 | 178 | .259 | .334 | .336 | 89 | -14 | | | 21 | .957 | -35 | 2-159,S-123/3 | -3.6 |

■ BUD SHARPE   Sharpe, Bayard Heston b: 8/6/1881, West Chester, Pa. d: 5/31/16, Haddock, Ga. BL/TR, Deb: 4/14/05

1905	Bos-N	46	170	8	31	3	2	0	11	7		.182	.215	.224	31	-15			0	.904	2	O-42/C-3,1	-1.5
1910	Bos-N	115	439	30	105	14	3	0	29	14	31	.239	.264	.285	58	-25			4	.987	7	*1-113	-1.9
Total	2	165	625	40	139	17	6	0	41	21	33	.222	.249	.269	50	-41			4	.987	9	1-118/O-42,C	-3.5
Team	2	161	609	38	136	17	5	0	40	21	31	.223	.250	.268	51	-39			4	.987	9	1-114/O-42,C	-3.4

■ MIKE SHARPERSON   Sharperson, Michael Tyrone b: 10/4/61, Orangeburg, S.C. BR/TR, 6'3", 190 lbs. Deb: 4/6/87

| 1995 | Atl-N | 7 | 7 | 1 | 1 | 1 | 0 | 0 | 2 | 0 | 2 | .143 | .143 | .286 | 9 | -1 | 0 | 0 | 0 | .000 | -0 | /3-1 | -0.1 |
| Total | 8 | 557 | 1203 | 149 | 337 | 61 | 5 | 10 | 123 | 139 | 154 | .280 | .357 | .364 | 103 | 8 | 22 | 14 | | .952 | -0 | 3-256,2-156/S10 | 1.1 |

■ AL SHAW   Shaw, Alfred "Shoddy" b: 10/3/1874, Burslem, England d: 3/25/58, Uhrichsville, Ohio BR/TR, 5'8", 170 lbs. Deb: 6/8/01

| 1909 | Bos-N | 18 | 41 | 1 | 4 | 0 | 0 | 0 | 0 | 5 | | .098 | .213 | .098 | -3 | -5 | | | 0 | .975 | 4 | C-14 | 0.0 |
| Total | 4 | 181 | 459 | 31 | 92 | 9 | 3 | 1 | 32 | 35 | | .200 | .267 | .240 | 53 | -26 | | | 6 | .961 | 21 | C-158/1-10,3S | 0.8 |

■ MARTY SHAY   Shay, Arthur Joseph b: 4/25/1896, Boston, Mass. d: 2/20/51, Worcester, Mass. BR/TR, 5'7.5", 148 lbs. Deb: 9/16/16

| 1924 | Bos-N | 19 | 68 | 4 | 16 | 3 | 1 | 0 | 2 | 5 | | .235 | .297 | .309 | 65 | -3 | 2 | 1 | 0 | .950 | -12 | 2-19/S-1 | -1.5 |
| Total | 2 | 21 | 75 | 4 | 18 | 3 | 1 | 0 | 2 | 5 | 6 | .240 | .296 | .307 | 66 | -4 | 2 | 1 | | .929 | -12 | /2-19,S-3 | -1.5 |

■ DAVE SHEAN   Shean, David William b: 7/9/1883, Arlington, Mass. d: 5/22/63, Boston, Mass. BR/TR, 5'11", 175 lbs. Deb: 9/10/06

1909	Bos-N	75	267	32	66	11	4	1	29	17		.247	.297	.330	90	-4			14	.956	8	2-72	0.3
1910	Bos-N	150	543	52	130	12	7	3	36	42	45	.239	.294	.304	71	-21			16	.953	43	*2-148	2.0
1912	Bos-N	4	10	1	3	0	0	0	0	1	2	.300	.417	.300	96	0			0	.917	-1	/S-4	-0.1
Total	9	630	2167	225	495	59	23	6	166	155	133	.228	.284	.285	70	-82			66	.961	55	2-554/S-38,103	-1.9
Team	3	229	820	85	199	23	11	4	65	60	47	.243	.297	.312	77	-24			30	.954	49	2-220/S-4	2.2

■ RAY SHEARER   Shearer, Ray Solomon b: 9/19/29, Jacobus, Pa. d: 2/21/82, York, Pa. BR/TR, 6', 200 lbs. Deb: 9/18/57

| 1957 | Mil-N | 2 | 2 | 1 | 1 | 0 | 0 | 0 | 0 | 1 | 1 | .500 | .667 | .500 | 237 | 1 | 0 | 0 | 0 | .000 | -0 | /O-1 | 0.0 |

■ EARL SHEELY   Sheely, Earl Homer "Whitey" b: 2/12/1893, Bushnell, Ill. d: 9/16/52, Seattle, Wash. BR/TR, 6'3.5", 195 lbs. Deb: 4/14/21 F

| 1931 | Bos-N | 147 | 538 | 30 | 147 | 15 | 2 | 1 | 77 | 34 | 21 | .273 | .319 | .314 | 73 | -20 | | | 0 | .992 | -3 | *1-143 | -3.6 |
| Total | 9 | 1234 | 4471 | 572 | 1340 | 244 | 27 | 48 | 747 | 563 | 205 | .300 | .383 | .399 | 104 | 45 | | | 33 | .991 | -14 | *1-1220 | -5.5 |

■ STEVE SHEMO   Shemo, Stephen Michael b: 4/9/15, Swoyersville, Pa. d: 4/13/92, Eden, N.C. BR/TR, 5'11", 175 lbs. Deb: 4/18/44

1944	Bos-N	18	31	3	9	2	0	0	1	1	3	.290	.324	.355	84	-1			0	.966	3	2-16/3-2	0.3
1945	Bos-N	17	46	4	11	1	0	0	7	1	3	.239	.255	.261	43	-4			0	.921	-6	2-12/3-3,S	-0.9
Total	2	35	77	7	20	3	0	0	8	2	6	.260	.278	.299	60	-4			0	.948	-3	/2-28,3-5,S	-0.6

■ ART SHIRES   Shires, Charles Arthur "Art The Great" b: 8/13/07, Italy, Tex. d: 7/13/67, Italy, Tex. BL/TR, 6'1", 195 lbs. Deb: 8/20/28

| 1932 | Bos-N | 82 | 298 | 32 | 71 | 9 | 3 | 5 | 30 | 25 | 21 | .238 | .299 | .339 | 74 | -11 | | | 1 | .988 | -2 | 1-80 | -2.0 |
| Total | 4 | 290 | 986 | 118 | 287 | 45 | 12 | 11 | 119 | 81 | 62 | .291 | .347 | .395 | 95 | -8 | | | 8 | .988 | -1 | 1-256/2-3 | -3.5 |

■ VINCE SHUPE   Shupe, Vincent William b: 9/5/21, E.Canton, Ohio d: 4/5/62, Canton, Ohio BL/TL, 5'11", 180 lbs. Deb: 7/7/45

| 1945 | Bos-N | 78 | 283 | 22 | 76 | 8 | 0 | 0 | 15 | 17 | 16 | .269 | .312 | .297 | 69 | -11 | | | 3 | .989 | 1 | 1-77 | -1.5 |

■ OSCAR SIEMER   Siemer, Oscar Sylvester "Cotton" b: 8/14/01, St.Louis, Mo. d: 12/5/59, St.Louis, Mo. BR/TR, 5'9", 162 lbs. Deb: 5/20/25

1925	Bos-N	16	46	5	14	0	1	0	6	1	0	.304	.319	.413	94	-1	0	0	0	.900	-2	C-16	-0.2
1926	Bos-N	31	73	3	15	1	0	0	5	2	7	.205	.227	.219	22	-8			0	.920	-2	C-30	-0.9
Total	2	47	119	8	29	1	1	0	11	3	7	.244	.262	.294	51	-9	0	0	0	.913	-4	/C-46	-1.1

■ AL SIMMONS   Simmons, Aloysius Harry "Bucketfoot Al" (b: Aloys Szymanski)
b: 5/22/02, Milwaukee, Wis. d: 5/26/56, Milwaukee, Wis. BR/TR, 5'11", 190 lbs. Deb: 4/15/24 CH

| 1939 | Bos-N | 93 | 330 | 39 | 93 | 17 | 5 | 7 | 43 | 22 | 40 | .282 | .331 | .427 | 110 | 3 | | | 0 | .982 | -0 | O-82 | 0.0 |
| Total | 20 | 2215 | 8759 | 1507 | 2927 | 539 | 149 | 307 | 1827 | 615 | 737 | .334 | .380 | .498 | 132 | 361 | | | 88 | .982 | 53 | *O-2142/1-1 | 25.6 |

■ TED SIMMONS Simmons, Ted Lyle b: 8/9/49, Highland Park, Mich. BB/TR, 6', 200 lbs. Deb: 9/21/68

YEAR	TM/L	G	AB	R	H	2B	3B	HR	RBI	BB	SO	AVG	OBP	SLG	PRO+	BR/A	SB	CS	SBR	FA	FR	G/POS	TPR
1986	Atl-N	76	127	14	32	5	0	4	25	12	14	.252	.321	.386	89	-2	1	0	0	.964	-3	1-14,C-10/3	-0.5
1987	Atl-N	73	177	20	49	8	0	4	30	21	23	.277	.354	.390	92	-2	1	1	-0	.984	-1	1-28,C-15/3	-0.4
1988	Atl-N	78	107	6	21	6	0	2	11	15	9	.196	.295	.308	70	-4	0	0	0	.993	-1	1-19,C-10	-0.6
Total	21	2456	8680	1074	2472	483	47	248	1389	855	694	.285	.352	.437	118	208	21	33		.987	-79	*C-1771,D-279,1/03	16.8
Team	3	227	411	40	102	19	0	10	66	48	46	.248	.328	.367	86	-7	2	1		.981	-5	/1-61,C-35,3	-1.5

■ MATT SINATRO Sinatro, Matthew Stephen b: 3/22/60, Hartford, Conn. BR/TR, 5'9", 175 lbs. Deb: 9/22/81

YEAR	TM/L	G	AB	R	H	2B	3B	HR	RBI	BB	SO	AVG	OBP	SLG	PRO+	BR/A	SB	CS	SBR	FA	FR	G/POS	TPR
1981	Atl-N	12	32	4	9	1	1	0	4	5	4	.281	.378	.375	111	1	1	0	0	1.000	4	C-12	0.6
1982	Atl-N	37	81	10	11	2	0	1	4	4	9	.136	.176	.198	4	-10	0	1	-1	1.000	4	C-35	-0.7
1983	Atl-N	7	12	0	2	0	0	0	2	2	1	.167	.286	.167	26	-1	0	0	0	.967	2	/C-7	0.0
1984	Atl-N	2	4	0	0	0	0	0	0	0	0	.000	.000	.000	-93	-1	0	0	0	1.000	-0	/C-2	-0.2
Total	10	140	252	20	48	6	1	1	21	17	35	.190	.244	.234	34	-22	2	1	0	.996	19	C-135	-0.1
Team	4	58	129	14	22	3	1	1	10	11	14	.171	.236	.233	30	-12	1	1	-0	.996	9	/C-56	-0.3

■ HOSEA SINER Siner, Hosea John b: 3/20/1885, Shelburn, Ind. d: 6/10/48, Sullivan, Ind. BR/TR, 5'10.5", 185 lbs. Deb: 7/28/09

YEAR	TM/L	G	AB	R	H	2B	3B	HR	RBI	BB	SO	AVG	OBP	SLG	PRO+	BR/A	SB	CS	SBR	FA	FR	G/POS	TPR
1909	Bos-N	10	23	1	3	0	0	0	1	2		.130	.200	.130	3	-3	0			.909	-1	/3-5,2-1,S	-0.4

■ GEORGE SISLER Sisler, George Harold "Georgeous George"
b: 3/24/1893, Manchester, Ohio d: 3/26/73, Richmond Heights, Mo. BL/TL, 5'11", 170 lbs. Deb: 6/28/15 FMCH

YEAR	TM/L	G	AB	R	H	2B	3B	HR	RBI	BB	SO	AVG	OBP	SLG	PRO+	BR/A	SB	CS	SBR	FA	FR	G/POS	TPR
1928	Bos-N	118	491	71	167	26	4	4	68	30	15	.340	.380	.434	119	13	11			.988	7	*1-118/P-1	0.9
1929	Bos-N	154	629	67	205	40	8	2	79	33	17	.326	.363	.424	98	-2	6			.982	3	*1-154	-1.3
1930	Bos-N	116	431	54	133	15	7	3	67	23	15	.309	.346	.397	82	-12	7			.987	5	*1-107	-1.6
Total	15	2055	8267	1284	2812	425	164	102	1175	472	327	.340	.379	.468	124	254	375			.987	88	*1-1971/O-37,P23	22.7
Team	3	388	1551	192	505	81	19	9	214	86	47	.326	.364	.420	100	-2	24			.985	16	1-379/P-1	-2.0

■ SIBBY SISTI Sisti, Sebastian Daniel b: 7/26/20, Buffalo, N.Y. BR/TR, 5'11", 175 lbs. Deb: 7/21/39 C

YEAR	TM/L	G	AB	R	H	2B	3B	HR	RBI	BB	SO	AVG	OBP	SLG	PRO+	BR/A	SB	CS	SBR	FA	FR	G/POS	TPR
1939	Bos-N	63	215	19	49	7	1	1	11	12	38	.228	.269	.284	52	-15	4			.994	0	2-34,3-17,S	-1.2
1940	Bos-N	123	459	73	115	19	5	6	34	36	64	.251	.311	.353	87	-9	4			.936	-2	*3-102,2-16	-0.8
1941	Bos-N	140	541	72	140	24	3	1	45	38	76	.259	.309	.320	81	-15	7			.916	-8	*3-137/2-2,S	-2.0
1942	Bos-N	129	407	50	86	11	4	4	35	45	55	.211	.296	.287	73	-14	5			.970	-4	*2-124/O-1	-1.1
1946	Bos-N	1	0	0	0	0	0	0	0	0	0	—	—	—	—	0	0			.000	0	/3-1	0.0
1947	Bos-N	56	153	22	43	8	0	2	15	20	17	.281	.371	.373	100	1	2			.947	-9	S-51/2-1	-0.6
1948	*Bos-N	83	221	30	54	6	2	0	21	31	34	.244	.340	.290	73	-7	0			.972	-5	2-44,S-26	-0.9
1949	Bos-N	101	268	39	69	12	0	5	22	34	42	.257	.343	.358	93	-2	1			.989	-13	O-48,2-21,S/3	-1.5
1950	Bos-N	69	105	21	18	3	1	2	11	16	19	.171	.287	.276	52	-7	1			.931	0	S-23,2-19,3/10	-0.6
1951	Bos-N	114	362	46	101	20	2	2	38	32	50	.279	.341	.362	96	-2	4	5	-2	.944	-23	S-55,2-52/310	-2.2
1952	Bos-N	90	245	19	52	10	1	4	24	14	43	.212	.255	.310	58	-15	2	0	1	.966	-12	2-33,O-23,S/3	-2.5
1953	Mil-N	38	23	8	5	1	0	0	4	5	2	.217	.357	.261	69	-1	0	0	0	1.000	4	2-13/S-6,3	0.3
1954	Mil-N	9	0	2	0	0	0	0	0	0	0	—	—	—	—	0	0	0	0	.000	0	R	0.0
Total	13	1016	2999	401	732	121	19	27	260	283	440	.244	.313	.324	79	-85	30	5		.973	-72	2-359,3-290,S/O1	-13.1

■ JIMMY SLAGLE Slagle, James Franklin "Rabbit" or "Shorty" b: 7/11/1873, Worthville, Pa. d: 5/10/56, Chicago, Ill. BL/TR, 5'7", 144 lbs. Deb: 4/17/1899

YEAR	TM/L	G	AB	R	H	2B	3B	HR	RBI	BB	SO	AVG	OBP	SLG	PRO+	BR/A	SB	CS	SBR	FA	FR	G/POS	TPR
1901	Bos-N	66	255	35	69	7	0	0	7	34		.271	.359	.298	84	-4	14			.935	-2	O-66	-1.1
Total	10	1298	4996	779	1340	124	56	2	344	619		.268	.352	.317	97	3	273			.950	22	*O-1292	-5.7

■ ENOS SLAUGHTER Slaughter, Enos Bradsher "Country" b: 4/27/16, Roxboro, N.C. BL/TR, 5'9", 192 lbs. Deb: 4/19/38 H

YEAR	TM/L	G	AB	R	H	2B	3B	HR	RBI	BB	SO	AVG	OBP	SLG	PRO+	BR/A	SB	CS	SBR	FA	FR	G/POS	TPR
1959	Mil-N	11	18	0	3	0	0	0	1	3	3	.167	.286	.167	27	-2	0	0	0	1.000	-1	/O-5	-0.3
Total	19	2380	7946	1247	2383	413	148	169	1304	1018	538	.300	.382	.453	122	256	71	15		.980	-0	*O-2064	16.3

■ HANK SMALL Small, George Henry b: 7/31/53, Atlanta, Ga. BR/TR, 6'3", 205 lbs. Deb: 9/27/78

YEAR	TM/L	G	AB	R	H	2B	3B	HR	RBI	BB	SO	AVG	OBP	SLG	PRO+	BR/A	SB	CS	SBR	FA	FR	G/POS	TPR
1978	Atl-N	1	4	0	0	0	0	0	0	0	0	.000	.000	.000	-90	-1	0	0	0	1.000	0	/1-1	-0.1

■ ROY SMALLEY Smalley, Roy Frederick Sr. b: 6/9/26, Springfield, Mo. BR/TR, 6'3", 190 lbs. Deb: 4/20/48 F

YEAR	TM/L	G	AB	R	H	2B	3B	HR	RBI	BB	SO	AVG	OBP	SLG	PRO+	BR/A	SB	CS	SBR	FA	FR	G/POS	TPR
1954	Mil-N	25	36	5	8	0	0	1	7	4	9	.222	.317	.306	67	-2	0	0	0	.950	4	/S-9,2-7,1	0.3
Total	11	872	2644	277	601	103	33	61	305	257	541	.227	.300	.360	77	-93	4	0	1	.966	3	S-820/2-8,13	-3.4

■ EDGAR SMITH Smith, Albert Edgar b: 10/15/1860, North Haven, Conn. TR, 6', 200 lbs. Deb: 6/20/1883

YEAR	TM/L	G	AB	R	H	2B	3B	HR	RBI	BB	SO	AVG	OBP	SLG	PRO+	BR/A	SB	CS	SBR	FA	FR	G/POS	TPR
1883	Bos-N	30	115	10	25	5	3	0	16	5	11	.217	.250	.313	68	-4				.905	-0	O-30/C-1	-0.4

■ POP SMITH Smith, Charles Marvin b: 10/12/1856, Digby, N.S., Canada d: 4/18/27, Boston, Mass. BR/TR, 5'11", 170 lbs. Deb: 5/1/1880 U

YEAR	TM/L	G	AB	R	H	2B	3B	HR	RBI	BB	SO	AVG	OBP	SLG	PRO+	BR/A	SB	CS	SBR	FA	FR	G/POS	TPR
1889	Bos-N	59	208	21	54	13	4	0	32	23	30	.260	.345	.361	92	-3	11			.890	-0	S-59	0.1
1890	Bos-N	134	463	82	106	16	12	1	53	80	81	.229	.353	.322	90	-5	39			.918	-20	*2-134/S-1	-1.5
Total	12	1112	4238	643	941	141	87	24	264	325	345	.222	.287	.313	86	-64	169			.903	70	2-713,S-336/3OPC	3.5
Team	2	193	671	103	160	29	16	1	85	103	111	.238	.351	.334	91	-8	50			.918	-20	2-134/S-60	-1.4

■ EARL SMITH Smith, Earl Sutton "Oil" b: 2/14/1897, Hot Springs, Ark. d: 6/8/63, Little Rock, Ark. BL/TR, 5'10.5", 180 lbs. Deb: 4/24/19

YEAR	TM/L	G	AB	R	H	2B	3B	HR	RBI	BB	SO	AVG	OBP	SLG	PRO+	BR/A	SB	CS	SBR	FA	FR	G/POS	TPR
1923	Bos-N	72	191	22	55	15	1	3	19	22	10	.288	.364	.424	112	3	0	1	-1	.975	-4	C-54	0.2
1924	Bos-N	33	59	1	16	3	0	0	8	6	3	.271	.338	.322	81	-1	0	1	-1	.946	-1	C-13	-0.2
Total	12	860	2264	225	686	115	19	46	355	247	106	.303	.374	.432	111	37	18	9		.971	-20	C-720/2-1	5.6
Team	2	105	250	23	71	18	1	3	27	28	13	.284	.358	.400	105	2	0	2		.968	-5	/C-67	0.0

■ ELMER SMITH Smith, Elmer Ellsworth b: 3/23/1868, Pittsburgh, Pa. d: 11/3/45, Pittsburgh, Pa. BL/TL, 5'11", 178 lbs. Deb: 9/10/1886

YEAR	TM/L	G	AB	R	H	2B	3B	HR	RBI	BB	SO	AVG	OBP	SLG	PRO+	BR/A	SB	CS	SBR	FA	FR	G/POS	TPR
1901	Bos-N	16	57	5	10	2	1	0	3	6		.175	.254	.246	41	-4	2			.833	-3	O-15	-0.8
Total	14	1234	4684	912	1454	196	136	37	638	636		.310	.398	.434	126	191	232			.921	-15	*O-1086,P-149	9.5

■ FRED SMITH Smith, Fred Vincent b: 7/29/1886, Cleveland, Ohio d: 5/28/61, Cleveland, Ohio BR/TR, 5'11.5", 185 lbs. Deb: 4/17/13 F

YEAR	TM/L	G	AB	R	H	2B	3B	HR	RBI	BB	SO	AVG	OBP	SLG	PRO+	BR/A	SB	CS	SBR	FA	FR	G/POS	TPR
1913	Bos-N	92	285	35	65	9	3	0	27	29	55	.228	.302	.281	65	-12	7			.920	-14	3-59,2-14,S/O	-2.7
Total	4	438	1422	143	321	39	25	8	158	133	219	.226	.296	.305	63	-73	58			.932	-3	3-253,S-157/2O1	-6.2

■ HARRY SMITH Smith, Harry Thomas b: 10/31/1874, Yorkshire, England d: 2/17/33, Salem, N.J. BR/TR, Deb: 7/11/01 M

YEAR	TM/L	G	AB	R	H	2B	3B	HR	RBI	BB	SO	AVG	OBP	SLG	PRO+	BR/A	SB	CS	SBR	FA	FR	G/POS	TPR
1908	Bos-N	41	130	13	32	2	2	1	16	7		.246	.295	.315	96	-1	2			.975	0	C-38	0.3
1909	Bos-N	43	113	9	19	4	1	0	4	5		.168	.203	.221	30	-9	3			.972	2	C-31,M	-0.5
1910	Bos-N	70	147	8	35	4	0	1	15	5	14	.238	.263	.286	57	-8	5			.949	3	C-38	-0.2
Total	10	343	1004	83	214	22	7	2	89	55	14	.213	.262	.255	54	-56	23			.967	-9	C-290/O-5	-3.8
Team	3	154	390	30	86	10	3	2	35	17	14	.221	.257	.277	62	-19	10			.965	5	C-107	-0.4

■ JACK SMITH Smith, Jack b: 6/23/1895, Chicago, Ill. d: 5/2/72, Westchester, Ill. BL/TL, 5'8", 165 lbs. Deb: 9/30/15

YEAR	TM/L	G	AB	R	H	2B	3B	HR	RBI	BB	SO	AVG	OBP	SLG	PRO+	BR/A	SB	CS	SBR	FA	FR	G/POS	TPR
1926	Bos-N	96	322	46	100	15	2	2	25	28	12	.311	.369	.388	114	7	11			.973	2	O-83	0.3
1927	Bos-N	84	183	27	58	6	4	1	24	16	12	.317	.375	.410	119	5	8			.950	-0	O-48	0.2
1928	Bos-N	96	254	30	71	9	2	1	32	21	14	.280	.335	.343	82	-7	6			.988	1	O-65	-1.0
1929	Bos-N	19	20	2	5	0	0	0	2	2	2	.250	.318	.250	45	-2	0			.833	-3	/O-9	-0.5
Total	15	1406	4532	783	1301	182	71	40	382	334	348	.287	.339	.385	103	18	228			.961	-36	*O-1219	-9.5
Team	4	295	779	105	234	30	8	4	83	67	40	.300	.358	.375	102	3	25			.969	-1	O-205	-1.0

■ STUB SMITH Smith, James A. b: 11/26/1876, Elmwood, Ill. BL/TR, 5'6", 145 lbs. Deb: 9/10/1898

YEAR	TM/L	G	AB	R	H	2B	3B	HR	RBI	BB	SO	AVG	OBP	SLG	PRO+	BR/A	SB	CS	SBR	FA	FR	G/POS	TPR
1898	Bos-N	3	10	1	1	0	0	0	0	0		.100	.100	.100	-41	-2	0			.933	1	/S-3	-0.1

■ RED SMITH Smith, James Carlisle b: 4/6/1890, Greenville, S.C. d: 10/11/66, Atlanta, Ga. BR/TR, 5'11", 165 lbs. Deb: 9/5/11

YEAR	TM/L	G	AB	R	H	2B	3B	HR	RBI	BB	SO	AVG	OBP	SLG	PRO+	BR/A	SB	CS	SBR	FA	FR	G/POS	TPR
1914	Bos-N	60	207	30	65	17	1	3	37	28	24	.314	.401	.449	153	14	4			.937	10	3-60	2.8
1915	Bos-N	157	549	66	145	34	4	2	65	67	49	.264	.345	.352	116	12	10	5	0	.947	-6	*3-157	1.4
1916	Bos-N	150	509	48	132	16	10	3	60	53	55	.259	.333	.348	114	9	13			.928	-4	*3-150	1.1
1917	Bos-N	147	505	60	149	31	6	2	62	53	61	.295	.369	.392	142	26	16			.925	-21	*3-147	0.9
1918	Bos-N	119	429	55	128	20	3	2	65	45	47	.298	.373	.373	133	18	8			.922	4	*3-119	2.7
1919	Bos-N	87	241	24	59	6	0	1	25	40	22	.245	.359	.282	98	2	6			.981	-0	O-48,3-23	0.0
Total	9	1117	3907	477	1087	208	49	27	514	420	415	.278	.353	.377	120	100	117	5		.932	-2	*3-1050/O-48	12.8
Team	6	720	2440	283	678	124	24	13	314	286	258	.278	.359	.364	125	81	57	5		.931	-17	3-656/O-48	8.9

■ JIMMY SMITH Smith, James Lawrence "Greenfield Jimmy" b: 5/15/1895, Pittsburgh, Pa. d: 1/1/74, Pittsburgh, Pa. BB/TR, 5'9", 152 lbs. Deb: 9/26/14

YEAR	TM/L	G	AB	R	H	2B	3B	HR	RBI	BB	SO	AVG	OBP	SLG	PRO+	BR/A	SB	CS	SBR	FA	FR	G/POS	TPR
1918	Bos-N	34	102	8	23	3	4	1	14	3	13	.225	.255	.363	91	-2	1			1.000	-1	2-10/S-9,O3	-0.2
Total	8	370	1127	119	247	32	15	12	108	63	186	.219	.265	.306	57	-69	18			.910	-16	S-199,2-123/3O	-7.8

■ DWIGHT SMITH Smith, John Dwight b: 11/8/63, Tallahassee, Fla. BL/TR, 5'11", 175 lbs. Deb: 5/1/89

YEAR	TM/L	G	AB	R	H	2B	3B	HR	RBI	BB	SO	AVG	OBP	SLG	PRO+	BR/A	SB	CS	SBR	FA	FR	G/POS	TPR
1995	*Atl-N	103	131	16	33	8	2	3	21	13	35	.252	.329	.412	92	-2	0	3	-2	.923	-4	O-25	-0.8
Total	7	712	1654	228	466	83	20	43	210	133	292	.282	.340	.434	106	13	41	34		.964	-34	O-455/D-5	-3.7

■ KEN SMITH Smith, Kenneth Earl b: 2/12/58, Youngstown, Ohio BL/TR, 6'1", 195 lbs. Deb: 9/22/81

YEAR	TM/L	G	AB	R	H	2B	3B	HR	RBI	BB	SO	AVG	OBP	SLG	PRO+	BR/A	SB	CS	SBR	FA	FR	G/POS	TPR
1981	Atl-N	5	3	0	1	1	0	0	0	0	1	.333	.333	.667	174	0	0	0	0	1.000	0	/1-4	0.1
1982	Atl-N	48	41	6	12	1	0	0	3	6	13	.293	.383	.317	94	-0	0	0	0	1.000	-1	/1-6,O-3	-0.2
1983	Atl-N	30	12	2	2	0	0	1	2	1	5	.167	.231	.417	71	-1	1	0	0	1.000	2	1-13	0.2
Total	3	83	56	8	15	2	0	1	5	7	19	.268	.349	.357	93	-0	1	0	0	1.000	1	/1-23,O-3	0.1

■ LONNIE SMITH Smith, Lonnie b: 12/22/55, Chicago, Ill. BR/TR, 5'9", 170 lbs. Deb: 9/2/78

YEAR	TM/L	G	AB	R	H	2B	3B	HR	RBI	BB	SO	AVG	OBP	SLG	PRO+	BR/A	SB	CS	SBR	FA	FR	G/POS	TPR
1988	Atl-N	43	114	14	27	3	0	3	9	10	25	.237	.298	.342	79	-3	4	2	0	.968	-1	O-35	-0.6
1989	Atl-N	134	482	89	152	34	4	21	79	76	95	.315	**.420**	.533	166	44	25	12	0	.993	9	*O-132	5.2
1990	Atl-N	135	466	72	142	27	9	9	42	58	69	.305	.389	.459	125	17	10	10	-3	.956	5	*O-122	1.7
1991	*Atl-N	122	353	58	97	19	1	7	44	50	64	.275	.379	.394	111	7	9	5	-0	.965	-8	O-99	-0.3
1992	*Atl-N	84	158	23	39	8	2	6	33	17	37	.247	.331	.437	109	2	4	0	1	.954	0	O-35	0.3
Total	17	1613	5170	909	1488	273	58	98	533	623	849	.288	.374	.420	117	138	370	140	27	.964	-12	*O-1356/D-60	11.5
Team	5	518	1573	256	457	91	16	46	207	211	290	.291	.384	.456	129	67	52	29	-2	.971	5	O-423	6.3

■ BOB SMITH Smith, Robert Eldridge b: 4/22/1895, Rogersville, Tenn. d: 7/19/87, Waycross, Ga. BR/TR, 5'10", 175 lbs. Deb: 4/19/23

YEAR	TM/L	G	AB	R	H	2B	3B	HR	RBI	BB	SO	AVG	OBP	SLG	PRO+	BR/A	SB	CS	SBR	FA	FR	G/POS	TPR
1923	Bos-N	115	375	30	94	16	3	0	40	17	35	.251	.285	.309	59	-23	4	9	-4	.944	14	*S-101/2-8	-0.3
1924	Bos-N	106	347	32	79	12	3	2	38	15	26	.228	.260	.297	51	-25	5	2	0	.958	8	S-80,3-23	-0.6
1925	Bos-N	58	174	17	49	9	4	0	23	5	6	.282	.302	.379	80	-6	2	2	-1	.906	3	S-21,2-15,P/O	0.0
1926	Bos-N	40	84	10	25	6	2	0	13	2	4	.298	.314	.417	105	-0	0			.972	2	P-33	0.0
1927	Bos-N	54	109	10	27	3	1	1	10	2	4	.248	.261	.321	60	-7	0			.966	2	P-41	0.0
1928	Bos-N	39	92	11	23	2	0	1	8	1	6	.250	.258	.304	49	-7	2			.965	3	P-38	0.0
1929	Bos-N	39	99	12	17	4	2	1	8	2	8	.172	.188	.283	16	-14	1			.986	4	P-34/S-5	0.2
1930	Bos-N	39	81	7	19	2	0	0	4	0	5	.235	.235	.259	20	-10	0			.984	2	P-38	0.0
1933	Bos-N	14	20	1	4	0	1	0	2	0	1	.200	.200	.300	45	-2	0			1.000	1	P-14	0.0
1934	Bos-N	42	36	5	9	1	0	0	3	0	1	.250	.250	.278	44	-3	0			1.000	1	P-39	0.0
1935	Bos-N	47	63	3	17	0	0	0	4	1	5	.270	.281	.270	53	-4	0			.980	-1	P-46	0.0
1936	Bos-N	35	45	1	10	2	0	0	4	0	4	.222	.222	.267	33	-4	0			1.000	1	P-35	0.0
1937	Bos-N	19	10	1	2	0	0	0	0	1	1	.200	.273	.200	33	-1	0			1.000	-1	P-18	0.0
Total	15	742	1689	154	409	64	17	5	166	52	110	.242	.265	.309	53	-117	16	13		.981	42	P-435,S-208/23O	-0.5
Team	13	647	1535	140	375	57	16	5	157	46	106	.244	.267	.312	54	-105	14	13		.980	39	P-349,S-207/32O	-0.7

■ FRED SNODGRASS Snodgrass, Frederick Carlisle "Snow" b: 10/19/1887, Ventura, Cal. d: 4/5/74, Ventura, Cal. BR/TR, 5'11.5", 175 lbs. Deb: 6/4/08

YEAR	TM/L	G	AB	R	H	2B	3B	HR	RBI	BB	SO	AVG	OBP	SLG	PRO+	BR/A	SB	CS	SBR	FA	FR	G/POS	TPR
1915	Bos-N	23	79	10	22	2	0	0	9	7	9	.278	.352	.304	104	1	0	4	-2	.938	-2	O-18/1-5	-0.5
1916	Bos-N	112	382	33	95	13	5	1	32	34	54	.249	.318	.317	100	0	14			.983	13	*O-110	0.9
Total	9	923	3101	453	852	143	42	11	351	386	359	.275	.367	.359	110	53	215	16		.965	24	O-818/1-60,C23	3.1
Team	2	135	461	43	117	15	5	1	41	41	63	.254	.324	.315	100	1	14	4		.977	12	O-128/1-5	0.4

■ POP SNYDER Snyder, Charles N. b: 10/6/1854, Washington, D.C. d: 10/29/24, Washington, D.C. BR/TR, 5'11.5", 184 lbs. Deb: 6/16/1873 MU

YEAR	TM/L	G	AB	R	H	2B	3B	HR	RBI	BB	SO	AVG	OBP	SLG	PRO+	BR/A	SB	CS	SBR	FA	FR	G/POS	TPR
1878	Bos-N	60	226	21	48	5	0	0	14	1	19	.212	.216	.235	44	-14				**.912**	5	*C-58/O-2	-0.7
1879	Bos-N	81	329	42	78	16	3	2	35	5	31	.237	.249	.322	85	-6				**.925**	**24**	*C-80/O-2	1.9
1881	Bos-N	62	219	14	50	8	0	0	16	3	23	.228	.239	.265	61	-9				.897	3	*C-60/O-1,S2	-0.4
Total	3 n	133	523	77	118	13	4	2	3	9	3	.226	.239	.277	67	-19	0	0	0			C-132/O-4D	-1.2
Total	15	797	3122	355	737	110	39	7	142	75	118	.236	.256	.303	73	-104	30	0	9	.904	148	C-744/1-45,OS2	7.5
Team	3	203	774	77	176	29	3	2	65	9	73	.227	.236	.280	66	-29	0	0	0	.913	32	C-198/O-5,2S	0.8

■ PETE SOMMERS Sommers, Joseph Andrews b: 10/26/1866, Cleveland, Ohio d: 7/22/08, Cleveland, Ohio BR/TR, 5'11.5", 181 lbs. Deb: 4/27/1887

YEAR	TM/L	G	AB	R	H	2B	3B	HR	RBI	BB	SO	AVG	OBP	SLG	PRO+	BR/A	SB	CS	SBR	FA	FR	G/POS	TPR
1888	Bos-N	4	13	1	3	1	0	0	0	0	3	.231	.231	.308	69	-0	0			.880	-0	/C-4	-0.1
Total	4	98	339	35	67	13	4	3	24	16	43	.198	.242	.286	50	-24	8			.860	-15	/C-86,O-7,1	-2.8

■ BILL SOUTHWORTH Southworth, William Frederick b: 11/10/45, Madison, Wis. BR/TR, 6'2", 205 lbs. Deb: 10/2/64

YEAR	TM/L	G	AB	R	H	2B	3B	HR	RBI	BB	SO	AVG	OBP	SLG	PRO+	BR/A	SB	CS	SBR	FA	FR	G/POS	TPR
1964	Mil-N	3	7	2	2	0	0	1	2	0	3	.286	.444	.714	219	1	0	0	0	1.000	-1	/3-2	0.0

■ BILLY SOUTHWORTH Southworth, William Harrison b: 3/9/1893, Harvard, Neb. d: 11/15/69, Columbus, Ohio BL/TR, 5'9", 170 lbs. Deb: 8/4/13 MC

YEAR	TM/L	G	AB	R	H	2B	3B	HR	RBI	BB	SO	AVG	OBP	SLG	PRO+	BR/A	SB	CS	SBR	FA	FR	G/POS	TPR
1921	Bos-N	141	569	86	175	25	15	7	79	36	13	.308	.351	.441	115	11	22	20	-5	.975	9	*O-141	0.4
1922	Bos-N	43	158	27	51	4	4	4	18	18	1	.323	.392	.475	128	7	4	1	1	.955	5	O-41	0.9
1923	Bos-N	153	611	95	195	29	16	6	78	61	23	.319	.383	.448	124	21	14	16	-5	.943	6	*O-151/2-2	1.1
Total	13	1192	4359	661	1296	173	91	52	561	402	148	.297	.359	.415	111	69	138	85	-10	.965	23	*O-1115/2-2	-0.8
Team	3	337	1338	208	421	58	35	17	175	115	37	.315	.371	.448	120	39	40	37	-10	.958	20	O-333/2-2	2.4

■ AL SPALDING Spalding, Albert Goodwill b: 9/2/1850, Byron, Ill. d: 9/9/15, San Diego, Cal. BR/TR, 6'1", 170 lbs. Deb: 5/5/1871 MH

YEAR	TM/L	G	AB	R	H	2B	3B	HR	RBI	BB	SO	AVG	OBP	SLG	PRO+	BR/A	SB	CS	SBR	FA	FR	G/POS	TPR
1871	Bos-n	31	144	43	39	10	1	1	31	8	1	.271	.309	.375	92	-2	2					*P-31/O-2	0.3
1872	Bos-n	48	244	60	87	13	5	0	48	3	1	.357	.364	.451	142	10						*P-48/O-2	0.6
1873	Bos-n	60	322	83	106	13	2	1	59	3	1	.329	.335	.391	104	-1						*P-60,O-12	0.8
1874	Bos-n	71	359	80	119	15	1	0		3		.331	.337	.379	121	6						*P-71	0.0
1875	Bos-n	74	343	68	107	12	3	0		4		.312	.320	.364	131	10						*P-72,O-10/1	0.8
Total	5 n	284	1412	334	458	63	12	2	138	21	3	.324	.334	.390	120	23						P-282/O-26,1	2.5
Total	3	127	550	83	158	21	8	0	79	9	19	.287	.299	.355	99	-4				.948	5	/P-65,1-48,2O3	-0.5

■ AL SPANGLER Spangler, Albert Donald b: 7/8/33, Philadelphia, Pa. BL/TL, 6', 175 lbs. Deb: 9/16/59 C

YEAR	TM/L	G	AB	R	H	2B	3B	HR	RBI	BB	SO	AVG	OBP	SLG	PRO+	BR/A	SB	CS	SBR	FA	FR	G/POS	TPR
1959	Mil-N	6	12	3	5	0	1	0	0	1	1	.417	.462	.583	192	2	1	0	0	1.000	-1	/O-4	0.1
1960	Mil-N	101	105	26	28	5	2	0	6	14	17	.267	.358	.352	103	1	6	2	1	.989	-14	O-92	-1.4

YEAR	TM/L	G	AB	R	H	2B	3B	HR	RBI	BB	SO	AVG	OBP	SLG	PRO+	BR/A	SB	CS	SBR	FA	FR	G/POS	TPR
1961	Mil-N	68	97	23	26	2	0	0	6	28	9	.268	.432	.289	102	2	4	2	0	1.000	-7	O-44	-0.6
Total	13	912	2267	307	594	87	26	21	175	295	234	.262	.350	.351	100	10	37	32	-8	.973	-45	O-714	-8.2
Team	3	175	214	52	59	7	3	0	12	43	27	.276	.399	.336	108	5	11	4	1	.994	-22	O-140	-1.9

■ CHET SPENCER Spencer, Chester Arthur b: 3/4/1883, S.Webster, Ohio d: 11/10/38, Portsmouth, Ohio BL/TR, 6', 180 lbs. Deb: 8/22/06

YEAR	TM/L	G	AB	R	H	2B	3B	HR	RBI	BB	SO	AVG	OBP	SLG	PRO+	BR/A	SB	CS	SBR	FA	FR	G/POS	TPR
1906	Bos-N	8	27	1	4	1	0	0	0	0		.148	.148	.185	4	-3	0			.875	-1	/O-8	-0.5

■ ED SPERBER Sperber, Edwin George b: 1/21/1895, Cincinnati, Ohio d: 1/5/76, Cincinnati, Ohio BL/TL, 5'11", 175 lbs. Deb: 4/16/24

YEAR	TM/L	G	AB	R	H	2B	3B	HR	RBI	BB	SO	AVG	OBP	SLG	PRO+	BR/A	SB	CS	SBR	FA	FR	G/POS	TPR
1924	Bos-N	24	59	8	17	2	0	1	12	10	9	.288	.400	.373	113	2	3	1	0	.897	-3	O-17	-0.2
1925	Bos-N	2	2	0	0	0	0	0	0	0	0	.000	.000	.000	-99	-1	0	0	0	.000	0	H	-0.1
Total	2	26	61	8	17	2	0	1	12	10	9	.279	.389	.361	106	1	3	1	0	.984	-3	/O-17	-0.3

■ CHARLIE SPIKES Spikes, Leslie Charles b: 1/23/51, Bogalusa, La. BR/TR, 6'3", 220 lbs. Deb: 9/1/72

YEAR	TM/L	G	AB	R	H	2B	3B	HR	RBI	BB	SO	AVG	OBP	SLG	PRO+	BR/A	SB	CS	SBR	FA	FR	G/POS	TPR
1979	Atl-N	66	93	12	26	8	0	3	21	5	30	.280	.316	.462	102	-0	0	0	0	.842	-3	O-15	-0.4
1980	Atl-N	41	36	6	10	1	0	0	2	3	18	.278	.350	.306	82	-1	0	0	0	1.000	-2	/O-7	-0.3
Total	9	670	2039	240	502	72	12	65	256	154	388	.246	.306	.389	96	-14	27	25	-7	.969	-2	O-533/D-32	-4.9
Team	2	107	129	18	36	9	0	3	23	8	48	.279	.326	.419	97	-1	0	0	0	.870	-5	/O-22	-0.7

■ AL SPOHRER Spohrer, Alfred Ray b: 12/3/02, Philadelphia, Pa. d: 7/17/72, Plymouth, N.H. BR/TR, 5'10.5", 175 lbs. Deb: 4/13/28

YEAR	TM/L	G	AB	R	H	2B	3B	HR	RBI	BB	SO	AVG	OBP	SLG	PRO+	BR/A	SB	CS	SBR	FA	FR	G/POS	TPR
1928	Bos-N	51	124	15	27	3	0	0	9	5	11	.218	.254	.242	32	-12	1			.976	-5	C-48	-1.5
1929	Bos-N	114	342	42	93	21	8	2	48	26	35	.272	.327	.398	82	-11	1			.954	-10	*C-109	-1.0
1930	Bos-N	112	356	44	113	22	8	2	37	22	24	.317	.361	.441	96	-3	3			.957	-18	*C-108	-1.0
1931	Bos-N	114	350	23	84	17	5	0	27	22	27	.240	.285	.317	64	-18	2			.982	-0	*C-111	-1.1
1932	Bos-N	104	335	31	90	12	2	0	33	15	26	.269	.300	.316	69	-15	2			.991	10	*C-100	0.1
1933	Bos-N	67	184	11	46	6	1	1	12	11	13	.250	.292	.310	78	-6	3			.972	-6	C-65	-0.9
1934	Bos-N	100	265	25	59	15	0	0	17	14	18	.223	.262	.279	49	-20	1			.977	0	C-98	-1.5
1935	Bos-N	92	260	22	63	7	1	1	16	9	12	.242	.273	.288	55	-17	0			.958	-10	C-90	-2.3
Total	8	756	2218	213	575	103	25	6	199	124	166	.259	.301	.336	70	-101	13			.972	-39	C-731	-9.3
Team	8	754	2216	213	575	103	25	6	199	124	166	.259	.301	.337	70	-101	13			.972	-39	C-729	-9.2

■ HARRY SPRATT Spratt, Henry Lee b: 7/10/1887, Broadford, Va. d: 7/3/69, Washington, D.C. BL/TR, 5'8.5", 175 lbs. Deb: 4/13/11

YEAR	TM/L	G	AB	R	H	2B	3B	HR	RBI	BB	SO	AVG	OBP	SLG	PRO+	BR/A	SB	CS	SBR	FA	FR	G/POS	TPR
1911	Bos-N	62	154	22	37	4	4	2	13	13	25	.240	.299	.357	77	-5	1			.892	-8	S-26/2-5,3O	-1.2
1912	Bos-N	27	89	6	23	3	2	3	15	7	11	.258	.313	.438	102	-0	2			.842	-13	S-23	-1.2
Total	2	89	243	28	60	7	6	5	28	20	36	.247	.304	.387	86	-6	3			.871	-22	/S-49,2-5,O3	-2.4

■ MARV STAEHLE Staehle, Marvin Gustave b: 3/13/42, Oak Park, Ill. BL/TR, 5'10", 172 lbs. Deb: 9/15/64

YEAR	TM/L	G	AB	R	H	2B	3B	HR	RBI	BB	SO	AVG	OBP	SLG	PRO+	BR/A	SB	CS	SBR	FA	FR	G/POS	TPR
1971	Atl-N	22	36	5	4	0	0	0	1	5	4	.111	.238	.111	2	-5	0	0	0	1.000	4	/2-7,3-1	0.0
Total	7	185	455	53	94	12	1	1	33	54	35	.207	.296	.244	50	-30	4	4		.971	-8	2-125/S-6,3	-3.3

■ GENERAL STAFFORD Stafford, James Joseph "Jamsey" b: 7/9/1868, Webster, Mass. d: 9/18/23, Worcester, Mass. BR/TR, 5'8", 165 lbs. Deb: 8/27/1890 F

YEAR	TM/L	G	AB	R	H	2B	3B	HR	RBI	BB	SO	AVG	OBP	SLG	PRO+	BR/A	SB	CS	SBR	FA	FR	G/POS	TPR
1898	Bos-N	37	123	21	32	2	0	1	8	4		.260	.289	.301	66	-6	3			.909	-3	O-35/1-1	-1.1
1899	Bos-N	55	182	29	55	4	2	3	40	7		.302	.328	.396	89	-4	9			.956	-9	O-41/2-5,S	-1.4
Total	8	568	2128	341	583	60	19	21	290	164		.274	.331	.350	82	-56	117			.911	-66	O-251,2-160,S/3P1	-10.6
Team	2	92	305	50	87	6	2	4	48	11		.285	.312	.357	80	-10	12			.936	-12	/O-76,S-5,21	-2.5

■ CHICK STAHL Stahl, Charles Sylvester b: 1/10/1873, Avila, Ind. d: 3/28/07, W.Baden, Ind. BL/TL, 5'10", 160 lbs. Deb: 4/19/1897 M

YEAR	TM/L	G	AB	R	H	2B	3B	HR	RBI	BB	SO	AVG	OBP	SLG	PRO+	BR/A	SB	CS	SBR	FA	FR	G/POS	TPR
1897	*Bos-N	114	469	112	166	30	13	4	97	38		.354	.406	.499	130	19	18			.928	-3	*O-111	0.6
1898	Bos-N	125	467	72	144	21	8	3	52	46		.308	.375	.407	118	10	6			.968	-2	*O-125	0.0
1899	Bos-N	148	576	122	202	23	19	7	52	72		.351	.426	.493	139	30	33			.969	6	*O-148/P-1	2.2
1900	Bos-N	136	553	88	163	23	16	5	82	34		.295	.336	.421	96	-7	27			**.968**	9	*O-135	-0.7
Total	10	1304	5069	858	1546	219	118	36	622	470		.305	.369	.416	121	133	189			.961	-7	*O-1295/P-1	3.9
Team	4	523	2065	394	675	97	56	19	283	190		.327	.387	.456	121	52	84			.960	11	O-519/P-1	2.1

■ EDDIE STANKY Stanky, Edward Raymond "The Brat" or "Muggsy" b: 9/3/16, Philadelphia, Pa. BR/TR, 5'8", 170 lbs. Deb: 4/21/43 MC

YEAR	TM/L	G	AB	R	H	2B	3B	HR	RBI	BB	SO	AVG	OBP	SLG	PRO+	BR/A	SB	CS	SBR	FA	FR	G/POS	TPR
1948	*Bos-N†	67	247	49	79	14	2	2	29	61	13	.320	.455	.417	140	18	3			.981	5	2-66	2.6
1949	Bos-N	138	506	90	144	24	5	1	42	113	41	.285	.417	.358	116	19	3			.979	-9	*2-135	1.6
Total	11	1259	4301	811	1154	185	35	29	364	996	374	.268	.410	.348	109	116	48			.975	4	*2-1152/S-51,3	18.4
Team	2	205	753	139	223	38	7	3	71	174	54	.296	.429	.377	124	37	6			.980	-4	2-201	4.2

■ JOE STANLEY Stanley, Joseph Bernard b: 4/2/1881, Washington, D.C. d: 9/13/67, Detroit, Mich. BB/TR, 5'9.5", 150 lbs. Deb: 9/11/1897 F

YEAR	TM/L	G	AB	R	H	2B	3B	HR	RBI	BB	SO	AVG	OBP	SLG	PRO+	BR/A	SB	CS	SBR	FA	FR	G/POS	TPR
1903	Bos-N	86	308	40	77	12	5	1	47	18		.250	.306	.331	85	-6	10			.902	3	O-77/P-1,S	-0.7
1904	Bos-N	3	8	0	0	0	0	0	0	0		.000	.000	.000	-99	-2	0			.800	1	/O-3	-0.2
Total	7	216	694	77	148	15	10	2	76	51		.213	.275	.272	66	-28	20			.918	-6	O-189/P-3,S	-4.7
Team	2	89	316	40	77	12	5	1	47	18		.244	.299	.323	81	-8	10			.899	4	/O-80,S-1,P	-0.9

■ CHARLIE STARR Starr, Charles Watkin b: 8/30/1878, Pike Co., Ohio d: 10/18/37, Pasadena, Cal. TR, Deb: 4/29/05

YEAR	TM/L	G	AB	R	H	2B	3B	HR	RBI	BB	SO	AVG	OBP	SLG	PRO+	BR/A	SB	CS	SBR	FA	FR	G/POS	TPR
1909	Bos-N	61	216	16	48	2	3	0	6	31		.222	.333	.259	80	-4	7			.931	-9	2-54/S-6,3	-1.5
Total	3	110	375	33	79	4	3	0	20	51		.211	.315	.237	72	-10	13			.932	-18	/2-84,S-11,3	-3.3

■ HARRY STEINFELDT Steinfeldt, Harry M. b: 9/29/1877, St.Louis, Mo. d: 8/17/14, Bellevue, Ky. BR/TR, 5'9.5", 180 lbs. Deb: 4/22/1898

YEAR	TM/L	G	AB	R	H	2B	3B	HR	RBI	BB	SO	AVG	OBP	SLG	PRO+	BR/A	SB	CS	SBR	FA	FR	G/POS	TPR
1911	Bos-N	19	63	5	16	4	0	1	8	6	3	.254	.338	.365	89	-1	1			.810	-5	3-19	-0.6
Total	14	1646	5896	758	1576	284	90	27	762	471	32	.267	.330	.360	101	-4	194			.926	38	*3-1386,2-187/OS1	7.4

■ FRED STEM Stem, Frederick Boothe b: 9/22/1885, Oxford, N.C. d: 9/5/64, Darlington, S.C. BL/TR, 6'2", 160 lbs. Deb: 9/15/08

YEAR	TM/L	G	AB	R	H	2B	3B	HR	RBI	BB	SO	AVG	OBP	SLG	PRO+	BR/A	SB	CS	SBR	FA	FR	G/POS	TPR
1908	Bos-N	20	72	9	20	0	1	0	3	2		.278	.297	.306	94	-1	1			.995	-1	1-19	-0.2
1909	Bos-N	73	245	13	51	2	3	0	11	12		.208	.254	.241	51	-14	5			.989	10	1-68	-0.5
Total	2	93	317	22	71	2	4	0	14	14		.224	.263	.256	60	-15	6			.990	10	/1-87	-0.7

■ CASEY STENGEL Stengel, Charles Dillon "The Old Professor"
b: 7/30/1890, Kansas City, Mo. d: 9/29/75, Glendale, Cal. BL/TL, 5'11", 175 lbs. Deb: 9/17/12 MCH

YEAR	TM/L	G	AB	R	H	2B	3B	HR	RBI	BB	SO	AVG	OBP	SLG	PRO+	BR/A	SB	CS	SBR	FA	FR	G/POS	TPR
1924	Bos-N	131	461	57	129	20	6	5	39	45	39	.280	.348	.382	100	0	13	13	-4	.978	-7	*O-126	-1.9
1925	Bos-N	12	13	0	1	0	0	0	2	1	2	.077	.143	.077	-46	-3	0	1	-1	1.000	-0	/O-1	-0.4
Total	14	1277	4288	575	1219	182	89	60	535	437	453	.284	.356	.410	119	107	131	43		.964	-9	*O-1183	1.9
Team	2	143	474	57	130	20	6	5	41	46	41	.274	.342	.373	96	-3	13	14		.978	-7	O-127	-2.3

■ JACK STIVETTS Stivetts, John Elmer "Happy Jack" b: 3/31/1868, Ashland, Pa. d: 4/18/30, Ashland, Pa. BR/TR, 6'2", 185 lbs. Deb: 6/26/1889

YEAR	TM/L	G	AB	R	H	2B	3B	HR	RBI	BB	SO	AVG	OBP	SLG	PRO+	BR/A	SB	CS	SBR	FA	FR	G/POS	TPR
1892	*Bos-N	71	240	40	71	14	2	3	36	27	28	.296	.369	.408	124	6	8			.904	-0	P-54,O-18/1	0.0
1893	Bos-N	50	172	32	51	5	6	3	25	12	14	.297	.342	.448	101	-1	6			.955	-4	P-38/O-8,3	-0.2
1894	Bos-N	68	244	55	80	12	7	8	64	16	21	.328	.369	.533	107	0	3			.943	-4	P-45,O-16/1	-0.1
1895	Bos-N	46	158	20	30	6	4	0	24	6	18	.190	.220	.278	26	-19	1			.961	-1	P-38/1-5,O	-0.3
1896	Bos-N	67	221	42	76	9	6	3	49	12	10	.344	.380	.480	119	5	4			.946	-6	P-42,O-12/13	-0.2
1897	*Bos-N	61	199	41	73	9	9	2	37	15		.367	.417	.533	141	11	2			.926	-3	O-29,P-18/21	0.1
1898	Bos-N	41	111	16	28	1	1	2	16	10		.252	.314	.333	81	-3	1			.909	-5	O-14,1-10/S2P	-0.8
Total	11	601	1991	347	592	84	46	35	314	133	136	.297	.344	.438	104	-7	31			.924	-17	P-388,O-141/1S32	-1.9
Team	7	404	1345	246	409	56	35	21	251	98	91	.304	.353	.445	104	-1	25			.939	-24	P-237/O-99,1S23	-1.5

YEAR	TM/L	G	AB	R	H	2B	3B	HR	RBI	BB	SO	AVG	OBP	SLG	PRO+	BR/A	SB	CS	SBR	FA	FR	G/POS	TPR

■ HARRY STOVEY　Stovey, Harry Duffield (b: Harry Duffield Stowe)　b: 12/20/1856, Philadelphia, Pa.　d: 9/20/37, New Bedford, Mass.　BR/TR, 5'11.5", 175 lbs.　Deb: 5/1/1880　M

1891	Bos-N	134	544	118	152	31	**20**	**16**	95	78	69	.279	.372	**.498**	136	21	57			.910	9	*O-134/1-1	2.2
1892	Bos-N	38	146	21	24	8	1	0	12	14	19	.164	.252	.233	43	-11	20			.901	0	O-38	-1.1
Total	14	1486	6138	1492	1770	347	174	122	549	662	343	.288	.361	.461	141	293	509			.896	40	O-944,1-550/P	21.4
Team	2	172	690	139	176	39	21	16	107	92	88	.255	.347	.442	118	10	77			.908	9	O-172/1-1	1.1

■ PAUL STRAND　Strand, Paul Edward　b: 12/19/1893, Carbonado, Wash.　d: 7/2/74, Salt Lake City, Utah　BL/TL, 6'0.5", 190 lbs.　Deb: 5/15/13

1913	Bos-N	7	6	0	1	0	0	0	0	0	0	.167	.167	.167	-5	-1	0			.875	0	/P-7	0.0
1914	Bos-N	18	24	2	8	2	0	0	3	0	2	.333	.333	.417	123	1	0			.813	-0	P-16	0.0
1915	Bos-N	24	22	3	2	0	0	0	2	0	4	.091	.091	.091	-47	-4	0			.750	-1	/P-6,O-5	-0.2
Total	4	96	219	20	49	11	4	0	18	4	15	.224	.244	.311	41	-18	3			.989	-7	/O-49,P-29	-2.4
Team	3	49	52	5	11	2	0	0	5	0	6	.212	.212	.250	38	-4	0			.821	-1	/P-29,O-5	-0.2

■ GABBY STREET　Street, Charles Evard "Old Sarge"　b: 9/30/1882, Huntsville, Ala.　d: 2/6/51, Joplin, Mo.　BR/TR, 5'11", 180 lbs.　Deb: 9/13/04　MC

| 1905 | Bos-N | 3 | 12 | 0 | 2 | 0 | 0 | 0 | | | | .167 | .167 | .167 | -1 | -1 | 0 | | | .778 | -2 | /C-3 | -0.4 |
| Total | 8 | 504 | 1501 | 98 | 312 | 44 | 11 | 2 | 105 | 119 | | .208 | .273 | .256 | 66 | -60 | 17 | | | .974 | 32 | C-493 | 2.0 |

■ JOE STRIPP　Stripp, Joseph Valentine "Jersey Joe"　b: 2/3/03, Harrison, N.J.　d: 6/10/89, Orlando, Fla.　BR/TR, 5'11.5", 175 lbs.　Deb: 7/2/28

| 1938 | Bos-N | 59 | 229 | 19 | 63 | 10 | 0 | 1 | 19 | 10 | 7 | .275 | .305 | .332 | 84 | -6 | 2 | | | .966 | 1 | 3-58 | -0.4 |
| Total | 11 | 1146 | 4211 | 575 | 1238 | 219 | 43 | 24 | 464 | 280 | 226 | .294 | .340 | .384 | 96 | -27 | 50 | | | .961 | 21 | 3-914,1-163/OS2 | 1.7 |

■ ALLIE STROBEL　Strobel, Albert Irving　b: 6/11/1884, Boston, Mass.　d: 2/10/55, Hollywood, Fla.　BR/TR, 6', 160 lbs.　Deb: 8/29/05

1905	Bos-N	5	19	1	2	0	0	0	2	0		.105	.105	.105	-38	-3	0			1.000	-0	/3-4,O-1	-0.4
1906	Bos-N	100	317	28	64	10	3	1	24	29		.202	.273	.262	69	-12	2			.946	-6	2-93/S-6,O	-1.8
Total	2	105	336	29	66	10	3	1	26	29		.196	.264	.253	63	-15	2			1.000	-6	/2-93,S-6,3O	-2.2

■ BOBBY STURGEON　Sturgeon, Robert Howard　b: 8/6/19, Clinton, Ind.　BR/TR, 6', 175 lbs.　Deb: 4/16/40

| 1948 | Bos-N | 34 | 78 | 10 | 17 | 3 | 1 | 0 | 4 | 4 | 5 | .218 | .256 | .282 | 46 | -6 | 0 | | | .938 | -3 | 2-18/S-4,3 | -0.9 |
| Total | 6 | 420 | 1220 | 106 | 313 | 48 | 12 | 1 | 80 | 34 | 79 | .257 | .277 | .318 | 68 | -56 | 7 | | | .951 | 14 | S-283,2-102/3 | -2.2 |

■ ANDY SULLIVAN　Sullivan, Andrew R.　b: 8/30/1884, Southborough, Mass　d: 2/14/20, Framingham, Mass.　TR ,　Deb: 9/13/04

| 1904 | Bos-N | 1 | 1 | 0 | 0 | 0 | 0 | 0 | 0 | 0 | 1 | .000 | .500 | .000 | 61 | 0 | 0 | | | 1.000 | -0 | /S-1 | 0.0 |

■ DENNY SULLIVAN　Sullivan, Dennis J.　b: 6/26/1858, Boston, Mass.　d: 12/31/25, Boston, Mass.　TR , 5'9", 170 lbs.　Deb: 8/25/1879

| 1880 | Bos-N | 1 | 4 | 1 | 1 | 0 | 0 | 0 | 1 | 0 | 1 | .250 | .250 | .250 | 72 | -0 | | | | .857 | -1 | /C-1 | -0.1 |
| Total | 2 | 6 | 23 | 6 | 6 | 2 | 0 | 0 | 3 | 1 | 2 | .261 | .292 | .348 | 110 | 0 | | | | .908 | -4 | /3-4,C-1,O | -0.4 |

■ JOHN SULLIVAN　Sullivan, John Lawrence　b: 3/21/1890, Williamsport, Pa.　d: 4/1/66, Milton, Pa.　BR/TR, 5'11", 180 lbs.　Deb: 4/18/20

1920	Bos-N	81	250	36	74	14	4	1	28	29	29	.296	.374	.396	126	9	3	2	-0	.977	-2	O-66/1-6	0.3
1921	Bos-N	5	5	0	0	0	0	0	0	0	0	.000	.000	.000	-99	-1	0	0	0	.000	0	H	-0.1
Total	2	162	495	64	153	28	8	5	69	48	55	.309	.374	.428	123	16	6	7	-2	.969	-9	O-132/1-6	-0.3
Team	2	86	255	36	74	14	4	1	28	29	29	.290	.367	.388	122	8	3	2	-0	.977	-2	/O-66,1-6	0.2

■ MARTY SULLIVAN　Sullivan, Martin C.　b: 10/20/1862, Lowell, Mass.　d: 1/6/1894, Lowell, Mass.　BR/TR ,　Deb: 4/30/1887

1890	Bos-N	121	505	82	144	19	7	6	61	56	48	.285	.355	.386	108	3	33			.951	4	*O-120/3-1	0.3
1891	Bos-N	17	67	15	15	1	0	2	7	5	3	.224	.288	.328	71	-3	7			.926	-2	O-17	-0.5
Total	5	398	1618	280	441	56	32	26	220	162	168	.273	.341	.395	104	3	99			.909	-7	O-392/1-5,3P	-1.4
Team	2	138	572	97	159	20	7	8	68	61	51	.278	.349	.379	103	0	40			.949	2	/O-137/3-1	-0.2

■ BILLY SULLIVAN　Sullivan, William Joseph Sr.　b: 2/1/1875, Oakland, Wis.　d: 1/28/65, Newberg, Ore.　BR/TR, 5'9", 155 lbs.　Deb: 9/13/1899　FM

1899	Bos-N	22	74	10	20	2	0	2	12	1		.270	.308	.378	80	-2	2			.952	5	C-22	0.4
1900	Bos-N	72	238	36	65	6	0	8	41	9		.273	.302	.399	83	-7	4			.974	-5	C-66/S-1,2	-0.1
Total	16	1147	3647	363	777	119	33	21	378	170		.213	.254	.281	63	-172	98			.976	-8	*C-1122/1-4,032S	-8.3
Team	2	94	312	46	85	8	0	10	53	10		.272	.304	.394	82	-10	6			.968	5	/C-88,2-1,S	0.3

■ BUTCH SUTCLIFFE　Sutcliffe, Charles Inigo　b: 7/22/15, Fall River, Mass.　d: 3/2/94, Fall River, Mass.　BR/TR, 5'8.5", 165 lbs.　Deb: 8/28/38

| 1938 | Bos-N | 4 | 4 | 1 | 1 | 0 | 0 | 0 | 2 | 2 | | .250 | .500 | .250 | 124 | 0 | 0 | | | .800 | 0 | /C-3 | 0.1 |

■ EZRA SUTTON　Sutton, Ezra Ballou　b: 9/17/1850, Palmyra, N.Y.　d: 6/20/07, Braintree, Mass.　BR/TR, 5'8.5", 153 lbs.　Deb: 5/4/1871

1877	Bos-N	58	253	43	74	10	6	0	39	4	10	.292	.304	.379	110	2				.882	-9	S-36,3-22	-0.4
1878	Bos-N	60	239	31	54	9	3	1	29	2	14	.226	.232	.301	69	-9				.888	-1	*3-59/S-1	-0.7
1879	Bos-N	84	339	54	84	13	4	0	34	2	18	.248	.252	.310	82	-7				.884	-12	S-51,3-33	-1.4
1880	Bos-N	76	288	41	72	9	2	0	25	7	7	.250	.268	.295	94	-2				.896	4	S-39,3-37	0.6
1881	Bos-N	83	333	43	97	12	4	0	31	13	9	.291	.318	.351	116	6				.877	-3	*3-81/S-2	0.4
1882	Bos-N	81	319	44	80	8	1	2	38	24	25	.251	.303	.301	94	-1				.856	-5	*3-77/S-4	-0.3
1883	Bos-N	94	414	101	134	28	15	3	73	17	12	.324	.350	.486	147	22				.866	-1	*3-93/O-1,S	1.8
1884	Bos-N	110	468	102	**162**	28	7	3	61	29	22	.346	.384	.456	164	34				**.908**	-4	*3-110	2.7
1885	Bos-N	110	457	78	143	23	8	4	47	17	25	.313	.338	.425	151	24				.875	-0	*3-91,S-16/21	2.4
1886	Bos-N	116	499	83	138	21	6	3	48	26	21	.277	.312	.361	108	5	18			.859	-5	O-43,S-28,32	0.0
1887	Bos-N	77	326	58	99	14	9	3	46	13	6	.304	.342	.429	113	5	17			.875	15	S-37,O-18,23	1.7
1888	Bos-N	28	110	16	24	3	1	1	16	7	3	.218	.237	.291	80	-2	10			.859	-5	3-27/S-1	-0.7
Total	5 n	232	1080	253	344	39	24	6	65	5	3	.319	.322	.413	123	22	5					3-202/S-28,P2O1	1.1
Total	13	1031	4281	739	1231	190	73	21	518	164	174	.288	.315	.381	118	88	45			.871	-30	3-677,S-216/O21	6.6
Team	12	977	4045	694	1161	178	66	20	487	161	172	.287	.316	.378	117	78	45			.874	-27	3-669,S-216/O21	6.1

■ CHARLIE SWEASY　Sweasy, Charles James (b: Charles James Swasey)　b: 11/2/1847, Newark, N.J.　d: 3/30/08, Newark, N.J.　BR/TR, 5'9", 172 lbs.　Deb: 5/19/1871　M

1873	Bos-n	1	4	0	1	0	0	0	0	0	0	.250	.250	.250	44	-0						/2-1	0.0
Total	5 n	55	228	26	47	2	0	0	10	9	1	.206	.236	.215	49	-11						/2-51,O-2	-1.1
Total	2	111	437	41	83	8	2	0	18	9	28	.190	.206	.217	44	-24				.855	-6	2-110/O-1	-2.4

■ BILL SWEENEY　Sweeney, William John　b: 3/6/1886, Covington, Ky.　d: 5/26/48, Cambridge, Mass.　BR/TR, 5'11", 175 lbs.　Deb: 6/14/07

1907	Bos-N	58	191	24	50	2	0	0	18	15		.262	.316	.272	85	-3	8			.871	0	3-23,S-15,O/21	-0.3
1908	Bos-N	127	418	44	102	15	3	0	40	45		.244	.317	.294	97	-0	17			.930	12	*3-123/S-3,2	1.8
1909	Bos-N	138	493	44	120	19	3	1	36	37		.243	.296	.300	81	-11	25			.903	8	*3-112,S-26	0.1
1910	Bos-N	150	499	43	133	22	4	5	46	61	28	.267	.349	.357	101	1	25			.903	-1	*S-110,3-21,1	0.5
1911	Bos-N	137	523	92	164	33	6	3	63	77	26	.314	.404	.417	120	15	33			.944	11	*2-136	2.4
1912	Bos-N	153	593	88	204	31	13	1	100	68	34	.344	.416	.445	133	29	27			.959	**27**	*2-153	5.0
1913	Bos-N	139	502	65	129	17	6	0	47	66	50	.257	.347	.315	88	-6	18			.939	1	*2-137	-0.7
Total	8	1039	3692	442	1004	153	40	11	389	423	153	.272	.349	.344	100	8	172			.949	69	2-566,3-279,S/10	7.9
Team	7	902	3219	396	902	139	35	10	350	369	138	.280	.356	.354	105	25	153			.948	58	2-432,3-279,S/10	8.8

■ CHUCK TANNER　Tanner, Charles William　b: 7/4/29, New Castle, Pa.　BL/TL, 6', 185 lbs.　Deb: 4/12/55　FM

| 1955 | Mil-N | 97 | 243 | 27 | 60 | 9 | 3 | 6 | 27 | 27 | 32 | .247 | .322 | .383 | 91 | -3 | 0 | 0 | 0 | .981 | -4 | O-62 | -1.0 |
| 1956 | Mil-N | 60 | 63 | 6 | 15 | 2 | 0 | 1 | 4 | 10 | 10 | .238 | .342 | .317 | 84 | -3 | 0 | 0 | 0 | .800 | -3 | /O-8 | -0.4 |

YEAR	TM/L	G	AB	R	H	2B	3B	HR	RBI	BB	SO	AVG	OBP	SLG	PRO+	BR/A	SB	CS	SBR	FA	FR	G/POS	TPR
1957	Mil-N	22	69	5	17	3	0	2	6	5	4	.246	.297	.377	86	-2	0	0	0	1.000	-0	O-18	-0.3
Total	8	396	885	98	231	39	5	21	105	82	93	.261	.325	.388	93	-10	2	2	-1	.983	-13	O-202	-3.2
Team	3	179	375	38	92	14	3	9	37	42	46	.245	.321	.371	89	-6	0	0	0	.980	-7	/O-88	-1.7

■ TONY TARASCO Tarasco, Anthony Giacinto b: 12/9/70, New York, N.Y. BL/TR, 6', 185 lbs. Deb: 4/30/93

YEAR	TM/L	G	AB	R	H	2B	3B	HR	RBI	BB	SO	AVG	OBP	SLG	PRO+	BR/A	SB	CS	SBR	FA	FR	G/POS	TPR
1993	*Atl-N	24	35	6	8	2	0	0	2	0	5	.229	.250	.286	43	-3	0	1	-1	1.000	-3	O-12	-0.6
1994	Atl-N	87	132	16	36	6	0	5	19	9	17	.273	.319	.432	91	-2	5	0	2	1.000	-8	O-45	-0.8
Total	3	237	605	86	153	26	4	19	61	60	100	.253	.323	.403	88	-11	29	4	6	.983	-4	O-173	-1.2
Team	2	111	167	22	44	8	0	5	21	9	22	.263	.305	.401	82	-5	5	1	1	1.000	-10	/O-57	-1.4

■ POP TATE Tate, Edward Christopher "Dimples" b: 12/22/1860, Richmond, Va. d: 6/25/32, Richmond, Va. BR/TL, 5'10", 178 lbs. Deb: 9/26/1885

YEAR	TM/L	G	AB	R	H	2B	3B	HR	RBI	BB	SO	AVG	OBP	SLG	PRO+	BR/A	SB	CS	SBR	FA	FR	G/POS	TPR
1885	Bos-N	4	13	1	2	0	0	0	2	1	3	.154	.214	.154	21	-1				.865	1	/C-4	0.0
1886	Bos-N	31	106	13	24	3	1	0	3	7	17	.226	.274	.274	70	-4	0			.885	-4	C-31	-0.3
1887	Bos-N	60	231	34	60	5	3	0	27	8	9	.260	.296	.307	68	-10	7			.924	13	C-53/O-8	0.7
1888	Bos-N	41	148	18	34	7	1	1	6	8	7	.230	.278	.311	86	-2	3			.854	-3	C-41/O-1	-0.1
Total	6	227	822	101	179	22	9	2	65	41	73	.218	.269	.274	58	-43	17			.905	3	C-202/1-18,O	-1.9
Team	4	136	498	66	120	15	5	1	38	24	36	.241	.284	.297	72	-17	10			.889	8	C-129/O-9	0.3

■ BEN TAYLOR Taylor, Benjamin Eugene b: 9/30/27, Metropolis, Ill. BL/TL, 6', 175 lbs. Deb: 7/29/51

YEAR	TM/L	G	AB	R	H	2B	3B	HR	RBI	BB	SO	AVG	OBP	SLG	PRO+	BR/A	SB	CS	SBR	FA	FR	G/POS	TPR
1955	Mil-N	12	10	2	1	0	0	0	0	2	4	.100	.250	.100	-3	-1	0	0	0	1.000	-0	/1-1	-0.2
Total	3	52	121	16	28	2	1	3	6	11	31	.231	.306	.339	73	-5	1	1		.976	-2	/1-30	-0.9

■ ED TAYLOR Taylor, Edward James b: 11/17/01, Chicago, Ill. d: 1/30/92, Chula Vista, Cal. BR/TR, 5'6.5", 160 lbs. Deb: 4/14/26

YEAR	TM/L	G	AB	R	H	2B	3B	HR	RBI	BB	SO	AVG	OBP	SLG	PRO+	BR/A	SB	CS	SBR	FA	FR	G/POS	TPR
1926	Bos-N	92	272	37	73	8	2	0	33	38	26	.268	.368	.313	93	-1	4			.945	-1	3-62,S-33	0.4

■ ZACK TAYLOR Taylor, James Wren b: 7/27/1898, Yulee, Fla. d: 9/19/74, Orlando, Fla. BR/TR, 5'11.5", 180 lbs. Deb: 6/15/20 MC

YEAR	TM/L	G	AB	R	H	2B	3B	HR	RBI	BB	SO	AVG	OBP	SLG	PRO+	BR/A	SB	CS	SBR	FA	FR	G/POS	TPR
1926	Bos-N	125	432	36	110	22	3	0	42	28	27	.255	.303	.319	74	-17	1			.985	2	*C-123	-0.7
1927	Bos-N	30	96	8	23	2	1	1	14	8	5	.240	.298	.313	69	-4	0			.988	12	C-27	0.9
1928	Bos-N	125	399	36	100	15	1	2	30	33	29	.251	.313	.308	66	-20	2			.985	-12	*C-124	-2.1
1929	Bos-N	34	101	8	25	7	0	0	10	7	9	.248	.303	.317	56	-7	0			.965	6	C-31	0.2
Total	16	918	2865	258	748	113	28	9	311	161	192	.261	.304	.329	68	-135	9			.977	1	C-856	-8.3
Team	4	314	1028	88	258	46	5	3	96	76	70	.251	.306	.314	69	-48	3			.983	8	C-305	-1.7

■ HAWK TAYLOR Taylor, Robert Dale b: 4/3/39, Metropolis, Ill. BR/TR, 6'2", 190 lbs. Deb: 6/9/57

YEAR	TM/L	G	AB	R	H	2B	3B	HR	RBI	BB	SO	AVG	OBP	SLG	PRO+	BR/A	SB	CS	SBR	FA	FR	G/POS	TPR
1957	Mil-N	7	1	2	0	0	0	0	0	0	0	.000	.000	.000	-99	-0	0	0	0	.000	0	/C-1	0.0
1958	Mil-N	4	8	1	1	1	0	0	0	0	3	.125	.125	.250	-4	-1	0	0	0	1.000	-0	/O-4	-0.2
1961	Mil-N	20	26	1	5	0	0	1	1	3	11	.192	.276	.308	58	-2	0	1	-1	1.000	0	/O-5,C-1	-0.2
1962	Mil-N	20	47	3	12	0	0	0	2	2	10	.255	.286	.255	48	-3	0	1	-1	.960	1	O-11	-0.3
1963	Mil-N	16	29	1	2	0	0	0	0	1	12	.069	.100	.069	-51	-6	0	0	0	1.000	-0	/O-8	-0.7
Total	11	394	724	56	158	25	0	16	82	36	146	.218	.259	.319	62	-38	0	3	-2	.984	-1	C-131/O-62,1	-4.2
Team	5	67	111	8	20	1	0	1	3	6	36	.180	.222	.216	21	-12	0	2	-1	.981	1	/O-28,C-2	-1.4

■ FRED TENNEY Tenney, Frederick b: 11/26/1871, Georgetown, Mass. d: 7/3/52, Boston, Mass. BL/TL, 5'9", 155 lbs. Deb: 6/16/1894 M

YEAR	TM/L	G	AB	R	H	2B	3B	HR	RBI	BB	SO	AVG	OBP	SLG	PRO+	BR/A	SB	CS	SBR	FA	FR	G/POS	TPR
1894	Bos-N	27	86	23	34	7	1	2	21	12	9	.395	.469	.570	139	5	6			.893	-0	C-20/O-6,1	0.5
1895	Bos-N	49	173	35	47	9	1	1	21	24	5	.272	.360	.353	78	-6	6			.885	-4	O-28,C-21	-0.8
1896	Bos-N	88	348	64	117	14	3	2	49	36	12	.336	.400	.411	108	4	18			.957	1	O-60,C-27	0.3
1897	*Bos-N	132	566	125	180	24	3	1	85	49		.318	.376	.376	93	-6	34			.988	5	*1-128/O-4	0.0
1898	Bos-N	117	488	106	160	25	5	0	62	33		.328	.370	.400	114	8	23			.980	5	*1-117/C-1	1.1
1899	Bos-N	150	603	115	209	19	17	1	67	63		.347	.411	.439	122	17	28			.978	10	*1-150	2.5
1900	Bos-N	112	437	77	122	13	5	1	56	39		.279	.346	.339	80	-13	17			.981	9	*1-111	-0.4
1901	Bos-N	115	451	66	127	13	1	1	22	37		.282	.340	.322	85	-9	15			.976	7	*1-113/C-2	-0.3
1902	Bos-N	134	489	88	154	18	3	2	30	73		.315	.409	.376	141	28	21			**.985**	13	*1-134	3.9
1903	Bos-N	122	447	79	140	22	3	3	41	70		.313	.415	.396	137	26	21			.974	8	*1-122	3.1
1904	Bos-N	147	533	76	144	17	9	1	37	57		.270	.351	.341	118	13	17			.986	8	*1-144/O-4	1.9
1905	Bos-N	149	549	84	158	18	3	0	28	67		.288	.368	.332	111	11	17			.982	22	*1-148/P-1M	2.9
1906	Bos-N	143	544	61	154	12	8	1	28	58		.283	.357	.340	121	15	17			.983	10	*1-143,M	2.2
1907	Bos-N	150	554	83	151	18	8	0	26	82		.273	.371	.334	121	17	15			.989	9	*1-149,M	2.5
1911	Bos-N	102	369	52	97	13	4	1	36	50	17	.263	.352	.328	84	-7	5			.985	2	1-96/O-2M	-0.5
Total	17	1994	7595	1278	2231	270	77	22	688	874	43	.294	.371	.358	109	107	285			.983	124	*1-1810,O-104/CP	20.9
Team	15	1737	6637	1134	1994	242	74	17	609	750	43	.300	.376	.367	110	104	260			.982	105	*1-1556,O-104/CP	18.9

■ FRANK TEPEDINO Tepedino, Frank Ronald b: 11/23/47, Brooklyn, N.Y. BL/TL, 5'11", 192 lbs. Deb: 5/12/67

YEAR	TM/L	G	AB	R	H	2B	3B	HR	RBI	BB	SO	AVG	OBP	SLG	PRO+	BR/A	SB	CS	SBR	FA	FR	G/POS	TPR
1973	Atl-N	74	148	20	45	5	0	4	29	13	21	.304	.360	.419	107	1	0	0	0	.992	2	1-58	0.1
1974	Atl-N	78	169	11	39	5	1	0	16	9	13	.231	.274	.272	51	-11	1	2	-1	.988	1	1-46	-1.4
1975	Atl-N	8	7	0	0	0	0	0	0	1	2	.000	.125	.000	-61	-2	0	0	0	.000	0	H	-0.2
Total	8	265	507	50	122	13	1	6	58	33	61	.241	.290	.306	65	-24	4	5		.989	4	1-134/O-15	-3.1
Team	3	160	324	31	84	10	1	4	45	23	36	.259	.310	.333	75	-11	1	2		.990	3	1-104	-1.5

■ ZEB TERRY Terry, Zebulon Alexander b: 6/17/1891, Denison, Tex. d: 3/14/88, Los Angeles, Cal. BR/TR, 5'8", 129 lbs. Deb: 4/12/16

YEAR	TM/L	G	AB	R	H	2B	3B	HR	RBI	BB	SO	AVG	OBP	SLG	PRO+	BR/A	SB	CS	SBR	FA	FR	G/POS	TPR
1918	Bos-N	28	105	17	32	2	2	0	8	8	14	.305	.360	.362	125	3	1			.977	8	S-27	1.4
Total	7	640	2327	254	605	90	24	2	216	179	133	.260	.318	.322	78	-64	32			.956	-5	S-322,2-310/3	-6.5

■ TOMMY THEVENOW Thevenow, Thomas Joseph b: 9/6/03, Madison, Ind. d: 7/29/57, Madison, Ind. BR/TR, 5'10", 155 lbs. Deb: 9/4/24

YEAR	TM/L	G	AB	R	H	2B	3B	HR	RBI	BB	SO	AVG	OBP	SLG	PRO+	BR/A	SB	CS	SBR	FA	FR	G/POS	TPR
1937	Bos-N	21	34	5	4	0	1	0	2	4	2	.118	.211	.176	7	-4	0			.969	1	S-12/3-6,2	-0.3
Total	15	1229	4164	380	1030	124	32	2	456	210	222	.247	.285	.294	52	-292	23			.950	9	S-848,2-188,3/1	-17.9

■ ANDRES THOMAS Thomas, Andres Perez (b: Andres Perez (Thomas)) b: 11/10/63, Boca Chica, D.R. BR/TR, 6'1", 185 lbs. Deb: 9/3/85

YEAR	TM/L	G	AB	R	H	2B	3B	HR	RBI	BB	SO	AVG	OBP	SLG	PRO+	BR/A	SB	CS	SBR	FA	FR	G/POS	TPR
1985	Atl-N	15	18	6	5	0	0	0	2	0	2	.278	.278	.278	53	-1	0	0	0	.920	3	S-10	0.2
1986	Atl-N	102	323	26	81	17	2	6	32	8	49	.251	.269	.372	71	-14	4	6	-2	.958	26	S-97	1.8
1987	Atl-N	82	324	29	75	11	0	5	39	14	50	.231	.268	.312	50	-23	6	5	-1	.953	9	S-81	-0.8
1988	Atl-N	153	606	54	153	22	2	13	68	14	95	.252	.271	.360	76	-20	7	3	0	.959	-8	*S-150	-1.7
1989	Atl-N	141	554	41	118	18	0	13	57	12	62	.213	.230	.316	53	-35	3	3	-1	.956	6	*S-138	-2.0
1990	Atl-N	84	278	26	61	8	0	5	30	11	43	.219	.249	.302	48	-20	2	1	0	.967	3	S-72/3-5	-1.2
Total	6	577	2103	182	493	76	4	42	228	59	301	.234	.256	.334	61	-113	22	18	-4	.958	38	S-548/3-5	-3.7

■ FRANK THOMAS Thomas, Frank Joseph b: 6/11/29, Pittsburgh, Pa. BR/TR, 6'3", 205 lbs. Deb: 8/17/51

YEAR	TM/L	G	AB	R	H	2B	3B	HR	RBI	BB	SO	AVG	OBP	SLG	PRO+	BR/A	SB	CS	SBR	FA	FR	G/POS	TPR
1961	Mil-N	124	423	58	120	13	3	25	67	29	70	.284	.338	.506	128	15	2	4	-2	.954	-0	*O-109,1-11	0.7
1965	Mil-N	15	33	3	7	3	0	0	1	2	11	.212	.257	.303	57	-2	0	0	0	.979	-1	/1-6,O-3	-0.3
Total	16	1766	6285	792	1671	262	31	286	962	484	894	.266	.323	.454	108	52	15	22	-9	.978	-31	*O-1045,3-394,1/2	-5.1
Team	2	139	456	61	127	16	3	25	68	31	81	.279	.333	.491	123	13	2	4	-2	.954	-1	O-112/1-17	0.4

■ HERB THOMAS Thomas, Herbert Mark b: 5/26/02, Sampson City, Fla. d: 12/4/91, Starke, Fla. BR/TR, 5'4.5", 157 lbs. Deb: 8/28/24

YEAR	TM/L	G	AB	R	H	2B	3B	HR	RBI	BB	SO	AVG	OBP	SLG	PRO+	BR/A	SB	CS	SBR	FA	FR	G/POS	TPR
1924	Bos-N	32	127	12	28	4	1	1	8	9	8	.220	.288	.291	58	-8	5	2	0	.983	8	O-32	-0.1
1925	Bos-N	5	17	2	4	0	1	0	0	2	0	.235	.350	.353	88	-0	0	1	-1	.963	-1	/2-5	-0.2

YEAR TM/L	G	AB	R	H	2B	3B	HR	RBI	BB	SO	AVG	OBP	SLG	PRO+	BR/A	SB	CS	SBR	FA	FR	G/POS	TPR
1927 Bos-N	24	74	11	17	6	1	0	6	3	9	.230	.269	.338	67	-4	2			.972	-11	2-17/S-2	-1.4
Total 3	74	235	27	52	11	4	1	15	15	18	.221	.285	.315	63	-13	7	3		.976	-4	/O-35,2-22,S	-1.8
Team 3	61	218	25	49	10	3	1	14	14	17	.225	.287	.312	63	-12	7	3		.983	-4	/O-32,2-22,S	-1.7

■ LEE THOMAS
Thomas, James Leroy b: 2/5/36, Peoria, Ill. BL/TR, 6'2", 198 lbs. Deb: 4/22/61 C

YEAR TM/L	G	AB	R	H	2B	3B	HR	RBI	BB	SO	AVG	OBP	SLG	PRO+	BR/A	SB	CS	SBR	FA	FR	G/POS	TPR
1966 Atl-N	39	126	11	25	1	1	6	15	10	15	.198	.263	.365	71	-5	1	1	-0	.987	2	1-36	-0.6
Total 8	1027	3324	405	847	111	22	106	428	332	397	.255	.328	.397	99	-6	25	11	1	.975	-7	O-485,1-425	-6.4

■ ROY THOMAS
Thomas, Roy Allen b: 3/24/1874, Norristown, Pa. d: 11/20/59, Norristown, Pa. BL/TL, 5'11", 150 lbs. Deb: 4/14/1899 FC

YEAR TM/L	G	AB	R	H	2B	3B	HR	RBI	BB	SO	AVG	OBP	SLG	PRO+	BR/A	SB	CS	SBR	FA	FR	G/POS	TPR
1909 Bos-N	82	281	36	74	9	1	0	11	47		.263	.369	.302	104	3	5			.976	-2	O-76	-0.1
Total 13	1470	5296	1011	1537	100	53	7	299	1042		.290	.413	.333	124	240	244			.972	71	*O-1434/1-14,P	22.8

■ WALT THOMAS
Thomas, William Walter "Tommy" b: 4/28/1884, Foot Of Ten, Pa. d: 6/6/50, Altoona, Pa. BR/TR, 5'8", Deb: 9/18/08

YEAR TM/L	G	AB	R	H	2B	3B	HR	RBI	BB	SO	AVG	OBP	SLG	PRO+	BR/A	SB	CS	SBR	FA	FR	G/POS	TPR
1908 Bos-N	5	13	2	2	0	0	0	1	3		.154	.313	.154	51	-1	2			.864	-1	/S-5	-0.2

■ DON THOMPSON
Thompson, Donald Newlin b: 12/28/23, Swepsonville, N.C. BL/TL, 6', 185 lbs. Deb: 4/24/49

YEAR TM/L	G	AB	R	H	2B	3B	HR	RBI	BB	SO	AVG	OBP	SLG	PRO+	BR/A	SB	CS	SBR	FA	FR	G/POS	TPR
1949 Bos-N	7	11	0	2	0	0	0	0	0	2	.182	.182	.182	-2	-2	0			.800	-0	/O-2	-0.2
Total 4	217	307	52	67	8	0	1	19	31	32	.218	.296	.254	46	-23	4			.984	-35	O-173	-6.7

■ MILT THOMPSON
Thompson, Milton Bernard b: 1/5/59, Washington, D.C. BL/TR, 5'11", 170 lbs. Deb: 9/4/84

YEAR TM/L	G	AB	R	H	2B	3B	HR	RBI	BB	SO	AVG	OBP	SLG	PRO+	BR/A	SB	CS	SBR	FA	FR	G/POS	TPR
1984 Atl-N	25	99	16	30	1	0	2	4	11	11	.303	.373	.374	103	1	14	2	3	.956	3	O-25	0.6
1985 Atl-N	73	182	17	55	7	2	0	6	7	36	.302	.339	.363	91	-2	9	4	0	.964	-5	O-49	-0.9
Total 12	1297	3695	488	1022	154	37	47	354	329	622	.277	.339	.376	95	-20	213	65	25	.983	6	*O-1045	-1.4
Team 2	98	281	33	85	8	2	2	10	18	47	.302	.351	.367	95	-1	23	6	3	.961	-2	/O-74	-0.3

■ TOMMY THOMPSON
Thompson, Rupert Lockhart b: 5/19/10, Elkhart, Ill. d: 5/24/71, Auburn, Cal. BL/TR, 5'9.5", 155 lbs. Deb: 9/3/33

YEAR TM/L	G	AB	R	H	2B	3B	HR	RBI	BB	SO	AVG	OBP	SLG	PRO+	BR/A	SB	CS	SBR	FA	FR	G/POS	TPR
1933 Bos-N	24	97	6	18	1	0	0	6	4	6	.186	.218	.196	21	-10	0			1.000	2	O-24	-1.0
1934 Bos-N	105	343	40	91	12	3	0	37	13	19	.265	.300	.318	71	-15	2			.964	10	O-82	-0.8
1935 Bos-N	112	297	34	81	7	1	4	30	36	17	.273	.353	.343	96	-1	2			.965	1	O-85	-0.2
1936 Bos-N	106	266	37	76	9	0	4	36	31	12	.286	.362	.365	103	2	3			1.000	0	O-39,1-25	-0.2
Total 6	397	1107	142	294	34	4	9	119	108	63	.266	.335	.328	84	-23	7			.975	13	O-253/1-26	-2.2
Team 4	347	1003	117	266	29	4	8	109	84	54	.265	.326	.326	83	-23	7			.975	14	O-230/1-25	-2.2

■ BOBBY THOMSON
Thomson, Robert Brown "The Staten Island Scot" b: 10/25/23, Glasgow, Scotland BR/TR, 6'2", 185 lbs. Deb: 9/9/46

YEAR TM/L	G	AB	R	H	2B	3B	HR	RBI	BB	SO	AVG	OBP	SLG	PRO+	BR/A	SB	CS	SBR	FA	FR	G/POS	TPR
1954 Mil-N	43	99	7	23	3	0	2	15	12	29	.232	.315	.323	71	-4	0	0	0	.980	1	O-26	-0.5
1955 Mil-N	101	343	40	88	12	3	12	56	34	52	.257	.324	.414	99	-1	2	1	0	.969	0	O-91	-0.5
1956 Mil-N	142	451	59	106	10	4	20	74	43	75	.235	.304	.408	95	-5	2	4	-2	.974	-4	*O-136/3-3	-1.7
1957 Mil-N	41	148	15	35	5	3	4	23	8	27	.236	.285	.392	86	-4	2	1	0	.988	-1	O-38	-0.7
Total 15	1779	6305	903	1705	267	74	264	1026	559	804	.270	.333	.462	111	77	38	20		.980	20	*O-1506,3-184/21	1.7
Team 4	327	1041	121	252	30	10	38	168	97	183	.242	.309	.400	93	-14	6	6		.975	-4	O-291/3-3	-3.4

■ BOB THORPE
Thorpe, Benjamin Robert b: 11/19/26, Caryville, Fla. BR/TR, 6'1.5", 190 lbs. Deb: 4/19/51

YEAR TM/L	G	AB	R	H	2B	3B	HR	RBI	BB	SO	AVG	OBP	SLG	PRO+	BR/A	SB	CS	SBR	FA	FR	G/POS	TPR
1951 Bos-N	2	2	1	1	0	1	0	1	0	0	.500	.500	1.500	448	1	0	0	0	.000	0	H	0.1
1952 Bos-N	81	292	20	76	8	2	3	26	5	42	.260	.275	.332	70	-13	3	1	0	.972	0	O-72	-1.6
1953 Mil-N	27	37	1	6	1	0	0	5	1	6	.162	.184	.189	-3	-6	0	1	-1	1.000	-5	O-18	-1.1
Total 3	110	331	22	83	9	3	3	32	6	48	.251	.266	.323	64	-17	3	2	-0	.975	-5	/O-90	-2.6

■ JIM THORPE
Thorpe, James Francis b: 5/28/1887, Prague, Okla. d: 3/28/53, Long Beach, Cal. BR/TR, 6'1", 185 lbs. Deb: 4/14/13

YEAR TM/L	G	AB	R	H	2B	3B	HR	RBI	BB	SO	AVG	OBP	SLG	PRO+	BR/A	SB	CS	SBR	FA	FR	G/POS	TPR
1919 Bos-N	60	156	16	51	7	3	1	25	6	30	.327	.360	.429	143	7	7			.926	-7	O-38/1-2	-0.2
Total 6	289	698	91	176	20	18	7	82	27	122	.252	.286	.362	99	-3	29			.951	-25	O-199/1-2	-4.3

■ COTTON TIERNEY
Tierney, James Arthur b: 2/10/1894, Kansas City, Kan. d: 4/18/53, Kansas City, Mo. BR/TR, 5'8", 175 lbs. Deb: 9/23/20

YEAR TM/L	G	AB	R	H	2B	3B	HR	RBI	BB	SO	AVG	OBP	SLG	PRO+	BR/A	SB	CS	SBR	FA	FR	G/POS	TPR
1924 Bos-N	136	505	38	131	16	1	6	58	22	37	.259	.296	.331	71	-22	11	8	-2	.964	-1	*2-115,3-22	-2.1
Total 6	630	2299	266	681	119	30	31	331	109	187	.296	.332	.415	93	-29	28	31		.966	-50	2-447,3-118/OS1	-7.3

■ BOB TILLMAN
Tillman, John Robert b: 3/24/37, Nashville, Tenn. BR/TR, 6'4", 205 lbs. Deb: 4/15/62

YEAR TM/L	G	AB	R	H	2B	3B	HR	RBI	BB	SO	AVG	OBP	SLG	PRO+	BR/A	SB	CS	SBR	FA	FR	G/POS	TPR
1968 Atl-N	86	236	16	52	4	0	5	20	16	55	.220	.278	.301	74	-8	1	0	0	.990	-1	C-75	-0.4
1969 *Atl-N	69	190	18	37	5	0	12	29	18	47	.195	.264	.411	86	-4	0	0	0	.988	-10	C-69	-1.2
1970 Atl-N	71	223	19	53	5	0	11	30	20	66	.238	.300	.408	83	-6	0	0	0	.988	-2	C-70	-0.5
Total 9	775	2329	189	540	68	10	79	282	228	510	.232	.302	.371	85	-49	1	0	0	.988	-31	C-725	-4.9
Team 3	226	649	53	142	14	0	28	79	54	168	.219	.282	.370	81	-18	1	0	0	.989	-12	C-214	-2.1

■ JOHN TITUS
Titus, John Franklin "Silent John" b: 2/21/1876, St.Clair, Pa. d: 1/8/43, St.Clair, Pa. BL/TL, 5'9", 156 lbs. Deb: 6/8/03

YEAR TM/L	G	AB	R	H	2B	3B	HR	RBI	BB	SO	AVG	OBP	SLG	PRO+	BR/A	SB	CS	SBR	FA	FR	G/POS	TPR
1912 Bos-N	96	345	56	112	23	6	2	48	49	20	.325	.422	.443	134	19	5			.965	-5	O-96	0.9
1913 Bos-N	87	269	33	80	14	2	5	38	35	22	.297	.392	.420	129	12	4			.919	-7	O-75	0.2
Total 11	1402	4960	738	1401	253	72	38	561	620	116	.282	.373	.385	127	181	140			.959	7	*O-1356	13.0
Team 2	183	614	89	192	37	8	7	86	84	42	.313	.409	.433	132	30	9			.947	-11	O-171	1.1

■ JIM TOBIN
Tobin, James Anthony "Abba Dabba" b: 12/27/12, Oakland, Cal. d: 5/19/69, Oakland, Cal. BR/TR, 6', 185 lbs. Deb: 4/30/37 F

YEAR TM/L	G	AB	R	H	2B	3B	HR	RBI	BB	SO	AVG	OBP	SLG	PRO+	BR/A	SB	CS	SBR	FA	FR	G/POS	TPR
1940 Bos-N	20	43	5	12	3	0	0	3	1	10	.279	.295	.349	82	-1	0			.957	-1	P-15	0.0
1941 Bos-N	43	103	6	19	5	0	0	9	10	31	.184	.257	.233	40	-8	1			.966	4	P-33	0.0
1942 Bos-N	47	114	14	28	2	0	6	15	16	23	.246	.344	.421	126	4	0			.947	6	P-37	0.0
1943 Bos-N	46	107	8	30	4	0	2	12	6	16	.280	.319	.374	101	-0	0			.927	2	P-33/1-1	0.0
1944 Bos-N★	62	116	13	22	5	1	2	18	16	28	.190	.288	.302	63	-6	0			.972	7	P-43	0.0
1945 Bos-N	41	77	9	11	3	0	3	12	15	22	.143	.290	.299	64	-4	0			**1.000**	2	P-27	0.0
Total 9	396	796	81	183	35	3	17	102	80	162	.230	.303	.345	82	-20	1			.965	17	P-287/1-1	0.0
Team 6	259	560	55	122	22	1	13	69	64	130	.218	.300	.330	80	-15	1			.960	20	P-188/1-1	0.0

■ EARL TORGESON
Torgeson, Clifford Earl "The Earl Of Snohomish" b: 1/1/24, Snohomish, Wash. d: 11/8/90, Everett, Wash. BL/TL, 6'3", 180 lbs. Deb: 4/15/47 C

YEAR TM/L	G	AB	R	H	2B	3B	HR	RBI	BB	SO	AVG	OBP	SLG	PRO+	BR/A	SB	CS	SBR	FA	FR	G/POS	TPR
1947 Bos-N	128	399	73	112	20	6	16	78	82	59	.281	.403	.481	137	24	11			.984	-1	*1-117	1.9
1948 *Bos-N	134	438	70	111	23	5	10	67	81	54	.253	.372	.397	110	9	19			.993	1	*1-129	0.9
1949 Bos-N	25	100	17	26	5	1	4	19	13	4	.260	.345	.450	118	2	4			.988	-3	1-25	-0.1
1950 Bos-N	156	576	**120**	167	30	3	23	87	119	69	.290	.412	.472	141	39	15			.986	-0	*1-156	3.4
1951 Bos-N	155	581	99	153	21	4	24	92	102	70	.263	.375	.437	127	24	20	11	-1	.988	-1	*1-155	1.5
1952 Bos-N	122	382	49	88	17	0	5	34	81	38	.230	.366	.314	94	0	11	7	-1	.989	-1	*1-105/O-5	-0.6
Total 15	1668	4969	848	1318	215	46	149	740	980	653	.265	.387	.417	118	162	133	39		.989	-39	*1-1416/O-6	6.6
Team 6	720	2476	428	657	116	19	82	377	478	294	.265	.385	.427	123	97	80	18		.988	-5	1-687/O-5	7.0

■ RED TORPHY
Torphy, Walter Anthony b: 11/6/1891, Fall River, Mass. d: 2/11/80, Fall River, Mass. BR/TR, 5'11", 169 lbs. Deb: 9/25/20

YEAR TM/L	G	AB	R	H	2B	3B	HR	RBI	BB	SO	AVG	OBP	SLG	PRO+	BR/A	SB	CS	SBR	FA	FR	G/POS	TPR
1920 Bos-N	3	15	1	3	2	0	0	2	0	1	.200	.200	.333	54	-1	0	0	0	.969	-1	/1-3	-0.2

■ FRANK TORRE
Torre, Frank Joseph b: 12/30/31, Brooklyn, N.Y. BL/TL, 6'3", 205 lbs. Deb: 4/20/56 F

YEAR TM/L	G	AB	R	H	2B	3B	HR	RBI	BB	SO	AVG	OBP	SLG	PRO+	BR/A	SB	CS	SBR	FA	FR	G/POS	TPR
1956 Mil-N	111	159	17	41	6	0	0	16	11	4	.258	.306	.296	67	-7	1	0	0	.993	6	1-89	-0.4
1957 *Mil-N	129	364	46	99	19	5	5	40	29	19	.272	.341	.393	104	2	0	0	0	**.996**	1	*1-117	-0.3
1958 *Mil-N	138	372	41	115	22	5	6	55	42	14	.309	.390	.444	131	17	2	0	1	**.994**	6	*1-122	1.8
1959 Mil-N	115	263	23	60	15	1	1	33	35	12	.228	.326	.304	75	-9	0	0	0	.994	-0	1-87	-1.4

YEAR TM/L	G	AB	R	H	2B	3B	HR	RBI	BB	SO	AVG	OBP	SLG	PRO+	BR/A	SB	CS	SBR	FA	FR	G/POS	TPR
1960 Mil-N	21	44	2	9	1	0	0	5	3	2	.205	.255	.227	36	-4	0	0	0	1.000	-1	1-17	-0.6
Total 7	714	1482	150	404	78	15	13	179	155	64	.273	.352	.372	101	5	4	1	1	.993	19	1-564	0.2
Team 5	514	1202	129	324	63	11	12	149	120	51	.270	.345	.370	99	-1	3	0	1	.995	11	1-432	-0.9

■ JOE TORRE Torre, Joseph Paul b: 7/18/40, Brooklyn, N.Y. BR/TR, 6'2", 212 lbs. Deb: 9/25/60 FM

YEAR TM/L	G	AB	R	H	2B	3B	HR	RBI	BB	SO	AVG	OBP	SLG	PRO+	BR/A	SB	CS	SBR	FA	FR	G/POS	TPR
1960 Mil-N	2	2	0	1	0	0	0	0	0	1	.500	.500	.500	189	0	0	0	0	.000	0	H	0.0
1961 Mil-N	113	406	40	113	21	4	10	42	28	60	.278	.331	.424	105	2	3	5	-2	.982	-8	*C-112	-0.3
1962 Mil-N	80	220	23	62	8	1	5	26	24	24	.282	.358	.395	105	2	1	0	0	.986	6	C-63	1.0
1963 Mil-N☆	142	501	57	147	19	4	14	71	42	79	.293	.354	.431	126	17	1	5	-3	.994	-7	*C-105,1-37/O	1.0
1964 Mil-N★	154	601	87	193	36	5	20	109	36	67	.321	.366	.498	140	31	2	4	-2	**.995**	-8	C-96,1-70	2.4
1965 Mil-N★	148	523	68	152	21	1	27	80	61	79	.291	.373	.489	140	28	0	1	-1	.991	-6	*C-100,1-49	2.6
1966 Atl-N★	148	546	83	172	20	3	36	101	60	61	.315	.385	.560	157	41	0	4	-2	.984	-3	*C-114,1-36	4.2
1967 Atl-N★	135	477	67	132	18	1	20	68	49	75	.277	.348	.444	127	16	2	2	-1	.991	-5	*C-114,1-23	1.7
1968 Atl-N	115	424	45	115	11	2	10	55	34	72	.271	.333	.377	112	7	1	0	0	**.996**	-11	C-92,1-29	0.1
Total 18	2209	7874	996	2342	344	59	252	1185	779	1094	.297	.367	.452	129	299	23	29	-11	.990	-93	C-903,1-787,3/O	19.6
Team 9	1037	3700	470	1087	154	21	142	552	334	518	.294	.358	.462	130	144	10	21	-10	.990	-41	C-796,1-244/O	12.7

■ WALT TRAGESSER Tragesser, Walter Joseph b: 6/14/1887, Lafayette, Ind. d: 12/14/70, Lafayette, Ind. BR/TR, 6', 175 lbs. Deb: 7/30/13

YEAR TM/L	G	AB	R	H	2B	3B	HR	RBI	BB	SO	AVG	OBP	SLG	PRO+	BR/A	SB	CS	SBR	FA	FR	G/POS	TPR
1913 Bos-N	2	0	0	0	0	0	0	0	0	0	—	—	—	—	0	0			1.000	-0	/C-2	0.0
1915 Bos-N	7	7	1	0	0	0	0	0	0	2	.000	.000	.000	-99	-2	0			.944	1	/C-7	-0.1
1916 Bos-N	41	54	3	11	1	0	0	4	5	10	.204	.283	.222	59	-2	0			.971	4	C-29	0.3
1917 Bos-N	98	297	23	66	10	2	0	25	15	36	.222	.264	.269	68	-12	5			.971	-2	C-94	-0.7
1918 Bos-N	7	1	0	0	0	0	0	0	0	0	.000	.000	.000	-99	-0	0			.833	1	/C-7	0.0
1919 Bos-N	20	40	3	7	2	0	0	3	2	10	.175	.233	.225	39	-3	1			.959	-0	C-14	-0.3
Total 7	272	689	54	148	31	3	6	66	35	125	.215	.260	.295	67	-29	14			.961	-6	C-239	-2.0
Team 6	175	399	30	84	13	2	0	32	22	58	.211	.259	.253	60	-19	6			.969	3	C-153	-0.8

■ JEFF TREADWAY Treadway, Hugh Jeffery b: 1/22/63, Columbus, Ga. BL/TR, 5'10", 170 lbs. Deb: 9/4/87

YEAR TM/L	G	AB	R	H	2B	3B	HR	RBI	BB	SO	AVG	OBP	SLG	PRO+	BR/A	SB	CS	SBR	FA	FR	G/POS	TPR
1989 Atl-N	134	473	58	131	18	3	8	40	30	38	.277	.320	.378	96	-3	3	2	-0	.981	3	*2-123/3-6	0.5
1990 Atl-N	128	474	56	134	20	2	11	59	25	42	.283	.323	.403	93	-5	3	4	-2	.976	10	*2-122	0.6
1991 *Atl-N	106	306	41	98	17	2	3	32	23	19	.320	.372	.418	115	6	2	2	-1	.960	-8	2-93	0.0
1992 *Atl-N	61	126	5	28	6	1	0	5	9	16	.222	.274	.286	55	-7	1	2	-1	.993	0	2-45/3-1	-0.8
Total 9	762	2119	244	596	103	14	28	208	140	184	.281	.329	.383	94	-17	14	13		.975	-1	2-556/3-57,D	-0.5
Team 4	429	1379	160	391	61	8	22	136	87	115	.284	.328	.387	96	-9	9	10		.975	6	2-383/3-7	0.3

■ ALEX TREVINO Trevino, Alejandro (Castro) b: 8/26/57, Monterrey, Mex. BR/TR, 5'11", 170 lbs. Deb: 9/11/78 F

YEAR TM/L	G	AB	R	H	2B	3B	HR	RBI	BB	SO	AVG	OBP	SLG	PRO+	BR/A	SB	CS	SBR	FA	FR	G/POS	TPR
1984 Atl-N	79	266	36	65	16	0	3	28	16	27	.244	.290	.338	71	-10	5	2	0	.989	7	C-79	0.0
Total 13	939	2430	245	604	117	10	23	244	205	317	.249	.312	.333	81	-61	19	11	-1	.979	16	C-742/3-53,2O1	-1.6

■ SAM TROTT Trott, Samuel W. b: 3/1859, Maryland d: 6/5/25, Catonsville, Md. BL/TL, 5'9", 190 lbs. Deb: 5/29/1880 M

YEAR TM/L	G	AB	R	H	2B	3B	HR	RBI	BB	SO	AVG	OBP	SLG	PRO+	BR/A	SB	CS	SBR	FA	FR	G/POS	TPR
1880 Bos-N	39	125	14	26	4	1	0	9	3	5	.208	.227	.256	65	-4				.893	6	C-36/O-4	0.2
Total 8	360	1354	166	338	73	22	3	74	54	44	.250	.280	.343	93	-11	9	0	3	.906	6	C-272/2-65,O1S3	1.2

■ TOMMY TUCKER Tucker, Thomas Joseph "Foghorn" b: 10/28/1863, Holyoke, Mass. d: 10/22/35, Montague, Mass. BB/TR, 5'11", 165 lbs. Deb: 4/16/1887

YEAR TM/L	G	AB	R	H	2B	3B	HR	RBI	BB	SO	AVG	OBP	SLG	PRO+	BR/A	SB	CS	SBR	FA	FR	G/POS	TPR
1890 Bos-N	132	539	104	159	17	8	1	62	56	22	.295	.387	.362	110	7	43			**.979**	-2	*1-132	-0.1
1891 Bos-N	140	548	103	148	16	5	2	69	37	30	.270	.349	.328	87	-10	26			.976	-3	*1-140/P-1	-1.9
1892 *Bos-N	149	542	85	153	15	7	1	62	45	35	.282	.365	.341	104	3	22			.972	-12	*1-149	-1.5
1893 Bos-N	121	486	83	138	13	2	7	91	27	31	.284	.347	.362	82	-15	8			.980	-11	*1-121	-2.4
1894 Bos-N	123	500	112	165	24	6	3	100	53	21	.330	.412	.420	94	-5	18			**.985**	2	*1-123/O-1	-0.2
1895 Bos-N	125	462	87	115	19	6	3	73	61	29	.249	.360	.335	74	-18	15			.978	6	*1-125	-0.8
1896 Bos-N	122	474	74	144	27	5	2	72	30	29	.304	.363	.395	94	-5	6			.985	3	*1-122	0.0
1897 Bos-N	4	14	0	3	2	0	0	4	2		.214	.313	.357	72	-1	0			.957	1	/1-4	0.0
Total 13	1687	6479	1084	1882	240	85	42	848	479	223	.290	.364	.373	101	12	352			.978	-8	*1-1669/O-20,P	-4.5
Team 8	916	3565	648	1025	133	39	19	533	311	197	.288	.369	.363	92	-43	138			.979	-18	1-916/P-1,O	-6.9

■ GEORGE TWOMBLY Twombly, George Frederick "Silent George" b: 6/4/1892, Boston, Mass. d: 2/17/75, Lexington, Mass. BR/TR, 5'9", 165 lbs. Deb: 7/9/14 F

YEAR TM/L	G	AB	R	H	2B	3B	HR	RBI	BB	SO	AVG	OBP	SLG	PRO+	BR/A	SB	CS	SBR	FA	FR	G/POS	TPR
1917 Bos-N	32	102	8	19	1	1	0	9	18	5	.186	.314	.216	68	-3	4			.943	-5	O-29/1-1	-1.1
Total 5	150	417	35	88	1	7	0	33	41	41	.211	.289	.247	62	-18	21			.967	-9	O-123/1-1	-3.7

■ FRED TYLER Tyler, Frederick Franklin "Clancy" b: 12/16/1891, Derry, N.H. d: 10/14/45, E.Derry, N.H. BR/TR, 5'10.5", 180 lbs. Deb: 4/14/14 F

YEAR TM/L	G	AB	R	H	2B	3B	HR	RBI	BB	SO	AVG	OBP	SLG	PRO+	BR/A	SB	CS	SBR	FA	FR	G/POS	TPR
1914 Bos-N	6	19	2	2	0	0	0	2	1	5	.105	.150	.105	-24	-3	0			1.000	-1	/C-6	-0.3

■ JOHNNIE TYLER Tyler, John Anthony "Ty Ty" or "Katz" (b: John Tylka)
b: 7/30/06, Mt.Pleasant, Pa. d: 7/11/72, Mt.Pleasant, Pa. BB/TR, 6', 175 lbs. Deb: 9/16/34

YEAR TM/L	G	AB	R	H	2B	3B	HR	RBI	BB	SO	AVG	OBP	SLG	PRO+	BR/A	SB	CS	SBR	FA	FR	G/POS	TPR
1934 Bos-N	3	6	0	1	0	0	0	1	0	3	.167	.167	.167	-11	-1	0			1.000	1	/O-1	0.0
1935 Bos-N	13	47	7	16	2	1	2	11	4	3	.340	.404	.553	168	4	0			.893	-0	O-11	0.4
Total 2	16	53	7	17	2	1	2	12	4	6	.321	.379	.509	148	3	0			.906	1	/O-12	0.4

■ BOB UECKER Uecker, Robert George b: 1/26/35, Milwaukee, Wis. BR/TR, 6'1", 190 lbs. Deb: 4/13/62

YEAR TM/L	G	AB	R	H	2B	3B	HR	RBI	BB	SO	AVG	OBP	SLG	PRO+	BR/A	SB	CS	SBR	FA	FR	G/POS	TPR
1962 Mil-N	33	64	5	16	2	0	1	8	7	15	.250	.324	.328	78	-2	0	0	0	.982	4	C-24	0.3
1963 Mil-N	13	16	3	4	2	0	0	0	2	5	.250	.333	.375	105	0	0	0	0	.958	1	/C-6	0.1
1967 Atl-N	62	158	14	23	2	0	3	13	19	51	.146	.237	.215	31	-14	0	1	-1	.972	5	C-59	-0.8
Total 6	297	731	65	146	22	0	14	74	96	167	.200	.295	.287	63	-35	0	3	-2	.981	14	C-271	-1.3
Team 3	108	238	22	43	6	0	4	21	28	71	.181	.267	.256	49	-16	0	1	-1	.974	10	/C-89	-0.4

■ MIKE ULISNEY Ulisney, Michael Edward "Slugs" b: 9/28/17, Greenwald, Pa. BR/TR, 5'9", 165 lbs. Deb: 5/5/45

YEAR TM/L	G	AB	R	H	2B	3B	HR	RBI	BB	SO	AVG	OBP	SLG	PRO+	BR/A	SB	CS	SBR	FA	FR	G/POS	TPR
1945 Bos-N	11	18	4	7	1	0	1	4	1	0	.389	.421	.611	184	2	0			.714	-2	/C-4	0.0

■ LUKE URBAN Urban, Louis John b: 3/22/1898, Fall River, Mass. d: 12/7/80, Somerset, Mass. BR/TR, 5'8", 168 lbs. Deb: 7/19/27

YEAR TM/L	G	AB	R	H	2B	3B	HR	RBI	BB	SO	AVG	OBP	SLG	PRO+	BR/A	SB	CS	SBR	FA	FR	G/POS	TPR
1927 Bos-N	35	111	11	32	5	0	0	10	3	6	.288	.313	.333	79	-4	1			.947	-8	C-34	-0.9
1928 Bos-N	15	17	0	3	0	0	0	2	0	1	.176	.222	.176	6	-2	0			1.000	1	C-10	-0.1
Total 2	50	128	11	35	5	0	0	12	3	7	.273	.301	.313	69	-6	1			.955	-7	/C-44	-1.0

■ BILLY URBANSKI Urbanski, William Michael b: 6/5/03, Linoleumville, N.Y d: 7/12/73, Perth Amboy, N.J. BR/TR, 5'8", 165 lbs. Deb: 7/4/31

YEAR TM/L	G	AB	R	H	2B	3B	HR	RBI	BB	SO	AVG	OBP	SLG	PRO+	BR/A	SB	CS	SBR	FA	FR	G/POS	TPR
1931 Bos-N	82	303	22	72	13	4	0	17	10	32	.238	.274	.307	58	-18	3			.961	11	3-68,S-19	-0.2
1932 Bos-N	136	563	80	153	25	8	8	46	28	60	.272	.307	.387	89	-10	8			.946	1	*S-136	0.3
1933 Bos-N	144	566	65	142	21	4	0	35	33	48	.251	.298	.302	78	-17	4			.953	-4	*S-143	-1.1
1934 Bos-N	146	605	104	177	30	6	7	53	56	37	.293	.357	.397	110	9	4			**.961**	-10	*S-146	0.7
1935 Bos-N	132	514	53	118	17	0	4	30	40	32	.230	.286	.286	59	-30	3			.939	-27	*S-129	-5.0
1936 Bos-N	122	494	55	129	17	5	0	26	31	42	.261	.310	.316	74	-18	2			.937	-18	S-80,3-38	-3.0
1937 Bos-N	1	1	0	0	0	0	0	0	0	1	.000	.000	.000	-99	-0	0			.000	0	H	0.0
Total 7	763	3046	379	791	123	27	19	207	198	252	.260	.309	.337	81	-85	24			.949	-47	S-653,3-106	-8.3

■ SANDY VALDESPINO Valdespino, Hilario (Borroto) b: 1/14/39, San Jose De Las Lajas, Cuba BL/TL, 5'8", 170 lbs. Deb: 4/12/65

YEAR TM/L	G	AB	R	H	2B	3B	HR	RBI	BB	SO	AVG	OBP	SLG	PRO+	BR/A	SB	CS	SBR	FA	FR	G/POS	TPR
1968 Atl-N	36	86	8	20	1	0	1	4	10	20	.233	.320	.279	81	-2	0	0	0	.976	1	O-20	-0.2
Total 7	382	765	96	176	23	3	7	67	57	129	.230	.288	.295	66	-33	14	10		.974	-10	O-217	-5.8

YEAR	TM/L	G	AB	R	H	2B	3B	HR	RBI	BB	SO	AVG	OBP	SLG	PRO+	BR/A	SB	CS	SBR	FA	FR	G/POS	TPR

■ BILL Van DYKE   Van Dyke, William Jennings   b: 12/15/1863, Paris, Ill.   d: 5/5/33, ElPaso, Tex.   BR/TR, 5'8", 170 lbs.   Deb: 4/17/1890

| 1893 | Bos-N | 3 | 12 | 2 | 3 | 1 | 0 | 0 | 1 | 0 | 1 | .250 | .250 | .333 | 50 | -1 | 1 | | | 1.000 | -1 | /O-3 | -0.1 |
| Total | 3 | 136 | 530 | 78 | 134 | 15 | 11 | 2 | 2 | 25 | 2 | .253 | .290 | .334 | 81 | -16 | 74 | | | .924 | -8 | O-117/3-18,2C | -2.3 |

■ PETE VARNEY   Varney, Richard Fred   b: 4/10/49, Roxbury, Mass.   BR/TR, 6'3", 235 lbs.   Deb: 8/26/73

| 1976 | Atl-N | 5 | 10 | 0 | 1 | 0 | 0 | 0 | 0 | 0 | 2 | .100 | .100 | .100 | -41 | -2 | 0 | 0 | 0 | 1.000 | -1 | /C-5 | -0.2 |
| Total | 4 | 69 | 190 | 18 | 47 | 7 | 1 | 5 | 15 | 10 | 47 | .247 | .289 | .374 | 86 | -4 | 2 | 0 | | .988 | 1 | /C-67,D-2 | 0.1 |

■ JIM VATCHER   Vatcher, James Ernest   b: 5/27/66, Santa Monica, Cal.   BR/TR, 5'9", 165 lbs.   Deb: 5/30/90

| 1990 | Atl-N | 21 | 27 | 2 | 7 | 1 | 1 | 0 | 3 | 1 | 9 | .259 | .286 | .370 | 75 | -1 | 0 | 0 | 0 | 1.000 | -1 | /O-6 | -0.2 |
| Total | 3 | 87 | 109 | 11 | 27 | 3 | 1 | 1 | 11 | 12 | 27 | .248 | .322 | .321 | 77 | -3 | 1 | 0 | 0 | .980 | -11 | /O-54 | -1.5 |

■ FREDDIE VELAZQUEZ   Velazquez, Federico Antonio (Velasquez)   b: 12/6/37, Santo Domingo, D.R.   BR/TR, 6'1", 185 lbs.   Deb: 4/20/69

| 1973 | Atl-N | 15 | 23 | 2 | 8 | 1 | 0 | 0 | 3 | 1 | 3 | .348 | .375 | .391 | 105 | 0 | 0 | 0 | 0 | .975 | 2 | C-11 | 0.2 |
| Total | 2 | 21 | 39 | 3 | 10 | 3 | 0 | 0 | 5 | 2 | 6 | .256 | .293 | .333 | 71 | -2 | 0 | 0 | 0 | .985 | 1 | /C-16 | 0.0 |

■ PAT VELTMAN   Veltman, Arthur Patrick   b: 3/24/06, Mobile, Ala.   d: 10/1/80, San Antonio, Tex.   BR/TR, 6', 175 lbs.   Deb: 4/17/26

| 1931 | Bos-N | 1 | 1 | 0 | 0 | 0 | 0 | 0 | 0 | 0 | 0 | .000 | .000 | .000 | -99 | -0 | 0 | | | .000 | 0 | H | 0.0 |
| Total | 6 | 23 | 38 | 4 | 5 | 0 | 1 | 0 | 2 | 4 | 3 | .132 | .214 | .184 | 7 | -5 | 0 | | | 1.000 | -2 | /C-12,O-1,S | -0.6 |

■ EMIL VERBAN   Verban, Emil Matthew "Dutch" or "Antelope"   b: 8/27/15, Lincoln, Ill.   d: 6/8/89, Quincy, Ill.   BR/TR, 5'11", 165 lbs.   Deb: 4/18/44

| 1950 | Bos-N | 4 | 5 | 1 | 0 | 0 | 0 | 0 | 0 | 0 | 0 | .000 | .000 | .000 | -99 | -1 | 0 | | | .833 | 1 | /2-2 | 0.0 |
| Total | 7 | 853 | 2911 | 301 | 793 | 99 | 26 | 1 | 241 | 108 | 74 | .272 | .301 | .325 | 73 | -113 | 21 | | | .971 | 1 | 2-802/S-3,O3 | -6.7 |

■ MICKEY VERNON   Vernon, James Barton   b: 4/22/18, Marcus Hook, Pa.   BL/TL, 6'2", 180 lbs.   Deb: 7/8/39   MC

| 1959 | Mil-N | 74 | 91 | 8 | 20 | 4 | 0 | 3 | 14 | 7 | 20 | .220 | .283 | .363 | 77 | -3 | 0 | 0 | 0 | .983 | 1 | 1-10/O-4 | -0.3 |
| Total | 20 | 2409 | 8731 | 1196 | 2495 | 490 | 120 | 172 | 1311 | 955 | 869 | .286 | .359 | .428 | 116 | 186 | 137 | 90 | | .990 | -32 | *1-2237/O-4 | 3.7 |

■ ZOILO VERSALLES   Versalles, Zoilo Casanova (Rodriguez) "Zorro"   b: 12/18/39, Veldado, Cuba   d: 6/9/95, Bloomington, Minn.   BR/TR, 5'10", 150 lbs.   Deb: 8/1/59

| 1971 | Atl-N | 66 | 194 | 21 | 37 | 11 | 0 | 5 | 22 | 11 | 40 | .191 | .234 | .325 | 53 | -12 | 2 | 1 | 0 | .902 | -14 | 3-30,S-24/2 | -2.6 |
| Total | 12 | 1400 | 5141 | 650 | 1246 | 230 | 63 | 95 | 471 | 318 | 810 | .242 | .292 | .367 | 82 | -133 | 97 | 48 | 0 | .956 | -20 | *S-1265/3-65,2 | -4.8 |

■ OZZIE VIRGIL   Virgil, Osvaldo Jose Jr.   b: 12/7/56, Mayaguez, P.R.   BR/TR, 6'1", 205 lbs.   Deb: 10/5/80   F

1986	Atl-N	114	359	45	80	9	0	15	48	63	73	.223	.345	.373	93	-2	1	0	0	.984	14	*C-111	2.0
1987	Atl-N★	123	429	57	106	13	1	27	72	47	81	.247	.331	.471	104	2	0	1	-1	.989	-2	*C-122	0.8
1988	Atl-N	107	320	23	82	10	0	9	31	22	54	.256	.314	.372	92	-3	2	0	1	.990	-11	C-96	-0.8
Total	11	739	2258	258	549	84	6	98	307	248	453	.243	.326	.416	101	1	4	5	-2	.987	8	C-677/D-7	2.9
Team	3	344	1108	125	268	32	1	51	151	132	208	.242	.331	.411	97	-4	3	1	0	.987	1	C-329	2.0

■ PHIL VOYLES   Voyles, Philip Vance   b: 5/12/1900, Murphy, N.C.   d: 11/3/72, Marlborough, Mass.   BL/TR, 5'11.5", 175 lbs.   Deb: 9/4/29

| 1929 | Bos-N | 20 | 68 | 9 | 16 | 0 | 2 | 0 | 14 | 6 | 8 | .235 | .297 | .294 | 49 | -5 | 0 | | | .922 | -2 | O-20 | -0.8 |

■ BILL WAGNER   Wagner, William Joseph   b: 1/2/1894, Jesup, Iowa   d: 1/11/51, Waterloo, Iowa   BR/TR, 6', 187 lbs.   Deb: 7/16/14

| 1918 | Bos-N | 13 | 47 | 2 | 10 | 0 | 0 | 1 | 7 | 4 | 5 | .213 | .275 | .277 | 71 | -2 | 0 | | | .917 | -5 | C-13 | -0.6 |
| Total | 5 | 93 | 242 | 19 | 50 | 7 | 4 | 1 | 18 | 21 | 37 | .207 | .273 | .281 | 69 | -9 | 1 | | | .947 | -5 | /C-71,1-12 | -1.1 |

■ NORM WALLEN   Wallen, Norman Edward (b: Norman Edward Walentoski)   b: 2/13/17, Milwaukee, Wis.   BR/TR, 5'11.5", 175 lbs.   Deb: 4/20/45

| 1945 | Bos-N | 4 | 15 | 1 | 2 | 0 | 1 | 0 | 1 | 1 | 1 | .133 | .188 | .267 | 25 | -2 | 0 | | | .800 | -2 | /3-4 | -0.3 |

■ JOE WALSH   Walsh, Joseph Patrick "Tweet"   b: 3/13/17, Roxbury, Mass.   BR/TR, 5'10", 155 lbs.   Deb: 7/1/38

| 1938 | Bos-N | 4 | 8 | 0 | 0 | 0 | 0 | 0 | 0 | 0 | 2 | .000 | .000 | .000 | -99 | -2 | 0 | | | .900 | -2 | /S-4 | -0.4 |

■ BUCKY WALTERS   Walters, William Henry   b: 4/19/09, Philadelphia, Pa.   d: 4/20/91, Abington, Pa.   BR/TR, 6'1", 180 lbs.   Deb: 9/18/31   MC

1931	Bos-N	9	38	2	8	2	0	0	0	3		.211	.211	.263	28	-4	0			.947	2	/3-6,2-3	-0.3
1932	Bos-N	22	75	8	14	3	1	0	4	2	18	.187	.208	.253	24	-8	0			.910	2	3-22	-0.5
1950	Bos-N	1	2	0	0	0	0	0	0	0	0	.000	.000	.000	-99	-1	0			1.000	-0	/P-1	0.0
Total	19	715	1966	227	477	99	16	23	234	114	303	.243	.288	.344	69	-90	12			.974	28	P-428,3-184/2O	-2.2
Team	3	32	115	10	22	5	1	0	4	2	21	.191	.205	.252	23	-13	0			.919	2	/3-28,2-3,P	-0.8

■ LLOYD WANER   Waner, Lloyd James "Little Poison"   b: 3/16/06, Harrah, Okla.   d: 7/22/82, Oklahoma City, Okla.   BL/TR, 5'9", 150 lbs.   Deb: 4/12/27   FH

| 1941 | Bos-N | 19 | 51 | 7 | 21 | 1 | 0 | 0 | 4 | 2 | 0 | .412 | .434 | .431 | 151 | 3 | 1 | | | .969 | -1 | O-15 | 0.2 |
| Total | 18 | 1993 | 7772 | 1201 | 2459 | 281 | 118 | 27 | 598 | 420 | 173 | .316 | .353 | .393 | 99 | -13 | 67 | | | .983 | 76 | *O-1818/2-2,3 | -3.4 |

■ PAUL WANER   Waner, Paul Glee "Big Poison"   b: 4/16/03, Harrah, Okla.   d: 8/29/65, Sarasota, Fla.   BL/TL, 5'8.5", 153 lbs.   Deb: 4/13/26   FCH

1941	Bos-N	95	294	40	82	10	2	2	46	47	14	.279	.378	.347	110	6	1			.965	-4	O-77/1-7	-0.3
1942	Bos-N	114	333	43	86	17	1	1	39	62	20	.258	.376	.324	108	6	2			.969	-8	O-94	-0.7
Total	20	2549	9459	1627	3152	605	191	113	1309	1091	376	.333	.404	.473	133	464	104			.975	40	*O-2288/1-73	36.1
Team	2	209	627	83	168	27	3	3	85	109	34	.268	.377	.335	109	12	3			.967	-12	O-171/1-7	-1.0

■ JOHN WARNER   Warner, John Joseph   b: 8/15/1872, New York, N.Y.   d: 12/21/43, Far Rockaway, N.Y.   BL/TR, 5'11", 165 lbs.   Deb: 4/23/1895

| 1895 | Bos-N | 3 | 7 | 2 | 1 | 0 | 0 | 0 | 1 | 1 | 0 | .143 | .333 | .143 | 24 | -1 | 0 | | | .917 | 1 | /C-3 | 0.0 |
| Total | 14 | 1073 | 3494 | 348 | 870 | 81 | 35 | 6 | 303 | 181 | 33 | .249 | .303 | .297 | 74 | -118 | 83 | | | .966 | 74 | *C-1032/1-8,O2 | 5.3 |

■ RABBIT WARSTLER   Warstler, Harold Burton   b: 9/13/03, N.Canton, Ohio   d: 5/31/64, N.Canton, Ohio   BR/TR, 5'7.5", 150 lbs.   Deb: 7/24/30

1936	Bos-N	74	304	27	64	6	0	0	17	22	33	.211	.266	.230	37	-27	2			.948	13	S-74	-0.9
1937	Bos-N	149	555	57	124	20	3	3	36	51	62	.223	.294	.276	60	-31	4			.942	-11	*S-149	-3.1
1938	Bos-N	142	467	37	108	10	4	0	40	48	38	.231	.303	.270	65	-22	3			.937	-7	*S-135/2-7	-1.9
1939	Bos-N	114	342	34	83	11	3	0	24	24	31	.243	.292	.292	62	-19	2			.953	1	S-49,2-43,3	-1.1
1940	Bos-N	33	57	6	12	0	0	0	4	10	5	.211	.328	.211	54	-3	0			.974	-1	2-24/3-2,S	-0.3
Total	11	1205	4088	431	935	133	36	11	332	405	414	.229	.300	.287	59	-243	42			.942	49	S-705,2-442/3	-11.3
Team	5	512	1725	161	391	47	7	3	121	155	169	.227	.292	.267	57	-102	11			.942	-5	S-408/2-74,3	-7.3

■ LINK WASEM   Wasem, Lincoln William   b: 1/30/11, Birmingham, Ohio   d: 3/6/79, S.Laguna, Cal.   BR/TR, 5'9.5", 180 lbs.   Deb: 5/5/37

| 1937 | Bos-N | 2 | 1 | 0 | 0 | 0 | 0 | 0 | 0 | 0 | 0 | .000 | .000 | .000 | -99 | -0 | 0 | | | 1.000 | 0 | /C-2 | 0.0 |

■ CLAUDELL WASHINGTON   Washington, Claudell   b: 8/31/54, Los Angeles, Cal.   BL/TL, 6', 190 lbs.   Deb: 7/5/74

1981	Atl-N	85	320	37	93	22	3	5	37	15	47	.291	.330	.425	110	3	12	6	0	.993	2	O-79	0.2
1982	*Atl-N	150	563	94	150	24	6	16	80	50	107	.266	.326	.416	104	3	33	10	4	.950	-4	*O-139	-0.2
1983	Atl-N	134	496	75	138	24	8	9	44	35	103	.278	.326	.413	96	-3	31	9	4	.974	2	*O-128	-0.1
1984	Atl-N★	120	416	62	119	21	2	17	61	59	77	.286	.376	.469	127	16	21	9	1	.967	-5	*O-107	0.8
1985	Atl-N	122	398	62	110	14	6	15	43	40	66	.276	.344	.455	115	7	14	4	2	.962	-14	O-99	-0.8
1986	Atl-N	40	137	17	37	11	0	5	14	14	26	.270	.338	.460	112	2	4	7	-3	.957	-5	O-38	-0.3
Total	17	1912	6787	926	1884	334	69	164	824	468	1266	.278	.328	.420	106	40	312	134		.973	-37	*O-1685/D-75	-4.7
Team	6	651	2330	347	647	116	25	67	279	213	426	.278	.341	.435	110	28	115	45		.967	-25	O-590	-0.9

YEAR	TM/L	G	AB	R	H	2B	3B	HR	RBI	BB	SO	AVG	OBP	SLG	PRO+	BR/A	SB	CS	SBR	FA	FR	G/POS	TPR

■ BOB WATSON Watson, Robert Jose "Bull" b: 4/10/46, Los Angeles, Cal. BR/TR, 6'2", 205 lbs. Deb: 9/9/66 C

1982	Atl-N	57	114	16	28	3	1	5	22	14	20	.246	.328	.421	104	1	1	1	-0	1.000	-4	1-27/O-2	-0.5
1983	Atl-N	65	149	14	46	9	0	6	37	18	23	.309	.383	.490	131	6	0	2	-1	.984	-3	1-34	0.0
1984	Atl-N	49	85	4	18	4	0	2	12	9	12	.212	.287	.329	68	-4	0	0	0	.983	1	1-19	-0.4
Total	19	1832	6185	802	1826	307	41	184	989	653	796	.295	.367	.447	130	247	27	28	-9	.991	-26	*1-1088,O-570/DC	12.1
Team	3	171	348	34	92	16	1	13	71	41	55	.264	.342	.428	107	3	1	3	-2	.989	-6	/1-80,O-2	-0.9

■ BERT WEEDEN Weeden, Charles Albert b: 12/21/1882, Northwood, N.H. d: 1/7/39, Northwood, N.H. BL/TL, 6', 200 lbs. Deb: 6/4/11

| 1911 | Bos-N | 1 | 1 | 0 | 0 | 0 | 0 | 0 | 0 | 0 | 0 | .000 | .000 | .000 | -93 | -0 | 0 | | | .000 | 0 | H | 0.0 |

■ JIMMY WELSH Welsh, James Daniel b: 10/9/02, Denver, Colo. d: 10/30/70, Oakland, Cal. BL/TR, 6'1", 174 lbs. Deb: 4/14/25

1925	Bos-N	122	484	69	151	25	8	7	63	20	24	.312	.350	.440	110	5	7	4	-0	.960	6	*O-116/2-3	0.4
1926	Bos-N	134	490	69	136	18	11	3	57	33	28	.278	.333	.378	100	-1	6			.965	10	*O-129	0.0
1927	Bos-N	131	497	72	143	26	7	9	54	23	27	.288	.330	.423	109	4	11			.969	13	*O-129/1-1	0.9
1929	Bos-N	53	186	24	54	8	7	2	16	13	9	.290	.350	.441	98	-1	1			.979	9	O-51	0.4
1930	Bos-N	113	422	51	116	21	9	3	36	29	23	.275	.327	.389	75	-18	5			.980	11	*O-110	-1.3
Total	6	715	2684	387	778	127	47	35	288	156	144	.290	.340	.411	98	-14	37	4		.971	42	O-687/2-3,1	-1.5
Team	5	553	2079	285	600	98	42	24	226	118	111	.289	.336	.411	98	-10	30	4		.970	49	O-535/2-3,1	0.4

■ STAN WENTZEL Wentzel, Stanley Aaron b: 1/13/17, Lorane, Pa. d: 11/28/91, St.Lawrence, Pa. BR/TR, 6'1", 200 lbs. Deb: 9/23/45

| 1945 | Bos-N | 4 | 19 | 3 | 4 | 0 | 1 | 0 | 6 | 0 | 3 | .211 | .211 | .316 | 45 | -1 | 1 | | | 1.000 | -1 | /O-4 | -0.3 |

■ JIM WESSINGER Wessinger, James Michael b: 9/25/55, Utica, N.Y. BR/TR, 5'10", 165 lbs. Deb: 8/4/79

| 1979 | Atl-N | 10 | 7 | 2 | 0 | 0 | 0 | 0 | 0 | 1 | 4 | .000 | .125 | .000 | -59 | -2 | 0 | 0 | 0 | .833 | 1 | /2-2 | -0.1 |

■ MAX WEST West, Max Edward b: 11/28/16, Dexter, Mo. BL/TR, 6'1.5", 182 lbs. Deb: 4/19/38

1938	Bos-N	123	418	47	98	16	5	10	63	38	38	.234	.300	.368	92	-6	5			.986	-9	*O-109/1-7	-1.9
1939	Bos-N	130	449	67	128	26	6	19	82	51	55	.285	.364	.497	139	23	1			.974	-7	*O-124	1.2
1940	Bos-N★	139	524	72	137	27	5	7	72	65	54	.261	.344	.372	103	3	2			.975	1	*O-102,1-36	-0.5
1941	Bos-N	138	484	63	134	28	4	12	68	72	68	.277	.373	.426	130	20	5			.981	1	*O-132	1.9
1942	Bos-N	134	452	54	115	22	0	16	56	68	59	.254	.354	.409	126	15	4			.991	-1	1-85,O-50	0.7
1946	Bos-N	1	1	0	0	0	0	0	0	0	0	.000	.000	.000	-99	-0	0			1.000	0	/1-1	0.0
Total	7	824	2676	338	681	136	20	77	380	353	340	.254	.344	.407	114	50	19			.975	-15	O-591,1-161	0.1
Team	6	665	2328	303	612	119	20	64	341	294	275	.263	.348	.414	118	55	17			.977	-10	O-517,1-129	1.4

■ OSCAR WESTERBERG Westerberg, Oscar William b: 7/8/1882, Alameda, Cal. d: 4/17/09, Alameda, Cal. BB/TR, Deb: 9/5/07

| 1907 | Bos-N | 2 | 6 | 0 | 2 | 0 | 0 | 0 | 1 | 1 | | .333 | .429 | .333 | 139 | 0 | 0 | | | 1.000 | -1 | /S-2 | 0.0 |

■ AL WESTON Weston, Alfred John b: 12/11/05, Lynn, Mass. BR/TR, 6', 195 lbs. Deb: 7/7/29

| 1929 | Bos-N | 3 | 3 | 0 | 0 | 0 | 0 | 0 | 0 | 0 | 2 | .000 | .000 | .000 | -99 | -1 | 0 | | | .000 | 0 | H | -0.1 |

■ JEFF WETHERBY Wetherby, Jeffrey Barrett b: 10/18/63, Granada Hills, Cal. BL/TL, 6'2", 195 lbs. Deb: 6/7/89

| 1989 | Atl-N | 52 | 48 | 5 | 10 | 2 | 1 | 1 | 7 | 4 | 6 | .208 | .269 | .354 | 75 | -2 | 1 | 0 | 0 | 1.000 | -2 | /O-9 | -0.4 |

■ BERT WHALING Whaling, Albert James b: 6/22/1888, Los Angeles, Cal. d: 1/21/65, Sawtelle, Cal. BR/TR, 6', 185 lbs. Deb: 4/22/13

1913	Bos-N	79	211	22	51	8	2	0	25	10	32	.242	.283	.299	65	-10	3			.990	1	C-77	-0.4
1914	Bos-N	60	172	18	36	7	0	0	12	21	28	.209	.303	.250	65	-7	2			.981	12	C-59	1.0
1915	Bos-N	72	190	10	42	6	2	0	13	8	38	.221	.264	.274	66	-8	0	1	-1	.986	1	C-69	-0.3
Total	3	211	573	50	129	21	4	0	50	39	98	.225	.283	.276	65	-25	5	1		.986	14	C-205	0.3

■ BOBBY WHEELOCK Wheelock, Warren H. b: 8/6/1864, Charlestown, Mass. d: 3/13/28, Boston, Mass. BR/TR, 5'8", 160 lbs. Deb: 5/19/1887

| 1887 | Bos-N | 48 | 166 | 32 | 42 | 4 | 2 | 1 | 15 | 15 | 15 | .253 | .315 | .337 | 81 | -4 | 20 | | | .878 | -7 | O-28,S-20/2 | -0.9 |
| Total | 3 | 236 | 854 | 138 | 201 | 25 | 4 | 3 | 54 | 118 | 70 | .235 | .330 | .285 | 80 | -18 | 106 | | | .894 | 11 | S-208/O-28,2 | 0.4 |

■ TOM WHELAN Whelan, Thomas Joseph b: 1/3/1894, Lynn, Mass. d: 6/26/57, Boston, Mass. BR/TR, 5'11", 175 lbs. Deb: 8/13/20

| 1920 | Bos-N | 1 | 1 | 0 | 0 | 0 | 0 | 0 | 0 | 1 | 1 | .000 | .500 | .000 | 54 | 0 | 0 | 0 | 0 | 1.000 | 0 | /1-1 | 0.0 |

■ PETE WHISENANT Whisenant, Thomas Peter b: 12/14/29, Asheville, N.C. BR/TR, 6'2", 200 lbs. Deb: 4/16/52 C

| 1952 | Bos-N | 24 | 52 | 3 | 10 | 2 | 0 | 1 | 4 | 13 | | .192 | .250 | .231 | 35 | -5 | 1 | 1 | -0 | .973 | 2 | O-14 | -0.3 |
| Total | 8 | 475 | 988 | 140 | 221 | 46 | 8 | 37 | 134 | 86 | 196 | .224 | .287 | .399 | 80 | -30 | 17 | 5 | 2 | .988 | -20 | O-343/3-1,C2 | -6.3 |

■ LARRY WHISENTON Whisenton, Larry b: 7/3/56, St.Louis, Mo. BL/TL, 6'1", 190 lbs. Deb: 9/17/77

1977	Atl-N	4	4	1	1	0	0	0	1	0	3	.250	.250	.250	31	-0	0	0	0	.000	0	H	-0.1
1978	Atl-N	6	16	1	3	1	0	0	2	1	2	.188	.235	.250	32	-1	0	0	0	1.000	-1	/O-4	-0.2
1979	Atl-N	13	37	3	9	2	1	0	1	3	3	.243	.300	.351	72	-1	1	0	0	1.000	3	O-13	0.1
1981	Atl-N	9	5	1	1	0	0	0	0	2	1	.200	.429	.200	81	0	0	0	0	.000	-1	/O-2	-0.1
1982	*Atl-N	84	143	21	34	7	2	4	17	23	33	.238	.343	.399	103	1	2	2	-1	.964	0	O-34	-0.3
Total	5	116	205	27	48	10	3	4	21	29	42	.234	.329	.371	90	-1	3	2	-0	.968	-1	/O-53	-0.6

■ CHARLIE WHITE White, Charles b: 8/12/28, Kinston, N.C. BL/TR, 5'11", 192 lbs. Deb: 4/18/54

1954	Mil-N	50	93	14	22	4	0	1	8	9	8	.237	.304	.312	65	-5	0	0	0	.981	-2	C-28	-0.6
1955	Mil-N	12	30	3	7	1	0	0	4	5	7	.233	.361	.267	74	-1	0	0	0	1.000	-2	C-10	-0.2
Total	2	62	123	17	29	5	0	1	12	14	15	.236	.319	.301	67	-6	0	0	0	.986	-4	/C-38	-0.8

■ DEACON WHITE White, James Laurie b: 12/7/1847, Caton, N.Y. d: 7/7/39, Aurora, Ill. BL/TR, 5'11", 175 lbs. Deb: 5/4/1871 FM

1873	Bos-n	60	310	79	121	20	8	0	64	0	2	.390	.390	.506	149	16						*C-56/O-9	1.2
1874	Bos-n	70	350	75	106	4	7	3		4		.303	.311	.380	112	3						*C-55,O-12/12	0.3
1875	Bos-n	80	372	77	136	20	4	1		9		.366	.369	.449	175	26						*C-72/O-7,1	2.4
1877	Bos-N	59	266	51	103	14	11	2	49	8	3	.387	.405	.545	190	26				.963	1	1-35,O-19/C	2.3
Total	5 n	261	1286	292	447	53	26	5	107	14	4	.348	.355	.441	144	58	8	0	2			C-223/O-31,21	4.7
Total	15	1299	5335	849	1619	217	73	18	756	292	215	.303	.344	.382	123	138	46	0	14	.853	-33	3-826,C-226,1O/2PS	10.6
Team	3 n	210	1032	231	363	44	19	4	64	6	2	.352	.355	.443	145	0	6	2	1	.963	0	C-183/O-28,12	3.9

■ JACK WHITE White, John Wallace b: 1/19/1878, Traders Point, Ind. d: 9/30/63, Indianapolis, Ind BR/TR, 5'6", Deb: 6/26/04

| 1904 | Bos-N | 2 | 5 | 1 | 0 | 0 | 0 | 0 | 0 | 0 | | .000 | .000 | .000 | -99 | -1 | 0 | | | 1.000 | 1 | /O-1 | -0.1 |

■ SAMMY WHITE White, Samuel Charles b: 7/7/28, Wenatchee, Wash. d: 8/5/91, Princeville, Hawaii BR/TR, 6'3", 195 lbs. Deb: 9/26/51

| 1961 | Mil-N | 21 | 63 | 1 | 14 | 1 | 0 | 1 | 5 | 2 | 9 | .222 | .246 | .286 | 43 | -5 | 0 | 0 | 0 | .974 | 4 | C-20 | 0.0 |
| Total | 11 | 1043 | 3502 | 324 | 916 | 167 | 20 | 66 | 421 | 218 | 381 | .262 | .307 | .377 | 79 | -109 | 14 | 15 | | .984 | 30 | *C-1027 | -4.0 |

■ SAM WHITE White, Samuel Lambeth b: 8/23/1892, Greater Preston, Yorkshire, England d: 11/11/29, Philadelphia, Pa. BL/TR, 6', 185 lbs. Deb: 9/8/19

| 1919 | Bos-N | 1 | 1 | 0 | 0 | 0 | 0 | 0 | 0 | 0 | 0 | .000 | .000 | .000 | -99 | -0 | 0 | | | 1.000 | 2 | /C-1 | 0.1 |

■ ED WHITED Whited, Edward Morris b: 2/9/64, Bristol, Pa. BR/TR, 6'3", 195 lbs. Deb: 7/5/89

| 1989 | Atl-N | 36 | 74 | 5 | 12 | 3 | 0 | 1 | 4 | 6 | 15 | .162 | .225 | .243 | 33 | -6 | 1 | 0 | 0 | .914 | -0 | 3-29/1-3 | -0.7 |

YEAR	TM/L	G	AB	R	H	2B	3B	HR	RBI	BB	SO	AVG	OBP	SLG	PRO+	BR/A	SB	CS	SBR	FA	FR	G/POS	TPR

■ GIL WHITEHOUSE   Whitehouse, Gilbert Arthur   b: 10/15/1893, Somerville, Mass.   d: 2/14/26, Brewer, Me.   BB/TR, 5'10", 170 lbs.   Deb: 6/20/12

| 1912 | Bos-N | 2 | 3 | 0 | 0 | 0 | 0 | 0 | 0 | 0 | 3 | .000 | .000 | .000 | -98 | -1 | 0 | | | .667 | -1 | /C-2 | -0.2 |
| Total | 2 | 37 | 123 | 16 | 27 | 6 | 2 | 6 | 9 | 6 | 19 | .220 | .262 | .301 | 53 | -9 | 3 | | | .846 | -2 | /O-28,C-3,P | -1.3 |

■ GURDON WHITELEY   Whiteley, Gurdon W.   b: 10/5/1859, Ashaway, R.I.   d: 11/24/24, Cranston, R.I.   5'11", 190 lbs.   Deb: 8/7/1884

| 1885 | Bos-N | 33 | 135 | 14 | 25 | 2 | 2 | 1 | 7 | 1 | 25 | .185 | .191 | .252 | 44 | -8 | | | | .781 | -2 | O-32/C-1 | -1.0 |
| Total | 2 | 41 | 169 | 18 | 30 | 2 | 2 | 1 | 7 | 2 | 33 | .178 | .187 | .231 | 34 | -12 | | | | .785 | -1 | /O-40,C-1 | -1.3 |

■ PINKY WHITNEY   Whitney, Arthur Carter   b: 1/2/05, San Antonio, Tex.   d: 9/1/87, Center, Tex.   BR/TR, 5'10", 165 lbs.   Deb: 4/11/28

1933	Bos-N	100	382	42	94	17	2	8	49	25	23	.246	.296	.364	95	-4	2			.971	1	3-85,2-18	0.4
1934	Bos-N	146	563	58	146	26	2	12	79	25	54	.259	.294	.377	85	-14	7			**.968**	3	*3-111,2-36/S	-0.5
1935	Bos-N	126	458	41	125	23	4	4	60	24	36	.273	.312	.367	89	-8	2			.958	6	3-74,2-49	0.4
1936	Bos-N	10	40	1	7	0	0	0	5	2	4	.175	.233	.175	12	-5	0			.971	1	3-10	-0.3
Total	12	1539	5765	696	1701	303	56	93	927	400	438	.295	.343	.415	96	-43	45			.961	63	*3-1358,2-119/1S	8.2
Team	4	382	1443	142	372	66	8	24	193	76	117	.258	.299	.365	87	-31	11			.966	11	3-280,2-103/S	0.0

■ FRANK WHITNEY   Whitney, Frank Thomas "Jumbo"   b: 2/18/1856, Brockton, Mass.   d: 10/30/43, Baltimore, Md.   BR/TR, 5'7.5", 152 lbs.   Deb: 5/17/1876   F

| 1876 | Bos-N | 34 | 139 | 27 | 33 | 7 | 1 | 0 | 15 | 1 | 3 | .237 | .243 | .302 | 79 | -3 | | | | .818 | 3 | O-34/2-1 | -0.1 |

■ JIM WHITNEY   Whitney, James Evans "Grasshopper Jim"   b: 11/10/1857, Conklin, N.Y.   d: 5/21/1891, Binghamton, N.Y.   BL/TR, 6'2", 172 lbs.   Deb: 5/2/1881

1881	Bos-N	75	282	37	72	17	3	0	32	19	18	.255	.302	.337	106	3				.808	-9	*P-66,O-15/1	-0.5
1882	Bos-N	61	251	49	81	18	7	5	48	24	13	.323	.382	.510	183	24				.886	-3	P-49/O-9,1	-0.1
1883	Bos-N	96	409	78	115	27	10	5	57	25	29	.281	.323	.433	124	11				.921	-4	P-62,O-40/1	0.0
1884	Bos-N	66	270	41	70	17	5	3	40	16	38	.259	.301	.393	117	5				**1.000**	-1	P-38,O-15,1/3	-0.4
1885	Bos-N	72	290	35	68	8	4	0	36	17	24	.234	.277	.290	86	-4				.901	5	P-51,O-17/1	-0.3
Total	10	550	2144	316	559	113	39	18	279	161	211	.261	.313	.375	112	30	20			.900	-9	*P-413,O-130/13	-1.8
Team	5	370	1502	240	406	87	29	13	213	101	122	.270	.316	.393	123	39	0			.894	-12	P-266/O-96,13	-1.3

■ ERNIE WHITT   Whitt, Leo Ernest   b: 6/13/52, Detroit, Mich.   BL/TR, 6'2", 200 lbs.   Deb: 9/12/76

| 1990 | Atl-N | 67 | 180 | 14 | 31 | 8 | 0 | 2 | 10 | 23 | 27 | .172 | .266 | .250 | 40 | -14 | 0 | 2 | -1 | .991 | 2 | C-59 | -1.1 |
| Total | 15 | 1328 | 3774 | 447 | 938 | 176 | 15 | 134 | 534 | 436 | 491 | .249 | .327 | .410 | 98 | -9 | 22 | 26 | | .991 | 36 | *C-1246/D-11 | 7.9 |

■ POSSUM WHITTED   Whitted, George Bostic   b: 2/4/1890, Durham, N.C.   d: 10/16/62, Wilmington, N.C.   BR/TR, 5'8.5", 168 lbs.   Deb: 9/16/12

| 1914 | *Bos-N | 66 | 218 | 36 | 57 | 11 | 4 | 2 | 31 | 18 | 18 | .261 | .326 | .376 | 109 | 2 | 10 | | | .967 | 4 | O-38,2-15/13S | 0.5 |
| Total | 11 | 1025 | 3630 | 440 | 978 | 145 | 60 | 23 | 451 | 215 | 310 | .269 | .313 | .361 | 95 | -27 | 116 | | | .975 | 27 | O-651,3-177/12S | -3.9 |

■ AL WICKLAND   Wickland, Albert   b: 1/27/1888, Chicago, Ill.   d: 3/14/80, Port Washington, Wis.   BL/TL, 5'7", 155 lbs.   Deb: 8/21/13

| 1918 | Bos-N | 95 | 332 | 55 | 87 | 7 | 13 | 4 | 32 | 53 | 39 | .262 | .367 | .398 | 139 | 17 | 12 | | | .975 | 3 | O-95 | 1.6 |
| Total | 5 | 444 | 1468 | 212 | 397 | 58 | 38 | 12 | 144 | 207 | 184 | .270 | .364 | .386 | 109 | 22 | 58 | | | .968 | -1 | O-424 | 0.2 |

■ WHITEY WIETELMANN   Wietelmann, William Frederick   b: 3/15/19, Zanesville, Ohio   BB/TR, 6', 170 lbs.   Deb: 9/6/39   C

1939	Bos-N	23	69	2	14	1	0	0	5	2	9	.203	.225	.217	21	-8	1			.953	2	S-22/2-1	-0.5
1940	Bos-N	35	41	3	8	1	0	0	1	5	5	.195	.283	.220	43	-3	0			.962	3	2-15/3-9,S	0.0
1941	Bos-N	16	33	1	3	0	0	0	1	2		.091	.118	.091	-43	-6	0			1.000	3	2-10/S-5,3	-0.3
1942	Bos-N	13	34	4	7	2	0	0	4	5		.206	.289	.265	64	-1	0			.941	-1	S-11/2-1	-0.1
1943	Bos-N	153	534	33	115	14	1	0	39	46	40	.215	.281	.245	53	-31	9			.957	20	*S-153	0.0
1944	Bos-N	125	417	46	100	18	1	2	32	33	25	.240	.300	.302	67	-18	0			.954	-6	*S-103,2-23/3	-1.6
1945	Bos-N	123	428	53	116	15	3	4	33	39	27	.271	.335	.348	89	-6	4			.972	3	2-87,S-39/3P	0.4
1946	Bos-N	44	78	7	16	0	0	0	5	14	8	.205	.326	.205	52	-4	0			.915	-6	S-16/3-8,2P	-0.9
Total	9	580	1762	170	409	55	6	7	122	156	131	.232	.298	.282	63	-85	14			.952	3	S-374,2-155/3P1	-4.9
Team	8	532	1634	149	379	51	5	6	115	144	121	.232	.297	.280	64	-78	14			.955	18	S-352,2-141/3P	-3.0

■ CLAUDE WILBORN   Wilborn, Claude Edward   b: 9/1/12, Woodsdale, N.C.   d: 11/13/92, Roxboro, N.C.   BL/TR, 6'1", 180 lbs.   Deb: 9/8/40

| 1940 | Bos-N | 5 | 7 | 0 | 0 | 0 | 0 | 0 | 0 | 0 | 1 | .000 | .000 | .000 | -99 | -2 | 0 | | | .500 | 1 | /O-3 | -0.4 |

■ JOE WILHOIT   Wilhoit, Joseph William   b: 12/20/1885, Hiawatha, Kan.   d: 9/25/30, Santa Barbara, Cal.   BL/TR, 6'2", 175 lbs.   Deb: 4/12/16

1916	Bos-N	116	383	44	88	13	4	2	38	27	45	.230	.282	.300	82	-8	18			.979	2	*O-108	-1.4
1917	Bos-N	54	186	20	51	5	0	1	10	17	15	.274	.335	.317	107	2	5			.928	-3	O-52	-0.4
Total	4	283	782	93	201	23	9	3	73	75	82	.257	.323	.321	101	2	28			.969	-11	O-234/1-1	-2.3
Team	2	170	569	64	139	18	4	3	48	44	60	.244	.300	.306	90	-7	23			.964	-1	O-160	-1.8

■ JERRY WILLARD   Willard, Gerald Duane   b: 3/14/60, Oxnard, Cal.   BL/TR, 6'2", 195 lbs.   Deb: 4/11/84

1991	*Atl-N	17	14	1	3	0	0	1	4	2	5	.214	.313	.429	100	-0	0	0	0	1.000	0	/C-1	0.0
1992	Atl-N	26	23	2	8	1	0	2	7	1	3	.348	.375	.652	175	2	0	0	0	1.000	0	/C-1	0.3
Total	8	346	783	82	195	29	1	25	114	83	161	.249	.323	.384	95	-5	1	1		.988	-11	C-247/D-7,13	-0.6
Team	2	43	37	3	11	1	0	3	11	3	8	.297	.350	.568	146	2	0	0	0	1.000	1	/C-2	0.3

■ EARL WILLIAMS   Williams, Earl Baxter   b: 1/27/03, Cumberland Gap, Tenn.   d: 3/10/58, Knoxville, Tenn.   BR/TR, 6'0.5", 185 lbs.   Deb: 5/27/28

| 1928 | Bos-N | 3 | 2 | 0 | 0 | 0 | 0 | 0 | 0 | 0 | 1 | .000 | .000 | .000 | -99 | -1 | 0 | | | 1.000 | 0 | /C-1 | -0.1 |

■ EARL WILLIAMS   Williams, Earl Craig   b: 7/14/48, Newark, N.J.   BR/TR, 6'3", 220 lbs.   Deb: 9/13/70

1970	Atl-N	10	19	4	7	4	0	0	5	3	4	.368	.455	.579	165	2	0	0	0	1.000	1	/1-4,3-3	0.3
1971	Atl-N	145	497	64	129	14	1	33	87	42	80	.260	.326	.491	121	12	0	1	-1	.981	-8	C-72,3-42,1	0.4
1972	Atl-N	151	565	72	146	24	2	28	87	62	118	.258	.338	.457	113	9	0	0	0	.980	-19	*C-116,3-21,1	-0.7
1975	Atl-N	111	383	42	92	13	0	11	50	34	63	.240	.307	.360	82	-10	0	0	0	.989	-5	1-90,C-11	-2.1
1976	Atl-N	61	184	18	39	3	0	9	26	19	33	.212	.289	.375	82	-5	0	0	0	.995	-9	C-38,1-17	-1.4
Total	8	889	3058	361	756	115	6	138	457	298	574	.247	.321	.424	105	14	2	5	-2	.984	-60	C-456,1-327/3D	-5.4
Team	5	478	1648	200	413	58	3	81	255	160	298	.251	.323	.437	106	9	0	1	-1	.982	-39	C-237,1-162/3	-3.5

■ ART WILSON   Wilson, Arthur Earl "Dutch"   b: 12/11/1885, Macon, Ill.   d: 6/12/60, Chicago, Ill.   BR/TR, 5'8", 170 lbs.   Deb: 9/29/08

1918	Bos-N	89	280	15	69	8	2	0	19	24	31	.246	.310	.289	87	-4	5			.977	-10	C-85	-0.8
1919	Bos-N	71	191	14	49	8	1	0	16	25	19	.257	.346	.309	102	1	2			.977	-2	C-64/1-1	0.5
1920	Bos-N	16	19	0	1	0	0	0	0	1	1	.053	.143	.053	-44	-4	0	0	0	1.000	-2	/3-6,C-2	-0.5
Total	14	812	2056	237	536	96	22	24	226	292	289	.261	.357	.364	106	28	50	0		.972	-18	C-738/3-6,1	6.4
Team	3	176	490	29	119	16	3	0	35	50	51	.243	.318	.288	87	-6	7	0		.976	-14	C-151/3-6,1	-0.8

■ CHARLIE WILSON   Wilson, Charles Woodrow "Swamp Baby"   b: 1/13/05, Clinton, S.C.   d: 12/19/70, Rochester, N.Y.   BB/TR, 5'10.5", 178 lbs.   Deb: 4/14/31

| 1931 | Bos-N | 16 | 58 | 7 | 11 | 4 | 0 | 1 | 11 | 3 | 5 | .190 | .230 | .310 | 45 | -5 | 0 | | | .917 | -2 | 3-14 | -0.6 |
| Total | 4 | 57 | 186 | 15 | 40 | 7 | 3 | 2 | 14 | 8 | 16 | .215 | .247 | .317 | 50 | -13 | 0 | | | .935 | -10 | /S-25,3-22 | -1.9 |

■ FRANK WILSON   Wilson, Francis Edward "Squash"   b: 4/20/01, Malden, Mass.   d: 11/25/74, Leicester, Mass.   BL/TR, 6', 185 lbs.   Deb: 6/20/24

1924	Bos-N	61	215	20	51	7	1	1	15	23	22	.237	.311	.284	63	-11	3	4	-2	.973	3	O-55	-1.3
1925	Bos-N	12	31	3	13	1	1	0	4	1	1	.419	.486	.516	171	4	2	1	0	1.000	1	O-10	0.3
1926	Bos-N	87	236	22	56	11	2	3	19	20	21	.237	.300	.309	70	-10	3			.934	1	O-56	-1.3
Total	4	168	488	46	120	19	4	5	38	48	44	.246	.315	.307	72	-19	8	5		.958	4	O-122	-2.5
Team	3	160	482	45	120	19	4	1	38	47	44	.249	.317	.311	74	-17	8	5		.958	5	O-121	-2.3

YEAR	TM/L	G	AB	R	H	2B	3B	HR	RBI	BB	SO	AVG	OBP	SLG	PRO+	BR/A	SB	CS	SBR	FA	FR	G/POS	TPR

■ CASEY WISE Wise, Kendall Cole b: 9/8/32, Lafayette, Ind. BB/TR, 6′, 170 lbs. Deb: 4/16/57

1958	*Mil-N	31	71	8	14	1	0	0	4	4	8	.197	.240	.211	23	-8	1	1	-0	1.000	0	2-10/S-7,3	-0.7
1959	Mil-N	22	76	11	13	2	0	1	5	10	5	.171	.267	.237	39	-7	0	0	0	.989	-7	2-20/S-5	-1.3
Total	4	126	321	37	56	6	3	3	17	29	36	.174	.243	.240	31	-32	2	1	0	.968	-2	/2-78,S-27,3	-2.8
Team	2	53	147	19	27	3	0	1	5	14	13	.184	.255	.224	31	-15	1	1	-0	.992	-7	/2-30,S-12,3	-2.0

■ NICK WISE Wise, Nicholas Joseph b: 6/15/1866, Boston, Mass. d: 1/15/23, Boston, Mass. BR/TR, 5′11″, 194 lbs. Deb: 6/20/1888

| 1888 | Bos-N | 1 | 3 | 0 | 0 | 0 | 0 | 0 | 0 | 0 | 0 | .000 | .000 | .000 | -98 | -1 | 0 | | | .000 | -0 | /O-1,C-1 | -0.1 |

■ SAM WISE Wise, Samuel Washington "Modoc" b: 8/18/1857, Akron, Ohio d: 1/22/10, Akron, Ohio BL/TR, 5′10.5″, 170 lbs. Deb: 7/30/1881

1882	Bos-N	78	298	44	66	11	4	4	34	5	45	.221	.234	.326	77	-8				.852	-13	*S-72/3-6	-1.5
1883	Bos-N	96	406	73	110	25	7	4	58	13	74	.271	.294	.397	105	2				.823	-2	*S-96	-0.2
1884	Bos-N	114	426	60	91	15	9	4	41	25	104	.214	.257	.319	81	-9				.884	6	*S-107/2-7	-0.2
1885	Bos-N	107	424	71	120	20	10	4	46	25	61	.283	.323	.406	139	18				.858	13	*S-79,2-22/O	3.1
1886	Bos-N	96	387	71	112	19	12	4	72	33	61	.289	.345	.432	140	19	31			.956	-24	1-57,2-20,S/O	-1.0
1887	Bos-N	113	467	103	156	27	17	9	92	36	44	.334	.390	.522	151	32	43			.869	-6	S-72,O-27,2	2.2
1888	Bos-N	105	417	66	100	19	12	4	40	34	66	.240	.306	.372	113	6	33			.888	10	S-89/3-6,102	1.7
Total	12	1175	4715	834	1281	221	112	49	672	389	643	.272	.332	.397	115	90	203			.859	-33	S-563,2-448/130	6.8
Team	7	709	2825	488	755	136	71	33	383	171	455	.267	.312	.401	118	60	107			.861	-16	S-533/2-67,103	4.4

■ HARRY WOLVERTON Wolverton, Harry Sterling "Fighting Harry" b: 12/6/1873, Mt.Vernon, Ohio d: 2/4/37, Oakland, Cal. BL/TR, 5′11″, 205 lbs. Deb: 9/25/1898 M

| 1905 | Bos-N | 122 | 463 | 38 | 104 | 15 | 7 | 2 | 55 | 22 | | .225 | .276 | .300 | 73 | -16 | 10 | | | .934 | 4 | *3-122 | -0.8 |
| Total | 9 | 783 | 3001 | 346 | 833 | 95 | 53 | 7 | 352 | 166 | | .278 | .326 | .352 | 96 | -17 | 83 | | | .909 | 6 | 3-756/S-1 | 0.4 |

■ SID WOMACK Womack, Sidney Kirk "Tex" b: 10/2/1896, Greensburg, La. d: 8/28/58, Jackson, Miss. BR/TR, 5′10.5″, 185 lbs. Deb: 8/15/26

| 1926 | Bos-N | 1 | 3 | 0 | 0 | 0 | 0 | 0 | 1 | 0 | 0 | .000 | .000 | .000 | -99 | -1 | 0 | | | 1.000 | 0 | /C-1 | -0.1 |

■ WOODY WOODWARD Woodward, William Frederick b: 9/23/42, Miami, Fla. BR/TR, 6′2″, 185 lbs. Deb: 9/9/63

1963	Mil-N	10	2	1	0	0	0	0	0	0	0	.000	.000	.000	-99	-1	0	0	0	1.000	3	/S-5	0.2
1964	Mil-N	77	115	18	24	2	1	0	11	6	28	.209	.260	.243	43	-9	0	1	-1	.958	13	2-40,S-18/31	0.6
1965	Mil-N	112	265	17	55	7	4	0	11	10	50	.208	.236	.264	41	-21	2	2	-1	.977	11	*S-107/2-8	-0.6
1966	Atl-N	144	455	46	120	23	3	0	43	37	54	.264	.325	.327	81	-11	2	2	-1	.973	-6	2-79,S-73	-0.7
1967	Atl-N	136	429	30	97	15	2	0	25	37	51	.226	.289	.270	62	-21	0	6	-4	.982	9	*2-120,S-16	-0.7
1968	Atl-N	12	24	2	4	1	0	0	1	1	6	.167	.200	.208	23	-2	1	0	0	.973	3	S-6,3-2,2	0.2
Total	9	880	2187	208	517	79	14	1	148	169	301	.236	.295	.287	64	-103	14	15	-5	.974	23	S-521,2-278/31	-2.9
Team	6	491	1290	114	300	48	10	0	91	91	189	.233	.287	.285	62	-64	5	11	-5	.977	32	2-248,S-225/31	-1.0

■ CHUCK WORKMAN Workman, Charles Thomas b: 1/6/15, Leeton, Mo. d: 1/3/53, Kansas City, Mo. BL/TR, 6′, 175 lbs. Deb: 9/18/38

1943	Bos-N	153	615	71	153	17	1	10	67	53	72	.249	.311	.328	86	-11	12			.988	6	*O-149/1-3,3	-1.5
1944	Bos-N	140	418	46	87	18	3	11	53	42	41	.208	.287	.344	74	-15	1			.983	-3	*O-103,3-19	-2.3
1945	Bos-N	139	514	77	141	16	2	25	87	51	58	.274	.347	.459	122	14	9			.910	-17	*3-107,O-24	-0.1
1946	Bos-N	25	48	5	8	2	0	2	7	3	11	.167	.231	.333	58	-3	0			.920	-1	O-12	-0.5
Total	6	526	1749	213	423	57	7	50	230	161	202	.242	.311	.368	91	-24	24			.985	-8	O-329,3-128/1	-4.8
Team	4	457	1595	199	389	53	6	48	214	149	182	.244	.314	.375	94	-16	22			.983	-14	O-288,3-127/1	-4.4

■ RED WORTHINGTON Worthington, Robert Lee b: 4/24/06, Alhambra, Cal. d: 12/8/63, Sepulveda, Cal. BR/TR, 5′11″, 170 lbs. Deb: 4/14/31

1931	Bos-N	128	491	47	143	25	10	4	44	26	38	.291	.328	.407	100	-1	1			.988	-3	*O-124	-1.3
1932	Bos-N	105	435	62	132	35	8	8	61	15	24	.303	.330	.476	118	9	1			.987	-1	*O-104	0.1
1933	Bos-N	17	45	3	7	4	0	0	1	3		.156	.174	.244	20	-5	0			.900	-1	O-10	-0.7
1934	Bos-N	41	65	6	16	5	0	0	6	6	5	.246	.319	.323	78	-2	0			.920	-1	O-11	-0.3
Total	4	292	1037	118	298	69	18	12	111	48	71	.287	.321	.423	103	1	2			.981	-7	O-249	-2.2
Team	4	291	1036	118	298	69	18	12	111	48	70	.288	.322	.424	103	1	2			.981	-7	O-249	-2.2

■ AL WRIGHT Wright, Albert Edgar "A-1" b: 11/11/12, San Francisco, Cal BR/TR, 6′1.5″, 170 lbs. Deb: 4/25/33

| 1933 | Bos-N | 4 | 1 | 0 | 1 | 0 | 0 | 0 | 0 | 0 | 0 | 1.000 | 1.000 | 1.000 | 515 | 1 | 0 | | | .500 | -0 | /2-3 | 0.0 |

■ AB WRIGHT Wright, Albert Owen b: 11/16/05, Terlton, Okla. BR/TR, 6′1.5″, 190 lbs. Deb: 4/20/35

| 1944 | Bos-N | 71 | 195 | 20 | 50 | 9 | 0 | 7 | 35 | 18 | 31 | .256 | .326 | .410 | 102 | 0 | 0 | | | .968 | -4 | O-47 | -0.6 |
| Total | 2 | 138 | 355 | 37 | 88 | 20 | 1 | 9 | 53 | 28 | 48 | .248 | .310 | .386 | 85 | -9 | 2 | | | .974 | -11 | /O-94 | -2.3 |

■ GEORGE WRIGHT Wright, George b: 1/28/1847, Yonkers, N.Y. d: 8/21/37, Boston, Mass. BR/TR, 5′9.5″, 150 lbs. Deb: 5/5/1871 FMH

1871	Bos-n	16	80	33	33	7	5	0	11	6	1	.412	.453	.625	200	10	9					S-15/1-1	0.6
1872	Bos-n	48	255	87	87	16	5	2	33	3	1	.341	.349	.467	141	10						*S-48	0.9
1873	Bos-n	59	325	99	126	13	7	3	48	8	2	.388	.402	.498	151	17						*S-59	1.0
1874	Bos-n	60	313	76	106	11	15	2		7		.339	.353	.489	156	18						*S-60	1.2
1875	Bos-n	79	406	105	135	18	7	1		2		.333	.336	.419	154	20						*S-79/P-2	1.4
1876	Bos-N	70	335	72	100	18	6	1	34	8	9	.299	.315	.397	134	11				.888	13	*S-68/2-2,P	2.1
1877	Bos-N	61	290	58	80	15	1	0	35	9	15	.276	.298	.334	95	-2				.878	7	*2-58/S-3	0.8
1878	Bos-N	59	267	35	60	5	1	0	12	6	22	.225	.242	.251	58	-13				.947	11	*S-59	0.1
1880	Bos-N	1	4	2	1	0	0	0	0	0	0	.250	.250	.250	72	-0				1.000	-0	/S-1	0.0
1881	Bos-N	7	25	4	5	0	0	0	0	0	3	.200	.286	.200	58	-1				.963	-3	/S-7	-0.3
Total	5 n	262	1379	400	487	65	39	8	92	26	4	.353	.365	.474	154	75						S-261/P-2,1	5.1
Total	7	329	1494	264	383	54	20	2	132	43	103	.256	.277	.323	93	-11				.911	42	S-269/2-60,P	3.9
Team	5	198	921	171	246	38	8	1	81	26	47	.267	.287	.329	96	-4				.914	29	S-138/2-60,P	2.7

■ SAM WRIGHT Wright, Samuel b: 11/25/1848, New York, N.Y. d: 5/6/28, Boston, Mass. BR/TR, 5′7.5″, 146 lbs. Deb: 4/21/1875 F

1876	Bos-N	2	8	0	1	0	0	0	0	0	0	.125	.125	.125	-16	-1				.778	-0	/S-2	-0.1
1881	Bos-N	1	4	0	1	0	0	0	0	0	0	.250	.250	.250	60	-0				.667	-1	/S-1	-0.1
Total	3	12	46	0	5	0	0	0	0	0	5	.109	.109	.109	-27	-6				.843	-3	/S-12	-0.8
Team	2	3	12	0	2	0	0	0	0	0	0	.167	.167	.167	9	-1				.733	-1	/S-3	-0.2

■ HARRY WRIGHT Wright, William Henry b: 1/10/1835, Sheffield, England d: 10/3/1895, Atlantic City, N.J. BR/TR, 5′9.5″, 157 lbs. Deb: 5/5/1871 FMH

1871	Bos-n	31	147	42	44	5	2	0	26	13	2	.299	.356	.361	103	1	7					*O-30/P-9,SM	0.2
1872	Bos-n	48	208	39	54	6	0	0	22	9	2	.260	.290	.288	75	-7						*O-48/P-7M	-0.2
1873	Bos-n	58	266	57	67	8	3	2	33	10	3	.252	.277	.327	72	-11						*O-58/P-12M	-0.5
1874	Bos-n	40	184	44	56	9	2	2		4		.304	.319	.408	123	4						*O-40/P-6,CM	0.4
1875	Bos-n	1	4	1	1	0	0	0		0		.250	.250	.250	71	-0						/O-1,M	0.0
1876	Bos-N	1	3	0	0	0	0	0	0	0	0	.000	.000	.000	-98	-1				.000	-0	/O-1,M	-0.1
1877	Bos-N	1	0	0	0	0	0	0	0	0	1	.000	.000	.000	-97	-1				.667	1	/O-1,M	0.0
Total	5 n	178	809	183	222	28	7	4	81	36	7	.274	.305	.341	89	-14						O-177/P-34,CS	-0.1
Total	2	2	7	0	0	0	0	0	0	0	2	.000	.000	.000	-97	-1				.667	0	/O-2	-0.1

■ JIM WYNN Wynn, James Sherman b: 3/12/42, Hamilton, Ohio BR/TR, 5′9″, 170 lbs. Deb: 7/10/63

| 1976 | Atl-N | 148 | 449 | 75 | 93 | 19 | 1 | 17 | 66 | 127 | 111 | .207 | .382 | .367 | 107 | 9 | 16 | 6 | 1 | .971 | 11 | *O-138 | 1.6 |
| Total | 15 | 1920 | 6653 | 1105 | 1665 | 285 | 39 | 291 | 964 | 1224 | 1427 | .250 | .369 | .436 | 129 | 289 | 225 | 101 | | .981 | 110 | *O-1810/D-30,S3 | 33.2 |

YEAR	TM/L	G	AB	R	H	2B	3B	HR	RBI	BB	SO	AVG	OBP	SLG	PRO+	BR/A	SB	CS	SBR	FA	FR	G/POS	TPR

■ GEORGE YEAGER   Yeager, George J. "Doc"   b: 6/5/1874, Cincinnati, Ohio   d: 7/5/40, Cincinnati, Ohio   BR/TR, 5'10", 190 lbs.   Deb: 9/25/1896

YEAR	TM/L	G	AB	R	H	2B	3B	HR	RBI	BB	SO	AVG	OBP	SLG	PRO+	BR/A	SB	CS	SBR	FA	FR	G/POS	TPR
1896	Bos-N	2	5	1	1	0	0	0	0	0	1	.200	.200	.200	5	-1	0			1.000	-0	/1-2	-0.1
1897	*Bos-N	30	95	20	23	2	3	2	15	7		.242	.294	.389	75	-4	2			.970	1	C-13,O-10/23	-0.2
1898	Bos-N	68	221	37	59	13	1	3	24	16		.267	.328	.376	96	-2	1			.951	-3	C-37,1-17/OS	-0.2
1899	Bos-N	3	8	1	1	0	0	0	0	1		.125	.222	.125	-3	-1	0			1.000	0	/O-2,C-1	-0.1
Total	6	217	705	90	168	25	6	5	73	45	1	.238	.290	.312	69	-30	7			.953	-1	C-134/1-28,O23S	-1.8
Team	4	103	329	59	84	15	4	5	39	24	1	.255	.314	.371	86	-8	3			.950	-3	/C-51,O-21,12S3	-0.6

■ HERMAN YOUNG   Young, Herman John   b: 4/14/1886, Boston, Mass.   d: 12/13/66, Ipswich, Mass.   BR/TR, 5'8", 155 lbs.   Deb: 6/11/11

YEAR	TM/L	G	AB	R	H	2B	3B	HR	RBI	BB	SO	AVG	OBP	SLG	PRO+	BR/A	SB	CS	SBR	FA	FR	G/POS	TPR
1911	Bos-N	9	25	2	6	0	0	0	0	0	3	.240	.269	.240	40	-2	0			.905	4	/3-5,S-3	0.2

■ GUY ZINN   Zinn, Guy   b: 2/13/1887, Hallbrook, W.Va.   d: 10/6/49, Clarksburg, W.Va.   BL/TR, 5'10.5", 170 lbs.   Deb: 9/11/11

YEAR	TM/L	G	AB	R	H	2B	3B	HR	RBI	BB	SO	AVG	OBP	SLG	PRO+	BR/A	SB	CS	SBR	FA	FR	G/POS	TPR
1913	Bos-N	36	138	15	41	8	2	1	15	4	23	.297	.322	.406	105	0	3			.948	4	O-35	0.3
Total	5	314	1103	136	297	51	23	15	139	109	77	.269	.338	.398	98	-6	28			.927	-17	O-294	-3.7

■ PAUL ZUVELLA   Zuvella, Paul   b: 10/31/58, San Mateo, Cal.   BR/TR, 6', 178 lbs.   Deb: 9/4/82

YEAR	TM/L	G	AB	R	H	2B	3B	HR	RBI	BB	SO	AVG	OBP	SLG	PRO+	BR/A	SB	CS	SBR	FA	FR	G/POS	TPR
1982	Atl-N	2	1	0	0	0	0	0	0	0	0	.000	.000	.000	-96	-0	0	0	0	.800	1	/S-1	0.1
1983	Atl-N	3	5	0	0	0	0	0	0	2	1	.000	.375	.000	11	-0	0	0	0	.750	-2	/S-2	-0.2
1984	Atl-N	11	25	2	5	1	0	0	1	2	3	.200	.259	.240	38	-2	0	0	0	1.000	1	/2-6,S-6	-0.1
1985	Atl-N	81	190	16	48	8	1	0	4	16	14	.253	.311	.305	69	-8	2	0	1	.986	9	2-42,S-33/3	0.5
Total	9	209	491	41	109	17	2	2	20	34	50	.222	.275	.277	52	-32	2	0	1	.959	5	S-133/2-55,3D	-1.7
Team	4	97	221	18	53	9	1	0	5	20	18	.240	.306	.290	63	-10	2	0	1	.988	9	/2-48,S-42,3	0.3

CHAPTER 8

The Pitcher Register

The Braves Pitcher Register consists of the central pitching statistics of every man who has pitched for the team since 1871, without exception. Pitcher batting is expressed in Batting Runs in the Pitcher Batting column, and in the columns for base hits and batting average. Pitcher defense is expressed in Fielding Runs in the Pitcher Defense column.

The pitchers are listed alphabetically by surname and, when more than one pitcher bears the name, alphabetically by *given* name—not by "use name," by which we mean the name he may have had applied to him during his playing career. This is the standard method of alphabetizing used in other biographical reference works, and in the case of baseball it makes it easier to find a lesser-known player with a common surname like Smith or Johnson. On the whole, we have been conservative in ascribing nicknames, doing so only when the player was in fact known by that name during his playing days.

Each page of the Pitcher Register is topped at the corner by a finding aid: in capital letters, the surname of, first, the pitcher whose entry heads up the page and, second, the player whose entry concludes it. Pitcher batting and pitcher defense, because the win-denominated numbers they produce are so small, are not sorted for single-season leaders (although the all-time leaders in these categories, single season and lifetime, will be found in the separate section called "All-Time Leaders"). Symbols denoting All Star Game selection and/or play appear to the right of the team/league column. An additional finding aid is an asterisk alongside the team for which a player appeared in postseason competition, thus making for easy cross-reference to the earlier section on postseason play.

The record of a man who pitched in more than one season is given in one line for each season, plus a career total line and a Braves total line. Refer to the preceding Player Index, and ultimately to *Total Baseball*, for complete seasonal data for Braves when they wore the uniforms of other clubs. If he pitched for another team in addition to the Braves, only his total for the Braves is shown in a given year. A man who pitched in only one year has no additional career total line since it would be identical to his seasonal listing.

In *Total Baseball 1*, fractional innings were calculated for teams in the Annual Record but were rounded off to the nearest whole inning for individuals, in accordance with baseball scoring practice. In 1981, this rounding-off procedure cost Sammy Stewart of Baltimore an ERA title, as Oakland's Steve McCatty won the crown despite hav-

ing a higher ERA when fractional innings were counted; this singular occurrence led to a change in baseball scoring practice. In the first edition our data base conformed to the 1976-1982 practice for all of pitching history, excepting those men who pitched only one-third of an inning in an entire season. In the second edition of *Total Baseball* we recalculated all fractional innings pitched: look for a superscript figure, either a one or a two, in the IP column to indicate thirds of innings.

Pitching records for the National Association are included in the Pitcher Register because the editors, like most baseball historians, regard it as a major league, inasmuch as it was the only professional league of its day and supplied the National League of 1876 with most of its personnel. In *Total Braves*, we benefit from the SABR research project which to date has produced games started, complete games, shutouts, saves, innings pitched, hits, bases on balls and, for 1871-1873, strikeouts, earned runs, and ERA. For the years 1874-1875 we have estimated ERA based on the teams' average of 40 percent of runs allowed being earned. In future editions we may have actual earned-run data, but for now this estimation produces reasonable results. Unless Major League Baseball reverses the position it adopted in 1969 and restores the NA to official major league status, we will continue the practice of carrying separate totals for the National Association rather than integrating them into the career marks of those pitchers whose major league tenures began before 1876 and concluded in that year or after it.

Gaps remain elsewhere in the official record of baseball and in the ongoing process of sabermetric reconstruction. The reader will note occasional blank elements in biographical lines; these are not typographical lapses but signs that the information does not exist or has not yet been found. However, unlike the case of batting records, there are no incomplete statistical columns for pitchers except in the National Association years of 1874-1875 and Pitcher Defense 1871-1875. Where official statistics did not exist or the raw data have not survived, as with batters facing pitchers before 1908 in the American League and before 1903 in the National, we have constructed figures from the available raw data. For example, to obtain a pitcher's BFP—Batters Facing Pitchers—for calculating Opponents' On Base Percentage or Batting Average, we have subtracted league base hits from league at-bats, divided by league innings pitched, multiplied by the pitcher's innings and added his hits and walks allowed and hit-by-pitch, if available. Research in this area continues, and we hope one day to eliminate the need for inferential data all the way back to 1871.

For a key to the team and league abbreviations used in the Pitcher Register go to the last page of the book. For a guide to the other procedures and abbreviations employed in the Pitcher Register, review the comments on the prodigiously extended pitching record below.

YEAR	TM/L	W	L	PCT	G	GS	CG	SH	SV	IP	H	HR	BB	SO	RAT	ERA	ERA+	OAV	OOB	BH	AVG	PB	PR	/A	PD	TPI
● **RIP VAN WINKLE**					Van Winkle, Rip "Half Moon" (Also Played in 1874 as Geoffrey Crayon)																					
					b: 4/30/1820, Plattekill, N.Y.					d: 12/12/80, Hudson, N.Y.			BL/TR, 5'5", 145 lbs.			Deb: 5/7/1874 MUCHF ◆										
1874	Bos-n	27	30	.474	57	57	56	1	0	498	502	5	18		9.4	3.90	104	.258	.270	40	.167	-3	5	3		-0.1
1875	Bos-n	29	22	.569	52	51	50	2	1	450	491	4	25		10.3	4.02	106	.260	.272	50	.200	1	7	7		0.5
1883	Bos-N	5	18	.217	27	23	19	0	1	196	207	7	76	77	13.0	3.44	101	.274	.340	18	.180	-0	-3	1	0	-0.4
1884	Bos-N	5	3	.625	7	7	6	0	0	60	76	0	11	17	13.0	4.35	104	.311	.341	9	.225	2	3	1	0	0.1
1890	Bos-N	0	0	—	1	1	1	0	0	0	5	2	2	0	∞	∞	-97	1.000	1.000	1	.250	0	-2	-2	0	-0.2
1907	Bos-N	16	13	.552	35	34	18	0	2	251	224	19	78	170	10.8	2.76	126	.236	.293	30	.250	1	17	20	2	2.2
1908	Bos-N	16	12	.571	36	35	14	1	5	278	224	15	48	205	8.8	2.20	130	.215	.250	25	.200	1	24	20	-3	2.2
1909	Bos-N	25	7	.781	36	35	18	0	5	273	202	24	82	208		2.21	164	.201	.261	20	.147	-1	42	43	1	4.2
1910	Bos-N	18	12	.600	37	36	19	0	2	291	230	21	83	283	9.4	2.81	135	.211	.267	38	.277	4	40	32	1	3.6
1911	Bos-N	20	10	.667	36	35	21	0	4	286	210	18	61	289	8.6	1.76	188	.202	.246	40	.296	4	54	49	-1	5.5
1912	Bos-N	21	12	.636	35	35	13	0	3	262	215	23	77	249	10.0	2.92	116	.219	.275	34	.281	3	18	14	1	1.7
1914	Bos-N	11	11	.500	32	32	12	0	5	236	199	19	75	201	10.4	3.20	126	.226	.287	22	.227	-1	11	22	1	2.2
1915	Bos-N	22	9	.710	36	36	15	0	5	280	217	11	88	243	9.8	2.38	155	.211	.274	33	.311	3	39	41	1	4.2
1956	Mil-N☆	7	3	.700	13	13	5	0	3	96	79	7	28	72	10.0	3.00	140	.218	.274	11	.196	1	10	13	3	1.5
1967	*Atl-N★	0	1	.000	1	1	0	0	0	⅓	5	2	1	1	180.0	108.00	1200	.833	.857	0	.000	0	-2	-2	0	-0.2
Total	2 n	56	52	.519	109	108	106	3	1	948	993	9	43		9.8	3.96	105	.259	.271	90	.184	-2	12	7		0.4
Total	14	190	128	.597	384	375	180	1	38	2903	2486	199	803	2338	10.2	2.76	134	.226	.285	294	.224	23	304	313	6	33.6
Team	13	166	111	.599	332	323	128	1	35	2509	2162	168	710	2015	10.2	2.72	138	.224	.286	243	.223	20	249	258	3	32.9

Looking at the biographical line for any pitcher, we see first his use name in full capitals, then his given name and nickname (and any other name he may have used or been born with, such as the matronymic of a Latin American player). His date and place of birth follow "b" and his date and place of death follow "d"; years through 1900 are expressed fully, in four digits, and years after 1900 are expressed in only their last two digits. Then come his manner of batting and throwing, abbreviated for a left-handed batter who throws right as BL/TR (a switch-hitter would be shown as BB for "bats both" and a switch thrower as TB for "throws both"). Next, and for most pitchers last, is the pitcher's debut date in the major leagues.

Some pitchers continue in major league baseball after their pitching days are through, as managers, coaches, or even umpires. A pitcher whose biographical line concludes with an M served as a major league manager, not necessarily with the Braves; one whose line bears a C served as a major league coach; and one with a U served as an umpire. (In the last case we have placed a U on the biographical line only for those pitchers who umpired in at least six games in a year, for in the nineteenth century—and especially in the years of the National Association—there were literally hundreds of players who were pressed into service as umpires for a game or two; it would be misleading to accord such pitchers the same code we give to Bob Emslie or Bill Dinneen.) The select few who have been enshrined in the Baseball Hall of Fame are noted with an H. An F in this line denotes family connection—father-son-grandfather-grandson or brother.

A black diamond appears at the end of the biographical line for pitchers who also appear in the Player Register by virtue of their having played in 100 or more games at another position, including pinch hitter, or having played more than half of their total major league games at another position, or having played more games at a position other than pitcher in at least one year.

The explanations for the statistical column heads follow; for more technical information about formulas and calculations, see the next-to-last page. The vertical rules in the column-header line separate the stats into six logical groupings: year, team, league; wins and losses; game-related counting stats; inning-related counting stats; basic calculated averages; pitcher batting; sabermetric figures of more complex calculation; and run-denominated Linear Weights stats for pitching, fielding, and Total Pitcher Index.

Note that the TPI (Total Pitcher Index) has been revised to employ the Relief Ranking formula for all pitchers, not just relievers. The principal effect will be to calculate Pitcher Wins for relievers instead of Adjusted Pitcher Runs. The TPI will still be the sum of pitching, batting, fielding, and baserunning runs, but the Pitcher Runs will be expressed as Ranking Runs rather than Adjusted Pitching Runs. The net effect will be to raise the TPIs of relief closers and, to a lesser extent, starters who average a high number of innings per start, and to lower somewhat the TPIs of mopup relievers (few saves, few decisions) and starters with many no-decision games.

We have made an upward adjustment to overall league performance in the Federal League of 1914-15 and the Union Association of 1884 (thus lowering individual ratings), because while both leagues are regarded as major leagues, there can be no doubt that their caliber of play was not equivalent to that in the rival leagues of those years. Suffice it to say here that league earned run averages were reduced by 20 percent for the UA and 10 percent for the FL. Few Braves extended their careers into the UA or FL.

YEAR	Year in which a man pitched
*	Denotes postseason play, World Series or League Championship Series.
★	Named to All Star Game, played
☆	Named to All Star Game, did not play
†	Named to All Star Game, replaced because of injury
TM/L	Team and League
W	Wins
L	Losses
PCT	Win Percentage (Wins divided by decisions)
G	Games pitched
GS	Games Started

CG   Complete Games

SH   Shutouts (Complete-game shutouts only)

SV   Saves (Employing definition in force at the time, and 1969 definition for years prior to 1969)

IP   Innings Pitched (Fractional innings included, as discussed above)

H   Hits allowed

HR   Home Runs allowed

BB   Bases on Balls allowed

SO   Strikeouts

RAT   Ratio (Hits allowed plus walks allowed per nine innings)

ERA   Earned Run Average (In a handful of cases, a pitcher will have faced one or more batters for his full season's work yet failed to retire any of them [thus having an innings-pitched figure of zero]; if any of the men he put on base came around to score earned runs, these runs produced an infinite ERA, expressed in the pitcher's record as ∞. (see Van Winkle's 1890 season)

ERA⁺ Adjusted Earned Run Average normalized to league average and adjusted for home-park factor. (See comments for /A.)

OAV   Opponents' Batting Average

OOB   Opponents' On Base Percentage

BH   Base Hits (as a batter)

AVG   Batting Average

PB   Pitcher Batting (Expressed in Batting Runs. Pitcher Batting is park-adjusted and weighted, for those who played primarily at other positions, by the ratio of games pitched to games played. For more technical data about Runs Per Win and Batting Run formulas, see the next-to-last page.)

PR   Pitching Runs (Linear Weights measure of runs saved *beyond* what a league-average pitcher might have saved, defined as zero. New to this edition, the formula used to calculate Relief Ranking is now employed for all pitchers; this creates small differences for starters but large differences for relievers, especially closers. Oc-

casionally the curious figure of − 0 will appear in this column, or in the columns of other Linear Weights measures of batting, fielding, and the TPI. This "negative zero" figure signifies a run contribution that falls below the league average, but to so small a degree that it cannot be said to have cost the team a run.

/A   Adjusted (This signifies that the stat to the immediate left, in this instance Pitching Runs, is here normalized to league average and adjusted for home-park factor. A mark of 100 is a league-average performance, and superior marks exceed 100. An innovation for this edition is to use three-year averages for pitching park factors. If a team moved, or the park changed dramatically, then two-year averages are employed; if the park was used for only one year, then of course only that run-scoring data is used.)

PD   Pitcher Defense (Expressed in Fielding Runs. See comment above on PB.)

TPI   Total Pitcher Index (The sum, expressed in wins beyond league average, of a pitcher's Pitching Runs, Batting Runs—in the AL since 1973—and Fielding Runs, all divided by the Runs Per Win factor for that year, which is generally around 10, historically in the 9–11 range.)

Total For players whose careers include play in the National Association as well as other major leagues, two totals are given, as described above and as illustrated in Rip Van Winkle's record, where the record of his years in the National Association is shown alongside the notation "Total 2 n," where *2* stands for the number of years totaled and *n* stands for National Association. For players whose careers began in 1876 or later, the lifetime record is shown alongside the notation "Total x," where *x* stands for the number of post-1875 years totaled.

Team The totals for a player while he was a Brave, from the Boston Red Stockings of 1876 onward. In cases where a player served two or more teams in the NA, he will receive an additional Team line, such as "Team 2n."

YEAR	TM/L	W	L	PCT	G	GS	CG	SH	SV	IP	H	HR	BB	SO	RAT	ERA	ERA+	OAV	OOB	BH	AVG	PB	PR	/A	PD	TPI
● TED ABERNATHY	Abernathy, Theodore Wade b: 3/6/33, Stanley, N.C. BR/TR, 6'4", 215 lbs. Deb: 4/13/55																									
1966	Atl-N	4	4	.500	38	0	0	0	4	65^{1}	58	5	36	42	12.9	3.86	94	.247	.347	2	.250	1	-2	-2	1	-0.1
Total	14	63	69	.477	681	34	7	2	148	1147^{2}	1010	70	592	765	12.9	3.46	106	.241	.341	25	.138	-4	12	26	27	8.7
● JIM ACKER	Acker, James Justin b: 9/24/58, Freer, Tex. BR/TR, 6'2", 212 lbs. Deb: 4/7/83																									
1986	Atl-N	3	8	.273	21	14	0	0	0	95	100	7	26	37	12.0	3.79	105	.274	.324	3	.107	-1	-1	2	1	0.2
1987	Atl-N	4	9	.308	68	0	0	0	14	114^{2}	109	11	51	68	12.9	4.16	104	.253	.338	3	.214	0	-1	2	1	0.5
1988	Atl-N	0	4	.000	21	1	0	0	0	42	45	6	14	25	12.9	4.71	78	.280	.341	2	.400	1	-6	-5	0	-0.3
1989	Atl-N	0	6	.000	59	0	0	0	2	97^{2}	84	5	20	68	9.7	2.67	137	.237	.280	1	.143	-0	9	11	1	0.7
Total	10	33	49	.402	467	32	0	0	30	904^{1}	918	82	329	482	12.7	3.97	102	.267	.337	9	.167	0	-5	10	8	2.0
Team	4	7	27	.206	169	15	0	0	16	349^{1}	338	29	111	198	11.7	3.71	107	.258	.319	9	.167	0	1	10	3	1.1
● JACK AKER	Aker, Jackie Delane b: 7/13/40, Tulare, Cal. BR/TR, 6'2", 190 lbs. Deb: 5/3/64 C																									
1974	Atl-N	0	1	.000	17	0	0	0	0	16^{2}	17	3	9	7	14.0	3.78	100	.298	.394	0	.000	-0	-0	-0	0	0.0
Total	11	47	45	.511	495	0	0	0	123	746	679	64	274	404	12.0	3.28	105	.247	.324	7	.076	-5	14	13	13	5.4
● JAY ALDRICH	Aldrich, Jay Robert b: 4/14/61, Alexandria, La. BR/TR, 6'3", 210 lbs. Deb: 6/5/87																									
1989	Atl-N	1	2	.333	8	0	0	0	0	12^{1}	7	0	6	7	9.5	2.19	167	.167	.271	0	.000	-0	2	2	-0	0.4
Total	3	6	5	.545	62	0	0	0	2	108^{2}	119	12	39	46	13.3	4.72	89	.283	.348	0	.000	-0	-7	-6	-1	-1.2
● DOYLE ALEXANDER	Alexander, Doyle Lafayette b: 9/4/50, Cordova, Ala. BR/TR, 6'3", 205 lbs. Deb: 6/26/71																									
1980	Atl-N	14	11	.560	35	35	7	1	0	231^{2}	227	20	74	114	11.8	4.20	89	.256	.316	15	.181	0	-15	-12	3	-0.8
1986	Atl-N	6	6	.500	17	17	2	0	0	117^{1}	135	9	17	74	11.7	3.84	104	.287	.312	8	.211	1	-2	2	-1	0.2
1987	Atl-N	5	10	.333	16	16	3	0	0	117^{2}	115	21	27	64	11.0	4.13	105	.257	.302	1	.029	-3	-1	3	-2	-0.1
Total	19	194	174	.527	561	464	98	18	3	3367^{2}	3376	324	978	1528	11.8	3.76	102	.261	.316	44	.166	1	38	32	5	5.0
Team	3	25	27	.481	68	68	12	1	0	466^{2}	477	50	118	252	11.6	4.09	97	.264	.312	24	.154	-2	-18	-7	0	-0.7
● FRANK ALLEN	Allen, Frank Leon b: 8/26/1889, Newbern, Ala. d: 7/30/33, Gainesville, Ala. BR/TL, 5'9", 175 lbs. Deb: 4/24/12																									
1916	Bos-N	8	2	.800	19	14	7	2	1	113	102	1	31	63	10.9	2.07	120	.244	.302	7	.206	3	7	5	-1	0.7
1917	Bos-N	3	11	.214	29	14	2	0	0	112	124	3	47	56	14.2	3.94	65	.297	.376	5	.172	2	-15	-17	-2	-2.1
Total	6	50	67	.427	180	127	60	10	3	970^{1}	893	26	373	457	12.1	2.93	98	.252	.330	39	.135	1	-5	-7	-8	-1.5
Team	2	11	13	.458	48	28	9	2	1	225	226	4	78	119	12.6	3.00	84	.270	.340	12	.190	5	-8	-12	-3	-1.4
● JOSE ALVAREZ	Alvarez, Jose Lino b: 4/12/56, Tampa, Fla. BR/TR, 5'10", 170 lbs. Deb: 10/1/81																									
1981	Atl-N	0	0	—	1	0	0	0	0	2	0	0	0	2	0.0	0.00	—	.000	.000	0	—	0	1	1	-0	0.0
1982	Atl-N	0	0	—	7	0	0	0	0	7^{2}	8	1	2	6	11.7	4.70	79	.308	.357	0	—	0	-1	-1	0	0.0
1988	Atl-N	5	6	.455	60	0	0	0	3	102^{1}	88	7	53	81	12.9	2.99	123	.240	.346	3	.375	1	5	8	1	1.1
1989	Atl-N	3	3	.500	30	0	0	0	2	50^{1}	44	4	24	45	12.3	2.86	128	.237	.327	0	.000	-0	4	4	1	0.6
Total	4	8	9	.471	98	0	0	0	5	162^{1}	140	12	79	134	12.5	2.99	123	.240	.337	3	.273	1	9	12	2	1.7
● BILL ANDERSON	Anderson, William Edward "Lefty" b: 11/28/1895, Boston, Mass. d: 3/13/83, Medford, Mass. BR/TL, 6'1", 165 lbs. Deb: 9/10/25																									
1925	Bos-N	0	0	—	2	0	0	0	0	2^{2}	5	0	2	1	23.6	10.13	40	.500	.583	0	.000	-0	-2	-2	-0	0.0
● NATE ANDREWS	Andrews, Nathan Hardy b: 9/30/13, Pembroke, N.C. d: 4/26/91, Winston-Salem, N.C. BR/TR, 6', 195 lbs. Deb: 5/1/37																									
1943	Bos-N	14	20	.412	36	34	23	3	0	283^{2}	253	11	75	80	10.6	2.57	133	.238	.291	14	.156	-0	26	27	2	3.4
1944	Bos-N☆	16	15	.516	37	34	16	2	2	257^{1}	263	14	74	76	11.9	3.22	119	.261	.312	10	.114	-4	11	17	1	1.8
1945	Bos-N	7	12	.368	21	19	8	0	0	137^{2}	160	9	52	26	13.9	4.58	84	.295	.356	9	.209	0	-12	-11	-0	-1.4
Total	8	41	54	.432	127	97	50	5	2	773^{1}	798	40	236	216	12.1	3.46	106	.265	.321	35	.146	-4	10	17	4	2.3
Team	3	37	47	.440	94	87	47	5	2	678^{2}	676	34	201	182	11.7	3.22	113	.258	.313	33	.149	-4	25	32	3	3.8
● JOHNNY ANTONELLI	Antonelli, John August b: 4/12/30, Rochester, N.Y. BL/TL, 6', 190 lbs. Deb: 7/4/48																									
1948	Bos-N	0	0	—	4	0	0	0	1	4	2	0	3	0	11.3	2.25	170	.143	.294	0	—	0	1	1	0	0.1
1949	Bos-N	3	7	.300	22	10	3	1	0	96	99	6	42	48	13.4	3.56	106	.273	.351	3	.120	-1	5	2	-1	0.0
1950	Bos-N	2	3	.400	20	6	2	1	0	57^{2}	81	2	22	33	16.7	5.93	65	.335	.399	2	.125	-1	-11	-13	0	-1.0
1953	Mil-N	12	12	.500	31	26	11	2	1	175^{1}	167	15	71	131	12.3	3.18	123	.242	.314	11	.177	0	22	14	1	1.9
1961	Mil-N	1	0	1.000	9	0	0	0	0	10^{2}	16	2	3	8	16.0	7.59	49	.340	.380	0	.000	-0	-4	-5	-0	-0.4
Total	12	126	110	.534	377	268	102	25	21	1992^{1}	1870	185	687	1162	11.7	3.34	116	.247	.313	121	.178	15	141	118	-1	15.7
Team	5	18	22	.450	86	42	16	4	2	343^{2}	365	25	141	220	13.4	3.88	100	.269	.341	16	.154	-2	12	-0	1	0.6
● PAUL ASSENMACHER	Assenmacher, Paul Andre b: 12/10/60, Detroit, Mich. BL/TL, 6'3", 195 lbs. Deb: 4/12/86																									
1986	Atl-N	7	3	.700	61	0	0	0	7	68^{1}	61	5	26	56	11.5	2.50	159	.241	.312	0	.000	-0	9	11	1	2.0
1987	Atl-N	1	1	.500	52	0	0	0	2	54^{2}	58	8	24	39	13.7	5.10	85	.260	.335	0	.000	-0	-6	-5	-1	-0.3
1988	Atl-N	8	7	.533	64	0	0	0	5	79^{1}	72	4	32	71	11.9	3.06	120	.251	.328	1	.333	1	3	5	0	1.2
1989	Atl-N	1	3	.250	49	0	0	0	0	57^{2}	55	2	16	64	11.2	3.59	102	.249	.303	0	.000	-0	-1	0	0	0.0
Total	10	48	36	.571	622	1	0	0	48	680	624	56	250	638	11.8	3.40	117	.245	.316	3	.083	-0	31	44	0	6.8
Team	4	17	14	.548	226	0	0	0	14	260	246	19	98	230	12.0	3.46	112	.250	.320	1	.067	0	6	12	1	2.9
● AL AUTRY	Autry, Albert b: 2/29/52, Modesto, Cal. BR/TR, 6'5", 225 lbs. Deb: 9/14/76																									
1976	Atl-N	1	0	1.000	1	1	0	0	0	5	4	2	3	3	12.6	5.40	70	.222	.333	0	.000	-0	-1	-1	-0	-0.2
● STEVE AVERY	Avery, Steven Thomas b: 4/14/70, Trenton, Mich. BL/TL, 6'4", 180 lbs. Deb: 6/13/90																									
1990	Atl-N	3	11	.214	21	20	1	1	0	99	121	7	45	75	15.3	5.64	72	.302	.375	4	.133	-1	-20	-18	2	-2.1
1991	*Atl-N	18	8	.692	35	35	3	1	0	210^{1}	189	21	65	137	11.0	3.38	115	.240	.300	17	.215	3	7	12	-0	1.8
1992	*Atl-N	11	11	.500	35	35	2	2	0	233^{2}	216	14	71	129	11.1	3.20	114	.246	.302	13	.171	2	8	12	-0	1.2
1993	*Atl-N★	18	6	.750	35	35	3	1	0	223^{1}	216	14	43	125	10.4	2.94	136	.261	.297	12	.160	1	27	27	2	2.9
1994	Atl-N	8	3	.727	24	24	1	0	0	151^{2}	127	15	55	122	11.0	4.04	105	.227	.301	5	.102	-2	3	3	0	0.1
1995	*Atl-N	7	13	.350	29	29	3	1	0	173^{1}	165	22	52	141	11.6	4.67	91	.252	.312	11	.208	3	-10	-9	2	-0.4
Total	6	65	52	.556	179	178	13	6	0	1091^{1}	1034	93	331	729	11.4	3.75	106	.252	.310	62	.171	6	16	28	5	3.5
● JOHNNY BABICH	Babich, John Charles b: 5/14/13, Albion, Cal. BR/TR, 6'1.5", 185 lbs. Deb: 6/19/34																									
1936	Bos-N	0	0	—	3	0	0	0	0	6	11	1	6	1	27.0	10.50	37	.440	.563	0	.000	-0	-4	-4	0	0.0
Total	5	30	45	.400	112	87	34	3	1	592	657	38	220	231	13.5	4.93	85	.279	.343	36	.171	-5	-49	-50	3	-5.4
● HARVEY BAILEY	Bailey, Harvey Francis b: 11/24/1876, Adrian, Mich. d: 7/10/22, Toledo, Ohio TL, 6', 160 lbs. Deb: 6/30/1899																									
1899	Bos-N	6	4	.600	12	11	8	0	0	86^{2}	83	7	35	26	12.9	3.95	105	.252	.334	8	.235	0	-1	2	-1	0.1
1900	Bos-N	0	0	—	4	1	0	0	0	20	24	0	11	9	16.6	4.95	83	.296	.394	2	.222	0	-3	-2	1	0.1
Total	2	6	4	.600	16	12	8	0	0	106^{2}	107	7	46	35	13.6	4.13	100	.260	.346	10	.233	0	-4	0	-0	0.2
● MIKE BALAS	Balas, Mitchell Francis (b: Mitchell Francis Balaski) b: 5/17/10, Lowell, Mass. BR/TR, 6', 195 lbs. Deb: 4/27/38																									
1938	Bos-N	0	0	—	1	0	0	0	0	1^{1}	3	0	0	0	20.3	6.75	51	.375	.375	0	—	0	-0	-0	-0	0.0
● BILL BANKS	Banks, William John (b: William John Yerrick) b: 2/26/1874, Danville, Pa. d: 9/8/36, Danville, Pa. BR/TR, 5'11", 150 lbs. Deb: 9/27/1895																									
1895	Bos-N	1	0	1.000	1	1	1	0	0	7	7	0	4	4	14.1	0.00	—	.259	.355	0	.000	-1	4	4	0	0.5
1896	Bos-N	0	3	.000	4	3	2	0	0	23	42	2	13	6	22.3	10.57	43	.389	.463	3	.273	0	-16	-15	-1	-1.4
Total	2	1	3	.250	5	4	3	0	0	30	49	2	17	10	20.4	8.10	58	.363	.442	3	.214	-1	-12	-11	-1	-0.9

● JIMMY BANNON Bannon, James Henry "Foxy Grandpa" b: 5/5/1871, Amesbury, Mass. d: 3/24/48, Glen Rock, N.J. BR/TR, 5'5", 160 lbs. Deb: 6/15/1893 F♦

YEAR	TM/L	W	L	PCT	G	GS	CG	SH	SV	IP	H	HR	BB	SO	RAT	ERA	ERA+	OAV	OOB	BH	AVG	PB	PR	/A	PD	TPI
1894	Bos-N	0	0	—	1	0	0	0	0	2	4	1	1	0	22.5	0.00	—	.400	.455	166	.336	0	1	1	0	0.0
1895	Bos-N	0	0	—	1	0	0	0	0	3	4	0	2	1	18.0	6.00	85	.308	.400	171	.350	0	-0	-0	0	0.0
Total	3	0	1	.000	3	1	0	0	0	9	18	2	8	2	28.0	12.00	42	.400	.509	459	.320	1	-7	-7	-0	-1.0
Team	2	0	0	—	2	0	0	0	0	5	8	1	3	1	19.8	3.60	148	.348	.423	337	.343	1	1	1	0	0.0

● STEVE BARBER Barber, Stephen David b: 2/22/39, Takoma Park, Md. BL/TL, 6', 200 lbs. Deb: 4/21/60

YEAR	TM/L	W	L	PCT	G	GS	CG	SH	SV	IP	H	HR	BB	SO	RAT	ERA	ERA+	OAV	OOB	BH	AVG	PB	PR	/A	PD	TPI
1970	Atl-N	0	1	.000	5	2	0	0	0	14^2	17	3	5	11	14.1	4.91	87	.288	.354	1	.250	0	-1	-1	-0	-0.1
1971	Atl-N	3	1	.750	39	3	0	0	2	75	92	6	25	40	14.3	4.80	77	.301	.357	2	.154	-0	-11	-9	0	-0.5
1972	Atl-N	0	0	—	5	0	0	0	0	15^2	18	1	6	6	14.4	5.74	66	.290	.362	1	.200	-0	-4	-3	1	0.1
Total	15	121	106	.533	466	272	59	21	13	1999	1818	125	950	1309	12.7	3.36	105	.245	.334	65	.115	-6	54	34	10	5.1
Team	3	3	2	.600	49	5	0	0	2	105^1	127	10	36	57	14.3	4.96	77	.297	.358	4	.182	-0	-17	-13	1	-0.5

● FRANK BARBERICH Barberich, Frank Frederick b: 2/3/1882, Newtown, N.Y. d: 5/1/65, Ocala, Fla. BB/TR, 5'10.5", 175 lbs. Deb: 9/17/07

YEAR	TM/L	W	L	PCT	G	GS	CG	SH	SV	IP	H	HR	BB	SO	RAT	ERA	ERA+	OAV	OOB	BH	AVG	PB	PR	/A	PD	TPI
1907	Bos-N	1	1	.500	2	2	1	0	0	12^1	19	0	5	1	17.5	5.84	44	.358	.414	0	.000	-0	-5	-5	0	-0.7
Total	2	1	1	.500	4	2	1	0	0	17^1	26	0	7	1	17.1	6.23	41	.356	.412	0	.000	-1	-7	-7	0	-0.7

● LEN BARKER Barker, Leonard Harold b: 7/7/55, Fort Knox, Ky. BR/TR, 6'5", 225 lbs. Deb: 9/14/76

YEAR	TM/L	W	L	PCT	G	GS	CG	SH	SV	IP	H	HR	BB	SO	RAT	ERA	ERA+	OAV	OOB	BH	AVG	PB	PR	/A	PD	TPI
1983	Atl-N	1	3	.250	6	6	0	0	0	33	31	0	14	21	12.3	3.82	102	.248	.324	1	.125	-0	-1	0	1	0.1
1984	Atl-N	7	8	.467	21	20	1	0	0	126^1	120	10	38	95	11.4	3.85	100	.254	.312	2	.053	-1	-4	0	3	0.2
1985	Atl-N	2	9	.182	20	18	0	0	0	73^2	84	10	37	47	14.9	6.35	61	.288	.370	0	.000	-2	-23	-21	-1	-3.0
Total	11	74	76	.493	248	194	35	7	5	1323^2	1289	96	513	975	12.4	4.34	93	.256	.327	3	.048	-3	-59	-48	1	-6.1
Team	3	10	20	.333	47	44	1	0	0	233	235	20	89	163	12.6	4.64	83	.264	.333	3	.048	-3	-27	-20	3	-2.7

● JESSE BARNES Barnes, Jesse Lawrence "Nubby" b: 8/26/1892, Perkins, Okla. d: 9/9/61, Santa Rosa, N.Mex. BL/TR, 6', 170 lbs. Deb: 7/30/15 F

YEAR	TM/L	W	L	PCT	G	GS	CG	SH	SV	IP	H	HR	BB	SO	RAT	ERA	ERA+	OAV	OOB	BH	AVG	PB	PR	/A	PD	TPI
1915	Bos-N	3	0	1.000	9	3	2	0	0	45^1	41	1	10	16	10.9	1.39	186	.244	.302	3	.176	0	7	6	-1	0.3
1916	Bos-N	6	15	.286	33	18	9	3	1	163	154	3	37	55	10.8	2.37	105	.254	.302	9	.188	0	4	2	4	0.7
1917	Bos-N	13	21	.382	50	33	27	2	1	295	261	3	50	107	9.6	2.68	95	.241	.277	24	.238	4	1	-4	3	0.3
1923	Bos-N	10	14	.417	31	23	12	5	2	195^1	204	8	43	41	11.4	2.76	144	.270	.310	10	.147	-4	27	27	3	2.9
1924	Bos-N	15	20	.429	37	32	21	**4**	0	267^2	292	7	53	49	11.6	3.23	118	.284	.319	20	.222	-1	19	18	1	2.1
1925	Bos-N	11	16	.407	32	28	17	0	0	216^1	255	14	63	55	13.3	4.53	88	.297	.346	16	.198	-1	-6	-13	-2	-1.5
Total	13	152	150	.503	422	313	180	26	13	2569^2	2686	88	515	653	11.3	3.22	104	.273	.310	195	.214	1	74	41	20	6.3
Team	6	58	86	.403	192	137	88	14	4	1182^2	1207	36	256	323	11.2	3.07	108	.268	.310	82	.202	-1	52	34	8	4.8

● VIRGIL BARNES Barnes, Virgil Jennings "Zeke" b: 3/5/1897, Ontario, Kan. d: 7/24/58, Wichita, Kan. BR/TR, 6', 165 lbs. Deb: 9/25/19 F

YEAR	TM/L	W	L	PCT	G	GS	CG	SH	SV	IP	H	HR	BB	SO	RAT	ERA	ERA+	OAV	OOB	BH	AVG	PB	PR	/A	PD	TPI
1928	Bos-N	2	7	.222	16	10	1	0	0	60^1	86	3	26	7	16.7	5.82	67	.344	.406	1	.059	-2	-12	-13	-1	-1.8
Total	9	61	59	.508	205	135	58	7	11	1094	1192	46	293	275	12.3	3.66	105	.282	.329	40	.108	-31	38	22	1	-0.9

● GEORGE BARNICLE Barnicle, George Bernard "Barney" b: 8/26/17, Fitchburg, Mass. d: 10/10/90, Largo, Fla. BR/TR, 6'2", 175 lbs. Deb: 9/6/39

YEAR	TM/L	W	L	PCT	G	GS	CG	SH	SV	IP	H	HR	BB	SO	RAT	ERA	ERA+	OAV	OOB	BH	AVG	PB	PR	/A	PD	TPI
1939	Bos-N	2	2	.500	6	1	0	0	0	18^1	16	1	8	15	11.8	4.91	75	.235	.316	0	.000	-1	-2	-2	0	-0.5
1940	Bos-N	1	0	1.000	13	2	1	0	0	32^2	28	1	31	11	17.9	7.44	50	.233	.414	0	.000	-1	-13	-14	1	-0.5
1941	Bos-N	0	1	.000	1	1	0	0	0	6^2	5	0	4	2	13.5	6.75	53	.238	.385	0	.000	-0	-2	-2	0	-0.3
Total	3	3	3	.500	20	4	1	0	0	57^2	49	2	43	28	15.5	6.55	56	.234	.382	0	.000	-2	-17	-18	1	-1.3

● RED BARRETT Barrett, Charles Henry b: 2/14/15, Santa Barbara, Cal d: 7/28/90, Wilson, N.C. BR/TR, 5'11", 183 lbs. Deb: 9/15/37

YEAR	TM/L	W	L	PCT	G	GS	CG	SH	SV	IP	H	HR	BB	SO	RAT	ERA	ERA+	OAV	OOB	BH	AVG	PB	PR	/A	PD	TPI
1943	Bos-N	12	18	.400	38	31	14	3	0	255	240	11	63	64	10.8	3.18	107	.250	.298	11	.136	-4	6	7	1	0.4
1944	Bos-N	9	16	.360	42	30	11	1	2	230^1	257	13	63	54	12.6	4.06	94	.279	.327	13	.173	-1	-12	-6	2	-0.6
1945	Bos-N	2	3	.400	9	5	2	0	2	38	43	6	16	13	14.2	4.74	81	.281	.353	2	.222	-0	-4	-4	1	-0.4
1947	Bos-N	11	12	.478	36	30	12	3	1	210^2	200	16	53	53	10.9	3.55	110	.244	.292	8	.111	-2	12	8	-0	0.5
1948	*Bos-N	7	8	.467	34	13	3	0	0	128^1	132	9	26	40	11.1	3.65	105	.268	.305	7	.179	-1	4	3	1	0.3
1949	Bos-N	1	1	.500	23	0	0	0	0	44^1	58	4	10	17	14.2	5.68	66	.326	.368	1	.200	-0	-8	-9	1	-0.3
Total	11	69	69	.500	253	149	67	11	7	1263^1	1292	78	312	333	11.5	3.53	105	.264	.309	54	.136	-16	28	26	5	1.6
Team	6	42	58	.420	182	109	42	7	5	906^2	930	59	231	241	11.6	3.74	100	.264	.311	42	.149	-8	-1	-1	6	-0.1

● FRANK BARRETT Barrett, Francis Joseph "Red" b: 7/1/13, Ft.Lauderdale, Fla BR/TR, 6'2", 173 lbs. Deb: 10/1/39

YEAR	TM/L	W	L	PCT	G	GS	CG	SH	SV	IP	H	HR	BB	SO	RAT	ERA	ERA+	OAV	OOB	BH	AVG	PB	PR	/A	PD	TPI
1946	Bos-N	2	4	.333	23	0	0	0	1	35^1	35	2	17	12	13.5	5.09	67	.252	.338	0	.000	-1	-7	-7	1	-1.0
Total	5	15	17	.469	104	2	0	0	12	217^2	211	8	90	90	12.5	3.51	98	.260	.336	9	.167	-1	-2	-2	1	-0.9

● DICK BARRETT Barrett, Tracy Souter "Kewpie Dick" (a.k.a. Richard Oliver 1933 And Richard Oliver Barrett 1934-43)
b: 9/28/06, Montoursville, Pa d: 10/30/66, Seattle, Wash. BR/TR, 5'9", 175 lbs. Deb: 6/27/33

YEAR	TM/L	W	L	PCT	G	GS	CG	SH	SV	IP	H	HR	BB	SO	RAT	ERA	ERA+	OAV	OOB	BH	AVG	PB	PR	/A	PD	TPI
1934	Bos-N	1	3	.250	15	3	0	0	0	32^1	50	2	12	14	17.3	6.68	57	.365	.416	1	.143	-0	-9	-10	1	-1.0
Total	5	35	58	.376	141	91	32	3	2	729	753	29	320	271	13.4	4.28	86	.266	.343	40	.180	1	-49	-50	4	-4.9

● JOE BATCHELDER Batchelder, Joseph Edmund "Win" b: 7/11/1898, Wenham, Mass. d: 5/5/89, Beverly, Mass. BR/TL, 5'7", 165 lbs. Deb: 9/29/23

YEAR	TM/L	W	L	PCT	G	GS	CG	SH	SV	IP	H	HR	BB	SO	RAT	ERA	ERA+	OAV	OOB	BH	AVG	PB	PR	/A	PD	TPI
1923	Bos-N	1	0	1.000	4	1	1	0	0	9	12	2	1	2	14.0	7.00	57	.353	.389	0	.000	-0	-3	-3	-0	-0.3
1924	Bos-N	0	0	—	3	0	0	0	0	4^2	4	0	2	2	11.6	3.86	99	.235	.316	0	.000	-0	0	-0	0	0.0
1925	Bos-N	0	0	—	4	0	0	0	0	7	10	0	1	2	14.1	5.14	78	.357	.379	0	.000	-0	-1	-1	0	0.0
Total	3	1	0	1.000	11	1	1	0	0	20^2	26	2	4	6	13.5	5.66	70	.329	.369	0	.000	-0	-4	-4	0	-0.3

● MIKE BEARD Beard, Michael Richard b: 6/21/50, Little Rock, Ark. BL/TL, 6'1", 185 lbs. Deb: 9/7/74

YEAR	TM/L	W	L	PCT	G	GS	CG	SH	SV	IP	H	HR	BB	SO	RAT	ERA	ERA+	OAV	OOB	BH	AVG	PB	PR	/A	PD	TPI
1974	Atl-N	0	0	—	6	0	0	0	0	9^1	5	1	1	7	6.8	2.89	131	.156	.206	0	—	0	1	1	0	0.0
1975	Atl-N	4	0	1.000	34	2	0	0	0	70^1	71	4	28	27	12.9	3.20	118	.265	.339	1	.111	-0	3	4	0	0.2
1976	Atl-N	0	2	.000	30	0	0	0	1	33^2	38	1	14	8	13.9	4.28	89	.299	.369	0	.000	-0	-3	-2	1	0.0
1977	Atl-N	0	0	—	4	0	0	0	0	4^2	14	3	2	1	30.9	9.64	46	.452	.485	0	—	0	-3	-3	0	0.0
Total	4	4	2	.667	74	2	0	0	1	118	128	9	45	43	13.4	3.74	102	.279	.348	1	.100	-0	-2	1	1	0.2

● JOHNNY BEAZLEY Beazley, John Andrew "Nig" b: 5/25/18, Nashville, Tenn. d: 4/21/90, Nashville, Tenn. BR/TR, 6'1.5", 190 lbs. Deb: 9/28/41

YEAR	TM/L	W	L	PCT	G	GS	CG	SH	SV	IP	H	HR	BB	SO	RAT	ERA	ERA+	OAV	OOB	BH	AVG	PB	PR	/A	PD	TPI
1947	Bos-N	2	0	1.000	9	2	2	0	0	28^2	30	1	19	12	15.4	4.40	89	.273	.380	0	.000	-1	-1	-2	-0	-0.2
1948	Bos-N	0	1	.000	3	2	0	0	0	16	19	2	7	4	14.6	4.50	85	.284	.351	0	.000	-1	-1	-1	-0	-0.1
1949	Bos-N	0	0	—	1	0	0	0	0	2	0	0	0	0	0.0	0.00	—	.000	.000	0	—	0	1	1	-0	0.0
Total	6	31	12	.721	76	46	21	3	3	374	349	13	157	147	12.3	3.01	116	.247	.325	18	.150	-1	18	20	-1	2.8
Team	3	2	1	.667	13	4	2	0	0	46^2	49	3	26	16	14.5	4.24	91	.268	.359	0	.000	-1	-1	-2	-0	-0.3

● STEVE BEDROSIAN Bedrosian, Stephen Wayne b: 12/6/57, Methuen, Mass. BR/TR, 6'3", 200 lbs. Deb: 8/14/81

YEAR	TM/L	W	L	PCT	G	GS	CG	SH	SV	IP	H	HR	BB	SO	RAT	ERA	ERA+	OAV	OOB	BH	AVG	PB	PR	/A	PD	TPI
1981	Atl-N	1	2	.333	15	1	0	0	0	24^1	15	2	15	9	11.5	4.44	81	.169	.295	0	.000	-0	-3	-2	-0	-0.3
1982	*Atl-N	8	6	.571	64	3	0	0	11	137^2	102	7	57	123	10.7	2.42	154	.206	.293	1	.038	-2	18	20	-0	2.1
1983	Atl-N	9	10	.474	70	1	0	0	19	120	100	11	51	114	11.6	3.60	108	.229	.315	2	.105	-1	0	4	0	0.6
1984	Atl-N	9	6	.600	40	4	0	0	11	83^2	65	5	33	81	10.6	2.37	163	.210	.289	2	.118	-1	11	14	-1	2.7
1985	Atl-N	7	15	.318	37	37	0	0	0	206^2	198	17	111	134	13.7	3.83	100	.254	.351	5	.078	-4	-6	0	-2	-0.5
1993	Atl-N	5	2	.714	49	0	0	0	0	49^2	34	4	14	33	9.1	1.63	246	.194	.262	0	.000	-0	13	13	-0	1.6
1994	Atl-N	0	2	.000	46	0	0	0	0	46	41	4	18	43	11.9	3.33	128	.243	.323	1	.500	0	5	5	-0	0.2
1995	Atl-N	1	2	.333	29	0	0	0	0	28	40	6	12	22	17.0	6.11	69	.354	.421	0	—	0	-6	-6	-0	-0.6
Total	14	76	79	.490	732	46	0	0	184	1191	1026	114	518	921	11.9	3.38	114	.232	.317	15	.098	-7	46	64	-9	8.2
Team	8	40	45	.471	350	46	0	0	41	696	595	56	311	559	12.0	3.26	119	.232	.320	11	.083	-8	34	48	-4	5.8

YEAR TM/L	W	L	PCT	G	GS	CG	SH	SV	IP	H	HR	BB	SO	RAT	ERA	ERA+	OAV	OOB	BH	AVG	PB	PR	/A	PD	TPI
● RICK BEHENNA Behenna, Richard Kipp b: 3/6/60, Miami, Fla. BR/TR, 6'2", 170 lbs. Deb: 4/12/83																									
1983 Atl-N	3	3	.500	14	6	0	0	0	37^1	37	7	12	17	12.1	4.58	85	.255	.316	4	.333	2	-4	-3	-0	-0.3
Total 3	3	10	.231	26	17	0	0	0	92^2	105	15	42	36	14.6	6.12	66	.287	.365	4	.333	2	-23	-21	-1	-3.3
● RAY BENGE Benge, Raymond Adelphia b: 4/22/02, Jacksonville, Tex. BR/TR, 5'9.5", 160 lbs. Deb: 9/26/25																									
1936 Bos-N	7	9	.438	21	19	2	0	0	115	161	6	38	32	15.7	5.79	66	.333	.382	6	.140	-3	-23	-25	-2	-3.2
Total 12	101	130	.437	346	249	102	12	19	1875^1	2177	132	598	655	13.5	4.52	95	.292	.347	124	.188	-17	-89	-46	-18	-7.5
● LARRY BENTON Benton, Lawrence James b: 11/20/1897, St.Louis, Mo. d: 4/3/53, Amberley, Ohio BR/TR, 5'11", 165 lbs. Deb: 4/25/23																									
1923 Bos-N	5	9	.357	35	9	1	0	0	128	141	4	57	42	14.2	4.99	80	.293	.373	5	.161	-1	-14	-14	1	-1.3
1924 Bos-N	5	7	.417	30	13	4	0	1	128	129	4	64	41	13.8	4.15	92	.274	.365	3	.091	-3	-4	-5	-0	-0.7
1925 Bos-N	14	7	.667	31	21	16	2	1	183^1	170	6	70	49	11.9	3.09	130	.249	.320	14	.241	2	24	19	-1	2.0
1926 Bos-N	14	14	.500	43	27	12	1	1	231^2	244	10	81	103	12.9	3.85	92	.280	.346	12	.154	-4	-1	-8	-3	-1.4
1927 Bos-N	4	2	.667	11	10	3	0	0	60^1	72	3	27	25	15.1	4.48	83	.310	.387	4	.222	1	-4	-5	-1	-0.4
1935 Bos-N	2	3	.400	29	0	0	0	0	72	103	6	24	21	16.0	6.88	55	.338	.388	4	.200	0	-23	-25	-1	-1.5
Total 13	127	128	.498	455	258	122	13	22	2297	2559	109	691	670	12.8	4.03	98	.288	.341	122	.165	-17	14	-16	-8	-2.2
Team 6	44	42	.512	179	80	36	3	3	803^1	859	33	323	281	13.5	4.22	90	.282	.355	42	.176	-4	-21	-38	-5	-3.3
● JUAN BERENGUER Berenguer, Juan Bautista b: 11/30/54, Aguadulce, Pan. BR/TR, 5'11", 215 lbs. Deb: 8/17/78																									
1991 Atl-N	0	3	.000	49	0	0	0	17	64^1	43	5	20	53	9.2	2.24	174	.189	.263	0	.000	-1	10	12	-0	1.2
1992 Atl-N	3	1	.750	28	0	0	0	1	33^1	35	7	16	19	14.0	5.13	71	.269	.354	0	.000	-0	-6	-5	-0	-0.7
Total 15	67	62	.519	490	95	5	2	32	1205^1	1034	116	604	975	12.5	3.90	103	.232	.328	2	.083	-1	7	14	-11	-1.5
Team 2	3	4	.429	77	0	0	0	18	97^2	78	12	36	72	10.9	3.23	118	.218	.296	0	.000	-1	4	6	-1	0.5
● HUCK BETTS Betts, Walter Martin b: 2/18/1897, Millsboro, Del. d: 6/13/87, Millsboro, Del. BR/TR, 5'11", 170 lbs. Deb: 4/26/20																									
1932 Bos-N	13	11	.542	31	27	16	3	1	221^2	229	9	35	32	10.7	2.80	134	.267	.295	19	.241	2	27	24	-2	2.4
1933 Bos-N	11	11	.500	35	26	17	2	4	242	225	9	55	40	10.4	2.79	110	.248	.290	17	.224	2	15	7	4	1.4
1934 Bos-N	17	10	.630	40	27	10	2	3	213	258	17	42	69	12.8	4.06	94	.296	.330	13	.188	1	0	-6	-2	-0.7
1935 Bos-N	2	9	.182	44	19	2	1	0	159^2	213	9	40	40	14.4	5.47	69	.321	.362	7	.159	-0	-26	-30	1	-1.7
Total 10	61	68	.473	307	125	53	8	16	1366^1	1581	83	321	323	12.7	3.93	98	.292	.334	86	.197	-2	-18	-9	-0	0.5
Team 4	43	41	.512	150	99	45	8	8	836^1	925	44	172	181	11.9	3.63	99	.280	.317	56	.209	4	16	-5	1	1.4
● VERN BICKFORD Bickford, Vernon Edgell b: 8/17/20, Hellier, Ky. d: 5/6/60, Concord, Va. BR/TR, 6', 185 lbs. Deb: 4/24/48																									
1948 *Bos-N	11	5	.688	33	22	10	1	1	146	125	9	63	60	11.8	3.27	117	.226	.309	10	.204	1	11	9	-1	0.9
1949 Bos-N★	16	11	.593	37	36	15	2	0	230^2	246	20	106	101	14.0	4.25	89	.273	.354	15	.185	-1	-5	-12	2	-1.1
1950 Bos-N	19	14	.576	40	39	**27**	2	0	**311^2**	293	25	122	126	12.2	3.47	111	.248	.321	16	.138	-4	23	13	-1	0.7
1951 Bos-N	11	9	.550	25	20	12	3	0	164^2	146	7	76	76	12.5	3.12	118	.240	.330	6	.115	-2	15	10	3	1.2
1952 Bos-N	7	12	.368	26	22	7	1	0	161^1	165	7	64	62	12.9	3.74	97	.269	.340	9	.176	-0	-0	-2	1	-0.2
1953 Mil-N	2	5	.286	20	9	2	0	1	58	60	8	35	25	15.1	5.28	74	.279	.385	1	.067	-1	-6	-9	1	-0.9
Total 7	66	57	.537	182	149	73	9	2	1076^1	1040	76	467	450	12.8	3.71	102	.254	.335	57	.156	-7	36	7	3	0.2
Team 6	66	56	.541	181	148	73	9	2	1072^1	1035	76	466	450	12.8	3.69	102	.254	.334	57	.157	-7	38	10	3	0.6
● MIKE BIELECKI Bielecki, Michael Joseph b: 7/31/59, Baltimore, Md. BR/TR, 6'3", 200 lbs. Deb: 9/14/84																									
1991 Atl-N	0	0	—	2	0	0	0	0	1^2	2	0	2	3	21.6	0.00	—	.286	.444	0	—	0	1	1	0	0.0
1992 Atl-N	2	4	.333	19	14	1	1	0	80^2	77	2	27	62	11.7	2.57	143	.254	.317	3	.125	-1	8	10	1	0.7
1994 Atl-N	2	0	1.000	19	1	0	0	0	27	28	2	12	18	13.7	4.00	106	.277	.360	0	.000	-0	1	1	0	0.0
Total 12	63	63	.500	257	173	7	4	1	1098^1	1117	99	442	652	12.9	4.29	92	.265	.338	21	.078	-14	-63	-42	3	-6.4
Team 3	4	4	.500	40	15	1	1	0	109^1	107	4	41	83	12.3	2.88	132	.260	.330	3	.111	-1	10	11	1	0.7
● AL BLANCHE Blanche, Prosby Albert (b: Prosper Belangio) b: 9/21/09, Somerville, Mass. BR/TR, 6', 178 lbs. Deb: 8/23/35																									
1935 Bos-N	0	0	—	6	0	0	0	0	17^1	14	0	5	4	9.9	1.56	243	.230	.288	1	.167	-0	5	4	0	0.0
1936 Bos-N	0	1	.000	11	0	0	0	1	16	20	1	8	4	16.3	6.19	62	.303	.387	1	.250	0	-4	-4	1	-0.2
Total 2	0	1	.000	17	0	0	0	1	33^1	34	1	13	8	13.0	3.78	101	.268	.340	2	.200	-0	1	0	1	-0.2
● KEVIN BLANKENSHIP Blankenship, Kevin De Wayne b: 1/26/63, Anaheim, Cal. BR/TR, 6', 180 lbs. Deb: 9/20/88																									
1988 Atl-N	0	1	.000	2	2	0	0	0	10^2	7	0	7	5	12.7	3.38	109	.194	.341	0	.000	-0	0	0	-0	0.0
Total 3	1	3	.250	8	5	0	0	0	33^1	31	3	16	16	13.0	4.59	83	.244	.333	0	.000	-1	-4	-3	-1	-0.8
● WADE BLASINGAME Blasingame, Wade Allen b: 11/22/43, Deming, N.Mex. BL/TL, 6'1", 185 lbs. Deb: 9/17/63																									
1963 Mil-N	0	0	—	2	0	0	0	0	3	7	0	2	6	27.0	12.00	27	.467	.529	0	—	0	-3	-3	0	0.0
1964 Mil-N	9	5	.643	28	13	3	1	2	116^2	113	15	51	70	12.7	4.24	83	.257	.334	7	.175	3	-9	-9	0	-0.7
1965 Mil-N	16	10	.615	38	36	10	1	1	224^2	200	17	116	117	12.9	3.77	94	.244	.341	15	.185	3	-6	-6	1	-0.2
1966 Atl-N	3	7	.300	16	12	0	0	0	67^2	71	5	25	34	13.0	5.32	68	.272	.340	5	.217	1	-13	-13	-0	-1.6
1967 Atl-N	1	0	1.000	10	4	0	0	0	25^1	27	1	21	20	17.4	4.62	72	.287	.422	1	.143	0	-4	-4	0	0.0
Total 10	46	51	.474	222	128	16	2	5	863^2	891	75	372	512	13.5	4.52	77	.271	.350	44	.166	14	-96	-101	4	-8.5
Team 5	29	22	.569	94	65	13	2	3	437^1	418	38	215	247	13.2	4.24	83	.256	.346	28	.185	9	-34	-35	2	-2.5
● TERRY BLOCKER Blocker, Terry Fennell b: 8/18/59, Columbia, S.C. BL/TL, 6'2", 195 lbs. Deb: 4/11/85 ♦																									
1989 Atl-N	0	0	—	1	0	0	0	0	1	0	0	2	0	18.0	0.00	—	.000	.500	7	.226	0	0	0	0	0.0
● JOE BOEVER Boever, Joseph Martin b: 10/4/60, Kirkwood, Mo. BR/TR, 6'1", 200 lbs. Deb: 7/19/85																									
1987 Atl-N	1	0	1.000	14	0	0	0	0	18^1	29	4	12	18	20.1	7.36	59	.367	.451	0	—	0	-7	-6	-0	-0.3
1988 Atl-N	0	2	.000	16	0	0	0	1	20^1	12	1	1	7	6.2	1.77	208	.182	.206	0	—	0	4	4	0	0.5
1989 Atl-N	4	11	.267	66	0	0	0	21	82^1	78	6	34	68	12.4	3.94	93	.252	.328	0	.000	-0	-4	-3	1	-0.5
1990 Atl-N	1	3	.250	33	0	0	0	8	42^1	40	6	35	35	15.9	4.68	86	.252	.387	0	.000	-0	-4	-3	-1	-0.5
Total 11	34	43	.442	503	0	0	0	47	739^1	734	73	337	535	13.2	3.90	103	.261	.344	2	.125	-0	9	9	-1	1.2
Team 4	6	16	.273	129	0	0	0	30	163^1	159	17	82	128	13.4	4.24	90	.259	.349	0	.000	-0	-11	-8	0	-0.8
● RAY BOGGS Boggs, Raymond Joseph "Lefty" b: 12/12/04, Reamsville, Kan. d: 11/27/89, Grand Junction, Colo. BL/TL, 6'0.5", 170 lbs. Deb: 9/1/28																									
1928 Bos-N	0	0	—	4	0	0	0	0	5	2	0	7	0	21.6	5.40	72	.167	.545	0	—	0	-1	-1	-0	0.0
● TOMMY BOGGS Boggs, Thomas Winton b: 10/25/55, Poughkeepsie, N.Y. BR/TR, 6'2", 200 lbs. Deb: 7/19/76																									
1978 Atl-N	2	8	.200	16	12	1	1	0	59	80	8	26	21	16.3	6.71	60	.323	.389	3	.167	0	-21	-17	-2	-2.7
1979 Atl-N	0	2	.000	3	3	0	0	0	12^2	21	0	4	1	18.5	6.39	63	.362	.413	1	.250	0	-4	-3	0	-0.4
1980 Atl-N	12	9	.571	32	26	4	3	0	192^1	180	14	46	84	10.8	3.42	109	.249	.298	10	.159	-2	4	7	-2	0.3
1981 Atl-N	3	13	.188	25	24	2	0	0	142^2	140	11	54	81	12.4	4.10	87	.265	.336	7	.152	-1	-10	-8	-1	-1.0
1982 Atl-N	2	2	.500	10	10	0	0	0	46^1	43	2	22	29	13.0	3.30	113	.253	.345	4	.235	0	2	2	-0	0.2
1983 Atl-N	0	0	—	5	0	0	0	0	6^1	8	1	1	5	12.8	5.68	68	.320	.346	0	—	0	-1	-1	-0	0.0
Total 9	20	44	.313	114	94	10	4	0	584	612	47	201	278	12.7	4.22	89	.273	.337	25	.169	-2	-41	-31	-5	-4.3
Team 6	19	34	.358	91	75	7	4	0	459^1	472	36	153	221	12.5	4.15	90	.269	.332	25	.169	-2	-30	-21	-5	-3.6
● TOMMY BOND Bond, Thomas Henry b: 4/2/1856, Granard, Ireland d: 1/24/41, Boston, Mass. BR/TR, 5'7.5", 160 lbs. Deb: 5/5/1874 MU♦																									
1877 Bos-N	**40**	17	**.702**	58	58	58	**6**	0	521	530	5	36	**170**	**9.8**	**2.11**	133	.249	**.261**	59	.228	-4	**41**	41	3	3.5
1878 Bos-N	**40**	19	**.678**	**59**	59	**57**	**9**	0	**532^2**	571	5	33	**182**	10.2	2.06	115	.269	.280	50	.212	-4	15	18	2	1.3
1879 Bos-N	43	19	.694	64	64	59	**11**	0	555^1	543	8	24	155	**9.2**	**1.96**	**126**	.251	.259	62	.241	2	33	**32**	7	**3.8**
1880 Bos-N	26	29	.473	63	57	49	3	0	493	559	1	45	118	11.0	2.67	85	.274	.290	62	.220	-2	-16	-22	10	-1.4

YEAR	TM/L	W	L	PCT	G	GS	CG	SH	SV	IP	H	HR	BB	SO	RAT	ERA	ERA+	OAV	OOB	BH	AVG	PB	PR	/A	PD	TPI
1881	Bos-N	0	3	.000	3	3	2	0	0	25^1	40	3	2	2	14.9	4.26	62	.360	.372	2	.200	-0	-4	-5	1	-0.4
Total	2 n	41	48	.461	95	94	92	7	0	849	910	19	20	0	9.9	2.51	109	.248	.252	132	.246	2	25	21		2.0
Total	8	193	115	.627	322	314	294	35	0	2779^2	2857	32	178	860	9.8	2.25	110	.255	.267	340	.236	-9	71	70	30	7.7
Team	5	149	87	.631	247	241	225	29	0	2127^1	2243	22	140	627	10.1	2.21	112	.262	.274	235	.225	-9	68	64	23	6.8

● **PEDRO BORBON** Borbon, Pedro Felix (Marte) b: 11/15/67, Mao, D.R. BR/TL, 6'1", 205 lbs. Deb: 10/2/92 F

YEAR	TM/L	W	L	PCT	G	GS	CG	SH	SV	IP	H	HR	BB	SO	RAT	ERA	ERA+	OAV	OOB	BH	AVG	PB	PR	/A	PD	TPI
1992	Atl-N	0	1	.000	2	0	0	0	0	1^1	2	0	1	1	20.3	6.75	54	.333	.429	0	—	0	-0	-0	0	-0.3
1993	Atl-N	0	0	—	3	0	0	0	0	1^2	3	0	3	2	32.4	21.60	19	.429	.600	0	—	0	-3	-3	-0	0.0
1995	*Atl-N	2	2	.500	41	0	0	0	2	32	29	2	17	33	13.2	3.09	137	.240	.338	0	.000	-0	4	4	0	0.5
Total	3	2	3	.400	46	0	0	0	2	35	34	2	21	36	14.4	4.11	102	.254	.359	0	.000	-0	0	0	0	0.2

● **JOE BORDEN** Borden, Joseph Emley (a.k.a. Joseph Emley Josephs In 1875)
b: 5/9/1854, Jacobstown, N.J. d: 10/14/29, Yeadon, Pa. BR/TR, 5'9", 140 lbs. Deb: 7/24/1875

YEAR	TM/L	W	L	PCT	G	GS	CG	SH	SV	IP	H	HR	BB	SO	RAT	ERA	ERA+	OAV	OOB	BH	AVG	PB	PR	/A	PD	TPI
1876	Bos-N	11	12	.478	29	24	16	2	1	218^1	257	4	51	34	12.7	2.89	78	.276	.313	25	.207	-3	-14	-15	-2	-1.7

● **JAKE BOULTES** Boultes, Jacob John b: 8/6/1884, St.Louis, Mo. d: 12/24/55, St.Louis, Mo. TR, 6'3", Deb: 4/18/07

YEAR	TM/L	W	L	PCT	G	GS	CG	SH	SV	IP	H	HR	BB	SO	RAT	ERA	ERA+	OAV	OOB	BH	AVG	PB	PR	/A	PD	TPI
1907	Bos-N	5	9	.357	24	12	11	0	0	139^2	140	1	50	49	12.8	2.71	94	.266	.338	9	.132	-2	-4	-2	4	0.0
1908	Bos-N	3	5	.375	17	5	1	0	0	74^2	80	7	8	28	10.7	3.01	80	.274	.296	3	.143	-0	-5	-5	-0	-0.7
1909	Bos-N	0	0	—	1	0	0	0	0	8	9	2	0	1	11.3	6.75	42	.290	.313	1	.333	0	-4	-3	-0	0.0
Total	3	8	14	.364	42	17	12	0	0	222^1	229	10	58	78	12.0	2.96	85	.269	.324	13	.141	-2	-13	-11	4	-0.7

● **JIM BOUTON** Bouton, James Alan b: 3/8/39, Newark, N.J. BR/TR, 6', 185 lbs. Deb: 4/22/62

YEAR	TM/L	W	L	PCT	G	GS	CG	SH	SV	IP	H	HR	BB	SO	RAT	ERA	ERA+	OAV	OOB	BH	AVG	PB	PR	/A	PD	TPI
1978	Atl-N	1	3	.250	5	5	0	0	0	29	25	4	21	10	14.3	4.97	82	.234	.359	0	.000	-1	-4	-3	-0	-0.5
Total	10	62	63	.496	304	144	34	11	6	1238^2	1131	127	435	720	11.5	3.57	99	.243	.311	35	.101	-13	5	-5	-1	-1.4

● **LARRY BRADFORD** Bradford, Larry b: 12/21/49, Chicago, Ill. BR/TL, 6'1", 200 lbs. Deb: 9/24/77

YEAR	TM/L	W	L	PCT	G	GS	CG	SH	SV	IP	H	HR	BB	SO	RAT	ERA	ERA+	OAV	OOB	BH	AVG	PB	PR	/A	PD	TPI
1977	Atl-N	0	0	—	2	0	0	0	0	2^2	3	1	0	1	10.1	3.38	132	.273	.273	0	—	0	0	0	0	0.0
1979	Atl-N	1	0	1.000	21	0	0	0	2	19	11	0	10	11	10.4	0.95	427	.172	.293	0	.000	-0	6	7	0	0.5
1980	Atl-N	3	4	.429	56	0	0	0	4	55^1	49	3	22	32	11.7	2.44	153	.243	.320	0	.000	-0	7	8	-0	1.1
1981	Atl-N	2	0	1.000	25	0	0	0	1	26^2	26	1	12	14	12.8	3.71	96	.268	.349	1	1.000	0	-1	-0	0	0.0
Total	4	6	4	.600	104	0	0	0	7	103^2	89	5	44	58	11.7	2.52	150	.238	.321	1	.200	-0	13	14	1	1.6

● **FOGHORN BRADLEY** Bradley, George H. b: 7/1/1855, Milford, Mass. d: 4/3/1900, Philadelphia, Pa. BR/TR, Deb: 8/23/1876 U

YEAR	TM/L	W	L	PCT	G	GS	CG	SH	SV	IP	H	HR	BB	SO	RAT	ERA	ERA+	OAV	OOB	BH	AVG	PB	PR	/A	PD	TPI
1876	Bos-N	9	10	.474	22	21	16	1	1	173^1	201	1	16	16	11.3	2.49	91	.263	.279	19	.232	-1	-4	-5	-1	-0.5

● **KING BRADY** Brady, James Ward b: 5/28/1881, Elmer, N.J. d: 8/21/47, Albany, N.Y. BR/TR, 6', 190 lbs. Deb: 9/21/05

YEAR	TM/L	W	L	PCT	G	GS	CG	SH	SV	IP	H	HR	BB	SO	RAT	ERA	ERA+	OAV	OOB	BH	AVG	PB	PR	/A	PD	TPI
1912	Bos-N	0	0	—	1	0	0	0	0	2^2	5	0	3	0	27.0	20.25	18	.313	.421	0	.000	-0	-5	-5	0	0.0
Total	5	3	2	.600	8	5	4	1	0	49^2	64	0	10	20	13.4	3.08	89	.306	.338	2	.111	-1	-2	-2	-1	0.0

● **BILL BRADY** Brady, William Aloysius "King" b: 8/18/1889, New York, N.Y. TR, 6'2", Deb: 7/9/12

YEAR	TM/L	W	L	PCT	G	GS	CG	SH	SV	IP	H	HR	BB	SO	RAT	ERA	ERA+	OAV	OOB	BH	AVG	PB	PR	/A	PD	TPI
1912	Bos-N	0	0	—	1	0	0	0	0	1	2	0	0	0	18.0	0.00	—	.500	.500	0	—	0	0	0	-0	0.0

● **ED BRANDT** Brandt, Edward Arthur "Big Ed" b: 2/17/05, Spokane, Wash. d: 11/1/44, Spokane, Wash. BL/TL, 6'1", 190 lbs. Deb: 4/26/28

YEAR	TM/L	W	L	PCT	G	GS	CG	SH	SV	IP	H	HR	BB	SO	RAT	ERA	ERA+	OAV	OOB	BH	AVG	PB	PR	/A	PD	TPI
1928	Bos-N	9	21	.300	38	31	12	1	0	225^1	234	22	109	84	14.0	5.07	77	.273	.359	17	.243	5	-27	-29	2	-2.6
1929	Bos-N	8	13	.381	26	21	13	0	0	167^2	196	12	83	50	15.2	5.53	85	.302	.385	15	.234	2	-15	-16	2	-1.2
1930	Bos-N	4	11	.267	41	13	4	1	1	147^1	168	15	59	65	13.9	5.01	99	.291	.356	12	.240	1	-1	-1	2	0.1
1931	Bos-N	18	11	.621	33	29	23	3	2	250	228	11	77	112	11.1	2.92	130	.244	.304	21	.256	5	26	24	3	3.6
1932	Bos-N	16	16	.500	35	31	19	2	1	254	271	11	57	79	11.8	3.97	95	.275	.318	19	.207	-0	-3	-6	1	-0.5
1933	Bos-N	18	14	.563	41	32	23	4	4	287^2	256	10	77	104	10.5	2.60	118	.245	.298	30	.309	9	24	15	-0	2.7
1934	Bos-N	16	14	.533	40	28	20	3	5	255	249	13	83	106	11.9	3.53	108	.254	.315	23	.240	4	15	8	-3	1.1
1935	Bos-N	5	19	.208	29	25	12	0	0	174^2	224	12	66	61	15.0	5.00	76	.319	.378	13	.210	-0	-19	-24	1	-2.6
Total	11	121	146	.453	378	278	150	18	17	2268^1	2342	134	778	877	12.5	3.86	101	.269	.332	187	.236	30	34	5	6	4.2
Team	8	94	119	.441	283	210	126	14	13	1761^2	1826	106	611	661	12.6	4.01	96	.271	.334	150	.245	26	1	-30	8	0.6

● **JOHN BRAUN** Braun, John Paul b: 12/26/39, Madison, Wis. BR/TR, 6'5", 218 lbs. Deb: 10/2/64

YEAR	TM/L	W	L	PCT	G	GS	CG	SH	SV	IP	H	HR	BB	SO	RAT	ERA	ERA+	OAV	OOB	BH	AVG	PB	PR	/A	PD	TPI
1964	Mil-N	0	0	—	1	0	0	0	0	2	2	0	1	1	13.5	0.00	—	.286	.375	0	—	0	1	1	-0	0.0

● **GARLAND BRAXTON** Braxton, Edgar Garland b: 6/10/1900, Snow Camp, N.C. d: 2/25/66, Norfolk, Va. BB/TL, 5'11", 152 lbs. Deb: 5/27/21

YEAR	TM/L	W	L	PCT	G	GS	CG	SH	SV	IP	H	HR	BB	SO	RAT	ERA	ERA+	OAV	OOB	BH	AVG	PB	PR	/A	PD	TPI
1921	Bos-N	1	3	.250	17	2	0	0	0	37^1	44	0	17	16	15.2	4.82	76	.310	.391	0	.000	-1	-4	-5	1	-0.5
1922	Bos-N	1	2	.333	25	4	2	0	0	66^2	75	3	24	15	13.9	3.38	118	.286	.355	1	.063	-2	5	5	-1	0.0
Total	10	50	53	.485	282	70	28	2	32	938	1014	38	276	412	12.6	4.13	101	.278	.332	40	.156	-8	8	2	-5	1.1
Team	2	2	5	.286	42	6	2	0	0	104	119	3	41	31	14.4	3.89	99	.295	.368	1	.043	-3	1	-0	0	-0.5

● **JIM BRITTON** Britton, James Allan b: 3/25/44, N.Tonawanda, N.Y. BR/TR, 6'5", 225 lbs. Deb: 9/20/67

YEAR	TM/L	W	L	PCT	G	GS	CG	SH	SV	IP	H	HR	BB	SO	RAT	ERA	ERA+	OAV	OOB	BH	AVG	PB	PR	/A	PD	TPI
1967	Atl-N	0	2	.000	2	2	0	0	0	13^1	15	2	2	4	11.5	6.08	55	.278	.304	0	.000	-0	-4	-4	-0	-0.6
1968	Atl-N	4	6	.400	34	9	2	2	3	90	81	1	34	61	11.7	3.10	97	.245	.320	3	.143	-0	-1	-1	0	-0.2
1969	*Atl-N	7	5	.583	24	13	2	1	1	88	69	10	49	60	12.1	3.78	95	.218	.323	4	.190	0	-2	-2	-1	-0.3
Total	4	13	16	.448	76	30	4	3	4	237	214	23	112	148	12.5	4.03	83	.243	.332	7	.127	-2	-18	-18	-2	-2.4
Team	3	11	13	.458	60	24	4	3	4	191^1	165	13	85	125	11.9	3.62	91	.236	.320	7	.152	-0	-7	-7	-1	-1.1

● **TONY BRIZZOLARA** Brizzolara, Anthony John b: 1/14/57, Santa Monica, Cal. BR/TR, 6'5", 215 lbs. Deb: 5/19/79

YEAR	TM/L	W	L	PCT	G	GS	CG	SH	SV	IP	H	HR	BB	SO	RAT	ERA	ERA+	OAV	OOB	BH	AVG	PB	PR	/A	PD	TPI
1979	Atl-N	6	9	.400	20	19	2	0	0	107^1	133	6	33	64	14.2	5.28	77	.303	.356	1	.029	-3	-18	-15	0	-2.1
1983	Atl-N	1	0	1.000	14	0	0	0	1	20^1	22	2	6	17	12.4	3.54	109	.278	.329	0	—	0	0	1	-0	0.0
1984	Atl-N	1	2	.333	10	4	0	0	0	29	33	4	13	17	14.3	5.28	73	.284	.357	0	.000	-1	-5	-5	0	-0.5
Total	3	8	11	.421	44	23	2	0	1	156^2	188	12	52	98	14.0	5.06	79	.297	.353	1	.024	-4	-24	-19	-0	-2.6

● **BUSTER BROWN** Brown, Charles Edward "Yank" b: 8/31/1881, Boone, Iowa d: 2/9/14, Sioux City, Iowa BR/TR, 6', 180 lbs. Deb: 6/22/05

YEAR	TM/L	W	L	PCT	G	GS	CG	SH	SV	IP	H	HR	BB	SO	RAT	ERA	ERA+	OAV	OOB	BH	AVG	PB	PR	/A	PD	TPI
1909	Bos-N	4	8	.333	18	17	8	2	0	123^1	108	1	56	32	12.5	3.14	90	.244	.339	7	.146	-2	-7	-4	1	-0.5
1910	Bos-N	9	23	.281	46	29	16	1	2	263	251	4	94	88	11.9	2.67	125	.268	.337	16	.198	0	11	19	1	2.5
1911	Bos-N	8	18	.308	42	25	13	0	2	241	258	11	116	76	14.3	4.29	89	.284	.371	21	.250	3	-24	-13	0	-0.9
1912	Bos-N	4	15	.211	31	21	12	0	0	168^1	146	7	66	68	11.4	4.01	89	.239	.315	13	.213	1	-11	-8	0	-0.7
1913	Bos-N	0	0	—	2	0	0	0	0	13^1	19	0	3	3	16.2	4.73	70	.396	.453	0	.000	-0	-2	-2	-0	0.0
Total	9	51	103	.331	234	165	106	10	4	1451^2	1368	36	631	501	12.8	3.21	96	.258	.343	95	.182	3	-41	-18	8	0.4
Team	5	25	64	.281	139	92	49	3	4	809	782	23	335	267	12.7	3.54	98	.265	.345	57	.204	3	-34	-8	2	0.4

● **BOB BROWN** Brown, Robert Murray b: 4/1/11, Dorchester, Mass. d: 8/3/90, Pembroke, Mass. BR/TR, 6'0.5", 190 lbs. Deb: 4/21/30

YEAR	TM/L	W	L	PCT	G	GS	CG	SH	SV	IP	H	HR	BB	SO	RAT	ERA	ERA+	OAV	OOB	BH	AVG	PB	PR	/A	PD	TPI
1930	Bos-N	0	0	—	3	0	0	0	0	6	10	0	8	1	27.0	10.50	47	.417	.563	0	.000	-0	-4	-4	0	0.0
1931	Bos-N	0	1	.000	3	1	0	0	0	6^1	9	0	3	2	17.1	8.53	44	.375	.444	1	.500	0	-3	-3	0	-0.4
1932	Bos-N	14	7	.667	35	28	9	0	1	213	187	6	104	110	12.4	3.30	114	.238	.329	13	.194	-0	14	11	-1	0.9
1933	Bos-N	0	0	—	5	0	0	0	0	6^2	6	0	3	3	12.2	2.70	114	.250	.333	0	.000	-0	0	0	-0	0.0
1934	Bos-N	1	3	.250	16	8	2	1	0	58^1	59	2	36	21	15.1	5.71	67	.262	.371	5	.238	0	-11	-12	-1	-0.8
1935	Bos-N	1	8	.111	15	10	2	1	0	65	79	2	36	17	15.9	6.37	59	.302	.386	2	.105	-1	-17	-19	-1	-2.3
1936	Bos-N	0	2	.000	2	2	0	0	0	8^1	10	1	3	5	14.0	5.40	71	.278	.333	0	.000	-0	-1	-1	0	-0.3
Total	7	16	21	.432	79	49	13	2	1	363^2	360	11	193	159	13.8	4.48	84	.261	.354	21	.183	-2	-22	-28	-3	-2.9

YEAR TM/L	W	L	PCT	G	GS	CG	SH	SV	IP	H	HR	BB	SO	RAT	ERA	ERA+	OAV	OOB	BH	AVG	PB	PR	/A	PD	TPI
● **BOB BRUCE**	Bruce, Robert James b: 5/16/33, Detroit, Mich. BR/TR, 6'3", 210 lbs. Deb: 9/14/59																								
1967 Atl-N	2	3	.400	12	7	1	0	1	38^{2}	42	3	15	22	13.5	4.89	68	.269	.337	2	.167	0	-7	-7	-1	-0.9
Total 9	49	71	.408	219	167	26	6	1	1122^{1}	1146	95	340	733	12.3	3.85	91	.263	.323	52	.150	6	-28	-43	-2	-4.2
● **GEORGE BRUNET**	Brunet, George Stuart "Lefty" b: 6/8/35, Houghton, Mich. d: 10/25/91, Poza Rica, Mex. BR/TL, 6'1", 210 lbs. Deb: 9/14/56																								
1960 Mil-N	2	0	1.000	17	6	0	0	0	49^{2}	53	6	22	39	13.8	5.07	68	.275	.352	1	.091	-1	-7	-9	0	-0.4
1961 Mil-N	0	0	—	5	0	0	0	0	5	7	1	2	0	16.2	5.40	69	.412	.474	0	—	0	-1	-1	0	0.0
Total 15	69	93	.426	324	213	39	15	4	1431^{2}	1303	133	581	921	12.0	3.62	92	.244	.320	37	.089	-14	-31	-46	-4	-5.7
Team 2	2	0	1.000	22	6	0	0	0	54^{2}	60	7	24	39	14.0	5.10	68	.286	.362	1	.091	-1	-8	-10	0	-0.4
● **TOD BRYNAN**	Brynan, Charles Ruley b: 7/1863, Philadelphia, Pa. d: 5/10/25, Philadelphia, Pa. BR/TR, Deb: 6/22/1888																								
1891 Bos-N	0	1	.000	1	1	0	0	0	1	4	0	3	0	63.0	54.00	7	.571	.700	0	—	0	-6	-6	-0	-1.9
Total 2	2	2	.500	4	4	2	0	0	26	33	2	10	11	15.6	8.31	37	.289	.357	2	.182	0	-16	-15	-1	-2.8
● **CHARLIE BUFFINTON**	Buffinton, Charles G. b: 6/14/1861, Fall River, Mass. d: 9/23/07, Fall River, Mass. BR/TR, 6'1", 180 lbs. Deb: 5/17/1882 M♦																								
1882 Bos-N	2	3	.400	5	5	4	1	0	42	53	2	14	17	14.4	4.07	70	.296	.347	13	.260	0	-5	-6	1	-0.5
1883 Bos-N	25	14	.641	43	41	34	4	1	333	346	4	51	188	10.7	3.03	102	.254	.281	81	.238	0	4	3	-1	0.1
1884 Bos-N	48	16	.750	67	67	63	8	0	587	506	15	76	417	8.9	2.15	135	.219	.244	94	.267	12	54	48	3	5.7
1885 Bos-N	22	27	.449	51	50	49	6	0	434^{1}	425	10	112	242	11.1	2.88	93	.246	.292	81	.240	5	-3	-9	6	0.0
1886 Bos-N	7	10	.412	18	17	16	0	0	151	203	4	39	47	14.4	4.59	70	.308	.346	51	.290	4	-21	-23	-1	-1.8
Total 11	233	152	.605	414	396	351	30	3	3404	3344	87	856	1700	11.2	2.96	114	.246	.292	543	.245	27	162	161	35	20.3
Team 5	104	70	.598	184	180	166	19	1	1547^{1}	1533	35	292	911	10.6	2.83	103	.246	.280	320	.255	21	29	13	8	3.5
● **BOB BUHL**	Buhl, Robert Ray b: 8/12/28, Saginaw, Mich. BR/TR, 6'2", 190 lbs. Deb: 4/17/53																								
1953 Mil-N	13	8	.619	30	18	8	3	0	154^{1}	133	9	73	83	12.2	2.97	132	.235	.326	6	.113	-3	23	16	1	1.8
1954 Mil-N	2	7	.222	31	14	2	1	3	110^{1}	117	5	65	57	15.0	4.00	93	.277	.376	1	.032	-3	1	-3	-0	-0.6
1955 Mil-N	13	11	.542	38	27	11	1	1	201^{2}	168	13	109	117	12.4	3.21	117	.227	.327	6	.105	-4	18	12	-1	0.9
1956 Mil-N	18	8	.692	38	33	13	2	0	216^{2}	190	18	105	86	12.3	3.32	104	.236	.326	7	.096	-4	11	3	0	0.0
1957 *Mil-N	18	7	**.720**	34	31	14	2	0	216^{2}	191	15	121	117	13.0	2.74	128	.241	.341	6	.082	-3	27	18	-2	1.4
1958 Mil-N	5	2	.714	11	10	3	0	1	73	74	5	30	27	12.9	3.45	102	.260	.332	5	.200	0	4	1	1	0.2
1959 Mil-N	15	9	.625	31	25	12	**4**	0	198	181	19	74	105	11.7	2.86	124	.243	.313	4	.057	-5	24	15	3	1.5
1960 Mil-N★	16	9	.640	36	33	11	2	0	238^{2}	202	23	103	121	11.6	3.09	111	.229	.312	14	.157	-2	18	9	3	1.0
1961 Mil-N	9	10	.474	32	28	9	1	0	188^{1}	180	23	98	77	13.5	4.11	91	.256	.351	4	.067	-4	-2	-8	1	-1.0
1962 Mil-N	0	1	.000	1	1	0	0	0	2	6	0	4	1	45.0	22.50	17	.545	.667	0	.000	-0	-4	-4	-0	-1.1
Total 15	166	132	.557	457	369	111	20	6	2587	2446	238	1105	1268	12.5	3.55	103	.251	.330	76	.089	-43	75	36	8	0.3
Team 10	109	72	.602	282	220	83	16	5	1599^{2}	1442	130	782	791	12.6	3.27	110	.242	.332	53	.100	-26	120	59	5	4.1
● **LEW BURDETTE**	Burdette, Selva Lewis b: 11/22/26, Nitro, W.Va. BR/TR, 6'2", 190 lbs. Deb: 9/26/50 C																								
1951 Bos-N	0	0	—	3	0	0	0	0	4^{1}	6	0	5	1	24.9	6.23	59	.375	.545	0	.000	-0	-1	-1	0	0.0
1952 Bos-N	6	11	.353	45	9	5	0	7	137	138	8	47	47	12.3	3.61	100	.265	.328	4	.114	-0	2	-0	1	0.0
1953 Mil-N	15	5	.750	46	13	6	1	8	175	177	7	56	58	12.2	3.24	121	.264	.326	9	.170	-1	20	13	2	1.5
1954 Mil-N	15	14	.517	38	32	13	4	0	238	224	17	62	79	11.0	2.76	135	.251	.302	7	.089	-5	35	26	1	2.5
1955 Mil-N	13	8	.619	42	33	11	2	0	230	253	25	73	70	13.0	4.03	93	.280	.337	20	.233	3	0	-7	2	-0.1
1956 Mil-N	19	10	.655	39	35	16	**6**	1	256^{1}	234	22	52	110	10.1	**2.70**	128	.241	.282	16	.186	1	30	22	1	2.6
1957 *Mil-N★	17	9	.654	37	33	14	1	0	256^{2}	260	25	59	78	11.3	3.72	94	.264	.307	13	.148	1	5	-6	2	-0.3
1958 *Mil-N	20	10	**.667**	40	36	19	3	0	275^{1}	279	18	50	113	10.9	2.91	121	.264	.301	24	.242	9	**32**	19	3	3.1
1959 Mil-N★	**21**	15	.583	41	39	20	**4**	1	289^{2}	312	38	38	105	10.9	4.07	87	.273	.297	21	.202	6	-4	-17	0	-1.3
1960 Mil-N	19	13	.594	45	32	**18**	4	4	275^{2}	277	19	35	83	10.3	3.36	102	.260	.287	16	.176	5	12	2	5	1.2
1961 Mil-N	18	11	.621	40	36	14	3	0	**272^{1}**	295	31	33	92	10.9	4.00	94	.273	.296	21	.204	5	1	-8	2	0.0
1962 Mil-N	10	9	.526	37	19	6	1	2	143^{2}	172	26	23	59	12.3	4.89	78	.298	.327	9	.176	0	-15	-17	1	-1.9
1963 Mil-N	6	5	.545	15	13	4	1	0	84	71	15	24	28	10.3	3.64	88	.228	.285	1	.038	-0	-3	-4	-0	-0.6
Total 18	203	144	.585	626	373	158	33	31	3067^{1}	3186	289	628	1074	11.4	3.66	99	.268	.308	185	.183	30	68	-18	19	3.4
Team 13	179	120	.599	468	330	146	30	23	2638	2698	251	557	923	11.2	3.53	102	.265	.305	161	.178	24	114	21	19	6.7
● **BILLY BURKE**	Burke, William Ignatius b: 7/11/1889, Clinton, Mass. d: 2/9/67, Worcester, Mass. BL/TL, 5'10", 165 lbs. Deb: 4/30/10																								
1910 Bos-N	1	0	1.000	19	1	1	0	0	64	68	1	29	22	13.9	4.08	82	.302	.387	4	.190	-1	-7	-5	-1	-0.2
1911 Bos-N	0	1	.000	2	1	0	0	0	3^{1}	6	0	5	1	29.7	18.90	20	.429	.579	1	1.000	0	-6	-6	-0	-1.1
Total 2	1	1	.500	21	2	1	0	0	67^{1}	74	1	34	23	14.7	4.81	70	.310	.400	5	.227	-0	-13	-11	-2	-1.3
● **GUY BUSH**	Bush, Guy Terrell "The Mississippi Mudcat" b: 8/23/01, Aberdeen, Miss. d: 7/2/85, Shannon, Miss. BR/TR, 6', 175 lbs. Deb: 9/17/23																								
1936 Bos-N	4	5	.444	15	11	5	0	0	90^{1}	98	2	20	28	11.8	3.39	113	.281	.320	3	.120	-1	6	4	1	0.4
1937 Bos-N	8	15	.348	32	20	11	1	1	180^{2}	201	8	48	56	12.4	3.54	101	.282	.328	6	.111	-2	8	1	1	0.0
Total 17	176	136	.564	542	308	151	16	34	2722	2950	152	859	850	12.7	3.86	103	.277	.334	143	.161	-22	64	40	12	3.7
Team 2	12	20	.375	47	31	16	1	1	271	299	10	68	84	12.2	3.49	105	.282	.325	9	.114	-3	14	5	1	0.4
● **CECIL BUTLER**	Butler, Cecil Dean "Slewfoot" b: 10/23/37, Dallas, Ga. BR/TR, 6'4", 195 lbs. Deb: 4/23/62																								
1962 Mil-N	2	0	1.000	9	2	1	0	0	31	26	4	9	22	10.2	2.61	145	.217	.271	0	.000	-1	5	4	0	0.2
1964 Mil-N	0	0	—	2	0	0	0	0	4^{1}	7	2	0	2	14.5	8.31	42	.368	.368	0	—	0	-2	-2	0	0.0
Total 2	2	0	1.000	11	2	1	0	0	35^{1}	33	6	9	24	10.7	3.31	114	.237	.284	0	.000	-1	2	2	0	0.2
● **JOE CALLAHAN**	Callahan, Joseph Thomas b: 10/8/16, E.Boston, Mass. d: 5/24/49, S.Boston, Mass. BR/TR, 6'2", 170 lbs. Deb: 9/13/39																								
1939 Bos-N	1	0	1.000	4	1	1	0	0	17^{1}	17	0	3	8	10.9	3.12	119	.250	.292	0	.000	-0	2	1	0	0.1
1940 Bos-N	0	2	.000	6	2	0	0	0	15	20	1	13	3	19.8	10.20	36	.351	.471	0	.000	-1	-11	-11	1	-1.2
Total 2	1	2	.333	10	3	1	0	0	32^{1}	37	1	16	11	15.0	6.40	58	.296	.380	0	.000	-1	-9	-10	1	-1.1
● **JACK CAMERON**	Cameron, John William "Happy Jack" b: 9/1884, Nova Scotia, Can. d: 8/17/51, Boston, Mass. Deb: 9/13/06 ♦																								
1906 Bos-N	0	0	—	2	1	0	0	0	6	4	0	6	2	15.0	0.00	—	.211	.400	11	.180	-0	2	2	0	0.0
● **RICK CAMP**	Camp, Rick Lamar b: 6/10/53, Trion, Ga. BR/TR, 6', 198 lbs. Deb: 9/15/76																								
1976 Atl-N	0	1	.000	5	1	0	0	0	11^{1}	13	0	2	6	11.9	6.35	60	.302	.333	0	.000	-0	-4	-3	1	-0.2
1977 Atl-N	6	3	.667	54	0	0	0	10	78^{2}	89	6	47	51	15.7	4.00	111	.283	.377	0	.000	-1	-1	4	-0	0.4
1978 Atl-N	2	4	.333	42	4	0	0	0	74^{1}	99	5	32	23	16.2	3.75	108	.329	.399	0	.000	-1	-1	2	-0	0.1
1980 Atl-N	6	4	.600	77	0	0	0	22	108^{1}	92	3	29	33	10.4	1.91	196	.235	.294	1	.111	-0	20	22	4	3.4
1981 Atl-N	9	3	.750	48	0	0	0	17	76	68	5	12	47	9.6	1.78	202	.239	.272	0	.000	-1	14	**15**	0	3.1
1982 *Atl-N	11	13	.458	51	21	3	0	5	177^{1}	199	18	52	68	12.8	3.65	102	.291	.342	1	.024	-3	-1	1	1	-0.1
1983 Atl-N	10	9	.526	40	16	1	0	0	140	146	16	38	61	12.1	3.79	102	.270	.323	3	.077	-2	-3	1	0	0.0
1984 Atl-N	8	6	.571	31	21	1	0	0	148^{2}	134	11	63	69	12.0	3.27	118	.245	.325	5	.111	-2	5	10	0	0.7
1985 Atl-N	4	6	.400	66	2	0	0	3	127^{2}	130	8	61	49	13.8	3.95	97	.263	.349	3	.231	1	-5	-1	-2	-0.2
Total 9	56	49	.533	414	65	5	0	57	942^{1}	970	72	336	407	12.7	3.37	114	.269	.335	13	.074	-8	25	51	3	7.2
● **DAVE CAMPBELL**	Campbell, David Alan b: 9/3/51, Princeton, Ind. BR/TR, 6'3", 210 lbs. Deb: 5/6/77																								
1977 Atl-N	0	6	.000	65	0	0	0	13	88^{2}	78	7	33	42	11.6	3.05	146	.239	.315	1	.083	-1	9	14	-2	1.1
1978 Atl-N	4	4	.500	53	0	0	0	1	69^{1}	67	10	49	45	15.7	4.80	84	.258	.385	0	—	0	-9	-6	0	-0.7
Total 2	4	10	.286	118	0	0	0	14	158	145	17	82	87	13.4	3.82	112	.247	.348	1	.083	-1	-1	8	-2	0.4

YEAR TM/L		W	L	PCT	G	GS	CG	SH	SV	IP	H	HR	BB	SO	RAT	ERA	ERA+	OAV	OOB	BH	AVG	PB	PR	/A	PD	TPI

● HUGH CANAVAN Canavan, Hugh Edward "Hugo" b: 5/13/1897, Worcester, Mass. d: 9/4/67, Boston, Mass. BL/TL, 5'8", 160 lbs. Deb: 4/23/18

| 1918 | Bos-N | 0 | 4 | .000 | 11 | 3 | 3 | 0 | 0 | 46² | 70 | 0 | 15 | 18 | 17.4 | 6.36 | 42 | .366 | .427 | 2 | .095 | -0 | -19 | -19 | 1 | -1.4 |

● BEN CANTWELL Cantwell, Benjamin Caldwell b: 4/13/02, Milan, Tenn. d: 12/4/62, Salem, Mo. BR/TR, 6'1", 168 lbs. Deb: 8/19/27

1928	Bos-N	3	3	.500	22	9	3	0	0	90	112	7	36	18	15.0	5.10	77	.304	.369	5	.172	-1	-11	-12	1	-0.7
1929	Bos-N	4	13	.235	27	20	8	0	2	157	171	11	52	25	12.9	4.47	105	.280	.338	9	.180	-0	4	4	4	0.7
1930	Bos-N	9	15	.375	31	21	10	0	2	173¹	213	15	45	43	13.4	4.88	101	.312	.355	19	.302	2	2	1	4	0.7
1931	Bos-N	7	9	.438	33	16	9	2	2	156¹	160	4	34	32	11.2	3.63	104	.262	.301	13	.228	0	4	3	3	0.6
1932	Bos-N	13	11	.542	37	9	3	1	5	146	133	6	33	33	10.5	2.96	127	.247	.296	14	.280	2	15	13	3	2.6
1933	Bos-N	20	10	**.667**	40	29	18	2	2	254²	242	12	54	57	10.6	2.62	117	.249	.291	12	.141	-1	20	13	4	1.8
1934	Bos-N	5	11	.313	27	19	6	1	5	143¹	163	8	34	45	12.5	4.33	88	.285	.327	12	.279	1	-4	-8	2	-0.5
1935	Bos-N	4	25	.138	39	24	13	0	0	210²	235	15	44	54	12.0	4.61	82	.282	.320	19	.284	4	-14	-19	2	-1.7
1936	Bos-N	9	9	.500	34	12	4	0	2	133¹	127	8	35	42	11.2	3.04	126	.252	.306	8	.195	-1	15	12	3	1.7
Total	11	76	108	.413	316	163	75	6	21	1534	1640	90	382	348	12.0	3.91	100	.275	.321	116	.231	8	25	-2	28	5.0
Team	9	74	106	.411	290	159	74	6	20	1464²	1556	86	367	329	11.9	3.87	101	.273	.320	111	.229	7	31	4	26	5.2

● BUZZ CAPRA Capra, Lee William b: 10/1/47, Chicago, Ill. BR/TR, 5'10", 168 lbs. Deb: 9/15/71

1974	Atl-N☆	16	8	.667	39	27	11	5	1	217	163	13	84	137	10.4	**2.28**	**166**	**.208**	.287	11	.164	0	32	36	-3	3.7
1975	Atl-N	4	7	.364	12	12	5	0	0	78¹	77	8	28	35	12.2	4.25	89	.257	.322	1	.043	-2	-5	-4	1	-0.7
1976	Atl-N	0	1	.000	5	0	0	0	0	9¹	9	0	6	4	14.5	8.68	44	.265	.375	0	—	-0	-5	-5	0	-0.5
1977	Atl-N	6	11	.353	45	16	0	0	0	139¹	142	28	80	100	14.6	5.36	83	.263	.362	4	.111	-2	-22	-14	-1	-1.7
Total	7	31	37	.456	142	61	16	5	5	544¹	479	60	258	362	12.4	3.87	100	.237	.326	19	.135	-2	-12	1	-1	-0.3
Team	4	26	27	.491	101	55	16	5	1	444	391	49	198	276	12.1	3.73	107	.236	.320	16	.127	-3	-1	12	-2	0.8

● BEN CARDONI Cardoni, Armand Joseph "Big Ben" b: 8/21/20, Jessup, Pa. d: 4/2/69, Jessup, Pa. BR/TR, 6'3", 195 lbs. Deb: 8/22/43

1943	Bos-N	0	0	—	11	0	0	0	1	28	38	1	14	5	17.0	6.43	53	.336	.414	0	.000	-1	-9	-9	0	-0.2
1944	Bos-N	0	6	.000	22	5	1	0	0	75²	83	5	37	24	14.4	3.93	97	.284	.367	4	.235	-0	-3	-1	-1	-0.1
1945	Bos-N	0	0	—	3	0	0	0	0	4	6	0	3	5	22.5	9.00	43	.300	.417	0	—	0	-2	-2	-0	0.0
Total	3	0	6	.000	36	5	1	0	1	107²	127	6	54	34	15.4	4.76	78	.299	.382	4	.167	-1	-14	-13	-1	-0.3

● DON CARDWELL Cardwell, Donald Eugene b: 12/7/35, Winston-Salem, N.C. BR/TR, 6'4", 210 lbs. Deb: 4/21/57

| 1970 | Atl-N | 2 | 1 | .667 | 16 | 2 | 1 | 1 | 0 | 23 | 31 | 5 | 13 | 10 | 17.6 | 9.00 | 48 | .326 | .413 | 2 | .400 | 1 | -13 | -12 | 1 | -1.2 |
| Total | 14 | 102 | 138 | .425 | 410 | 301 | 72 | 17 | 7 | 2122² | 2009 | 225 | 671 | 1211 | 11.8 | 3.92 | 95 | .250 | .315 | 94 | .135 | 2 | -59 | -47 | 10 | -2.7 |

● EDDIE CARNETT Carnett, Edwin Elliott "Lefty" b: 10/21/16, Springfield, Mo. BL/TL, 6', 185 lbs. Deb: 4/19/41 ♦

| 1941 | Bos-N | 0 | 0 | — | 2 | 0 | 0 | 0 | 0 | 1¹ | 4 | 0 | 3 | 2 | 47.3 | 20.25 | 18 | .500 | .636 | 0 | — | 0 | -2 | -2 | 0 | 0.0 |
| Total | 3 | 0 | 0 | — | 6 | 0 | 0 | 0 | 0 | 5¹ | 7 | 1 | 3 | 4 | 16.9 | 8.44 | 40 | .304 | .385 | 142 | .268 | 1 | -3 | -3 | 0 | 0.0 |

● PAT CARNEY Carney, Patrick Joseph "Doc" b: 8/7/1876, Holyoke, Mass. d: 1/9/53, Worcester, Mass. BL/TL, 6', 200 lbs. Deb: 9/20/01 ♦

1902	Bos-N	0	1	.000	2	1	0	0	0	5	6	1	3	2	18.0	9.00	31	.300	.417	141	.270	0	-3	-3	-0	-0.6
1903	Bos-N	4	5	.444	10	9	9	0	0	78	93	2	31	29	14.5	4.04	79	.284	.349	94	.240	2	-7	-7	-0	-0.6
1904	Bos-N	0	4	.000	4	2	1	0	0	26¹	40	1	12	5	18.1	5.81	47	.364	.431	57	.204	0	-9	-9	-0	-1.1
Total	3	4	10	.286	16	12	10	0	0	109¹	139	4	46	37	15.6	4.69	66	.303	.372	308	.247	2	-19	-20	-1	-2.3

● CLAY CARROLL Carroll, Clay Palmer "Hawk" b: 5/2/41, Clanton, Ala. BR/TR, 6'1", 200 lbs. Deb: 9/2/64

1964	Mil-N	2	0	1.000	11	1	0	0	0	20¹	15	1	3	17	8.0	1.77	199	.200	.231	0	.000	-0	4	4	1	0.5
1965	Mil-N	0	1	.000	19	1	0	0	1	34²	35	3	13	16	12.7	4.41	80	.269	.340	0	.000	-1	-3	-3	-0	-0.2
1966	Atl-N	8	7	.533	73	3	0	0	11	144¹	127	8	29	67	10.0	2.37	154	.236	.280	3	.100	-2	20	20	1	2.3
1967	Atl-N	6	12	.333	42	7	1	0	0	93	111	6	29	35	13.8	5.52	66	.304	.360	1	.063	-2	-22	-23	1	-4.0
1968	Atl-N	0	1	.000	10	0	0	0	0	22¹	26	1	6	10	12.9	4.84	62	.310	.356	0	.000	-0	-5	-5	0	-0.2
Total	15	96	73	.568	731	26	1	0	143	1353¹	1296	67	442	681	11.8	2.94	120	.257	.321	27	.130	-5	93	90	17	13.5
Team	5	16	21	.432	155	12	1	0	13	314²	314	19	80	145	11.5	3.66	95	.263	.314	4	.069	-4	-6	-6	3	-1.6

● CHUCK CARY Cary, Charles Douglas b: 3/3/60, Whittier, Cal. BL/TL, 6'4", 210 lbs. Deb: 8/22/85

1987	Atl-N	1	1	.500	13	0	0	0	1	16²	17	3	4	15	11.9	3.78	115	.266	.319	0	.000	-0	1	1	0	0.1
1988	Atl-N	0	0	—	7	0	0	0	0	8¹	8	1	4	7	14.0	6.48	57	.250	.351	0	—	0	-3	-3	-0	0.0
Total	8	14	26	.350	134	47	4	0	3	410¹	390	50	158	322	12.2	4.17	96	.250	.322	0	.000	-0	-9	-7	-4	-0.8
Team	2	1	1	.500	20	0	0	0	1	25	25	4	8	22	12.6	4.68	88	.260	.330	0	.000	-0	-2	-2	0	0.1

● TONY CASTILLO Castillo, Antonio Jose (Jimenez) b: 3/1/63, Quibor, Venez. BL/TL, 5'10", 177 lbs. Deb: 8/14/88

1989	Atl-N	0	1	.000	12	0	0	0	0	9¹	8	0	4	5	11.6	4.82	76	.222	.300	0	.000	-0	-1	-1	0	-0.1
1990	Atl-N	5	1	.833	52	3	0	0	1	76²	93	5	20	64	13.4	4.23	95	.302	.347	1	.143	0	-4	-2	1	-0.7
1991	Atl-N	1	1	.500	7	0	0	0	0	8²	13	3	5	8	18.7	7.27	53	.342	.419	0	—	0	-3	-3	-0	-0.7
Total	7	18	13	.581	259	6	0	0	16	342¹	348	29	121	220	12.5	3.52	122	.269	.335	1	.083	-0	28	30	2	2.6
Team	3	6	3	.667	71	3	0	0	1	94²	114	8	29	77	13.7	4.56	87	.298	.350	1	.125	-0	-9	-6	1	-0.8

● RED CAUSEY Causey, Cecil Algernon b: 8/11/1893, Georgetown, Fla. d: 11/11/60, Avon Park, Fla. BR/TR, 6'1", 160 lbs. Deb: 4/26/18

| 1919 | Bos-N | 4 | 5 | .444 | 10 | 10 | 3 | 0 | 0 | 69 | 81 | 1 | 20 | 14 | 13.3 | 4.57 | 63 | .308 | .359 | 2 | .095 | -2 | -13 | -13 | 0 | -1.7 |
| Total | 5 | 39 | 35 | .527 | 131 | 80 | 35 | 3 | 6 | 649² | 666 | 18 | 230 | 139 | 12.6 | 3.59 | 89 | .273 | .340 | 33 | .157 | -9 | -31 | -29 | -3 | -4.5 |

● ROME CHAMBERS Chambers, Richard Jerome b: 8/31/1875, Weaverville, N.C. d: 8/30/02, Weaverville, N.C. BL/TL, 6'2", 173 lbs. Deb: 5/7/00

| 1900 | Bos-N | 0 | 0 | — | 1 | 0 | 0 | 0 | 1 | 4 | 5 | 0 | 5 | 2 | 22.5 | 11.25 | 37 | .313 | .476 | 0 | .000 | -0 | -3 | -3 | -0 | -0.2 |

● TINY CHAPLIN Chaplin, James Bailey b: 7/13/05, Los Angeles, Cal. d: 3/25/39, National City, Cal BR/TR, 6'1", 195 lbs. Deb: 4/13/28

| 1936 | Bos-N | 10 | 15 | .400 | 40 | 31 | 14 | 0 | 2 | 231² | 273 | 21 | 62 | 86 | 13.1 | 4.12 | 93 | .294 | .340 | 17 | .202 | -0 | -3 | -7 | 2 | -0.6 |
| Total | 4 | 15 | 23 | .395 | 87 | 43 | 18 | 0 | 4 | 371 | 428 | 31 | 102 | 118 | 13.1 | 4.25 | 94 | .290 | .340 | 21 | .176 | -1 | -2 | -10 | 1 | -1.0 |

● BILL CHAPPELLE Chappelle, William Hogan "Big Bill" b: 3/22/1884, Waterloo, N.Y. d: 12/31/44, Mineola, N.Y. BR/TR, 6'2", 206 lbs. Deb: 8/20/08

1908	Bos-N	2	4	.333	13	7	3	1	0	70¹	60	0	17	23	10.4	1.79	135	.233	.290	1	.048	-1	4	5	1	0.4
1909	Bos-N	1	1	.500	5	3	2	0	0	29	31	0	11	18	13.3	1.86	152	.279	.350	4	.364	2	2	3	1	0.6
Total	3	7	7	.500	35	16	9	1	1	177²	167	1	59	62	11.9	2.38	113	.251	.321	5	.089	-3	5	6	1	0.3
Team	2	3	5	.375	18	10	5	1	0	99¹	91	0	28	31	11.2	1.81	140	.247	.308	5	.156	1	7	8	2	1.0

● DAVE CHEADLE Cheadle, David Baird b: 2/19/52, Greensboro, N.C. BL/TL, 6'2", 203 lbs. Deb: 9/16/73

| 1973 | Atl-N | 0 | 1 | .000 | 2 | 0 | 0 | 0 | 0 | 2 | 2 | 1 | 3 | 2 | 22.5 | 18.00 | 22 | .250 | .455 | 0 | — | 0 | -3 | -3 | -0 | -1.1 |

● LARRY CHENEY Cheney, Laurance Russell b: 5/2/1886, Belleville, Kan. d: 1/6/69, Daytona Beach, Fla. BR/TR, 6'1.5", 185 lbs. Deb: 9/9/11

| 1919 | Bos-N | 0 | 2 | .000 | 8 | 2 | 0 | 0 | 0 | 33 | 35 | 0 | 15 | 13 | 13.6 | 3.55 | 84 | .294 | .373 | 2 | .182 | 0 | -1 | -1 | 0 | -0.1 |
| Total | 9 | 116 | 100 | .537 | 313 | 225 | 132 | 20 | 19 | 1881¹ | 1605 | 36 | 733 | 926 | 11.5 | 2.70 | 109 | .234 | .313 | 115 | .186 | 9 | 49 | 52 | 0 | 6.8 |

● BOB CHIPMAN Chipman, Robert Howard "Mr. Chips" b: 10/11/18, Brooklyn, N.Y. d: 11/8/73, Huntington, N.Y. BL/TL, 6'2", 190 lbs. Deb: 9/28/41

1950	Bos-N	7	7	.500	27	12	4	0	1	124	127	10	37	40	12.2	4.43	87	.262	.319	6	.154	-1	-4	-8	-3	-1.1
1951	Bos-N	4	3	.571	33	0	0	0	4	52	59	5	19	17	13.8	4.85	76	.284	.349	1	.100	-1	-5	-7	-0	-1.0
1952	Bos-N	1	1	.500	29	0	0	0	0	41²	28	5	20	16	10.4	2.81	129	.188	.284	2	.400	1	4	4	0	0.3
Total	12	51	46	.526	293	87	29	7	14	880²	889	60	386	322	13.1	3.72	100	.261	.338	32	.128	-8	13	1	-2	-1.4
Team	3	12	11	.522	89	12	4	0	5	217²	214	20	76	73	12.2	4.22	89	.254	.320	9	.167	-1	-5	-11	-3	-1.8

YEAR TM/L	W	L	PCT	G	GS	CG	SH	SV	IP	H	HR	BB	SO	RAT	ERA	ERA+	OAV	OOB	BH	AVG	PB	PR	/A	PD	TPI
● **JIM CLANCY** Clancy, James b: 12/18/55, Chicago, Ill. BR/TR, 6'4", 220 lbs. Deb: 7/26/77																									
1991 *Atl-N	3	2	.600	24	0	0	0	3	34^2	36	3	14	17	13.2	5.71	68	.267	.340	0	.000	-0	-8	-7	0	-1.1
Total 15	140	167	.456	472	381	74	11	10	2517^1	2513	244	947	1422	12.5	4.23	98	.261	.329	9	.148	-0	-62	-26	-8	-6.4
● **TERRY CLARK** Clark, Terry Lee b: 10/18/60, Los Angeles, Cal. BR/TR, 6'2", 190 lbs. Deb: 7/7/88																									
1995 Atl-N	0	0	—	3	0	0	0	0	3^2	3	0	5	2	19.6	4.91	86	.231	.444	0	—	0	-0	-0	0	0.0
Total 4	8	13	.381	61	18	2	1	1	151^2	185	11	57	68	14.4	4.87	85	.312	.373	1	.500	0	-12	-13	0	-0.5
● **DAD CLARKSON** Clarkson, Arthur Hamilton b: 8/31/1866, Cambridge, Mass. d: 2/5/11, Somerville, Mass. BR/TR, 5'10", 165 lbs. Deb: 8/20/1891 F																									
1892 Bos-N	1	0	1.000	1	1	1	0	0	7	5	0	3	0	10.3	1.29	273	.192	.276	0	.000	-0	2	2	-0	0.2
Total 6	39	39	.500	96	81	63	2	0	704^2	873	26	325	133	15.8	4.90	99	.298	.376	44	.161	-14	-6	-3	2	-0.8
● **JOHN CLARKSON** Clarkson, John Gibson b: 7/1/1861, Cambridge, Mass. d: 2/4/09, Belmont, Mass. BR/TR, 5'10", 155 lbs. Deb: 5/2/1882 FH																									
1888 Bos-N	33	20	.623	54	54	53	3	0	**483**^{1}	448	17	119	223	10.7	2.76	103	.236	.284	40	.195	3	5	5	3	0.9
1889 Bos-N	**49**	19	**.721**	**73**	72	**68**	**8**	1	**620**	589	16	203	**284**	**11.7**	**2.73**	**153**	.243	**.306**	54	.206	0	**89**	**99**	11	**10.1**
1890 Bos-N	26	18	.591	44	44	43	2	0	383	370	14	140	138	12.4	3.27	115	.246	.317	43	.249	3	13	21	-1	2.0
1891 Bos-N	33	19	.635	55	51	47	3	**3**	460^2	435	18	154	141	11.8	2.79	131	.240	.305	42	.225	3	28	44	4	4.8
1892 Bos-N	8	6	.571	16	16	15	4	0	145^2	115	4	60	48	11.1	2.35	150	.208	.292	13	.228	1	15	19	0	1.7
Total 12	328	178	.648	531	518	485	37	5	4536^1	4295	161	1191	1978	11.0	2.81	134	.240	.291	432	.219	9	371	480	46	48.7
Team 5	149	82	.645	242	237	226	20	4	2092^2	1957	69	676	834	11.6	2.82	128	.239	.302	192	.217	11	150	187	17	19.5
● **BILL CLARKSON** Clarkson, William Henry "Blackie" b: 9/27/1898, Portsmouth, Va. d: 8/27/71, Raleigh, N.C. BR/TR, 5'11", 160 lbs. Deb: 5/2/27																									
1928 Bos-N	0	2	.000	19	1	0	0	0	34^2	53	2	22	8	19.7	6.75	58	.349	.434	0	.000	-0	-11	-11	1	-0.5
1929 Bos-N	0	1	.000	2	1	0	0	0	7	16	0	4	0	25.7	10.29	45	.485	.541	1	.500	0	-4	-4	0	-0.4
Total 3	3	12	.200	51	9	2	0	2	134	171	5	79	39	16.9	5.44	72	.319	.408	2	.080	-1	-22	-23	1	-1.6
Team 2	0	3	.000	21	2	0	0	0	41^2	69	2	26	8	20.7	7.34	55	.373	.453	1	.200	-0	-15	-15	1	-0.9
● **MARTY CLARY** Clary, Martin Keith b: 4/3/62, Detroit, Mich. BR/TR, 6'4", 190 lbs. Deb: 9/5/87																									
1987 Atl-N	0	1	.000	7	1	0	0	0	14^2	20	2	4	7	15.3	6.14	71	.328	.379	0	.000	-0	-3	-3	-0	-0.2
1989 Atl-N	4	3	.571	18	17	2	1	0	108^2	103	6	31	30	11.2	3.15	116	.249	.303	5	.161	0	4	6	0	0.5
1990 Atl-N	1	10	.091	33	14	0	0	0	101^2	128	9	39	44	14.9	5.67	71	.308	.368	0	.000	-3	-21	-18	1	-2.0
Total 3	5	14	.263	58	32	2	1	0	225	251	17	74	81	13.1	4.48	86	.282	.339	5	.083	-2	-20	-15	1	-1.7
● **TONY CLONINGER** Cloninger, Tony Lee b: 8/13/40, Lincoln Co., N.C. BR/TR, 6', 210 lbs. Deb: 6/15/61 C																									
1961 Mil-N	7	2	.778	19	10	3	0	0	84	84	16	33	51	12.6	5.25	71	.258	.328	5	.167	-0	-11	-14	1	-1.3
1962 Mil-N	8	3	.727	24	15	4	1	0	111	113	10	46	69	13.0	4.30	88	.264	.337	4	.103	-2	-4	-6	0	-0.7
1963 Mil-N	9	11	.450	41	18	4	2	1	145^1	131	17	63	100	12.1	3.78	85	.239	.320	5	.135	-0	-8	-9	-2	-1.4
1964 Mil-N	19	14	.576	38	34	15	3	2	242^2	206	20	82	163	10.8	3.56	99	.231	.298	21	.241	3	-1	-1	-0	0.2
1965 Mil-N	24	11	.686	40	38	16	1	1	279	247	20	119	211	11.9	3.29	107	.236	.316	17	.162	2	8	7	-1	0.9
1966 Atl-N	14	11	.560	39	38	11	1	1	257^2	253	29	116	178	13.1	4.12	88	.258	.340	26	.234	10	-15	-14	-0	-0.3
1967 Atl-N	4	7	.364	16	16	1	0	0	76^2	85	13	31	55	13.6	5.17	64	.285	.353	5	.200	1	-15	-16	-0	-2.0
1968 Atl-N	1	3	.250	8	1	0	0	0	19	15	0	11	7	12.3	4.26	70	.227	.338	0	.000	-0	-3	-3	0	-0.6
Total 12	113	97	.538	352	247	63	13	6	1767^2	1643	180	798	1120	12.6	4.07	88	.247	.330	119	.192	21	-96	-98	-2	-9.0
Team 8	86	62	.581	225	170	54	8	5	1215^1	1134	125	501	834	12.2	3.94	90	.247	.324	83	.189	13	-49	-55	-2	-5.2
● **BRAD CLONTZ** Clontz, John Bradley b: 4/25/71, Stuart, Va. BR/TR, 6'1", 180 lbs. Deb: 4/26/95																									
1995 *Atl-N	8	1	.889	59	0	0	0	4	69	71	5	22	55	12.7	3.65	116	.269	.334	0	.000	-0	4	4	0	0.6
● **AL CLOSTER** Closter, Alan Edward b: 6/15/43, Creighton, Neb. BL/TL, 6'2", 190 lbs. Deb: 4/19/66																									
1973 Atl-N	0	0	—	4	0	0	0	0	4^1	7	1	4	2	22.8	14.54	27	.389	.500	0	—	0	-5	-5	0	0.0
Total 4	2	2	.500	21	1	0	0	0	35^1	43	6	23	26	17.3	6.62	50	.303	.407	0	.000	-1	-12	-13	1	-0.8
● **GENE COCREHAM** Cocreham, Eugene b: 11/14/1884, Luling, Tex. d: 12/27/45, Luling, Tex. BR/TR, 6'3.5", 192 lbs. Deb: 9/25/13																									
1913 Bos-N	0	1	.000	1	1	0	0	0	8^1	13	0	4	3	19.4	7.56	43	.371	.450	0	.000	-1	-4	-4	0	-0.4
1914 Bos-N	3	4	.429	15	3	1	0	0	44^2	48	2	27	15	15.1	4.84	57	.296	.397	1	.100	-0	-10	-10	-1	-1.7
1915 Bos-N	0	0	—	1	0	0	0	0	1^2	3	0	0	0	16.2	5.40	48	.429	.429	0	—	0	-0	-1	-0	0.0
Total 3	3	5	.375	17	4	1	0	0	54^2	64	2	31	18	15.8	5.27	54	.314	.407	1	.071	-1	-15	-15	-2	-2.1
● **KEVIN COFFMAN** Coffman, Kevin Reese b: 1/19/65, Austin, Tex. BR/TR, 6'2", 175 lbs. Deb: 9/5/87																									
1987 Atl-N	2	3	.400	5	5	0	0	0	25^1	31	2	22	14	19.9	4.62	94	.313	.452	1	.100	-0	-2	-1	1	-0.1
1988 Atl-N	2	6	.250	18	11	0	0	0	67	62	3	54	24	16.1	5.78	64	.251	.393	5	.227	2	-17	-16	0	-1.5
Total 3	4	11	.267	31	18	0	0	0	110^2	119	5	95	47	18.0	6.42	61	.281	.420	7	.189	1	-34	-31	2	-2.9
Team 2	4	9	.308	23	16	0	0	0	92^1	93	5	76	38	17.2	5.46	71	.269	.410	6	.188	1	-19	-16	2	-1.6
● **DICK COFFMAN** Coffman, Samuel Richard b: 12/18/06, Veto, Ala. d: 3/24/72, Athens, Ala. BR/TR, 6'2", 195 lbs. Deb: 4/28/27 F																									
1940 Bos-N	1	5	.167	31	0	0	0	3	48^1	63	4	11	11	14.2	5.40	69	.323	.365	1	.083	-1	-8	-9	-1	-1.2
Total 15	72	95	.431	472	132	47	8	38	1460^1	1782	92	463	372	14.1	4.65	96	.302	.357	51	.127	-22	-61	-33	-2	-4.3
● **DAVE COLE** Cole, David Bruce b: 8/29/30, Williamsport, Md. BR/TR, 6'2", 175 lbs. Deb: 9/9/50																									
1950 Bos-N	0	1	.000	4	0	0	0	0	8	7	0	3	8	12.4	1.13	342	.259	.355	0	.000	-0	3	2	-0	0.2
1951 Bos-N	2	4	.333	23	7	1	0	0	67^2	64	3	64	33	17.3	4.26	86	.254	.409	6	.353	4	-2	-4	0	0.0
1952 Bos-N	1	1	.500	22	3	0	0	0	44^2	38	2	42	22	16.7	4.03	90	.241	.409	0	.000	-1	-1	-2	0	-0.2
1953 Mil-N	0	1	.000	10	0	0	0	0	14^2	17	1	14	13	19.0	8.59	46	.279	.413	1	.500	1	-7	-8	0	-0.3
Total 6	6	18	.250	84	27	3	1	0	237^1	221	16	199	119	16.2	4.93	79	.253	.395	14	.230	5	-25	-27	1	-2.1
Team 4	3	7	.300	59	10	1	0	0	135	126	6	123	76	17.0	4.47	83	.253	.407	7	.250	4	-8	-12	1	-0.3
● **DON COLLINS** Collins, Donald Edward b: 9/15/52, Lyons, Ga. BR/TL, 6'2", 195 lbs. Deb: 5/4/77																									
1977 Atl-N	3	9	.250	40	6	0	0	2	70^2	82	8	41	27	15.8	5.09	87	.299	.392	0	.000	-1	-9	-5	-1	-1.1
Total 2	3	9	.250	44	6	0	0	2	76^2	91	8	48	27	16.4	5.28	84	.303	.401	0	.000	-1	-12	-7	-1	-1.1
● **GENE CONLEY** Conley, Donald Eugene b: 11/10/30, Muskogee, Okla. BR/TR, 6'8", 225 lbs. Deb: 4/17/52																									
1952 Bos-N	0	3	.000	4	3	0	0	0	12^2	23	4	9	6	24.2	7.82	46	.397	.493	2	.400	1	-6	-6	-0	-1.1
1954 Mil-N★	14	9	.609	28	27	12	2	0	194^1	171	17	79	113	11.9	2.96	126	.240	.322	12	.156	-2	24	16	-1	1.5
1955 Mil-N★	11	7	.611	22	21	10	0	0	158	152	23	52	107	11.7	4.16	90	.254	.315	11	.204	-1	-2	-7	-0	-0.8
1956 Mil-N	8	9	.471	31	19	5	1	3	158^1	169	13	52	68	12.7	3.13	111	.276	.335	7	.156	-1	11	6	-1	0.5
1957 *Mil-N	9	9	.500	35	18	6	1	1	148	133	9	64	61	12.1	3.16	111	.244	.325	9	.196	1	12	6	-0	0.7
1958 Mil-N	0	6	.000	26	7	0	0	2	72	89	8	17	53	13.8	4.88	72	.309	.356	3	.188	1	-7	-11	0	-0.8
Total 11	91	96	.487	276	214	69	13	9	1588^2	1606	162	511	888	12.2	3.82	101	.264	.324	105	.192	8	20	6	-6	0.1
Team 6	42	43	.494	146	95	33	4	6	743^1	737	74	273	408	12.4	3.56	101	.262	.331	44	.181	-0	32	4	-2	-0.0
● **JOHN CONNOR** Connor, John b: 8/1854, Scotland d: 10/13/32, Boston, Mass. Deb: 7/26/1884																									
1884 Bos-N	1	4	.200	7	7	7	0	0	60	70	1	18	29	13.2	3.15	92	.275	.322	2	.080	-3	-1	-2	0	-0.3
Total 2	2	8	.200	12	12	12	0	0	104	127	1	32	48	13.9	3.81	79	.290	.341	4	.095	-4	-9	-9	-1	-1.2

YEAR	TM/L	W	L	PCT	G	GS	CG	SH	SV	IP	H	HR	BB	SO	RAT	ERA	ERA+	OAV	OOB	BH	AVG	PB	PR	/A	PD	TPI
● JIM CONSTABLE Constable, Jimmy Lee "Sheriff" b: 6/14/33, Jonesborough, Tenn. BB/TL, 6'1", 185 lbs. Deb: 6/24/56																										
1962	Mil-N	1	1	.500	3	2	1	1	1	18	14	1	4	12	9.0	2.00	190	.222	.269	0	.000	-0	4	4	-1	0.4
Total	5	3	4	.429	56	6	1	1	2	98	109	8	41	59	14.4	4.87	78	.291	.371	4	.235	2	-11	-11	-1	-0.4
● DICK CONWAY Conway, Richard Butler b: 4/25/1865, Lowell, Mass. d: 9/9/26, Lowell, Mass. BL/TR, 5'7.5", 140 lbs. Deb: 7/22/1886 F																										
1887	Bos-N	9	15	.375	26	26	25	0	0	222^1	249	10	86	45	13.8	4.66	87	.276	.343	36	.248	2	-14	-15	1	-1.0
1888	Bos-N	4	2	.667	6	6	6	0	0	53	49	2	8	12	10.4	2.38	120	.240	.282	4	.160	-1	3	3	-0	0.2
Total	3	15	24	.385	41	41	39	0	0	352	404	18	137	121	14.2	4.78	78	.279	.347	47	.230	1	-40	-41	2	-3.0
Team	2	13	17	.433	32	32	31	0	0	275^1	298	12	94	57	13.2	4.22	91	.269	.333	40	.235	1	-12	-12	0	-0.8
● JOHNNY COONEY Cooney, John Walter b: 3/18/01, Cranston, R.I. d: 7/8/86, Sarasota, Fla. BR/TL, 5'10", 165 lbs. Deb: 4/19/21 FMC♦																										
1921	Bos-N	0	1	.000	8	1	0	0	0	20^2	19	3	10	9	12.6	3.92	93	.241	.326	1	.200	-0	-0	-1	0	0.0
1922	Bos-N	1	2	.333	4	3	1	0	0	25	19	0	6	7	9.4	2.16	185	.224	.283	0	.000	-1	5	5	0	0.4
1923	Bos-N	3	5	.375	23	8	5	2	0	98	92	3	22	23	10.7	3.31	121	.246	.293	25	.379	4	8	7	-2	0.7
1924	Bos-N	8	9	.471	34	19	12	2	2	181	176	4	50	67	11.4	3.18	120	.260	.314	33	.254	2	14	13	-1	1.1
1925	Bos-N	14	14	.500	31	29	20	2	0	245^2	267	18	50	65	11.7	3.48	115	.274	.312	33	.320	5	22	14	1	2.4
1926	Bos-N	3	3	.500	19	8	3	1	0	83^1	106	0	29	23	15.3	4.00	89	.320	.387	38	.302	3	-2	-4	0	0.1
1928	Bos-N	3	7	.300	24	6	2	0	1	89^2	106	7	31	18	13.8	4.32	91	.303	.360	7	.171	-0	-3	-4	3	-0.1
1929	Bos-N	2	3	.400	14	2	1	0	3	45	57	4	22	11	15.8	5.00	94	.315	.389	23	.319	2	-1	-2	1	0.1
1930	Bos-N	0	0	—	2	0	0	0	0	7	16	2	3	1	25.7	18.00	27	.471	.526	0	.000	-1	-10	-10	1	0.0
Total	9	34	44	.436	159	76	44	7	6	795^1	858	41	223	224	12.4	3.72	106	.278	.331	965	.286	15	32	19	4	4.7
● BILL COONEY Cooney, William A. "Cush" b: 4/7/1883, Boston, Mass. d: 11/6/28, Roxbury, Mass. TR, Deb: 9/22/09 ♦																										
1909	Bos-N	0	0	—	3	0	0	0	0	6^1	4	0	2	3	8.5	1.42	199	.182	.250	3	.300	0	1	1	-0	0.0
● MORT COOPER Cooper, Morton Cecil b: 3/2/13, Atherton, Mo. d: 11/17/58, Little Rock, Ark. BR/TR, 6'2", 210 lbs. Deb: 9/14/38 F																										
1945	Bos-N†	7	4	.636	20	11	4	1	1	78	77	4	27	45	12.1	3.35	115	.257	.320	6	.231	1	4	4	0	0.7
1946	Bos-N☆	13	11	.542	28	27	15	4	1	199	181	16	39	83	**9.9**	3.12	110	.239	**.276**	14	.209	1	6	7	-3	0.6
1947	Bos-N	2	5	.286	10	7	2	0	0	46^2	48	2	13	15	12.2	4.05	96	.271	.328	0	.000	-1	0	-1	-1	-0.3
Total	11	128	75	.631	295	239	128	33	14	1840^2	1666	85	571	913	11.1	2.97	123	.240	.300	127	.194	6	132	143	-20	12.9
Team	3	22	20	.524	58	45	21	5	2	323^2	306	22	79	143	10.8	3.31	109	.248	.295	20	.189	1	10	10	-4	1.0
● ENSIGN COTTRELL Cottrell, Ensign Stover b: 8/29/1888, Hoosick Falls, N.Y d: 2/27/47, Syracuse, N.Y. BL/TL, 5'9.5", 173 lbs. Deb: 6/21/11																										
1914	Bos-N	0	1	.000	1	1	0	0	0	1	2	0	3	1	45.0	9.00	31	.333	.556	0	—	0	-1	-1	0	-0.5
Total	5	1	2	.333	12	2	1	0	0	37^1	58	2	14	12	17.6	4.82	61	.354	.408	1	.083	-0	-8	-8	-0	-0.8
● JOE COWLEY Cowley, Joseph Alan b: 8/15/58, Lexington, Ky. BR/TR, 6'5", 210 lbs. Deb: 4/13/82																										
1982	Atl-N	1	2	.333	17	8	0	0	0	52^1	53	6	16	27	12.0	4.47	83	.265	.323	3	.200	-0	-5	-4	-0	-0.2
Total	5	33	25	.569	95	76	8	1	0	469^1	414	69	232	332	12.7	4.20	96	.235	.329	4	.222	1	-7	-8	-1	-1.7
● BILL COYLE Coyle, William Claude b: Pittsburgh, Pa. TR, Deb: 7/7/1893																										
1893	Bos-N	0	1	.000	2	1	0	0	0	8	14	1	3	2	19.1	9.00	55	.368	.415	0	.000	-1	-4	-4	0	-0.4
● CHARLIE COZART Cozart, Charles Rhubin b: 10/17/19, Lenoir, N.C. BR/TL, 6', 190 lbs. Deb: 4/17/45																										
1945	Bos-N	1	0	1.000	5	0	0	0	0	8	10	2	15	4	28.1	10.13	38	.303	.521	0	.000	-0	-6	-6	1	-0.5
● DOC CRANDALL Crandall, James Otis b: 10/8/1887, Wadena, Ind. d: 8/17/51, Bell, Cal. BR/TR, 5'10.5", 180 lbs. Deb: 4/24/08 ♦																										
1918	Bos-N	1	2	.333	5	3	3	0	0	34	39	1	4	4	11.6	2.38	113	.307	.333	8	.286	1	1	1	0	0.3
Total	10	102	62	.622	302	134	91	9	25	1546^2	1538	52	379	606	11.4	2.92	101	.261	.310	253	.285	54	-1	5	1	6.6
● RAY CRONE Crone, Raymond Hayes b: 8/7/31, Memphis, Tenn. BR/TR, 6'2", 185 lbs. Deb: 4/13/54																										
1954	Mil-N	1	0	1.000	19	2	1	0	1	49	44	6	19	33	11.8	2.02	184	.247	.323	2	.200	-0	11	9	-0	0.2
1955	Mil-N	10	9	.526	33	15	6	1	0	140^1	117	11	42	76	10.2	3.46	108	.227	.285	7	.159	-1	9	5	0	0.4
1956	Mil-N	11	10	.524	35	21	6	0	2	169^2	173	19	44	73	11.6	3.87	89	.263	.311	6	.122	1	-2	-8	-1	-0.9
1957	Mil-N	3	1	.750	11	5	2	0	0	42^1	54	8	15	15	14.7	4.46	78	.312	.367	2	.182	1	-3	-5	1	-0.2
Total	5	30	30	.500	137	61	17	1	4	546	554	60	173	260	12.1	3.87	95	.263	.321	18	.115	-3	2	-12	2	-2.0
Team	4	25	20	.556	98	43	15	1	3	401^1	388	44	120	197	11.4	3.57	101	.255	.310	17	.149	1	15	2	-0	-0.5
● CAL CRUM Crum, Calvin N. b: 7/27/1890, Cooks Mills, Ill. d: 12/7/45, Tulsa, Okla. BR/TR, 6'1", 175 lbs. Deb: 4/17/17																										
1917	Bos-N	0	0	—	1	0	0	0	0	1	1	0	1	0	18.0	0.00	—	.250	.400	0	—	0	0	0	0	0.0
1918	Bos-N	0	1	.000	1	1	0	0	0	2^1	6	0	3	0	38.6	15.43	17	.600	.714	0	.000	-0	-3	-3	0	-0.9
Total	2	0	1	.000	2	1	0	0	0	3^1	7	0	4	0	32.4	10.80	24	.500	.632	0	.000	-0	-3	-3	1	-0.9
● DICK CRUTCHER Crutcher, Richard Louis b: 11/25/1889, Frankfort, Ky. d: 6/19/52, Frankfort, Ky. BR/TR, 5'9", 148 lbs. Deb: 4/14/14																										
1914	Bos-N	5	7	.417	33	15	5	1	0	158^2	169	4	66	48	13.7	3.46	80	.293	.371	8	.148	-1	-12	-12	1	-0.9
1915	Bos-N	2	2	.500	14	4	1	0	2	43^2	50	1	16	17	14.0	4.33	60	.309	.378	3	.231	1	-8	-8	0	-0.7
Total	2	7	9	.438	47	19	6	1	2	202^1	219	5	82	65	13.7	3.65	75	.296	.373	11	.164	-0	-19	-21	1	-1.6
● BRUCE CUNNINGHAM Cunningham, Bruce Lee b: 9/29/05, San Francisco, Cal. d: 3/8/84, Hayward, Cal. BR/TR, 5'10.5", 165 lbs. Deb: 5/7/29																										
1929	Bos-N	4	6	.400	17	8	4	0	1	91^2	100	7	32	22	13.2	4.52	104	.282	.344	4	.148	-0	2	2	1	0.2
1930	Bos-N	5	6	.455	36	6	2	0	0	106^2	121	7	41	28	13.7	5.48	90	.289	.352	6	.194	0	-6	-6	3	-0.2
1931	Bos-N	3	12	.200	33	16	6	1	1	136^2	157	7	54	32	14.0	4.48	85	.296	.363	3	.071	-4	-9	-10	4	-1.0
1932	Bos-N	1	0	1.000	18	3	0	0	0	47	50	1	19	21	14.0	3.45	109	.281	.363	2	.222	2	2	2	1	0.3
Total	4	13	24	.351	104	33	12	1	2	382	428	22	146	103	13.7	4.64	93	.289	.356	15	.138	-2	-11	-14	9	-0.7
● NIG CUPPY Cuppy, George Joseph (b: George Koppe) b: 7/3/1869, Logansport, Ind. d: 7/27/22, Elkhart, Ind. BR/TR, 5'7", 160 lbs. Deb: 4/16/1892																										
1900	Bos-N	8	4	.667	17	13	9	0	1	105^1	107	8	24	23	11.7	3.08	134	.263	.314	11	.262	1	7	12	-1	1.2
Total	10	162	98	.623	302	262	224	9	5	2283	2520	62	609	504	12.6	3.48	127	.275	.325	223	.233	6	200	239	6	22.5
● SAMMY CURRAN Curran, Simon Francis b: 10/30/1874, Dorchester, Mass. d: 5/19/36, Dorchester, Mass. TL, Deb: 8/1/02																										
1902	Bos-N	0	0	—	1	0	0	0	0	6^2	6	0	0	3	8.1	1.35	209	.240	.240	0	.000	-0	1	1	-0	-0.1
● CLIFF CURTIS Curtis, Clifton Garfield b: 7/3/1883, Delaware, Ohio d: 4/23/43, Utica, Ohio BR/TR, 6'2", 180 lbs. Deb: 8/23/09																										
1909	Bos-N	4	5	.444	10	9	8	2	0	83	53	1	30	22	9.2	1.41	200	.191	.275	1	.034	-3	11	13	1	1.3
1910	Bos-N	6	24	.200	43	37	12	2	2	251	251	9	124	75	13.9	3.55	94	.277	.371	12	.146	-4	-14	-6	6	-0.6
1911	Bos-N	1	8	.111	12	9	5	0	1	77	79	4	34	23	13.4	4.44	86	.265	.344	7	.250	-0	-9	-5	1	-0.5
Total	5	28	61	.315	136	94	39	5	6	744^2	707	22	317	236	12.8	3.31	101	.259	.344	39	.159	-10	-13	3	9	-0.1
Team	3	11	37	.229	65	55	25	4	3	411	383	14	188	120	12.9	3.28	101	.258	.348	20	.144	-7	-12	1	7	0.2
● JACK CURTIS Curtis, Jack Patrick b: 1/11/37, Rhodhiss, N.C. BL/TL, 5'10", 175 lbs. Deb: 4/22/61																										
1962	Mil-N	4	4	.500	30	5	0	0	1	75^2	82	8	27	40	13.2	4.16	91	.282	.347	4	.222	2	-2	-3	-1	-0.2
Total	3	14	19	.424	69	35	6	0	1	279	328	33	89	108	13.6	4.84	84	.297	.352	15	.183	5	-26	-24	-1	-1.3
● JOHN DAGENHARD Dagenhard, John Douglas b: 4/25/17, Magnolia, Ohio BR/TR, 6'2", 195 lbs. Deb: 9/28/43																										
1943	Bos-N	1	0	1.000	2	1	1	0	0	11	9	0	4	2	12.3	0.00	—	.225	.326	0	.000	-0	4	4	1	0.5

YEAR TM/L	W	L	PCT	G	GS	CG	SH	SV	IP	H	HR	BB	SO	RAT	ERA	ERA+	OAV	OOB	BH	AVG	PB	PR	/A	PD	TPI
● **BRUCE DalCANTON** DalCanton, John Bruce b: 6/15/42, California, Pa. BR/TR, 6'2", 205 lbs. Deb: 9/3/67 C																									
1975 Atl-N	2	7	.222	26	9	0	0	3	67	63	2	24	38	12.5	3.36	112	.248	.327	2	.105	-1	2	3	1	0.4
1976 Atl-N	3	5	.375	42	1	0	0	1	73^1	67	6	42	36	13.6	3.56	106	.244	.348	2	.222	0	-0	2	1	0.3
Total 11	51	49	.510	316	83	15	2	19	931^1	894	48	391	485	12.6	3.67	99	.253	.331	17	.113	-3	-12	-5	-3	-1.7
Team 2	5	12	.294	68	10	0	0	4	140^1	130	8	66	74	13.1	3.46	109	.246	.338	4	.143	-1	1	5	2	0.7
● **BILL DALEY** Daley, William b: 6/27/1868, Poughkeepsie, N.Y d: 5/4/22, Poughkeepsie, N.Y. TL , Deb: 7/17/1889																									
1889 Bos-N	3	3	.500	9	7	4	0	0	48	34	1	43	40	14.8	4.31	97	.193	.357	3	.150	-1	-2	-1	3	0.1
Total 3	29	16	.644	62	43	33	2	4	409^2	399	14	291	218	15.6	3.49	117	.245	.366	30	.159	-8	25	27	3	1.6
● **MIKE DAVEY** Davey, Michael Gerard b: 6/2/52, Spokane, Wash. BR/TL, 6'2", 190 lbs. Deb: 8/13/77																									
1977 Atl-N	0	0	—	16	0	0	0	2	16	19	1	9	7	15.8	5.06	88	.302	.389	0	.000	-0	-2	-1	-0	-0.1
1978 Atl-N	0	0	—	3	0	0	0	0	2^2	1	0	1	0	6.8	0.00	—	.125	.222	0	—	0	1	1	-0	0.0
Total 2	0	0	—	19	0	0	0	2	18^2	20	1	10	7	14.5	4.34	101	.282	.370	0	.000	-0	-1	0	-0	-0.1
● **TED DAVIDSON** Davidson, Thomas Eugene b: 10/4/39, Las Vegas, Nev. BR/TL, 6', 192 lbs. Deb: 7/24/65																									
1968 Atl-N	0	0	—	4	0	0	0	0	6^2	10	2	4	3	18.9	6.75	44	.345	.424	0	—	0	-3	-3	0	0.0
Total 4	11	7	.611	114	1	0	0	5	195^1	189	21	54	124	11.3	3.69	101	.256	.309	0	.000	-3	-5	1	1	0.4
● **GEORGE DAVIS** Davis, George Allen "Iron" b: 3/9/1890, Lancaster, N.Y. d: 6/4/61, Buffalo, N.Y. BB/TR, 5'10.5", 175 lbs. Deb: 7/16/12																									
1913 Bos-N	0	0	—	2	0	0	0	0	8	7	1	5	3	13.5	4.50	73	.241	.353	0	.000	-0	-1	-1	-0	-0.1
1914 Bos-N	3	3	.500	9	6	4	1	0	55^2	42	1	26	26	11.5	3.40	81	.215	.317	3	.167	0	-4	-4	-2	-0.6
1915 Bos-N	3	3	.500	15	9	4	0	0	73^1	85	2	19	26	13.3	3.80	68	.304	.356	6	.261	1	-9	-10	0	-0.6
Total 4	7	10	.412	36	22	13	1	0	191	195	7	78	77	13.3	4.48	66	.274	.354	11	.180	-0	-33	-33	-3	-2.9
Team 3	6	6	.500	26	15	8	1	0	137	134	4	50	55	12.5	3.68	73	.266	.340	9	.209	1	-13	-15	-2	-1.3
● **DAISY DAVIS** Davis, John Henry Albert b: 11/28/1858, Boston, Mass. d: 11/5/02, Lynn, Mass. TR , Deb: 5/6/1884																									
1884 Bos-N	1	3	.250	4	4	3	0	0	31	50	2	8	13	16.8	7.84	37	.355	.389	0	.000	-3	-17	-17	0	-1.6
1885 Bos-N	5	6	.455	11	11	10	1	0	94^1	110	2	28	30	13.2	4.29	63	.280	.328	7	.189	-0	-15	-17	-1	-1.7
Total 2	16	21	.432	40	39	33	2	0	323^2	356	5	71	186	12.3	3.78	81	.269	.313	22	.157	-5	-25	-26	-2	-2.9
Team 2	6	9	.400	15	15	13	1	0	125^1	160	4	36	43	14.1	5.17	53	.300	.344	7	.132	-3	-32	-34	-1	-3.3
● **MARK DAVIS** Davis, Mark William b: 10/19/60, Livermore, Cal. BL/TL, 6'4", 205 lbs. Deb: 9/12/80																									
1992 Atl-N	1	0	1.000	14	0	0	0	0	16^2	22	3	13	15	19.4	7.02	52	.314	.429	0	.000	-0	-7	-6	-1	-0.4
Total 14	51	84	.378	605	85	4	2	96	1128^2	1047	125	529	993	12.8	4.15	88	.248	.335	26	.156	5	-52	-61	-4	-2.8
● **KEN DAYLEY** Dayley, Kenneth Grant b: 2/25/59, Jerome, Idaho BL/TL, 6', 175 lbs. Deb: 5/13/82																									
1982 Atl-N	5	6	.455	20	11	0	0	0	71^1	79	9	25	34	13.1	4.54	82	.286	.346	5	.250	1	-7	-6	-2	-1.0
1983 Atl-N	5	8	.385	24	16	0	0	0	104^2	100	12	39	70	12.1	4.30	90	.257	.328	7	.219	1	-8	-5	-2	-0.7
1984 Atl-N	0	3	.000	4	4	0	0	0	18^2	28	5	6	10	16.9	5.30	73	.341	.393	2	.500	1	-4	-3	0	-0.4
Total 11	33	45	.423	385	33	0	0	39	573^2	564	42	225	406	12.5	3.64	103	.261	.332	17	.210	3	1	7	-5	0.7
Team 3	10	17	.370	48	31	0	0	0	194^2	207	26	70	114	12.9	4.48	85	.277	.341	14	.250	3	-19	-14	-4	-2.1
● **JEFF DEDMON** Dedmon, Jeffrey Linden b: 3/4/60, Torrance, Cal. BL/TR, 6'2", 200 lbs. Deb: 9/2/83																									
1983 Atl-N	0	0	—	5	0	0	0	0	4	10	1	0	3	22.5	13.50	29	.455	.455	0	—	0	-4	-4	0	0.0
1984 Atl-N	4	3	.571	54	0	0	0	4	81	86	5	35	51	13.7	3.78	102	.277	.354	0	.000	-1	-2	1	2	0.2
1985 Atl-N	6	3	.667	60	0	0	0	0	86	84	5	49	41	14.0	4.08	94	.264	.364	1	.111	-0	-5	-2	3	0.1
1986 Atl-N	6	6	.500	57	0	0	0	3	99^2	90	8	39	58	12.0	2.98	133	.242	.320	2	.125	-1	8	11	2	1.4
1987 Atl-N	3	4	.429	53	3	0	0	4	89^2	82	8	42	40	12.5	3.91	111	.246	.332	4	.250	1	2	4	1	0.6
Total 6	20	16	.556	250	3	0	0	12	394	387	30	186	210	13.3	3.84	105	.261	.348	7	.149	-0	-3	8	9	2.4
Team 5	19	16	.543	229	3	0	0	11	360^1	352	27	165	193	13.1	3.77	106	.260	.343	7	.149	-0	-1	9	8	2.3
● **JIM DELAHANTY** Delahanty, James Christopher b: 6/20/1879, Cleveland, Ohio d: 10/17/53, Cleveland, Ohio BR/TR, 5'10.5", 170 lbs. Deb: 4/19/01 F♦																									
1904 Bos-N	0	0	—	1	0	0	0	0	3^1	5	0	1	0	16.2	0.00	—	.357	.400	142	.285	0	1	1	0	0.0
1905 Bos-N	0	0	—	1	1	0	0	0	2	5	1	0	0	22.5	4.50	69	.500	.500	119	.258	0	-0	-0	0	0.0
Total 2	0	0	—	2	1	0	0	0	5^1	10	1	1	0	18.6	1.69	171	.417	.440	1159	.283	1	1	1	0	0.0
● **ART DELANEY** Delaney, Arthur Dewey "Swede" (b: Arthur Dewey Helenius) b: 1/5/1895, Chicago, Ill. d: 5/2/70, Hayward, Cal. BR/TR, 5'10.5", 178 lbs. Deb: 4/16/24																									
1928 Bos-N	9	17	.346	39	22	8	0	2	192^1	197	11	56	45	11.9	3.79	103	.267	.319	9	.143	-3	4	3	1	0.1
1929 Bos-N	3	5	.375	20	8	3	1	0	75	103	6	35	17	16.7	6.12	76	.336	.405	3	.143	0	-12	-12	-1	-1.0
Total 3	13	22	.371	67	31	12	1	2	287^1	319	17	97	64	13.1	4.26	96	.285	.343	14	.154	-2	-3	-5	0	-0.6
Team 2	12	22	.353	59	30	11	1	2	267^1	300	17	91	62	13.2	4.44	93	.287	.345	12	.143	-2	-7	-10	0	-0.9
● **AL DEMAREE** Demaree, Albert Wentworth b: 9/8/1884, Quincy, Ill. d: 4/30/62, Los Angeles, Cal. BL/TR, 6', 170 lbs. Deb: 9/26/12																									
1919 Bos-N	6	6	.500	25	13	6	0	3	128	147	8	35	34	12.9	3.80	75	.300	.348	2	.048	-5	-13	-13	-2	-2.0
Total 8	80	72	.526	232	173	84	15	9	1424	1350	34	337	514	10.9	2.77	100	.256	.304	54	.118	-20	6	0	-16	-4.9
● **RUBE DESSAU** Dessau, Frank Rolland b: 3/29/1883, New Galilee, Pa. d: 5/6/52, York, Pa. BB/TR, 5'11", 175 lbs. Deb: 9/22/07																									
1907 Bos-N	0	1	.000	2	2	1	0	0	9^1	13	0	10	1	23.1	10.61	24	.394	.545	0	.000	-0	-8	-8	-0	-0.8
Total 2	2	4	.333	21	2	1	0	1	60^2	80	0	39	25	18.5	6.53	45	.338	.443	1	.053	-1	-24	-24	-2	-2.5
● **ADRIAN DEVINE** Devine, Paul Adrian b: 12/2/51, Galveston, Tex. BR/TR, 6'4", 205 lbs. Deb: 6/27/73																									
1973 Atl-N	2	3	.400	24	1	0	0	4	32^1	45	6	12	15	16.4	6.40	61	.338	.401	1	.250	0	-10	-9	-1	-1.5
1975 Atl-N	1	0	1.000	5	2	0	0	0	16^1	19	2	7	8	14.9	4.41	86	.284	.360	0	.000	-1	-1	-1	-0	-0.2
1976 Atl-N	5	6	.455	48	1	0	0	9	73	72	3	26	48	12.2	3.21	118	.255	.320	0	.000	-2	2	5	-1	0.6
1978 Atl-N	5	4	.556	31	6	0	0	3	65^1	84	3	25	26	15.0	5.92	68	.323	.382	1	.091	-1	-17	-14	0	-1.9
1979 Atl-N	1	2	.333	40	0	0	0	0	66^2	84	8	25	22	15.0	3.24	125	.311	.374	0	.000	-1	4	6	-0	0.1
Total 7	26	22	.542	217	12	0	0	31	387^1	455	34	135	194	14.0	4.21	95	.296	.357	2	.049	-3	-19	-9	0	-1.9
Team 5	14	15	.483	148	10	0	0	16	253^2	304	22	95	119	14.4	4.40	90	.300	.364	2	.049	-3	-22	-13	-2	-2.9
● **CARLOS DIAZ** Diaz, Carlos Antonio b: 1/7/58, Kaneohe, Hawaii BR/TL, 6', 170 lbs. Deb: 6/30/82																									
1982 Atl-N	3	2	.600	19	0	0	0	1	25^1	31	3	9	16	14.2	4.62	81	.307	.364	0	.000	-0	-3	-3	0	-0.5
Total 5	13	6	.684	179	0	0	0	4	258	249	17	97	207	12.1	3.21	111	.253	.320	0	.000	-1	12	10	-0	0.7
● **WALT DICKSON** Dickson, Walter R. "Hickory" b: 12/3/1878, New Summerfield, Tex. d: 12/9/18, Ardmore, Okla. BR/TR, 5'11.5", 175 lbs. Deb: 4/26/10																									
1912 Bos-N	3	19	.136	36	20	9	1	1	189	233	2	61	47	14.1	3.86	93	.320	.375	10	.167	-1	-9	-6	2	-0.6
1913 Bos-N	6	7	.462	19	15	8	0	0	128	118	4	45	47	11.5	3.23	102	.249	.316	8	.178	-1	-0	1	-1	-0.2
Total 5	26	50	.342	134	79	40	4	2	700	759	17	222	202	12.7	3.60	86	.288	.345	30	.135	-12	-41	-38	0	-4.8
Team 2	9	26	.257	55	35	17	1	1	317	351	6	106	94	13.1	3.61	96	.292	.351	18	.171	-2	-10	-5	1	-0.8
● **GEORGE DIEHL** Diehl, George Krause b: 2/25/18, Emmaus, Pa. d: 8/24/86, Kingsport, Tenn. BR/TR, 6'2", 196 lbs. Deb: 4/19/42																									
1942 Bos-N	0	0	—	1	0	0	0	0	3^2	2	0	2	0	12.3	2.45	136	.167	.333	0	.000	-0	0	0	0	0.0
1943 Bos-N	0	0	—	1	0	0	0	0	4	4	0	3	1	15.8	4.50	76	.267	.389	0	.000	-0	-0	-0	1	0.1
Total 2	0	0	—	2	0	0	0	0	7^2	6	0	5	1	14.1	3.52	96	.222	.364	0	.000	-0	-0	-0	1	0.1

YEAR	TM/L	W	L	PCT	G	GS	CG	SH	SV	IP	H	HR	BB	SO	RAT	ERA	ERA+	OAV	OOB	BH	AVG	PB	PR	/A	PD	TPI
● BILL DINNEEN	Dinneen, William Henry "Big Bill" b: 4/5/1876, Syracuse, N.Y. d: 1/13/55, Syracuse, N.Y. BR/TR, 6'1", 190 lbs. Deb: 4/22/1898 U																									
1900	Bos-N	20	14	.588	40	37	33	1	0	320^2	304	11	105	107	11.7	3.12	133	.250	.314	35	.280	2	21	**36**	2	**3.6**
1901	Bos-N	15	18	.455	37	34	31	0	0	309^1	295	8	77	141	11.0	2.94	123	.250	.299	31	.211	0	13	23	-1	2.1
Total	12	170	177	.490	391	352	306	23	7	3074^2	2957	78	829	1127	11.3	3.01	107	.254	.308	219	.192	-6	38	71	-15	4.8
Team	2	35	32	.522	77	71	64	1	0	630	599	19	182	248	11.4	3.03	128	.250	.307	66	.243	2	34	59	0	5.7
● PAT DOBSON	Dobson, Patrick Edward b: 2/12/42, Depew, N.Y. BR/TR, 6'3", 190 lbs. Deb: 5/31/67 C																									
1973	Atl-N	3	7	.300	12	10	1	1	0	57^2	73	1	19	23	14.5	4.99	79	.315	.369	1	.067	-1	-9	-7	0	-1.2
Total	11	122	129	.486	414	279	74	14	19	2120^1	2043	197	665	1301	11.6	3.54	100	.255	.314	39	.123	-8	10	-1	-3	-1.1
● COZY DOLAN	Dolan, Patrick Henry b: 12/3/1872, Cambridge, Mass. d: 3/29/07, Louisville, Ky. BL/TL, 5'10", 160 lbs. Deb: 4/26/1895 ♦																									
1895	Bos-N	11	7	.611	25	21	18	3	1	198^1	215	11	67	47	13.4	4.27	120	.272	.340	20	.241	-1	11	18	4	1.5
1896	Bos-N	1	4	.200	6	5	3	0	0	41	55	1	27	14	18.7	4.83	94	.318	.419	2	.143	-1	-2	-1	-0	-0.3
1905	Bos-N	0	1	.000	2	0	0	0	0	4	7	2	1	1	18.0	9.00	34	.368	.400	119	.275	1	-3	-3	-0	-0.5
1906	Bos-N	0	1	.000	2	0	0	0	0	12	12	1	6	7	13.5	4.50	60	.300	.391	136	.248	0	-2	-2	-1	-0.2
Total	4	12	13	.480	35	26	21	3	1	255^1	289	15	101	69	14.3	4.44	109	.283	.357	855	.269	-2	4	12	3	0.5
● ART DOLL	Doll, Arthur James "Moose" b: 5/7/13, Chicago, Ill. d: 4/28/78, Calumet City, Ill. BR/TR, 6'1", 190 lbs. Deb: 9/21/35 ♦																									
1936	Bos-N	0	1	.000	1	1	0	0	0	8	11	1	2	2	15.8	3.38	114	.355	.412	0	.000	-0	1	0	-0	0.0
1938	Bos-N	0	0	—	3	0	0	0	0	4	4	0	3	1	15.8	2.25	153	.286	.412	1	1.000	1	1	1	0	0.1
Total	2	0	1	.000	4	1	0	0	0	12	15	1	5	3	15.8	3.00	123	.333	.412	2	.154	0	1	1	0	0.1
● ED DONNELLY	Donnelly, Edward "Big Ed" or "Ned" (b: Edward O'Donnell) b: 7/29/1880, Hampton, N.Y. d: 11/28/57, Rutland, Vt. BR/TR, 6'1", 205 lbs. Deb: 9/19/11																									
1911	Bos-N	3	2	.600	5	4	4	1	0	36^2	33	0	9	16	10.8	2.45	156	.236	.291	1	.071	-1	4	6	-0	0.6
1912	Bos-N	5	10	.333	37	18	10	0	0	184^1	225	10	72	67	14.7	4.35	82	.304	.370	19	.275	3	-19	-16	1	-0.8
Total	2	8	12	.400	42	22	14	1	0	221	258	10	81	83	14.1	4.03	90	.293	.357	20	.241	1	-15	-10	1	-0.2
● BLIX DONNELLY	Donnelly, Sylvester Urban b: 1/21/14, Olivia, Minn. d: 6/20/76, Olivia, Minn. BR/TR, 5'10", 178 lbs. Deb: 5/6/44																									
1951	Bos-N	0	1	.000	6	0	0	0	0	7^1	8	1	6	3	18.4	7.36	50	.286	.429	0	.000	-0	-3	-3	0	-0.4
Total	8	27	36	.429	190	75	27	7	12	691^2	659	52	306	296	12.8	3.49	109	.257	.340	32	.159	-1	27	24	-8	0.7
● DICK DONOVAN	Donovan, Richard Edward b: 12/7/27, Boston, Mass. BL/TR, 6'3", 205 lbs. Deb: 4/24/50																									
1950	Bos-N	0	2	.000	10	3	0	0	0	29^2	28	4	34	9	19.4	8.19	47	.255	.438	1	.167	1	-13	-14	-0	-0.7
1951	Bos-N	0	0	—	8	2	0	0	0	13^2	17	0	11	4	18.4	5.27	70	.298	.412	1	.333	1	-2	-2	0	0.2
1952	Bos-N	0	2	.000	7	2	0	0	1	13	18	1	12	6	22.2	5.54	65	.346	.485	0	.000	-0	-3	-3	1	-0.4
Total	15	122	99	.552	345	273	101	25	5	2017^1	1988	198	495	880	11.3	3.67	104	.258	.306	113	.163	24	45	31	-0	7.3
Team	3	0	4	.000	25	7	0	0	1	56^1	63	5	57	19	19.8	6.87	55	.288	.443	2	.167	2	-18	-20	1	-0.9
● BILL DONOVAN	Donovan, Willard Earl b: 7/6/16, Maywood, Ill. BB/TL, 6'2", 198 lbs. Deb: 4/19/42																									
1942	Bos-N	3	6	.333	31	10	2	0	0	89^1	97	2	32	23	13.0	3.43	97	.283	.344	6	.240	1	-1	-1	2	0.3
1943	Bos-N	1	0	1.000	7	0	0	0	0	14^2	17	0	9	1	16.0	1.84	185	.304	.400	1	.333	0	3	3	1	0.3
Total	2	4	6	.400	38	10	2	0	0	104	114	2	41	24	13.4	3.20	105	.286	.352	7	.250	1	1	2	3	0.6
● GUS DORNER	Dorner, Augustus b: 8/18/1876, Chambersburg, Pa. d: 5/4/56, Chambersburg, Pa. BR/TR, 5'10", 176 lbs. Deb: 9/17/02																									
1906	Bos-N	8	25	.242	34	32	29	0	0	273^1	264	5	103	104	12.6	3.65	74	.260	.338	14	.140	-4	-31	-29	3	-3.5
1907	Bos-N	12	16	.429	36	31	24	2	0	271^1	253	4	92	85	11.9	3.12	82	.255	.327	12	.130	-3	-19	-17	-3	-2.4
1908	Bos-N	8	19	.296	38	28	14	3	0	216^1	176	3	77	41	11.1	3.54	68	.224	.305	12	.179	-1	-28	-27	2	-3.3
1909	Bos-N	1	2	.333	5	2	0	0	1	24^2	17	1	17	7	13.1	2.55	110	.198	.343	1	.167	-0	0	1	-0	0.0
Total	6	36	69	.343	131	106	76	8	1	910^1	842	18	330	275	12.1	3.37	78	.250	.326	46	.149	-9	-80	-74	1	-9.5
Team	4	29	62	.319	113	93	67	5	1	785^2	710	13	289	237	12.0	3.40	76	.247	.325	39	.147	-9	-79	-73	1	-9.2
● PAUL DOYLE	Doyle, Paul Sinnott b: 10/2/39, Philadelphia, Pa. BL/TL, 5'11", 172 lbs. Deb: 5/28/69																									
1969	*Atl-N	2	0	1.000	36	0	0	0	4	39	31	4	16	25	10.8	2.08	174	.231	.313	0	.000	-0	7	7	1	0.5
Total	3	5	3	.625	87	0	0	0	11	90^1	85	11	46	65	13.2	3.79	96	.259	.352	0	.000	-1	-1	-2	3	-0.8
● MOE DRABOWSKY	Drabowsky, Myron Walter b: 7/21/35, Ozanna, Poland BR/TR, 6'2", 200 lbs. Deb: 8/7/56 C																									
1961	Mil-N	0	2	.000	16	0	0	0	2	25^1	26	4	18	5	16.0	4.62	81	.277	.398	1	.250	0	-2	-2	0	-0.2
Total	17	88	105	.456	589	154	33	6	55	1641	1441	182	702	1162	12.1	3.71	101	.236	.321	68	.162	-0	-5	4	-5	2.9
● BOB DRESSER	Dresser, Robert Nicholson b: 10/4/1878, Newton, Mass. d: 7/27/24, Duxbury, Mass. BL/TL, Deb: 8/13/02																									
1902	Bos-N	0	1	.000	1	1	1	0	0	9	12	0	0	8	12.0	3.00	94	.316	.316	1	.250	0	-0	-0	-0	0.0
● TOM EARLEY	Earley, Thomas Francis Aloysius b: 2/19/17, Roxbury, Mass. d: 4/5/88, Nantucket, Mass. BR/TR, 6', 180 lbs. Deb: 9/27/38																									
1938	Bos-N	1	0	1.000	2	1	1	0	0	11	8	2	1	4	8.2	3.27	105	.186	.222	0	.000	-1	1	0	-0	-0.1
1939	Bos-N	1	4	.200	14	2	0	0	1	40	49	1	19	9	15.7	4.72	78	.304	.385	3	.300	1	-4	-5	1	-0.4
1940	Bos-N	2	0	1.000	4	1	1	1	0	16^1	16	1	3	5	11.6	3.86	96	.267	.323	2	.400	1	-0	-0	-0	0.1
1941	Bos-N	6	8	.429	33	13	6	1	3	138^2	120	9	46	54	11.0	2.53	141	.233	.300	11	.234	1	17	16	-1	1.7
1942	Bos-N	6	11	.353	27	18	6	0	1	112^2	120	10	55	28	14.1	4.71	71	.276	.359	4	.118	-1	-18	-17	0	-2.4
1945	Bos-N	2	1	.667	11	2	1	0	0	41	36	4	19	4	12.1	4.61	83	.235	.320	3	.214	1	-4	-4	0	-0.2
Total	6	18	24	.429	91	37	15	2	5	359^2	349	27	143	104	12.5	3.78	94	.256	.330	23	.202	2	-7	-9	-0	-1.3
● MAL EASON	Eason, Malcolm Wayne "Kid" b: 3/13/1879, Brookville, Pa. d: 4/16/70, Douglas, Ariz. BR/TR, 6', 175 lbs. Deb: 10/1/00 U																									
1902	Bos-N	9	11	.450	27	26	20	2	0	206^1	237	4	59	50	13.4	2.75	103	.288	.344	6	.083	-6	1	2	-1	-0.6
Total	6	36	72	.333	125	113	90	10	1	944^1	1015	20	289	273	12.8	3.39	85	.278	.338	43	.121	-19	-47	-54	2	-7.7
● JAMIE EASTERLY	Easterly, James Morris b: 2/17/53, Houston, Tex. BL/TL, 5'9", 180 lbs. Deb: 4/6/74																									
1974	Atl-N	0	0	—	3	0	0	0	0	2^2	6	0	4	0	33.8	16.88	22	.400	.526	0	—	0	-4	-4	0	0.0
1975	Atl-N	2	9	.182	21	13	0	0	0	68^2	73	5	42	34	15.3	4.98	76	.275	.379	1	.056	-2	-10	-9	-1	-1.5
1976	Atl-N	1	1	.500	4	4	0	0	0	22	23	0	13	11	14.7	4.91	77	.280	.379	1	.111	-0	-3	-3	0	-0.3
1977	Atl-N	2	4	.333	22	5	0	0	1	58^2	72	5	30	37	16.1	6.14	72	.303	.387	4	.267	1	-15	-11	-1	-1.1
1978	Atl-N	3	6	.333	37	6	0	0	1	78	91	9	45	42	15.9	5.65	72	.299	.393	4	.211	0	-18	-14	0	-1.5
1979	Atl-N	0	0	—	4	0	0	0	0	2^2	7	0	3	3	33.8	13.50	30	.467	.556	0	—	0	-3	-3	0	0.0
Total	13	23	33	.411	321	36	0	0	14	611^1	663	48	319	350	14.7	4.62	87	.283	.373	10	.161	-1	-49	-40	-0	-3.9
Team	6	8	20	.286	91	28	0	0	2	232^2	272	19	137	127	16.1	5.72	71	.296	.391	10	.164	-1	-53	-44	-2	-4.4
● GARY EAVE	Eave, Gary Louis b: 7/22/63, Monroe, La. BR/TR, 6'4", 200 lbs. Deb: 4/12/88																									
1988	Atl-N	0	0	—	5	0	0	0	0	5	7	0	3	0	18.0	9.00	41	.333	.417	0	—	0	-3	-3	-0	0.0
1989	Atl-N	2	0	1.000	3	3	0	0	0	20^2	15	0	12	9	12.2	1.31	279	.200	.318	0	.000	-1	5	5	-1	0.4
Total	3	2	3	.400	16	8	0	0	0	55^2	49	5	35	25	14.1	3.56	107	.236	.354	0	.000	-1	1	2	-1	0.3
Team	2	2	0	1.000	8	3	0	0	0	25^2	22	0	15	9	13.3	2.81	130	.229	.339	0	.000	-1	2	2	-1	0.4
● EDDIE EAYRS	Eayrs, Edwin b: 11/10/1890, Blackstone, Mass. d: 11/30/69, Warwick, R.I. BL/TL, 5'7", 160 lbs. Deb: 6/30/13 ♦																									
1920	Bos-N	1	2	.333	7	3	0	0	0	26^1	36	1	12	7	17.1	5.47	56	.346	.424	80	.328	2	-7	-7	1	-0.5

YEAR	TM/L	W	L	PCT	G	GS	CG	SH	SV	IP	H	HR	BB	SO	RAT	ERA	ERA+	OAV	OOB	BH	AVG	PB	PR	/A	PD	TPI
1921	Bos-N	0	0	—	2	0	0	0	0	4^2	9	0	9	1	34.7	17.36	21	.391	.563	1	.067	-2	-7	-7	-0	-0.2
Total	3	1	2	.333	11	3	0	0	0	39	53	1	27	13	18.9	6.23	50	.338	.441	83	.306	0	-13	-14	0	-0.7
Team	2	1	2	.333	9	3	0	0	0	31	45	1	21	8	19.7	7.26	43	.354	.453	81	.313	0	-14	-14	1	-0.7

● **JOHN EDELMAN** Edelman, John Rogers b: 7/27/35, Philadelphia, Pa. BR/TR, 6'3", 185 lbs. Deb: 6/2/55

YEAR	TM/L	W	L	PCT	G	GS	CG	SH	SV	IP	H	HR	BB	SO	RAT	ERA	ERA+	OAV	OOB	BH	AVG	PB	PR	/A	PD	TPI
1955	Mil-N	0	0	—	5	0	0	0	0	5^2	7	0	8	3	23.8	11.12	34	.304	.484	0	—	0	-4	-5	0	0.0

● **FOSTER EDWARDS** Edwards, Foster Hamilton "Eddie" b: 9/1/03, Holstein, Iowa d: 1/4/80, Orleans, Mass. BR/TR, 6'3", 175 lbs. Deb: 7/2/25

YEAR	TM/L	W	L	PCT	G	GS	CG	SH	SV	IP	H	HR	BB	SO	RAT	ERA	ERA+	OAV	OOB	BH	AVG	PB	PR	/A	PD	TPI
1925	Bos-N	0	0	—	1	0	0	0	0	2	6	0	1	1	31.5	9.00	45	.545	.583	0	—	0	-1	-1	-0	0.0
1926	Bos-N	2	0	1.000	3	3	1	0	0	25	20	0	13	4	11.9	0.72	492	.230	.330	0	.000	-2	9	8	-0	0.4
1927	Bos-N	2	8	.200	29	11	1	0	0	92	95	2	45	37	14.0	4.99	74	.274	.362	1	.045	-2	-11	-13	-1	-1.5
1928	Bos-N	2	1	.667	21	3	2	0	0	49^1	67	2	23	17	16.8	5.66	69	.327	.400	1	.091	-1	-9	-10	0	-0.6
Total	5	6	9	.400	56	17	4	0	0	170	193	4	84	60	14.9	4.76	79	.292	.377	2	.048	-5	-16	-19	-1	-1.7
Team	4	6	9	.400	54	17	4	0	0	168^1	188	4	82	59	14.7	4.60	82	.289	.373	2	.048	-5	-13	-16	-1	-1.7

● **JUAN EICHELBERGER** Eichelberger, Juan Tyrone b: 10/21/53, St.Louis, Mo. BR/TR, 6'3", 205 lbs. Deb: 9/7/78

YEAR	TM/L	W	L	PCT	G	GS	CG	SH	SV	IP	H	HR	BB	SO	RAT	ERA	ERA+	OAV	OOB	BH	AVG	PB	PR	/A	PD	TPI
1988	Atl-N	2	0	1.000	20	0	0	0	0	37^1	44	3	10	13	13.0	3.86	95	.297	.342	0	.000	-0	-2	-1	1	0.0
Total	7	26	36	.419	125	79	14	1	0	603^1	575	50	283	281	12.9	4.10	87	.254	.339	14	.103	-4	-29	-35	-2	-3.8

● **MARK EICHHORN** Eichhorn, Mark Anthony b: 11/21/60, San Jose, Cal. BR/TR, 6'4", 200 lbs. Deb: 8/30/82

YEAR	TM/L	W	L	PCT	G	GS	CG	SH	SV	IP	H	HR	BB	SO	RAT	ERA	ERA+	OAV	OOB	BH	AVG	PB	PR	/A	PD	TPI
1989	Atl-N	5	5	.500	45	0	0	0	0	68^1	70	6	19	49	11.9	4.35	84	.275	.327	0	.000	-0	-6	-5	2	-0.5
Total	10	47	41	.534	539	7	0	0	32	855^1	789	46	259	616	11.4	2.93	144	.247	.311	0	.000	-0	116	122	12	14.5

● **DAVE EILERS** Eilers, David Louis b: 12/3/36, Oldenburg, Tex. BR/TR, 5'11", 188 lbs. Deb: 7/27/64

YEAR	TM/L	W	L	PCT	G	GS	CG	SH	SV	IP	H	HR	BB	SO	RAT	ERA	ERA+	OAV	OOB	BH	AVG	PB	PR	/A	PD	TPI
1964	Mil-N	0	0	—	6	0	0	0	0	7^2	11	1	1	1	15.3	4.70	75	.333	.371	0	—	0	-1	-1	-0	0.0
1965	Mil-N	0	0	—	6	0	0	0	0	3^2	8	1	0	1	19.6	12.27	29	.421	.421	0	—	0	-4	-4	0	0.0
Total	4	8	6	.571	81	0	0	0	3	123^1	146	14	29	52	13.3	4.45	78	.297	.345	1	.111	-0	-13	-14	-0	-1.1
Team	2	0	0	—	12	0	0	0	0	11^1	19	2	1	2	16.7	7.15	49	.365	.389	0	—	0	-5	-5	-0	0.0

● **GLENN ELLIOTT** Elliott, Herbert Glenn "Lefty" b: 11/11/19, Sapulpa, Okla d: 7/27/69, Portland, Ore. BB/TL, 5'10", 170 lbs. Deb: 4/17/47

YEAR	TM/L	W	L	PCT	G	GS	CG	SH	SV	IP	H	HR	BB	SO	RAT	ERA	ERA+	OAV	OOB	BH	AVG	PB	PR	/A	PD	TPI
1947	Bos-N	0	1	.000	11	0	0	0	1	19	18	4	11	8	13.7	4.74	82	.269	.372	1	.500	0	-1	-2	0	0.0
1948	Bos-N	1	0	1.000	1	1	0	0	0	3	5	0	1	2	18.0	3.00	128	.357	.400	0	.000	-0	0	0	-0	0.0
1949	Bos-N	3	4	.429	22	6	1	0	0	68^1	70	7	27	15	12.8	3.95	96	.269	.338	1	.059	-1	1	-1	1	-0.2
Total	3	4	5	.444	34	7	1	0	1	90^1	93	11	39	25	13.2	4.08	93	.273	.347	2	.095	-1	-0	-3	1	-0.2

● **JUMBO ELLIOTT** Elliott, James Thomas b: 10/22/1900, St.Louis, Mo. d: 1/7/70, Terre Haute, Ind. BR/TL, 6'3", 235 lbs. Deb: 4/21/23

YEAR	TM/L	W	L	PCT	G	GS	CG	SH	SV	IP	H	HR	BB	SO	RAT	ERA	ERA+	OAV	OOB	BH	AVG	PB	PR	/A	PD	TPI
1934	Bos-N	1	1	.500	7	3	0	0	0	15^1	19	2	9	6	17.0	5.87	65	.284	.377	1	.250	0	-3	-3	-0	-0.4
Total	10	63	74	.460	252	144	51	8	12	1206^2	1338	70	414	453	13.3	4.24	100	.283	.344	68	.163	-8	-29	2	-21	-4.1

● **DICK ERRICKSON** Errickson, Richard Merriwell "Lief" b: 3/5/14, Vineland, N.J. BL/TR, 6'1", 175 lbs. Deb: 4/27/38

YEAR	TM/L	W	L	PCT	G	GS	CG	SH	SV	IP	H	HR	BB	SO	RAT	ERA	ERA+	OAV	OOB	BH	AVG	PB	PR	/A	PD	TPI
1938	Bos-N	9	7	.563	34	10	6	1	6	122^2	113	1	56	40	12.5	3.15	109	.246	.330	4	.114	-1	9	4	2	0.5
1939	Bos-N	6	9	.400	28	11	3	0	1	128^1	143	6	54	33	13.9	4.00	92	.293	.365	10	.227	1	-1	-4	2	-0.2
1940	Bos-N	12	13	.480	34	29	17	3	4	236^1	241	8	90	34	12.6	3.16	118	.270	.338	13	.157	-2	18	15	1	1.4
1941	Bos-N	6	12	.333	38	23	5	2	1	165^2	192	12	62	45	14.0	4.78	75	.287	.351	8	.178	-0	-21	-22	1	-2.2
1942	Bos-N	2	5	.286	21	4	0	0	1	59^1	76	8	20	15	14.6	5.01	67	.309	.361	2	.125	-1	-11	-11	-1	-1.4
Total	5	36	47	.434	168	77	31	6	13	736^1	804	36	290	176	13.5	3.85	93	.282	.350	37	.162	-5	-9	-21	5	-2.1
Team	5	35	46	.432	155	77	31	6	13	712^1	765	35	282	167	13.3	3.84	94	.278	.347	37	.166	-4	-7	-19	4	-1.9

● **GEORGE ESTOCK** Estock, George John b: 11/2/24, Stirling, N.J. BR/TR, 6', 185 lbs. Deb: 4/21/51

YEAR	TM/L	W	L	PCT	G	GS	CG	SH	SV	IP	H	HR	BB	SO	RAT	ERA	ERA+	OAV	OOB	BH	AVG	PB	PR	/A	PD	TPI
1951	Bos-N	0	1	.000	37	1	0	0	3	60^1	56	2	37	11	13.9	4.33	85	.258	.366	2	.286	1	-2	-4	0	0.0

● **CHICK EVANS** Evans, Charles Franklin b: 10/15/1889, Arlington, Vt. d: 9/2/16, Schenectady, N.Y. BR/TR, Deb: 9/19/09

YEAR	TM/L	W	L	PCT	G	GS	CG	SH	SV	IP	H	HR	BB	SO	RAT	ERA	ERA+	OAV	OOB	BH	AVG	PB	PR	/A	PD	TPI
1909	Bos-N	0	3	.000	4	3	1	0	0	21^2	25	0	14	11	16.2	4.57	62	.305	.406	0	.000	-1	-5	-4	-0	-0.7
1910	Bos-N	1	1	.500	13	1	0	0	2	31	28	1	27	12	16.8	5.23	64	.275	.439	1	.100	-1	-8	-7	0	-0.5
Total	2	1	4	.200	17	4	1	0	2	52^2	53	1	41	23	16.6	4.96	63	.288	.425	1	.053	-2	-12	-11	0	-1.2

● **PETE FALCONE** Falcone, Peter Frank b: 10/1/53, Brooklyn, N.Y. BL/TL, 6'2", 185 lbs. Deb: 4/13/75

YEAR	TM/L	W	L	PCT	G	GS	CG	SH	SV	IP	H	HR	BB	SO	RAT	ERA	ERA+	OAV	OOB	BH	AVG	PB	PR	/A	PD	TPI
1983	Atl-N	9	4	.692	33	15	2	0	0	106^2	102	14	60	59	13.8	3.63	107	.256	.355	3	.115	-1	-0	3	-2	0.0
1984	Atl-N	5	7	.417	35	16	2	1	2	120	115	15	57	55	12.9	4.13	93	.252	.335	7	.212	1	-7	-4	-1	-0.4
Total	10	70	90	.438	325	217	25	7	7	1435^1	1385	152	671	865	13.0	4.07	90	.257	.341	62	.149	-6	-71	-63	-20	-8.9
Team	2	14	11	.560	68	31	4	1	2	226^2	217	29	117	114	13.3	3.89	99	.254	.345	10	.169	-0	-7	-1	-3	-0.4

● **ED FALLENSTEIN** Fallenstein, Edward Joseph "Jack" (b: Edward Joseph Valestin)
b: 12/22/08, Newark, N.J. d: 11/24/71, Orange, N.J. BR/TR, 6'3", 180 lbs. Deb: 4/16/31

YEAR	TM/L	W	L	PCT	G	GS	CG	SH	SV	IP	H	HR	BB	SO	RAT	ERA	ERA+	OAV	OOB	BH	AVG	PB	PR	/A	PD	TPI
1933	Bos-N	2	1	.667	9	4	1	1	0	35	43	1	13	5	14.7	3.60	85	.305	.368	3	.375	1	-1	-2	-0	-0.1
Total	2	2	1	.667	33	4	1	1	0	76^2	99	3	39	20	16.3	5.52	67	.320	.398	4	.308	1	-16	-16	-0	-0.1

● **KERBY FARRELL** Farrell, Major Kerby b: 9/3/13, Leapwood, Tenn. d: 12/17/75, Nashville, Tenn. BL/TL, 5'11", 172 lbs. Deb: 4/24/43 MC♦

YEAR	TM/L	W	L	PCT	G	GS	CG	SH	SV	IP	H	HR	BB	SO	RAT	ERA	ERA+	OAV	OOB	BH	AVG	PB	PR	/A	PD	TPI
1943	Bos-N	0	1	.000	5	0	0	0	0	23	24	1	9	4	12.9	4.30	79	.276	.344	75	.268	1	-2	-2	-0	0.0

● **GEORGE FERGUSON** Ferguson, George Cecil "Cecil" b: 8/19/1886, Ellsworth, Ind. d: 9/5/43, Orlando, Fla. BR/TR, 5'10", 165 lbs. Deb: 4/19/06

YEAR	TM/L	W	L	PCT	G	GS	CG	SH	SV	IP	H	HR	BB	SO	RAT	ERA	ERA+	OAV	OOB	BH	AVG	PB	PR	/A	PD	TPI
1908	Bos-N	11	11	.500	37	20	13	3	0	208	168	1	84	98	11.3	2.47	98	.230	.316	11	.169	1	-2	-1	-3	-0.4
1909	Bos-N	5	23	.179	36	30	19	3	0	226^2	235	2	83	87	13.1	3.73	76	.282	.355	15	.205	1	-28	-23	0	-2.5
1910	Bos-N	7	7	.500	26	14	10	1	0	123	110	3	58	40	12.8	3.80	87	.254	.351	7	.175	-1	-11	-7	-0	-0.8
1911	Bos-N	1	3	.250	6	3	0	0	0	24	40	3	12	4	19.5	9.75	39	.388	.452	2	.286	1	-17	-16	-0	-1.9
Total	6	29	46	.387	142	73	47	8	8	698	659	12	281	298	12.6	3.34	83	.261	.343	41	.188	3	-55	-44	-2	-5.3
Team	4	24	44	.353	105	67	42	7	0	581^2	553	9	237	229	12.6	3.54	79	.263	.345	35	.189	2	-58	-47	-3	-5.6

● **WES FERRELL** Ferrell, Wesley Cheek b: 2/2/08, Greensboro, N.C. d: 12/9/76, Sarasota, Fla. BR/TR, 6'2", 195 lbs. Deb: 9/9/27 F♦

YEAR	TM/L	W	L	PCT	G	GS	CG	SH	SV	IP	H	HR	BB	SO	RAT	ERA	ERA+	OAV	OOB	BH	AVG	PB	PR	/A	PD	TPI
1941	Bos-N	2	1	.667	4	3	1	0	0	14	13	1	9	10	14.8	5.14	69	.241	.359	2	.500	2	-2	-2	-0	-0.3
Total	15	193	128	.601	374	323	227	17	13	2623	2845	132	1040	985	13.4	4.04	117	.275	.343	329	.280	100	147	195	6	32.3

● **LOU FETTE** Fette, Louis Henry William b: 3/15/07, Alma, Mo. d: 1/3/81, Warrensburg, Mo. BR/TR, 6'1.5", 200 lbs. Deb: 4/26/37

YEAR	TM/L	W	L	PCT	G	GS	CG	SH	SV	IP	H	HR	BB	SO	RAT	ERA	ERA+	OAV	OOB	BH	AVG	PB	PR	/A	PD	TPI
1937	Bos-N	20	10	.667	35	33	23	**5**	0	259	243	5	81	70	11.4	2.88	124	.251	.311	22	.239	3	30	20	0	2.5
1938	Bos-N	11	13	.458	33	32	17	3	1	239^2	235	11	79	83	11.9	3.15	109	.258	.320	16	.188	0	17	7	2	0.9
1939	Bos-N★	10	10	.500	27	26	11	**6**	0	146	123	7	61	35	11.4	2.96	125	.229	.309	3	.061	-4	16	12	3	1.3
1940	Bos-N	0	5	.000	7	5	0	0	0	32^1	38	0	18	2	15.9	5.57	67	.302	.393	3	.375	1	-6	-7	-1	-0.8
1945	Bos-N	0	2	.000	5	1	0	0	0	11	16	1	7	4	19.6	5.73	67	.356	.453	0	.000	-0	-2	-2	0	-0.4
Total	5	41	40	.506	109	97	51	14	1	691	658	24	248	194	11.9	3.15	113	.253	.321	44	.186	-0	55	32	4	3.5
Team	5	41	40	.506	107	97	51	14	1	688	655	24	246	194	11.9	3.17	113	.253	.321	44	.186	-0	54	31	4	3.5

● **DANA FILLINGIM** Fillingim, Dana b: 11/6/1893, Columbus, Ga. d: 2/3/61, Tuskegee, Ala. BL/TR, 5'10", 175 lbs. Deb: 8/2/15

YEAR	TM/L	W	L	PCT	G	GS	CG	SH	SV	IP	H	HR	BB	SO	RAT	ERA	ERA+	OAV	OOB	BH	AVG	PB	PR	/A	PD	TPI
1918	Bos-N	7	6	.538	14	13	10	4	0	113	99	0	28	29	10.5	2.23	120	.243	.300	9	.214	0	7	6	-0	0.7
1919	Bos-N	6	13	.316	32	18	9	0	2	186^1	185	2	39	50	10.9	3.38	85	.270	.312	16	.246	1	-10	-11	2	-0.7
1920	Bos-N	12	21	.364	37	31	22	2	0	272	292	8	79	66	12.4	3.11	98	.287	.340	16	.174	-2	1	-2	5	0.2
1921	Bos-N	15	10	.600	44	22	11	**3**	1	239^2	249	10	56	54	11.5	3.45	106	.272	.316	21	.247	5	9	5	-1	0.8
1922	Bos-N	5	9	.357	25	12	5	1	2	117	143	6	37	25	13.9	4.54	88	.311	.363	6	.158	-2	-6	-7	-1	-0.9

YEAR TM/L	W	L	PCT	G	GS	CG	SH	SV	IP	H	HR	BB	SO	RAT	ERA	ERA+	OAV	OOB	BH	AVG	PB	PR	/A	PD	TPI
1923 Bos-N	1	9	.100	35	12	1	0	0	100^{1}	141	6	36	27	16.0	5.20	77	.345	.399	7	.226	1	-13	-14	-0	-1.1
Total 8	47	73	.392	200	113	59	10	5	1076^{1}	1170	32	313	270	12.5	3.56	93	.287	.340	77	.209	4	-21	-30	5	-1.8
Team 6	46	68	.404	187	108	58	10	5	1028^{1}	1109	32	275	251	12.2	3.51	94	.285	.334	75	.212	4	-13	-22	6	-1.0

● HANK FISCHER Fischer, Henry William "Bulldog" b: 1/11/40, Yonkers, N.Y. BR/TR, 6', 190 lbs. Deb: 4/16/62

YEAR TM/L	W	L	PCT	G	GS	CG	SH	SV	IP	H	HR	BB	SO	RAT	ERA	ERA+	OAV	OOB	BH	AVG	PB	PR	/A	PD	TPI
1962 Mil-N	2	3	.400	29	0	0	0	4	37^{1}	43	4	20	29	15.2	5.30	72	.291	.375	0	.000	-0	-6	-6	-0	-0.9
1963 Mil-N	4	3	.571	31	6	1	0	0	74^{1}	74	8	28	72	13.0	4.96	65	.262	.340	2	.105	-0	-14	-14	-1	-1.4
1964 Mil-N	11	10	.524	37	28	9	5	2	168^{1}	177	17	39	99	11.7	4.01	88	.265	.309	8	.154	1	-9	-9	-1	-1.1
1965 Mil-N	8	9	.471	31	19	2	0	0	122^{2}	126	18	39	79	12.3	3.89	91	.270	.331	4	.108	-1	-5	-5	-2	-1.0
1966 Atl-N	2	3	.400	14	8	0	0	0	48^{1}	55	3	14	22	13.0	3.91	93	.296	.348	0	.000	-2	-2	-1	-1	-0.4
Total 6	30	39	.435	168	77	14	5	7	546^{2}	587	60	174	369	12.8	4.23	84	.275	.334	18	.118	-3	-43	-41	-5	-5.5
Team 5	27	28	.491	142	61	12	5	6	451	475	50	140	301	12.5	4.23	83	.272	.330	14	.112	-2	-35	-36	-5	-4.8

● TOM FISHER Fisher, Thomas Chalmers "Red" b: 11/1/1880, Anderson, Ind. d: 9/3/72, Anderson, Ind. BR/TR, 5'10.5", 185 lbs. Deb: 4/17/04 F

YEAR TM/L	W	L	PCT	G	GS	CG	SH	SV	IP	H	HR	BB	SO	RAT	ERA	ERA+	OAV	OOB	BH	AVG	PB	PR	/A	PD	TPI
1904 Bos-N	6	16	.273	31	21	19	2	0	214	257	5	82	84	14.7	4.25	65	.302	.370	21	.212	3	-36	-35	-5	-3.4

● PATSY FLAHERTY Flaherty, Patrick Joseph b: 6/29/1876, Mansfield, Pa. d: 1/23/68, Alexandria, La. BL/TL, 5'8", 165 lbs. Deb: 9/8/1899 ♦

YEAR TM/L	W	L	PCT	G	GS	CG	SH	SV	IP	H	HR	BB	SO	RAT	ERA	ERA+	OAV	OOB	BH	AVG	PB	PR	/A	PD	TPI
1907 Bos-N	12	15	.444	27	25	23	0	0	217	197	4	59	34	10.9	2.70	95	.248	.306	22	.191	2	-5	-3	2	0.1
1908 Bos-N	12	18	.400	31	31	21	0	0	244	221	6	81	50	11.4	3.25	74	.236	.303	12	.140	-0	-24	-23	2	-2.6
1911 Bos-N	0	2	.000	4	2	1	0	0	14	21	0	8	0	20.6	7.07	54	.350	.451	27	.287	1	-6	-5	-0	-0.6
Total 9	67	84	.444	173	150	125	7	2	1302^{2}	1292	25	331	271	11.6	3.10	89	.259	.312	123	.197	10	-49	-50	14	-2.5
Team 3	24	35	.407	62	58	45	0	0	475	439	10	148	84	11.5	3.11	81	.245	.309	61	.207	2	-35	-31	4	-3.1

● CURRY FOLEY Foley, Charles Joseph b: 1/14/1856, Milltown, Ireland d: 10/20/1898, Boston, Mass. TL, 5'10", 160 lbs. Deb: 5/13/1879 ♦

YEAR TM/L	W	L	PCT	G	GS	CG	SH	SV	IP	H	HR	BB	SO	RAT	ERA	ERA+	OAV	OOB	BH	AVG	PB	PR	/A	PD	TPI
1879 Bos-N	9	9	.500	21	16	16	1	0	161^{2}	175	1	15	57	10.6	2.51	99	.252	.268	46	.315	5	-0	-0	-2	0.2
1880 Bos-N	14	14	.500	36	28	21	1	0	238	264	1	40	68	11.5	3.89	58	.274	.303	97	.292	8	-40	-43	1	-3.6
Total 5	27	27	.500	69	50	39	2	0	442^{2}	511	3	64	127	11.7	3.54	68	.273	.297	373	.286	14	-53	-56	-2	-4.6
Team 2	23	23	.500	57	44	37	2	0	399^{2}	439	2	55	125	11.1	3.33	71	.265	.288	143	.299	13	-40	-43	-1	-3.4

● GENE FORD Ford, Eugene Matthew b: 6/23/12, Ft.Dodge, Iowa d: 9/7/70, Emmetsburg, Iowa BR/TR, 6'2", 195 lbs. Deb: 6/17/36

YEAR TM/L	W	L	PCT	G	GS	CG	SH	SV	IP	H	HR	BB	SO	RAT	ERA	ERA+	OAV	OOB	BH	AVG	PB	PR	/A	PD	TPI
1936 Bos-N	0	0	—	2	1	0	0	0	2	2	0	3	0	22.5	13.50	28	.250	.455	0	—	0	-2	-2	0	0.0
Total 2	0	0	—	6	1	0	0	0	16	23	1	15	2	21.4	10.69	44	.338	.458	1	.167	-0	-11	-11	0	0.0

● WENTY FORD Ford, Percival Edmund Wentworth b: 11/25/46, Nassau, Bahamas d: 7/8/80, Nassau, Bahamas BR/TR, 5'11", 165 lbs. Deb: 9/10/73

YEAR TM/L	W	L	PCT	G	GS	CG	SH	SV	IP	H	HR	BB	SO	RAT	ERA	ERA+	OAV	OOB	BH	AVG	PB	PR	/A	PD	TPI
1973 Atl-N	1	2	.333	4	2	1	0	0	16^{1}	17	3	8	4	14.3	5.51	71	.279	.371	2	.400	1	-3	-3	0	-0.4

● TERRY FORSTER Forster, Terry Jay b: 1/14/52, Sioux Falls, S.D. BL/TL, 6'3", 210 lbs. Deb: 4/11/71

YEAR TM/L	W	L	PCT	G	GS	CG	SH	SV	IP	H	HR	BB	SO	RAT	ERA	ERA+	OAV	OOB	BH	AVG	PB	PR	/A	PD	TPI
1983 Atl-N	3	2	.600	56	0	0	0	13	79^{1}	60	3	31	54	10.6	2.16	180	.217	.301	4	.500	2	13	15	1	1.7
1984 Atl-N	2	0	1.000	25	0	0	0	5	26^{2}	30	1	7	10	12.5	2.70	143	.297	.343	2	.667	1	3	3	0	0.5
1985 Atl-N	2	3	.400	46	0	0	0	1	59^{1}	49	7	28	37	11.7	2.28	169	.222	.309	0	.000	-0	9	10	-1	0.8
Total 16	54	65	.454	614	39	5	0	127	1105^{2}	1034	51	457	791	12.3	3.23	114	.251	.330	31	.397	11	48	57	16	11.5
Team 3	7	5	.583	127	0	0	0	19	165^{1}	139	11	66	101	11.3	2.29	169	.232	.311	6	.400	2	24	29	0	3.0

● JOHN FOX Fox, John Joseph b: 2/7/1859, Roxbury, Mass. d: 4/18/1893, Boston, Mass. Deb: 6/2/1881

YEAR TM/L	W	L	PCT	G	GS	CG	SH	SV	IP	H	HR	BB	SO	RAT	ERA	ERA+	OAV	OOB	BH	AVG	PB	PR	/A	PD	TPI
1881 Bos-N	6	8	.429	17	16	12	0	0	124^{1}	144	0	39	30	13.2	3.33	80	.279	.329	21	.178	-4	-8	-9	1	-1.1
Total 4	13	28	.317	45	43	38	0	0	356^{2}	440	4	98	104	13.7	4.16	76	.287	.331	42	.176	-8	-42	-40	0	-4.0

● TERRY FOX Fox, Terrence Edward b: 7/31/35, Chicago, Ill. BR/TR, 6', 175 lbs. Deb: 9/4/60

YEAR TM/L	W	L	PCT	G	GS	CG	SH	SV	IP	H	HR	BB	SO	RAT	ERA	ERA+	OAV	OOB	BH	AVG	PB	PR	/A	PD	TPI
1960 Mil-N	0	0	—	5	0	0	0	0	8^{1}	6	0	6	5	13.0	4.32	79	.200	.333	0	.000	-0	-1	-1	-0	0.0
Total 7	29	19	.604	248	0	0	0	59	397	379	34	124	185	11.7	2.99	125	.254	.316	8	.123	1	31	33	4	5.7

● FRED FRANKHOUSE Frankhouse, Frederick Meloy b: 4/9/04, Port Royal, Pa. d: 8/17/89, Port Royal, Pa. BR/TR, 5'11", 175 lbs. Deb: 9/11/27

YEAR TM/L	W	L	PCT	G	GS	CG	SH	SV	IP	H	HR	BB	SO	RAT	ERA	ERA+	OAV	OOB	BH	AVG	PB	PR	/A	PD	TPI
1930 Bos-N	7	6	.538	27	11	3	1	0	110^{2}	138	13	43	30	14.9	5.61	88	.313	.377	14	.359	4	-8	-8	-0	-0.4
1931 Bos-N	8	8	.500	26	15	6	0	1	127^{1}	125	4	43	50	12.1	4.03	94	.252	.315	6	.150	-0	-2	-3	1	-0.3
1932 Bos-N	4	6	.400	37	6	3	0	6	108^{2}	113	7	45	35	13.3	3.56	106	.278	.355	3	.100	-1	4	2	3	0.4
1933 Bos-N	16	15	.516	43	30	14	2	2	244^{2}	249	12	77	83	12.1	3.16	97	.267	.324	19	.237	4	5	-3	4	0.5
1934 Bos-N★	17	9	.654	37	31	13	2	1	233^{2}	239	10	77	78	12.3	3.20	120	.262	.322	17	.200	2	22	16	-0	1.8
1935 Bos-N	11	15	.423	40	29	10	1	0	230^{2}	278	12	81	64	14.2	4.76	80	.293	.352	20	.263	6	-19	-25	3	-1.4
1939 Bos-N	0	2	.000	23	0	0	0	4	38	37	3	18	12	13.3	2.61	142	.253	.339	0	.000	-1	6	5	-1	0.2
Total 13	106	97	.522	402	216	81	10	12	1888	2033	111	701	622	13.2	3.92	100	.275	.341	132	.208	12	18	-0	18	2.1
Team 7	63	61	.508	233	122	49	6	8	1093^{2}	1179	61	384	352	13.0	3.88	96	.275	.338	79	.221	13	7	-17	10	0.8

● CHICK FRASER Fraser, Charles Carrolton b: 3/17/1871, Chicago, Ill. d: 5/8/40, Wendell, Idaho BR/TR, 5'10.5", 188 lbs. Deb: 4/19/1896 C

YEAR TM/L	W	L	PCT	G	GS	CG	SH	SV	IP	H	HR	BB	SO	RAT	ERA	ERA+	OAV	OOB	BH	AVG	PB	PR	/A	PD	TPI
1905 Bos-N	14	21	.400	39	38	35	2	0	334^{1}	320	8	149	130	13.0	3.28	94	.254	.340	35	.224	3	-10	-7	-1	-0.3
Total 14	175	212	.452	433	389	342	22	6	3356	3460	69	1332	1098	13.4	3.68	92	.267	.345	235	.179	-15	-109	-108	29	-9.4

● VIC FRASIER Frasier, Victor Patrick b: 8/5/04, Ruston, La. d: 1/10/77, Jacksonville, Tex. BR/TR, 6', 182 lbs. Deb: 4/18/31

YEAR TM/L	W	L	PCT	G	GS	CG	SH	SV	IP	H	HR	BB	SO	RAT	ERA	ERA+	OAV	OOB	BH	AVG	PB	PR	/A	PD	TPI
1937 Bos-N	0	0	—	3	0	0	0	0	8	12	1	1	2	14.6	5.63	64	.364	.382	0	.000	-0	-2	-2	0	0.0
Total 6	23	38	.377	126	68	21	2	4	579	686	37	291	170	15.4	5.77	75	.293	.373	33	.177	-3	-88	-94	4	-7.2

● JIMMY FREEMAN Freeman, Jimmy Lee b: 6/29/51, Carlsbad, N.Mex. BL/TL, 6'4", 180 lbs. Deb: 9/1/72

YEAR TM/L	W	L	PCT	G	GS	CG	SH	SV	IP	H	HR	BB	SO	RAT	ERA	ERA+	OAV	OOB	BH	AVG	PB	PR	/A	PD	TPI
1972 Atl-N	2	2	.500	6	6	1	0	0	36	40	5	22	18	15.5	6.00	63	.278	.373	1	.077	-0	-10	-9	-1	-1.0
1973 Atl-N	0	2	.000	13	5	0	0	1	37^{1}	50	7	25	20	18.1	7.71	51	.327	.421	2	.154	-0	-17	-16	-1	-1.0
Total 2	2	4	.333	19	11	1	0	1	73^{1}	90	12	47	38	16.8	6.87	56	.303	.398	3	.115	-1	-27	-25	-2	-2.0

● MARVIN FREEMAN Freeman, Marvin b: 4/10/63, Chicago, Ill. BR/TR, 6'7", 200 lbs. Deb: 9/16/86

YEAR TM/L	W	L	PCT	G	GS	CG	SH	SV	IP	H	HR	BB	SO	RAT	ERA	ERA+	OAV	OOB	BH	AVG	PB	PR	/A	PD	TPI
1990 Atl-N	1	0	1.000	9	0	0	0	0	15^{2}	7	0	3	12	6.9	1.72	234	.130	.203	0	—	0	4	4	-0	0.2
1991 Atl-N	1	0	1.000	34	0	0	0	1	48	37	2	13	34	9.8	3.00	130	.214	.277	0	.000	-1	4	5	-1	0.0
1992 *Atl-N	7	5	.583	58	0	0	0	3	64^{1}	61	7	29	41	12.7	3.22	114	.251	.333	2	.500	1	2	3	-1	0.6
1993 Atl-N	2	0	1.000	21	0	0	0	0	23^{2}	24	1	10	25	13.3	6.08	66	.261	.340	0	—	0	-5	-5	-1	-0.5
Total 9	28	19	.596	194	54	0	0	5	462	461	42	191	311	13.0	4.21	104	.261	.339	11	.111	-3	-16	8	-3	0.9
Team 4	11	5	.688	122	0	0	0	4	151^{2}	129	10	55	112	11.3	3.44	111	.230	.305	2	.182	-0	4	6	-2	0.3

● DANNY FRISELLA Frisella, Daniel Vincent "Bear" b: 3/4/46, San Francisco, Cal. d: 1/1/77, Phoenix, Ariz. BL/TR, 6', 195 lbs. Deb: 7/27/67

YEAR TM/L	W	L	PCT	G	GS	CG	SH	SV	IP	H	HR	BB	SO	RAT	ERA	ERA+	OAV	OOB	BH	AVG	PB	PR	/A	PD	TPI
1973 Atl-N	1	2	.333	42	0	0	0	8	45	40	5	23	27	12.8	4.20	94	.241	.337	1	.500	0	-3	-1	-0	-0.1
1974 Atl-N	3	4	.429	36	1	0	0	6	41^{2}	37	4	28	27	14.0	5.18	73	.240	.357	0	.000	0	-7	-7	-0	-1.2
Total 10	34	40	.459	351	17	0	0	57	609^{1}	529	53	286	471	12.1	3.32	106	.235	.323	14	.179	1	14	13	0	3.1
Team 2	4	6	.400	78	1	0	0	14	86^{2}	77	9	51	54	13.4	4.67	83	.241	.347	1	.333	0	-10	-8	-1	-1.3

● SAM FROCK Frock, Samuel William b: 12/23/1882, Baltimore, Md. d: 11/3/25, Baltimore, Md. BR/TR, 6', 168 lbs. Deb: 9/21/07

YEAR TM/L	W	L	PCT	G	GS	CG	SH	SV	IP	H	HR	BB	SO	RAT	ERA	ERA+	OAV	OOB	BH	AVG	PB	PR	/A	PD	TPI
1907 Bos-N	1	2	.333	5	3	3	1	0	33^{1}	28	1	11	12	11.1	2.97	86	.243	.320	1	.071	-1	-2	-2	-2	-0.4
1910 Bos-N	12	19	.387	45	29	13	2	2	255^{1}	245	8	91	170	12.0	3.21	104	.262	.330	16	.190	-3	-5	3	1	0.2
1911 Bos-N	0	1	.000	4	1	1	0	0	16	29	0	5	8	19.7	5.63	68	.426	.473	1	.200	-0	-4	-3	0	-0.2
Total 4	15	23	.395	63	37	20	3	3	343	348	9	113	202	12.4	3.23	99	.274	.339	20	.171	-5	-11	-1	0	-0.4
Team 3	13	22	.371	54	33	17	3	2	304^{2}	302	9	107	190	12.3	3.31	99	.270	.338	18	.175	-4	-11	-1	-0	-0.4

● **FRANK FUNK** Funk, Franklin Ray b: 8/30/35, Washington, D.C. BR/TR, 6', 175 lbs. Deb: 9/3/60 C

YEAR TM/L	W	L	PCT	G	GS	CG	SH	SV	IP	H	HR	BB	SO	RAT	ERA	ERA+	OAV	OOB	BH	AVG	PB	PR	/A	PD	TPI
1963 Mil-N	3	3	.500	25	0	0	0	0	43^{2}	42	3	13	19	11.5	2.68	120	.258	.316	0	.000	-0	3	3	-1	0.2
Total 4	20	17	.541	137	0	0	0	18	248^{1}	210	26	85	150	11.0	3.01	125	.233	.305	3	.067	-3	23	21	-1	2.9

● **FRANK GABLER** Gabler, Frank Harold "The Great Gabbo" b: 11/6/11, E.Highlands, Cal. d: 11/1/67, Long Beach, Cal. BR/TR, 6'1", 175 lbs. Deb: 4/19/35

YEAR TM/L	W	L	PCT	G	GS	CG	SH	SV	IP	H	HR	BB	SO	RAT	ERA	ERA+	OAV	OOB	BH	AVG	PB	PR	/A	PD	TPI
1937 Bos-N	4	7	.364	19	9	2	1	2	76	84	7	16	19	11.8	5.09	70	.283	.319	4	.182	0	-10	-13	-0	-1.6
1938 Bos-N	0	0	—	1	0	0	0	0	0^{1}	3	0	1	0	108.0	81.00	4	1.000	1.000	0	—	0	-3	-3	0	0.0
Total 4	16	23	.410	113	31	10	1	8	376^{1}	457	37	107	109	13.6	5.26	76	.303	.351	21	.196	1	-47	-53	-2	-3.6
Team 2	4	7	.364	20	9	2	1	2	76^{1}	87	7	17	19	12.3	5.42	66	.290	.328	4	.182	0	-13	-16	-0	-1.6

● **GENE GARBER** Garber, Henry Eugene b: 11/13/47, Lancaster, Pa. BR/TR, 5'10", 175 lbs. Deb: 6/17/69

YEAR TM/L	W	L	PCT	G	GS	CG	SH	SV	IP	H	HR	BB	SO	RAT	ERA	ERA+	OAV	OOB	BH	AVG	PB	PR	/A	PD	TPI
1978 Atl-N	4	4	.500	43	0	0	0	22	78^{1}	58	11	13	61	8.4	2.53	160	.204	.244	1	.091	-0	9	13	1	2.3
1979 Atl-N	6	16	.273	68	0	0	0	25	106	121	10	24	56	12.7	4.33	94	.283	.328	3	.300	1	-7	-3	1	-0.6
1980 Atl-N	5	5	.500	68	0	0	0	7	82^{1}	95	6	24	51	13.0	3.83	98	.288	.336	1	.500	0	-2	-1	2	0.1
1981 Atl-N	4	6	.400	35	0	0	0	2	58^{2}	49	2	20	34	10.6	2.61	137	.214	.277	0	.000	-1	6	6	2	1.3
1982 *Atl-N	8	10	.444	69	0	0	0	30	119^{1}	100	4	32	68	10.1	2.34	160	.231	.288	2	.133	0	17	18	2	4.1
1983 Atl-N	4	5	.444	43	0	0	0	9	60^{2}	72	8	23	45	14.4	4.60	84	.300	.366	0	.000	0	-7	-5	2	-0.6
1984 Atl-N	3	6	.333	62	0	0	0	11	106	103	7	24	55	11.0	3.06	126	.254	.299	2	.143	-0	6	9	1	1.0
1985 Atl-N	6	6	.500	59	0	0	0	1	97^{1}	98	8	25	66	11.6	3.61	107	.263	.313	1	.200	0	-0	3	1	0.4
1986 Atl-N	5	5	.500	61	0	0	0	24	78	76	3	20	56	11.2	2.54	157	.260	.310	1	.167	0	10	12	1	2.6
1987 Atl-N	8	10	.444	49	0	0	0	10	69^{1}	87	7	28	48	15.1	4.41	98	.311	.375	0	.000	-0	-3	-1	2	0.0
Total 19	96	113	.459	931	9	4	0	218	1510	1464	123	445	940	11.6	3.34	116	.257	.314	17	.148	-0	59	92	20	16.7
Team 10	53	73	.421	557	0	0	0	141	856	859	66	233	540	11.7	3.34	117	.261	.313	11	.147	0	30	53	14	10.6

● **JIM GARRY** Garry, James Thomas b: 9/21/1869, Great Barrington, Mass. d: 1/15/17, Pittsfield, Mass. TL , Deb: 5/2/1893

YEAR TM/L	W	L	PCT	G	GS	CG	SH	SV	IP	H	HR	BB	SO	RAT	ERA	ERA+	OAV	OOB	BH	AVG	PB	PR	/A	PD	TPI
1893 Bos-N	0	1	.000	1	0	0	0	0	1	5	0	4	2	81.0	63.00	8	.625	.750	0	.000	-0	-6	-6	0	-2.1

● **HANK GASTRIGHT** Gastright, Henry Carl (b: Henry Carl Gastreich) b: 3/29/1865, Covington, Ky. d: 10/9/37, Cold Springs, Ky. BR/TR, 6'2", 190 lbs. Deb: 4/19/1889

YEAR TM/L	W	L	PCT	G	GS	CG	SH	SV	IP	H	HR	BB	SO	RAT	ERA	ERA+	OAV	OOB	BH	AVG	PB	PR	/A	PD	TPI
1893 Bos-N	12	4	.750	19	18	16	0	0	156	179	9	76	27	15.2	5.13	96	.279	.364	13	.191	-3	-8	-3	-2	-0.6
Total 7	72	63	.533	171	142	121	6	2	1301^{1}	1337	39	584	514	13.7	4.20	92	.258	.339	101	.186	-8	-23	-51	-7	-4.3

● **AUBREY GATEWOOD** Gatewood, Aubrey Lee b: 11/17/38, Little Rock, Ark. BR/TR, 6'1", 170 lbs. Deb: 9/11/63

YEAR TM/L	W	L	PCT	G	GS	CG	SH	SV	IP	H	HR	BB	SO	RAT	ERA	ERA+	OAV	OOB	BH	AVG	PB	PR	/A	PD	TPI
1970 Atl-N	0	0	—	3	0	0	0	0	2	4	0	2	0	31.5	4.50	95	.364	.500	0	—	0	-0	-0	0	0.0
Total 4	8	9	.471	68	13	1	0	0	178^{1}	166	9	67	75	11.9	2.78	122	.250	.322	5	.119	-1	15	12	-1	0.8

● **DINTY GEARIN** Gearin, Dennis John b: 10/15/1897, Providence, R.I. d: 3/11/59, Providence, R.I. BL/TL, 5'4", 148 lbs. Deb: 8/6/23

YEAR TM/L	W	L	PCT	G	GS	CG	SH	SV	IP	H	HR	BB	SO	RAT	ERA	ERA+	OAV	OOB	BH	AVG	PB	PR	/A	PD	TPI
1924 Bos-N	0	1	.000	1	1	0	0	0	0	3	0	2	0	—	∞	—	1.000	1.000	0	—	0	-5	-5	0	-0.4
Total 2	2	4	.333	13	6	3	0	0	53	56	4	28	13	14.3	3.74	100	.281	.370	5	.313	1	1	0	-1	0.1

● **JOE GENEWICH** Genewich, Joseph Edward b: 1/15/1897, Elmira, N.Y. d: 12/21/85, Lockport, N.Y. BR/TR, 6', 174 lbs. Deb: 9/13/22

YEAR TM/L	W	L	PCT	G	GS	CG	SH	SV	IP	H	HR	BB	SO	RAT	ERA	ERA+	OAV	OOB	BH	AVG	PB	PR	/A	PD	TPI
1922 Bos-N	0	2	.000	6	2	1	0	0	23	29	2	11	4	15.7	7.04	57	.319	.392	1	.167	-0	-8	-8	-0	-0.6
1923 Bos-N	13	14	.481	43	24	12	1	1	227^{1}	272	15	46	54	12.9	3.72	107	.303	.341	19	.247	2	7	7	2	1.1
1924 Bos-N	10	19	.345	34	27	11	2	1	200^{1}	258	4	65	43	14.9	5.21	73	.329	.386	10	.167	-2	-30	-31	-0	-4.0
1925 Bos-N	12	10	.545	34	21	10	0	0	169	185	4	41	34	12.4	3.99	100	.279	.327	15	.273	1	5	0	-1	0.1
1926 Bos-N	8	16	.333	37	26	12	2	2	216	239	6	63	59	12.8	3.88	92	.288	.342	11	.164	-1	-1	-8	1	-0.8
1927 Bos-N	11	8	.579	40	19	7	0	1	181	199	7	54	38	12.7	3.83	97	.279	.332	11	.193	-1	2	-2	0	-0.3
1928 Bos-N	3	7	.300	13	11	4	0	0	80^{2}	88	14	18	15	12.2	4.13	95	.280	.325	1	.038	-3	-1	-2	1	-0.4
Total 9	73	92	.442	272	166	71	7	12	1401^{2}	1610	77	402	316	13.1	4.29	91	.293	.345	96	.207	-4	-35	-58	5	-6.0
Team 7	57	76	.429	207	130	57	5	5	1097^{1}	1270	52	298	247	13.1	4.18	91	.296	.346	68	.195	-4	-26	-44	2	-4.9

● **GARY GENTRY** Gentry, Gary Edward b: 10/6/46, Phoenix, Ariz. BR/TR, 6', 183 lbs. Deb: 4/10/69

YEAR TM/L	W	L	PCT	G	GS	CG	SH	SV	IP	H	HR	BB	SO	RAT	ERA	ERA+	OAV	OOB	BH	AVG	PB	PR	/A	PD	TPI
1973 Atl-N	4	6	.400	16	14	3	0	1	86^{2}	74	7	35	42	11.4	3.43	115	.231	.308	7	.233	1	2	5	-1	0.5
1974 Atl-N	0	0	—	3	1	0	0	0	6^{2}	4	1	2	0	9.5	1.35	280	.167	.259	0	.000	-0	2	2	-0	0.0
1975 Atl-N	1	1	.500	7	2	0	0	0	20	25	3	8	10	14.8	4.95	76	.313	.375	0	.000	-1	-3	-3	0	-0.3
Total 7	46	49	.484	157	138	25	8	2	902^{2}	770	90	369	615	11.6	3.56	103	.231	.312	27	.095	-12	8	9	-1	-0.6
Team 3	5	7	.417	26	17	3	0	1	113^{1}	103	11	45	52	11.9	3.57	109	.242	.318	7	.194	-0	1	4	-1	0.2

● **LEFTY GEORGE** George, Thomas Edward b: 8/13/1886, Pittsburgh, Pa. d: 5/13/55, York, Pa. BL/TL, 6', 155 lbs. Deb: 4/14/11

YEAR TM/L	W	L	PCT	G	GS	CG	SH	SV	IP	H	HR	BB	SO	RAT	ERA	ERA+	OAV	OOB	BH	AVG	PB	PR	/A	PD	TPI
1918 Bos-N	1	5	.167	9	5	4	0	0	54^{1}	56	0	21	22	13.3	2.32	116	.281	.359	2	.091	-2	3	2	2	0.3
Total 4	7	21	.250	52	26	14	2	0	243	285	5	98	74	14.9	3.85	82	.281	.355	14	.152	-2	-19	-19	1	-1.9

● **LEFTY GERVAIS** Gervais, Lucien Edward b: 7/6/1890, Grover, Wis. d: 10/19/50, Los Angeles, Cal. BL/TL, 5'10", 165 lbs. Deb: 4/17/13

YEAR TM/L	W	L	PCT	G	GS	CG	SH	SV	IP	H	HR	BB	SO	RAT	ERA	ERA+	OAV	OOB	BH	AVG	PB	PR	/A	PD	TPI
1913 Bos-N	0	1	.000	5	2	1	0	0	15^{2}	18	0	4	1	12.6	5.74	57	.383	.431	0	.000	-0	-4	-4	-0	-0.3

● **CHARLIE GETZIEN** Getzien, Charles H. "Pretzels" b: 2/14/1864, Germany d: 6/19/32, Chicago, Ill. BR/TR, 5'10", 172 lbs. Deb: 8/13/1884

YEAR TM/L	W	L	PCT	G	GS	CG	SH	SV	IP	H	HR	BB	SO	RAT	ERA	ERA+	OAV	OOB	BH	AVG	PB	PR	/A	PD	TPI
1890 Bos-N	23	17	.575	40	40	39	4	0	350	342	5	82	140	11.0	3.19	118	.248	.292	34	.231	5	15	22	-2	2.2
1891 Bos-N	4	5	.444	11	9	7	0	0	89	112	4	23	29	13.7	3.84	95	.296	.337	7	.171	1	-5	-2	1	0.0
Total 9	145	139	.511	296	292	277	11	1	2539^{2}	2670	95	602	1070	11.7	3.46	99	.259	.302	209	.198	8	-17	-9	-13	-1.5
Team 2	27	22	.551	51	49	46	4	0	439	454	9	105	169	11.5	3.32	112	.258	.301	41	.218	6	10	20	-2	2.2

● **BOB GIGGIE** Giggie, Robert Thomas b: 8/13/33, Dorchester, Mass. BR/TR, 6'1", 200 lbs. Deb: 4/18/59

YEAR TM/L	W	L	PCT	G	GS	CG	SH	SV	IP	H	HR	BB	SO	RAT	ERA	ERA+	OAV	OOB	BH	AVG	PB	PR	/A	PD	TPI
1959 Mil-N	1	0	1.000	13	0	0	0	1	20	24	2	10	15	15.3	4.05	87	.316	.395	0	.000	-0	-0	-1	1	0.0
1960 Mil-N	0	0	—	3	0	0	0	0	4^{1}	5	0	4	5	18.7	4.15	83	.278	.409	0	—	0	-0	-0	-0	0.0
Total 3	3	1	.750	30	2	0	0	1	57^{1}	70	8	32	32	16.2	5.18	74	.313	.401	0	.000	-1	-8	-8	0	-0.7
Team 2	1	0	1.000	16	0	0	0	1	24^{1}	29	2	14	20	15.9	4.07	87	.309	.398	0	.000	-0	-0	-1	1	0.0

● **BILLY GING** Ging, William Joseph b: 11/7/1872, Elmira, N.Y. d: 9/14/50, Elmira, N.Y. BR/TR, 5'10", 170 lbs. Deb: 9/25/1899

YEAR TM/L	W	L	PCT	G	GS	CG	SH	SV	IP	H	HR	BB	SO	RAT	ERA	ERA+	OAV	OOB	BH	AVG	PB	PR	/A	PD	TPI
1899 Bos-N	1	0	1.000	1	1	1	0	0	8	5	0	5	2	11.3	1.13	370	.179	.303	0	.000	-0	2	3	-0	0.2

● **TOM GLAVINE** Glavine, Thomas Michael b: 3/25/66, Concord, Mass. BL/TL, 6'1", 190 lbs. Deb: 8/17/87

YEAR TM/L	W	L	PCT	G	GS	CG	SH	SV	IP	H	HR	BB	SO	RAT	ERA	ERA+	OAV	OOB	BH	AVG	PB	PR	/A	PD	TPI
1987 Atl-N	2	4	.333	9	9	0	0	0	50^{1}	55	5	33	20	16.3	5.54	78	.279	.391	2	.125	-0	-8	-7	1	-0.7
1988 Atl-N	7	17	.292	34	34	1	0	0	195^{1}	201	12	63	84	12.5	4.56	81	.270	.333	11	.183	1	-24	-19	2	-1.9
1989 Atl-N	14	8	.636	29	29	6	4	0	186	172	20	40	90	10.4	3.68	99	.243	.285	10	.149	0	-4	-1	1	0.1
1990 Atl-N	10	12	.455	33	33	1	0	0	214^{1}	232	18	78	129	13.1	4.28	94	.281	.343	7	.113	0	-12	-6	1	-0.4
1991 *Atl-N★	**20**	11	.645	34	34	**9**	1	0	246^{2}	201	17	69	192	9.9	2.55	**152**	.222	.279	17	.230	4	31	**37**	3	**5.5**
1992 *Atl-N★	**20**	8	.714	33	33	7	**5**	0	225	197	6	70	129	10.8	2.76	133	.235	.295	19	.247	4	19	22	-0	3.3
1993 *Atl-N☆	**22**	6	.786	36	36	4	2	0	239^{1}	236	16	90	120	12.3	3.20	126	.259	.327	14	.173	1	22	22	0	2.5
1994 Atl-N	13	9	.591	25	25	2	0	0	165^{1}	173	10	70	140	13.3	3.97	107	.268	.341	10	.179	1	4	5	2	0.9
1995 *Atl-N	16	7	.696	29	29	3	1	0	198^{2}	182	9	66	127	11.5	3.08	137	.246	.312	14	.222	3	24	25	3	3.4
Total 9	124	82	.602	262	262	33	13	0	1721	1649	113	579	1031	11.8	3.52	112	.253	.317	104	.187	14	53	80	13	12.7

● **HAL GOLDSMITH** Goldsmith, Harold Eugene b: 8/18/1898, Peconic, N.Y. d: 10/20/85, Riverhead, N.Y. BR/TR, 6', 174 lbs. Deb: 6/23/26

YEAR TM/L	W	L	PCT	G	GS	CG	SH	SV	IP	H	HR	BB	SO	RAT	ERA	ERA+	OAV	OOB	BH	AVG	PB	PR	/A	PD	TPI
1926 Bos-N	5	7	.417	19	15	5	0	0	101	135	2	28	16	14.6	4.37	81	.333	.377	8	.211	0	-6	-9	1	-0.8
1927 Bos-N	1	3	.250	22	5	1	0	1	71^{2}	83	4	26	13	13.7	3.52	106	.289	.348	5	.238	0	3	2	0	0.1

YEAR	TM/L	W	L	PCT	G	GS	CG	SH	SV	IP	H	HR	BB	SO	RAT	ERA	ERA+	OAV	OOB	BH	AVG	PB	PR	/A	PD	TPI
1928	Bos-N	0	0	—	4	0	0	0	0	8^1	14	2	1	1	16.2	3.24	121	.359	.375	0	.000	-0	1	1	0	0.0
Total	4	6	10	.375	47	20	6	0	1	185	235	9	56	30	14.2	4.04	90	.315	.364	13	.210	0	-3	-8	1	-0.7
Team	3	6	10	.375	45	20	6	0	1	181	232	8	55	30	14.3	3.98	91	.317	.365	13	.213	1	-2	-7	1	-0.7
● **LUIS GOMEZ** Gomez, Luis (Sanchez) b: 8/19/51, Guadalajara, Mex. BR/TR, 5'9", 150 lbs. Deb: 4/28/74 ♦																										
1981	Atl-N	0	0	—	1	0	0	0	0	1	3	0	2	0	45.0	27.00	13	.500	.625	7	.200	0	-3	-3	-0	0.0
● **RALPH GOOD** Good, Ralph Nelson "Holy" b: 4/25/1886, Monticello, Me. d: 11/24/65, Waterville, Maine BR/TR, 6', 165 lbs. Deb: 7/1/10																										
1910	Bos-N	0	0	—	2	0	0	0	0	9	6	0	2	4	10.0	2.00	166	.188	.278	0	.000	-0	1	1	0	0.0
● **CHARLIE GORIN** Gorin, Charles Perry b: 2/6/28, Waco, Tex. BL/TL, 5'10", 165 lbs. Deb: 5/29/54																										
1954	Mil-N	0	1	.000	5	0	0	0	0	9^2	5	0	6	12	10.2	1.86	200	.152	.282	0	.000	-0	2	2	-0	0.1
1955	Mil-N	0	0	—	2	0	0	0	0	0^1	1	0	3	0	108.0	54.00	7	.500	.800	0	—	0	-2	-2	0	0.0
Total	2	0	1	.000	7	0	0	0	0	10	6	0	9	12	13.5	3.60	103	.171	.341	0	.000	-0	1	0	-0	0.1
● **SKINNY GRAHAM** Graham, Kyle b: 8/14/1899, Oak Grove, Ala. d: 12/1/73, Oak Grove, Ala. BR/TR, 6'2", 172 lbs. Deb: 9/3/24																										
1924	Bos-N	0	4	.000	5	4	1	0	0	33	33	0	11	15	12.0	3.82	100	.287	.349	0	.000	-1	0	0	-0	-0.1
1925	Bos-N	7	12	.368	34	23	5	0	1	157	177	6	62	32	13.9	4.41	91	.296	.365	6	.136	-2	-3	-7	-2	-1.1
1926	Bos-N	3	3	.500	15	4	1	0	0	36^1	54	3	19	7	18.6	7.93	45	.370	.449	2	.167	-1	-17	-18	0	-2.4
Total	4	11	22	.333	67	37	9	0	2	278	334	11	125	61	15.1	5.02	79	.314	.390	10	.122	-5	-27	-32	-3	-4.3
Team	3	10	19	.345	54	31	7	0	1	226^1	264	9	92	54	14.4	4.89	80	.307	.378	8	.127	-4	-19	-25	-2	-3.6
● **MARK GRANT** Grant, Mark Andrew b: 10/24/63, Aurora, Ill. BR/TR, 6'2", 205 lbs. Deb: 4/27/84																										
1990	Atl-N	1	2	.333	33	1	0	0	3	52^1	61	4	18	40	13.8	4.64	87	.293	.352	1	.250	1	-5	-4	-0	-0.2
Total	8	22	32	.407	233	58	2	1	8	638^2	676	72	235	382	13.0	4.31	87	.277	.343	7	.067	-3	-39	-40	-2	-4.1
● **TOMMY GREENE** Greene, Ira Thomas b: 4/6/67, Lumberton, N.C. BR/TR, 6'5", 225 lbs. Deb: 9/10/89																										
1989	Atl-N	1	2	.333	4	4	1	1	0	26^1	22	5	6	17	9.6	4.10	89	.234	.280	1	.100	-1	-2	-1	-0	-0.2
1990	Atl-N	1	0	1.000	5	2	0	0	0	12^1	14	3	9	4	17.5	8.03	50	.286	.407	0	.000	-0	-6	-5	-0	-0.4
Total	7	38	24	.613	117	95	11	5	0	619	581	60	236	450	12.0	4.10	93	.248	.319	46	.219	14	-18	-18	-6	-1.1
Team	2	2	2	.500	9	6	1	1	0	38^2	36	8	15	21	12.1	5.35	70	.252	.327	1	.091	-1	-8	-7	-1	-0.6
● **KENT GREENFIELD** Greenfield, Kent b: 7/1/02, Guthrie, Ky. d: 3/14/78, Guthrie, Ky. BR/TR, 6'1", 180 lbs. Deb: 9/28/24																										
1927	Bos-N	11	14	.440	27	26	11	1	0	190	203	3	59	59	12.6	3.84	97	.282	.341	11	.172	-2	2	-3	-0	-0.5
1928	Bos-N	3	11	.214	32	23	5	0	0	143^2	173	6	60	30	14.9	5.32	73	.307	.378	2	.053	-4	-21	-23	1	-2.2
1929	Bos-N	0	0	—	6	2	0	0	0	15^2	33	1	15	7	28.7	10.91	43	.465	.568	0	.000	-1	-11	-11	1	0.0
Total	6	41	48	.461	152	102	36	2	1	775^1	871	36	297	242	13.8	4.54	85	.290	.358	24	.101	-18	-46	-58	-0	-6.9
Team	3	14	25	.359	65	51	16	1	0	349^1	409	10	134	96	14.3	4.77	80	.302	.370	13	.121	-7	-30	-36	1	-2.7
● **HANK GRIFFIN** Griffin, James Linton "Pepper" b: 7/11/1886, Whitehouse, Tex. d: 2/11/50, Terrell, Tex. BR/TR, 6', 165 lbs. Deb: 5/5/11																										
1911	Bos-N	0	6	.000	15	6	1	0	0	82^2	96	3	34	30	14.8	5.23	73	.305	.383	7	.233	-0	-17	-13	0	-0.8
1912	Bos-N	0	0	—	3	0	0	0	0	1^2	3	0	3	0	37.8	27.00	13	.750	.875	0	—	0	-4	-4	-0	0.0
Total	2	0	6	.000	19	7	1	0	0	85^1	100	4	40	31	15.5	5.80	66	.310	.397	7	.233	-0	-23	-19	0	-0.8
Team	2	0	6	.000	18	6	1	0	0	84^1	99	3	37	30	15.3	5.66	68	.310	.394	7	.233	-0	-21	-17	0	-0.8
● **BURLEIGH GRIMES** Grimes, Burleigh Arland "Ol' Stubblebeard" b: 8/18/1893, Emerald, Wis. d: 12/6/85, Clear Lake, Wis. BR/TR, 5'10", 175 lbs. Deb: 9/10/16 MCH																										
1930	Bos-N	3	5	.375	11	9	1	0	0	49	72	4	22	15	17.8	7.35	67	.353	.424	3	.188	-0	-13	-13	0	-1.6
Total	19	270	212	.560	616	497	314	35	18	4179^2	4412	148	1295	1512	12.5	3.53	107	.273	.331	380	.248	52	118	121	58	24.0
● **SKIP GUINN** Guinn, Drannon Eugene b: 10/25/44, St.Charles, Mo. BR/TL, 5'10", 180 lbs. Deb: 5/7/68																										
1968	Atl-N	0	0	—	3	0	0	0	0	5	3	0	3	4	10.8	3.60	83	.167	.286	0	—	0	-0	-0	-0	0.0
Total	3	1	2	.333	35	0	0	0	1	36^2	38	3	27	40	16.2	5.40	64	.262	.382	0	.000	-0	-8	-8	-0	-0.9
● **MICKEY HAEFNER** Haefner, Milton Arnold b: 10/9/12, Lenzburg, Ill. d: 1/3/95, New Athens, Ill. BL/TL, 5'8", 160 lbs. Deb: 4/22/43																										
1950	Bos-N	0	2	.000	8	2	1	0	0	24	23	3	12	10	13.1	5.63	68	.247	.333	2	.286	1	-4	-5	-0	-0.3
Total	8	78	91	.462	261	179	91	13	13	1466^2	1414	76	577	508	12.5	3.50	102	.252	.326	84	.188	8	31	13	1	3.0
● **HAL HAID** Haid, Harold Augustine b: 12/21/1897, Barberton, Ohio d: 8/13/52, Los Angeles, Cal. BR/TR, 5'10.5", 150 lbs. Deb: 9/5/19																										
1931	Bos-N	0	2	.000	27	0	0	0	1	56	59	3	16	20	12.5	4.50	84	.263	.321	1	.125	-1	-4	-4	2	0.0
Total	6	14	15	.483	119	12	8	0	12	307^1	330	15	123	103	13.7	4.16	106	.275	.349	9	.125	-3	10	9	2	2.1
● **DAD HALE** Hale, Ray Luther b: 2/18/1880, Allegan, Mich. d: 2/1/46, Allegan, Mich. BR/TR, 5'10", 180 lbs. Deb: 4/21/02																										
1902	Bos-N	1	4	.200	8	6	3	0	0	47	69	1	18	12	16.9	6.32	45	.340	.396	0	.000	-1	-18	-18	-0	-1.8
Total	1	1	5	.167	11	8	4	0	0	61	90	1	24	18	17.1	5.90	51	.341	.400	0	.000	-2	-20	-19	-1	-2.0
● **BOB HALL** Hall, Robert Lewis b: 12/22/23, Swissvale, Pa. d: 3/12/83, St.Petersburg, Fla BR/TR, 6'2", 195 lbs. Deb: 4/23/49																										
1949	Bos-N	6	4	.600	31	6	2	0	0	74^1	77	7	41	43	14.4	4.36	87	.272	.366	8	.364	3	-3	-5	-2	-0.5
1950	Bos-N	0	2	.000	21	4	0	0	0	50^1	58	8	33	22	16.6	6.97	55	.293	.399	1	.083	-1	-16	-17	-0	-0.7
Total	3	9	18	.333	89	27	8	1	1	276^2	307	32	146	133	14.9	5.40	77	.284	.371	15	.208	2	-37	-38	-3	-2.6
Team	2	6	6	.500	52	10	2	0	0	124^2	135	15	74	65	15.3	5.41	70	.281	.380	9	.265	2	-18	-22	-3	-1.2
● **PRESTON HANNA** Hanna, Preston Lee b: 9/10/54, Pensacola, Fla. BR/TR, 6'1", 195 lbs. Deb: 9/13/75																										
1975	Atl-N	0	0	—	4	0	0	0	0	5^2	7	0	5	2	22.2	1.59	238	.304	.467	0	—	0	1	1	-0	0.0
1976	Atl-N	0	0	—	5	0	0	0	0	8	11	0	4	3	16.9	4.50	84	.333	.405	0	.000	-0	-1	-1	-0	0.0
1977	Atl-N	2	6	.250	17	9	1	0	1	60	69	6	34	37	15.8	4.95	90	.285	.378	1	.071	-0	-7	-3	1	-0.3
1978	Atl-N	7	13	.350	29	28	0	0	0	140^1	132	10	93	90	14.6	5.13	79	.251	.367	9	.184	1	-24	-17	-0	-2.1
1979	Atl-N	1	1	.500	6	4	0	0	0	24^1	27	1	15	15	15.5	2.96	137	.284	.382	0	.000	-0	2	3	1	0.3
1980	Atl-N	2	0	1.000	32	2	0	0	0	79^1	63	3	44	35	12.5	3.18	118	.224	.335	2	.143	0	4	5	-1	0.0
1981	Atl-N	2	1	.667	20	1	0	0	0	35^1	45	2	23	22	17.3	6.37	56	.341	.439	1	.250	0	-11	-11	2	-0.7
1982	Atl-N	3	0	1.000	20	1	0	0	0	36	36	3	28	17	16.0	3.75	99	.277	.405	2	.400	1	-1	-0	-1	0.0
Total	8	17	25	.405	156	47	2	0	1	437^1	444	28	279	253	15.1	4.61	86	.269	.378	15	.161	1	-45	-31	1	-3.5
Team	8	17	21	.447	133	45	1	0	1	389	390	25	246	221	14.9	4.49	88	.267	.376	15	.161	1	-37	-23	2	-2.8
● **JIM HARDIN** Hardin, James Warren b: 8/6/43, Morris Chapel, Tenn. d: 3/9/91, Key West, Fla. BR/TR, 6', 175 lbs. Deb: 6/23/67																										
1972	Atl-N	5	2	.714	26	9	1	0	2	79^2	93	11	24	25	13.4	4.41	86	.287	.340	2	.095	1	-8	-5	-1	-0.5
Total	6	43	32	.573	164	100	28	7	4	751^2	691	70	202	408	11.0	3.18	104	.244	.300	24	.103	-3	14	11	-5	0.9
● **STEVE HARGAN** Hargan, Steven Lowell b: 9/8/42, Ft.Wayne, Ind. BR/TR, 6'3", 180 lbs. Deb: 8/3/65																										
1977	Atl-N	0	3	.000	16	5	0	0	0	36^2	49	3	16	18	16.0	6.87	65	.325	.389	0	.000	-1	-12	-10	1	-0.7
Total	12	87	107	.448	354	215	56	17	4	1632	1593	125	614	891	12.4	3.92	91	.257	.328	42	.129	-7	-77	-64	6	-7.6
● **DICK HARLEY** Harley, Henry Risk b: 8/18/1874, Springfield, Ohio d: 5/16/61, Springfield, Ohio BR/TR, Deb: 4/15/05																										
1905	Bos-N	2	5	.286	9	4	4	1	0	65^2	72	5	19	19	12.6	4.66	67	.286	.338	1	.045	-2	-12	-11	2	-1.1
● **RORIC HARRISON** Harrison, Roric Edward b: 9/20/46, Los Angeles, Cal. BR/TR, 6'3", 195 lbs. Deb: 4/18/72																										
1973	Atl-N	11	8	.579	38	22	3	0	5	177^1	161	15	98	130	13.3	4.16	94	.242	.342	3	.056	-2	-10	-5	-1	-0.8

YEAR TM/L	W	L	PCT	G	GS	CG	SH	SV	IP	H	HR	BB	SO	RAT	ERA	ERA+	OAV	OOB	BH	AVG	PB	PR	/A	PD	TPI
1974 Atl-N	6	11	.353	20	20	3	0	0	126	148	12	49	46	14.3	4.71	80	.294	.360	7	.184	2	-15	-13	-2	-1.6
1975 Atl-N	3	4	.429	15	7	2	0	1	54^{2}	58	7	19	22	12.7	4.77	79	.266	.325	3	.200	1	-7	-6	0	-0.7
Total 5	30	35	.462	140	70	12	0	10	590	590	45	257	319	13.1	4.24	87	.261	.340	15	.121	2	-43	-35	-5	-4.4
Team 3	20	23	.465	73	49	8	0	6	358	367	34	166	198	13.6	4.45	87	.265	.346	13	.121	1	-32	-24	-3	-3.1

● BOB HARTMAN Hartman, Robert Louis b: 8/28/37, Kenosha, Wis. BR/TL, 5'11", 185 lbs. Deb: 4/26/59

YEAR TM/L	W	L	PCT	G	GS	CG	SH	SV	IP	H	HR	BB	SO	RAT	ERA	ERA+	OAV	OOB	BH	AVG	PB	PR	/A	PD	TPI
1959 Mil-N	0	0	—	3	0	0	0	0	1^{2}	6	0	2	1	43.2	27.00	13	.545	.615	0	—	0	-4	-4	-0	0.0
Total 2	0	1	.000	11	2	0	0	0	19	20	1	10	12	14.2	5.21	74	.256	.341	0	.000	-1	-3	-3	-0	0.0

● TOM HAUSMAN Hausman, Thomas Matthew b: 3/31/53, Mobridge, S.D. BR/TR, 6'5", 200 lbs. Deb: 4/26/75

YEAR TM/L	W	L	PCT	G	GS	CG	SH	SV	IP	H	HR	BB	SO	RAT	ERA	ERA+	OAV	OOB	BH	AVG	PB	PR	/A	PD	TPI
1982 Atl-N	0	0	—	3	0	0	0	0	3^{2}	6	0	4	2	24.5	4.91	76	.500	.625	0	—	0	-1	-0	0	0.0
Total 7	15	23	.395	160	33	2	0	3	441	439	37	121	180	11.8	3.80	96	.262	.317	7	.111	-2	-7	-8	2	-0.6

● SCOTT HAWLEY Hawley, Marvin Hiram b: Painesville, Ohio d: 4/28/04, Alliance, Ohio Deb: 9/22/1894

YEAR TM/L	W	L	PCT	G	GS	CG	SH	SV	IP	H	HR	BB	SO	RAT	ERA	ERA+	OAV	OOB	BH	AVG	PB	PR	/A	PD	TPI
1894 Bos-N	0	1	.000	1	1	1	0	0	7	10	0	7	1	24.4	7.71	74	.333	.487	0	.000	-1	-2	-2	0	-0.2

● BUNNY HEARN Hearn, Bunn b: 5/21/1891, Chapel Hill, N.C. d: 10/10/59, Wilson, N.C. BL/TL, 5'11", 190 lbs. Deb: 9/17/10

YEAR TM/L	W	L	PCT	G	GS	CG	SH	SV	IP	H	HR	BB	SO	RAT	ERA	ERA+	OAV	OOB	BH	AVG	PB	PR	/A	PD	TPI
1918 Bos-N	5	6	.455	17	12	9	1	0	126^{1}	119	2	29	30	10.5	2.49	108	.256	.300	8	.178	-1	4	3	1	0.2
1920 Bos-N	0	3	.000	11	4	2	0	0	43	54	3	11	9	13.8	5.65	54	.329	.375	2	.143	-1	-12	-12	0	-0.9
Total 6	13	24	.351	66	40	24	2	0	399^{2}	429	14	100	111	12.0	3.56	78	.287	.333	24	.180	-2	-32	-34	-1	-2.8
Team 2	5	9	.357	28	16	11	1	0	169^{1}	173	5	40	39	11.4	3.30	84	.275	.319	10	.169	-2	-8	-10	1	-0.7

● BUNNY HEARN Hearn, Elmer Lafayette b: 1/13/04, Brooklyn, N.Y. d: 3/31/74, Venice, Fla. BL/TL, 5'8", 160 lbs. Deb: 4/13/26

YEAR TM/L	W	L	PCT	G	GS	CG	SH	SV	IP	H	HR	BB	SO	RAT	ERA	ERA+	OAV	OOB	BH	AVG	PB	PR	/A	PD	TPI
1926 Bos-N	4	9	.308	34	12	3	0	2	117^{1}	121	2	56	40	13.6	4.22	84	.276	.358	3	.100	-2	-5	-9	2	-0.9
1927 Bos-N	0	2	.000	8	0	0	0	0	12^{2}	16	0	9	5	17.8	4.26	87	.327	.431	2	.400	1	-0	-1	0	0.0
1928 Bos-N	1	0	1.000	7	0	0	0	0	10	6	0	8	8	13.5	6.30	62	.167	.333	0	.000	-0	-3	-3	-0	-0.3
1929 Bos-N	2	0	1.000	10	1	0	0	0	18^{1}	18	2	9	12	13.3	4.42	106	.277	.365	0	.000	0	1	1	1	0.1
Total 4	7	11	.389	59	13	3	0	2	158^{1}	161	4	82	65	13.9	4.38	85	.273	.363	5	.132	-2	-8	-12	2	-1.1

● FRANK HEIFER Heifer, Franklin "Heck" b: 1/18/1854, Reading, Pa. d: 8/29/1893, Reading, Pa. 5'10.5", 175 lbs. Deb: 6/4/1875 ♦

YEAR TM/L	W	L	PCT	G	GS	CG	SH	SV	IP	H	HR	BB	SO	RAT	ERA	ERA+	OAV	OOB	BH	AVG	PB	PR	/A	PD	TPI
1875 Bos-n	0	0	—	2	0	0	0	1	2^{1}	7	0	0		27.0	*7.71*	31	.500	.500	14	.275	1	-1	-1		-0.1

● BOB HENDLEY Hendley, Charles Robert b: 4/30/39, Macon, Ga. BR/TL, 6'2", 190 lbs. Deb: 6/23/61

YEAR TM/L	W	L	PCT	G	GS	CG	SH	SV	IP	H	HR	BB	SO	RAT	ERA	ERA+	OAV	OOB	BH	AVG	PB	PR	/A	PD	TPI
1961 Mil-N	5	7	.417	19	13	3	0	0	97	96	8	39	44	12.5	3.90	96	.262	.333	1	.032	-3	1	-2	1	-0.4
1962 Mil-N	11	13	.458	35	29	7	2	1	200	188	17	59	112	11.1	3.60	105	.247	.301	7	.119	1	8	4	1	0.6
1963 Mil-N	9	9	.500	41	24	7	3	3	169^{1}	153	16	64	105	11.6	3.93	82	.244	.315	5	.106	-1	-12	-13	1	-1.4
Total 7	48	52	.480	216	126	25	6	12	879^{1}	864	99	329	522	12.3	3.97	90	.257	.325	23	.095	-6	-34	-38	0	-3.5
Team 3	25	29	.463	95	66	17	5	4	466^{1}	437	41	162	261	11.6	3.78	95	.249	.313	13	.095	-3	-3	-11	3	-1.2

● DON HENDRICKSON Hendrickson, Donald William b: 7/14/15, Kewanna, Ind. d: 1/19/77, Norfolk, Va. BR/TR, 6'2", 204 lbs. Deb: 7/4/45

YEAR TM/L	W	L	PCT	G	GS	CG	SH	SV	IP	H	HR	BB	SO	RAT	ERA	ERA+	OAV	OOB	BH	AVG	PB	PR	/A	PD	TPI
1945 Bos-N	4	8	.333	37	2	1	0	5	73^{1}	74	8	39	14	14.0	4.91	78	.261	.353	3	.167	-0	-9	-9	-1	-1.5
1946 Bos-N	0	1	.000	2	0	0	0	0	2	4	0	2	2	27.0	4.50	76	.364	.462	0	.000	-0	-0	-0	-0	-0.1
Total 2	4	9	.308	39	2	1	0	5	75^{1}	78	8	41	16	14.3	4.90	78	.265	.357	3	.158	-0	-9	-9	-1	-1.6

● DWAYNE HENRY Henry, Dwayne Allen b: 2/16/62, Elkton, Md. BR/TR, 6'3", 205 lbs. Deb: 9/7/84

YEAR TM/L	W	L	PCT	G	GS	CG	SH	SV	IP	H	HR	BB	SO	RAT	ERA	ERA+	OAV	OOB	BH	AVG	PB	PR	/A	PD	TPI
1989 Atl-N	0	2	.000	12	0	0	0	1	12^{2}	12	2	5	16	12.1	4.26	86	.250	.321	0	—	0	-1	-1	-0	-0.2
1990 Atl-N	2	2	.500	34	0	0	0	0	38^{1}	41	3	25	34	15.5	5.63	72	.273	.377	0	—	0	-8	-7	-1	-0.7
Total 11	14	15	.483	256	1	0	0	14	334^{2}	298	26	216	275	14.1	4.65	84	.241	.357	1	.167	-0	-29	-27	-3	-2.2
Team 2	2	4	.333	46	0	0	0	1	51	53	5	30	50	14.6	5.29	74	.268	.364	0	—	0	-9	-8	-1	-0.9

● RON HERBEL Herbel, Ronald Samuel b: 1/16/38, Denver, Colo. BR/TR, 6'1", 195 lbs. Deb: 9/10/63

YEAR TM/L	W	L	PCT	G	GS	CG	SH	SV	IP	H	HR	BB	SO	RAT	ERA	ERA+	OAV	OOB	BH	AVG	PB	PR	/A	PD	TPI
1971 Atl-N	0	1	.000	25	0	0	0	1	51^{2}	61	6	23	22	15.3	5.23	71	.300	.383	1	.091	-1	-10	-9	0	-0.3
Total 9	42	37	.532	331	79	11	3	16	894	945	81	285	447	12.6	3.83	94	.273	.332	6	.029	-15	-25	-25	7	-1.5

● RAMON HERNANDEZ Hernandez, Ramon (Gonzalez) b: 8/31/40, Carolina, P.R. BB/TL, 5'9", 170 lbs. Deb: 4/11/67

YEAR TM/L	W	L	PCT	G	GS	CG	SH	SV	IP	H	HR	BB	SO	RAT	ERA	ERA+	OAV	OOB	BH	AVG	PB	PR	/A	PD	TPI
1967 Atl-N	0	2	.000	46	0	0	0	5	51^{2}	60	5	14	28	13.2	4.18	79	.296	.347	0	.000	-0	-5	-5	1	-0.3
Total 9	23	15	.605	337	0	0	0	46	430^{1}	399	23	135	255	11.5	3.03	115	.245	.308	5	.125	1	25	22	1	4.3

● FRANK HERSHEY Hershey, Frank b: 12/13/1877, Gorham, N.Y. d: 12/15/49, Canandaigua, N.Y. TR , 175 lbs. Deb: 4/20/05

YEAR TM/L	W	L	PCT	G	GS	CG	SH	SV	IP	H	HR	BB	SO	RAT	ERA	ERA+	OAV	OOB	BH	AVG	PB	PR	/A	PD	TPI
1905 Bos-N	0	1	.000	1	1	0	0	0	4	5	0	2	1	15.8	6.75	46	.313	.389	0	.000	-0	-2	-2	-0	-0.3

● JOE HESKETH Hesketh, Joseph Thomas b: 2/15/59, Lackawanna, N.Y. BR/TL, 6'2", 170 lbs. Deb: 8/7/84

YEAR TM/L	W	L	PCT	G	GS	CG	SH	SV	IP	H	HR	BB	SO	RAT	ERA	ERA+	OAV	OOB	BH	AVG	PB	PR	/A	PD	TPI
1990 Atl-N	0	2	.000	31	0	0	0	5	31	30	5	12	21	12.5	5.81	69	.248	.321	0	.000	-0	-7	-6	-0	-0.6
Total 11	60	47	.561	339	114	4	2	21	961^{2}	947	85	378	726	12.5	3.78	107	.259	.330	6	.070	-2	16	26	-1	0.5

● OTTO HESS Hess, Otto C. b: 10/10/1878, Bern, Switzerland d: 2/25/26, Tucson, Ariz. BL/TL, 6'1", 170 lbs. Deb: 8/3/02 ♦

YEAR TM/L	W	L	PCT	G	GS	CG	SH	SV	IP	H	HR	BB	SO	RAT	ERA	ERA+	OAV	OOB	BH	AVG	PB	PR	/A	PD	TPI
1912 Bos-N	12	17	.414	33	31	21	0	0	254	270	3	90	80	13.3	3.76	95	.283	.354	23	.245	3	-10	-5	-4	-0.6
1913 Bos-N	7	17	.292	29	27	19	2	0	218^{1}	231	12	70	80	12.7	3.83	86	.279	.340	26	.313	8	-15	-13	1	-0.5
1914 Bos-N	5	6	.455	14	11	7	1	1	89	89	2	33	24	12.8	3.03	91	.271	.347	11	.234	1	-2	-3	2	0.0
1915 Bos-N	0	1	.000	4	1	1	0	0	14	16	0	6	5	15.4	3.86	67	.286	.375	2	.400	1	-2	-2	-0	-0.1
Total 10	70	90	.438	198	165	129	18	5	1418	1355	25	448	580	12.0	2.98	98	.257	.324	154	.216	14	-11	-11	-2	0.4
Team 4	24	41	.369	80	70	48	3	1	575^{1}	606	17	199	189	13.0	3.68	90	.280	.348	62	.271	13	-29	-23	-1	-1.2

● JOE HEVING Heving, Joseph William b: 9/2/1900, Covington, Ky. d: 4/11/70, Covington, Ky. BR/TR, 6'1", 185 lbs. Deb: 4/29/30 F

YEAR TM/L	W	L	PCT	G	GS	CG	SH	SV	IP	H	HR	BB	SO	RAT	ERA	ERA+	OAV	OOB	BH	AVG	PB	PR	/A	PD	TPI
1945 Bos-N	1	0	1.000	3	0	0	0	0	5^{1}	5	0	3	1	15.2	3.38	114	.294	.429	0	.000	-0	0	0	1	0.1
Total 13	76	48	.613	430	40	17	3	63	1038^{2}	1136	64	380	429	13.3	3.90	108	.279	.344	47	.170	-4	40	36	14	4.2

● JIM HICKEY Hickey, James Robert "Sid" b: 10/22/20, N.Abington, Mass. BR/TR, 6'1", 204 lbs. Deb: 4/25/42

YEAR TM/L	W	L	PCT	G	GS	CG	SH	SV	IP	H	HR	BB	SO	RAT	ERA	ERA+	OAV	OOB	BH	AVG	PB	PR	/A	PD	TPI
1942 Bos-N	0	1	.000	1	1	0	0	0	1^{1}	4	1	2	0	40.5	20.25	16	.500	.600	0	.000	-0	-3	-3	-0	-1.0
1944 Bos-N	0	0	—	8	0	0	0	0	9^{1}	15	0	5	3	20.3	4.82	79	.366	.447	0	.000	-0	-1	-1	0	0.0
Total 2	0	1	.000	9	1	0	0	0	10^{2}	19	1	7	3	22.8	6.75	56	.388	.474	0	.000	-0	-4	-4	0	-1.0

● CHARLIE HICKMAN Hickman, Charles Taylor "Cheerful Charlie" or "Piano Legs"
b: 3/4/1876, Taylortown, Dunkard Township, Pa. d: 4/19/34, Morgantown, W.Va. BR/TR, 5'11.5", 215 lbs. Deb: 9/8/1897 ♦

YEAR TM/L	W	L	PCT	G	GS	CG	SH	SV	IP	H	HR	BB	SO	RAT	ERA	ERA+	OAV	OOB	BH	AVG	PB	PR	/A	PD	TPI
1897 *Bos-N	0	0	—	2	0	0	0	1	7^{2}	10	0	5	0	17.6	5.87	76	.313	.405	2	.667	2	-1	-1	0	0.1
1898 Bos-N	1	2	.333	6	3	3	1	2	33	22	0	13	9	9.5	2.18	169	.188	.269	15	.259	0	5	6	-1	0.4
1899 Bos-N	6	0	1.000	11	9	5	2	1	66^{1}	52	3	40	14	13.6	4.48	93	.216	.346	25	.397	6	-5	-2	-1	0.2
Total 6	10	8	.556	30	22	15	3	4	185	175	4	94	37	13.7	4.28	86	.249	.347	1176	.295	11	-14	-12	-1	-0.2
Team 3	7	2	.778	19	12	8	3	4	107	84	3	58	23	12.6	3.87	104	.215	.329	42	.339	7	-1	2	-2	0.7

● GARRY HILL Hill, Garry Alton b: 11/3/46, Rutherfordton, N.C. BR/TR, 6'2", 195 lbs. Deb: 6/12/69

YEAR TM/L	W	L	PCT	G	GS	CG	SH	SV	IP	H	HR	BB	SO	RAT	ERA	ERA+	OAV	OOB	BH	AVG	PB	PR	/A	PD	TPI
1969 Atl-N	0	1	.000	1	1	0	0	0	2^{1}	6	1	1	2	27.0	15.43	23	.462	.500	0	—	0	-3	-3	0	-0.8

● MILT HILL Hill, Milton Giles b: 8/22/65, Atlanta, Ga. BR/TR, 6', 180 lbs. Deb: 8/1/91

YEAR TM/L	W	L	PCT	G	GS	CG	SH	SV	IP	H	HR	BB	SO	RAT	ERA	ERA+	OAV	OOB	BH	AVG	PB	PR	/A	PD	TPI
1994 Atl-N	0	0	—	10	0	0	0	0	11^{1}	18	3	6	10	19.1	7.94	53	.367	.436	0	—	0	-5	-5	-0	0.0
Total 4	5	1	.833	78	0	0	0	1	117	133	14	39	79	13.3	5.08	80	.294	.351	0	.000	-0	-14	-13	-1	-0.8

YEAR	TM/L	W	L	PCT	G	GS	CG	SH	SV	IP	H	HR	BB	SO	RAT	ERA	ERA+	OAV	OOB	BH	AVG	PB	PR	/A	PD	TPI

● **HERB HIPPAUF**   Hippauf, Herbert August b: 5/9/39, New York, N.Y. d: 7/17/95, Santa Clara, Cal.   BR/TL, 6′, 180 lbs.   Deb: 4/27/66

| 1966 | Atl-N | 0 | 1 | .000 | 3 | 0 | 0 | 0 | 0 | 2² | 6 | 0 | 1 | 1 | 23.6 | 13.50 | 27 | .462 | .500 | 0 | — | 0 | -3 | -3 | -0 | -0.9 |

● **GEORGE HODSON**   Hodson, George S. b: 6/1870, Pennsylvania   Deb: 8/9/1894

| 1894 | Bos-N | 4 | 4 | .500 | 12 | 11 | 8 | 0 | 0 | 74 | 103 | 4 | 35 | 12 | 17.4 | 5.84 | 97 | .326 | .402 | 3 | .100 | -4 | -4 | -1 | -1 | -0.5 |
| Total | 2 | 5 | 6 | .455 | 16 | 13 | 9 | 0 | 0 | 91 | 130 | 8 | 44 | 18 | 17.7 | 6.53 | 84 | .332 | .406 | 3 | .086 | -5 | -13 | -10 | -2 | -1.6 |

● **BILLY HOEFT**   Hoeft, William Frederick b: 5/17/32, Oshkosh, Wis. BL/TL, 6′3″, 205 lbs.   Deb: 4/18/52

| 1964 | Mil-N | 4 | 0 | 1.000 | 42 | 0 | 0 | 0 | 4 | 73¹ | 76 | 9 | 18 | 47 | 11.7 | 3.80 | 93 | .271 | .318 | 2 | .222 | 1 | -2 | -2 | 0 | 0.0 |
| Total | 15 | 97 | 101 | .490 | 505 | 200 | 75 | 17 | 33 | 1847¹ | 1820 | 173 | 685 | 1140 | 12.4 | 3.94 | 98 | .259 | .327 | 107 | .202 | 24 | -15 | -15 | -11 | -1.4 |

● **JOE HOERNER**   Hoerner, Joseph Walter b: 11/12/36, Dubuque, Iowa BR/TL, 6′1″, 200 lbs.   Deb: 9/27/63

1972	Atl-N	1	3	.250	25	0	0	0	2	23¹	34	4	8	19	16.6	6.56	58	.351	.406	0	.000	-0	-8	-7	-0	-1.4
1973	Atl-N	2	2	.500	20	0	0	0	2	12²	17	1	4	10	14.9	6.39	61	.333	.382	0	—	0	-4	-3	-0	-1.2
Total	14	39	34	.534	493	0	0	0	99	562²	519	50	181	412	11.6	2.99	119	.249	.314	6	.102	-1	35	36	-7	4.9
Team	2	3	5	.375	45	0	0	0	4	36	51	5	12	29	16.0	6.50	59	.345	.398	0	.000	-0	-12	-11	-1	-2.6

● **BRAD HOGG**   Hogg, Carter Bradley b: 3/26/1888, Buena Vista, Ga. d: 4/2/35, Buena Vista, Ga.   BR/TR, 6′, 185 lbs.   Deb: 9/1/11

1911	Bos-N	0	3	.000	8	3	2	0	1	25²	33	0	14	8	16.8	6.66	57	.337	.425	4	.444	1	-9	-8	0	-0.7
1912	Bos-N	1	1	.500	10	1	0	0	1	31	37	2	16	12	16.0	6.97	51	.308	.399	1	.091	-1	-12	-12	-1	-0.8
Total	5	20	29	.408	71	50	33	4	3	448	446	13	152	149	12.3	3.70	85	.271	.338	40	.247	5	-40	-27	-0	-1.5
Team	2	1	4	.200	18	4	2	0	2	56²	70	2	30	20	16.4	6.83	54	.321	.410	5	.250	0	-22	-20	-0	-1.5

● **BOBBY HOGUE**   Hogue, Robert Clinton b: 4/5/21, Miami, Fla. d: 12/22/87, Miami, Fla.   BR/TR, 5′10″, 195 lbs.   Deb: 4/24/48

1948	Bos-N	8	2	.800	40	1	0	0	4	86¹	88	4	19	43	11.4	3.23	119	.265	.309	2	.095	-1	7	6	-1	0.4
1949	Bos-N	2	2	.500	33	0	0	0	3	72	78	4	25	23	13.1	3.13	121	.280	.343	6	.286	1	7	5	2	0.6
1950	Bos-N	3	5	.375	36	1	0	0	7	62²	69	8	31	15	14.9	5.03	77	.280	.370	3	.231	1	-6	-8	1	-1.0
1951	Bos-N	0	0	—	3	0	0	0	0	5	4	1	3	0	12.6	5.40	68	.235	.350	1	.500	-1	-1	-0	0	0.0
Total	5	18	16	.529	172	3	0	0	17	326²	336	25	142	108	13.4	3.97	96	.271	.350	17	.233	3	-0	-6	1	-1.4
Team	4	13	9	.591	112	2	0	0	12	226	239	17	78	81	12.9	3.74	102	.273	.339	12	.211	1	7	2	1	0.0

● **BONNIE HOLLINGSWORTH**   Hollingsworth, John Burnette b: 12/26/1895, Jacksboro, Tenn. d: 1/4/90, Knoxville, Tenn.   BR/TR, 5′10″, 170 lbs.   Deb: 5/30/22

| 1928 | Bos-N | 0 | 2 | .000 | 7 | 2 | 0 | 0 | 0 | 22¹ | 32 | 2 | 13 | 10 | 17.3 | 5.24 | 75 | .341 | .426 | 1 | .167 | -0 | -3 | -3 | 0 | -0.2 |
| Total | 4 | 4 | 9 | .308 | 36 | 11 | 2 | 0 | 0 | 117¹ | 127 | 5 | 81 | 50 | 16.3 | 4.91 | 78 | .291 | .406 | 3 | .097 | -2 | -12 | -14 | -1 | -1.0 |

● **DICK HOOVER**   Hoover, Richard Lloyd b: 12/11/25, Columbus, Ohio d: 4/12/81, Lake Placid, Fla.   BL/TL, 6′, 170 lbs.   Deb: 4/16/52

| 1952 | Bos-N | 0 | 0 | — | 2 | 0 | 0 | 0 | 0 | 4² | 8 | 1 | 3 | 0 | 21.2 | 7.71 | 47 | .348 | .423 | 0 | — | 0 | -2 | -2 | -0 | 0.0 |

● **TOM HOUSE**   House, Thomas Ross b: 4/29/47, Seattle, Wash. BL/TL, 5′11″, 190 lbs.   Deb: 6/23/71 C

1971	Atl-N	1	0	1.000	11	0	0	0	0	20²	20	3	3	11	10.5	3.05	122	.263	.300	2	.400	1	1	2	0	0.1
1972	Atl-N	0	0	—	8	0	0	0	2	9¹	7	1	6	7	13.5	2.89	131	.226	.368	0	.000	-0	1	1	0	0.0
1973	Atl-N	4	2	.667	52	0	0	0	4	67¹	58	13	31	42	12.2	4.68	84	.243	.335	2	.200	-0	-8	-6	-0	-0.5
1974	Atl-N	6	2	.750	56	0	0	0	11	102²	74	5	27	64	9.1	1.93	196	.203	.264	4	.400	1	19	21	1	2.4
1975	Atl-N	7	7	.500	58	0	0	0	11	79¹	79	2	36	36	13.3	3.18	119	.262	.344	1	.111	-0	4	5	1	1.1
Total	8	29	23	.558	289	21	4	0	33	536	516	49	182	261	12.1	3.79	102	.256	.324	9	.257	-5	-5	5	1	1.3
Team	5	18	11	.621	185	1	0	0	28	279¹	238	23	103	160	11.3	3.06	124	.235	.311	9	.257	1	17	23	2	3.1

● **JAY HOWELL**   Howell, Jay Canfield b: 11/26/55, Miami, Fla.   BR/TR, 6′3″, 205 lbs.   Deb: 8/10/80

| 1993 | Atl-N | 3 | 3 | .500 | 54 | 0 | 0 | 0 | 3 | 58¹ | 48 | 3 | 16 | 37 | 9.9 | 2.31 | 173 | .229 | .283 | 0 | — | 0 | 11 | 11 | -0 | 1.0 |
| Total | 15 | 58 | 53 | .523 | 568 | 21 | 2 | 0 | 155 | 844² | 782 | 57 | 291 | 666 | 11.6 | 3.34 | 114 | .246 | .313 | 0 | .000 | -1 | 56 | 43 | 2 | 11.0 |

● **AL HRABOSKY**   Hrabosky, Alan Thomas b: 7/21/49, Oakland, Cal.   BR/TL, 5′11″, 185 lbs.   Deb: 6/16/70

1980	Atl-N	4	2	.667	45	0	0	0	1	59²	50	8	31	31	12.2	3.62	103	.223	.318	0	.000	-0	-0	1	-2	-0.1
1981	Atl-N	1	1	.500	24	0	0	0	1	33²	24	1	9	13	8.8	1.07	335	.207	.264	0	.000	-0	9	9	-1	0.5
1982	Atl-N	2	1	.667	31	0	0	0	5	37¹	41	5	17	20	14.0	5.54	67	.285	.360	1	.333	-0	-8	-8	-1	-0.8
Total	13	64	35	.646	545	1	0	0	97	722	619	50	315	548	11.8	3.10	121	.234	.318	8	.143	-4	49	52	-9	8.2
Team	3	7	4	.636	100	0	0	0	7	130²	115	14	57	64	11.8	3.51	105	.238	.318	1	.200	-0	1	3	-3	-0.4

● **TOM HUGHES**   Hughes, Thomas L. "Salida Tom" b: 1/28/1884, Coal Creek, Colo. d: 11/1/61, Los Angeles, Cal.   BR/TR, 6′2″, 175 lbs.   Deb: 9/18/06

1914	Bos-N	2	0	1.000	2	2	1	0	0	17	14	0	4	11	9.5	2.65	104	.226	.273	0	.000	-1	0	0	1	0.0
1915	Bos-N	16	14	.533	**50**	25	17	4	**9**	280¹	208	4	58	171	8.9	2.12	122	.213	.265	9	.100	-3	20	15	-2	1.1
1916	Bos-N	16	3	**.842**	40	13	7	1	5	161	121	2	51	97	10.1	2.35	106	.215	.290	10	.192	-3	5	2	-1	0.4
1917	Bos-N	5	3	.625	11	8	6	2	0	74	54	1	30	40	10.6	1.95	131	.216	.307	0	.000	-3	6	5	-0	0.4
1918	Bos-N	0	2	.000	3	3	1	0	0	18¹	17	0	6	9	11.3	3.44	78	.250	.311	2	.333	1	-1	-2	0	0.0
Total	9	56	39	.589	160	85	55	9	17	863	703	14	235	476	10.1	2.56	102	.229	.291	37	.130	-4	8	4	-4	1.2
Team	5	39	22	.639	106	51	32	7	14	550²	414	7	149	328	9.6	2.22	115	.216	.280	21	.117	-4	30	21	-3	1.7

● **HARRY HULIHAN**   Hulihan, Harry Joseph b: 4/18/1899, Rutland, Vt. d: 9/11/80, Rutland, Vt.   BR/TL, 5′11″, 170 lbs.   Deb: 8/16/22

| 1922 | Bos-N | 2 | 3 | .400 | 7 | 6 | 2 | 0 | 0 | 40 | 40 | 0 | 26 | 16 | 15.7 | 3.15 | 127 | .274 | .398 | 2 | .154 | -0 | 4 | 4 | -1 | 0.3 |

● **JOHNNY HUTCHINGS**   Hutchings, John Richard Joseph b: 4/14/16, Chicago, Ill. d: 4/27/63, Indianapolis, Ind.   BB/TR, 6′2″, 250 lbs.   Deb: 4/26/40

1941	Bos-N	1	6	.143	36	7	1	1	2	95²	110	6	22	36	12.8	4.14	86	.287	.333	4	.148	-0	-5	-6	0	-0.4
1942	Bos-N	1	0	1.000	20	3	0	0	0	65²	66	2	34	27	14.0	4.39	76	.260	.352	1	.050	-2	-8	-8	-1	-0.4
1944	Bos-N	1	4	.200	14	7	1	0	1	56²	55	3	26	26	13.0	3.97	96	.252	.335	1	.067	-1	-2	-1	-1	-0.2
1945	Bos-N	7	6	.538	57	12	3	2	3	185	173	21	75	99	12.3	3.75	102	.244	.320	13	.241	2	1	2	0	0.3
1946	Bos-N	0	1	.000	1	1	0	0	0	3	5	1	1	1	18.0	9.00	38	.357	.400	0	.000	-0	-2	-2	-0	-0.5
Total	6	12	18	.400	155	34	5	3	6	471	474	36	180	212	12.7	3.96	93	.260	.330	21	.162	-1	-15	-14	-2	-1.2
Team	5	10	17	.370	128	30	5	3	6	406	409	33	158	189	12.8	4.01	92	.259	.331	19	.162	-1	-16	-15	-1	-1.2

● **IRA HUTCHINSON**   Hutchinson, Ira Kendall b: 8/31/10, Chicago, Ill. d: 8/21/73, Chicago, Ill.   BR/TR, 5′10.5″, 180 lbs.   Deb: 9/24/33

1937	Bos-N	4	6	.400	31	8	1	0	0	91²	99	4	35	29	13.3	3.73	96	.286	.353	3	.115	-1	2	-1	1	-0.2
1938	Bos-N	9	8	.529	36	12	4	1	4	151	150	3	61	38	12.8	2.74	125	.258	.332	9	.173	-1	18	12	1	1.3
1944	Bos-N	9	7	.563	40	8	1	1	1	119²	136	8	53	22	14.4	4.21	91	.296	.373	4	.138	-1	-8	-5	1	-0.7
1945	Bos-N	2	3	.400	11	0	0	0	1	28²	33	2	8	4	13.2	5.02	76	.277	.328	0	.000	-1	-4	-4	1	-0.7
Total	8	34	33	.507	209	32	7	2	13	610²	628	33	249	179	13.1	3.76	100	.270	.344	24	.140	-7	2	-1	5	-0.1
Team	4	24	24	.500	118	28	6	2	6	391	418	17	157	93	13.4	3.59	101	.278	.349	16	.138	-5	8	1	3	-0.3

● **BILL JAMES**   James, William Lawrence "Seattle Bill" b: 3/12/1892, Iowa Hill, Cal. d: 3/10/71, Oroville, Cal.   BR/TR, 6′3″, 196 lbs.   Deb: 4/17/13

1913	Bos-N	6	10	.375	24	14	10	1	0	135²	134	4	57	73	13.1	2.79	118	.264	.347	12	.255	1	6	8	0	1.0
1914	*Bos-N	26	7	**.788**	46	37	30	4	2	332¹	261	7	118	156	10.6	1.90	145	.225	.304	33	.256	4	**33**	**32**	-1	**3.6**
1915	Bos-N	5	4	.556	13	10	4	0	0	68¹	68	3	22	23	12.1	3.03	86	.269	.332	1	.048	-0	-2	-3	1	-0.5
1919	Bos-N	0	0	—	1	0	0	0	0	5¹	6	0	2	1	13.5	3.38	85	.273	.333	0	.000	-0	-0	-0	-0	-0.1
Total	4	37	21	.638	84	61	44	5	2	541²	469	14	199	253	11.5	2.28	126	.242	.319	46	.231	4	37	35	1	4.1

● PAT JARVIS Jarvis, Robert Patrick b: 3/18/41, Carlyle, Ill. BR/TR, 5'10.5", 180 lbs. Deb: 8/4/66

YEAR TM/L	W	L	PCT	G	GS	CG	SH	SV	IP	H	HR	BB	SO	RAT	ERA	ERA+	OAV	OOB	BH	AVG	PB	PR	/A	PD	TPI
1966 Atl-N	6	2	.750	10	9	3	1	0	62^1	46	1	12	41	8.5	2.31	157	.206	.250	0	.000	-2	9	9	-1	0.8
1967 Atl-N	15	10	.600	32	30	7	1	0	194	195	15	62	118	12.1	3.66	91	.260	.320	6	.085	-3	-6	-7	-2	-1.4
1968 Atl-N	16	12	.571	34	34	14	1	0	256	202	15	50	157	8.9	2.60	115	.214	.255	12	.141	0	11	11	-3	1.0
1969 *Atl-N	13	11	.542	37	33	4	1	0	217^1	204	25	73	123	11.5	4.43	81	.246	.308	8	.113	-2	-20	-20	-0	-2.3
1970 Atl-N	16	16	.500	36	34	11	1	0	254	240	21	72	173	11.1	3.61	119	.247	.299	15	.183	-0	12	19	2	2.4
1971 Atl-N	6	14	.300	35	23	3	3	1	162^1	162	16	51	68	12.0	4.10	90	.261	.320	5	.106	-2	-12	-7	1	-1.0
1972 Atl-N	11	7	.611	37	6	0	0	2	98^2	94	7	44	56	12.6	4.10	92	.260	.341	3	.125	-0	-7	-3	1	-0.5
Total 8	85	73	.538	249	169	42	8	3	1284	1180	106	380	755	11.0	3.58	101	.243	.300	49	.121	-10	-11	3	-3	-0.9
Team 7	83	72	.535	221	169	42	8	3	1244^2	1143	100	364	736	11.0	3.59	100	.243	.299	49	.122	-10	-13	1	-2	-1.0

● LARRY JASTER Jaster, Larry Edward b: 1/13/44, Midland, Mich. BL/TL, 6'3.5", 205 lbs. Deb: 9/17/65

YEAR TM/L	W	L	PCT	G	GS	CG	SH	SV	IP	H	HR	BB	SO	RAT	ERA	ERA+	OAV	OOB	BH	AVG	PB	PR	/A	PD	TPI
1970 Atl-N	1	1	.500	14	0	0	0	0	22^1	33	5	8	9	16.5	6.85	63	.359	.410	0	.000	-0	-7	-6	1	-0.5
1972 Atl-N	1	1	.500	5	1	0	0	0	12^1	12	4	8	6	14.6	5.11	74	.267	.377	0	.000	-0	-2	-2	-0	-0.3
Total 7	35	33	.515	138	80	15	7	3	598	579	69	178	313	11.6	3.64	93	.256	.314	29	.170	3	-16	-17	-7	-2.2
Team 2	2	2	.500	19	1	0	0	0	34^2	45	9	16	15	15.8	6.23	66	.328	.399	0	.000	-0	-9	-8	1	-0.8

● AL JAVERY Javery, Alva William "Beartracks" b: 6/5/18, Worcester, Mass. d: 9/13/77, Woodstock, Conn. BR/TR, 6'3", 183 lbs. Deb: 4/23/40

YEAR TM/L	W	L	PCT	G	GS	CG	SH	SV	IP	H	HR	BB	SO	RAT	ERA	ERA+	OAV	OOB	BH	AVG	PB	PR	/A	PD	TPI
1940 Bos-N	2	4	.333	29	4	1	0	1	83^1	99	2	36	42	14.8	5.51	68	.293	.364	2	.087	-1	-15	-17	-2	-1.4
1941 Bos-N	10	11	.476	34	23	9	1	1	160^2	181	5	65	54	14.1	4.31	83	.283	.355	6	.103	-4	-12	-13	1	-1.8
1942 Bos-N	12	16	.429	42	37	19	5	0	261	251	8	78	85	11.4	3.03	110	.251	.307	9	.105	-5	8	9	2	0.6
1943 Bos-N★	17	16	.515	41	35	19	5	0	**303**	288	13	99	134	11.6	3.21	106	.248	.309	17	.163	-3	6	7	2	0.7
1944 Bos-N☆	10	19	.345	40	33	11	3	3	254	248	12	118	137	13.0	3.54	108	.262	.345	12	.152	-3	2	8	-2	0.3
1945 Bos-N	2	7	.222	17	14	2	1	0	77^1	92	4	51	18	16.6	6.28	61	.295	.394	6	.207	-0	-21	-21	1	-2.0
1946 Bos-N	0	1	.000	2	1	0	0	0	3^1	5	0	5	0	27.0	13.50	25	.417	.588	0	.000	-0	-4	-4	-0	-0.9
Total 7	53	74	.417	205	147	61	15	5	1142^2	1164	44	452	470	12.9	3.80	94	.264	.335	52	.137	-15	-37	-31	2	-4.5

● JOEY JAY Jay, Joseph Richard b: 8/15/35, Middletown, Conn. BB/TR, 6'4", 228 lbs. Deb: 7/21/53

YEAR TM/L	W	L	PCT	G	GS	CG	SH	SV	IP	H	HR	BB	SO	RAT	ERA	ERA+	OAV	OOB	BH	AVG	PB	PR	/A	PD	TPI
1953 Mil-N	1	0	1.000	3	1	1	1	0	10	6	0	5	4	9.9	0.00	—	.188	.297	0	.000	-0	5	4	-0	0.3
1954 Mil-N	1	0	1.000	15	1	0	0	0	18	21	2	16	13	19.0	6.50	57	.304	.442	0	—	0	-5	-6	-0	-0.3
1955 Mil-N	0	0	—	12	1	0	0	0	19	23	2	13	3	17.1	4.74	79	.324	.429	2	.667	1	-1	-2	-1	0.0
1957 Mil-N	0	0	—	1	0	0	0	1	0^2	0	0	0	0	0.0	0.00	—	.000	.000	0	—	0	0	0	0	0.1
1958 Mil-N	7	5	.583	18	12	6	3	0	96^2	60	8	43	74	9.7	2.14	164	.177	.272	3	.094	-1	19	15	0	1.7
1959 Mil-N	6	11	.353	34	19	4	1	0	136^1	130	11	64	88	13.1	4.09	87	.248	.336	3	.086	-1	-2	-8	2	-0.9
1960 Mil-N	9	8	.529	32	11	3	0	1	133^1	128	10	59	90	13.0	3.24	106	.254	.339	7	.156	0	8	3	-0	0.3
1966 Atl-N	0	4	.000	9	8	0	0	1	29^2	39	4	20	19	18.2	7.89	46	.315	.414	1	.125	-0	-14	-14	-0	-1.7
Total 13	99	91	.521	310	203	63	16	7	1546^1	1460	153	607	999	12.2	3.77	99	.251	.325	55	.114	-10	-1	-5	-6	-2.4
Team 8	24	28	.462	124	53	14	5	3	443^2	407	37	220	291	13.0	3.69	96	.244	.338	16	.127	-2	10	-8	1	-0.5

● GEORGE JEFFCOAT Jeffcoat, George Edward b: 12/24/13, New Brookland, S.C d: 10/13/78, Leesville, S.C. BR/TR, 5'11.5", 175 lbs. Deb: 4/20/36 F

YEAR TM/L	W	L	PCT	G	GS	CG	SH	SV	IP	H	HR	BB	SO	RAT	ERA	ERA+	OAV	OOB	BH	AVG	PB	PR	/A	PD	TPI
1943 Bos-N	1	2	.333	8	1	0	0	0	17^2	15	1	10	10	12.7	3.06	112	.217	.316	2	.500	1	1	1	0	0.2
Total 4	7	11	.389	70	9	4	1	3	169^2	159	12	100	86	14.2	4.51	89	.248	.358	5	.128	-2	-11	-9	-1	-1.0

● VIRGIL JESTER Jester, Virgil Milton b: 7/23/27, Denver, Colo. BR/TR, 5'11", 188 lbs. Deb: 6/18/52

YEAR TM/L	W	L	PCT	G	GS	CG	SH	SV	IP	H	HR	BB	SO	RAT	ERA	ERA+	OAV	OOB	BH	AVG	PB	PR	/A	PD	TPI
1952 Bos-N	3	5	.375	19	8	4	1	0	73	80	5	23	25	12.8	3.33	108	.283	.339	4	.211	1	3	2	-1	0.2
1953 Mil-N	0	0	—	2	0	0	0	0	2	4	1	4	0	36.0	22.50	17	.400	.571	0	—	0	-4	-4	0	0.0
Total 2	3	5	.375	21	8	4	1	0	75	84	6	27	25	13.4	3.84	94	.287	.349	4	.211	1	-1	-2	-1	0.2

● GERMAN JIMENEZ Jimenez, German (Camarena) b: 12/5/62, Santiago, Mex. BL/TL, 5'11", 200 lbs. Deb: 6/28/88

YEAR TM/L	W	L	PCT	G	GS	CG	SH	SV	IP	H	HR	BB	SO	RAT	ERA	ERA+	OAV	OOB	BH	AVG	PB	PR	/A	PD	TPI
1988 Atl-N	1	6	.143	15	9	0	0	0	55^2	65	4	12	26	12.6	5.01	73	.294	.333	1	.059	-1	-10	-8	-1	-1.2

● ART JOHNSON Johnson, Arthur Henry "Lefty" b: 7/16/16, Winchester, Mass. BL/TL, 6'2", 185 lbs. Deb: 9/22/40

YEAR TM/L	W	L	PCT	G	GS	CG	SH	SV	IP	H	HR	BB	SO	RAT	ERA	ERA+	OAV	OOB	BH	AVG	PB	PR	/A	PD	TPI
1940 Bos-N	0	1	.000	2	1	0	0	0	6	10	0	3	1	21.0	10.50	35	.345	.424	0	.000	-0	-4	-5	0	-0.6
1941 Bos-N	7	15	.318	43	18	6	0	1	183^1	189	7	71	70	13.0	3.53	101	.270	.342	8	.145	-2	2	1	0	-0.1
1942 Bos-N	0	0	—	4	0	0	0	0	6^1	4	0	5	0	14.2	1.42	235	.190	.370	0	.000	-0	1	1	-0	0.0
Total 3	7	16	.304	49	19	6	0	1	195^2	203	7	79	71	13.3	3.68	97	.271	.346	8	.140	-2	-1	-2	1	-0.7

● ERNIE JOHNSON Johnson, Ernest Thorwald b: 6/16/24, Brattleboro, Vt. BR/TR, 6'4", 195 lbs. Deb: 4/28/50

YEAR TM/L	W	L	PCT	G	GS	CG	SH	SV	IP	H	HR	BB	SO	RAT	ERA	ERA+	OAV	OOB	BH	AVG	PB	PR	/A	PD	TPI
1950 Bos-N	2	0	1.000	16	1	0	0	0	20^2	37	1	13	15	21.8	6.97	55	.394	.467	1	.500	0	-6	-7	1	-0.4
1952 Bos-N	6	3	.667	29	10	2	1	1	92	100	7	31	45	13.0	4.11	88	.270	.329	2	.091	-0	-4	-5	1	-0.4
1953 Mil-N	4	3	.571	36	1	0	0	0	81	79	4	22	36	11.6	2.67	147	.263	.320	1	.071	-1	15	11	0	0.7
1954 Mil-N	5	2	.714	40	4	1	0	2	99^1	77	11	34	68	10.1	2.81	133	.219	.290	3	.231	0	14	10	1	0.8
1955 Mil-N	5	7	.417	40	2	0	0	4	92	81	5	55	43	13.5	3.42	110	.240	.349	2	.100	-1	6	3	-0	0.3
1956 Mil-N	4	3	.571	36	0	0	0	6	51	54	9	21	26	13.4	3.71	93	.270	.342	1	.250	0	0	-1	0	-0.2
1957 *Mil-N	7	3	.700	30	0	0	0	4	65	67	9	26	44	13.0	3.88	90	.265	.336	6	.353	3	0	-3	1	0.0
1958 Mil-N	3	1	.750	15	0	0	0	1	23^1	35	4	10	13	17.7	8.10	43	.357	.422	0	.000	0	-11	-12	0	-1.8
Total 9	40	23	.635	273	19	3	1	19	574^2	587	56	231	319	13.0	3.77	98	.266	.340	18	.180	2	13	-5	5	-1.1
Team 8	36	22	.621	242	18	3	1	18	524^1	530	50	212	290	12.9	3.74	98	.264	.338	16	.170	1	14	-3	5	-1.0

● JOE JOHNSON Johnson, Joseph Richard b: 10/30/61, Brookline, Mass. BR/TR, 6'2", 195 lbs. Deb: 7/25/85

YEAR TM/L	W	L	PCT	G	GS	CG	SH	SV	IP	H	HR	BB	SO	RAT	ERA	ERA+	OAV	OOB	BH	AVG	PB	PR	/A	PD	TPI
1985 Atl-N	4	4	.500	15	14	1	0	0	85^2	95	9	24	34	12.8	4.10	94	.285	.339	1	.043	-1	-5	-2	-2	-0.5
1986 Atl-N	6	7	.462	17	15	2	0	0	87	101	8	35	49	14.3	4.97	80	.289	.358	3	.115	-1	-12	-10	2	-1.2
Total 3	20	18	.526	62	58	3	0	0	327^1	367	30	99	149	13.1	4.48	92	.286	.342	4	.082	-2	-19	-13	-2	-2.1
Team 2	10	11	.476	32	29	3	0	0	172^2	196	17	59	83	13.6	4.53	86	.287	.349	4	.082	-2	-17	-12	-0	-1.7

● KEN JOHNSON Johnson, Kenneth Travis b: 6/16/33, W.Palm Beach, Fla. BR/TR, 6'4", 210 lbs. Deb: 9/13/58

YEAR TM/L	W	L	PCT	G	GS	CG	SH	SV	IP	H	HR	BB	SO	RAT	ERA	ERA+	OAV	OOB	BH	AVG	PB	PR	/A	PD	TPI
1965 Mil-N	13	8	.619	29	26	8	1	2	179^2	165	15	37	123	10.3	3.21	110	.240	.282	7	.115	-2	7	6	-3	0.2
1966 Atl-N	14	8	.636	32	31	11	2	0	215^2	213	24	46	105	10.8	3.30	110	.262	.301	10	.143	0	7	8	0	0.8
1967 Atl-N	13	9	.591	29	29	6	0	0	210^1	191	19	38	85	10.1	2.74	121	.244	.285	9	.127	-0	15	14	-2	1.2
1968 Atl-N	5	8	.385	31	16	1	0	0	135	145	10	25	57	11.9	3.47	86	.279	.324	7	.175	-0	-7	-7	-1	-0.8
1969 Atl-N	0	1	.000	9	2	0	0	1	29	32	4	9	20	12.7	4.97	73	.283	.336	0	.000	-0	-4	-4	0	-0.2
Total 13	91	106	.462	334	231	50	7	9	1737^1	1670	157	413	1042	11.1	3.46	101	.253	.302	61	.114	-12	18	8	5	0.2
Team 5	45	34	.570	130	104	26	3	3	769^2	746	72	155	390	10.8	3.22	106	.256	.298	33	.133	-2	17	17	-6	1.2

● BOB JOHNSON Johnson, Robert Dale b: 4/25/43, Aurora, Ill. BL/TR, 6'4", 220 lbs. Deb: 9/19/69

YEAR TM/L	W	L	PCT	G	GS	CG	SH	SV	IP	H	HR	BB	SO	RAT	ERA	ERA+	OAV	OOB	BH	AVG	PB	PR	/A	PD	TPI
1977 Atl-N	0	1	.000	15	0	0	0	0	22^1	24	7	14	16	16.1	7.25	61	.270	.381	1	.333	0	-8	-7	-1	-0.3
Total 7	28	34	.452	183	76	18	2	12	692^1	644	82	269	507	12.3	3.48	102	.249	.327	15	.096	-4	9	6	-7	-0.2

● SI JOHNSON Johnson, Silas Kenneth b: 10/5/06, Danway, Ill. d: 5/12/94, Sheridan, Ill. BR/TR, 5'11.5", 185 lbs. Deb: 5/2/28

YEAR TM/L	W	L	PCT	G	GS	CG	SH	SV	IP	H	HR	BB	SO	RAT	ERA	ERA+	OAV	OOB	BH	AVG	PB	PR	/A	PD	TPI
1946 Bos-N	6	5	.545	28	12	5	1	1	127	134	8	35	41	12.3	2.76	124	.272	.325	5	.135	-2	9	9	-1	0.5
1947 Bos-N	6	8	.429	36	10	3	0	2	112^2	124	7	34	27	12.7	4.23	92	.275	.327	1	.033	-3	-2	-4	3	-0.5
Total 17	101	165	.380	492	272	108	13	15	2281^1	2510	120	687	840	12.8	4.09	92	.279	.333	87	.123	-37	-76	-79	-17	-14.1
Team 2	12	13	.480	64	22	8	1	3	239^2	258	15	69	68	12.5	3.45	106	.273	.326	6	.090	-5	7	5	2	0.0

YEAR	TM/L	W	L	PCT	G	GS	CG	SH	SV	IP	H	HR	BB	SO	RAT	ERA	ERA+	OAV	OOB	BH	AVG	PB	PR	/A	PD	TPI

● DAVE JOLLY Jolly, David "Gabby" b: 10/14/24, Stony Point, N.C. d: 5/27/63, Durham, N.C. BR/TR, 6', 165 lbs. Deb: 5/9/53

1953	Mil-N	0	1	.000	24	0	0	0	0	38¹	34	4	27	23	14.6	3.52	111	.239	.365	1	.500	1	3	2	0	0.1
1954	Mil-N	11	6	.647	47	1	0	0	10	111¹	87	6	64	62	12.4	2.43	154	.215	.326	9	.290	3	20	16	0	3.0
1955	Mil-N	2	3	.400	36	0	0	0	1	58¹	58	6	51	23	17.0	5.71	66	.258	.397	1	.167	0	-11	-13	1	-0.9
1956	Mil-N	2	3	.400	29	0	0	0	7	45²	39	7	35	20	14.6	3.74	92	.228	.359	0	.000	-0	0	-1	-1	-0.3
1957	Mil-N	1	1	.500	23	0	0	0	1	37²	37	4	21	27	14.6	5.02	70	.264	.372	3	.600	1	-5	-6	0	-0.2
Total	5	16	14	.533	159	1	0	0	19	291¹	255	27	198	155	14.2	3.77	98	.236	.357	14	.292	5	8	-3	0	1.7

● JOHNNY JONES Jones, John Paul "Admiral" b: 8/25/1892, Arcadia, La. d: 6/5/80, Ruston, La. BR/TR, 6'1", 151 lbs. Deb: 4/24/19

| 1920 | Bos-N | 1 | 0 | 1.000 | 3 | 1 | 0 | 0 | 0 | 9² | 16 | 1 | 5 | 6 | 19.6 | 6.52 | 47 | .372 | .438 | 1 | .250 | 1 | -4 | -4 | 0 | -0.3 |
| Total | 2 | 1 | 0 | 1.000 | 5 | 1 | 0 | 0 | 1 | 16¹ | 25 | 1 | 8 | 9 | 18.7 | 6.06 | 49 | .347 | .420 | 1 | .143 | 0 | -5 | -6 | 0 | -0.4 |

● KEN JONES Jones, Kenneth Frederick "Broadway" b: 4/13/03, Dover, N.J. d: 5/15/91, Hartford, Conn. BR/TR, 6'3", 193 lbs. Deb: 5/19/24

| 1930 | Bos-N | 0 | 1 | .000 | 8 | 1 | 0 | 0 | 0 | 19² | 28 | 1 | 4 | 4 | 14.6 | 5.95 | 83 | .359 | .390 | 1 | .200 | -0 | -2 | -2 | 0 | -0.1 |
| Total | 2 | 0 | 1 | .000 | 9 | 1 | 0 | 0 | 0 | 21² | 29 | 1 | 5 | 4 | 14.1 | 5.40 | 90 | .341 | .378 | 1 | .200 | -0 | -1 | -1 | 0 | -0.1 |

● PERCY JONES Jones, Percy Lee b: 10/28/1899, Harwood, Tex. d: 3/18/79, Dallas, Tex. BR/TL, 5'11.5", 175 lbs. Deb: 8/6/20

| 1929 | Bos-N | 7 | 15 | .318 | 35 | 22 | 11 | 1 | 0 | 188¹ | 219 | 15 | 84 | 69 | 14.7 | 4.64 | 101 | .298 | .373 | 9 | .148 | -3 | 2 | 1 | 1 | -0.1 |
| Total | 9 | 53 | 57 | .482 | 251 | 117 | 49 | 8 | 6 | 1026 | 1137 | 53 | 494 | 381 | 14.7 | 4.34 | 95 | .288 | .373 | 63 | .194 | -5 | -24 | -24 | 1 | -1.5 |

● SHELDON JONES Jones, Sheldon Leslie "Available" b: 2/2/22, Tecumseh, Neb. d: 4/18/91, Greenville, N.C. BR/TR, 6', 180 lbs. Deb: 9/9/46

| 1952 | Bos-N | 1 | 4 | .200 | 39 | 4 | 0 | 0 | 0 | 70 | 81 | 8 | 31 | 40 | 14.5 | 4.76 | 76 | .286 | .359 | 1 | .125 | -0 | -8 | -9 | 0 | -0.6 |
| Total | 8 | 54 | 57 | .486 | 260 | 101 | 33 | 4 | 12 | 920 | 909 | 90 | 413 | 413 | 13.3 | 3.96 | 100 | .258 | .342 | 35 | .136 | -7 | 4 | 1 | -3 | -0.5 |

● IKE KAMP Kamp, Alphonse Francis b: 9/5/1900, Roxbury, Mass. d: 2/25/55, Boston, Mass. BB/TL, 6', 170 lbs. Deb: 9/16/24

1924	Bos-N	0	1	.000	1	1	0	0	0	7	9	0	5	4	18.0	5.14	74	.360	.467	0	.000	-0	-1	-1	0	-0.1
1925	Bos-N	2	4	.333	24	4	1	0	0	58¹	68	0	35	20	15.9	5.09	79	.301	.395	2	.167	-0	-5	-7	0	-0.6
Total	2	2	5	.286	25	5	1	0	0	65¹	77	0	40	24	16.1	5.10	78	.307	.402	2	.154	-0	-6	-8	1	-0.7

● ANDY KARL Karl, Anton Andrew b: 4/8/14, Mt.Vernon, N.Y. d: 4/8/89, LaJolla, Cal. BR/TR, 6'1.5", 175 lbs. Deb: 4/24/43

| 1947 | Bos-N | 2 | 3 | .400 | 27 | 0 | 0 | 0 | 0 | 35 | 41 | 2 | 13 | 5 | 13.9 | 3.86 | 101 | .318 | .380 | 1 | .167 | -0 | 1 | 0 | 2 | 0.2 |
| Total | 5 | 18 | 23 | .439 | 191 | 4 | 1 | 0 | 26 | 422² | 451 | 16 | 130 | 107 | 12.5 | 3.51 | 104 | .279 | .334 | 16 | .168 | -0 | 7 | 7 | 6 | 0.0 |

● RAY KEATING Keating, Raymond Herbert b: 7/21/1891, Bridgeport, Conn. d: 12/28/63, Sacramento, Cal. BR/TR, 5'11", 185 lbs. Deb: 9/12/12

| 1919 | Bos-N | 7 | 11 | .389 | 22 | 14 | 9 | 1 | 0 | 136 | 129 | 2 | 45 | 48 | 11.6 | 2.98 | 96 | .261 | .325 | 7 | .152 | -1 | -1 | -2 | 2 | -0.2 |
| Total | 7 | 30 | 51 | .370 | 130 | 92 | 50 | 4 | 1 | 751² | 706 | 13 | 293 | 349 | 12.2 | 3.29 | 88 | .254 | .329 | 42 | .170 | -2 | -35 | -33 | 5 | -2.7 |

● DICK KELLEY Kelley, Richard Anthony b: 1/8/40, Boston, Mass d: 12/12/91, Northridge, Cal. BR/TL, 6', 175 lbs. Deb: 4/15/64

1964	Mil-N	0	0	—	2	0	0	0	0	2	2	0	3	2	22.5	18.00	20	.250	.455	0	—	0	-3	-3	-0	0.0
1965	Mil-N	1	1	.500	21	4	0	0	0	45	37	5	20	31	11.4	3.00	117	.226	.310	0	.000	-1	3	3	-0	0.0
1966	Atl-N	7	5	.583	20	13	2	2	0	81	75	6	21	50	11.4	3.22	113	.247	.302	1	.036	-3	3	4	-2	0.1
1967	Atl-N	2	9	.182	39	9	1	1	2	98	88	8	42	75	12.0	3.77	88	.247	.328	4	.250	1	-4	-5	1	-0.3
1968	Atl-N	2	4	.333	31	11	1	1	0	98	86	4	45	78	12.1	2.76	109	.238	.324	1	.043	-1	3	3	1	0.2
Total	7	18	30	.375	188	61	5	5	5	519²	453	39	215	369	11.8	3.39	100	.237	.319	12	.096	-5	1	-1	2	-0.2
Team	5	12	19	.387	113	37	4	4	3	324	288	23	131	231	11.8	3.31	101	.241	.319	6	.080	-3	1	1	0	-0.0

● TOM KELLEY Kelley, Thomas Henry b: 1/5/44, Manchester, Conn. BR/TR, 6', 191 lbs. Deb: 5/5/64

1971	Atl-N	9	5	.643	28	20	5	0	0	143	140	8	69	68	13.2	2.96	125	.262	.347	2	.047	-4	8	12	-1	0.7
1972	Atl-N	5	7	.417	27	14	2	1	0	116¹	122	12	65	59	14.5	4.56	83	.272	.364	3	.088	-2	-14	-10	-3	-1.4
1973	Atl-N	0	1	.000	7	0	0	0	0	12²	13	0	7	4	14.2	2.84	138	.289	.385	0	.000	-0	1	2	-0	0.1
Total	7	20	22	.476	104	45	9	1	0	408	400	38	207	234	13.4	3.75	97	.260	.349	11	.095	-6	-13	-4	-5	-1.6
Team	3	14	13	.519	62	34	7	1	0	272	275	20	141	132	13.8	3.64	103	.267	.356	5	.063	-6	-5	4	-3	-0.6

● KING KELLY Kelly, Michael Joseph b: 12/31/1857, Troy, N.Y. d: 11/8/1894, Boston, Mass. BR/TR, 5'10", 170 lbs. Deb: 5/1/1878 MH ♦

1887	Bos-N	1	0	1.000	3	0	0	0	0	13	17	1	14	0	21.5	3.46	117	.298	.437	156	.322	1	1	1	0	0.1
1892	*Bos-N	0	0	—	1	0	0	0	0	4	4	0	2	0	22.5	1.50	234	.308	.455	53	.189	0	1	1	-0	0.1
Total	7	2	2	.500	12	0	0	0	0	45²	63	5	30	4	19.1	4.14	92	.312	.411	1813	.308	4	-3	-2	0	-0.3
Team	2	1	0	1.000	4	0	0	0	0	19	25	1	18	0	21.8	2.84	137	.301	.442	209	.273	1	2	2	0	0.1

● ART KENNEY Kenney, Arthur Joseph b: 4/29/16, Milford, Mass. BL/TL, 6', 175 lbs. Deb: 7/1/38

| 1938 | Bos-N | 0 | 0 | — | 2 | 0 | 0 | 0 | 0 | 2¹ | 3 | 0 | 8 | 2 | 42.4 | 15.43 | 22 | .300 | .611 | 0 | — | 0 | -3 | -3 | 0 | 0.0 |

● CHARLIE KERFELD Kerfeld, Charles Patrick b: 9/28/63, Knob Knoster, Mo. BR/TR, 6'6", 225 lbs. Deb: 7/27/85

| 1990 | Atl-N | 3 | 1 | .750 | 25 | 0 | 0 | 0 | 2 | 30² | 31 | 2 | 23 | 27 | 15.8 | 5.58 | 72 | .270 | .391 | 0 | — | 0 | -6 | -5 | -1 | -0.8 |
| Total | 4 | 18 | 9 | .667 | 123 | 6 | 0 | 0 | 9 | 201² | 189 | 12 | 117 | 155 | 13.8 | 4.20 | 88 | .256 | .360 | 1 | .038 | -2 | -10 | -11 | -2 | -2.6 |

● RICK KESTER Kester, Richard Lee b: 7/7/46, Iola, Kan. BR/TR, 6', 190 lbs. Deb: 8/18/68

1968	Atl-N	0	0	—	5	0	0	0	0	6¹	8	0	3	9	15.6	5.68	53	.308	.379	0	—	0	-2	-2	-0	0.0
1969	Atl-N	0	0	—	1	0	0	0	0	2	5	1	0	2	22.5	13.50	27	.455	.455	0	—	0	-2	-2	-0	0.0
1970	Atl-N	0	0	—	15	0	0	0	0	32¹	36	3	19	20	15.3	5.57	77	.283	.377	0	.000	-1	-5	-5	-1	-0.2
Total	3	0	0	—	21	0	0	0	0	40²	49	4	22	31	15.7	5.98	68	.299	.382	0	.000	-1	-10	-9	-1	-0.2

● JOHN KILEY Kiley, John Frederick b: 7/1/1859, Dedham, Mass. d: 12/18/40, Norwood, Mass. BL/TL, 5'7", 147 lbs. Deb: 5/1/1884 ♦

| 1891 | Bos-N | 0 | 1 | .000 | 1 | 1 | 0 | 0 | 0 | 8 | 13 | 3 | 5 | 1 | 20.3 | 6.75 | 54 | .351 | .429 | 0 | .000 | -0 | -3 | -3 | 0 | -0.2 |

● FRANK KILLEN Killen, Frank Bissell "Lefty" b: 11/30/1870, Pittsburgh, Pa. d: 12/3/39, Pittsburgh, Pa. BL/TL, 6'1", 200 lbs. Deb: 8/27/1891

| 1899 | Bos-N | 7 | 5 | .583 | 12 | 12 | 11 | 0 | 0 | 99¹ | 108 | 3 | 26 | 23 | 12.4 | 4.26 | 98 | .276 | .326 | 7 | .171 | -2 | -4 | -1 | -0 | -0.3 |
| Total | 10 | 164 | 131 | .556 | 321 | 300 | 253 | 13 | 0 | 2511¹ | 2730 | 55 | 822 | 725 | 13.0 | 3.78 | 109 | .272 | .332 | 241 | .241 | 44 | 104 | 92 | 5 | 12.9 |

● RON KLINE Kline, Ronald Lee b: 3/9/32, Callery, Pa. BR/TR, 6'3", 205 lbs. Deb: 4/21/52

| 1970 | Atl-N | 0 | 0 | — | 5 | 0 | 0 | 0 | 0 | 6¹ | 9 | 4 | 2 | 3 | 15.6 | 7.11 | 60 | .321 | .367 | 0 | — | 0 | -2 | -2 | -0 | -0.1 |
| Total | 17 | 114 | 144 | .442 | 736 | 203 | 44 | 8 | 108 | 2078 | 2113 | 218 | 731 | 989 | 12.5 | 3.75 | 101 | .266 | .331 | 45 | .092 | -28 | 1 | 13 | -5 | 3.7 |

● STEVE KLINE Kline, Steven Jack b: 10/6/47, Wenatchee, Wash. BR/TR, 6'3", 205 lbs. Deb: 7/10/70

| 1977 | Atl-N | 0 | 0 | — | 16 | 0 | 0 | 0 | 0 | 20¹ | 21 | 4 | 12 | 10 | 14.6 | 6.64 | 67 | .259 | .355 | 0 | — | 0 | -6 | -5 | -0 | -0.1 |
| Total | 6 | 43 | 45 | .489 | 129 | 105 | 34 | 6 | 1 | 750¹ | 708 | 61 | 184 | 240 | 10.9 | 3.26 | 101 | .249 | .298 | 21 | .124 | -1 | 14 | 3 | 5 | 1.3 |

● FRED KLOBEDANZ Klobedanz, Frederick Augustus "Duke" b: 6/13/1871, Waterbury, Conn. d: 4/12/40, Waterbury, Conn. BL/TL, 5'11", 190 lbs. Deb: 8/20/1896

1896	Bos-N	6	4	.600	10	9	9	0	0	80²	69	5	31	26	11.9	3.01	151	.229	.316	13	.317	2	12	14	-1	1.5
1897	*Bos-N	26	7	**.788**	38	37	30	2	0	309¹	344	13	125	92	14.3	4.60	97	.279	.357	48	.324	9	-10	-4	-4	0.1
1898	Bos-N	19	10	.655	35	33	25	0	0	270²	281	13	99	51	13.0	3.89	95	.266	.336	27	.213	-0	-6	-1	-0	-0.6
1899	Bos-N	1	4	.200	5	5	4	0	0	33¹	39	2	9	8	13.5	4.86	86	.291	.345	2	.182	-1	-4	-3	1	-0.2
1902	Bos-N	1	0	1.000	1	1	1	0	0	8	9	0	2	4	13.5	1.13	251	.281	.343	1	.500	1	2	2	-0	0.3
Total	5	53	25	.679	89	85	69	2	0	702	742	33	266	181	13.5	4.12	101	.269	.343	91	.277	13	-8	2	-6	1.1

YEAR TM/L	W	L	PCT	G	GS	CG	SH	SV	IP	H	HR	BB	SO	RAT	ERA	ERA+	OAV	OOB	BH	AVG	PB	PR	/A	PD	TPI
● STAN KLOPP Klopp, Stanley Harold "Betz" b: 12/22/10, Womelsdorf, Pa. d: 3/11/80, Robesonia, Pa. BR/TR, 6'1.5", 180 lbs. Deb: 4/30/44																									
1944 Bos-N	1	2	.333	24	0	0	0	0	46^{1}	47	1	33	17	15.5	4.27	89	.272	.388	2	.286	0	-3	-2	-1	-0.2
● ELMER KNETZER Knetzer, Elmer Ellsworth "Baron" b: 7/22/1885, Carrick, Pa. d: 10/3/75, Pittsburgh, Pa. BR/TR, 5'10", 180 lbs. Deb: 9/11/09																									
1916 Bos-N	0	2	.000	2	0	0	0	0	5	11	0	2	2	23.4	7.20	35	.524	.565	0	—	0	-3	-3	1	-0.8
Total 8	69	69	.500	220	134	82	13	6	1267^{1}	1206	30	484	535	12.1	3.15	93	.258	.330	42	.109	-25	-27	-32	2	-6.0
● JACK KNIGHT Knight, Elma Russell b: 1/12/1895, Pittsboro, Miss. d: 7/30/76, San Antonio, Tex. BL/TR, 6', 175 lbs. Deb: 9/20/22																									
1927 Bos-N	0	0	—	3	0	0	0	0	3	6	0	2	0	24.0	15.00	25	.429	.500	0	—	0	-4	-4	1	0.1
Total 4	10	18	.357	72	27	9	0	5	255	382	28	89	49	16.7	6.85	64	.353	.403	22	.216	0	-80	-70	4	-5.7
● ED KONETCHY Konetchy, Edward Joseph "Big Ed" b: 9/3/1885, LaCrosse, Wis. d: 5/27/47, Ft.Worth, Tex. BR/TR, 6'2.5", 195 lbs. Deb: 6/29/07 ◆																									
1918 Bos-N	0	1	.000	1	1	1	0	0	8	14	1	2	3	18.0	6.75	40	.378	.410	103	.236	0	-4	-4	-0	-0.4
Total 3	1	1	.500	3	1	1	0	0	16^{2}	19	1	7	6	14.0	4.32	67	.288	.356	2150	.281	1	-3	-3	-1	0.0
● JIM KONSTANTY Konstanty, Casimir James b: 3/2/17, Strykersville, N.Y. d: 6/11/76, Oneonta, N.Y. BR/TR, 6'1.5", 202 lbs. Deb: 6/18/44																									
1946 Bos-N	0	1	.000	10	1	0	0	0	15^{1}	17	2	7	9	14.1	5.28	65	.283	.358	0	.000	0	-3	-3	1	-0.1
Total 11	66	48	.579	433	36	14	2	74	945^{2}	957	88	269	268	11.7	3.46	112	.268	.320	33	.163	-5	54	44	2	7.0
● DAVE KOSLO Koslo, George Bernard (b: George Bernard Koslowski) b: 3/31/20, Menasha, Wis. d: 12/1/75, Menasha, Wis. BL/TL, 5'11", 180 lbs. Deb: 9/12/41																									
1954 Mil-N	1	1	.500	12	0	0	0	1	17^{1}	13	0	9	7	11.4	3.12	120	.228	.333	0	.000	-0	2	1	-1	0.1
1955 Mil-N	0	1	.000	1	0	0	0	0	0	1	1	0	0	—	∞	—	1.000	1.000	0	—	0	-1	-1	0	-0.1
Total 12	92	107	.462	348	189	74	15	22	1591^{1}	1597	121	538	606	12.2	3.68	105	.260	.321	56	.109	-15	34	32	2	2.4
Team 2	1	2	.333	13	0	0	0	1	17^{1}	14	1	9	7	11.9	3.63	102	.241	.343	0	.000	-0	1	0	-1	0.0
● FABIAN KOWALIK Kowalik, Fabian Lorenz b: 4/22/08, Falls City, Tex. d: 8/14/54, Karnes City, Tex. BR/TR, 5'11", 185 lbs. Deb: 9/4/32																									
1936 Bos-N	0	1	.000	1	1	1	0	0	9	18	0	2	0	20.0	8.00	48	.419	.444	2	.400	1	-4	-4	0	-0.3
Total 3	3	11	.214	51	12	4	0	2	167^{1}	218	10	63	42	15.3	5.43	78	.313	.373	23	.242	-0	-26	-22	-1	-1.9
● LEW KRAUSSE Krausse, Lewis Bernard Jr. b: 4/25/43, Media, Pa. BR/TR, 5'11", 186 lbs. Deb: 6/16/61 F																									
1974 Atl-N	4	3	.571	29	4	0	0	0	66^{2}	65	3	32	27	13.4	4.18	90	.258	.346	2	.333	2	-4	-3	-1	-0.2
Total 12	68	91	.428	321	167	21	5	21	1283^{2}	1205	137	493	721	12.2	4.00	85	.248	.322	47	.133	6	-81	-84	-9	-10.3
● RUBE KROH Kroh, Floyd Myron b: 8/25/1886, Friendship, N.Y. d: 3/17/44, New Orleans, La. BL/TL, 6'2", 186 lbs. Deb: 9/30/06																									
1912 Bos-N	0	0	—	3	1	0	0	0	6^{1}	8	0	6	1	19.9	5.68	63	.364	.500	1	.500	0	-2	-1	0	0.1
Total 6	14	9	.609	36	25	13	3	0	216^{1}	182	3	67	92	10.6	2.29	115	.231	.296	13	.181	-0	9	8	2	1.3
● FRANK LaCORTE LaCorte, Frank Joseph b: 10/13/51, San Jose, Cal. BR/TR, 6'1", 180 lbs. Deb: 9/8/75																									
1975 Atl-N	0	3	.000	3	2	0	0	0	13^{2}	13	1	6	10	12.5	5.27	72	.245	.322	0	.000	-1	-3	-2	0	-0.5
1976 Atl-N	3	12	.200	19	17	1	0	0	105^{1}	97	6	53	79	13.3	4.70	81	.249	.348	3	.091	-2	-14	-11	-0	-1.6
1977 Atl-N	1	8	.111	14	7	0	0	0	37	67	10	29	28	23.8	11.68	38	.394	.488	2	.200	-0	-32	-30	0	-5.3
1978 Atl-N	0	1	.000	2	2	0	0	0	14^{2}	9	0	4	7	8.0	3.68	110	.180	.241	0	.000	-0	-0	1	-0	0.0
1979 Atl-N	0	0	—	6	0	0	0	0	8^{1}	9	2	5	6	15.1	7.56	54	.273	.368	0	.000	-0	-4	-3	-0	0.0
Total 10	23	44	.343	253	32	1	0	26	490	457	49	258	372	13.3	5.01	72	.249	.345	8	.104	-4	-75	-77	-7	-11.2
Team 5	4	24	.143	44	28	1	0	0	179	195	19	97	130	15.1	6.23	63	.281	.375	5	.094	-3	-52	-45	-1	-7.4
● FRANK LaMANNA LaManna, Frank "Hank" b: 8/22/19, Watertown, Pa. d: 9/1/80, Syracuse, N.Y. BR/TR, 6'2.5", 195 lbs. Deb: 4/16/40																									
1940 Bos-N	1	0	1.000	5	1	1	0	0	13^{1}	13	1	8	3	14.2	4.73	79	.271	.375	1	.200	0	-1	-1	0	-0.1
1941 Bos-N	5	4	.556	35	4	0	0	1	72^{2}	77	5	56	23	16.6	5.33	67	.285	.410	9	.281	1	-14	-14	1	-1.4
1942 Bos-N	0	1	.000	5	0	0	0	0	6^{2}	5	1	3	2	10.8	5.40	62	.208	.296	0	.000	-0	-2	-2	-0	-0.3
Total 3	6	5	.545	45	5	1	0	1	92^{2}	95	7	67	28	15.8	5.24	68	.278	.398	10	.256	1	-17	-17	1	-1.8
● HENRY LAMPE Lampe, Henry Joseph b: 9/19/1872, Boston, Mass. d: 9/16/36, Dorchester, Mass. BR/TL, 5'11.5", 175 lbs. Deb: 5/14/1894																									
1894 Bos-N	0	1	.000	2	1	0	0	0	5^{1}	17	5	7	1	40.5	11.81	48	.531	.615	0	.000	-0	-4	-4	0	-0.4
Total 2	0	3	.000	9	4	2	0	0	49^{1}	85	8	40	19	23.0	8.03	61	.373	.468	2	.111	-1	-17	-17	0	-0.9
● WALT LANFRANCONI Lanfranconi, Walter Oswald b: 11/9/16, Barre, Vt. d: 8/18/86, Barre, Vt. BR/TR, 5'7.5", 155 lbs. Deb: 9/12/41																									
1947 Bos-N	4	4	.500	36	4	1	0	1	64	65	2	27	18	12.9	2.95	132	.272	.346	0	.000	-1	**8**	**7**	1	0.8
Total 2	4	5	.444	38	5	1	0	1	70	72	2	29	19	13.0	2.96	131	.273	.345	0	.000	-1	8	7	1	0.8
● JOHNNY LANNING Lanning, John Young "Tobacco Chewin' Johnny" b: 9/6/10, Asheville, N.C. d: 11/8/89, Asheville, N.C. BR/TR, 6'1", 185 lbs. Deb: 4/17/36 F																									
1936 Bos-N	7	11	.389	28	20	3	1	0	153	154	9	55	33	12.3	3.65	105	.263	.326	7	.135	-2	6	3	-2	0.0
1937 Bos-N	5	7	.417	32	11	4	1	2	116^{2}	107	10	40	37	11.4	3.93	91	.236	.300	4	.121	-1	-0	-5	-0	-0.5
1938 Bos-N	8	7	.533	32	18	4	1	0	138	146	5	52	39	13.0	3.72	92	.267	.332	9	.188	-1	1	-4	-1	-0.6
1939 Bos-N	5	6	.455	37	6	3	0	4	129	120	6	53	45	12.2	3.42	108	.252	.329	6	.143	-1	7	4	0	0.2
1947 Bos-N	0	0	—	3	0	0	0	0	3^{2}	4	0	6	0	24.5	9.82	40	.400	.625	0	—	0	-2	-2	0	0.0
Total 11	58	60	.492	278	104	30	4	13	1071	1078	55	358	295	12.1	3.58	101	.261	.321	47	.146	-7	19	5	-1	1.1
Team 5	25	31	.446	132	55	14	3	6	540^{1}	531	30	206	154	12.3	3.71	98	.256	.325	26	.149	-5	12	-4	-2	-0.9
● GENE LANSING Lansing, Eugene Hewitt "Jigger" b: 1/11/1898, Albany, N.Y. d: 1/18/45, Rensselaer, N.Y. BR/TR, 6'1", 185 lbs. Deb: 4/27/22																									
1922 Bos-N	0	1	.000	15	1	0	0	0	40^{2}	46	1	22	14	15.0	5.98	67	.301	.389	0	.000	-1	-8	-9	-0	-0.3
● FRANK LARY Lary, Frank Strong "Mule" or "The Yankee Killer" b: 4/10/30, Northport, Ala. BR/TR, 5'11", 180 lbs. Deb: 9/14/54 F																									
1964 Mil-N	1	0	1.000	5	2	0	0	0	12^{1}	15	4	0	4	10.9	4.38	80	.306	.306	0	.000	-0	-1	-1	1	0.0
Total 12	128	116	.525	350	292	126	21	11	2162^{1}	2123	197	616	1099	11.8	3.49	113	.257	.316	130	.177	5	95	112	3	13.9
● AL LAWSON Lawson, Alfred William b: 3/24/1869, London, England d: 11/29/54, San Antonio, Tex. BR/TR, 5'11", 161 lbs. Deb: 5/13/1890																									
1890 Bos-N	0	1	.000	1	1	1	0	0	9	12	0	4	1	16.0	4.00	94	.308	.372	0	.000	-0	-0	-0	0	0.0
● BOB LAWSON Lawson, Robert Baker b: 8/23/1876, Brookneal, Va. d: 10/28/52, Durham, N.C. BR/TR, 5'10", 170 lbs. Deb: 5/7/01																									
1901 Bos-N	2	2	.500	6	4	4	0	0	46	45	0	28	12	14.9	3.33	109	.254	.365	4	.148	-0	-0	1	1	0.2
Total 2	2	4	.333	9	6	5	0	0	59	66	0	31	17	15.6	3.66	100	.281	.376	5	.152	-1	-2	-0	1	0.0
● JACK LEARY Leary, John J. b: 1858, New Haven, Conn. TL, 5'11", 186 lbs. Deb: 8/21/1880 ◆																									
1880 Bos-N	0	1	.000	1	1	0	0	0	3	8	0	0	1	24.0	15.00	15	.727	.727	0	.000	-0	-4	-4	0	-0.8
Total 4	3	9	.250	14	12	8	0	0	94^{2}	123	1	20	23	13.6	4.56	59	.301	.333	125	.232	-2	-21	-20	-0	-2.0
● BILL LEE Lee, William Crutcher "Big Bill" b: 10/21/09, Plaquemine, La. d: 6/15/77, Plaquemine, La. BR/TR, 6'3", 195 lbs. Deb: 4/29/34																									
1945 Bos-N	6	3	.667	16	13	6	1	0	106^{1}	112	6	36	12	12.5	2.79	137	.279	.338	4	.129	-1	12	12	1	1.0
1946 Bos-N	10	9	.526	25	21	8	0	0	140	148	7	45	32	12.5	4.18	82	.273	.330	8	.170	-1	-12	-12	1	-1.4
Total 14	169	157	.518	462	378	182	29	13	2864	2953	138	893	998	12.2	3.54	106	.266	.322	165	.168	-10	78	66	14	6.2
Team 2	16	12	.571	41	34	14	1	0	246^{1}	260	13	81	44	12.5	3.58	101	.275	.333	12	.154	-1	-0	1	2	-0.4
● CHARLIE LEIBRANDT Leibrandt, Charles Louis b: 10/4/56, Chicago, Ill. BR/TL, 6'3", 200 lbs. Deb: 9/17/79																									
1990 Atl-N	9	11	.450	24	24	5	2	0	162^{1}	164	9	35	76	11.3	3.16	128	.261	.304	9	.180	1	11	16	1	2.1
1991 *Atl-N	15	13	.536	36	36	1	1	0	229^{2}	212	18	56	128	10.7	3.49	111	.245	.294	3	.043	-4	5	10	4	1.2

YEAR TM/L	W	L	PCT	G	GS	CG	SH	SV	IP	H	HR	BB	SO	RAT	ERA	ERA+	OAV	OOB	BH	AVG	PB	PR	/A	PD	TPI
1992 *Atl-N	15	7	.682	32	31	5	2	0	193	191	9	42	104	11.1	3.36	109	.258	.302	7	.121	-1	3	6	3	0.9
Total 14	140	119	.541	394	346	52	18	2	2308	2390	172	656	1121	12.0	3.71	108	.268	.321	32	.120	-5	60	77	25	10.4
Team 3	39	31	.557	92	91	11	5	0	585	567	36	133	308	11.0	3.35	115	.254	.300	19	.107	-5	20	32	8	4.2

● **DENNY LEMASTER** Lemaster, Denver Clayton b: 2/25/39, Corona, Cal. BR/TL, 6'1", 185 lbs. Deb: 7/15/62

YEAR TM/L	W	L	PCT	G	GS	CG	SH	SV	IP	H	HR	BB	SO	RAT	ERA	ERA+	OAV	OOB	BH	AVG	PB	PR	/A	PD	TPI
1962 Mil-N	3	4	.429	17	12	4	1	0	86^2	75	11	32	69	11.4	3.01	126	.233	.308	4	.121	-1	9	8	-2	0.3
1963 Mil-N	11	14	.440	46	31	10	1	1	237	199	30	85	190	10.8	3.04	106	.227	.296	14	.189	3	7	5	-3	0.5
1964 Mil-N	17	11	.607	39	35	9	3	1	221	216	27	75	185	12.0	4.15	85	.252	.315	9	.134	0	-15	-15	0	-1.8
1965 Mil-N	7	13	.350	32	23	4	1	0	146^1	140	12	58	111	12.4	4.43	80	.251	.325	4	.089	-1	-14	-15	-0	-2.0
1966 Atl-N	11	8	.579	27	27	10	3	0	171	170	25	41	139	11.2	3.74	97	.258	.303	7	.119	-1	-2	-2	-2	-0.5
1967 Atl-N†	9	9	.500	31	31	8	2	0	215^1	184	20	72	148	10.8	3.34	99	.229	.295	7	.104	-2	1	-1	-1	-0.3
Total 11	90	105	.462	357	249	66	14	8	1787^2	1703	184	600	1305	11.7	3.58	96	.249	.312	72	.130	1	-18	-28	-13	-4.8
Team 6	58	59	.496	192	159	45	11	2	1077^1	984	125	363	842	11.4	3.63	95	.242	.306	45	.130	-2	-16	-20	-7	-3.8

● **MAX LEON** Leon, Maximino (Molino) b: 2/4/50, Pozo Hondo, Aculo, Mexico BR/TR, 6', 170 lbs. Deb: 7/18/73

YEAR TM/L	W	L	PCT	G	GS	CG	SH	SV	IP	H	HR	BB	SO	RAT	ERA	ERA+	OAV	OOB	BH	AVG	PB	PR	/A	PD	TPI
1973 Atl-N	2	2	.500	12	1	1	0	0	27	30	6	9	18	14.0	5.33	74	.278	.350	2	.286	0	-5	-4	-0	-0.6
1974 Atl-N	4	7	.364	34	2	1	1	3	75	68	5	14	38	10.0	2.64	143	.242	.280	2	.133	-1	8	9	1	1.4
1975 Atl-N	2	1	.667	50	1	0	0	6	85	90	5	33	53	13.8	4.13	91	.274	.352	3	.333	1	-5	-3	1	0.0
1976 Atl-N	2	4	.333	30	0	0	0	3	36	32	2	15	16	12.3	2.75	138	.234	.318	0	.000	-0	3	4	-1	0.7
1977 Atl-N	4	4	.500	31	9	0	0	1	81^2	89	9	25	44	13.6	3.97	112	.280	.349	6	.316	1	-1	4	0	0.5
1978 Atl-N	0	0	—	5	0	0	0	0	5^2	6	1	4	1	17.5	6.35	64	.273	.407	0	—	0	-2	-1	-0	0.0
Total 6	14	18	.438	162	13	2	1	13	310^1	315	28	100	170	12.7	3.71	107	.264	.332	13	.250	1	-1	9	1	2.0

● **DIXIE LEVERETT** Leverett, Gorham Vance b: 3/29/1894, Georgetown, Tex. d: 2/20/57, Beaverton, Ore. BR/TR, 5'11", 190 lbs. Deb: 5/6/22

YEAR TM/L	W	L	PCT	G	GS	CG	SH	SV	IP	H	HR	BB	SO	RAT	ERA	ERA+	OAV	OOB	BH	AVG	PB	PR	/A	PD	TPI
1929 Bos-N	3	7	.300	24	12	3	0	1	97^2	135	5	30	28	15.7	6.36	74	.339	.393	6	.188	-0	-18	-18	-0	-1.6
Total 5	29	34	.460	122	77	33	4	6	637	725	25	221	193	13.6	4.51	92	.291	.353	50	.234	6	-25	-27	-1	-0.8

● **TED LEWIS** Lewis, Edward Morgan "Parson" b: 12/25/1872, Machynlleth, Wales d: 5/24/36, Durham, N.H. BR/TR, 5'10.5", 158 lbs. Deb: 7/6/1896

YEAR TM/L	W	L	PCT	G	GS	CG	SH	SV	IP	H	HR	BB	SO	RAT	ERA	ERA+	OAV	OOB	BH	AVG	PB	PR	/A	PD	TPI
1896 Bos-N	1	4	.200	6	5	4	0	0	41^2	37	2	27	12	13.8	3.24	140	.236	.348	2	.111	-2	5	6	1	0.4
1897 *Bos-N	21	12	.636	38	34	30	2	1	290	316	11	125	65	14.0	3.85	116	.275	.351	28	.248	-2	15	20	-5	1.2
1898 Bos-N	26	8	**.765**	41	33	29	1	2	313^1	267	9	109	72	11.1	2.90	127	.229	.300	37	.282	4	25	28	-1	2.9
1899 Bos-N	17	11	.607	29	25	23	2	0	234^2	245	10	73	60	12.5	3.49	119	.269	.328	25	.260	0	10	17	-4	1.4
1900 Bos-N	13	12	.520	30	22	19	1	0	209	215	11	86	66	13.1	4.13	100	.265	.339	10	.137	-4	-10	-0	-3	-0.6
Total 6	94	64	.595	183	153	136	7	4	1405	1379	57	511	378	12.4	3.53	113	.255	.324	123	.223	-5	49	71	-13	4.9
Team 5	78	47	.624	144	119	105	6	3	1088^2	1080	43	420	275	12.7	3.53	117	.258	.330	102	.237	-3	44	71	-12	5.3

● **DON LIDDLE** Liddle, Donald Eugene b: 5/25/25, Mt.Carmel, Ill. BL/TL, 5'10", 165 lbs. Deb: 4/17/53

YEAR TM/L	W	L	PCT	G	GS	CG	SH	SV	IP	H	HR	BB	SO	RAT	ERA	ERA+	OAV	OOB	BH	AVG	PB	PR	/A	PD	TPI
1953 Mil-N	7	6	.538	31	15	4	0	2	128^2	119	6	55	63	12.3	3.08	127	.248	.328	3	.088	-2	17	12	-1	0.9
Total 4	28	18	.609	117	54	13	3	4	427^2	397	42	203	198	12.8	3.75	106	.250	.339	17	.152	1	16	10	-2	0.7

● **DEREK LILLIQUIST** Lilliquist, Derek Jansen b: 2/20/66, Winter Park, Fla. BL/TL, 6', 200 lbs. Deb: 4/13/89

YEAR TM/L	W	L	PCT	G	GS	CG	SH	SV	IP	H	HR	BB	SO	RAT	ERA	ERA+	OAV	OOB	BH	AVG	PB	PR	/A	PD	TPI
1989 Atl-N	8	10	.444	32	30	0	0	0	165^2	202	16	34	79	12.9	3.97	92	.301	.337	12	.190	0	-9	-6	-1	-0.7
1990 Atl-N	2	8	.200	12	11	0	0	0	61^2	75	10	19	34	13.9	6.28	64	.301	.353	8	.348	4	-17	-15	-1	-1.9
Total 7	25	34	.424	257	52	1	1	17	480	527	58	134	260	12.6	4.11	97	.282	.333	23	.213	4	-12	-7	-4	-0.3
Team 2	10	18	.357	44	41	0	0	0	227^1	277	26	53	113	13.2	4.59	82	.301	.341	20	.233	4	-26	-21	-2	-2.6

● **VIVE LINDAMAN** Lindaman, Vivan Alexander b: 10/28/1877, Charles City, Iowa d: 2/13/27, Charles City, Iowa BR/TR, 6'1", 200 lbs. Deb: 4/14/06

YEAR TM/L	W	L	PCT	G	GS	CG	SH	SV	IP	H	HR	BB	SO	RAT	ERA	ERA+	OAV	OOB	BH	AVG	PB	PR	/A	PD	TPI
1906 Bos-N	12	23	.343	39	37	32	2	0	307^1	303	4	90	115	11.8	2.43	111	.264	.324	14	.132	-2	7	9	-2	0.7
1907 Bos-N	11	15	.423	34	28	24	2	1	260	252	10	108	90	13.0	3.63	70	.265	.349	11	.122	-2	-34	-31	-2	-3.5
1908 Bos-N	12	16	.429	43	30	21	2	1	270^2	246	7	70	68	10.8	2.36	102	.249	.306	15	.176	0	0	2	-3	-0.2
1909 Bos-N	1	6	.143	15	6	6	1	0	66	75	1	28	13	14.2	4.64	61	.299	.371	6	.273	1	-15	-13	-1	-1.4
Total 4	36	60	.375	131	101	83	7	2	904	876	22	296	286	12.0	2.92	88	.263	.329	46	.152	-3	-41	-34	-8	-4.4

● **ERNIE LINDEMANN** Lindemann, Ernest b: 6/10/1883, New York, N.Y. d: 12/27/51, Brooklyn, N.Y. BR/TR, Deb: 6/28/07

YEAR TM/L	W	L	PCT	G	GS	CG	SH	SV	IP	H	HR	BB	SO	RAT	ERA	ERA+	OAV	OOB	BH	AVG	PB	PR	/A	PD	TPI
1907 Bos-N	0	0	—	1	1	0	0	0	6^1	6	0	4	3	14.2	5.68	45	.286	.400	1	.500	0	-2	-2	0	0.1

● **CARL LINDQUIST** Lindquist, Carl Emil b: 5/9/19, Morris Run, Pa. BR/TR, 6'2", 185 lbs. Deb: 9/27/43

YEAR TM/L	W	L	PCT	G	GS	CG	SH	SV	IP	H	HR	BB	SO	RAT	ERA	ERA+	OAV	OOB	BH	AVG	PB	PR	/A	PD	TPI
1943 Bos-N	0	2	.000	2	2	0	0	0	13	17	3	4	1	14.5	6.23	55	.315	.362	0	.000	-1	-4	-4	0	-0.5
1944 Bos-N	0	0	—	5	0	0	0	0	8^2	8	1	2	4	10.4	3.12	123	.222	.263	0	.000	-0	0	1	-0	0.0
Total 2	0	2	.000	7	2	0	0	0	21^2	25	4	6	5	12.9	4.98	72	.278	.323	0	.000	-1	-4	-3	-0	-0.5

● **DICK LITTLEFIELD** Littlefield, Richard Bernard b: 3/18/26, Detroit, Mich. BL/TL, 6', 180 lbs. Deb: 7/7/50

YEAR TM/L	W	L	PCT	G	GS	CG	SH	SV	IP	H	HR	BB	SO	RAT	ERA	ERA+	OAV	OOB	BH	AVG	PB	PR	/A	PD	TPI
1958 Mil-N	0	1	.000	4	0	0	0	1	6^1	7	2	1	7	12.8	4.26	83	.280	.333	0	—	0	-0	-1	-0	-0.1
Total 9	33	54	.379	243	83	16	2	9	761^2	750	91	413	495	13.9	4.71	86	.260	.355	28	.145	-5	-65	-56	-9	-7.2

● **BOB LOGAN** Logan, Robert Dean "Lefty" b: 2/10/10, Thompson, Neb. d: 5/20/78, Indianapolis, Ind. BR/TL, 5'10", 170 lbs. Deb: 4/18/35

YEAR TM/L	W	L	PCT	G	GS	CG	SH	SV	IP	H	HR	BB	SO	RAT	ERA	ERA+	OAV	OOB	BH	AVG	PB	PR	/A	PD	TPI
1945 Bos-N	7	11	.389	34	25	5	1	1	187	213	9	53	53	12.9	3.18	121	.283	.331	13	.213	1	13	14	0	1.4
Total 5	7	15	.318	57	25	5	1	4	222^2	245	9	81	67	13.3	3.15	122	.277	.339	13	.200	1	16	17	0	1.3

● **RED LONG** Long, Nelson b: 9/28/1876, Burlington, Ont., Canada d: 8/11/29, Hamilton, Ont., Can BR/TR, 6'1", 190 lbs. Deb: 9/11/02

YEAR TM/L	W	L	PCT	G	GS	CG	SH	SV	IP	H	HR	BB	SO	RAT	ERA	ERA+	OAV	OOB	BH	AVG	PB	PR	/A	PD	TPI
1902 Bos-N	0	0	—	1	1	1	0	0	8	4	0	3	5	9.0	1.13	251	.148	.258	0	.000	-0	1	2	-0	0.0

● **TOM LOVETT** Lovett, Thomas Joseph b: 12/7/1863, Providence, R.I. d: 3/19/28, Providence, R.I. BR , 5'8", 162 lbs. Deb: 6/4/1885

YEAR TM/L	W	L	PCT	G	GS	CG	SH	SV	IP	H	HR	BB	SO	RAT	ERA	ERA+	OAV	OOB	BH	AVG	PB	PR	/A	PD	TPI
1894 Bos-N	8	6	.571	15	13	10	0	0	104	155	12	36	23	16.8	5.97	95	.341	.394	7	.143	-5	-7	-3	-1	-0.8
Total 6	88	59	.599	162	149	132	9	1	1305^1	1341	48	444	439	12.7	3.94	94	.257	.322	106	.185	-13	-28	-34	-5	-4.1

● **BOBBY LOWE** Lowe, Robert Lincoln "Link" b: 7/10/1868, Pittsburgh, Pa. d: 12/8/51, Detroit, Mich. BR/TR, 5'10", 150 lbs. Deb: 4/19/1890 M◆

YEAR TM/L	W	L	PCT	G	GS	CG	SH	SV	IP	H	HR	BB	SO	RAT	ERA	ERA+	OAV	OOB	BH	AVG	PB	PR	/A	PD	TPI
1891 Bos-N	0	0	—	1	0	0	0	0	1	3	0	1	0	36.0	9.00	41	.500	.571	129	.260	0	-1	-1	-0	0.0

● **RED LUCAS** Lucas, Charles Frederick "The Nashville Narcissus"
b: 4/28/02, Columbia, Tenn. d: 7/9/86, Nashville, Tenn. BL/TR, 5'9.5", 170 lbs. Deb: 4/19/23 ◆

YEAR TM/L	W	L	PCT	G	GS	CG	SH	SV	IP	H	HR	BB	SO	RAT	ERA	ERA+	OAV	OOB	BH	AVG	PB	PR	/A	PD	TPI
1924 Bos-N	1	4	.200	27	4	1	0	0	83^2	112	5	18	30	14.6	5.16	74	.332	.377	11	.333	2	-12	-12	1	-0.4
Total 15	157	135	.538	396	301	204	22	7	2542	2736	136	455	602	11.4	3.72	107	.275	.308	404	.281	98	92	77	-9	18.5

● **RICK LUECKEN** Luecken, Richard Fred b: 11/15/60, McAllen, Tex. BR/TR, 6'6", 210 lbs. Deb: 6/6/89

YEAR TM/L	W	L	PCT	G	GS	CG	SH	SV	IP	H	HR	BB	SO	RAT	ERA	ERA+	OAV	OOB	BH	AVG	PB	PR	/A	PD	TPI
1990 Atl-N	1	4	.200	36	0	0	0	1	53	73	5	30	35	18.0	5.77	70	.336	.424	1	.333	1	-12	-10	0	-0.9
Total 2	3	5	.375	56	0	0	0	2	77^2	98	9	44	51	16.8	5.10	78	.316	.406	1	.333	1	-11	-10	-0	-0.8

● **DOLF LUQUE** Luque, Adolfo Domingo De Guzman "The Pride Of Havana" b: 8/4/1890, Havana, Cuba d: 7/3/57, Havana, Cuba BR/TR, 5'7", 160 lbs. Deb: 5/20/14 C

YEAR TM/L	W	L	PCT	G	GS	CG	SH	SV	IP	H	HR	BB	SO	RAT	ERA	ERA+	OAV	OOB	BH	AVG	PB	PR	/A	PD	TPI
1914 Bos-N	0	1	.000	2	1	1	0	0	8^2	5	0	4	1	9.3	4.15	66	.167	.265	0	.000	-0	-1	-1	-1	-0.2
1915 Bos-N	0	0	—	2	1	0	0	0	5	6	0	4	3	18.0	3.60	72	.286	.400	0	.000	-0	-0	-1	0	0.0
Total 20	194	179	.520	550	365	206	26	28	3220^1	3231	113	918	1130	11.7	3.24	117	.265	.318	237	.227	37	245	200	13	26.3
Team 2	0	1	.000	4	2	1	0	0	13^2	11	0	8	4	12.5	3.95	68	.216	.322	0	.000	-1	-2	-2	-0	-0.2

● **AL LYONS** Lyons, Albert Harold b: 7/18/18, St.Joseph, Mo. d: 12/20/65, Inglewood, Cal. BR/TR, 6'2", 195 lbs. Deb: 4/19/44

YEAR TM/L	W	L	PCT	G	GS	CG	SH	SV	IP	H	HR	BB	SO	RAT	ERA	ERA+	OAV	OOB	BH	AVG	PB	PR	/A	PD	TPI
1948 Bos-N	1	0	1.000	7	0	0	0	0	12^2	17	1	8	5	17.8	7.82	49	.309	.397	2	.167	0	-5	-6	1	-0.2
Total 4	3	3	.500	39	1	0	0	0	100	125	9	59	46	16.9	6.30	59	.307	.400	17	.293	5	-29	-28	2	-1.2

● DANNY MacFAYDEN MacFayden, Daniel Knowles "Deacon Danny" b: 6/10/05, N.Truro, Mass. d: 8/26/72, Brunswick, Me. BR/TR, 5'11", 170 lbs. Deb: 8/25/26

YEAR TM/L	W	L	PCT	G	GS	CG	SH	SV	IP	H	HR	BB	SO	RAT	ERA	ERA+	OAV	OOB	BH	AVG	PB	PR	/A	PD	TPI
1935 Bos-N	5	13	.278	28	20	7	1	0	151^2	200	8	34	46	14.2	5.10	74	.314	.354	8	.157	-1	-18	-22	2	-2.1
1936 Bos-N	17	13	.567	37	31	21	2	0	266^2	268	5	66	86	11.4	2.87	134	.259	.307	8	.096	-5	34	29	3	2.7
1937 Bos-N	14	14	.500	32	32	16	2	0	246	250	5	60	70	11.4	2.93	123	.268	.313	13	.157	-2	27	18	1	1.8
1938 Bos-N	14	9	.609	29	29	19	5	0	219^2	208	6	64	58	11.3	2.95	116	.247	.304	9	.117	-4	20	12	-1	0.6
1939 Bos-N	8	14	.364	33	28	8	0	2	191^2	221	11	59	46	13.3	3.90	95	.291	.345	12	.179	-1	0	-4	1	-0.4
1943 Bos-N	2	1	.667	10	1	0	0	0	21^1	31	1	9	5	17.3	5.91	58	.344	.410	1	.250	0	-6	-6	-0	-0.8
Total 17	132	159	.454	465	332	158	18	9	2706	2981	112	872	797	13.0	3.96	101	.281	.340	129	.142	-34	58	11	10	0.1
Team 6	60	64	.484	169	141	71	10	2	1097	1178	36	292	311	12.2	3.45	106	.274	.324	51	.140	-13	58	26	6	1.8

● KEN MacKENZIE MacKenzie, Kenneth Purvis b: 3/10/34, Gore Bay, Ont., Can. BR/TL, 6', 185 lbs. Deb: 5/2/60

YEAR TM/L	W	L	PCT	G	GS	CG	SH	SV	IP	H	HR	BB	SO	RAT	ERA	ERA+	OAV	OOB	BH	AVG	PB	PR	/A	PD	TPI
1960 Mil-N	0	1	.000	9	0	0	0	0	8^1	9	2	3	9	13.0	6.48	53	.281	.343	0	.000	-0	-3	-3	-0	-0.3
1961 Mil-N	0	1	.000	5	0	0	0	0	7	8	1	2	5	14.1	5.14	73	.296	.367	0	.000	-0	-1	-1	0	-0.1
Total 6	8	10	.444	129	1	0	0	5	208^1	231	33	63	142	13.0	4.80	78	.278	.334	4	.111	-2	-27	-24	-1	-2.1
Team 2	0	2	.000	14	0	0	0	0	15^1	17	3	5	14	13.5	5.87	61	.288	.354	0	.000	-0	-3	-4	0	-0.4

● MAX MACON Macon, Max Cullen b: 10/14/15, Pensacola, Fla. d: 8/5/89, Jupiter, Fla. BL/TL, 6'3", 175 lbs. Deb: 4/21/38 ♦

YEAR TM/L	W	L	PCT	G	GS	CG	SH	SV	IP	H	HR	BB	SO	RAT	ERA	ERA+	OAV	OOB	BH	AVG	PB	PR	/A	PD	TPI
1944 Bos-N	0	0	—	1	0	0	0	0	3	10	2	1	1	33.0	21.00	18	.556	.579	100	.273	0	-6	-6	0	0.0
1947 Bos-N	0	0	—	1	0	0	0	0	2	1	0	1	1	9.0	0.00	—	.167	.286	0	.000	-0	1	1	0	0.0
Total 6	17	19	.472	81	29	9	2	3	297^1	307	20	128	90	13.5	4.24	85	.267	.345	133	.265	5	-23	-21	1	-2.9
Team 2	0	0	—	2	0	0	0	0	5	11	2	2	2	23.4	12.60	31	.458	.500	100	.272	0	-5	-5	0	0.0

● HARRY MacPHERSON MacPherson, Harry William b: 7/10/26, N.Andover, Mass. BR/TR, 5'10", 150 lbs. Deb: 8/14/44

YEAR TM/L	W	L	PCT	G	GS	CG	SH	SV	IP	H	HR	BB	SO	RAT	ERA	ERA+	OAV	OOB	BH	AVG	PB	PR	/A	PD	TPI
1944 Bos-N	0	0	—	1	0	0	0	0	1	0	0	1	1	9.0	0.00	—	.000	.250	0	—	0	0	0	0	0.0

● KID MADDEN Madden, Michael Joseph b: 10/22/1866, Portland, Me. d: 3/16/1896, Portland, Maine TL, 5'7.5", 130 lbs. Deb: 5/6/1887

YEAR TM/L	W	L	PCT	G	GS	CG	SH	SV	IP	H	HR	BB	SO	RAT	ERA	ERA+	OAV	OOB	BH	AVG	PB	PR	/A	PD	TPI
1887 Bos-N	21	14	.600	37	37	36	3	0	321	317	20	122	81	12.9	3.79	107	.251	.327	32	.242	4	10	10	-2	0.9
1888 Bos-N	7	11	.389	20	18	17	1	0	165	142	6	24	53	9.9	2.95	97	.228	.273	11	.164	-2	-2	-2	1	-0.3
1889 Bos-N	10	10	.500	22	19	18	1	1	178	194	7	71	64	14.2	4.40	95	.269	.348	25	.291	2	-8	-5	0	-0.2
Total 5	54	50	.519	122	109	97	7	2	958	987	41	336	284	13.2	3.92	97	.259	.332	106	.245	10	-15	-11	4	-0.1
Team 3	38	35	.521	79	74	71	5	1	664	653	33	217	198	12.5	3.74	101	.251	.320	68	.239	5	1	3	-1	0.4

● GREG MADDUX Maddux, Gregory Alan b: 4/14/66, San Angelo, Tex. BR/TR, 6', 150 lbs. Deb: 9/3/86 F

YEAR TM/L	W	L	PCT	G	GS	CG	SH	SV	IP	H	HR	BB	SO	RAT	ERA	ERA+	OAV	OOB	BH	AVG	PB	PR	/A	PD	TPI
1993 *Atl-N	20	10	.667	36	36	**8**	1	0	**267**	228	14	52	197	**9.6**	**2.36**	**170**	.232	**.274**	15	.165	-1	**50**	**49**	7	6.1
1994 Atl-N★	**16**	6	.727	25	25	**10**	**3**	0	**202**	150	4	31	156	**8.3**	**1.56**	**272**	**.207**	**.245**	14	.222	2	**60**	**60**	3	**7.3**
1995 *Atl-N☆	**19**	2	**.905**	28	28	**10**	**3**	0	**209^2**	147	8	23	181	**7.5**	**1.63**	**259**	.197	**.225**	11	.153	-0	**59**	**61**	6	**6.7**
Total 10	150	93	.617	301	297	70	20	0	2120^2	1877	108	561	1471	10.6	2.88	137	.238	.294	130	.182	6	216	250	46	33.4
Team 3	55	18	.753	89	89	28	7	0	678^2	525	26	106	534	8.6	1.90	219	.214	.251	40	.177	1	169	170	15	20.1

● MICKEY MAHLER Mahler, Michael James b: 7/30/52, Montgomery, Ala. BB/TL, 6'3", 189 lbs. Deb: 9/13/77 F

YEAR TM/L	W	L	PCT	G	GS	CG	SH	SV	IP	H	HR	BB	SO	RAT	ERA	ERA+	OAV	OOB	BH	AVG	PB	PR	/A	PD	TPI
1977 Atl-N	1	2	.333	5	5	0	0	0	23	31	4	9	14	16.0	6.26	71	.326	.390	3	.500	2	-6	-5	-0	-0.4
1978 Atl-N	4	11	.267	34	21	1	0	0	134^2	130	16	66	92	13.6	4.68	87	.255	.349	4	.098	-2	-16	-9	-1	-1.3
1979 Atl-N	5	11	.313	26	18	1	0	0	100	123	11	47	71	15.6	5.85	69	.304	.381	3	.111	-1	-24	-20	-0	-2.9
Total 8	14	32	.304	122	58	3	1	4	406	429	40	190	262	14.1	4.68	86	.274	.359	13	.144	-1	-41	-29	-3	-3.3
Team 3	10	24	.294	65	44	2	0	0	257^2	284	31	122	177	14.6	5.27	77	.282	.365	10	.135	-2	-46	-34	-2	-4.6

● RICK MAHLER Mahler, Richard Keith b: 8/5/53, Austin, Tex. BR/TR, 6'1", 202 lbs. Deb: 4/20/79 F

YEAR TM/L	W	L	PCT	G	GS	CG	SH	SV	IP	H	HR	BB	SO	RAT	ERA	ERA+	OAV	OOB	BH	AVG	PB	PR	/A	PD	TPI
1979 Atl-N	0	0	—	15	0	0	0	0	22	28	4	11	12	16.0	6.14	66	.311	.386	1	.500	0	-6	-5	-0	0.0
1980 Atl-N	0	0	—	2	0	0	0	0	3^2	2	0	0	1	4.9	2.45	152	.154	.154	0	—	0	0	1	0	0.0
1981 Atl-N	8	6	.571	34	14	1	0	2	112^1	109	5	43	54	12.3	2.80	128	.258	.328	4	.148	-1	9	10	1	1.2
1982 *Atl-N	9	10	.474	39	33	5	2	0	205^1	213	18	62	105	12.1	4.21	89	.272	.327	11	.190	2	-14	-11	2	-0.6
1983 Atl-N	0	0	—	10	0	0	0	0	14^1	16	0	9	7	15.7	5.02	77	.296	.397	0	.000	-0	-2	-2	-0	0.0
1984 Atl-N	13	10	.565	38	29	9	1	0	222	209	13	62	106	11.1	3.12	123	.251	.305	21	.296	5	12	18	2	2.6
1985 Atl-N	17	15	.531	39	39	6	1	0	266^2	272	24	79	107	11.9	3.48	111	.268	.322	14	.156	-1	3	11	1	1.3
1986 Atl-N	14	18	.438	39	39	7	1	0	237^2	283	25	95	137	14.4	4.88	81	.301	.367	16	.193	2	-31	-24	2	-2.6
1987 Atl-N	8	13	.381	39	28	3	1	0	197	212	24	85	95	13.7	4.98	87	.283	.357	11	.169	1	-20	-14	2	-1.0
1988 Atl-N	9	16	.360	39	34	5	0	0	249	279	17	42	131	11.9	3.69	100	.282	.317	9	.125	-2	-7	-0	1	-0.1
1991 Atl-N	1	1	.500	13	2	0	0	0	28^2	33	2	13	10	15.1	5.65	69	.282	.364	1	.200	0	-6	-6	0	-0.3
Total 13	96	111	.464	392	271	43	9	6	1951^1	2069	165	606	952	12.5	3.99	96	.275	.332	104	.179	7	-77	-33	10	-0.5
Team 11	79	89	.470	307	218	36	6	2	1558^2	1656	132	501	765	12.6	4.00	97	.276	.334	88	.185	7	-61	-23	10	0.5

● MIKE MAHONEY Mahoney, George W. "Big Mike" b: 12/5/1873, Boston, Mass. d: 1/3/40, Boston, Mass. BR, 6'4", 220 lbs. Deb: 5/18/1897 ♦

YEAR TM/L	W	L	PCT	G	GS	CG	SH	SV	IP	H	HR	BB	SO	RAT	ERA	ERA+	OAV	OOB	BH	AVG	PB	PR	/A	PD	TPI
1897 Bos-N	0	0	—	1	0	0	0	0	1	3	0	1	1	36.0	18.00	25	.500	.571	1	.500	0	-2	-2	0	0.0

● WILLARD MAINS Mains, Willard Eben "Grasshopper" b: 7/7/1868, N.Windham, Maine d: 5/23/23, Bridgton, Maine TR, 6'2", 190 lbs. Deb: 8/3/1888

YEAR TM/L	W	L	PCT	G	GS	CG	SH	SV	IP	H	HR	BB	SO	RAT	ERA	ERA+	OAV	OOB	BH	AVG	PB	PR	/A	PD	TPI
1896 Bos-N	3	2	.600	8	5	3	0	1	42^2	43	1	31	13	16.0	5.48	83	.261	.384	6	.273	-0	-5	-4	-0	-0.4
Total 3	16	17	.485	42	32	24	0	1	267^2	261	5	154	96	14.5	3.53	118	.249	.353	32	.258	1	8	19	3	1.8

● JOHN MALARKEY Malarkey, John S. "Liz" b: 5/4/1872, Springfield, Ohio d: 10/29/49, Cincinnati, Ohio TR, 5'11", 155 lbs. Deb: 9/21/1894

YEAR TM/L	W	L	PCT	G	GS	CG	SH	SV	IP	H	HR	BB	SO	RAT	ERA	ERA+	OAV	OOB	BH	AVG	PB	PR	/A	PD	TPI
1902 Bos-N	8	10	.444	21	19	17	1	1	170^1	158	0	58	39	11.4	2.59	109	.246	.309	13	.210	2	4	4	2	0.9
1903 Bos-N	11	16	.407	32	27	25	2	0	253	266	5	96	98	13.3	3.09	104	.272	.344	14	.161	1	5	3	2	0.6
Total 6	21	37	.362	80	59	51	3	3	566	629	10	227	179	13.9	3.64	96	.281	.353	35	.169	-2	-8	-9	2	0.1
Team 2	19	26	.422	53	46	42	3	1	423^1	424	5	154	137	12.5	2.89	106	.262	.330	27	.181	3	9	8	4	1.5

● CHARLIE MALONEY Maloney, Charles Michael b: 5/22/1886, Cambridge, Mass. d: 1/17/67, Arlington, Mass. BR/TR, 5'8", 155 lbs. Deb: 8/10/08

YEAR TM/L	W	L	PCT	G	GS	CG	SH	SV	IP	H	HR	BB	SO	RAT	ERA	ERA+	OAV	OOB	BH	AVG	PB	PR	/A	PD	TPI
1908 Bos-N	0	0	—	1	0	0	0	0	2	3	0	1	0	18.0	4.50	54	.429	.500	0	—	0	-0	-0	0	0.0

● LEO MANGUM Mangum, Leo Allan "Blackie" b: 5/24/1896, Durham, N.C. d: 7/9/74, Lima, Ohio BR/TR, 6'1", 187 lbs. Deb: 7/11/24

YEAR TM/L	W	L	PCT	G	GS	CG	SH	SV	IP	H	HR	BB	SO	RAT	ERA	ERA+	OAV	OOB	BH	AVG	PB	PR	/A	PD	TPI
1932 Bos-N	0	0	—	7	0	0	0	0	10^1	17	1	0	3	14.8	5.23	72	.333	.333	0	.000	-0	-2	-2	1	0.1
1933 Bos-N	4	3	.571	25	5	2	1	0	84	93	2	11	28	11.1	3.32	92	.280	.303	2	.091	-2	0	-2	2	-0.2
1934 Bos-N	5	3	.625	29	3	1	0	1	94^1	127	9	23	28	14.3	5.72	67	.315	.352	9	.281	2	-17	-20	1	-1.2
1935 Bos-N	0	0	—	3	0	0	0	0	4^2	6	0	2	0	15.4	3.86	98	.300	.364	0	—	0	0	-0	-0	0.0
Total 7	11	10	.524	85	16	4	1	1	258^1	343	15	72	78	14.5	5.37	68	.318	.362	15	.200	0	-43	-49	4	-2.9
Team 4	9	6	.600	64	8	3	1	1	193^1	243	12	36	59	13.0	4.61	76	.301	.331	11	.196	-0	-19	-24	4	-1.3

● JACK MANNING Manning, John E. b: 12/20/1853, Braintree, Mass. d: 8/15/29, Boston, Mass. BR/TR, 5'8.5", 158 lbs. Deb: 4/23/1873 M♦

YEAR TM/L	W	L	PCT	G	GS	CG	SH	SV	IP	H	HR	BB	SO	RAT	ERA	ERA+	OAV	OOB	BH	AVG	PB	PR	/A	PD	TPI
1875 Bos-n	15	2	.882	27	17	8	1	7	139^2	153	1	14		10.8	*2.19*	108	.258	.275	94	.274	4	4	3		0.4
1876 Bos-N	18	5	.783	34	20	13	0	**5**	197^1	213	1	32	24	11.2	2.14	105	.252	.279	76	.264	3	4	2	0	0.4
1878 Bos-N	1	0	1.000	3	1	1	0	0	11^1	24	1	5	2	23.0	14.29	17	.393	.439	63	.254	0	-15	-15	0	-0.9
Total 2 n	19	18	.514	49	37	26	1	7	319^1	384	4	24		11.5	*2.87*	95	.266	.278	197	.292	11	-4	-5		0.3
Total 3	19	9	.679	47	25	16	0	6	252^2	320	3	44	32	13.0	3.53	66	.284	.311	725	.257	7	-32	-34	1	-1.8
Team 2	19	5	.792	37	21	14	0	5	208^2	237	2	37	26	11.8	2.80	81	.261	.290	139	.259	3	-12	-13	0	-0.5

● DICK MANVILLE Manville, Richard Wesley b: 12/25/26, Des Moines, Iowa BR/TR, 6'4", 192 lbs. Deb: 4/30/50

YEAR TM/L	W	L	PCT	G	GS	CG	SH	SV	IP	H	HR	BB	SO	RAT	ERA	ERA+	OAV	OOB	BH	AVG	PB	PR	/A	PD	TPI
1950 Bos-N	0	0	—	1	0	0	0	0	2	0	0	3	2	13.5	0.00	—	.000	.300	0	—	0	1	1	-0	0.0
Total 2	0	0	—	12	0	0	0	0	19	25	2	15	8	18.9	7.11	54	.329	.440	1	.500	0	-7	-7	0	0.1

YEAR TM/L	W	L	PCT	G	GS	CG	SH	SV	IP	H	HR	BB	SO	RAT	ERA	ERA+	OAV	OOB	BH	AVG	PB	PR	/A	PD	TPI

● PAUL MARAK Marak, Paul Patrick b: 8/2/65, Lakenheath, England BR/TR, 6'2", 175 lbs. Deb: 9/1/90

| 1990 Atl-N | 1 | 2 | .333 | 7 | 7 | 1 | 1 | 0 | 39 | 39 | 2 | 19 | 15 | 14.1 | 3.69 | 109 | .267 | .363 | 1 | .091 | -0 | 0 | 1 | 1 | 0.2 |

● RUBE MARQUARD Marquard, Richard William b: 10/9/1889, Cleveland, Ohio d: 6/1/80, Baltimore, Md. BB/TL, 6'3", 180 lbs. Deb: 9/25/08 H

1922 Bos-N	11	15	.423	39	24	7	0	1	198	255	12	66	57	14.6	5.09	79	.322	.374	14	.222	-1	-22	-24	1	-2.6
1923 Bos-N	11	14	.440	38	29	11	3	0	239	265	16	65	78	12.5	3.73	107	.288	.337	12	.140	-6	7	7	0	0.0
1924 Bos-N	1	2	.333	6	6	1	0	0	36	33	3	13	10	11.8	3.00	127	.254	.326	3	.273	0	3	3	-0	0.3
1925 Bos-N	2	8	.200	26	8	0	0	0	72	105	5	27	19	16.5	5.75	70	.341	.394	3	.136	-1	-12	-14	-2	-1.9
Total 18	201	177	.532	536	404	197	30	19	3306²	3233	107	858	1593	11.2	3.08	103	.260	.310	198	.179	-17	53	36	-31	-2.2
Team 4	25	39	.391	109	67	19	3	1	545	658	30	171	164	13.7	4.44	90	.306	.358	32	.176	-8	-23	-28	-1	-4.2

● MIKE MARSHALL Marshall, Michael Grant b: 1/15/43, Adrian, Mich. BR/TR, 5'10", 180 lbs. Deb: 5/31/67 ♦

1976 Atl-N	2	1	.667	24	0	0	0	6	36²	35	4	14	17	12.3	3.19	119	.259	.333	1	.167	0	1	2	0	0.4
1977 Atl-N	1	0	1.000	4	0	0	0	0	6	12	1	2	6	21.0	9.00	49	.400	.438	1	1.000	0	-3	-3	-0	-0.4
Total 14	97	112	.464	723	24	3	1	188	1386²	1281	79	514	880	11.9	3.14	118	.249	.321	35	.196	6	84	87	17	20.8
Team 2	3	1	.750	28	0	0	0	6	42²	47	5	16	23	13.5	4.01	97	.285	.352	2	.286	1	-2	-1	0	0.0

● RAY MARTIN Martin, Raymond Joseph b: 3/13/25, Norwood, Mass. BR/TR, 6'2", 177 lbs. Deb: 8/15/43

1943 Bos-N	0	0	—	2	0	0	0	0	3¹	3	0	1	1	10.8	8.10	42	.231	.286	0	.000	-0	-2	-2	0	0.0
1947 Bos-N	1	0	1.000	1	1	1	0	0	9	7	0	4	2	11.0	1.00	389	.212	.297	0	.000	-0	3	3	0	0.4
1948 Bos-N	0	0	—	2	0	0	0	0	2¹	0	1	0	3	3.9	0.00	—	.000	.125	—	—	1	1	1	-0	0.0
Total 3	1	0	1.000	5	1	1	0	0	14²	10	0	6	3	9.8	2.45	154	.189	.271	0	.000	-0	2	2	1	0.4

● BOBBY MATHEWS Mathews, Robert T. b: 11/21/1851, Baltimore, Md. d: 4/17/1898, Baltimore, Md. BR/TR, 5'5½", 140 lbs. Deb: 5/4/1871 U♦

1881 Bos-N	1	0	1.000	5	1	1	0	2	23	22	0	11	5	12.9	2.35	113	.239	.320	12	.169	-1	1	1	-0	0.0
1882 Bos-N	19	15	.559	34	32	31	0	0	285	278	5	22	153	9.5	2.87	100	.232	.246	38	.225	-2	1	-0	-4	-0.6
Total 5 n	131	112	.539	255	253	236	9	0	2222	2583	19	197	147	11.3	2.76	116	.261	.275	234	.213	-27	89	107		5.9
Total 10	166	136	.550	323	315	289	10	3	2734¹	3008	50	336	1199	11.2	3.00	100	.261	.285	267	.192	-37	-3	-3	-11	-3.2
Team 2	20	15	.571	39	33	32	0	2	308	300	5	33	158	9.7	2.83	101	.233	.252	50	.208	-3	2	1	-4	-0.6

● AL MATTERN Mattern, Alonzo Albert b: 6/16/1883, W.Rush, N.Y. d: 11/6/58, West Rush, N.Y. BL/TR, 5'10", 165 lbs. Deb: 9/16/08

1908 Bos-N	1	2	.333	5	3	1	1	0	30¹	30	0	6	8	10.7	2.08	116	.265	.303	1	.125	-0	1	1	-0	0.0
1909 Bos-N	15	21	.417	47	32	24	2	3	316¹	322	4	108	98	12.3	2.85	99	.268	.330	17	.168	-1	-9	-1	3	0.1
1910 Bos-N	16	19	.457	51	37	17	6	1	305	288	5	121	94	12.2	2.98	112	.257	.332	16	.163	-4	2	12	1	0.9
1911 Bos-N	4	15	.211	33	21	11	0	0	186¹	228	13	63	51	14.1	4.97	77	.320	.376	11	.175	-2	-33	-24	2	-2.1
1912 Bos-N	0	1	.000	2	1	0	0	0	6¹	10	0	1	3	15.6	7.11	50	.313	.333	0	.000	-0	-3	-2	0	-0.3
Total 5	36	58	.383	138	94	53	9	4	844¹	878	22	299	254	12.7	3.37	95	.276	.340	45	.165	-8	-41	-15	5	-1.4

● JOE MATTHEWS Matthews, John Joseph "Lefty" b: 9/29/1898, Baltimore, Md. d: 2/8/68, Hagerstown, Md. BB/TL, 6', 170 lbs. Deb: 9/18/22

| 1922 Bos-N | 0 | 1 | .000 | 3 | 1 | 0 | 0 | 0 | 10 | 5 | 1 | 6 | 0 | 10.8 | 3.60 | 111 | .143 | .286 | 0 | .000 | -0 | 1 | 0 | -0 | 0.0 |

● RICK MATULA Matula, Richard Carlton b: 11/22/53, Wharton, Tex. BR/TR, 6', 190 lbs. Deb: 4/8/79

1979 Atl-N	8	10	.444	28	28	1	0	0	171¹	193	14	64	67	13.7	4.15	98	.286	.350	5	.094	-3	-8	-2	1	-0.4
1980 Atl-N	11	13	.458	33	30	3	1	0	176²	195	17	60	62	13.0	4.58	82	.286	.343	6	.105	-3	-19	-17	1	-2.2
1981 Atl-N	0	0	—	5	0	0	0	0	7	8	1	2	0	12.9	6.43	56	.286	.333	0	.000	-0	-2	-2	0	0.0
Total 3	19	23	.452	66	58	4	1	0	355	396	32	126	129	13.3	4.41	88	.286	.347	11	.099	-6	-30	-21	2	-2.6

● LARRY MAXIE Maxie, Larry Hans b: 10/10/40, Upland, Cal. BR/TR, 6'4", 220 lbs. Deb: 8/30/69

| 1969 Atl-N | 0 | 0 | — | 2 | 0 | 0 | 0 | 0 | 3 | 1 | 0 | 1 | 1 | 9.0 | 3.00 | 120 | .111 | .273 | 0 | — | 0 | 0 | 0 | 0 | 0.0 |

● DARRELL MAY May, Darrell Kevin b: 6/13/72, San Bernardino, Cal. BL/TL, 6'2", 170 lbs. Deb: 9/10/95

| 1995 Atl-N | 0 | 0 | — | 2 | 0 | 0 | 0 | 0 | 4 | 10 | 0 | 0 | 1 | 22.5 | 11.25 | 38 | .500 | .500 | 0 | — | 0 | -3 | -3 | 0 | 0.0 |

● BILL McAFEE McAfee, William Fort b: 9/7/07, Smithville, Ga. d: 7/8/58, Culpeper, Va. BR/TR, 6'2", 186 lbs. Deb: 5/12/30

| 1931 Bos-N | 0 | 1 | .000 | 18 | 1 | 0 | 0 | 0 | 29² | 39 | 2 | 10 | 9 | 14.9 | 6.37 | 59 | .333 | .386 | 0 | .000 | -0 | -8 | -9 | 0 | -0.3 |
| Total 5 | 10 | 4 | .714 | 83 | 7 | 2 | 0 | 5 | 186² | 237 | 12 | 81 | 44 | 15.5 | 5.69 | 78 | .313 | .382 | 9 | .173 | 0 | -28 | -26 | 1 | -1.5 |

● DICK McBRIDE McBride, James Dickson b: 1845, Philadelphia, Pa. d: 10/10/16, Philadelphia, Pa. TR, 5'9", 150 lbs. Deb: 5/20/1871 M

| 1876 Bos-N | 0 | 4 | .000 | 4 | 4 | 3 | 0 | 0 | 33 | 53 | 1 | 5 | 2 | 15.8 | 2.73 | 83 | .353 | .374 | 3 | .188 | -1 | -2 | -2 | -0 | -0.3 |
| Total 5 n | 149 | 74 | .668 | 233 | 233 | 224 | 10 | 0 | 2048² | 2367 | 18 | 167 | 84 | 11.1 | 2.86 | 115 | .261 | .275 | 305 | .259 | -2 | 75 | 98 | | 6.9 |

● TOMMY McCARTHY McCarthy, Thomas Francis Michael b: 7/24/1863, Boston, Mass. d: 8/5/22, Boston, Mass. BR/TR, 5'7", 170 lbs. Deb: 7/10/1884 MH♦

| 1894 Bos-N | 0 | 0 | — | 1 | 0 | 0 | 0 | 0 | 2 | 1 | 0 | 3 | 0 | 18.0 | 4.50 | 126 | .143 | .400 | 188 | .349 | -1 | -0 | -0 | 0 | 0.0 |
| Total 6 | 0 | 7 | .000 | 13 | 6 | 5 | 0 | 0 | 69¹ | 83 | 3 | 26 | 21 | 14.1 | 4.93 | 54 | .279 | .337 | 1496 | .292 | -1 | -17 | -17 | 1 | -1.4 |

● TOM McCARTHY McCarthy, Thomas Patrick b: 5/22/1884, Ft.Wayne, Ind. d: 3/28/33, Mishawaka, Ind. TR, 5'7", 170 lbs. Deb: 5/10/08

1908 Bos-N	7	3	.700	14	11	7	2	0	94	77	0	28	27	10.1	1.63	148	.235	.298	6	.171	0	8	8	0	1.0
1909 Bos-N	0	5	.000	8	7	3	0	0	46¹	47	3	28	11	15.0	3.50	81	.272	.379	2	.125	-0	-5	-3	0	-0.4
Total 2	7	9	.438	25	20	10	2	0	150	133	3	65	42	12.1	2.34	108	.248	.332	8	.140	-1	2	3	1	-0.0
Team 2	7	8	.467	22	18	10	2	0	140¹	124	3	56	38	11.7	2.24	113	.248	.327	8	.157	-0	3	5	1	0.6

● BILL McCARTHY McCarthy, William Thomas b: 4/11/1882, Ashland, Mass. d: 5/29/39, Boston, Mass. BR/TR, 5'11", 180 lbs. Deb: 4/21/06

| 1906 Bos-N | 0 | 0 | — | 1 | 0 | 0 | 0 | 0 | 2 | 2 | 0 | 3 | 0 | 22.5 | 9.00 | 30 | .182 | .357 | 0 | .000 | -0 | -1 | -1 | -0 | 0.0 |

● JIM McCLOSKEY McCloskey, James Ellwood "Irish" b: 5/26/10, Danville, Pa. d: 8/18/71, Jersey City, N.J. BL/TL, 5'9.5", 180 lbs. Deb: 4/21/36

| 1936 Bos-N | 0 | 0 | — | 4 | 1 | 0 | 0 | 0 | 8 | 14 | 1 | 3 | 2 | 20.3 | 11.25 | 34 | .378 | .439 | 0 | .000 | -0 | -6 | -7 | 0 | 0.0 |

● DENNY McLAIN McLain, Dennis Dale b: 3/29/44, Chicago, Ill. BR/TR, 6'1", 185 lbs. Deb: 9/21/63

| 1972 Atl-N | 3 | 5 | .375 | 15 | 8 | 2 | 0 | 1 | 54 | 60 | 12 | 18 | 21 | 13.2 | 6.50 | 58 | .279 | .338 | 2 | .167 | 0 | -18 | -16 | -1 | -2.3 |
| Total 10 | 131 | 91 | .590 | 280 | 264 | 105 | 29 | 2 | 1886 | 1646 | 242 | 548 | 1282 | 10.6 | 3.39 | 101 | .234 | .292 | 82 | .133 | -9 | -1 | 5 | -10 | -2.8 |

● JOEY McLAUGHLIN McLaughlin, Joey Richard b: 7/11/56, Tulsa, Okla. BR/TR, 6'2", 205 lbs. Deb: 6/11/77

1977 Atl-N	0	0	—	3	2	0	0	0	6	10	3	3	0	19.5	15.00	30	.385	.448	0	.000	-0	-7	-7	0	0.0
1979 Atl-N	5	3	.625	37	0	0	0	5	69	54	3	34	40	11.6	2.48	163	.224	.322	2	.182	-0	10	12	-1	1.5
Total 7	29	28	.509	250	12	0	0	36	448²	440	46	198	268	12.9	3.85	110	.262	.341	2	.167	-0	5	19	-0	2.8
Team 2	5	3	.625	40	2	0	0	5	75	64	6	37	40	12.2	3.48	117	.240	.334	2	.167	-0	2	5	-0	1.5

● BO McLAUGHLIN McLaughlin, Michael Duane b: 10/23/53, Oakland, Cal. BR/TR, 6'5", 210 lbs. Deb: 7/20/76

| 1979 Atl-N | 1 | 1 | .500 | 37 | 1 | 0 | 0 | 0 | 49² | 63 | 2 | 16 | 45 | 14.7 | 4.89 | 83 | .303 | .358 | 0 | .000 | -1 | -6 | -5 | -1 | -0.3 |
| Total 6 | 10 | 20 | .333 | 156 | 21 | 5 | 2 | 9 | 313 | 335 | 22 | 123 | 188 | 13.6 | 4.49 | 80 | .275 | .348 | 0 | .000 | -3 | -25 | -32 | 0 | -2.2 |

● DON McMAHON McMahon, Donald John b: 1/4/30, Brooklyn, N.Y. d: 7/22/87, Los Angeles, Cal. BR/TR, 6'2", 222 lbs. Deb: 6/30/57 C

1957 *Mil-N	2	3	.400	32	0	0	0	0	46²	33	0	29	46	12.0	1.54	227	.196	.315	2	.250	1	12	10	-0	1.6
1958 *Mil-N☆	7	2	.778	38	0	0	0	8	58²	50	4	29	37	12.4	3.68	96	.235	.332	1	.111	0	2	-1	-0	-0.2
1959 Mil-N	5	3	.625	60	0	0	0	15	80²	81	5	37	55	13.3	2.57	138	.259	.339	2	.222	1	12	9	-1	1.1
1960 Mil-N	3	6	.333	48	0	0	0	10	63²	66	9	32	50	14.1	5.94	58	.263	.351	0	.000	-1	-15	-18	0	-3.0
1961 Mil-N	6	4	.600	53	0	0	0	5	92	84	4	51	55	13.4	2.84	132	.249	.351	3	.188	-0	12	9	1	1.2

YEAR TM/L	W	L	PCT	G	GS	CG	SH	SV	IP	H	HR	BB	SO	RAT	ERA	ERA+	OAV	OOB	BH	AVG	PB	PR	/A	PD	TPI
1962 Mil-N	0	1	.000	2	0	0	0	0	3	3	1	0	3	9.0	6.00	63	.250	.250	0	—	0	-1	-1	-0	-0.2
Total 18	90	68	.570	874	2	0	0	153	1310^2	1054	105	579	1003	11.4	2.96	119	.221	.310	23	.137	-1	96	83	-1	10.2
Team 6	23	19	.548	233	0	0	0	50	344^2	317	23	178	246	13.1	3.34	107	.245	.339	8	.151	1	22	9	-0	0.5

● GREG McMICHAEL McMichael, Gregory Winston b: 12/1/66, Knoxville, Tenn. BR/TR, 6'3", 215 lbs. Deb: 4/12/93

YEAR TM/L	W	L	PCT	G	GS	CG	SH	SV	IP	H	HR	BB	SO	RAT	ERA	ERA+	OAV	OOB	BH	AVG	PB	PR	/A	PD	TPI
1993 *Atl-N	2	3	.400	74	0	0	0	19	91^2	68	3	29	89	9.5	2.06	195	.206	.270	0	.000	-0	20	20	2	2.0
1994 Atl-N	4	6	.400	51	0	0	0	21	58^2	66	1	19	47	13.0	3.84	111	.280	.333	0	.000	-0	2	3	-1	0.5
1995 *Atl-N	7	2	.778	67	0	0	0	2	80^2	64	8	32	74	10.7	2.79	152	.213	.289	0	.000	-0	12	13	-1	1.2
Total 3	13	11	.542	192	0	0	0	42	231	198	12	80	210	10.8	2.77	150	.229	.294	0	.000	-1	35	35	-0	3.7

● CRAIG McMURTRY McMurtry, Joe Craig b: 11/5/59, Troy, Tex. BR/TR, 6'5", 195 lbs. Deb: 4/10/83

YEAR TM/L	W	L	PCT	G	GS	CG	SH	SV	IP	H	HR	BB	SO	RAT	ERA	ERA+	OAV	OOB	BH	AVG	PB	PR	/A	PD	TPI
1983 Atl-N	15	9	.625	36	35	6	3	0	224^2	204	13	88	105	11.7	3.08	126	.243	.315	6	.086	-4	14	20	3	2.0
1984 Atl-N	9	17	.346	37	30	0	0	0	183^1	184	16	102	99	14.1	4.32	89	.268	.363	6	.115	-1	-15	-10	4	-1.0
1985 Atl-N	0	3	.000	17	6	0	0	1	45	56	6	27	28	16.8	6.60	58	.306	.398	1	.071	-1	-15	-14	1	-0.9
1986 Atl-N	1	6	.143	37	5	0	0	0	79^2	82	7	43	50	14.3	4.74	84	.265	.359	2	.125	-0	-9	-7	0	-0.6
Total 8	28	42	.400	212	79	6	3	4	667^2	650	54	336	349	13.4	4.08	96	.259	.348	15	.098	-6	-29	-13	10	0.3
Team 4	25	35	.417	127	76	6	3	1	532^2	526	42	260	282	13.4	4.06	96	.261	.346	15	.099	-6	-26	-10	8	-0.5

● TIM McNAMARA McNamara, Timothy Augustine b: 11/20/1898, Millville, Mass. d: 11/5/94, N.Smithfield, R.I. BR/TR, 5'11", 170 lbs. Deb: 4/27/22

YEAR TM/L	W	L	PCT	G	GS	CG	SH	SV	IP	H	HR	BB	SO	RAT	ERA	ERA+	OAV	OOB	BH	AVG	PB	PR	/A	PD	TPI
1922 Bos-N	3	4	.429	24	5	4	2	0	70^2	55	2	26	16	10.4	2.42	165	.225	.303	2	.118	-1	**13**	**12**	-0	1.0
1923 Bos-N	3	13	.188	32	16	3	0	0	139^1	185	8	29	32	14.1	4.91	81	.320	.357	7	.179	1	-14	-14	-2	-1.5
1924 Bos-N	8	12	.400	35	21	6	2	0	179	242	9	31	35	13.9	5.18	74	.334	.364	6	.140	-1	-26	-27	1	-2.6
1925 Bos-N	0	0	—	1	0	0	0	0	0^2	6	0	2	1	108.0	81.00	5	.857	.889	0	—	0	-6	-6	0	0.0
Total 5	14	29	.326	98	42	13	4	0	395^2	495	19	92	88	13.6	4.78	82	.314	.355	15	.152	-1	-36	-38	-2	-3.1
Team 4	14	29	.326	92	42	13	4	0	389^2	488	19	88	84	13.5	4.71	83	.314	.354	15	.152	-1	-33	-35	-2	-3.1

● ED McNICHOL McNichol, Edwin Briggs b: 1/10/1879, Martins Ferry, O. d: 11/1/52, Salineville, O. BR/TR, 5'5", 170 lbs. Deb: 7/9/04

YEAR TM/L	W	L	PCT	G	GS	CG	SH	SV	IP	H	HR	BB	SO	RAT	ERA	ERA+	OAV	OOB	BH	AVG	PB	PR	/A	PD	TPI
1904 Bos-N	2	12	.143	17	15	12	1	0	122	120	3	74	39	14.7	4.28	64	.262	.371	4	.093	-4	-21	-21	-2	-2.6

● MIKE McQUEEN McQueen, Michael Robert b: 8/30/50, Oklahoma City, Okla BL/TL, 5'11", 190 lbs. Deb: 10/2/69

YEAR TM/L	W	L	PCT	G	GS	CG	SH	SV	IP	H	HR	BB	SO	RAT	ERA	ERA+	OAV	OOB	BH	AVG	PB	PR	/A	PD	TPI
1969 Atl-N	0	0	—	1	1	0	0	0	3	2	0	3	3	15.0	3.00	120	.182	.357	0	—	0	0	0	-0	0.0
1970 Atl-N	1	5	.167	22	8	1	0	1	66	67	10	31	54	13.5	5.59	77	.266	.349	6	.300	2	-11	-10	-1	-0.7
1971 Atl-N	4	1	.800	17	3	0	0	1	56	47	7	23	38	11.6	3.54	105	.228	.312	4	.211	0	-0	1	-1	0.0
1972 Atl-N	0	5	.000	23	7	1	0	1	78^1	79	11	44	40	14.2	4.60	82	.260	.355	2	.087	-2	-10	-7	-1	-0.7
Total 5	5	11	.313	73	19	2	0	3	218^1	212	32	112	140	13.5	4.66	84	.255	.346	13	.206	1	-24	-18	-4	-1.4
Team 4	5	11	.313	63	19	2	0	3	203^1	195	28	101	135	13.3	4.60	85	.252	.342	12	.194	1	-22	-15	-3	-1.4

● HUGH McQUILLAN McQuillan, Hugh A. "Handsome Hugh" b: 9/15/1897, New York, N.Y. d: 8/26/47, New York, N.Y. BR/TR, 6', 170 lbs. Deb: 7/26/18

YEAR TM/L	W	L	PCT	G	GS	CG	SH	SV	IP	H	HR	BB	SO	RAT	ERA	ERA+	OAV	OOB	BH	AVG	PB	PR	/A	PD	TPI
1918 Bos-N	1	0	1.000	1	1	1	0	0	9	7	0	5	1	12.0	3.00	90	.219	.324	1	.250	0	-0	-0	0	0.0
1919 Bos-N	2	3	.400	16	7	2	0	1	60	66	3	14	13	12.2	3.45	83	.288	.332	4	.222	0	-4	-4	-1	-0.4
1920 Bos-N	11	15	.423	38	26	17	1	5	225^2	230	3	70	53	12.0	3.55	86	.273	.330	19	.257	6	-10	-13	2	-0.6
1921 Bos-N	13	17	.433	45	31	13	2	5	250	284	9	90	94	13.5	4.00	91	.291	.352	18	.205	1	-6	-10	0	-0.9
1922 Bos-N	5	10	.333	28	17	7	0	0	136	154	3	56	33	14.0	4.24	94	.299	.369	7	.167	-1	-2	-4	1	-0.4
1927 Bos-N	3	5	.375	13	11	2	0	0	78	109	2	24	17	15.6	5.54	67	.332	.381	5	.227	0	-14	-16	0	-1.3
Total 10	88	94	.484	279	203	95	10	16	1561^2	1703	67	489	446	12.7	3.83	95	.284	.340	103	.195	0	-10	-32	1	-2.2
Team 6	35	50	.412	141	93	42	3	11	758^2	850	20	259	211	13.3	4.01	87	.291	.350	54	.218	7	-36	-46	3	-3.6

● BILL McTIGUE McTigue, William Patrick "Rebel" b: 1/3/1891, Nashville, Tenn. d: 5/8/20, Nashville, Tenn. BL/TL, 6'1.5", 175 lbs. Deb: 5/2/11 ♦

YEAR TM/L	W	L	PCT	G	GS	CG	SH	SV	IP	H	HR	BB	SO	RAT	ERA	ERA+	OAV	OOB	BH	AVG	PB	PR	/A	PD	TPI
1911 Bos-N	0	5	.000	14	8	0	0	0	37	37	3	49	23	21.4	7.05	54	.280	.481	1	.083	-1	-15	-13	-1	-1.7
1912 Bos-N	2	0	1.000	10	1	1	0	0	34^2	39	0	18	17	14.8	5.45	66	.289	.373	1	.077	-1	-8	-7	1	-0.4
Total 3	2	5	.286	27	9	1	0	0	77	81	3	72	41	18.1	6.19	59	.284	.432	2	.077	-2	-24	-22	0	-2.1
Team 2	2	5	.286	24	9	1	0	0	71^2	76	3	67	40	18.2	6.28	59	.285	.432	2	.080	-2	-23	-20	-0	-2.1

● CAL McVEY McVey, Calvin Alexander b: 8/30/1850, Montrose, Iowa d: 8/20/26, San Francisco, Cal BR/TR, 5'9", 170 lbs. Deb: 5/5/1871 M♦

YEAR TM/L	W	L	PCT	G	GS	CG	SH	SV	IP	H	HR	BB	SO	RAT	ERA	ERA+	OAV	OOB	BH	AVG	PB	PR	/A	PD	TPI
1875 Bos-n	1	0	1.000	3	2	0	0	1	11	15	0	1		13.1	3.27	72	.294	.308	137	.352	2	-1	-1		0.0
Total 3	9	12	.429	31	17	12	0	4	165^1	220	3	15	36	12.8	3.76	73	.295	.309	393	.328	10	-21	-19	-1	-1.5

● LARRY McWILLIAMS McWilliams, Larry Dean b: 2/10/54, Wichita, Kan. BL/TL, 6'5", 180 lbs. Deb: 7/17/78

YEAR TM/L	W	L	PCT	G	GS	CG	SH	SV	IP	H	HR	BB	SO	RAT	ERA	ERA+	OAV	OOB	BH	AVG	PB	PR	/A	PD	TPI
1978 Atl-N	9	3	.750	15	15	3	1	0	99^1	84	11	35	42	11.0	2.81	144	.224	.294	2	.063	-2	8	14	1	1.6
1979 Atl-N	3	2	.600	13	13	1	0	0	66^1	69	4	22	32	12.9	5.56	73	.272	.339	5	.208	1	-13	-11	1	-0.5
1980 Atl-N	9	14	.391	30	30	4	1	0	163^2	188	27	39	77	12.9	4.95	76	.285	.332	8	.157	-0	-25	-22	-0	-2.8
1981 Atl-N	2	1	.667	6	5	2	1	0	37^2	31	2	8	23	9.3	3.11	115	.230	.273	1	.100	-0	2	2	1	0.2
1982 Atl-N	2	3	.400	27	2	0	0	0	37^2	52	3	20	24	17.7	6.21	60	.327	.409	1	.167	0	-11	-10	2	-1.1
1987 Atl-N	0	1	.000	9	2	0	0	0	20^1	25	2	7	13	15.0	5.75	76	.301	.370	1	.200	0	-4	-3	0	-0.1
Total 13	78	90	.464	370	224	34	13	3	1558^1	1548	137	542	940	12.4	3.99	93	.259	.326	60	.135	-8	-66	-48	8	-4.9
Team 6	25	24	.510	100	67	10	3	0	425	449	49	131	211	12.6	4.53	85	.270	.329	18	.141	-1	-43	-31	5	-2.7

● JOUETT MEEKIN Meekin, George Jouett b: 2/21/1867, New Albany, Ind. d: 12/14/44, New Albany, Ind. BR/TR, 6'1", 180 lbs. Deb: 6/13/1891

YEAR TM/L	W	L	PCT	G	GS	CG	SH	SV	IP	H	HR	BB	SO	RAT	ERA	ERA+	OAV	OOB	BH	AVG	PB	PR	/A	PD	TPI
1899 Bos-N	7	6	.538	13	13	12	0	0	108	111	0	23	23	11.3	2.83	147	.266	.307	7	.171	-1	12	16	-2	1.3
Total 10	153	133	.535	324	308	270	9	2	2603^1	2831	67	1058	900	13.8	4.07	102	.273	.345	267	.243	29	55	27	-22	2.2

● KENT MERCKER Mercker, Kent Franklin b: 2/1/68, Indianapolis, Ind. BL/TL, 6'1", 175 lbs. Deb: 9/22/89

YEAR TM/L	W	L	PCT	G	GS	CG	SH	SV	IP	H	HR	BB	SO	RAT	ERA	ERA+	OAV	OOB	BH	AVG	PB	PR	/A	PD	TPI
1989 Atl-N	0	0	—	2	1	0	0	0	4^1	8	0	6	4	29.1	12.46	29	.400	.538	0	.000	-0	-4	-4	-0	0.0
1990 Atl-N	4	7	.364	36	0	0	0	7	48^1	43	6	24	39	12.8	3.17	127	.236	.332	0	.000	-0	3	5	-1	1.0
1991 *Atl-N	5	3	.625	50	4	0	0	6	73^1	56	5	35	62	11.3	2.58	151	.211	.305	1	.100	-0	9	11	-1	1.2
1992 *Atl-N	3	2	.600	53	0	0	0	6	68^1	51	4	35	49	11.7	3.42	107	.207	.313	0	.000	-0	1	2	-2	-0.1
1993 *Atl-N	3	1	.750	43	6	0	0	0	66	52	2	36	59	12.3	2.86	140	.212	.318	0	.000	-1	9	8	-1	0.2
1994 Atl-N	9	4	.692	20	17	2	1	0	112^1	90	16	45	111	10.8	3.45	123	.220	.297	2	.054	-2	10	10	0	0.8
1995 *Atl-N	7	8	.467	29	26	0	0	0	143	140	16	61	102	12.8	4.15	102	.258	.336	5	.104	-2	0	1	0	0.0
Total 7	31	25	.554	233	54	2	1	19	515^2	440	49	242	426	12.1	3.49	116	.230	.320	8	.068	-7	27	33	-5	3.1

● ANDY MESSERSMITH Messersmith, John Alexander b: 8/6/45, Toms River, N.J. BR/TR, 6'1", 200 lbs. Deb: 7/4/68

YEAR TM/L	W	L	PCT	G	GS	CG	SH	SV	IP	H	HR	BB	SO	RAT	ERA	ERA+	OAV	OOB	BH	AVG	PB	PR	/A	PD	TPI
1976 Atl-N†	11	11	.500	29	28	12	3	1	207^1	166	14	74	135	10.5	3.04	125	.219	.290	12	.179	0	11	17	1	2.0
1977 Atl-N	5	4	.556	16	16	1	0	0	102^1	101	12	39	69	12.5	4.40	101	.256	.326	4	.118	-0	-6	1	-0	0.0
Total 12	130	99	.568	344	295	98	27	15	2230^1	1719	174	831	1625	10.5	2.86	121	.212	.289	124	.170	20	172	145	-1	17.1
Team 2	16	15	.516	45	44	13	3	1	309^2	267	26	113	204	11.2	3.49	115	.231	.302	16	.158	0	5	18	1	2.0

● FRANK MILLER Miller, Frank Lee "Bullet" b: 5/13/1886, Allegan, Mich. d: 2/19/74, Allegan, Mich. BR/TR, 6', 188 lbs. Deb: 7/12/13

YEAR TM/L	W	L	PCT	G	GS	CG	SH	SV	IP	H	HR	BB	SO	RAT	ERA	ERA+	OAV	OOB	BH	AVG	PB	PR	/A	PD	TPI
1922 Bos-N	11	13	.458	31	23	14	2	1	200	213	7	60	65	12.4	3.51	114	.279	.333	8	.118	-5	13	11	1	0.8
1923 Bos-N	0	3	.000	8	6	0	0	1	39^1	54	2	11	6	15.6	4.58	87	.335	.389	1	.143	-0	-3	-3	-1	-0.3
Total 7	52	66	.441	163	127	68	14	4	1010	944	21	254	359	10.9	3.01	104	.253	.306	38	.117	-19	7	15	1	-1.4
Team 2	11	16	.407	39	29	14	2	2	239^1	267	9	71	71	12.9	3.69	108	.289	.343	9	.120	-5	11	8	-0	0.5

● STU MILLER Miller, Stuart Leonard b: 12/26/27, Northampton, Mass. BR/TR, 5'11.5", 165 lbs. Deb: 8/12/52

YEAR TM/L	W	L	PCT	G	GS	CG	SH	SV	IP	H	HR	BB	SO	RAT	ERA	ERA+	OAV	OOB	BH	AVG	PB	PR	/A	PD	TPI
1968 Atl-N	0	0	—	2	0	0	0	0	1^1	1	0	4	1	33.8	27.00	11	.500	.833	0	—	0	-4	-4	0	0.0
Total 16	105	103	.505	704	93	24	5	154	1694	1522	140	600	1164	11.5	3.24	115	.242	.312	49	.133	-2	107	89	22	17.0

YEAR	TM/L	W	L	PCT	G	GS	CG	SH	SV	IP	H	HR	BB	SO	RAT	ERA	ERA+	OAV	OOB	BH	AVG	PB	PR	/A	PD	TPI
● ART MILLS Mills, Arthur Grant b: 3/2/03, Utica, N.Y. d: 7/23/75, Utica, N.Y. BR/TR, 5'10", 155 lbs. Deb: 4/16/27 FC																										
1927	Bos-N	0	1	.000	15	1	0	0	0	37^{2}	41	1	18	7	14.8	3.82	97	.287	.378	0	.000	-1	0	-0	1	0.0
1928	Bos-N	0	0	—	4	0	0	0	0	7^{2}	17	3	8	0	31.7	12.91	30	.472	.587	0	.000	-0	-8	-8	-0	0.0
Total	2	0	1	.000	19	1	0	0	0	45^{1}	58	4	26	7	17.7	5.36	70	.324	.424	0	.000	-1	-7	-8	1	0.0
● GEORGE MOGRIDGE Mogridge, George Anthony b: 2/18/1889, Rochester, N.Y. d: 3/4/62, Rochester, N.Y. BL/TL, 6'2", 165 lbs. Deb: 8/17/11																										
1926	Bos-N	6	10	.375	39	10	2	0	3	142	173	6	36	46	13.4	4.50	79	.311	.356	8	.174	-1	-11	-15	2	-1.4
1927	Bos-N	6	4	.600	20	1	0	0	5	48^{2}	48	4	15	26	12.0	3.70	100	.257	.319	3	.200	-0	1	0	1	0.1
Total	15	132	131	.502	398	261	138	20	20	2265^{2}	2352	77	565	678	11.9	3.23	109	.273	.323	137	.182	-8	95	75	11	8.0
Team	2	12	14	.462	59	11	2	0	8	190^{2}	221	10	51	72	13.1	4.30	84	.297	.346	11	.180	-1	-9	-15	3	-1.3
● JOHN MONTEFUSCO Montefusco, John Joseph "Count" b: 5/25/50, Long Branch, N.J. BR/TR, 6'1", 180 lbs. Deb: 9/3/74																										
1981	Atl-N	2	3	.400	26	9	0	0	1	77^{1}	75	9	27	34	11.9	3.49	103	.260	.324	1	.067	-1	-0	1	0	0.0
Total	13	90	83	.520	298	244	32	11	5	1652^{1}	1604	135	513	1081	11.7	3.54	102	.255	.314	44	.097	-10	20	16	-12	0.5
● DONNIE MOORE Moore, Donnie Ray b: 2/13/54, Lubbock, Tex. d: 7/18/89, Anaheim, Cal. BL/TR, 6', 185 lbs. Deb: 9/14/75																										
1982	*Atl-N	3	1	.750	16	0	0	0	1	27^{2}	32	1	7	17	13.3	4.23	88	.294	.347	0	.000	-0	-2	-2	0	-0.2
1983	Atl-N	2	3	.400	43	0	0	0	6	68^{2}	72	6	10	41	10.7	3.67	106	.279	.306	4	.500	1	-0	2	-1	0.2
1984	Atl-N	4	5	.444	47	0	0	0	16	64^{1}	63	3	18	47	11.5	2.94	131	.258	.312	0	.000	-0	5	7	0	1.3
Total	13	43	40	.518	416	4	0	0	89	655	698	53	186	416	12.3	3.67	110	.276	.328	16	.281	5	12	27	-1	8.0
Team	3	9	9	.500	106	0	0	0	23	160^{2}	167	10	35	105	11.5	3.47	111	.273	.316	4	.333	1	2	7	-0	1.3
● HIKER MORAN Moran, Albert Thomas b: 1/1/12, Rochester, N.Y. BR/TR, 6'4.5", 185 lbs. Deb: 9/29/38																										
1938	Bos-N	0	0	—	1	0	0	0	0	3	1	0	1	0	6.0	0.00	—	.111	.200	0	.000	-0	1	1	-0	0.0
1939	Bos-N	1	1	.500	6	2	1	0	0	20	21	3	11	4	14.4	4.50	82	.276	.368	1	.200	1	-1	-2	-0	-0.1
Total	2	1	1	.500	7	2	1	0	0	23	22	3	12	4	13.3	3.91	94	.259	.351	1	.167	0	-0	-1	-1	-0.1
● FORREST MORE More, Forrest b: 9/30/1883, Hayden, Ind. d: 8/17/68, Columbus, Ind. BR/TR, 6', 180 lbs. Deb: 4/15/09																										
1909	Bos-N	1	5	.167	10	4	3	0	0	48^{2}	47	0	20	10	13.1	4.44	64	.270	.359	1	.067	-1	-10	-9	0	-1.1
● SETH MOREHEAD Morehead, Seth Marvin "Moe" b: 8/15/34, Houston, Tex. BL/TL, 6'0.5", 195 lbs. Deb: 4/27/57																										
1961	Mil-N	1	0	1.000	12	0	0	0	0	15^{1}	16	4	7	13	14.1	6.46	58	.271	.358	0	—	0	-4	-5	-0	-0.3
Total	5	5	19	.208	132	24	3	0	5	318^{1}	357	34	110	184	13.4	4.81	80	.282	.343	9	.145	-1	-33	-34	-4	-3.2
● ROGER MORET Moret, Rogelio (Torres) b: 9/16/49, Guayama, P.R. BB/TL, 6'4", 175 lbs. Deb: 9/13/70																										
1976	Atl-N	3	5	.375	27	12	1	0	1	77^{1}	84	7	27	30	13.0	5.00	76	.280	.341	3	.130	-1	-13	-10	-0	-1.2
Total	9	47	27	.635	168	82	24	5	12	723^{1}	656	61	339	408	12.5	3.66	107	.245	.332	5	.100	-2	4	22	-6	1.1
● CY MORGAN Morgan, Cyril Arlon b: 11/11/1895, Lakeville, Mass. d: 9/11/46, Lakeville, Mass. BR/TR, 6', 170 lbs. Deb: 6/8/21																										
1921	Bos-N	1	1	.500	17	0	0	0	1	30^{1}	37	0	17	8	16.3	6.53	56	.314	.404	0	.000	-1	-9	-10	1	-0.6
1922	Bos-N	0	0	—	2	0	0	0	0	1^{1}	8	0	2	0	67.5	27.00	15	.667	.714	0	—	0	-3	-3	-0	0.0
Total	2	1	1	.500	19	0	0	0	1	31^{2}	45	0	19	8	18.5	7.39	50	.346	.433	0	.000	-1	-13	-13	1	-0.6
● JIM MORONEY Moroney, James Francis b: 12/4/1885, Boston, Mass. d: 2/26/29, Philadelphia, Pa. BL/TL, 6'1", 175 lbs. Deb: 4/24/06																										
1906	Bos-N	0	3	.000	3	3	3	0	0	27	28	1	12	11	15.3	5.33	50	.259	.365	1	.100	-1	-8	-8	0	-0.8
Total	3	2	6	.250	25	8	5	0	2	92^{2}	96	2	40	29	14.6	3.69	83	.288	.388	4	.154	-1	-7	-7	-1	-0.8
● JOHN MORRILL Morrill, John Francis "Honest John" b: 2/19/1855, Boston, Mass. d: 4/2/32, Boston, Mass. BR/TR, 5'10.5", 155 lbs. Deb: 4/24/1876 M◆																										
1880	Bos-N	0	0	—	3	0	0	0	0	10^{2}	9	0	1	0	8.4	0.84	269	.273	.294	81	.237	0	2	2	0	0.0
1881	Bos-N	0	1	.000	3	0	0	0	1	5^{2}	9	0	1	0	15.9	6.35	42	.333	.357	90	.289	1	-2	-2	-0	-0.4
1882	Bos-N	0	0	—	1	0	0	0	0	2	3	0	0	2	13.5	0.00	—	.375	.375	101	.289	0	1	1	0	0.0
1883	Bos-N	1	0	1.000	2	1	1	0	0	13	15	0	4	5	13.2	2.77	112	.268	.317	129	.319	1	1	0	-0	0.1
1884	Bos-N	0	1	.000	7	1	1	0	**2**	23	34	0	6	13	15.7	7.43	39	.315	.351	114	.260	1	-11	-12	0	-0.5
1886	Bos-N	0	0	—	1	0	0	0	0	4	5	0	0	2	11.3	0.00	—	.313	.313	106	.247	0	1	1	0	0.0
Total	7	1	2	.333	18	2	2	0	3	58^{2}	75	0	12	22	13.3	4.30	66	.301	.333	1275	.260	4	-9	-10	0	-0.8
Team	6	1	2	.333	17	2	2	0	3	58^{1}	75	0	12	22	13.4	4.32	65	.302	.335	621	.273	4	-9	-10	0	-0.8
● JIM MORRISON Morrison, James Forrest b: 9/23/52, Pensacola, Fla. BR/TR, 5'11", 182 lbs. Deb: 9/18/77 ◆																										
1988	Atl-N	0	0	—	3	0	0	0	0	3^{2}	3	0	2	1	12.3	0.00	—	.214	.313	14	.152	0	1	1	-0	0.0
● GUY MORRISON Morrison, Walter Guy b: 8/29/1895, Hinton, W.Va. d: 8/14/34, Grand Rapids, Mich BR/TR, 5'11", 185 lbs. Deb: 8/31/27																										
1927	Bos-N	1	2	.333	11	3	1	0	0	34^{1}	40	1	15	6	14.4	4.46	83	.296	.367	1	.125	1	-2	-3	1	0.0
1928	Bos-N	0	0	—	1	0	0	0	0	3	4	1	3	0	21.0	12.00	33	.308	.438	0	—	0	-3	-3	0	0.0
Total	2	1	2	.333	12	3	1	0	0	37^{1}	44	2	18	6	14.9	5.06	74	.297	.373	1	.125	1	-5	-6	1	0.0
● CARL MORTON Morton, Carl Wendle b: 1/18/44, Kansas City, Mo. d: 4/12/83, Tulsa, Okla. BR/TR, 6', 200 lbs. Deb: 4/11/69																										
1973	Atl-N	15	10	.600	38	37	10	4	0	256^{1}	254	18	70	112	11.5	3.41	115	.259	.311	17	.181	4	7	15	0	1.8
1974	Atl-N	16	12	.571	38	38	7	1	0	274^{2}	293	10	89	113	12.6	3.15	120	.277	.334	10	.112	-4	14	19	-1	1.4
1975	Atl-N	17	16	.515	39	39	11	2	0	277^{2}	302	19	82	78	12.5	3.50	108	.278	.330	15	.160	-1	4	8	0	0.9
1976	Atl-N	4	9	.308	26	24	1	1	0	140^{1}	172	6	45	42	14.2	4.17	91	.306	.362	8	.178	-0	-10	-6	2	-0.3
Total	8	87	92	.486	255	242	51	13	1	1648^{2}	1753	120	565	650	12.8	3.73	102	.275	.336	86	.156	3	-15	13	6	1.5
Team	4	52	47	.525	141	138	29	8	0	949	1021	53	286	345	12.5	3.47	110	.277	.331	50	.155	-1	15	37	1	3.8
● RAY MOSS Moss, Raymond Earl b: 12/5/01, Chattanooga, Tenn. BR/TR, 6'1", 185 lbs. Deb: 4/17/26																										
1931	Bos-N	1	3	.250	12	5	0	0	0	45	56	2	16	14	14.4	4.60	82	.306	.362	2	.133	-1	-4	-4	-0	-0.4
Total	6	22	18	.550	112	42	13	3	2	416	474	29	189	109	14.6	4.95	91	.289	.367	22	.148	-5	-18	-21	-4	-2.3
● JOE MUICH Muich, Ignatius Andrew b: 11/23/03, St.Louis, Mo. d: 7/2/93, St.Louis, Mo. BR/TR, 6'2", 175 lbs. Deb: 9/4/24																										
1924	Bos-N	0	0	—	3	0	0	0	0	9	19	1	5	1	24.0	11.00	35	.432	.490	0	.000	-1	-7	-7	-0	-0.1
● DICK MULLIGAN Mulligan, Richard Charles b: 3/18/18, Swoyersville, Pa. d: 12/15/92, Victoria, Tex. BL/TL, 6', 167 lbs. Deb: 9/24/41																										
1946	Bos-N	1	0	1.000	4	0	0	0	0	15^{1}	6	1	9	4	8.8	2.35	146	.122	.259	0	.000	0	2	2	-0	0.1
1947	Bos-N	0	0	—	1	0	0	0	0	2	4	0	1	1	22.5	9.00	43	.400	.455	0	—	0	-1	-1	-0	0.0
Total	3	3	3	.500	25	6	2	0	1	81	82	1	39	23	13.9	4.44	79	.268	.358	0	.000	-1	-8	-8	-0	-0.7
Team	2	1	0	1.000	5	0	0	0	0	17^{1}	10	1	10	5	10.4	3.12	112	.169	.290	0	.000	0	1	1	-0	0.1
● RED MURFF Murff, John Robert b: 4/1/21, Burlington, Tex. BR/TR, 6'3", 195 lbs. Deb: 4/21/56																										
1956	Mil-N	0	0	—	14	1	0	0	1	24^{1}	25	3	7	18	11.8	4.44	78	.272	.323	1	.200	0	-2	-3	0	0.0
1957	Mil-N	2	2	.500	12	1	0	0	2	26	31	3	11	13	14.5	4.85	72	.301	.368	0	.000	-1	-3	-4	0	-0.6
Total	2	2	2	.500	26	2	0	0	3	50^{1}	56	6	18	31	13.2	4.65	75	.287	.347	1	.091	-1	-5	-7	1	-0.6
● AMBY MURRAY Murray, Joseph Ambrose b: 6/4/13, Fall River, Mass. BL/TL, 5'7", 150 lbs. Deb: 7/5/36																										
1936	Bos-N	0	0	—	4	1	0	0	0	11	15	1	3	2	14.7	4.09	94	.319	.360	1	.250	0	-0	-0	0	0.0
● MATT MURRAY Murray, Matthew Michael b: 9/26/70, Boston, Mass. BL/TR, 6'6", 240 lbs. Deb: 8/12/95																										
1995	Atl-N	0	2	.000	4	1	0	0	0	10^{2}	10	3	5	3	13.5	6.75	63	.256	.356	1	.500	0	-3	-3	0	-0.4
Total	1	0	3	.000	6	2	0	0	0	14	21	4	8	4	19.3	9.64	45	.350	.435	1	.500	0	-8	-8	0	-1.5

● JIM NASH Nash, James Edwin b: 2/9/45, Hawthorne, Nev. BR/TR, 6'5", 230 lbs. Deb: 7/3/66

YEAR TM/L	W	L	PCT	G	GS	CG	SH	SV	IP	H	HR	BB	SO	RAT	ERA	ERA+	OAV	OOB	BH	AVG	PB	PR	/A	PD	TPI
1970 Atl-N	13	9	.591	34	33	6	2	0	212^1	211	22	90	153	13.0	4.07	105	.257	.334	7	.087	-3	-1	5	0	0.2
1971 Atl-N	9	7	.563	32	19	2	0	2	133	166	17	50	65	14.6	4.94	75	.314	.374	7	.149	-1	-22	-18	-1	-2.3
1972 Atl-N	1	1	.500	11	4	0	0	1	31^1	35	2	25	10	17.2	5.46	69	.307	.432	2	.222	0	-7	-6	-0	-0.4
Total 7	68	64	.515	201	167	36	11	4	1107^1	1050	108	401	771	11.9	3.58	96	.250	.318	38	.101	-11	-18	-16	-10	-4.6
Team 3	23	17	.575	77	56	8	2	3	376^2	412	41	165	228	13.9	4.49	90	.282	.356	16	.118	-4	-29	-19	-2	-2.5

● BILLY NASH Nash, William Mitchell b: 6/24/1865, Richmond, Va. d: 11/15/29, E.Orange, N.J. BR/TR, 5'8.5", 167 lbs. Deb: 8/5/1884 MU♦

YEAR TM/L	W	L	PCT	G	GS	CG	SH	SV	IP	H	HR	BB	SO	RAT	ERA	ERA+	OAV	OOB	BH	AVG	PB	PR	/A	PD	TPI
1889 Bos-N	0	0	—	1	0	0	0	0	1	0	0	1	0	9.0	0.00	—	.000	.250	132	.274	0	0	0	-0	0.0
Total 2	0	0	—	2	0	0	0	0	1^1	1	0	1	0	13.5	0.00	—	.200	.333	1606	.275	1	1	1	-0	0.0

● JULIO NAVARRO Navarro, Julio (Ventura) "Whiplash" b: 1/9/36, Vieques, P.R. BR/TR, 5'11", 190 lbs. Deb: 9/3/62 F

YEAR TM/L	W	L	PCT	G	GS	CG	SH	SV	IP	H	HR	BB	SO	RAT	ERA	ERA+	OAV	OOB	BH	AVG	PB	PR	/A	PD	TPI
1970 Atl-N	0	0	—	17	0	0	0	1	26^1	24	7	1	21	8.9	4.10	105	.233	.248	1	.167	-0	-0	1	0	0.0
Total 6	7	9	.438	130	1	0	0	17	212^1	191	32	70	151	11.4	3.65	99	.241	.309	5	.147	-0	1	-1	1	0.1

● ART NEHF Nehf, Arthur Neukom b: 7/31/1892, Terre Haute, Ind. d: 12/18/60, Phoenix, Ariz. BL/TL, 5'9.5", 176 lbs. Deb: 8/13/15

YEAR TM/L	W	L	PCT	G	GS	CG	SH	SV	IP	H	HR	BB	SO	RAT	ERA	ERA+	OAV	OOB	BH	AVG	PB	PR	/A	PD	TPI
1915 Bos-N	5	4	.556	12	10	6	4	0	78^1	60	0	21	39	9.7	2.53	103	.214	.276	4	.143	-1	2	1	0	0.0
1916 Bos-N	7	5	.583	22	13	6	1	0	121	110	1	20	36	9.9	2.01	124	.244	.281	5	.125	-0	8	6	-1	0.5
1917 Bos-N	17	8	.680	38	23	17	5	0	233^1	197	4	39	101	9.3	2.16	118	.231	.268	12	.171	5	14	10	-0	1.7
1918 Bos-N	15	15	.500	32	31	**28**	2	0	284^1	274	2	76	96	11.3	2.69	100	.259	.312	16	.168	1	2	-0	3	0.6
1919 Bos-N	8	9	.471	22	19	13	1	0	168^2	151	6	40	53	10.5	3.09	92	.242	.294	13	.206	2	-3	-4	1	-0.1
Total 15	184	120	.605	451	320	182	28	13	2707^2	2715	107	640	844	11.3	3.20	105	.265	.310	192	.210	34	85	45	17	9.7
Team 5	52	41	.559	126	96	70	13	0	885^2	792	13	196	325	10.3	2.52	105	.243	.290	50	.169	7	23	12	4	2.7

● GARY NEIBAUER Neibauer, Gary Wayne b: 10/29/44, Billings, Mont. BR/TR, 6'3", 200 lbs. Deb: 4/12/69

YEAR TM/L	W	L	PCT	G	GS	CG	SH	SV	IP	H	HR	BB	SO	RAT	ERA	ERA+	OAV	OOB	BH	AVG	PB	PR	/A	PD	TPI
1969 *Atl-N	1	2	.333	29	0	0	0	0	57^2	42	9	31	42	11.5	3.90	92	.204	.311	0	.000	-1	-2	-2	-0	-0.2
1970 Atl-N	0	3	.000	7	0	0	0	0	12^2	11	0	8	9	13.5	4.97	86	.239	.352	0	.000	-0	-1	-1	-0	-0.2
1971 Atl-N	1	0	1.000	6	1	0	0	1	21	14	3	9	6	10.3	2.14	173	.187	.282	0	.000	-1	3	4	0	0.2
1972 Atl-N	0	0	—	8	0	0	0	0	17^1	27	6	6	8	17.7	7.27	52	.360	.415	0	.000	-0	-7	-7	-0	-0.1
1973 Atl-N	2	1	.667	16	1	0	0	0	21^1	24	3	19	9	19.0	7.17	55	.282	.425	1	.250	1	-8	-8	-1	-0.9
Total 5	4	8	.333	75	4	0	0	1	148^2	135	22	87	81	13.8	4.78	78	.242	.350	2	.069	-1	-20	-17	-2	-1.6
Team 5	4	6	.400	66	2	0	0	1	130	118	21	73	74	13.6	4.71	80	.242	.347	1	.040	-1	-16	-14	-1	-1.2

● KID NICHOLS Nichols, Charles Augustus b: 9/14/1869, Madison, Wis. d: 4/11/53, Kansas City, Mo. BB/TR, 5'10.5", 175 lbs. Deb: 4/23/1890 MH

YEAR TM/L	W	L	PCT	G	GS	CG	SH	SV	IP	H	HR	BB	SO	RAT	ERA	ERA+	OAV	OOB	BH	AVG	PB	PR	/A	PD	TPI
1890 Bos-N	27	19	.587	48	47	47	**7**	0	424	374	8	112	222	10.5	2.23	168	.229	.284	43	.247	1	63	**72**	0	6.7
1891 Bos-N	30	17	.638	52	48	45	5	**3**	425^1	413	15	103	240	11.3	2.39	**153**	.245	.295	36	.197	-3	**45**	**60**	6	**5.8**
1892 *Bos-N	35	16	.686	53	51	49	5	0	453	404	15	121	187	10.6	2.84	124	.229	.282	39	.198	1	22	34	-1	3.2
1893 Bos-N	34	14	.708	52	44	43	1	1	425	426	15	118	94	11.8	3.52	140	.253	.308	39	.220	-2	54	67	-2	5.5
1894 Bos-N	32	13	.711	50	46	40	**3**	0	407	488	23	121	113	13.7	4.75	120	.294	.345	50	.294	3	26	42	0	3.5
1895 Bos-N	26	16	.619	47	42	42	1	**3**	379^2	417	15	86	140	12.0	3.41	149	.275	.316	37	.236	-4	58	**71**	-0	5.7
1896 Bos-N	**30**	14	.682	49	43	37	3	1	372^1	387	14	101	102	12.0	2.83	161	.266	.316	28	.190	-3	**63**	**71**	2	**6.6**
1897 *Bos-N	**31**	11	.738	**46**	40	37	2	**3**	**368**	362	9	68	127	**10.6**	2.64	**169**	.255	**.291**	39	.265	4	**68**	**75**	-2	**7.3**
1898 Bos-N	**31**	12	.721	**50**	42	40	5	**4**	388	316	7	85	138	**9.6**	2.13	173	**.221**	**.272**	38	.241	3	**64**	**67**	-2	**6.9**
1899 Bos-N	21	19	.525	42	37	37	4	1	343^1	326	11	82	108	10.9	2.99	139	.250	.298	26	.191	-5	33	45	-1	3.9
1900 Bos-N	13	16	.448	29	27	25	**4**	0	231^1	215	11	72	53	11.6	3.07	134	.246	.311	18	.200	-2	16	27	-1	2.6
1901 Bos-N	19	16	.543	38	34	33	4	0	321	306	8	90	143	11.4	3.22	112	.250	.306	46	.282	9	4	14	-1	2.3
Total 15	361	208	.634	620	561	531	48	17	5056^1	4912	156	1268	1868	11.2	2.95	139	.250	.300	471	.226	-0	531	653	-9	60.9
Team 12	329	183	.643	556	501	475	44	16	4538	4434	151	1159	1667	11.3	3.00	143	.251	.302	439	.231	1	517	646	-2	60.0

● CHET NICHOLS Nichols, Chester Raymond Jr. b: 2/22/31, Pawtucket, R.I. d: 3/27/95, Lincoln, R.I. BB/TL, 6'1.5", 195 lbs. Deb: 4/19/51 F

YEAR TM/L	W	L	PCT	G	GS	CG	SH	SV	IP	H	HR	BB	SO	RAT	ERA	ERA+	OAV	OOB	BH	AVG	PB	PR	/A	PD	TPI
1951 Bos-N	11	8	.579	33	19	12	3	2	156	142	4	69	71	12.2	**2.88**	127	.246	.327	7	.137	-2	19	14	2	1.5
1954 Mil-N	9	11	.450	35	20	5	1	1	122^1	132	5	65	55	14.8	4.41	84	.286	.379	3	.086	-3	-5	-9	1	-1.5
1955 Mil-N	9	8	.529	34	21	6	0	1	144	139	20	67	44	12.9	4.00	94	.253	.335	8	.154	-2	1	-4	2	-0.5
1956 Mil-N	0	1	.000	2	0	0	0	0	4	9	1	3	2	27.0	6.75	51	.563	.632	0	.000	-0	-1	-1	0	-0.3
Total 9	34	36	.486	189	71	23	4	10	603^1	600	45	280	266	13.2	3.64	105	.264	.346	22	.127	-8	22	11	8	0.7
Team 4	29	28	.509	104	60	23	4	4	426^1	422	30	204	172	13.3	3.74	99	.263	.348	18	.129	-7	13	-1	4	-0.8

● TRICKY NICHOLS Nichols, Frederick C. b: 7/26/1850, Bridgeport, Conn. d: 8/22/1897, Bridgeport, Conn. BR/TR, 5'7.5", 150 lbs. Deb: 4/21/1875

YEAR TM/L	W	L	PCT	G	GS	CG	SH	SV	IP	H	HR	BB	SO	RAT	ERA	ERA+	OAV	OOB	BH	AVG	PB	PR	/A	PD	TPI
1876 Bos-N	1	0	1.000	1	1	1	0	0	9	7	0	0	0	7.0	1.00	226	.200	.200	0	.000	-1	1	1	0	0.1
Total 5	24	44	.353	72	65	60	1	0	593	724	4	82	126	12.2	3.37	76	.287	.309	55	.161	-10	-45	-53	-1	-5.4

● ROD NICHOLS Nichols, Rodney Lea b: 12/29/64, Burlington, Iowa BR/TR, 6'2", 190 lbs. Deb: 7/30/88

YEAR TM/L	W	L	PCT	G	GS	CG	SH	SV	IP	H	HR	BB	SO	RAT	ERA	ERA+	OAV	OOB	BH	AVG	PB	PR	/A	PD	TPI
1995 Atl-N	0	0	—	5	0	0	0	0	6^2	14	3	5	3	25.7	5.40	78	.424	.500	0	—	0	-1	-1	0	0.0
Total 7	11	31	.262	100	48	6	1	1	412^2	460	42	121	214	13.0	4.43	91	.282	.337	0	—	0	-20	-18	-1	-2.2

● DAVID NIED Nied, David Glen b: 12/22/68, Dallas, Texas BR/TR, 6'2", 175 lbs. Deb: 9/1/92

YEAR TM/L	W	L	PCT	G	GS	CG	SH	SV	IP	H	HR	BB	SO	RAT	ERA	ERA+	OAV	OOB	BH	AVG	PB	PR	/A	PD	TPI
1992 Atl-N	3	0	1.000	6	2	0	0	0	23	10	0	5	19	5.9	1.17	312	.130	.183	2	.286	0	6	6	-0	0.9
Total 4	17	16	.515	46	40	3	1	0	236^1	257	25	97	142	13.7	4.87	98	.281	.354	10	.143	-2	-21	-3	-2	0.3

● JOE NIEKRO Niekro, Joseph Franklin b: 11/7/44, Martins Ferry, Ohio BR/TR, 6'1", 190 lbs. Deb: 4/16/67 F

YEAR TM/L	W	L	PCT	G	GS	CG	SH	SV	IP	H	HR	BB	SO	RAT	ERA	ERA+	OAV	OOB	BH	AVG	PB	PR	/A	PD	TPI
1973 Atl-N	2	4	.333	20	0	0	0	3	24	23	2	11	12	12.8	4.13	95	.277	.362	1	.333	0	-1	-1	1	-0.1
1974 Atl-N	3	2	.600	27	2	0	0	0	43	36	5	18	31	11.7	3.56	106	.237	.326	0	.000	-1	0	1	1	0.1
Total 22	221	204	.520	702	500	107	29	16	3584	3466	276	1262	1747	12.0	3.59	97	.255	.321	152	.156	6	14	-38	-3	-5.4
Team 2	5	6	.455	47	2	0	0	3	67	59	7	29	43	12.1	3.76	102	.251	.338	1	.125	-0	-1	1	1	0.0

● PHIL NIEKRO Niekro, Philip Henry b: 4/1/39, Blaine, Ohio BR/TR, 6'1", 180 lbs. Deb: 4/15/64 F

YEAR TM/L	W	L	PCT	G	GS	CG	SH	SV	IP	H	HR	BB	SO	RAT	ERA	ERA+	OAV	OOB	BH	AVG	PB	PR	/A	PD	TPI
1964 Mil-N	0	0	—	10	0	0	0	0	15	15	1	7	8	13.8	4.80	73	.273	.365	0	—	0	-2	-2	-0	0.0
1965 Mil-N	2	3	.400	41	1	0	0	6	74^2	73	5	26	49	12.3	2.89	122	.258	.327	1	.100	-0	5	5	1	0.5
1966 Atl-N	4	3	.571	28	0	0	0	2	50^1	48	4	23	17	13.1	4.11	88	.249	.335	0	.000	-1	-3	-3	2	-0.3
1967 Atl-N	11	9	.550	46	20	10	1	9	207	164	9	55	129	9.8	**1.87**	**178**	.218	.277	7	.123	-0	35	33	1	3.8
1968 Atl-N	14	12	.538	37	34	15	5	2	257	228	16	45	140	9.7	2.59	116	.239	.277	8	.104	-1	11	11	3	1.5
1969 *Atl-N★	23	13	.639	40	35	21	4	1	284^1	235	21	57	193	9.4	2.56	141	.221	.264	20	.211	3	33	33	2	4.8
1970 Atl-N	12	18	.400	34	32	10	3	0	229^2	222	40	68	168	11.6	4.27	100	.248	.305	12	.152	-1	-6	0	2	0.1
1971 Atl-N	15	14	.517	42	36	18	4	2	268^2	248	27	70	173	10.8	2.98	124	.245	.296	14	.152	-2	14	22	2	2.3
1972 Atl-N	16	12	.571	38	36	17	1	0	282^1	254	22	53	164	9.9	3.06	124	.236	.275	18	.194	1	12	23	1	2.5
1973 Atl-N	13	10	.565	42	30	9	1	4	245	214	21	89	131	11.3	3.31	119	.234	.306	10	.122	-1	10	17	2	1.7
1974 Atl-N	**20**	13	.606	41	39	**18**	6	1	**302^1**	249	19	88	195	10.2	2.38	159	.225	.286	20	.192	-0	**42**	**47**	0	**5.2**
1975 Atl-N☆	15	15	.500	39	37	13	1	0	275^2	285	29	72	144	12.0	3.20	118	.269	.322	17	.172	-0	13	18	1	1.9
1976 Atl-N	17	11	.607	38	37	10	2	0	270^2	249	18	101	173	11.9	3.29	115	.242	.315	18	.191	1	6	15	1	1.7
1977 Atl-N	16	20	.444	44	43	**20**	2	0	**330^1**	315	26	164	**262**	13.3	4.03	110	.255	.346	19	.174	-3	-5	15	2	1.4
1978 Atl-N★	19	18	.514	44	42	**22**	4	1	**334^1**	295	16	102	248	11.0	2.88	141	.235	.299	27	.225	2	26	**43**	4	**5.7**
1979 Atl-N	**21**	20	.512	44	44	**23**	1	0	**342**	311	41	113	208	11.4	3.39	119	.241	.307	24	.195	1	13	25	3	3.4
1980 Atl-N	15	18	.455	40	38	11	3	1	275	256	30	85	176	11.3	3.63	103	.249	.308	12	.133	-2	-1	3	1	0.2
1981 Atl-N	7	7	.500	22	22	3	3	0	139^1	120	6	56	62	11.4	3.10	115	.233	.310	4	.077	-4	6	7	0	0.3
1982 *Atl-N☆	17	4	**.810**	35	35	4	2	0	234^1	225	23	73	144	11.6	3.61	103	.255	.314	17	.195	2	-0	3	1	0.6

YEAR	TM/L	W	L	PCT	G	GS	CG	SH	SV	IP	H	HR	BB	SO	RAT	ERA	ERA+	OAV	OOB	BH	AVG	PB	PR	/A	PD	TPI
1983	Atl-N	11	10	.524	34	33	2	0	0	201^{2}	212	18	105	128	14.2	3.97	98	.276	.364	12	.185	0	-8	-2	0	-0.2
1987	Atl-N	0	0	—	1	1	0	0	0	3	6	0	6	0	36.0	15.00	29	.429	.600	0	.000	-0	-4	-4	-0	0.0
Total	24	318	274	.537	864	716	245	45	29	5404^{1}	5044	482	1809	3342	11.6	3.35	115	.247	.312	260	.169	-6	192	299	28	35.4
Team	21	268	230	.538	740	595	226	43	29	4622^{2}	4224	392	1458	2912	11.3	3.20	119	.243	.305	260	.169	-6	198	309	28	37.1
● **JOHNNY NIGGELING**	Niggeling, John Arnold b: 7/10/03, Remsen, Iowa d: 9/16/63, LeMars, Iowa BR/TR, 6', 170 lbs. Deb: 4/30/38																									
1938	Bos-N	1	0	1.000	2	0	0	0	0	2	4	0	1	1	22.5	9.00	38	.400	.455	0	—	0	-1	-1	-0	-0.5
1946	Bos-N	2	5	.286	8	8	3	0	0	58	54	2	21	24	11.8	3.26	105	.243	.311	2	.111	-1	1	1	0	0.0
Total	9	64	69	.481	184	161	81	12	0	1250^{2}	1111	60	516	620	12.0	3.22	113	.236	.316	59	.140	-14	63	58	-7	4.2
Team	2	3	5	.375	10	8	3	0	0	60	58	2	22	25	12.2	3.45	99	.250	.318	2	.111	-1	-0	-0	0	-0.5
● **LOU NORTH**	North, Louis Alexander b: 6/15/1891, Elgin, Ill. d: 5/16/74, Shelton, Conn. BR/TR, 5'11", 175 lbs. Deb: 8/22/13																									
1924	Bos-N	1	2	.333	9	4	1	0	0	35^{1}	45	1	19	11	16.3	5.35	71	.321	.403	1	.111	-1	-6	-6	-1	-0.6
Total	7	21	16	.568	172	25	8	0	13	463	509	24	200	199	14.0	4.43	82	.287	.363	27	.197	-1	-34	-42	0	-3.0
● **JAKE NORTHROP**	Northrop, George Howard "Jerky" b: 3/5/1888, Monroeton, Pa. d: 11/16/45, Monroeton, Pa. BL/TR, 5'11", 170 lbs. Deb: 7/29/18																									
1918	Bos-N	5	1	.833	7	4	4	1	0	40	26	0	3	4	6.5	1.35	199	.183	.200	2	.154	-1	6	6	0	0.9
1919	Bos-N	1	5	.167	11	3	2	0	0	37^{1}	43	2	10	9	13.0	4.58	62	.301	.351	4	.500	3	-7	-7	1	-0.7
Total	2	6	6	.500	18	7	6	1	0	77^{1}	69	2	13	13	9.7	2.91	95	.242	.278	6	.286	2	-1	-1	1	0.2
● **DON NOTTEBART**	Nottebart, Donald Edward b: 1/23/36, West Newton, Mass. BR/TR, 6'1", 190 lbs. Deb: 7/1/60																									
1960	Mil-N	1	0	1.000	5	1	0	0	1	15^{1}	14	0	15	8	17.0	4.11	83	.233	.387	0	.000	-1	-1	-1	1	-0.1
1961	Mil-N	6	7	.462	38	11	2	0	3	126^{1}	117	11	48	66	11.9	4.06	92	.251	.323	7	.184	0	-0	-4	2	-0.2
1962	Mil-N	2	2	.500	39	0	0	0	2	64	64	4	20	36	12.4	3.23	117	.258	.324	2	.333	1	5	4	2	0.5
Total	9	36	51	.414	296	89	16	2	21	928^{1}	902	69	283	525	11.7	3.65	96	.256	.315	32	.134	-3	-8	-13	11	-1.6
Team	3	9	9	.500	82	12	2	0	6	205^{2}	195	15	83	110	12.4	3.81	98	.252	.329	9	.184	1	4	-2	4	0.2
● **WIN NOYES**	Noyes, Winfield Charles b: 6/16/1889, Pleasanton, Neb. d: 4/8/69, Cashmere, Wash. BR/TR, 6', 180 lbs. Deb: 5/19/13																									
1913	Bos-N	0	0	—	11	0	0	0	0	20^{2}	22	1	6	5	13.9	4.79	69	.289	.372	1	.250	0	-4	-3	0	0.0
Total	3	11	15	.423	49	29	14	1	1	246^{2}	254	7	98	93	13.2	3.76	78	.280	.356	10	.135	-3	-25	-22	-1	-2.2
● **BILLY O'DELL**	O'Dell, William Oliver b: 2/10/33, Whitmire, S.C. BB/TL, 5'11", 170 lbs. Deb: 6/20/54																									
1965	Mil-N	10	6	.625	62	1	0	0	18	111^{1}	87	10	30	78	9.6	2.18	161	.215	.272	4	.174	1	17	17	-0	3.0
1966	Atl-N	2	3	.400	24	0	0	0	6	41^{1}	44	3	18	20	13.9	2.40	152	.272	.352	2	.250	0	6	6	-0	0.8
Total	13	105	100	.512	479	199	63	13	48	1817	1697	137	556	1133	11.4	3.29	109	.246	.306	66	.125	-7	85	59	-12	3.8
Team	2	12	9	.571	86	1	0	0	24	152^{2}	131	13	48	98	10.8	2.24	159	.231	.296	6	.194	1	22	22	-1	3.8
● **DAVE ODOM**	Odom, David Everett "Blimp" or "Porky" b: 6/5/18, Dinuba, Cal. d: 11/19/87, Myrtle Beach, Fla. BR/TR, 6'1", 220 lbs. Deb: 5/31/43																									
1943	Bos-N	0	3	.000	22	3	1	0	2	54^{2}	54	3	30	17	14.5	5.27	65	.269	.374	0	.000	-2	-11	-11	-1	-1.0
● **BLUE MOON ODOM**	Odom, Johnny Lee b: 5/29/45, Macon, Ga. BR/TR, 6', 185 lbs. Deb: 9/5/64 ♦																									
1975	Atl-N	1	7	.125	15	10	0	0	0	56	78	5	28	30	17.0	7.07	53	.342	.414	1	.077	-1	-21	-21	0	-2.5
Total	13	84	85	.497	295	229	40	15	1	1509	1362	103	788	857	13.0	3.70	89	.244	.341	79	.195	26	-45	-71	5	-5.8
● **JOE OESCHGER**	Oeschger, Joseph Carl b: 5/24/1892, Chicago, Ill. d: 7/28/86, Rohnert Park, Cal BR/TR, 6' ", 190 lbs. Deb: 4/21/14																									
1919	Bos-N	4	2	.667	7	7	4	1	0	56^{2}	63	0	21	16	13.5	2.54	112	.300	.366	2	.091	-1	2	2	-1	-0.1
1920	Bos-N	15	13	.536	38	30	20	5	0	299	294	10	99	80	12.1	3.46	88	.265	.329	18	.178	-3	-11	-14	-3	-1.8
1921	Bos-N	20	14	.588	46	36	19	**3**	0	299	303	11	97	68	12.5	3.52	104	.274	.341	28	.255	2	9	4	2	0.9
1922	Bos-N	6	21	.222	46	23	10	1	1	195^{2}	234	8	81	51	14.9	5.06	79	.303	.375	12	.190	-0	-21	-23	1	-2.6
1923	Bos-N	5	15	.250	44	19	6	1	2	166^{1}	227	4	54	33	15.5	5.68	70	.330	.383	12	.231	-0	-31	-31	0	-3.2
Total	12	82	116	.414	365	197	99	18	8	1818	1936	61	651	535	13.1	3.81	88	.281	.349	99	.165	-18	-96	-89	-8	-11.1
Team	5	50	65	.435	181	115	59	11	3	1016^{2}	1121	33	352	248	13.4	4.10	87	.288	.353	72	.207	-2	-52	-62	-1	-6.8
● **JOE OGRODOWSKI**	Ogrodowski, Joseph Anthony b: 11/20/06, Hoytville, Pa. d: 6/24/59, Elmira, N.Y. BR/TR, 5'11", 165 lbs. Deb: 4/27/25																									
1925	Bos-N	0	0	—	1	0	0	0	0	1	6	0	3	0	81.0	54.00	7	.600	.692	0	—	0	-6	-6	-0	0.0
● **CHI-CHI OLIVO**	Olivo, Federico Emilio (Maldonado) b: 3/18/28, Guayubin, D.R. d: 2/3/77, Guayubin, D.R. BR/TR, 6'2", 215 lbs. Deb: 6/5/61 F																									
1961	Mil-N	0	0	—	3	0	0	0	0	2	3	1	5	1	36.0	18.00	21	.500	.727	0	—	0	-3	-3	-0	0.0
1964	Mil-N	2	1	.667	38	0	0	0	5	60	55	7	21	45	11.4	3.75	94	.247	.311	1	.250	0	-1	-2	1	0.0
1965	Mil-N	0	1	.000	8	0	0	0	0	13	12	1	5	11	11.8	1.38	254	.267	.340	0	—	0	3	3	-0	0.2
1966	Atl-N	5	4	.556	47	0	0	0	7	66	59	4	19	41	10.8	4.23	86	.240	.297	1	.111	-0	-5	-4	-1	-0.8
Total	4	7	6	.538	96	0	0	0	12	141	129	13	50	98	11.5	3.96	90	.248	.315	2	.154	-0	-6	-6	-1	-0.6
● **GREGG OLSON**	Olson, Greggory William b: 10/11/66, Scribner, Neb. BR/TR, 6'4", 210 lbs. Deb: 9/2/88																									
1994	Atl-N	0	2	.000	16	0	0	0	1	14^{2}	19	1	13	10	20.3	9.20	46	.317	.446	0	.000	-0	-8	-8	-1	-1.1
Total	8	20	26	.435	359	0	0	0	164	398	328	15	190	378	11.8	2.67	151	.225	.317	0	.000	0	62	61	1	13.7
● **ED OLWINE**	Olwine, Edward R. b: 5/28/58, Greenville, Ohio BL/TL, 6'2", 165 lbs. Deb: 6/2/86																									
1986	Atl-N	0	0	—	37	0	0	0	1	47^{2}	35	5	17	37	10.0	3.40	117	.207	.283	1	.333	1	2	3	-0	0.0
1987	Atl-N	0	1	.000	27	0	0	0	1	23^{1}	25	4	8	12	13.1	5.01	87	.269	.333	0	—	0	-2	-2	-0	-0.1
1988	Atl-N	0	0	—	16	0	0	0	1	18^{2}	22	4	4	5	13.0	6.75	54	.286	.329	0	—	0	-7	-6	-1	-0.1
Total	3	0	1	.000	80	0	0	0	3	89^{2}	82	13	29	54	11.4	4.52	89	.242	.307	1	.333	1	-8	-5	-1	-0.2
● **RANDY O'NEAL**	O'Neal, Randall Jeffrey b: 8/30/60, Ashland, Ky. BR/TR, 6'2", 195 lbs. Deb: 9/12/84																									
1987	Atl-N	4	2	.667	16	10	0	0	0	61	79	12	24	33	15.5	5.61	78	.316	.380	2	.105	-1	-10	-9	1	-0.7
Total	7	17	19	.472	142	46	2	0	3	440^{2}	461	48	149	248	12.6	4.35	91	.272	.334	4	.080	-3	-19	-19	5	-0.6
● **WAYNE OSBORNE**	Osborne, Wayne Harold "Ossie" or "Fish Hook" b: 10/11/12, Watsonville, Cal. d: 3/13/87, Vancouver, Wash. BL/TR, 6'2.5", 172 lbs. Deb: 4/18/35																									
1936	Bos-N	1	1	.500	5	3	0	0	0	20	31	1	9	8	18.0	5.85	66	.352	.412	2	.250	0	-4	-4	0	-0.4
Total	2	1	1	.500	7	3	0	0	0	21^{1}	32	1	9	9	17.3	5.91	65	.348	.406	2	.250	0	-4	-5	0	-0.4
● **DAN OSINSKI**	Osinski, Daniel b: 11/17/33, Chicago, Ill. BR/TR, 6'2", 195 lbs. Deb: 4/11/62																									
1965	Mil-N	0	3	.000	61	0	0	0	6	83	81	4	40	54	13.2	2.82	125	.261	.348	1	.167	-0	7	6	-0	0.3
Total	8	29	28	.509	324	21	5	2	18	589^{2}	556	47	264	400	12.6	3.34	107	.250	.331	12	.122	-3	16	15	1	1.8
● **PHIL PAINE**	Paine, Phillips Steere "Flip" b: 6/8/30, Chepachet, R.I. d: 2/19/78, Lebanon, Pa. BR/TR, 6'2", 181 lbs. Deb: 7/14/51																									
1951	Bos-N	2	0	1.000	21	0	0	0	0	35^{1}	36	2	20	17	15.3	3.06	120	.271	.382	0	.000	-1	4	2	-0	0.0
1954	Mil-N	1	0	1.000	11	0	0	0	0	14	14	1	12	11	17.4	3.86	97	.292	.443	0	—	0	0	-0	-0	-0.1
1955	Mil-N	2	0	1.000	15	0	0	0	0	25^{1}	20	2	14	26	12.1	2.49	151	.225	.330	1	.333	0	4	4	0	0.3
1956	Mil-N	0	0	—	1	0	0	0	0	0	3	0	0	0	—	∞	—	1.000	1.000	0	—	0	-2	-2	0	-0.2
1957	Mil-N	0	0	—	1	0	0	0	0	2	1	0	3	2	18.0	0.00	—	.143	.400	0	—	0	1	1	0	0.0
Total	6	10	1	.909	95	0	0	0	1	150	144	12	80	101	14.0	3.36	116	.260	.364	3	.214	-0	10	9	-0	0.4
Team	5	5	0	1.000	49	0	0	0	0	76^{2}	74	5	49	56	15.0	3.17	117	.264	.383	1	.143	-0	7	5	-0	0.0
● **DAVID PALMER**	Palmer, David William b: 10/19/57, Glens Falls, N.Y. BR/TR, 6'1", 205 lbs. Deb: 9/9/78																									
1986	Atl-N	11	10	.524	35	35	2	0	0	209^{2}	181	17	102	170	12.4	3.65	109	.234	.327	12	.182	1	2	8	2	1.1

YEAR	TM/L	W	L	PCT	G	GS	CG	SH	SV	IP	H	HR	BB	SO	RAT	ERA	ERA+	OAV	OOB	BH	AVG	PB	PR	/A	PD	TPI
1987	Atl-N	8	11	.421	28	28	0	0	0	152^1	169	17	64	111	14.2	4.90	89	.281	.357	6	.125	-0	-14	-9	1	-1.0
Total	10	64	59	.520	212	176	10	4	2	1085	1036	78	434	748	12.4	3.78	99	.252	.327	48	.149	2	-11	-6	5	-0.3
Team	2	19	21	.475	63	63	2	0	0	362	350	34	166	281	13.1	4.18	99	.255	.340	18	.158	1	-12	-2	2	0.1

● EMILIO PALMERO Palmero, Emilio Antonio "Pal" b: 6/13/1895, Guanabacoa, Cuba d: 7/15/70, Toledo, Ohio BL/TL, 5'11", 157 lbs. Deb: 9/21/15

YEAR	TM/L	W	L	PCT	G	GS	CG	SH	SV	IP	H	HR	BB	SO	RAT	ERA	ERA+	OAV	OOB	BH	AVG	PB	PR	/A	PD	TPI
1928	Bos-N	0	1	.000	3	1	0	0	0	6^2	14	0	2	0	21.6	5.40	72	.452	.485	0	.000	-0	-1	-1	-0	-0.2
Total	5	6	15	.286	41	17	5	0	0	141	172	4	83	48	17.0	5.17	77	.319	.420	10	.208	1	-19	-19	2	-2.5

● JIM PANTHER Panther, James Edward b: 3/1/45, Burlington, Iowa BR/TR, 6'1", 190 lbs. Deb: 4/5/71

YEAR	TM/L	W	L	PCT	G	GS	CG	SH	SV	IP	H	HR	BB	SO	RAT	ERA	ERA+	OAV	OOB	BH	AVG	PB	PR	/A	PD	TPI
1973	Atl-N	2	3	.400	23	0	0	0	0	30^2	45	3	9	8	15.8	7.63	52	.363	.406	0	—	0	-14	-13	-1	-1.9
Total	3	7	13	.350	85	4	0	0	0	130	156	12	60	56	15.3	5.26	61	.303	.381	1	.111	-0	-30	-29	-1	-4.4

● MILT PAPPAS Pappas, Milton Stephen "Gimpy" (b: Miltiades Stergios Papastegios) b: 5/11/39, Detroit, Mich. BR/TR, 6'3", 190 lbs. Deb: 8/10/57

YEAR	TM/L	W	L	PCT	G	GS	CG	SH	SV	IP	H	HR	BB	SO	RAT	ERA	ERA+	OAV	OOB	BH	AVG	PB	PR	/A	PD	TPI
1968	Atl-N	10	8	.556	22	19	3	1	0	121^1	111	8	22	75	10.1	2.37	126	.246	.285	6	.162	2	8	8	-1	1.5
1969	*Atl-N	6	10	.375	26	24	1	0	0	144	149	14	44	72	12.3	3.63	99	.267	.325	7	.156	3	-0	-0	-0	0.2
1970	Atl-N	2	2	.500	11	3	1	0	0	35^2	44	6	7	25	13.4	6.06	71	.293	.333	0	.000	-1	-8	-7	0	-0.8
Total	17	209	164	.560	520	465	129	43	4	3186	3046	298	858	1728	11.2	3.40	110	.252	.306	132	.123	-14	86	120	0	12.4
Team	3	18	20	.474	59	46	5	1	0	301	304	28	73	172	11.5	3.41	101	.262	.311	13	.141	3	-0	1	-1	0.9

● JEFF PARRETT Parrett, Jeffrey Dale b: 8/26/61, Indianapolis, Ind. BR/TR, 6'3", 200 lbs. Deb: 4/11/86

YEAR	TM/L	W	L	PCT	G	GS	CG	SH	SV	IP	H	HR	BB	SO	RAT	ERA	ERA+	OAV	OOB	BH	AVG	PB	PR	/A	PD	TPI
1990	Atl-N	1	1	.500	20	0	0	0	1	27	27	1	19	17	15.7	3.00	134	.281	.405	1	1.000	0	2	3	0	0.3
1991	Atl-N	1	2	.333	18	0	0	0	1	21^1	31	2	12	14	18.1	6.33	61	.326	.402	0	—	0	-6	-6	1	-0.7
Total	9	53	40	.570	440	11	0	0	22	658^1	608	59	314	552	12.7	3.84	102	.249	.336	4	.111	-1	-2	6	-3	1.0
Team	2	2	3	.400	38	0	0	0	2	48^1	58	3	31	31	16.8	4.47	89	.304	.404	1	1.000	1	-4	-3	1	-0.4

● JIGGS PARSON Parson, William Edwin b: 12/28/1885, Parker, S.Dak. d: 5/19/67, Los Angeles, Cal. BR/TR, 6'2", 180 lbs. Deb: 5/16/10

YEAR	TM/L	W	L	PCT	G	GS	CG	SH	SV	IP	H	HR	BB	SO	RAT	ERA	ERA+	OAV	OOB	BH	AVG	PB	PR	/A	PD	TPI
1910	Bos-N	0	2	.000	10	4	0	0	0	35^1	35	2	26	7	16.0	3.82	87	.278	.409	1	.083	-1	-3	-2	-0	-0.2
1911	Bos-N	0	1	.000	7	0	0	0	0	25	36	2	15	7	19.8	6.48	59	.375	.478	2	.200	-0	-9	-7	-1	-0.3
Total	2	0	3	.000	17	4	0	0	0	60^1	71	4	41	14	17.6	4.92	72	.320	.439	3	.136	-2	-12	-9	-1	-0.5

● CHARLIE PARSONS Parsons, Charles James b: 7/18/1863, Cherry Flats, Pa. d: 3/24/36, Mansfield, Pa. BL/TL, 5'10", 160 lbs. Deb: 5/29/1886

YEAR	TM/L	W	L	PCT	G	GS	CG	SH	SV	IP	H	HR	BB	SO	RAT	ERA	ERA+	OAV	OOB	BH	AVG	PB	PR	/A	PD	TPI
1886	Bos-N	0	2	.000	2	2	2	0	0	16	20	0	4	5	13.5	3.94	81	.308	.348	3	.375	1	-1	-1	-1	-0.1
Total	3	1	4	.200	8	7	6	0	0	59	83	0	16	12	15.9	4.58	84	.314	.365	9	.333	2	-4	-5	-1	-0.3

● MIKE PAYNE Payne, Michael Earl b: 11/15/61, Woonsocket, R.I. BR/TR, 5'11", 165 lbs. Deb: 8/22/84

YEAR	TM/L	W	L	PCT	G	GS	CG	SH	SV	IP	H	HR	BB	SO	RAT	ERA	ERA+	OAV	OOB	BH	AVG	PB	PR	/A	PD	TPI
1984	Atl-N	0	1	.000	3	1	0	0	0	5^2	7	0	3	3	15.9	6.35	61	.333	.417	0	.000	-0	-2	-2	0	-0.3

● RED PEERY Peery, George Allan b: 8/15/06, Payson, Utah d: 5/6/85, Salt Lake City, Ut. BL/TL, 5'11", 160 lbs. Deb: 9/22/27

YEAR	TM/L	W	L	PCT	G	GS	CG	SH	SV	IP	H	HR	BB	SO	RAT	ERA	ERA+	OAV	OOB	BH	AVG	PB	PR	/A	PD	TPI
1929	Bos-N	0	1	.000	9	1	0	0	0	44	53	1	9	3	12.7	5.11	91	.305	.339	3	.214	1	-2	-2	-0	0.0
Total	2	0	1	.000	10	1	0	0	0	45	53	1	10	3	12.6	5.00	93	.298	.335	3	.214	1	-2	-2	0	0.0

● ALEJANDRO PENA Pena, Alejandro (Vasquez) b: 6/25/59, Cambiaso, D.R. BR/TR, 6'1", 205 lbs. Deb: 9/14/81

YEAR	TM/L	W	L	PCT	G	GS	CG	SH	SV	IP	H	HR	BB	SO	RAT	ERA	ERA+	OAV	OOB	BH	AVG	PB	PR	/A	PD	TPI
1991	*Atl-N	2	0	1.000	15	0	0	0	11	19^1	11	1	3	13	6.5	1.40	278	.167	.203	0	.000	-0	5	5	-0	1.3
1992	Atl-N	1	6	.143	41	0	0	0	15	42	40	7	13	34	11.4	4.07	90	.255	.312	0	.000	-0	-3	-2	-1	-0.6
1995	*Atl-N	0	0	—	14	0	0	0	0	13	11	1	4	18	10.4	4.15	102	.224	.283	0	—	0	0	0	0	0.0
Total	14	56	51	.523	499	72	12	7	74	1053^2	955	73	330	834	11.1	3.10	117	.240	.301	20	.110	-5	70	63	-7	7.5
Team	3	3	6	.333	70	0	0	0	26	74^1	62	9	20	65	9.9	3.39	113	.228	.281	0	.000	-0	2	4	-1	0.7

● HUB PERDUE Perdue, Herbert Rodney "The Gallatin Squash" b: 6/7/1882, Bethpage, Tenn. d: 10/31/68, Gallatin, Tex. BR/TR, 5'10.5", 192 lbs. Deb: 4/19/11

YEAR	TM/L	W	L	PCT	G	GS	CG	SH	SV	IP	H	HR	BB	SO	RAT	ERA	ERA+	OAV	OOB	BH	AVG	PB	PR	/A	PD	TPI
1911	Bos-N	6	10	.375	24	19	9	0	1	137^1	180	10	41	40	14.7	4.98	77	.321	.372	10	.208	-1	-24	-18	-0	-1.9
1912	Bos-N	13	16	.448	37	30	20	1	3	249	295	11	54	101	12.7	3.80	94	.303	.341	12	.138	-5	-11	-6	-4	-1.5
1913	Bos-N	16	13	.552	38	32	16	3	1	212^1	201	7	39	91	10.3	3.26	101	.249	.287	7	.104	-5	-1	0	-7	-1.1
1914	Bos-N	2	5	.286	9	9	2	0	0	51	60	5	11	13	13.1	5.82	47	.311	.357	1	.071	-0	-17	-17	0	-2.0
Total	5	51	64	.443	161	122	64	5	7	918^1	1037	43	199	317	12.3	3.85	85	.293	.334	42	.140	-13	-73	-60	-15	-10.0
Team	4	37	44	.457	108	90	47	4	5	649^2	736	33	145	245	12.4	4.03	86	.290	.332	30	.139	-11	-53	-41	-11	-6.5

● PASCUAL PEREZ Perez, Pascual Gross (b: Pascual Gross (Perez)) b: 5/17/57, San Cristobal, D.R. BR/TR, 6'2", 163 lbs. Deb: 5/7/80 F

YEAR	TM/L	W	L	PCT	G	GS	CG	SH	SV	IP	H	HR	BB	SO	RAT	ERA	ERA+	OAV	OOB	BH	AVG	PB	PR	/A	PD	TPI
1982	*Atl-N	4	4	.500	16	11	0	0	0	79^1	85	4	17	29	11.6	3.06	122	.276	.314	3	.167	1	5	6	0	0.7
1983	Atl-N★	15	8	.652	33	33	7	1	0	215^1	213	20	51	144	11.2	3.43	113	.260	.307	12	.160	-1	5	11	1	1.2
1984	Atl-N	14	8	.636	30	30	4	1	0	211^2	208	26	51	145	11.1	3.74	103	.260	.307	5	.076	-2	-4	3	3	0.4
1985	Atl-N	1	13	.071	22	22	0	0	0	95^1	115	10	57	57	16.3	6.14	63	.297	.389	3	.120	-0	-27	-24	-1	-3.2
Total	11	67	68	.496	207	193	21	4	0	1244^1	1167	107	344	822	11.1	3.44	110	.249	.303	41	.120	-5	25	47	6	4.8
Team	4	34	33	.507	101	96	11	2	0	601^2	621	60	176	375	12.0	3.92	98	.268	.322	23	.125	-2	-21	-5	3	-0.9

● GAYLORD PERRY Perry, Gaylord Jackson b: 9/15/38, Williamston, N.C. BR/TR, 6'4", 215 lbs. Deb: 4/14/62 FH

YEAR	TM/L	W	L	PCT	G	GS	CG	SH	SV	IP	H	HR	BB	SO	RAT	ERA	ERA+	OAV	OOB	BH	AVG	PB	PR	/A	PD	TPI
1981	Atl-N	8	9	.471	23	23	3	0	0	150^2	182	9	24	60	12.5	3.94	91	.304	.335	12	.250	3	-8	-6	-1	-0.5
Total	22	314	265	.542	777	690	303	53	11	5350^1	4938	399	1379	3534	10.8	3.11	117	.245	.297	141	.131	-16	311	305	21	34.4

● DAN PETRY Petry, Daniel Joseph b: 11/13/58, Palo Alto, Cal. BR/TR, 6'4", 200 lbs. Deb: 7/8/79

YEAR	TM/L	W	L	PCT	G	GS	CG	SH	SV	IP	H	HR	BB	SO	RAT	ERA	ERA+	OAV	OOB	BH	AVG	PB	PR	/A	PD	TPI
1991	Atl-N	0	0	—	10	0	0	0	0	24^1	29	2	14	9	16.3	5.55	70	.296	.389	1	.200	0	-5	-4	0	0.0
Total	13	125	104	.546	370	300	52	11	1	2080^1	1984	218	852	1063	12.5	3.95	102	.253	.330	1	.200	0	24	16	23	4.9

● BIG JEFF PFEFFER Pfeffer, Francis Xavier b: 3/31/1882, Champaign, Ill. d: 12/19/54, Kankakee, Ill. BR/TR, 6'1", 185 lbs. Deb: 4/15/05 F

YEAR	TM/L	W	L	PCT	G	GS	CG	SH	SV	IP	H	HR	BB	SO	RAT	ERA	ERA+	OAV	OOB	BH	AVG	PB	PR	/A	PD	TPI
1906	Bos-N	13	22	.371	35	35	33	4	0	302^1	270	4	114	158	11.9	2.95	91	.246	.325	31	.196	3	-11	-9	2	-0.3
1907	Bos-N	6	8	.429	19	16	12	1	0	144	129	3	61	65	12.3	3.00	85	.253	.341	15	.250	3	-8	-7	-0	-0.4
1908	Bos-N	0	0	—	4	0	0	0	0	10	18	1	8	3	23.4	12.60	19	.383	.473	0	.000	-0	-11	-11	-0	-0.1
1911	Bos-N	7	5	.583	26	6	4	1	2	97	116	3	57	24	16.1	4.73	81	.301	.391	9	.196	1	-14	-10	0	-1.0
Total	6	31	39	.443	112	69	59	6	2	695^2	660	14	292	317	12.7	3.30	87	.260	.342	66	.204	8	-40	-34	-0	-1.4
Team	4	26	35	.426	84	57	49	6	2	553^1	533	11	240	250	12.9	3.45	82	.261	.346	55	.207	7	-45	-38	1	-1.8

● TAYLOR PHILLIPS Phillips, William Taylor "Tay" b: 6/18/33, Atlanta, Ga. BL/TL, 5'11", 185 lbs. Deb: 6/8/56

YEAR	TM/L	W	L	PCT	G	GS	CG	SH	SV	IP	H	HR	BB	SO	RAT	ERA	ERA+	OAV	OOB	BH	AVG	PB	PR	/A	PD	TPI
1956	Mil-N	5	3	.625	23	6	3	0	2	87^2	69	6	33	36	11.2	2.26	153	.223	.311	0	.000	-2	15	12	2	1.1
1957	Mil-N	3	2	.600	27	6	0	0	2	73	82	3	40	36	15.2	5.55	63	.300	.392	2	.100	-1	-14	-17	0	-1.2
Total	6	16	22	.421	147	45	9	1	6	438^2	460	42	211	233	14.2	4.82	78	.275	.364	6	.053	-9	-46	-51	4	-3.5
Team	2	8	5	.615	50	12	3	0	4	160^2	151	9	73	72	13.0	3.75	93	.259	.349	2	.049	-3	1	-5	2	-0.1

● WILEY PIATT Piatt, Wiley Harold "Iron Man" b: 7/13/1874, Blue Creek, Ohio d: 9/20/46, Cincinnati, Ohio BL/TL, 5'10", 175 lbs. Deb: 4/22/1898

YEAR	TM/L	W	L	PCT	G	GS	CG	SH	SV	IP	H	HR	BB	SO	RAT	ERA	ERA+	OAV	OOB	BH	AVG	PB	PR	/A	PD	TPI
1903	Bos-N	9	14	.391	25	23	18	0	0	181	198	5	61	100	13.1	3.18	101	.280	.340	16	.225	2	2	1	-3	0.0
Total	6	86	79	.521	182	170	139	12	1	1390^1	1481	27	455	517	13.0	3.61	97	.272	.337	130	.239	13	4	-15	-20	-1.8

● RON PICHE Piche, Ronald Jacques b: 5/22/35, Verdun, Que., Canada BR/TR, 5'11", 165 lbs. Deb: 5/30/60 C

YEAR	TM/L	W	L	PCT	G	GS	CG	SH	SV	IP	H	HR	BB	SO	RAT	ERA	ERA+	OAV	OOB	BH	AVG	PB	PR	/A	PD	TPI
1960	Mil-N	3	5	.375	37	0	0	0	9	48	48	3	23	38	13.9	3.56	96	.258	.349	0	.000	-0	1	-1	-1	-0.2
1961	Mil-N	2	2	.500	12	1	1	0	1	23^1	20	1	16	16	13.9	3.47	108	.238	.360	0	.000	-1	1	1	0	0.1
1962	Mil-N	3	2	.600	14	8	2	0	0	52	54	6	29	28	14.9	4.85	78	.273	.374	1	.056	-1	-5	-6	1	-0.6
1963	Mil-N	1	1	.500	37	1	0	0	0	53	53	4	25	40	13.2	3.40	95	.256	.336	0	.000	-1	-1	-1	1	0.0
Total	6	10	16	.385	134	11	3	0	12	221^1	216	23	123	157	14.1	4.19	84	.255	.354	1	.024	-3	-13	-16	1	-2.2
Team	4	9	10	.474	100	10	3	0	10	176^1	175	14	93	122	14.0	3.88	91	.259	.354	1	.027	-3	-3	-7	2	-0.7

YEAR	TM/L	W	L	PCT	G	GS	CG	SH	SV	IP	H	HR	BB	SO	RAT	ERA	ERA+	OAV	OOB	BH	AVG	PB	PR	/A	PD	TPI
● CLARENCE PICKREL	Pickrel, Clarence Douglas b: 3/28/11, Gretna, Va. d: 11/4/83, Rocky Mount, Va. BR/TR, 6'1", 180 lbs. Deb: 4/22/33																									
1934	Bos-N	0	0	—	10	1	0	0	0	16	24	0	7	9	17.4	5.06	76	.333	.392	0	.000	-0	-2	-2	-1	-0.1
Total	2	1	0	1.000	19	1	0	0	0	29^{2}	44	0	10	15	16.7	4.55	85	.344	.396	0	.000	-0	-3	-2	-1	-0.2
● AL PIECHOTA	Piechota, Aloysius Edward "Pie" b: 1/19/14, Chicago, Ill. BR/TR, 6', 195 lbs. Deb: 5/7/40																									
1940	Bos-N	2	5	.286	21	8	2	0	0	61	68	6	41	18	16.1	5.75	65	.278	.381	4	.200	1	-13	-14	-0	-1.3
1941	Bos-N	0	0	—	1	0	0	0	0	1	0	0	1	0	9.0	0.00	—	.000	.250	0	—	0	0	0	-0	0.0
Total	2	2	5	.286	22	8	2	0	0	62	68	6	42	18	16.0	5.66	66	.274	.379	4	.200	1	-13	-13	-0	-1.3
● AL PIEROTTI	Pierotti, Albert Felix b: 10/24/1895, Boston, Mass. d: 2/12/64, Everett, Mass. BR/TR, 5'10.5", 195 lbs. Deb: 8/9/20																									
1920	Bos-N	1	1	.500	6	2	2	0	0	25	23	2	9	12	11.5	2.88	106	.250	.317	2	.250	0	1	0	-0	0.0
1921	Bos-N	0	1	.000	2	0	0	0	0	1^{2}	3	0	3	1	32.4	21.60	17	.375	.545	0	.000	-0	-3	-3	0	-1.3
Total	2	1	2	.333	8	2	2	0	0	26^{2}	26	2	12	13	12.8	4.05	76	.260	.339	2	.222	-0	-3	-3	-0	-1.3
● TOGIE PITTINGER	Pittinger, Charles Reno b: 1/12/1872, Greencastle, Pa. d: 1/14/09, Greencastle, Pa. BL/TR, 6'2", 175 lbs. Deb: 4/26/00																									
1900	Bos-N	2	9	.182	18	13	8	0	0	114	135	7	54	27	15.6	5.13	80	.293	.377	6	.130	-4	-18	-13	-1	-1.4
1901	Bos-N	13	16	.448	34	33	27	1	0	281^{1}	288	7	76	129	11.9	3.01	120	.263	.316	11	.110	-8	10	19	3	1.2
1902	Bos-N	27	16	.628	46	40	36	7	0	389^{1}	360	4	128	174	11.7	2.52	112	.245	.313	20	.136	-8	11	13	-2	0.2
1903	Bos-N	18	22	.450	44	39	35	3	1	351^{2}	396	12	143	140	14.2	3.48	92	.294	.369	14	.109	-9	-8	-11	-3	-2.1
1904	Bos-N	15	21	.417	38	38	35	5	0	335^{1}	298	1	144	146	12.2	2.66	104	.242	.329	13	.107	-9	3	4	5	0.0
Total	8	115	113	.504	262	228	187	23	3	2040^{2}	2017	39	734	832	12.6	3.10	98	.260	.332	92	.124	-43	-23	-13	-3	-6.2
Team	5	75	84	.472	180	163	141	16	1	1471^{2}	1477	31	545	616	12.8	3.08	102	.264	.336	64	.118	-38	-2	11	2	-2.1
● JUAN PIZARRO	Pizarro, Juan Ramon (Cordova) b: 2/7/37, Santurce, P.R. BL/TL, 5'11", 190 lbs. Deb: 5/4/57																									
1957	*Mil-N	5	6	.455	24	10	3	0	0	99^{1}	99	16	51	68	13.7	4.62	76	.261	.350	9	.250	3	-8	-12	-1	-1.0
1958	*Mil-N	6	4	.600	16	10	7	1	1	96^{2}	75	12	47	84	11.7	2.70	130	.212	.312	8	.250	3	13	9	1	1.2
1959	Mil-N	6	2	.750	29	14	6	2	0	133^{2}	117	13	70	126	13.1	3.77	94	.237	.342	5	.122	-0	3	-3	0	-0.2
1960	Mil-N	6	7	.462	21	17	3	0	0	114^{2}	105	13	72	88	14.2	4.55	75	.244	.357	11	.275	3	-10	-14	-1	-1.2
Total	18	131	105	.555	488	245	79	17	28	2034^{1}	1807	201	888	1522	12.1	3.43	104	.237	.320	133	.202	29	55	33	-5	4.6
Team	4	23	19	.548	90	51	19	3	1	444^{1}	396	54	240	366	13.2	3.93	89	.239	.341	33	.221	9	-2	-21	-1	-1.2
● BILL POSEDEL	Posedel, William John "Sailor Bill" or "Barnacle Bill" b: 8/2/06, San Francisco, Cal. d: 11/28/89, Livermore, Cal. BR/TR, 5'11", 175 lbs. Deb: 4/23/38 C																									
1939	Bos-N	15	13	.536	33	29	18	5	0	220^{2}	221	8	78	73	12.2	3.92	94	.268	.331	8	.110	-4	0	-5	-1	-1.1
1940	Bos-N	12	17	.414	35	32	18	0	1	233	263	16	81	86	13.3	4.13	90	.288	.346	14	.171	1	-7	-11	-0	-1.1
1941	Bos-N	4	4	.500	18	9	3	0	0	57^{1}	61	6	30	10	14.4	4.87	73	.279	.368	8	.320	2	-8	-8	-0	-0.8
1946	Bos-N	2	0	1.000	19	0	0	0	4	28^{1}	34	4	13	9	14.9	6.99	49	.304	.376	0	.000	-0	-11	-11	-0	-1.2
Total	5	41	43	.488	138	87	45	6	6	679^{1}	757	48	248	227	13.4	4.56	82	.286	.349	40	.176	0	-55	-63	-4	-7.1
Team	4	33	34	.493	105	70	39	5	5	539^{1}	579	34	202	178	13.1	4.27	86	.280	.344	30	.164	-1	-26	-36	-2	-4.2
● NELS POTTER	Potter, Nelson Thomas "Nellie" b: 8/23/11, Mt.Morris, Ill. d: 9/30/90, Mt.Morris, Ill. BL/TR, 5'11", 180 lbs. Deb: 4/25/36																									
1948	*Bos-N	5	2	.714	18	7	3	0	2	85	77	4	8	47	9.0	2.33	165	.245	.264	11	.379	3	15	14	1	1.6
1949	Bos-N	6	11	.353	41	3	1	0	7	96^{2}	99	6	30	57	12.1	4.19	90	.265	.321	3	.130	-0	-2	-4	1	-0.7
Total	12	92	97	.487	349	177	89	6	22	1686	1721	123	582	747	12.4	3.99	99	.265	.328	128	.228	11	-23	-6	3	1.3
Team	2	11	13	.458	59	10	4	0	9	181^{2}	176	10	38	104	10.7	3.32	115	.256	.296	14	.269	3	14	10	2	0.9
● JIM PRENDERGAST	Prendergast, James Bartholomew b: 8/23/17, Brooklyn, N.Y. d: 8/23/94, Amherst, N.Y. BL/TL, 6'1", 208 lbs. Deb: 4/25/48																									
1948	Bos-N	1	1	.500	10	2	0	0	1	16^{2}	30	1	5	3	18.9	10.26	37	.380	.417	0	.000	-1	-12	-12	0	-1.4
● BOB PRIDDY	Priddy, Robert Simpson b: 12/10/39, Pittsburgh, Pa. BR/TR, 6'1", 200 lbs. Deb: 9/20/62																									
1969	Atl-N	0	0	—	1	0	0	0	0	2	1	0	1	1	9.0	0.00	—	.143	.250	0	—	0	1	1	-0	0.0
1970	Atl-N	5	5	.500	41	0	0	0	8	73	75	9	24	32	12.6	5.42	79	.269	.333	3	.200	0	-11	-9	1	-1.3
1971	Atl-N	4	9	.308	40	0	0	0	4	64	71	8	44	36	16.3	4.22	88	.289	.399	2	.182	0	-5	-4	1	-0.7
Total	9	24	38	.387	249	29	3	0	18	536	518	60	198	294	12.2	4.00	87	.257	.327	13	.137	1	-33	-30	-2	-3.6
Team	3	9	14	.391	82	0	0	0	12	139	147	17	69	69	14.2	4.79	84	.276	.364	5	.192	0	-16	-12	1	-2.0
● HUB PRUETT	Pruett, Hubert Shelby "Shucks" b: 9/1/1900, Malden, Mo. d: 1/28/82, Ladue, Mo. BL/TL, 5'10.5", 165 lbs. Deb: 4/26/22																									
1932	Bos-N	1	5	.167	18	7	4	0	0	63	76	3	30	27	16.0	5.14	73	.308	.396	2	.105	-1	-9	-10	2	-0.7
Total	7	29	48	.377	211	69	28	1	13	745	816	28	396	357	15.1	4.63	92	.286	.380	36	.170	-3	-38	-29	10	-2.1
● CHARLIE PULEO	Puleo, Charles Michael b: 2/7/55, Glen Ridge, N.J. BR/TR, 6'3", 200 lbs. Deb: 9/16/81																									
1986	Atl-N	1	2	.333	5	3	1	0	0	24^{1}	13	4	12	18	9.6	2.96	134	.160	.277	2	.333	0	2	3	-0	0.4
1987	Atl-N	6	8	.429	35	16	1	0	0	123^{1}	122	11	40	99	12.0	4.23	103	.262	.325	5	.179	1	-2	2	-2	0.1
1988	Atl-N	5	5	.500	53	3	0	0	1	106^{1}	101	9	47	70	12.8	3.47	106	.251	.333	3	.231	0	-0	2	-0	0.2
1989	Atl-N	1	1	.500	15	1	0	0	0	29	26	2	16	17	13.0	4.66	78	.245	.344	0	.000	-0	-4	-3	-1	-0.3
Total	8	29	39	.426	180	76	3	1	2	633	621	59	319	387	13.6	4.25	90	.261	.351	22	.144	-1	-41	-30	-2	-3.8
Team	4	13	16	.448	108	23	2	0	1	283	262	26	115	204	12.2	3.88	103	.248	.326	10	.208	2	-4	3	-3	0.4
● EWALD PYLE	Pyle, Herbert Ewald "Lefty" b: 8/27/10, St.Louis, Mo. BL/TL, 6'0.5", 175 lbs. Deb: 4/23/39																									
1945	Bos-N	0	1	.000	4	2	0	0	0	13^{2}	16	1	18	10	22.4	7.24	53	.302	.479	2	.333	1	-5	-5	-0	-0.3
Total	5	11	21	.344	67	36	5	1	1	270^{1}	277	16	150	122	14.4	5.03	71	.262	.357	12	.143	-2	-44	-43	-0	-4.2
● BILL QUARLES	Quarles, William H. b: 1869, Petersburg, Va. d: 3/25/1897, Petersburg, Va. 6'3", Deb: 5/21/1891																									
1893	Bos-N	2	1	.667	3	3	3	0	0	27	31	2	5	6	12.7	4.67	106	.279	.322	2	.222	0	-0	1	-0	0.0
Total	2	3	2	.600	6	5	5	0	0	49	63	3	17	16	15.4	6.24	70	.303	.367	2	.100	-2	-11	-10	-1	-0.8
● JACK QUINN	Quinn, John Picus (b: John Quinn Picus) b: 7/5/1883, Janesville, Pa. d: 4/17/46, Pottsville, Pa. BR/TR, 6' ", 196 lbs. Deb: 4/15/09																									
1913	Bos-N	4	3	.571	8	7	6	1	0	56^{1}	55	1	7	33	10.1	2.40	137	.261	.288	4	.200	1	5	6	2	1.1
Total	23	247	218	.531	756	444	243	28	57	3920^{1}	4238	102	860	1329	11.9	3.29	113	.280	.323	248	.184	-16	140	182	40	23.6
● CHARLEY RADBOURN	Radbourn, Charles Gardner "Old Hoss" b: 12/11/1854, Rochester, N.Y. d: 2/5/1897, Bloomington, Ill. BR/TR, 5'9", 168 lbs. Deb: 5/5/1880 H♦																									
1886	Bos-N	27	31	.466	58	58	57	3	0	509^{1}	521	18	111	218	11.2	3.00	106	.254	.292	60	.237	8	17	11	2	1.9
1887	Bos-N	24	23	.511	50	50	48	1	0	425	505	20	133	87	13.8	4.55	89	.286	.340	40	.229	2	-23	-23	-3	-2.1
1888	Bos-N	7	16	.304	24	24	24	1	0	207	187	8	45	64	10.4	2.87	99	.234	.282	17	.215	1	-0	-0	-1	-0.1
1889	Bos-N	20	11	.645	33	31	28	1	0	277	282	14	72	99	11.8	3.67	113	.256	.306	23	.189	-1	11	15	2	1.4
Total	11	309	195	.613	528	503	489	35	2	4535^{1}	4335	117	875	1830	10.4	2.67	120	.241	.278	585	.235	40	302	267	7	28.7
Team	4	78	81	.491	165	163	157	6	0	1418^{1}	1495	60	361	468	12.0	3.58	100	.261	.309	140	.223	10	5	1	1	1.1
● PAT RAGAN	Ragan, Don Carlos Patrick b: 11/15/1888, Blanchard, Iowa d: 9/4/56, Los Angeles, Cal. BR/TR, 5'10.5", 185 lbs. Deb: 4/21/09 C																									
1915	Bos-N	16	12	.571	33	26	13	3	0	227	208	2	59	81	10.9	2.46	105	.255	.311	12	.150	-0	7	3	-2	0.0
1916	Bos-N	9	9	.500	28	23	14	3	0	182	143	3	47	94	9.4	2.08	120	.218	.270	13	.217	3	11	8	1	1.3
1917	Bos-N	6	9	.400	30	13	5	1	1	147^{2}	138	6	35	61	10.6	2.93	87	.250	.295	6	.125	-1	-4	-6	0	-0.8
1918	Bos-N	8	17	.320	30	25	15	2	0	206^{1}	212	4	54	68	11.8	3.23	83	.270	.320	13	.183	-2	-11	-12	-0	-1.6

YEAR TM/L	W	L	PCT	G	GS	CG	SH	SV	IP	H	HR	BB	SO	RAT	ERA	ERA+	OAV	OOB	BH	AVG	PB	PR	/A	PD	TPI
1919 Bos-N	0	2	.000	4	3	0	0	0	12^{2}	16	0	3	3	13.5	7.11	40	.281	.317	1	.250	0	-6	-6	0	-0.8
Total 11	77	104	.425	283	182	93	12	6	1608^{1}	1555	38	470	680	11.5	2.99	97	.260	.317	84	.154	-13	-8	-18	-2	-4.8
Team 5	39	49	.443	125	90	47	9	1	775^{2}	717	15	198	307	10.8	2.74	95	.250	.301	45	.171	-1	-2	-13	-1	-1.9

● ED RAKOW Rakow, Edward Charles "Rock" b: 5/30/36, Pittsburgh, Pa. BB/TR, 5'11", 178 lbs. Deb: 4/22/60

YEAR TM/L	W	L	PCT	G	GS	CG	SH	SV	IP	H	HR	BB	SO	RAT	ERA	ERA+	OAV	OOB	BH	AVG	PB	PR	/A	PD	TPI
1967 Atl-N	3	2	.600	17	3	0	0	0	39^{1}	36	4	15	25	11.9	5.26	63	.240	.313	0	.000	-1	-8	-8	-1	-1.2
Total 7	36	47	.434	195	90	20	3	5	761^{1}	771	88	304	484	13.0	4.33	92	.264	.339	19	.084	-13	-46	-31	4	-3.1

● CLAUDE RAYMOND Raymond, Joseph Claude Marc "Frenchy" b: 5/7/37, St.Jean, Que., Canada BR/TR, 5'10", 175 lbs. Deb: 4/15/59

YEAR TM/L	W	L	PCT	G	GS	CG	SH	SV	IP	H	HR	BB	SO	RAT	ERA	ERA+	OAV	OOB	BH	AVG	PB	PR	/A	PD	TPI
1961 Mil-N	1	0	1.000	13	0	0	0	2	20^{1}	22	2	9	13	14.2	3.98	94	.275	.356	0	.000	-0	0	-1	0	0.0
1962 Mil-N	5	5	.500	26	0	0	0	10	42^{2}	37	5	15	40	11.4	2.74	138	.236	.310	0	.000	-1	6	5	-1	1.2
1963 Mil-N	4	6	.400	45	0	0	0	5	53^{1}	57	12	27	44	14.9	5.40	60	.268	.361	2	.500	2	-13	-13	1	-2.3
1967 Atl-N	4	1	.800	28	0	0	0	5	34^{1}	33	2	11	14	11.5	2.62	127	.260	.319	0	.000	-0	3	3	0	0.5
1968 Atl-N	3	5	.375	36	0	0	0	10	60^{1}	56	4	18	37	11.2	2.83	106	.256	.315	1	.143	-0	1	1	0	0.2
1969 Atl-N	2	2	.500	33	0	0	0	1	48	56	4	13	15	13.3	5.25	69	.298	.350	2	.286	0	-9	-9	-1	-0.8
Total 12	46	53	.465	449	7	2	0	83	721	711	75	225	497	12.0	3.66	96	.261	.324	11	.109	-2	-7	-13	-0	-1.4
Team 6	19	19	.500	181	0	0	0	33	259	261	29	93	163	12.6	3.86	88	.265	.335	5	.161	1	-12	-13	0	-1.2

● JEFF REARDON Reardon, Jeffrey James b: 10/1/55, Dalton, Mass. BR/TR, 6'1", 195 lbs. Deb: 8/25/79

YEAR TM/L	W	L	PCT	G	GS	CG	SH	SV	IP	H	HR	BB	SO	RAT	ERA	ERA+	OAV	OOB	BH	AVG	PB	PR	/A	PD	TPI
1992 *Atl-N	3	0	1.000	14	0	0	0	3	15^{2}	14	0	2	7	9.8	1.15	318	.241	.279	0	—	0	4	4	-0	1.0
Total 16	73	77	.487	880	0	0	0	367	1132^{1}	1000	109	358	877	11.0	3.16	121	.236	.299	5	.088	-3	80	83	-18	11.5

● RON REED Reed, Ronald Lee b: 11/2/42, LaPorte, Ind. BR/TR, 6'6", 215 lbs. Deb: 9/26/66

YEAR TM/L	W	L	PCT	G	GS	CG	SH	SV	IP	H	HR	BB	SO	RAT	ERA	ERA+	OAV	OOB	BH	AVG	PB	PR	/A	PD	TPI
1966 Atl-N	1	1	.500	2	2	0	0	0	8^{1}	7	1	4	6	11.9	2.16	168	.226	.314	0	.000	-0	1	1	-0	0.3
1967 Atl-N	1	1	.500	3	3	0	0	0	21^{1}	21	1	3	11	11.0	2.95	112	.262	.306	0	.000	-1	1	1	1	0.1
1968 Atl-N★	11	10	.524	35	28	6	1	0	201^{2}	189	10	49	111	10.9	3.35	89	.246	.297	10	.161	1	-8	-8	0	-0.7
1969 *Atl-N	18	10	.643	36	33	7	1	0	241^{1}	227	24	56	160	10.8	3.47	104	.246	.294	10	.125	-2	3	4	-1	0.1
1970 Atl-N	7	10	.412	21	18	6	0	0	134^{2}	140	16	39	68	12.1	4.41	97	.266	.319	4	.091	-2	-5	-2	1	-0.4
1971 Atl-N	13	14	.481	32	32	8	1	0	222^{1}	221	26	54	129	11.2	3.72	100	.261	.306	11	.149	-3	-6	-0	-1	-0.4
1972 Atl-N	11	15	.423	31	30	11	1	0	213	222	18	60	111	12.2	3.93	96	.270	.325	13	.178	-1	-11	-3	1	-0.4
1973 Atl-N	4	11	.267	20	19	2	0	1	116^{1}	133	7	31	64	12.9	4.41	89	.287	.335	9	.200	-0	-10	-6	1	-0.6
1974 Atl-N	10	11	.476	28	28	6	2	0	186	171	16	41	78	10.4	3.39	112	.243	.286	6	.105	-3	5	8	-2	0.3
1975 Atl-N	4	5	.444	10	10	1	0	0	74^{2}	93	1	16	40	13.1	4.22	89	.304	.339	6	.231	1	-5	-4	-0	-0.3
Total 19	146	140	.510	751	236	55	8	103	2477^{2}	2374	182	633	1481	11.1	3.46	107	.252	.303	98	.158	-6	32	68	-3	6.8
Team 10	80	88	.476	218	203	47	6	1	1419^{2}	1424	120	353	778	11.4	3.74	98	.260	.309	69	.146	-10	-35	-10	1	-2.0

● EARL REID Reid, Earl Percy b: 6/8/13, Bangor, Ala. d: 5/11/84, Cullman, Ala. BL/TR, 6'3", 190 lbs. Deb: 5/8/46

YEAR TM/L	W	L	PCT	G	GS	CG	SH	SV	IP	H	HR	BB	SO	RAT	ERA	ERA+	OAV	OOB	BH	AVG	PB	PR	/A	PD	TPI
1946 Bos-N	1	0	1.000	2	0	0	0	0	3	4	0	3	2	21.0	3.00	114	.308	.438	0	—	0	0	0	-0	0.0

● BOBBY REIS Reis, Robert Joseph Thomas b: 1/2/09, Woodside, N.Y. d: 5/1/73, St.Paul, Minn. BR/TR, 6'1", 175 lbs. Deb: 9/19/31 ♦

YEAR TM/L	W	L	PCT	G	GS	CG	SH	SV	IP	H	HR	BB	SO	RAT	ERA	ERA+	OAV	OOB	BH	AVG	PB	PR	/A	PD	TPI
1936 Bos-N	6	5	.545	35	5	3	0	0	138^{2}	152	7	74	25	15.0	4.48	86	.283	.375	13	.217	1	-7	-10	4	-0.2
1937 Bos-N	0	0	—	4	0	0	0	0	5	3	0	5	0	14.4	1.80	199	.158	.333	21	.244	1	1	1	-0	0.0
1938 Bos-N	1	6	.143	16	2	1	0	0	57^{2}	61	5	41	20	16.9	4.99	69	.271	.397	9	.184	-0	-8	-10	0	-1.0
Total 4	10	13	.435	69	9	5	0	2	242^{2}	262	12	144	52	15.5	4.27	88	.277	.379	70	.233	3	-8	-14	5	-0.4
Team 3	7	11	.389	55	7	4	0	0	201^{1}	216	12	120	45	15.5	4.56	81	.277	.380	43	.221	1	-14	-19	4	-1.2

● TOMMY REIS Reis, Thomas Edward b: 8/6/14, Newport, Ky. BR/TR, 6'2", 180 lbs. Deb: 4/27/38

YEAR TM/L	W	L	PCT	G	GS	CG	SH	SV	IP	H	HR	BB	SO	RAT	ERA	ERA+	OAV	OOB	BH	AVG	PB	PR	/A	PD	TPI
1938 Bos-N	0	0	—	4	0	0	0	0	6^{1}	8	1	1	4	12.8	7.11	48	.296	.321	0	—	0	-2	-3	-0	0.0

● ED REULBACH Reulbach, Edward Marvin "Big Ed" b: 12/1/1882, Detroit, Mich. d: 7/17/61, Glens Falls, N.Y. BR/TR, 6'1", 190 lbs. Deb: 5/16/05

YEAR TM/L	W	L	PCT	G	GS	CG	SH	SV	IP	H	HR	BB	SO	RAT	ERA	ERA+	OAV	OOB	BH	AVG	PB	PR	/A	PD	TPI
1916 Bos-N	7	6	.538	21	11	6	0	0	109^{1}	99	1	41	47	11.9	2.47	101	.251	.328	3	.091	-1	2	0	5	0.5
1917 Bos-N	0	1	.000	5	2	0	0	0	22^{1}	21	0	15	9	14.9	2.82	90	.256	.378	0	.000	1	-0	-1	1	0.2
Total 13	182	106	.632	399	300	201	40	13	2632^{1}	2118	33	892	1138	10.7	2.28	122	.224	.299	127	.147	-11	159	146	22	17.7
Team 2	7	7	.500	26	13	6	0	0	131^{2}	120	1	56	56	12.4	2.53	99	.252	.337	3	.083	-1	2	-0	7	0.7

● ARMANDO REYNOSO Reynoso, Armando Martin (Gutierrez) b: 5/1/66, San Luis Potosi, Mex. BR/TR, 6', 186 lbs. Deb: 8/11/91

YEAR TM/L	W	L	PCT	G	GS	CG	SH	SV	IP	H	HR	BB	SO	RAT	ERA	ERA+	OAV	OOB	BH	AVG	PB	PR	/A	PD	TPI
1991 Atl-N	2	1	.667	6	5	0	0	0	23^{1}	26	4	10	10	15.0	6.17	63	.299	.390	0	.000	-0	-6	-6	2	-0.5
1992 Atl-N	1	0	1.000	3	1	0	0	1	7^{2}	11	2	2	2	16.4	4.70	78	.393	.452	0	.000	-0	-1	-1	0	-0.1
Total 5	25	23	.521	68	63	5	0	1	365^{1}	413	45	133	194	14.0	4.61	105	.291	.361	15	.126	-4	-22	10	9	1.7
Team 2	3	1	.750	9	6	0	0	1	31	37	6	12	12	15.4	5.81	66	.322	.405	0	.000	-1	-7	-7	2	-0.6

● FLINT RHEM Rhem, Charles Flint "Shad" b: 1/24/01, Rhems, S.C. d: 7/30/69, Columbia, S.C. BR/TR, 6'2", 180 lbs. Deb: 9/6/24

YEAR TM/L	W	L	PCT	G	GS	CG	SH	SV	IP	H	HR	BB	SO	RAT	ERA	ERA+	OAV	OOB	BH	AVG	PB	PR	/A	PD	TPI
1934 Bos-N	8	8	.500	25	20	5	1	0	152^{2}	164	5	38	56	11.9	3.60	106	.273	.317	3	.058	-5	8	4	1	0.0
1935 Bos-N	0	5	.000	10	6	0	0	0	40^{1}	61	4	11	10	16.1	5.36	71	.341	.379	0	.000	-1	-6	-7	0	-0.8
Total 12	105	97	.520	294	229	91	8	10	1725^{1}	1958	113	529	534	13.1	4.20	98	.287	.340	88	.144	-28	-39	-20	-3	-6.8
Team 2	8	13	.381	35	26	5	1	0	193	225	9	49	66	12.8	3.96	96	.289	.331	3	.048	-7	2	-3	1	-0.8

● WOODY RICH Rich, Woodrow Earl b: 3/9/16, Morganton, N.C. d: 4/18/83, Morganton, N.C. BL/TR, 6'2", 185 lbs. Deb: 4/22/39

YEAR TM/L	W	L	PCT	G	GS	CG	SH	SV	IP	H	HR	BB	SO	RAT	ERA	ERA+	OAV	OOB	BH	AVG	PB	PR	/A	PD	TPI
1944 Bos-N	1	1	.500	7	2	1	0	0	25	32	3	12	6	16.9	5.76	66	.327	.416	1	.125	-1	-6	-5	0	-0.4
Total 4	6	4	.600	33	16	5	0	1	117^{1}	127	8	50	42	14.2	5.06	89	.280	.361	8	.205	-1	-9	-7	2	-0.1

● RUSTY RICHARDS Richards, Russell Earl b: 1/27/65, Houston, Tex. BL/TR, 6'4", 200 lbs. Deb: 9/20/89

YEAR TM/L	W	L	PCT	G	GS	CG	SH	SV	IP	H	HR	BB	SO	RAT	ERA	ERA+	OAV	OOB	BH	AVG	PB	PR	/A	PD	TPI
1989 Atl-N	0	0	—	2	2	0	0	0	9^{1}	10	2	6	4	16.4	4.82	76	.278	.395	0	.000	-0	-1	-1	0	0.0
1990 Atl-N	0	0	—	1	0	0	0	0	1	2	1	1	0	27.0	27.00	15	.400	.500	0	—	0	-3	-3	0	0.0
Total 2	0	0	—	3	2	0	0	0	10^{1}	12	3	7	4	17.4	6.97	53	.293	.408	0	.000	-0	-4	-4	0	0.0

● LEW RICHIE Richie, Lewis A. b: 8/23/1883, Ambler, Pa. d: 8/15/36, South Montain, Pa. BR/TR, 5'8", 165 lbs. Deb: 5/8/06

YEAR TM/L	W	L	PCT	G	GS	CG	SH	SV	IP	H	HR	BB	SO	RAT	ERA	ERA+	OAV	OOB	BH	AVG	PB	PR	/A	PD	TPI
1909 Bos-N	7	7	.500	22	13	9	2	2	131^{2}	118	2	44	42	11.1	2.32	121	.247	.312	5	.114	-2	4	7	-3	0.2
1910 Bos-N	0	3	.000	4	2	0	0	0	16^{1}	20	0	9	7	16.0	2.76	121	.317	.403	0	.000	-1	1	1	1	0.2
Total 8	74	65	.532	241	136	86	20	9	1359^{1}	1190	21	495	437	11.4	2.54	115	.246	.320	65	.147	-7	60	58	-11	4.0
Team 2	7	10	.412	26	15	9	2	2	148	138	2	53	49	11.7	2.37	121	.255	.323	5	.104	-3	5	8	-3	0.4

● LEE RICHMOND Richmond, J Lee b: 5/5/1857, Sheffield, Ohio d: 10/1/29, Toledo, Ohio TL, 5'10", 155 lbs. Deb: 9/27/1879 ♦

YEAR TM/L	W	L	PCT	G	GS	CG	SH	SV	IP	H	HR	BB	SO	RAT	ERA	ERA+	OAV	OOB	BH	AVG	PB	PR	/A	PD	TPI
1879 Bos-N	1	0	1.000	1	1	1	0	0	9	4	0	1	11	5.0	2.00	124	.114	.139	2	.333	0	0	0	0	0.1
Total 6	75	100	.429	191	179	161	8	3	1583	1763	27	269	552	11.6	3.06	95	.269	.298	262	.257	7	-66	-28	-1	-1.9

● JAY RITCHIE Ritchie, Jay Seay b: 11/20/36, Salisbury, N.C. BR/TR, 6'4", 190 lbs. Deb: 8/4/64

YEAR TM/L	W	L	PCT	G	GS	CG	SH	SV	IP	H	HR	BB	SO	RAT	ERA	ERA+	OAV	OOB	BH	AVG	PB	PR	/A	PD	TPI
1966 Atl-N	0	1	.000	22	0	0	0	4	35^{1}	32	3	12	33	11.2	4.08	89	.241	.303	2	.500	1	-2	-2	0	0.0
1967 Atl-N	4	6	.400	52	0	0	0	2	82^{1}	75	6	29	57	11.8	3.17	105	.245	.319	3	.300	1	2	1	1	0.4
Total 5	8	13	.381	167	2	0	0	8	291^{1}	301	23	94	212	12.4	3.49	101	.269	.329	7	.200	1	-3	1	0	-0.2
Team 2	4	7	.364	74	0	0	0	6	117^{2}	107	9	41	90	11.6	3.44	99	.244	.314	5	.357	2	0	-0	1	0.4

● BEN RIVERA Rivera, Bienvenido Santana b: 1/11/68, San Pedro De Macoris, D.R. BR/TR, 6'6", 210 lbs. Deb: 4/9/92

YEAR TM/L	W	L	PCT	G	GS	CG	SH	SV	IP	H	HR	BB	SO	RAT	ERA	ERA+	OAV	OOB	BH	AVG	PB	PR	/A	PD	TPI
1992 Atl-N	0	1	.000	8	0	0	0	0	15^{1}	21	1	13	11	21.1	4.70	78	.339	.468	0	.000	-0	-2	-2	0	-0.1
Total 3	23	17	.575	67	49	5	2	0	318^{1}	314	32	152	219	13.5	4.52	85	.258	.345	8	.086	-3	-23	-24	-2	-3.8

● CHARLIE ROBERTSON Robertson, Charles Culbertson b: 1/31/1896, Dexter, Tex. d: 8/23/84, Fort Worth, Tex. BL/TR, 6', 175 lbs. Deb: 5/13/19

YEAR TM/L	W	L	PCT	G	GS	CG	SH	SV	IP	H	HR	BB	SO	RAT	ERA	ERA+	OAV	OOB	BH	AVG	PB	PR	/A	PD	TPI
1927 Bos-N	7	17	.292	28	22	6	0	0	154^1	188	2	46	49	13.9	4.72	79	.308	.360	12	.240	1	-14	-17	-1	-2.4
1928 Bos-N	2	5	.286	13	7	3	0	1	59^1	73	5	16	17	13.5	5.31	74	.308	.352	0	.000	-1	-9	-9	-1	-1.1
Total 8	49	80	.380	166	142	60	6	1	1005	1149	38	377	310	13.8	4.44	90	.296	.361	68	.208	-2	-42	-49	-13	-7.6
Team 2	9	22	.290	41	29	9	0	1	213^2	261	7	62	66	13.8	4.89	77	.308	.358	12	.179	-1	-23	-27	-2	-3.5

● HUMBERTO ROBINSON Robinson, Humberto Valentino b: 6/25/30, Colon, Panama BR/TR, 6'1", 155 lbs. Deb: 4/20/55

YEAR TM/L	W	L	PCT	G	GS	CG	SH	SV	IP	H	HR	BB	SO	RAT	ERA	ERA+	OAV	OOB	BH	AVG	PB	PR	/A	PD	TPI
1955 Mil-N	3	1	.750	13	2	1	0	2	38	31	1	25	19	14.2	3.08	122	.235	.373	1	.077	-1	4	3	0	0.2
1956 Mil-N	0	0	—	1	0	0	0	0	2	1	0	2	0	13.5	0.00	—	.167	.375	0	—	0	1	1	0	0.0
1958 Mil-N	2	4	.333	19	0	0	0	1	41^2	30	4	13	26	9.7	3.02	116	.203	.276	1	.167	1	4	2	1	0.5
Total 5	8	13	.381	102	7	2	0	4	213	189	17	90	114	12.0	3.25	119	.241	.323	6	.158	0	16	14	2	1.6
Team 3	5	5	.500	33	2	1	0	3	81^2	62	5	40	45	11.9	2.98	122	.217	.325	2	.105	-1	9	6	1	0.7

● STEVE ROSER Roser, Emerson Corey b: 1/25/18, Rome, N.Y. BR/TR, 6'4", 220 lbs. Deb: 5/5/44

YEAR TM/L	W	L	PCT	G	GS	CG	SH	SV	IP	H	HR	BB	SO	RAT	ERA	ERA+	OAV	OOB	BH	AVG	PB	PR	/A	PD	TPI
1946 Bos-N	1	1	.500	14	1	0	0	1	35	33	1	18	18	13.1	3.60	95	.250	.340	0	.000	-1	-1	-1	-0	-0.1
Total 3	6	5	.545	45	8	1	0	2	149^1	147	5	64	64	12.7	4.04	86	.261	.336	4	.093	-3	-10	-9	-1	-2.6

● NORMIE ROY Roy, Norman Brooks "Jumbo" b: 11/15/28, Newton, Mass. BR/TR, 6', 200 lbs. Deb: 4/23/50

YEAR TM/L	W	L	PCT	G	GS	CG	SH	SV	IP	H	HR	BB	SO	RAT	ERA	ERA+	OAV	OOB	BH	AVG	PB	PR	/A	PD	TPI
1950 Bos-N	4	3	.571	19	6	2	0	1	59^2	72	7	39	25	17.0	5.13	75	.305	.408	3	.167	0	-7	-8	0	-0.9

● DICK RUDOLPH Rudolph, Richard "Baldy" b: 8/25/1887, New York, N.Y. d: 10/20/49, Bronx, N.Y. BR/TR, 5'9.5", 160 lbs. Deb: 9/30/10 C

YEAR TM/L	W	L	PCT	G	GS	CG	SH	SV	IP	H	HR	BB	SO	RAT	ERA	ERA+	OAV	OOB	BH	AVG	PB	PR	/A	PD	TPI
1913 Bos-N	14	13	.519	33	22	17	2	0	249^1	258	4	59	109	11.5	2.92	112	.276	.320	21	.239	4	8	10	5	1.9
1914 *Bos-N	26	10	.722	42	36	31	6	0	336^1	288	9	61	138	**9.4**	2.35	117	.238	.276	15	.125	-1	16	15	2	1.7
1915 Bos-N	22	19	.537	44	43	30	3	1	341^1	304	4	64	147	9.9	2.37	109	.242	.282	23	.198	6	14	8	1	1.7
1916 Bos-N	19	12	.613	41	38	27	5	3	312	266	7	38	133	**8.9**	2.16	115	.235	**.261**	16	.158	1	16	11	6	1.9
1917 Bos-N	13	13	.500	31	30	22	5	0	242^2	252	1	54	96	11.5	3.41	75	.272	.314	20	.230	3	-19	-23	1	-2.1
1918 Bos-N	9	10	.474	21	20	15	3	0	154	144	2	30	48	10.2	2.57	104	.255	.292	10	.185	-1	3	2	1	0.3
1919 Bos-N	13	18	.419	37	32	24	2	2	273^2	282	2	54	76	11.1	2.17	132	.276	.314	17	.193	3	23	21	0	2.9
1920 Bos-N	4	8	.333	18	11	3	0	0	89	104	4	24	24	13.3	4.04	75	.294	.346	5	.185	-0	-9	-10	0	-1.2
1922 Bos-N	0	2	.000	3	3	1	0	0	16	22	2	5	3	15.2	5.06	79	.328	.375	2	.400	1	-2	-2	0	-0.1
1923 Bos-N	1	2	.333	4	4	1	1	0	19^1	27	0	10	3	17.7	3.72	107	.333	.413	0	.000	-1	1	1	0	0.0
1927 Bos-N	0	0	—	1	0	0	0	0	1^1	1	0	1	0	13.5	0.00	—	.200	.333	0	—	0	1	1	-0	0.0
Total 13	121	108	.528	279	240	172	27	8	2049	1971	35	402	786	10.5	2.66	104	.258	.298	131	.188	14	44	25	15	6.3
Team 11	121	107	.531	275	239	171	27	6	2035	1948	35	400	777	10.5	2.62	105	.258	.297	129	.186	13	52	33	16	7.0

● BOB RUSH Rush, Robert Ransom b: 12/21/25, Battle Creek, Mich BR/TR, 6'4", 205 lbs. Deb: 4/22/48

YEAR TM/L	W	L	PCT	G	GS	CG	SH	SV	IP	H	HR	BB	SO	RAT	ERA	ERA+	OAV	OOB	BH	AVG	PB	PR	/A	PD	TPI
1958 *Mil-N	10	6	.625	28	20	5	2	0	147^1	142	13	31	84	10.6	3.42	103	.253	.293	9	.200	2	9	2	-2	0.2
1959 Mil-N	5	6	.455	31	9	1	1	0	101^1	102	5	23	64	11.2	2.40	148	.257	.299	6	.188	0	17	13	-1	1.3
1960 Mil-N	2	0	1.000	10	0	0	0	1	15	24	2	5	8	17.4	4.20	82	.369	.414	1	.333	1	-1	-1	-0	-0.1
Total 13	127	152	.455	417	321	118	16	8	2410^2	2327	177	789	1244	11.8	3.65	109	.251	.313	140	.173	0	88	90	7	11.2
Team 3	17	12	.586	69	29	6	3	1	263^2	268	20	59	156	11.2	3.07	115	.262	.304	16	.200	2	25	13	-2	1.4

● JOHN RUSSELL Russell, John William b: 1/5/61, Oklahoma City, Okla. BR/TR, 6', 200 lbs. Deb: 6/22/84 ♦

YEAR TM/L	W	L	PCT	G	GS	CG	SH	SV	IP	H	HR	BB	SO	RAT	ERA	ERA+	OAV	OOB	BH	AVG	PB	PR	/A	PD	TPI
1989 Atl-N	0	0	—	1	0	0	0	0	0^1	0	0	0	0	0.0	0.00	—	.000	.000	29	.182	0	0	0	0	0.0

● DICK RUTHVEN Ruthven, Richard David b: 3/27/51, Sacramento, Cal. BR/TR, 6'3", 190 lbs. Deb: 4/17/73

YEAR TM/L	W	L	PCT	G	GS	CG	SH	SV	IP	H	HR	BB	SO	RAT	ERA	ERA+	OAV	OOB	BH	AVG	PB	PR	/A	PD	TPI
1976 Atl-N☆	14	17	.452	36	36	8	4	0	240^1	255	14	90	142	13.2	4.19	90	.275	.345	13	.171	-0	-19	-11	2	-1.1
1977 Atl-N	7	13	.350	25	23	6	2	0	151	158	14	62	84	13.2	4.23	105	.267	.338	12	.267	3	-5	4	-2	0.6
1978 Atl-N	2	6	.250	13	13	2	1	0	81	78	8	28	45	11.8	4.11	98	.257	.319	2	.083	-2	-5	-1	-0	-0.2
Total 14	123	127	.492	355	332	61	17	1	2109	2155	165	767	1145	12.6	4.14	92	.267	.333	123	.183	6	-123	-75	-4	-8.1
Team 3	23	36	.390	74	72	16	7	0	472^1	491	36	180	271	13.0	4.19	96	.270	.338	27	.186	1	-29	-8	1	-0.7

● CYCLONE RYAN Ryan, Daniel R. b: 1866, Cappagh White, Ireland d: 1/30/17, Medfield, Mass. TR, 6', 200 lbs. Deb: 8/8/1887 ♦

YEAR TM/L	W	L	PCT	G	GS	CG	SH	SV	IP	H	HR	BB	SO	RAT	ERA	ERA+	OAV	OOB	BH	AVG	PB	PR	/A	PD	TPI
1891 Bos-N	0	0	—	1	0	0	0	0	3	2	0	1	0	9.0	0.00	—	.182	.250	0	.000	-0	1	1	0	0.0
Total 2	0	1	.000	3	1	0	0	0	5^1	7	1	7	0	23.6	10.13	39	.318	.483	7	.212	-0	-4	-4	0	-1.2

● ROSY RYAN Ryan, Wilfred Patrick Dolan b: 3/15/1898, Worcester, Mass. d: 12/10/80, Scottsdale, Ariz. BL/TR, 6', 185 lbs. Deb: 9/7/19

YEAR TM/L	W	L	PCT	G	GS	CG	SH	SV	IP	H	HR	BB	SO	RAT	ERA	ERA+	OAV	OOB	BH	AVG	PB	PR	/A	PD	TPI
1925 Bos-N	2	8	.200	37	7	1	0	2	122^2	152	7	52	48	15.0	6.31	64	.303	.368	11	.282	3	-28	-31	-1	-2.0
1926 Bos-N	0	2	.000	7	2	0	0	0	19	29	1	7	1	17.1	7.58	47	.392	.444	1	.200	-0	-8	-9	-0	-0.8
Total 10	52	47	.525	248	73	29	1	19	881	941	33	278	315	12.6	4.14	91	.277	.333	51	.190	1	-22	-38	-5	-1.3
Team 2	2	10	.167	44	9	1	0	2	141^2	181	8	59	49	15.2	6.48	61	.314	.378	12	.273	3	-36	-40	-1	-2.8

● RAY SADECKI Sadecki, Raymond Michael b: 12/26/40, Kansas City, Kan. BL/TL, 5'11", 180 lbs. Deb: 5/19/60

YEAR TM/L	W	L	PCT	G	GS	CG	SH	SV	IP	H	HR	BB	SO	RAT	ERA	ERA+	OAV	OOB	BH	AVG	PB	PR	/A	PD	TPI
1975 Atl-N	2	3	.400	25	5	0	0	1	66^1	73	3	21	24	13.3	4.21	90	.286	.350	3	.200	0	-4	-3	-1	-0.3
Total 18	135	131	.508	563	328	85	20	7	2500^2	2456	240	922	1614	12.3	3.78	97	.258	.326	151	.191	19	-61	-32	-30	-4.9

● BOB SADOWSKI Sadowski, Robert b: 2/19/38, Pittsburgh, Pa. BR/TR, 6'2", 195 lbs. Deb: 6/19/63 F

YEAR TM/L	W	L	PCT	G	GS	CG	SH	SV	IP	H	HR	BB	SO	RAT	ERA	ERA+	OAV	OOB	BH	AVG	PB	PR	/A	PD	TPI
1963 Mil-N	5	7	.417	19	18	5	1	0	116^2	99	8	30	72	10.3	2.62	123	.231	.289	2	.057	-2	9	8	1	0.6
1964 Mil-N	9	10	.474	51	18	5	0	5	166^2	159	18	56	96	12.0	4.10	86	.251	.319	8	.154	0	-11	-11	3	-1.0
1965 Mil-N	5	9	.357	34	13	3	0	3	123	117	11	35	78	11.3	4.32	82	.250	.306	3	.086	-2	-11	-11	-1	-1.5
Total 4	20	27	.426	115	54	13	1	8	439^2	416	41	130	257	11.5	3.87	90	.250	.311	13	.101	-4	-20	-20	2	-2.3
Team 3	19	26	.422	104	49	13	1	8	406^1	375	37	121	246	11.3	3.74	92	.245	.307	13	.107	-4	-12	-14	2	-1.9

● JOHNNY SAIN Sain, John Franklin b: 9/25/17, Havana, Ark. BR/TR, 6'2", 200 lbs. Deb: 4/24/42 C

YEAR TM/L	W	L	PCT	G	GS	CG	SH	SV	IP	H	HR	BB	SO	RAT	ERA	ERA+	OAV	OOB	BH	AVG	PB	PR	/A	PD	TPI
1942 Bos-N	4	7	.364	40	3	0	0	6	97	79	8	63	68	13.6	3.90	86	.228	.354	2	.074	-2	-6	-6	1	-0.8
1946 Bos-N	20	14	.588	37	**24**	24	3	2	265	225	8	87	129	10.7	2.21	155	.230	.294	28	.298	5	35	36	3	**5.9**
1947 Bos-N★	21	12	.636	38	35	22	3	1	266	265	19	79	132	11.8	3.52	111	.255	.310	37	.346	12	16	11	1	2.6
1948 *Bos-N★	**24**	15	.615	42	39	**28**	4	1	**314^2**	297	19	83	137	11.0	2.60	147	.245	.296	25	.217	3	**47**	43	-2	5.3
1949 Bos-N	10	17	.370	37	36	16	1	0	243	285	15	75	73	13.5	4.81	78	.291	.344	20	.206	1	-21	-28	-2	-2.7
1950 Bos-N	20	13	.606	37	37	25	3	0	278^1	294	34	70	96	11.8	3.94	98	.269	.314	21	.206	4	6	-3	-2	-0.2
1951 Bos-N	5	13	.278	26	22	6	1	1	160^1	195	16	45	63	13.6	4.21	87	.299	.347	11	.212	3	-4	-10	0	-0.7
Total 11	139	116	.545	412	245	140	16	51	2125^2	2145	180	619	910	11.8	3.49	106	.261	.315	190	.245	40	94	50	-2	11.4
Team 7	104	91	.533	257	206	121	15	11	1624^1	1640	119	502	698	12.0	3.49	107	.260	.317	144	.242	27	73	45	-0	9.4

● RANDY ST.CLAIRE St.Claire, Randy Anthony b: 8/23/60, Glens Falls, N.Y. BR/TR, 6'2", 190 lbs. Deb: 9/11/84 F

YEAR TM/L	W	L	PCT	G	GS	CG	SH	SV	IP	H	HR	BB	SO	RAT	ERA	ERA+	OAV	OOB	BH	AVG	PB	PR	/A	PD	TPI
1991 *Atl-N	0	0	—	19	0	0	0	0	28^2	31	4	9	30	12.6	4.08	95	.282	.336	1	.500	0	-1	-1	0	0.1
1992 Atl-N	0	0	—	10	0	0	0	0	15^1	17	1	8	7	14.7	5.87	62	.283	.368	0	—	0	-4	-4	0	0.0
Total 9	12	6	.667	162	0	0	0	9	252	252	28	93	160	12.5	4.14	92	.260	.328	4	.267	1	-11	-10	1	0.3
Team 2	0	0	—	29	0	0	0	0	44	48	5	17	37	13.3	4.70	81	.282	.348	1	.500	0	-5	-4	1	0.1

● MANNY SALVO Salvo, Manuel "Gyp" b: 6/30/13, Sacramento, Cal. BR/TR, 6'4", 210 lbs. Deb: 4/22/39

YEAR TM/L	W	L	PCT	G	GS	CG	SH	SV	IP	H	HR	BB	SO	RAT	ERA	ERA+	OAV	OOB	BH	AVG	PB	PR	/A	PD	TPI
1940 Bos-N	10	9	.526	21	20	14	**5**	0	160^2	151	9	43	60	11.0	3.08	121	.248	.300	6	.103	-3	14	11	-1	0.8
1941 Bos-N	7	16	.304	35	27	11	2	0	195	192	9	93	67	13.3	4.06	88	.255	.340	7	.113	-0	-9	-11	-0	-1.2
1942 Bos-N	7	8	.467	25	14	6	1	0	130^2	129	7	41	25	12.0	3.03	110	.260	.322	5	.122	-1	4	4	-1	0.2
1943 Bos-N	0	1	.000	1	1	0	0	0	5	5	0	6	1	19.8	7.20	47	.250	.423	2	1.000	2	-2	-2	-0	-0.2

YEAR	TM/L	W	L	PCT	G	GS	CG	SH	SV	IP	H	HR	BB	SO	RAT	ERA	ERA+	OAV	OOB	BH	AVG	PB	PR	/A	PD	TPI
1943	Bos-N	5	6	.455	20	13	5	1	0	93^2	94	6	25	25	11.5	3.27	105	.261	.311	6	.214	0	1	2	-1	0.2
Total	5	33	50	.398	135	93	40	9	1	721^1	723	42	284	247	12.8	3.69	98	.261	.334	30	.129	-4	-4	-7	-3	-1.2
Team	5	29	40	.420	102	75	36	9	0	585	571	31	208	178	12.2	3.46	102	.255	.322	26	.136	-2	8	5	-4	-0.2

● **AL SANTORINI** Santorini, Alan Joel b: 5/19/48, Irvington, N.J. BR/TR, 6', 190 lbs. Deb: 9/10/68

YEAR	TM/L	W	L	PCT	G	GS	CG	SH	SV	IP	H	HR	BB	SO	RAT	ERA	ERA+	OAV	OOB	BH	AVG	PB	PR	/A	PD	TPI
1968	Atl-N	0	1	.000	1	1	0	0	0	3	4	1	0	0	12.0	0.00	—	.286	.286	0	—	0	1	1	-0	0.4
Total	6	17	38	.309	127	70	5	4	3	493^1	533	36	194	268	13.5	4.29	83	.276	.346	15	.109	-4	-38	-40	-3	-4.5

● **SID SCHACHT** Schacht, Sidney b: 2/3/18, Bogota, N.J. d: 3/30/91, Ft.Lauderdale, Fla. BR/TR, 5'11", 170 lbs. Deb: 4/23/50

YEAR	TM/L	W	L	PCT	G	GS	CG	SH	SV	IP	H	HR	BB	SO	RAT	ERA	ERA+	OAV	OOB	BH	AVG	PB	PR	/A	PD	TPI
1951	Bos-N	0	2	.000	5	0	0	0	0	4^2	6	0	2	1	15.4	1.93	191	.300	.364	0	—	0	1	1	-0	0.3
Total	2	0	2	.000	19	1	0	0	1	21^1	44	6	21	12	27.4	14.34	31	.411	.508	0	.000	-0	-24	-23	-1	-0.1

● **HAL SCHACKER** Schacker, Harold b: 4/6/25, Brooklyn, N.Y. BR/TR, 6', 190 lbs. Deb: 5/9/45

YEAR	TM/L	W	L	PCT	G	GS	CG	SH	SV	IP	H	HR	BB	SO	RAT	ERA	ERA+	OAV	OOB	BH	AVG	PB	PR	/A	PD	TPI
1945	Bos-N	0	1	.000	6	0	0	0	0	15^1	14	2	9	6	13.5	5.28	73	.241	.343	0	.000	0	-3	-2	-0	-0.2

● **JASON SCHMIDT** Schmidt, Jason David b: 1/29/73, Kelso, Wash. BR/TR, 6'5", 185 lbs. Deb: 4/28/95

YEAR	TM/L	W	L	PCT	G	GS	CG	SH	SV	IP	H	HR	BB	SO	RAT	ERA	ERA+	OAV	OOB	BH	AVG	PB	PR	/A	PD	TPI
1995	Atl-N	2	2	.500	9	2	0	0	0	25	27	2	18	19	16.6	5.76	73	.287	.407	1	.200	0	-4	-4	0	-0.5

● **DAN SCHNEIDER** Schneider, Daniel Louis b: 8/29/42, Evansville, Ind. BL/TL, 6'3", 170 lbs. Deb: 5/12/63

YEAR	TM/L	W	L	PCT	G	GS	CG	SH	SV	IP	H	HR	BB	SO	RAT	ERA	ERA+	OAV	OOB	BH	AVG	PB	PR	/A	PD	TPI
1963	Mil-N	1	0	1.000	30	3	0	0	0	43^2	36	2	20	19	11.5	3.09	104	.225	.311	0	.000	-1	1	1	-1	-0.2
1964	Mil-N	1	2	.333	13	5	0	0	0	36^1	38	6	13	14	12.6	5.45	65	.270	.331	0	.000	-1	-8	-8	1	-0.6
1966	Atl-N	0	0	—	14	0	0	0	0	26^1	35	1	5	11	14.0	3.42	106	.324	.360	4	.500	1	1	1	-0	0.1
Total	5	2	5	.286	117	8	0	0	2	166^1	185	16	70	86	14.0	4.71	72	.287	.359	5	.172	-0	-24	-24	1	-1.9
Team	3	2	2	.500	57	8	0	0	0	106^1	109	9	38	44	12.5	3.98	86	.267	.330	4	.174	-0	-6	-7	-1	-0.7

● **RON SCHUELER** Schueler, Ronald Richard b: 4/18/48, Catharine, Kan. BR/TR, 6'4", 205 lbs. Deb: 4/16/72 C

YEAR	TM/L	W	L	PCT	G	GS	CG	SH	SV	IP	H	HR	BB	SO	RAT	ERA	ERA+	OAV	OOB	BH	AVG	PB	PR	/A	PD	TPI
1972	Atl-N	5	8	.385	37	18	3	0	2	144^2	122	16	60	96	11.4	3.67	103	.227	.307	8	.190	0	-3	2	-1	0.1
1973	Atl-N	8	7	.533	39	20	4	2	2	186	179	24	66	124	11.9	3.87	102	.255	.319	11	.177	-1	-4	1	-1	-0.1
Total	8	40	48	.455	291	86	13	2	11	912^1	861	96	393	563	12.6	4.08	94	.253	.334	27	.159	-3	-40	-25	-2	-2.7
Team	2	13	15	.464	76	38	7	2	4	330^2	301	40	126	220	11.7	3.78	102	.243	.314	19	.183	-1	-8	3	-2	0.0

● **DAVE SCHULER** Schuler, David Paul b: 10/4/53, Framingham, Mass. BR/TL, 6'4", 210 lbs. Deb: 9/17/79

YEAR	TM/L	W	L	PCT	G	GS	CG	SH	SV	IP	H	HR	BB	SO	RAT	ERA	ERA+	OAV	OOB	BH	AVG	PB	PR	/A	PD	TPI
1985	Atl-N	0	0	—	9	0	0	0	0	10^2	19	4	3	10	18.6	6.75	57	.404	.440	0	—	0	-4	-3	-0	0.0
Total	3	0	1	.000	18	0	0	0	0	25	34	8	5	17	14.0	5.40	72	.337	.368	0	—	0	-4	-4	-1	0.2

● **DON SCHWALL** Schwall, Donald Bernard b: 3/2/36, Wilkes-Barre, Pa. BR/TR, 6'6", 200 lbs. Deb: 5/21/61

YEAR	TM/L	W	L	PCT	G	GS	CG	SH	SV	IP	H	HR	BB	SO	RAT	ERA	ERA+	OAV	OOB	BH	AVG	PB	PR	/A	PD	TPI
1966	Atl-N	3	3	.500	11	8	0	0	0	45^1	44	2	19	27	12.9	4.37	83	.256	.337	0	.000	-2	-4	-4	-0	-0.6
1967	Atl-N	0	0	—	1	0	0	0	0	0^2	0	0	1	0	13.5	0.00	—	.000	.500	0	—	0	0	0	-0	0.0
Total	7	49	48	.505	172	103	18	5	4	743	710	50	391	408	13.7	3.72	102	.257	.354	34	.145	-5	-1	5	4	1.0
Team	2	3	3	.500	12	8	0	0	0	46	44	2	20	27	12.9	4.30	84	.254	.338	0	.000	-2	-4	-3	-1	-0.6

● **JACK SCOTT** Scott, John William b: 4/18/1892, Ridgeway, N.C. d: 11/30/59, Durham, N.C. BL/TR, 6'2.5", 199 lbs. Deb: 9/6/16

YEAR	TM/L	W	L	PCT	G	GS	CG	SH	SV	IP	H	HR	BB	SO	RAT	ERA	ERA+	OAV	OOB	BH	AVG	PB	PR	/A	PD	TPI
1917	Bos-N	1	2	.333	7	3	3	0	0	39^2	36	0	5	21	10.0	1.82	141	.255	.295	2	.125	-1	4	3	-1	0.1
1919	Bos-N	6	6	.500	19	12	7	0	1	103^2	109	3	39	44	12.9	3.13	91	.275	.341	7	.175	-1	-2	-3	-3	-0.7
1920	Bos-N	10	21	.323	44	33	22	3	1	291	308	6	85	94	12.6	3.53	87	.277	.336	21	.212	0	-13	-15	-4	-2.0
1921	Bos-N	15	13	.536	**47**	29	16	2	3	233^2	258	9	57	83	12.4	3.70	99	.283	.330	30	.341	10	2	-1	-1	0.7
Total	12	103	109	.486	356	196	115	11	19	1814^2	1969	94	493	657	12.4	3.85	96	.281	.332	187	.275	44	-13	-30	-9	0.3
Team	4	32	42	.432	117	77	48	5	5	668	711	18	186	242	12.4	3.42	94	.278	.332	60	.247	9	-9	-16	-9	-1.9

● **SOCKS SEIBOLD** Seibold, Harry b: 4/3/1896, Philadelphia, Pa. d: 9/21/65, Philadelphia, Pa. BR/TR, 5'8.5", 162 lbs. Deb: 9/18/15 ♦

YEAR	TM/L	W	L	PCT	G	GS	CG	SH	SV	IP	H	HR	BB	SO	RAT	ERA	ERA+	OAV	OOB	BH	AVG	PB	PR	/A	PD	TPI
1929	Bos-N	12	17	.414	33	27	16	1	1	205^2	228	17	80	54	13.6	4.73	99	.285	.352	20	.286	4	-0	-1	-1	0.2
1930	Bos-N	15	16	.484	36	33	20	1	2	251	288	16	85	70	13.4	4.12	120	.290	.348	19	.211	0	24	23	-3	2.1
1931	Bos-N	10	18	.357	33	29	10	3	0	206^1	226	12	65	50	12.8	4.67	81	.279	.335	9	.129	-4	-18	-20	0	-2.7
1932	Bos-N	3	10	.231	28	20	6	1	0	136^2	173	12	41	33	14.2	4.68	80	.309	.358	7	.152	-2	-12	-14	2	-1.1
1933	Bos-N	1	4	.200	11	5	1	0	1	36^2	43	0	14	10	14.0	3.68	83	.295	.356	1	.111	0	-1	-3	0	-0.3
Total	8	48	86	.358	191	135	64	8	5	1063^2	1179	60	405	296	13.5	4.43	91	.284	.350	76	.192	-0	-45	-48	-1	-5.6
Team	5	41	65	.387	141	114	53	6	4	836^1	958	57	285	217	13.5	4.48	96	.290	.348	56	.196	-1	-8	-16	-1	-1.8

● **FRANK SEXTON** Sexton, Frank Joseph b: 7/8/1872, Brockton, Mass. d: 1/4/38, Brighton, Mass. 160 lbs. Deb: 6/21/1895

YEAR	TM/L	W	L	PCT	G	GS	CG	SH	SV	IP	H	HR	BB	SO	RAT	ERA	ERA+	OAV	OOB	BH	AVG	PB	PR	/A	PD	TPI
1895	Bos-N	1	5	.167	7	5	4	0	0	49	59	2	22	14	15.2	5.69	90	.294	.369	5	.227	-1	-5	-3	-1	-0.4

● **BOB SHAW** Shaw, Robert John b: 6/29/33, Bronx, N.Y. BR/TR, 6'2", 195 lbs. Deb: 8/11/57 C

YEAR	TM/L	W	L	PCT	G	GS	CG	SH	SV	IP	H	HR	BB	SO	RAT	ERA	ERA+	OAV	OOB	BH	AVG	PB	PR	/A	PD	TPI
1962	Mil-N★	15	9	.625	38	29	12	3	2	225	223	20	44	124	11.2	2.80	136	.260	.305	10	.137	1	29	25	-0	2.6
1963	Mil-N	7	11	.389	48	16	3	3	13	159	144	10	55	105	11.5	2.66	121	.243	.312	5	.122	0	11	10	-2	1.2
Total	11	108	98	.524	430	223	55	14	32	1778	1837	149	511	880	12.2	3.52	105	.267	.323	69	.133	-7	38	34	-2	2.1
Team	2	22	20	.524	86	45	15	6	15	384	367	30	99	229	11.3	2.74	130	.253	.308	15	.132	1	40	35	-2	3.8

● **BILL SHERDEL** Sherdel, William Henry "Wee Willie" b: 8/15/1896, McSherrystown, Pa d: 11/14/68, McSherrystown, Pa BL/TL, 5'10", 160 lbs. Deb: 4/22/18

YEAR	TM/L	W	L	PCT	G	GS	CG	SH	SV	IP	H	HR	BB	SO	RAT	ERA	ERA+	OAV	OOB	BH	AVG	PB	PR	/A	PD	TPI
1930	Bos-N	6	5	.545	21	14	7	0	1	119^1	131	10	30	26	12.3	4.75	104	.283	.329	4	.095	-4	3	2	-1	-0.2
1931	Bos-N	6	10	.375	27	16	8	0	0	137^2	163	13	35	34	13.0	4.25	89	.294	.337	14	.304	4	-6	-7	-2	-0.6
1932	Bos-N	0	0	—	1	0	0	0	0	1^2	3	0	1	0	21.6	0.00	—	.375	.444	0	—	0	1	1	-0	0.0
Total	15	165	146	.531	514	273	159	11	26	2709^1	3018	149	661	839	12.4	3.72	103	.285	.330	214	.223	27	55	38	-25	4.4
Team	3	12	15	.444	49	30	15	0	1	258^2	297	23	66	60	12.7	4.45	97	.289	.334	18	.205	-0	-2	-4	-3	-0.8

● **STEVE SHIELDS** Shields, Stephen Mack b: 11/30/58, Gadsden, Ala. BR/TR, 6'5", 230 lbs. Deb: 6/1/85

YEAR	TM/L	W	L	PCT	G	GS	CG	SH	SV	IP	H	HR	BB	SO	RAT	ERA	ERA+	OAV	OOB	BH	AVG	PB	PR	/A	PD	TPI
1985	Atl-N	1	2	.333	23	6	0	0	0	68	86	9	32	29	15.8	5.16	75	.320	.394	2	.111	-1	-12	-10	-1	-0.6
1986	Atl-N	0	0	—	6	0	0	0	0	12^2	13	4	7	6	14.2	7.11	56	.271	.364	0	.000	-0	-5	-4	-0	0.0
Total	5	8	8	.500	102	6	0	0	3	219	269	32	91	126	14.9	5.26	77	.308	.375	2	.105	-1	-33	-29	-1	-2.4
Team	2	1	2	.333	29	6	0	0	0	80^2	99	13	39	35	15.5	5.47	71	.312	.389	2	.105	-1	-17	-14	-1	-0.6

● **MILT SHOFFNER** Shoffner, Milburn James b: 11/13/05, Sherman, Tex. d: 1/19/78, Madison, Ohio BL/TL, 6'1.5", 184 lbs. Deb: 7/20/29

YEAR	TM/L	W	L	PCT	G	GS	CG	SH	SV	IP	H	HR	BB	SO	RAT	ERA	ERA+	OAV	OOB	BH	AVG	PB	PR	/A	PD	TPI
1937	Bos-N	3	1	.750	6	5	3	1	1	42^2	38	1	9	13	10.1	2.53	142	.239	.284	2	.125	1	7	5	1	0.6
1938	Bos-N	8	7	.533	26	15	9	1	1	139^2	147	7	36	49	11.9	3.54	97	.270	.317	12	.211	3	4	-2	-2	-0.1
1939	Bos-N	4	6	.400	25	11	7	0	1	132^1	133	4	42	51	12.0	3.13	118	.265	.324	7	.159	-0	12	8	0	0.6
Total	7	25	26	.490	134	51	22	2	3	577	647	34	214	180	13.6	4.59	85	.287	.352	32	.156	-0	-35	-43	-2	-2.7
Team	3	15	14	.517	57	31	19	2	3	314^2	318	12	87	113	11.7	3.23	110	.264	.316	21	.179	3	22	12	-1	1.1

● **CLYDE SHOUN** Shoun, Clyde Mitchell "Hardrock" b: 3/20/12, Mountain City, Tenn. d: 3/20/68, Mountain Home, Tenn. BL/TL, 6'1", 188 lbs. Deb: 8/7/35

YEAR	TM/L	W	L	PCT	G	GS	CG	SH	SV	IP	H	HR	BB	SO	RAT	ERA	ERA+	OAV	OOB	BH	AVG	PB	PR	/A	PD	TPI
1947	Bos-N	5	3	.625	26	3	1	1	1	73^2	73	6	21	23	11.5	4.40	89	.254	.305	3	.158	-1	-3	-4	-1	-0.6
1948	Bos-N	5	1	.833	36	2	1	0	4	74	77	7	20	25	11.8	4.01	96	.267	.315	4	.190	0	-0	-1	-2	-0.3
1949	Bos-N	0	0	—	1	0	0	0	0	1	1	0	0	0	9.0	0.00	—	.250	.250	0	—	0	0	0	-0	0.0
Total	14	73	59	.553	454	85	34	3	29	1287	1325	81	404	483	12.2	3.91	96	.267	.324	73	.202	1	-27	-25	-9	-3.6
Team	3	10	4	.714	63	5	2	1	5	148^2	151	13	41	48	11.6	4.18	92	.261	.310	7	.175	-0	-3	-5	-4	-0.9

● **ELMER SINGLETON** Singleton, Bert Elmer "Smoky" b: 6/26/18, Ogden, Utah BR/TR, 6'2", 174 lbs. Deb: 8/20/45

YEAR	TM/L	W	L	PCT	G	GS	CG	SH	SV	IP	H	HR	BB	SO	RAT	ERA	ERA+	OAV	OOB	BH	AVG	PB	PR	/A	PD	TPI
1945	Bos-N	1	4	.200	7	5	1	0	0	37^1	35	1	14	14	12.1	4.82	79	.248	.321	0	.000	-1	-4	-4	-0	-0.6

YEAR TM/L	W	L	PCT	G	GS	CG	SH	SV	IP	H	HR	BB	SO	RAT	ERA	ERA+	OAV	OOB	BH	AVG	PB	PR	/A	PD	TPI
1946 Bos-N	0	1	.000	15	2	0	0	1	33^2	27	3	21	17	13.1	3.74	92	.221	.340	0	.000	-1	-1	-1	0	-0.1
Total 8	11	17	.393	145	19	2	0	4	327^2	322	33	146	160	13.0	4.83	83	.258	.338	9	.132	-3	-32	-29	3	-1.9
Team 2	1	5	.167	22	7	1	0	1	71	62	4	35	31	12.5	4.31	84	.236	.330	0	.000	-2	-5	-5	-0	-0.7

● DOUG SISK Sisk, Douglas Randall b: 9/26/57, Renton, Wash. BR/TR, 6'2", 210 lbs. Deb: 9/6/82

YEAR TM/L	W	L	PCT	G	GS	CG	SH	SV	IP	H	HR	BB	SO	RAT	ERA	ERA+	OAV	OOB	BH	AVG	PB	PR	/A	PD	TPI
1990 Atl-N	0	0	—	3	0	0	0	0	2^1	1	0	4	1	19.3	3.86	105	.143	.455	0	—	0	-0	0	0	0.0
1991 Atl-N	2	1	.667	14	0	0	0	0	14^1	21	1	8	5	18.2	5.02	77	.333	.408	0	—	0	-2	-2	0	-0.3
Total 9	22	20	.524	332	0	0	0	33	523^1	527	15	267	195	14.0	3.27	112	.268	.361	4	.105	-1	29	23	2	1.8
Team 2	2	1	.667	17	0	0	0	0	16^2	22	1	12	6	18.4	4.86	80	.314	.415	0	—	0	-2	-2	0	-0.3

● GEORGE SISLER Sisler, George Harold "Georgeous George"
b: 3/24/1893, Manchester, Ohio d: 3/26/73, Richmond Heights, Mo. BL/TL, 5'11", 170 lbs. Deb: 6/28/15 FMCH ♦

YEAR TM/L	W	L	PCT	G	GS	CG	SH	SV	IP	H	HR	BB	SO	RAT	ERA	ERA+	OAV	OOB	BH	AVG	PB	PR	/A	PD	TPI
1928 Bos-N	0	0	—	1	0	0	0	0	1	0	0	1	0	9.0	0.00	—	.000	.333	167	.340	0	0	0	-0	0.0
Total 7	5	6	.455	24	12	9	1	3	111	91	0	52	63	12.1	2.35	123	.231	.330	2812	.340	7	8	7	1	1.3

● CRAIG SKOK Skok, Craig Richard b: 9/1/47, Dobbs Ferry, N.Y. BR/TL, 6', 190 lbs. Deb: 5/4/73

YEAR TM/L	W	L	PCT	G	GS	CG	SH	SV	IP	H	HR	BB	SO	RAT	ERA	ERA+	OAV	OOB	BH	AVG	PB	PR	/A	PD	TPI
1978 Atl-N	3	2	.600	43	0	0	0	2	62	64	8	27	28	13.2	4.35	93	.266	.340	2	.250	0	-5	-2	-0	-0.2
1979 Atl-N	1	3	.250	44	0	0	0	2	54^1	58	7	17	30	12.9	3.98	102	.282	.345	0	.000	-0	-1	0	0	0.1
Total 4	4	7	.364	107	0	0	0	5	150	170	19	58	85	13.9	4.86	83	.289	.355	2	.182	0	-20	-14	-0	-1.4
Team 2	4	5	.444	87	0	0	0	4	116^1	122	15	44	58	13.1	4.18	97	.273	.342	2	.182	0	-7	-2	0	-0.1

● LOU SLEATER Sleater, Louis Mortimer b: 9/8/26, St.Louis, Mo. BL/TL, 5'10", 185 lbs. Deb: 4/25/50

YEAR TM/L	W	L	PCT	G	GS	CG	SH	SV	IP	H	HR	BB	SO	RAT	ERA	ERA+	OAV	OOB	BH	AVG	PB	PR	/A	PD	TPI
1956 Mil-N	2	2	.500	25	1	0	0	2	45^2	42	6	27	32	13.6	3.15	110	.240	.342	5	.500	2	3	2	1	0.5
Total 7	12	18	.400	131	21	7	1	5	300^2	306	32	172	152	14.5	4.70	83	.263	.362	21	.204	3	-28	-26	-2	-2.2

● JACK SMITH Smith, Jack Hatfield b: 11/15/35, Pikeville, Ky. BR/TR, 6', 185 lbs. Deb: 9/10/62

YEAR TM/L	W	L	PCT	G	GS	CG	SH	SV	IP	H	HR	BB	SO	RAT	ERA	ERA+	OAV	OOB	BH	AVG	PB	PR	/A	PD	TPI
1964 Mil-N	2	2	.500	22	0	0	0	0	31	28	3	11	19	11.3	3.77	93	.237	.302	1	.333	0	-1	-1	1	0.0
Total 3	2	2	.500	34	0	0	0	1	49^1	48	5	17	31	12.2	4.56	76	.254	.322	1	.167	-0	-5	-6	1	-0.1

● PETE SMITH Smith, Peter John b: 2/27/66, Abington, Mass. BR/TR, 6'3", 200 lbs. Deb: 9/8/87

YEAR TM/L	W	L	PCT	G	GS	CG	SH	SV	IP	H	HR	BB	SO	RAT	ERA	ERA+	OAV	OOB	BH	AVG	PB	PR	/A	PD	TPI
1987 Atl-N	1	2	.333	6	6	0	0	0	31^2	39	3	14	11	15.1	4.83	90	.307	.376	1	.091	-1	-3	-2	-1	-0.3
1988 Atl-N	7	15	.318	32	32	5	3	0	195^1	183	15	88	124	12.5	3.69	100	.250	.331	6	.113	-1	-5	-0	-3	-0.4
1989 Atl-N	5	14	.263	28	27	1	0	0	142	144	13	57	115	12.7	4.75	77	.263	.333	4	.098	-0	-20	-17	-1	-2.3
1990 Atl-N	5	6	.455	13	13	3	0	0	77	77	11	24	56	11.8	4.79	84	.260	.316	2	.087	-1	-9	-6	-1	-1.0
1991 Atl-N	1	3	.250	14	10	0	0	0	48	48	5	22	29	13.1	5.06	77	.262	.341	2	.167	0	-7	-6	1	-0.4
1992 *Atl-N	7	0	1.000	12	11	2	1	0	79	63	3	28	43	10.4	2.05	178	.217	.286	1	.038	-1	13	14	-0	1.1
1993 Atl-N	4	8	.333	20	14	0	0	0	90^2	92	15	36	53	12.9	4.37	92	.270	.343	6	.222	1	-3	-4	0	-0.3
Total 9	35	60	.368	157	136	12	4	0	819^1	821	98	318	507	12.6	4.40	88	.263	.333	27	.116	-3	-60	-48	-4	-6.0
Team 7	30	48	.385	125	113	11	4	0	663^2	646	65	269	431	12.4	4.10	93	.257	.329	22	.114	-4	-34	-21	-4	-3.6

● BOB SMITH Smith, Robert Eldridge b: 4/22/1895, Rogersville, Tenn. d: 7/19/87, Waycross, Ga. BR/TR, 5'10", 175 lbs. Deb: 4/19/23 ♦

YEAR TM/L	W	L	PCT	G	GS	CG	SH	SV	IP	H	HR	BB	SO	RAT	ERA	ERA+	OAV	OOB	BH	AVG	PB	PR	/A	PD	TPI
1925 Bos-N	5	3	.625	13	10	6	0	0	92^2	110	6	36	19	14.2	4.47	90	.304	.367	49	.282	3	-2	-5	-0	-0.1
1926 Bos-N	10	13	.435	33	23	14	4	1	201^1	199	10	75	44	12.2	3.75	94	.269	.336	25	.298	7	2	-5	2	0.5
1927 Bos-N	10	18	.357	41	32	16	1	3	260^2	297	9	75	81	12.9	3.76	99	.301	.351	27	.248	4	4	-1	2	0.6
1928 Bos-N	13	17	.433	38	25	14	0	2	244^1	274	11	74	59	12.9	3.87	101	.289	.342	23	.250	3	3	1	3	0.7
1929 Bos-N	11	17	.393	34	29	19	1	3	231	256	20	71	65	12.8	4.68	100	.285	.338	17	.172	-1	1	0	1	0.1
1930 Bos-N	10	14	.417	38	24	14	2	5	219^2	247	25	85	84	13.7	4.26	116	.290	.357	19	.235	-1	17	16	2	1.6
1933 Bos-N	4	3	.571	14	4	3	1	1	58^2	68	3	7	16	11.5	3.22	95	.296	.316	4	.200	1	1	-1	1	0.0
1934 Bos-N	6	9	.400	39	5	3	0	5	121^2	133	9	36	26	12.5	4.66	82	.277	.328	9	.250	1	-8	-11	1	-1.1
1935 Bos-N	8	18	.308	46	20	8	2	5	203^1	232	13	61	58	13.1	3.94	96	.285	.337	17	.270	2	2	-3	-1	-0.2
1936 Bos-N	6	7	.462	35	11	5	2	8	136	142	3	35	36	11.8	3.77	102	.264	.311	10	.222	0	4	1	1	0.2
1937 Bos-N	0	1	.000	18	0	0	0	3	44	52	6	6	14	12.3	4.09	88	.295	.326	2	.200	0	-1	-2	-1	-0.1
Total 13	106	139	.433	435	229	128	16	40	2246^1	2472	132	670	618	12.7	3.94	100	.283	.335	409	.242	23	40	4	12	4.8
Team 11	83	120	.409	349	183	102	13	36	1813^1	2010	115	561	502	12.8	4.06	99	.286	.340	202	.248	20	23	-12	11	2.2

● TOM SMITH Smith, Thomas Edward b: 12/5/1871, Boston, Mass. d: 3/2/29, Dorchester, Mass. BR/TR, 5'7.5", 165 lbs. Deb: 6/6/1894

YEAR TM/L	W	L	PCT	G	GS	CG	SH	SV	IP	H	HR	BB	SO	RAT	ERA	ERA+	OAV	OOB	BH	AVG	PB	PR	/A	PD	TPI
1894 Bos-N	0	0	—	2	0	0	0	1	6	8	2	6	2	27.0	15.00	38	.320	.514	0	.000	-0	-6	-6	-0	-0.2
Total 4	4	7	.364	25	13	9	0	1	138	166	5	89	38	17.7	6.33	72	.294	.406	17	.224	-0	-27	-27	-0	-1.2

● ZANE SMITH Smith, Zane William b: 12/28/60, Madison, Wis. BL/TL, 6'2", 195 lbs. Deb: 9/10/84

YEAR TM/L	W	L	PCT	G	GS	CG	SH	SV	IP	H	HR	BB	SO	RAT	ERA	ERA+	OAV	OOB	BH	AVG	PB	PR	/A	PD	TPI
1984 Atl-N	1	0	1.000	3	3	0	0	0	20	16	1	13	16	13.0	2.25	171	.219	.337	5	.556	2	3	4	0	0.4
1985 Atl-N	9	10	.474	42	18	2	2	0	147	135	4	80	85	13.3	3.80	101	.254	.355	6	.162	-0	-3	1	2	0.3
1986 Atl-N	8	16	.333	38	32	3	1	1	204^2	209	8	105	139	14.0	4.05	98	.275	.367	5	.085	-3	-7	-2	3	-0.2
1987 Atl-N	15	10	.600	36	36	9	3	0	242	245	19	91	130	12.7	4.09	106	.266	.335	10	.132	-1	-0	7	1	0.8
1988 Atl-N	5	10	.333	23	22	3	0	0	140^1	159	8	44	59	13.2	4.30	86	.292	.348	7	.167	0	-13	-10	3	-0.6
1989 Atl-N	1	12	.077	17	17	0	0	0	99	102	5	33	58	12.5	4.45	82	.267	.329	5	.179	-0	-11	-9	2	-0.9
Total 12	96	109	.468	344	275	34	15	3	1836	1876	115	562	964	12.1	3.68	106	.269	.326	83	.158	1	28	47	17	5.8
Team 6	39	58	.402	159	128	17	6	1	853	866	45	366	487	13.2	4.06	98	.270	.348	38	.151	-2	-32	-9	12	-0.2

● JOHN SMOLTZ Smoltz, John Andrew b: 5/15/67, Detroit, Mich. BR/TR, 6'3", 210 lbs. Deb: 7/23/88

YEAR TM/L	W	L	PCT	G	GS	CG	SH	SV	IP	H	HR	BB	SO	RAT	ERA	ERA+	OAV	OOB	BH	AVG	PB	PR	/A	PD	TPI
1988 Atl-N	2	7	.222	12	12	0	0	0	64	74	10	33	37	15.3	5.48	67	.285	.369	2	.118	-0	-14	-13	-1	-1.7
1989 Atl-N★	12	11	.522	29	29	5	0	0	208	160	15	72	168	10.1	2.94	124	.212	.282	7	.113	1	13	16	2	2.1
1990 Atl-N	14	11	.560	34	34	6	2	0	231^1	206	20	90	170	11.6	3.85	105	.240	.313	12	.162	1	-2	5	1	0.7
1991 *Atl-N	14	13	.519	36	36	5	0	0	229^2	206	16	77	148	11.2	3.80	102	.243	.308	7	.108	-1	-3	2	0	0.2
1992 *Atl-N★	15	12	.556	35	35	9	3	0	246^2	206	17	80	**215**	10.6	2.85	129	.224	.289	12	.160	2	18	22	-1	2.6
1993 *Atl-N★	15	11	.577	35	35	3	1	0	243^2	208	23	100	208	11.6	3.62	111	.230	.311	13	.183	3	11	11	-0	1.3
1994 Atl-N	6	10	.375	21	21	1	0	0	134^2	120	15	48	113	11.5	4.14	102	.239	.310	6	.162	2	1	1	0	0.3
1995 *Atl-N	12	7	.632	29	29	2	1	0	192^2	166	15	72	193	11.3	3.18	133	.232	.306	6	.107	-1	21	23	-1	1.8
Total 8	90	82	.523	231	231	31	7	0	1550^2	1346	131	572	1252	11.3	3.53	111	.233	.306	65	.142	7	46	68	0	7.3

● EDDIE SOLOMON Solomon, Eddie "Buddy" b: 2/9/51, Perry, Ga. d: 1/12/86, Macon, Ga. BR/TR, 6'3", 190 lbs. Deb: 9/2/73

YEAR TM/L	W	L	PCT	G	GS	CG	SH	SV	IP	H	HR	BB	SO	RAT	ERA	ERA+	OAV	OOB	BH	AVG	PB	PR	/A	PD	TPI
1977 Atl-N	6	6	.500	18	16	0	0	0	88^2	110	10	34	54	14.8	4.57	97	.305	.368	4	.129	-1	-6	-1	-0	-0.3
1978 Atl-N	4	6	.400	37	8	0	0	2	106	98	12	50	64	12.7	4.08	99	.247	.335	4	.138	-1	-6	-0	-0	-0.1
1979 Atl-N	7	14	.333	31	30	4	0	0	186	184	19	51	96	11.7	4.21	96	.254	.308	13	.203	1	-10	-3	-1	-0.4
Total 10	36	42	.462	191	95	8	0	4	718	764	76	247	337	12.9	4.00	97	.274	.337	39	.177	-1	-28	-8	-3	-1.6
Team 3	17	26	.395	86	54	4	0	2	380^2	392	41	135	214	12.7	4.26	97	.265	.330	21	.169	-1	-22	-5	-2	-0.8

● ELIAS SOSA Sosa, Elias (Martinez) b: 6/10/50, LaVega, D.R. BR/TR, 6'2", 190 lbs. Deb: 9/8/72

YEAR TM/L	W	L	PCT	G	GS	CG	SH	SV	IP	H	HR	BB	SO	RAT	ERA	ERA+	OAV	OOB	BH	AVG	PB	PR	/A	PD	TPI
1975 Atl-N	2	2	.500	43	0	0	0	2	62^1	70	3	29	31	14.7	4.48	84	.294	.378	1	.143	-0	-6	-5	-0	-0.4
1976 Atl-N	4	4	.500	21	0	0	0	3	35^1	41	3	13	32	14.0	5.35	71	.287	.350	1	.143	-0	-7	-6	-0	-1.5
Total 12	59	51	.536	601	3	0	0	83	918	873	64	334	538	12.0	3.32	111	.255	.325	12	.130	-3	37	39	-3	5.1
Team 2	6	6	.500	64	0	0	0	5	97^2	111	6	42	63	14.5	4.79	79	.291	.368	2	.143	-1	-13	-11	-0	-1.9

● BILL SOWDERS Sowders, William Jefferson "Little Bill"
b: 11/29/1864, Louisville, Ky. d: 2/2/51, Indianapolis, Ind. BR/TR, 6', 155 lbs. Deb: 4/24/1888 F

YEAR TM/L	W	L	PCT	G	GS	CG	SH	SV	IP	H	HR	BB	SO	RAT	ERA	ERA+	OAV	OOB	BH	AVG	PB	PR	/A	PD	TPI
1888 Bos-N	19	15	.559	36	35	34	2	0	317	278	3	73	132	10.2	2.07	138	.226	.275	18	.148	-4	27	27	1	2.3

YEAR TM/L	W	L	PCT	G	GS	CG	SH	SV	IP	H	HR	BB	SO	RAT	ERA	ERA+	OAV	OOB	BH	AVG	PB	PR	/A	PD	TPI
1889 Bos-N	1	2	.333	7	4	3	0	2	42	53	3	23	10	16.7	5.14	81	.299	.386	4	.235	-0	-5	-5	1	-0.2
Total 3	29	30	.492	71	61	55	2	2	517^2	542	8	149	205	12.3	3.34	94	.260	.314	44	.186	-4	-7	-11	2	-2.0
Team 2	20	17	.541	43	39	37	2	2	359	331	6	96	142	11.0	2.43	123	.235	.289	22	.158	-4	22	23	2	2.1

● WARREN SPAHN

Spahn, Warren Edward b: 4/23/21, Buffalo, N.Y. BL/TL, 6', 175 lbs. Deb: 4/19/42 CH

YEAR TM/L	W	L	PCT	G	GS	CG	SH	SV	IP	H	HR	BB	SO	RAT	ERA	ERA+	OAV	OOB	BH	AVG	PB	PR	/A	PD	TPI
1942 Bos-N	0	0	—	4	2	1	0	0	15^2	25	0	11	7	20.7	5.74	58	.368	.456	1	.167	-0	-4	-4	-0	0.0
1946 Bos-N	8	5	.615	24	16	8	0	1	125^2	107	6	36	67	10.3	2.94	117	.228	.285	7	.163	-1	7	7	-2	0.4
1947 Bos-N★	21	10	.677	40	35	22	**7**	3	**289^2**	245	15	84	123	**10.3**	**2.33**	**167**	.226	**.283**	16	.163	1	**56**	**50**	-2	5.1
1948 *Bos-N	15	12	.556	36	35	16	3	1	257	237	19	77	114	11.0	3.71	103	.242	.298	15	.167	2	7	3	0	0.5
1949 Bos-N★	**21**	14	.600	38	38	**25**	4	0	**302^1**	283	27	86	**151**	11.1	3.07	123	.245	.299	18	.162	-0	33	24	-2	2.3
1950 Bos-N☆	**21**	17	.553	41	39	25	1	1	293	248	22	111	**191**	11.1	3.16	122	.227	.299	23	.217	4	32	22	0	3.1
1951 Bos-N☆	22	14	.611	39	36	**26**	**7**	0	310^2	278	20	109	**164**	11.2	2.98	123	.238	.304	22	.190	5	34	24	-2	2.9
1952 Bos-N☆	14	19	.424	40	35	19	5	3	290	263	19	73	**183**	10.6	2.98	121	.240	.291	18	.161	2	24	20	1	2.7
1953 Mil-N★	**23**	7	.767	35	32	24	5	3	265^2	211	14	70	148	**9.6**	**2.10**	**187**	**.217**	**.270**	23	.219	5	**65**	54	2	**6.6**
1954 Mil-N★	21	12	.636	39	34	23	1	3	283^1	262	24	86	136	11.1	3.14	118	.245	.302	21	.208	6	29	18	1	2.7
1955 Mil-N	17	14	.548	39	32	16	1	1	245^2	249	25	65	110	11.6	3.26	115	.265	.314	17	.210	5	21	14	0	2.1
1956 Mil-N★	20	11	.645	39	35	20	3	3	281^1	249	25	52	128	9.7	2.78	124	.238	.276	22	.210	6	**31**	21	-1	2.9
1957 *Mil-N☆	**21**	11	.656	39	35	**18**	4	3	271	241	23	78	111	10.7	2.69	130	.237	.293	13	.138	1	**36**	24	0	3.0
1958 *Mil-N★	**22**	11	**.667**	38	36	**23**	2	1	**290**	257	29	76	150	**10.4**	3.07	115	.237	.288	36	.333	18	28	14	4	**3.9**
1959 Mil-N☆	**21**	15	.583	40	36	**21**	**4**	0	**292**	282	21	70	143	10.9	2.96	120	.253	.298	24	.231	7	32	19	-1	2.8
1960 Mil-N	**21**	10	.677	40	33	**18**	4	2	267^2	254	24	74	154	11.2	3.50	98	.250	.303	14	.147	3	8	-2	3	0.3
1961 Mil-N★	**21**	13	.618	38	34	**21**	**4**	0	262^2	236	24	64	115	**10.4**	**3.02**	124	.243	**.293**	21	.223	10	**30**	21	3	**3.9**
1962 Mil-N☆	18	14	.563	34	34	**22**	0	0	269^1	248	25	55	118	10.2	3.04	125	.246	.287	18	.184	4	27	23	1	3.1
1963 Mil-N☆	23	7	.767	33	33	**22**	7	0	259^2	241	23	49	102	10.1	2.60	124	.248	.284	16	.178	5	20	18	4	3.2
1964 Mil-N	6	13	.316	38	25	4	1	4	173^2	204	23	52	78	13.4	5.29	67	.297	.348	11	.186	2	-34	-34	-1	-3.5
Total 21	363	245	.597	750	665	382	63	29	5243^2	4830	434	1434	2583	10.8	3.09	118	.244	.297	363	.194	88	470	330	9	47.0
Team 20	356	229	.609	714	635	374	63	29	5046	4620	408	1378	2493	10.8	3.05	120	.243	.296	356	.196	86	480	339	9	48.0

● AL SPALDING

Spalding, Albert Goodwill b: 9/2/1850, Byron, Ill. d: 9/9/15, San Diego, Cal. BR/TR, 6'1", 170 lbs. Deb: 5/5/1871 MH♦

YEAR TM/L	W	L	PCT	G	GS	CG	SH	SV	IP	H	HR	BB	SO	RAT	ERA	ERA+	OAV	OOB	BH	AVG	PB	PR	/A	PD	TPI
1871 Bos-n	**19**	10	**.655**	**31**	31	**22**	**1**	0	**257^1**	333	2	38	**23**	**13.0**	**3.36**	**124**	**.268**	**.290**	39	.271	2	**25**	**23**		**1.6**
1872 Bos-n	**38**	8	**.826**	**48**	48	**41**	**3**	0	**404^2**	412	0	27	**27**	**9.8**	**1.98**	**188**	**.240**	**.252**	87	.357	19	**78**	**79**		**7.1**
1873 Bos-n	**41**	14	**.745**	**60**	55	**48**	**1**	**2**	**497^2**	643	5	28	**31**	**12.1**	**2.46**	**135**	**.283**	**.292**	106	.329	19	**44**	**47**		**4.3**
1874 Bos-n	**52**	16	**.765**	**71**	69	**65**	**4**	0	**616^1**	753	1	23		**11.3**	**2.35**	**126**	**.273**	**.279**	119	.331	22	**44**	**42**		**4.6**
1875 Bos-n	**55**	5	**.917**	**72**	63	**52**	**7**	**8**	**575**	571	1	14		**9.2**	**1.52**	**156**	**.244**	**.249**	107	.312	22	**60**	**54**		**6.0**
Total 5 n	205	53	.795	282	266	228	16	10	2351	2712	9	130	81	10.9	2.22	142	.263	.272	458	.324	84	251	244		23.6
Total 2	48	12	.800	65	61	53	8	1	539^2	559	6	26	41	9.8	1.78	138	.249	.257	158	.287	9	32	40	5	4.6
Team 5 n	205	53	.795	282	266	228	16	10	2351	2712	9	130	81	10.9	2.22	142	.263	.272	458	.324	0	251	244	0	23.6

● CLIFF SPECK

Speck, Robert Clifford b: 8/8/56, Portland, Ore. BR/TR, 6'4", 195 lbs. Deb: 7/30/86

YEAR TM/L	W	L	PCT	G	GS	CG	SH	SV	IP	H	HR	BB	SO	RAT	ERA	ERA+	OAV	OOB	BH	AVG	PB	PR	/A	PD	TPI
1986 Atl-N	2	1	.667	13	1	0	0	0	28^1	25	2	15	21	13.0	4.13	96	.238	.339	0	.000	-0	-1	-0	0	0.0

● CHICK STAHL

Stahl, Charles Sylvester b: 1/10/1873, Avila, Ind. d: 3/28/07, W.Baden, Ind. BL/TL, 5'10", 160 lbs. Deb: 4/19/1897 M♦

YEAR TM/L	W	L	PCT	G	GS	CG	SH	SV	IP	H	HR	BB	SO	RAT	ERA	ERA+	OAV	OOB	BH	AVG	PB	PR	/A	PD	TPI
1899 Bos-N	0	0	—	1	0	0	0	0	2	2	0	3	0	22.5	9.00	46	.250	.455	202	.351	0	-1	-1	0	0.0

● HARRY STALEY

Staley, Henry Eli b: 11/3/1866, Jacksonville, Ill. d: 1/12/10, Battle Creek, Mich BR/TR, 5'10", 175 lbs. Deb: 6/23/1888

YEAR TM/L	W	L	PCT	G	GS	CG	SH	SV	IP	H	HR	BB	SO	RAT	ERA	ERA+	OAV	OOB	BH	AVG	PB	PR	/A	PD	TPI
1891 Bos-N	20	8	.714	31	30	26	1	0	252^1	236	11	69	114	11.0	2.50	146	.238	.290	17	.167	-2	24	33	-1	2.7
1892 *Bos-N	22	10	.688	37	35	31	3	0	299^2	273	10	97	93	11.2	3.03	116	.233	.293	16	.131	-6	8	16	-2	0.7
1893 Bos-N	18	10	.643	36	31	23	0	0	263	344	22	81	61	14.7	5.13	96	.307	.356	30	.265	3	-14	-6	-1	-0.4
1894 Bos-N	12	10	.545	27	21	18	0	0	208^2	305	15	61	32	16.0	6.81	83	.337	.382	20	.235	0	-35	-26	-3	-2.1
Total 8	136	119	.533	283	257	231	10	1	2269	2468	92	601	746	12.4	3.80	105	.269	.317	174	.182	-19	51	51	-9	2.7
Team 4	72	38	.655	131	117	98	4	0	1023^2	1158	58	308	300	13.0	4.21	104	.276	.329	83	.197	-5	-16	17	-7	0.9

● JOE STANLEY

Stanley, Joseph Bernard b: 4/2/1881, Washington, D.C. d: 9/13/67, Detroit, Mich. BB/TR, 5'9.5", 150 lbs. Deb: 9/11/1897 F♦

YEAR TM/L	W	L	PCT	G	GS	CG	SH	SV	IP	H	HR	BB	SO	RAT	ERA	ERA+	OAV	OOB	BH	AVG	PB	PR	/A	PD	TPI
1903 Bos-N	0	0	—	1	0	0	0	0	4	4	0	4	4	20.3	9.00	36	.286	.474	77	.250	0	-3	-3	-0	0.0
Total 3	0	0	—	3	0	0	0	0	7^2	7	1	5	4	16.4	9.39	33	.259	.412	148	.213	0	-5	-5	-1	0.0

● MIKE STANTON

Stanton, William Michael b: 6/2/67, Houston, Tex. BL/TL, 6'1", 190 lbs. Deb: 8/24/89

YEAR TM/L	W	L	PCT	G	GS	CG	SH	SV	IP	H	HR	BB	SO	RAT	ERA	ERA+	OAV	OOB	BH	AVG	PB	PR	/A	PD	TPI
1989 Atl-N	0	1	.000	20	0	0	0	7	24	17	0	8	27	9.4	1.50	243	.207	.278	0	—	0	5	6	-0	0.6
1990 Atl-N	0	3	.000	7	0	0	0	2	7	16	1	4	7	27.0	18.00	22	.444	.512	0	—	0	-11	-11	0	-3.7
1991 *Atl-N	5	5	.500	74	0	0	0	7	78	62	6	21	54	9.7	2.88	135	.217	.273	3	.500	2	7	9	1	1.5
1992 *Atl-N	5	4	.556	65	0	0	0	8	63^2	59	6	20	44	11.5	4.10	89	.247	.310	1	.500	0	-4	-3	0	-0.5
1993 *Atl-N	4	6	.400	63	0	0	0	27	52	51	4	29	43	13.8	4.67	86	.255	.349	0	—	0	-4	-4	0	-1.1
1994 Atl-N	3	1	.750	49	0	0	0	3	45^2	41	2	26	35	13.8	3.55	120	.248	.361	2	.667	1	3	4	1	0.5
1995 Atl-N	1	1	.500	26	0	0	0	1	19^1	31	3	6	13	17.7	5.59	76	.369	.418	0	—	0	-3	-3	0	-0.3
Total 7	19	21	.475	326	0	0	0	55	310^2	294	25	122	233	12.3	3.94	101	.252	.327	6	.545	3	-2	2	2	-3.0
Team 7	18	21	.462	304	0	0	0	55	289^2	277	22	114	223	12.4	4.01	98	.254	.329	6	.545	3	-6	-3	2	-3.0

● RAY STARR

Starr, Raymond Francis "Iron Man" b: 4/23/06, Nowata, Okla. d: 2/9/63, Baylis, Ill. BR/TR, 6'1", 178 lbs. Deb: 9/11/32

YEAR TM/L	W	L	PCT	G	GS	CG	SH	SV	IP	H	HR	BB	SO	RAT	ERA	ERA+	OAV	OOB	BH	AVG	PB	PR	/A	PD	TPI
1933 Bos-N	0	1	.000	9	1	0	0	0	28	32	4	9	15	13.5	3.86	79	.296	.356	1	.143	0	-2	-2	0	0.0
Total 7	37	35	.514	138	88	35	9	4	699	670	33	279	189	12.4	3.53	96	.255	.329	26	.123	-7	-8	-11	-1	-2.2

● BILL STEMMEYER

Stemmeyer, William "Cannon Ball" b: 5/6/1865, Cleveland, Ohio d: 5/3/45, Cleveland, Ohio BR/TR, 6'2", 190 lbs. Deb: 10/3/1885

YEAR TM/L	W	L	PCT	G	GS	CG	SH	SV	IP	H	HR	BB	SO	RAT	ERA	ERA+	OAV	OOB	BH	AVG	PB	PR	/A	PD	TPI
1885 Bos-N	1	1	.500	2	2	2	1	0	11	7	0	11	8	14.7	0.00	—	.194	.383	3	.429	1	3	3	0	0.8
1886 Bos-N	22	18	.550	41	41	41	0	0	348^2	300	11	144	239	11.5	3.02	106	.218	.292	41	.277	9	11	7	-3	1.2
1887 Bos-N	6	8	.429	15	14	14	0	**1**	119^1	138	4	41	41	13.7	5.20	78	.274	.331	12	.255	2	-15	-15	-2	-1.3
Total 4	29	29	.500	60	59	59	1	1	495	482	15	205	295	12.5	3.67	92	.241	.312	60	.283	14	-11	-16	-4	-0.1
Team 3	29	27	.518	58	57	57	1	1	479	445	15	196	288	12.1	3.49	97	.232	.304	56	.277	13	-0	-5	-4	0.7

● JOE STEWART

Stewart, Joseph Lawrence "Ace" b: 3/11/1879, Monroe, N.C. d: 2/9/13, Youngstown, Ohio TR, 5'11", 175 lbs. Deb: 9/13/04

YEAR TM/L	W	L	PCT	G	GS	CG	SH	SV	IP	H	HR	BB	SO	RAT	ERA	ERA+	OAV	OOB	BH	AVG	PB	PR	/A	PD	TPI
1904 Bos-N	0	0	—	2	0	0	0	0	9^1	12	0	4	1	16.4	9.64	29	.286	.362	1	.200	-0	-7	-7	-0	0.0

● JACK STIVETTS

Stivetts, John Elmer "Happy Jack" b: 3/31/1868, Ashland, Pa. d: 4/18/30, Ashland, Pa. BR/TR, 6'2", 185 lbs. Deb: 6/26/1889 ♦

YEAR TM/L	W	L	PCT	G	GS	CG	SH	SV	IP	H	HR	BB	SO	RAT	ERA	ERA+	OAV	OOB	BH	AVG	PB	PR	/A	PD	TPI
1892 *Bos-N	35	16	.686	54	48	45	3	1	415^2	346	12	171	180	11.4	3.03	116	.217	.297	71	.296	15	12	22	1	3.7
1893 Bos-N	20	12	.625	38	34	29	1	1	283^2	315	17	115	61	14.0	4.41	112	.273	.344	51	.297	7	8	17	-2	1.7
1894 Bos-N	26	14	.650	45	39	30	0	0	338	429	27	127	76	15.2	4.90	116	.306	.369	80	.328	10	16	29	-3	3.0
1895 Bos-N	17	17	.500	38	34	30	0	0	291	341	15	89	111	13.7	4.64	110	.288	.344	30	.190	-7	5	15	-1	0.5
1896 Bos-N	22	14	.611	42	36	31	2	0	329	353	20	99	71	12.6	4.10	111	.272	.327	76	.344	11	9	16	-3	2.1
1897 *Bos-N	11	4	.733	18	15	10	0	0	129^1	147	5	43	27	13.6	3.41	131	.284	.345	73	.367	7	13	15	1	2.1
1898 Bos-N	0	1	.000	2	1	1	0	0	12	17	2	7	1	18.0	8.25	45	.333	.414	28	.252	0	-6	-6	0	-0.3
Total 11	203	132	.606	388	333	278	14	4	2887^2	2905	131	1155	1223	13.0	3.74	121	.255	.329	592	.297	65	141	247	0	28.2
Team 7	131	78	.627	237	207	176	6	2	1798^2	1948	98	651	527	13.3	4.12	113	.271	.336	409	.304	43	57	108	-7	12.8

● OTIS STOCKSDALE

Stocksdale, Otis Hinkley "Old Gray Fox"
b: 8/7/1871, Arcadia, Md. d: 3/15/33, Pennsville, N.J. BL/TR, 5'10.5", 180 lbs. Deb: 7/24/1893

YEAR TM/L	W	L	PCT	G	GS	CG	SH	SV	IP	H	HR	BB	SO	RAT	ERA	ERA+	OAV	OOB	BH	AVG	PB	PR	/A	PD	TPI
1895 Bos-N	2	2	.500	4	4	1	0	0	23	31	2	8	2	15.3	5.87	87	.316	.368	4	.267	-0	-3	-2	-0	-0.3
Total 4	15	31	.326	54	46	30	0	1	347	521	23	136	48	17.8	6.20	80	.341	.405	63	.310	5	-49	-48	1	-4.7

YEAR TM/L	W	L	PCT	G	GS	CG	SH	SV	IP	H	HR	BB	SO	RAT	ERA	ERA+	OAV	OOB	BH	AVG	PB	PR	/A	PD	TPI
● GEORGE STONE	Stone, George Heard b: 7/9/46, Ruston, La. BL/TL, 6'3", 205 lbs. Deb: 9/15/67																								
1967 Atl-N	0	0	—	2	1	0	0	0	7^1	8	0	1	5	11.0	4.91	68	.267	.290	0	.000	-0	-1	-1	0	0.0
1968 Atl-N	7	4	.636	17	10	2	0	0	75	63	9	19	52	9.8	2.76	108	.222	.271	9	.333	3	2	2	-1	0.5
1969 *Atl-N	13	10	.565	36	20	3	0	3	165^1	166	20	48	102	11.9	3.65	99	.260	.317	11	.186	1	-1	-1	-1	0.0
1970 Atl-N	11	11	.500	35	30	9	2	0	207^1	218	27	50	131	11.9	3.86	111	.267	.314	17	.236	4	4	10	3	1.6
1971 Atl-N	6	8	.429	27	24	4	2	0	172^2	186	19	35	110	11.8	3.60	103	.274	.315	11	.177	-0	-3	2	-0	0.1
1972 Atl-N	6	11	.353	31	16	2	1	1	111	143	18	44	63	15.5	5.51	69	.315	.380	5	.200	1	-25	-21	1	-2.8
Total 9	60	57	.513	203	145	24	5	5	1020^2	1119	122	270	590	12.4	3.89	96	.278	.326	72	.212	10	-31	-19	4	-1.2
Team 6	43	44	.494	148	101	20	5	4	738^2	784	93	197	463	12.2	3.90	97	.270	.321	53	.215	9	-24	-10	2	-0.6
● ALLYN STOUT	Stout, Allyn McClelland "Fish Hook" b: 10/31/04, Peoria, Ill. d: 12/22/74, Sikeston, Mo. BR/TR, 5'10", 167 lbs. Deb: 5/16/31																								
1943 Bos-N	1	0	1.000	9	0	0	0	1	9^1	17	1	4	3	20.3	6.75	51	.378	.429	0	.000	-0	-3	-3	-0	-0.5
Total 6	20	20	.500	180	29	8	0	11	457^2	546	28	177	185	14.5	4.54	85	.299	.365	18	.149	-3	-35	-34	-1	-3.3
● PAUL STRAND	Strand, Paul Edward b: 12/19/1893, Carbonado, Wash. d: 7/2/74, Salt Lake City, Utah BL/TL, 6'0.5", 190 lbs. Deb: 5/15/13 ♦																								
1913 Bos-N	0	0	—	7	0	0	0	0	17	22	1	12	6	18.0	2.12	155	.393	.500	1	.167	-0	2	2	0	0.0
1914 Bos-N	6	2	.750	16	3	1	0	1	55^1	47	1	23	33	11.5	2.44	113	.235	.317	8	.333	2	2	2	-0	0.5
1915 Bos-N	1	1	.500	6	2	2	0	1	22^2	26	0	3	13	11.5	2.38	109	.295	.319	2	.091	-0	1	1	-1	-0.1
Total 3	7	3	.700	29	5	3	0	2	95	95	2	38	52	12.7	2.37	119	.276	.350	49	.224	2	5	5	-1	0.4
● OSCAR STREIT	Streit, Oscar William b: 7/7/1873, Florence, Ala. d: 10/10/35, Birmingham, Ala. BL/TL, 6'5", 190 lbs. Deb: 4/21/1899																								
1899 Bos-N	1	0	1.000	2	1	1	0	0	14^2	15	1	15	0	19.6	6.75	62	.263	.432	0	.000	-1	-5	-4	0	-0.3
Total 2	1	7	.125	10	8	5	0	0	66^1	87	4	40	10	17.9	5.56	65	.316	.412	4	.154	-0	-14	-14	-1	-1.4
● NICK STRINCEVICH	Strincevich, Nicholas "Jumbo" b: 3/1/15, Gary, Ind. BR/TR, 6'1", 180 lbs. Deb: 4/23/40																								
1940 Bos-N	4	8	.333	32	14	5	0	1	128^2	142	17	63	54	14.9	5.53	67	.278	.367	5	.116	-2	-24	-26	-2	-2.5
1941 Bos-N	0	0	—	3	0	0	0	0	3^1	7	0	6	1	37.8	10.80	33	.412	.583	0	—	0	-3	-3	0	0.0
Total 8	46	49	.484	203	103	46	4	6	889^2	958	52	270	274	12.7	4.05	93	.273	.329	43	.158	-4	-34	-26	-0	-1.3
Team 2	4	8	.333	35	14	5	0	1	132	149	17	69	55	15.5	5.66	66	.283	.375	5	.116	-2	-27	-29	-2	-2.5
● DUTCH STRYKER	Stryker, Sterling Alpa b: 7/29/1895, Atlantic Highlands, N.J. d: 11/5/64, Red Bank, N.J. BR/TR, 5'11.5", 180 lbs. Deb: 4/16/24																								
1924 Bos-N	3	8	.273	20	10	2	0	0	73^1	90	4	22	22	13.9	6.01	64	.314	.365	5	.217	-0	-17	-18	2	-2.1
Total 2	3	8	.273	22	10	2	0	0	75^1	98	4	23	22	14.6	6.57	58	.326	.375	5	.217	-0	-23	-23	2	-2.1
● GEORGE STULTZ	Stultz, George Irvin b: 6/30/1873, Louisville, Ky. d: 3/19/55, Louisville, Ky. 5'10", 150 lbs. Deb: 9/22/1894																								
1894 Bos-N	1	0	1.000	1	1	1	0	0	9	4	0	5	1	9.0	0.00	—	.133	.257	1	.333	-0	5	6	1	0.6
● JIM SULLIVAN	Sullivan, James E. b: 4/25/1869, Charlestown, Mass. d: 11/30/01, Roxbury, Mass. BR/TR, 5'10", 155 lbs. Deb: 4/22/1891																								
1891 Bos-N	0	0	—	1	0	0	0	0	0^1	2	0	5	0	189.0	81.00	5	.667	.875	0	—	0	-3	-3	-0	0.0
1895 Bos-N	11	9	.550	21	19	16	0	0	179^1	236	10	58	46	15.6	4.82	106	.312	.373	15	.176	-6	-1	6	-2	-0.2
1896 Bos-N	11	12	.478	31	26	21	1	1	225^1	268	12	68	33	13.7	4.03	113	.293	.346	19	.216	-2	8	13	-3	0.5
1897 *Bos-N	4	5	.444	13	9	8	1	2	89	91	1	26	17	12.0	3.94	113	.263	.318	6	.182	-3	4	5	-1	0.1
Total 4	26	27	.491	67	55	46	2	3	503	607	24	162	97	14.2	4.35	108	.295	.354	40	.190	-11	8	20	-6	0.3
Team 4	26	26	.500	66	54	45	2	3	494	597	23	157	96	14.2	4.35	109	.296	.353	40	.194	-11	8	21	-7	0.4
● JOE SULLIVAN	Sullivan, Joe b: 9/26/10, Mason City, Ill. d: 4/8/85, Sequim, Wash. BL/TL, 5'11", 175 lbs. Deb: 4/20/35																								
1939 Bos-N	6	9	.400	31	11	7	0	2	113^2	114	3	50	46	13.1	3.64	101	.266	.346	12	.300	3	3	1	0	0.4
1940 Bos-N	10	14	.417	36	22	7	0	1	177^1	157	9	89	64	12.9	3.55	105	.240	.339	14	.197	-0	6	3	0	0.4
1941 Bos-N	2	2	.500	16	2	0	0	0	52^1	60	3	26	11	15.1	4.13	86	.290	.374	1	.067	-1	-3	-3	1	-0.3
Total 5	30	37	.448	150	55	20	0	5	588	601	25	298	216	14.0	4.01	99	.265	.355	43	.207	1	7	-3	0	0.3
Team 3	18	25	.419	83	35	14	0	3	343^1	331	15	165	121	13.3	3.67	101	.257	.347	27	.214	2	6	1	1	0.5
● MIKE SULLIVAN	Sullivan, Michael Joseph "Big Mike" b: 10/23/1866, Boston, Mass. d: 6/14/06, Boston, Mass. BL , 6'1", 210 lbs. Deb: 6/17/1889																								
1898 Bos-N	0	1	.000	3	2	0	0	0	12	19	1	9	1	21.8	12.00	31	.358	.460	1	.333	0	-11	-11	-0	-0.7
1899 Bos-N	1	0	1.000	1	1	1	0	0	9	10	1	4	1	15.0	5.00	83	.278	.366	1	.333	0	-1	-1	-0	-0.1
Total 11	54	66	.450	163	121	99	1	4	1123^1	1311	46	577	286	15.8	5.11	84	.285	.375	97	.196	-21	-100	-102	-5	-9.5
Team 2	1	1	.500	4	3	1	0	0	21	29	2	13	2	18.9	9.00	43	.326	.423	2	.333	0	-12	-12	-1	-0.8
● MAX SURKONT	Surkont, Matthew Constantine b: 6/16/22, Central Falls, R.I. d: 10/8/86, Largo, Fla. BR/TR, 6', 205 lbs. Deb: 4/19/49																								
1950 Bos-N	5	2	.714	9	6	2	0	0	55^2	63	5	20	21	13.7	3.23	119	.285	.350	10	.435	5	6	4	-1	0.9
1951 Bos-N	12	16	.429	37	33	11	2	1	237	230	21	89	110	12.4	3.99	92	.252	.323	11	.151	0	-1	-8	-3	-1.1
1952 Bos-N	12	13	.480	31	29	12	3	0	215	201	19	76	125	11.7	3.77	96	.245	.311	7	.111	-1	-1	-4	-1	-0.6
1953 Mil-N	11	5	.688	28	24	11	2	0	170	168	22	64	83	12.3	4.18	94	.255	.321	16	.286	7	2	-5	1	0.3
Total 9	61	76	.445	236	149	53	7	8	1194^1	1209	134	481	571	12.9	4.38	89	.262	.335	63	.176	8	-48	-63	-5	-6.1
Team 4	40	36	.526	105	92	36	7	1	677^2	662	67	249	339	12.3	3.90	96	.253	.321	44	.205	12	6	-13	-3	-0.5
● BRUCE SUTTER	Sutter, Howard Bruce b: 1/8/53, Lancaster, Pa. BR/TR, 6'2", 190 lbs. Deb: 5/9/76																								
1985 Atl-N	7	7	.500	58	0	0	0	23	88^1	91	13	29	52	12.5	4.48	86	.267	.330	0	.000	-0	-9	-6	-0	-1.4
1986 Atl-N	2	0	1.000	16	0	0	0	3	18^2	17	3	9	16	12.5	4.34	92	.243	.329	0	.000	-0	-1	-1	0	-0.1
1988 Atl-N	1	4	.200	38	0	0	0	14	45^1	49	4	11	40	12.1	4.76	77	.275	.321	0	.000	0	-7	-5	-0	-1.0
Total 12	68	71	.489	661	0	0	0	300	1042^1	879	77	309	861	10.4	2.83	135	.230	.289	9	.088	-5	91	116	4	20.8
Team 3	10	11	.476	112	0	0	0	40	152^1	157	20	49	108	12.4	4.55	84	.267	.327	0	.000	-0	-17	-13	-0	-2.5
● BILL SWIFT	Swift, William Vincent b: 1/10/08, Elmira, N.Y. d: 2/23/69, Bartow, Fla. BR/TR, 6'1.5", 192 lbs. Deb: 4/12/32																								
1940 Bos-N	1	1	.500	4	0	0	0	1	9^1	12	0	7	7	18.3	2.89	129	.308	.413	0	.000	-0	1	1	0	0.2
Total 11	95	82	.537	336	163	78	7	20	1637^2	1682	103	351	636	11.4	3.58	108	.263	.305	134	.227	18	49	49	-25	4.6
● JOHN TABER	Taber, John Pardon b: 6/28/1868, Acushnet, Mass. d: 2/21/40, Boston, Mass. BR/TR, 5'8", Deb: 4/30/1890																								
1890 Bos-N	0	1	.000	2	1	1	0	1	13	11	0	8	3	13.2	4.15	90	.220	.328	0	.000	-1	-1	-1	0	-0.1
● ROY TALCOTT	Talcott, Le Roy Everett b: 1/16/20, Brookline, Mass. BR/TR, 6'1.5", 180 lbs. Deb: 6/24/43																								
1943 Bos-N	0	0	—	1	0	0	0	0	0^2	1	0	2	0	40.5	27.00	13	.333	.600	0	—	0	-2	-2	0	0.0
● FRED TENNEY	Tenney, Frederick b: 11/26/1871, Georgetown, Mass. d: 7/3/52, Boston, Mass. BL/TL, 5'9", 155 lbs. Deb: 6/16/1894 M♦																								
1905 Bos-N	0	0	—	1	0	0	0	0	2	5	0	1	0	27.0	4.50	69	.417	.462	158	.288	0	-0	-0	0	0.0
● DUANE THEISS	Theiss, Duane Charles b: 11/20/53, Zanesville, Ohio BR/TR, 6'3", 185 lbs. Deb: 8/5/77																								
1977 Atl-N	1	1	.500	17	0	0	0	0	20^2	26	1	16	7	18.7	6.53	68	.338	.457	0	.000	-0	-6	-5	0	-0.4
1978 Atl-N	0	0	—	3	0	0	0	0	6^1	3	0	3	3	9.9	1.42	285	.158	.304	0	.000	-0	2	2	0	0.0
Total 2	1	1	.500	20	0	0	0	0	27	29	1	19	10	16.7	5.33	82	.302	.427	0	.000	-0	-5	-3	0	-0.4
● BERT THIEL	Thiel, Maynard Bert b: 5/4/26, Marion, Wis. BR/TR, 5'10", 185 lbs. Deb: 4/17/52																								
1952 Bos-N	1	1	.500	4	0	0	0	0	7	11	1	4	6	21.9	7.71	47	.344	.447	0	—	0	-3	-3	-0	-0.8
● TOM THOBE	Thobe, Thomas Neal b: 9/3/69, Covington, Ky. BL/TL, 6'6", 195 lbs. Deb: 9/12/95 F																								
1995 Atl-N	0	0	—	3	0	0	0	0	3^1	7	0	0	2	18.9	10.80	39	.412	.412	0	—	0	-2	-2	-0	0.0

YEAR TM/L	W	L	PCT	G	GS	CG	SH	SV	IP	H	HR	BB	SO	RAT	ERA	ERA+	OAV	OOB	BH	AVG	PB	PR	/A	PD	TPI
● FULLER THOMPSON	Thompson, Fuller Weidner b: 5/1/1889, Los Angeles, Cal. d: 2/19/72, Los Angeles, Cal. BR/TR, 5'11.5", 164 lbs. Deb: 8/19/11																								
1911 Bos-N	0	0	—	3	0	0	0	0	4^2	5	0	2	0	13.5	3.86	99	.294	.368	0	—	0	-0	-0	0	0.0
● MIKE THOMPSON	Thompson, Michael Wayne b: 9/6/49, Denver, Colo. BR/TR, 6'3", 190 lbs. Deb: 5/19/71																								
1974 Atl-N	0	0	—	1	1	0	0	0	4	7	0	2	2	20.3	4.50	84	.412	.474	1	1.000	0	-0	-0	0	0.1
1975 Atl-N	0	6	.000	16	10	0	0	0	51^2	60	2	32	42	16.0	4.70	80	.305	.402	1	.071	-1	-6	-5	1	-0.6
Total 4	1	15	.063	54	29	0	0	0	164^2	158	6	128	113	15.9	4.86	73	.263	.396	4	.098	-1	-24	-24	1	-2.3
Team 2	0	6	.000	17	11	0	0	0	55^2	67	2	34	44	16.3	4.69	80	.313	.407	2	.133	-1	-7	-6	1	-0.5
● BOBBY TIEFENAUER	Tiefenauer, Bobby Gene b: 10/10/29, Desloge, Mo. BR/TR, 6'2", 185 lbs. Deb: 7/14/52 C																								
1963 Mil-N	1	1	.500	12	0	0	0	2	29^2	20	1	4	22	7.3	1.21	265	.194	.224	0	.000	-0	7	7	1	0.6
1964 Mil-N	4	6	.400	46	0	0	0	13	73	61	6	15	48	9.7	3.21	110	.225	.273	0	.000	-1	3	3	-1	0.2
1965 Mil-N	0	1	.000	6	0	0	0	0	7	8	1	3	7	15.4	7.71	46	.286	.375	0	—	0	-3	-3	0	-0.4
Total 10	9	25	.265	179	0	0	0	23	316	312	29	87	204	11.7	3.84	94	.260	.317	1	.026	-1	-7	-9	-2	-1.2
Team 3	5	8	.385	64	0	0	0	15	109^2	89	8	22	77	9.4	2.95	116	.221	.269	0	.000	-1	6	6	0	0.4
● JIM TOBIN	Tobin, James Anthony "Abba Dabba" b: 12/27/12, Oakland, Cal. d: 5/19/69, Oakland, Cal. BR/TR, 6', 185 lbs. Deb: 4/30/37 F♦																								
1940 Bos-N	7	3	.700	15	11	9	0	0	96^1	102	8	24	29	11.8	3.83	97	.264	.307	12	.279	3	0	-1	-1	0.2
1941 Bos-N	12	12	.500	33	26	20	3	0	238	229	12	60	61	10.9	3.10	115	.253	.300	19	.184	3	14	12	4	2.0
1942 Bos-N	12	21	.364	37	33	**28**	1	0	**287^2**	283	20	96	71	12.0	3.97	84	.257	.320	28	.246	14	-21	-20	6	-0.1
1943 Bos-N	14	14	.500	33	30	24	1	0	250	241	12	69	52	11.2	2.66	128	.251	.303	30	.280	6	20	21	2	3.5
1944 Bos-N★	18	19	.486	43	36	**28**	5	3	299^1	271	18	97	83	11.2	3.01	127	.240	.302	22	.190	5	20	27	7	4.7
1945 Bos-N	9	14	.391	27	25	16	0	0	196^2	220	10	56	38	12.9	3.84	100	.282	.334	11	.143	5	-1	-0	2	0.7
Total 9	105	112	.484	287	227	156	12	5	1900	1929	107	557	498	11.9	3.44	106	.262	.316	183	.230	54	39	45	16	13.0
Team 6	72	83	.465	188	161	125	10	3	1368	1346	80	402	334	11.6	3.34	108	.256	.311	122	.218	35	32	39	20	11.0
● PABLO TORREALBA	Torrealba, Pablo Arnoldo (Torrealba) b: 4/28/48, Barquisimeto, Ven. BL/TL, 5'9", 175 lbs. Deb: 4/9/75																								
1975 Atl-N	0	1	.000	6	0	0	0	0	6^2	7	0	3	5	13.5	1.35	279	.250	.323	1	1.000	0	2	2	1	0.4
1976 Atl-N	0	2	.000	36	0	0	0	2	53	67	0	22	33	15.6	3.57	106	.315	.387	0	.000	-0	-0	1	1	0.1
Total 5	6	13	.316	111	13	4	1	5	239^1	275	12	104	113	14.6	3.27	120	.291	.366	1	.200	-0	16	17	2	1.4
Team 2	0	3	.000	42	0	0	0	2	59^2	74	0	25	38	15.4	3.32	114	.307	.379	1	.200	-0	1	3	2	0.5
● LOU TOST	Tost, Louis Eugene b: 6/1/11, Cumberland, Wash. d: 2/22/67, Santa Clara, Cal. BL/TL, 6', 175 lbs. Deb: 4/20/42																								
1942 Bos-N	10	10	.500	35	22	5	1	0	147^2	146	12	52	43	12.3	3.53	94	.256	.322	9	.176	0	-4	-3	-1	-0.5
1943 Bos-N	0	1	.000	3	1	0	0	0	6^2	10	2	4	3	18.9	5.40	63	.357	.438	0	.000	-0	-1	-1	0	-0.2
Total 3	10	11	.476	39	23	5	1	0	155^1	159	14	56	46	12.7	3.65	92	.263	.330	9	.173	-0	-6	-5	-1	-0.7
Team 2	10	11	.476	38	23	5	1	0	154^1	156	14	56	46	12.6	3.62	92	.260	.328	9	.173	-0	-5	-5	-1	-0.7
● CLAY TOUCHSTONE	Touchstone, Clayland Maffitt b: 1/24/03, Moore, Pa. d: 4/28/49, Beaumont, Tex. BR/TR, 5'9", 175 lbs. Deb: 9/4/28																								
1928 Bos-N	0	0	—	5	0	0	0	0	8	15	0	2	1	20.3	4.50	87	.417	.462	0	.000	-0	-0	-1	0	0.0
1929 Bos-N	0	0	—	1	0	0	0	0	2^2	6	1	0	1	20.3	16.88	28	.429	.429	1	1.000	0	-4	-4	-0	0.0
Total 3	0	0	—	12	0	0	0	0	20^2	35	2	8	6	19.6	6.53	57	.368	.429	1	.250	0	-6	-6	0	0.0
Team 2	0	0	—	6	0	0	0	0	10^2	21	1	2	2	20.3	7.59	54	.420	.453	1	.333	0	-4	-4	0	0.0
● IRA TOWNSEND	Townsend, Ira Dance "Pat" b: 1/9/1894, Weimar, Tex. d: 7/21/65, Schulenberg, Tex. BR/TR, 6'1", 180 lbs. Deb: 8/25/20																								
1920 Bos-N	0	0	—	4	1	0	0	0	6^2	10	0	2	1	17.6	1.35	226	.370	.433	0	.000	-0	1	1	-0	0.0
1921 Bos-N	0	0	—	4	0	0	0	0	7^1	11	1	4	0	20.9	6.14	59	.344	.447	0	.000	-0	-2	-2	0	0.0
Total 2	0	0	—	8	1	0	0	0	14	21	1	6	1	19.3	3.86	87	.356	.441	0	.000	-1	-1	-1	0	0.0
● LEO TOWNSEND	Townsend, Leo Alphonse "Lefty" b: 1/15/1891, Mobile, Ala. d: 12/3/76, Mobile, Ala. BL/TL, 5'10", 160 lbs. Deb: 9/8/20																								
1920 Bos-N	2	2	.500	7	1	1	0	0	24^1	18	1	2	0	7.4	1.48	206	.220	.238	1	.167	0	4	4	0	0.7
1921 Bos-N	0	1	.000	1	1	0	0	0	1^1	2	0	3	0	33.8	27.00	14	.400	.625	0	—	0	-3	-3	0	-1.2
Total 2	2	3	.400	8	2	1	0	0	25^2	20	1	5	0	8.8	2.81	110	.230	.272	1	.167	0	1	1	0	-0.5
● BOB TROWBRIDGE	Trowbridge, Robert b: 6/27/30, Hudson, N.Y. d: 4/3/80, Hudson, N.Y. BR/TR, 6'1", 190 lbs. Deb: 4/22/56																								
1956 Mil-N	3	2	.600	19	4	1	0	0	50^2	38	4	34	40	13.1	2.66	130	.210	.341	0	.000	-1	6	4	0	0.4
1957 *Mil-N	7	5	.583	32	16	3	1	1	126	118	9	52	75	12.2	3.64	96	.248	.323	4	.103	-2	3	-2	-1	-0.4
1958 Mil-N	1	3	.250	27	4	0	0	1	55	53	4	26	31	13.1	3.93	90	.252	.338	1	.111	-1	0	-2	-1	-0.3
1959 Mil-N	1	0	1.000	16	0	0	0	1	30^1	45	2	10	22	16.3	5.93	60	.344	.390	0	.000	-0	-7	-8	-0	-0.4
Total 5	13	13	.500	116	25	4	1	5	330^1	324	25	156	201	13.2	3.95	91	.260	.344	6	.078	-5	-3	-13	-1	-1.1
Team 4	12	10	.545	94	24	4	1	3	262	254	19	122	168	13.1	3.78	93	.255	.338	5	.085	-3	3	-8	-1	-0.7
● TOMMY TUCKER	Tucker, Thomas Joseph "Foghorn" b: 10/28/1863, Holyoke, Mass. d: 10/22/35, Montague, Mass. BB/TR, 5'11", 165 lbs. Deb: 4/16/1887 ♦																								
1891 Bos-N	0	0	—	1	0	0	0	0	1	3	0	0	0	27.0	9.00	41	.500	.500	148	.270	0	-1	-1	-0	0.0
Total 2	0	0	—	2	0	0	0	0	3^1	7	0	0	2	18.9	5.40	59	.412	.412	1882	.290	0	-1	-1	-0	0.0
● TOM TUCKEY	Tuckey, Thomas H. "Tabasco Tom" b: 10/7/1883, Birmingham, England d: 10/17/50, New York, N.Y. TL , 6'3", Deb: 8/11/08																								
1908 Bos-N	3	3	.500	8	8	3	1	0	72	60	2	20	26	10.5	2.50	96	.265	.336	1	.050	-2	-1	-1	0	-0.2
1909 Bos-N	0	9	.000	17	10	4	0	0	90^2	104	1	22	16	12.8	4.27	66	.295	.342	4	.138	-1	-17	-15	1	-1.4
Total 2	3	12	.200	25	18	7	1	0	162^2	164	3	42	42	11.8	3.49	76	.284	.340	5	.102	-3	-18	-15	1	-1.6
● JIM TURNER	Turner, James Riley "Milkman Jim" b: 8/6/03, Antioch, Tenn. BL/TR, 6', 185 lbs. Deb: 4/30/37 C																								
1937 Bos-N	20	11	.645	33	30	**24**	**5**	1	256^2	228	13	52	69	**9.8**	**2.38**	**150**	.235	**.274**	24	.250	4	**44**	34	-0	**4.5**
1938 Bos-N☆	14	18	.438	35	34	22	3	0	268	267	21	54	71	10.9	3.46	99	.259	.299	22	.229	4	10	-1	4	0.7
1939 Bos-N	4	11	.267	25	22	9	0	0	157^2	181	10	51	50	13.5	4.28	86	.293	.351	13	.236	2	-6	-10	1	-0.5
Total 9	69	60	.535	231	119	69	8	20	1132	1123	67	283	329	11.3	3.22	111	.260	.307	87	.218	12	70	45	6	7.6
Team 3	38	40	.487	93	86	55	8	1	682^1	676	44	157	190	11.1	3.24	109	.258	.303	59	.239	11	47	23	5	4.7
● LEFTY TYLER	Tyler, George Albert b: 12/14/1889, Derry, N.H. d: 9/29/53, Lowell, Mass. BL/TL, 6', 175 lbs. Deb: 9/20/10 F																								
1910 Bos-N	0	0	—	2	0	0	0	0	11^1	11	1	6	6	13.5	2.38	140	.275	.370	2	.500	1	1	1	-0	0.1
1911 Bos-N	7	10	.412	28	20	10	1	0	165^1	150	11	109	90	14.6	5.06	76	.243	.365	10	.164	-1	-31	-23	3	-1.8
1912 Bos-N	12	22	.353	42	29	15	1	0	256^1	262	8	126	144	14.0	4.18	86	.276	.367	19	.198	-1	-22	-17	4	-1.8
1913 Bos-N	16	17	.485	39	34	**28**	4	2	290^1	245	2	108	143	11.3	2.79	118	.235	.313	21	.206	4	13	16	7	2.9
1914 *Bos-N	16	13	.552	38	34	21	5	2	271^1	247	7	101	140	12.0	2.69	103	.249	.327	19	.202	1	3	2	-2	0.1
1915 Bos-N	10	9	.526	32	24	15	1	0	204^2	182	6	84	89	11.9	2.86	91	.243	.324	23	.261	8	-2	-6	-1	0.2
1916 Bos-N	17	9	.654	34	28	21	6	1	249^1	200	6	58	117	9.4	2.02	123	.226	.276	19	.204	7	17	13	2	2.5
1917 Bos-N	14	12	.538	32	28	22	4	1	239	203	1	86	98	11.1	2.52	101	.240	.314	31	.231	4	5	1	3	1.1
Total 12	127	116	.523	323	265	179	30	7	2230	1990	51	829	1003	11.6	2.95	101	.245	.320	189	.217	30	9	11	21	7.7
Team 8	92	92	.500	247	197	132	22	6	1687^2	1500	42	678	827	11.9	3.06	97	.245	.326	144	.214	23	-16	-16	15	3.3
● JIM TYNG	Tyng, James Alexander b: 3/27/1856, Philadelphia, Pa. d: 10/30/31, New York, N.Y. 5'9", 155 lbs. Deb: 9/23/1879																								
1879 Bos-N	1	2	.333	3	3	3	0	0	27	35	0	6	7	13.7	5.00	50	.292	.325	5	.357	1	-8	-8	0	-0.5
Total 2	1	2	.333	4	3	3	0	1	31	43	0	8	9	15.1	4.94	51	.305	.347	5	.333	1	-8	-8	0	-0.5
● ARNOLD UMBACH	Umbach, Arnold William b: 12/6/42, Williamsburg, Va. BR/TR, 6'1", 180 lbs. Deb: 10/3/64																								
1964 Mil-N	1	0	1.000	1	1	0	0	0	8^1	11	0	4	7	16.2	3.24	109	.333	.405	0	.000	0	0	0	-0	0.0

YEAR TM/L	W	L	PCT	G	GS	CG	SH	SV	IP	H	HR	BB	SO	RAT	ERA	ERA+	OAV	OOB	BH	AVG	PB	PR	/A	PD	TPI
1966 Atl-N	0	2	.000	22	3	0	0	0	40^{2}	40	1	18	23	13.3	3.10	117	.256	.341	1	.200	0	2	2	-0	0.1
Total 2	1	2	.333	23	4	0	0	0	49	51	1	22	30	13.8	3.12	116	.270	.352	1	.125	0	3	3	-0	0.1

● **BILL UPHAM** Upham, William Lawrence b: 4/4/1888, Akron, Ohio d: 9/14/59, Newark, N.J. BB/TR, 6', 178 lbs. Deb: 4/10/15

YEAR TM/L	W	L	PCT	G	GS	CG	SH	SV	IP	H	HR	BB	SO	RAT	ERA	ERA+	OAV	OOB	BH	AVG	PB	PR	/A	PD	TPI
1918 Bos-N	1	1	.500	3	2	2	0	0	20^{2}	28	2	1	8	12.6	5.23	51	.326	.333	2	.222	0	-6	-6	-0	-0.5
Total 2	7	9	.438	36	13	6	2	5	141^{2}	157	2	41	54	12.6	3.37	81	.282	.332	6	.133	-2	-10	-10	2	-1.1

● **CECIL UPSHAW** Upshaw, Cecil Lee b: 10/22/42, Spearsville, La. d: 2/7/95, Lawrenceville, Ga. BR/TR, 6'6", 205 lbs. Deb: 10/1/66

YEAR TM/L	W	L	PCT	G	GS	CG	SH	SV	IP	H	HR	BB	SO	RAT	ERA	ERA+	OAV	OOB	BH	AVG	PB	PR	/A	PD	TPI
1966 Atl-N	0	0	—	1	0	0	0	0	3	0	0	3	2	9.0	0.00	—	.000	.273	1	1.000	0	1	1	-0	0.0
1967 Atl-N	2	3	.400	30	0	0	0	8	45^{1}	42	4	8	31	10.7	2.58	129	.247	.297	1	.167	1	4	4	0	0.6
1968 Atl-N	8	7	.533	52	0	0	0	13	116^{2}	98	6	24	74	9.7	2.47	121	.229	.276	4	.174	0	7	7	-0	1.1
1969 *Atl-N	6	4	.600	62	0	0	0	27	105^{1}	102	7	29	57	11.3	2.91	124	.259	.311	5	.238	2	8	8	1	1.5
1971 Atl-N	11	6	.647	49	0	0	0	17	82	95	5	28	56	13.7	3.51	106	.292	.352	0	.000	-2	-0	2	-1	0.2
1972 Atl-N	3	5	.375	42	0	0	0	13	53^{2}	50	5	19	23	11.7	3.69	103	.249	.317	1	.143	-0	-1	1	1	0.2
1973 Atl-N	0	1	.000	5	0	0	0	0	3^{2}	8	0	2	3	24.5	9.82	40	.444	.500	0	—	0	-3	-2	0	-0.6
Total 9	34	36	.486	348	0	0	0	86	563	545	37	177	323	11.9	3.13	112	.258	.322	12	.160	1	19	23	2	3.2
Team 7	30	26	.536	241	0	0	0	78	409^{2}	395	27	113	246	11.4	3.01	114	.256	.312	12	.164	1	16	20	0	3.0

● **SERGIO VALDEZ** Valdez, Sergio Sanchez (b: Sergio Sanchez (Valdez)) b: 9/7/64, Elias Pina, D.R. BR/TR, 6', 165 lbs. Deb: 9/10/86

YEAR TM/L	W	L	PCT	G	GS	CG	SH	SV	IP	H	HR	BB	SO	RAT	ERA	ERA+	OAV	OOB	BH	AVG	PB	PR	/A	PD	TPI
1989 Atl-N	1	2	.333	19	1	0	0	0	32^{2}	31	5	17	26	13.2	6.06	60	.246	.336	1	1.000	0	-9	-9	-1	-0.8
1990 Atl-N	0	0	—	6	0	0	0	0	5^{1}	6	0	3	3	15.2	6.75	60	.273	.360	0	—	0	-2	-2	0	0.0
Total 8	12	20	.375	116	31	1	0	0	302^{2}	332	46	109	190	13.3	5.06	77	.279	.343	4	.121	-1	-39	-38	-1	-4.1
Team 2	1	2	.333	25	1	0	0	0	38	37	5	20	29	13.5	6.16	60	.250	.339	1	1.000	0	-11	-10	-0	-0.8

● **ROBERTO VARGAS** Vargas, Roberto Enrique (Velez) b: 5/29/29, Santurce, P.R. BL/TL, 5'11", 170 lbs. Deb: 4/17/55

YEAR TM/L	W	L	PCT	G	GS	CG	SH	SV	IP	H	HR	BB	SO	RAT	ERA	ERA+	OAV	OOB	BH	AVG	PB	PR	/A	PD	TPI
1955 Mil-N	0	0	—	25	0	0	0	2	24^{2}	39	4	14	13	19.7	8.76	43	.355	.432	1	.500	0	-13	-14	1	-0.1

● **BILL VARGUS** Vargus, William Fay b: 11/11/1899, N.Scituate, Mass. d: 2/12/79, Hyannis, Mass. BL/TL, 6', 165 lbs. Deb: 6/23/25

YEAR TM/L	W	L	PCT	G	GS	CG	SH	SV	IP	H	HR	BB	SO	RAT	ERA	ERA+	OAV	OOB	BH	AVG	PB	PR	/A	PD	TPI
1925 Bos-N	1	1	.500	11	2	1	0	0	36^{1}	45	1	13	5	14.9	3.96	101	.302	.366	3	.250	0	1	0	0	0.0
1926 Bos-N	0	0	—	4	0	0	0	0	3	4	0	1	0	15.0	3.00	118	.333	.385	0	—	0	0	0	0	0.0
Total 2	1	1	.500	15	2	1	0	0	39^{1}	49	1	14	5	14.9	3.89	102	.304	.367	3	.250	0	2	0	0	0.0

● **CHARLIE VAUGHAN** Vaughan, Charles Wayne b: 10/6/47, Mercedes, Tex. BR/TL, 6'1.5", 185 lbs. Deb: 9/3/66

YEAR TM/L	W	L	PCT	G	GS	CG	SH	SV	IP	H	HR	BB	SO	RAT	ERA	ERA+	OAV	OOB	BH	AVG	PB	PR	/A	PD	TPI
1966 Atl-N	1	0	1.000	1	1	0	0	0	7	8	0	3	6	14.1	2.57	141	.296	.367	1	.250	0	1	1	0	0.1
1969 Atl-N	0	0	—	1	0	0	0	0	1	1	0	3	1	36.0	18.00	20	.250	.571	0	—	0	-2	-2	0	0.0
Total 2	1	0	1.000	2	1	0	0	0	8	9	0	6	7	16.9	4.50	81	.290	.405	1	.250	0	-1	-1	0	0.1

● **AL VEIGEL** Veigel, Allen Francis b: 1/30/17, Dover, Ohio BR/TR, 6'1", 180 lbs. Deb: 9/21/39

YEAR TM/L	W	L	PCT	G	GS	CG	SH	SV	IP	H	HR	BB	SO	RAT	ERA	ERA+	OAV	OOB	BH	AVG	PB	PR	/A	PD	TPI
1939 Bos-N	0	1	.000	2	2	0	0	0	2^{2}	3	0	5	1	27.0	6.75	55	.250	.471	0	.000	-0	-1	-1	-0	-0.3

● **LEE VIAU** Viau, Leon A. b: 7/5/1866, Corinth, Vt. d: 12/17/47, Hopewell, N.J. BR/TR, 5'4", 160 lbs. Deb: 4/22/1888

YEAR TM/L	W	L	PCT	G	GS	CG	SH	SV	IP	H	HR	BB	SO	RAT	ERA	ERA+	OAV	OOB	BH	AVG	PB	PR	/A	PD	TPI
1892 Bos-N	1	0	1.000	1	1	1	0	0	9	5	0	4	1	9.0	0.00	—	.156	.250	0	.000	-0	3	4	-0	0.3
Total 5	83	77	.519	178	162	146	5	1	1442	1441	37	526	554	12.6	3.33	105	.251	.320	82	.139	-27	16	25	-1	-1.9

● **BILL VOISELLE** Voiselle, William Symmes "Big Bill" or "Ninety-Six" b: 1/29/19, Greenwood, S.C. BR/TR, 6'4", 200 lbs. Deb: 9/1/42

YEAR TM/L	W	L	PCT	G	GS	CG	SH	SV	IP	H	HR	BB	SO	RAT	ERA	ERA+	OAV	OOB	BH	AVG	PB	PR	/A	PD	TPI
1947 Bos-N	8	7	.533	22	20	7	0	0	131^{1}	146	10	51	59	13.6	4.32	90	.280	.345	9	.170	-1	-4	-6	1	-0.6
1948 *Bos-N	13	13	.500	37	30	9	2	2	215^{2}	226	18	90	89	13.3	3.63	106	.272	.345	7	.097	-4	8	5	-3	-0.1
1949 Bos-N	7	8	.467	30	22	5	4	1	169^{1}	170	14	78	63	13.2	4.04	94	.263	.343	7	.115	-2	0	-5	1	-0.5
Total 9	74	84	.468	245	190	74	13	3	1373^{1}	1370	115	588	645	12.9	3.83	98	.258	.334	68	.147	-10	-6	-10	-6	-2.2
Team 3	28	28	.500	89	72	21	6	3	516^{1}	542	42	219	211	13.4	3.94	97	.271	.345	23	.124	-6	4	-6	-1	-1.2

● **JAKE VOLZ** Volz, Jacob Phillip "Silent Jake" b: 4/4/1878, San Antonio, Tex. d: 8/11/62, San Antonio, Tex. BR/TR, 5'10", 175 lbs. Deb: 9/28/01

YEAR TM/L	W	L	PCT	G	GS	CG	SH	SV	IP	H	HR	BB	SO	RAT	ERA	ERA+	OAV	OOB	BH	AVG	PB	PR	/A	PD	TPI
1905 Bos-N	0	2	.000	3	2	0	0	0	8^{2}	12	0	8	1	21.8	10.38	30	.364	.500	0	.000	-0	-7	-7	-1	-1.3
Total 3	2	4	.333	11	7	2	0	0	38^{1}	34	3	29	12	15.5	6.10	44	.241	.382	1	.100	-1	-14	-14	-2	-2.3

● **TONY Von FRICKEN** Von Fricken, Anthony b: 5/30/1870, Brooklyn, N.Y. d: 3/22/47, Troy, N.Y. BB/TR, 5'11.5", 160 lbs. Deb: 5/9/1890

YEAR TM/L	W	L	PCT	G	GS	CG	SH	SV	IP	H	HR	BB	SO	RAT	ERA	ERA+	OAV	OOB	BH	AVG	PB	PR	/A	PD	TPI
1890 Bos-N	0	1	.000	1	1	1	0	0	8	23	0	8	2	34.9	10.13	37	.489	.564	0	.000	-1	-6	-6	-0	-0.5

● **TERRELL WADE** Wade, Hawatha Terrell b: 1/25/73, Rembert, S.C. BL/TL, 6'3", 205 lbs. Deb: 9/12/95

YEAR TM/L	W	L	PCT	G	GS	CG	SH	SV	IP	H	HR	BB	SO	RAT	ERA	ERA+	OAV	OOB	BH	AVG	PB	PR	/A	PD	TPI
1995 Atl-N	0	1	.000	3	0	0	0	0	4	3	1	4	3	15.8	4.50	94	.214	.389	0	—	0	-0	-0	-0	0.0

● **BOB WALK** Walk, Robert Vernon b: 11/26/56, Van Nuys, Cal. BR/TR, 6'4", 208 lbs. Deb: 5/26/80

YEAR TM/L	W	L	PCT	G	GS	CG	SH	SV	IP	H	HR	BB	SO	RAT	ERA	ERA+	OAV	OOB	BH	AVG	PB	PR	/A	PD	TPI
1981 Atl-N	1	4	.200	12	8	0	0	0	43^{1}	41	6	23	16	13.3	4.57	78	.250	.342	1	.143	-0	-5	-5	-1	-0.6
1982 *Atl-N	11	9	.550	32	27	3	1	0	164^{1}	179	19	59	84	13.4	4.87	77	.280	.347	10	.196	2	-23	-21	-2	-2.4
1983 Atl-N	0	0	—	1	1	0	0	0	3^{2}	7	0	2	4	22.1	7.36	53	.412	.474	0	.000	-0	-2	-1	0	0.0
Total 14	105	81	.565	350	259	16	6	5	1666	1671	143	606	848	12.5	4.03	91	.263	.330	74	.145	1	-66	-67	-1	-8.0
Team 3	12	13	.480	45	36	3	1	0	211^{1}	227	25	84	104	13.5	4.85	76	.277	.348	11	.186	1	-30	-27	-2	-3.0

● **MURRAY WALL** Wall, Murray Wesley b: 9/19/26, Dallas, Tex. d: 10/8/71, Lone Oak, Tex. BR/TR, 6'3", 185 lbs. Deb: 7/4/50

YEAR TM/L	W	L	PCT	G	GS	CG	SH	SV	IP	H	HR	BB	SO	RAT	ERA	ERA+	OAV	OOB	BH	AVG	PB	PR	/A	PD	TPI
1950 Bos-N	0	0	—	1	0	0	0	0	4	6	0	2	2	18.0	9.00	43	.333	.400	0	.000	-0	-2	-2	-0	0.0
Total 4	13	14	.481	91	1	0	0	14	193	196	25	63	82	12.4	4.20	96	.270	.333	5	.109	-3	-8	-4	5	0.1

● **LEFTY WALLACE** Wallace, James Harold b: 8/12/21, Evansville, Ind. d: 7/28/82, Evansville, Ind. BL/TL, 5'11", 160 lbs. Deb: 5/5/42

YEAR TM/L	W	L	PCT	G	GS	CG	SH	SV	IP	H	HR	BB	SO	RAT	ERA	ERA+	OAV	OOB	BH	AVG	PB	PR	/A	PD	TPI
1942 Bos-N	1	3	.250	19	3	1	0	0	49^{1}	39	3	24	20	11.9	3.83	87	.217	.316	2	.143	-0	-3	-3	-1	-0.3
1945 Bos-N	1	0	1.000	5	3	1	0	0	20	18	1	9	4	12.6	4.50	85	.240	.329	0	.000	-1	-2	-1	0	-0.1
1946 Bos-N	3	3	.500	27	8	2	0	0	75^{1}	76	5	31	27	12.9	4.18	82	.253	.325	1	.056	-1	-6	-6	2	-0.4
Total 3	5	6	.455	51	14	4	0	0	144^{2}	133	9	64	51	12.5	4.11	84	.240	.323	3	.079	-2	-11	-10	1	-0.8

● **ED WALSH** Walsh, Edward Augustine "Big Ed" b: 5/14/1881, Plains, Pa. d: 5/26/59, Pompano Beach, Fla BR/TR, 6'1", 193 lbs. Deb: 5/7/04 FMUCH

YEAR TM/L	W	L	PCT	G	GS	CG	SH	SV	IP	H	HR	BB	SO	RAT	ERA	ERA+	OAV	OOB	BH	AVG	PB	PR	/A	PD	TPI
1917 Bos-N	0	1	.000	4	3	1	0	0	18	22	0	9	4	16.0	3.50	73	.314	.400	1	.250	1	-2	-2	0	0.0
Total 14	195	126	.607	430	315	250	57	34	2964^{1}	2346	23	617	1736	9.2	1.82	145	.218	.264	210	.193	14	310	270	83	43.3

● **BUCKY WALTERS** Walters, William Henry b: 4/19/09, Philadelphia, Pa. d: 4/20/91, Abington, Pa. BR/TR, 6'1", 180 lbs. Deb: 9/18/31 MC♦

YEAR TM/L	W	L	PCT	G	GS	CG	SH	SV	IP	H	HR	BB	SO	RAT	ERA	ERA+	OAV	OOB	BH	AVG	PB	PR	/A	PD	TPI
1950 Bos-N	0	0	—	1	0	0	0	0	4	5	0	2	0	15.8	4.50	86	.313	.389	0	.000	-0	-0	-0	-0	0.0
Total 16	198	160	.553	428	398	242	42	4	3104^{2}	2990	154	1121	1107	12.1	3.30	115	.253	.321	477	.243	57	152	168	27	28.6

● **DUANE WARD** Ward, Roy Duane b: 5/28/64, Park View, N.Mex. BR/TR, 6'4", 215 lbs. Deb: 4/12/86

YEAR TM/L	W	L	PCT	G	GS	CG	SH	SV	IP	H	HR	BB	SO	RAT	ERA	ERA+	OAV	OOB	BH	AVG	PB	PR	/A	PD	TPI
1986 Atl-N	0	1	.000	10	0	0	0	0	16	22	2	8	8	16.9	7.31	54	.349	.423	0	.000	-0	-6	-6	1	-0.3
Total 9	32	37	.464	462	2	0	0	121	666^{2}	551	32	286	679	11.5	3.28	123	.228	.314	0	.000	-0	53	55	2	8.1

● **MULE WATSON** Watson, John Reeves b: 10/15/1896, Homer, La. d: 8/25/49, Shreveport, La. BR/TR, 6'1.5", 185 lbs. Deb: 7/4/18

YEAR TM/L	W	L	PCT	G	GS	CG	SH	SV	IP	H	HR	BB	SO	RAT	ERA	ERA+	OAV	OOB	BH	AVG	PB	PR	/A	PD	TPI
1920 Bos-N	0	0	—	1	0	0	0	0	3	0	0	0	0	0.0	0.00	—	.000	.000	0	.000	-0	1	1	0	0.0
1920 Bos-N	5	4	.556	12	10	4	2	0	71^{2}	79	0	17	16	12.2	3.77	81	.298	.343	3	.130	-1	-5	-6	-0	-0.8
1921 Bos-N	14	13	.519	44	31	15	1	2	259^{1}	269	11	57	48	11.6	3.85	95	.270	.314	12	.138	-4	-2	-6	-1	-1.0
1922 Bos-N	8	14	.364	41	29	8	1	1	201	262	9	59	53	14.6	4.70	85	.317	.366	13	.197	-0	-13	-16	-0	-1.5

YEAR TM/L	W	L	PCT	G	GS	CG	SH	SV	IP	H	HR	BB	SO	RAT	ERA	ERA+	OAV	OOB	BH	AVG	PB	PR	/A	PD	TPI
1923 Bos-N	1	2	.333	11	4	1	0	1	31^{1}	42	2	20	10	17.8	5.17	77	.339	.431	2	.250	-0	-4	-4	0	-0.4
Total 7	50	53	.485	178	126	53	8	4	941^{2}	1062	44	256	208	12.8	4.03	89	.293	.342	53	.165	-8	-38	-45	-3	-4.9
Team 5	28	33	.459	109	74	28	4	4	566^{1}	652	22	153	127	13.0	4.20	88	.293	.343	30	.162	-6	-23	-30	-1	-3.7
● **KEN WEAFER** Weafer, Kenneth Albert "Al" b: 2/6/14, Woburn, Mass. BR/TR, 6'0.5", 183 lbs. Deb: 5/29/36																									
1936 Bos-N	0	0	—	1	0	0	0	0	3	6	1	3	0	27.0	12.00	32	.375	.474	0	.000	-0	-3	-3	-0	0.0
● **ORLIE WEAVER** Weaver, Orville Forest b: 6/4/1886, Newport, Ky. d: 11/28/70, New Orleans, La. BR/TR, 6', 180 lbs. Deb: 9/14/10																									
1911 Bos-N	3	12	.200	27	17	4	0	0	121	140	9	84	50	17.2	6.47	59	.303	.418	5	.122	-2	-41	-36	-2	-4.1
Total 2	6	15	.286	40	23	7	1	0	196^{2}	203	11	116	92	15.1	5.03	71	.276	.383	8	.113	-4	-37	-32	-4	-4.1
● **ROY WEIR** Weir, William Franklin "Bill" b: 2/25/11, Portland, Maine d: 9/30/89, Anaheim, Cal. BL/TL, 5'8.5", 170 lbs. Deb: 6/25/36																									
1936 Bos-N	4	3	.571	12	7	3	2	0	57^{1}	53	0	24	29	12.1	2.83	136	.241	.316	5	.278	2	8	6	1	1.0
1937 Bos-N	1	1	.500	10	4	1	0	0	33	27	0	19	8	12.5	3.82	94	.227	.333	0	.000	-1	0	-1	1	-0.1
1938 Bos-N	1	0	1.000	5	0	0	0	0	13^{1}	14	4	6	3	13.5	6.75	51	.269	.345	1	.333	0	-4	-5	0	-0.3
1939 Bos-N	0	0	—	2	0	0	0	0	2^{2}	1	0	1	2	6.8	0.00	—	.125	.222	0	.000	-0	1	1	0	0.0
Total 4	6	4	.600	29	11	4	2	0	106^{1}	95	4	50	42	12.3	3.55	104	.238	.323	6	.188	1	5	2	2	0.6
● **JOHNNY WERTS** Werts, Henry Levi b: 4/20/1898, Pomaria, S.C. d: 9/24/90, Newberry, S.C. BR/TR, 5'10", 180 lbs. Deb: 4/14/26																									
1926 Bos-N	11	9	.550	32	23	7	1	0	189^{1}	212	6	47	65	12.8	3.28	108	.287	.338	17	.266	4	11	6	2	1.2
1927 Bos-N	4	10	.286	42	15	4	0	1	164^{1}	204	5	52	39	14.2	4.55	82	.315	.369	7	.163	-0	-11	-15	-1	-1.3
1928 Bos-N	0	2	.000	10	2	0	0	0	18^{1}	31	2	8	5	19.1	10.31	38	.369	.424	1	.333	0	-13	-13	0	-1.1
1929 Bos-N	0	0	—	4	0	0	0	1	6	13	1	4	2	25.5	10.50	45	.433	.500	1	1.000	0	-4	-4	-0	-0.1
Total 4	15	21	.417	88	40	11	1	2	378	460	14	111	111	13.9	4.29	85	.307	.360	26	.234	4	-17	-27	1	-1.3
● **FRANK WEST** West, J. Franklin b: 1/1874, Johnstown, Pa. d: 9/6/32, Wilmerding, Pa. 180 lbs. Deb: 7/11/1894																									
1894 Bos-N	0	0	—	1	0	0	0	0	3	5	0	2	1	21.0	9.00	63	.357	.438	0	.000	-0	-1	-1	-0	0.0
● **BOB WHITCHER** Whitcher, Robert Arthur b: 4/29/17, Berlin, N.H. BL/TL, 5'8", 165 lbs. Deb: 8/20/45																									
1945 Bos-N	0	2	.000	6	3	0	0	0	15^{2}	12	1	12	6	13.8	2.87	133	.235	.381	1	.333	0	2	2	-0	0.2
● **ERNIE WHITE** White, Ernest Daniel b: 9/5/16, Pacolet Mills, S.C d: 5/22/74, Augusta, Ga. BR/TL, 5'11.5", 175 lbs. Deb: 5/9/40 C																									
1946 Bos-N	0	1	.000	12	1	0	0	0	23^{2}	22	1	12	8	12.9	4.18	82	.256	.347	1	.250	0	-2	-2	-1	-0.1
1947 Bos-N	0	0	—	1	1	0	0	0	4	1	0	1	1	4.5	0.00	—	.083	.154	1	1.000	0	2	2	-0	0.0
1948 Bos-N	0	2	.000	15	0	0	0	2	23	13	0	17	8	11.7	1.96	196	.167	.316	0	.000	-0	5	5	-1	0.4
Total 7	30	21	.588	108	57	24	5	6	489^{1}	425	28	188	244	11.5	2.78	130	.231	.306	34	.209	2	41	45	-8	4.2
Team 3	0	3	.000	28	2	0	0	2	50^{2}	36	1	30	17	11.7	2.84	129	.205	.320	2	.250	0	5	5	-2	0.3
● **KIRBY WHITE** White, Oliver Kirby "Red" or "Buck" b: 1/3/1884, Hillsboro, Ohio d: 4/22/43, Hillsboro, Ohio BL/TR, 6', 190 lbs. Deb: 5/4/09																									
1909 Bos-N	6	13	.316	23	19	11	1	0	148^{1}	134	5	80	53	13.0	3.22	88	.245	.343	8	.160	-1	-10	-6	-1	-1.0
1910 Bos-N	1	2	.333	3	3	3	0	0	26	15	2	12	6	10.4	1.38	240	.188	.316	2	.333	1	5	6	0	0.8
Total 3	17	25	.405	58	44	21	4	2	330^{2}	294	10	168	102	12.8	3.24	93	.247	.345	22	.214	3	-15	-9	-4	-1.4
Team 2	7	15	.318	26	22	14	1	0	174^{1}	149	7	92	59	12.6	2.94	98	.238	.339	10	.179	-0	-5	-1	-1	-0.2
● **STEVE WHITE** White, Stephen Vincent b: 12/21/1884, Dorchester, Mass. d: 1/29/75, Braintree, Mass. BR/TR, 5'10", 160 lbs. Deb: 5/29/12																									
1912 Bos-N	0	0	—	3	0	0	0	0	6	9	0	5	2	22.5	6.00	60	.429	.556	0	.000	-0	-2	-2	0	0.0
Total 1	0	0	—	4	0	0	0	0	6^{2}	11	1	5	3	23.0	5.40	66	.458	.567	0	.000	-0	-1	-1	-0	0.0
● **WILL WHITE** White, William Henry "Whoop-La" b: 10/11/1854, Caton, N.Y. d: 8/31/11, Port Carling, Ont., Canada BB/TR, 5'9.5", 175 lbs. Deb: 7/20/1877 FM																									
1877 Bos-N	2	1	.667	3	3	3	1	0	27	27	0	2	7	9.7	3.00	94	.243	.257	3	.200	-1	-1	-1	-1	-0.2
Total 10	229	166	.580	403	401	394	36	0	3542^{2}	3440	65	496	1041	10.2	2.28	120	.239	.268	271	.183	-33	198	179	-17	12.2
● **JIM WHITNEY** Whitney, James Evans "Grasshopper Jim" b: 11/10/1857, Conklin, N.Y. d: 5/21/1891, Binghamton, N.Y. BL/TR, 6'2", 172 lbs. Deb: 5/2/1881 ♦																									
1881 Bos-N	**31**	33	.484	**66**	63	**57**	6	0	**552^{1}**	548	6	90	162	10.4	2.48	107	.248	.277	72	.255	11	18	11	-4	1.9
1882 Bos-N	24	21	.533	49	48	46	3	0	420	404	3	41	180	9.5	2.64	109	.237	.255	81	.323	23	12	11	1	3.1
1883 Bos-N	37	21	.638	62	56	54	1	**2**	514	492	7	35	**345**	9.2	2.24	138	.238	.251	115	.281	20	51	49	0	6.0
1884 Bos-N	23	14	.622	38	37	35	6	0	336	272	12	27	270	8.0	2.09	138	.207	.223	70	.259	10	33	30	4	4.0
1885 Bos-N	18	32	.360	51	50	50	2	0	441^{1}	503	14	37	200	11.0	2.98	90	.272	.286	68	.234	7	-8	-14	6	-0.2
Total 10	191	204	.484	413	396	377	25	2	3496^{1}	3598	79	411	1571	10.4	2.97	105	.253	.275	559	.261	89	60	55	15	14.7
Team 5	133	121	.524	266	254	242	18	2	2263^{2}	2219	42	230	1157	9.7	2.49	114	.243	.261	406	.270	71	108	86	8	14.8
● **WHITEY WIETELMANN** Wietelmann, William Frederick b: 3/15/19, Zanesville, Ohio BB/TR, 6', 170 lbs. Deb: 9/6/39 C♦																									
1945 Bos-N	0	0	—	1	0	0	0	0	1	6	0	2	0	72.0	54.00	7	.667	.727	116	.271	0	-6	-6	-0	0.0
1946 Bos-N	0	0	—	3	0	0	0	0	6^{2}	9	1	4	2	18.9	8.10	42	.310	.412	16	.205	0	-3	-3	-0	0.0
Total 2	0	0	—	4	0	0	0	0	7^{2}	15	1	6	2	25.8	14.09	25	.395	.489	409	.232	1	-9	-9	-0	0.0
● **KAISER WILHELM** Wilhelm, Irvin Key b: 1/26/1874, Wooster, Ohio d: 5/21/36, Rochester, N.Y. BR/TR, 6', 162 lbs. Deb: 4/18/03 MUC																									
1904 Bos-N	14	20	.412	39	36	30	3	0	288	316	8	74	73	12.4	3.69	75	.285	.333	7	.070	-8	-30	-30	1	-3.9
1905 Bos-N	3	23	.115	34	27	23	0	0	242^{1}	287	7	75	76	13.6	4.53	68	.295	.349	16	.160	-2	-41	-39	2	-3.7
Total 9	56	105	.348	216	157	118	12	5	1432^{1}	1495	34	418	444	12.2	3.44	81	.274	.328	78	.154	-12	-108	-102	11	-10.6
Team 2	17	43	.283	73	63	53	3	0	530^{1}	603	15	149	149	13.0	4.07	72	.290	.341	23	.115	-11	-71	-68	3	-7.6
● **HOYT WILHELM** Wilhelm, James Hoyt b: 7/26/23, Huntersville, N.C. BR/TR, 6', 195 lbs. Deb: 4/19/52 H																									
1969 Atl-N	2	0	1.000	8	0	0	0	4	12^{1}	5	0	4	14	7.3	0.73	494	.119	.213	0	.000	-0	4	4	0	1.0
1970 Atl-N☆	6	4	.600	50	0	0	0	13	78^{1}	69	7	39	67	12.5	3.10	138	.234	.325	1	.091	-0	8	10	0	1.6
1971 Atl-N	0	0	—	3	0	0	0	0	2^{1}	6	2	1	1	27.0	15.43	24	.500	.538	0	—	0	-3	-3	0	0.0
Total 21	143	122	.540	1070	52	20	5	227	2254^{1}	1757	150	778	1610	10.4	2.52	146	.216	.290	38	.088	-21	310	288	5	40.0
Team 3	8	4	.667	61	0	0	0	17	93	80	9	44	82	12.2	3.10	135	.229	.319	1	.083	-0	9	11	1	2.6
● **CARL WILLEY** Willey, Carlton Francis b: 6/6/31, Cherryfield, Me. BR/TR, 6', 175 lbs. Deb: 4/30/58																									
1958 *Mil-N	9	7	.563	23	19	9	**4**	0	140	110	14	53	74	10.6	2.70	130	.215	.291	5	.104	-2	19	13	-2	0.9
1959 Mil-N	5	9	.357	26	15	5	2	0	117	126	12	31	51	12.2	4.15	85	.273	.322	4	.103	-1	-3	-8	-1	-1.1
1960 Mil-N	6	7	.462	28	21	2	1	0	144^{2}	136	19	65	109	12.9	4.35	79	.248	.335	7	.146	1	-10	-15	-1	-1.2
1961 Mil-N	6	12	.333	35	22	4	0	0	159^{2}	147	20	65	91	12.1	3.83	98	.247	.323	1	.019	-6	4	-2	3	-0.5
1962 Mil-N	2	5	.286	30	6	0	0	1	73^{1}	95	9	20	40	14.2	5.40	70	.319	.364	3	.273	1	-12	-13	-0	-1.1
Total 8	38	58	.396	199	117	28	11	1	875^{2}	830	105	326	493	12.1	3.76	95	.250	.320	26	.099	-9	1	-17	-3	-2.6
Team 5	28	40	.412	142	83	20	7	1	634^{2}	614	74	234	365	12.2	3.94	91	.254	.324	20	.100	-7	-1	-25	-1	-3.0
● **ACE WILLIAMS** Williams, Robert Fulton b: 3/18/17, Montclair, N.J. BR/TL, 6'2", 174 lbs. Deb: 7/15/40																									
1940 Bos-N	0	0	—	5	0	0	0	0	9	21	0	12	5	34.0	16.00	23	.375	.493	0	.000	-0	-12	-12	0	0.0
1946 Bos-N	0	0	—	1	0	0	0	0	0	1	0	1	0	—	—	—	1.000	1.000	0	—	0	0	0	0	0.0
Total 2	0	0	—	6	0	0	0	0	9	22	0	13	5	36.0	16.00	23	.386	.507	0	.000	-0	-12	-12	0	0.0
● **POP WILLIAMS** Williams, Walter Merrill b: 5/19/1874, Bowdoinham, Me. d: 8/4/59, Topsham, Maine BL/TR, 5'11", 190 lbs. Deb: 9/14/1898																									
1903 Bos-N	4	5	.444	10	10	9	1	0	83	97	3	37	20	15.5	4.12	78	.295	.381	10	.238	-0	-8	-8	-1	-0.8
Total 3	16	25	.390	46	46	40	2	0	377^{1}	418	5	113	127	13.1	3.20	90	.282	.340	38	.217	4	-10	-13	2	-0.4

YEAR	TM/L	W	L	PCT	G	GS	CG	SH	SV	IP	H	HR	BB	SO	RAT	ERA	ERA+	OAV	OOB	BH	AVG	PB	PR	/A	PD	TPI
● **VIC WILLIS**	Willis, Victor Gazaway b: 4/12/1876, Cecil Co., Md. d: 8/3/47, Elkton, Md. BR/TR, 6'2", 185 lbs. Deb: 4/20/1898 H																									
1898	Bos-N	25	13	.658	41	38	29	1	0	311	264	5	148	160	12.8	2.84	130	.228	.331	17	.145	-6	27	30	-0	2.5
1899	Bos-N	27	8	.771	41	38	35	**5**	2	342^2	277	6	117	120	11.1	**2.50**	**167**	**.221**	.303	29	.216	-4	52	**63**	0	5.3
1900	Bos-N	10	17	.370	32	29	22	2	0	236	258	11	106	53	14.3	4.19	98	.277	.359	12	.136	-6	-13	-2	-2	-0.9
1901	Bos-N	20	17	.541	38	35	33	**6**	0	305^1	262	6	78	133	10.3	2.36	**153**	.230	.286	20	.187	-1	33	**43**	-1	4.6
1902	Bos-N	27	20	.574	**51**	46	**45**	4	**3**	**410**	372	6	101	**225**	10.7	2.20	129	.242	.295	23	.153	-6	27	29	4	3.1
1903	Bos-N	12	18	.400	33	32	29	2	0	278	256	3	88	125	11.5	2.98	108	.251	.317	24	.188	-1	9	7	3	0.8
1904	Bos-N	18	25	.419	43	43	**39**	2	0	350	357	7	109	196	12.3	2.85	97	.266	.327	27	.182	1	-4	-4	7	0.4
1905	Bos-N	12	29	.293	41	41	36	4	0	342	340	7	107	149	12.1	3.21	97	.265	.328	20	.153	-3	-8	-4	6	-0.1
Total	13	249	205	.548	513	471	388	50	11	3996	3621	66	1212	1651	11.2	2.63	118	.243	.307	248	.166	-33	172	208	27	22.0
Team	8	151	147	.507	320	302	268	26	5	2575	2386	51	854	1161	11.8	2.82	120	.247	.317	172	.171	-25	122	159	17	15.7
● **ZEKE WILSON**	Wilson, Frank Ealton b: 12/24/1869, Benton, Ala. d: 4/26/28, Montgomery, Ala. BR/TR, 5'10", 165 lbs. Deb: 4/23/1895																									
1895	Bos-N	2	4	.333	6	6	4	0	0	45	54	1	27	5	16.2	5.20	98	.293	.384	6	.316	1	-2	-0	1	0.1
Total	5	52	44	.542	119	105	83	3	1	874	1042	26	266	194	13.8	4.03	106	.293	.347	82	.215	-8	13	25	14	2.5
● **JIM WILSON**	Wilson, James Alger b: 2/20/22, San Diego, Cal. d: 9/2/86, Newport Beach, Cal BR/TR, 6'1.5", 200 lbs. Deb: 4/18/45																									
1951	Bos-N	7	7	.500	20	15	5	0	1	110	131	14	40	33	14.3	5.40	68	.294	.357	7	.179	0	-18	-21	-1	-2.4
1952	Bos-N	12	14	.462	33	33	14	0	0	234	234	19	90	104	12.6	4.23	85	.262	.333	14	.163	-0	-13	-16	-1	-1.8
1953	Mil-N	4	9	.308	20	18	5	0	0	114	107	16	43	71	12.1	4.34	90	.243	.315	6	.167	1	-1	-5	1	-0.3
1954	Mil-N☆	8	2	.800	27	19	6	4	0	127^2	129	12	36	52	12.0	3.52	106	.266	.323	7	.159	0	8	3	1	0.3
Total	12	86	89	.491	257	217	75	19	2	1539	1479	151	608	692	12.4	4.01	93	.254	.327	99	.181	4	-21	-45	-5	-4.0
Team	4	31	32	.492	100	85	30	4	1	585^2	601	61	209	260	12.7	4.32	86	.266	.332	34	.166	1	-24	-39	-0	-4.2
● **ROY WITHERUP**	Witherup, Foster Leroy b: 7/26/1886, N.Washington, Pa. d: 12/23/41, New Bethlehem, Pa. BR/TR, 6', 185 lbs. Deb: 5/14/06																									
1906	Bos-N	0	3	.000	8	3	3	0	0	46	59	2	19	14	15.5	6.26	43	.322	.389	2	.133	-1	-19	-18	-1	-1.2
Total	3	3	12	.200	26	17	12	0	0	162^1	189	3	47	71	13.2	4.44	55	.298	.348	6	.115	-3	-35	-36	-2	-3.2
● **MARK WOHLERS**	Wohlers, Mark Edward b: 1/23/70, Holyoke, Mass. BR/TR, 6'4", 207 lbs. Deb: 8/17/91																									
1991	*Atl-N	3	1	.750	17	0	0	0	2	19^2	17	1	13	13	14.6	3.20	121	.239	.372	0	.000	-0	1	1	0	0.3
1992	*Atl-N	1	2	.333	32	0	0	0	4	35^1	28	0	14	17	11.0	2.55	144	.235	.321	0	.000	-0	4	4	0	0.5
1993	*Atl-N	6	2	.750	46	0	0	0	0	48	37	2	22	45	11.3	4.50	89	.218	.311	0	—	0	-2	-3	0	-0.3
1994	Atl-N	7	2	.778	51	0	0	0	1	51	51	1	33	58	14.8	4.59	92	.264	.372	1	1.000	0	-2	-2	0	-0.2
1995	*Atl-N	7	3	.700	65	0	0	0	25	64^2	51	2	24	90	10.6	2.09	203	.211	.285	0	.000	-0	15	15	-1	3.4
Total	5	24	10	.706	211	0	0	0	32	218^2	184	6	106	223	12.1	3.38	120	.231	.326	1	.143	-0	15	17	0	3.7
● **BRAD WOODALL**	Woodall, David Bradley b: 6/25/69, Atlanta, Ga. BB/TL, 6', 175 lbs. Deb: 7/22/94																									
1994	Atl-N	0	1	.000	1	1	0	0	0	6	5	2	2	2	10.5	4.50	94	.227	.292	1	.500	0	-0	-0	1	0.1
1995	Atl-N	1	1	.500	9	0	0	0	0	10^1	13	1	8	5	18.3	6.10	69	.310	.420	1	1.000	0	-2	-2	0	-0.3
Total	2	1	2	.333	10	1	0	0	0	16^1	18	3	10	7	15.4	5.51	77	.281	.378	2	.667	1	-2	-2	1	-0.2
● **GEORGE WOODEND**	Woodend, George Anthony b: 12/9/17, Hartford, Conn. d: 2/6/80, Hartford, Conn. BR/TR, 6', 200 lbs. Deb: 4/22/44																									
1944	Bos-N	0	0	—	3	0	0	0	0	2	5	0	5	0	45.0	13.50	28	.556	.714	0	—	0	-2	-2	0	0.0
● **GEORGE WRIGHT**	Wright, George b: 1/28/1847, Yonkers, N.Y. d: 8/21/37, Boston, Mass. BR/TR, 5'9.5", 150 lbs. Deb: 5/5/1871 FMH♦																									
1875	Bos-n	0	1	.000	2	0	0	0	0	4	5	0	0		11.3	*2.25*	105	.263	.263	135	.333	1	0	0		0.0
1876	Bos-N	0	0	—	1	0	0	0	0	1	1	0	0	1	9.0	0.00	—	.250	.250	100	.299	0	0	0	0	0.0
● **ED WRIGHT**	Wright, Henderson Edward b: 5/15/19, Dyersburg, Tenn. BR/TR, 6'1", 180 lbs. Deb: 7/29/45																									
1945	Bos-N	8	3	.727	15	12	7	1	0	111^1	104	7	33	24	11.1	2.51	153	.254	.310	5	.128	-2	16	16	-1	1.2
1946	Bos-N	12	9	.571	36	21	8	2	0	176^1	164	8	71	44	12.1	3.52	97	.250	.325	18	.305	6	-2	-2	0	0.4
1947	Bos-N	3	3	.500	23	6	1	0	0	64^2	80	9	35	14	16.3	6.40	61	.305	.391	3	.130	-0	-17	-18	-0	-1.5
1948	Bos-N	0	0	—	3	0	0	0	0	4^2	9	0	2	2	21.2	1.93	199	.474	.524	0	—	0	1	1	0	0.0
Total	5	25	16	.610	101	39	16	3	1	398^1	412	30	161	93	13.1	4.00	92	.271	.344	27	.211	3	-15	-14	-2	-0.8
Team	4	23	15	.605	77	39	16	3	0	357	357	24	141	84	12.7	3.71	98	.265	.336	26	.215	4	-2	-2	-1	0.1
● **HARRY WRIGHT**	Wright, William Henry b: 1/10/1835, Sheffield, England d: 10/3/1895, Atlantic City, N.J. BR/TR, 5'9.5", 157 lbs. Deb: 5/5/1871 FMH♦																									
1871	Bos-n	1	0	1.000	9	0	0	0	**3**	18^2	34	0	4	0	18.3	6.27	66	.337	.362	44	.299	1	-4	-4		-0.2
1872	Bos-n	1	0	1.000	7	0	0	0	**1**	25^2	26	0	0	1	9.1	2.10	177	.241	.241	54	.260	0	**5**	**5**		0.1
1873	Bos-n	2	2	.500	12	5	0	0	1	38^1	65	0	7	0	16.9	4.23	78	.330	.353	67	.252	1	-4	-4		-0.3
1874	Bos-n	0	2	.000	6	2	0	0	**3**	16^2	24	0	4		15.1	*2.70*	110	.338	.373	56	.304	2	1	0		0.1
Total	4 n	4	4	.500	34	7	0	0	8	99^1	149	0	15	<u>1</u>	14.9	*3.81*	78	.312	.333	222	.274	5	-9	-9		-0.3
● **AL YEARGIN**	Yeargin, James Almond b: 10/16/01, Mauldin, S.C. d: 5/8/37, Greenville, S.C. BR/TR, 5'11", 170 lbs. Deb: 10/1/22																									
1922	Bos-N	0	1	.000	1	1	1	0	0	7	5	1	2	1	9.0	1.29	311	.192	.250	0	.000	-0	2	2	0	0.2
1924	Bos-N	1	11	.083	32	12	6	0	0	141^1	162	7	42	34	13.2	5.09	75	.293	.346	6	.143	-2	-19	-20	4	-1.3
Total	2	1	12	.077	33	13	7	0	0	148^1	167	8	44	35	13.0	4.91	78	.288	.342	6	.133	-2	-17	-18	4	-1.1
● **CY YOUNG**	Young, Denton True b: 3/29/1867, Gilmore, Ohio d: 11/4/55, Newcomerstown, Ohio BR/TR, 6'2", 210 lbs. Deb: 8/6/1890 MH																									
1911	Bos-N	4	5	.444	11	11	8	2	0	80	83	4	15	35	11.4	3.71	103	.268	.308	2	.080	-2	-3	1	0	-0.1
Total	22	511	316	.618	906	815	749	76	17	7356^2	7092	138	1217	2803	10.4	2.63	138	.252	.286	623	.210	-22	754	820	19	79.9
● **HARLEY YOUNG**	Young, Harlan Edward "Cy The Third" b: 9/28/1883, Portland, Ind. d: 3/26/75, Jacksonville, Fla. BR/TR, 6'2", Deb: 4/21/08																									
1908	Bos-N	0	1	.000	6	2	1	0	0	27^1	29	0	4	12	11.9	3.29	73	.269	.313	2	.200	0	-3	-3	-0	-0.1
● **IRV YOUNG**	Young, Irving Melrose "Young Cy" or "Cy The Second" b: 7/21/1877, Columbia Falls, Maine d: 1/14/35, Brewer, Maine BL/TL, 5'10", 170 lbs. Deb: 4/14/05																									
1905	Bos-N	20	21	.488	43	42	**41**	7	0	**378**	337	6	71	156	9.9	2.90	107	.241	.282	14	.103	-8	4	8	4	0.4
1906	Bos-N	16	25	.390	43	41	**37**	4	0	**358^1**	349	7	83	151	11.0	2.91	92	.263	.309	12	.096	-7	-11	-9	3	-1.5
1907	Bos-N	10	23	.303	40	32	22	3	1	245^1	287	5	58	86	13.1	3.96	64	.306	.354	13	.162	-1	-41	-38	1	-4.9
1908	Bos-N	4	9	.308	16	11	7	1	0	85	94	2	19	32	12.2	2.86	84	.289	.332	5	.156	-1	-5	-4	-1	-0.9
Total	6	63	95	.399	209	161	120	21	4	1384^2	1361	23	316	560	11.1	3.11	88	.260	.307	60	.126	-18	-62	-57	6	-8.5
Team	4	50	78	.391	142	126	107	15	1	1066^2	1067	20	231	425	11.2	3.15	88	.268	.312	44	.118	-17	-52	-43	7	-6.9
● **TOM ZACHARY**	Zachary, Jonathan Thompson Walton (a.k.a. Zach Walton In 1918) b: 5/7/1896, Graham, N.C. d: 1/24/69, Burlington, N.C. BL/TL, 6'1", 187 lbs. Deb: 7/11/18																									
1930	Bos-N	11	5	.688	24	22	10	1	0	151^1	192	9	50	57	14.4	4.58	108	.317	.369	13	.241	2	7	6	-1	0.6
1931	Bos-N	11	15	.423	33	28	16	3	2	229	243	8	53	64	11.7	3.10	122	.272	.314	14	.167	-1	19	17	2	2.0
1932	Bos-N	12	11	.522	32	24	12	1	0	212	231	5	55	67	12.2	3.10	121	.280	.326	21	.273	5	18	16	-2	1.9
1933	Bos-N	7	9	.438	26	20	6	2	2	125	134	1	35	22	12.2	3.53	87	.276	.325	5	.119	-2	-3	-6	0	-1.0
1934	Bos-N	1	2	.333	5	4	2	1	0	24	27	1	8	4	13.1	3.38	113	.278	.333	0	.000	-1	2	1	-0	0.0
Total	19	186	191	.493	533	409	186	24	22	3126^1	3580	119	914	720	13.1	3.73	106	.294	.345	254	.226	25	116	82	-2	10.3
Team	5	42	42	.500	120	98	46	8	4	741^1	827	24	201	214	12.5	3.48	111	.284	.331	53	.200	3	44	33	-1	3.5
● **STEVE ZIEM**	Ziem, Stephen Graeling b: 10/24/61, Milwaukee, Wis. BR/TR, 6'2", 210 lbs. Deb: 4/30/87																									
1987	Atl-N	0	1	.000	2	0	0	0	0	2^1	4	0	1	0	19.3	7.71	56	.364	.417	0	—	0	-1	-1	-0	-0.3

CHAPTER 9

The Annual Roster

This valuable presentation of a team's personnel history and development makes its first appearance in *Total Braves*. The reader may see at a glance who played for the franchise in each year of its existence, how many games he played at various positions, how effectively he played or managed, how he came to join the club, and where his travels may have taken him next.

Each page of the Annual Roster is topped at the corner by a finding aid: first, the year of the Braves team that heads up the page; second, the year which concludes that page. Remember that major league teams which may have played in Boston or Milwaukee in leagues other than the National League or National Association are excluded; these teams are not of the same franchise as the Braves, which has a direct (and, uniquely, unbroken) line of descent from the first year of the first professional league, with the Boston Red Stockings of 1871.

In compact style, the year-by-year flow of stars and spares may be traced, and reference to other sections of this book for additional data becomes simple enough. The expanded record of every player in these lists may be found in the Player Register, Pitcher Register, and Player Index. Superior players may be found as well in the All-Time Leaders section to follow, or in the capsule biographies of Braves Greats.

Below is a sample entry from the Annual Roster.

Name	G	AB/IP	P/E	G/POS	From	To
◆ **1914 BOSTON** (158 94-59 1) ATT: 382,913						
George Stallings				M		
Ted Cather	50	161	.738	LF-48	xStL-N	
Gene Cocreham	15	45	4.84	P-15(3-4)	B	
Wilson Collins	27	37	.554	LF-19	B	C
Joe Connolly	120	469	.886	LF-118	B	
Ensign Cottrell	1	1	9.00	P-1(0-1)	Phi-A	NY-A
Dick Crutcher	33	159	3.46	P-33(5-7)	A	
George Davis	9	56	3.40	P-9(3-3)	B	
Charlie Deal	79	293	.546	3-74,S-1	B	StL-F
Josh Devore	51	151	.608	LF-42	xPhi-N	C
Oscar Dugey	58	122	.505	RF-16,2-16,3-1	B	Phi-N
Johnny Evers	139	611	.728	2-139	Chi-N	
Larry Gilbert	72	261	.717	RF-60	A	
Hank Gowdy	128	426	.684	C-115,1-9	B	
Tommy Griffith	16	50	.244	RF-14	B	Cin-N
Otto Hess	31	89	3.03	P-14(5-6),1-5	B	
Tom Hughes	2	2	2.65	P-2(2-0)	NY-A	
Bill James	49	332	1.90	P-46(26-7)	B	
Clarence Kraft	3	3	.667	1-1	A	C
Dolf Luque	2	9	4.15	P-2(0-1)	A	
Les Mann	126	425	.668	CF-123	B	Chi-F
Rabbit Maranville	156	664	.632	S-156	B	
Jack Martin	33	94	.499	3-26,1-1,2-1	NY-A	xPhi-N
Billy Martin	1	3	.000	S-1	A	C
Herbie Moran	41	178	.646	RF-41	xCin-N	
Jim Murray	39	121	.581	LF-32	StL-A	C
Hub Perdue	9	51	5.82	P-9(2-5)	B	xStL-N
Dick Rudolph	43	336	2.35	P-42(26-10)	B	
Butch Schmidt	147	614	.706	1-147	B	
Red Smith	60	251	.850	3-60	xBro-N	
Paul Strand	18	55	2.44	P-16(6-2)	B	
Fred Tyler	6	21	.255	C-6	A	C
Lefty Tyler	38	271	2.69	P-38(16-13)	B	
Bert Whaling	60	199	.553	C-59	B	
Possum Whitted	66	258	.703	CF-38,2-15,1-4,3-4,S-3	xStL-N	Phi-N
Coach: Fred Mitchell						

Note that to the right of the team year and city is a parenthetical grouping of three figures, representing games played, won-lost mark, and place in the standings. The manager is listed immediately below, and his won-lost record is identical to the team's record if he was the only manager that season, as George Stallings was for the Miracle Braves. (In seasons characterized by managerial changes, the won-lost mark of each manager is presented.) Coaches, if any, are listed at the end of each seasonal entry.

The column headings otherwise describe players by use name (proper names are available in the Registers), followed by games played ("G"). Next comes a measure of appearance frequency, AB/IP: at bats for position players, innings pitched for pitchers.

The "P/E" column contains a dual measure of efficiency: Production (on base average plus slugging percentage) for position players, Earned Run Average for pitchers. Other measures might have appeared here, but these are the single best shorthand means of identifying batting or pitching excellence. Note that Production is expressed, for all but superlative seasons, as numbers less than 1.000 (three figures to the right of a decimal point), while ERA is expressed as a whole number followed by a decimal and two decimal places.

"G/POS" stands for games by position, expressed in descending order of frequency. If a man pitched and played a regular position, the statistic provided in the "P/E" column will be determined by which position he played more often. In G/POS for outfielders, the position is shown as left, center, or right field based on which outfield position he played more often. (If game data is missing for more than two games, "OF" is the abbreviation shown.) Beyond the expected abbreviations, note that "H" stands for a pinch hitter who did not take the field and "R" for a pinch runner who did not have a plate appearance.

In the column marked "From," the letter "A" signifies a player's major league debut, as with Dolf Luque of the 1914 Braves. "B" means he played for the Braves as his last or only club the previous year, as with Hank Gowdy. If he came from another major league club, that club is shown in abbreviated form; if the abbreviation is preceded by an "x," then he has come to the Braves during the season, as with Josh Devore. A key to these abbreviations may be found on the final page of this book.

In the column marked "To," the letter "C" signifies that this season marked the close of his major league career (see Jim Murray). If the player moved on to another club during the season, the abbreviation for that club is preceded by an "x" (see Jack Martin). If the column is blank, the reader knows the player returned to the Braves the following season.

Name	G	AB/IP	P/E	G/POS	From	To
♦ 1871 BOSTON (31 20-10 3) ATT: 32,600						
Harry Wright				M		
Ross Barnes	31	170	1.027	2-16,S-15,3-1	A	
Frank Barrows	18	86	.349	LF-17,2-1	A	C
Dave Birdsall	29	156	.682	RF-27,C-7	A	
Fred Cone	19	85	.654	LF-19	A	C
Charlie Gould	31	154	.709	1-30,RF-1	A	
Sam Jackson	16	77	.602	2-14,CF-1	A	Atl-n
Cal McVey	29	154	.991	C-29,RF-5	A	
Harry Schafer	31	152	.692	3-31,2-1	A	
Al Spalding	31	257	3.36	P-31(19-10),CF-9	A	
George Wright	16	86	1.078	S-15,1-1	A	
Harry Wright	31	160	.717	CF-30,P-9(1-0),S-1	A	
♦ 1872 BOSTON (48 39-8 1) ATT: 38,400						
Harry Wright				M		
Ross Barnes	45	239	1.017	2-45	B	
Dave Birdsall	16	77	.418	C-12,LF-8	B	
Charlie Gould	45	216	.647	1-44,RF-2	B	Bal-n
Andy Leonard	46	243	.765	LF-38,3-6,2-4	Oly-n	
Cal McVey	46	237	.688	C-40,RF-9	B	Bal-n
Fraley Rogers	45	205	.646	RF-42,1-6	A	
Harry Schafer	48	226	.695	3-43,LF-5	B	
Al Spalding	48	405	1.98	P-48(38-8),CF-7	B	
George Wright	48	258	.816	S-48	B	
Harry Wright	48	217	.579	CF-48,P-7(1-0)	B	
♦ 1873 BOSTON (60 43-16 1) ATT: 46,000						
Harry Wright				M		
Bob Addy	31	153	.800	RF-31	xPhi-n	Har-n
Ross Barnes	60	340	1.058	2-47,3-13	B	
Dave Birdsall	3	12	.167	RF-3	B	C
Andy Leonard	58	306	.718	LF-45,2-12,1-2,3-1	B	
Jack Manning	32	160	.602	1-29,RF-5	B	Bal-n
Jim O'Rourke	57	294	.842	1-32,RF-22,C-9	Man-n	
Fraley Rogers	1	6	1.000	1-1	B	C
Harry Schafer	60	298	.611	3-47,LF-13	B	
Al Spalding	60	498	2.46	P-60(41-14),CF-12	B	
Charlie Sweasy	1	4	.500	2-1	Cle-n	Bal-n
Deacon White	60	310	.897	C-56,RF-9	Cle-n	
George Wright	59	333	.901	S-59	B	
Harry Wright	58	276	.606	CF-58,P-12(2-2)	B	
♦ 1874 BOSTON (71 52-18 1) ATT: 49,000						
Harry Wright				M		
Ross Barnes	51	267	.784	2-51	B	
Tommy Beals	19	97	.505	2-12,RF-9	Was-n	
George Hall	47	224	.709	CF-47	Bal-n	Ath-n
Andy Leonard	71	342	.722	LF-51,S-11,2-11	B	
Cal McVey	70	341	.850	RF-57,C-23	Bal-n	
Jim O'Rourke	70	334	.754	1-70	B	
Harry Schafer	71	325	.585	3-71	B	
Al Spalding	71	616	2.35	P-71(52-16),CF-6	B	
Deacon White	70	354	.691	C-58,RF-21,1-1,2-1	B	
George Wright	60	320	.842	S-60	B	
Harry Wright	40	188	.727	CF-40,P-6(0-2),C-2	B	
♦ 1875 BOSTON (82 71-8 1) ATT: 53,000						
Harry Wright				M		
Ross Barnes	78	400	.828	2-78	B	Chi-N
Tommy Beals	36	166	.588	2-31,CF-6	B	Chi-N
Frank Heifer	11	51	.667	1-7,LF-6,P-2	A	C
Juice Latham	16	77	.623	1-16	xNH-n	
Andy Leonard	80	395	.720	LF-73,S-3,3-3,2-1	B	
Jack Manning	77	345	.596	RF-58,P-27(15-2),1-2,3-2	Har-n	
Cal McVey	82	390	.860	1-54,CF-17,C-11,P-3(1-0)	B	Chi-N
Jim O'Rourke	75	374	.739	CF-45,3-27,1-3	B	
Harry Schafer	51	216	.616	3-50,RF-1	B	
Al Spalding	74	575	1.52	P-72(55-5),RF-10,1-2	B	Chi-N
Deacon White	80	374	.818	C-72,RF-7,1-1	B	Chi-N
George Wright	79	408	.755	S-79,P-2(0-1)	B	
Harry Wright	1	4	.500	RF-1	B	
♦ 1876 BOSTON (70 39-31 4) ATT: 57,000						
Harry Wright				M		
Joe Borden	32	218	2.89	P-29(11-12),RF-16	Phi-n	C
Foghorn Bradley	22	173	2.49	P-22(9-10),RF-4	A	C
Lew Brown	45	198	.556	C-45,CF-1	A	
Andy Leonard	64	307	.617	LF-35,2-30	B	
Jack Manning	70	295	.611	RF-56,P-34(18-5),S-1,2-1	B	Cin-N
Dick McBride	4	33	2.73	P-4(0-4),RF-1	Ath-n	C
Tim McGinley	9	40	.300	CF-6,C-3	NH-n	C
John Morrill	66	281	.565	2-37,C-23,CF-5,1-3	A	
Tim Murnane	69	316	.635	1-65,LF-3,2-1	Phi-n	
Tricky Nichols	1	9	1.00	P-1(1-0)	NH-n	StL-N
Jim O'Rourke	70	327	.778	CF-68,1-2,C-1	B	
Bill Parks	1	4	.000	LF-1	Phi-n	C
Harry Schafer	70	290	.552	3-70	B	
Frank Whitney	34	140	.545	LF-34,2-1	A	C
George Wright	70	343	.712	S-68,2-2,P-1	B	
Sam Wright	2	8	.250	S-2	NH-n	Cin-N
Harry Wright	1	3	.000	RF-1	B	
♦ 1877 BOSTON (61 42-18 1) ATT: 45,369						
Harry Wright				M		
Tommy Bond	61	521	2.11	P-58(40-17),RF-3	Har-N	
Lew Brown	58	227	.667	C-55,1-4	B	Pro-N
Andy Leonard	58	277	.605	LF-37,S-21	B	
John Morrill	61	248	.649	3-30,1-18,RF-11,2-3	B	
Tim Murnane	35	146	.673	CF-30,1-5	B	Pro-N
Jim O'Rourke	61	285	.852	CF-60,1-1	B	
Harry Schafer	33	141	.617	RF-23,3-9,S-1	B	
Ezra Sutton	58	257	.683	S-36,3-22	Phi-N	
Deacon White	59	274	.950	1-35,RF-19,C-7	Chi-N	Cin-N
Will White	3	27	3.00	P-3(2-1)	A	Cin-N

Name	G	AB/IP	P/E	G/POS	From	To
George Wright	61	299	.632	2-58,S-3	B	
Harry Wright	1	4	.000	CF-1	B	C
♦ 1878 BOSTON (60 41-19 1) ATT: 44,885						
Harry Wright				M		
Tommy Bond	59	533	2.06	P-59(40-19),RF-2	B	
Jack Burdock	60	249	.627	2-60	Har-N	
Andy Leonard	60	265	.596	LF-60	B	Cin-N
Jack Manning	60	258	.585	RF-59,P-3(1-0)	Cin-N	Cin-N
John Morrill	60	238	.527	1-59,CF-1,3-1	B	
Jim O'Rourke	60	260	.704	CF-57,1-2,C-2	B	Pro-N
Harry Schafer	2	8	.250	RF-2	B	C
Pop Snyder	60	227	.450	C-58,RF-2	Lou-N	
Ezra Sutton	60	241	.534	3-59,S-1	B	
George Wright	59	273	.493	S-59	B	Pro-N
♦ 1879 BOSTON (84 54-30 2) ATT: 36,501						
Harry Wright				M		
Tommy Bond	65	555	1.96	P-64(43-19),RF-5,1-1	B	
Jack Burdock	84	368	.542	2-84	B	
Ed Cogswell	49	244	.721	1-49	A	Tro-N
Curry Foley	35	162	2.51	P-21(9-9),RF-17,1-2	A	
Bill Hawes	38	157	.468	RF-34,C-5	A	Cin-U
Sadie Houck	80	360	.677	RF-47,S-33	A	
Charley Jones	83	384	.877	LF-83	Cin-N	
John Morrill	84	362	.671	3-51,1-33	B	
John O'Rourke	72	325	.877	CF-71	A	
Lee Richmond	1	9	2.00	P-1(1-0)	A	Wor-N
Pop Snyder	81	334	.571	C-80,RF-2	B	
Ezra Sutton	84	341	.562	S-51,3-33	B	
Jim Tyng	3	27	5.00	P-3(1-2)	A	Phi-N
♦ 1880 BOSTON (86 40-44 6) ATT: 34,000						
Harry Wright				M		
John Bergh	11	42	.513	C-11	Phi-N	C
Tommy Bond	76	493	2.67	P-63(26-29),RF-26,3-1,1-1	B	
Jack Burdock	86	364	.609	2-86	B	
Steve Dignan	8	34	.676	RF-8	A	xWor-N
Curry Foley	80	238	3.89	P-36(14-14),RF-35,1-25	B	Buf-N
Sadie Houck	12	47	.298	RF-12	B	xPro-N
Charley Jones	66	291	.755	LF-66	B	Cin-a
Jack Leary	1	4	.250	RF-1,P-1(0-1)	A	Det-N
John Morrill	86	353	.609	1-46,3-40,P-3	B	
Dan O'Leary	3	12	.667	RF-3	Pro-N	Det-N
Jim O'Rourke	86	384	.756	RF-37,1-19,S-17,3-10,C-9	Pro-N	Buf-N
John O'Rourke	81	331	.739	CF-81	B	NY-a
Phil Powers	37	131	.358	C-37,LF-2	Chi-N	Cle-N
John Richmond	32	131	.546	S-31,CF-1	Syr-N	
Denny Sullivan	1	4	.500	C-1	Pro-N	C
Ezra Sutton	76	295	.563	S-39,3-37	B	
Sam Trott	39	128	.483	C-36,CF-4	A	Det-N
George Wright	1	4	.500	S-1	Pro-N	
♦ 1881 BOSTON (83 38-45 6) ATT: 34,343						
Harry Wright				M		
Ross Barnes	69	311	.634	S-63,2-7	Cin-N	C
Tommy Bond	3	25	4.26	P-3(0-3)	B	Wor-N
Jack Burdock	73	289	.575	2-72,S-1	B	
Bill Crowley	72	293	.588	CF-72	Buf-N	Phi-a
Pat Deasley	43	152	.562	C-28,RF-7,S-7,1-2	A	
John Fox	30	124	3.33	P-17(6-8),RF-12,1-6	A	Bal-a
Joe Hornung	83	329	.598	LF-83	Buf-N	
Fred Lewis	27	121	.536	RF-27	A	Phi-N
Bobby Mathews	19	71	.366	CF-18,P-5(1-0)	xPro-N	
John Morrill	81	323	.695	1-74,2-4,P-3(0-1),3-2	B	
Quinn	1	4	.500	1-1	A	xWor-N
John Richmond	27	104	.685	CF-25,S-2	Cle-N	Cle-N
Pop Snyder	62	222	.504	C-60,RF-1,S-1,2-1	B	Cin-a
Ezra Sutton	83	346	.669	3-81,S-2	B	
Jim Whitney	75	552	2.48	P-66(31-33),RF-15,1-2	A	
George Wright	7	28	.486	S-7	B	Pro-N
Sam Wright	1	4	.500	S-1	Cin-N	C
♦ 1882 BOSTON (85 45-39 3) ATT: 50,971						
John Morrill				M		
Charlie Buffinton	15	52	.568	RF-7,P-5(2-3),1-4	A	
Jack Burdock	83	328	.560	2-83	B	
Pat Deasley	67	271	.580	C-56,RF-14,S-1	B	StL-a
Joe Hornung	85	390	.707	LF-84,1-1	B	
Pete Hotaling	84	394	.617	CF-84	Wor-N	Cle-N
Bobby Mathews	45	285	2.87	P-34(19-15),RF-13,S-1	B	Phi-a
Hal McClure	2	6	.667	RF-2	A	C
John Morrill	83	367	.748	1-76,S-3,2-2,CF-1,3-1,P-1	B	
Ed Rowen	83	346	.592	RF-48,C-34,S-6,3-1	A	Phi-a
Ezra Sutton	81	343	.604	3-77,S-4	B	
Jim Whitney	61	420	2.64	P-49(24-21),RF-9,1-6	B	
Sam Wise	78	303	.560	S-72,3-6	Det-N	
♦ 1883 BOSTON (98 63-35 1) ATT: 138,284						
Jack Burdock				M(54 30-24 4)		
John Morrill				M(44 33-11 1)		
Lew Brown	14	57	.633	1-14	Pro-N	xLou-a
Charlie Buffinton	86	347	.538	RF-51,P-43(25-14),1-2	B	
Jack Burdock	96	414	.828	2-96	B	
Mert Hackett	46	180	.619	C-44,CF-4	A	
Mike Hines	63	238	.538	C-59,RF-7	B	
Joe Hornung	98	454	.737	LF-98,3-1	B	
John Morrill	97	419	.748	1-81,CF-7,3-6,S-2, 2-2,P-2(1-0)	B	
Paul Radford	72	267	.484	RF-72	A	Pro-N
Edgar Smith	30	120	.563	CF-30,C-1	A	C
Ezra Sutton	94	431	.836	3-93,RF-1,S-1	B	
Jim Whitney	96	514	2.24	P-62(37-21),CF-40,1-2	B	
Sam Wise	96	419	.690	S-96	B	

♦ **1884 BOSTON** (116 73-38 2) ATT: 146,777

Name	G	AB/IP	P/E	G/POS	From	To
John Morrill				M		
Bill Annis	27	96	.375	CF-27	A	C
Marty Barrett	3	6	.000	C-3	A	xInd-a
Charlie Buffinton	87	587	2.15	P-67(48-16),CF-13,1-11	B	
Jack Burdock	87	376	.677	2-87,3-1	B	
John Connor	7	60	3.15	P-7(1-4)	A	Buf-N
Bill Crowley	108	440	.703	RF-108	Cle-N	Buf-N
Daisy Davis	4	31	7.84	P-4(1-3),CF-1	xStL-a	
Tom Gunning	12	46	.308	C-12	A	
Mert Hackett	72	270	.491	C-71,3-1	B	
Mike Hines	35	135	.390	C-35	B	
Joe Hornung	115	535	.691	LF-110,1-6	B	
Jim Manning	89	364	.596	CF-73,S-9,2-9,3-3	A	
Gene Moriarity	4	16	.125	CF-4	A	xInd-a
John Morrill	111	468	.664	1-91,2-17,P-7(0-1), 3-2,LF-1	B	
Ezra Sutton	110	497	.839	3-110	B	
Jim Whitney	66	336	2.09	P-38(23-14),CF-15, 1-15,3-1	B	
Sam Wise	114	451	.576	S-107,2-7	B	

♦ **1885 BOSTON** (113 46-66 5) ATT: 110,290

Name	G	AB/IP	P/E	G/POS	From	To
John Morrill				M		
Charlie Buffinton	82	434	2.88	P-51(22-27),CF-18,1-15	B	
Jack Burdock	45	177	.352	2-45	B	
Bill Collver	1	4	.000	RF-1	A	C
Daisy Davis	11	94	4.29	P-11(5-6)	B	C
Pat Dealy	35	132	.527	C-29,3-3,LF-2,S-2,1-1	Stp-U	
Tom Gunning	48	179	.408	C-48	B	
Mert Hackett	34	117	.457	C-34	B	KC-N
Walter Hackett	35	128	.411	2-20,S-15	Bos-U	C
Mike Hines	14	60	.587	RF-14	B	xBro-a
Joe Hornung	25	110	.493	LF-25	B	
Dick Johnston	26	111	.604	CF-26	Ric-a	
Jim Manning	84	325	.563	CF-83,S-1	B	xDet-N
Tommy McCarthy	40	153	.405	LF-40	Bos-U	Phi-N
John Morrill	111	458	.677	1-92,2-17,3-2	B	
Billy Nash	26	96	.569	3-19,2-8	Ric-a	
Tom Poorman	56	234	.587	RF-56	Tol-a	
Blondie Purcell	21	90	.497	LF-21	xPhi-a	Bal-a
Bill Stemmeyer	2	11	0.00	P-2(1-1)	A	
Ezra Sutton	110	474	.762	3-91,S-16,2-2,1-1	B	
Pop Tate	4	14	.368	C-4	A	
Gurdon Whiteley	33	136	.443	RF-32,C-1	Cle-N	C
Jim Whitney	72	441	2.98	P-51(18-32),CF-17,1-5	B	KC-N
Sam Wise	107	449	.729	S-79,2-22,LF-6	B	

♦ **1886 BOSTON** (118 56-61 5) ATT: 133,682

Name	G	AB/IP	P/E	G/POS	From	To
John Morrill				M		
Myron Allen	1	3	.000	2-1	NY-N	Cle-a
Charlie Buffinton	44	182	.654	1-19,P-18(7-10),RF-9	B	Phi-N
Jack Burdock	59	232	.508	2-59	B	
Con Daily	50	199	.595	C-49,LF-1	Pro-N	
Pat Dealy	15	50	.771	C-14,LF-1	B	Was-N
Tom Gunning	27	101	.513	C-27	B	Phi-N
Joe Hornung	94	434	.583	LF-94	B	
Dick Johnston	109	416	.579	CF-109	B	
John Morrill	117	486	.715	S-55,1-42,2-20,P-1	B	
Billy Nash	109	441	.672	3-90,S-17,LF-2	B	
Charlie Parsons	2	16	3.94	P-2(0-2)	A	NY-a
Tom Poorman	88	390	.659	RF-88	B	Phi-a
Charley Radbourn	66	509	3.00	P-58(27-31),RF-6	Pro-N	
Bill Stemmeyer	41	349	3.02	P-41(22-18)	B	
Ezra Sutton	116	525	.673	LF-43,S-28,3-28,2-18	B	
Pop Tate	31	113	.548	C-31	B	
Sam Wise	96	420	.777	1-57,2-20,S-18,RF-1	B	

♦ **1887 BOSTON** (127 61-60 5) ATT: 261,000

Name	G	AB/IP	P/E	G/POS	From	To
King Kelly				M(95 49-43 5)		
John Morrill				M(32 12-17 5)		
Jack Burdock	65	259	.603	2-65	B	
Dick Conway	42	222	4.66	P-26(9-15),RF-16	Bal-a	
Con Daily	36	131	.429	C-36	B	Ind-N
Joe Hornung	98	457	.657	LF-98	B	
Dick Johnston	127	523	.674	CF-127	B	
King Kelly	116	540	.880	RF-61,2-30,C-24, P-3(1-0),S-2,3-2	Chi-N	
Kid Madden	37	321	3.79	P-37(21-14),RF-1	A	
John Morrill	127	542	.769	1-127	B	
Billy Nash	121	537	.810	3-117,LF-5	B	
Tom O'Rourke	22	86	.425	C-21,RF-1,3-1	A	
Charley Radbourn	51	425	4.55	P-50(24-23),RF-2	B	
Bill Stemmeyer	15	119	5.20	P-15(6-8)	B	Cle-a
Ezra Sutton	77	345	.771	S-37,LF-18,2-13,3-11	B	
Pop Tate	60	243	.604	C-53,RF-8	B	
Bobby Wheelock	48	181	.652	RF-28,S-20,2-4	A	Col-a
Sam Wise	113	510	.913	S-72,RF-27,2-16	B	

♦ **1888 BOSTON** (137 70-64 4) ATT: 265,015

Name	G	AB/IP	P/E	G/POS	From	To
John Morrill				M		
Tom Brown	107	451	.668	RF-107	Ind-N	
Jack Burdock	22	82	.434	2-22	B	xBro-a
John Clarkson	55	483	2.76	P-54(33-20),RF-1	Chi-N	
Dick Conway	7	53	2.38	P-6(4-2),RF-1	B	C
Ed Glenn	20	69	.418	LF-19,3-1	xKC-a	C
Bill Higgins	14	55	.404	2-14	A	StL-a
Mike Hines	4	18	.472	LF-3,C-1	Pro-N	C
Joe Hornung	107	449	.587	LF-107	B	Bal-a
Dick Johnston	135	601	.786	CF-135	B	
King Kelly	107	475	.848	C-76,RF-34	B	
Billy Klusman	28	112	.467	2-28	A	StL-a
Kid Madden	20	165	2.95	P-20(7-11)	B	
John Morrill	135	543	.570	1-133,2-2	B	Was-N
Billy Nash	135	580	.747	3-105,2-31	B	
Tom O'Rourke	20	75	.362	C-20,RF-1	B	NY-N
Joe Quinn	38	158	.778	2-38	StL-N	
Charley Radbourn	24	207	2.87	P-24(7-16)	B	
Irv Ray	50	213	.588	S-48,2-3	A	
Pete Sommers	4	13	.538	C-4	NY-a	Chi-N
Bill Sowders	36	317	2.07	P-36(19-15)	A	
Ezra Sutton	28	119	.568	3-27,S-1	B	C
Pop Tate	41	158	.589	C-41,RF-1	B	Bal-a
Nick Wise	1	3	.000	RF-1,C-1	A	C
Sam Wise	105	457	.678	S-89,3-6,1-5,LF-4,2-2	B	Was-N

♦ **1889 BOSTON** (133 83-45 2) ATT: 283,257

Name	G	AB/IP	P/E	G/POS	From	To
Jim Hart				M		
Charlie Bennett	82	270	.624	C-82	Det-N	
Dan Brouthers	126	565	.969	1-126	Det-N	Bos-P
Tom Brown	90	422	.645	LF-90	B	Bos-P
John Clarkson	73	620	2.73	P-73(49-19),RF-2,3-1	B	
Bill Daley	9	48	4.31	P-9(3-3)	A	Bos-P
Charlie Ganzel	73	292	.632	C-39,RF-26,1-7,S-6,3-1	Det-N	
Jerry Hurley	1	4	.000	RF-1,C-1	A	Pit-P
Dick Johnston	132	582	.586	CF-132	B	Bos-P
King Kelly	125	574	.824	RF-113,C-23	B	Bos-P
Kid Madden	24	178	4.40	P-22(10-10),RF-2	B	Bos-P
Billy Nash	128	562	.722	3-128,P-1	B	Bos-P
Joe Quinn	112	474	.635	S-63,2-47,3-2	B	Bos-P
Charley Radbourn	35	277	3.67	P-33(20-11),CF-2,3-1	B	Bos-P
Irv Ray	9	37	.712	S-5,3-4	B	xBal-a
Hardy Richardson	132	589	.803	2-86,LF-46	Det-N	Bos-P
Pop Smith	59	235	.705	S-59	xPit-N	
Bill Sowders	7	42	5.14	P-7(1-2)	B	xPit-N

♦ **1890 BOSTON** (134 76-57 5) ATT: 147,539

Name	G	AB/IP	P/E	G/POS	From	To
Frank Selee				M		
Charlie Bennett	85	355	.698	C-85	B	
Steve Brodie	132	591	.755	RF-132	A	
John Clarkson	45	383	3.27	P-44(26-18),LF-1	B	
Patsy Donovan	32	150	.564	CF-32	A	xBro-N
Charlie Ganzel	38	170	.650	C-22,RF-15,S-3,2-1	B	
Charlie Getzien	41	350	3.19	P-40(23-17),LF-1	Ind-N	
Lou Hardie	47	203	.614	C-25,LF-15,3-7,S-1,1-1	Chi-N	Bal-a
Paul Hines	69	309	.701	CF-69,1-1	xPit-N	Was-a
Al Lawson	1	9	4.00	P-1(0-1)	A	xPit-N
Herman Long	101	475	.675	S-101	KC-a	
Bobby Lowe	52	235	.757	S-24,CF-15,3-12	A	
Chippy McGarr	121	525	.587	3-115,S-5,RF-1	Bal-a	Cle-N
Kid Nichols	49	424	2.23	P-48(27-19),RF-2	A	
Al Schellhase	9	30	.305	RF-5,C-2,S-1,3-1	A	Lou-a
Pop Smith	134	552	.675	2-134,S-1	B	Was-a
Marty Sullivan	121	561	.743	LF-120,3-1	Ind-N	
John Taber	2	13	4.15	P-2(0-1)	A	C
Tommy Tucker	132	620	.749	1-132	Bal-a	
Tony VonFricken	1	8	10.13	P-1(0-1)	A	C

♦ **1891 BOSTON** (140 87-51 1) ATT: 184,472

Name	G	AB/IP	P/E	G/POS	From	To
Frank Selee				M		
Charlie Bennett	75	301	.664	C-75	B	
Steve Brodie	133	596	.670	CF-133	B	StL-N
Tod Bryan	1	1	54.00	P-1(0-1)	Chi-N	C
John Clarkson	55	461	2.79	P-55(33-19),CF-1	B	
Charlie Ganzel	70	280	.680	C-59,RF-13	B	
Charlie Getzien	14	89	3.84	P-11(4-5),LF-3	B	xCle-N
Joe Kelley	12	47	.588	LF-12	A	Pit-N
King Kelly	16	59	.572	C-11,RF-6	xBos-a	
John Kiley	1	8	6.75	P-1(0-1)	Was-a	C
Fred Lake	5	9	.476	C-4,RF-1	A	Lou-N
Herman Long	139	665	.785	S-139	B	
Bobby Lowe	125	559	.696	LF-107,2-17,S-2,3-1,P-1	B	
Billy Nash	140	616	.750	3-140	Bos-P	
Kid Nichols	52	425	2.39	P-52(30-17)	B	
Joe Quinn	124	542	.601	2-124	Bos-P	
George Rooks	5	20	.425	LF-5	A	C
Cyclone Ryan	1	3	0.00	P-1	NY-a	C
Harry Staley	31	252	2.50	P-31(20-8)	xPit-N	
Harry Stovey	134	624	.870	RF-134,1-1	Bos-P	
Jim Sullivan	1	0	81.00	P-1	A	xCol-a
Marty Sullivan	17	73	.616	LF-17	B	xCle-N
Tommy Tucker	140	614	.677	1-140,P-1	B	

♦ **1892 BOSTON** (152 102-48 2) ATT: 146,421

Name	G	AB/IP	P/E	G/POS	From	To
Frank Selee				M(75 52-22 1) 1st half		
Frank Selee				M(77 50-26 2) 2nd half		
Charlie Bennett	35	141	.618	C-35	B	
Dan Burke	1	4	.000	C-1	Syr-a	C
Dad Clarkson	1	7	1.29	P-1(1-0)	NY-N	StL-N
John Clarkson	16	146	2.35	P-16(8-6)	B	xCle-N
Joe Daly	1	0	†	C-1	Cle-N	C
Hugh Duffy	147	673	.774	CF-146,3-2	Bos-a	
Charlie Ganzel	54	217	.675	C-51,LF-2,1-1	B	
King Kelly	78	320	.522	C-72,LF-2,3-2,1-2,P-1	B	NY-N
Herman Long	151	698	.712	S-141,LF-12,3-1	B	
Bobby Lowe	124	520	.632	LF-90,3-14,S-13,2-10	B	
Tommy McCarthy	152	700	.657	RF-152	StL-a	
Billy Nash	135	588	.688	3-135,LF-1	B	
Kid Nichols	57	453	2.84	P-53(35-16),LF-5	B	
Joe Quinn	143	574	.529	2-143	B	StL-N
Harry Staley	38	300	3.03	P-37(22-10),RF-1	B	
Jack Stivetts	71	416	3.03	P-54(35-16),LF-18,1-1	StL-a	
Harry Stovey	38	163	.484	LF-38	B	xBal-N
Tommy Tucker	149	613	.707	1-149	B	
Lee Viau	1	9	0.00	P-1(1-0)	xLou-N	C

♦ **1893 BOSTON** (131 86-43 1) ATT: 193,300

Name	G	AB/IP	P/E	G/POS	From	To
Frank Selee				M		
Charlie Bennett	60	233	.656	C-60	B	C
Cliff Carroll	120	531	.636	RF-120	StL-N	C

Name	G	AB/IP	P/E	G/POS	From	To
Bill Coyle	2	8	9.00	P-2(0-1)	A	C
Hugh Duffy	131	611	.876	CF-131	B	
Charlie Ganzel	73	305	.652	C-40,RF-23,1-10	B	
Jim Garry	1	1	63.00	P-1(0-1)	A	C
Hank Gastright	20	156	5.13	P-19(12-4),CF-1	xPit-N	Bro-N
Herman Long	128	630	.758	S-123,2-5	B	
Bobby Lowe	126	585	.803	2-121,S-5	B	
Tommy McCarthy	116	529	.894	LF-108,2-7,S-3	B	
Bill Merritt	39	154	.899	C-37,LF-2	Lou-N	
Billy Nash	128	572	.832	3-128	B	
Kid Nichols	53	425	3.52	P-52(34-14),RF-1	B	
Bill Quarles	3	27	4.67	P-3(2-1)	Was-a	C
Harry Staley	36	263	5.13	P-36(18-10)	B	
Jack Stivetts	50	284	4.41	P-38(20-12),RF-8,3-3	B	
Tommy Tucker	121	533	.709	1-121	B	
Bill VanDyke	3	12	.583	LF-3	StL-N	C

♦ 1894 BOSTON (133 83-49 3) ATT: 152,800

Name	G	AB/IP	P/E	G/POS	From	To
Frank Selee				M		
Jimmy Bannon	128	566	.928	RF-128,P-1	StL-N	
Frank Connaughton	46	190	.864	S-33,C-7,LF-4	A	NY-N
Hugh Duffy	125	616	1.196	CF-124,S-2	B	
Charlie Ganzel	70	289	.710	C-59,1-7,RF-3,S-2,2-1	B	
Scott Hawley	1	7	7.71	P-1(0-1)	A	C
George Hodson	12	74	5.84	P-12(4-4)	A	Phi-N
Henry Lampe	2	5	11.81	P-2(0-1)	A	Phi-N
Herman Long	104	522	.881	S-98,LF-5,2-3	B	
Tom Lovett	15	104	5.97	P-15(8-6)	Bro-N	C
Bobby Lowe	133	678	.921	2-130,S-2,3-1	B	
Tommy McCarthy	127	613	.909	LF-127,S-2,2-1,P-1	B	
Bill Merritt	10	36	.681	C-8,CF-1	B	xPit-N
Billy Nash	132	609	.804	3-132	B	
Kid Nichols	51	407	4.75	P-50(32-13),LF-1	B	
Jack Ryan	53	216	.729	C-51,1-2	Lou-a	
Tom Smith	2	6	15.00	P-2	A	Phi-N
Harry Staley	28	209	6.81	P-27(12-10),CF-1	B	StL-N
Jack Stivetts	68	338	4.90	P-45(26-14),LF-16,1-4	B	
George Stultz	1	9	0.00	P-1(1-0)	A	C
Fred Tenney	27	100	1.039	C-20,LF-6,1-1	A	
Tommy Tucker	123	572	.832	1-123,CF-1	B	
Frank West	1	3	9.00	P-1	A	C

♦ 1895 BOSTON (133 71-60 5) ATT: 242,000

Name	G	AB/IP	P/E	G/POS	From	To
Frank Selee				M		
Bill Banks	1	7	0.00	P-1(1-0)	A	
Jimmy Bannon	123	560	.898	RF-122,P-1	B	
Jimmy Collins	11	44	.671	RF-10	A	xLou-N
Cozy Dolan	26	198	4.27	P-25(11-7),CF-1	A	
Hugh Duffy	130	614	.907	CF-130	B	
Charlie Ganzel	80	307	.642	C-76,S-2,1-2	B	
Joe Harrington	18	75	.787	2-18	A	
Herman Long	124	590	.803	S-122,2-2	B	
Bobby Lowe	99	475	.780	2-99	B	
Tommy McCarthy	117	542	.732	LF-109,2-9	B	Bro-N
Billy Nash	132	596	.800	3-132	B	Phi-N
Kid Nichols	48	380	3.41	P-47(26-16),LF-1	B	
Charlie Nyce	9	40	.868	S-9	A	C
Jack Ryan	49	203	.641	C-43,2-5,RF-1	B	
Frank Sexton	9	49	5.69	P-7(1-5),LF-1,2-1	A	C
Jack Stivetts	46	291	4.64	P-38(17-17),1-5,CF-2	B	
Otis Stocksdale	5	23	5.87	P-4(2-2),1-2	xWas-N	Bal-N
Jim Sullivan	22	179	4.82	P-21(11-9),RF-1	Col-a	
Fred Tenney	49	200	.713	LF-28,C-21	B	
Tommy Tucker	125	553	.695	1-125	B	
John Warner	3	9	.476	C-3	A	xLou-N
Zeke Wilson	6	45	5.20	P-6(2-4)	A	xCle-N

♦ 1896 BOSTON (132 74-57 4) ATT: 240,000

Name	G	AB/IP	P/E	G/POS	From	To
Frank Selee				M		
Bill Banks	4	23	10.57	P-4(0-3)	B	C
Jimmy Bannon	89	384	.623	RF-76,2-6,S-5,3-3	B	C
Marty Bergen	65	263	.684	C-63,1-1	A	
Jimmy Collins	84	350	.772	3-80,S-4	Lou-N	
Cozy Dolan	6	41	4.83	P-6(1-4)	B	Chi-N
Hugh Duffy	131	601	.754	LF-120,2-9,S-2	B	
Charlie Ganzel	47	195	.596	C-41,1-3,S-2	B	
Billy Hamilton	131	641	.940	CF-131	Phi-N	
Joe Harrington	54	221	.538	3-49,S-4,2-1	B	C
Fred Klobedanz	11	81	3.01	P-10(6-4)	A	
Ted Lewis	6	42	3.24	P-6(1-4)	A	
Herman Long	120	544	.845	S-120	B	
Bobby Lowe	73	335	.774	2-73	B	
Willard Mains	10	43	5.48	P-8(3-2)	Mil-a	C
Dan McGann	43	188	.857	2-43	A	Bal-N
Kid Nichols	51	372	2.83	P-49(30-14),RF-2	B	
Jack Ryan	8	32	.219	C-8	B	Bro-N
Jack Stivetts	67	329	4.10	P-42(22-14),RF-12,1-5,3-1	B	
Jim Sullivan	31	225	4.03	P-31(11-12)	B	
Fred Tenney	88	406	.811	RF-60,C-27	B	
Tommy Tucker	122	526	.757	1-122	B	
George Yeager	2	5	.400	1-2	A	

♦ 1897 BOSTON (135 93-39 1) ATT: 334,800

Name	G	AB/IP	P/E	G/POS	From	To
Frank Selee				M		
Bob Allen	34	140	.795	S-32,CF-1,2-1	Phi-N	Cin-N
Marty Bergen	87	351	.613	C-85,CF-1	B	
Jimmy Collins	134	585	.882	3-134	B	
Hugh Duffy	134	621	.885	LF-129,2-6,S-2	B	
Charlie Ganzel	30	113	.662	C-27,1-2	B	C
Billy Hamilton	127	591	.875	CF-126	B	
Charlie Hickman	2	8	5.87	P-2	A	
Fred Klobedanz	48	309	4.60	P-38(26-7),RF-2	B	
Fred Lake	19	65	.560	C-18	Lou-N	Pit-N
Ted Lewis	38	290	3.85	P-38(21-12)	B	
Herman Long	107	492	.802	S-107,LF-1	B	
Bobby Lowe	123	548	.774	2-123	B	
Mike Mahoney	2	2	1.000	C-1,P-1	A	StL-N
Kid Nichols	46	368	2.64	P-46(31-11)	B	
Chick Stahl	114	515	.905	RF-111	B	
Jack Stivetts	61	217	.949	RF-29,P-18(11-4),2-2,1-2	B	
Jim Sullivan	13	89	3.94	P-13(4-5)	B	C
Fred Tenney	132	646	.753	1-128,RF-4	B	
Tommy Tucker	4	16	.670	1-4	B	xWas-N
George Yeager	30	105	.684	C-13,RF-10,2-4,3-1	B	

♦ 1898 BOSTON (152 102-47 1) ATT: 229,275

Name	G	AB/IP	P/E	G/POS	From	To
Frank Selee				M		
Marty Bergen	120	469	.661	C-117,1-2	B	
Kitty Bransfield	5	9	.667	C-4,1-1	A	Pit-N
Jimmy Collins	152	657	.856	3-152	B	
Hugh Duffy	152	645	.738	LF-152,3-1,1-1,C-1	B	
Billy Hamilton	110	508	.933	CF-110	B	
Charlie Hickman	19	61	.576	LF-7,1-6,P-6(1-2)	B	
Bill Keister	10	30	.400	S-4,2-4,RF-1	Bal-N	Bal-N
Fred Klobedanz	43	271	3.89	P-35(19-10),1-6,CF-2	B	
Hi Ladd	1	4	.500	LF-1	xPit-N	C
Ted Lewis	42	313	2.90	P-41(26-8),2-1	B	
Herman Long	144	645	.676	S-142,2-2	B	
Bobby Lowe	147	611	.649	2-145,S-2	B	
Kid Nichols	51	388	2.13	P-50(31-12),1-1	B	
Dave Pickett	14	51	.682	LF-14	A	C
Stub Smith	3	10	.200	S-3	A	
General Stafford	37	132	.590	RF-35,1-1	xLou-N	
Chick Stahl	125	529	.782	RF-125	B	
Jack Stivetts	41	125	.647	RF-14,1-10,S-4,2-2,P-2(0-1)	B	Cle-N
Mike Sullivan	3	12	12.00	P-3(0-1)	NY-N	
Fred Tenney	117	536	.770	1-117,C-1	B	
Vic Willis	41	311	2.84	P-41(25-13)	A	
George Yeager	68	244	.703	C-37,1-17,LF-9,S-2	B	

♦ 1899 BOSTON (153 95-57 2) ATT: 200,384

Name	G	AB/IP	P/E	G/POS	From	To
Frank Selee				M		
Harvey Bailey	12	87	3.95	P-12(6-4)	A	
Marty Bergen	72	272	.625	C-72	B	C
Boileryard Clarke	60	243	.553	C-60	Bal-N	
Jimmy Collins	151	660	.721	3-151	B	
Hugh Duffy	147	641	.705	LF-147	B	
Charlie Frisbee	42	169	.756	CF-40	A	NY-N
Billy Ging	1	8	1.13	P-1(1-0)	A	C
Billy Hamilton	84	375	.796	CF-81	B	
Mike Hickey	1	3	.667	2-1	A	C
Charlie Hickman	19	66	4.48	P-11(6-0),LF-7,1-1	B	NY-N
Frank Killen	12	99	4.26	P-12(7-5)	xWas-N	Chi-N
Fred Klobedanz	5	33	4.86	P-5(1-4)	B	
Charlie Kuhns	7	20	.628	S-3,3-3	Pit-N	C
Ted Lewis	29	235	3.49	P-29(17-11)	B	
Herman Long	145	651	.697	S-143,1-2	B	
Bobby Lowe	152	614	.650	2-148,S-4	B	
Jouett Meekin	13	108	2.83	P-13(7-6)	xNY-N	Pit-N
Bill Merritt	1	3	.333	C-1	Pit-N	C
Kid Nichols	42	343	2.99	P-42(21-19)	B	
General Stafford	55	201	.724	CF-41,2-5,S-5	B	xWas-N
Chick Stahl	148	661	.919	RF-148,P-1	B	
Oscar Streit	2	15	6.75	P-2(1-0)	A	Cle-A
Mike Sullivan	1	9	5.00	P-1(1-0)	A	
Billy Sullivan	22	78	.686	C-22	A	
Fred Tenney	150	691	.851	1-150	B	
Vic Willis	41	343	2.50	P-41(27-8)	B	Cle-A
George Yeager	3	9	.347	CF-2,C-1	B	

♦ 1900 BOSTON (142 66-72 4) ATT: 202,000

Name	G	AB/IP	P/E	G/POS	From	To
Frank Selee				M		
Harvey Bailey	4	20	4.95	P-4	B	C
Shad Barry	81	277	.667	LF-24,S-18,2-16,1-10,3-1	Was-N	
Rome Chambers	1	4	11.25	P-1	A	C
Boileryard Clarke	81	291	.703	C-67,1-8	B	Was-A
Jack Clements	16	46	.774	C-10	Cle-N	C
Jimmy Collins	142	639	.747	3-141,S-1	B	Bos-A
Joe Connor	7	21	.496	C-7	StL-N	Mil-A
Nig Cuppy	17	105	3.08	P-17(8-4)	StL-N	Bos-A
Bill Dinneen	44	321	3.12	P-40(20-14)	Was-N	
Hugh Duffy	55	202	.769	LF-49,2-1	B	Mil-A
Buck Freeman	117	461	.808	RF-91,1-19	Was-N	Bos-A
Billy Hamilton	136	635	.845	CF-136	B	
Ted Lewis	30	209	4.13	P-30(13-12)	B	Bos-A
Herman Long	125	550	.716	S-125	B	
Bobby Lowe	127	514	.665	2-127	B	
Kid Nichols	29	231	3.07	P-29(13-16)	B	
Togie Pittinger	18	114	5.13	P-18(2-9)	A	
Chick Stahl	136	597	.757	RF-135	B	Bos-A
Billy Sullivan	72	251	.702	C-66,S-1,2-1	B	Chi-A
Fred Tenney	112	492	.685	1-111	B	
Vic Willis	32	236	4.19	P-32(10-17)	B	

♦ 1901 BOSTON (140 69-69 5) ATT: 146,502

Name	G	AB/IP	P/E	G/POS	From	To
Frank Selee				M		
Shad Barry	11	43	.458	LF-11	B	xPhi-N
Fred Brown	7	14	.286	LF-5	A	
Pat Carney	13	59	.703	RF-13	A	
Duff Cooley	63	263	.639	LF-53,1-10	Pit-N	
Fred Crolius	49	222	.591	RF-49	A	Pit-N
Gene DeMontreville	140	619	.685	2-120,3-20	Bro-N	
Bill Dinneen	54	309	2.94	P-37(15-18),LF-3,1-2	B	Bos-A
Daff Gammons	28	103	.457	LF-23,2-2,3-1	A	C
George Grossart	7	26	.231	LF-7	A	C
Billy Hamilton	102	425	.760	CF-99	B	C
John Hinton	4	15	.277	3-4	A	C
Malachi Kittridge	114	427	.616	C-113	Was-N	

Name	G	AB/IP	P/E	G/POS	From	To
Bob Lawson	10	46	3.33	P-6(2-2),LF-3,3-1	A	Bal-A
Herman Long	138	559	.537	S-138	B	
Bobby Lowe	129	519	.583	3-111,2-18	B	Chi-N
Billy Lush	7	30	.563	CF-7	Was-N	
Pat Moran	52	191	.512	C-28,1-13,3-4,S-3,RF-3,2-1	A	
Frank Murphy	45	185	.623	LF-45	A	xNY-N
Kid Nichols	55	321	3.22	P-38(19-16),LF-7,1-5	B	StL-N
Togie Pittinger	34	281	3.01	P-34(13-16)	B	
Joe Rickert	13	64	.456	LF-13	Pit-N	C
Jimmy Slagle	66	296	.657	RF-66	xPhi-N	Chi-N
Elmer Smith	16	64	.500	RF-15	xPit-N	C
Fred Tenney	115	508	.662	1-113,C-2	B	
Vic Willis	38	305	2.36	P-38(20-17)	B	

♦ 1902 BOSTON (142 73-64 3) ATT: 116,960

Name	G	AB/IP	P/E	G/POS	From	To
Al Buckenberger				M		
Fred Brown	2	6	.833	RF-2	B	C
Pat Carney	137	580	.668	RF-137,P-2(0-1)	B	
Duff Cooley	135	596	.711	LF-127,1-7	B	
Ernie Courtney	48	183	.528	LF-39,S-3	A	xBal-A
Sammy Curran	1	7	1.35	P-1	A	C
Gene DeMontreville	124	519	.592	2-112,S-10	B	Was-A
Charlie Dexter	48	207	.613	S-22,2-19,CF-7,3-1	xChi-N	
Bob Dresser	1	9	3.00	P-1(0-1)	A	C
Mal Eason	27	206	2.75	P-27(9-11)	xChi-N	Det-A
Ed Gremminger	140	572	.661	3-140	Cle-N	
Dad Hale	8	47	6.32	P-8(1-4)	A	xBal-A
Malachi Kittridge	80	286	.590	C-72	B	
Fred Klobedanz	1	8	1.13	P-1(1-0)	B	C
Herman Long	120	484	.551	S-107,2-13	B	NY-A
Red Long	1	8	1.13	P-1	A	C
Billy Lush	120	502	.608	CF-116,3-1	B	Det-A
John Malarkey	22	170	2.59	P-21(8-10),2-1	Chi-N	
Pat Moran	80	278	.614	C-71,1-3,RF-1	B	
Togie Pittinger	46	389	2.52	P-46(27-16)	B	
Fred Tenney	134	596	.785	1-134	B	
Vic Willis	52	410	2.20	P-51(27-20)	B	

♦ 1903 BOSTON (140 58-80 6) ATT: 143,155

Name	G	AB/IP	P/E	G/POS	From	To
Al Buckenberger				M		
Ed Abbaticchio	136	562	.597	2-116,S-17	Phi-N	
Harry Aubrey	96	357	.514	S-94,2-1,LF-1	A	C
Frank Bonner	48	187	.528	2-24,S-22	Phi-A	C
Pat Carney	110	429	.596	RF-92,P-10(4-5),1-1	B	
Duff Cooley	138	600	.720	LF-126,1-13	B	
Charlie Dexter	123	536	.603	CF-106,S-9,C-6	B	C
Ed Gremminger	140	555	.688	3-140	B	Det-A
Malachi Kittridge	32	116	.523	C-30	B	xWas-A
John Malarkey	32	253	3.09	P-32(11-16)	B	C
Tom McCreery	23	93	.595	CF-23	xBro-N	C
Pat Moran	109	436	.737	C-107,1-1	B	
Wiley Piatt	27	181	3.18	P-25(9-14)	Chi-A	C
Togie Pittinger	44	352	3.48	P-44(18-22)	B	
Joe Stanley	86	337	.637	RF-77,P-1,S-1	Was-N	
Fred Tenney	122	541	.811	1-122	B	
Pop Williams	14	83	4.12	P-10(4-5),LF-2	xPhi-N	C
Vic Willis	39	278	2.98	P-33(12-18),1-6	B	

♦ 1904 BOSTON (155 55-98 7) ATT: 140,694

Name	G	AB/IP	P/E	G/POS	From	To
Al Buckenberger				M		
Ed Abbaticchio	154	637	.646	S-154	B	
George Barclay	24	99	.537	RF-24	xStL-N	
Rip Cannell	100	378	.540	RF-93	A	
Pat Carney	78	300	.476	RF-71,P-4(0-4),1-1	B	C
Duff Cooley	122	494	.684	LF-116,1-6	B	Det-A
Jim Delahanty	142	541	.721	3-113,2-18,LF-9,P-1	NY-N	
Tom Fisher	39	214	4.25	P-31(6-16),CF-6	A	C
Phil Geier	149	647	.599	CF-137,3-7,2-5,S-1	Mil-A	
Bill Lauterborn	20	71	.590	2-20	A	
Doc Marshall	13	45	.500	C-10,LF-1	xNY-N	C
Gene McAuliffe	1	2	1.000	C-1	A	C
Ed McNichol	17	122	4.28	P-17(2-12)	A	C
Pat Moran	113	423	.566	C-72,3-39,1-2	B	
Tom Needham	84	282	.664	C-77,CF-1	A	
Kid O'Hara	8	33	.510	RF-8	A	C
Togie Pittinger	38	335	2.66	P-38(15-21)	B	Phi-N
Fred Raymer	114	453	.496	2-114	Chi-N	
Joe Stanley	3	8	.000	RF-3	B	Was-A
Joe Stewart	2	9	9.64	P-2	A	C
Andy Sullivan	1	2	.500	S-1	A	C
Fred Tenney	147	621	.692	1-144,RF-4	B	
Jack White	1	5	.000	LF-1	A	C
Kaiser Wilhelm	39	288	3.69	P-39(14-20)	Pit-N	
Vic Willis	52	350	2.85	P-43(18-25),1-6	B	

♦ 1905 BOSTON (156 51-103 7) ATT: 150,003

Name	G	AB/IP	P/E	G/POS	From	To
Fred Tenney				M		
Ed Abbaticchio	153	658	.700	S-152,CF-1	B	Pit-N
George Barclay	29	112	.391	LF-28	B	C
Rip Cannell	154	630	.597	CF-154	B	C
Jim Delahanty	125	506	.664	LF-124,P-1	B	Cin-N
Cozy Dolan	112	472	.675	RF-111,P-2(0-1),1-2	xCin-N	
Chick Fraser	48	334	3.28	P-39(14-21),1-4,CF-2	Phi-N	Cin-N
Dick Harley	9	66	4.66	P-9(2-5)	A	C
Frank Hershey	1	4	6.75	P-1(0-1)	A	C
Bill Lauterborn	67	219	.438	3-29,2-23,S-3,CF-2	B	C
Bill McCarthy	1	3	.000	C-1	A	Cin-N
Pat Moran	85	279	.611	C-78	B	Chi-N
Dave Murphy	3	12	.364	S-2,3-1	A	C
Tom Needham	83	301	.563	C-77,CF-3,1-2	B	
Fred Raymer	137	522	.479	2-134,1-1,LF-1	B	C
Bud Sharpe	46	180	.438	RF-42,C-3,1-1	A	
Gabby Street	3	12	.333	C-3	xCin-N	xCin-N
Allie Strobel	5	21	.211	3-4,LF-1	A	

Name	G	AB/IP	P/E	G/POS	From	To
Fred Tenney	149	632	.700	1-148,P-1	B	
Jake Volz	3	9	10.38	P-3(0-2)	Bos-A	Cin-N
Kaiser Wilhelm	38	242	4.53	P-34(3-23),CF-4	B	Bro-N
Vic Willis	43	342	3.21	P-41(12-29)	B	Pit-N
Harry Wolverton	122	505	.576	3-122	Phi-N	NY-A
Irv Young	43	378	2.90	P-43(20-21)	A	

♦ 1906 BOSTON (152 49-102 8) ATT: 143,280

Name	G	AB/IP	P/E	G/POS	From	To
Fred Tenney				M		
Johnny Bates	140	559	.664	CF-140	A	
Dave Brain	139	574	.626	3-139	Pit-N	
Al Bridwell	120	518	.548	S-119,RF-1	Cin-N	
Sam Brown	71	256	.505	C-35,LF-13,3-12,1-3,2-2	A	
Jack Cameron	18	63	.387	LF-16,P-2	A	C
Frank Connaughton	12	48	.475	S-11,2-1	NY-N	C
Ernie Diehl	3	11	1.091	LF-2,S-1	Pit-N	
Cozy Dolan	152	619	.617	RF-144,2-7,P-2(0-1),1-1	xCin-N	
Gus Dorner	34	273	3.65	P-34(8-25)	xCin-N	
Gene Good	34	135	.398	LF-34	A	C
Del Howard	147	591	.637	LF-87,2-45,S-14,1-2	Pit-N	
Vive Lindaman	39	307	2.43	P-39(12-23)	A	
Tommy Madden	4	16	.579	LF-4	A	NY-N
Bill McCarthy	1	2	9.00	P-1	A	C
Jim Moroney	3	27	5.33	P-3(0-3)	A	Phi-N
Tom Needham	83	302	.472	C-76,2-5,1-2,3-1,CF-1	B	
Jack O'Neill	61	186	.465	C-48,1-2,RF-1	Chi-N	C
Big Jeff Pfeffer	60	302	2.95	P-35(13-22),RF-14	Chi-N	
Jack Schulte	2	7	.000	S-2	A	C
Chet Spencer	8	27	.333	CF-8	A	C
Allie Strobel	100	360	.535	2-93,S-6,CF-1	B	C
Fred Tenney	143	624	.698	1-143	B	
Roy Witherup	8	46	6.26	P-8(0-3)	A	Was-A
Irv Young	43	358	2.91	P-43(16-25)	B	

♦ 1907 BOSTON (152 58-90 7) ATT: 203,221

Name	G	AB/IP	P/E	G/POS	From	To
Fred Tenney				M		
Tom Asmussen	2	6	.000	C-2	A	C
Jim Ball	10	38	.433	C-10	A	
Frank Barberich	2	12	5.84	P-2(1-1)	A	Bos-A
Johnny Bates	126	504	.695	RF-120	B	
Ginger Beaumont	150	632	.790	CF-149	Pit-N	
Jake Boultes	29	140	2.71	P-24(5-9),S-2,3-2,CF-1	A	
Dave Brain	133	552	.745	3-130,LF-3	B	Cin-N
Al Bridwell	140	586	.551	S-140	B	NY-N
Sam Brown	70	231	.471	C-63,1-2	B	C
Bob Brush	2	2	.000	1-1	A	C
Frank Burke	43	145	.437	LF-36	NY-N	C
Rube Dessau	2	9	10.61	P-2(0-1)	A	Bro-N
Gus Dorner	36	271	3.12	P-36(12-16)	B	
Patsy Flaherty	41	217	2.70	P-27(12-15),LF-8	Pit-N	
Sam Frock	5	33	2.97	P-5(1-2)	A	Pit-N
Izzy Hoffman	19	92	.663	RF-19	Was-A	C
Del Howard	50	203	.662	LF-45,2-3	B	xChi-N
Joe Knotts	3	10	.111	C-3	A	C
Vive Lindaman	34	260	3.63	P-34(11-15)	B	
Ernie Lindemann	1	6	5.68	P-1	A	C
Tom Needham	86	289	.510	C-78,1-1	B	NY-N
Jess Orndorff	5	17	.235	C-5	A	C
Big Jeff Pfeffer	21	144	3.00	P-19(6-8)	B	
Newt Randall	75	284	.545	LF-73	xChi-N	C
Claude Ritchey	144	572	.645	2-144	Pit-N	
Bill Sweeney	58	206	.588	3-23,S-15,LF-11,2-5,1-1	xChi-N	
Fred Tenney	150	659	.705	1-149	B	NY-N
Oscar Westerberg	2	7	.762	S-2	A	C
Irv Young	40	245	3.96	P-40(10-23)	B	

♦ 1908 BOSTON (156 63-91 6) ATT: 253,750

Name	G	AB/IP	P/E	G/POS	From	To
Joe Kelley				M		
Jim Ball	6	17	.192	C-6	B	C
Johnny Bates	127	495	.639	LF-117	B	
Ginger Beaumont	125	532	.674	CF-121	B	
Beals Becker	43	180	.607	RF-43	xPit-N	
Jake Boultes	18	75	3.01	P-17(3-5)	B	
Frank Bowerman	86	274	.554	C-63,1-11	NY-N	
George Browne	138	590	.550	RF-138	NY-N	Chi-N
Bill Chappelle	13	70	1.79	P-13(2-4)	A	
Bill Dahlen	144	588	.604	S-144	NY-N	
Gus Dorner	38	216	3.54	P-38(8-19)	B	
George Ferguson	38	208	2.47	P-37(11-11)	NY-N	
Patsy Flaherty	32	244	3.25	P-31(12-18)	B	Phi-N
Peaches Graham	75	250	.658	C-62,2-5	Chi-N	
Jack Hannifin	90	296	.553	3-35,2-22,S-15,LF-7	xNY-N	C
Joe Kelley	73	263	.680	LF-51,1-11	Cin-N	C
Vive Lindaman	43	271	2.36	P-43(12-16)	B	
Charlie Maloney	1	2	4.50	P-1	A	C
Al Mattern	5	30	2.08	P-5(1-2)	A	
Tom McCarthy	14	94	1.63	P-14(7-3)	xPit-N	
Dan McGann	135	552	.612	1-121,2-9	NY-N	C
Herbie Moran	8	34	.639	LF-8	xPhi-A	
Big Jeff Pfeffer	4	10	12.60	P-4	B	Chi-N
Claude Ritchey	121	500	.687	2-120	B	
Harry Smith	41	143	.610	C-38	Pit-N	
Fred Stem	20	76	.603	1-19	B	
Bill Sweeney	127	481	.612	3-123,S-3,2-1	B	
Walt Thomas	5	17	.466	S-5	A	C
Tom Tuckey	8	72	2.50	P-8(3-3)	A	
Harley Young	6	27	3.29	P-6(0-1)	xPit-N	C
Irv Young	16	85	2.86	P-16(4-9)	B	xPit-N

♦ 1909 BOSTON (155 45-108 8) ATT: 195,188

Name	G	AB/IP	P/E	G/POS	From	To
Frank Bowerman				M(76 22-54 8)		
Harry Smith				M(79 23-54 8)		
Chick Autry	65	236	.495	1-61,LF-4	xCin-N	C
Johnny Bates	63	266	.744	LF-60	B	xPhi-N

Name	G	AB/IP	P/E	G/POS	From	To
Ginger Beaumont	123	456	.631	CF-111	B	Chi-N
Fred Beck	96	364	.518	CF-57,1-33	A	
Beals Becker	152	645	.631	RF-152	B	NY-N
Jake Boultes	1	8	6.75	P-1	B	C
Frank Bowerman	33	102	.460	C-27	B	C
Buster Brown	18	123	3.14	P-18(4-8)	xPhi-N	
Bill Chappelle	5	29	1.86	P-5(1-1)	B	xCin-N
Jack Coffey	73	274	.462	S-73	A	Det-A
Bill Cooney	5	6	1.42	P-3,2-1,S-1	A	
Cliff Curtis	10	83	1.41	P-10(4-5)	A	
Bill Dahlen	69	231	.636	S-49,2-6,3-2	B	Bro-N
Bill Dam	1	3	1.667	LF-1	A	C
Ernie Diehl	1	4	1.250	LF-1	A	C
Gus Dorner	5	25	2.55	P-5(1-2)	B	C
Chick Evans	4	22	4.57	P-4(0-3)	A	
George Ferguson	36	227	3.73	P-36(5-23)	B	
Gus Getz	40	153	.465	3-36,2-2,S-2	A	
Peaches Graham	92	306	.587	C-76,RF-6,S-1,3-1	B	
Vive Lindaman	15	66	4.64	P-15(1-6)	B	C
Al Mattern	47	316	2.85	P-47(15-21)	B	
Tom McCarthy	9	46	3.50	P-8(0-5)	B	C
Herbie Moran	8	36	.591	LF-8	B	
Forrest More	10	49	4.44	P-10(1-5)	xStL-N	C
Bill Rariden	13	48	.384	C-13	A	
Lew Richie	22	132	2.32	P-22(7-7)	xPhi-N	
Claude Ritchey	30	97	.426	2-25	B	C
Al Shaw	18	47	.310	C-14	Chi-A	C
Dave Shean	75	300	.627	2-72	xPhi-N	
Hosea Siner	10	25	.330	3-5,2-1,S-1	A	C
Harry Smith	43	120	.425	C-31	B	
Charlie Starr	61	260	.593	2-54,S-6,3-3	Pit-N	xPhi-N
Fred Stem	73	272	.495	1-68	B	C
Bill Sweeney	138	539	.596	3-112,S-26	B	
Roy Thomas	82	339	.671	LF-76	Pit-N	Phi-I
Tom Tuckey	17	91	4.27	P-17(0-9)	B	C
Kirby White	23	148	3.22	P-23(6-13)	A	

♦ 1910 BOSTON (157 53-100 8) ATT: 149,027

Name	G	AB/IP	P/E	G/POS	From	To
Fred Lake				M		
Ed Abbaticchio	52	198	.587	S-46,2-1	xPit-N	C
Fred Beck	154	607	.722	CF-134,1-19	B	Cin-N
Buster Brown	46	263	2.67	P-46(9-23)	B	
Joe Burg	13	54	.785	3-12,S-1	A	C
Billy Burke	20	64	4.08	P-19(1-0)	A	
Bill Collins	151	656	.599	LF-151	A	
Bill Cooney	8	14	.607	RF-2	B	C
Cliff Curtis	43	251	3.55	P-43(6-24)	B	
Rowdy Elliott	3	2	.000	C-1	A	Chi-N
Chick Evans	13	31	5.23	P-13(1-1)	B	C
George Ferguson	26	123	3.80	P-26(7-7)	B	
Sam Frock	45	255	3.21	P-45(12-19)	xPit-N	
Gus Getz	54	154	.440	3-22,2-13,LF-8,S-4	B	Bro-N
Ralph Good	2	9	2.00	P-2	A	C
Wilbur Good	23	98	.882	CF-23	Cle-A	
Peaches Graham	110	384	.699	C-87,3-2,1-1,RF-1	B	
Buck Herzog	106	445	.672	3-105	NY-N	
Art Kruger	1	1	.000	H	xCle-A	xCle-A
Fred Lake	3	2	.500	H	Pit-N	C
Fred Liese	5	5	.200	H	A	C
Doc Martel	10	34	.311	1-10	Phi-N	C
Al Mattern	51	305	2.98	P-51(16-19)	B	
Doc Miller	130	534	.711	RF-130	xChi-N	
Herbie Moran	20	82	.400	LF-20	B	Bro-N
Jiggs Parson	10	35	3.82	P-10(0-2)	A	
Bill Rariden	49	156	.593	C-49	B	
Lew Richie	4	14	2.76	P-4(0-3)	B	xChi-N
Jim Riley	1	2	.500	LF-1	A	C
Rube Sellers	12	39	.446	LF-9	A	C
Bud Sharpe	115	473	.549	1-113	B	xPit-N
Dave Shean	150	602	.598	2-148	B	Chi-N
Harry Smith	70	157	.549	C-38	B	C
Bill Sweeney	150	579	.705	S-110,3-21,1-17	B	
Lefty Tyler	2	11	2.38	P-2	A	
Kirby White	3	26	1.38	P-3(1-2)	B	xPit-N

♦ 1911 BOSTON (156 44-107 8) ATT: 116,000

Name	G	AB/IP	P/E	G/POS	From	To
Fred Tenney				M		
Al Bridwell	51	225	.721	S-51	xNY-N	
Buster Brown	42	241	4.29	P-42(8-18)	B	
Billy Burke	2	3	18.90	P-2(0-1)	B	C
Art Butler	27	76	.469	3-14,2-4,S-1	A	Pit-N
Josh Clarke	32	151	.753	LF-30	Cle-A	C
Bill Collins	17	48	.360	CF-13,3-1	B	xChi-N
Cliff Curtis	12	77	4.44	P-12(1-8)	B	xChi-N
Mike Donlin	56	248	.800	CF-56	xNY-N	Pit-N
Ed Donnelly	5	37	2.45	P-5(3-2)	A	
George Ferguson	6	24	9.75	P-6(1-3)	B	C
Patsy Flaherty	38	103	.769	CF-19,P-4(0-2)	Phi-N	C
Sam Frock	4	16	5.63	P-4(0-1)	B	C
Wilbur Good	43	181	.674	CF-43	B	xChi-N
Hank Gowdy	29	104	.695	1-26,C-1	xNY-N	
Peaches Graham	33	103	.736	C-26	B	xChi-N
Hank Griffin	15	83	5.23	P-15(0-6)	A	xChi-N
Buck Herzog	79	356	.857	S-74,3-4	B	xNY-N
Brad Hogg	8	26	6.66	P-8(0-3)	A	
Ben Houser	20	79	.639	1-20	Phi-A	
Scotty Ingerton	136	575	.644	3-58,LF-43,1-17,2-11,S-4	A	C
George Jackson	39	167	.853	LF-39	A	
Bill Jones	24	67	.688	CF-18	A	
Al Kaiser	66	217	.528	LF-58	xChi-N	
Jay Kirke	20	94	.909	LF-14,1-3,2-1,S-1,3-1	Det-A	
Johnny Kling	75	278	.600	C-71,3-1	xChi-N	
Al Mattern	33	186	4.97	P-33(4-15)	B	
Ed McDonald	54	220	.657	3-53,S-1	A	
Bill McTigue	14	37	7.05	P-14(0-5)	A	

Name	G	AB/IP	P/E	G/POS	From	To
Doc Miller	146	632	.821	RF-146	B	
Jiggs Parson	7	25	6.48	P-7(0-1)	B	C
Hub Perdue	24	137	4.98	P-24(6-10)	A	
Big Jeff Pfeffer	33	97	4.73	P-26(7-5),CF-3,1-1	Chi-N	C
Bill Rariden	70	271	.553	C-65,3-3,2-1	B	
Harry Spratt	62	171	.657	S-26,2-5,3-4,CF-4	A	
Harry Steinfeldt	19	71	.703	3-19	Chi-N	C
Bill Sweeney	137	613	.820	2-136	B	
Fred Tenney	102	432	.680	1-96,CF-2	NY-N	C
Fuller Thompson	3	5	3.86	P-3	A	C
Lefty Tyler	28	165	5.06	P-28(7-10)	B	
Orlie Weaver	27	121	6.47	P-27(3-12)	xChi-N	C
Bert Weeden	1	1	.000	H	A	C
Cy Young	11	80	3.71	P-11(4-5)	xCle-A	C
Herman Young	9	28	.509	3-5,S-3	A	C

♦ 1912 BOSTON (155 52-101 8) ATT: 121,000

Name	G	AB/IP	P/E	G/POS	From	To
Johnny Kling				M		
King Brady	1	3	20.25	P-1	Bos-A	C
Bill Brady	1	1	0.00	P-1	A	C
Al Bridwell	31	116	.572	S-31	B	Chi-N
Buster Brown	31	168	4.01	P-31(4-15)	B	
Vin Campbell	145	681	.725	CF-144	Pit-N	Ind-F
Art Devlin	124	498	.734	1-69,S-26,3-26,LF-1	NY-N	
Walt Dickson	36	189	3.86	P-36(3-19)	NY-N	
Ed Donnelly	38	184	4.35	P-37(5-10)	B	C
Mike Gonzalez	1	3	.333	C-1	A	Cin-N
Hank Gowdy	44	115	.834	C-22,1-7	B	
Hank Griffin	3	2	27.00	P-3	B	C
Otto Hess	33	254	3.76	P-33(12-17)	Cle-A	
Brad Hogg	10	31	6.97	P-10(1-1)	B	Chi-N
Ben Houser	108	360	.760	1-83	B	C
George Jackson	110	456	.692	LF-107	B	
Bill Jones	3	2	1.000	H	B	C
Al Kaiser	4	14	.000	LF-4	B	Ind-F
Jay Kirke	103	378	.745	LF-72,3-14,S-2,1-1	B	
Johnny Kling	81	274	.761	C-74	B	Cin-N
Rube Kroh	3	6	5.68	P-3	Chi-N	C
Rabbit Maranville	26	101	.524	S-26	A	
Al Mattern	2	6	7.11	P-2(0-1)	B	C
Ed McDonald	121	540	.712	3-118	B	Chi-N
Bill McTigue	10	35	5.45	P-10(2-0)	B	
Doc Miller	51	224	.600	RF-50	B	xPhi-N
Frank O'Rourke	61	216	.325	S-59,3-1	A	Bro-N
Hub Perdue	37	249	3.80	P-37(13-16)	B	
Bill Rariden	79	274	.536	C-73	B	
Joe Schultz	4	12	.583	2-4	A	
Art Schwind	1	2	1.000	3-1	A	C
Dave Shean	4	12	.717	S-4	Chi-N	Cin-N
Harry Spratt	27	96	.751	S-23	B	C
Bill Sweeney	153	699	.861	2-153	B	
John Titus	96	415	.865	RF-96	xPhi-N	
Lefty Tyler	42	256	4.18	P-42(12-22)	B	
Steve White	3	6	6.00	P-3	xWas-A	C
Gil Whitehouse	2	3	.000	C-2	A	New-F

♦ 1913 BOSTON (154 69-82 5) ATT: 208,000

Name	G	AB/IP	P/E	G/POS	From	To
George Stallings				M		
Buster Brown	2	13	4.72	P-2	B	C
Drummond Brown	15	37	.802	C-12	A	KC-F
Art Bues	2	1	.000	2-1,3-1	A	Chi-N
Bill Calhoun	6	13	.154	1-3	A	C
Otis Clymer	14	41	.834	CF-11	xChi-N	C
Gene Cocreham	1	8	7.56	P-1(0-1)	A	
Wilson Collins	16	3	.667	LF-9	A	
Joe Connolly	126	513	.788	LF-124	A	
George Davis	2	8	4.50	P-2	NY-A	
Charlie Deal	10	41	.692	2-10	xDet-A	
Art Devlin	73	245	.637	3-69	B	C
Rex DeVogt	3	6	.000	C-3	A	C
Walt Dickson	19	128	3.23	P-19(6-7)	B	Pit-F
Oscar Dugey	5	9	.583	3-2,2-1,S-1	A	
Lefty Gervais	6	16	5.74	P-5(0-1)	A	C
Hank Gowdy	3	5	1.550	C-2	A	
Tommy Griffith	37	139	.624	RF-35	A	
Otto Hess	35	218	3.83	P-29(7-17)	B	
George Jackson	3	11	.600	CF-3	B	C
Bill James	24	136	2.79	P-24(6-10)	A	
Jay Kirke	18	43	.582	RF-13	B	Cle-A
Bris Lord	73	247	.663	RF-62	Phi-A	C
Les Mann	120	435	.660	CF-120	A	
Rabbit Maranville	143	659	.638	S-143	A	
Jeff McCleskey	2	4	.250	3-2	A	C
Tex McDonald	62	167	.864	3-31,2-6,RF-1	xCin-N	Pit-F
Bill McKechnie	1	5	.200	CF-1	Pit-N	xNY-A
Bill McTigue	1	0	†	R	B	Det-A
Fred Mitchell	4	4	.667	H	NY-A	C
Hap Myers	140	597	.659	1-135	Bos-A	Bro-F
Win Noyes	11	21	4.79	P-11	A	Phi-A
Hub Perdue	38	212	3.26	P-38(16-13)	B	
Jack Quinn	9	56	2.40	P-8(4-3)	NY-A	Bal-F
Bill Rariden	95	286	.649	C-87	B	Ind-F
Dick Rudolph	35	249	2.92	P-33(14-13)	NY-N	
Butch Schmidt	22	82	.756	1-22	NY-N	
Joe Schultz	9	23	.556	RF-5,2-1	A	Bro-N
Cy Seymour	39	83	.465	RF-18	NY-N	C
Fred Smith	92	326	.582	3-59,2-14,S-11,LF-4	A	Buf-F
Paul Strand	7	17	2.12	P-7	A	
Bill Sweeney	139	584	.662	2-137	B	Chi-N
John Titus	87	317	.812	RF-75	B	C
Walt Tragesser	2	0	†	C-2	A	
Lefty Tyler	43	290	2.79	P-39(16-17)	B	
Bert Whaling	79	233	.581	C-77	A	
Guy Zinn	36	147	.727	CF-35	NY-A	Bal-F

1914 BOSTON (158 94-59 1) ATT: 382,913

Name	G	AB/IP	P/E	G/POS	From	To
George Stallings				M		
Ted Cather	50	161	.738	LF-48	xStL-N	
Gene Cocreham	15	45	4.84	P-15(3-4)	B	
Wilson Collins	27	37	.554	LF-19	B	C
Joe Connolly	120	469	.886	LF-118	B	
Ensign Cottrell	1	1	9.00	P-1(0-1)	Phi-A	NY-A
Dick Crutcher	33	159	3.46	P-33(5-7)	A	
George Davis	9	56	3.40	P-9(3-3)	B	
Charlie Deal	79	293	.546	3-74,S-1	B	StL-F
Josh Devore	51	151	.608	LF-42	xPhi-N	C
Oscar Dugey	58	122	.505	RF-16,2-16,3-1	B	Phi-N
Johnny Evers	139	611	.728	2-139	Chi-N	
Larry Gilbert	72	261	.717	RF-60	A	
Hank Gowdy	128	426	.684	C-115,1-9	B	
Tommy Griffith	16	50	.244	RF-14	B	Cin-N
Otto Hess	31	89	3.03	P-14(5-6),1-5	B	
Tom Hughes	2	17	2.65	P-2(2-0)	NY-A	
Bill James	49	332	1.90	P-46(26-7)	B	
Clarence Kraft	3	3	.667	1-1	A	C
Dolf Luque	2	9	4.15	P-2(0-1)	A	
Les Mann	126	425	.668	CF-123	B	Chi-F
Rabbit Maranville	156	664	.632	S-156	B	
Jack Martin	33	94	.499	3-26,1-1,2-1	NY-A	xPhi-N
Billy Martin	1	3	.000	S-1	A	C
Herbie Moran	41	178	.646	RF-41	xCin-N	
Jim Murray	39	121	.581	LF-32	StL-A	C
Hub Perdue	9	51	5.82	P-9(2-5)	B	xStL-N
Dick Rudolph	43	336	2.35	P-42(26-10)	B	
Butch Schmidt	147	614	.706	1-147	B	
Red Smith	60	251	.850	3-60	xBro-N	
Paul Strand	18	55	2.44	P-16(6-2)	B	
Fred Tyler	6	21	.255	C-6	A	C
Lefty Tyler	38	271	2.69	P-38(16-13)	B	
Bert Whaling	60	199	.553	C-59	B	
Possum Whitted	66	258	.703	CF-38,2-15,1-4,3-4,S-3	xStL-N	Phi-N

Coach: Fred Mitchell

1915 BOSTON (157 83-69 2) ATT: 376,283

Name	G	AB/IP	P/E	G/POS	From	To
George Stallings				M		
Jesse Barnes	9	45	1.39	P-9(3-0)	A	
Earl Blackburn	3	8	.542	C-3	Cin-N	
Ted Cather	40	126	.633	LF-32	B	C
Gene Cocreham	1	2	5.40	P-1	B	C
Zip Collins	5	16	.875	LF-4	xPit-N	
Pete Compton	35	127	.635	CF-31	xStL-F	
Joe Connolly	104	356	.784	LF-93	B	
Dick Crutcher	14	44	4.33	P-14(2-2)	B	C
George Davis	15	73	3.80	P-15(3-3)	B	C
Dick Egan	83	256	.652	RF-24,2-22,S-10,1-9,3-4	xBro-N	
Johnny Evers	83	349	.670	2-82	B	
Ed Fitzpatrick	105	374	.648	2-71,RF-29	A	
Larry Gilbert	45	120	.419	RF-27	B	C
Hank Gowdy	118	365	.671	C-114	B	
Otto Hess	5	14	3.86	P-4(0-1),1-1	B	C
Tom Hughes	50	280	2.12	P-50(16-14)	B	
Bill James	14	68	3.03	P-13(5-4)	B	
Fletcher Low	1	4	1.000	3-1	A	C
Dolf Luque	3	5	3.60	P-2	B	Cin-N
Sherry Magee	156	655	.742	CF-135,1-21	Phi-N	
Rabbit Maranville	149	579	.632	S-149	B	
Herbie Moran	130	505	.576	RF-123	B	C
Art Nehf	12	78	2.53	P-12(5-4)	A	
Pat Ragan	33	227	2.46	P-33(16-12)	xBro-N	
Dick Rudolph	45	341	2.37	P-44(22-19)	B	
Butch Schmidt	127	524	.670	1-127	B	C
Joe Shannon	5	11	.400	LF-4,2-1	A	C
Red Shannon	1	3	.000	2-1	A	Phi-A
Red Smith	157	636	.697	3-157	B	
Fred Snodgrass	23	93	.656	CF-18,1-5	xNY-N	
Paul Strand	24	23	2.38	P-6(1-1),LF-5	B	Phi-A
Walt Tragesser	7	7	.000	C-7	B	
Lefty Tyler	45	205	2.86	P-32(10-9)	B	
Bert Whaling	72	205	.537	C-69	B	C

Coach: Fred Mitchell

1916 BOSTON (158 89-63 3) ATT: 313,495

Name	G	AB/IP	P/E	G/POS	From	To
George Stallings				M		
Frank Allen	19	113	2.07	P-19(8-2)	Pit-F	
Fred Bailey	6	10	.200	LF-2	A	
Jesse Barnes	33	163	2.37	P-33(6-15)	B	
Earl Blackburn	47	123	.710	C-44	B	Chi-N
Larry Chappell	20	56	.551	LF-14	xCle-A	
Zip Collins	93	296	.530	CF-78	B	
Pete Compton	34	109	.489	CF-30	B	xPit-N
Joe Connolly	62	130	.629	LF-31	B	C
Dick Egan	83	271	.562	2-59,S-12,3-8	B	C
Johnny Evers	71	294	.570	2-71	B	
Ed Fitzpatrick	83	248	.544	2-46,RF-28	B	
Hank Gowdy	118	393	.618	C-116	B	
Tom Hughes	40	161	2.35	P-40(16-3)	B	
Elmer Knetzer	2	5	7.20	P-2(0-2)	Pit-F	xCin-N
Ed Konetchy	158	636	.693	1-158	Pit-F	
Sherry Magee	122	485	.649	LF-120,1-2,S-1	B	
Rabbit Maranville	155	680	.620	S-155	B	
Joe Mathes	2	0	†	2-2	StL-F	C
Art Nehf	23	121	2.01	P-22(7-5)	B	
Pat Ragan	31	182	2.08	P-28(9-9)	B	
Ed Reulbach	21	109	2.47	P-21(7-6)	New-F	
Art Rico	4	4	.000	C-4	A	
Dick Rudolph	41	312	2.16	P-41(19-12)	B	
Red Smith	150	584	.680	3-150	B	
Fred Snodgrass	112	436	.635	CF-110	B	
Walt Tragesser	41	61	.506	C-29	B	C
Lefty Tyler	39	249	2.02	P-34(17-9)	B	

Name	G	AB/IP	P/E	G/POS	From	To
Joe Wilhoit	116	426	.582	RF-108	A	

Coach: Fred Mitchell

1917 BOSTON (158 72-81 6) ATT: 174,253

Name	G	AB/IP	P/E	G/POS	From	To
George Stallings				M		
Frank Allen	29	112	3.94	P-29(3-11)	B	C
Fred Bailey	50	124	.525	CF-27	B	
Jesse Barnes	53	295	2.68	P-50(13-21)	B	NY-N
Larry Chappell	4	2	.000	CF-1	B	C
Zip Collins	9	27	.370	RF-5	B	Phi-A
Sam Covington	17	75	.537	1-17	StL-A	
Cal Crum	1	1	0.00	P-1	A	
Johnny Evers	24	98	.495	2-24	B	xPhi-N
Ed Fitzpatrick	63	203	.661	2-22,RF-19,3-15	B	C
Hank Gowdy	49	176	.548	C-49	B	
Tom Hughes	13	74	1.95	P-11(5-3)	B	
Fred Jacklitsch	1	0	†	C-1	Bal-F	C
Joe Kelly	116	489	.567	LF-116	Chi-N	
Ed Konetchy	130	526	.710	1-129	B	
Sherry Magee	72	277	.635	LF-65,1-2	B	xCin-N
Rabbit Maranville	142	613	.668	S-142	B	
Mike Massey	31	114	.516	2-25	A	C
Chief Meyers	25	77	.737	C-24	xBro-N	C
Art Nehf	38	233	2.16	P-38(17-8)	B	
Ray Powell	88	388	.673	CF-88	Det-A	
Pat Ragan	30	148	2.93	P-30(6-9)	B	
Johnny Rawlings	122	429	.655	2-96,S-17,3-1,LF-1	KC-F	
Wally Rehg	87	378	.669	RF-86	Bos-A	
Ed Reulbach	5	22	2.82	P-5(0-1)	B	C
Art Rico	13	14	.643	C-11,LF-2	B	C
Dick Rudolph	32	243	3.41	P-31(13-13)	B	
Hank Schreiber	2	7	.571	S-1,3-1	Chi-A	Cin-N
Jack Scott	7	40	1.82	P-7(1-2)	Pit-N	
Red Smith	147	585	.761	3-147	B	
Walt Tragesser	98	323	.534	C-94	B	
George Twombly	32	127	.530	CF-29,1-1	Cin-N	Was-A
Lefty Tyler	61	239	2.52	P-32(14-12),1-11	B	Chi-N
Ed Walsh	4	18	3.50	P-4(0-1)	Chi-A	C
Joe Wilhoit	54	212	.652	RF-52	B	xPit-N

1918 BOSTON (124 53-71 7) ATT: 84,938

Name	G	AB/IP	P/E	G/POS	From	To
George Stallings				M		
Fred Bailey	4	4	.500	H	B	C
Doc Bass	2	1	2.000	H	A	C
Hugh Canavan	16	47	6.36	P-11(0-4),LF-2	A	C
Chet Chadbourne	27	119	.598	CF-27	KC-F	C
Rip Conway	14	28	.397	2-5,3-1	A	C
Sam Covington	3	3	.667	H	B	C
Doc Crandall	14	34	2.38	P-5(1-2),RF-3	StL-A	C
Cal Crum	1	2	15.43	P-1(0-1)	B	C
Dana Fillingim	14	113	2.23	P-14(7-6)	Phi-A	
Lefty George	10	54	2.32	P-9(1-5)	Cin-N	C
Bunny Hearn	17	126	2.49	P-17(5-6)	Pit-F	
John Henry	43	115	.509	C-38	Was-A	C
Buck Herzog	118	526	.559	2-99,1-12,S-7	NY-N	
Tom Hughes	3	18	3.44	P-3(0-2)	B	C
Jim Kelly	35	162	.766	LF-35	Pit-F	C
Joe Kelly	47	166	.562	LF-45	B	
Ed Konetchy	119	487	.598	1-112,CF-6,P-1(0-1)	B	Bro-N
Rabbit Maranville	11	42	.749	S-11	B	
Roy Massey	66	230	.703	CF-45,3-2,1-1,S-1	A	C
Hugh McQuillan	1	9	3.00	P-1(1-0)	A	
Tom Miller	2	2	.000	H	A	
Buzz Murphy	9	36	1.147	LF-9	A	Was-A
Art Nehf	35	284	2.69	P-32(15-15),LF-2	B	
Jake Northrop	7	40	1.35	P-7(5-1)	A	
Ray Powell	53	222	.624	CF-53	B	
Pat Ragan	30	206	3.23	P-30(8-17)	B	
Johnny Rawlings	111	460	.504	S-71,2-20,RF-18	B	
Wally Rehg	40	140	.584	LF-38	B	Cin-N
Dick Rudolph	21	154	2.57	P-21(9-10)	B	
Red Smith	119	500	.746	3-119	B	
Jimmy Smith	34	112	.617	2-10,S-9,CF-6,3-5	NY-N	Cin-N
Zeb Terry	28	118	.722	S-27	Chi-A	Pit-N
Walt Tragesser	7	1	.000	C-7	B	
Bill Upham	3	21	5.23	P-3(1-1)	Bro-F	C
Bill Wagner	13	52	.551	C-13	Pit-N	C
Al Wickland	95	399	.765	RF-95	Pit-F	NY-A
Art Wilson	89	311	.600	C-85	Chi-N	

Coach: Jack Slattery

1919 BOSTON (140 57-82 6) ATT: 167,401

Name	G	AB/IP	P/E	G/POS	From	To
George Stallings				M		
Gene Bailey	4	6	.667	CF-3	Phi-A	
Lena Blackburne	31	92	.647	3-24,1-1,2-1,S-1	Cin-N	xPhi-N
Tony Boeckel	95	405	.632	3-93	xPit-N	
Dixie Carroll	15	59	.747	CF-13	A	C
Red Causey	10	69	4.57	P-10(4-5)	xNY-N	Phi-N
Larry Cheney	8	33	3.55	P-8(0-2)	xBro-N	xPhi-N
Lloyd Christenbury	7	34	.656	LF-7	A	
Walton Cruise	73	266	.525	LF-66	xStL-N	
Al Demaree	25	128	3.80	P-25(6-6)	NY-N	C
Dana Fillingim	32	186	3.38	P-32(6-13)	B	
Hod Ford	10	32	.576	S-8,3-2	A	
Hank Gowdy	78	245	.677	C-74,1-1	B	
Buck Herzog	73	307	.683	2-70,1-1	B	xChi-N
Walter Holke	137	570	.667	1-136	NY-N	
Bill James	1	5	3.38	P-1	B	C
Ray Keating	24	136	2.98	P-22(7-11)	NY-A	C
Joe Kelly	18	66	.310	LF-16	B	C
Lee King	2	1	.000	H	Phi-A	C
Les Mann	40	160	.770	LF-40	xChi-N	
Rabbit Maranville	131	529	.696	S-131	B	
Hugh McQuillan	20	60	3.45	P-16(2-3),RF-3	B	
Tom Miller	7	6	.667	H	B	C

Name	G	AB/IP	P/E	G/POS	From	To
Art Nehf	23	169	3.09	P-22(8-9),RF-1	B	xNY-N
Jake Northrop	11	37	4.58	P-11(1-5)	B	C
Dizzy Nutter	18	56	.479	CF-12	A	C
Joe Oeschger	7	57	2.54	P-7(4-2)	xNY-N	
Mickey O'Neil	11	32	.456	C-11	B	
Charlie Pick	34	128	.632	2-21,3-5,LF-3,1-2	xChi-N	
Ray Powell	123	526	.628	RF-122	B	
Pat Ragan	4	13	7.11	P-4(0-2)	B	xNY-N
Johnny Rawlings	77	307	.607	2-58,LF-10,S-5	B	
Joe Riggert	63	270	.764	CF-61	StL-N	C
Dick Rudolph	37	274	2.17	P-37(13-18)	B	
Jack Scott	24	104	3.13	P-19(6-6),RF-1	B	
Red Smith	87	294	.641	CF-48,3-23	B	C
Jim Thorpe	60	168	.789	LF-38,1-2	xNY-N	C
Walt Tragesser	20	44	.458	C-14	B	xPhi-N
Sam White	1	1	.000	C-1	A	C
Art Wilson	71	226	.655	C-64,1-1	B	

Coach: Jack Slattery

♦ **1920 BOSTON** (153 62-90 7) ATT: 162,483

Name	G	AB/IP	P/E	G/POS	From	To
George Stallings				M		
Gene Bailey	13	29	.269	LF-8	B	xBos-A
Tony Boeckel	153	630	.663	3-149,S-3,2-1	B	
Lloyd Christenbury	65	125	.564	CF-14,S-7,2-6,3-2	B	
Walton Cruise	91	331	.699	RF-82	B	
Oscar Dugey	5	0	†	R	Phi-N	C
Eddie Eayrs	87	284	.787	LF-63,P-7(1-2)	Pit-N	
Dana Fillingim	38	272	3.11	P-37(12-21)	B	
Hod Ford	88	287	.635	2-59,S-18,1-4	B	
Hank Gowdy	80	241	.627	C-74	B	
Bunny Hearn	11	43	5.65	P-11(0-3)	B	C
Walter Holke	144	603	.707	1-143	B	
Johnny Jones	3	10	6.52	P-3(1-0)	NY-N	C
Les Mann	115	477	.693	LF-110	B	StL-N
Rabbit Maranville	134	534	.676	S-133	B	Pit-N
Hugh McQuillan	38	226	3.55	P-38(11-15)	B	
Joe Oeschger	38	299	3.46	P-38(15-13)	B	
Mickey O'Neil	112	343	.665	C-105,2-1	B	
Charlie Pick	95	427	.683	2-94	B	C
Al Pierotti	6	25	2.88	P-6(1-1)	A	
Ray Powell	147	666	.595	CF-147	B	
Johnny Rawlings	5	6	.000	2-1	B	xPhi-N
Dick Rudolph	18	89	4.04	P-18(4-8)	B	
Jack Scott	44	291	3.53	P-44(10-21)	B	
John Sullivan	81	290	.770	RF-66,1-6	A	
Red Torphy	3	15	.533	1-3	A	C
Ira Townsend	4	7	1.35	P-4	A	
Leo Townsend	7	24	1.48	P-7(2-2)	A	
Mule Watson	1	3	0.00	P-1	Phi-A	xPit-N
Mule Watson	12	72	3.77	P-12(5-4)	xPit-N	
Tom Whelan	1	2	.500	1-1	A	C
Art Wilson	16	21	.195	3-6,C-2	B	Cle-A

Coach: Oscar Dugey

♦ **1921 BOSTON** (153 79-74 4) ATT: 318,627

Name	G	AB/IP	P/E	G/POS	From	To
Fred Mitchell				M		
Walter Barbare	134	600	.698	S-121,2-8,3-2	Pit-N	
Tony Boeckel	153	663	.811	3-153	B	
Garland Braxton	17	37	4.82	P-17(1-3)	A	
Lloyd Christenbury	62	151	.953	2-32,S-2,3-2	B	
Johnny Cooney	8	21	3.92	P-8(0-1)	A	
Walton Cruise	108	403	.932	LF-102,1-2	B	
Eddie Eayrs	15	5	17.36	P-2	B	xBro-N
Dana Fillingim	45	240	3.45	P-44(15-10)	B	
Hod Ford	152	614	.688	2-119,S-33	B	
Frank Gibson	63	133	.708	C-41	Det-A	
Hank Gowdy	64	188	.771	C-53	B	
Walter Holke	150	621	.621	1-150	B	
Hugh McQuillan	45	250	4.00	P-45(13-17)	B	
Cy Morgan	17	30	6.53	P-17(1-1)	A	
Fred Nicholson	83	271	.860	LF-59,1-4,2-2	Pit-N	
Al Nixon	55	152	.629	LF-43	Bro-N	
Joe Oeschger	46	299	3.52	P-46(20-14)	B	
Mickey O'Neil	98	313	.639	C-95	B	
Al Pierotti	2	2	21.60	P-2(0-1)	B	C
Ray Powell	149	699	.830	CF-149	B	
Jack Scott	51	234	3.70	P-47(15-13)	B	Cin-N
Billy Southworth	141	642	.792	RF-141	Pit-N	
John Sullivan	5	5	.000	H	B	xChi-N
Ira Townsend	4	7	6.14	P-4	B	C
Leo Townsend	1	1	27.00	P-1(0-1)	B	C
Mule Watson	44	259	3.85	P-44(14-13)	B	

Coach: Dick Rudolph

♦ **1922 BOSTON** (154 53-100 8) ATT: 167,965

Name	G	AB/IP	P/E	G/POS	From	To
Fred Mitchell				M		
Walter Barbare	106	408	.537	2-45,3-38,1-14	B	C
Tony Boeckel	119	450	.759	3-106	B	
Garland Braxton	25	67	3.38	P-25(1-2)	B	NY-A
Lloyd Christenbury	71	177	.666	LF-32,2-5,3-2	B	
Johnny Cooney	4	25	2.16	P-4(1-2)	B	
Walton Cruise	104	413	.772	RF-100,1-2	B	
Dana Fillingim	25	117	4.54	P-25(5-9)	B	
Hod Ford	143	574	.680	S-115,2-28	B	
Gil Gallagher	7	23	.178	S-6	A	C
Joe Genewich	6	23	7.04	P-6(0-2)	A	
Frank Gibson	66	179	.760	C-29,1-20	B	
Hank Gowdy	92	254	.780	C-72,1-1	B	
Snake Henry	18	71	.508	1-18	A	
Walter Holke	105	424	.651	1-105	B	Phi-N
Harry Hulihan	7	40	3.15	P-7(2-3)	A	
Larry Kopf	126	528	.630	2-78,S-33,3-13	Cin-N	
Gene Lansing	15	41	5.98	P-15(0-1)	A	C
Rube Marquard	39	198	5.09	P-39(11-15)	Cin-N	
Joe Matthews	3	10	3.60	P-3(0-1)	A	C

Name	G	AB/IP	P/E	G/POS	From	To
Tim McNamara	24	71	2.42	P-24(3-4)	A	
Hugh McQuillan	32	136	4.24	P-28(5-10)	B	xNY-N
Frank Miller	31	200	3.51	P-31(11-13)	Pit-N	
Cy Morgan	2	1	27.00	P-2	B	C
Fred Nicholson	78	257	.678	RF-63	B	C
Al Nixon	86	331	.637	LF-79	B	
Joe Oeschger	46	196	5.06	P-46(6-21)	B	
Mickey O'Neil	83	271	.526	C-79	B	
Ray Powell	142	619	.778	CF-136	B	
Bunny Roser	32	132	.643	LF-32	A	C
Dick Rudolph	3	16	5.06	P-3(0-2)	B	
Billy Southworth	43	182	.867	RF-41	B	
Mule Watson	41	201	4.70	P-41(8-14)	B	
Al Yeargin	1	7	1.29	P-1(0-1)	A	

Coach: Dick Rudolph

♦ **1923 BOSTON** (155 54-100 7) ATT: 227,802

Name	G	AB/IP	P/E	G/POS	From	To
Fred Mitchell				M		
Bill Bagwell	56	101	.774	LF-22	A	Phi-A
Jesse Barnes	31	195	2.76	P-31(10-14)	xNY-N	
Joe Batchelder	4	9	7.00	P-4(1-0)	A	
Larry Benton	35	128	4.99	P-35(5-9)	A	
Tony Boeckel	148	633	.762	3-147,S-1	B	C
Jocko Conlon	59	171	.537	2-36,S-6,3-4	A	C
Johnny Cooney	42	98	3.31	P-23(3-5),CF-11,1-1	B	
Dee Cousineau	1	2	2.000	C-1	A	
Walton Cruise	21	43	.531	LF-9	B	
Bob Emmerich	13	27	.237	CF-8	A	C
Gus Felix	139	573	.697	LF-123,2-5,3-4	A	
Dana Fillingim	36	100	5.20	P-35(1-9)	B	Phi-N
Hod Ford	111	425	.692	2-95,S-19	B	Phi-N
Joe Genewich	43	227	3.72	P-43(13-14)	B	
Frank Gibson	41	57	.706	C-20	B	
Hank Gowdy	23	66	.541	C-15	B	xNY-N
Snake Henry	11	10	.311	H	B	C
Al Hermann	31	96	.516	2-15,3-5,1-4	A	
Larry Kopf	39	157	.649	S-37,2-4	B	C
Rube Marquard	38	239	3.73	P-38(11-14)	B	
Stuffy McInnis	154	670	.735	1-154	Cle-A	
Tim McNamara	32	139	4.91	P-32(3-13)	B	
Frank Miller	8	39	4.58	P-8(0-3)	B	C
Al Nixon	88	358	.671	CF-80	B	Phi-N
Joe Oeschger	44	166	5.68	P-44(5-15)	B	NY-N
Mickey O'Neil	96	328	.520	C-95	B	
Ernie Padgett	4	13	.490	S-2,2-1	A	
Ray Powell	97	395	.806	CF-84	B	
Dick Rudolph	4	19	3.72	P-4(1-2)	B	
Earl Smith	72	216	.789	C-54	xNY-N	
Bob Smith	115	406	.594	S-101,2-8	A	
Billy Southworth	153	692	.831	RF-151,2-2	B	NY-N
Mule Watson	11	31	5.17	P-11(1-2)	B	xNY-N

Coach: Dick Rudolph

♦ **1924 BOSTON** (154 53-100 8) ATT: 177,478

Name	G	AB/IP	P/E	G/POS	From	To
Dave Bancroft				M		
Dave Bancroft	79	362	.694	S-79	NY-N	
Jesse Barnes	37	268	3.23	P-37(15-20)	B	
Joe Batchelder	3	5	3.86	P-3	B	
Larry Benton	30	128	4.15	P-30(5-7)	B	
Johnny Cooney	55	181	3.18	P-34(8-9),CF-16,1-1	B	
Dee Cousineau	3	2	.000	C-3	B	
Walton Cruise	9	9	1.333	H	B	C
Bill Cunningham	114	476	.676	LF-109	NY-N	C
Gus Felix	59	225	.544	CF-51	B	
Dinty Gearin	1	0	/	P-1(0-1)	xNY-N	C
Joe Genewich	34	200	5.21	P-34(10-19)	B	
Frank Gibson	90	241	.783	C-46,1-10,3-2	B	
Skinny Graham	5	33	3.82	P-5(0-4)	A	
Al Hermann	1	1	.000	H	B	C
Ike Kamp	1	7	5.14	P-1(0-1)	A	
John Kelleher	1	1	.000	H	Chi-N	C
Hunter Lane	7	16	.192	3-4,2-1	A	C
Wade Lefler	1	1	.000	H	A	xWas-A
Red Lucas	33	84	5.16	P-27(1-4),3-2	NY-N	
Les Mann	32	112	.755	RF-28	Cin-N	
Rube Marquard	6	36	3.00	P-6(1-2)	B	
Stuffy McInnis	146	611	.671	1-146	B	Pit-N
Tim McNamara	35	179	5.18	P-35(8-12)	B	
Joe Muich	3	9	11.00	P-3	A	C
Lou North	9	35	5.35	P-9(1-2)	xStL-N	C
Mickey O'Neil	106	382	.538	C-106	B	
Ernie Padgett	138	548	.657	3-113,2-29	B	
Eddie Phillips	3	3	.000	C-1	A	Det-A
Ray Powell	74	213	.673	CF-46	B	C
Marty Shay	19	74	.606	2-19,S-1	Chi-N	C
Earl Smith	33	66	.660	C-13	B	xPit-N
Bob Smith	106	368	.556	S-80,3-23	B	
Ed Sperber	24	74	.773	RF-17	A	
Casey Stengel	131	518	.730	RF-126	NY-N	
Dutch Stryker	20	73	6.01	P-20(3-8)	A	Bro-N
Herb Thomas	32	139	.579	CF-32	B	
Cotton Tierney	136	539	.626	2-115,3-22	Phi-N	Bro-N
Frank Wilson	61	241	.595	LF-55	A	
Al Yeargin	32	141	5.09	P-32(1-11)	B	C

Coach: Dick Rudolph

♦ **1925 BOSTON** (153 70-83 5) ATT: 313,528

Name	G	AB/IP	P/E	G/POS	From	To
Dave Bancroft				M		
Bill Anderson	2	3	10.13	P-2	A	C
Dave Bancroft	128	560	.826	S-125	B	
Jesse Barnes	32	216	4.53	P-32(11-16)	B	Bro-N
Joe Batchelder	4	7	5.14	P-4	B	C
Larry Benton	32	183	3.09	P-31(14-7)	B	
Dick Burrus	152	652	.845	1-151	Phi-A	
Johnny Cooney	54	246	3.48	P-31(14-14),1-3,LF-1	B	

Name	G	AB/IP	P/E	G/POS	From	To
Dee Cousineau	1	0	†	C-1	B	C
Foster Edwards	1	2	9.00	P-1	A	
Gus Felix	121	507	.762	CF-114	B	Bro-N
Doc Gautreau	68	319	.676	2-68	xPhi-A	
Joe Genewich	34	169	3.99	P-34(12-10)	B	
Frank Gibson	104	341	.715	C-86,1-2	B	
Skinny Graham	34	157	4.41	P-34(7-12)	B	
Dave Harris	92	377	.694	LF-90	A	
Andy High	60	251	.762	3-60,2-1	xBro-N	
Shanty Hogan	9	22	.747	RF-5	A	
Abie Hood	5	23	.842	2-5	A	C
Ike Kamp	24	58	5.09	P-24(2-4)	B	C
Hod Kibbie	11	46	.665	2-8,S-3	A	C
Red Lucas	6	23	.377	2-6	B	Cin-N
Les Mann	60	199	.851	RF-57	B	
Rube Marquard	26	72	5.75	P-26(2-8)	B	C
William Marriott	103	411	.628	3-89,LF-1	Chi-N	Bro-N
Tim McNamara	1	1	81.00	P-1	B	NY-N
Bernie Neis	106	400	.748	CF-87	Bro-N	
Joe Ogrodowski	1	1	54.00	P-1	A	C
Mickey O'Neil	70	249	.682	C-69	B	Bro-N
Ernie Padgett	86	274	.735	2-47,S-18,3-7	B	Cle-A
Rosy Ryan	38	123	6.31	P-37(2-8)	NY-N	
Oscar Siemer	16	48	.732	C-16	A	
Bob Smith	58	181	.681	S-21,2-15,P-13(5-3),CF-1	B	
Ed Sperber	2	2	.000	H	B	C
Casey Stengel	12	15	.220	RF-1	B	C
Herb Thomas	5	20	.703	2-5	B	
Bill Vargus	11	36	3.96	P-11(1-1)	A	
Jimmy Welsh	122	521	.790	RF-116,2-3	A	
Frank Wilson	12	36	1.002	LF-10	B	
Coach: Dick Rudolph						

♦ 1926 BOSTON (153 66-86 7) ATT: 303,598

Name	G	AB/IP	P/E	G/POS	From	To
Dave Bancroft				M		
Dave Bancroft	127	541	.783	S-123,3-2	B	
Larry Benton	45	232	3.85	P-43(14-14)	B	
Eddie Brown	153	650	.770	CF-153	Bro-N	
Dick Burrus	131	540	.659	1-128	B	
Johnny Cooney	64	147	.724	1-31,P-19(3-3),RF-1	B	
Foster Edwards	3	25	0.72	P-3(2-0)	B	
Doc Gautreau	79	317	.687	2-74	B	
Joe Genewich	37	216	3.88	P-37(8-16)	B	
Frank Gibson	24	52	.818	C-13	B	
Hal Goldsmith	19	101	4.37	P-19(5-7)	A	
Skinny Graham	15	36	7.93	P-15(3-3)	B	Det-A
Bunny Hearn	34	117	4.22	P-34(4-9)	B	
Andy High	130	533	.737	3-81,2-49	B	
Shanty Hogan	4	14	.786	C-4	B	
Jimmy Johnston	23	67	.674	3-14,2-2,LF-1	Bro-N	xNY-N
Les Mann	50	141	.766	LF-46	B	
George Mogridge	40	142	4.50	P-39(6-10),1-1	StL-A	
Eddie Moore	54	212	.629	2-39,S-14,3-1	xPit-N	
Bernie Neis	30	103	.589	LF-23	B	Cle-A
Harry Riconda	4	14	.452	3-4	Phi-A	Bro-N
Rosy Ryan	7	19	7.58	P-7(0-2)	B	NY-A
Oscar Siemer	31	77	.446	C-30	B	C
Jack Smith	96	359	.758	CF-83	xStL-N	
Bob Smith	40	201	3.75	P-33(10-13)	B	
Ed Taylor	92	327	.681	3-62,S-33	A	C
Zack Taylor	125	470	.622	C-123	Bro-N	
Bill Vargus	4	3	3.00	P-4	B	C
Jimmy Welsh	134	563	.711	RF-129	B	
Johnny Werts	32	189	3.28	P-32(11-9)	A	
Frank Wilson	87	265	.609	LF-56	B	Cle-A
Sid Womack	1	3	.000	C-1	A	C
Coaches: Lore Bader, Art Devlin, Dick Rudolph						

♦ 1927 BOSTON (155 60-94 7) ATT: 288,685

Name	G	AB/IP	P/E	G/POS	From	To
Dave Bancroft				M		
Dave Bancroft	111	427	.629	S-104,3-1	B	Bro-N
Larry Benton	11	60	4.48	P-11(4-2)	B	xNY-N
Eddie Brown	155	605	.741	LF-150,1-1	B	
Dick Burrus	72	248	.752	1-61	B	
Earl Clark	13	49	.600	LF-13	A	
Johnny Cooney	10	1	.000	H	B	
Foster Edwards	33	92	4.99	P-29(2-8)	B	
Doc Farrell	110	457	.655	S-57,2-40,3-18	xNY-N	
Jack Fournier	122	433	.790	1-102	Bro-N	C
Doc Gautreau	87	270	.634	2-57	B	
Joe Genewich	40	181	3.83	P-40(11-8)	B	
Frank Gibson	60	173	.487	C-47	B	C
Hal Goldsmith	22	72	3.52	P-22(1-3)	B	
Sid Graves	7	21	.650	CF-5	A	C
Kent Greenfield	27	190	3.84	P-27(11-14)	xNY-N	
Bunny Hearn	8	13	4.26	P-8(0-2)	B	
Andy High	113	422	.769	3-89,2-8,S-2	B	StL-N
Shanty Hogan	71	246	.734	C-61	B	NY-N
Jack Knight	3	3	15.00	P-3	Phi-N	C
Les Mann	29	75	.671	RF-24	B	xNY-N
Dinny McNamara	11	11	.000	CF-3	A	
Hugh McQuillan	13	78	5.54	P-13(3-5)	xNY-N	C
Art Mills	15	38	3.82	P-15(0-1)	A	
George Mogridge	20	49	3.70	P-20(6-4)	B	C
Eddie Moore	112	442	.726	3-52,2-39,CF-16,S-1	B	
Guy Morrison	11	34	4.46	P-11(1-2)	A	
Lance Richbourg	115	491	.731	RF-110	Was-A	
Charlie Robertson	28	154	4.72	P-28(7-17)	StL-A	
Dick Rudolph	1	1	0.00	P-1	B	C
Jack Smith	84	207	.785	RF-48	B	
Bob Smith	54	261	3.76	P-41(10-18)	B	
Zack Taylor	30	105	.611	C-27	B	xNY-N
Herb Thomas	24	82	.607	2-17,S-2	B	xNY-N
Luke Urban	35	116	.646	C-34	A	
Jimmy Welsh	131	556	.752	CF-129,1-1	B	NY-N

Name	G	AB/IP	P/E	G/POS	From	To
Johnny Werts	42	164	4.55	P-42(4-10)	B	
Coach: Dick Rudolph						

♦ 1928 BOSTON (153 50-103 7) ATT: 227,001

Name	G	AB/IP	P/E	G/POS	From	To
Jack Slattery				M(31 11-20 7)		
Rogers Hornsby				M(122 39-83 7)		
Virgil Barnes	16	60	5.82	P-16(2-7)	xNY-N	C
Les Bell	153	656	.736	3-153	StL-N	
Ray Boggs	4	5	5.40	P-4	A	C
Ed Brandt	39	225	5.07	P-38(9-21)	A	
Eddie Brown	142	569	.645	LF-129,1-1	B	C
Dick Burrus	64	159	.747	1-32	B	C
Ben Cantwell	22	90	5.10	P-22(2-3)	xNY-N	
Earl Clark	28	121	.741	CF-27	B	
Bill Clarkson	19	35	6.75	P-19(0-2)	xNY-N	
Jimmy Cooney	18	53	.307	S-11,2-4	Phi-N	C
Johnny Cooney	33	90	4.32	P-24(3-7),1-3,CF-2	B	
Bill Cronin	3	3	.333	C-3	A	
Art Delaney	39	192	3.79	P-39(9-17)	StL-N	
Doc Farrell	134	533	.534	S-132,2-1	B	
Charlie Fitzberger	7	7	.571	H	A	C
Howard Freigau	52	123	.695	S-14,2-11	xBro-N	C
Doc Gautreau	23	22	.798	2-4,S-1	B	C
Joe Genewich	13	81	4.13	P-13(3-7)	B	xNY-N
Hal Goldsmith	4	8	3.24	P-4	B	StL-N
Kent Greenfield	32	144	5.32	P-32(3-11)	B	
Dave Harris	7	19	.387	LF-6	B	Chi-A
Bunny Hearn	7	10	6.30	P-7(1-0)	B	
Bonnie Hollingsworth	7	22	5.24	P-7(0-2)	Bro-N	C
Rogers Hornsby	140	619	1.130	2-140	NY-N	Chi-N
Dinny McNamara	9	5	.500	RF-3	B	C
Art Mills	4	8	12.91	P-4	B	C
Eddie Moore	68	244	.606	LF-54,2-1	B	Bro-N
Guy Morrison	1	3	12.00	P-1	B	C
Heinie Mueller	42	182	.574	CF-41	NY-N	
Emilio Palmero	3	7	5.40	P-3(0-1)	Was-A	C
Lance Richbourg	148	685	.828	RF-148	B	
Charlie Robertson	13	59	5.31	P-13(2-5)	B	C
George Sisler	118	537	.814	1-118,P-1	xWas-A	
Jack Smith	96	289	.677	CF-65	B	
Bob Smith	39	244	3.87	P-38(13-17)	B	
Al Spohrer	51	130	.496	C-48	xNY-N	
Zack Taylor	125	442	.621	C-124	NY-N	
Clay Touchstone	5	8	4.50	P-5	A	
Luke Urban	15	19	.399	C-10	B	C
Johnny Werts	10	18	10.31	P-10(0-2)	B	
Earl Williams	3	2	.000	C-1	A	C
Coach: Art Devlin						

♦ 1929 BOSTON (154 56-98 8) ATT: 372,351

Name	G	AB/IP	P/E	G/POS	From	To
Judge Fuchs				M		
Red Barron	10	22	.465	LF-6	A	C
Les Bell	139	553	.786	3-127,2-1,S-1	B	Chi-N
Buzz Boyle	17	66	.719	LF-17	A	
Ed Brandt	29	168	5.53	P-26(8-13)	B	
Ben Cantwell	27	157	4.47	P-27(4-13)	B	
Earl Clark	84	303	.740	CF-74	B	
Bill Clarkson	2	7	10.29	P-2(0-1)	B	C
Pat Collins	7	11	.375	C-6	NY-A	C
Johnny Cooney	41	76	.758	CF-16,P-14(2-3)	B	
Bill Cronin	6	9	.222	C-6	B	
Jack Cummings	3	6	.333	C-3	xNY-N	C
Bruce Cunningham	19	92	4.52	P-17(4-6),LF-1	A	
Art Delaney	20	75	6.12	P-20(3-5)	B	C
Joe Dugan	60	139	.730	3-24,S-5,2-2,LF-2	NY-A	Det-A
Bill Dunlap	10	33	1.071	LF-9	A	
Johnny Evers	1	0	†	2-1	Chi-A	C
Doc Farrell	5	8	.250	2-1,S-1	B	xNY-N
Hank Gowdy	10	16	.875	C-9	NY-N	
Kent Greenfield	6	16	10.91	P-6	B	xBro-N
George Harper	136	538	.822	LF-130	StL-N	C
Bunny Hearn	10	18	4.42	P-10(2-0)	B	C
Bernie James	46	113	.746	2-32,CF-1	A	
Percy Jones	36	188	4.64	P-35(7-15)	Chi-N	Pit-N
Lou Legett	39	84	.376	C-28	A	Bos-A
Dixie Leverett	24	98	6.36	P-24(3-7)	Chi-A	
Freddie Maguire	138	544	.620	2-138,S-1	Chi-N	
Rabbit Maranville	146	634	.710	S-145,2-1	StL-N	
Heinie Mueller	46	109	.549	CF-24	B	StL-A
Red Peery	10	44	5.11	P-9(0-1)	Pit-N	C
Henry Peploski	6	12	.473	3-2	A	C
Lance Richbourg	139	616	.766	RF-134	B	
Gene Robertson	8	31	.596	3-6,S-1	xNY-A	
Socks Seibold	33	206	4.73	P-33(12-17)	Phi-A	
George Sisler	154	686	.788	1-154	B	
Jack Smith	19	24	.568	CF-9	B	C
Bob Smith	39	231	4.68	P-34(11-17),S-5	B	
Al Spohrer	114	382	.725	C-109	B	
Zack Taylor	34	114	.620	C-31	B	xChi-N
Clay Touchstone	1	3	16.88	P-1	B	Chi-A
Phil Voyles	20	79	.591	CF-20	A	C
Jimmy Welsh	53	212	.791	CF-51	xNY-N	
Johnny Werts	4	6	10.50	P-4	B	C
Al Weston	3	3	.000	H	A	C
Coaches: Johnny Evers, Hank Gowdy						

♦ 1930 BOSTON (154 70-84 6) ATT: 464,835

Name	G	AB/IP	P/E	G/POS	From	To
Bill McKechnie				M		
Wally Berger	151	625	.990	LF-145	A	
Buzz Boyle	1	1	.000	CF-1	B	Bro-N
Ed Brandt	41	147	5.01	P-41(4-11)	B	
Bob Brown	3	6	10.50	P-3	A	
Ben Cantwell	34	173	4.88	P-31(9-15)	B	

Name	G	AB/IP	P/E	G/POS	From	To
Buster Chatham	112	463	.740	3-92,S-17	A	
Earl Clark	82	245	.727	CF-63	B	
Johnny Cooney	4	7	18.00	P-2	B	Bro-N
Bill Cronin	66	189	.592	C-64	B	
Bruce Cunningham	37	107	5.48	P-36(5-6)	B	
Bill Dunlap	16	29	.172	RF-7	B	C
Fred Frankhouse	27	111	5.61	P-27(7-6)	xStL-N	
Hank Gowdy	16	29	.550	C-15	B	C
Burleigh Grimes	11	49	7.35	P-11(3-5)	Pit-N	xStL-N
Bernie James	8	11	.455	2-7	B	NY-N
Ken Jones	8	20	5.95	P-8(0-1)	Det-A	C
Owen Kahn	1	0	†	R	A	C
Freddie Maguire	146	557	.625	2-146	B	
Rabbit Maranville	142	628	.711	S-138,3-4	B	
Randy Moore	83	204	.690	CF-34,3-13	Chi-A	
Johnny Neun	81	243	.818	1-55	Det-A	
Billy Rhiel	20	51	.459	3-13,2-2	Bro-N	Det-A
Lance Richbourg	130	557	.726	RF-128	B	
Gene Robertson	21	67	.453	3-17	B	C
Red Rollings	52	137	.572	3-28,2-10	Bos-A	C
Socks Seibold	36	251	4.12	P-36(15-16)	B	
Bill Sherdel	21	119	4.75	P-21(6-5)	xStL-N	
George Sisler	116	470	.743	1-107	B	C
Bob Smith	39	220	4.26	P-38(10-14)	B	Chi-N
Al Spohrer	112	388	.802	C-108	B	
Jimmy Welsh	113	465	.716	CF-110	B	C
Tom Zachary	25	151	4.58	P-24(11-5)	xNY-A	

Coaches: Johnny Evers, Hank Gowdy, George Sisler

◆ 1931 BOSTON (156 64-90 7) ATT: 515,005

Name	G	AB/IP	P/E	G/POS	From	To
Bill McKechnie				M		
Wally Berger	156	678	.892	CF-156,1-1	B	
Al Bool	49	96	.466	C-37	Pit-N	C
Ed Brandt	34	250	2.92	P-33(18-11)	B	
Bob Brown	3	6	8.53	P-3(0-1)	B	
Ben Cantwell	40	156	3.63	P-33(7-9)	B	
Buster Chatham	17	50	.638	S-6,3-6	B	C
Earl Clark	16	59	.576	LF-14	B	
Bill Cronin	51	116	.548	C-50	B	C
Bruce Cunningham	34	137	4.48	P-33(3-12)	B	
Bill Dreesen	48	204	.649	3-47	A	C
Fred Frankhouse	26	127	4.03	P-26(8-8)	B	
Hal Haid	27	56	4.50	P-27(0-2)	StL-N	Chi-A
Bill Hunnefield	11	23	.571	3-5,2-4	xCle-A	xNY-N
Freddie Maguire	148	544	.532	2-148	B	C
Rabbit Maranville	145	636	.646	S-137,2-11	B	
Bill McAfee	18	30	6.37	P-18(0-1)	Chi-N	Was-A
Randy Moore	83	209	.670	LF-29,3-22,2-1	B	
Ray Moss	12	45	4.60	P-12(1-3)	xBro-N	C
Johnny Neun	79	117	.590	1-36	B	C
Lance Richbourg	97	311	.719	RF-71	B	Chi-N
Johnny Scalzi	2	1	.000	H	A	C
Wes Schulmerich	95	359	.785	RF-87	A	
Socks Seibold	33	206	4.67	P-33(10-18)	B	
Earl Sheely	147	586	.633	1-143	Pit-N	C
Bill Sherdel	27	138	4.25	P-27(6-10)	B	
Al Spohrer	114	373	.602	C-111	B	
Billy Urbanski	82	333	.581	3-68,S-19	A	
Pat Veltman	1	1	.000	H	NY-N	NY-N
Bucky Walters	9	38	.474	3-6,2-3	A	
Charlie Wilson	16	62	.540	3-14	A	StL-N
Red Worthington	128	524	.736	LF-124	A	
Tom Zachary	33	229	3.10	P-33(11-15)	B	

Coaches: Johnny Evers, Hank Gowdy, Duffy Lewis

◆ 1932 BOSTON (155 77-77 5) ATT: 507,606

Name	G	AB/IP	P/E	G/POS	From	To
Bill McKechnie				M		
Bill Akers	36	105	.674	3-20,2-5,S-5	Det-A	C
Wally Berger	145	639	.815	CF-134,1-11	B	
Huck Betts	31	222	2.80	P-31(13-11)	Phi-N	
Ed Brandt	35	254	3.97	P-35(16-16)	B	
Bob Brown	35	213	3.30	P-35(14-7)	B	
Ben Cantwell	37	146	2.96	P-37(13-11)	B	
Earl Clark	50	47	.578	LF-16	B	
Bruce Cunningham	18	47	3.45	P-18(1-0)	B	C
Ox Eckhardt	8	8	.500	H	A	Bro-N
Hod Ford	40	106	.692	2-20,S-16,3-2	xStL-N	
Fred Frankhouse	40	109	3.56	P-37(4-6)	B	
Pinky Hargrave	82	244	.746	C-73	Was-A	
Dutch Holland	39	169	.743	LF-39	A	
Buck Jordan	49	219	.767	1-49	Was-A	
Fritz Knothe	89	388	.626	3-87	A	
Freddy Leach	84	244	.624	CF-50	NY-N	C
Leo Mangum	7	10	5.23	P-7	NY-N	
Rabbit Maranville	149	635	.579	2-149	B	
Randy Moore	107	372	.713	RF-41,3-31,1-22,C-1	B	
Hub Pruett	18	63	5.14	P-18(1-5)	NY-N	C
Wes Schulmerich	119	439	.735	RF-101	B	
Johnny Schulte	10	12	.919	C-10	xStL-A	C
Socks Seibold	28	137	4.68	P-28(3-10)	B	
Bill Sherdel	1	2	0.00	P-1	B	xStL-N
Art Shires	82	328	.638	1-80	Was-A	C
Al Spohrer	104	354	.616	C-100	B	
Billy Urbanski	136	614	.695	S-136	B	
Bucky Walters	22	83	.461	3-22	B	Bos-A
Red Worthington	105	460	.806	LF-104	B	
Tom Zachary	33	212	3.10	P-32(12-11)	B	

Coaches: Johnny Evers, Hank Gowdy, Duffy Lewis

◆ 1933 BOSTON (156 83-71 4) ATT: 517,803

Name	G	AB/IP	P/E	G/POS	From	To
Bill McKechnie				M		
Wally Berger	137	574	.932	CF-136	B	
Huck Betts	35	242	2.79	P-35(11-11)	B	
Ed Brandt	47	288	2.60	P-41(18-14)	B	
Bob Brown	6	7	2.70	P-5	B	

Name	G	AB/IP	P/E	G/POS	From	To
Ben Cantwell	49	255	2.62	P-40(20-10)	B	
Earl Clark	7	26	.791	LF-6	B	StL-A
Ed Fallenstein	11	35	3.60	P-9(2-1)	Phi-N	C
Hod Ford	5	18	.289	S-5	B	C
Fred Frankhouse	43	245	3.16	P-43(16-15)	B	
Dick Gyselman	58	166	.575	3-42,2-5,S-1	A	
Pinky Hargrave	45	80	.419	C-25	B	C
Shanty Hogan	96	347	.590	C-95	NY-N	
Dutch Holland	13	34	.678	LF-7	B	Cle-A
Buck Jordan	152	643	.713	1-150	B	
Fritz Knothe	44	176	.594	3-33,S-9	B	xPhi-N
Hal Lee	88	341	.602	LF-87	xPhi-N	
Leo Mangum	25	84	3.32	P-25(4-3)	B	
Rabbit Maranville	143	532	.539	2-142	B	
Randy Moore	135	548	.781	RF-122,1-10	B	
Joe Mowry	86	276	.567	LF-64	A	
Wes Schulmerich	29	91	.665	RF-21	B	xPhi-N
Socks Seibold	11	37	3.68	P-11(1-4)	B	C
Bob Smith	14	59	3.22	P-14(4-3)	xCin-N	
Al Spohrer	67	199	.602	C-65	B	
Ray Starr	9	28	3.86	P-9(0-1)	xNY-N	Cin-N
Tommy Thompson	24	102	.414	CF-24	A	
Billy Urbanski	144	618	.600	S-143	B	
Pinky Whitney	100	414	.660	3-85,2-18	xPhi-N	
Red Worthington	17	46	.418	RF-10	B	
Al Wright	4	1	2.000	2-3	A	C
Tom Zachary	27	125	3.53	P-26(7-9)	B	

Coaches: Hank Gowdy, Duffy Lewis

◆ 1934 BOSTON (152 78-73 4) ATT: 303,205

Name	G	AB/IP	P/E	G/POS	From	To
Bill McKechnie				M		
Dick Barrett	15	32	6.68	P-15(1-3)	Phi-A	Chi-N
Wally Berger	150	668	.899	CF-150	B	
Huck Betts	40	213	4.06	P-40(17-10)	B	
Ed Brandt	48	255	3.53	P-40(16-14)	B	
Bob Brown	16	58	5.71	P-16(1-3)	B	
Ben Cantwell	29	143	4.33	P-27(5-11)	B	
Jumbo Elliott	7	15	5.87	P-7(1-1)	xPhi-N	C
Elbie Fletcher	8	4	1.000	1-1	A	
Fred Frankhouse	37	234	3.20	P-37(17-9)	B	
Dick Gyselman	24	38	.461	3-15,2-2	B	C
Shanty Hogan	92	302	.653	C-90	B	
Buck Jordan	124	535	.771	1-117	B	
Hal Lee	139	574	.758	LF-128,2-4	B	
Les Mallon	42	188	.697	2-42	Phi-N	
Leo Mangum	29	94	5.72	P-29(5-3)	B	
Dan McGee	7	26	.376	S-7	A	C
Marty McManus	119	472	.702	2-73,3-37	Bos-A	C
Randy Moore	123	466	.740	RF-72,1-37	B	
Joe Mowry	25	83	.535	RF-20,2-1	B	
Clarence Pickrel	10	16	5.06	P-10	Phi-N	C
Flint Rhem	25	153	3.60	P-25(8-8)	xStL-N	
Bob Smith	42	122	4.66	P-39(6-9)	B	
Al Spohrer	100	280	.541	C-98	B	
Tommy Thompson	105	369	.618	RF-82	B	
Johnnie Tyler	3	6	.333	CF-1	A	
Billy Urbanski	146	677	.754	S-146	B	
Pinky Whitney	146	597	.671	3-111,2-36,S-2	B	
Red Worthington	41	72	.643	RF-11	B	xStL-N
Tom Zachary	5	24	3.38	P-5(1-2)	B	xBro-N

Coaches: Jewel Ens, Hank Gowdy, Duffy Lewis

◆ 1935 BOSTON (153 38-115 8) ATT: 232,754

Name	G	AB/IP	P/E	G/POS	From	To
Bill McKechnie				M		
Larry Benton	29	72	6.88	P-29(2-3)	Cin-N	C
Wally Berger	150	644	.903	CF-149	B	
Huck Betts	44	160	5.47	P-44(2-9)	B	C
Al Blanche	6	17	1.56	P-6	A	
Ed Brandt	31	175	5.00	P-29(5-19)	B	Bro-N
Bob Brown	16	65	6.37	P-15(1-8)	B	
Ben Cantwell	41	211	4.61	P-39(4-25)	B	
Joe Coscarart	86	305	.576	3-41,S-27,2-15	A	
Art Doll	3	10	.200	C-3	A	
Elbie Fletcher	39	157	.589	1-39	B	
Fred Frankhouse	40	231	4.76	P-40(11-15)	B	Bro-N
Shanty Hogan	59	188	.780	C-56	B	Was-A
Buck Jordan	130	491	.690	1-95,3-8,RF-2	B	
Hal Lee	112	445	.708	LF-110	B	
Bill Lewis	6	5	.200	C-1	StL-N	
Danny MacFayden	28	152	5.10	P-28(5-13)	xCin-N	
Les Mallon	116	448	.679	2-73,3-36,RF-1	B	C
Leo Mangum	3	5	3.86	P-3	B	C
Rabbit Maranville	23	71	.365	2-20	B	C
Randy Moore	125	435	.692	RF-78,1-21	B	Bro-N
Ed Moriarty	8	34	.853	2-8	A	
Joe Mowry	81	152	.685	LF-45	B	C
Ray Mueller	42	101	.621	C-40	A	
Flint Rhem	10	40	5.36	P-10(0-5)	B	StL-N
Babe Ruth	28	92	.789	LF-26	NY-A	C
Bob Smith	47	203	3.94	P-46(8-18)	B	
Al Spohrer	92	275	.562	C-90	B	C
Tommy Thompson	112	343	.697	RF-85	B	
Johnnie Tyler	13	53	.957	LF-11	B	C
Billy Urbanski	132	566	.572	S-129	B	
Pinky Whitney	126	491	.679	3-74,2-49	B	

Coaches: Hank Gowdy, Duffy Lewis

◆ 1936 BOSTON (157 71-83 6) ATT: 340,585

Name	G	AB/IP	P/E	G/POS	From	To
Bill McKechnie				M		
Johnny Babich	3	6	10.50	P-3	Bro-N	Phi-A
Ray Benge	21	115	5.79	P-21(7-9)	Bro-N	xPhi-N
Wally Berger	138	595	.844	CF-133	B	
Al Blanche	11	16	6.19	P-11(0-1)	B	C
Bob Brown	2	8	5.40	P-2(0-2)	B	C
Guy Bush	15	90	3.39	P-15(4-5)	xPit-N	

Name	G	AB/IP	P/E	G/POS	From	To
Ben Cantwell	35	133	3.04	P-34(9-9)	B	NY-N
Tiny Chaplin	40	232	4.12	P-40(10-15)	NY-N	C
Joe Coscarart	104	400	.594	3-97,S-6,2-1	B	C
Tony Cuccinello	150	641	.776	2-150	Bro-N	
Art Doll	1	8	3.38	P-1(0-1)	B	
Gene Ford	2	2	13.50	P-2	A	Chi-A
Mickey Haslin	36	109	.697	3-17,2-7	xPhi-N	NY-N
Buck Jordan	138	610	.781	1-136		C
Fabian Kowalik	2	9	8.00	P-1(0-1)	xPhi-N	C
Johnny Lanning	28	153	3.65	P-28(7-11)	A	
Swede Larsen	3	1	.000	2-2	A	C
Hal Lee	152	626	.655	LF-150	B	C
Bill Lewis	29	74	.758	C-21	B	C
Al Lopez	128	470	.654	C-127,1-1	Bro-N	
Danny MacFayden	37	267	2.87	P-37(17-13)	B	
Jim McCloskey	4	8	11.25	P-4	A	C
Gene Moore	151	691	.784	RF-151	StL-N	
Ed Moriarty	6	6	.333	H	B	C
Ray Mueller	24	77	.504	C-23	B	
Amby Murray	4	11	4.09	P-4	A	C
Wayne Osborne	5	20	5.85	P-5(1-1)	Pit-N	C
Andy Pilney	3	2	.000	H	A	C
Bobby Reis	37	139	4.48	P-35(6-5),CF-2	Bro-N	
Bob Smith	35	136	3.77	P-35(6-7)	B	
Tommy Thompson	106	304	.727	CF-39,1-25	B	Chi-A
Billy Urbanski	122	536	.626	S-80,3-38	B	
Rabbit Warstler	74	329	.496	S-74	xPhi-A	C
Ken Weafer	1	3	12.00	P-1	A	C
Roy Weir	13	57	2.83	P-12(4-3)	B	
Pinky Whitney	10	43	.408	3-10	B	xPhi-N

Coach: Hank Gowdy

♦ **1937 BOSTON** (152 79-73 5) ATT: 385,339

Name	G	AB/IP	P/E	G/POS	From	To
Bill McKechnie				M		
Wally Berger	30	126	.848	LF-28	B	xNY-N
Guy Bush	33	181	3.54	P-32(8-15)	B	StL-N
Tony Cuccinello	152	647	.746	2-151	B	
Vince DiMaggio	132	539	.699	CF-130	A	
Gil English	79	295	.694	3-71	xDet-A	
Lou Fette	36	259	2.88	P-35(20-10)	A	
Elbie Fletcher	148	605	.629	1-148	B	
Vic Frasier	3	8	5.63	P-3	Det-A	Chi-A
Frank Gabler	19	76	5.09	P-19(4-7)	xNY-N	
Debs Garms	125	521	.653	LF-81,3-36	StL-A	
Ira Hutchinson	31	92	3.73	P-31(4-6)	Chi-A	
Roy Johnson	85	299	.735	LF-63,3-1	xNY-A	
Buck Jordan	8	8	.500	H	B	xCin-N
Johnny Lanning	32	117	3.93	P-32(5-7)	B	
Al Lopez	105	378	.551	C-102	B	
Danny MacFayden	32	246	2.93	P-32(14-14)	B	
Eddie Mayo	65	199	.583	3-50	NY-N	
Beauty McGowan	9	13	.237	RF-2	StL-A	C
Gene Moore	148	631	.814	RF-148	B	
Ray Mueller	64	210	.670	C-57	B	
Bobby Reis	45	99	.646	CF-18,P-4,1-4	B	
Johnny Riddle	2	4	.250	C-2	xWas-A	
Milt Shoffner	6	43	2.53	P-6(3-1)	Cle-A	
Bob Smith	19	44	4.09	P-18(0-1)	B	C
Tommy Thevenow	21	39	.387	S-12,3-6,2-2	Cin-N	Pit-N
Jim Turner	39	257	2.38	P-33(20-11)	A	
Billy Urbanski	1	1	.000	H	B	C
Rabbit Warstler	149	630	.567	S-149	B	
Link Wasem	2	1	.000	C-2	A	C
Roy Weir	10	33	3.82	P-10(1-1)	B	

Coaches: Hank Gowdy, Mike Kelly

♦ **1938 BOSTON** (153 77-75 5) ATT: 341,149

Name	G	AB/IP	P/E	G/POS	From	To
Casey Stengel				M		
Mike Balas	1	1	6.75	P-1	A	C
Johnny Cooney	120	466	.660	RF-110,1-13	Bro-N	
Tony Cuccinello	147	616	.697	2-147	B	
Vince DiMaggio	150	611	.682	CF-149,2-1	B	Cin-N
Art Doll	3	4	2.25	P-3	B	C
Tom Earley	2	11	3.27	P-2(1-0)	A	
Gil English	53	182	.636	3-43,LF-3,2-2,S-2	A	Bro-N
Dick Errickson	34	123	3.15	P-34(9-7)	A	
Lou Fette	33	240	3.15	P-33(11-13)	B	
Elbie Fletcher	147	596	.729	1-146	B	
Frank Gabler	1	0	81.00	P-1	B	xChi-A
Debs Garms	117	474	.736	LF-63,3-54,2-1	B	
Jim Hitchcock	28	79	.363	S-24,3-2	A	C
Ira Hutchinson	36	151	2.74	P-36(9-8)	B	Bro-N
Roy Johnson	7	30	.372	LF-7	B	C
Bob Kahle	8	3	.667	H	A	C
Tom Kane	2	4	.500	2-2	A	C
Art Kenney	2	2	15.43	P-2	A	C
Johnny Lanning	32	138	3.72	P-32(8-7)	B	
Al Lopez	71	256	.619	C-71	B	
Danny MacFayden	29	220	2.95	P-29(14-9)	B	
Harl Maggert	66	99	.769	LF-10,3-8	A	C
Eddie Mayo	8	15	.695	3-6,S-2	B	Phi-A
Ralph McLeod	6	7	.714	LF-1	A	C
Gene Moore	54	198	.738	RF-47	B	Bro-N
Hiker Moran	1	3	0.00	P-1	A	
Ray Mueller	83	296	.636	C-75	B	Pit-N
Johnny Niggeling	2	2	9.00	P-2(1-0)	A	Cin-N
Bobby Reis	34	58	4.99	P-16(1-6),LF-10,S-3,C-1,2-1	B	C
Tommy Reis	4	6	7.11	P-4	xPhi-N	C
Johnny Riddle	19	61	.626	C-19	B	Cin-N
Milt Shoffner	27	140	3.54	P-26(8-7)	B	
Joe Stripp	59	245	.637	3-58	xStL-N	C
Butch Sutcliffe	4	6	.750	C-3	A	C
Jim Turner	35	268	3.46	P-35(14-18)	B	
Joe Walsh	4	8	.000	S-4	A	C
Rabbit Warstler	142	520	.573	S-135,2-7	B	
Roy Weir	5	13	6.75	P-5(1-0)	B	
Max West	123	459	.668	LF-109,1-7	A	

Coaches: Mike Kelly, George Kelly

♦ **1939 BOSTON** (152 63-88 7) ATT: 285,994

Name	G	AB/IP	P/E	G/POS	From	To
Casey Stengel				M		
Stan Andrews	13	27	.490	C-10	A	
Red Barkley	12	12	.083	S-7,3-4	StL-A	Bro-N
George Barnicle	6	18	4.91	P-6(2-2)	A	
Joe Callahan	4	17	3.12	P-4(1-0)	A	
Chet Clemens	9	24	.467	LF-7	A	
Johnny Cooney	118	402	.635	CF-116,1-2	B	
Tony Cuccinello	81	342	.747	2-80	B	
Tom Earley	14	40	4.72	P-14(1-4)	B	
Dick Errickson	28	128	4.00	P-28(6-9)	B	
Lou Fette	27	146	2.96	P-27(10-10)	B	
Elbie Fletcher	35	126	.629	1-31	B	xPit-N
Fred Frankhouse	23	38	2.61	P-23(0-2)	Bro-N	C
Debs Garms	132	566	.742	RF-96,3-37	B	Pit-N
Buddy Hassett	147	638	.696	1-123,RF-23	Bro-N	
Oliver Hill	2	2	1.500	H	A	C
Ralph Hodgin	32	51	.484	RF-9	A	Chi-A
Otto Huber	11	23	.591	2-4,3-4	A	C
Johnny Lanning	37	129	3.42	P-37(5-6)	B	Pit-N
Al Lopez	131	463	.688	C-129	B	
Danny MacFayden	33	192	3.90	P-33(8-14)	B	Pit-N
Hank Majeski	106	394	.689	3-99	A	
Phil Masi	46	124	.692	C-42	A	
Eddie Miller	77	324	.677	S-77	Cin-N	
Hiker Moran	6	20	4.50	P-6(1-1)	B	C
Jimmy Outlaw	65	144	.593	CF-39,3-2	Cin-N	Det-A
Bill Posedel	33	221	3.92	P-33(15-13)	Bro-N	
Chet Ross	11	33	.783	RF-8	A	
Bama Rowell	21	62	.488	CF-16	A	
Bill Schuster	2	3	.000	S-1,3-1	Pit-N	Chi-A
Milt Shoffner	25	132	3.13	P-25(4-6)	B	xCin-N
Al Simmons	93	358	.758	LF-82	Was-A	xCin-N
Sibby Sisti	63	232	.552	2-34,3-17,S-10	A	
Joe Sullivan	33	114	3.64	P-31(6-9)	Det-A	
Jim Turner	25	158	4.28	P-25(4-11)	B	Cin-N
Al Veigel	2	3	6.75	P-2(0-1)	A	C
Rabbit Warstler	114	370	.585	S-49,2-43,3-21	B	
Roy Weir	2	3	0.00	P-2	B	C
Max West	130	513	.861	RF-124	B	
Whitey Wietelmann	23	71	.443	S-22,2-1	A	

Coaches: Mike Kelly, George Kelly

♦ **1940 BOSTON** (152 65-87 7) ATT: 241,616

Name	G	AB/IP	P/E	G/POS	From	To
Casey Stengel				M		
Stan Andrews	19	33	.364	C-14	B	Bro-N
George Barnicle	13	33	7.44	P-13(1-0)	B	
Ray Berres	85	256	.469	C-85	xPit-N	
Sig Broskie	11	23	.623	C-11	A	C
Joe Callahan	6	15	10.20	P-6(0-2)	B	C
Dick Coffman	31	48	5.40	P-31(1-5)	NY-N	Phi-N
Johnny Cooney	108	404	.736	CF-99,1-7	B	
Tony Cuccinello	34	135	.660	3-33	B	xNY-N
Tom Earley	4	16	3.86	P-4(2-0)	B	
Dick Errickson	34	236	3.16	P-34(12-13)	B	
Lou Fette	7	32	5.57	P-7(0-5)	B	xBro-N
Al Glossop	60	165	.639	2-18,3-18,S-1	xNY-N	Phi-N
Buddy Gremp	4	10	.444	1-3	A	
Buddy Hassett	124	485	.566	1-98,RF-13	B	
Al Javery	29	83	5.51	P-29(2-4)	A	
Art Johnson	2	6	10.50	P-2(0-1)	A	
Frank LaManna	5	13	4.72	P-5(1-0)	A	
Bob Loane	13	25	.655	CF-10	Was-A	C
Al Lopez	36	126	.715	C-36	B	xPit-N
Hank Majeski	3	3	.000	H	B	
Don Manno	3	7	1.000	RF-2	A	
Phil Masi	63	152	.531	C-52	B	
Eddie Miller	151	617	.748	S-151	B	
Gene Moore	103	392	.743	RF-94	xBro-N	
Al Piechota	21	61	5.75	P-21(2-5)	B	
Bill Posedel	35	233	4.13	P-35(12-17)	B	
Mel Preibisch	11	43	.537	CF-11	A	
Chet Ross	149	632	.812	LF-149	B	
Bama Rowell	130	508	.726	2-115,RF-7	B	
Manny Salvo	21	161	3.08	P-21(10-9)	NY-N	
Les Scarsella	18	64	.760	1-15	Cin-N	C
Sibby Sisti	123	507	.664	3-102,2-16	B	
Nick Strincevich	33	129	5.53	P-32(4-8)	A	
Joe Sullivan	36	177	3.55	P-36(10-14)	B	
Bill Swift	4	9	2.89	P-4(1-1)	Pit-N	Bro-N
Jim Tobin	20	96	3.83	P-15(7-3)	Pit-N	
Rabbit Warstler	33	68	.539	2-24,3-2,S-1	B	xChi-N
Max West	139	590	.716	CF-102,1-36	B	
Whitey Wietelmann	35	46	.502	2-15,3-9,S-3	B	
Claude Wilborn	5	7	.000	RF-3	A	C
Ace Williams	5	9	16.00	P-5	A	

Coaches: Johnny Cooney, George Kelly

♦ **1941 BOSTON** (156 62-92 7) ATT: 263,680

Name	G	AB/IP	P/E	G/POS	From	To
Casey Stengel				M		
Earl Averill	8	19	.328	CF-4	Det-A	C
George Barnicle	1	7	6.75	P-1(0-1)	B	C
Ray Berres	120	302	.494	C-120	B	NY-N
Buster Bray	4	12	.348	CF-3	A	C
Eddie Carnett	2	1	20.25	P-2	A	Chi-A
Johnny Cooney	123	478	.743	CF-111,1-4	B	
Babe Dahlgren	44	183	.728	1-39,3-5	NY-A	xChi-N
Frank Demaree	48	127	.667	RF-28	xNY-N	
John Dudra	14	28	.989	2-5,3-5,3-5,1-1,S-1	A	C
Tom Earley	34	139	2.53	P-33(6-8)	B	

Name	G	AB/IP	P/E	G/POS	From	To
Dick Errickson	38	166	4.78	P-38(6-12)	B	
Wes Ferrell	4	14	5.14	P-4(2-1)	Bro-N	C
Buddy Gremp	37	83	.568	1-21,2-6,C-3	B	
Buddy Hassett	118	449	.699	1-99	B	NY-A
Johnny Hutchings	36	96	4.14	P-36(1-6)	xCin-N	
Al Javery	34	161	4.31	P-34(10-11)	B	
Art Johnson	44	183	3.53	P-43(7-15)	B	
Frank LaManna	47	73	5.33	P-35(5-4),CF-4	B	
Hank Majeski	19	56	.397	3-11	B	NY-A
Don Manno	22	33	.442	LF-5,3-3,1-1	B	C
Phil Masi	87	198	.625	C-83	B	
Eddie Miller	154	630	.614	S-154	B	
Al Montgomery	42	63	.534	C-30	A	C
Gene Moore	129	447	.742	RF-110	B	Was-A
Al Piechota	1	1	0.00	P-1	B	C
Bill Posedel	18	57	4.87	P-18(4-4)	B	
Mel Preibisch	5	5	.200	LF-2	B	C
Skippy Roberge	55	179	.507	2-46,3-5,S-2	A	
Chet Ross	29	59	.394	LF-12	B	
Bama Rowell	138	524	.705	2-112,LF-14,3-2	B	
Manny Salvo	35	195	4.06	P-35(7-16)	B	
Sibby Sisti	140	588	.628	3-137,2-2,S-2	B	
Nick Strincevich	3	3	10.80	P-3	B	xPit-N
Joe Sullivan	16	52	4.13	P-16(2-2)	B	xPit-N
Jim Tobin	43	238	3.10	P-33(12-12)	B	
Lloyd Waner	19	53	.865	CF-15	xPit-N	xCin-N
Paul Waner	95	341	.725	RF-77,1-7	xBro-N	
Max West	138	560	.798	LF-132	B	
Whitey Wietelmann	16	36	.209	2-10,S-5,3-2	B	

Coaches: Johnny Cooney, George Kelly

♦ 1942 BOSTON (150 59-89 7) ATT: 285,332

Name	G	AB/IP	P/E	G/POS	From	To
Casey Stengel				M		
Johnny Cooney	74	226	.527	RF-54,1-23	B	Bro-N
Tony Cuccinello	40	114	.525	3-20,2-14	NY-N	
Frank Demaree	64	208	.589	LF-49	B	StL-N
Ducky Detweiler	12	46	.757	3-12	A	
George Diehl	1	4	2.45	P-1	A	
Bill Donovan	31	89	3.43	P-31(3-6)	A	
Tom Earley	27	113	4.71	P-27(6-11)	B	
Dick Errickson	21	59	5.01	P-21(2-5)	B	xChi-N
Nanny Fernandez	145	620	.650	3-98,LF-44	A	
Buddy Gremp	72	222	.581	1-62,3-1	B	C
Jim Hickey	1	1	20.25	P-1(0-1)	A	
Tommy Holmes	141	633	.710	CF-140	A	
Johnny Hutchings	20	66	4.39	P-20(1-0)	B	
Al Javery	42	261	3.03	P-42(12-16)	B	
Art Johnson	4	6	1.42	P-4	B	C
Clyde Kluttz	72	220	.632	C-57	A	
Frank LaManna	10	7	5.40	P-5(0-1)	B	C
Ernie Lombardi	105	347	.886	C-85	Cin-N	NY-N
Phil Masi	57	99	.589	C-39,RF-4	B	
Frank McElyea	7	4	.000	LF-1	A	C
Eddie Miller	142	570	.616	S-142	B	Cin-N
Skippy Roberge	74	189	.531	2-29,3-27,S-6	B	
Chet Ross	76	237	.564	LF-57	B	
Johnny Sain	40	97	3.90	P-40(4-7)	A	
Manny Salvo	25	131	3.03	P-25(7-8)	B	
Mike Sandlock	2	1	2.000	S-2	A	
Sibby Sisti	129	469	.584	2-124,CF-1	B	
Warren Spahn	4	16	5.74	P-4	A	
Jim Tobin	47	288	3.97	P-37(12-21)	B	
Lou Tost	35	148	3.53	P-35(10-10)	A	
Lefty Wallace	19	49	3.83	P-19(1-3)	A	
Paul Waner	114	404	.701	RF-94	B	Bro-N
Max West	134	525	.764	1-85,LF-50	B	
Whitey Wietelmann	13	38	.554	S-11,2-1	B	

Coaches: Johnny Cooney, George Kelly

♦ 1943 BOSTON (153 68-85 6) ATT: 271,289

Name	G	AB/IP	P/E	G/POS	From	To
Bob Coleman				M(46 21-25 6)		
Casey Stengel				M(107 47-60 6)		
Nate Andrews	36	284	2.57	P-36(14-20)	Cle-A	
Red Barrett	38	255	3.18	P-38(12-18)	Cin-N	
Bill Brubaker	13	21	1.055	3-5,1-3	Pit-N	C
Joe Burns	52	148	.514	3-34,RF-4	A	Phi-A
Ben Cardoni	11	28	6.43	P-11	A	
Connie Creeden	5	5	.650	H	A	C
Tony Cuccinello	13	22	.136	3-4,2-2,S-1	B	xChi-A
John Dagenhard	2	11	0.00	P-2(1-0)	A	C
George Diehl	1	4	4.50	P-1	B	C
Bill Donovan	7	15	1.84	P-7(1-0)	B	C
Buck Etchison	10	21	.855	1-6	B	
Kerby Farrell	85	303	.632	1-69,P-5(0-1)	A	Chi-A
Sam Gentile	8	5	.900	H	A	C
Ben Geraghty	8	1	.000	2-1,S-1,3-1	Bro-N	
Heinie Heltzel	29	93	.401	3-29	A	Phi-N
Tommy Holmes	152	697	.712	CF-152	B	
Al Javery	41	303	3.21	P-41(17-16)	B	
George Jeffcoat	8	13	3.06	P-8(1-2)	Bro-N	C
Eddie Joost	124	496	.550	3-67,2-60,S-1	Cin-N	
Clyde Kluttz	66	227	.577	C-55	B	
Carl Lindquist	2	13	6.23	P-2(0-2)	A	
Danny MacFayden	10	21	5.91	P-10(2-1)	B	Was-A
Ray Martin	2	3	8.10	P-2	A	
Phil Masi	80	268	.692	C-73	B	
Johnny McCarthy	78	327	.765	1-78	NY-N	
Butch Nieman	101	375	.737	LF-93	A	
Dave Odom	22	55	5.27	P-22(0-3)	A	C
Hugh Poland	44	146	.455	C-38	xNY-N	
Chet Ross	94	313	.633	LF-73	B	
Connie Ryan	132	531	.550	2-100,3-30	NY-N	
Manny Salvo	1	5	7.20	P-1(0-1)	B	xPhi-N
Manny Salvo	20	94	3.27	P-20(5-6)	xPhi-N	C
Allyn Stout	9	9	6.75	P-9(1-0)	NY-N	C

Name	G	AB/IP	P/E	G/POS	From	To
Roy Talcott	1	1	27.00	P-1	A	C
Jim Tobin	46	250	2.66	P-33(14-14),1-1	B	
Lou Tost	3	7	5.40	P-3(0-1)	B	Pit-N
Whitey Wietelmann	153	591	.527	S-153	B	
Chuck Workman	153	679	.640	RF-149,1-3,3-1	Cle-A	

Coaches: Bob Coleman, George Kelly

♦ 1944 BOSTON (155 65-89 6) ATT: 208,691

Name	G	AB/IP	P/E	G/POS	From	To
Bob Coleman				M		
Nate Andrews	37	257	3.22	P-37(16-15)	B	
Red Barrett	42	230	4.06	P-42(9-16)	B	
Pat Capri	7	1	.000	2-1	A	C
Ben Cardoni	29	76	3.93	P-22(0-6)	B	
Chet Clemens	19	19	.616	LF-7	B	C
Dick Culler	8	32	.259	S-8	Chi-A	
Frank Drews	46	169	.613	2-46	A	
Buck Etchison	109	348	.637	1-85	B	C
Ben Geraghty	11	17	.544	2-4,3-3	B	C
Roland Gladu	21	70	.624	3-15,LF-3	A	C
Jim Hickey	8	9	4.82	P-8	B	C
Stew Hofferth	66	192	.507	C-47	A	
Tommy Holmes	155	705	.828	CF-155	B	
Warren Huston	33	64	.531	3-20,2-5,S-4	Phi-A	C
Johnny Hutchings	14	57	3.97	P-14(1-4)	B	
Ira Hutchinson	40	120	4.21	P-40(9-7)	StL-N	
Al Javery	40	254	3.54	P-40(10-19)	B	
Stan Klopp	24	46	4.27	P-24(1-2)	A	C
Clyde Kluttz	81	247	.694	C-58	B	
Carl Lindquist	5	9	3.12	P-5	B	C
Max Macon	106	380	.651	1-72,LF-22,P-1	Bro-N	
Harry MacPherson	1	1	0.00	P-1	A	C
Phil Masi	89	286	.757	C-63,1-12,3-2	B	
Butch Nieman	134	517	.759	LF-126	B	
Gene Patton	1	0	†	R	A	C
Damon Phillips	140	531	.630	3-90,S-60	Cin-N	
Hugh Poland	8	23	.304	C-6	B	
Woody Rich	7	25	5.76	P-7(1-1)	Bos-A	C
Chet Ross	54	168	.697	LF-38	B	
Connie Ryan	88	381	.780	2-80,3-14	B	
Mike Sandlock	30	37	.350	3-22,S-7	B	Bro-N
Steve Shemo	18	35	.667	2-16,3-2	A	
Jim Tobin	62	299	3.01	P-43(18-19)	B	
Whitey Wietelmann	125	463	.602	S-103,2-23,3-1	B	
George Woodend	3	2	13.50	P-3	A	C
Chuck Workman	140	473	.631	RF-103,3-19	B	
Ab Wright	71	216	.736	LF-47	Cle-A	C

Coaches: Benny Bengough, Tom Sheehan

♦ 1945 BOSTON (154 67-85 6) ATT: 374,178

Name	G	AB/IP	P/E	G/POS	From	To
Bob Coleman				M(94 42-51 7)		
Del Bissonette				M(60 25-34 6)		
Morrie Aderholt	31	111	.819	LF-24,2-1	xBro-N	C
Nate Andrews	22	138	4.58	P-21(7-12)	B	Cin-N
Red Barrett	9	38	4.74	P-9(2-3)	B	xStL-N
Ben Cardoni	3	4	9.00	P-3	B	C
Mort Cooper	20	78	3.35	P-20(7-4)	xStL-N	
Charlie Cozart	5	8	10.13	P-5(1-0)	A	C
Dick Culler	136	587	.628	S-126,3-6	B	
Frank Drews	49	169	.527	2-48	B	C
Tom Earley	13	41	4.61	P-11(2-1)	B	C
Lou Fette	5	11	5.73	P-5(0-2)	Bro-N	C
Carden Gillenwater	144	600	.755	CF-140	Bro-N	
Don Hendrickson	37	73	4.91	P-37(4-8)	A	
Joe Heving	3	5	3.38	P-3(1-0)	Cle-A	C
Stew Hofferth	50	185	.597	C-45	B	
Tommy Holmes	154	713	.997	RF-154	B	
Johnny Hutchings	57	185	3.75	P-57(7-6)	B	
Ira Hutchinson	11	29	5.02	P-11(2-3)	B	C
Al Javery	17	77	6.28	P-17(2-7)	B	
Eddie Joost	35	158	.624	2-19,3-16	B	Phi-A
Clyde Kluttz	25	84	.684	C-19	B	xNY-N
Bill Lee	16	106	2.79	P-16(6-3)	xPhi-N	
Bob Logan	34	187	3.18	P-34(7-11)	Cin-N	C
Joe Mack	66	303	.643	1-65	A	C
Phil Masi	114	420	.766	C-95,1-7	B	
Joe Medwick	66	231	.669	LF-38,1-15	xNY-N	Bro-N
Tommy Nelson	40	127	.374	3-20,2-12	A	C
Butch Nieman	97	291	.839	LF-57	B	C
Ewald Pyle	4	14	7.24	P-4(0-1)	xNY-N	C
Bill Ramsey	78	145	.699	LF-43	A	C
Hal Schacker	6	15	5.28	P-6(0-1)	A	C
Steve Shemo	17	47	.516	2-12,3-3,S-1	B	C
Vince Shupe	78	305	.609	1-77	A	C
Elmer Singleton	7	37	4.82	P-7(1-4)	A	
Jim Tobin	41	197	3.84	P-27(9-14)	B	xDet-A
Mike Ulisney	11	19	1.032	C-4	A	C
Lefty Wallace	6	20	4.50	P-5(1-0)	B	
Norm Wallen	4	16	.454	3-4	A	C
Stan Wentzel	4	19	.526	CF-4	A	
Bob Whitcher	9	16	2.87	P-6(0-2)	A	C
Whitey Wietelmann	123	471	.683	2-87,S-39,3-2,P-1	B	
Chuck Workman	139	580	.806	3-107,RF-24	B	
Ed Wright	15	111	2.51	P-15(8-3)	A	

Coaches: Benny Bengough, Del Bissonette

♦ 1946 BOSTON (154 81-72 4) ATT: 969,673

Name	G	AB/IP	P/E	G/POS	From	To
Billy Southworth				M		
Frank Barrett	23	35	5.09	P-23(2-4)	Bos-A	Pit-N
Johnny Barrett	24	55	.702	CF-17	xPit-N	C
Bob Brady	3	6	.533	C-1	A	
Mort Cooper	28	199	3.12	P-28(13-11)	B	
Dick Culler	134	553	.641	S-132	B	
Alvin Dark	15	13	.692	S-12,LF-1	A	
Ducky Detweiler	1	1	.000	H	B	C
Nanny Fernandez	115	413	.635	3-81,S-18,LF-14	B	

Name	G	AB/IP	P/E	G/POS	From	To
Carden Gillenwater	99	270	.637	CF-78	B	Was-A
Don Hendrickson	2	2	4.50	P-2(0-1)	B	C
Billy Herman	75	301	.849	2-44,1-22,3-5	xBro-N	Pit-N
Stew Hofferth	20	65	.505	C-15	B	
Tommy Holmes	149	642	.801	RF-146	B	
Johnny Hopp	129	492	.827	1-68,CF-58	StL-N	
Johnny Hutchings	1	3	9.00	P-1(0-1)	B	C
Al Javery	2	3	13.50	P-2(0-1)	B	C
Si Johnson	28	127	2.76	P-28(6-5)	xPhi-N	
Jim Konstanty	10	15	5.28	P-10(0-1)	Cin-N	Phi-N
Bill Lee	25	140	4.18	P-25(10-9)	B	Chi-N
Danny Litwhiler	79	275	.800	LF-65,3-2	xStL-N	
Phil Masi	133	462	.715	C-124	B	
Johnny McCarthy	2	9	.476	1-2	B	NY-N
Mike McCormick	59	177	.650	CF-48	xCin-N	
Dick Mulligan	4	15	2.35	P-4(1-0)	xPhi-N	
Tommy Neill	13	49	.609	LF-13	A	
Johnny Niggeling	8	58	3.26	P-8(2-5)	xWas-A	C
Ken O'Dea	12	41	.594	C-12	xStL-N	C
Don Padgett	44	104	.638	C-26	xBro-N	Phi-N
Damon Phillips	2	2	1.000	H	B	C
Hugh Poland	4	6	.500	C-2	B	Phi-N
Bill Posedel	19	28	6.99	P-19(2-0)	B	C
Earl Reid	2	3	3.00	P-2(1-0)	A	C
Skippy Roberge	48	181	.595	3-48	B	C
Steve Roser	14	35	3.60	P-14(1-1)	xNY-A	C
Bama Rowell	95	329	.737	LF-85	B	
Connie Ryan	143	568	.652	2-120,3-24	B	
Johnny Sain	40	265	2.21	P-37(20-14)	B	
Ray Sanders	80	314	.727	1-77	StL-N	
Elmer Singleton	16	34	3.74	P-15(0-1)	B	Pit-N
Sibby Sisti	1	0	†	3-1	B	
Warren Spahn	24	126	2.94	P-24(8-5)	B	
Lefty Wallace	27	75	4.18	P-27(3-3)	B	C
Max West	1	1	.000	1-1	B	xCin-N
Ernie White	14	24	4.18	P-12(0-1)	StL-N	
Whitey Wietelmann	44	92	.531	S-16,3-8,2-4,P-3	B	Pit-N
Ace Williams	1	0	0.00	P-1	B	C
Chuck Workman	25	53	.564	CF-12	B	xPit-N
Ed Wright	36	176	3.52	P-36(12-9)	B	

Coaches: Johnny Cooney, Jake Flowers, Bob Keely

◆ 1947 BOSTON (154 86-68 3) ATT: 1,277,361

Name	G	AB/IP	P/E	G/POS	From	To
Billy Southworth				M		
Red Barrett	36	211	3.55	P-36(11-12)	StL-N	
Johnny Beazley	9	29	4.40	P-9(2-0)	StL-N	
Bob Brady	1	1	.000	H	B	C
Hank Camelli	52	170	.560	C-51	Pit-N	C
Mort Cooper	10	47	4.05	P-10(2-5)	B	xNY-N
Dick Culler	77	241	.589	S-77	B	Chi-N
Glenn Elliott	11	19	4.74	P-11(0-1)	A	
Bob Elliott	150	645	.927	3-148	Pit-N	
Nanny Fernandez	83	237	.535	S-62,RF-8,3-6	B	Pit-N
Tommy Holmes	150	676	.776	RF-147	B	
Johnny Hopp	134	502	.734	CF-125	B	Pit-N
Si Johnson	36	113	4.23	P-36(6-8)	B	C
Andy Karl	27	35	3.86	P-27(2-3)	Phi-N	C
Walt Lanfranconi	37	64	2.95	P-36(4-4)	Chi-N	C
Johnny Lanning	3	4	9.82	P-3	Pit-N	C
Danny Litwhiler	91	254	.731	LF-66	B	
Max Macon	1	2	0.00	P-1	B	C
Ray Martin	1	9	1.00	P-1(1-0)	B	
Phil Masi	126	470	.820	C-123	B	
Frank McCormick	81	225	.871	1-46	xPhi-N	
Mike McCormick	92	315	.744	CF-79	B	
Dick Mulligan	1	2	9.00	P-1	B	C
Danny Murtaugh	3	9	.347	2-2,3-2	Phi-N	Pit-N
Tommy Neill	7	12	.733	LF-2	B	C
Bama Rowell	113	414	.696	LF-100,2-7,3-4	B	Phi-N
Connie Ryan	150	627	.722	2-150,S-1	B	
Johnny Sain	40	266	3.52	P-38(21-12)	B	
Clyde Shoun	26	74	4.40	P-26(5-3)	xCin-N	
Sibby Sisti	56	181	.744	S-51,2-1	B	
Warren Spahn	41	290	2.33	P-40(21-10)	B	
Earl Torgeson	128	484	.885	1-117	A	
Bill Voiselle	22	131	4.32	P-22(8-7)	xNY-N	
Ernie White	1	4	0.00	P-1	B	
Ed Wright	23	65	6.40	P-23(3-3)	B	

Coaches: Johnny Cooney, Bob Keely, Ernie White

◆ 1948 BOSTON (154 91-62 1) ATT: 1,455,439

Name	G	AB/IP	P/E	G/POS	From	To
Billy Southworth				M		
Johnny Antonelli	4	4	2.25	P-4	A	
Red Barrett	34	128	3.65	P-34(7-8)	B	
Johnny Beazley	3	16	4.50	P-3(0-1)	B	
Vern Bickford	33	146	3.27	P-33(11-5)	A	
Paul Burris	2	4	1.000	C-2	A	
Clint Conatser	90	259	.754	CF-76	A	
Alvin Dark	137	579	.786	S-133	B	
Glenn Elliott	1	3	3.00	P-1(1-0)	B	
Bob Elliott	151	675	.897	3-150	B	
Jeff Heath	115	419	.986	LF-106	StL-A	
Bobby Hogue	40	86	3.23	P-40(8-2)	A	
Tommy Holmes	139	639	.814	RF-137	B	
Danny Litwhiler	13	40	.718	LF-8	B	xCin-N
Al Lyons	16	13	7.82	P-7(1-0),RF-4	Pit-N	C
Ray Martin	2	2	0.00	P-2	B	C
Phil Masi	113	423	.661	C-109	B	
Frank McCormick	75	194	.678	1-50	B	C
Mike McCormick	115	383	.780	LF-100	B	Bro-N
Nels Potter	18	85	2.33	P-18(5-2)	xPhi-A	
Jim Prendergast	10	17	10.26	P-10(1-1)	A	C
Marv Rickert	3	14	.670	LF-3	xCin-N	
Jim Russell	89	374	.771	CF-84	Pit-N	
Connie Ryan	51	148	.571	2-40,3-4	B	

Name	G	AB/IP	P/E	G/POS	From	To
Johnny Sain	43	315	2.60	P-42(24-15)	B	
Bill Salkeld	78	250	.792	C-59	Pit-N	
Ray Sanders	5	5	.650	H	B	
Clyde Shoun	36	74	4.01	P-36(5-1)	B	
Sibby Sisti	83	261	.630	2-44,S-26	B	
Warren Spahn	37	257	3.71	P-36(15-12)	B	
Eddie Stanky	67	312	.872	2-66	Bro-N	
Bobby Sturgeon	34	82	.538	2-18,S-4,3-4	Chi-N	C
Earl Torgeson	134	531	.770	1-129	B	
Bill Voiselle	37	216	3.63	P-37(13-13)	B	
Ernie White	16	23	1.96	P-15(0-2)	B	C
Ed Wright	3	5	1.93	P-3	B	Phi-A

Coaches: Johnny Cooney, Freddie Fitzsimmons, Bob Keely, Ernie White

◆ 1949 BOSTON (157 75-79 4) ATT: 1,081,795

Name	G	AB/IP	P/E	G/POS	From	To
Billy Southworth				M(111 55-54 4)		
Johnny Cooney				M(46 20-25 4)		
Johnny Antonelli	22	96	3.56	P-22(3-7)	B	
Red Barrett	23	44	5.68	P-23(1-1)	B	C
Johnny Beazley	1	2	0.00	P-1	B	C
Vern Bickford	37	231	4.25	P-37(16-11)	B	
Clint Conatser	53	167	.687	RF-44	B	C
Del Crandall	67	239	.660	C-63	A	
Alvin Dark	130	572	.673	S-125,3-4	B	NY-N
Glenn Elliott	22	68	3.95	P-22(3-4)	B	C
Bob Elliott	139	578	.862	3-130	B	
Elbie Fletcher	122	518	.798	1-121	Pit-N	C
Bob Hall	31	74	4.36	P-31(6-4)	A	
Jeff Heath	36	126	1.002	LF-31	B	C
Bobby Hogue	33	72	3.13	P-33(2-2)	B	
Tommy Holmes	117	425	.740	RF-103	B	
Steve Kuczek	1	1	3.000	H	A	C
Al Lakeman	3	7	.452	1-2	Phi-N	Det-A
Mickey Livingston	28	69	.587	C-22	xNY-N	Bro-N
Phil Masi	37	120	.531	C-37	B	xPit-N
Nels Potter	41	97	4.19	P-41(6-11)	B	C
Pete Reiser	84	258	.812	CF-63,3-4	Bro-N	
Marv Rickert	100	301	.791	LF-75,1-12	B	Pit-N
Jim Russell	130	486	.684	CF-120	B	Bro-N
Connie Ryan	85	233	.727	3-25,S-18,2-16,1-3	B	
Johnny Sain	39	243	4.81	P-37(10-17)	B	
Bill Salkeld	66	209	.796	C-63	B	Chi-A
Ray Sanders	9	25	.470	1-7	B	C
Ed Sauer	79	234	.688	LF-71	xStL-N	C
Clyde Shoun	1	1	0.00	P-1	B	xChi-A
Sibby Sisti	101	311	.701	LF-48,2-21,S-18,3-1	B	
Warren Spahn	40	302	3.07	P-38(21-14)	B	
Eddie Stanky	138	628	.775	2-135	B	NY-N
Don Thompson	7	11	.364	RF-2	A	Bro-N
Earl Torgeson	25	113	.795	1-25	B	
Bill Voiselle	30	169	4.04	P-30(7-8)	B	Chi-N

Coaches: Jimmy Brown, Johnny Cooney, Bob Keely

◆ 1950 BOSTON (156 83-71 4) ATT: 944,391

Name	G	AB/IP	P/E	G/POS	From	To
Billy Southworth				M		
Bob Addis	16	31	.608	RF-7	A	
Johnny Antonelli	20	58	5.93	P-20(2-3)	B	
Vern Bickford	40	312	3.47	P-40(19-14)	B	
Paul Burris	10	25	.426	C-8	B	
Bob Chipman	27	124	4.43	P-27(7-7)	Chi-N	
Dave Cole	4	8	1.13	P-4(0-1)	A	
Walker Cooper	102	373	.917	C-88	xCin-N	
Del Crandall	79	274	.567	C-75,1-1	B	
Dick Donovan	10	30	8.19	P-10(0-2)	A	
Bob Elliott	142	602	.898	3-137	B	
Sid Gordon	134	562	.960	LF-123,3-10	NY-N	
Mickey Haefner	8	24	5.63	P-8(0-2)	xChi-A	C
Bob Hall	21	50	6.97	P-21(0-2)	B	Pit-N
Roy Hartsfield	107	450	.694	2-96	A	
Bobby Hogue	36	63	5.03	P-36(3-5)	B	
Tommy Holmes	105	363	.821	RF-88	B	
Sam Jethroe	141	642	.780	CF-141	A	
Ernie Johnson	16	21	6.97	P-16(2-0)	A	
Buddy Kerr	155	571	.606	S-155	NY-N	
Walt Linden	3	6	1.100	C-3	A	C
Dick Manville	1	2	0.00	P-1	A	Chi-N
Willard Marshall	105	336	.652	RF-85	NY-N	
Gene Mauch	48	137	.614	2-28,3-7,S-5	Chi-N	
Luis Olmo	69	173	.691	RF-55,3-1	Bro-N	
Pete Reiser	53	98	.637	LF-24,3-1	B	Pit-N
Normie Roy	19	60	5.13	P-19(4-3)	A	C
Connie Ryan	20	87	.673	2-20	B	xCin-N
Johnny Sain	37	278	3.94	P-37(20-13)	B	
Sibby Sisti	69	123	.563	S-23,2-19,3-13,1-1,RF-1	B	
Warren Spahn	41	293	3.16	P-41(21-17)	B	
Max Surkont	9	56	3.23	P-9(5-2)	Chi-A	
Earl Torgeson	156	704	.885	1-156	B	
Emil Verban	4	5	.000	2-2	xChi-N	C
Murray Wall	1	4	9.00	P-1	A	Bos-A
Bucky Walters	1	4	4.50	P-1	Cin-N	C

Coaches: Jimmy Brown, Johnny Cooney, Bob Keely, Bucky Walters

◆ 1951 BOSTON (155 76-78 4) ATT: 487,475

Name	G	AB/IP	P/E	G/POS	From	To
Billy Southworth				M(60 28-31 5)		
Tommy Holmes				M(95 48-47 4)		
Bob Addis	85	211	.634	LF-46	B	Chi-N
Vern Bickford	25	165	3.12	P-25(11-9)	B	
Lew Burdette	3	4	6.23	P-3	NY-A	
Bob Chipman	33	52	4.85	P-33(4-3)	B	
Dave Cole	23	68	4.26	P-23(2-4)	B	
Walker Cooper	109	372	.884	C-90	B	
Blix Donnelly	6	7	7.36	P-6(0-1)	Phi-N	C
Dick Donovan	8	14	5.27	P-8	B	
Bob Elliott	136	547	.819	3-127	B	NY-N
George Estock	37	60	4.33	P-37(0-1)	A	C

Name	G	AB/IP	P/E	G/POS	From	To
Sid Gordon	150	641	.883	LF-122,3-34	B	
Roy Hartsfield	120	497	.678	2-114	B	
Bobby Hogue	3	5	5.40	P-3	B	xStL-A
Tommy Holmes	27	32	.491	LF-3	B	Bro-N
Sam Jethroe	148	644	.816	CF-140	B	
Buddy Kerr	69	200	.509	S-63,2-5	B	C
Johnny Logan	62	193	.570	S-58	A	
Luis Marquez	68	138	.528	CF-43	A	Chi-N
Willard Marshall	136	523	.784	RF-136	B	
Gene Mauch	19	28	.433	S-10,3-3,2-2	B	StL-N
Ray Mueller	28	79	.462	C-23	Pit-N	C
Chet Nichols	33	156	2.88	P-33(11-8)	A	
Luis Olmo	21	60	.500	LF-16	B	C
Phil Paine	21	35	3.06	P-21(2-0)	A	
Johnny Sain	26	160	4.21	P-26(5-13)	B	xNY-A
Ebba St.Claire	72	233	.713	C-62	A	
Sid Schacht	5	5	1.93	P-5(0-2)	xStL-A	C
Sibby Sisti	114	399	.703	S-55,2-52,3-6,1-1,RF-1	B	
Warren Spahn	42	311	2.98	P-39(22-14)	B	
Max Surkont	37	237	3.99	P-37(12-16)	B	
Bob Thorpe	2	2	2.000	H	A	
Earl Torgeson	155	690	.812	1-155	B	
Jim Wilson	20	110	5.40	P-20(7-7)	Phi-A	

Coaches: Jimmy Brown, Johnny Cooney, Bob Keely, Bucky Walters

◆ 1952 BOSTON (155 64-89 7) ATT: 281,278

Name	G	AB/IP	P/E	G/POS	From	To
Tommy Holmes				M(35 13-22 7)		
Charlie Grimm				M(120 51-67 7)		
Vern Bickford	26	161	3.74	P-26(7-12)	B	
Lew Burdette	45	137	3.61	P-45(6-11)	B	
Paul Burris	55	178	.535	C-50	B	
Bob Chipman	29	42	2.81	P-29(1-1)	B	C
Buzz Clarkson	14	28	.486	S-6,3-2	A	C
Dave Cole	22	45	4.03	P-22(1-1)	B	
Gene Conley	4	13	7.82	P-4(0-3)	A	
Walker Cooper	102	375	.643	C-89	B	
George Crowe	73	240	.712	1-55	A	
Jack Cusick	49	84	.406	S-28,3-3	Chi-N	C
Jack Daniels	106	256	.535	RF-87	A	C
Jack Dittmer	93	355	.546	2-90	A	
Dick Donovan	7	13	5.54	P-7(0-2)	B	Det-A
Sid Gordon	144	606	.866	LF-142,3-2	B	
Roy Hartsfield	38	116	.650	2-29	B	C
Dick Hoover	2	5	7.71	P-2	A	C
Virgil Jester	19	73	3.33	P-19(3-5)	A	
Sam Jethroe	151	688	.675	CF-151	B	Pit-N
Ernie Johnson	29	92	4.11	P-29(6-3)	B	
Sheldon Jones	39	70	4.76	P-39(1-4)	NY-N	Chi-N
Billy Klaus	7	5	.200	S-4	A	
Johnny Logan	117	500	.702	S-117	B	
Willard Marshall	21	70	.681	RF-16	B	xCin-N
Eddie Mathews	145	593	.767	3-142	A	
Billy Reed	15	55	.514	2-14	A	C
Ebba St.Claire	39	117	.554	C-34	B	
Sibby Sisti	90	269	.565	2-33,RF-23,S-18,3-9	B	
Warren Spahn	52	290	2.98	P-40(14-19)	B	
Max Surkont	31	215	3.77	P-31(12-13)	B	
Bert Thiel	4	7	7.71	P-4(1-1)	A	C
Bob Thorpe	81	302	.607	RF-72	B	
Earl Torgeson	122	471	.681	1-105,RF-5	B	Phi-N
Pete Whisenant	24	56	.481	LF-14	A	StL-N
Jim Wilson	33	234	4.23	P-33(12-14)	B	

Coaches: Johnny Cooney, Bob Keely, Bucky Walters

◆ 1953 MILWAUKEE (157 92-62 2) ATT: 1,826,397

Name	G	AB/IP	P/E	G/POS	From	To
Charlie Grimm				M		
Joe Adcock	157	640	.787	1-157	Cin-N	
Johnny Antonelli	31	175	3.18	P-31(12-12)	B	NY-N
Vern Bickford	20	58	5.28	P-20(2-5)	B	Bal-A
Bill Bruton	151	668	.636	CF-150	A	
Bob Buhl	30	154	2.97	P-30(13-8)	A	
Lew Burdette	46	175	3.24	P-46(15-5)	B	
Paul Burris	2	1	.000	C-2	B	C
Dave Cole	10	15	8.59	P-10(0-1)	B	Chi-N
Walker Cooper	53	151	.615	C-35	B	Pit-N
Del Crandall	116	420	.759	C-108	B	
George Crowe	47	45	.810	1-9	B	
Jack Dittmer	138	525	.660	2-138	B	
Sid Gordon	140	541	.834	LF-137	B	Pit-N
Harry Hanebrink	51	87	.603	2-21,3-1	A	
Joey Jay	3	10	0.00	P-3(1-0)	A	
Virgil Jester	2	2	22.50	P-2	B	C
Ernie Johnson	36	81	2.67	P-36(4-3)	B	
Dave Jolly	24	38	3.52	P-24(0-1)	A	
Billy Klaus	2	2	.000	H	B	Bos-A
Don Liddle	31	129	3.08	P-31(7-6)	A	NY-N
Johnny Logan	150	668	.724	S-150	B	
Eddie Mathews	157	681	1.033	3-157	B	
Andy Pafko	140	568	.803	RF-139	Bro-N	
Jim Pendleton	120	261	.785	LF-105,S-7	A	
Mel Roach	5	2	.000	2-1	A	
Ebba St.Claire	33	83	.541	C-27	B	NY-N
Sibby Sisti	38	28	.618	2-13,S-6,3-4	B	
Warren Spahn	38	266	2.10	P-35(23-7)	B	
Max Surkont	28	170	4.18	P-28(11-5)	B	Pit-N
Bob Thorpe	27	39	.373	LF-18	B	C
Jim Wilson	20	114	4.34	P-20(4-9)	B	

Coaches: Johnny Cooney, Bob Keely, Bucky Walters

◆ 1954 MILWAUKEE (154 89-65 3) ATT: 2,131,388

Name	G	AB/IP	P/E	G/POS	From	To
Charlie Grimm				M		
Hank Aaron	122	509	.771	LF-116	A	
Joe Adcock	133	562	.887	1-133	B	
Bill Bruton	142	619	.701	CF-141	B	
Bob Buhl	31	110	4.00	P-31(2-7)	B	
Lew Burdette	39	238	2.76	P-38(15-14)	B	
Sam Calderone	22	34	.903	C-16	NY-N	C
Gene Conley	28	194	2.96	P-28(14-9)	B	
Del Crandall	138	514	.732	C-136	B	
Ray Crone	19	49	2.02	P-19(1-0)	A	
Jack Dittmer	66	219	.703	2-55	B	
Charlie Gorin	5	10	1.86	P-5(0-1)	A	
Joey Jay	15	18	6.50	P-15(1-0)	B	
Ernie Johnson	40	99	2.81	P-40(5-2)	B	
Dave Jolly	48	111	2.43	P-47(11-6)	B	
Dave Koslo	12	17	3.12	P-12(1-1)	xBal-A	
Johnny Logan	154	638	.715	S-154	B	
Eddie Mathews	138	601	1.031	3-127,LF-10	B	
Catfish Metkovich	68	142	.717	1-18,RF-13	Chi-N	C
Chet Nichols	35	144	4.41	P-35(9-11)	B	
Danny O'Connell	146	604	.685	2-103,3-35,1-8,S-1	Pit-N	
Andy Pafko	138	570	.767	RF-138	B	
Phil Paine	11	14	3.86	P-11(1-0)	B	
Jim Pendleton	71	179	.503	LF-50	B	
Billy Queen	3	2	.000	RF-1	A	C
Mel Roach	3	4	.000	1-1	B	
Sibby Sisti	9	0	†	R	B	C
Roy Smalley	25	42	.623	S-9,2-7,1-2	Chi-N	Phi-N
Warren Spahn	41	283	3.14	P-39(21-12)	B	
Bobby Thomson	43	113	.639	LF-26	NY-N	
Charlie White	50	102	.616	C-28	A	
Jim Wilson	27	128	3.52	P-27(8-2)	B	Bal-A

Coaches: Johnny Cooney, Bob Keely, Sibby Sisti, Bucky Walters

◆ 1955 MILWAUKEE (154 85-69 2) ATT: 2,005,836

Name	G	AB/IP	P/E	G/POS	From	To
Charlie Grimm				M		
Hank Aaron	153	665	.908	RF-126,2-27	B	
Joe Adcock	84	324	.808	1-78	B	
Bill Bruton	149	685	.728	CF-149	B	
Bob Buhl	38	202	3.21	P-38(13-11)	B	
Lew Burdette	45	230	4.03	P-42(13-8)	B	
Gene Conley	22	158	4.16	P-22(11-7)	B	
Del Crandall	133	494	.760	C-131	B	
Ray Crone	33	140	3.46	P-33(10-9)	B	
George Crowe	104	354	.870	1-79	B	Cin-N
Jack Dittmer	38	77	.379	2-28	B	
John Edelman	5	6	11.12	P-5	A	C
Charlie Gorin	2	0	54.00	P-2	B	C
Joey Jay	12	19	4.74	P-12	B	
Ernie Johnson	40	92	3.42	P-40(5-7)	B	
Dave Jolly	36	58	5.71	P-36(2-3)	B	
Dave Koslo	1	0	/	P-1(0-1)	B	C
Johnny Logan	154	680	.806	S-154	B	
Eddie Mathews	141	616	1.018	3-137	B	
Chet Nichols	34	144	4.00	P-34(9-8)	B	
Danny O'Connell	124	491	.593	2-114,3-7,S-1	B	
Andy Pafko	86	267	.674	RF-58,3-12	B	
Phil Paine	15	25	2.49	P-15(2-0)	B	
Jim Pendleton	8	10	.000	S-1,3-1,CF-1	B	
Del Rice	27	78	.570	C-22	xStL-N	
Humberto Robinson	13	38	3.08	P-13(3-1)	A	
Bob Roselli	6	11	.697	C-2	A	
Warren Spahn	40	246	3.26	P-39(17-14)	B	
Chuck Tanner	97	275	.705	LF-62	A	
Ben Taylor	12	12	.350	1-1	Det-A	C
Bobby Thomson	101	383	.738	LF-91	B	
Roberto Vargas	25	25	8.76	P-25	A	C
Charlie White	12	36	.628	C-10	B	C

Coaches: Johnny Cooney, Bob Keely, Bucky Walters

◆ 1956 MILWAUKEE (155 92-62 2) ATT: 2,046,331

Name	G	AB/IP	P/E	G/POS	From	To
Charlie Grimm				M(46 24-22 5)		
Fred Haney				M(109 68-40 2)		
Hank Aaron	153	660	.927	RF-152	B	
Joe Adcock	137	500	.936	1-129	B	
Toby Atwell	15	34	.665	C-10	xPit-N	C
Bill Bruton	147	578	.727	CF-145	B	
Bob Buhl	38	217	3.32	P-38(18-8)	B	
Lew Burdette	45	256	2.70	P-39(19-10)	B	
Gene Conley	31	158	3.13	P-31(8-9)	B	
Wes Covington	75	157	.716	LF-35	A	
Del Crandall	112	358	.767	C-109	B	
Ray Crone	35	170	3.87	P-35(11-10)	B	
Jack Dittmer	44	112	.614	2-42	B	Det-A
Earl Hersh	7	13	.692	LF-2	A	C
Ernie Johnson	36	51	3.71	P-36(4-3)	B	
Dave Jolly	29	46	3.74	P-29(2-3)	B	
Johnny Logan	148	631	.773	S-148	B	
Felix Mantilla	35	56	.649	S-15,3-3	A	
Eddie Mathews	151	651	.894	3-150	B	
Red Murff	14	24	4.44	P-14	A	
Chet Nichols	2	4	6.75	P-2(0-1)	B	Bos-A
Danny O'Connell	139	598	.666	2-138,3-4,S-1	B	
Andy Pafko	45	104	.706	LF-37	B	
Phil Paine	1	0	/	P-1	B	
Jim Pendleton	14	12	.083	S-3,3-2,1-1,2-1	B	Pit-N
Taylor Phillips	23	88	2.26	P-23(5-3)	A	
Del Rice	71	208	.601	C-65	B	
Humberto Robinson	1	2	0.00	P-1	B	
Bob Roselli	4	2	2.500	C-3	B	
Lou Sleater	25	46	3.15	P-25(2-2)	KC-A	Det-A
Warren Spahn	39	281	2.78	P-39(20-11)	B	
Chuck Tanner	60	73	.660	LF-8	B	
Bobby Thomson	142	505	.712	LF-136,3-3	B	
Frank Torre	111	175	.601	1-89	A	
Bob Trowbridge	19	51	2.66	P-19(3-2)	A	

Coaches: Fred Haney, Bob Keely, Johnny Riddle, Charlie Root

◆ 1957 MILWAUKEE (155 95-59 1) ATT: 2,215,404

Name	G	AB/IP	P/E	G/POS	From	To
Fred Haney				M		
Hank Aaron	151	675	.979	RF-150	B	
Joe Adcock	65	231	.893	1-56	B	
Bill Bruton	79	332	.760	CF-79	B	
Bob Buhl	34	217	2.74	P-34(18-7)	B	
Lew Burdette	41	257	3.72	P-37(17-9)	B	
Dick Cole	15	19	.307	2-10,1-1,3-1	Pit-N	C
Gene Conley	35	148	3.16	P-35(9-9)	B	
Wes Covington	96	371	.882	LF-89	B	
Del Crandall	118	420	.719	C-102,RF-9,1-1	B	
Ray Crone	11	42	4.46	P-11(3-1)	B	xNY-N
John DeMerit	33	34	.294	CF-13	A	
Harry Hanebrink	6	8	.661	3-2	B	
Bob Hazle	41	155	1.126	RF-40	Cin-N	
Joey Jay	1	1	0.00	P-1	B	
Ernie Johnson	30	65	3.88	P-30(7-3)	B	
Dave Jolly	23	38	5.02	P-23(1-1)	B	C
Nippy Jones	30	83	.685	1-20,RF-1	Phi-N	C
Johnny Logan	129	541	.722	S-129	B	
Bobby Malkmus	13	25	.382	2-7	A	Was-A
Felix Mantilla	71	200	.661	S-35,2-13,3-7,CF-1	B	
Eddie Mathews	148	666	.928	3-147	B	
Don McMahon	32	47	1.54	P-32(2-3)	A	
Red Murff	12	26	4.85	P-12(2-2)	B	C
Danny O'Connell	48	207	.625	2-48	B	xNY-N
Andy Pafko	83	235	.734	RF-69	B	
Phil Paine	1	2	0.00	P-1	B	StL-N
Taylor Phillips	27	73	5.55	P-27(3-2)	B	Chi-N
Juan Pizarro	25	99	4.62	P-24(5-6)	A	
Del Rice	54	163	.748	C-48	B	
Mel Roach	7	7	.333	2-5	B	
Carl Sawatski	58	118	.764	C-28	Chi-A	
Red Schoendienst	93	426	.783	2-92,CF-2	xNY-N	
Ray Shearer	2	3	1.167	LF-1	A	C
Warren Spahn	39	271	2.69	P-39(21-11)	B	
Chuck Tanner	22	74	.674	LF-18	B	xChi-A
Hawk Taylor	7	1	.000	C-1	A	
Bobby Thomson	41	160	.677	LF-38	B	xNY-N
Frank Torre	129	411	.734	1-117	B	
Bob Trowbridge	32	126	3.64	P-32(7-5)	B	

Coaches: Bob Keely, Johnny Riddle, Charlie Root, Connie Ryan

◆ 1958 MILWAUKEE (154 92-62 1) ATT: 1,971,101

Name	G	AB/IP	P/E	G/POS	From	To
Fred Haney				M		
Hank Aaron	153	664	.933	RF-153	B	
Joe Adcock	105	349	.828	1-71,LF-22	B	
Bill Bruton	100	361	.699	CF-96	B	
Bob Buhl	11	73	3.45	P-11(5-2)	B	
Lew Burdette	47	275	2.91	P-40(20-10)	B	
Gene Conley	26	72	4.88	P-26(0-6)	B	Phi-N
Wes Covington	90	324	1.005	LF-82	B	
Del Crandall	131	485	.807	C-124	B	
John DeMerit	3	3	1.333	CF-2	B	
Eddie Haas	9	16	.795	CF-3	Chi-N	
Harry Hanebrink	63	150	.571	LF-33,3-7	B	Phi-N
Bob Hazle	20	66	.482	RF-20	B	xDet-A
Joey Jay	18	97	2.14	P-18(7-5)	B	
Ernie Johnson	15	23	8.10	P-15(3-1)	B	Bal-A
Joe Koppe	16	10	.944	S-3	A	Phi-N
Dick Littlefield	4	6	4.26	P-4(0-1)	Chi-N	C
Johnny Logan	145	590	.613	S-144	B	
Felix Mantilla	85	252	.630	CF-43,2-21,S-5,3-2	B	
Eddie Mathews	149	649	.812	3-149	B	
Don McMahon	38	59	3.68	P-38(7-2)	B	
Andy Pafko	95	185	.657	LF-93	B	
Juan Pizarro	16	97	2.70	P-16(6-4)	B	
Del Rice	43	132	.577	C-38	B	
Mel Roach	44	147	.764	2-27,LF-7,1-1	B	
Humberto Robinson	19	42	3.02	P-19(2-4)	B	Cle-A
Bob Roselli	1	1	.000	H	B	Chi-N
Bob Rush	28	147	3.42	P-28(10-6)	Chi-N	
Carl Sawatski	10	13	.350	C-3	B	xPhi-N
Red Schoendienst	106	465	.642	2-105	B	
Warren Spahn	41	290	3.07	P-38(22-11)	B	
Hawk Taylor	4	8	.375	LF-4	B	
Frank Torre	138	430	.833	1-122	B	
Bob Trowbridge	27	55	3.93	P-27(1-3)	B	
Carl Willey	23	140	2.70	P-23(9-7)	A	
Casey Wise	31	76	.451	2-10,S-7,3-1	Chi-N	

Coaches: John Fitzpatrick, Billy Herman, George Susce, Whit Wyatt

◆ 1959 MILWAUKEE (157 86-70 2) ATT: 1,749,112

Name	G	AB/IP	P/E	G/POS	From	To
Fred Haney				M		
Hank Aaron	154	693	1.042	RF-152,3-5	B	
Joe Adcock	115	444	.879	1-89,LF-21	B	
Bobby Avila	51	204	.663	2-51	xBos-A	C
Ray Boone	13	20	.768	1-3	xKC-A	
Bill Bruton	133	522	.736	CF-133	B	
Bob Buhl	31	198	2.86	P-31(15-9)	B	
Lew Burdette	52	290	4.07	P-41(21-15)	B	
Chuck Cottier	10	28	.389	2-10	A	
Wes Covington	103	405	.728	LF-94	B	
Del Crandall	150	581	.744	C-146	B	
John DeMerit	11	6	.533	LF-4	B	
Bob Giggie	13	20	4.05	P-13(1-0)	A	
Bob Hartman	3	2	27.00	P-3	A	Cle-A
Joey Jay	34	136	4.09	P-34(6-11)	B	
Johnny Logan	138	540	.782	S-138	B	
Stan Lopata	25	51	.261	C-11,1-2	Phi-N	
Felix Mantilla	103	274	.539	2-60,S-23,3-9,CF-7	B	
Eddie Mathews	148	682	.984	3-148	B	
Lee Maye	51	150	.774	LF-44	A	
Don McMahon	60	81	2.57	P-60(5-3)	B	
Joe Morgan	13	26	.541	2-7	A	xKC-A
Johnny O'Brien	44	133	.532	2-37	StL-N	C
Andy Pafko	71	158	.617	LF-64	B	C
Jim Pisoni	9	26	.439	CF-9	KC-A	xNY-A
Juan Pizarro	29	134	3.77	P-29(6-2)	B	
Del Rice	13	32	.465	C-9	B	Chi-N
Mel Roach	19	33	.248	2-8,LF-4,3-1	B	
Bob Rush	31	101	2.40	P-31(5-6)	B	
Red Schoendienst	5	3	.000	2-4	B	
Enos Slaughter	11	21	.452	LF-5	xNY-A	C
Warren Spahn	40	292	2.96	P-40(21-15)	B	
Al Spangler	6	14	1.045	CF-4	A	
Frank Torre	115	307	.630	1-87	B	
Bob Trowbridge	16	30	5.93	P-16(1-0)	B	KC-A
Mickey Vernon	74	99	.645	1-10,LF-4	Cle-A	Pit-N
Carl Willey	26	117	4.15	P-26(5-9)	B	
Casey Wise	22	86	.504	2-20,S-5	B	Det-A

Coaches: John Fitzpatrick, Billy Herman, George Susce, Whit Wyatt

◆ 1960 MILWAUKEE (154 88-66 2) ATT: 1,497,799

Name	G	AB/IP	P/E	G/POS	From	To
Chuck Dressen				M		
Hank Aaron	153	664	.925	RF-153,2-2	B	
Joe Adcock	138	570	.857	1-136	B	
Ray Boone	7	17	.804	1-4	B	xBos-A
George Brunet	17	50	5.07	P-17(2-0)	xKC-A	
Bill Bruton	151	677	.760	CF-149	B	Det-A
Bob Buhl	36	239	3.09	P-36(16-9)	B	
Lew Burdette	46	276	3.36	P-45(19-13)	B	
Chuck Cottier	95	254	.579	2-92	B	Det-A
Wes Covington	95	299	.709	LF-72	B	
Del Crandall	142	596	.771	C-141	B	
Alvin Dark	50	152	.726	LF-25,1-10,3-4,2-3	xPhi-N	C
Terry Fox	5	8	4.32	P-5	A	Det-A
Len Gabrielson	4	4	.250	LF-1	A	
Bob Giggie	3	4	4.15	P-3	B	xKC-A
Eddie Haas	32	37	.699	LF-2	B	C
Joey Jay	32	133	3.24	P-32(9-8)	B	Cin-N
Mike Krsnich	4	9	.778	LF-3	A	
Charlie Lau	21	61	.498	C-16	Det-A	
Johnny Logan	136	537	.643	S-136	B	
Stan Lopata	7	9	.347	C-4	B	C
Ken MacKenzie	9	8	6.48	P-9(0-1)	A	
Felix Mantilla	63	159	.660	2-26,S-25,CF-8	B	
Eddie Mathews	153	671	.952	3-153	B	
Lee Maye	41	92	.736	LF-19	B	
Don McMahon	48	64	5.94	P-48(3-6)	B	
Don Nottebart	5	5	4.11	P-5(1-0)	B	
Ron Piche	37	48	3.56	P-37(3-5)	A	
Juan Pizarro	23	115	4.55	P-21(6-7)	B	Chi-A
Mel Roach	48	152	.783	LF-21,2-20,1-1,3-1	B	
Bob Rush	10	15	4.20	P-10(2-0)	B	xChi-A
Red Schoendienst	68	246	.630	2-62	B	StL-N
Warren Spahn	40	268	3.50	P-40(21-10)	B	
Al Spangler	101	122	.711	LF-92	B	
Frank Torre	21	50	.483	1-17	B	Phi-N
Joe Torre	2	2	1.000	H	A	
Carl Willey	28	145	4.35	P-28(6-7)	B	

Coaches: George Myatt, Andy Pafko, Bob Scheffing, Whit Wyatt

◆ 1961 MILWAUKEE (155 83-71 4) ATT: 1,101,441

Name	G	AB/IP	P/E	G/POS	From	To
Chuck Dressen				M(130 71-58 3)		
Birdie Tebbetts				M(25 12-13 4)		
Hank Aaron	155	671	.979	RF-154,3-2	B	
Joe Adcock	152	629	.862	1-148	B	
Johnny Antonelli	9	11	7.59	P-9(1-0)	xCle-A	C
Frank Bolling	148	658	.710	2-148	Det-A	
Bob Boyd	36	43	.506	1-3	xKC-A	C
George Brunet	5	5	5.40	P-5	B	Hou-N
Bob Buhl	32	188	4.11	P-32(9-10)	B	
Lew Burdette	42	272	4.00	P-40(18-11)	B	
Neil Chrisley	10	10	.522	H	Det-A	C
Gino Cimoli	37	131	.582	CF-31	xPit-N	KC-A
Tony Cloninger	19	84	5.25	P-19(7-2)	A	
Wes Covington	9	23	.499	LF-5	B	xChi-A
Del Crandall	15	32	.526	C-5	B	
John DeMerit	32	80	.509	RF-21	B	NY-N
Moe Drabowsky	16	25	4.62	P-16(0-2)	Chi-N	Cin-N
Bob Hendley	19	97	3.90	P-19(5-7)	A	
Mack Jones	28	119	.620	CF-26	A	
Charlie Lau	28	102	.598	C-25	B	xPit-N
Johnny Logan	18	20	.308	S-2	B	xPit-N
Ken MacKenzie	5	7	5.14	P-5(0-1)	B	NY-N
Felix Mantilla	45	105	.578	S-19,2-10,CF-10,3-6	B	NY-N
Billy Martin	6	6	.000	H	Cin-N	xMin-A
Eddie Mathews	152	672	.940	3-151	B	
Lee Maye	110	417	.779	RF-96	B	
Don McMahon	53	92	2.84	P-53(6-4)	B	
Roy McMillan	154	588	.602	S-154	Cin-N	
Seth Morehead	12	15	6.46	P-12(1-0)	Chi-N	C
Don Nottebart	38	126	4.06	P-38(6-7)	B	
Chi-Chi Olivo	3	2	18.00	P-3	A	
Ron Piche	12	23	3.47	P-12(2-2)	B	
Claude Raymond	13	20	3.98	P-13(1-0)	Chi-A	
Mel Roach	13	42	.500	LF-9,1-2	B	xChi-N
Phil Roof	1	0	†	C-1	A	
Warren Spahn	39	263	3.02	P-38(21-13)	B	
Al Spangler	68	125	.721	LF-44	B	Hou-N
Hawk Taylor	20	29	.584	LF-5,C-1	B	
Frank Thomas	124	464	.844	LF-109,1-11	xChi-N	NY-N
Joe Torre	113	441	.755	C-112	B	
Sammy White	21	68	.532	C-20	Bos-A	Phi-N
Carl Willey	35	160	3.83	P-35(6-12)	B	

Coaches: George Myatt, Andy Pafko, Whit Wyatt

♦ 1962 MILWAUKEE (162 86-76 5) ATT: 766,921

Name	G	AB/IP	P/E	G/POS	From	To
Birdie Tebbetts				M		
Hank Aaron	156	667	1.012	CF-153,1-1	B	
Tommie Aaron	141	382	.689	1-110,LF-42,2-1,3-1	A	
Joe Adcock	121	447	.841	1-112	B	
Ken Aspromonte	34	88	.665	2-12,3-6	xCle-A	Chi-N
Howie Bedell	58	150	.487	LF-45	A	Phi-N
Gus Bell	79	228	.758	LF-58	xNY-N	
Ethan Blackaby	6	14	.445	LF-3	A	
Frank Bolling	122	452	.734	2-119	B	
Bob Buhl	1	2	22.50	P-1(0-1)	B	xChi-N
Lew Burdette	39	144	4.89	P-37(10-9)	B	
Cecil Butler	9	31	2.61	P-9(2-0)	A	
Tony Cloninger	24	111	4.30	P-24(8-3)	B	
Jim Constable	3	18	2.00	P-3(1-1)	Was-A	SF-N
Del Crandall	107	388	.768	C-90,1-5	B	
Jack Curtis	30	76	4.16	P-30(4-4)	xChi-N	Cle-A
Hank Fischer	29	37	5.30	P-29(2-3)	A	
Bob Hendley	36	200	3.60	P-35(11-13)	B	
Lou Johnson	61	129	.802	LF-55	LA-A	LA-N
Mack Jones	91	386	.775	RF-91	B	
Lou Klimchock	8	8	.000	H	KC-A	Was-A
Mike Krsnich	11	12	.250	LF-3,1-1,3-1	B	C
Denny Lemaster	17	87	3.01	P-17(3-4)	A	
Eddie Mathews	152	643	.880	3-140,1-7	B	
Lee Maye	99	378	.654	CF-94	B	
Don McMahon	2	3	6.00	P-2(0-1)	B	xHou-N
Roy McMillan	137	544	.688	S-135	B	
Denis Menke	50	166	.548	2-20,3-15,S-9,1-2,LF-1	A	
Don Nottebart	39	64	3.23	P-39(2-2)	B	Hou-N
Ron Piche	16	52	4.85	P-14(3-2)	B	
Claude Raymond	26	43	2.74	P-26(5-5)	B	
Amado Samuel	76	224	.546	S-36,2-28,3-3	A	
Bob Shaw	38	225	2.80	P-38(15-9)	KC-A	
Warren Spahn	36	269	3.04	P-34(18-14)	B	
Hawk Taylor	20	49	.541	LF-11	B	
Joe Torre	80	248	.753	C-63	B	
Bob Uecker	33	71	.652	C-24	A	
Carl Willey	30	73	5.40	P-30(2-5)	B	NY-N

Coaches: Bill Adair, Jimmy Dykes, Andy Pafko, Whit Wyatt

♦ 1963 MILWAUKEE (163 84-78 6) ATT: 773,018

Name	G	AB/IP	P/E	G/POS	From	To
Bobby Bragan				M		
Hank Aaron	161	714	.980	RF-161	B	
Tommie Aaron	72	151	.542	1-45,LF-14,2-6,3-1	B	
Gus Bell	3	3	.667	H	B	
Wade Blasingame	2	3	12.00	P-2	A	
Frank Bolling	142	606	.612	2-141	B	
Lew Burdette	17	84	3.64	P-15(6-5)	B	xStL-N
Rico Carty	2	2	.000	H	A	
Ty Cline	72	190	.544	CF-62	Cle-A	
Tony Cloninger	41	145	3.78	P-41(9-11)	B	
Del Crandall	86	282	.504	C-75,1-7	B	SF-N
Don Dillard	67	127	.650	LF-30	Cle-A	
Hank Fischer	31	74	4.96	P-31(4-3)	B	
Frank Funk	26	44	2.68	P-25(3-3)	Cle-A	C
Len Gabrielson	46	129	.599	LF-22,1-16,3-3	B	
Bob Hendley	46	169	3.93	P-41(9-9)	B	SF-N
Mack Jones	93	263	.660	CF-80	B	
Lou Klimchock	24	41	.413	1-12	xWas-A	
Norm Larker	64	176	.539	1-42	Hou-N	xSF-N
Denny Lemaster	46	237	3.04	P-46(11-14)	B	
Eddie Mathews	158	675	.854	3-121,LF-42	B	
Lee Maye	124	487	.758	CF-111	B	
Roy McMillan	100	346	.617	S-94	B	
Denis Menke	146	572	.636	S-82,3-51,2-22,1-1,LF-1	B	
Bubba Morton	15	31	.437	LF-9	xDet-A	Cal-A
Gene Oliver	95	331	.739	1-55,LF-35,C-2	xStL-N	
Ron Piche	37	53	3.40	P-37(1-1)	B	Cal-A
Claude Raymond	45	53	5.40	P-45(4-6)	B	Hou-N
Bob Sadowski	19	117	2.62	P-19(5-7)	A	
Amado Samuel	15	18	.412	S-7,2-4	B	NY-N
Dan Schneider	30	44	3.09	P-30(1-0)	A	
Bob Shaw	48	159	2.66	P-48(7-11)	B	SF-N
Warren Spahn	33	260	2.60	P-33(23-7)	B	
Hawk Taylor	16	30	.169	LF-8	B	NY-N
Bobby Tiefenauer	12	30	1.21	P-12(1-1)	Hou-N	
Joe Torre	142	556	.785	C-105,1-37,LF-2	B	
Bob Uecker	13	18	.708	C-6	B	StL-N
Woody Woodward	10	2	.000	S-5	A	

Coaches: Ken Silvestri, Dixie Walker, Jo-Jo White, Whit Wyatt

♦ 1964 MILWAUKEE (162 88-74 5) ATT: 910,911

Name	G	AB/IP	P/E	G/POS	From	To
Bobby Bragan				M		
Hank Aaron	145	634	.908	RF-139,2-11	B	
Sandy Alomar	19	53	.509	S-19	A	
Felipe Alou	121	455	.705	CF-92,1-18	SF-N	
Ed Bailey	95	309	.708	C-80	SF-N	SF-N
Gus Bell	3	3	.000	H	B	C
Ethan Blackaby	9	13	.237	RF-5	B	C
Wade Blasingame	29	117	4.24	P-28(9-5)	B	
Frank Bolling	120	387	.526	2-117	B	
John Braun	1	2	0.00	P-1	A	C
Cecil Butler	2	4	8.31	P-2	B	C
Clay Carroll	11	20	1.77	P-11(2-0)	A	
Rico Carty	133	505	.945	LF-121	B	
Ty Cline	101	132	.759	CF-54,1-6	B	
Tony Cloninger	38	243	3.56	P-38(19-14)	B	
Mike DeLa Hoz	78	206	.748	2-25,3-25,S-8	Cle-A	
Dave Eilers	6	4	4.70	P-6	A	
Hank Fischer	38	168	4.01	P-37(11-10)	B	
Len Gabrielson	24	39	.442	1-12,RF-2	B	xChi-N
Billy Hoeft	42	73	3.80	P-42(4-0)	SF-N	Chi-N
Dick Kelley	2	2	18.00	P-2	A	
Lou Klimchock	10	22	.792	3-4,2-2	B	
Gary Kolb	36	71	.460	RF-14,3-7,2-6,C-2	StL-N	
Frank Lary	5	12	4.38	P-5(1-0)	xNY-A	NY-N
Denny Lemaster	39	221	4.15	P-39(17-11)	B	
Eddie Mathews	141	590	.758	3-128,1-7	B	
Lee Maye	153	627	.794	CF-135,3-5	B	
Roy McMillan	8	13	.615	S-8	B	xNY-N
Denis Menke	151	588	.852	S-141,2-15,3-6	B	
Phil Niekro	10	15	4.80	P-10	A	
Gene Oliver	93	298	.797	1-76,C-1	B	
Chi-Chi Olivo	38	60	3.75	P-38(2-1)	B	
Merritt Ranew	9	17	.235	C-3	xChi-N	Cal-A
Phil Roof	1	2	.000	C-1	B	Cal-A
Bob Sadowski	51	167	4.10	P-51(9-10)	B	
Dan Schneider	14	36	5.45	P-13(1-2)	B	
Jack Smith	22	31	3.77	P-22(2-2)	LA-N	C
Bill Southworth	3	9	1.159	3-2	A	C
Warren Spahn	39	174	5.29	P-38(6-13)	B	NY-N
Bobby Tiefenauer	46	73	3.21	P-46(4-6)	B	
Joe Torre	154	646	.864	C-96,1-70	B	
Arnold Umbach	1	8	3.24	P-1(1-0)	A	
Woody Woodward	77	124	.504	2-40,S-18,3-7,1-1	B	

Coaches: Ken Silvestri, Dixie Walker, Jo-Jo White, Whit Wyatt

♦ 1965 MILWAUKEE (162 86-76 5) ATT: 555,584

Name	G	AB/IP	P/E	G/POS	From	To
Bobby Bragan				M		
Hank Aaron	150	639	.943	RF-148	B	
Tommie Aaron	8	17	.423	1-6	B	
Sandy Alomar	67	116	.536	S-39,2-19	B	
Felipe Alou	143	599	.821	LF-91,1-69,3-2,S-1	B	
Jim Beauchamp	4	4	.250	1-2	xHou-N	
Johnny Blanchard	10	12	.650	LF-1	xKC-A	C
Wade Blasingame	38	225	3.77	P-38(16-10)	B	
Frank Bolling	148	577	.658	2-147	B	
Clay Carroll	19	35	4.41	P-19(0-1)	B	
Rico Carty	83	293	.852	LF-73	B	
Ty Cline	123	240	.487	CF-86,1-5	B	Chi-N
Tony Cloninger	41	279	3.29	P-40(24-11)	B	
Billy Cowan	19	27	.407	LF-10	xNY-N	Phi-N
Mike DeLa Hoz	81	188	.625	S-41,3-22,2-10,1-1	B	
Don Dillard	20	19	.474	LF-1	B	C
Dave Eilers	6	4	12.27	P-6	B	xNY-N
Hank Fischer	32	123	3.89	P-31(8-9)	B	
Jesse Gonder	31	57	.456	C-13	xNY-N	Pit-N
Ken Johnson	29	180	3.21	P-29(13-8)	xHou-N	
Mack Jones	143	546	.824	CF-133	B	
Dick Kelley	22	45	3.00	P-21(1-1)	B	
Lou Klimchock	34	42	.199	1-4	B	NY-N
Gary Kolb	24	28	.545	LF-13	B	xNY-N
Denny Lemaster	32	146	4.43	P-32(7-13)	B	
Eddie Mathews	156	626	.811	3-153	B	
Lee Maye	15	56	.792	CF-13	B	xHou-N
Denis Menke	71	202	.707	S-54,1-8,3-4	B	
Phil Niekro	42	75	2.89	P-41(2-3)	B	
Billy O'Dell	62	111	2.18	P-62(10-6),1-1	SF-N	
Gene Oliver	122	432	.819	C-64,1-52,LF-1	B	
Chi-Chi Olivo	8	13	1.38	P-8(0-1)	B	
Dan Osinski	61	83	2.82	P-61(0-3)	LA-A	Bos-A
Bob Sadowski	34	123	4.32	P-34(5-9)	B	Bos-A
Frank Thomas	15	36	.560	1-6,LF-3	xHou-N	Chi-N
Bobby Tiefenauer	6	7	7.71	P-6(0-1)	B	xNY-A
Joe Torre	148	594	.863	C-100,1-49	B	
Woody Woodward	112	280	.501	S-107,2-8	B	

Coaches: Ken Silvestri, Dixie Walker, Jo-Jo White, Whit Wyatt

♦ 1966 ATLANTA (163 85-77 5) ATT: 1,539,801

Name	G	AB/IP	P/E	G/POS	From	To
Bobby Bragan				M(112 52-59 7)		
Billy Hitchcock				M(51 33-18 5)		
Hank Aaron	158	688	.899	RF-158,2-2	B	
Ted Abernathy	38	65	3.86	P-38(4-4)	xChi-N	Cin-N
Sandy Alomar	31	45	.225	2-21,S-5	B	NY-N
Felipe Alou	154	706	.895	1-90,LF-79,3-3,S-1	B	
Lee Bales	12	16	.125	2-7,3-3	A	Hou-N
Wade Blasingame	18	68	5.32	P-16(3-7)	B	
Frank Bolling	75	245	.503	2-67	B	C
Clay Carroll	73	144	2.37	P-73(8-7)	B	
Rico Carty	151	588	.864	LF-126,C-17,1-2,3-1	B	
Ty Cline	42	77	.556	RF-19,1-6	xChi-N	
Tony Cloninger	47	258	4.12	P-39(14-11)	B	
Mike DeLa Hoz	71	117	.552	3-30,2-8,S-1	B	
Hank Fischer	14	48	3.91	P-14(2-3)	B	xCin-N
Adrian Garrett	4	3	.000	RF-1	A	Chi-N
Gary Geiger	78	151	.816	CF-49	Bos-A	
John Herrnstein	17	18	.444	LF-5	xChi-N	C
Herb Hippauf	3	3	13.50	P-3(0-1)	A	C
Pat Jarvis	10	62	2.31	P-10(6-2)	A	
Joey Jay	9	30	7.89	P-9(0-4)	xCin-N	C
Ken Johnson	32	216	3.30	P-32(14-8)	B	
Mack Jones	118	470	.806	CF-112,1-1	B	
Dick Kelley	20	81	3.22	P-20(7-5)	B	
Marty Keough	17	18	.170	1-4,LF-3	Cin-N	xChi-N
George Kopacz	6	10	.100	1-2	A	Pit-N
Denny Lemaster	27	171	3.74	P-27(11-8)	B	Hou-N
Eddie Mathews	134	517	.762	3-127	B	
Denis Menke	138	545	.772	S-106,3-39,1-7	B	
Felix Millan	37	93	.631	2-25,S-1,3-1	A	
Phil Niekro	28	50	4.11	P-28(4-3)	B	
Billy O'Dell	26	41	2.40	P-24(2-3)	B	xPit-N
Gene Oliver	76	209	.633	C-48,1-5,LF-2	B	
Chi-Chi Olivo	47	66	4.23	P-47(5-4)	B	
Ron Reed	2	8	2.16	P-2(1-1)	A	
Jay Ritchie	22	35	4.08	P-22(0-1)	Bos-A	
Bill Robinson	6	11	.727	RF-5	A	NY-A
Ed Sadowski	3	10	.311	C-3	LA-A	C
Dan Schneider	14	26	3.42	P-14	B	Hou-N
Don Schwall	11	45	4.37	P-11(3-3)	xPit-N	

Name	G	AB/IP	P/E	G/POS	From	To
Lee Thomas	39	139	.628	1-36	Bos-A	xChi-N
Joe Torre	148	614	.945	C-114,1-36	B	
Arnold Umbach	22	41	3.10	P-22(0-2)	B	C
Cecil Upshaw	1	3	0.00	P-1	A	
Charlie Vaughan	1	7	2.57	P-1(1-0)	A	
Woody Woodward	144	516	.652	2-79,S-73	B	

Coaches: Billy Hitchcock, Grover Resinger, Ken Silvestri, Jo-Jo White, Whit Wyatt

◆ 1967 ATLANTA (162 77-85 7) ATT: 1,389,222

Name	G	AB/IP	P/E	G/POS	From	To
Billy Hitchcock				M(159 77-82 7)		
Ken Silvestri				M(3 0-3 7)		
Hank Aaron	155	669	.946	RF-152,2-1	B	
Felipe Alou	140	617	.727	1-85,CF-56	B	
Jim Beauchamp	4	4	.000	H	B	Cin-N
Wade Blasingame	10	25	4.62	P-10(1-0)	B	xHou-N
Clete Boyer	154	619	.718	3-150,S-6	NY-A	
Jim Britton	2	13	6.07	P-2(0-2)	A	
Bob Bruce	12	39	4.89	P-12(2-3)	Hou-N	C
Clay Carroll	42	93	5.52	P-42(6-12)	B	
Rico Carty	134	496	.731	LF-112,1-9	B	
Glen Clark	4	4	.000	H	A	C
Ty Cline	10	9	.111	LF-1	B	xSF-N
Tony Cloninger	16	77	5.17	P-16(4-7)	B	
Mike DeLa Hoz	74	147	.511	2-23,3-22,S-1	B	Cin-N
Tito Francona	82	280	.652	1-56,LF-6		xPhi-N
Cito Gaston	9	27	.320	CF-7	A	SD-N
Gary Geiger	69	140	.498	CF-38	B	Hou-N
Remy Hermoso	11	28	.665	S-9,2-2	A	Mon-N
Ramon Hernandez	46	52	4.18	P-46(0-2)	A	Chi-N
Pat Jarvis	32	194	3.66	P-32(15-10)	B	
Ken Johnson	29	210	2.74	P-29(13-9)	B	
Mack Jones	140	534	.791	CF-126	B	Cin-N
Dick Kelley	39	98	3.77	P-39(2-9)	B	
Charlie Lau	52	49	.554	H	xBal-A	C
Denny Lemaster	31	215	3.34	P-31(9-9)	B	Hou-N
Mike Lum	9	27	.490	CF-6	A	
Marty Martinez	44	87	.731	S-25,2-9,C-3,3-2,1-1	Min-A	
Denis Menke	129	491	.661	S-124,3-3	B	Hou-N
Felix Millan	41	144	.613	2-41	B	
Dave Nicholson	10	29	.459	LF-7	Hou-N	C
Phil Niekro	46	207	1.87	P-46(11-9)	B	
Gene Oliver	17	57	.692	C-14	B	xPhi-N
Ed Rakow	17	39	5.26	P-17(3-2)	Det-A	C
Claude Raymond	28	34	2.62	P-28(4-1)		xHou-N
Ron Reed	3	21	2.95	P-3(1-1)	B	
Jay Ritchie	52	82	3.17	P-52(4-6)	B	Cin-N
Don Schwall	1	1	0.00	P-1	B	C
George Stone	2	7	4.91	P-2	A	
Joe Torre	135	534	.792	C-114,1-23	B	
Bob Uecker	62	180	.452	C-59	xPhi-N	C
Cecil Upshaw	30	45	2.58	P-30(2-3)	B	
Woody Woodward	136	476	.559	2-120,S-16	B	

Coaches: Bill Adair, Jim Fanning, Bob Kennedy, Ken Silvestri, Whit Wyatt

◆ 1968 ATLANTA (163 81-81 5) ATT: 1,126,540

Name	G	AB/IP	P/E	G/POS	From	To
Lum Harris				M		
Hank Aaron	160	676	.855	RF-151,1-14	B	
Tommie Aaron	98	307	.607	LF-62,1-28,3-1	B	
Felipe Alou	160	718	.805	CF-158	B	
Dusty Baker	6	5	.800	CF-3	A	
Clete Boyer	71	291	.586	3-69	B	
Jim Britton	34	90	3.10	P-34(4-6)	B	
Clay Carroll	10	22	4.84	P-10(0-1)	B	xCin-N
Wayne Causey	16	39	.351	2-6,S-2,3-2	xCal-A	C
Tony Cloninger	8	19	4.26	P-8(1-3)	B	xCin-N
Ted Davidson	4	7	6.75	P-4	xCin-N	C
Tito Francona	122	400	.725	LF-65,1-33	B	
Ralph Garr	11	8	.661	H	A	
Gil Garrido	18	57	.444	S-17	SF-N	
Skip Guinn	7	5	3.60	P-3	A	Hou-N
Walt Hriniak	9	26	.692	C-9	A	
Sonny Jackson	105	392	.551	S-99	Hou-N	
Pat Jarvis	34	256	2.60	P-34(16-12)	B	
Deron Johnson	127	383	.603	1-97,3-21	Cin-N	Phi-N
Ken Johnson	31	135	3.47	P-31(5-8)	B	
Bob Johnson	59	198	.599	3-48,2-4	xCin-N	StL-N
Dick Kelley	31	98	2.76	P-31(2-4)	B	SD-N
Rick Kester	5	6	5.68	P-5	A	
Mike Lum	122	256	.599	LF-95	B	
Marty Martinez	113	395	.553	S-54,3-37,2-16,C-14	B	Hou-N
Felix Millan	149	615	.663	2-145	B	
Stu Miller	2	1	27.00	P-2	Bal-A	C
Phil Niekro	37	257	2.59	P-37(14-12)	B	
Mike Page	20	29	.385	RF-6	A	C
Milt Pappas	22	121	2.37	P-22(10-8)	xCin-N	
Claude Raymond	36	60	2.83	P-36(3-5)	B	
Ron Reed	35	202	3.35	P-35(11-10)	B	
Al Santorini	1	3	0.00	P-1(0-1)	A	SD-N
George Stone	17	75	2.76	P-17(7-4)	B	
Bob Tillman	86	257	.579	C-75	NY-A	
Joe Torre	115	464	.710	C-92,1-29	B	StL-N
Cecil Upshaw	52	117	2.47	P-52(8-7)	B	
Sandy Valdespino	36	97	.599	LF-20	Min-A	Hou-N
Woody Woodward	12	25	.408	S-6,3-2,2-1	B	xCin-N

Coaches: Jim Busby, Fritz Dorish, Billy Goodman, Satchell Paige, Ken Silvestri

◆ 1969 ATLANTA (162 93-69 1W) ATT: 1,458,320

Name	G	AB/IP	P/E	G/POS	From	To
Lum Harris				M		
Hank Aaron	147	639	1.005	RF-144,1-4	B	
Tommie Aaron	49	66	.652	1-16,LF-8	B	
Felipe Alou	123	509	.665	CF-116	B	Oak-A
Bob Aspromonte	82	215	.654	LF-24,3-23,S-18,2-2	Hou-N	
Dusty Baker	3	7	.000	CF-3	A	
Clete Boyer	144	562	.701	3-141	B	
Jim Breazeale	2	3	.667	1-1	A	
Jim Britton	24	88	3.78	P-24(7-5)	B	Mon-N
Oscar Brown	7	4	.500	CF-3	A	
Rico Carty	104	339	.954	LF-79	B	
Orlando Cepeda	154	636	.755	1-153	StL-N	
Bob Didier	114	397	.628	C-114	A	
Paul Doyle	36	39	2.08	P-36(2-0)	A	Cal-A
Darrell Evans	12	28	.490	3-6	A	
Tito Francona	51	105	.761	LF-15,1-7	B	xOak-A
Ralph Garr	22	29	.535	LF-7	B	
Gil Garrido	82	251	.523	S-81	B	
Tony Gonzalez	89	357	.805	CF-82	xSD-N	
Garry Hill	1	2	15.43	P-1(0-1)	A	C
Walt Hriniak	7	9	.476	C-6	B	xSD-N
Sonny Jackson	98	363	.608	S-97	B	
Pat Jarvis	37	217	4.43	P-37(13-11)	B	
Ken Johnson	9	29	4.97	P-9(0-1)	B	xNY-A
Rick Kester	1	2	13.50	P-1	B	
Mike Lum	121	187	.665	LF-89	B	
Larry Maxie	2	3	3.00	P-2	A	C
Mike McQueen	1	3	3.00	P-1	A	
Felix Millan	162	708	.656	2-162	B	
Gary Neibauer	29	58	3.90	P-29(1-2)	A	
Phil Niekro	40	284	2.56	P-40(23-13)	B	
Milt Pappas	26	144	3.62	P-26(6-10)	B	
Bob Priddy	1	2	0.00	P-1	xCal-A	
Claude Raymond	33	48	5.25	P-33(2-2)	B	xMon-N
Ron Reed	37	241	3.47	P-36(18-10)	B	
George Stone	36	165	3.65	P-36(13-10)	B	
Bob Tillman	69	209	.675	C-69	B	
Cecil Upshaw	62	105	2.91	P-62(6-4)	B	
Charlie Vaughan	1	1	18.00	P-1	B	C
Hoyt Wilhelm	8	12	0.73	P-8(2-0)	xCal-A	

Coaches: Jim Busby, Fritz Dorish, Billy Goodman, Satchell Paige, Ken Silvestri

◆ 1970 ATLANTA (162 76-86 5W) ATT: 1,078,848

Name	G	AB/IP	P/E	G/POS	From	To
Lum Harris				M		
Hank Aaron	150	598	.962	RF-125,1-11	B	
Tommie Aaron	44	66	.576	1-16,LF-12	B	
Bob Aspromonte	62	142	.522	3-30,S-4,1-1,LF-1	B	NY-N
Dusty Baker	13	27	.638	LF-11	B	
Steve Barber	5	15	4.91	P-5(0-1)	xChi-N	
Clete Boyer	134	525	.689	3-126,S-5	B	
Oscar Brown	28	57	1.005	CF-25	A	
Don Cardwell	16	23	6.90	P-16(2-1)	xNY-N	C
Rico Carty	136	560	1.040	LF-133	B	
Orlando Cepeda	148	627	.911	1-148	B	
Bob Didier	57	183	.383	C-57	B	
Darrell Evans	12	52	.809	3-12	B	
Ralph Garr	37	102	.629	RF-21	B	
Gil Garrido	101	389	.601	S-80,2-26	B	
Aubrey Gatewood	3	2	4.50	P-3	Cal-A	C
Tony Gonzalez	123	487	.712	CF-119	B	xCal-N
Jimmie Hall	39	49	.628	LF-28	xChi-N	C
Sonny Jackson	103	380	.670	S-87	B	
Pat Jarvis	36	254	3.61	P-36(16-16)	B	
Larry Jaster	14	22	6.85	P-14(1-1)	Mon-N	
Rick Kester	15	32	5.57	P-15	B	C
Hal King	89	239	.826	C-62	Hou-N	
Ron Kline	5	6	7.11	P-5	Bos-A	C
Mike Lum	123	316	.705	LF-98	B	
Mike McQueen	22	66	5.59	P-22(1-5)	B	
Felix Millan	142	642	.734	2-142	B	
Jim Nash	34	212	4.07	P-34(13-9)	Oak-A	
Julio Navarro	17	26	4.10	P-17	Det-A	C
Gary Neibauer	7	13	4.97	P-7(0-3)	B	
Phil Niekro	34	230	4.27	P-34(12-18)	B	
Milt Pappas	11	36	6.06	P-11(2-2)	B	xChi-N
Bob Priddy	41	73	5.42	P-41(5-5)	B	
Ron Reed	22	135	4.41	P-21(7-10)	B	
George Stone	35	207	3.86	P-35(11-11)	B	
Bob Tillman	71	245	.708	C-70	B	C
Hoyt Wilhelm	50	78	3.10	P-50(6-4)	B	xChi-N
Earl Williams	10	24	1.033	1-4,3-3	A	

Coaches: Jim Busby, Fritz Dorish, Billy Goodman, Ken Silvestri

◆ 1971 ATLANTA (162 82-80 3W) ATT: 1,006,320

Name	G	AB/IP	P/E	G/POS	From	To
Lum Harris				M		
Hank Aaron	139	573	1.082	1-71,RF-60	B	
Tommie Aaron	25	56	.532	1-11,3-7	B	C
Dusty Baker	29	64	.496	RF-18	B	
Steve Barber	39	75	4.80	P-39(3-1)	B	
Clete Boyer	30	108	.741	3-25,S-1	B	C
Jim Breazeale	10	22	.524	1-4	B	
Oscar Brown	27	46	.563	CF-15	B	
Orlando Cepeda	71	276	.827	1-63	B	
Bob Didier	51	171	.507	C-50	B	
Darrell Evans	89	305	.774	3-72,LF-3	B	
Leo Foster	9	10	.000	S-3	A	
Ralph Garr	154	693	.815	LF-153	B	
Gil Garrido	79	143	.540	S-32,3-28,2-18	B	
Ron Herbel	25	52	5.23	P-25(0-1)	NY-N	C
Tom House	11	21	3.05	P-11(1-0)	A	
Sonny Jackson	149	593	.627	CF-145	B	
Pat Jarvis	35	162	4.10	P-35(6-14)	B	
Tom Kelley	28	143	2.96	P-28(9-5)	Cle-A	
Hal King	86	233	.649	C-60	B	Tex-A
Tony LaRussa	9	8	.661	2-9	xOak-A	Chi-N
Mike Lum	145	512	.734	RF-125,1-1	B	
Mike McQueen	17	56	3.54	P-17(4-1)	B	
Felix Millan	143	635	.698	2-141	B	
Jim Nash	33	133	4.94	P-32(9-7)	B	
Gary Neibauer	6	21	2.14	P-6(1-0)	B	
Phil Niekro	42	269	2.98	P-42(15-14)	B	
Marty Perez	130	445	.580	S-126,2-1	Cal-A	

Name	G	AB/IP	P/E	G/POS	From	To
Bob Priddy	40	64	4.22	P-40(4-9)	B	C
Ron Reed	32	222	3.72	P-32(13-14)	B	
Marv Staehle	22	42	.349	2-7,3-1	Mon-N	C
George Stone	30	173	3.60	P-27(6-8)	B	
Cecil Upshaw	49	82	3.51	P-49(11-6)	B	
Zoilo Versalles	66	210	.559	3-30,S-24,2-1	Was-A	C
Hoyt Wilhelm	3	2	15.43	P-3	Chi-N	xLA-N
Earl Williams	145	550	.817	C-72,3-42,1-31	B	

Coaches: Jim Busby, Fritz Dorish, Eddie Mathews, Connie Ryan, Ken Silvestri

◆ 1972 ATLANTA (155 70-84 4W) ATT: 752,973

Name	G	AB/IP	P/E	G/POS	From	To
Lum Harris				M(105 47-57 4)		
Eddie Mathews				M(50 23-27 4)		
Hank Aaron	129	544	.906	1-109,RF-15	B	
Dusty Baker	127	503	.892	CF-123	B	
Steve Barber	5	16	5.74	P-5	B	xCal-A
Larvell Blanks	33	94	.804	2-18,S-4,3-2	A	
Jim Breazeale	52	91	.744	1-16,3-1	B	Chi-A
Oscar Brown	76	168	.567	LF-59	B	
Rico Carty	86	315	.780	LF-78	B	Tex-A
Paul Casanova	49	140	.501	C-43	Was-A	
Orlando Cepeda	28	91	.828	1-22	B	xOak-A
Bob Didier	13	44	.749	C-11	B	Det-A
Darrell Evans	125	521	.809	3-123	B	
Jimmy Freeman	8	36	6.00	P-6(2-2)	A	
Ralph Garr	134	594	.790	LF-131	B	
Gil Garrido	40	87	.648	2-21,S-10,3-3	B	C
Rod Gilbreath	18	41	.556	2-7,3-4	A	
Jim Hardin	26	80	4.41	P-26(5-2)	NY-A	C
Joe Hoerner	25	23	6.56	P-25(1-3)	xPhi-N	
Tom House	8	9	2.89	P-8	B	
Sonny Jackson	60	133	.612	S-17,CF-10,3-6	B	
Pat Jarvis	37	99	4.10	P-37(11-7)	B	Mon-N
Larry Jaster	5	12	5.11	P-5(1-1)	B	C
Tom Kelley	27	116	4.56	P-27(5-7)	B	
Mike Lum	123	424	.674	RF-109,1-2	B	
Denny McLain	15	54	6.50	P-15(3-5)	xOak-A	C
Mike McQueen	23	78	4.60	P-23(0-5)	B	Cin-N
Felix Millan	125	534	.607	2-120	B	NY-N
Jim Nash	11	31	5.46	P-11(1-1)	B	xPhi-N
Gary Neibauer	8	17	7.27	P-8	B	xPhi-N
Phil Niekro	38	282	3.06	P-38(16-12)	B	
Rowland Office	2	6	.900	CF-1	A	
Marty Perez	141	518	.542	S-141	B	
Ron Reed	31	213	3.93	P-31(11-15)	B	
Ron Schueler	37	145	3.67	P-37(5-8)	A	
George Stone	33	111	5.51	P-31(6-11)	B	NY-N
Cecil Upshaw	42	54	3.69	P-42(3-5)	B	
Earl Williams	151	637	.795	C-116,3-21,1-20	B	Bal-A

Coaches: Lew Burdette, Jim Busby, Eddie Mathews, Ken Silvestri

◆ 1973 ATLANTA (162 76-85 5W) ATT: 800,655

Name	G	AB/IP	P/E	G/POS	From	To
Eddie Mathews				M		
Hank Aaron	120	465	1.048	LF-105	B	
Dusty Baker	159	686	.818	CF-156	B	
Larvell Blanks	17	19	.485	3-3,2-2,S-2	B	
Oscar Brown	22	62	.505	LF-13	B	C
Paul Casanova	82	248	.589	C-78	B	
Dave Cheadle	2	2	18.00	P-2(0-1)	A	C
Al Closter	4	4	14.54	P-4	NY-A	C
Adrian Devine	24	32	6.40	P-24(2-3)	A	
Dick Dietz	83	191	.910	1-36,C-20	LA-N	C
Pat Dobson	12	58	4.99	P-12(3-7)	Bal-A	xNY-A
Darrell Evans	161	733	.964	3-146,1-20	B	
Wenty Ford	4	16	5.51	P-4(1-2)	A	C
Leo Foster	3	7	.500	S-1	B	
Jimmy Freeman	14	37	7.71	P-13(0-2)	B	C
Danny Frisella	42	45	4.20	P-42(1-2)	NY-N	
Ralph Garr	148	698	.738	RF-148	B	
Gary Gentry	17	87	3.43	P-16(4-6)	NY-N	
Rod Gilbreath	29	82	.684	3-22	B	
Chuck Goggin	64	100	.698	2-19,LF-6,S-5,C-1	xPit-N	Bos-A
Roric Harrison	39	177	4.16	P-38(11-8)	Bal-A	
Joe Hoerner	20	13	6.39	P-20(2-2)	B	xKC-A
Tom House	52	67	4.68	P-52(4-2)	B	
Larry Howard	4	10	.425	C-2	xHou-N	C
Sonny Jackson	117	234	.541	LF-56,S-36	B	
Davey Johnson	157	651	.917	2-156	Bal-A	
Tom Kelley	7	13	2.84	P-7(0-1)	B	C
Max Leon	16	27	5.33	P-12(2-2)	A	
Mike Lum	138	568	.816	1-84,LF-64	B	
Norm Miller	9	12	1.420	LF-1	xHou-N	
Carl Morton	40	256	3.41	P-38(15-10)	Mon-N	
Gary Neibauer	16	21	7.17	P-16(2-1)	Phi-N	C
Joe Niekro	20	24	4.13	P-20(2-4)	Det-A	
Phil Niekro	42	245	3.31	P-42(13-10)	B	
Johnny Oates	93	351	.603	C-86	Bal-A	
Jim Panther	23	31	7.63	P-23(2-3)	Tex-A	C
Joe Pepitone	3	12	.780	1-3	xChi-N	C
Marty Perez	141	567	.666	S-139	B	
Jack Pierce	11	21	.145	1-6	A	
Ron Reed	21	116	4.41	P-20(4-11)	B	
Ron Schueler	39	186	3.87	P-39(8-7)	B	Phi-N
Frank Tepedino	74	165	.779	1-58	NY-A	
Cecil Upshaw	5	4	9.82	P-5(0-1)	B	xHou-N
Freddie Velazquez	15	24	.766	C-11	Sea-A	C

Coaches: Lew Burdette, Jim Busby, Roy Hartsfield, Connie Ryan, Ken Silvestri

◆ 1974 ATLANTA (163 88-74 3W) ATT: 981,085

Name	G	AB/IP	P/E	G/POS	From	To
Eddie Mathews				M(99 50-49 4)		
Clyde King				M(64 38-25 3)		
Hank Aaron	112	382	.834	LF-89	B	Mil-A
Jack Aker	17	17	3.78	P-17(0-1)	Chi-N	xNY-A
Dusty Baker	149	656	.761	RF-148	B	
Mike Beard	6	9	2.89	P-6	A	

Name	G	AB/IP	P/E	G/POS	From	To
Larvell Blanks	3	8	.500	S-2	B	
Buzz Capra	39	217	2.28	P-39(16-8)	NY-N	
Paul Casanova	42	113	.440	C-33	B	C
Vic Correll	73	231	.703	C-59	Bos-A	
Jamie Easterly	3	3	16.88	P-3	A	
Darrell Evans	160	710	.801	3-160	B	
Leo Foster	72	124	.497	S-43,2-10,3-3,RF-1	B	NY-N
Danny Frisella	36	42	5.18	P-36(3-4)	B	SD-N
John Fuller	3	3	.667	CF-1	A	C
Ralph Garr	143	645	.887	LF-139	B	
Gary Gentry	3	7	1.35	P-3	B	
Rod Gilbreath	3	9	.833	2-2	B	
Roric Harrison	20	126	4.71	P-20(6-11)	B	
Tom House	56	103	1.93	P-56(6-2)	B	
Sonny Jackson	5	7	.857	RF-1	B	C
Davey Johnson	136	540	.751	1-73,2-71	B	
Lew Krausse	29	67	4.18	P-29(4-3)	StL-N	C
Max Leon	34	75	2.64	P-34(4-7)	B	
Mike Lum	106	411	.687	1-60,RF-50	B	
Norm Miller	42	48	.560	RF-4	B	C
Carl Morton	38	275	3.15	P-38(16-12)	B	
Ivan Murrell	73	139	.591	LF-32,1-13	SD-N	C
Joe Niekro	27	43	3.56	P-27(3-2)	B	Hou-N
Phil Niekro	41	302	2.38	P-41(20-13)	B	
Johnny Oates	100	327	.548	C-91	B	
Rowland Office	131	268	.647	CF-119	B	
Marty Perez	127	491	.655	2-102,S-14,3-6	B	
Jack Pierce	6	10	.311	1-2	B	Det-A
Ron Reed	28	186	3.39	P-28(10-11)	B	
Craig Robinson	145	506	.548	S-142	Phi-N	
Frank Tepedino	78	181	.546	1-46	B	
Mike Thompson	1	4	4.50	P-1	xStL-N	

Coaches: Jim Busby, Eddie Haas, Connie Ryan, Ken Silvestri, Herm Starrette

◆ 1975 ATLANTA (161 67-94 5W) ATT: 534,672

Name	G	AB/IP	P/E	G/POS	From	To
Clyde King				M(134 58-76 5)		
Connie Ryan				M(27 9-18 5)		
Dusty Baker	142	567	.770	RF-136	B	LA-N
Bob Beall	20	38	.642	1-8	A	
Mike Beard	34	70	3.20	P-34(4-0)	B	
Rob Belloir	43	118	.525	S-38,2-1	A	
Larvell Blanks	141	517	.587	S-129,2-12	B	Cle-A
Buzz Capra	12	78	4.25	P-12(4-7)	B	
Vic Correll	103	375	.667	C-97	B	
Bruce DalCanton	26	67	3.36	P-26(2-7)	xKC-A	
Adrian Devine	5	16	4.41	P-5(1-0)	B	
Jamie Easterly	21	69	4.98	P-21(2-9)	B	
Darrell Evans	156	681	.769	3-156,1-3	B	
Ralph Garr	151	678	.713	LF-148	B	Chi-A
Cito Gaston	64	159	.720	CF-35,1-1	SD-N	
Gary Gentry	7	20	4.95	P-7(1-1)	B	C
Rod Gilbreath	90	237	.623	2-52,3-10,S-1	B	
Ed Goodson	47	80	.507	1-13,3-1	xSF-N	LA-N
Preston Hanna	4	6	1.59	P-4	B	
Roric Harrison	15	55	4.77	P-15(3-4)	B	xCle-A
Tom House	58	79	3.18	P-58(7-7)	B	Bos-A
Davey Johnson	1	1	3.000	H	B	Phi-N
Frank LaCorte	3	14	5.27	P-3(0-2)	A	
Max Leon	50	85	4.13	P-50(2-1)	B	
Mike Lum	124	406	.630	1-60,CF-38	B	Cin-N
Dave May	82	230	.853	RF-53	Mil-A	
Carl Morton	39	278	3.50	P-39(17-16)	B	
Phil Niekro	39	276	3.20	P-39(15-15)	B	
Joe Nolan	4	5	.650	C-1	NY-N	
Johnny Oates	8	19	.541	C-6	B	xPhi-N
Blue Moon Odom	15	56	7.07	P-15(1-7)	xCle-A	Chi-A
Rowland Office	126	388	.699	CF-107	B	
Marty Perez	120	508	.657	2-116,S-7	B	
Biff Pocoroba	67	211	.646	C-62	A	
Ron Reed	10	75	4.22	P-10(4-5)	B	xStL-N
Craig Robinson	10	17	.118	S-7	B	xSF-N
Ray Sadecki	25	66	4.21	P-25(2-3)	xStL-N	xKC-A
Elias Sosa	43	62	4.48	P-43(2-2)	xStL-N	
Frank Tepedino	8	8	.125	H	B	C
Mike Thompson	16	52	4.70	P-16(0-6)	B	C
Pablo Torrealba	6	7	1.35	P-6(0-1)	A	
Earl Williams	111	424	.667	1-90,C-11	Bal-A	

Coaches: Jim Busby, Eddie Haas, Connie Ryan, Ken Silvestri, Herm Starrette

◆ 1976 ATLANTA (162 70-92 6W) ATT: 818,179

Name	G	AB/IP	P/E	G/POS	From	To
Dave Bristol				M		
Brian Asselstine	11	36	.538	CF-9	A	
Al Autry	1	5	5.40	P-1(1-0)	A	C
Mike Beard	30	34	4.28	P-30(0-2)	B	
Rob Belloir	30	69	.495	S-12,3-10,2-5	B	
Rick Camp	5	11	6.35	P-5(0-1)	A	
Buzz Capra	5	9	8.68	P-5(0-1)	B	
Darrel Chaney	153	564	.657	S-151,2-1,3-1	Cin-N	
Vic Correll	69	224	.652	C-65	B	
Terry Crowley	7	7	.000	H	Cin-N	xBal-A
Bruce DalCanton	42	73	3.56	P-42(3-5)	B	Chi-A
Adrian Devine	48	73	3.21	P-48(5-6)	B	Tex-A
Jamie Easterly	4	22	9.41	P-4(1-1)	B	
Mike Eden	5	8	.000	2-2	A	Chi-A
Darrell Evans	44	169	.514	1-36,3-7	B	xSF-N
Cito Gaston	69	147	.764	LF-28,1-2	B	
Rod Gilbreath	116	452	.660	2-104,3-7,S-1	B	
Preston Hanna	5	8	4.50	P-5	B	
Ken Henderson	133	505	.751	RF-122	Chi-A	Tex-A
Frank LaCorte	21	105	4.70	P-19(3-12)	B	
Lee Lacy	50	190	.666	2-44,CF-5,3-1	LA-N	xLA-N
Max Leon	30	36	2.75	P-30(2-4)	B	
Mike Marshall	24	37	3.19	P-24(2-1)	xLA-N	
Dave May	105	243	.611	LF-60	B	Tex-A
Andy Messersmith	29	207	3.04	P-29(11-11)	LA-N	

Name	G	AB/IP	P/E	G/POS	From	To
Willie Montanez	103	442	.773	1-103	xSF-N	
Junior Moore	20	32	.695	3-6,2-1,LF-1	A	
Roger Moret	27	77	5.00	P-27(3-5)	Bos-A	Tex-A
Carl Morton	27	140	4.17	P-26(4-9)	B	C
Dale Murphy	19	72	.687	C-19	A	
Phil Niekro	38	271	3.29	P-38(17-11)	B	
Rowland Office	99	407	.719	CF-92	B	
Tom Paciorek	111	350	.718	RF-84,1-12,3-1	LA-N	
Marty Perez	31	109	.631	2-18,S-17,3-2	B	xSF-N
Biff Pocoroba	54	196	.598	C-54	B	
Craig Robinson	15	23	.644	2-5,S-2,3-1	xSF-N	
Pat Rockett	4	5	.400	S-2	A	
Jerry Royster	149	605	.620	3-148,S-2	LA-N	
Dick Ruthven	37	240	4.19	P-36(14-17)	Phi-N	
Elias Sosa	21	35	5.35	P-21(4-4)	B	xLA-N
Pablo Torrealba	36	53	3.57	P-36(0-2)	B	Oak-A
Pete Varney	5	10	.200	C-5	xChi-A	C
Earl Williams	61	208	.664	C-38,1-17	B	xMon-N
Jim Wynn	148	584	.749	LF-138	LA-N	NY-A

Coaches: Vern Benson, Chris Cannizzaro, Eddie Haas, Herm Starrette

♦ 1977 ATLANTA (162 61-101 6W) ATT: 872,464

Name	G	AB/IP	P/E	G/POS	From	To
Dave Bristol				M(29 8-21 6)		
Ted Turner				M(1 0-1 6)		
Vern Benson				M(1 1-0 6)		
Dave Bristol				M(131 52-79 6)		
Brian Asselstine	83	134	.618	CF-35	B	
Mike Beard	4	5	9.64	P-4	B	C
Rob Belloir	6	1	1.000	S-3	B	
Barry Bonnell	100	403	.707	CF-75,3-32	A	
Larry Bradford	2	3	3.38	P-2	A	
Jeff Burroughs	154	671	.885	RF-154	Tex-A	
Rick Camp	54	79	4.00	P-54(6-3)	B	
Dave Campbell	65	89	3.05	P-65(0-6)	A	
Buzz Capra	45	139	5.36	P-45(6-11)	B	C
Darrel Chaney	74	231	.558	S-41,2-24	B	
Don Collins	40	71	5.09	P-40(3-9)	A	Cle-A
Vic Correll	54	170	.720	C-49	B	Cin-N
Mike Davey	16	16	5.06	P-16	A	
Jamie Easterly	23	59	6.14	P-22(2-4)	B	
Cito Gaston	56	93	.735	LF-9,1-5	B	
Rod Gilbreath	128	463	.670	2-122,3-1	B	
Preston Hanna	17	60	4.95	P-17(2-6)	B	
Steve Hargan	16	37	6.87	P-16(0-3)	xTex-A	C
Bob Johnson	15	22	7.25	P-15(0-1)	Cle-A	C
Steve Kline	16	20	6.64	P-16	Cle-A	C
Frank LaCorte	14	37	11.68	P-14(1-8)	B	
Max Leon	33	82	3.97	P-31(4-4)	B	
Mickey Mahler	5	23	6.26	P-5(1-2)	A	
Mike Marshall	4	6	9.00	P-4(1-0)	B	xTex-A
Gary Matthews	148	627	.800	LF-145	SF-N	
Joey McLaughlin	3	6	15.00	P-3	A	
Andy Messersmith	16	102	4.40	P-16(5-4)	B	NY-A
Willie Montanez	136	582	.788	1-134	B	NY-N
Junior Moore	112	408	.668	3-104,2-1	B	Chi-A
Dale Murphy	18	76	.842	C-18	B	
Phil Niekro	44	330	4.03	P-44(16-20)	B	
Joe Nolan	62	96	.806	C-19	B	
Rowland Office	124	461	.595	CF-104,1-1	B	
Tom Paciorek	72	164	.615	1-32,LF-9,3-1	B	
Biff Pocoroba	113	387	.844	C-100	B	
Craig Robinson	27	30	.475	S-23	B	C
Pat Rockett	93	297	.633	S-84	B	
Jerry Royster	140	491	.567	3-56,S-51,2-38,CF-1	B	
Dick Ruthven	25	151	4.23	P-25(7-13)	B	
Eddie Solomon	18	89	4.57	P-18(6-6)	StL-N	
Duane Theiss	17	21	6.53	P-17(1-1)	A	
Larry Whisenton	4	4	.500	H	A	

Coaches: Vern Benson, Chris Cannizzaro, Eddie Haas, Johnny Sain

♦ 1978 ATLANTA (162 69-93 6W) ATT: 904,494

Name	G	AB/IP	P/E	G/POS	From	To
Bobby Cox				M		
Brian Asselstine	39	122	.771	RF-35	B	
Bob Beall	108	225	.672	1-40,LF-8	B	
Rob Belloir	2	1	3.000	S-1,3-1	B	C
Bruce Benedict	22	58	.616	C-22	A	
Tommy Boggs	16	59	6.71	P-16(2-8)	Tex-A	
Barry Bonnell	117	326	.593	CF-105,3-15	B	
Jim Bouton	5	29	4.97	P-5(1-3)	Hou-N	C
Jeff Burroughs	153	611	.965	LF-146	B	
Rick Camp	42	74	3.75	P-42(2-4)	B	
Dave Campbell	53	69	4.80	P-53(4-4)	B	C
Darrel Chaney	89	274	.602	S-77,3-8,2-1	B	
Mike Davey	3	3	0.00	P-3	B	C
Adrian Devine	31	65	5.92	P-31(5-4)	Tex-A	
Jamie Easterly	37	78	5.65	P-37(3-6)	B	
Gene Garber	44	78	2.53	P-43(4-4)	xPhi-N	
Cito Gaston	60	124	.511	RF-29,1-4	B	xPit-N
Rod Gilbreath	116	356	.632	3-62,2-39	B	C
Preston Hanna	29	140	5.13	P-29(7-13)	B	
Bob Horner	89	359	.860	3-89	A	
Glenn Hubbard	44	179	.628	2-44	A	
Frank LaCorte	2	15	3.68	P-2(0-1)	B	
Max Leon	6	6	6.35	P-5	B	C
Jerry Maddox	7	15	.481	3-5	A	C
Mickey Mahler	34	135	4.68	P-34(4-11)	B	
Gary Matthews	129	542	.831	RF-127	B	
Larry McWilliams	15	99	2.81	P-15(9-3)	A	
Eddie Miller	6	24	.440	CF-5	Tex-A	
Dale Murphy	151	583	.681	1-129,C-21	B	
Phil Niekro	45	334	2.88	P-44(19-18)	B	
Joe Nolan	95	249	.686	C-61	B	
Rowland Office	146	439	.653	CF-136	B	C
Tom Paciorek	5	9	.667	1-2	B	xSea-A
Biff Pocoroba	92	327	.648	C-79	B	

Name	G	AB/IP	P/E	G/POS	From	To
Pat Rockett	55	157	.368	S-51	B	C
Jerry Royster	140	600	.666	2-75,S-60,3-1	B	
Chico Ruiz	18	48	.660	2-14,3-1	A	
Dick Ruthven	13	81	4.11	P-13(2-6)	B	xPhi-N
Craig Skok	43	62	4.35	P-43(3-2)	Tex-A	
Hank Small	1	4	.000	1-1	A	C
Eddie Solomon	38	106	4.08	P-37(4-6)	B	
Duane Theiss	3	6	1.42	P-3	B	C
Larry Whisenton	6	17	.485	RF-4	B	

Coaches: Cloyd Boyer, Tom Burgess, Chris Cannizzaro, Pete Ward

♦ 1979 ATLANTA (160 66-94 6W) ATT: 769,465

Name	G	AB/IP	P/E	G/POS	From	To
Bobby Cox				M		
Brian Asselstine	8	11	.282	LF-1	B	
Bob Beall	17	19	.544	1-3	B	Pit-N
Bruce Benedict	76	241	.613	C-76	B	
Tommy Boggs	3	13	6.39	P-3(0-2)	B	
Barry Bonnell	127	412	.736	LF-124,3-1	B	Tor-A
Larry Bradford	21	19	0.95	P-21(1-0)	B	
Tony Brizzolara	20	107	5.28	P-20(6-9)	A	
Jeff Burroughs	116	475	.696	LF-110	B	
Darrel Chaney	63	137	.485	S-39,2-5,3-4,C-1	B	C
Adrian Devine	40	67	3.24	P-40(1-2)	B	Tex-A
Jamie Easterly	4	3	13.50	P-4	B	Mil-A
Pepe Frias	140	510	.612	S-137	Mon-N	Tex-A
Gene Garber	68	106	4.33	P-68(6-16)	B	
Preston Hanna	6	24	2.96	P-6(1-1)	B	
Bob Horner	121	515	.900	3-82,1-45	B	
Glenn Hubbard	97	357	.587	2-91	B	
Frank LaCorte	6	8	7.56	P-6	B	xHou-N
Mike Lum	111	242	.666	1-51,LF-3	Cin-N	
Mike Macha	6	14	.368	3-3	A	Tor-A
Mickey Mahler	26	100	5.85	P-26(5-11)	B	Pit-N
Rick Mahler	15	22	6.14	P-15	A	
Gary Matthews	156	695	.867	RF-156	B	
Rick Matula	28	171	4.15	P-28(8-10)	A	
Joey McLaughlin	37	69	2.48	P-37(5-3)	B	Tor-A
Bo McLaughlin	37	50	4.89	P-37(1-1)	xHou-N	Oak-A
Larry McWilliams	13	66	5.56	P-13(3-2)	B	
Eddie Miller	27	123	.669	CF-27	B	
Dale Murphy	104	429	.813	1-76,C-27	B	
Phil Niekro	44	342	3.39	P-44(21-20)	B	
Joe Nolan	89	261	.700	C-74	B	
Rowland Office	124	307	.656	CF-97	B	Mon-N
Biff Pocoroba	28	46	.843	C-7	B	
Jerry Royster	154	676	.690	3-80,2-77	B	
Craig Skok	44	54	3.98	P-44(1-3)	B	C
Eddie Solomon	32	186	4.21	P-31(7-14)	B	Pit-N
Charlie Spikes	66	100	.779	LF-15	Det-A	
Jim Wessinger	10	8	.125	2-2	A	C
Larry Whisenton	13	41	.651	LF-13	B	

Coaches: Tommie Aaron, Cloyd Boyer, Bobby Dews, Alex Grammas

♦ 1980 ATLANTA (161 81-80 4W) ATT: 1,048,411

Name	G	AB/IP	P/E	G/POS	From	To
Bobby Cox				M		
Doyle Alexander	35	232	4.20	P-35(14-11)	Tex-A	SF-N
Brian Asselstine	87	235	.716	CF-61	B	
Bruce Benedict	120	402	.624	C-120	B	
Larvell Blanks	88	243	.515	S-56,3-43,2-1	Tex-A	C
Tommy Boggs	32	192	3.42	P-32(12-9)	B	
Larry Bradford	56	55	2.44	P-56(3-4)	B	
Jeff Burroughs	99	318	.802	LF-73	B	Sea-A
Rick Camp	77	108	1.91	P-77(6-4)	B	
Chris Chambliss	158	661	.781	1-158	NY-A	
Gary Cooper	21	2	.000	LF-13	A	C
Gene Garber	68	82	3.83	P-68(5-5)	B	
Luis Gomez	121	307	.452	S-119	Tor-A	
Preston Hanna	32	79	3.18	P-32(2-0)	B	
Terry Harper	21	61	.538	LF-18	A	
Bob Horner	124	495	.839	3-121,1-1	B	
Al Hrabosky	45	60	3.62	P-45(4-2)	KC-A	
Glenn Hubbard	117	487	.699	2-117	B	
Mike Lum	93	103	.587	LF-19,1-10	B	
Rick Mahler	2	4	2.45	P-2	B	
Gary Matthews	155	619	.746	RF-143	B	Phi-N
Rick Matula	33	177	4.58	P-33(11-13)	B	
Larry McWilliams	30	164	4.95	P-30(9-14)	B	
Eddie Miller	11	19	.316	CF-9	B	
Dale Murphy	156	633	.859	CF-154,1-1	B	
Bill Nahorodny	59	167	.701	C-54,1-1	Chi-A	
Phil Niekro	40	275	3.63	P-40(15-18)	B	
Joe Nolan	17	24	.652	C-6	B	xCin-N
Biff Pocoroba	70	96	.737	C-10	B	
Rafael Ramirez	50	174	.644	S-46	A	
Jerry Royster	123	435	.628	2-49,3-48,LF-41	B	
Chico Ruiz	25	29	.841	3-16,S-4,2-2	B	C
Charlie Spikes	41	40	.656	RF-7	B	C

Coaches: Tommie Aaron, Cloyd Boyer, Bobby Dews, John Sullivan

♦ 1981 ATLANTA (107 50-56 5W) ATT: 535,418

Name	G	AB/IP	P/E	G/POS	From	To
Bobby Cox				M(55 25-29 4) 1st half		
Bobby Cox				M(52 25-27 5) 2nd half		
Jose Alvarez	1	2	0.00	P-1	A	
Brian Asselstine	56	91	.680	RF-16	B	C
Steve Bedrosian	15	24	4.44	P-15(1-2)	A	
Bruce Benedict	90	339	.707	C-90	B	
Tommy Boggs	25	143	4.10	P-25(3-13)	B	
Larry Bradford	25	27	3.71	P-25(2-0)	B	C
Brett Butler	40	145	.669	LF-37	A	
Rick Camp	48	76	1.78	P-48(9-3)	B	
Chris Chambliss	107	454	.749	1-107	B	
Gene Garber	35	59	2.61	P-35(4-6)	B	
Luis Gomez	35	41	.517	S-21,3-9,2-3,P-1	B	
Albert Hall	6	3	.333	LF-2	A	
Preston Hanna	20	35	6.37	P-20(2-1)	B	

Name	G	AB/IP	P/E	G/POS	From	To
Terry Harper	40	85	.713	RF-27	B	
Bob Horner	79	336	.808	3-79	B	
Al Hrabosky	24	34	1.07	P-24(1-1)	B	
Glenn Hubbard	99	400	.652	2-98	B	
Brook Jacoby	11	10	.400	3-3	A	
Rufino Linares	78	265	.666	LF-60	A	
Mike Lum	10	13	.322	LF-1	B	xChi-N
Rick Mahler	34	112	2.80	P-34(8-6)	B	
Rick Matula	5	7	6.43	P-5	B	C
Larry McWilliams	6	38	3.11	P-6(2-1)	B	
Eddie Miller	50	146	.553	LF-36	B	Det-A
John Montefusco	26	77	3.49	P-26(2-3)	SF-N	SD-N
Dale Murphy	104	416	.717	CF-103,1-3	B	
Bill Nahorodny	14	14	.593	C-3,1-1	B	Cle-A
Phil Niekro	22	139	3.10	P-22(7-7)	B	
Larry Owen	13	17	.059	C-10	A	
Gaylord Perry	24	151	3.94	P-23(8-9)	NY-A	Sea-A
Biff Pocoroba	57	140	.478	3-21,C-9	B	
Bob Porter	17	16	.732	H	A	
Rafael Ramirez	95	342	.580	S-95	B	
Jerry Royster	64	105	.529	3-24,2-13	B	
Paul Runge	10	31	.651	S-10	A	
Matt Sinatro	12	37	.753	C-12	A	
Ken Smith	5	3	1.000	1-4	A	
Bob Walk	12	43	4.57	P-12(1-4)		Phi-N
Claudell Washington	85	349	.755	RF-79		NY-N
Larry Whisenton	9	7	.629	LF-2	B	

Coaches: Tommie Aaron, Cloyd Boyer, Bobby Dews, John Sullivan

♦ 1982 ATLANTA (162 89-73 1W) ATT: 1,801,985
Joe Torre M

Name	G	AB/IP	P/E	G/POS	From	To
Jose Alvarez	7	8	4.70	P-7	B	
Steve Bedrosian	64	138	2.42	P-64(8-6)	B	
Bruce Benedict	118	436	.620	C-118	B	
Tommy Boggs	10	46	3.30	P-10(2-2)	B	
Brett Butler	89	268	.516	CF-77	B	
Rick Camp	51	177	3.65	P-51(11-13)	B	
Chris Chambliss	157	597	.776	1-151	B	
Joe Cowley	17	52	4.47	P-17(1-2)	A	NY-A
Ken Dayley	20	71	4.54	P-20(5-6)	A	
Carlos Diaz	19	25	4.62	P-19(3-2)	A	xNY-N
Gene Garber	69	119	2.34	P-69(8-10)	B	
Albert Hall	5	0	†	R	B	
Preston Hanna	20	36	3.75	P-20(3-0)	B	xOak-A
Terry Harper	48	167	.698	LF-41	B	
Tom Hausman	3	4	4.91	P-3	xNY-N	C
Bob Horner	140	572	.852	3-137	B	
Al Hrabosky	31	37	5.54	P-31(2-1)	B	C
Glenn Hubbard	145	618	.676	2-144	B	
Randy Johnson	27	56	.700	2-13,3-4	A	
Rufino Linares	77	200	.704	LF-53	B	
Rick Mahler	39	205	4.21	P-39(9-10)	B	
Larry McWilliams	27	38	6.21	P-27(2-3)	B	xPit-N
Donnie Moore	16	28	4.23	P-16(3-1)	Mil-A	
Dale Murphy	162	698	.887	CF-162	B	
Phil Niekro	35	234	3.61	P-35(17-4)	B	
Larry Owen	2	3	1.000	C-2	B	
Pascual Perez	16	79	3.06	P-16(4-4)	Pit-N	
Biff Pocoroba	56	134	.734	C-36,3-2	B	
Bob Porter	24	29	.254	LF-4,1-1	B	C
Rafael Ramirez	157	669	.700	S-157	B	
Jerry Royster	108	293	.738	3-62,LF-25,2-16,S-10	B	
Paul Runge	4	2	.000	H	B	
Matt Sinatro	37	87	.374	C-35	B	
Ken Smith	48	47	.700	1-6,LF-3	B	
Bob Walk	32	164	4.87	P-32(11-9)	B	
Claudell Washington	150	626	.748	RF-139	B	
Bob Watson	57	130	.749	1-27,LF-2	xNY-A	
Larry Whisenton	84	168	.742	LF-34	B	C
Paul Zuvella	2	1	.000	S-1	A	

Coaches: Tommie Aaron, Bob Gibson, Sonny Jackson, Dal Maxvill, Joe Pignatano, Rube Walker

♦ 1983 ATLANTA (162 88-74 2W) ATT: 2,119,935
Joe Torre M

Name	G	AB/IP	P/E	G/POS	From	To
Len Barker	6	33	3.82	P-6(1-3)	xCle-A	
Steve Bedrosian	70	120	3.60	P-70(9-10)	B	
Rick Behenna	14	37	4.58	P-14(3-3)	A	xCle-A
Bruce Benedict	134	492	.735	C-134	B	
Tommy Boggs	5	6	5.68	P-5	B	Tex-A
Tony Brizzolara	14	20	3.54	P-14(1-0)	B	
Brett Butler	151	613	.741	LF-143	B	Cle-A
Rick Camp	40	140	3.79	P-40(10-9)	B	
Chris Chambliss	131	513	.850	1-126	B	
Ken Dayley	25	105	4.30	P-24(5-8)	B	
Jeff Dedmon	5	4	13.50	P-5	A	
Pete Falcone	33	107	3.63	P-33(9-4)	NY-N	
Terry Forster	56	79	2.16	P-56(3-2)	LA-N	
Gene Garber	43	61	4.60	P-43(4-5)	B	
Albert Hall	10	10	.200	LF-4	B	
Terry Harper	80	224	.716	RF-60	B	
Bob Horner	104	439	.913	3-104,1-1	B	
Glenn Hubbard	148	592	.741	2-148	B	
Brook Jacoby	4	9	.000	3-2	B	Cle-A
Randy Johnson	86	169	.637	3-53,2-4	B	
Mike Jorgensen	57	57	.690	1-19,LF-6	xNY-N	
Brad Komminsk	19	41	.595	RF-13	A	
Rick Mahler	10	14	5.02	P-10	B	
Craig McMurtry	36	225	3.08	P-36(15-9)	A	
Donnie Moore	43	69	3.67	P-43(2-3)	B	
Dale Murphy	162	687	.936	CF-160	B	
Phil Niekro	34	202	3.97	P-34(11-10)	B	NY-A
Larry Owen	17	17	.235	C-16	B	
Pascual Perez	33	215	3.43	P-33(15-8)	B	
Gerald Perry	27	45	.919	1-7,LF-1	A	
Biff Pocoroba	55	133	.700	C-34	B	
Rafael Ramirez	152	668	.706	S-152	B	
Jerry Royster	91	303	.636	3-47,2-26,LF-18,S-13	B	
Paul Runge	5	10	.583	2-2	B	
Matt Sinatro	7	14	.452	C-7	B	
Ken Smith	30	13	.647	1-13	B	C
Bob Walk	1	4	7.36	P-1	B	Pit-N
Claudell Washington	134	538	.739	RF-128	B	
Bob Watson	65	170	.873	1-34	B	
Paul Zuvella	3	8	.375	S-2	A	

Coaches: Tommie Aaron, Bob Gibson, Sonny Jackson, Dal Maxvill, Joe Pignatano, Rube Walker

♦ 1984 ATLANTA (162 80-82 2W) ATT: 1,724,892
Joe Torre M

Name	G	AB/IP	P/E	G/POS	From	To
Len Barker	21	126	3.85	P-21(7-8)	B	
Steve Bedrosian	40	84	2.37	P-40(9-6)	B	
Bruce Benedict	95	340	.601	C-95	B	
Tony Brizzolara	10	29	5.28	P-10(1-2)	B	C
Rick Camp	31	149	3.27	P-31(8-6)	B	
Chris Chambliss	135	454	.717	1-109	B	
Ken Dayley	5	19	5.30	P-4(0-3)	B	xStL-N
Jeff Dedmon	54	81	3.78	P-54(4-3)	B	
Pete Falcone	35	120	4.13	P-35(5-7)	B	C
Terry Forster	25	27	2.70	P-25(2-0)	B	
Gene Garber	62	106	3.06	P-62(3-6)	B	
Albert Hall	87	153	.647	LF-66	B	
Terry Harper	40	108	.402	LF-29	B	
Bob Horner	32	129	.779	3-32	B	
Glenn Hubbard	120	461	.714	2-117	B	
Randy Johnson	91	322	.703	3-81	B	C
Mike Jorgensen	31	30	.653	1-8,RF-4	B	xStL-N
Brad Komminsk	90	334	.593	RF-80	B	
Rufino Linares	34	66	.592	LF-13	B	Cal-A
Rick Mahler	38	222	3.12	P-38(13-10)	B	
Craig McMurtry	40	183	4.32	P-37(9-17)	B	
Donnie Moore	47	64	2.94	P-47(4-5)	B	Cal-A
Dale Murphy	162	691	.920	CF-160	B	
Ken Oberkfell	50	193	.602	3-45,2-4	xStL-N	
Mike Payne	3	6	6.35	P-3(0-1)	A	C
Pascual Perez	32	212	3.74	P-30(14-8)	B	
Gerald Perry	122	419	.750	1-64,LF-53	B	
Biff Pocoroba	4	4	.500	H	B	C
Rafael Ramirez	145	629	.624	S-145	B	
Jerry Royster	81	247	.554	2-29,3-17,S-16,LF-11	B	SD-N
Paul Runge	28	103	.662	2-22,S-7,3-3	B	
Matt Sinatro	2	4	.000	C-2	B	Oak-A
Zane Smith	3	20	2.25	P-3(1-0)	A	
Milt Thompson	25	111	.746	LF-25	B	
Alex Trevino	79	289	.628	C-79	xCin-N	SF-N
Claudell Washington	120	479	.845	RF-107	B	
Bob Watson	49	94	.617	1-19	B	C
Paul Zuvella	11	27	.499	2-6,S-6	B	

Coaches: Bob Gibson, Dal Maxvill, Joe Pignatano, Rube Walker

♦ 1985 ATLANTA (162 66-96 5W) ATT: 1,350,137
Eddie Haas M(121 50-71 5)
Bobby Wine M(41 16-25 5)

Name	G	AB/IP	P/E	G/POS	From	To
Len Barker	20	74	6.35	P-20(2-9)	B	Mil-A
Steve Bedrosian	37	207	3.83	P-37(7-15)	B	Phi-N
Bruce Benedict	70	237	.512	C-70	B	
Rick Camp	66	128	3.95	P-66(4-6)	B	C
Rick Cerone	96	316	.572	C-91	NY-A	Mil-A
Chris Chambliss	101	189	.638	1-39	B	
Jeff Dedmon	60	86	4.08	P-60(6-3)	B	
Terry Forster	46	59	2.28	P-46(2-3)	B	Cal-A
Gene Garber	59	97	3.61	P-59(6-6)	B	
Albert Hall	54	57	.477	LF-13	B	
Terry Harper	138	542	.735	LF-131	B	
Bob Horner	130	540	.836	1-87,3-40	B	
Glenn Hubbard	142	512	.639	2-140	B	
Joe Johnson	15	86	4.10	P-15(4-4)	A	
Brad Komminsk	106	343	.642	RF-92	B	
Rick Mahler	39	267	3.48	P-39(17-15)	B	
Craig McMurtry	17	45	6.60	P-17(0-3)	B	
Dale Murphy	162	712	.929	CF-161	B	
Ken Oberkfell	134	472	.720	3-117,2-16	B	
Larry Owen	26	82	.683	C-25	B	KC-A
Pascual Perez	22	95	6.14	P-22(1-13)	B	Mon-N
Gerald Perry	110	262	.557	1-55,LF-1	B	
John Rabb	3	2	.000	LF-1	SF-N	Sea-A
Rafael Ramirez	138	595	.607	S-133	B	
Paul Runge	50	110	.640	3-28,S-5,2-2	B	
Dave Schuler	9	11	6.75	P-9	Cal-A	C
Steve Shields	23	68	5.16	P-23(1-2)	A	
Zane Smith	43	147	3.80	P-42(9-10)	B	
Bruce Sutter	58	88	4.48	P-58(7-7)	StL-N	
Andres Thomas	15	19	.556	S-10	A	
Milt Thompson	73	193	.701	RF-49	B	Phi-N
Claudell Washington	122	441	.799	RF-99	B	
Paul Zuvella	81	210	.616	2-42,S-33,3-5	B	NY-A

Coaches: Bobby Dews, Clarence Jones, Leo Mazzone, Joe Pignatano, Johnny Sain, Brian Snitker, Bobby Wine

♦ 1986 ATLANTA (161 72-89 6W) ATT: 1,387,181
Chuck Tanner M

Name	G	AB/IP	P/E	G/POS	From	To
Jim Acker	21	95	3.79	P-21(3-8)	xTor-A	
Doyle Alexander	18	117	3.84	P-17(6-6)	xTor-A	
Paul Assenmacher	61	68	2.50	P-61(7-3)	A	
Bruce Benedict	64	182	.599	C-57	B	

Name	G	AB/IP	P/E	G/POS	From	To
Chris Chambliss	97	138	.813	1-20	B	NY-A
Jeff Dedmon	57	100	2.98	P-57(6-6),LF-1	B	
Gene Garber	61	78	2.54	P-61(5-5)	B	
Ken Griffey	80	313	.856	LF-77,1-1	xNY-A	
Albert Hall	16	57	.589	RF-14	B	
Terry Harper	106	298	.725	LF-83	B	Det-A
Bob Horner	141	581	.813	1-139	B	StL-N
Glenn Hubbard	143	488	.647	2-142	B	
Joe Johnson	17	87	4.97	P-17(6-7)	B	xTor-A
Brad Komminsk	5	5	.800	3-2,RF-2	B	Mil-A
Rick Mahler	40	238	4.88	P-39(14-18)	B	
Craig McMurtry	40	80	4.74	P-37(1-6)	B	Tex-A
Omar Moreno	118	386	.627	RF-97	KC-A	C
Darryl Motley	5	11	.573	RF-3	xKC-A	
Dale Murphy	160	692	.825	CF-159	B	
Ken Oberkfell	151	596	.736	3-130,2-41	B	
Ed Olwine	37	48	3.40	P-37	A	
David Palmer	35	210	3.65	P-35(11-10)	Mon-N	
Gerald Perry	29	80	.732	LF-21,1-1	B	
Charlie Puleo	5	24	2.96	P-5(1-2)	Cin-N	
Rafael Ramirez	134	530	.610	S-86,3-57,LF-3	B	
Paul Runge	7	10	.650	2-5	B	
Bill Sample	92	221	.771	RF-56,2-1	NY-A	C
Steve Shields	6	13	7.11	P-6	B	xKC-A
Ted Simmons	76	144	.707	1-14,C-10,3-9	Mil-A	
Zane Smith	43	205	4.05	P-38(8-16)	B	
Cliff Speck	13	28	4.13	P-13(2-1)	A	C
Bruce Sutter	16	19	4.34	P-16(2-0)	B	
Andres Thomas	102	335	.640	S-97	B	
Ozzie Virgil	114	431	.718	C-111	Phi-N	
Duane Ward	10	16	7.31	P-10(0-1)	A	xTor-A
Claudell Washington	40	153	.798	RF-38	B	xNY-A

Coaches: Tony Bartirome, Al Monchak, Rich Morales, Russ Nixon, Johnny Sain, Bob Skinner, Willie Stargell

♦ 1987 ATLANTA (161 69-92 5W) ATT: 1,217,402

Name	G	AB/IP	P/E	G/POS	From	To
Chuck Tanner				M		
Jim Acker	68	115	4.16	P-68(4-9)	B	
Doyle Alexander	16	118	4.13	P-16(5-10)	B	xDet-A
Paul Assenmacher	52	55	5.10	P-52(1-1)	B	
Terry Bell	1	1	.000	H	KC-A	C
Bruce Benedict	37	114	.466	C-35	B	
Jeff Blauser	51	187	.679	S-50	A	
Joe Boever	14	18	7.36	P-14(1-0)	StL-N	
Chuck Cary	13	17	3.78	P-13(1-1)	Det-A	
Marty Clary	7	15	6.14	P-7(0-1)	A	
Kevin Coffman	5	25	4.62	P-5(2-3)	A	
Trench Davis	6	3	.000	H	Pit-N	C
Jeff Dedmon	53	90	3.91	P-53(3-4)	B	Cle-A
Mike Fischlin	1	0	†	R	NY-A	C
Ron Gant	21	86	.659	2-20	A	
Gene Garber	49	69	4.41	P-49(8-10)	B	xKC-A
Tom Glavine	9	50	5.54	P-9(2-4)	A	
Ken Griffey	122	451	.817	LF-107,1-3	B	
Albert Hall	92	337	.781	CF-69	B	
Glenn Hubbard	141	533	.762	2-139	B	Oak-A
Dion James	134	494	.871	CF-126	Mil-A	
Rick Mahler	40	197	4.98	P-39(8-13)	B	
Larry McWilliams	9	20	5.75	P-9(0-1)	Pit-N	StL-N
Darryl Motley	6	8	.000	LF-2	B	C
Dale Murphy	159	693	1.000	RF-159	B	
Graig Nettles	112	201	.647	3-40,1-6	SD-N	Mon-N
Phil Niekro	1	3	15.00	P-1	xCle-A	C
Ken Oberkfell	135	566	.706	3-126,2-11	B	
Ed Olwine	27	23	5.01	P-27(0-1)	B	
Randy O'Neal	17	61	5.61	P-16(4-2)	Det-A	xStL-N
David Palmer	28	152	4.90	P-28(8-11)	B	Phi-N
Gerald Perry	142	590	.742	1-136,LF-7	B	
Charlie Puleo	36	123	4.23	P-35(6-8)	B	
Rafael Ramirez	56	194	.648	S-38,3-12	B	Hou-N
Gary Roenicke	67	187	.809	LF-44,1-9	NY-A	
Paul Runge	27	54	.714	3-10,S-9,2-2	B	
Ted Simmons	73	200	.743	1-28,C-15,3-2	B	
Pete Smith	6	32	4.83	P-6(1-2)	A	
Zane Smith	41	242	4.09	P-36(15-10)	B	
Andres Thomas	82	343	.579	S-81	B	
Ozzie Virgil	123	486	.802	C-122	B	
Steve Ziem	2	2	7.71	P-2(0-1)	A	C

Coaches: Tony Bartirome, J. Dal Canton, Al Monchak, Rich Morales, Russ Nixon, Bob Skinner, Willie Stargell

♦ 1988 ATLANTA (160 54-106 6W) ATT: 848,089

Name	G	AB/IP	P/E	G/POS	From	To
Chuck Tanner				M(39 12-27 6)		
Russ Nixon				M(121 42-79 6)		
Jim Acker	21	42	4.71	P-21(0-4)	B	
Jose Alvarez	61	102	2.99	P-60(5-6)	B	
Paul Assenmacher	64	79	3.06	P-64(8-7)	B	
Bruce Benedict	90	262	.569	C-89	B	
Kevin Blankenship	2	11	3.38	P-2(0-1)	A	xChi-N
Jeff Blauser	18	74	.674	2-9,S-8	B	
Terry Blocker	66	210	.533	CF-61	NY-N	
Joe Boever	16	20	1.77	P-16(0-2)	B	
Chuck Cary	7	8	6.48	P-7	B	NY-A
Kevin Coffman	19	67	5.78	P-18(2-6)	B	Chi-N
Jody Davis	2	8	.875	C-2	xChi-N	
Gary Eave	5	5	9.00	P-5	A	
Juan Eichelberger	20	37	3.86	P-20(2-0)	Cle-A	C
Ron Gant	146	618	.757	2-122,3-22	B	
Damaso Garcia	21	64	.342	2-13	Tor-A	Mon-N
Tom Glavine	42	195	4.56	P-34(7-17)	B	
Tommy Gregg	11	31	.835	LF-7	xPit-N	
Ken Griffey	69	212	.615	LF-42,1-11	B	xCin-N
Albert Hall	85	257	.614	CF-63	B	Pit-N
Dion James	132	449	.705	LF-120	B	
German Jimenez	15	56	5.01	P-15(1-6)	A	C
Mark Lemke	16	64	.567	2-16	A	
Rick Mahler	39	249	3.69	P-39(9-16)	B	Cin-N
Jim Morrison	51	105	.474	3-20,LF-4,P-3	xDet-A	C
Dale Murphy	156	671	.735	RF-156	B	
Ken Oberkfell	120	469	.696	3-113,2-1	B	xPit-N
Ed Olwine	16	19	6.75	P-16	B	C
Gerald Perry	141	595	.745	1-141	B	
Charlie Puleo	53	106	3.47	P-53(5-5)	B	
Gary Roenicke	49	122	.577	LF-35,1-1	B	C
Jerry Royster	68	111	.428	CF-26,3-10,2-2,S-2	NY-A	C
Paul Runge	52	91	.610	3-19,2-7,S-6	B	C
Ted Simmons	78	123	.603	1-19,C-10	B	C
Lonnie Smith	43	125	.640	LF-35	KC-A	
Pete Smith	32	195	3.69	P-32(7-15)	B	
Zane Smith	27	140	4.30	P-23(5-10)	B	
John Smoltz	12	64	5.48	P-12(2-7)	A	
Bruce Sutter	38	45	4.76	P-38(1-4)	B	
Andres Thomas	153	627	.630	S-150	B	
Ozzie Virgil	107	350	.686	C-96	B	Tor-A

Coaches: Tony Bartirome, J. Dal Canton, Clarence Jones, Roy Majtyka, Al Monchak, Bob Skinner, Brian Snitker, Willie Stargell

♦ 1989 ATLANTA (161 63-97 6W) ATT: 984,930

Name	G	AB/IP	P/E	G/POS	From	To
Russ Nixon				M		
Jim Acker	59	98	2.67	P-59(0-6)	B	xTor-A
Jay Aldrich	8	12	2.19	P-8(1-2)	xMil-A	Bal-A
Jose Alvarez	30	50	2.86	P-30(3-3)	B	C
Paul Assenmacher	49	58	3.59	P-49(1-3)	B	xChi-N
Bruce Benedict	66	186	.530	C-65	B	C
Geronimo Berroa	81	143	.639	RF-34	B	
Jeff Blauser	142	507	.737	3-78,2-39,S-30,CF-2	B	
Terry Blocker	26	32	.508	RF-8,P-1	B	C
Joe Boever	66	82	3.94	P-66(4-11)	B	
Francisco Cabrera	4	14	.571	1-2,C-1	xTor-A	
Tony Castillo	12	9	4.82	P-12(0-1)	xTor-A	
Marty Clary	18	109	3.15	P-18(4-3)	B	
Jody Davis	78	257	.489	C-72,1-2	B	
Drew Denson	12	39	.585	1-12	A	Chi-A
Gary Eave	3	21	1.31	P-3(2-0)	B	Sea-A
Mark Eichhorn	45	68	4.35	P-45(5-5)	Tor-A	Cal-A
Darrell Evans	107	323	.664	1-50,3-28	Det-A	C
Ron Gant	75	285	.573	3-53,CF-14	B	
Tom Glavine	30	186	3.68	P-29(14-8)	B	
Tommy Greene	4	26	4.10	P-4(1-2)	A	
Tommy Gregg	102	298	.626	RF-48,1-37	B	
Dwayne Henry	12	13	4.26	P-12(0-2)	Tex-A	
Dion James	63	200	.675	LF-46,1-8	B	xCle-A
David Justice	16	56	.644	RF-16	A	
Mark Lemke	14	60	.614	2-14	B	
Derek Lilliquist	36	166	3.97	P-32(8-10)	A	
Kelly Mann	7	25	.532	C-7	A	
Oddibe McDowell	76	308	.836	CF-68	xCle-A	
Kent Mercker	2	4	12.46	P-2	A	
John Mizerock	11	27	.444	C-11	Hou-N	C
Dale Murphy	154	647	.670	CF-151	B	
Gerald Perry	72	303	.677	1-72	B	KC-A
Charlie Puleo	15	29	4.66	P-15(1-1)	B	C
Rusty Richards	2	9	4.82	P-2	A	
Ed Romero	7	19	.737	2-4,S-2,3-1	xBos-A	xMil-A
John Russell	74	169	.459	C-45,RF-14,1-2,3-2,P-1	Phi-N	Tex-A
Lonnie Smith	134	577	.953	LF-132	B	
Pete Smith	29	142	4.75	P-28(5-14)	B	
Zane Smith	21	99	4.45	P-17(1-12)	B	xMon-N
John Smoltz	33	208	2.94	P-29(12-11)	B	
Mike Stanton	20	24	1.50	P-20(0-1)	A	
Andres Thomas	141	571	.546	S-138	B	
Jeff Treadway	134	514	.699	2-123,3-6	Cin-N	
Sergio Valdez	19	33	6.06	P-19(1-2)	Mon-N	
Jeff Wetherby	52	55	.623	LF-9	A	C
Ed Whited	36	82	.468	3-29,1-3	A	C

Coaches: J. Dal Canton, Clarence Jones, Roy Majtyka, Brian Snitker, Bobby Wine

♦ 1990 ATLANTA (162 65-97 6W) ATT: 980,129

Name	G	AB/IP	P/E	G/POS	From	To
Russ Nixon				M(65 25-40 6)		
Bobby Cox				M(97 40-57 6)		
Steve Avery	21	99	5.64	P-21(3-11)	A	
Mike Bell	36	48	.758	1-24	A	
Geronimo Berroa	7	5	.200	LF-3	B	Cin-N
Jeff Blauser	115	429	.747	S-93,2-14,3-9,CF-1	B	
Joe Boever	33	42	4.68	P-33(1-3)	B	xPhi-N
Francisco Cabrera	63	143	.785	1-48,C-3	B	
Tony Castillo	52	77	4.23	P-52(5-1)	B	
Marty Clary	33	102	5.67	P-33(1-10)	B	C
Jody Davis	12	31	.233	1-6,C-4	B	C
Nick Esasky	9	38	.428	1-9	Bos-A	C
Marvin Freeman	9	16	1.72	P-9(1-0)	xPhi-N	
Ron Gant	152	631	.899	CF-146	B	
Tom Glavine	34	214	4.28	P-33(10-12)	B	
Mark Grant	33	52	4.64	P-33(1-2)	xSD-N	Sea-A
Tommy Greene	5	12	8.03	P-5(1-0)	B	xPhi-N
Tommy Gregg	124	261	.712	1-50,RF-20	B	
Dwayne Henry	34	38	5.63	P-34(2-2)	B	Hou-N
Joe Hesketh	31	31	5.81	P-31(0-2)	xMon-N	xBos-A
Alexis Infante	20	32	.140	2-10,3-4,S-3	Tor-A	
David Justice	127	504	.909	1-69,RF-61	B	
Charlie Kerfeld	25	31	5.58	P-25(3-1)	xHou-N	C
Jimmy Kremers	29	79	.369	C-27	A	C
Charlie Leibrandt	24	162	3.16	P-24(9-11)	KC-A	
Mark Lemke	102	266	.569	3-45,2-44,S-1	B	
Derek Lilliquist	13	62	6.28	P-12(2-8)	B	xSD-N
Rick Luecken	36	53	5.77	P-36(1-4)	KC-A	xTor-A
Kelly Mann	11	28	.429	C-10	B	C
Paul Marak	7	39	3.69	P-7(1-2)	A	C

Name	G	AB/IP	P/E	G/POS	From	To
Oddibe McDowell	113	329	.653	CF-72	B	Tex-A
Kent Mercker	36	48	3.17	P-36(4-7)	B	
Dale Murphy	97	394	.733	RF-97	B	xPhi-N
Greg Olson	100	332	.713	C-97,3-1	Min-A	
Jeff Parrett	20	27	3.00	P-20(1-1)	xPhi-N	
Jim Presley	140	577	.699	3-133,1-17	Sea-A	SD-N
Rusty Richards	1	1	27.00	P-1	B	C
Victor Rosario	9	8	.393	S-3,2-1	A	C
Doug Sisk	3	2	3.86	P-3	Bal-A	
Lonnie Smith	135	537	.848	LF-122	B	
Pete Smith	13	77	4.79	P-13(5-6)	B	
John Smoltz	38	231	3.85	P-34(14-11)	B	
Mike Stanton	7	7	18.00	P-7(0-3)	B	
Andres Thomas	84	290	.551	S-72,3-5	B	C
Jeff Treadway	128	511	.726	2-122	B	
Sergio Valdez	6	5	6.75	P-6	B	xCle-A
Jim Vatcher	21	28	.656	RF-6	xPhi-N	SD-N
Ernie Whitt	67	204	.516	C-59	B	Bal-A

Coaches: Pat Corrales, J. Dal Canton, Clarence Jones, Roy Majtyka, Leo Mazzone, Brian Snitker, Jimy Williams, Bobby Wine

♦ **1991 ATLANTA** (162 94-68 1W) ATT: 2,140,217

Name	G	AB/IP	P/E	G/POS	From	To
Bobby Cox				M		
Steve Avery	37	210	3.38	P-35(18-8)	B	
Mike Bell	17	32	.421	1-14	B	C
Rafael Belliard	149	385	.583	S-145	Pit-N	
Juan Berenguer	49	64	2.24	P-49(0-3)	Min-A	
Damon Berryhill	1	1	.000	C-1	xChi-N	
Mike Bielecki	2	2	0.00	P-2	xChi-N	
Jeff Blauser	129	415	.769	S-85,2-32,3-18	B	
Sid Bream	91	298	.740	1-85	Pit-N	
Francisco Cabrera	44	102	.719	C-17,1-14	B	
Vinny Castilla	12	6	.400	S-12	A	
Tony Castillo	7	9	7.27	P-7(1-1)	B	xNY-N
Jim Clancy	24	35	5.71	P-24(3-2)	xHou-N	C
Marvin Freeman	34	48	3.00	P-34(1-0)	B	
Ron Gant	154	642	.836	CF-148	B	
Tom Glavine	36	247	2.55	P-34(20-11)	B	
Tommy Gregg	72	120	.583	LF-14,1-13	B	
Mike Heath	49	150	.518	C-45	Det-A	C
Danny Heep	14	13	.962	1-1,LF-1	Bos-A	C
Brian Hunter	97	291	.748	1-85,LF-6	A	
David Justice	109	469	.884	RF-106	B	
Charlie Leibrandt	36	230	3.49	P-36(15-13)	B	
Mark Lemke	136	308	.621	2-110,3-15	B	
Rick Mahler	13	29	5.65	P-13(1-1)	xMon-N	C
Kent Mercker	50	73	2.58	P-50(5-3)	B	
Keith Mitchell	48	74	.801	LF-34	A	Sea-A
Otis Nixon	124	460	.700	LF-115	Mon-N	
Greg Olson	133	464	.664	C-127	B	
Jeff Parrett	18	21	6.33	P-18(1-2)	B	Oak-A
Alejandro Pena	15	19	1.40	P-15(2-0)	xNY-N	
Terry Pendleton	153	644	.884	3-148	StL-N	
Dan Petry	10	24	5.55	P-10	xDet-A	xBos-A
Armando Reynoso	6	23	6.17	P-6(2-1)	A	
Rico Rossy	5	1	.000	S-1	A	KC-A
Randy St.Claire	19	29	4.08	P-19	Min-A	
Deion Sanders	54	122	.616	LF-44	NY-A	
Doug Sisk	14	14	5.02	P-14(2-1)	B	C
Lonnie Smith	122	416	.772	LF-99	B	
Pete Smith	14	48	5.06	P-14(1-3)	B	
John Smoltz	38	230	3.80	P-36(14-13)	B	
Mike Stanton	74	78	2.88	P-74(5-5)	B	
Jeff Treadway	106	336	.790	2-93	B	
Jerry Willard	17	16	.741	C-1	Chi-A	
Mark Wohlers	17	20	3.20	P-17(3-1)	A	

Coaches: Jim Beauchamp, Pat Corrales, Clarence Jones, Leo Mazzone, Jimy Williams

♦ **1992 ATLANTA** (162 98-64 1W) ATT: 3,077,400

Name	G	AB/IP	P/E	G/POS	From	To
Bobby Cox				M		
Steve Avery	35	234	3.20	P-35(11-11)	B	
Rafael Belliard	144	315	.494	S-139,2-1	B	
Juan Berenguer	28	33	5.13	P-28(3-1)	B	xKC-A
Damon Berryhill	101	328	.655	C-84	B	
Mike Bielecki	19	81	2.57	P-19(2-4)	B	Cle-A
Jeff Blauser	123	403	.814	S-106,2-21,3-1	B	
Pedro Borbon	2	1	6.75	P-2(0-1)	A	
Sid Bream	125	426	.758	1-120	B	
Francisco Cabrera	12	11	1.264	C-1	B	
Vinny Castilla	9	18	.646	3-4,S-4	B	Col-N
Mark Davis	14	17	7.02	P-14(1-0)	xKC-A	Phi-N
Marvin Freeman	58	64	3.22	P-58(7-5)	B	
Ron Gant	153	602	.739	LF-147	B	
Tom Glavine	35	225	2.76	P-33(20-8)	B	
Tommy Gregg	18	20	.721	CF-9	B	Cin-N
Brian Hunter	102	268	.789	1-92,RF-6	B	
David Justice	144	571	.809	RF-140	B	
Ryan Klesko	13	15	.067	1-5	A	
Charlie Leibrandt	32	193	3.36	P-32(15-7)	B	Tex-A
Mark Lemke	155	491	.613	2-145,3-13	B	
Javy Lopez	9	16	.875	C-9	A	
Steve Lyons	11	14	.286	RF-6,2-2	Bos-A	xMon-N
Kent Mercker	53	68	3.42	P-53(3-2)	B	
David Nied	6	23	1.17	P-6(3-0)	A	Col-N
Melvin Nieves	12	21	.549	LF-6	A	SD-N
Otis Nixon	120	502	.696	CF-111	B	
Greg Olson	95	340	.645	C-94	B	
Alejandro Pena	41	42	4.07	P-41(1-6)	B	Pit-N
Terry Pendleton	160	689	.822	3-158	B	
Jeff Reardon	14	16	1.15	P-14(3-0)	xBos-A	Cin-N
Armando Reynoso	3	8	4.70	P-3(1-0)	B	Col-N
Ben Rivera	8	15	4.70	P-8(0-1)	A	xPhi-N
Randy St.Claire	10	15	5.87	P-10	B	Tor-A
Deion Sanders	97	325	.842	CF-75	B	

Name	G	AB/IP	P/E	G/POS	From	To
Lonnie Smith	84	182	.768	LF-35	B	Pit-N
Pete Smith	12	79	2.05	P-12(7-0)	B	
John Smoltz	36	247	2.85	P-35(15-12)	B	
Mike Stanton	65	64	4.10	P-65(5-4)	B	
Jeff Treadway	61	136	.560	2-45,3-1	B	Cle-A
Jerry Willard	26	24	1.027	C-1	B	xMon-N
Mark Wohlers	32	35	2.55	P-32(1-2)	B	

Coaches: Jim Beauchamp, Pat Corrales, Clarence Jones, Leo Mazzone, Jimy Williams

♦ **1993 ATLANTA** (162 104-58 1W) ATT: 3,884,720

Name	G	AB/IP	P/E	G/POS	From	To
Bobby Cox				M		
Steve Avery	35	223	2.94	P-35(18-6)	B	
Steve Bedrosian	49	50	1.63	P-49(5-2)	Min-A	
Rafael Belliard	91	89	.582	S-58,2-24	B	
Damon Berryhill	115	363	.675	C-105	B	Bos-A
Jeff Blauser	161	710	.841	S-161	B	
Pedro Borbon	3	2	21.60	P-3	B	
Sid Bream	117	311	.750	1-90	B	Hou-N
Francisco Cabrera	70	91	.729	1-12,C-2	B	C
Ramon Caraballo	6	0	†	2-5	A	StL-N
Marvin Freeman	21	24	6.08	P-21(2-0)	B	Col-N
Ron Gant	157	682	.858	LF-155	B	Cin-N
Tom Glavine	36	239	3.20	P-36(22-6)	B	
Jay Howell	54	58	2.31	P-54(3-3)	LA-N	Tex-A
Brian Hunter	37	85	.359	1-29,RF-2	B	Pit-N
Chipper Jones	8	4	1.750	S-3	A	
David Justice	157	670	.873	RF-157	B	
Ryan Klesko	22	20	1.215	1-3,LF-2	B	
Mark Lemke	151	569	.679	2-150	B	
Javy Lopez	8	17	1.162	C-7	B	
Greg Maddux	36	267	2.36	P-36(20-10)	Chi-N	
Fred McGriff	68	291	1.005	1-66	xSD-N	
Greg McMichael	74	92	2.06	P-74(2-3)	A	
Kent Mercker	43	66	2.86	P-43(3-1)	B	
Otis Nixon	134	532	.669	CF-116	B	Bos-A
Greg Olson	83	295	.614	C-81	B	C
Bill Pecota	72	65	.731	3-23,2-4,RF-1	NY-N	
Terry Pendleton	161	682	.722	3-161	B	
Deion Sanders	95	294	.775	CF-60	B	
Pete Smith	20	91	4.37	P-20(4-8)	B	NY-N
John Smoltz	35	244	3.62	P-35(15-11)	B	
Mike Stanton	63	52	4.67	P-63(4-6)	B	
Tony Tarasco	24	37	.536	RF-12	A	
Mark Wohlers	46	48	4.50	P-46(6-2)	B	

Coaches: Jim Beauchamp, Pat Corrales, Clarence Jones, Leo Mazzone, Jimy Williams

♦ **1994 ATLANTA** (114 68-46 2E) ATT: 2,539,240

Name	G	AB/IP	P/E	G/POS	From	To
Bobby Cox				M		
Steve Avery	24	152	4.04	P-24(8-3)	B	
Steve Bedrosian	46	46	3.33	P-46(0-2)	B	
Rafael Belliard	46	127	.583	S-26,2-18	B	
Mike Bielecki	19	27	4.00	P-19(2-0)	Cle-A	Cal-A
Jeff Blauser	96	434	.715	S-96	B	
Jarvis Brown	17	16	.533	CF-9	SD-N	Bal-A
Dave Gallagher	89	177	.622	LF-77,1-1	NY-N	Phi-N
Tom Glavine	26	165	3.97	P-25(13-9)	B	
Milt Hill	10	11	7.94	P-10	Cin-N	xSea-A
David Justice	104	424	.959	RF-102	B	
Mike Kelly	30	80	.806	LF-25	A	
Roberto Kelly	63	281	.787	CF-63	xCin-N	Mon-N
Ryan Klesko	92	276	.913	LF-74,1-6	B	
Mark Lemke	104	394	.726	2-103	B	
Javy Lopez	80	303	.720	C-75	B	
Greg Maddux	25	202	1.56	P-25(16-6)	B	
Fred McGriff	113	478	1.014	1-112	B	
Greg McMichael	51	59	3.84	P-51(4-6)	B	
Kent Mercker	20	112	3.45	P-20(9-4)	B	
Mike Mordecai	4	5	1.400	S-4	A	
Charlie O'Brien	51	172	.797	C-48	NY-N	
Jose Oliva	19	66	1.042	3-16	A	
Gregg Olson	16	15	9.20	P-16(0-2)	Bal-A	Cle-A
Bill Pecota	64	130	.625	3-31,2-1,LF-1	B	C
Terry Pendleton	77	324	.678	3-77	B	Fla-N
Deion Sanders	46	211	.749	CF-46	B	xCin-N
John Smoltz	21	135	4.14	P-21(6-10)	B	
Mike Stanton	49	46	3.55	P-49(3-1)	B	
Tony Tarasco	87	144	.751	LF-45	B	Mon-N
Mark Wohlers	51	51	4.59	P-51(7-2)	B	
Brad Woodall	1	6	4.50	P-1(0-1)	A	

Coaches: Jim Beauchamp, Pat Corrales, Clarence Jones, Leo Mazzone, Jimy Williams

♦ **1995 ATLANTA** (144 90-54 1E) ATT: 2,561,831

Name	G	AB/IP	P/E	G/POS	From	To
Bobby Cox				M		
Steve Avery	29	173	4.67	P-29(7-13)	B	
Steve Bedrosian	29	28	6.11	P-29(1-2)	B	
Rafael Belliard	75	192	.500	S-40,2-32	B	
Jeff Blauser	115	504	.661	S-115	B	
Pedro Borbon	41	32	3.09	P-41(2-2)	B	
Terry Clark	3	4	4.91	P-3	Hou-N	xBal-A
Brad Clontz	59	69	3.65	P-59(8-1)	A	
Mike Devereaux	29	57	.644	LF-27	xChi-A	
Ed Giovanola	13	17	.307	2-7,3-3,S-1	A	
Tom Glavine	29	199	3.08	P-29(16-7)	B	
Marquis Grissom	139	606	.695	CF-136	Mon-N	
Chipper Jones	140	602	.805	3-123,LF-20	B	
David Justice	120	491	.848	RF-120	B	
Mike Kelly	97	153	.574	LF-83	B	
Ryan Klesko	107	381	1.007	LF-102,1-4	B	
Brian Kowitz	10	28	.468	RF-8	A	
Mark Lemke	116	453	.683	2-115	B	
Javy Lopez	100	352	.845	C-93	B	
Greg Maddux	28	210	1.63	P-28(19-2)	B	

Name	G	AB/IP	P/E	G/POS	From	To
Darrell May	2	4	11.25	P-2	A	
Fred McGriff	144	604	.853	1-144	B	
Greg McMichael	67	81	2.79	P-67(7-2)	B	
Kent Mercker	29	143	4.15	P-29(7-8)	B	
Mike Mordecai	69	87	.837	2-21,1-9,3-6,S-6,CF-1	B	
Matt Murray	4	11	6.75	P-4(0-2)	A	xBos-A
Rod Nichols	5	7	5.40	P-5	LA-N	
Charlie O'Brien	67	233	.742	C-64	B	
Jose Oliva	48	116	.537	3-25,1-1	B	xStL-N
Alejandro Pena	14	13	4.15	P-14	xFla-N	
Eddie Perez	7	13	.923	C-5,1-1	A	
Luis Polonia	28	57	.700	LF-15	xNY-A	

Name	G	AB/IP	P/E	G/POS	From	To
Jason Schmidt	9	25	5.76	P-9(2-2)	A	
Mike Sharperson	7	7	.429	3-1	LA-N	
Dwight Smith	103	147	.741	RF-25	Bal-A	
John Smoltz	29	193	3.18	P-29(12-7)	B	
Mike Stanton	26	19	5.59	P-26(1-1)	B	xBos-A
Tom Thobe	3	3	10.80	P-3	A	
Terrell Wade	3	4	4.50	P-3(0-1)	A	
Mark Wohlers	65	65	2.09	P-65(7-3)	B	
Brad Woodall	9	10	6.10	P-9(1-1)	B	

Coaches: Jim Beauchamp, Pat Corrales, Clarence Jones, Leo Mazzone, Jimy Williams

CHAPTER 10

The All-Time Leaders

This section is divided into two parts: lifetime leaders and single-season leaders. Both groups command our attention and convey the pleasures of the game, which lie as much in contemplation of the past as in experiencing the present: Henry Aaron, 755; Babe Ruth, 714; Willie Mays, 660—this is no mere aggregation of names and numbers, as in a telephone directory . . . it comprises the romance and lore of the home run, and of baseball itself. Bob Gibson, 1.12, 1968; Nolan Ryan, 383; Greg Maddux, 1.56, 1994 . . . you can fill in the blanks that tell the story of pitching's most glorious seasons.

What follows are the all-time great Braves achievements, in both the traditional statistics and the new. For most categories we will give the top 20 lifetime and the top 10 single season. Some categories will be dominated by players of a certain era (for example, slugging average by batters of the 1920s and 1930s, earned run average by pitchers of 1900–1919). So, for many stats we will offer a second kind of ranking, broken down into six distinct eras of baseball, with the top five leaders in each. For example, breaking down single-season home runs this way on a major-league level would produce lists topped by these men:

> 1876–1892: Ned Williamson, 27, 1884
> 1893–1919: Babe Ruth, 29, 1919
> 1920–1941: Babe Ruth, 60, 1927
> 1942–1960: Ralph Kiner, 54, 1949
> 1961–1976: Roger Maris, 61, 1961
> 1977–1995: George Foster, 52, 1977

To be eligible for a lifetime pitching category that is stated as an average, a man must have pitched 750 or more innings, or 375 or more innings if he is a relief pitcher, for the Braves. For a counting statistic, he must simply have attained the necessary quantity to crack the list. For a single-season category expressed as an average, he must have pitched one inning per league scheduled game or have attained the necessary quantity (wins, strikeouts, saves) to head a counted list.

To be eligible for a lifetime batting category that is stated as an average, a man must have played in 500 or more games; for counting stats such as strikeouts, a Rob Deer earned his place on the major-league list before he played his 1,000th game. For Pitcher Batting Average, the criterion is 750 innings pitched or 50 hits. And to reach the single-season batting lists, a man must have 3.1 plate appearances per scheduled game.

We provide tables of the top fielding performances, too, sorted by position as you would expect (and including only games played at the position). But we go one step further and rank several *batting* categories by position, thus recognizing and illustrating the greater demands for fielding skill at such positions as shortstop, catcher, and second base, and the comparatively plentiful supply of batting talent in the outfield and at first base. As we establish a 500-game minimum for inclusion in all but a few batting and baserunning categories, we likewise establish for these positional rankings a minimum of 500 games played at the position.

For the three principal categories—Total Player Rating, Total Pitcher Index, and Total Baseball Ranking—ties are calculated to as many decimal places as needed to break them, but averages are shown to only three places. When two or more players are tied in an averaged category with a narrow base of data, such as a season's won-lost percentage, the reader can presume a numerical dead heat. But where there is a tie for batting average, earned run average, or any of the sabermetric measures, the reader may assume that the man listed above the other(s) has the minutely higher average.

Here are the stats carried in this section that are not carried in the Registers, with definitions where the terms are not self-explanatory:

Batting, Baserunning, Fielding

Runs (Scored) Per Game   Broken down by era
Home Run Percentage   Home runs per 100 at bats
Bases on Balls Percentage   Walks (most) per 100 appearances (at bats plus walks)
At-Bats Per Strikeout   Broken down by era
Relative Batting Average   Normalized to league average
Isolated Power   Slugging average minus batting average
Extra Base Hits
Pinch Hits
Pinch Hit Batting Average
Pinch Hit Home Runs
Strikeout Percentage
Total Player Rating Per 150 Games   Highlighting the achievements of modern players and those with comparatively short careers (though at least 500 games)
Total Chances Per Game   Broken down by position
Chances Accepted Per Game   Broken down by position
Putouts   Broken down by position
Putouts Per Game   Broken down by position
Assists   Broken down by position
Assists Per Game   Broken down by position
Double Plays   Broken down by position

Pitching

Wins Above Team   How many wins a pitcher garnered beyond those expected of an average pitcher for that team; the formula is weighted so that a pitcher on a good team has a chance to compete with pitchers on poor teams who otherwise would benefit from the larger potential spread between their team's won-lost percentage and their own; see next-to-last page for more information.
Wins Above League   A pitcher's won-lost record restated by adding his Pitching Wins above the league average to the record that a league-average pitcher would have had with the same number of decisions (for example, Tom Glavine goes 20–10 with 7 Pitching Wins; applying the 7 wins to a 15–15 mark in the same 30 decisions results in a WAL of 22–8).
Percentage of Team Wins
Relief Games
Pitchers' Batting Runs
Pitchers' Fielding Runs
Relief Wins   This statistic, like the relief stats below, includes only games in relief.
Relief Losses
Relief Innings Pitched
Relief Points   Relief wins plus saves minus losses

Games

1	Hank Aaron	3076
2	Eddie Mathews	2223
3	Dale Murphy	1926
4	Rabbit Maranville	1795
5	Fred Tenney	1737
6	Herman Long	1646
7	Bobby Lowe	1410
8	Del Crandall	1394
9	Johnny Logan	1351
10	Tommy Holmes	1289
11	Mike Lum	1225
12	John Morrill	1219
13	Joe Adcock	1207
14	Glenn Hubbard	1196
15	Billy Nash	1186
16	Hugh Duffy	1152
17	Jerry Royster	1118
18	Wally Berger	1057
19	Bill Bruton	1052
20	Joe Torre	1037

At Bats

1	Hank Aaron	11628
2	Eddie Mathews	8049
3	Dale Murphy	7098
4	Herman Long	6777
5	Rabbit Maranville	6724
6	Fred Tenney	6637
7	Bobby Lowe	5617
8	Tommy Holmes	4956
9	Johnny Logan	4931
10	John Morrill	4759
11	Hugh Duffy	4656
12	Del Crandall	4583
13	Billy Nash	4561
14	Joe Adcock	4232
15	Wally Berger	4153
16	Bill Bruton	4079
17	Ezra Sutton	4045
18	Glenn Hubbard	4016
19	Joe Torre	3700
20	Bob Horner	3571

Runs

1	Hank Aaron	2107
2	Eddie Mathews	1452
3	Herman Long	1291
4	Fred Tenney	1134
5	Dale Murphy	1103
6	Bobby Lowe	999
7	Hugh Duffy	996
8	Billy Nash	855
9	Rabbit Maranville	801
10	John Morrill	800
11	Tommy Holmes	696
12	Ezra Sutton	694
13	Wally Berger	651
	Billy Hamilton	651
15	Tommy Tucker	648
16	Johnny Logan	624
17	Bill Bruton	622
18	Joe Adcock	564
19	Joe Hornung	560
20	Del Crandall	552

Runs per Game (by era)

1876-1892

1	Joe Hornung	.79
2	Billy Nash	.72
3	Ezra Sutton	.71
4	Sam Wise	.69
5	John Morrill	.66

1893-1919

1	Billy Hamilton	.94
2	Hugh Duffy	.86
3	Tommy McCarthy	.82
4	Herman Long	.78
5	Chick Stahl	.75

1920-1941

1	Wally Berger	.62
2	Lance Richbourg	.56
3	Ray Powell	.53
4	Buck Jordan	.53
5	Jimmy Welsh	.52

1942-1960

1	Eddie Mathews	.65
2	Bob Elliott	.61
3	Earl Torgeson	.59
4	Bill Bruton	.59
5	Sid Gordon	.55

1961-1976

1	Hank Aaron	.68
2	Ralph Garr	.59
3	Felipe Alou	.55
4	Darrell Evans	.52
5	Lee Maye	.52

1977-1995

1	Ron Gant	.60
2	David Justice	.58
3	Gary Matthews	.58
4	Dale Murphy	.57
5	Bob Horner	.57

Hits

1	Hank Aaron	3600
2	Eddie Mathews	2201
3	Fred Tenney	1994
4	Dale Murphy	1901
5	Herman Long	1900
6	Rabbit Maranville	1696
7	Bobby Lowe	1606
8	Hugh Duffy	1544
9	Tommy Holmes	1503
10	Johnny Logan	1329
11	Billy Nash	1283
12	Wally Berger	1263
13	John Morrill	1247
14	Joe Adcock	1206
15	Del Crandall	1176
16	Ezra Sutton	1161
17	Bill Bruton	1126
18	Joe Torre	1087
19	Tommy Tucker	1025
20	Ralph Garr	1022

Doubles

1	Hank Aaron	600
2	Eddie Mathews	338
3	Dale Murphy	306
4	Herman Long	295
5	Tommy Holmes	291
6	Wally Berger	248
7	Rabbit Maranville	244
8	Fred Tenney	242
9	John Morrill	234
10	Hugh Duffy	220
11	Johnny Logan	207
12	Billy Nash	199
13	Joe Adcock	197
14	Glenn Hubbard	196
15	Bobby Lowe	186
16	Ezra Sutton	178
17	Bill Bruton	167
	Del Crandall	167
19	Felipe Alou	163
20	Bob Horner	160

Triples

1	Rabbit Maranville	103
2	Hank Aaron	96
3	Herman Long	91
4	John Morrill	80
5	Bill Bruton	79
6	Fred Tenney	74
7	Hugh Duffy	73
8	Bobby Lowe	71
	Sam Wise	71
10	Eddie Mathews	70
11	Billy Nash	69
12	Ray Powell	67
13	Ezra Sutton	66
14	Joe Hornung	58
15	Chick Stahl	56
16	Dick Johnston	54
17	Wally Berger	52
18	Lance Richbourg	48
19	Tommy Holmes	47
20	Jimmy Collins	43

Triples (by era)

1876-1892

1	John Morrill	80
2	Sam Wise	71
3	Billy Nash	69
4	Ezra Sutton	66
5	Joe Hornung	58

1893-1919

1	Rabbit Maranville	103
2	Herman Long	91
3	Fred Tenney	74
4	Hugh Duffy	73
5	Bobby Lowe	71

1920-1941

1	Ray Powell	67
2	Wally Berger	52
3	Lance Richbourg	48
4	Jimmy Welsh	42
5	Billy Southworth	35

Home Runs (by era) — continued

1942-1960

1	Bill Bruton	79
2	Eddie Mathews	70
3	Tommy Holmes	47
4	Johnny Logan	40
5	2 players tied	25

1961-1976

1	Hank Aaron	96
2	Ralph Garr	40
3	Felix Millan	26
4	Mack Jones	22
5	Joe Torre	21

1977-1995

1	Dale Murphy	37
2	Jerry Royster	30
3	Ron Gant	27
4	Claudell Washington	25
5	Jeff Blauser	23

Home Runs

1	Hank Aaron	733
2	Eddie Mathews	493
3	Dale Murphy	371
4	Joe Adcock	239
5	Bob Horner	215
6	Wally Berger	199
7	Del Crandall	170
8	David Justice	154
9	Ron Gant	147
10	Joe Torre	142
11	Darrell Evans	131
12	Rico Carty	109
13	Bob Elliott	101
14	Sid Gordon	100
15	Felipe Alou	94
16	Johnny Logan	92
17	Jeff Burroughs	88
	Tommy Holmes	88
	Herman Long	88
20	Mack Jones	84

Home Runs (by era)

1876-1892

1	Billy Nash	51
2	John Morrill	41
3	Sam Wise	33
4	Joe Hornung	29
5	King Kelly	28

1893-1919

1	Herman Long	88
2	Bobby Lowe	70
3	Hugh Duffy	69
4	Jimmy Collins	34
5	Tommy McCarthy	24

1920-1941

1	Wally Berger	199
2	Max West	64
3	Gene Moore	42
4	Ray Powell	35
5	2 players tied	30

1942-1960

1	Eddie Mathews	493
2	Joe Adcock	239
3	Del Crandall	170
4	Bob Elliott	101
5	Sid Gordon	100

1961-1976

1	Hank Aaron	733
2	Joe Torre	142
3	Darrell Evans	131
4	Rico Carty	109
5	Felipe Alou	94

1977-1995

1	Dale Murphy	371
2	Bob Horner	215
3	David Justice	154
4	Ron Gant	147
5	Jeff Burroughs	88

Home Run Percentage

1	Hank Aaron	6.30
2	Eddie Mathews	6.12
3	Bob Horner	6.02
4	David Justice	5.67
5	Joe Adcock	5.65
6	Dale Murphy	5.23
7	Jeff Burroughs	5.05
8	Sid Gordon	4.96
9	Wally Berger	4.79
10	Ron Gant	4.61
11	Darrell Evans	4.52
12	Mack Jones	4.12
13	Rico Carty	3.97
14	Bob Elliott	3.90
15	Joe Torre	3.84
16	Del Crandall	3.71
17	Gary Matthews	3.63
18	Dusty Baker	3.47
19	Clete Boyer	3.45
20	Earl Torgeson	3.31

Home Run Pctg. (by era)

1876-1892

1	Sam Wise	1.17
2	Billy Nash	1.12
3	Dick Johnston	1.11
4	Joe Hornung	0.94
5	John Morrill	0.86

1893-1919

1	Hugh Duffy	1.48
2	Herman Long	1.30
3	Jimmy Collins	1.28
4	Bobby Lowe	1.25
5	Tommy McCarthy	1.09

1920-1941

1	Wally Berger	4.79
2	Max West	2.75
3	Gene Moore	1.96
4	Eddie Miller	1.51
5	Tony Cuccinello	1.33

1942-1960

1	Eddie Mathews	6.12
2	Joe Adcock	5.65
3	Sid Gordon	4.96
4	Bob Elliott	3.90
5	Del Crandall	3.71

1961-1976

1	Hank Aaron	6.30
2	Darrell Evans	4.52
3	Mack Jones	4.12
4	Rico Carty	3.97
5	Joe Torre	3.84

1977-1995

1	Bob Horner	6.02
2	David Justice	5.67
3	Dale Murphy	5.23
4	Jeff Burroughs	5.05
5	Ron Gant	4.61

Total Bases

1	Hank Aaron	6591
2	Eddie Mathews	4158
3	Dale Murphy	3394
4	Herman Long	2641
5	Fred Tenney	2435
6	Rabbit Maranville	2215
7	Wally Berger	2212
8	Joe Adcock	2164
9	Tommy Holmes	2152
10	Bobby Lowe	2144
11	Hugh Duffy	2117
12	Johnny Logan	1892
13	Del Crandall	1887
14	Bob Horner	1813
15	Billy Nash	1773
16	John Morrill	1764
17	Joe Torre	1709
18	Bill Bruton	1595
19	Ezra Sutton	1531
20	Ron Gant	1489

Runs Batted In

1	Hank Aaron	2202
2	Eddie Mathews	1388
3	Dale Murphy	1143
4	Herman Long	964
5	Hugh Duffy	927
6	Bobby Lowe	872
7	Billy Nash	809
8	Joe Adcock	760
9	Wally Berger	746
10	Bob Horner	652
11	Del Crandall	628
12	John Morrill	625
13	Fred Tenney	609
14	Tommy Holmes	580
15	Rabbit Maranville	558
16	Joe Torre	552
17	Tommy Tucker	533
18	Johnny Logan	521
19	David Justice	497
20	Ezra Sutton	487

Runs Batted In (by era)

1876-1892

1	Billy Nash	809
2	John Morrill	625
3	Ezra Sutton	487
4	Sam Wise	383
5	Jack Burdock	349

1893-1919

1	Herman Long	964
2	Hugh Duffy	927
3	Bobby Lowe	872
4	Fred Tenney	609
5	Rabbit Maranville	558

1920-1941

1	Wally Berger	746
2	Max West	341
3	Tony Cuccinello	311
4	Tony Boeckel	298
5	Randy Moore	287

1942-1960

1	Eddie Mathews	1388
2	Joe Adcock	760
3	Del Crandall	628
4	Tommy Holmes	580
5	Johnny Logan	521

1961-1976

1	Hank Aaron	2202
2	Joe Torre	552
3	Rico Carty	451
4	Darrell Evans	424
5	Mike Lum	365

1977-1995

1	Dale Murphy	1143
2	Bob Horner	652
3	David Justice	497
4	Ron Gant	480
5	Glenn Hubbard	403

Runs Batted In per Game

1	Hugh Duffy	.80
2	Jimmy Collins	.72
3	Hank Aaron	.72
4	Wally Berger	.71
5	Tommy McCarthy	.70
6	Billy Nash	.68
7	Bob Horner	.68
8	Bob Elliott	.65
9	David Justice	.64
10	Sid Gordon	.64
11	Joe Adcock	.63
12	Eddie Mathews	.62
13	Bobby Lowe	.62
14	Dale Murphy	.59
15	Herman Long	.59
16	Tommy Tucker	.58
17	Charlie Ganzel	.58
18	Ron Gant	.56
19	Jeff Burroughs	.55
20	Terry Pendleton	.55

Walks

1	Eddie Mathews	1376
2	Hank Aaron	1297
3	Dale Murphy	912
4	Fred Tenney	750
5	Billy Nash	598
6	Darrell Evans	563
7	Rabbit Maranville	561
8	Billy Hamilton	545
9	Herman Long	536
10	Glenn Hubbard	487
11	Earl Torgeson	478
12	Tommy Holmes	476
13	Hugh Duffy	457
14	Bob Elliott	441
15	David Justice	431
16	Bobby Lowe	420
17	Johnny Logan	417
18	Joe Adcock	377
19	Del Crandall	374
20	Jeff Blauser	373

Walk Percentage

1	Billy Hamilton	17.26
2	Darrell Evans	16.28
3	Earl Torgeson	16.18
4	Jeff Burroughs	15.15
5	Eddie Mathews	14.60
6	Bob Elliott	14.56
7	David Justice	13.69
8	Sid Gordon	13.17
9	Lonnie Smith	11.83
10	Tommy McCarthy	11.73
11	Billy Nash	11.59
12	Dale Murphy	11.39
13	Max West	11.21
14	Biff Pocoroba	11.10
15	Denis Menke	11.01
16	Connie Ryan	10.91
17	Glenn Hubbard	10.82
18	Jeff Blauser	10.51
19	Rico Carty	10.50
20	Red Smith	10.49

Strikeouts

1	Dale Murphy	1581
2	Eddie Mathews	1387
3	Hank Aaron	1294
4	Joe Adcock	732
5	Jeff Blauser	637
6	John Morrill	632
7	Ron Gant	600
8	Glenn Hubbard	570
9	Wally Berger	544
10	Bill Bruton	536
11	Joe Torre	518
12	Rabbit Maranville	515
13	Darrell Evans	502
	Mack Jones	502
15	Bob Horner	489
16	David Justice	470
17	Ray Powell	461
18	Sam Wise	455
19	Sibby Sisti	440
20	Del Crandall	437

At Bats per Strikeout

1	Tommy Holmes	42.0
2	Johnny Cooney	30.6
3	Randy Moore	27.5
4	Buck Jordan	27.3
5	Frank Torre	23.6
6	Ezra Sutton	23.5
7	Felix Millan	20.8
8	Jimmy Welsh	18.7
9	Lance Richbourg	17.4
10	Walter Holke	17.0
11	Mickey O'Neil	15.1
12	Tony Boeckel	15.0
13	Bob Smith	14.5
14	Whitey Wietelmann	13.5
15	Tony Cuccinello	13.4
16	Biff Pocoroba	13.4
17	Al Spohrer	13.3
18	Sid Gordon	13.3
	Ken Oberkfell	13.3
20	Rabbit Maranville	13.1

Batting Average

1	Billy Hamilton	.338
2	Hugh Duffy	.332
3	Chick Stahl	.327
4	Ralph Garr	.317
5	Rico Carty	.317
6	Lance Richbourg	.311
7	Hank Aaron	.310
8	Jimmy Collins	.309
9	Wally Berger	.304
10	Tommy Holmes	.303
11	Buck Jordan	.301
12	Fred Tenney	.300
13	Tommy McCarthy	.296
14	Felipe Alou	.295
15	Bob Elliott	.295
16	Joe Torre	.294
17	Terry Pendleton	.293
18	Lonnie Smith	.291
19	Jimmy Welsh	.289
20	Sid Gordon	.289

Batting Average (by era)

1876-1892

1	Ezra Sutton	.287
2	Billy Nash	.281
3	Sam Wise	.267
4	Joe Hornung	.263
5	John Morrill	.262

1893-1919

1	Billy Hamilton	.338
2	Hugh Duffy	.332
3	Chick Stahl	.327
4	Jimmy Collins	.309
5	Fred Tenney	.300

1920-1941

1	Lance Richbourg	.311
2	Wally Berger	.304
3	Buck Jordan	.301
4	Jimmy Welsh	.289
5	Johnny Cooney	.286

1942-1960

1	Tommy Holmes	.303
2	Bob Elliott	.295
3	Sid Gordon	.289
4	Joe Adcock	.285
5	Bill Bruton	.276

1961-1976

1	Ralph Garr	.317
2	Rico Carty	.317
3	Hank Aaron	.310
4	Felipe Alou	.295
5	Joe Torre	.294

1977-1995

1	Terry Pendleton	.293
2	Lonnie Smith	.291
3	Gary Matthews	.288
4	Bob Horner	.278
5	Claudell Washington	.278

Batting Average (by position)

First Base

1	Buck Jordan	.301
2	Fred Tenney	.300
3	Tommy Tucker	.288
4	Joe Adcock	.285
5	Walter Holke	.283

Second Base

1	Bobby Lowe	.286
2	Felix Millan	.281
3	Tony Cuccinello	.278
4	Jack Burdock	.251
5	Frank Bolling	.247

Shortstop

1	Herman Long	.280
2	Johnny Logan	.270
3	Sam Wise	.267
4	Jeff Blauser	.263
5	Rafael Ramirez	.263

Third Base

1	Jimmy Collins	.309
2	Bob Elliott	.295
3	Terry Pendleton	.293
4	Ezra Sutton	.287
5	Tony Boeckel	.286

Outfield

1	Billy Hamilton	.338
2	Hugh Duffy	.332
3	Chick Stahl	.327
4	Ralph Garr	.317
5	Rico Carty	.317
6	Lance Richbourg	.311
7	Hank Aaron	.310
8	Wally Berger	.304
9	Tommy Holmes	.303
10	Tommy McCarthy	.296

Catcher

1	Joe Torre	.294
2	Phil Masi	.262
3	Hank Gowdy	.260
4	Al Spohrer	.259
5	Del Crandall	.257

Relative Batting Average

1	Ralph Garr	121.3
2	Rico Carty	121.3
3	Hank Aaron	117.5
4	Billy Hamilton	117.5
5	Hugh Duffy	114.9
6	Felipe Alou	114.0
7	Chick Stahl	113.6
8	Tommy Holmes	113.4
9	Joe Torre	112.7
10	Lonnie Smith	112.4
11	Ezra Sutton	111.0
12	Terry Pendleton	111.0
13	Fred Tenney	109.5
14	Bob Elliott	109.2
15	Felix Millan	108.3
16	Gary Matthews	108.0
17	Red Smith	107.8
18	Sid Gordon	107.6
19	Jimmy Collins	107.0
20	Buck Jordan	106.6

On Base Percentage

1	Billy Hamilton	.456
2	Bob Elliott	.398
3	Hugh Duffy	.394
4	Rico Carty	.391
5	Chick Stahl	.387
6	Sid Gordon	.385
	Earl Torgeson	.385
8	Lonnie Smith	.384
9	Tommy McCarthy	.382
10	Eddie Mathews	.381
11	Hank Aaron	.380
	Jeff Burroughs	.380
13	Fred Tenney	.376
14	David Justice	.375
15	Darrell Evans	.372
16	Tommy Tucker	.369
17	Billy Nash	.368
18	Tommy Holmes	.367
19	Jimmy Collins	.365
20	Wally Berger	.362

Slugging Average

1	Hank Aaron	.567
2	Wally Berger	.533
3	Eddie Mathews	.517
4	Joe Adcock	.511
5	Bob Horner	.508
6	Sid Gordon	.500
7	David Justice	.498
8	Rico Carty	.496
9	Bob Elliott	.485
10	Dale Murphy	.478
11	Jeff Burroughs	.472
12	Ron Gant	.466
13	Joe Torre	.462
14	Lonnie Smith	.456
15	Gary Matthews	.456
16	Chick Stahl	.456
17	Terry Pendleton	.455
18	Hugh Duffy	.455
19	Felipe Alou	.440
20	Mack Jones	.440

Production

1 Hank Aaron .... .947
2 Eddie Mathews .... .898
3 Wally Berger .... .894
4 Rico Carty .... .887
5 Sid Gordon .... .886
6 Bob Elliott .... .883
7 David Justice .... .873
8 Billy Hamilton .... .867
9 Joe Adcock .... .857
10 Jeff Burroughs .... .852
11 Bob Horner .... .851
12 Hugh Duffy .... .848
13 Chick Stahl .... .842
14 Lonnie Smith .... .841
15 Dale Murphy .... .832
16 Joe Torre .... .820
17 Gary Matthews .... .812
    Earl Torgeson .... .812
19 Tommy Holmes .... .801
20 Darrell Evans .... .798

Adjusted Production

1 Hank Aaron 159
2 Eddie Mathews 147
3 Wally Berger 144
4 Rico Carty 143
    Sid Gordon 143
6 Bob Elliott 141
7 Joe Adcock 133
8 David Justice 130
    Joe Torre 130
10 Lonnie Smith 129
11 Billy Hamilton 128
12 Bob Horner 126
13 Red Smith 125
14 Tommy Holmes 123
    Dale Murphy 123
    Earl Torgeson 123
17 Jeff Burroughs 121
    Chick Stahl 121
19 Felipe Alou 120
20 2 players tied 119

Batting Runs

1 Hank Aaron 879
2 Eddie Mathews 474
3 Dale Murphy 276
4 Wally Berger 194
5 Hugh Duffy 184
6 Billy Hamilton 180
7 Rico Carty 173
8 Bob Horner 149
9 Tommy Holmes 143
10 Fred Tenney 142
11 Joe Torre 141
12 Bob Elliott 138
13 David Justice 137
14 Joe Adcock 134
15 Darrell Evans 104
    Sid Gordon 104
17 Chick Stahl 86
18 Billy Nash 85
19 Jeff Burroughs 83
20 Felipe Alou 82

Adjusted Batting Runs

1 Hank Aaron 915
2 Eddie Mathews 552
3 Wally Berger 239
4 Dale Murphy 212
5 Joe Adcock 178
6 Rico Carty 161
7 Bob Elliott 159
8 Tommy Holmes 149
9 Joe Torre 144
10 Billy Hamilton 132
11 Sid Gordon 126
12 David Justice 119
13 Bob Horner 115
14 Hugh Duffy 111
15 Fred Tenney 104
16 Earl Torgeson 97
17 Felipe Alou 81
    Red Smith 81
19 Ezra Sutton 78
20 Darrell Evans 76

Batting Wins

1 Hank Aaron 91.2
2 Eddie Mathews 48.3
3 Dale Murphy 28.9
4 Wally Berger 18.9
5 Rico Carty 18.2
6 Billy Hamilton 16.2
7 Hugh Duffy 15.8
8 Bob Horner 15.6
9 Joe Torre 14.9
10 Tommy Holmes 14.6
11 David Justice 14.0
12 Fred Tenney 13.8
13 Bob Elliott 13.7
14 Joe Adcock 13.4
15 Darrell Evans 11.0
16 Sid Gordon 10.3
17 Felipe Alou 8.8
18 Jeff Burroughs 8.6
19 Lonnie Smith 8.4
20 Chick Stahl 7.8

Adjusted Batting Wins

1 Hank Aaron 94.9
2 Eddie Mathews 56.2
3 Wally Berger 23.3
4 Dale Murphy 22.2
5 Joe Adcock 17.8
6 Rico Carty 16.9
7 Bob Elliott 15.7
8 Joe Torre 15.3
9 Tommy Holmes 15.2
10 Sid Gordon 12.5
11 David Justice 12.1
12 Bob Horner 12.1
13 Billy Hamilton 11.9
14 Fred Tenney 10.1
15 Earl Torgeson 9.7
16 Hugh Duffy 9.6
17 Red Smith 9.1
18 Felipe Alou 8.7
19 Darrell Evans 8.0
20 Ezra Sutton 7.1

Runs Created

1 Hank Aaron 2463
2 Eddie Mathews 1673
3 Dale Murphy 1211
4 Herman Long 1092
5 Fred Tenney 1076
6 Hugh Duffy 1019
7 Bobby Lowe 864
8 Tommy Holmes 808
9 Wally Berger 806
10 Billy Nash 759
11 Rabbit Maranville 732
12 Joe Adcock 713
13 Billy Hamilton 639
14 Johnny Logan 636
15 Bob Horner 595
16 John Morrill 581
17 Joe Torre 577
18 Del Crandall 566
19 Tommy Tucker 546
20 Bill Bruton 528

Total Average

1 Billy Hamilton 1.106
2 Hank Aaron .... .962
3 Hugh Duffy .... .940
4 Eddie Mathews .... .931
5 Bob Elliott .... .900
6 Wally Berger .... .890
7 David Justice .... .883
8 Chick Stahl .... .882
9 Sid Gordon .... .881
10 Jeff Burroughs .... .862
11 Tommy McCarthy .... .849
    Earl Torgeson .... .849
13 Rico Carty .... .846
    Lonnie Smith .... .846
15 Darrell Evans .... .816
16 Dale Murphy .... .815
17 Joe Adcock .... .805
18 Bob Horner .... .801
    Billy Nash .... .801
20 Jimmy Collins .... .788

Runs Produced

1 Hank Aaron 3576
2 Eddie Mathews 2347
3 Herman Long 2167
4 Dale Murphy 1875
5 Hugh Duffy 1854
6 Bobby Lowe 1801
7 Fred Tenney 1726
8 Billy Nash 1613
9 John Morrill 1384
10 Rabbit Maranville 1336
11 Wally Berger 1198
12 Tommy Holmes 1188
13 Tommy Tucker 1162
14 Ezra Sutton 1161
15 Joe Adcock 1085
16 Johnny Logan 1053
17 Del Crandall 1010
18 Bob Horner 982
19 Jimmy Collins 920
20 Billy Hamilton 918

Clutch Hitting Index

1 Frank Torre 127
2 Red Smith 120
3 Charlie Ganzel 119
4 Billy Nash 117
5 Hugh Duffy 115
6 Biff Pocoroba 114
7 Tommy McCarthy 112
    Randy Moore 112
9 Jimmy Collins 111
10 Hank Gowdy 110
11 Hod Ford 109
    Dick Johnston 109
13 Bruce Benedict 108
    Bob Smith 108
15 Tony Cuccinello 107
    Bobby Lowe 107
    Earl Torgeson 107
18 Jack Burdock 106
    Ezra Sutton 106
    Tommy Tucker 106

Isolated Power

1 Hank Aaron .... .257
2 Eddie Mathews .... .243
3 Bob Horner .... .229
4 Wally Berger .... .229
5 Joe Adcock .... .226
6 David Justice .... .225
7 Sid Gordon .... .212
8 Dale Murphy .... .210
9 Jeff Burroughs .... .205
10 Ron Gant .... .205
11 Bob Elliott .... .190
12 Mack Jones .... .187
13 Darrell Evans .... .181
14 Rico Carty .... .179
15 Joe Torre .... .168
16 Gary Matthews .... .168
17 Lonnie Smith .... .166
18 Terry Pendleton .... .162
19 Dusty Baker .... .162
20 Earl Torgeson .... .162

Extra Base Hits

1 Hank Aaron 1429
2 Eddie Mathews 901
3 Dale Murphy 714
4 Wally Berger 499
5 Herman Long 474
6 Joe Adcock 458
7 Tommy Holmes 426
8 Bob Horner 382
9 Rabbit Maranville 370
10 Hugh Duffy 362
11 John Morrill 355
12 Del Crandall 354
13 Johnny Logan 339
14 Fred Tenney 333
15 Ron Gant 332
16 Bobby Lowe 327
17 Billy Nash 319
18 Joe Torre 317
19 Bill Bruton 294
20 David Justice 288

Pinch Hits

1 Mike Lum 70
2 Chris Chambliss 45
3 Cito Gaston 39
4 Biff Pocoroba 38
5 Tommy Gregg 36

Pinch Hit Average
(75 at-bats minimum)

1 Charlie Spikes .... .333
2 Cito Gaston .... .298
3 Bob Watson .... .288
4 Tommy Gregg .... .277
5 Chris Chambliss .... .273

Pinch Hit Home Runs

1 Joe Adcock 7
2 Mike Lum 6
    Tommy Gregg 6
4 Butch Nieman 5
5 Chris Chambliss 4
    Ted Simmons 4

Total Player Rating / 150g

1 Hank Aaron 4.42
2 Eddie Mathews 3.54
3 Wally Berger 3.05
4 Sid Gordon 2.75
5 Bob Elliott 2.59
6 Terry Pendleton 2.45
7 David Justice 2.39
8 Glenn Hubbard 2.38
9 Rico Carty 2.37
10 Darrell Evans 2.29
11 Jimmy Collins 2.20
12 Johnny Logan 1.94
13 Red Smith 1.85
14 Joe Torre 1.84
15 Lonnie Smith 1.82
16 Gene Moore 1.64
17 Tommy Holmes 1.64
18 Fred Tenney 1.63
19 Dale Murphy 1.61
20 Bill Sweeney 1.46

Stolen Bases

1 Herman Long 431
2 Hugh Duffy 331
3 Billy Hamilton 274
4 Bobby Lowe 260
    Fred Tenney 260
6 Hank Aaron 240
7 King Kelly 238
8 Billy Nash 232
9 Rabbit Maranville 194
10 Jerry Royster 174
11 Tommy McCarthy 160
    Dale Murphy 160
13 Ron Gant 157
14 Bill Sweeney 153
15 Bill Bruton 143
16 Tommy Tucker 138
17 Ralph Garr 137
18 Dick Johnston 132
19 Claudell Washington 115
20 Sam Wise 107

Stolen Base Average

1 Hank Aaron 77.2
2 Otis Nixon 75.5
3 Gary Matthews 71.1
4 Dale Murphy 70.5
5 Dusty Baker 69.9
6 Ron Gant 69.8
7 Bill Bruton 69.1
8 Ralph Garr 68.8
9 Felix Millan 65.9
10 Gerald Perry 65.6

Stolen Base Runs

1 Hank Aaron 29
2 Dale Murphy 8
3 Ron Gant 6
4 Bill Bruton 5
5 Ralph Garr 4
    Terry Pendleton 4
7 Gary Matthews 3
    Lee Maye 3
9 Dusty Baker 2
10 Darrell Evans 1
    Frank Torre 1

Stolen Base Wins

1 Hank Aaron 3.0
2 Dale Murphy 0.8
3 Ron Gant 0.6
4 Bill Bruton 0.5
5 Ralph Garr 0.4
6 Terry Pendleton 0.4
7 Gary Matthews 0.3
8 Lee Maye 0.3
9 Dusty Baker 0.2
10 Darrell Evans 0.1

Games

First Base
1 Fred Tenney 1556
2 Joe Adcock 1109
3 Tommy Tucker 916
4 John Morrill 875
5 Chris Chambliss 710

Second Base
1 Glenn Hubbard 1180
2 Bobby Lowe 1011
3 Felix Millan 776
4 Jack Burdock 759
5 Frank Bolling 739

Shortstop
1 Herman Long 1606
2 Rabbit Maranville 1466
3 Johnny Logan 1330
4 Rafael Ramirez 852
5 Jeff Blauser 744

Third Base
1 Eddie Mathews 2130
2 Billy Nash 1126
3 Darrell Evans 710
4 Bob Elliott 692
5 Bob Horner 684

Outfield
1 Hank Aaron 2756
2 Dale Murphy 1622
3 Tommy Holmes 1225
4 Hugh Duffy 1128
5 Bill Bruton 1042
6 Wally Berger 1031
7 Ray Powell 825
8 Ralph Garr 747
9 Rico Carty 722
10 David Justice 702

Catcher
1 Del Crandall 1305
2 Bruce Benedict 971
3 Phil Masi 840
4 Joe Torre 796
5 Hank Gowdy 731

Pitcher
1 Phil Niekro 740
2 Warren Spahn 714
3 Gene Garber 557
4 Kid Nichols 556
5 Lew Burdette 468

Fielding Average

First Base
1 Chris Chambliss 994
2 Joe Adcock 994
3 Walter Holke 994
4 Buck Jordan 990
5 Earl Torgeson 988

Second Base
1 Mark Lemke 986
2 Frank Bolling 984
3 Glenn Hubbard 983
4 Felix Millan 980
5 Tony Cuccinello 971

Shortstop
1 Eddie Miller 972
2 Johnny Logan 966
3 Jeff Blauser 966
4 Denis Menke 964
5 Andres Thomas 958

Third Base
1 Ken Oberkfell 967
2 Clete Boyer 966
3 Eddie Mathews 956
4 Terry Pendleton 956
5 Bob Elliott 951

Outfield
1 Johnny Cooney 989
2 Tommy Holmes 989
3 Sid Gordon 987
4 Mike Lum 986
5 Rowland Office 985
6 Dusty Baker 984
7 Dale Murphy 983
8 Mack Jones 981
9 Felipe Alou 981
10 Hank Aaron 980

Catcher
1 Bruce Benedict 990
2 Joe Torre 990
3 Del Crandall 989
4 Phil Masi 982
5 Hank Gowdy 973

Pitcher
1 Jesse Barnes 983
2 Bob Smith 980
3 Ed Brandt 978
4 Phil Niekro 972
5 Bob Buhl 972

Total Chances per Game

First Base
1 Walter Holke 10.93
2 John Morrill 10.75
3 Fred Tenney 10.74
4 Buck Jordan 10.54
5 Tommy Tucker 10.40

Second Base
1 Jack Burdock 6.48
2 Bobby Lowe 6.04
3 Tony Cuccinello 5.87
4 Glenn Hubbard 5.66
5 Connie Ryan 5.54

Shortstop
1 Herman Long 6.33
2 Rabbit Maranville 6.19
3 Eddie Miller 5.71
4 Billy Urbanski 5.47
5 Sam Wise 5.35

Third Base
1 Jimmy Collins 4.27
2 Billy Nash 4.05
3 Ezra Sutton 3.56
4 Darrell Evans 3.38
5 Red Smith 3.38

Outfield
1 Wally Berger 2.88
2 Jimmy Welsh 2.88
3 Dick Johnston 2.71
4 Ray Powell 2.71
5 Bill Bruton 2.66
6 Dusty Baker 2.49
7 Lance Richbourg 2.48
8 Hugh Duffy 2.47
9 Tommy Holmes 2.42
10 Billy Hamilton 2.40

Catcher
1 Joe Torre 5.82
2 Del Crandall 5.50
3 Bruce Benedict 5.44
4 Hank Gowdy 5.04
5 Mickey O'Neil 4.27

Pitcher
1 John Clarkson 2.89
2 Vic Willis 2.87
3 Togie Pittinger 2.81
4 Tommy Bond 2.73
5 Dick Rudolph 2.63

Chances Accepted per Game

First Base
1 Walter Holke 10.86
2 Fred Tenney 10.55
3 Buck Jordan 10.43
4 John Morrill 10.43
5 Tommy Tucker 10.18

Second Base
1 Jack Burdock 5.93
2 Bobby Lowe 5.73
3 Tony Cuccinello 5.70
4 Glenn Hubbard 5.57
5 Connie Ryan 5.38

Shortstop
1 Rabbit Maranville 5.86
2 Herman Long 5.76
3 Eddie Miller 5.55
4 Billy Urbanski 5.19
5 Johnny Logan 5.11

Third Base
1 Jimmy Collins 3.97
2 Billy Nash 3.65
3 Darrell Evans 3.19
4 Red Smith 3.14
5 Ezra Sutton 3.11

Outfield
1 Wally Berger 2.81
2 Jimmy Welsh 2.79
3 Bill Bruton 2.60
4 Ray Powell 2.60
5 Dick Johnston 2.46
6 Dusty Baker 2.45
7 Tommy Holmes 2.40
8 Lance Richbourg 2.40
9 Hugh Duffy 2.35
10 Dale Murphy 2.30

Catcher
1 Joe Torre 5.76
2 Del Crandall 5.44
3 Bruce Benedict 5.39
4 Hank Gowdy 4.91
5 Mickey O'Neil 4.15

Pitcher
1 Vic Willis 2.73
2 Tommy Bond 2.58
3 Togie Pittinger 2.58
4 John Clarkson 2.56
5 Dick Rudolph 2.55

Putouts

First Base
1 Fred Tenney 15233
2 Joe Adcock 9799
3 Tommy Tucker 8912
4 John Morrill 8768
5 Chris Chambliss 6552

Second Base
1 Bobby Lowe 2573
2 Glenn Hubbard 2518
3 Jack Burdock 2122
4 Felix Millan 1824
5 Frank Bolling 1560

Shortstop
1 Herman Long 3748
2 Rabbit Maranville 3570
3 Johnny Logan 2529
4 Rafael Ramirez 1437
5 Billy Urbanski 1386

Third Base
1 Eddie Mathews 2010
2 Billy Nash 1708
3 Jimmy Collins 1059
4 Ezra Sutton 885
5 Tony Boeckel 798

Outfield
1 Hank Aaron 5536
2 Dale Murphy 3618
3 Wally Berger 2820
4 Tommy Holmes 2817
5 Bill Bruton 2619
6 Hugh Duffy 2508
7 Ray Powell 2020
8 Billy Hamilton 1485
9 Ralph Garr 1456
10 Dusty Baker 1422

Catcher
1 Del Crandall 6398
2 Bruce Benedict 4651
3 Joe Torre 4189
4 Phil Masi 2693
5 Hank Gowdy 2681

Pitcher
1 Phil Niekro 340
2 Kid Nichols 293
3 Lew Burdette 217
4 Warren Spahn 214
5 Vic Willis 194

Putouts per Game

First Base
1 Walter Holke 10.29
2 John Morrill 10.03
3 Buck Jordan 9.80
4 Fred Tenney 9.79
5 Tommy Tucker 9.73

Second Base
1 Jack Burdock 2.80
2 Bobby Lowe 2.55
3 Connie Ryan 2.47
4 Felix Millan 2.36
5 Tony Cuccinello 2.33

Shortstop
1 Rabbit Maranville 2.44
2 Herman Long 2.34
3 Eddie Miller 2.31
4 Billy Urbanski 2.13
5 Johnny Logan 1.91

Third Base
1 Jimmy Collins 1.61
2 Billy Nash 1.52
3 Ezra Sutton 1.33
4 Tony Boeckel 1.24
5 Red Smith 1.09

Outfield
1 Wally Berger 2.74
2 Jimmy Welsh 2.63
3 Bill Bruton 2.52
4 Ray Powell 2.45
5 Dusty Baker 2.38
6 Lance Richbourg 2.32
7 Tommy Holmes 2.30
8 Dale Murphy 2.24
9 Hugh Duffy 2.23
10 Dick Johnston 2.23

Catcher
1 Joe Torre 5.27
2 Del Crandall 4.91
3 Bruce Benedict 4.79
4 Hank Gowdy 3.67
5 Phil Masi 3.21

Pitcher
1 Vic Willis 0.61
2 Kid Nichols 0.53
3 Tommy Bond 0.50
4 Bob Buhl 0.47
5 Lew Burdette 0.47

Assists

First Base
1 Fred Tenney 1174
2 Joe Adcock 691
3 Chris Chambliss 523
4 Earl Torgeson 455
5 Tommy Tucker 410

Second Base
1 Glenn Hubbard 4045
2 Bobby Lowe 3214
3 Jack Burdock 2373
4 Felix Millan 2198
5 Frank Bolling 1964

Shortstop
1 Herman Long 5490
2 Rabbit Maranville 5018
3 Johnny Logan 4260
4 Rafael Ramirez 2739
5 Billy Urbanski 2001

Third Base
1 Eddie Mathews 4251
2 Billy Nash 2398
3 Darrell Evans 1568
4 Jimmy Collins 1547
5 Bob Elliott 1398

Outfield
1 Hank Aaron 201
2 Hugh Duffy 138
3 Ray Powell 124
4 Dick Johnston 123
5 Tommy Holmes 114
6 Tommy McCarthy 109
7 Joe Hornung 108
8 Dale Murphy 102
9 Jimmy Welsh 88
10 Bill Bruton 83

Catcher
1 Hank Gowdy 905
2 Del Crandall 691
3 Mickey O'Neil 602
4 Bruce Benedict 577
5 Phil Masi 391
  Joe Torre 391

Pitcher
1 Warren Spahn 958
2 Kid Nichols 914
3 Phil Niekro 773
4 Vic Willis 677
5 Dick Rudolph 623

Assists per Game

First Base
1 Fred Tenney 0.76
2 Chris Chambliss 0.74
3 Earl Torgeson 0.67
4 Buck Jordan 0.64
5 Joe Adcock 0.63

Second Base
1 Glenn Hubbard 3.43
2 Tony Cuccinello 3.37
3 Bobby Lowe 3.18
4 Jack Burdock 3.13
5 Connie Ryan 2.91

Shortstop
1 Rabbit Maranville 3.43
2 Herman Long 3.42
3 Eddie Miller 3.24
4 Rafael Ramirez 3.22
5 Johnny Logan 3.21

Third Base

1	Jimmy Collins	2.36
2	Darrell Evans	2.21
3	Billy Nash	2.13
4	Terry Pendleton	2.10
5	Red Smith	2.06

Outfield

1	Dick Johnston	0.24
2	Tommy McCarthy	0.21
3	Jimmy Welsh	0.17
4	Joe Hornung	0.16
5	Ray Powell	0.16
6	Chick Stahl	0.16
7	Les Mann	0.15
8	Gene Moore	0.15
9	Hugh Duffy	0.13
10	Tommy Holmes	0.10
11	Max West	0.10

Catcher

1	Hank Gowdy	1.24
2	Mickey O'Neil	1.08
3	Bruce Benedict	0.60
4	Del Crandall	0.53
5	Joe Torre	0.50

Pitcher

1	Dick Rudolph	2.27
2	Togie Pittinger	2.17
3	John Clarkson	2.12
4	Vic Willis	2.12
5	Tommy Bond	2.08

Double Plays

First Base

1	Joe Adcock	940
2	Fred Tenney	835
3	Chris Chambliss	614
4	Earl Torgeson	538
5	Tommy Tucker	536

Second Base

1	Glenn Hubbard	881
2	Frank Bolling	482
3	Felix Millan	469
4	Bobby Lowe	416
5	Tony Cuccinello	378

Shortstop

1	Johnny Logan	863
2	Rabbit Maranville	794
3	Herman Long	692
4	Rafael Ramirez	627
5	Eddie Miller	388

Third Base

1	Eddie Mathews	366
2	Billy Nash	192
3	Darrell Evans	158
4	Bob Elliott	127
5	Bob Horner	104

Outfield

1	Hank Aaron	41
2	Tommy Holmes	37
3	Hugh Duffy	31
4	Dick Johnston	24
	Ray Powell	24
	Jimmy Welsh	24
7	Bill Bruton	22
8	Dale Murphy	21
9	Tommy McCarthy	20
10	Wally Berger	19

Catcher

1	Del Crandall	103
2	Hank Gowdy	83
3	Joe Torre	53
4	Bruce Benedict	50
5	Mickey O'Neil	40

Pitcher

1	Warren Spahn	80
2	Phil Niekro	71
3	Lew Burdette	47
4	Ben Cantwell	33
5	Kid Nichols	32

Fielding Runs

1	Glenn Hubbard	215
2	Rabbit Maranville	130
3	Fred Tenney	105
4	Hank Aaron	102
5	Johnny Logan	100
6	Jimmy Collins	85
7	Rafael Belliard	81
8	Herman Long	65
9	Darrell Evans	63
10	Terry Pendleton	59
11	Bill Sweeney	58
12	Tommy Holmes	54
13	Billy Nash	51
14	Jimmy Welsh	49
15	Bruce Benedict	47
16	Joe Hornung	43
	Dick Johnston	43
	Eddie Miller	43
	Dale Murphy	43
20	Gene Moore	40

Fielding Runs (by position)

First Base

1	Fred Tenney	111
2	John Morrill	38
3	Chris Chambliss	21
4	Walter Holke	3

Second Base

1	Glenn Hubbard	216
2	Bobby Lowe	41
3	Mark Lemke	20
4	Jack Burdock	4

Shortstop

1	Rabbit Maranville	161
2	Johnny Logan	101
3	Herman Long	68
4	Eddie Miller	43
5	Andres Thomas	38

Third Base

1	Jimmy Collins	88
2	Terry Pendleton	59
3	Darrell Evans	55
4	Billy Nash	52
5	Clete Boyer	24

Outfield

1	Hank Aaron	107
2	Tommy Holmes	55
3	Dale Murphy	49
	Jimmy Welsh	49
5	Joe Hornung	43
	Dick Johnston	43
7	Gene Moore	40
8	Wally Berger	39
9	David Justice	37
10	Bill Bruton	29
	Ray Powell	29

Catcher

1	Bruce Benedict	46
2	Del Crandall	30
3	Mickey O'Neil	26
4	Hank Gowdy	7

Pitcher

1	Phil Niekro	28
2	Ben Cantwell	26
3	Tommy Bond	22
4	Jim Tobin	20
5	Lew Burdette	19

Fielding Wins

1	Glenn Hubbard	22.4
2	Rabbit Maranville	13.5
3	Hank Aaron	10.6
4	Fred Tenney	10.2
5	Johnny Logan	10.1
6	Rafael Belliard	8.3
7	Jimmy Collins	7.6
8	Darrell Evans	6.6
9	Bill Sweeney	6.1
10	Terry Pendleton	6.1
11	Herman Long	5.8
12	Tommy Holmes	5.5
13	Bruce Benedict	4.9
14	Jimmy Welsh	4.6
15	Dale Murphy	4.5
16	Eddie Miller	4.4
17	Billy Nash	4.4
18	Gene Moore	4.0
19	Andres Thomas	4.0
20	Joe Hornung	3.9

Total Player Rating

1	Hank Aaron	90.7
2	Eddie Mathews	52.4
3	Wally Berger	21.5
4	Dale Murphy	20.7
5	Glenn Hubbard	19.0
6	Fred Tenney	18.9
7	Johnny Logan	17.5
8	Tommy Holmes	14.1
9	Rabbit Maranville	13.3
10	Darrell Evans	13.2
11	Rico Carty	13.1
12	Joe Torre	12.7
13	Bob Elliott	12.4
	David Justice	12.4
15	Billy Nash	10.5
16	Sid Gordon	10.4
17	Jimmy Collins	9.9
18	Terry Pendleton	9.0
19	Red Smith	8.9
20	Bill Sweeney	8.8
21	Dave Brain	7.9
22	Joe Adcock	7.8
23	Earl Torgeson	7.0
24	Dave Bancroft	6.8
25	Hank Gowdy	6.4
	Gene Moore	6.4
27	Lonnie Smith	6.3
28	Ron Gant	6.2
29	Ezra Sutton	6.1
30	Del Crandall	5.6
31	Bill Dahlen	5.2
	Herman Long	5.2
33	Eddie Miller	5.0
34	Davey Johnson	4.8
35	Billy Hamilton	4.5
	Charley Jones	4.5
37	Sam Wise	4.4
38	John O'Rourke	4.2
	Eddie Stanky	4.2
40	Pat Moran	4.0
	Claude Ritchey	4.0
42	King Kelly	3.9
43	Jeff Heath	3.4
44	Fred McGriff	3.3
45	Charlie Bennett	3.1
	Bob Horner	3.1
47	Sam Jethroe	3.0
48	Rafael Belliard	2.9
	Tony Cuccinello	2.9
50	2 players tied	2.8

Total Player Rating (alpha.)

Hank Aaron	90.7
Joe Adcock	7.8
Dave Bancroft	6.8
Rafael Belliard	2.9
Charlie Bennett	3.1
Wally Berger	21.5
Dave Brain	7.9
Rico Carty	13.1
Jimmy Collins	9.9
Del Crandall	5.6
Tony Cuccinello	2.9
Bill Dahlen	5.2
Bob Elliott	12.4
Darrell Evans	13.2
Ron Gant	6.2
Sid Gordon	10.4
Hank Gowdy	6.4
Billy Hamilton	4.5
Jeff Heath	3.4
Tommy Holmes	14.1
Bob Horner	3.1
Glenn Hubbard	19.0
Sam Jethroe	3.0
Davey Johnson	4.8
Charley Jones	4.5
David Justice	12.4
King Kelly	3.9
Johnny Logan	17.5
Herman Long	5.2
Rabbit Maranville	13.3
Eddie Mathews	52.4
Eddie Miller	5.0
Gene Moore	6.4
Pat Moran	4.0
Dale Murphy	20.7
Fred McGriff	3.3
Billy Nash	10.5
John O'Rourke	4.2
Terry Pendleton	9.0
Claude Ritchey	4.0
Red Smith	8.9
Lonnie Smith	6.3
Eddie Stanky	4.2
Ezra Sutton	6.1
Bill Sweeney	8.8
Fred Tenney	18.9
Earl Torgeson	7.0
Joe Torre	12.7
Sam Wise	4.4

Total Player Rating (by era)

1876-1892

1	Billy Nash	10.5
2	Ezra Sutton	6.1
3	Sam Wise	4.4
4	King Kelly	3.9
5	Charlie Bennett	3.1

1893-1919

1	Fred Tenney	18.9
2	Rabbit Maranville	13.3
3	Jimmy Collins	9.9
4	Red Smith	8.9
5	Bill Sweeney	8.8

1920-1941

1	Wally Berger	21.5
2	Dave Bancroft	6.8
3	Gene Moore	6.4
4	Eddie Miller	5.0
5	Tony Cuccinello	2.9

1942-1960

1	Eddie Mathews	52.4
2	Johnny Logan	17.5
3	Tommy Holmes	14.1
4	Bob Elliott	12.4
5	Sid Gordon	10.4

1961-1976

1	Hank Aaron	90.7
2	Darrell Evans	13.2
3	Rico Carty	13.1
4	Joe Torre	12.7
5	Felipe Alou	2.5

1977-1995

1	Dale Murphy	20.7
2	Glenn Hubbard	19.0
3	David Justice	12.4
4	Terry Pendleton	9.0
5	Lonnie Smith	6.3

Wins

1	Warren Spahn	356
2	Kid Nichols	329
3	Phil Niekro	268
4	Lew Burdette	179
5	Vic Willis	151
6	Tommy Bond	149
	John Clarkson	149
8	Jim Whitney	133
9	Jack Stivetts	131
10	Tom Glavine	124
11	Dick Rudolph	121
12	Bob Buhl	109
13	Charlie Buffinton	104
	Johnny Sain	104
15	Ed Brandt	94
16	Lefty Tyler	92
17	John Smoltz	90
18	Tony Cloninger	86
19	Pat Jarvis	83
	Bob Smith	83

Losses

1	Phil Niekro	230
2	Warren Spahn	229
3	Kid Nichols	183
4	Vic Willis	147
5	Jim Whitney	121
6	Lew Burdette	120
	Bob Smith	120
8	Ed Brandt	119
9	Dick Rudolph	107
10	Ben Cantwell	106
11	Lefty Tyler	92
12	Johnny Sain	91
13	Rick Mahler	89
14	Ron Reed	88
15	Tommy Bond	87
16	Jesse Barnes	86
17	Togie Pittinger	84
18	Jim Tobin	83
19	3 players tied	82

Winning Percentage

1	Harry Staley	.655
2	John Clarkson	.645
3	Kid Nichols	.643
4	Tommy Bond	.631
5	Jack Stivetts	.627
6	Ted Lewis	.624
7	Warren Spahn	.609
8	Bob Buhl	.602
9	Tom Glavine	.602
10	Lew Burdette	.599
11	Charlie Buffinton	.598
12	Tony Cloninger	.581
13	Ken Johnson	.570
14	Art Nehf	.559
15	Steve Avery	.556
16	Vern Bickford	.541
17	Phil Niekro	.538
18	Pat Jarvis	.535
19	Rick Camp	.533
	Johnny Sain	.533

Games

1	Phil Niekro	740
2	Warren Spahn	714
3	Gene Garber	557
4	Kid Nichols	556
5	Lew Burdette	468
6	Rick Camp	414
7	Steve Bedrosian	350
8	Bob Smith	349
9	Vic Willis	320
10	Rick Mahler	307
11	Mike Stanton	304
12	Ben Cantwell	290
13	Ed Brandt	283
14	Bob Buhl	282
15	Dick Rudolph	275
16	Jim Whitney	266
17	Tom Glavine	262
18	Johnny Sain	257
19	Tommy Bond	247
	Lefty Tyler	247

Games Started

1	Warren Spahn	635
2	Phil Niekro	595
3	Kid Nichols	501
4	Lew Burdette	330
5	Vic Willis	302
6	Tom Glavine	262
7	Jim Whitney	254
8	Tommy Bond	241
9	Dick Rudolph	239
10	John Clarkson	237
11	John Smoltz	231
12	Bob Buhl	220
13	Rick Mahler	218
14	Ed Brandt	210
15	Jack Stivetts	207
16	Johnny Sain	206
17	Ron Reed	203
18	Lefty Tyler	197
19	Bob Smith	183
20	Charlie Buffinton	180

Games Started (by era)

1876-1892

1	Jim Whitney	254
2	Tommy Bond	241
3	John Clarkson	237
4	Charlie Buffinton	180
5	Charley Radbourn	163

1893-1919

1	Kid Nichols	501
2	Vic Willis	302
3	Dick Rudolph	239
4	Jack Stivetts	207
5	Lefty Tyler	197

1920-1941

1	Ed Brandt	210
2	Bob Smith	183
3	Ben Cantwell	159
4	Danny MacFayden	141
5	Jesse Barnes	137

1942-1960

1	Warren Spahn	635
2	Lew Burdette	330
3	Bob Buhl	220
4	Johnny Sain	206
5	Jim Tobin	161

1961-1976

1	Phil Niekro	595
2	Ron Reed	203
3	Tony Cloninger	170
4	Pat Jarvis	169
5	Denny Lemaster	159

1977-1995

1	Tom Glavine	262
2	John Smoltz	231
3	Rick Mahler	218
4	Steve Avery	178
5	Zane Smith	128

Complete Games

1	Kid Nichols	475
2	Warren Spahn	374
3	Vic Willis	268
4	Jim Whitney	242
5	John Clarkson	226
	Phil Niekro	226
7	Tommy Bond	225
8	Jack Stivetts	176
9	Dick Rudolph	171
10	Charlie Buffinton	166
11	Charley Radbourn	157
12	Lew Burdette	146
13	Togie Pittinger	141
14	Lefty Tyler	132
15	Ed Brandt	126
16	Jim Tobin	125
17	Johnny Sain	121
18	Irv Young	107
19	Ted Lewis	105
20	Bob Smith	102

Complete Games (by era)

1876-1892

1	Jim Whitney	242
2	John Clarkson	226
3	Tommy Bond	225
4	Charlie Buffinton	166
5	Charley Radbourn	157

1893-1919

1	Kid Nichols	475
2	Vic Willis	268
3	Jack Stivetts	176
4	Dick Rudolph	171
5	Togie Pittinger	141

1920-1941

1	Ed Brandt	126
2	Bob Smith	102
3	Jesse Barnes	88
4	Ben Cantwell	74
5	Danny MacFayden	71

1942-1960

1	Warren Spahn	374
2	Lew Burdette	146
3	Jim Tobin	125
4	Johnny Sain	121
5	Bob Buhl	83

1961-1976

1	Phil Niekro	226
2	Tony Cloninger	54
3	Ron Reed	47
4	Denny Lemaster	45
5	Pat Jarvis	42

1977-1995

1	Rick Mahler	36
2	Tom Glavine	33
3	John Smoltz	31
4	Greg Maddux	28
5	Zane Smith	17

Shutouts

1	Warren Spahn	63
2	Kid Nichols	44
3	Phil Niekro	43
4	Lew Burdette	30
5	Tommy Bond	29
6	Dick Rudolph	27
7	Vic Willis	26
8	Lefty Tyler	22
9	John Clarkson	20
10	Charlie Buffinton	19
11	Jim Whitney	18
12	Bob Buhl	16
	Togie Pittinger	16
14	Al Javery	15
	Johnny Sain	15
	Irv Young	15
17	Jesse Barnes	14
	Ed Brandt	14
	Lou Fette	14
20	3 players tied	13

Saves

1	Gene Garber	141
2	Cecil Upshaw	78
3	Rick Camp	57
4	Mike Stanton	55
5	Don McMahon	50
6	Greg McMichael	42
7	Steve Bedrosian	41
8	Bruce Sutter	40
9	Bob Smith	36
10	Claude Raymond	33
11	Mark Wohlers	32
12	Joe Boever	30
13	Phil Niekro	29
	Warren Spahn	29
15	Tom House	28
16	Alejandro Pena	26
17	Billy O'Dell	24
18	Lew Burdette	23
	Donnie Moore	23
20	Ben Cantwell	20

Innings Pitched

1	Warren Spahn	5046.0
2	Phil Niekro	4622.2
3	Kid Nichols	4538.0
4	Lew Burdette	2638.0
5	Vic Willis	2575.0
6	Jim Whitney	2263.2
7	Tommy Bond	2127.1
8	John Clarkson	2092.2
9	Dick Rudolph	2035.0
10	Bob Smith	1813.1
11	Jack Stivetts	1798.2
12	Ed Brandt	1761.2
13	Tom Glavine	1721.0
14	Lefty Tyler	1687.2
15	Johnny Sain	1624.1
16	Bob Buhl	1599.2
17	Rick Mahler	1558.2
18	John Smoltz	1550.2
19	Charlie Buffinton	1547.1
20	Togie Pittinger	1471.2

Innings Pitched (by era)

1876-1892

1	Jim Whitney	2263.2
2	Tommy Bond	2127.1
3	John Clarkson	2092.2
4	Charlie Buffinton	1547.1
5	Charley Radbourn	1418.1

1893-1919

1	Kid Nichols	4538.0
2	Vic Willis	2575.0
3	Dick Rudolph	2035.0
4	Jack Stivetts	1798.2
5	Lefty Tyler	1687.2

1920-1941

1	Bob Smith	1813.1
2	Ed Brandt	1761.2
3	Ben Cantwell	1464.2
4	Jesse Barnes	1182.2
5	Joe Genewich	1097.1

1942-1960

1	Warren Spahn	5046.0
2	Lew Burdette	2638.0
3	Johnny Sain	1624.1
4	Bob Buhl	1599.2
5	Jim Tobin	1368.0

1961-1976

1	Phil Niekro	4622.2
2	Ron Reed	1419.2
3	Pat Jarvis	1244.2
4	Tony Cloninger	1215.1
5	Denny Lemaster	1077.1

1977-1995

1	Tom Glavine	1721.0
2	Rick Mahler	1558.2
3	John Smoltz	1550.2
4	Steve Avery	1091.1
5	Rick Camp	942.1

Hits per Game

1	John Smoltz	7.81
2	Lefty Tyler	8.00
3	Art Nehf	8.05
4	Bob Buhl	8.11
5	Gus Dorner	8.13
6	Denny Lemaster	8.22
7	Phil Niekro	8.22
8	Warren Spahn	8.24
9	Pat Jarvis	8.26
10	Pat Ragan	8.32
11	Vic Willis	8.34
12	Tony Cloninger	8.40
13	John Clarkson	8.42
14	Steve Avery	8.53
15	Dick Rudolph	8.62
16	Tom Glavine	8.62
17	Vern Bickford	8.69
18	Buster Brown	8.70
19	Vive Lindaman	8.72
20	Ken Johnson	8.72

Home Runs Allowed

1	Warren Spahn	408
2	Phil Niekro	392
3	Lew Burdette	251
4	Kid Nichols	151
5	Rick Mahler	132
6	John Smoltz	131
7	Bob Buhl	130
8	Tony Cloninger	125
	Denny Lemaster	125
10	Ron Reed	120
11	Johnny Sain	119
12	Bob Smith	115
13	Tom Glavine	113
14	Ed Brandt	106
15	Pat Jarvis	100
16	Jack Stivetts	98
17	Steve Avery	93
18	Ben Cantwell	86
19	Jim Tobin	80
20	Vern Bickford	76

Home Runs Allowed (by era)

1876-1892

1	John Clarkson	69
2	Charley Radbourn	60
3	Harry Staley	58
4	Jim Whitney	42
5	Charlie Buffinton	35

1893-1919

1	Kid Nichols	151
2	Jack Stivetts	98
3	Vic Willis	51
4	Ted Lewis	43
5	Lefty Tyler	42

1920-1941

1	Bob Smith	115
2	Ed Brandt	106
3	Ben Cantwell	86
4	Fred Frankhouse	61
5	Socks Seibold	57

1942-1960

1	Warren Spahn	408
2	Lew Burdette	251
3	Bob Buhl	130
4	Johnny Sain	119
5	Jim Tobin	80

1961-1976

1	Phil Niekro	392
2	Tony Cloninger	125
	Denny Lemaster	125
4	Ron Reed	120
5	Pat Jarvis	100

1977-1995

1	Rick Mahler	132
2	John Smoltz	131
3	Tom Glavine	113
4	Steve Avery	93
5	Rick Camp	72

Walks

1	Phil Niekro	1458
2	Warren Spahn	1378
3	Kid Nichols	1159
4	Vic Willis	854
5	Bob Buhl	782
6	Lefty Tyler	678
7	John Clarkson	676
8	Jack Stivetts	651
9	Ed Brandt	611
10	Tom Glavine	579
11	John Smoltz	572
12	Bob Smith	561
13	Lew Burdette	557
14	Togie Pittinger	545
15	Johnny Sain	502
16	Tony Cloninger	501
	Rick Mahler	501
18	Vern Bickford	466
19	Al Javery	452
20	Ted Lewis	420

Fewest Walks per Game

1876-1892

1	Tommy Bond	0.59
2	Jim Whitney	0.91
3	Charlie Buffinton	1.70
4	Charley Radbourn	2.29
5	Harry Staley	2.71

1893-1919

1	Dick Rudolph	1.77
2	Irv Young	1.95
3	Art Nehf	1.99
4	Pat Ragan	2.30
5	Kid Nichols	2.30

1920-1941

1	Huck Betts	1.85
2	Jesse Barnes	1.95
3	Ben Cantwell	2.26
4	Danny MacFayden	2.40
5	Dana Fillingim	2.41

1942-1960

1	Lew Burdette	1.90
2	Red Barrett	2.29
3	Warren Spahn	2.46
4	Jim Tobin	2.64
5	Johnny Sain	2.78

1961-1976

1	Ken Johnson	1.81
2	Ron Reed	2.24
3	Pat Jarvis	2.63
4	Carl Morton	2.71
5	Phil Niekro	2.84

1977-1995

1	Gene Garber	2.45
2	Steve Avery	2.73
3	Rick Mahler	2.89
4	Tom Glavine	3.03
5	Rick Camp	3.21

Ratio

1	Jim Whitney	9.7
2	Tommy Bond	10.1
3	Art Nehf	10.3
4	Dick Rudolph	10.5
5	Charlie Buffinton	10.6
6	Ken Johnson	10.8
	Pat Ragan	10.8
	Warren Spahn	10.8
9	Pat Jarvis	11.0
10	Jesse Barnes	11.2
	Lew Burdette	11.2
	Irv Young	11.2
13	Kid Nichols	11.3
	Phil Niekro	11.3
	John Smoltz	11.3
16	Steve Avery	11.4
	Denny Lemaster	11.4
	Ron Reed	11.4
19	3 players tied	11.6

Strikeouts

1	Phil Niekro	2912
2	Warren Spahn	2493
3	Kid Nichols	1667
4	John Smoltz	1252
5	Vic Willis	1161
6	Jim Whitney	1157
7	Tom Glavine	1031
8	Lew Burdette	923
9	Charlie Buffinton	911
10	Denny Lemaster	842
11	John Clarkson	834
	Tony Cloninger	834
13	Lefty Tyler	827
14	Bob Buhl	791
15	Ron Reed	778
16	Dick Rudolph	777
17	Rick Mahler	765
18	Pat Jarvis	736
19	Steve Avery	729
20	Johnny Sain	698

Strikeouts per Game

1	John Smoltz	7.27
2	Denny Lemaster	7.03
3	Tony Cloninger	6.18
4	Steve Avery	6.01
5	Gene Garber	5.68
6	Phil Niekro	5.67
7	Tom Glavine	5.39
8	Pat Jarvis	5.32
9	Charlie Buffinton	5.30
10	Zane Smith	5.14
11	Ron Reed	4.93
12	Jim Whitney	4.60
13	Ken Johnson	4.56
14	Bob Buhl	4.45
15	Warren Spahn	4.45
16	Rick Mahler	4.42
17	Lefty Tyler	4.41
18	Vic Willis	4.06
19	Rick Camp	3.89
20	Johnny Sain	3.87

Earned Run Average (by era)

1876-1892

1	Tommy Bond	2.21
2	Jim Whitney	2.49
3	John Clarkson	2.82
4	Charlie Buffinton	2.83
5	Charley Radbourn	3.58

1893-1919

1	Art Nehf	2.52
2	Dick Rudolph	2.62
3	Pat Ragan	2.74
4	Vic Willis	2.82
5	Vive Lindaman	2.92

1920-1941

1	Jesse Barnes	3.07
2	Danny MacFayden	3.45
3	Dana Fillingim	3.51
4	Huck Betts	3.63
5	Johnny Cooney	3.72

1942-1960

1	Warren Spahn	3.05
2	Bob Buhl	3.27
3	Jim Tobin	3.34
4	Johnny Sain	3.49
5	Lew Burdette	3.53

1961-1976

1	Phil Niekro	3.20
2	Ken Johnson	3.22
3	Carl Morton	3.47
4	Pat Jarvis	3.59
5	Denny Lemaster	3.63

1977-1995

1	Gene Garber	3.34
2	Rick Camp	3.37
3	Tom Glavine	3.52
4	John Smoltz	3.53
5	Steve Avery	3.75

Earned Run Average

1	Tommy Bond	2.21
2	Jim Whitney	2.49
3	Art Nehf	2.52
4	Dick Rudolph	2.62
5	Pat Ragan	2.74
6	John Clarkson	2.82
	Vic Willis	2.82
8	Charlie Buffinton	2.83
9	Vive Lindaman	2.92
10	Kid Nichols	3.00
11	Warren Spahn	3.05
12	Lefty Tyler	3.06
13	Jesse Barnes	3.07
14	Togie Pittinger	3.08
15	Irv Young	3.15
16	Phil Niekro	3.20
17	Ken Johnson	3.22
18	Bob Buhl	3.27
19	Gene Garber	3.34
	Jim Tobin	3.34

Adjusted Earned Run Average

1	Kid Nichols	143
2	John Clarkson	128
3	Warren Spahn	120
	Vic Willis	120
5	Phil Niekro	119
6	Gene Garber	117
	Ted Lewis	117
8	Rick Camp	114
	Jim Whitney	114
10	Jack Stivetts	113
11	Tommy Bond	112
	Tom Glavine	112
13	John Smoltz	111
14	Bob Buhl	110
	Carl Morton	110
16	Jesse Barnes	108
	Jim Tobin	108
18	Johnny Sain	107
19	4 players tied	106

Adjusted ERA (by era)

1876-1892

1	John Clarkson	128
2	Jim Whitney	114
3	Tommy Bond	112
4	Harry Staley	104
5	Charlie Buffinton	103

1893-1919

1	Kid Nichols	143
2	Vic Willis	120
3	Ted Lewis	117
4	Jack Stivetts	113
5	2 players tied	105

1920-1941

1	Jesse Barnes	108
2	Johnny Cooney	106
	Danny MacFayden	106
4	Ben Cantwell	101
5	2 players tied	99

1942-1960

1	Warren Spahn	120
2	Bob Buhl	110
3	Jim Tobin	108
4	Johnny Sain	107
5	2 players tied	102

1961-1976

1	Phil Niekro	119
2	Carl Morton	110
3	Ken Johnson	106
4	Pat Jarvis	100
5	Ron Reed	98

1977-1995

1	Gene Garber	117
2	Rick Camp	114
3	Tom Glavine	112
4	John Smoltz	111
5	Steve Avery	106

Pitching Runs

1	Kid Nichols	517
2	Warren Spahn	480
3	Phil Niekro	198
4	Greg Maddux	169
5	John Clarkson	150
6	Vic Willis	122
7	Bob Buhl	120
8	Lew Burdette	114
9	Jim Whitney	108
10	Johnny Sain	73
11	Tommy Bond	68
12	Danny MacFayden	58
13	Jack Stivetts	57
14	Lou Fette	54
15	Tom Glavine	53
16	Jesse Barnes	52
	Dick Rudolph	52
18	Jim Turner	47
19	John Smoltz	46
20	2 players tied	44

Adjusted Pitching Runs

1	Kid Nichols	646
2	Warren Spahn	339
3	Phil Niekro	309
4	John Clarkson	187
5	Greg Maddux	170
6	Vic Willis	159
7	Jack Stivetts	108
8	Jim Whitney	86
9	Tom Glavine	80
10	Ted Lewis	71
11	John Smoltz	68
12	Tommy Bond	64
13	Bob Buhl	59
	Bill Dinneen	59
15	Gene Garber	53
16	Rick Camp	51
17	Steve Bedrosian	48
18	Johnny Sain	45
19	Jim Tobin	39
20	Carl Morton	37

Pitching Wins

1	Warren Spahn	48.4
2	Kid Nichols	45.1
3	Phil Niekro	20.8
4	Greg Maddux	16.7
5	John Clarkson	13.6
6	Bob Buhl	12.1
7	Vic Willis	12.0
8	Lew Burdette	11.5
9	Jim Whitney	9.8
10	Johnny Sain	7.3
11	Tommy Bond	6.3
12	Danny MacFayden	5.7
13	Dick Rudolph	5.7
14	Tom Glavine	5.5
15	Lou Fette	5.4
16	Jesse Barnes	5.4
17	Jack Stivetts	4.8
18	John Smoltz	4.7
19	Jim Turner	4.7
20	Tom Zachary	4.3

Adjusted Pitching Wins

1	Kid Nichols	56.3
2	Warren Spahn	34.2
3	Phil Niekro	32.5
4	John Clarkson	16.9
5	Greg Maddux	16.8
6	Vic Willis	15.6
7	Jack Stivetts	9.0
8	Tom Glavine	8.3
9	Jim Whitney	7.8
10	John Smoltz	7.0
11	Ted Lewis	6.4
12	Tommy Bond	5.9
13	Bob Buhl	5.9
14	Bill Dinneen	5.6
15	Gene Garber	5.5
16	Rick Camp	5.4
17	Steve Bedrosian	5.0
18	Johnny Sain	4.5
19	Jim Tobin	4.0
20	Carl Morton	3.9

Opponents' Batting Average

1	John Smoltz	.233
2	John Clarkson	.239
3	Bob Buhl	.242
	Denny Lemaster	.242
5	Pat Jarvis	.243
	Art Nehf	.243
	Phil Niekro	.243
	Warren Spahn	.243
	Jim Whitney	.243
10	Lefty Tyler	.245
11	Charlie Buffinton	.246
12	Tony Cloninger	.247
	Gus Dorner	.247
	Vic Willis	.247
15	Pat Ragan	.250
16	Kid Nichols	.251
17	Steve Avery	.252
18	Tom Glavine	.253
19	Vern Bickford	.254
20	2 players tied	.256

Opponents' On Base Pctg.

1	Jim Whitney	.261
2	Tommy Bond	.274
3	Charlie Buffinton	.280
4	Art Nehf	.290
5	Warren Spahn	.296
6	Dick Rudolph	.297
7	Ken Johnson	.298
8	Pat Jarvis	.299
9	Pat Ragan	.301
10	John Clarkson	.302
	Kid Nichols	.302
12	Lew Burdette	.305
	Phil Niekro	.305
14	Denny Lemaster	.306
	John Smoltz	.306
16	Charley Radbourn	.309
	Ron Reed	.309
18	Steve Avery	.310
	Jesse Barnes	.310
20	2 players tied	.311

Wins Above Team

1	Warren Spahn	48.5
2	Phil Niekro	34.6
3	Kid Nichols	29.9
4	John Clarkson	21.0
5	Tom Glavine	19.3
6	Lew Burdette	15.5
7	Charlie Buffinton	15.4
8	Greg Maddux	13.5
9	Tony Cloninger	10.2
10	Larry Benton	9.0
	Art Nehf	9.0
12	Bob Buhl	8.7
13	Dick Rudolph	8.5
14	Fred Frankhouse	7.2
15	Vic Willis	7.0
16	Bill James	6.9
17	Pat Jarvis	6.3
18	Carl Morton	5.8
19	Ken Johnson	5.7
	Jim Tobin	5.7

Wins Above League

1	Warren Spahn	292.5
2	Kid Nichols	256.0
3	Phil Niekro	249.0
4	Lew Burdette	149.5
5	Vic Willis	149.0
6	Jim Whitney	127.0
7	Tommy Bond	118.0
8	John Clarkson	115.5
9	Dick Rudolph	114.0
10	Ed Brandt	106.5
11	Jack Stivetts	104.5
12	Tom Glavine	103.0
13	Bob Smith	101.5
14	Johnny Sain	97.5
15	Lefty Tyler	92.0
16	Bob Buhl	90.5
17	Ben Cantwell	90.0
18	Charlie Buffinton	87.0
19	John Smoltz	86.0
20	2 players tied	84.0

Relief Games

1	Gene Garber	557
2	Rick Camp	349
3	Steve Bedrosian	304
	Mike Stanton	304
5	Cecil Upshaw	241
6	Don McMahon	233
7	Paul Assenmacher	226
	Jeff Dedmon	226
9	Ernie Johnson	224
10	Mark Wohlers	211

Relief Wins

1	Gene Garber	53
2	Rick Camp	33
3	Ernie Johnson	31
4	Cecil Upshaw	30
5	Steve Bedrosian	29
6	Lew Burdette	26
7	Mark Wohlers	24
8	Don McMahon	23
9	3 players tied	19

Relief Losses

1	Gene Garber	73
2	Don McMahon	29
3	Steve Bedrosian	27
4	Cecil Upshaw	26
5	Rick Camp	24
6	Mike Stanton	21
7	Claude Raymond	19
8	Jim Acker	18
	Bob Smith	18
10	Ernie Johnson	15

Relief Innings Pitched

1	Gene Garber	856.0
2	Rick Camp	548.2
3	Ernie Johnson	480.0
4	Bob Smith	455.0
5	Steve Bedrosian	436.0
6	Cecil Upshaw	409.2
7	Jeff Dedmon	352.0
8	Don McMahon	344.2
9	Mike Stanton	289.2
10	Lew Burdette	283.0

Relief Points

1	Gene Garber	315
2	Cecil Upshaw	190
3	Rick Camp	156
4	Don McMahon	127
5	Mike Stanton	125
6	Steve Bedrosian	113
7	Mark Wohlers	102
8	Greg McMichael	99
9	Bob Smith	92
10	Bruce Sutter	89

Relief Ranking

1	Gene Garber	83
2	Steve Bedrosian	66
	Rick Camp	66
4	Greg McMichael	39
5	Billy O'Dell	38
6	Mark Wohlers	35
7	Kent Mercker	27
8	Paul Assenmacher	26
	Terry Forster	26
	Cecil Upshaw	26

Relievers' Runs

1	Steve Bedrosian	39
2	Greg McMichael	35
3	Gene Garber	30
4	Bob Smith	29
5	Rick Camp	25
6	Terry Forster	24
	Billy O'Dell	24
8	Don McMahon	22
9	Lew Burdette	19
10	Cecil Upshaw	16

Adjusted Relievers' Runs

1	Gene Garber	53
2	Steve Bedrosian	46
3	Rick Camp	41
4	Greg McMichael	35
5	Terry Forster	29
6	Billy O'Dell	24
7	Tom House	21
8	Cecil Upshaw	20
9	Kent Mercker	18
	Bob Smith	18

Clutch Pitching Index

1	Rick Camp	120
2	Tommy Bond	113
3	Bob Buhl	112
4	Vive Lindaman	111
	Togie Pittinger	111
6	Carl Morton	109
7	John Clarkson	107
	Al Mattern	107
9	Fred Frankhouse	105
	Danny MacFayden	105
11	Vern Bickford	104
	Gene Garber	104
	Ken Johnson	104
	Rick Mahler	104
	Johnny Sain	104
	Bob Smith	104
	Vic Willis	104
18	Jesse Barnes	103
	Dana Fillingim	103
20	4 players tied	102

Pitcher Batting Runs

1	Warren Spahn	86
2	Jim Whitney	71
3	Jack Stivetts	43
4	Jim Tobin	35
5	Johnny Sain	27
6	Ed Brandt	26
7	Lew Burdette	24
8	Lefty Tyler	23
9	Charlie Buffinton	21
10	Bob Smith	20
11	Johnny Cooney	15
12	Tom Glavine	14
13	Tony Cloninger	13
	Fred Frankhouse	13
	Dick Rudolph	13
16	John Clarkson	11
	Jim Turner	11
18	Charley Radbourn	10
19	5 players tied	7

Pitcher Fielding Runs

1	Phil Niekro	28
2	Ben Cantwell	26
3	Tommy Bond	23
4	Jim Tobin	20
5	Lew Burdette	19
6	John Clarkson	17
	Vic Willis	17
8	Dick Rudolph	16
9	Greg Maddux	15
	Lefty Tyler	15
11	Gene Garber	14
12	Tom Glavine	13
13	Zane Smith	12
14	Bob Smith	11
15	Fred Frankhouse	10
	Rick Mahler	10
17	Warren Spahn	9
18	6 players tied	8

Pitcher Batting Average

1	Jack Stivetts	.304
2	Johnny Cooney	.286
3	Jim Whitney	.270
4	Charlie Buffinton	.255
5	Bob Smith	.248
6	Ed Brandt	.245
7	Johnny Sain	.242
8	Ted Lewis	.237
9	Kid Nichols	.231
10	Ben Cantwell	.229
11	Tommy Bond	.225
12	Charley Radbourn	.223
13	Fred Frankhouse	.221
14	Hugh McQuillan	.218
	Jim Tobin	.218
16	John Clarkson	.217
17	Lefty Tyler	.214
18	Dana Fillingim	.212
19	Huck Betts	.209
20	Joe Oeschger	.207

Total Pitcher Index

1	Kid Nichols	60.0
2	Warren Spahn	48.0
3	Phil Niekro	37.1
4	Greg Maddux	20.1
5	John Clarkson	19.5
6	Vic Willis	15.7
7	Jim Whitney	14.8
8	Jack Stivetts	12.8
9	Tom Glavine	12.7
10	Jim Tobin	11.0
11	Gene Garber	10.6
12	Johnny Sain	9.4
13	John Smoltz	7.3
14	Rick Camp	7.2
15	Dick Rudolph	7.0
16	Tommy Bond	6.8
17	Lew Burdette	6.7
18	Steve Bedrosian	5.8
19	Bill Dinneen	5.7
20	Ted Lewis	5.3
21	Ben Cantwell	5.2
22	Jesse Barnes	4.8
23	Johnny Cooney	4.7
	Jim Turner	4.7
25	Charlie Leibrandt	4.2
26	Bob Buhl	4.1
	Bill James	4.1
28	Nate Andrews	3.8
	Carl Morton	3.8
	Billy O'Dell	3.8
	Bob Shaw	3.8
32	Greg McMichael	3.7
	Mark Wohlers	3.7
34	Steve Avery	3.5
	Charlie Buffinton	3.5
	Lou Fette	3.5
	Tom Zachary	3.5
38	Lefty Tyler	3.3
39	Tom House	3.1
	Kent Mercker	3.1
41	Terry Forster	3.0
	Cecil Upshaw	3.0
43	Paul Assenmacher	2.9
44	Art Nehf	2.7
45	Hoyt Wilhelm	2.6
46	Jeff Dedmon	2.3
47	Charlie Getzien	2.2
	Bob Smith	2.2
49	Bill Sowders	2.1
50	2 players tied	2.0

Total Pitcher Index (alpha.)

Nate Andrews	3.8
Paul Assenmacher	2.9
Steve Avery	3.5
Jesse Barnes	4.8
Steve Bedrosian	5.8
Tommy Bond	6.8
Charlie Buffinton	3.5
Bob Buhl	4.1
Lew Burdette	6.7
Rick Camp	7.2
Ben Cantwell	5.2
John Clarkson	19.5
Johnny Cooney	4.7
Jeff Dedmon	2.3
Bill Dinneen	5.7
Lou Fette	3.5
Terry Forster	3.0
Gene Garber	10.6
Charlie Getzien	2.2
Tom Glavine	12.7
Tom House	3.1
Bill James	4.1
Charlie Leibrandt	4.2
Ted Lewis	5.3
Greg Maddux	20.1
Kent Mercker	3.1
Carl Morton	3.8
Greg McMichael	3.7
Art Nehf	2.7
Kid Nichols	60.0
Phil Niekro	37.1
Billy O'Dell	3.8
Dick Rudolph	7.0
Johnny Sain	9.4
Bob Shaw	3.8
Bob Smith	2.2
John Smoltz	7.3
Bill Sowders	2.1
Warren Spahn	48.0
Jack Stivetts	12.8
Jim Tobin	11.0
Jim Turner	4.7
Lefty Tyler	3.3
Cecil Upshaw	3.0
Jim Whitney	14.8
Hoyt Wilhelm	2.6
Vic Willis	15.7
Mark Wohlers	3.7
Tom Zachary	3.5

Total Pitcher Index (by era)

1876-1892
1	John Clarkson	19.5
2	Jim Whitney	14.8
3	Tommy Bond	6.8
4	Charlie Buffinton	3.5
5	Charlie Getzien	2.2

1893-1919
1	Kid Nichols	60.0
2	Vic Willis	15.7
3	Jack Stivetts	12.8
4	Dick Rudolph	7.0
5	Bill Dinneen	5.7

1920-1941
1	Ben Cantwell	5.2
2	Jesse Barnes	4.8
3	Johnny Cooney	4.7
	Jim Turner	4.7
5	Lou Fette	3.5
	Tom Zachary	3.5

1942-1960
1	Warren Spahn	48.0
2	Jim Tobin	11.0
3	Johnny Sain	9.4
4	Lew Burdette	6.7
5	Bob Buhl	4.1

1961-1976
1	Phil Niekro	37.1
2	Carl Morton	3.8
	Billy O'Dell	3.8
	Bob Shaw	3.8
5	Tom House	3.1

1977-1995
1	Greg Maddux	20.1
2	Tom Glavine	12.7
3	Gene Garber	10.6
4	John Smoltz	7.3
5	Rick Camp	7.2

Total Baseball Ranking

1	Hank Aaron	90.7
2	Kid Nichols	60.0
3	Eddie Mathews	52.4
4	Warren Spahn	48.0
5	Phil Niekro	37.1
6	Wally Berger	21.5
7	Dale Murphy	20.7
8	Greg Maddux	20.1
9	John Clarkson	19.5
10	Glenn Hubbard	19.0
11	Fred Tenney	18.9
12	Johnny Logan	17.5
13	Vic Willis	15.7
14	Jim Whitney	14.8
15	Tommy Holmes	14.1
16	Rabbit Maranville	13.3
17	Darrell Evans	13.2
18	Rico Carty	13.1
19	Jack Stivetts	12.8
20	Tom Glavine	12.7
	Joe Torre	12.7
22	Bob Elliott	12.4
	David Justice	12.4
24	Jim Tobin	11.0
25	Gene Garber	10.6
26	Billy Nash	10.5
27	Sid Gordon	10.4
28	Jimmy Collins	9.9
29	Johnny Sain	9.4
30	Terry Pendleton	9.0
31	Red Smith	8.9
32	Bill Sweeney	8.8
33	Dave Brain	7.9
34	Joe Adcock	7.8
35	John Smoltz	7.3
36	Rick Camp	7.2
37	Dick Rudolph	7.0
	Earl Torgeson	7.0
39	Tommy Bond	6.8
	Dave Bancroft	6.8
41	Lew Burdette	6.7
42	Hank Gowdy	6.4
	Gene Moore	6.4
44	Lonnie Smith	6.3
45	Ron Gant	6.2
46	Ezra Sutton	6.1
47	Steve Bedrosian	5.8
48	Bill Dinneen	5.7
49	Del Crandall	5.6
50	Ted Lewis	5.3
51	Ben Cantwell	5.2
	Bill Dahlen	5.2
	Herman Long	5.2
54	Eddie Miller	5.0
55	Jesse Barnes	4.8
	Davey Johnson	4.8
57	Johnny Cooney	4.7
	Jim Turner	4.7
59	Billy Hamilton	4.5
	Charley Jones	4.5
61	Sam Wise	4.4
62	Charlie Leibrandt	4.2
	John O'Rourke	4.2
	Eddie Stanky	4.2
65	Bob Buhl	4.1
	Bill James	4.1
67	Pat Moran	4.0
	Claude Ritchey	4.0
69	King Kelly	3.9
70	Nate Andrews	3.8
	Carl Morton	3.8
	Billy O'Dell	3.8
	Bob Shaw	3.8
74	Greg McMichael	3.7
	Mark Wohlers	3.7
76	Steve Avery	3.5
	Charlie Buffinton	3.5
	Lou Fette	3.5
	Tom Zachary	3.5
80	Jeff Heath	3.4
81	Lefty Tyler	3.3
	Fred McGriff	3.3
83	Tom House	3.1
	Kent Mercker	3.1
	Charlie Bennett	3.1
	Bob Horner	3.1
87	Terry Forster	3.0
	Cecil Upshaw	3.0
	Sam Jethroe	3.0
90	Paul Assenmacher	2.9
	Rafael Belliard	2.9
	Tony Cuccinello	2.9
93	Ginger Beaumont	2.8
	Joe Connolly	2.8
95	Art Nehf	2.7
96	Hoyt Wilhelm	2.6
97	Felipe Alou	2.5
	Jeff Burroughs	2.5
99	Billy Southworth	2.4
100	3 players tied	2.3

Total Baseball Rank (alpha.)

Hank Aaron	90.7
Joe Adcock	7.8
Felipe Alou	2.5
Nate Andrews	3.8
Paul Assenmacher	2.9
Steve Avery	3.5
Dave Bancroft	6.8
Jesse Barnes	4.8
Ginger Beaumont	2.8
Steve Bedrosian	5.8
Rafael Belliard	2.9
Charlie Bennett	3.1
Wally Berger	21.5
Tommy Bond	6.8
Dave Brain	7.9
Charlie Buffinton	3.5
Bob Buhl	4.1
Lew Burdette	6.7
Jeff Burroughs	2.5
Rick Camp	7.2
Ben Cantwell	5.2
Rico Carty	13.1
John Clarkson	19.5
Jimmy Collins	9.9
Joe Connolly	2.8
Johnny Cooney	4.7
Del Crandall	5.6
Tony Cuccinello	2.9
Bill Dahlen	5.2
Bill Dinneen	5.7
Bob Elliott	12.4
Darrell Evans	13.2
Lou Fette	3.5
Terry Forster	3.0
Ron Gant	6.2
Gene Garber	10.6
Tom Glavine	12.7
Sid Gordon	10.4
Hank Gowdy	6.4
Billy Hamilton	4.5
Jeff Heath	3.4
Tommy Holmes	14.1
Bob Horner	3.1
Tom House	3.1
Glenn Hubbard	19.0
Bill James	4.1
Sam Jethroe	3.0
Davey Johnson	4.8
Charley Jones	4.5
David Justice	12.4
King Kelly	3.9
Charlie Leibrandt	4.2
Ted Lewis	5.3
Johnny Logan	17.5
Herman Long	5.2
Greg Maddux	20.1
Rabbit Maranville	13.3
Eddie Mathews	52.4
Kent Mercker	3.1
Eddie Miller	5.0
Gene Moore	6.4
Pat Moran	4.0
Carl Morton	3.8
Dale Murphy	20.7
Fred McGriff	3.3
Greg McMichael	3.7
Billy Nash	10.5
Art Nehf	2.7
Kid Nichols	60.0
Phil Niekro	37.1
Billy O'Dell	3.8
John O'Rourke	4.2
Terry Pendleton	9.0
Claude Ritchey	4.0
Dick Rudolph	7.0
Johnny Sain	9.4
Bob Shaw	3.8
Red Smith	8.9
Lonnie Smith	6.3
John Smoltz	7.3
Billy Southworth	2.4
Warren Spahn	48.0
Eddie Stanky	4.2
Jack Stivetts	12.8
Ezra Sutton	6.1
Bill Sweeney	8.8
Fred Tenney	18.9
Jim Tobin	11.0
Earl Torgeson	7.0
Joe Torre	12.7
Jim Turner	4.7
Lefty Tyler	3.3
Cecil Upshaw	3.0
Jim Whitney	14.8
Hoyt Wilhelm	2.6
Vic Willis	15.7
Sam Wise	4.4
Mark Wohlers	3.7
Tom Zachary	3.5

Total Baseball Rank (by era)

1876-1892
1	John Clarkson	19.5
2	Jim Whitney	14.8
3	Billy Nash	10.5
4	Tommy Bond	6.8
5	Ezra Sutton	6.1
6	Charley Jones	4.5
7	Sam Wise	4.4
8	John O'Rourke	4.2
9	King Kelly	3.9
10	Charlie Buffinton	3.5

1893-1919
1	Kid Nichols	60.0
2	Fred Tenney	18.9
3	Vic Willis	15.7
4	Rabbit Maranville	13.3
5	Jack Stivetts	12.8
6	Jimmy Collins	9.9
7	Red Smith	8.9
8	Bill Sweeney	8.8
9	Dave Brain	7.9
10	Dick Rudolph	7.0

1920-1941
1	Wally Berger	21.5
2	Dave Bancroft	6.8
3	Gene Moore	6.4
4	Ben Cantwell	5.2
5	Eddie Miller	5.0
6	Jesse Barnes	4.8
7	Johnny Cooney	4.7
	Jim Turner	4.7
9	Lou Fette	3.5
	Tom Zachary	3.5

1942-1960
1	Eddie Mathews	52.4
2	Warren Spahn	48.0
3	Johnny Logan	17.5
4	Tommy Holmes	14.1
5	Bob Elliott	12.4
6	Jim Tobin	11.0
7	Sid Gordon	10.4
8	Johnny Sain	9.4
9	Joe Adcock	7.8
10	Earl Torgeson	7.0

1961-1976
1	Hank Aaron	90.7
2	Phil Niekro	37.1
3	Darrell Evans	13.2
4	Rico Carty	13.1
5	Joe Torre	12.7
6	Davey Johnson	4.8
7	Carl Morton	3.8
	Billy O'Dell	3.8
	Bob Shaw	3.8
10	Tom House	3.1

1977-1995
1	Dale Murphy	20.7
2	Greg Maddux	20.1
3	Glenn Hubbard	19.0
4	Tom Glavine	12.7
5	David Justice	12.4
6	Gene Garber	10.6
7	Terry Pendleton	9.0
8	John Smoltz	7.3
9	Rick Camp	7.2
10	Lonnie Smith	6.3

At Bats

1	Ralph Garr, 1973	668
2	Felipe Alou, 1966	666
3	Felipe Alou, 1968	662
4	Felix Millan, 1969	652
5	Herman Long, 1892	646
6	Terry Pendleton, 1992	640
7	Ralph Garr, 1971	639
8	Gene Moore, 1936	637
9	Tommy Holmes, 1945	636
	Bill Bruton, 1955	636
11	Terry Pendleton, 1993	633
12	Tommy Holmes, 1944	631
	Hank Aaron, 1963	631
	Gary Matthews, 1979	631
15	George Sisler, 1929	629
	Tommy Holmes, 1943	629
	Hank Aaron, 1959	629
	Bill Bruton, 1960	629
19	Ralph Garr, 1975	625
20	2 players tied	624

Runs

1	Hugh Duffy, 1894	160
2	Bobby Lowe, 1894	158
3	Billy Hamilton, 1896	152
	Billy Hamilton, 1897	152
5	Herman Long, 1893	149
6	Hugh Duffy, 1893	147
7	Herman Long, 1894	136
8	Billy Nash, 1894	132
9	Dale Murphy, 1983	131
10	Bobby Lowe, 1893	130
	Jimmy Bannon, 1894	130
	Hugh Duffy, 1897	130
13	Herman Long, 1891	129
14	Hank Aaron, 1962	127
15	Hugh Duffy, 1892	125
	Fred Tenney, 1897	125
	Tommy Holmes, 1945	125
18	Hardy Richardson, 1889	122
	Chick Stahl, 1899	122
	Felipe Alou, 1966	122

Runs per Game

1876-1892

1	Jim O'Rourke, 1877	1.11
2	Joe Hornung, 1883	1.09
3	Ezra Sutton, 1883	1.07
4	Joe Hornung, 1884	1.03
5	King Kelly, 1887	1.03

1893-1919

1	Herman Long, 1894	1.31
2	Hugh Duffy, 1894	1.28
3	Billy Hamilton, 1897	1.20
4	Bobby Lowe, 1894	1.19
5	Herman Long, 1893	1.16

1920-1941

1	Ray Powell, 1921	.77
2	Billy Urbanski, 1934	.71
3	Lance Richbourg, 1928	.71
4	Rogers Hornsby, 1928	.71
5	Wally Berger, 1930	.65

1942-1960

1	Tommy Holmes, 1945	.81
2	Eddie Mathews, 1959	.80
3	Hank Aaron, 1957	.78
4	Earl Torgeson, 1950	.77
5	Eddie Mathews, 1955	.77

1961-1976

1	Hank Aaron, 1962	.81
2	Felipe Alou, 1966	.79
3	Hank Aaron, 1963	.75
4	Hank Aaron, 1961	.74
5	Hank Aaron, 1966	.74

1977-1995

1	Dale Murphy, 1983	.81
2	Dale Murphy, 1985	.73
3	Dale Murphy, 1987	.72
4	Ron Gant, 1993	.72
5	Fred McGriff, 1994	.72

Hits

1	Hugh Duffy, 1894	237
2	Tommy Holmes, 1945	224
3	Hank Aaron, 1959	223
4	Ralph Garr, 1971	219
5	Felipe Alou, 1966	218
6	Ralph Garr, 1974	214
7	Bobby Lowe, 1894	212
8	Felipe Alou, 1968	210
9	Fred Tenney, 1899	209
10	Lance Richbourg, 1928	206
11	George Sisler, 1929	205
12	Bill Sweeney, 1912	204
13	Hugh Duffy, 1893	203
14	Chick Stahl, 1899	202
15	Eddie Brown, 1926	201
	Hank Aaron, 1963	201
17	Dick Burrus, 1925	200
	Hank Aaron, 1956	200
	Ralph Garr, 1973	200
20	2 players tied	199

Doubles

1	Hugh Duffy, 1894	51
2	Tommy Holmes, 1945	47
3	Hank Aaron, 1959	46
4	Wally Berger, 1931	44
	Lee Maye, 1964	44
6	Rogers Hornsby, 1928	42
	Tommy Holmes, 1944	42
8	King Kelly, 1889	41
	Dick Burrus, 1925	41
10	George Sisler, 1929	40
	Hank Aaron, 1965	40
12	Wally Berger, 1935	39
	Alvin Dark, 1948	39
	Hank Aaron, 1961	39
	Terry Pendleton, 1992	39
16	Gene Moore, 1936	38
17	7 players tied	37

Triples (by era)

1876-1892

1	Dick Johnston, 1887	20
	Harry Stovey, 1891	20
3	Dick Johnston, 1888	18
4	Sam Wise, 1887	17
5	John Morrill, 1883	16

1893-1919

1	Chick Stahl, 1899	19
2	Fred Tenney, 1899	17
3	Hugh Duffy, 1894	16
	Chick Stahl, 1900	16
5	Ginger Beaumont, 1907	14

1920-1941

1	Ray Powell, 1921	18
2	Billy Southworth, 1923	16
3	Rabbit Maranville, 1920	15
	Billy Southworth, 1921	15
5	2 players tied	14

1942-1960

1	Bill Bruton, 1956	15
2	Bill Bruton, 1953	14
	Hank Aaron, 1956	14
4	Bill Bruton, 1960	13
5	Bill Bruton, 1955	12

1961-1976

1	Ralph Garr, 1974	17
2	Ralph Garr, 1975	11
3	Hank Aaron, 1961	10
4	4 players tied	8

1977-1995

1	Deion Sanders, 1992	14
2	Brett Butler, 1983	13
3	Lonnie Smith, 1990	9
4	5 players tied	8

Triples

1	Dick Johnston, 1887	20
	Harry Stovey, 1891	20
3	Chick Stahl, 1899	19
4	Dick Johnston, 1888	18
	Ray Powell, 1921	18
6	Sam Wise, 1887	17
	Fred Tenney, 1899	17
	Ralph Garr, 1974	17
9	John Morrill, 1883	16
	Hugh Duffy, 1894	16
	Chick Stahl, 1900	16
	Billy Southworth, 1923	16
13	Ezra Sutton, 1883	15
	Billy Nash, 1888	15
	Rabbit Maranville, 1920	15
	Billy Southworth, 1921	15
	Bill Bruton, 1956	15
18	6 players tied	14

Home Runs

1	Eddie Mathews, 1953	47
	Hank Aaron, 1971	47
3	Eddie Mathews, 1959	46
4	Hank Aaron, 1962	45
5	Hank Aaron, 1957	44
	Hank Aaron, 1963	44
	Hank Aaron, 1966	44
	Hank Aaron, 1969	44
	Dale Murphy, 1987	44
10	Davey Johnson, 1973	43
11	Eddie Mathews, 1955	41
	Darrell Evans, 1973	41
	Jeff Burroughs, 1977	41
14	Eddie Mathews, 1954	40
	Hank Aaron, 1960	40
	Hank Aaron, 1973	40
	David Justice, 1993	40
18	Hank Aaron, 1959	39
	Eddie Mathews, 1960	39
	Hank Aaron, 1967	39

Home Runs (by era)

1876-1892

1	Harry Stovey, 1891	16
2	John Morrill, 1887	12
	Dick Johnston, 1888	12
4	6 players tied	9

1893-1919

1	Hugh Duffy, 1894	18
2	Bobby Lowe, 1894	17
3	Jimmy Collins, 1898	15
4	Bobby Lowe, 1893	14
5	2 players tied	13

1920-1941

1	Wally Berger, 1930	38
2	Wally Berger, 1934	34
	Wally Berger, 1935	34
4	Wally Berger, 1933	27
5	Wally Berger, 1936	25

1942-1960

1	Eddie Mathews, 1953	47
2	Eddie Mathews, 1959	46
3	Hank Aaron, 1957	44
4	Eddie Mathews, 1955	41
5	2 players tied	40

1961-1976

1	Hank Aaron, 1971	47
2	Hank Aaron, 1962	45
3	Hank Aaron, 1963	44
	Hank Aaron, 1966	44
	Hank Aaron, 1969	44

1977-1995

1	Dale Murphy, 1987	44
2	Jeff Burroughs, 1977	41
3	David Justice, 1993	40
4	Dale Murphy, 1985	37
5	4 players tied	36

Home Run Percentage

1	Hank Aaron, 1971	9.49
2	Eddie Mathews, 1954	8.40
3	Joe Adcock, 1956	8.37
4	Eddie Mathews, 1955	8.22
5	Eddie Mathews, 1953	8.12
6	Hank Aaron, 1969	8.04
7	Fred McGriff, 1994	8.02
8	Dale Murphy, 1987	7.77
9	Eddie Mathews, 1959	7.74
10	Davey Johnson, 1973	7.69
11	Hank Aaron, 1962	7.60
12	Hank Aaron, 1972	7.57
13	Hank Aaron, 1970	7.36
14	Hank Aaron, 1966	7.30
15	Hank Aaron, 1957	7.15
16	Eddie Mathews, 1960	7.12
17	Jeff Burroughs, 1977	7.08
18	Hank Aaron, 1963	6.97
19	Darrell Evans, 1973	6.89
20	Wally Berger, 1930	6.85

Home Run Pctg.(by era)

1876-1892

1	Harry Stovey, 1891	2.94
2	Charley Jones, 1879	2.54
3	John Morrill, 1887	2.38
4	Tom Brown, 1888	2.14
5	Dick Johnston, 1888	2.05

1893-1919

1	Hugh Duffy, 1894	3.34
2	Bobby Lowe, 1894	2.77
3	Bobby Lowe, 1893	2.66
4	Jimmy Bannon, 1894	2.63
5	Herman Long, 1894	2.53

Home Runs (continued)

1920-1941

1	Wally Berger, 1930	6.85
2	Wally Berger, 1935	5.77
3	Wally Berger, 1934	5.53
4	Wally Berger, 1933	5.11
5	Wally Berger, 1936	4.68

1942-1960

1	Eddie Mathews, 1954	8.40
2	Joe Adcock, 1956	8.37
3	Eddie Mathews, 1955	8.22
4	Eddie Mathews, 1953	8.12
5	Eddie Mathews, 1959	7.74

1961-1976

1	Hank Aaron, 1971	9.49
2	Hank Aaron, 1969	8.04
3	Davey Johnson, 1973	7.69
4	Hank Aaron, 1962	7.60
5	Hank Aaron, 1972	7.57

1977-1995

1	Fred McGriff, 1994	8.02
2	Dale Murphy, 1987	7.77
3	Jeff Burroughs, 1977	7.08
4	David Justice, 1993	6.84
5	Bob Horner, 1979	6.78

Total Bases

1	Hank Aaron, 1959	400
2	Hugh Duffy, 1894	374
3	Hank Aaron, 1963	370
4	Hank Aaron, 1957	369
5	Tommy Holmes, 1945	367
6	Hank Aaron, 1962	366
7	Eddie Mathews, 1953	363
8	Hank Aaron, 1961	358
9	Felipe Alou, 1966	355
10	Eddie Mathews, 1959	352
11	Hank Aaron, 1967	344
12	Wally Berger, 1930	341
13	Hank Aaron, 1956	340
14	Wally Berger, 1934	336
15	Hank Aaron, 1960	334
16	Hank Aaron, 1969	332
	Dale Murphy, 1984	332
	Dale Murphy, 1985	332
19	Hank Aaron, 1971	331
	Darrell Evans, 1973	331

Runs Batted In

1	Hugh Duffy, 1894	145
2	Eddie Mathews, 1953	135
3	Jimmy Collins, 1897	132
	Hank Aaron, 1957	132
5	Wally Berger, 1935	130
	Hank Aaron, 1963	130
7	Hugh Duffy, 1897	129
8	Hank Aaron, 1962	128
9	Hank Aaron, 1966	127
10	Tommy McCarthy, 1894	126
	Hank Aaron, 1960	126
12	Eddie Mathews, 1960	124
13	Billy Nash, 1893	123
	Hank Aaron, 1959	123
15	Wally Berger, 1934	121
	Dale Murphy, 1983	121
17	Hank Aaron, 1961	120
	David Justice, 1993	120
19	Wally Berger, 1930	119
20	4 players tied	118

Runs Batted In per Game

1	Hugh Duffy, 1894	1.16
2	Tommy McCarthy, 1894	.99
3	Jimmy Collins, 1897	.99
4	Hugh Duffy, 1897	.96
5	Billy Nash, 1893	.96
6	Tommy McCarthy, 1893	.96
7	Dan Brouthers, 1889	.94
8	Jack Burdock, 1883	.92
9	Hugh Duffy, 1893	.90
10	Jimmy Bannon, 1894	.89
11	Hank Aaron, 1957	.87
12	Wally Berger, 1935	.87
13	Bobby Lowe, 1894	.86
14	Hugh Duffy, 1896	.86
15	Bobby Lowe, 1897	.86
16	John O'Rourke, 1879	.86
17	Eddie Mathews, 1953	.86
18	Chick Stahl, 1897	.85
19	Hank Aaron, 1971	.85
20	Herman Long, 1896	.83

Strikeout Percentage

1876-1892
1 Sam Wise, 1884 . . . . 24.41
2 John Morrill, 1884 . . . . . 19.86
3 John Morrill, 1885 . . . . . 19.80
4 John Morrill, 1886 . . . . . 18.84
5 Sam Wise, 1883 . . . . 18.23

1893-1919
1 Ed McDonald, 1912 . . . . . 19.83
2 Ray Powell, 1919 . . . . . . 16.81
3 Scotty Ingerton, 1911 . . . 13.05
4 Butch Schmidt, 1915 . . . . 12.88
5 Rabbit Maranville, 1915 . . 12.77

1920-1941
1 Vince DiMaggio, 1938 . . . . 24.81
2 Vince DiMaggio, 1937 . . . . 22.52
3 Chet Ross, 1940 . . . . 22.32
4 Wally Berger, 1936 . . . . . 15.73
5 Wally Berger, 1933 . . . . . . 14.58

1942-1960
1 Eddie Mathews, 1952 . . . . 21.78
2 Eddie Mathews, 1960 . . . . 20.62
3 Eddie Mathews, 1955 . . . . 19.64
4 Eddie Joost, 1943 . . . . . . 19.00
5 Joe Adcock, 1956 . . . . 18.94

1961-1976
1 Jim Wynn, 1976 . . . . 24.72
2 Mack Jones, 1965 . . . . . . 24.21
3 Mack Jones, 1967 . . . . . . 23.79
4 Eddie Mathews, 1963 . . . . 21.76
5 Earl Williams, 1972 . . . . . 20.88

1977-1995
1 Dale Murphy, 1978 . . . . . 27.36
2 Jeff Blauser, 1995 . . . . . . 24.83
3 Dale Murphy, 1989 . . . . . 24.74
4 Jim Presley, 1990 . . . . . . 24.03
5 Dale Murphy, 1987 . . . . . 24.03

Walks

1 Bob Elliott, 1948 131
2 Jim Wynn, 1976 127
3 Darrell Evans, 1974 126
4 Eddie Mathews, 1963 124
  Darrell Evans, 1973 124
6 Earl Torgeson, 1950 119
7 Jeff Burroughs, 1978 117
8 Dale Murphy, 1987 115
9 Eddie Stanky, 1949 113
  Eddie Mathews, 1954 113
11 Eddie Mathews, 1960 111
12 Billy Hamilton, 1896 110
13 Eddie Mathews, 1955 109
14 Billy Hamilton, 1900 107
  Rogers Hornsby, 1928 . . . 107
16 Billy Hamilton, 1897 105
  Darrell Evans, 1975 105
18 Earl Torgeson, 1951 102
19 Eddie Mathews, 1962 . . . 101
20 Eddie Mathews, 1953 99

Strikeouts

1 Dale Murphy, 1978 145
2 Dale Murphy, 1989 142
3 Dale Murphy, 1985 141
  Dale Murphy, 1986 141
5 Dale Murphy, 1987 136
6 Vince DiMaggio, 1938 134
  Dale Murphy, 1982 134
  Dale Murphy, 1984 134
9 Dale Murphy, 1980 133
10 Jim Presley, 1990 130
11 Chet Ross, 1940 127
12 Jeff Burroughs, 1977 126
13 Dale Murphy, 1988 125
14 Mack Jones, 1965 122
15 Eddie Mathews, 1963 119
16 Earl Williams, 1972 118
  Ron Gant, 1988 118
18 Ron Gant, 1993 117
19 Eddie Mathews, 1952 115
20 Eddie Mathews, 1960 113

At Bats per Strikeout

1876-1892
1 Deacon White, 1877 . . . . . 88.7
2 Dan Brouthers, 1889 . . . . . 80.8
3 Jack Manning, 1876 . . . . . 57.6
4 John Morrill, 1876 . . . . . . 55.6
5 Andy Leonard, 1877 . . . . . 54.4

1893-1919
1 Tommy McCarthy, 1893 . . 46.2
2 Herman Long, 1895 . . . . . 44.6
3 Hugh Duffy, 1893 . . . . 43.1
4 Tommy McCarthy, 1895 . . 37.7
5 Hugh Duffy, 1894 . . . . 35.9

1920-1941
1 Stuffy McInnis, 1924 . . . . . 96.8
2 Andy High, 1926 . . . . 52.9
3 Stuffy McInnis, 1923 . . . . . 50.6
4 Billy Southworth, 1921 . . . 43.8
5 Buddy Hassett, 1939 . . . . 42.1

1942-1960
1 Tommy Holmes, 1945 . . . . 70.7
2 Tommy Holmes, 1944 . . . . 57.4
3 Tommy Holmes, 1942 . . . . 55.8
4 Tommy Holmes, 1946 . . . . 40.6
5 Tommy Holmes, 1947 . . . . 38.6

1961-1976
1 Felix Millan, 1971 . . . . 26.2
2 Felix Millan, 1970 . . . . 25.7
3 Felix Millan, 1968 . . . . 21.9
4 Felipe Alou, 1969 . . . . 20.7
5 Felix Millan, 1969 . . . . 18.6

1977-1995
1 Ken Oberkfell, 1987 . . . . . 17.5
2 Bruce Benedict, 1981 . . . . 14.0
3 Pepe Frias, 1979 . . . . 13.2
4 Rafael Ramirez, 1983 . . . . 13.0
5 Ken Oberkfell, 1986 . . . . . 12.6

Batting Average

1 Hugh Duffy, 1894 440
2 Deacon White, 1877 387
3 Rogers Hornsby, 1928 387
4 Dan Brouthers, 1889 373
5 Billy Hamilton, 1898 369
6 Rico Carty, 1970 366
7 Billy Hamilton, 1896 365
8 Hugh Duffy, 1893 363
9 Jim O'Rourke, 1877 362
10 Hank Aaron, 1959 355
11 Abner Dalrymple, 1878 354
12 Chick Stahl, 1897 354
13 Ralph Garr, 1974 353
14 Tommy Holmes, 1945 352
15 Hugh Duffy, 1895 352
16 Chick Stahl, 1899 351
17 Jimmy Bannon, 1895 350
18 Tommy McCarthy, 1894 . . .349
19 Fred Tenney, 1899 347
20 Tommy McCarthy, 1893 . . .346

Batting Average (by era)

1876-1892
1 Deacon White, 1877 387
2 Dan Brouthers, 1889 373
3 Jim O'Rourke, 1877 362
4 Abner Dalrymple, 1878 354
5 Ezra Sutton, 1884 346

1893-1919
1 Hugh Duffy, 1894 440
2 Billy Hamilton, 1898 369
3 Billy Hamilton, 1896 365
4 Hugh Duffy, 1893 363
5 Chick Stahl, 1897 354

1920-1941
1 Rogers Hornsby, 1928 387
2 Dick Burrus, 1925 340
3 George Sisler, 1928 340
4 Lance Richbourg, 1928 337
5 Eddie Brown, 1926 328

1942-1960
1 Hank Aaron, 1959 355
2 Tommy Holmes, 1945 352
3 Johnny Hopp, 1946 333
4 Hank Aaron, 1956 328
5 Hank Aaron, 1958 326

1961-1976
1 Rico Carty, 1970 366
2 Ralph Garr, 1974 353
3 Ralph Garr, 1971 343
4 Rico Carty, 1964 330
5 Hank Aaron, 1964 328

1977-1995
1 Terry Pendleton, 1991 319
2 Fred McGriff, 1994 318
3 Lonnie Smith, 1989 315
4 Bob Horner, 1979 314
5 David Justice, 1994 313

Relative Batting Average

1 Deacon White, 1877 . . . . 1.405
2 Hugh Duffy, 1894 . . . . . . 1.395
3 Ezra Sutton, 1884 . . . . . . 1.380
4 Rico Carty, 1970 . . . . 1.372
5 Dan Brouthers, 1889 . . . . 1.370
6 Ralph Garr, 1974 . . . . 1.346
7 Abner Dalrymple, 1878 . . . 1.336
8 Rogers Hornsby, 1928 . . . 1.334
9 Billy Hamilton, 1898 . . . . . 1.330
10 Ralph Garr, 1971 . . . . 1.320
11 Jim O'Rourke, 1877 . . . . . 1.314
12 John O'Rourke, 1879 . . . . 1.314
13 Hank Aaron, 1959 . . . . . . 1.313
14 King Kelly, 1888 . . . . 1.296
15 Tommy Holmes, 1945 . . . . 1.289
16 Ginger Beaumont, 1907 . . 1.279
17 Jim Whitney, 1882 . . . . . . 1.273
18 Ezra Sutton, 1885 . . . . . . 1.269
19 Hugh Duffy, 1893 . . . . . . 1.269
20 Johnny Hopp, 1946 . . . . . 1.268

Batting Average (by position)

First Base
1 Dan Brouthers, 1889 373
2 Fred Tenney, 1899 347
3 Dick Burrus, 1925 340
4 George Sisler, 1928 340
5 Tommy Tucker, 1894 330

Second Base
1 Rogers Hornsby, 1928 387
2 Bobby Lowe, 1894 346
3 Bill Sweeney, 1912 344
4 Jack Burdock, 1883 330
5 Bill Sweeney, 1911 314

Shortstop
1 Herman Long, 1896 343
2 Herman Long, 1894 324
3 Alvin Dark, 1948 322
4 Herman Long, 1897 322
5 Dave Bancroft, 1925 319

Third Base
1 Ezra Sutton, 1884 346
2 Jimmy Collins, 1897 346
3 Jimmy Collins, 1898 328
4 Ezra Sutton, 1883 324
5 Terry Pendleton, 1991 319

Outfield
1 Hugh Duffy, 1894 440
2 Billy Hamilton, 1898 369
3 Rico Carty, 1970 366
4 Billy Hamilton, 1896 365
5 Hugh Duffy, 1893 363
6 Jim O'Rourke, 1877 362
7 Hank Aaron, 1959 355
8 Chick Stahl, 1897 354
9 Ralph Garr, 1974 353
10 Tommy Holmes, 1945 352

Catcher
1 Al Spohrer, 1930 317
2 Joe Torre, 1966 315
3 Phil Masi, 1947 304
4 Bruce Benedict, 1983 298
5 Del Crandall, 1960 294

On Base Percentage

1 Hugh Duffy, 1894 502
2 Rogers Hornsby, 1928 498
3 Billy Hamilton, 1898 480
4 Billy Hamilton, 1896 477
5 Dan Brouthers, 1889 462
6 Billy Hamilton, 1897 461
7 Rico Carty, 1970 456
8 Billy Hamilton, 1900 449
9 Jeff Burroughs, 1978 436
10 Tommy McCarthy, 1893 . . .429
11 Eddie Mathews, 1954 428
12 David Justice, 1994 428
13 Chick Stahl, 1899 426
14 Hugh Duffy, 1895 425
15 Bob Elliott, 1948 423
16 Dale Murphy, 1987 420
17 Lonnie Smith, 1989 420
18 Tommy Holmes, 1945 420
19 Jimmy Bannon, 1895 420
20 Tommy McCarthy, 1894 . . .419

Slugging Average

1 Hugh Duffy, 1894 694
2 Hank Aaron, 1971 669
3 Hank Aaron, 1959 636
4 Rogers Hornsby, 1928 632
5 Eddie Mathews, 1953 627
6 Fred McGriff, 1994 623
7 Hank Aaron, 1962 618
8 Wally Berger, 1930 614
9 Hank Aaron, 1969 607
10 Eddie Mathews, 1954 603
11 Eddie Mathews, 1955 601
12 Hank Aaron, 1957 600
13 Joe Adcock, 1956 597
14 Hank Aaron, 1961 594
15 Eddie Mathews, 1959 593
16 Hank Aaron, 1963 586
17 Rico Carty, 1970 584
18 Dale Murphy, 1987 580
19 Tommy Holmes, 1945 577
20 Hank Aaron, 1970 574

Production

1 Hugh Duffy, 1894 . . . . 1.196
2 Rogers Hornsby, 1928 . . . . 1.130
3 Hank Aaron, 1971 . . . . . . 1.082
4 Hank Aaron, 1959 . . . . . . 1.042
5 Rico Carty, 1970 . . . . 1.040
6 Eddie Mathews, 1953 . . . . 1.033
7 Eddie Mathews, 1954 . . . . 1.031
8 Eddie Mathews, 1955 . . . . 1.018
9 Fred McGriff, 1994 . . . . . . 1.014
10 Hank Aaron, 1962 . . . . . . 1.012
11 Hank Aaron, 1969 . . . . . . 1.005
12 Dale Murphy, 1987 . . . . . 1.000
13 Tommy Holmes, 1945 997
14 Wally Berger, 1930 990
15 Eddie Mathews, 1959 984
16 Hank Aaron, 1963 980
17 Hank Aaron, 1961 979
18 Hank Aaron, 1957 979
19 Dan Brouthers, 1889 969
20 Jeff Burroughs, 1978 965

Adjusted Production

1 Rogers Hornsby, 1928 . . . 204
2 Hank Aaron, 1971 190
3 Deacon White, 1877 190
4 Hank Aaron, 1959 188
5 Jim Whitney, 1882 183
6 Charley Jones, 1879 182
7 John O'Rourke, 1879 181
8 Hank Aaron, 1963 180
9 Hank Aaron, 1969 177
10 Wally Berger, 1933 177
11 Eddie Mathews, 1954 177
12 Eddie Mathews, 1953 175
13 Eddie Mathews, 1955 175
14 Tommy Holmes, 1945 175
15 Hugh Duffy, 1894 172
16 Eddie Mathews, 1959 172
17 Hank Aaron, 1962 171
18 Eddie Mathews, 1960 170
19 Hank Aaron, 1957 170
20 Hank Aaron, 1967 169

Batting Runs

1 Hugh Duffy, 1894 76
2 Rogers Hornsby, 1928 72
3 Hank Aaron, 1971 65
4 Hank Aaron, 1963 63
5 Tommy Holmes, 1945 63
6 Hank Aaron, 1959 63
7 Hank Aaron, 1969 56
8 Eddie Mathews, 1953 55
9 Darrell Evans, 1973 55
10 Rico Carty, 1970 54
11 Hank Aaron, 1962 54
12 Dale Murphy, 1987 53
13 Hank Aaron, 1967 50
14 Jeff Burroughs, 1978 50
15 Eddie Mathews, 1955 50
16 Dan Brouthers, 1889 50
17 Eddie Mathews, 1954 49
18 Eddie Mathews, 1959 48
19 Hank Aaron, 1957 48
20 Dale Murphy, 1985 48

Adjusted Batting Runs

1	Rogers Hornsby, 1928	80
2	Hank Aaron, 1959	75
3	Hank Aaron, 1963	64
4	Eddie Mathews, 1953	64
5	Tommy Holmes, 1945	62
6	Hugh Duffy, 1894	61
7	Eddie Mathews, 1959	59
8	Hank Aaron, 1971	58
9	Hank Aaron, 1962	58
10	Hank Aaron, 1957	58
11	Eddie Mathews, 1954	57
12	Eddie Mathews, 1955	56
13	Hank Aaron, 1969	56
14	Eddie Mathews, 1960	55
15	Hank Aaron, 1961	54
16	Hank Aaron, 1967	52
17	Wally Berger, 1933	49
18	Eddie Mathews, 1961	48
19	Rico Carty, 1970	48
20	Hank Aaron, 1958	47

Batting Wins

1	Rogers Hornsby, 1928	7.1
2	Hank Aaron, 1971	7.0
3	Hank Aaron, 1963	6.8
4	Hank Aaron, 1959	6.3
5	Tommy Holmes, 1945	6.3
6	Hank Aaron, 1969	5.9
7	Hugh Duffy, 1894	5.8
8	Darrell Evans, 1973	5.7
9	Hank Aaron, 1967	5.4
10	Rico Carty, 1970	5.4
11	Hank Aaron, 1962	5.4
12	Dale Murphy, 1987	5.3
13	Jeff Burroughs, 1978	5.3
14	Eddie Mathews, 1953	5.3
15	Lonnie Smith, 1989	5.0
16	Dale Murphy, 1985	5.0
17	Eddie Mathews, 1955	5.0
18	Hank Aaron, 1957	4.9
19	Eddie Mathews, 1959	4.9
20	Hank Aaron, 1965	4.9

Adjusted Batting Wins

1	Rogers Hornsby, 1928	7.8
2	Hank Aaron, 1959	7.6
3	Hank Aaron, 1963	7.0
4	Tommy Holmes, 1945	6.2
5	Hank Aaron, 1971	6.2
6	Eddie Mathews, 1953	6.1
7	Eddie Mathews, 1959	6.0
8	Hank Aaron, 1969	5.9
9	Hank Aaron, 1957	5.8
10	Hank Aaron, 1962	5.7
11	Eddie Mathews, 1960	5.7
12	Hank Aaron, 1967	5.6
13	Eddie Mathews, 1954	5.6
14	Eddie Mathews, 1955	5.6
15	Hank Aaron, 1961	5.3
16	Wally Berger, 1933	5.2
17	Hank Aaron, 1965	4.8
18	Eddie Mathews, 1961	4.7
19	Eddie Mathews, 1957	4.7
20	Rico Carty, 1970	4.7

Runs Created

1	Hugh Duffy, 1894	217
2	Billy Hamilton, 1896	160
3	Eddie Mathews, 1953	157
4	Hank Aaron, 1959	156
5	Tommy Holmes, 1945	156
6	Rogers Hornsby, 1928	154
7	Hank Aaron, 1963	149
8	Darrell Evans, 1973	143
9	Dale Murphy, 1987	143
10	Eddie Mathews, 1959	143
11	Bobby Lowe, 1894	141
12	Hank Aaron, 1962	140
13	Chick Stahl, 1899	139
14	Hank Aaron, 1971	137
15	Hank Aaron, 1957	136
16	Tommy McCarthy, 1894	133
17	Hank Aaron, 1961	132
18	Hugh Duffy, 1895	131
19	Eddie Mathews, 1954	131
20	Billy Hamilton, 1897	131

Total Average

1	Hugh Duffy, 1894	1.619
2	Rogers Hornsby, 1928	1.409
3	Billy Hamilton, 1896	1.316
4	Billy Hamilton, 1898	1.262
5	Hank Aaron, 1971	1.178
6	Eddie Mathews, 1954	1.169
7	Billy Hamilton, 1897	1.162
8	King Kelly, 1887	1.146
9	Dan Brouthers, 1889	1.145
10	Eddie Mathews, 1955	1.124
11	Jimmy Bannon, 1894	1.119
12	Eddie Mathews, 1953	1.119
13	Dale Murphy, 1987	1.106
14	Rico Carty, 1970	1.102
15	Hank Aaron, 1959	1.089
16	Tommy McCarthy, 1893	1.086
17	Tommy Holmes, 1945	1.078
18	Fred McGriff, 1994	1.063
19	Hank Aaron, 1963	1.063
20	Sam Wise, 1887	1.061

Runs Produced

1	Hugh Duffy, 1894	287
2	Hugh Duffy, 1893	259
3	Bobby Lowe, 1894	256
4	Hugh Duffy, 1897	248
5	Jimmy Bannon, 1894	231
	Tommy McCarthy, 1894	231
7	Jimmy Collins, 1897	229
8	Billy Nash, 1893	228
9	Dan Brouthers, 1889	216
	Dale Murphy, 1983	216
11	Tommy Holmes, 1945	214
12	Tommy McCarthy, 1893	213
13	Billy Nash, 1894	211
14	Billy Hamilton, 1897	210
	Hank Aaron, 1962	210
16	Tommy Tucker, 1894	209
	Fred Tenney, 1897	209
18	Hank Aaron, 1963	207
19	Hank Aaron, 1957	206
20	3 players tied	205

Clutch Hitting Index

1	Earl Sheely, 1931	151
2	Hugh Duffy, 1896	148
3	Tommy Bond, 1877	139
4	Bill Sweeney, 1912	138
5	Ed Konetchy, 1918	137
6	George Wright, 1877	136
7	Billy Nash, 1892	135
8	Jack Burdock, 1883	135
	Red Smith, 1918	135
10	Harry Schafer, 1876	134
11	Jimmy Collins, 1897	133
	Bobby Lowe, 1898	133
	Sherry Magee, 1916	133
14	Dan McGann, 1908	133
15	Herman Long, 1901	133
16	Harry Wolverton, 1905	132
17	Dan Brouthers, 1889	132
18	Tommy Bond, 1878	131
	Sam Wise, 1886	131
	Sherry Magee, 1915	131

Isolated Power

1	Hank Aaron, 1971	.341
2	Eddie Mathews, 1953	.325
3	Eddie Mathews, 1954	.313
4	Eddie Mathews, 1955	.313
5	Hank Aaron, 1969	.307
6	Joe Adcock, 1956	.306
7	Wally Berger, 1930	.305
8	Fred McGriff, 1994	.304
9	Hank Aaron, 1962	.296
10	Eddie Mathews, 1959	.286
11	Dale Murphy, 1987	.284
12	Hank Aaron, 1959	.281
13	Hank Aaron, 1957	.278
14	Darrell Evans, 1973	.276
15	Davey Johnson, 1973	.275
16	Hank Aaron, 1970	.275
17	Hank Aaron, 1960	.275
18	Eddie Mathews, 1960	.274
19	Hank Aaron, 1963	.268
20	Hank Aaron, 1961	.267

Extra Base Hits

1	Hank Aaron, 1959	92
2	Eddie Mathews, 1953	86
3	Hugh Duffy, 1894	85
4	Hank Aaron, 1961	83
5	Tommy Holmes, 1945	81
6	Wally Berger, 1930	79
	Hank Aaron, 1962	79
	Hank Aaron, 1967	79
9	Wally Berger, 1934	77
	Wally Berger, 1935	77
	Hank Aaron, 1957	77
	Hank Aaron, 1963	77
	Hank Aaron, 1969	77
14	Dale Murphy, 1984	76
15	Hank Aaron, 1956	74
	Darrell Evans, 1973	74
17	Hank Aaron, 1955	73
	Hank Aaron, 1965	73
19	3 players tied	72

Pinch Hits

1	Chris Chambliss, 1986	20
2	Tommy Gregg, 1990	18
3	Mike Lum, 1979	17
4	Charley Spikes, 1979	16
	Dwight Smith, 1995	16

Pinch Hit Average (20 at-bats minimum)

1	Milt Thompson, 1985	.433
2	Frank Tepedino, 1973	.417
2	Deion Sanders, 1993	.429
4	Rico Carty, 1969	.409
5	Bob Watson, 1983	.407

Pinch Hit Home Runs

1	Butch Nieman, 1945	5
2	Tommy Gregg, 1990	4
3	Jim Breazeale, 1972	3
	Mike Lum, 1979	3
	Jeff Burroughs, 1980	3
	Graig Nettles, 1987	3

Total Player Rating / 150g

1	Hank Aaron, 1959	6.43
2	Charley Jones, 1879	6.33
3	Eddie Mathews, 1959	6.28
4	Rogers Hornsby, 1928	6.21
5	Hank Aaron, 1963	6.06
6	Hank Aaron, 1967	5.90
7	Deacon White, 1877	5.85
8	Lonnie Smith, 1989	5.82
9	Terry Pendleton, 1991	5.78
10	Glenn Hubbard, 1985	5.70
11	Rabbit Maranville, 1914	5.67
12	Eddie Mathews, 1954	5.65
13	Dave Brain, 1907	5.64
14	Eddie Mathews, 1953	5.54
15	Jack Burdock, 1878	5.50
16	Hank Aaron, 1965	5.50
17	Billy Nash, 1888	5.44
18	Hank Aaron, 1961	5.42
19	Rabbit Maranville, 1919	5.38
20	Hank Aaron, 1969	5.31

Stolen Bases

1	King Kelly, 1887	84
2	Billy Hamilton, 1896	83
3	Otis Nixon, 1991	72
4	King Kelly, 1889	68
5	Billy Hamilton, 1897	66
6	Tom Brown, 1889	63
7	Herman Long, 1891	60
8	Harry Stovey, 1891	57
	Herman Long, 1892	57
	Hap Myers, 1913	57
11	King Kelly, 1888	56
12	Billy Hamilton, 1898	54
13	Tommy McCarthy, 1892	53
14	Dick Johnston, 1887	52
15	Hugh Duffy, 1892	51
16	Herman Long, 1890	49
17	Hugh Duffy, 1894	48
18	Hardy Richardson, 1889	47
	Jimmy Bannon, 1894	47
	Otis Nixon, 1993	47

Stolen Base Average

1	Lee Maye, 1961	90.9
2	Dusty Baker, 1973	88.9
3	Dale Murphy, 1983	88.2
4	Sam Jethroe, 1951	87.5
	Lee Maye, 1963	87.5
	Hank Aaron, 1966	87.5
7	Oddibe McDowell, 1990	86.7
8	Hank Aaron, 1963	86.1
9	Hank Aaron, 1965	85.7
10	Hank Aaron, 1968	84.8

Stolen Base Runs

1	Otis Nixon, 1991	9
2	Sam Jethroe, 1951	8
3	Dale Murphy, 1983	7
4	Hank Aaron, 1963	6
	Otis Nixon, 1993	6
6	Jerry Royster, 1979	6
7	Hank Aaron, 1968	5
8	Dusty Baker, 1973	5
9	Hank Aaron, 1965	5
10	Hank Aaron, 1966	5

Stolen Base Wins

1	Otis Nixon, 1991	0.9
2	Sam Jethroe, 1951	0.8
3	Dale Murphy, 1983	0.7
4	Hank Aaron, 1963	0.7
5	Otis Nixon, 1993	0.6
6	Hank Aaron, 1968	0.6
7	Jerry Royster, 1979	0.6
8	Dusty Baker, 1973	0.6
9	Hank Aaron, 1965	0.5
10	Hank Aaron, 1966	0.5

Fielding Average

First Base

1	Walter Holke, 1921	.997
2	Joe Adcock, 1962	.997
3	Chris Chambliss, 1981	.997
4	Fred McGriff, 1995	.996
5	Chris Chambliss, 1983	.996

Second Base

1	Mark Lemke, 1994	.994
2	Glenn Hubbard, 1981	.991
3	Mark Lemke, 1995	.990
4	Frank Bolling, 1962	.989
5	Glenn Hubbard, 1985	.989

Shortstop

1	Eddie Miller, 1942	.983
2	Roy McMillan, 1961	.975
3	Johnny Logan, 1953	.975
4	Johnny Logan, 1959	.975
5	Johnny Logan, 1952	.972

Third Base

1	Ken Oberkfell, 1987	.979
2	Ken Oberkfell, 1986	.976
3	Clete Boyer, 1967	.970
4	Bob Horner, 1982	.970
5	Pinky Whitney, 1934	.968

Outfield

1	Willard Marshall, 1951	1.000
2	Johnny Cooney, 1941	.996
3	Sid Gordon, 1952	.996
4	Dion James, 1987	.996
5	Rowland Office, 1974	.994
6	Marquis Grissom, 1995	.994
7	Claudell Washington, 1981	.993
8	Lonnie Smith, 1989	.993
9	Tommy Holmes, 1943	.993
10	Wally Berger, 1932	.993

Catcher

1	Greg Olson, 1992	.998
2	Damon Berryhill, 1992	.998
3	Shanty Hogan, 1933	.997
4	Joe Torre, 1968	.996
5	Del Crandall, 1956	.996

Pitcher

1	Kid Nichols, 1896	1.000
2	Jesse Barnes, 1917	.991
3	Dana Fillingim, 1920	.982
4	Lew Burdette, 1960	.980
5	Irv Young, 1905	.980

Total Chances per Game

First Base

1	Jake Goodman, 1878	12.45
2	Fred Tenney, 1905	11.76
3	Walter Holke, 1919	11.62
4	Ed Konetchy, 1918	11.59
5	Fred Tenney, 1907	11.54

Second Base

1	Jack Burdock, 1878	8.30
2	Jack Burdock, 1879	7.88
3	Jack Burdock, 1880	7.59
4	George Wright, 1877	7.47
5	Tony Cuccinello, 1936	6.47

Shortstop

1	Rabbit Maranville, 1919	6.89
2	Herman Long, 1893	6.81
3	Herman Long, 1896	6.74
4	Rabbit Maranville, 1914	6.71
5	Herman Long, 1894	6.64

Third Base

1	Harry Schafer, 1876	4.73
2	Billy Nash, 1892	4.52
3	Jimmy Collins, 1900	4.40
4	Billy Nash, 1887	4.34
5	Dave Brain, 1907	4.32

Outfield

1	Carden Gillenwater, 1945	3.46
2	Wally Berger, 1935	3.24
3	Jimmy Welsh, 1927	3.21
4	Dick Johnston, 1887	3.15
5	Jimmy Welsh, 1930	3.13
6	Wally Berger, 1931	3.10
7	Gus Felix, 1925	3.10
8	Otis Nixon, 1992	3.08
9	Wally Berger, 1936	3.07
10	Wally Berger, 1932	3.05

Catcher

1	Mert Hackett, 1884	9.35
2	Mike Hines, 1883	9.27
3	Lew Brown, 1877	8.65
4	Pop Snyder, 1878	8.24
5	Javy Lopez, 1994	7.96

Pitcher

1	Togie Pittinger, 1904	3.89
2	Vic Willis, 1905	3.88
3	Vic Willis, 1904	3.63
4	Patsy Flaherty, 1907	3.59
5	John Malarkey, 1902	3.57

Chances Accepted per Game

First Base

1	Jake Goodman, 1878	11.75
2	Fred Tenney, 1905	11.54
3	Walter Holke, 1919	11.54
4	Ed Konetchy, 1918	11.49
5	Elbie Fletcher, 1937	11.45

Second Base

1	Jack Burdock, 1878	7.62
2	Jack Burdock, 1879	7.18
3	Jack Burdock, 1880	7.01
4	George Wright, 1877	6.55
5	Tony Cuccinello, 1936	6.28

Shortstop

1	Rabbit Maranville, 1919	6.48
2	Rabbit Maranville, 1914	6.29
3	Rabbit Maranville, 1920	6.14
4	Herman Long, 1902	6.08
5	Dave Bancroft, 1925	6.07

Third Base

1	Jimmy Collins, 1900	4.11
2	Billy Nash, 1892	4.06
3	Dave Brain, 1907	3.95
4	Jimmy Collins, 1899	3.93
5	Jimmy Collins, 1897	3.86

Outfield

1	Carden Gillenwater, 1945	3.39
2	Wally Berger, 1935	3.13
3	Jimmy Welsh, 1927	3.11
4	Jimmy Welsh, 1930	3.06
5	Otis Nixon, 1992	3.05
6	Wally Berger, 1931	3.03
7	Wally Berger, 1932	3.03
8	Gus Felix, 1925	3.01
9	Wally Berger, 1936	2.96
10	Dick Johnston, 1887	2.94

Catcher

1	Mert Hackett, 1884	8.68
2	Mike Hines, 1883	8.22
3	Javy Lopez, 1994	7.92
4	Lew Brown, 1877	7.76
5	Pop Snyder, 1878	7.52

Pitcher

1	Vic Willis, 1905	3.71
2	Togie Pittinger, 1904	3.58
3	Vic Willis, 1904	3.47
4	Irv Young, 1905	3.44
5	Art Nehf, 1918	3.44

Putouts

First Base

1	Ed Konetchy, 1916	1626
	Chris Chambliss, 1980	1626
3	Fred Tenney, 1907	1587
	Elbie Fletcher, 1937	1587
5	Fred Tenney, 1905	1556

Second Base

1	Bill Sweeney, 1912	459
2	Dave Shean, 1910	408
3	Rabbit Maranville, 1932	402
4	Bobby Lowe, 1898	397
5	Connie Ryan, 1947	393

Shortstop

1	Rabbit Maranville, 1914	407
2	Eddie Miller, 1940	405
3	Rabbit Maranville, 1915	391
4	Ed Abbaticchio, 1905	386
	Rabbit Maranville, 1916	386

Third Base

1	Jimmy Collins, 1900	251
2	Jimmy Collins, 1898	243
3	Ed Gremminger, 1902	222
4	Tony Boeckel, 1920	219
5	Jimmy Collins, 1899	217
	Ed Gremminger, 1903	217

Outfield

1	Wally Berger, 1935	458
2	Wally Berger, 1931	457
3	Carden Gillenwater, 1945	451
4	Tommy Holmes, 1944	426
5	Vince DiMaggio, 1938	415
6	Sam Jethroe, 1952	413
7	Bill Bruton, 1955	412
8	Tommy Holmes, 1943	408
9	Dale Murphy, 1982	407
10	Eddie Brown, 1926	401

Catcher

1	Del Crandall, 1959	783
2	Del Crandall, 1960	764
3	Bruce Benedict, 1983	738
4	Greg Olson, 1991	721
5	Ozzie Virgil, 1986	682

Pitcher

1	Charlie Buffinton, 1884	40
2	Charley Radbourn, 1886	39
	Vic Willis, 1904	39
	Greg Maddux, 1993	39
5	Vic Willis, 1902	37
	Vic Willis, 1905	37

Putouts per Game

First Base

1	Jake Goodman, 1878	11.55
2	Ed Konetchy, 1918	10.95
3	Walter Holke, 1919	10.84
4	Elbie Fletcher, 1937	10.72
5	Walter Holke, 1920	10.69

Second Base

1	Jack Burdock, 1878	4.08
2	Jack Burdock, 1880	3.81
3	Jack Burdock, 1879	3.61
4	Bill Sweeney, 1912	3.00
5	George Wright, 1877	2.95

Shortstop

1	Rabbit Maranville, 1919	2.76
2	Al Bridwell, 1906	2.71
3	Eddie Miller, 1940	2.68
4	Herman Long, 1902	2.66
5	Rabbit Maranville, 1920	2.66

Third Base

1	Jimmy Collins, 1900	1.78
2	Billy Nash, 1887	1.77
3	Harry Schafer, 1876	1.74
4	Billy Nash, 1889	1.60
5	Jimmy Collins, 1898	1.60

Outfield

1	Carden Gillenwater, 1945	3.22
2	Wally Berger, 1935	3.07
3	Otis Nixon, 1992	3.00
4	Jimmy Welsh, 1930	2.99
5	Wally Berger, 1932	2.96
6	Wally Berger, 1931	2.93
7	Jimmy Welsh, 1927	2.92
8	Wally Berger, 1936	2.89
9	Gus Felix, 1925	2.88
10	Wally Berger, 1933	2.81

Catcher

1	Javy Lopez, 1994	7.45
2	Mert Hackett, 1884	7.21
3	Javy Lopez, 1995	6.72
4	Lew Brown, 1877	6.55
5	Mike Hines, 1883	6.47

Pitcher

1	Greg Maddux, 1993	1.08
2	Chick Fraser, 1905	0.92
3	Vic Willis, 1904	0.91
4	Vic Willis, 1905	0.90
5	John Smoltz, 1993	0.83

Assists

First Base

1	Fred Tenney, 1905	152
2	Chris Chambliss, 1982	138
3	Elbie Fletcher, 1938	126
4	Fred Tenney, 1906	118
5	Fred Tenney, 1904	115

Second Base

1	Tony Cuccinello, 1936	559
2	Glenn Hubbard, 1985	539
3	Tony Cuccinello, 1937	524
4	Glenn Hubbard, 1982	505
5	Dave Shean, 1910	493

Shortstop

1	Whitey Wietelmann, 1943	581
2	Rabbit Maranville, 1914	574
3	Bill Dahlen, 1908	553
4	Rabbit Maranville, 1929	536
5	Rafael Ramirez, 1982	528

Third Base

1	Darrell Evans, 1975	381
2	Jimmy Collins, 1899	376
3	Darrell Evans, 1974	367
4	Billy Nash, 1892	351
	Eddie Mathews, 1958	351

Outfield

1	Jimmy Bannon, 1894	43
2	Dick Johnston, 1887	34
3	Gene Moore, 1936	32
4	Dick Johnston, 1888	30
	Jimmy Bannon, 1895	30
	Ginger Beaumont, 1907	30
7	Dick Johnston, 1886	29
	Tommy McCarthy, 1892	29
9	Tommy McCarthy, 1893	28
	Tommy McCarthy, 1894	28

Catcher

1	Pat Moran, 1903	214
2	Hank Gowdy, 1916	158
3	Mickey O'Neil, 1920	153
4	Hank Gowdy, 1914	151
5	Hank Gowdy, 1915	148

Pitcher

1	John Clarkson, 1889	172
2	Tommy Bond, 1879	144
3	Tommy Bond, 1880	141
4	Jim Whitney, 1885	128
5	Charlie Buffinton, 1884	118
	Charlie Buffinton, 1885	118

Assists per Game

First Base

1	Fred Tenney, 1905	1.03
2	Chris Chambliss, 1982	0.91
3	Buddy Hassett, 1939	0.91
4	Chris Chambliss, 1981	0.88
5	Elbie Fletcher, 1938	0.86

Second Base

1	Glenn Hubbard, 1985	3.85
2	Tony Cuccinello, 1936	3.73
3	George Wright, 1877	3.60
4	Jack Burdock, 1879	3.57
5	Jack Burdock, 1878	3.53

Shortstop

1	Bill Dahlen, 1908	3.84
2	Herman Long, 1893	3.81
3	Whitey Wietelmann, 1943	3.80
4	Rabbit Maranville, 1919	3.73
5	Rabbit Maranville, 1929	3.70

Third Base

1	Billy Nash, 1892	2.60
2	Jimmy Collins, 1899	2.49
3	Dave Brain, 1907	2.48
4	Red Smith, 1918	2.45
5	Darrell Evans, 1975	2.44

Outfield

1	Jimmy Bannon, 1894	0.34
2	Dick Johnston, 1887	0.27
3	Dick Johnston, 1886	0.27
4	Jim O'Rourke, 1878	0.26
5	Tommy McCarthy, 1893	0.26
6	Jim Manning, 1885	0.25
7	Jimmy Bannon, 1895	0.25
8	Charley Jones, 1879	0.24
9	Tom Poorman, 1886	0.24
10	Bill Crowley, 1881	0.24

Catcher

1	Pat Moran, 1903	2.00
2	King Kelly, 1888	1.92
3	Tom Needham, 1904	1.82
4	Pop Snyder, 1879	1.77
5	Pop Snyder, 1881	1.75

Pitcher

1	Art Nehf, 1918	3.03
2	Togie Pittinger, 1904	3.00
3	Patsy Flaherty, 1907	2.81
4	Dana Fillingim, 1920	2.81
5	John Malarkey, 1902	2.81

Double Plays

First Base

1	Joe Adcock, 1953	146
2	Chris Chambliss, 1982	144
3	Chris Chambliss, 1980	140
4	Bob Horner, 1986	138
5	Buck Jordan, 1936	137
	Earl Torgeson, 1951	137

Second Base

1	Tony Cuccinello, 1936	128
2	Glenn Hubbard, 1985	127
3	Felix Millan, 1971	120
	Glenn Hubbard, 1986	120
5	Glenn Hubbard, 1987	114

Shortstop

1	Rafael Ramirez, 1982	130
2	Eddie Miller, 1940	122
3	Rafael Ramirez, 1983	116
4	Rafael Ramirez, 1985	115
5	Eddie Miller, 1941	112

Third Base

1	Darrell Evans, 1974	45
2	Darrell Evans, 1975	41
3	Les Bell, 1928	37
4	Jerry Royster, 1976	35
5	Eddie Mathews, 1953	33
	Darrell Evans, 1973	33

Outfield

1	Jimmy Bannon, 1894	12
	Ginger Beaumont, 1907	12
3	Phil Geier, 1904	11
4	Tommy McCarthy, 1894	10
	Vince DiMaggio, 1938	10
6	Dick Johnston, 1887	9
	Steve Brodie, 1891	9
8	George Browne, 1908	8
	Beals Becker, 1909	8
	Les Mann, 1914	8
	Joe Kelly, 1917	8
	Jimmy Welsh, 1926	8

Catcher

1	Hank Gowdy, 1916	19
2	Pat Moran, 1903	17
	Zack Taylor, 1926	17
4	Del Crandall, 1959	15
5	Ray Berres, 1941	13
	Del Crandall, 1953	13

Pitcher

1	Ben Cantwell, 1930	9
	Rick Mahler, 1985	9
3	Charley Radbourn, 1886	8
	John Clarkson, 1889	8
	Warren Spahn, 1963	8

Fielding Wins

1	Glenn Hubbard, 1985	6.5
2	Rabbit Maranville, 1914	5.6
3	Dave Shean, 1910	4.5
4	Bill Dahlen, 1908	4.3
5	Glenn Hubbard, 1986	4.3
6	Rabbit Maranville, 1919	3.2
7	Terry Pendleton, 1991	2.9
8	Rafael Belliard, 1992	2.9
9	Dave Brain, 1906	2.9
10	Glenn Hubbard, 1987	2.8
11	Dave Brain, 1907	2.8
12	Rafael Belliard, 1991	2.7
13	Andres Thomas, 1986	2.7
14	Bill Sweeney, 1912	2.6
15	Billy Nash, 1888	2.5
16	Rabbit Maranville, 1916	2.5
17	Darrell Evans, 1975	2.4
18	Johnny Logan, 1957	2.4
19	Herman Long, 1902	2.4
20	Carden Gillenwater, 1945	2.4

Fielding Runs

1	Glenn Hubbard, 1985	61.8
2	Rabbit Maranville, 1914	51.8
3	Dave Shean, 1910	42.5
4	Glenn Hubbard, 1986	41.0
5	Bill Dahlen, 1908	37.5
6	Rabbit Maranville, 1919	28.7
7	Glenn Hubbard, 1987	28.2
8	Terry Pendleton, 1991	27.9
9	Bill Sweeney, 1912	26.9
10	Rafael Belliard, 1992	26.6
11	Rafael Belliard, 1991	26.1
12	Andres Thomas, 1986	25.9
13	Dave Brain, 1906	25.7
14	Billy Nash, 1888	25.6
15	Dick Johnston, 1887	25.3
16	Bobby Lowe, 1896	24.9
17	Dave Brain, 1907	24.7
18	Billy Nash, 1892	24.2
19	Pop Snyder, 1879	23.9
	Johnny Logan, 1957	23.9

Fielding Runs

First Base

1	Fred Tenney, 1905	22
2	Chris Chambliss, 1982	14
3	Fred Tenney, 1902	13
4	Dick Burrus, 1926	12
5	Fred Tenney, 1899	10

Second Base

1	Glenn Hubbard, 1985	62
2	Dave Shean, 1910	42
3	Glenn Hubbard, 1986	41
4	Glenn Hubbard, 1987	28
5	Bill Sweeney, 1912	27

Shortstop

1	Rabbit Maranville, 1914	52
2	Bill Dahlen, 1908	38
3	Rabbit Maranville, 1919	29
4	Rafael Belliard, 1992	26
5	Rafael Belliard, 1991	26

Third Base

1	Terry Pendleton, 1991	28
2	Dave Brain, 1906	26
3	Billy Nash, 1892	25
4	Dave Brain, 1907	23
5	Darrell Evans, 1975	23

Outfield

1	Dick Johnston, 1887	25
2	Carden Gillenwater, 1945	24
3	Jimmy Bannon, 1894	18
4	Dale Murphy, 1988	18
5	Dick Johnston, 1886	17
6	Ralph Garr, 1971	16
7	Vince DiMaggio, 1937	16
8	Gene Moore, 1936	15
9	Tommy Holmes, 1942	15
10	Sherry Magee, 1915	15

Catcher

1	Pop Snyder, 1879	25
2	Pat Moran, 1903	19
3	Charlie Ganzel, 1895	17
4	Lew Brown, 1877	15
5	Del Crandall, 1953	15

Pitcher

1	John Clarkson, 1889	11
2	Tommy Bond, 1880	10
3	Tommy Bond, 1879	7
4	Lefty Tyler, 1913	7
5	Vic Willis, 1904	7

Total Player Rating

1	Hank Aaron, 1959	6.6
2	Hank Aaron, 1963	6.5
3	Eddie Mathews, 1959	6.2
4	Hank Aaron, 1967	6.1
5	Rabbit Maranville, 1914	5.9
	Terry Pendleton, 1991	5.9
7	Rogers Hornsby, 1928	5.8
	Eddie Mathews, 1953	5.8
9	Hank Aaron, 1961	5.6
10	Hank Aaron, 1962	5.5
	Hank Aaron, 1965	5.5
	Hank Aaron, 1968	5.5
13	Tommy Holmes, 1945	5.4
	Glenn Hubbard, 1985	5.4
	Dale Murphy, 1987	5.4
16	Eddie Mathews, 1963	5.3
17	Eddie Mathews, 1954	5.2
	Hank Aaron, 1969	5.2
	Darrell Evans, 1973	5.2
	Lonnie Smith, 1989	5.2

Total Player Rating (alpha.)

Hank Aaron, 1959	6.6
Hank Aaron, 1961	5.6
Hank Aaron, 1962	5.5
Hank Aaron, 1963	6.5
Hank Aaron, 1965	5.5
Hank Aaron, 1967	6.1
Hank Aaron, 1968	5.5
Hank Aaron, 1969	5.2
Darrell Evans, 1973	5.2
Tommy Holmes, 1945	5.4
Rogers Hornsby, 1928	5.8
Glenn Hubbard, 1985	5.4
Rabbit Maranville, 1914	5.9
Eddie Mathews, 1953	5.8
Eddie Mathews, 1954	5.2
Eddie Mathews, 1959	6.2
Eddie Mathews, 1963	5.3
Dale Murphy, 1987	5.4
Terry Pendleton, 1991	5.9
Lonnie Smith, 1989	5.2

Total Player Rating (by era)

1876-1892

1	Billy Nash, 1888	4.9
2	Charley Jones, 1879	3.5
3	King Kelly, 1888	3.4
4	Sam Wise, 1885	3.1
5	2 players tied	2.9

1893-1919

1	Rabbit Maranville, 1914	5.9
2	Dave Brain, 1907	5.0
	Bill Sweeney, 1912	5.0
4	Rabbit Maranville, 1919	4.7
5	Hugh Duffy, 1894	4.3

1920-1941

1	Rogers Hornsby, 1928	5.8
2	Wally Berger, 1933	4.7
3	Tony Cuccinello, 1936	4.5
4	Wally Berger, 1935	4.0
5	Dave Bancroft, 1925	3.8

1942-1960

1	Hank Aaron, 1959	6.6
2	Eddie Mathews, 1959	6.2
3	Eddie Mathews, 1953	5.8
4	Tommy Holmes, 1945	5.4
5	Eddie Mathews, 1954	5.2

1961-1976

1	Hank Aaron, 1963	6.5
2	Hank Aaron, 1967	6.1
3	Hank Aaron, 1961	5.6
4	3 players tied	5.5

1977-1995

1	Terry Pendleton, 1991	5.9
2	Glenn Hubbard, 1985	5.4
	Dale Murphy, 1987	5.4
4	Lonnie Smith, 1989	5.2
5	Dale Murphy, 1983	4.6

Wins

1	John Clarkson, 1889	49
2	Charlie Buffinton, 1884	48
3	Tommy Bond, 1879	43
4	Tommy Bond, 1877	40
	Tommy Bond, 1878	40
6	Jim Whitney, 1883	37
7	Kid Nichols, 1892	35
	Jack Stivetts, 1892	35
9	Kid Nichols, 1893	34
10	John Clarkson, 1888	33
	John Clarkson, 1891	33
12	Kid Nichols, 1894	32
13	Jim Whitney, 1881	31
	Kid Nichols, 1897	31
	Kid Nichols, 1898	31
16	Kid Nichols, 1891	30
	Kid Nichols, 1896	30
18	5 players tied	27

Wins (by era)

1876-1892

1	John Clarkson, 1889	49
2	Charlie Buffinton, 1884	48
3	Tommy Bond, 1879	43
4	Tommy Bond, 1877	40
	Tommy Bond, 1878	40

1893-1919

1	Kid Nichols, 1893	34
2	Kid Nichols, 1894	32
3	Kid Nichols, 1897	31
	Kid Nichols, 1898	31
5	Kid Nichols, 1896	30

1920-1941

1	Joe Oeschger, 1921	20
	Ben Cantwell, 1933	20
	Jim Turner, 1937	20
	Lou Fette, 1937	20
5	2 players tied	18

1942-1960

1	Johnny Sain, 1948	24
2	Warren Spahn, 1953	23
3	Warren Spahn, 1951	22
	Warren Spahn, 1958	22
5	9 players tied	21

1961-1976

1	Tony Cloninger, 1965	24
2	Warren Spahn, 1963	23
	Phil Niekro, 1969	23
4	Warren Spahn, 1961	21
5	Phil Niekro, 1974	20

1977-1995

1	Tom Glavine, 1993	22
2	Phil Niekro, 1979	21
3	Tom Glavine, 1991	20
	Tom Glavine, 1992	20
	Greg Maddux, 1993	20

Losses

1	Jim Whitney, 1881	33
2	Jim Whitney, 1885	32
3	Sam Weaver, 1878	31
	Charley Radbourn, 1886	31
5	Tommy Bond, 1880	29
	Vic Willis, 1905	29
7	Charlie Buffinton, 1885	27
8	Vic Willis, 1904	25
	Irv Young, 1906	25
	Gus Dorner, 1906	25
	Ben Cantwell, 1935	25
12	Cliff Curtis, 1910	24
13	Charley Radbourn, 1887	23
	Kaiser Wilhelm, 1905	23
	Vive Lindaman, 1906	23
	Irv Young, 1907	23
	George Ferguson, 1909	23
	Buster Brown, 1910	23
19	3 players tied	22

Winning Percentage

1	Greg Maddux, 1995	.905
2	Tom Hughes, 1916	.842
3	Phil Niekro, 1982	.810
4	Fred Klobedanz, 1897	.788
	Bill James, 1914	.788
6	Tom Glavine, 1993	.786
7	Jack Manning, 1876	.783
8	Vic Willis, 1899	.771
9	Warren Spahn, 1953	.767
	Warren Spahn, 1963	.767
11	Ted Lewis, 1898	.765
12	Charlie Buffinton, 1884	.750
	Steve Avery, 1993	.750
14	Kid Nichols, 1897	.738
15	Greg Maddux, 1994	.727
16	Dick Rudolph, 1914	.722
17	Kid Nichols, 1898	.721
18	John Clarkson, 1889	.721
19	Bob Buhl, 1957	.720
20	2 players tied	.714

Winning Percentage (by era)

1876-1892

1	Jack Manning, 1876	.783
2	Charlie Buffinton, 1884	.750
3	John Clarkson, 1889	.721
4	Harry Staley, 1891	.714
5	Tommy Bond, 1877	.702

1893-1919

1	Tom Hughes, 1916	.842
2	Fred Klobedanz, 1897	.788
	Bill James, 1914	.788
4	Vic Willis, 1899	.771
5	Ted Lewis, 1898	.765

1920-1941

1	Ben Cantwell, 1933	.667
	Lou Fette, 1937	.667
3	Fred Frankhouse, 1934	.654
4	Jim Turner, 1937	.645
5	Huck Betts, 1934	.630

1942-1960

1	Warren Spahn, 1953	.767
2	Bob Buhl, 1957	.720
3	Bob Buhl, 1956	.692
4	Warren Spahn, 1947	.677
	Warren Spahn, 1960	.677

1961-1976

1	Warren Spahn, 1963	.767
2	Tony Cloninger, 1965	.686
3	Buzz Capra, 1974	.667
4	Ron Reed, 1969	.643
5	Phil Niekro, 1969	.639

1977-1995

1	Greg Maddux, 1995	.905
2	Phil Niekro, 1982	.810
3	Tom Glavine, 1993	.786
4	Steve Avery, 1993	.750
5	Greg Maddux, 1994	.727

Games

1	Rick Camp, 1980	77
2	Mike Stanton, 1991	74
	Greg McMichael, 1993	74
4	John Clarkson, 1889	73
	Clay Carroll, 1966	73
6	Steve Bedrosian, 1983	70
7	Gene Garber, 1982	69
8	Gene Garber, 1979	68
	Gene Garber, 1980	68
	Jim Acker, 1987	68
11	Charlie Buffinton, 1884	67
	Greg McMichael, 1995	67
13	Jim Whitney, 1881	66
	Rick Camp, 1985	66
	Joe Boever, 1989	66
16	Dave Campbell, 1977	65
	Mike Stanton, 1992	65
	Mark Wohlers, 1995	65
19	3 players tied	64

Games (by era)

1876-1892

1	John Clarkson, 1889	73
2	Charlie Buffinton, 1884	67
3	Jim Whitney, 1881	66
4	Tommy Bond, 1879	64
5	Tommy Bond, 1880	63

1893-1919

1	Kid Nichols, 1893	52
2	Vic Willis, 1902	51
	Al Mattern, 1910	51
4	4 players tied	50

1920-1941

1	Jack Scott, 1921	47
2	Joe Oeschger, 1921	46
	Joe Oeschger, 1922	46
	Bob Smith, 1935	46
5	Hugh McQuillan, 1921	45

1942-1960

1	Don McMahon, 1959	60
2	Johnny Hutchings, 1945	57
3	Don McMahon, 1960	48
4	Dave Jolly, 1954	47
5	Lew Burdette, 1953	46

1961-1976

1	Clay Carroll, 1966	73
2	Billy O'Dell, 1965	62
	Cecil Upshaw, 1969	62
4	Dan Osinski, 1965	61
5	Tom House, 1975	58

1977-1995

1	Rick Camp, 1980	77
2	Mike Stanton, 1991	74
	Greg McMichael, 1993	74
4	Steve Bedrosian, 1983	70
5	Gene Garber, 1982	69

Games Started

1	John Clarkson, 1889	72
2	Charlie Buffinton, 1884	67
3	Tommy Bond, 1879	64
4	Jim Whitney, 1881	63
5	Tommy Bond, 1878	59
6	Tommy Bond, 1877	58
	Charley Radbourn, 1886	58
8	Tommy Bond, 1880	57
9	Jim Whitney, 1883	56
10	John Clarkson, 1888	54
11	John Clarkson, 1891	51
	Kid Nichols, 1892	51
13	Charlie Buffinton, 1885	50
	Jim Whitney, 1885	50
	Charley Radbourn, 1887	50
16	Jim Whitney, 1882	48
	Kid Nichols, 1891	48
	Jack Stivetts, 1892	48
19	Kid Nichols, 1890	47
20	2 players tied	46

Games Started (by era)

1876-1892
1	John Clarkson, 1889	72
2	Charlie Buffinton, 1884	67
3	Tommy Bond, 1879	64
4	Jim Whitney, 1881	63
5	Tommy Bond, 1878	59

1893-1919
1	Kid Nichols, 1894	46
	Vic Willis, 1902	46
3	Kid Nichols, 1893	44
4	3 players tied	43

1920-1941
1	Joe Oeschger, 1921	36
2	Jim Turner, 1938	34
3	Jack Scott, 1920	33
	Socks Seibold, 1930	33
	Lou Fette, 1937	33

1942-1960
1	Johnny Sain, 1948	39
	Warren Spahn, 1950	39
	Vern Bickford, 1950	39
	Lew Burdette, 1959	39
5	Warren Spahn, 1949	38

1961-1976
1	Phil Niekro, 1974	39
	Carl Morton, 1975	39
3	Tony Cloninger, 1965	38
	Tony Cloninger, 1966	38
	Carl Morton, 1974	38

1977-1995
1	Phil Niekro, 1979	44
2	Phil Niekro, 1977	43
3	Phil Niekro, 1978	42
4	Rick Mahler, 1985	39
	Rick Mahler, 1986	39

Complete Games

1	John Clarkson, 1889	68
2	Charlie Buffinton, 1884	63
3	Tommy Bond, 1879	59
4	Tommy Bond, 1877	58
5	Tommy Bond, 1878	57
	Jim Whitney, 1881	57
	Charley Radbourn, 1886	57
8	Jim Whitney, 1883	54
9	John Clarkson, 1888	53
10	Jim Whitney, 1885	50
11	Tommy Bond, 1880	49
	Charlie Buffinton, 1885	49
	Kid Nichols, 1892	49
14	Charley Radbourn, 1887	48
15	Kid Nichols, 1890	47
	John Clarkson, 1891	47
17	Jim Whitney, 1882	46
18	Kid Nichols, 1891	45
	Jack Stivetts, 1892	45
	Vic Willis, 1902	45

Complete Games (by era)

1876-1892
1	John Clarkson, 1889	68
2	Charlie Buffinton, 1884	63
3	Tommy Bond, 1879	59
4	Tommy Bond, 1877	58
5	3 players tied	57

1893-1919
1	Vic Willis, 1902	45
2	Kid Nichols, 1893	43
3	Kid Nichols, 1895	42
4	Irv Young, 1905	41
5	2 players tied	40

1920-1941
1	Jim Turner, 1937	24
2	Ed Brandt, 1931	23
	Ed Brandt, 1933	23
	Lou Fette, 1937	23
5	3 players tied	22

1942-1960
1	Jim Tobin, 1942	28
	Jim Tobin, 1944	28
	Johnny Sain, 1948	28
4	Vern Bickford, 1950	27
5	Warren Spahn, 1951	26

1961-1976
1	Warren Spahn, 1962	22
	Warren Spahn, 1963	22
3	Warren Spahn, 1961	21
	Phil Niekro, 1969	21
5	2 players tied	18

Innings Pitched

1	John Clarkson, 1889	620.0
2	Charlie Buffinton, 1884	587.0
3	Tommy Bond, 1879	555.1
4	Jim Whitney, 1881	552.1
5	Tommy Bond, 1878	532.2
6	Tommy Bond, 1877	521.0
7	Jim Whitney, 1883	514.0
8	Charley Radbourn, 1886	509.1
9	Tommy Bond, 1880	493.0
10	John Clarkson, 1888	483.1
11	John Clarkson, 1891	460.2
12	Kid Nichols, 1892	453.0
13	Jim Whitney, 1885	441.1
14	Charlie Buffinton, 1885	434.1
15	Kid Nichols, 1891	425.1
16	Charley Radbourn, 1887	425.0
	Kid Nichols, 1893	425.0
18	Kid Nichols, 1890	424.0
19	Jim Whitney, 1882	420.0
20	Jack Stivetts, 1892	415.2

Innings Pitched (by era)

1876-1892
1	John Clarkson, 1889	620.0
2	Charlie Buffinton, 1884	587.0
3	Tommy Bond, 1879	555.1
4	Jim Whitney, 1881	552.1
5	Tommy Bond, 1878	532.2

1893-1919
1	Kid Nichols, 1893	425.0
2	Vic Willis, 1902	410.0
3	Kid Nichols, 1894	407.0
4	Togie Pittinger, 1902	389.1
5	Kid Nichols, 1898	388.0

1920-1941
1	Joe Oeschger, 1920	299.0
	Joe Oeschger, 1921	299.0
3	Jack Scott, 1920	291.0
4	Ed Brandt, 1933	287.2
5	Dana Fillingim, 1920	272.0

1942-1960
1	Johnny Sain, 1948	314.2
2	Vern Bickford, 1950	311.2
3	Warren Spahn, 1951	310.2
4	Al Javery, 1943	303.0
5	Warren Spahn, 1949	302.1

1961-1976
1	Phil Niekro, 1974	302.1
2	Phil Niekro, 1969	284.1
3	Phil Niekro, 1972	282.1
4	Tony Cloninger, 1965	279.0
5	Carl Morton, 1975	277.2

Shutouts

1	Tommy Bond, 1879	11
2	Tommy Bond, 1878	9
3	Charlie Buffinton, 1884	8
	John Clarkson, 1889	8
5	Kid Nichols, 1890	7
	Togie Pittinger, 1902	7
	Irv Young, 1905	7
	Warren Spahn, 1947	7
	Warren Spahn, 1951	7
	Warren Spahn, 1963	7
11	11 players tied	6

Saves

1	Gene Garber, 1982	30
2	Cecil Upshaw, 1969	27
	Mike Stanton, 1993	27
4	Gene Garber, 1979	25
	Mark Wohlers, 1995	25
6	Gene Garber, 1986	24
7	Bruce Sutter, 1985	23
8	Gene Garber, 1978	22
	Rick Camp, 1980	22
10	Joe Boever, 1989	21
	Greg McMichael, 1994	21
12	Steve Bedrosian, 1983	19
	Greg McMichael, 1993	19
14	Billy O'Dell, 1965	18
15	Cecil Upshaw, 1971	17
	Rick Camp, 1981	17
	Juan Berenguer, 1991	17
18	Donnie Moore, 1984	16
19	Don McMahon, 1959	15
	Alejandro Pena, 1992	15

Innings Pitched

1	Phil Niekro, 1979	342.0
2	Phil Niekro, 1978	334.1
3	Phil Niekro, 1977	330.1
4	Phil Niekro, 1980	275.0
5	Greg Maddux, 1993	267.0

Hits per Game

1	Greg Maddux, 1995	6.31
2	Tom Hughes, 1915	6.68
3	Greg Maddux, 1994	6.68
4	Buzz Capra, 1974	6.76
5	Tom Hughes, 1916	6.76
6	John Smoltz, 1989	6.92
7	Bill James, 1914	7.07
8	Pat Ragan, 1916	7.07
9	Pat Jarvis, 1968	7.10
10	Phil Niekro, 1967	7.13
11	Warren Spahn, 1953	7.15
12	Andy Messersmith, 1976	7.21
13	Lefty Tyler, 1916	7.22
14	George Ferguson, 1908	7.27
15	Vic Willis, 1899	7.28
16	Jim Whitney, 1884	7.29
17	Gus Dorner, 1908	7.32
18	Kid Nichols, 1898	7.33
19	Tom Glavine, 1991	7.33
20	Phil Niekro, 1974	7.41

Hits per Game (by era)

1876-1892
1	Jim Whitney, 1884	7.29
2	Jack Stivetts, 1892	7.49
3	Bill Stemmeyer, 1886	7.74
4	Kid Madden, 1888	7.75
5	Charlie Buffinton, 1884	7.76

1893-1919
1	Tom Hughes, 1915	6.68
2	Tom Hughes, 1916	6.76
3	Bill James, 1914	7.07
4	Pat Ragan, 1916	7.07
5	Lefty Tyler, 1916	7.22

1920-1941
1	Bob Brown, 1932	7.90
2	Joe Sullivan, 1940	7.97
3	Jim Turner, 1937	7.99
4	Ed Brandt, 1933	8.01
5	Ed Brandt, 1931	8.21

1942-1960
1	Warren Spahn, 1953	7.15
2	Bob Buhl, 1955	7.50
3	Warren Spahn, 1947	7.61
4	Bob Buhl, 1960	7.62
5	Warren Spahn, 1950	7.62

1961-1976
1	Buzz Capra, 1974	6.76
2	Pat Jarvis, 1968	7.10
3	Phil Niekro, 1967	7.13
4	Andy Messersmith, 1976	7.21
5	Phil Niekro, 1974	7.41

1977-1995
1	Greg Maddux, 1995	6.31
2	Greg Maddux, 1994	6.68
3	John Smoltz, 1989	6.92
4	Tom Glavine, 1991	7.33
5	John Smoltz, 1992	7.52

Home Runs Allowed

1	Phil Niekro, 1979	41
2	Phil Niekro, 1970	40
3	Lew Burdette, 1959	38
4	Johnny Sain, 1950	34
5	Lew Burdette, 1961	31
6	Denny Lemaster, 1963	30
	Phil Niekro, 1980	30
8	Warren Spahn, 1958	29
	Tony Cloninger, 1966	29
	Phil Niekro, 1975	29
11	Buzz Capra, 1977	28
12	Jack Stivetts, 1894	27
	Warren Spahn, 1949	27
	Denny Lemaster, 1964	27
	George Stone, 1970	27
	Phil Niekro, 1971	27
	Larry McWilliams, 1980	27
18	4 players tied	26

Home Runs Allowed (by era)

1876-1892
1	Kid Madden, 1887	20
	Charley Radbourn, 1887	20
3	Charley Radbourn, 1886	18
	John Clarkson, 1891	18
5	John Clarkson, 1888	17

(by era) — continued

1893-1919
1	Jack Stivetts, 1894	27
2	Kid Nichols, 1894	23
3	Harry Staley, 1893	22
4	Jack Stivetts, 1896	20
5	Jack Stivetts, 1893	17

1920-1941
1	Bob Smith, 1930	25
2	Ed Brandt, 1928	22
3	Tiny Chaplin, 1936	21
	Jim Turner, 1938	21
5	Bob Smith, 1929	20

1942-1960
1	Lew Burdette, 1959	38
2	Johnny Sain, 1950	34
3	Warren Spahn, 1958	29
4	Warren Spahn, 1949	27
5	5 players tied	25

1961-1976
1	Phil Niekro, 1970	40
2	Lew Burdette, 1961	31
3	Denny Lemaster, 1963	30
4	Tony Cloninger, 1966	29
	Phil Niekro, 1975	29

1977-1995
1	Phil Niekro, 1979	41
2	Phil Niekro, 1980	30
3	Buzz Capra, 1977	28
4	Larry McWilliams, 1980	27
5	2 players tied	26

Walks

1	John Clarkson, 1889	203
2	Jack Stivetts, 1892	171
3	Phil Niekro, 1977	164
4	John Clarkson, 1891	154
5	Chick Fraser, 1905	149
6	Vic Willis, 1898	148
7	Bill Stemmeyer, 1886	144
	Togie Pittinger, 1904	144
9	Togie Pittinger, 1903	143
10	John Clarkson, 1890	140
11	Charley Radbourn, 1887	133
12	Togie Pittinger, 1902	128
13	Jack Stivetts, 1894	127
14	Lefty Tyler, 1912	126
15	Fred Klobedanz, 1897	125
	Ted Lewis, 1897	125
17	Cliff Curtis, 1910	124
18	Kid Madden, 1887	122
	Vern Bickford, 1950	122
20	4 players tied	121

Fewest Walks/Game (by era)

1876-1892
1	Tommy Bond, 1879	0.39
2	Sam Weaver, 1878	0.49
3	Tommy Bond, 1878	0.56
4	Jim Whitney, 1883	0.61
5	Tommy Bond, 1877	0.62

1893-1919
1	Dick Rudolph, 1916	1.10
2	Art Nehf, 1917	1.50
3	Jesse Barnes, 1917	1.53
4	Dick Rudolph, 1914	1.63
5	Hub Perdue, 1913	1.65

1920-1941
1	Huck Betts, 1932	1.42
2	Tim McNamara, 1924	1.56
3	Huck Betts, 1934	1.77
4	Jesse Barnes, 1924	1.78
5	Jim Turner, 1938	1.81

1942-1960
1	Lew Burdette, 1960	1.14
2	Lew Burdette, 1959	1.18
3	Lew Burdette, 1958	1.63
4	Warren Spahn, 1956	1.66
5	Mort Cooper, 1946	1.76

1961-1976
1	Lew Burdette, 1961	1.09
2	Phil Niekro, 1968	1.58
3	Ken Johnson, 1967	1.63
4	Phil Niekro, 1972	1.69
5	Warren Spahn, 1963	1.70

1977-1995
1	Greg Maddux, 1995	0.99
2	Greg Maddux, 1994	1.38
3	Gaylord Perry, 1981	1.43
4	Rick Mahler, 1988	1.52
5	Steve Avery, 1993	1.73

Ratio

1	Greg Maddux, 1995	7.47
2	Jim Whitney, 1884	8.01
3	Greg Maddux, 1994	8.33
4	Dick Rudolph, 1916	8.86
5	Tom Hughes, 1915	8.89
6	Charlie Buffinton, 1884	8.92
7	Pat Jarvis, 1968	8.93
8	Tommy Bond, 1879	9.19
9	Sam Weaver, 1878	9.21
10	Jim Whitney, 1883	9.23
11	Art Nehf, 1917	9.26
12	Pat Ragan, 1916	9.40
13	Phil Niekro, 1969	9.40
14	Lefty Tyler, 1916	9.42
15	Dick Rudolph, 1914	9.45
16	Bobby Mathews, 1882	9.47
17	Jim Whitney, 1882	9.54
18	Warren Spahn, 1953	9.55
19	Jesse Barnes, 1917	9.58
20	Kid Nichols, 1898	9.63

Strikeouts

1	Charlie Buffinton, 1884	417
2	Jim Whitney, 1883	345
3	John Clarkson, 1889	284
4	Jim Whitney, 1884	270
5	Phil Niekro, 1977	262
6	Phil Niekro, 1978	248
7	Charlie Buffinton, 1885	242
8	Kid Nichols, 1891	240
9	Bill Stemmeyer, 1886	239
10	Vic Willis, 1902	225
11	John Clarkson, 1888	223
12	Kid Nichols, 1890	222
13	Charley Radbourn, 1886	218
14	John Smoltz, 1992	215
15	Tony Cloninger, 1965	211
16	Phil Niekro, 1979	208
	John Smoltz, 1993	208
18	Jim Whitney, 1885	200
19	Greg Maddux, 1993	197
20	Vic Willis, 1904	196

Strikeouts (by era)

1876-1892

1	Charlie Buffinton, 1884	417
2	Jim Whitney, 1883	345
3	John Clarkson, 1889	284
4	Jim Whitney, 1884	270
5	Charlie Buffinton, 1885	242

1893-1919

1	Vic Willis, 1902	225
2	Vic Willis, 1904	196
3	Togie Pittinger, 1902	174
4	Tom Hughes, 1915	171
5	Sam Frock, 1910	170

1920-1941

1	Ed Brandt, 1931	112
2	Bob Brown, 1932	110
3	Ed Brandt, 1934	106
4	Ed Brandt, 1933	104
5	Larry Benton, 1926	103

1942-1960

1	Warren Spahn, 1950	191
2	Warren Spahn, 1952	183
3	Warren Spahn, 1951	164
4	Warren Spahn, 1960	154
5	Warren Spahn, 1949	151

1961-1976

1	Tony Cloninger, 1965	211
2	Phil Niekro, 1974	195
3	Phil Niekro, 1969	193
4	Denny Lemaster, 1963	190
5	Denny Lemaster, 1964	185

1977-1995

1	Phil Niekro, 1977	262
2	Phil Niekro, 1978	248
3	John Smoltz, 1992	215
4	Phil Niekro, 1979	208
	John Smoltz, 1993	208

Strikeouts per Game

1	John Smoltz, 1995	9.02
2	John Smoltz, 1992	7.84
3	Greg Maddux, 1995	7.77
4	John Smoltz, 1993	7.68
5	Tom Glavine, 1994	7.62
6	John Smoltz, 1994	7.55
7	Denny Lemaster, 1964	7.53
8	Steve Avery, 1995	7.32
9	Denny Lemaster, 1966	7.32
10	David Palmer, 1986	7.30
11	John Smoltz, 1989	7.27
12	Steve Avery, 1994	7.24
13	Jim Whitney, 1884	7.23
14	Denny Lemaster, 1963	7.22
15	Phil Niekro, 1977	7.14
16	Tom Glavine, 1991	7.01
17	Greg Maddux, 1994	6.95
18	Tony Cloninger, 1965	6.81
19	Johnny Antonelli, 1953	6.72
20	Phil Niekro, 1978	6.68

Strikeouts per Game (by era)

1876-1892

1	Jim Whitney, 1884	7.23
2	Charlie Buffinton, 1884	6.39
3	Bill Stemmeyer, 1886	6.17
4	Jim Whitney, 1883	6.04
5	Charlie Buffinton, 1883	5.08

1893-1919

1	Sam Frock, 1910	5.99
2	Tom Hughes, 1915	5.49
3	Tom Hughes, 1916	5.42
4	Lefty Tyler, 1912	5.06
5	Vic Willis, 1904	5.04

1920-1941

1	Bob Brown, 1932	4.65
2	Ed Brandt, 1931	4.03
3	Larry Benton, 1926	4.00
4	Ed Brandt, 1934	3.74
5	Bob Smith, 1930	3.44

1942-1960

1	Johnny Antonelli, 1953	6.72
2	Gene Conley, 1955	6.09
3	Warren Spahn, 1950	5.87
4	Warren Spahn, 1952	5.68
5	Gene Conley, 1954	5.23

1961-1976

1	Denny Lemaster, 1964	7.53
2	Denny Lemaster, 1966	7.32
3	Denny Lemaster, 1963	7.22
4	Tony Cloninger, 1965	6.81
5	Roric Harrison, 1973	6.60

1977-1995

1	John Smoltz, 1995	9.02
2	John Smoltz, 1992	7.84
3	Greg Maddux, 1995	7.77
4	John Smoltz, 1993	7.68
5	Tom Glavine, 1994	7.62

Earned Run Average

1	Greg Maddux, 1994	1.56
2	Greg Maddux, 1995	1.63
3	Phil Niekro, 1967	1.87
4	Bill James, 1914	1.90
5	Sam Weaver, 1878	1.95
6	Tommy Bond, 1879	1.96
7	Lefty Tyler, 1916	2.02
8	Tommy Bond, 1878	2.06
9	Bill Sowders, 1888	2.07
10	Pat Ragan, 1916	2.08
11	Jim Whitney, 1884	2.09
12	Warren Spahn, 1953	2.10
13	Tommy Bond, 1877	2.11
14	Tom Hughes, 1915	2.12
15	Kid Nichols, 1898	2.13
16	Jack Manning, 1876	2.14
17	Charlie Buffinton, 1884	2.15
18	Art Nehf, 1917	2.16
19	Dick Rudolph, 1916	2.16
20	Dick Rudolph, 1919	2.17

Earned Run Average (by era)

1876-1892

1	Sam Weaver, 1878	1.95
2	Tommy Bond, 1879	1.96
3	Tommy Bond, 1878	2.06
4	Bill Sowders, 1888	2.07
5	Jim Whitney, 1884	2.09

1893-1919

1	Bill James, 1914	1.90
2	Lefty Tyler, 1916	2.02
3	Pat Ragan, 1916	2.08
4	Tom Hughes, 1915	2.12
5	Kid Nichols, 1898	2.13

1920-1941

1	Jim Turner, 1937	2.38
2	Ed Brandt, 1933	2.60
3	Ben Cantwell, 1933	2.62
4	Jesse Barnes, 1923	2.76
5	Huck Betts, 1933	2.79

1942-1960

1	Warren Spahn, 1953	2.10
2	Johnny Sain, 1946	2.21
3	Warren Spahn, 1947	2.33
4	Nate Andrews, 1943	2.57
5	Johnny Sain, 1948	2.60

1961-1976

1	Phil Niekro, 1967	1.87
2	Buzz Capra, 1974	2.28
3	Phil Niekro, 1974	2.38
4	Phil Niekro, 1969	2.56
5	Phil Niekro, 1968	2.59

1977-1995

1	Greg Maddux, 1994	1.56
2	Greg Maddux, 1995	1.63
3	Greg Maddux, 1993	2.36
4	Tom Glavine, 1991	2.55
5	Tom Glavine, 1992	2.76

Adjusted Earned Run Average

1	Greg Maddux, 1994	272
2	Greg Maddux, 1995	259
3	Warren Spahn, 1953	187
4	Phil Niekro, 1967	178
5	Kid Nichols, 1898	173
6	Greg Maddux, 1993	170
7	Kid Nichols, 1897	169
8	Kid Nichols, 1890	168
9	Warren Spahn, 1947	167
10	Vic Willis, 1899	167
11	Buzz Capra, 1974	166
12	Kid Nichols, 1896	161
13	Phil Niekro, 1974	159
14	Johnny Sain, 1946	155
15	Vic Willis, 1901	153
16	Kid Nichols, 1891	153
17	John Clarkson, 1889	153
18	Tom Glavine, 1991	152
19	Jim Turner, 1937	150
20	Kid Nichols, 1895	150

Adjusted ERA (by era)

1876-1892

1	Kid Nichols, 1890	168
2	Kid Nichols, 1891	153
3	John Clarkson, 1889	153
4	Harry Staley, 1891	146
5	Jim Whitney, 1883	138

1893-1919

1	Kid Nichols, 1898	173
2	Kid Nichols, 1897	169
3	Vic Willis, 1899	167
4	Kid Nichols, 1896	161
5	Vic Willis, 1901	153

1920-1941

1	Jim Turner, 1937	150
2	Jesse Barnes, 1923	144
3	Huck Betts, 1932	134
4	Danny Mac Fayden, 1936	134
5	Ed Brandt, 1931	130

1942-1960

1	Warren Spahn, 1953	187
2	Warren Spahn, 1947	167
3	Johnny Sain, 1946	155
4	Johnny Sain, 1948	147
5	Lew Burdette, 1954	135

1961-1976

1	Phil Niekro, 1967	178
2	Buzz Capra, 1974	166
3	Phil Niekro, 1974	159
4	Phil Niekro, 1969	141
5	Bob Shaw, 1962	136

1977-1995

1	Greg Maddux, 1994	272
2	Greg Maddux, 1995	259
3	Greg Maddux, 1993	170
4	Tom Glavine, 1991	152
5	Phil Niekro, 1978	140

Pitching Runs

1	John Clarkson, 1889	88.7
2	Kid Nichols, 1897	68.4
3	Warren Spahn, 1953	64.5
4	Kid Nichols, 1898	63.5
5	Kid Nichols, 1896	63.5
6	Kid Nichols, 1890	63.2
7	Greg Maddux, 1994	59.5
8	Greg Maddux, 1995	59.4
9	Kid Nichols, 1895	57.8
10	Warren Spahn, 1947	55.7
11	Charlie Buffinton, 1884	54.5
12	Kid Nichols, 1893	54.3
13	Vic Willis, 1899	51.8
14	Jim Whitney, 1883	51.2
15	Greg Maddux, 1993	49.9
16	Johnny Sain, 1948	47.3
17	Kid Nichols, 1891	45.3
18	Jim Turner, 1937	43.6
19	Phil Niekro, 1974	41.5
20	Tommy Bond, 1877	40.6

Adjusted Pitching Runs

1	John Clarkson, 1889	98.9
2	Kid Nichols, 1897	74.9
3	Kid Nichols, 1890	71.8
4	Kid Nichols, 1895	71.3
5	Kid Nichols, 1896	70.9
6	Kid Nichols, 1898	67.3
7	Kid Nichols, 1893	67.1
8	Vic Willis, 1899	63.4
9	Greg Maddux, 1995	60.5
10	Greg Maddux, 1994	60.2
11	Kid Nichols, 1891	59.8
12	Warren Spahn, 1953	53.8
13	Warren Spahn, 1947	50.3
14	Jim Whitney, 1883	49.1
15	Greg Maddux, 1993	49.0
16	Charlie Buffinton, 1884	48.5
17	Phil Niekro, 1974	46.9
18	Kid Nichols, 1899	44.7
19	John Clarkson, 1891	44.2
20	Phil Niekro, 1978	43.3

Pitching Wins

1	John Clarkson, 1889	7.7
2	Warren Spahn, 1953	6.2
3	Kid Nichols, 1898	5.9
4	Kid Nichols, 1897	5.9
5	Greg Maddux, 1994	5.9
6	Greg Maddux, 1995	5.8
7	Kid Nichols, 1890	5.6
8	Warren Spahn, 1947	5.5
9	Kid Nichols, 1896	5.4
10	Greg Maddux, 1993	5.0
11	Charlie Buffinton, 1884	4.9
12	Johnny Sain, 1948	4.7
13	Vic Willis, 1899	4.7
14	Kid Nichols, 1895	4.7
15	Jim Whitney, 1883	4.5
16	Kid Nichols, 1893	4.5
17	Jim Turner, 1937	4.3
18	Phil Niekro, 1974	4.3
19	Kid Nichols, 1891	4.0
20	Johnny Sain, 1946	3.8

Adjusted Pitching Wins

1	John Clarkson, 1889	8.6
2	Kid Nichols, 1897	6.4
3	Kid Nichols, 1890	6.4
4	Kid Nichols, 1898	6.3
5	Kid Nichols, 1896	6.0
6	Greg Maddux, 1995	6.0
7	Greg Maddux, 1994	5.9
8	Kid Nichols, 1895	5.8
9	Vic Willis, 1899	5.7
10	Kid Nichols, 1893	5.5
11	Kid Nichols, 1891	5.3
12	Warren Spahn, 1953	5.2
13	Warren Spahn, 1947	4.9
14	Greg Maddux, 1993	4.9
15	Phil Niekro, 1974	4.9
16	Phil Niekro, 1978	4.6
17	Charlie Buffinton, 1884	4.3
18	Johnny Sain, 1948	4.3
19	Jim Whitney, 1883	4.3
20	Vic Willis, 1901	4.2

Opponents' Batting Average

1	Greg Maddux, 1995	.197
2	Greg Maddux, 1994	.207
3	Jim Whitney, 1884	.207
4	Buzz Capra, 1974	.208
5	John Smoltz, 1989	.212
6	Tom Hughes, 1915	.213
7	Pat Jarvis, 1968	.214
8	Tom Hughes, 1916	.215
9	Warren Spahn, 1953	.217
10	Jack Stivetts, 1892	.217
11	Phil Niekro, 1967	.218
12	Pat Ragan, 1916	.218
13	Bill Stemmeyer, 1886	.218
14	Andy Messersmith, 1976	.219
15	Charlie Buffinton, 1884	.219
16	Kid Nichols, 1898	.221
17	Vic Willis, 1899	.221
18	Phil Niekro, 1969	.221
19	Tom Glavine, 1991	.222
20	Gus Dorner, 1908	.224

Opponents' On Base Pctg.

1	Jim Whitney, 1884	.223
2	Greg Maddux, 1995	.225
3	Charlie Buffinton, 1884	.244
4	Greg Maddux, 1994	.245
5	Bobby Mathews, 1882	.246
6	Sam Weaver, 1878	.247
7	Jim Whitney, 1883	.251
8	Pat Jarvis, 1968	.255
9	Jim Whitney, 1882	.255
10	Tommy Bond, 1879	.259
11	Dick Rudolph, 1916	.261
12	Tommy Bond, 1877	.261
13	Phil Niekro, 1969	.264
14	Tom Hughes, 1915	.265
15	Curry Foley, 1879	.268
16	Art Nehf, 1917	.268
17	Pat Ragan, 1916	.270
18	Warren Spahn, 1953	.270
19	Kid Nichols, 1898	.272
20	Kid Madden, 1888	.273

Wins Above Team

1	Charlie Buffinton, 1884	14.9
2	John Clarkson, 1889	12.1
3	Tommy Bond, 1879	12.0
4	Warren Spahn, 1963	8.5
5	Bill James, 1914	8.4
6	John Clarkson, 1888	8.1
	Greg Maddux, 1995	8.1
8	Vic Willis, 1899	7.9
9	Kid Nichols, 1896	7.8
10	Warren Spahn, 1953	7.1
11	Jack Manning, 1876	7.0
12	Kid Nichols, 1894	6.8
	Tony Cloninger, 1965	6.8
14	Phil Niekro, 1982	6.4
15	Tom Glavine, 1993	6.3
16	Tom Hughes, 1916	6.2
17	Dick Rudolph, 1914	6.1
18	Irv Young, 1905	6.0
19	Jim Whitney, 1881	5.9
20	2 players tied	5.8

Wins Above League

1	John Clarkson, 1889	42.6
2	Charlie Buffinton, 1884	36.3
3	Tommy Bond, 1879	34.0
4	Jim Whitney, 1883	33.3
5	Jim Whitney, 1881	33.0
6	Tommy Bond, 1877	32.1
7	Tommy Bond, 1878	31.2
8	Charley Radbourn, 1886	30.0
9	John Clarkson, 1891	29.9
10	Kid Nichols, 1893	29.5
11	Kid Nichols, 1890	29.4
12	Kid Nichols, 1891	28.8
13	Kid Nichols, 1892	28.6
14	Kid Nichols, 1896	28.0
15	Kid Nichols, 1898	27.8
16	Jack Stivetts, 1892	27.6
17	Kid Nichols, 1897	27.4
18	John Clarkson, 1888	27.0
19	Kid Nichols, 1895	26.8
20	Vic Willis, 1902	26.5

Relief Games

1	Rick Camp, 1980	77
2	Mike Stanton, 1991	74
	Greg McMichael, 1993	74
4	Clay Carroll, 1966	70
5	Gene Garber, 1982	69
	Steve Bedrosian, 1983	69
7	Gene Garber, 1979	68
	Gene Garber, 1980	68
	Jim Acker, 1987	68
10	Greg McMichael, 1995	67

Relief Wins

1	Dave Jolly, 1954	11
	Cecil Upshaw, 1971	11
3	Billy O'Dell, 1965	10
4	Rick Camp, 1981	9
	Steve Bedrosian, 1983	9
6	8 players tied	8

Relief Losses

1	Gene Garber, 1979	16
2	Nels Potter, 1949	11
	Joe Boever, 1989	11
4	Gene Garber, 1982	10
	Steve Bedrosian, 1983	10
	Gene Garber, 1987	10
7	Bob Priddy, 1971	9
	Jim Acker, 1987	9
9	Don Hendrickson, 1945	8
	Clay Carroll, 1967	8

Relief Innings Pitched

1	Clay Carroll, 1966	137.1
2	Steve Bedrosian, 1982	122.0
3	Gene Garber, 1982	119.1
4	Rick Camp, 1985	118.2
5	Cecil Upshaw, 1968	116.2
6	Jim Acker, 1987	114.2
7	Steve Bedrosian, 1983	113.0
8	Rick Camp, 1980	108.1
9	Billy O'Dell, 1965	107.1
10	2 players tied	106.0

Relief Points

1	Gene Garber, 1982	66
2	Cecil Upshaw, 1969	62
3	Mark Wohlers, 1995	61
4	Mike Stanton, 1993	56
5	Bruce Sutter, 1985	53
	Gene Garber, 1986	53
7	Rick Camp, 1980	52
8	Billy O'Dell, 1965	51
9	Cecil Upshaw, 1971	50
10	Rick Camp, 1981	49

Relief Ranking

1	Gene Garber, 1982	35.5
2	Mark Wohlers, 1995	34.8
3	Steve Bedrosian, 1984	29.5
4	Billy O'Dell, 1965	29.4
5	Rick Camp, 1981	29.3
6	Rick Camp, 1980	28.4
7	Clay Carroll, 1966	25.8
8	Gene Garber, 1986	22.9
9	Dave Jolly, 1954	22.4
10	Steve Bedrosian, 1982	21.3

Relievers' Runs

1	Clay Carroll, 1966	23.0
2	Rick Camp, 1980	20.3
3	Greg McMichael, 1993	20.1
4	Tom House, 1974	19.3
5	Billy O'Dell, 1965	18.2
6	Steve Bedrosian, 1982	17.8
7	Dave Jolly, 1954	16.8
8	Gene Garber, 1982	16.7
9	Ernie Johnson, 1953	15.7
10	Mark Wohlers, 1995	15.0

Adjusted Relievers' Runs

1	Clay Carroll, 1966	23.5
2	Rick Camp, 1980	22.0
3	Tom House, 1974	21.1
4	Greg McMichael, 1993	19.9
5	Steve Bedrosian, 1982	19.6
6	Gene Garber, 1982	18.5
7	Billy O'Dell, 1965	18.0
8	Mark Wohlers, 1995	15.4
9	Rick Camp, 1981	15.2
10	Terry Forster, 1983	15.2

Clutch Pitching Index

1	Dick Rudolph, 1919	141.2
2	Mal Eason, 1902	135.8
3	Bob Buhl, 1957	134.8
4	Gene Conley, 1956	127.3
5	Vive Lindaman, 1906	126.3
6	Togie Pittinger, 1903	126.0
7	Dick Errickson, 1940	124.5
8	Rick Camp, 1982	124.3
9	Bob Logan, 1945	124.2
	Rick Mahler, 1981	124.2
11	Bob Shaw, 1962	123.2
12	Buster Brown, 1910	122.3
13	Kid Nichols, 1896	122.1
14	Phil Niekro, 1975	121.5
15	Bill James, 1914	121.2
16	Phil Niekro, 1967	120.8
17	Bob Buhl, 1959	120.3
18	Dick Crutcher, 1914	120.1
19	Bill Voiselle, 1948	120.0
20	Tommy Bond, 1878	118.6

Pitcher Batting Runs

1	Jim Whitney, 1882	22.3
2	Jim Whitney, 1883	18.1
3	Warren Spahn, 1958	16.0
4	Jack Stivetts, 1892	15.1
5	Jim Tobin, 1942	14.0
6	Johnny Sain, 1947	11.7
7	Jack Stivetts, 1896	11.5
8	Jim Whitney, 1881	11.0
9	Charlie Buffinton, 1884	10.8
10	Jack Stivetts, 1894	10.7
11	Kid Nichols, 1901	10.3
12	Jack Scott, 1921	10.3
13	Tony Cloninger, 1966	9.5
14	Warren Spahn, 1961	9.3
15	Bill Stemmeyer, 1886	9.2
16	Jim Whitney, 1884	8.8
17	Otto Hess, 1913	8.6
18	Ed Brandt, 1933	8.5
19	Fred Klobedanz, 1897	8.4
20	Charley Radbourn, 1886	7.6

Pitcher Fielding Runs

1	John Clarkson, 1889	11.3
2	Tommy Bond, 1880	9.8
3	Tommy Bond, 1879	7.3
4	Lefty Tyler, 1913	6.9
5	Vic Willis, 1904	6.8
	Jim Tobin, 1944	6.8
7	Greg Maddux, 1993	6.6
8	Vic Willis, 1905	6.4
9	Jim Whitney, 1885	6.1
10	Cliff Curtis, 1910	5.9
	Greg Maddux, 1995	5.9
12	Charlie Buffinton, 1885	5.7
	Dick Rudolph, 1916	5.7
14	Jim Tobin, 1942	5.6
15	Kid Nichols, 1891	5.5
16	Dana Fillingim, 1920	5.4
17	Ed Reulbach, 1916	5.3
18	Togie Pittinger, 1904	5.0
19	Dick Rudolph, 1913	4.6
20	Lew Burdette, 1960	4.5

Total Pitcher Index

1	John Clarkson, 1889	10.1
2	Kid Nichols, 1897	7.3
	Greg Maddux, 1994	7.3
4	Kid Nichols, 1898	6.9
5	Kid Nichols, 1890	6.7
	Greg Maddux, 1995	6.7
7	Kid Nichols, 1896	6.6
	Warren Spahn, 1953	6.6
9	Greg Maddux, 1993	6.1
10	Jim Whitney, 1883	6.0
11	Johnny Sain, 1946	5.9
12	Kid Nichols, 1891	5.8
13	Charlie Buffinton, 1884	5.7
	Kid Nichols, 1895	5.7
	Phil Niekro, 1978	5.7
16	Kid Nichols, 1893	5.5
	Tom Glavine, 1991	5.5
18	Vic Willis, 1899	5.3
	Johnny Sain, 1948	5.3
20	Phil Niekro, 1974	5.2

Total Pitcher Index (alpha.)

Charlie Buffinton, 1884	5.7
John Clarkson, 1889	10.1
Tom Glavine, 1991	5.5
Greg Maddux, 1993	6.1
Greg Maddux, 1994	7.3
Greg Maddux, 1995	6.7
Kid Nichols, 1890	6.7
Kid Nichols, 1891	5.8
Kid Nichols, 1893	5.5
Kid Nichols, 1895	5.7
Kid Nichols, 1896	6.6
Kid Nichols, 1897	7.3
Kid Nichols, 1898	6.9
Phil Niekro, 1974	5.2
Phil Niekro, 1978	5.7
Johnny Sain, 1946	5.9
Johnny Sain, 1948	5.3
Warren Spahn, 1953	6.6
Jim Whitney, 1883	6.0
Vic Willis, 1899	5.3

Total Pitcher Index (by era)

1876-1892

1	John Clarkson, 1889	10.1
2	Kid Nichols, 1890	6.7
3	Jim Whitney, 1883	6.0
4	Kid Nichols, 1891	5.8
5	Charlie Buffinton, 1884	5.7

1893-1919

1	Kid Nichols, 1897	7.3
2	Kid Nichols, 1898	6.9
3	Kid Nichols, 1896	6.6
4	Kid Nichols, 1895	5.7
5	Kid Nichols, 1893	5.5

1920-1941

1	Jim Turner, 1937	4.5
2	Ed Brandt, 1931	3.6
3	Jesse Barnes, 1923	2.9
4	Ed Brandt, 1933	2.7
	Danny Mac Fayden, 1936	2.7

1942-1960

1	Warren Spahn, 1953	6.6
2	Johnny Sain, 1946	5.9
3	Johnny Sain, 1948	5.3
4	Warren Spahn, 1947	5.1
5	Jim Tobin, 1944	4.7

1961-1976

1	Phil Niekro, 1974	5.2
2	Phil Niekro, 1969	4.8
3	Warren Spahn, 1961	3.9
4	Phil Niekro, 1967	3.8
5	Buzz Capra, 1974	3.7

1977-1995

1	Greg Maddux, 1994	7.3
2	Greg Maddux, 1995	6.7
3	Greg Maddux, 1993	6.1
4	Phil Niekro, 1978	5.7
5	Tom Glavine, 1991	5.5

Total Baseball Ranking

1	John Clarkson, 1889	10.1
2	Kid Nichols, 1897	7.3
	Greg Maddux, 1994	7.3
4	Kid Nichols, 1898	6.9
5	Kid Nichols, 1890	6.7
	Greg Maddux, 1995	6.7
7	Kid Nichols, 1896	6.6
	Warren Spahn, 1953	6.6
	Hank Aaron, 1959	6.6
10	Hank Aaron, 1963	6.5
11	Eddie Mathews, 1959	6.2
12	Greg Maddux, 1993	6.1
	Hank Aaron, 1967	6.1
14	Jim Whitney, 1883	6.0
15	Johnny Sain, 1946	5.9
	Rabbit Maranville, 1914	5.9
	Terry Pendleton, 1991	5.9
18	Kid Nichols, 1891	5.8
	Rogers Hornsby, 1928	5.8
	Eddie Mathews, 1953	5.8

Total Baseball Rank (alpha.)

Hank Aaron, 1959	6.6
Hank Aaron, 1963	6.5
Hank Aaron, 1967	6.1
John Clarkson, 1889	10.1
Rogers Hornsby, 1928	5.8
Greg Maddux, 1993	6.1
Greg Maddux, 1994	7.3
Greg Maddux, 1995	6.7
Rabbit Maranville, 1914	5.9
Eddie Mathews, 1953	5.8
Eddie Mathews, 1959	6.2
Kid Nichols, 1890	6.7
Kid Nichols, 1891	5.8
Kid Nichols, 1896	6.6
Kid Nichols, 1897	7.3
Kid Nichols, 1898	6.9
Terry Pendleton, 1991	5.9
Johnny Sain, 1946	5.9
Warren Spahn, 1953	6.6
Jim Whitney, 1883	6.0

Total Baseball Rank (by era)

1876-1892
1. John Clarkson, 1889 — 10.1
2. Kid Nichols, 1890 — 6.7
3. Jim Whitney, 1883 — 6.0
4. Kid Nichols, 1891 — 5.8
5. Charlie Buffinton, 1884 — 5.7

1893-1919
1. Kid Nichols, 1897 — 7.3
2. Kid Nichols, 1898 — 6.9
3. Kid Nichols, 1896 — 6.6
4. Rabbit Maranville, 1914 — 5.9
5. Kid Nichols, 1895 — 5.7

1920-1941
1. Rogers Hornsby, 1928 — 5.8
2. Wally Berger, 1933 — 4.7
3. Jim Turner, 1937 — 4.5
   Tony Cuccinello, 1936 — 4.5
5. Wally Berger, 1935 — 4.0

1942-1960
1. Warren Spahn, 1953 — 6.6
   Hank Aaron, 1959 — 6.6
3. Eddie Mathews, 1959 — 6.2
4. Johnny Sain, 1946 — 5.9
5. Eddie Mathews, 1953 — 5.8

1961-1976
1. Hank Aaron, 1963 — 6.5
2. Hank Aaron, 1967 — 6.1
3. Hank Aaron, 1961 — 5.6
4. 3 players tied — 5.5

1977-1995
1. Greg Maddux, 1994 — 7.3
2. Greg Maddux, 1995 — 6.7
3. Greg Maddux, 1993 — 6.1
4. Terry Pendleton, 1991 — 5.9
5. Phil Niekro, 1978 — 5.7

Braves All Stars

1933 NL
Wally Berger

1934 NL
Wally Berger
Fred Frankhouse

1935 NL
Wally Berger

1936 NL
Wally Berger*

1937 NL
Gene Moore*

1938 NL
Tony Cuccinello*
Jim Turner*

1939 NL
Lou Fette

1940 NL
Eddie Miller
Max West

1941 NL
Eddie Miller

1942 NL
Ernie Lombardi
Eddie Miller

1943 NL
Al Javery

1944 NL
Nate Andrews*
Al Javery*
Connie Ryan
Jim Tobin

1945 NL
Mort Cooper*
Tommy Holmes*
Phil Masi*

1946 NL
Mort Cooper*
Johnny Hopp
Phil Masi

1947 NL
Bob Elliott†
Phil Masi
Johnny Sain
Warren Spahn

1948 NL
Bob Elliott
Tommy Holmes
Phil Masi
Johnny Sain
Eddie Stanky†

1949 NL
Vern Bickford
Warren Spahn

1950 NL
Walker Cooper*
Warren Spahn*

1951 NL
Bob Elliott
Warren Spahn*

1952 NL
Warren Spahn*

1953 NL
Del Crandall†
Eddie Mathews
Warren Spahn

1954 NL
Gene Conley
Del Crandall*
Warren Spahn
Jim Wilson*

1955 NL
Hank Aaron
Gene Conley
Del Crandall
Johnny Logan
Eddie Mathews

1956 NL
Hank Aaron
Del Crandall†
Eddie Mathews*
Warren Spahn

1957 NL
Hank Aaron
Lew Burdette
Johnny Logan*
Eddie Mathews
Red Schoendienst
Warren Spahn*

1958 NL
Hank Aaron
Del Crandall
Johnny Logan
Eddie Mathews*
Don McMahon*
Warren Spahn

1959 NL (Game 1)
Hank Aaron
Lew Burdette
Del Crandall
Eddie Mathews
Warren Spahn*

1959 NL (Game 2)
Hank Aaron
Lew Burdette*
Del Crandall
Johnny Logan*
Eddie Mathews
Warren Spahn*

1960 NL (Game 1)
Hank Aaron
Joe Adcock
Bob Buhl
Del Crandall
Eddie Mathews

1960 NL (Game 2)
Hank Aaron
Joe Adcock
Bob Buhl*
Del Crandall
Eddie Mathews

1961 NL (Game 1)
Hank Aaron
Frank Bolling
Eddie Mathews
Warren Spahn

1961 NL (Game 2)
Hank Aaron
Frank Bolling
Eddie Mathews
Warren Spahn*

1962 NL (Game 1)
Hank Aaron†
Frank Bolling
Del Crandall
Bob Shaw
Warren Spahn*

1962 NL (Game 2)
Hank Aaron
Frank Bolling
Del Crandall
Eddie Mathews
Warren Spahn*

1963 NL
Hank Aaron
Warren Spahn*
Joe Torre*

1964 NL
Hank Aaron
Joe Torre

1965 NL
Hank Aaron
Joe Torre

1966 NL
Hank Aaron
Felipe Alou*
Joe Torre

1967 NL
Hank Aaron
Denny Lemaster†
Joe Torre

1968 NL
Hank Aaron
Felipe Alou
Ron Reed

1969 NL
Hank Aaron
Felix Millan
Phil Niekro

1970 NL
Hank Aaron
Rico Carty
Felix Millan†
Hoyt Wilhelm*

1971 NL
Hank Aaron
Felix Millan

1972 NL
Hank Aaron

1973 NL
Hank Aaron
Darrell Evans
Davey Johnson

1974 NL
Hank Aaron
Buzz Capra*
Ralph Garr

1975 NL
Phil Niekro*

1976 NL
Andy Messersmith†
Dick Ruthven*

1977 NL
Willie Montanez

1978 NL
Jeff Burroughs*
Phil Niekro
Biff Pocoroba

1979 NL
Gary Matthews

1980 NL
Dale Murphy

1981 NL
Bruce Benedict

1982 NL
Bob Horner
Dale Murphy
Phil Niekro*

1983 NL
Bruce Benedict
Glenn Hubbard
Dale Murphy
Pascual Perez

1984 NL
Dale Murphy
Rafael Ramirez*
Claudell Washington

1985 NL
Dale Murphy

1986 NL
Dale Murphy

1987 NL
Dale Murphy
Ozzie Virgil

1988 NL
Gerald Perry

1989 NL
John Smoltz

1990 NL
Greg Olson

1991 NL
Tom Glavine

1992 NL
Ron Gant
Tom Glavine
Terry Pendleton
John Smoltz

1993 NL
Steve Avery
Jeff Blauser
Tom Glavine*
David Justice
John Smoltz

1994 NL
David Justice
Greg Maddux
Fred McGriff

1995 NL
Greg Maddux*
Fred McGriff

* Named to All Star Game, did not play.
† Named to All Star Game, replaced because of injury.

Formulas and Technical Information

Batting Runs = $(.47)1B + (.78)2B + (1.09)3B + (1.40)HR + (.33)(BB + HB) - (.25)(AB - H) - (.50)(OOB)$

Clutch Hitting Index Calculated for individuals, actual RBIs over expected RBIs, adjusted for league average and slot in batting order; 100 is a league-average performance. The spot in the batting order is figured as: $5 - (9 \times BFPGP - BFPGT)$, where BFPGP is the batters facing pitcher per game for the player, or plate appearances divided by games, and BFPGT is the batters facing pitcher per game of the entire team. Expected RBIs are calculated as (.25 singles + .50 doubles + .75 triples + 1.75 homers) $\times$ LGAV $\times$ EXPSL where LGAV (league average) = league RBIs divided by (.25 singles + .50 doubles + .75 triples + 1.75 homers), and EXPSL (expected RBIs by slot number) = .88 for the leadoff batter, and for the remaining slots, descending to ninth, .90, .98, 1.08, 1.08, 1.04, 1.04, 1.04, and 1.02.

Calculated for teams, Clutch Hitting Index is actual runs scored over Batting Runs.

Clutch Pitching Index Expected runs allowed over actual runs allowed, with 100 being a league-average performance. Expected runs are figured on the basis of the pitcher's opposing at bats, hits, walks, and hit batsmen (doubles and triples are estimated at league average).

Fielding Runs Calculated to take account of the particular demands of the different positions. (For a full explanation, see *Total Baseball*.) For second basemen, shortstops and third basemen, the formula begins by calculating the league average for each position as follows:

$$\text{League Average} = \left(\frac{.20 (PO + 2A - E + DP) \text{ league at position}}{PO \text{ league total} - K \text{ league total}} \right)$$

where PO = putouts, A = assists, E = errors, DP = double plays, and K = strikeouts. Then we estimate the number of innings for each player at each position based upon each player's entire fielding record and his number of plate appearances. So, if the team played 1,500 innings and one player was calculated to have played 1,000 of those innings at a given position, his Fielding Runs (FR) would be calculated as:

$$FR = .20 (PO + 2A - E + DP) \text{ player} - \text{avg. pos. lg.} \times \left(\frac{PO - K}{\text{team} \quad \text{team}} \right) \frac{\text{innings, player}}{\text{innings, team}}$$

Assists are doubly weighted because more fielding skill is generally required to get one than to record a putout.

For catchers, the above formula is modified by removing strikeouts from their formulas and subtracting not only errors but also passed balls divided by two. Also incorporated in the catcher's Fielding Runs is one tenth of the adjusted Pitching Runs for the team, times the percentage of games behind the plate by that catcher.

For pitchers, the above formula is modified to subtract individual pitcher strikeouts from the total number of potential outs (otherwise, exceptional strikeout pitchers like Nolan Ryan or Bob Feller would see their Fielding Runs artificially depressed). Also, pitchers' chances are weighted less than infielders' assists because a pitcher's style may produce fewer ground balls. Thus the formula for pitchers is $.10(PO + 2A - E + DP)$, whereas for second basemen, shortstops, and third basemen it is $.20(PO + 2A - E + DP)$.

For first basemen, because putouts and double plays require so little skill in all but the odd case, these plays are eliminated, leaving only $.20(2A - E)$ in the numerator.

For outfielders, the formula becomes $.20(PO + 4A - E + 2DP)$. The weighting for assists is boosted here because a good outfielder can prevent runs through the threat of assists that are never made; for them, unlike infielders, the assist is essentially an elective play, like the stolen base.

Isolated Power Total bases minus hits, divided by at bats; or more simply, Slugging Average minus Batting Average.

On-Base Percentage The editors employ the version created by Allan Roth and Branch Rickey in the early 1950s: hits plus walks plus hit by pitch divided by at bats plus walks, without regard to sacrifice flies.

Park Factor Calculated separately for batters and pitchers and abbreviated PF. The computation of Park Factor is daunting and what follows is probably of interest to few readers but here's a taste; for the full explanation, consult the Glossary of *Total Baseball*.

Step 1: Find games, losses, and runs scored and allowed for each team at home and on the road. Take runs per game scored and allowed at home over runs per game scored and allowed on the road. This is the initial figure, but requires two corrections.

Step 2: The first correction is for innings pitched at home and on the road. First, find the team's home winning percentage (wins at home over games at home). Do the same for road games. Then calculate the Innings Pitched Corrector (IPC):

$$IPC = \frac{(18.5 - \text{Wins at home} / \text{Games at home})}{(18.5 - \text{Losses on road} / \text{Games on road})}$$

If the number is greater than 1, this means that the innings pitched on the road are higher because the other team is batting more often in the last of the ninth. The 18.5 figure is the average number of half innings per game if the home team always bats in the bottom of the ninth.

Step 3: Correct for the fact that the other road parks' total difference from the league average is offset by the park rating of the club being rated. Multiply this rating by the Other Parks Corrector (OPC):

$$OPC = \frac{\text{No. of teams}}{\text{No. of teams} - 1 + \text{Run Factor, team}}$$

Pitching Runs = Innings Pitched $\times$ (League ERA/9) - Earned Runs Allowed. An alternative version is: Innings Pitched/9 $\times$ (League ERA - Individual ERA).

Production = On-Base Percentage plus Slugging Average. When PRO, as it is abbreviated, is adjusted, the calculation is modified slightly to create a baseline of 100 for league average performance. For PRO/A, the equation is:

$$\frac{\text{Player On Base Pct.}}{\text{League On Base Pct.}} + \frac{\text{Player Slugging Avg.}}{\text{League Slugging Avg.}} - 1$$

Relief Ranking = Relief Runs x $(9 \times [\text{Wins} + \text{Losses} + \text{Saves}/4] / \text{Innings Pitched})$

Runs Created Bill James's formulation runs to fourteen separate versions; see the Glossary of *Total Baseball* for a full accounting. For 1963-1989, the years covered by the Player and Pitcher Registers, the formula is:

$$\frac{(H + BB + HBP - CS - GIDP) (TB + .26 [BB - IBB + HBP] + .52 [SH + SF + SB])}{AB + BB + HBP + SH + SF}$$

Runs per Win Calculated on a league-wide basis as the square root of $(2 \times \text{runs per inning})$ multiplied by 10. The runs per inning is multiplied by two to account for the scoring of each team. Historically, the average number of runs per inning is one-half, or 4.5 runs per game per team, so the Runs per Win equation is generally the square root of a number very close to one times 10 or 10 runs per win. In a year with a lot of scoring, the Runs per Win figure will move closer to 11 and in low scoring years the figure will move closer to 9, but 10 is a good estimate for any season.

For individuals, the Runs per Win calculation adjusts the runs per inning to reflect the contribution of the pitcher or batter. A pitcher who allows 45 runs less than average over the course of 25 games lowers the runs per game by 1.8, which is .2 runs per inning, so the Runs per Win figure is 10 times the square root of average runs per inning for both teams minus the pitcher's rating. (A pitcher who allowed 45 more runs than average would have his runs per inning added to the league average.) If the league average was one run per inning, then the Runs per Win for that pitcher would become the square root of .8 runs per inning times 10, which is 8.9. Dividing his 45 pitching runs by 8.9 runs per wins gives him 5.1 linear weights wins. Similarly a batter who produces 45 runs more than average in 150 games contributes .3 runs per game or .03 per inning, which is added to the league average of one run per inning. His Runs per Win equation becomes 10 times the square root of 1.03, which is 10.1. Dividing his 45 batter runs over 10.1 runs per win gives him 4.4 linear weights wins. Although the batter and pitcher contribute the same number of linear weights runs to their team, the pitcher comes out with more linear weights wins, and is statistically more valuable to his team, because he contributes his runs over fewer games and because, as the number of runs scored decreases, each run becomes more valuable.

Slugging Average = Total Bases divided by At Bats.

Total Average = (Total Bases + Walks + Stolen Bases + HBP - Caught Stealing) / (At Bats - Hits + Caught Stealing + GIDP)

Wins Above Team For a pitcher with a winning percentage better than his team (a positive WAT):

Pitcher Decisions $\times$ ([Pitcher pct. - Team pct.] / [2 - 2 $\times$ Team pct.])

For a pitcher with a winning percentage lower than his team's winning percentage (a negative WAT), the equation is:

Pitcher Decisions $\times$ ([Pitcher pct. - Team pct.] / [2 $\times$ Team pct.])

Team and League Abbreviations

These are the 146 franchises, seven principal leagues, and their abbreviations as used throughout this book.

NATIONAL ASSOCIATION, 1871–1875 (shown as n or NA)

Abbrev.	First	Last	Team
ATH n	1871	1875	Philadelphia Athletics
ATL n	1872	1875	Brooklyn Atlantics
BAL n	1872	1874	Baltimore Lord Baltimores
BOS n	1871	1875	Boston Red Stockings
CEN n	1875	1875	Philadelphia Centennials
CHI n	1871	1871	Chicago White Stockings
CHI n	1874	1875	Chicago White Stockings
CLE n	1871	1872	Cleveland Forest City
ECK n	1872	1872	Brooklyn Eckfords
HAR n	1874	1875	Hartford Dark Blues
KEK n	1871	1871	Fort Wayne Kekiongas
MAN n	1872	1872	Middletown (Conn.) Mansfields
MAR n	1873	1873	Baltimore Marylands
MUT n	1871	1875	New York Mutuals
NAT n	1872	1872	Washington, D.C., Nationals
NH n	1875	1875	New Haven Elm City
OLY n	1871	1872	Washington, D.C., Olympics
PHI n	1873	1875	Philadelphia White Stockings
RES n	1873	1873	Elizabeth (N.J.) Resolutes
ROK n	1871	1871	Rockford (Ill.) Forest City
RS n	1875	1875	St. Louis Red Stockings
STL n	1875	1875	St. Louis Brown Stockings
TRO n	1871	1872	Troy Haymakers
WAS n	1873	1873	Washington Washingtons
WAS n	1875	1875	Washington Washingtons
WES n	1875	1875	Keokuk (Iowa) Westerns

NATIONAL LEAGUE, 1876– (shown as N or NL)

Abbrev.	First	Last	Team
ATL N	1966		Atlanta
BAL N	1892	1899	Baltimore
BOS N	1876	1952	Boston (transferred to Milwaukee)
BRO N	1890	1957	Brooklyn (transferred to Los Angeles)
BUF N	1879	1885	Buffalo
CHI N	1876		Chicago
CIN N	1876	1880	Cincinnati
CIN N	1890		Cincinnati
CLE N	1879	1884	Cleveland
CLE N	1889	1899	Cleveland
COL N	1993		Colorado
DET N	1881	1888	Detroit
FLA N	1993		Florida
HAR N	1876	1877	Hartford (played in Brooklyn in 1877)
HOU N	1962		Houston
IND N	1878	1878	Indianapolis
IND N	1887	1889	Indianapolis
KC N	1886	1886	Kansas City
LA N	1958		Los Angeles
LOU N	1876	1877	Louisville
LOU N	1892	1899	Louisville
MIL N	1878	1878	Milwaukee
MIL N	1953	1965	Milwaukee (transferred to Atlanta)
MON N	1969		Montreal
NY N	1876	1876	New York (played in Brooklyn)
NY N	1883	1957	New York (transferred to San Francisco)
NY N	1962		New York
PHI N	1876	1876	Philadelphia
PHI N	1883		Philadelphia
PIT N	1887		Pittsburgh
PRO N	1878	1885	Providence
STL N	1876	1877	St. Louis
STL N	1885	1886	St. Louis
STL N	1892		St. Louis
SD N	1969		San Diego
SF N	1958		San Francisco
SYR N	1879	1879	Syracuse
TRO N	1879	1882	Troy (N.Y.)
WAS N	1886	1889	Washington, D.C.
WAS N	1892	1899	Washington, D.C.
WOR N	1880	1882	Worcester (Mass.)

AMERICAN ASSOCIATION, 1882-1891 (shown as a or AA)

Abbrev.	First	Last	Team
BAL a	1882	1889	Baltimore
BAL a	1890	1890	Baltimore (combined with Brooklyn, shown as BB)
BAL a	1891	1891	Baltimore (transferred to National League)
BOS a	1891	1891	Boston
BRO a	1884	1889	Brooklyn (transferred to National League)
BRO a	1890	1890	Brooklyn (combined with Baltimore, shown as BB)
CIN a	1882	1889	Cincinnati (transferred to National League)
CIN a	1891	1891	Cincinnati
CLE a	1887	1888	Cleveland (transferred to National League)
COL a	1883	1884	Columbus (Ohio)
COL a	1889	1891	Columbus (Ohio)
IND a	1884	1884	Indianapolis
KC a	1888	1889	Kansas City
LOU a	1882	1891	Louisville (transferred to National League)
MIL a	1891	1891	Milwaukee
NY a	1883	1887	New York
PHI a	1882	1891	Philadelphia
PIT a	1882	1886	Pittsburgh (transferred to National League)
RIC a	1884	1884	Richmond
ROC a	1890	1890	Rochester
STL a	1882	1891	St. Louis (transferred to National League)
SYR a	1890	1890	Syracuse
TOL a	1884	1884	Toledo
TOL a	1890	1890	Toledo
WAS a	1884	1884	Washington, D.C.
WAS a	1891	1891	Washington, D.C. (transferred to National League)

UNION ASSOCIATION, 1884 (shown as U or UA)

Abbrev.	First	Last	Team
ALT U	1884	1884	Altoona (Pa.)
BAL U	1884	1884	Baltimore
BOS U	1884	1884	Boston
CHI U	1884	1884	Chicago (combined with Pittsburgh, shown as CP)
CIN U	1884	1884	Cincinnati
KC U	1884	1884	Kansas City
MIL U	1884	1884	Milwaukee
PHI U	1884	1884	Philadelphia
PIT U	1884	1884	Pittsburgh (combined with Chicago, shown as CP)
STL U	1884	1884	St. Louis
STP U	1884	1884	St. Paul (Minn.)
WAS U	1884	1884	Washington, D.C.
WIL U	1884	1884	Wilmington (Del.)

PLAYERS LEAGUE, 1890 (shown as P or PL)

Abbrev.	First	Last	Team
BOS P	1890	1890	Boston
BRO P	1890	1890	Brooklyn
BUF P	1890	1890	Buffalo
CHI P	1890	1890	Chicago
CLE P	1890	1890	Cleveland
NY P	1890	1890	New York
PHI P	1890	1890	Philadelphia
PIT P	1890	1890	Pittsburgh

AMERICAN LEAGUE, 1901– (shown as A or AL)

Abbrev.	First	Last	Team
BAL A	1901	1902	Baltimore (replaced by New York)
BAL A	1954		Baltimore
BOS A	1901		Boston
CAL A	1965		California
CHI A	1901		Chicago
CLE A	1901		Cleveland
DET A	1901		Detroit
KC A	1955	1967	Kansas City (transferred to Oakland)
KC A	1969		Kansas City
LA A	1961	1964	Los Angeles (transferred to California)
MIL A	1901	1901	Milwaukee (replaced by St. Louis)
MIL A	1970		Milwaukee
MIN A	1961		Minnesota
NY A	1903		New York
OAK A	1968		Oakland
PHI A	1901	1954	Philadelphia (transferred to Kansas City)
STL A	1902	1953	St. Louis (transferred to Baltimore)
SEA A	1969	1969	Seattle (transferred to Milwaukee)
SEA A	1977		Seattle
TEX A	1972		Texas
TOR A	1977		Toronto
WAS A	1901	1960	Washington, D.C. (transferred to Minnesota)
WAS A	1961	1971	Washington, D.C. (transferred to Texas)

FEDERAL LEAGUE, 1914-1915 (shown as F or FL)

Abbrev.	First	Last	Team
BAL F	1914	1915	Baltimore
BRO F	1914	1915	Brooklyn
BUF F	1914	1915	Buffalo
CHI F	1914	1915	Chicago
IND F	1914	1914	Indianapolis (transferred to Newark)
KC F	1914	1915	Kansas City
NEW F	1915	1915	Newark
PIT F	1914	1915	Pittsburgh
STL F	1914	1915	St. Louis